W9-DER-899

WITHDRAWN

WITHDRAWN

THE
ANALOGY OF
THE FAERIE
QUEENE

THE
ANALOGY OF
THE FAERIE
QUEENE

JAMES NOHRNBERG

HE WHO CANNOT ATTRACT PAN,

APPROACHES PROTEUS

IN VAIN.

PRINCETON UNIVERSITY PRESS

PRINCETON, NEW JERSEY

PR
2358
N6

Copyright © 1976 by Princeton University Press

Published by Princeton University Press
Princeton, New Jersey
In the United Kingdom:
Princeton University Press
Guildford, Surrey

ALL RIGHTS RESERVED

Two excerpts are reprinted by permission of
Penguin Books Ltd.: Eugenio Montale, "The
Eel," from *The Penguin Book of Italian
Verse*, edited and translated by George M.
Kay, © George Kay, 1958, 1965 (pp. 404–
405), and a section of François Rabelais, *Gar-
gantua and Pantagruel*, translated by J. M.
Cohen, © J. M. Cohen, 1955 (pp. 509–510).

Library of Congress Cataloging in Publication Data
will be found on the last printed page of this book

Printed in the United States of America
by Princeton University Press
Princeton, New Jersey

TO

STEPHANIE

LOOKE HOW THE CROWNE . . .
(VI.x.13)

CONTENTS

IV. THE CONJUGATION OF THE WORLD

V. THE WORD OF GOD AND THE WORDS OF MEN

VI. IN DAEMOGORGON'S HALL: THE FORMING-POWER OF A RENAISSANCE IMAGINATION

PREFACE

The following study attempts to offer a critically unified commentary on *The Faerie Queene*. The distinguishing quality of Spenser's major poem is, quite simply, its manifold capacity, and observations on the poem may be sorted according to which element of this capacity is emphasized: the element that unifies and assimilates, or the one that diversifies and accommodates. On the one hand, we can study the poem's apt consecution of episodes, the repetitions in its imagery, the detailed correspondence of symbol and motif, and the overall concordance of theme. On the other hand, we can study the poem in terms of its mythopoeia, its continuous invention, and its vast creative speciation—that is, under the several heads of its imagination. The first emphasis will insure an exposition of the poem according to that analogical coherence that obtains over any congregation of vaguely homologous forms considered as a whole. The presiding deity here is Pan, the god of shepherds, but also the god of totalities—his more catholic functions are frequently recognized in the allegory of *The Shepheardes Calender*. The champion of the unity of *The Faerie Queene* naturally calls upon the poet's intention, expressed in the encyclopedic educational program that Spenser devised to contain his fable. The fable itself, however, often seems doomed to remain comparatively indeterminate— "By succession made perpetual," as the poet himself says, speaking of natural forms, but also of the life of the genus. This generativity—or copiousness—is the entering wedge for the other emphasis, upon the poem's virtuosity, and the conspicuous heterogeneity of its matter. Even the poem's allegoricalness is partly a function of the existence of internal *differentia per se*: the telling substitution that we call the "allegorical interpolant," the sign that gives the allegory away, also signals the poem's calculated foreignness to itself. The deliberate alienation of the fiction from the argument, characteristic of all allegory, produces a kind of *heterosis*: an increased vigor and capacity for growth resulting from cross-breeding. The manifold character of the poem is also owed to the "poetic theology" peculiar to romance, which we call "polydaemonism"; there is a broken analogy between polydaemonism and multi-fictionality. Finally, the capacity of the poem is an attribute of its *resourcefulness*. *The Faerie Queene* is our most re-sourceful poem, in its re-creation of a source in a way that seems to illustrate those nuances or details that belong to the allegorical or interpretive future of that source. In many senses, then, the poem is a House of Proteus, the return from which figures heavily at the end of Spenser's fourth book. Proteus symbolizes for Spenser that "euer-lasting store" of matter on which the world draws for its re-creation; the shepherd of the seas is an elemental, prolific nature. However, the first of Spenser's nature symbols was not Proteus, but Pan, who is also matter (as Silvanus, or *silva*), but matter in its universal aspect. And though Proteus is not Pan, and never takes a definitive total form, his manifestations may still issue in an apotheosis of formity. Thus the two emphases—the one on a universal spirit of comprehension, and the other on a deeply resourceful and sometimes perplexing spirit of variegation—are not exclusive: on the contrary.

The aphorism that I have taken from Pico della Mirandola for an epigraph warns that the one pole cannot exist without the other: "He who cannot attract Pan, approaches Proteus or Nature in vain."[1] A "canonic" impulse may inform a "variorum" appetite; the heterogeneous may seek its rationalization in the homologous; every plurality harbors an honorary totality. We might even go on to paraphrase Pico to mean, "He who has not conceived of an overall criticism of *The Faerie Queene* will be unable to generate and sustain a fully coherent commentary on it."

This work began as a study of the "unity of design" in *The Faerie Queene*. I was attracted to my topic by Pan, and I hoped to attract Pan to my topic. With the passing of time, I became aware that I was approaching Proteus as well. Nonetheless, I have preserved a principle feature of my original scheme, the study of Spenser's poem under the aegis of three "greater analogies," derived from comparisons between the "private" virtues of the poet's first three books and the "public" virtues of his second three. I still maintain that, among the endless harmonies of theme, fiction, and symbol evinced by the poem, there exists a demonstrable apposition of the two installments themselves; the structure of this apposition corresponds to the structure of my commentary.

The first chapter of this book treats the plan and organization of Spenser's poem. The second chapter begins with an account of the formal theory of allegory, and then studies Book I, which, because of the dominant biblical analogy, obtains a status somewhat independent of the poem as a whole—the Bible's title defines it as *sui generis*. The third chapter is a study of Books II and V, hinged upon the median essay, called "The Analogy of Good Order." The fourth chapter studies the massed center of the poem, Books III and IV: in a way, Book IV replenishes Book III,

---

[1] The first of Pico's Orphic Conclusions, in *Op. om.* (Basel, 1572–1573), p. 106; see Edgar Wind, *Pagan Mysteries in the Renaissance*, rev. edn. (reprint, New York, 1968), p. 191. For Pan as Nature, see below, Chap. II, n. 296; for the Orphic Proteus, see Chap. IV, n. 400 and text.

and their relation is studied formally in the essay on "The Analogy of Natural Plenitude." The book concludes with a study of Book VI, especially as it looks back to Book I—"The Analogy of Sufficient Grace"—and as it looks forward to the completion of the poem—"The Quest for the Faerie Queene." Two epilogia follow, under the general rubric "In Daemogorgon's Hall." These retrospective essays recur to the Mutabilitie cantos and the general theory of allegory, which are otherwise treated at the end of the first chapter and the beginning of the second, respectively. As their title indicates, these pieces comprise the book's "Chaos," the name sometimes given to a miscellaneous appendix at the end of a Renaissance encyclopedia.

Overall, my plan hopes to suggest the way in which Spenser's poem is gradually shaped by an analogy of inner and outer government, between the legends of temperance and justice; an analogy of sexual and social love, between the legends of chastity and friendship; and an analogy of theological and human grace, between the legends of holiness and courtesy. These are the poem's basic canons of coherence, or perhaps *analogies* of coherence. Near the end of Book VI we meet the poet Colin Clout, who has created a triple pattern of two concentric rings around a focal point occupied by his mistress. Mythography tells us that she stands in place of the goddess of love. Venus is also at the center of *The Faerie Queene*, and it appears that Spenser has created a similar pattern for *his* mistress, that is, for the poem itself.

My plan imposes upon the reader an obvious interruption of the *seriatim* order of the poem; Book V is studied immediately after Book II, and before any treatment of Books III and IV. Of the three analogies, it is the one between Books II and V that we are likely to discover first; only then do we recur to Books III and IV to see if the same pattern is at work there. If it is, we will be predisposed to find in Book VI analogies with Book I. Thus my order does represent the actual process of recognition, despite the obvious violence done to the sequence of development, and especially to the progressive education of the gentleman as I will be describing it. Many commentaries have already taken the path of the physical traveler, who assumes that because he is always facing forward he must also always be traveling in the same direction. This perception must submit to the correction of the mental traveler, who at some point parts company with his fellow to see the poem coming back against itself.

My scheme for Spenser's poem can help account for the experience of teachers who find that the first three books afford richer material than the second three. The earlier books are especially enriched by their declared relations to Scripture, to classic epic, and to the Italian *romanzi*. To a lesser extent, the later books also benefit from this external reference, but there much of the place of such allusion is taken by the developing internal relation between the two installments. Thus emerges the nice paradox that while the private virtues seek and institute relations with antecedents that are a prior public possession, the public virtues show an opposite and compensating movement of the poem back into itself—that is, into its private first half. If the private virtues of the first three books became "public" upon the publication of the first installment, then perhaps the public virtues of the second three books may have become "private" while Spenser constructed the second installment upon the convenient analogy of the first. Such a thesis makes the poem not only a revelation to the reader, but also to itself.

Early in my studies I became reconciled to the fact that this idea was not wholly susceptible of scientific verification. In the humanities the unrepeatable experiment may have as much to contribute as the repeatable one; results that everyone else would have gotten seem to have severe limits imposed upon their suggestibility. Comparative study, however, can hope to ensure that such results are not *merely* fantastic.

From the consideration of design, I sought to retrace my steps back into the poem, and into the poems out of which it was made, to find those connexities inherent in the poem's matter that seem to be determining its form. Thus what began as a *criticism* of the poem, in the sense of an analysis of its ostensible total form, evolved into a *commentary*, a divulging of the form's hidden allegorical content.

A note concerning the critical inheritance represented by my commentary: the founding father is the author (or text) known as Longinus. This author was particularly sensitive to the collapse of the poetic subject into the poetic object, that is, to the way in which the state of consciousness required to produce or experience a poem might usurp or arrogate to itself the place of the poem's theme. Spenser checks this process and, simultaneously, authorizes and augments it, by frequently co-opting allegorical theory for his actual practice in creating allegories. His poem becomes a true phenomenology of allegory, a treatise on the manifestations of allegory that is itself yet a further manifestation. The "curious" or provocative imagery of Book II provides an example of this compounding. In a legend of temperance, the stimulus of the imagery is quite properly tempered by rationalization. And yet this process is precisely what makes allegorical imagery so curious in the first place—and what makes the curious so potentially allegorical. Again, consider the heavenly sign Virgo, created by the retreat of Astraea, at the opening of the legend of justice. Virgo is a decidedly *allegorical* sign, because it was once something else. It is an image that has been displaced into, or superseded by, an abstraction. Or, it is an image of justice that has been canonized by being assumed into its own Platonic heaven of forms. For a completely different kind of example, one might consider how Spenser's protagonists become allegorical of *each other*. In the legend of friendship this is part of the goal: friends try to reach a "likeness" (German *Gleichnis*, "allegory") of their *alter* selves.

Everyone will be able to supply examples of "the poem about the poem within the poem," but an insistent reading of the text in this way will also yield a more general perception: the equation of the poem's more prominent internal agents with the various mental operators implied by the mere existence of the text. One oblique acknowledgment of this equation will suffice to illustrate it. Generally, Arthur seeks the fairy queen, but in a fine episode in Book II he takes time out to read a history book. In the most notable stanza here (II.x.68), the text suddenly offers to align Arthur's baffled search with the goal of "th'Authour selfe," who presumably wanted at some point to complete his project. In many senses the "Infant" is an unfinished man, and his "author" abruptly breaks off, as if he "could not at least attend / To finish it." So Arthur remains arrested at the penultimate subject of the history, which happens to be the reign of Arthur's progenitor. The father is Arthur's "author" in yet another sense: his name is *Uther*, called Pendragon. Meanwhile, in a parallel activity, Arthur's fellow Guyon is reading the faerie archives. They begin from the fore-thinker Prometheus, who originally formed "A man, of many parts" (II.x.70); this is yet another way of conceiving Arthur. As such an example indicates, the poem regularly comments on its own mode of being. My commentary merely hopes to amplify this already far-advanced thematizing of the poem's self-apperception.

This is perhaps the place to observe, contrary to what Hazlitt maintained,[2] that the allegory *will* bite you if you ignore it—the comparison is apparently to the Blatant Beast. Nor can I offer an obvious sop for this particular Cerberus, apart from an effort of comprehension: as with the Beast, the problem is really whether or not one wants to be bitten from behind. For example: a character in Book VI roams through the greenwood in search of his lost ladylove, whose name is Serena. Sooner or later it will strike us that the knight's restless pursuit is determined by a quest for serenity. The absent Serena thus takes on a numinous, nostalgic, and problematic quality that she would not otherwise have had. Calepine—

[2] In the *Lectures on the English Poets* (1818), William Hazlitt writes that ". . . some people will say . . . that they cannot understand it [Spenser's poem] on account of the allegory. They are afraid of the allegory, as if they thought it would bite them: they look at it as a child looks at a painted dragon, and think it will strangle them in its shining folds. This is very idle. If they do not meddle with the allegory, the allegory will not meddle with them." But the allegory in Book I becomes a "painted dragon"—or naive—only when innocence has been recovered, double meanings resolved, truth made whole, errors disentangled, and the world made safe for children —i.e., safe from dragons. See below, Chap. II, "The Siege of Paradise," sec. iii.

the name of the knight—suggests a Greek word, *chalepōs*, for "sore, grievous, afflicted," or simply "difficult"; as a result, Calepine's troubled mind
also attaches itself to an allegorical rationale (a kind of ironic decorum),
which in fact his proneness to being found in difficult situations already
badly wants. Whatever Calepine's frequent distress loses in immediacy
because of such qualification, it gains in perspective. The allegorical vision
is a "mediated vision," and, being enveiled, it is also a "mystery." Even
in Book VI, where the mystery seems to be well on its way to evaporating,
the cynosures and cells and retreats in the imagery continue to suggest
that Spenser's poem is intended for those willing to pause and reflect. In
part, this means reflecting on the nature of a sign, which is a sign precisely insofar as it is liable to interpretation, and even, we might hazard,
to misconstruction.

"The Learneds taske," as Spenser calls the office of the poet, is often for
scholars merely the grateful task of deferring to the superior learning of
others. Many studies before the present book have treated Spenser's poem
as a whole, and just as many more have plunged into the imagination of
its parts. To the better known of these studies I owe much of my larger
sense of what might be the aims of mine. At the outset, I would like to
draw attention to the essay of Northrop Frye, "The Structure of Imagery
in *The Faerie Queene*,"[3] from which my work took its beginning, and to
which I owe my greatest single debt. Scarcely less influential have been
the abundant references to Spenser's genre and symbolism in the same
author's *Anatomy of Criticism*. Further, Professor Frye was the director
for the Toronto dissertation upon which my book is based. I dare not
match my pipe with Tityrus his style, but I have followed him far off,
and his high steps adore.

Secondly, I wish to recognize here my indebtedness to Erik Erikson's
Freudian interpretation of character strengths and his theory of their
psychogenesis. I have appropriated both his concepts and his phraseology
for my argument about the sequence or development represented in Spenser's series of "legendary" virtues.

Equally important has been Edgar Wind's interpretation of pagan mysteries, his studies in their philosophy and iconography amplifying the
methods and results of Erwin Panofsky. Spenser has rather more than
his share of these mysteries, and the reader who lacks the will to investigate them may be a Spenserian by nature, but not, I think, by art. On the
first page of the poem we meet Una mounted on her ass; among other

[3] *University of Toronto Quarterly*, 30 (1961), pp. 109–127; reprinted in *Fables of
Identity: Studies in Poetic Mythology* (New York, 1963), pp. 69–87.

things this ass is an *onōs agon mysteria*, an ass bearing mysteries, and so the reader is given fair warning from the start.[4]

I would like to record my debts to contemporary Spenserians. Almost all owe something to the pioneering interpretations of C. S. Lewis, in *The Allegory of Love*. Beyond Lewis, I have felt particularly close to John Hankins' 1945 article on Spenser and Revelation, reprinted in his *Source and Meaning*; to Thomas Roche's *Kindly Flame*, on almost every aspect of Books III and IV; to A. Bartlett Giamatti, in *The Earthly Paradise in the Renaissance Epic*, and in his study, "Proteus Unbound: Some Versions of the Sea-God in the Renaissance"; to Harry Berger, Jr., in his essays on Book I and on Book VI; to Rosemond Tuve, on the medieval virtues tradition, in her *Allegorical Imagery*; to A. C. Hamilton, in his *Structure of Allegory in "The Faerie Queene,"* on many points, and especially classical wrath in Book II; and to Paul Alpers, in *The Poetry of "The Faerie Queene,"* on Ariosto, and on the analogizing of the reader to the subject of the text. Important links in my various arguments are also found in William Blisset's essay on the significance of Mutabilitie, in articles by John Steadman, and in Alastair Fowler's article on temperance symbolism in Book II, and his remarks on the center of Book V in his *Spenser and the Numbers of Time*. My work on the seminal reasons in the Garden of Adonis begins from Robert Ellrodt and William Nelson, and is anticipated and in part duplicated in John Hankins' book.

To Professors Hamilton and Alpers I also owe extraordinarily circumstantial reports of their readings of my manuscript. These reports have been very influential in the form finally taken by my work, and they have spared me many errors. In two cases I have had to choose between divided counsels: in one, I have continued to organize my book as a formally *conjugated* critique; in the other, I have allowed it to become an *extended* commentary—often extended beyond Spenser into the Renaissance. To find the concord of this discord, Pan and Proteus needs must agree to disagree.

Three books published since my thesis was written (in 1969) corroborated many of its ideas: Jane Aptekar's *Icons of Justice* (New York, 1969), Douglas Waters' *Duessa* (Missouri, 1972), and John Hankins' *Source and Meaning* (Oxford, 1972). I have been greatly encouraged by these remarkable studies, and in some places they have prompted me to make a further point of my own, with the aid of their rich citations. To a lesser extent perhaps, I have also overlapped with Michael Murrin's *Veil of*

---

[4] See Chap. II, nn. 146, 300, and 458, and cf. Hazlitt, in *Lectures on the English Poets*, rebuking Southey's description of Spenser as "High priest of all the Muses' mysteries": "On the contrary, no one was more apt to pry into mysteries which do not strictly belong to the Muses."

Allegory (Chicago, 1969), and Angus Fletcher's *Prophetic Moment* (Chicago, 1971). Humphrey Tonkin's study of Book VI, *Spenser's Courteous Pastoral* (Oxford, 1972), did not come to my attention until after the text of the present book was fixed, but it appears to agree with many of the conclusions drawn in my fifth chapter.

This book began with a project on literary Biblism, from which the present topic, quite early on, insisted on separating itself; this was in 1965, two years after the publication of William Nelson's *The Poetry of Edmund Spenser*—the study freshest in my mind as I began this one. My research was largely done during the three-year period that I was a member of the Society of Fellows at Harvard University, under the chairmanships of Harry Levin and Wassily Leontief. The publisher accepted the book in 1972; my revisions added two more years to the work. It is inevitable that this kind of study, prepared over six years of gainful employment, contains scholarly results that I am no longer the first to report. I have been chary of eliminating these where they answer to requirements of my larger argument.

Among my colleagues, my greatest debt is to Stephen Barney, whose ideas and suggestions turn up often in the following pages. Dr. Barney has read and commented on many parts of my study in a very fruitful way, has graciously allowed me to read his essays on Book I and Books III and IV, has generously lent me a chapter title for one of my essays, and has moreover done research for me in the British Museum that I was unable to do myself. I will only add here that I have found his friendship as valuable as his scholarship.

I would also like to thank my colleague Fred Nichols, for many ideas about Renaissance subjects and sources from his remarkable fund of knowledge and learning.

Next I would mention my debt to Susan Hagan, for one summer my dedicated research assistant, and a true Anamnestes to my Eumnestes. And my especial thanks to Prassede Calabi, who has checked many of my references and citations.

For readings and comments on drafts and versions, I would like to thank Northrop Frye, Douglas Bush, David Kalstone, Hershel Baker, William Blisset, Michael Holahan, René Graziani, H. MacCallum, W. McLeod, Mrs. A. Patterson, and Robert Kellogg; and likewise my students Richard Drake, David Quint, and Mrs. Patricia Parker; and for the opportunity to read pre-publication work on topics related to mine, I wish to thank Dr. Hamilton, Mr. Quint, Mrs. Parker, Mrs. Carol Schreier Rupprecht, Dr. Holahan, and Eric Rosenberg. I have profited greatly from the work of students in Yale College, and I have not hesitated to adopt many of their perceptions into my text where they supported an argument. Besides Mr. Rosenberg, I am sensible of particular debts to work by Richard Beubien, Suzanne Wofford, Donald Bivens, Erroll Mc-Donald, John Chasnoff, Walter Stiller, Willie Signal, Joseph Weiss, Robert Watson, Michael Salzman, and, more recently, Joyce Van Dyke.

For translations and help with translations, I wish to thank Professor Traugott Lawler, Dr. Nichols, David Quint, Susan Hagan, and Mr. Alan Cooper.

For many courtesies and much forebearance, my thanks to the staffs of the various libraries of Harvard and Yale.

For preparation of the manuscript, I would like to thank the secretarial staff of the Yale English Department, under Mrs. Dottie Nelson: Grace Michele, Wanda Fiack, and especially Gale Pollen and Linna Smelzer. And I would like to thank Mrs. Suzanne Burbank, my typist and friend over many years; she has typed much of my work more than once, and all of the notes for both the thesis and the book.

My thanks to the A. Whitney Griswold Fund at Yale, for a grant that helped defray some of the expense of preparing and checking the final manuscript.

I owe particular debts of thanks to the editors of Princeton University Press: to Joanna Hitchcock, for her courtesy and encouragement, from the Press's first response through publication; and to Connie Martin, for her dedicated copy-editing of the typescript. Only they can guess how much they have contributed.

Deep in the background of the present study is the late A.S.P. Wood-house, the chairman of the English Department when I first undertook graduate work at the University of Toronto. It was Professor Woodhouse who willed to Spenser studies the distinction between the order of nature and the order of grace, in a published lecture on *The Faerie Queene* that shortly became a classic in the field.[5] I have disposed of this famous patrimony rather freely here, with a boldness befitting one who claims to be an heir, rather than a mere trustee. My debt is not merely intellectual, however. Professor Woodhouse was personally very generous toward beginners: he found the support for their studies, and expressed his confidence in them when and where it mattered.

Finally, my thanks to my friends among my colleagues, my students, and my three families, for their advice, encouragement, and long-sufference. My father-in-law, Professor Harold Lamport, has not lived to see

[5] "Nature and Grace in *The Faerie Queene*," ELH, 16 (1949), pp. 194–228; reprinted in Paul Alpers, ed., *Elizabethan Poetry: Modern Essays in Criticism* (Oxford, 1967), pp. 345–379. See Chap. I, n. 187, below.

publication, but he followed the progress of the manuscript with un-dimmed enthusiasm from start to finish, and I am sorry to be unable to present him with the first copy of the book.

Leading up to a study like this one there is always a long trail of prede-cessors, scholars, teachers, sponsors, peers, students, and assistants. These eudoxi and willing helpers have occupied their salient positions all along the way, from the Interpreter's House to the Delectable Mountains; they should recognize themselves in whatever of the following may claim merit or distinction. I hardly need add that they bear no responsibility for the parts that are foolish, obscure, distracted, or in error: these are wholly mine.

We are told that there is no such thing as a finished book: rather, there are only abandoned ones. I owe it almost entirely to my wife that I have been able to abandon my "analogy" at what I believe to be the right time. Works of scholarship are not ultimately justified by faith, but I know that the spouse of one who aspires to write such a thing often must be. I have relied upon my wife's patience and devotion throughout, and I am thinking fondly of her now.

J. C. N.

ABBREVIATIONS

Titles of books of the Bible are abbreviated wherever possible. Classical titles are often abbreviated; forms are generally longer than those listed in Liddell and Scott, eds., *Greek-English Lexicon*, rev. Jones and McKenzie (Oxford, 1968), "Authors and Works," pp. xvi–xxxviii, and in Lewis and Short, *A Latin Dictionary* (Oxford, 1958), "Abbreviations," pp. vii–xi; their lists may be consulted for full titles. Titles of patristic works are also abbreviated, according to the pattern of patrological scholarship and works like Emile Mâle's *Religious Art in France of the Thirteenth Century*. Standard abbreviations, often of parts of titles, include *Comm.* (Commentarius, Commentarium), *Epist.* (Epistola, -ae), *Evang.* (Evangelium), *Frg.* (Fragmentum, -a), *Expos.* (Expositio), *Hom.* (Homilium, -ii), *Op. om.* (Opera omnia), *Sat.* (Satura, Satira, -ae), and *Tract.* (Tractatus, -es). In addition to titles like Virgil's *Aeneid* (*Aen.*) and Ovid's *Metamorphoses* (*Metam.*), I regularly shorten Aquinas, *Summa Theologica* (*Summa Theol.*), Boccaccio, *Genealogia Deorum Gentilium* (*G.D.G.*), Gregorius Lilius Giraldus, *Historiam de Deis Gentium* (*Hist. Deorum*), Natalis Comes, *Mythologiae* (*Mythol.*), and the following post-classical poetic texts:

Inferno, Purgatorio (Dante): *Inf., Purg.*

Canzonieri (Petrarch): *Canz.*

Orlando Innamorato (Boiardo): *Orl. Inn.*

Stanze per la Giostra (Politian): *Stanze*

Orlando Furioso (Ariosto): *O.F.*

Gerusalemne Liberata (Tasso): *Ger. Lib.*

The Faerie Queene (Spenser): *F.Q.*

Paradise Lost, Paradise Regained (Milton): *Par. Lost, Par. Reg.*

The titles of Shakespeare's plays are occasionally reduced to their initials. *Son.* is used for Sonnet. Other abbreviations include:

ANF: *The Ante-Nicene Fathers: Translation of the Writings of the Fathers down to A.D. 325.* Ed. Reverend Alexander Roberts and James Donaldson. American reprint of the Edinburgh edn. Revised by A. Cleveland Coxe. 10 vols. New York, 1899.

EETS: Editions of the Early English Text Society.

Loeb: Alternately, Loeb edn. Editions of the Loeb Classical Library, texts and translations of Greek and Latin authors.

NPNF: 1st Series: *A Select Library of the Nicene and Post-Nicene Fathers of the Christian Church*. Ed. Philip Schaff. 14 vols. Buffalo, New York, 1886–1890.

2nd Series: *A Select Library of the Nicene and Post-Nicene Fathers of the Christian Church*, A New Series. Ed. Philip Schaff and Henry Wace. 14 vols. (vols. 2–14: "second series"). New York, 1890–1900.

PG: *Patrologiae Cursus Completus . . . Series Graeca*. Ed. Jacques Paul Migne. 161 vols. in 166. Paris, 1857–1866.

PL: *Patrologiae Cursus Completus . . . Series [Latina]*. Ed. Migne. 217 vols.; vols. 218–221, Indices. Paris, 1844–1865.

NOTE

QUOTATIONS from Spenser's poems and E. K.'s apparatus to *The Shepheardes Calender* are from *The Poetical Works of Edmund Spenser*, ed. J. C. Smith and E. de Selincourt, Oxford Standard Authors (reprint New York, 1963). Spenser's *Vewe of the Present State of Ireland* is quoted and cited according to the text in Rudolf Gottfried, ed., *Spenser's Prose Works*, vol. 10 of *The Works of Edmund Spenser: A Variorum Edition*, ed. Edwin Greenlaw, Charles Grosvenor Osgood, Frederick Morgan Padelford, and Ray Heffner, in 10 vols. (Baltimore, 1932–1949). It has not been thought necessary to cite editions for texts of many standard authors (e.g., Dante, Petrarch, Boiardo, Ariosto, Tasso, Milton); the form of citation for their poems has been regularly condensed in imitation of standard forms for classical texts. Many classical texts are also cited without reference to specific editions. Line numbers for Shakespeare texts have been supplied from Marvin Spevack, *Harvard Concordance to Shakespeare* (Cambridge, Mass., 1973), which is keyed to G. M. Evans, gen. ed., *The Riverside Shakespeare* (Cambridge, Mass., 1974); the texts themselves are quoted from a variety of editions. Milton's prose, when the text is modernized, is quoted from Merritt Y. Hughes, ed., *Complete Poems and Major Prose* (New York, 1967). Chaucer texts and numbers are from F. N. Robinson's edn. of the *Complete Works* (Boston, 1933). Translations, except of brief passages, are acknowledged where they are the published work of others; exceptions are quotes from the series of the Ante-Nicene, Nicene, and Post-Nicene Fathers, and the Library of the Fathers; and from the *Summa Theologica* of St. Thomas Aquinas.

THE
ANALOGY OF
*THE FAERIE
QUEENE*

I

THE ONE AND THE MANY

... the art of composing a poem is like the nature of the universe, which is composed of contraries, such as appear in the law of music, for if there were no multiplicity there would be no whole, and no law, as Plotinus says.

(Tasso, *Discourses on the Heroic Poem*, III, *Prose*, ed. Mazzali, p. 589)

"Enough of buccaneers, and viceroys, and kings," cried out Cnemon, impatiently; "your discourse is wandering from the point I aim at. This episode has nothing to do with the main plot; come back to the performance of your promise; you are like the Pharian Proteus; not turning indeed into false and fleeting shapes, but trying to slip away from me."

(Heliodorus, *Ethiopica*, II, trans. Reverend Rowland Smith, *The Greek Romances*, p. 50)

For considering those who want to attain many things with regard to a single piece of writing, who can bring it to pass? His discourse not inapposite, not ill-matched; not departing from itself, inconstant to what it would be; not awkward, not barely coherent; yet retaining its polish—indeed, its ardor; on the one hand ornate; on the other, negligent (which, as in a woman with a face not made up, is on occasion more pleasing: so in a writer); and six hundred other variations besides, and the many qualities which are comprehended by the different kinds of writing? And in fact it seems to me that the oldest of Poets was feigned to be Proteus, when they say that he became now water, now fire, now a beast. They did not reckon him not to be single because he was able to become these things, but rather on this account, because they did not see how things of diverse feature, among themselves otherwise various, were so aptly joined.

(Peter Bembo, *Of Imitation*, to Giovanni Francesco Pico, in Pico della Mirandola, *Opera Omnia*, Basil, 1572–1573, pp. 194f.)

3

From Epic to Romance

[i]

THE formal epic takes precedence over other literary kinds naturally. When it is successful, it becomes the privileged and summary testament of a people and their epoch. To be an epic, a narrative poem must satisfy two basic requirements: it must contain the concept of a total action,[1] and it must possess a nearly determinative relation to a culture. Helen says that the things that happened to her happened because she and Paris were destined to become a song for ages to come.[2] It is a singularly vain and complacent thing to say, perhaps, but she is doubtless right in thinking that being the subject of song and story is second nature to her. Alkinoos says the same thing about the fall of Troy, in the *Odyssey*;[3] and so whatever Helen may mean, the bard means that the events of the Homeric epos, in the mind of his culture, are indistinguishable from the poem about them. In the epic, the fall of Troy is destined to be; in the culture that produced the epic, the poem itself seemed equally destined to be. Such an epic is one of the things that a culture intends.

Being culturally specific, the epic may become prescriptive, on matters ranging from mythology to etiquette. In this respect, the matter of epic, which is culturally homogenous and even monolithic and aggressive, differs from the matter of romance, which is basically more ecumenical. Many romances can be decomposed into folktale motifs; these have great combining powers, and they pass easily from one culture to another.[4] In themselves, romance fictions are not, unlike such potentially epic matter

---

[1] The phrase "total action" is taken from Northrop Frye, *The Return of Eden: Five Essays on Milton's Epics* (Toronto, 1965), p. 14, and the same author's *Anatomy of Criticism* (Princeton, 1957), pp. 318f. Many of my ideas about unity and multiplicity in the long poem of the Renaissance have been suggested by an article by D. S. Carne-Ross, "The One and the Many: A Reading of *Orlando Furioso*, Cantos 1 and 8," in *Arion*, 5 (1966), pp. 195-234; I have borrowed my chapter title from this piece.

[2] *Iliad* VI.357f.

[3] *Od.* VIII.579f. Penelope-like, the gods *wove* this catastrophe.

[4] For this idea, see Northrop Frye, *The Critical Path* (Bloomington and London, 1971), pp. 34f., and his "Myth, Fiction, and Displacement," in *Fables of Identity* (New York, 1963), pp. 30-32. Romances of course become expressions of social values and attitudes, though especially ideals that can be expressed in the form of wish-fulfillments. The interest of romance in a stylized code of manners might be classified as novelistic in tendency, but even the institution of chivalry, so important in medieval examples, seems nearly pre-societal: an institution in lieu of one, so to speak. Romance differs from epic above all regarding the machinery of necessity: when compared to epic, romance is always a myth of personal freedom.

5

as patriarchal and military saga, tied to the institutions of a particular people or culture. This tie and its maintenance form a typical epic subject, particularly in those epics where the fable entails the extension or relocation of a cultural domain. The exodus, the *translatio imperii*, the succession of dynasties, and the crusade are all epic matters that suggest a unifying cultural bias that could bend an entire work to its will. The romance is more universally periegetic, especially where it treats themes of exile and pilgrimage: the very vagabondage of its avatars implies a kind of release from the traumatic experience of a mass translation of rootedness or domain. Thus the first thing for us to notice about the Arthurian romances is the extraordinary development that they underwent "abroad," in France. Likewise, the Charlemagne romances—supposedly the "matter of France" —became widely diffused in Italy. Paradoxically and conversely, one of the *romanzi* of the Italian Renaissance achieved an authority among its international readership in some ways comparable to that of epic, even though its form lay outside of the specific epic requirements that the Renaissance believed Aristotle to have prescribed. Ariosto's *Orlando Furioso* was a work that contained enough recognizable epic quotation to suggest a re-creative use of classical predecessors, like the use that Virgil made of Homer; and it broached enough allegories to suggest an epic poet's intention to educate his audience through exemplary types of action. At the same time, it was romantic enough to become popular and translatable.

But did Ariosto's poem possess that sense of a "total action" of which we have just spoken? This question haunts the second essay of Torquato Tasso's three *Discourses on the Art of Poetry*,[5] where Tasso maintains that the fable of the heroic poem should possess integrity, magnitude, and unity.[6] From Tasso's indications we might derive the idea that the epic poem is a specific kind of monumental organization imposed upon an undifferentiated body of popular or received narrative, and this idea seems essentially correct. Aristotle himself describes the epic both as a nuclear story lengthened out by episodes, and as "a poem made up of many actions."[7] The contents of the greater store are accounts of strife and tales of adventure. In terms suggested by the first Renaissance commentary on the *Poetics*—that of Robortelli—the emphasis in epic construction falls not on the seriatim *taxis* of pure storytelling, but on the comprehensive

---

[5] There are two series of *discorsi* on the heroic poem by Tasso. The first set (first published in Venice in 1587) contains three essays; the second set (1594), called *Discourses on the Heroic Poem*, is in six books. My text for both is *Prose*, ed. Ettore Mazzali, Storia e Testi, 22 (Milan, 1959), pp. 349–410, 487–729.

[6] *Prose*, ed. Mazzali, p. 362.

[7] *Poetics* xxiii (1459a); xxvi (1462a); also xxiv (1459b).

thesis of a wrath or a quest;[8] these are the theses of the strife-subject and the adventure-subject respectively. In marshaling such a narrative, the poet "hurries to the crisis," that is, to an advanced point in the story taken as a whole, and then brings us up to date at his leisure.[9] The narrative already has some larger form of its own, which, insofar as it is suitable for epic treatment, is the total action. The epic treats the part of the total action that has the greatest implications for the whole.[10] By a kind of law the remainder of the greater saga, out of which the epic treatment is differentiated, almost inevitably becomes the subject for romance. The Joseph romance in the Bible develops to connect the Patriarchal saga to the Exodus-Conquest epos. The *Odyssey* seems to develop in the aftermath of the *Iliad*, the cyclic epics develop to occupy the space not taken up by the Homeric *massif*, and subsequently Darys and Dictys and the *roman de Troie* tradition attach themselves to the narrative as a whole. Similarly, *The Song of Roland* is "epic" in our terms, being linked to feudal institutions like the crusades, and concerned with a critical portion of the collective epos of the wars of Charlemagne. The prior adventures of the peers of Charlemagne become the kind of exploit vouched for by the good Bishop Turpin, who has about the same authority as Dares.

The epic must begin late in the total action if it is to limit its possible expansion. It moves *in medias res* with respect to the larger story pattern, and uses a decisive, proleptic, or representative episode to focus the epos as a whole—its reach exceeds its grasp. When the epic is conceived historically, an extended cycle of history passes through the nuclear episode and takes some of its ultimate shape from it. Some epics therefore develop a sophisticated kind of etiological tale, that is, a fiction explaining "how it came to be." Virgil's Aeneas, for example, puts his Roman destiny before a Carthaginian amour, causing the rejected lady to curse his descendants, and thus engenders the Punic Wars. Milton's Adam chooses to go along with Eve, and the English people, with a large inheritance of original sin, consent to the Restoration. Both examples illustrate the subordination of a tale to a thesis.

Unlike the *Aeneid* and *Paradise Lost*, the primary epic is organized fictionally, often around strife. (The "books" of the literary epic show a movement away from pure storytelling, toward a more thematic organi-

---

[8] My source is Baxter Hathaway, *The Age of Criticism: The Late Renaissance in Italy* (Ithaca, N.Y., 1962), pp. 169f., which cites Robortelli's *De Arte poetica explicationes* (1548), p. 268, with reference to the "predicaments" of Aristotle.

[9] Horace, *De Arte Poetica* (*Epist. ad Piso*) 148f.: "semper ad eventum festinat et in medias res/non secus ac notas . . ." (he always hastens on to the event; and he carries off his listener into the midst of things, not otherwise than as if it were known); and Frye, *Return of Eden*, p. 14.

[10] Frye, *Return of Eden*, p. 140.

zation.) The action of the primary epic has its germ in the retailing of a heroic "geste," or exploit. The geste often involves a foray into foreign or hostile territory, and the earlier epic often has a somewhat nomadic character. (The later epic is more likely to suggest a theme of colonization.) War song, ballad, lay, saga, and *chanson de geste* are all logically prior to the epic construction, but the stock-in-trade of the singer of tales is retained in the larger form. The recital still includes tales of exile, foreign service, local courts, war parties, border raids, raids for plunder, heroic last stands, feats of arms, blood feuds, and family revenge. Such a "matter" implies a continuously unsettled social order; it is not surprising that its historical origins are said to be the "wars of migration" involved in the larger movement of peoples.[11] The heroic construction is put on this material—which we may now call the strife-epos—when the protagonists are imagined as greater beings than we are, and when the epos is treated as part of a heroic age by a succeeding culture.

Apart from the mere notion of prowess, the organizing ideas of the strife-epos are offense and reprisal. They provide the negative basis for the heroic code. The positive basis is found in rules of heroic deference and demeanor, or heroic communal obligation. Heroic giving is a particularly rich source of motifs; it includes generosity and restitution, and even the yielding to superior force on the battlefield, or yielding to old age. The institutions of later epic are noticeably different; they are first of all more clearly institutional. The total action, likewise, becomes a more universal history. The emphasis in characterization moves from the individual hero to the office of heroism, and the clan or *comitatus* or patriarchal allegiance is replaced by an affirmation of the social contract. The theses of literary epic are nation-founding; the establishment of peoplehood, national boundaries, and the national faith; and the manifestation of national destinies.[12] An important subsidiary theme is epic reconnaissance, often the expression of the expansionary ideal of a new dynasty. Adam's survey of the whole fallen world at the end of *Paradise Lost* is an ironic example, with distinguished precedents in Camoëns and the Pentateuch.[13] The sources of the strife-epos are conflicts over possessions or territories, or dynastic struggles. There is also a more diffuse potential for conflict in the migration of peoples. The sources of epic characterization are thus located in concepts of heroic leadership: military, dynastic, or colonial.

The divine world in the epic takes on configurations similar to those in the human world. The *Iliad*, for example, begins with a social break-

---

[11] Arnold Toynbee, *A Study of History* (Oxford, 1963), vol. 8, *Heroic Ages*, pp. 1–87 with appendix. See also H. M. Chadwick, *The Heroic Age* (Cambridge, 1912).

[12] Frye, *Anatomy of Criticism*, p. 58.

[13] *Os Lusiadas*, cantos ix–x, with *Par. Lost* XI.376–411 (and *Par. Reg.* III.252ff.); and Deut. 1:19–22, 3:25–27, 32:49, 34:1–4 (cf. Numb. 13:17; 22:14, 29).

down in which Achilles, the type of the individual, comes to know his own separateness from the parent body of his society. As Homer's second book shows, this individuation echoes the Greek myths of a cataclysmic rebellion within a divine confederation or family. *Paradise Lost* similarly begins from the Judaeo-Christian myth of the fall of the proud, divisive Satan. After military defeat, Satan emerges as a typical colonial leader, and Milton compares the devils, who will one day be "wand'ring o'er the Earth" (I.365), to the barbarians overrunning the Roman empire. In *Beowulf* the struggle for order in a world of strife is directly projected into a contest between the voyaging hero and a descendent of the wanderer Cain —a treatment of conflict like the one between Marduk and Tiamat in the Babylonian Creation Epic, or God and the sea-monster in Job 26; that is, a cosmogonic struggle between *Schöpfung* and *Chaos*. The triumphal forms of the typical creation epic are only slightly less prominent in a parody like Pope's *Dunciad*.

The sources of action in the romance may be identified with adventure, and the sources of characterization with the concept of a preternatural being. In the epic, the heroic is shadowed by the divine; in the romance, it is shadowed by the daemonic, that is, by the kind of dynamistic forces that pass through nature and are controlled by magicians. The epic contest is typically between two leaders, or two concepts of leadership. The romance contest is more likely to be between two magics, or two concepts of magic. The romance adventure takes the form of contact with, or access to, a world governed by magical forces. Because the author who controls the story may be thought of as exercising control over these forces, one of the magics may be identified with the art of composing romance itself.

The tendencies of epic and romance should be evident in any motif common to both. A convenient example is the non-encounter in battle of two warriors. In the twentieth book of the *Iliad*, Achilles comes upon the Trojan Aeneas. It is apparent that Aeneas is no match for the Achaean, but he will not desert his post, and Aphrodite descends to remove her overly brave son from Achilles' path. Achilles, confronted by Aeneas' disappearance, stares momentarily, and concludes that Aeneas is beloved of the immortal gods. The motif is more complicated at the end of the twenty-first book, when Apollo not only rescues the beleaguered Agenor but also likens himself to that warrior; Apollo tempts Achilles into chasing him while the Trojans, taking advantage of Achilles' distraction, make good their withdrawal into the city. In both cases the emphasis is chiefly on divine intervention in the fortunes of battle.

We may contrast an episode in the *Aeneid*, where Turnus is reserved from the wrath of Aeneas.[14] Virgil has retained the Homeric motif of the fabrication of a Trojan, but transferred the benefits of the divine trick

---

[14] *Aen.* X.633–688.

9

to the Trojans' enemy. Turnus pursues the image of Aeneas, a phantasm
contrived to distract him from battle by Turnus' patron-deity, Juno. After
Turnus has followed the phantasm aboard a ship, which then cuts loose
from land, the image mysteriously vanishes into the clouds. At the end
of the poem Turnus' sister, Juturna, disguised as her brother's charioteer,
also delays the reckoning with Aeneas, but she ultimately abandons Turnus
to his fate, and flies off in the form of an owl.

Juturna is not wholly unlike a fay in one of the *romanzi*, and Virgil's
more magical treatment opens the way to Boiardo's, where the military-
epic attachment of the same motif becomes a mere pretext.[15] In the *Orlando Innamorato* the magician Malagigi has summoned up two demons;
each demon impersonates a warrior's second and challenges a rival knight
to combat. The demons divide the two knights, Rinaldo and Gradasso,
rather than bring them together, for when Rinaldo arrives at the seashore
appointed for the battle he finds his enemy Gradasso apparently de-
faulting on his challenge and fleeing aboard a little boat. Rinaldo boards
the craft and attempts to bring Gradasso to blows, but what he takes to be
his enemy vanishes into a cloud of smoke. The boat has already put out
from shore, and after a fifteen days' voyage it deposits the hero on an
island where the deeply infatuated Angelica—who is behind it all—has
contrived a splendid pleasance on the hero's behalf. As in Virgil, the
hero is chagrined by what has happened to him, and an attempt is made
to reason him out of his shame. In the *Aeneid*, however, the emphasis is
on departure from the epic context. In Boiardo, it is on entry into the
romance context.

The same motifs are sometimes recaptured for the epic. In Trissino's
"heroic poem," *L'Italia Liberata da Gotti*, Narses and the other rescuers
sent to Acratia's pleasure-isle are conveyed there by a magically propelled
boat, but the voyage no longer represents a species of errantry; rather it
is an errand, essentially a raid-deed.[16] In Tasso's epic, the image of the
virago Clorinda, fashioned by Satan, has the epic function: the preservation of a warrior for another day.[17] In a Spenserian example of the enchanted boat motif, the voyage provides for both the conveyance of the
hero over a psychological threshold of romance and the convergence of
two heroes—one a Mars—on an epic battle rendezvous.[18] But the destination, an enchanted island, shows that the affinities of Spenser's treatment
are decidedly with romance.

[15] *Orl. Inn.* I.v.32–55.

[16] Cantos iv–v. For a description of the action, see A. Bartlett Giamatti, *The
Earthly Paradise in the Renaissance Epic* (Princeton, 1966), pp. 173-178.

[17] *Ger. Lib.* VII.99.

[18] *F.Q.* II.vi, the Phedria episode; discussed below in Chap. III, "The Temper of
Occasion," sec. i.

If we contrast the original episode in Homer with the one in Boiardo, we find that the epic action is simplified and sustained, whereas the romance action is complicated and digressive. With respect to supernatural intervention, the epic example is the action of a patron-deity, whereas the romance example is a complexly mediated play of conjured forces and demons. With respect to conflict, the epic contrasts Greek and Trojan, and implies that Aeneas, who is kept by the gods in order to found a future people, may be a different kind of hero from Achilles. The romance illustrates the limitations of Rinaldo in the presence of magic and illusion, rather than the fortunes of battle and the power of the gods. The real conflict is between Rinaldo, under the enchantment of Disdain, and Angelica, under the enchantment of Love. Love himself, as Plato said, is an enchanter.

The most obvious contrast between romance and epic is the least susceptible of precise critical description. It is the proportion of fiction in each genre, not so much what is true and what is false, but what is authorized and what is apocryphal or palpably made up: fiction with an analogy to truth, and fiction with an analogy to lies. Without explaining why, almost every theorist will also say that the romance differs from the epic in the multiplicity of the actions it treats, for there is a further analogy between the true and the simple, and between the false and the multiplex or digressive. Certainly the immense simplification of the action of the *Iliad* is in marked contrast to the dilation of the storytelling in the *Odyssey*. The art of the *Iliad* observes aesthetic criteria analogous to the unifying shield of Achilles; the art of the *Odyssey* resembles the overelaborated, repeatedly woven shroud of Laertes. Both the critics Cinthio and Pigna note the analogy between the *Odyssey* and the *romanzi*:[19] the pleasures of uninhibited fabrication surely belong to it.

[ii]

Aristotle's emphasis on the literary work as a production, like a play, led cinquecento theorists of the heroic poem to seek unifying concepts that would make Ariosto's form somewhat answerable to the canon of unified action. Insofar as the theorist wishes to seek this kind of coherence, he will have to follow in these theorists' steps. In the descriptions that follow, the distinction between epic and romance is presented in a new form: as a distinction between alternative "ends" in a poem, between epic glorification (or edification) and romantic entertainment.

Aristotle calls the means to the unity of action "probability" and "neces-

---

[19] Cinthio, *Discorsi* (1554), p. 65, and Pigna, *I romanzi* (1554), pp. 18–20, as cited in Bernard Weinberg, *History of Literary Criticism in the Italian Renaissance* (Chicago, 1962), vol. 2, pp. 969f., and vol. 1, p. 445.

sity";[20] probability, in particular, both unifies an action and universalizes it. A number of other "unities" were employed to help organize the long poem—singleness of place, time, character, and exploit, according to Weinberg—but the theorists were apparently unwilling to specify that intimate connexity of beginning, middle, and end that only causality can supply.[21] We have already drawn on Robortelli's distinction between the taxic organization of the annalist, and the thesis organization of the poet; in the same place he says that poetry "seeks a connected series, and on account of their affinity, constitutes one action from many."[22] Thus Robortelli describes an aggregate unity, collected from without, rather than caused from within.

Tasso particularly addresses himself to Aristotelian requirements in the second *Discourse*. He argues that even the simple plot may be said to be compound or mixed "when it contains in itself things of diverse natures, such as wars, loves, enchantments and adventures, events either happy or unhappy, which carry with them either terror and commiseration or sympathy and merriment."[23] Tasso commends such a variety:

> This same, which is blameworthy in tragedy, is in my judgment, most praiseworthy in epic, and almost as necessary [to epic] as what the other derives from recognition or from the change of fortune. And for this reason the multiplicity and diversity of the episodes is observed by the epic; Aristotle himself blames the episodic fable, or rather blames it in tragedy solely, or by episodic fable does not intend the one in which the episodes are many and diverse, but the one in which these episodes are interpolated beyond verisimilitude and badly compounded with the fable, and on equal footing with it, being useless and idle in the extreme and not working to its principal end: for the variety of episodes in such [a poem] is praiseworthy insofar as the unity of the fable is not corrupted, and not praiseworthy insofar as the fable is confused. I am speaking of that unity which is mixed, not that which is simple and uniform and, in the heroic poem, less suitable.

An important phrase here describes the fable as "working to its principal end." This end is a unifying principle, and Tasso locates it very near the author's own intention, and even his integrity:

> If unity bears perfection in its nature, and multiplicity imperfection— whence the Pythagoreans count the former among the good and the latter among the evil, and whence the one is an attribute of form and the other

[20] *Poetics* ix (1451a): "kata to eikos ē to anankaion."
[21] Weinberg, *History of Criticism*, vol. 2, p. 803.
[22] Hathaway, *Age of Criticism*, pp. 169f., citing Robortelli, *De Arte poetica explicationes* (1548), p. 268.
[23] Tasso, *Prose*, ed. Mazzali, pp. 390f.

of matter—then will not unity in the heroic poem also carry greater perfection than multiplicity? Beyond this, I presume that the fable is the end
of the poet, as Aristotle affirms, and there have been none who deny it:
if the fable is one, the end will be one; if on the other hand the fables are
diverse, the ends will be diverse. But how much better the work where
the author has regard to a single end than one who proposes for himself
diverse ends, distractions in the soul and impediments in execution originating from the diversity of ends; how much better does the imitator of
one sole fable perform than the imitator of many actions. I would add
that from the multiplicity of fable indeterminacy is born; and this process
could go *ad infinitum*, when there is no end either fixed in advance or
determined by art.[24]

But it was the purposeful Tasso, rather than the dilatory Ariosto, who
suffered "distractions in the soul," and the same things that threaten the
health of his art seem to have threatened the health of the man.

Tasso assumes that the "end of the fable" and the "end of the poet" are
roughly in agreement: an endless fable argues a distracted poet. That the
two ends should be at odds was not intolerable to some cinquecento critics
however. Fornari, in his *Spositione*, says that the "end" of the *Furioso* is
the contrast of the Christian Charlemagne and the pagan Agramante,
and the "end" of its author is the celebration of Ruggiero, the fictional
ancestor of Ariosto's patron.[25] Pigna compares the somewhat misleading
title of the poem to that of the *Iliad*. Ariosto's title slights Ruggiero; Homer's does not name Achilles.[26] Also speaking of Ruggiero and Orlando,
Minturno says that Ariosto "chose to base on the romances a single work in
which these two heroes should be indicated as the chief and most glorious
of all, the one to give his name to the poem, the other as providing the
goal to which all might be directed."[27]

Minturno further suggests that there are really two possible poems—
he means epics—that might have been constructed from the materials of
the *Furioso*.[28] They would correspond to Homer's two poems, though
nothing in the *Furioso* evinces Homeric method. One poem would be
based on an Iliadic Orlando, his distraction and its alleviation being com-

[24] *Ibid.*, pp. 373f.

[25] *Spositione* (1549), p. 35, in Weinberg, *History of Criticism*, vol. 2, pp. 954ff.

[26] Pigna, *I romanzi* (1554), p. 77, in Weinberg, *History of Criticism*, vol. 2, pp.
954-957.

[27] Minturno, *L'Arte Poetica*, in Allan Gilbert, ed., *Literary Criticism: Plato to
Dryden* (Detroit, 1962), pp. 280f., translating Naples edn. of 1725, p. 28b.

[28] *L'Arte Poetica*, in Gilbert, *Literary Criticism*, pp. 277-280, translating Naples
edn. of 1725, p. 28a.

parable to the wrath of Achilles. The other poem would celebrate the illustrious deeds of an Odyssean Ruggiero, just as the *Odyssey* was composed in praise of Ulysses. This Aristotelian rewriting of the poem is shrewd enough, despite its lack of sympathy. Ruggiero, for example, goes through a vaguely Odyssean cycle that includes a Circean island paradise; an encounter with a water-monster distantly related to Polyphemus; shipwreck; and a "complex" dénouement involving disguises, recognitions, and ultimately union with the virtuous and loyal Bradamante.[29] Minturno's comparison of Orlando to Achilles also has something in it. The opening situation of the *Furioso* involves a brawl between Orlando and Rinaldo over Angelica. (Pigna asserts that Ariosto treats Angelica as the *Iliad* suggests,[30] though he could be thinking of Helen rather than Briseis.) More obvious is the thesis of a "fury"—the strong man on his bender. Each hero is transfigured by his rage, and attains the power of an elemental force. Achilles is on equal footing with the glutted river Scamander and gives battle to its offended god; Orlando, not doubting that he will reach the farther shore, plunges heedlessly into the Strait of Gibraltar.

Ariosto is preeminently the poet of Sidney's famous description, freely ranging among the "heros, demigods, cyclops, chimeras and furies" of his own wit.[31] His passage through this zodiac creates something like a comprehensive representation of Being; that is, an image of totality, analogous to the creation itself. In keeping with the principles cited above, any effective discussion of the poem will acknowledge alternative "ends" or structures in the poem, and will then concern itself with eliciting and relating them. As a kind of epic given—strife—there is the battle for Christendom. The pagan challenge is most memorably embodied in Rodomonte; his *aristeia* (best in battle) in the poem's sixteenth canto offers the greatest single threat to Charlemagne's beleaguered capital. This more or less continuous struggle provides a kind of base line from which the heroes are typically content to depart, carried away from public duty— like Turnus in the enchanted boat—in pursuit of various private phantoms. As Minturno implies, two large continuities stand out in the poem: a "matter" of Orlando and a "matter" of Ruggiero, the two outstanding champions on either side. One matter develops from the infatuation of the Christian hero; its theme of distraction is introduced with the flight of Angelica into the forest of Ardennes in the first canto. Its climax comes

[29] The technical use of "complex" in Renaissance discussion of the fable comes from Aristotle, *Poetics* x (1452a), and xii (1452b).

[30] According to Ralph Coplestone Williams, *The Theory of the Heroic Epic in Italian Criticism of the Sixteenth Century* (Baltimore, 1917), citing Pigna, *I romanzi* (1554), p. 78. Two pages later Pigna notes that the *Orlando Furioso* begins with the first line of the *Iliad* and ends like the *Aeneid*.

[31] My text for Sidney is Gilbert, *Literary Criticism*, p. 412.

when the hero discovers Angelica's infidelity, and the ironic peripety follows directly: the loss of Orlando's wits. The meaning of the opening forest of the poem becomes explicit in the conclusion Ariosto now draws in the remarks introducing the twenty-fourth canto (XXIV.2):

> Varii gli effetti son, ma la pazzia
> È tutt'una però, che li fa uscire;
> Gli è come una gran selva, ove la via
> Conviene a forza, a chi vi va, fallire
> Chi su, chi giú, chi qua, chi là, travia;

Various are the effects, but the madness is still all one, which causes them to issue; it is like a great forest, where the way is bound to fail, perforce, him who goes there: one about, one back, one here, one there, goes astray.[32]

"Che non è in somma amor, se non insania" (for love is nothing, in sum, if not madness; XXIV.1). This state of distraction also seems to be symbolized in the twelfth canto by a labyrinthine palace, contrived by the enchanter Atlante, in which knights willfully wander in search of supposedly abducted loves and stolen horses. Perhaps significantly, both Ruggiero and Orlando are drawn to its confines after each has rescued an attractive nude woman exposed to the Orco monster.

The *donnée* for the other continuity—where love implies finding one's identity rather than losing it—is the *enfance*, enamoring, and education of the pagan Ruggiero. In the fourth canto he is delivered, by his affianced, from a pleasure-palace contrived by his uncle Atlante; however, in the sixth and seventh cantos he is seduced by the enchantress Alcina into an equally imprisoning paradise on an Atlantic isle. The thematic importance of the latter is emphasized by the various allegories with which the poet has supplied the episode—its influence on Ariosto's successors also testifies to its central character. Ruggiero is carried to this remote spot by the hippogriff. The same aerial beast provides Astolfo's transportation to the other paradise of the poem, which is located on a mountaintop at the headwaters of the Nile. This second paradise is identified as Eden, and it is attached to the Orlando matter as Alcina's isle was to the Ruggiero matter. Astolfo

---

[32] Ariosto imitates Horace, *Sat.* II.3, ll. 43–53, on the universality of folly: "The school and sect of Chrysippus deem every man mad, whom vicious folly or the ignorance of truth drives blindly forward. This definition takes in whole nations, this even great kings, the wise man alone excepted. Now learn, why all those, who have fixed the name of madman upon you, are as senseless as yourself. As in woods (*silvis*), where a mistake (*error*) makes people wander about from the proper path; one goes out of the way to the right, another to the left; there is the same blunder (*error*) on both sides, only the illusion is different in different directions: in this manner imagine yourself mad. . . ." (Trans. C. Smart, New York edn., 1894.) As in Shakespeare's forest of Arden, "Love is merely a madness" (*As You Like It*, III.ii.400).

ascends the forbidden mountain preliminary to being conveyed to the moon, which turns out to be the repository of Orlando's departed wits. Thus the two principal paradisal places each involve a loss and recovery of self.

It might follow that the two paradises, as reserves, function as repositories of potential being. Ruggiero is urged not to leave his future offspring dormant in Alcina's paradise, and Orlando's wits are kept in a jar on the moon. The latter is particularly suggestive, since Plato refers to a none-too-serious link between the shifting of the desiring soul and a jar. In the *Gorgias* (493), Socrates reports that "some clever fellow, a Sicilian perhaps or Italian, writing in allegory, by a slight perversion of language named this part of the soul a jar, because it can be swayed and easily persuaded. . . ." Porphyry, whose treatise on the cave of the nymphs in the *Odyssey* had a Renaissance readership, solemnly explains the relevance of Plato's pun:

> Plato also says, that there are two openings, one of which affords a passage to souls ascending to the heavens, but the other to souls descending to the earth. And, according to the theologist, the Sun and Moon are the gates of souls, which ascend through the Sun and descend through the Moon. With Homer, likewise, there are two tubs,
>
> > From which the lots of every one he fills,
> > Blessings to these, to those distributes ills.
> > (Iliad XXIV.528f.)
>
> But Plato, in the Gorgias, by tubs intends to signify souls, some of which are malefic, but others beneficent, and some of which are rational, but others irrational. Souls, however, are tubs, because they contain in themselves energies and habits, as in a vessel.[33]

Astolfo's visit to the moon gives way to a visit to the Fates, where he beholds "future lives," including the fleece of the poet's patron, a descendant of the very progeny that Ruggiero was exhorted to beget.

Some agreement between the two matters may be observed as the dénouement approaches. The seaside cleansing and cure of Orlando in the thirty-ninth canto is followed in the forty-first—after a sufficiently admonitory dunking in the Mediterranean—by the baptism of the pagan Ruggiero. Orlando is once again available for public duty, and a combat in the fortieth canto confirms the declining fortunes of the pagans. Ruggiero's conversion to Christianity is regarded as equally fatal to their cause. The cure of the jealousy of Orlando's cousin Rinaldo in the forty-second canto furnishes the epilogue for the Orlando-Angelica branch: Rinaldo's drink-

---

[33] *On the Cave of the Nymphs*, 13, trans. Thomas Taylor, in *Select Works of Porphyry* (London, 1823), pp. 194f.

ing from the Waters of Disdain goes back to a motif introduced by Boiardo in the third canto of the *Orlando Innamorato* (Ariosto refers to it at the end of the first canto of the *Furioso*).[34] The final cantos of the poem contain a complex friendship-romance that celebrates Ruggiero; the poem is concluded with his marriage feast and the Turnus-like death of the challenger Rodomonte. Orlando has no part in this coda, which thus belongs to the Ruggiero-Bradamante branch exclusively. The poem begins with Orlando and ends with Ruggiero; they form two piers, as it were, supporting the vast cantilevered construction stretching between them.

The structure shows a departure from, and return to, epic. The epic strength of the distracted Orlando is wasted upon the complexities and errors of romance, and the romantic circuit traced by Ruggiero gradually makes him eligible for epic celebration. If the heroic potential of the cavaliers may be either enhanced or subverted by their romances, then romance itself is subject to two poles of sensibility: a romantic or sympathetic one, and an ironic or critical one. We have located one pole in the alleviation of Orlando's infatuation with Angelica, namely, the pole of ironic detachment and perception of folly. The author, being a man, is notably acute regarding the weakness and knavery of women; the stories of Gabrina and Origilla belong here, and also the interpolated tales of mine host, of Lydia in hell, and the two stories told to Rinaldo in the forty-third canto. The other pole, which we may associate with the lovers Ruggiero and Bradamante, is the pole of romantic commitment and ennobling dedication. Especially notable is the "faithful unto death" theme of the story of Zerbino and Isabella; it is repeated in the story of Brandimart and Fiordiligi. Stories of faithful friends belong here too, including that of Leone and Ruggiero. There is the friendship of Cloridano and Medoro, in which the death-defying bond also involves loyalty to a fallen leader. Medoro, the idealistic foot-soldier, is rewarded with Angelica, and for once she too seems capable of devotion.

The *débrouillard* Astolfo is the connecting link between the Orlando matter and the Ruggiero matter, for he is a guest in both paradises. A trapped romantic in the sixth canto—his hostess has imprisoned him in the form of a Venerean myrtle tree—he unsuccessfully warns Ruggiero of the perils of being one of Alcina's lovers. By the time he enters the Ethiopian kingdom of the thirty-third canto he is an accomplished ironist and a resourceful destroyer of illusions. Thus he passes from the one pole to the other. We meet him under the enchantment of Alcina, but by the tenth canto he is in the realm of Logostilla, who teaches her charges how to control romance, and prevent being controlled by it. He subsequently disenchants the palace where both Orlando and Ruggiero wander in search

---

[34] *Orl. Inn.* I.iii.32; *O.F.* I.78.

of imaginary dames. In the thirty-third canto he has reached the pole of authorial detachment, hobnobbing with the apostle John in the earthly paradise. He eats the fruit of knowledgeability that Eve ate, with no ill effects, and John informs him that paradise is the reward he has received for a favorable biography of a patron.

The reader experiences a curious elegiac *frisson* when late in the poem Astolfo disenchants the leaves from which he had once created a navy for cutting off the pagan retreat by sea. What is affecting here is not in the fiction itself, but rather in the sense of the author's withdrawing his support from the fiction, or from its proliferation of marvels. The unreflective heroic and epic element of the romance also finds its symbolic terminus. The heroes of Boiardo seemed unlikely ever to die, but Ariosto's characters are increasingly subject to the melancholy fact of mortality, in a line running from Atlante to Brandimart.[35] We mentioned the truly impressive battle-rage of Rodomonte at the siege of Paris. The same *enfant terrible* attempts a comeback at the end of the poem, but now, it would seem, he is the last of the furiosi. Voluble, dauntless, violently committed and committed to violence—and finally not too bright—his race of child-like giants is suddenly obsolescent and doomed to a swift extinction. As the comparison to the death of Turnus suggests, Ariosto follows Virgil in perfecting his own work by means of a symbol for the "death" of the heroics of the primary epic. The unconverted Rodomonti are survived by the more urbane, civic-minded, and flexible Ruggieri; the latter have had the sense to be born of a stock that will eventually produce a Renaissance princeling—that is to say, a patron.

As this last example shows, little in *Furioso* is free from a subversive kind of irony. Likewise the allegories, where their significances are prescribed by the author, are particularly concerned with seeing folly, and seeing one's way clear of it. The trip to the moon is an engaging romantic fiction; the survey from its vantage of what men have lost on earth provides the natural ironic sequel. Only the poets, we learn from the appended allegory of the Fates, can preserve a reputation, and yet all the things that the poets have said about Achilles and the others were exaggerations— or lies. Far from making the end of the poet and the end of the fable coincide, Ariosto is rarely unwilling to make a point at the expense of a character's reputation, or to sabotage the unity of mood in an affecting scene with a ridiculous or grotesque addition. Hence we have identified the ironic or satiric pole of sensibility with the author himself. Ultimately, the romantic pole must be located in the romance itself, for the efflorescence of the marvelous cannot be dissociated from storytelling for its own sake,

[35] The death of Atlante from grief, implied at *O.F.* IV.34, is confirmed at *O.F.* XXXVI.64, when his shade speaks up. Brandimart's death, at XLI.100, darkens everything around it.

as stylized as you please and devoid—though never for long—of the critical faculty, and the critical deflation.

Renaissance commentary does not organize the poem in quite this way. It does, however, treat the various stories the poem tells as presenting a conspectus of ethical examples, ranging from the most cautionary to the most edifying. At one point the poet tells a tale involving a cup that can reveal whether one's wife has remained chaste. The implications of the story are that most wives have not, and Rinaldo prudently refuses to make the test.[36] Ariosto is always suspicious of the appearance of virtue and the reliability of appearances, and yet the story of the magic cup warns us that some curiosity is destructive, and therefore ill-advised. Few characters in Ariosto offer a stronger lesson than the self-imprisoned Sospetto of the *Cinque Canti*: in the end nobility and honesty may have to be taken on faith, on the evidence of things unseen. These are roughly our critical and uncritical poles of sensibility, suitably moralized.

Perhaps the theorists have done better by the poem's dual structure; at least one of them, Fornari in his *Spositione*, treats the two paradises as among the most logical places for commentary to attach itself to the poem. We have taken the unifying view, as theorists must. But the famous question of Cardinal Ippolito—"Where did you find all these silly stories, Messer Lodovico?"—indicates that at least one cooler Renaissance head reacted to the poem as a mere aggregate.

Our first reference to Spenser's *Faerie Queene* tells us that the poet intended to "overgoe Ariosto."[37] The same ambition to improve on this model may be heard in Tasso's *Three Discourses*. They were written with the *Gerusalemne Liberata* in view, and they may be considered its program. The first essay treats the "invention," or the proper subject matter of the heroic poem. On the basis of characterizations common to both epic and romance, the heroic poem is allowed as a mixed genre. In the interests of credibility in matters human and divine, the subject of such a poem should be a history from the Christian epoch—this requirement, in our terms, is "epic." But the history should also be from a somewhat legendary age, to permit the poet the greatest possible latitude for fabrication—a requirement of "romance." Epics may be made from amorous romance, we are told; better, however, are "the histories of a time neither too modern nor too remote. . . . Such are the times of Charlemagne, Arthur, or those that shortly preceded or followed them—hence it has come

---

[36] *O.F.* XLII.104, XLIII.6-8, with reference to the prohibition on Adam.

[37] In the third of the *Three Proper and Wittie Familiar Letters*; in *The Poetical Works of Edmund Spencer*, ed. J. C. Smith and E. de Selincourt, Oxford Standard Authors (New York, 1963), p. 628.

about that their feats provided material to so many writers." Further, Tasso commends as an especially worthy subject "those deeds undertaken either for dignity of empire, or for the exaltation of the faith of Christ."[38]

The second essay, as noted earlier, treats the unification of the fable; Tasso prescribes the more specifically epic form that this indifferently epic or romantic subject matter ought to take. The essay's epigraph might be taken from Godfrey's dream, in Tasso's poem, where the leader of the first crusade is told that his counsellor will show the messengers how to recover the wayward warrior Rinaldo (XIV.18):

> e sarà lor dimostro il modo e l'arte
> di liberarlo e di condurlo a vui.
> Cosí al fin tutti i tuoi compagni erranti
> ridurrà il Ciel sotto i tuoi segni santi.

and he will show them the way and the art to release him and conduct him to you. Thus Heaven finally will reduce all your errant company beneath your holy banners.

The poem's title informs us that its subject, like that of the *Iliad*, is the siege of an Asian city by Europeans, and that it treats an action derived from history, as does the *Italia Liberata da Gotti* of the poet's predecessor Trissino. Jerusalem itself is the ostensible focus of the poem—a city central to the faith and encompassed by a devoted host. The "epic" relevance of the first crusade to Tasso's own culture is clear enough, if we consider either the Mediterranean imperial history that climaxed in the Battle of Lepanto, or the ecclesiastical history that saw the successful consolidating campaign of Post-Tridentine Catholicism. At Troy the object of recovery was a wayward bride; Tasso's poem ends with the conversion of the repentant enchantress Armida. Typologically, the Church is a bride, and also a Jerusalem. Godfrey, like Virgil's Aeneas, is cast in a somewhat priestly role. The potential analogy is that of the vicar of Christ reclaiming spiritual territory, as Christ redeems the Church.[39]

In outline, the unity of Tasso's fable is eclectic and composed: "it seeks

---

[38] *Prose*, ed. Mazzali, pp. 358, 362; similarly in the second book of the second set of *Discorsi*, in *Prose*, pp. 539f.

[39] This comparison will not appeal to all. That the Church is the bride of the Pope is implied by Dante, *Inf.* XIX.56. For a similar parallel, see Trissino's dedication of his *Liberata* poem to Charles V: the emperor is one who "as if he were Justinian, holds laws in himself, as Dante says; deals with the excessive and the useless, frees Italy from the bondage of the Goths, takes Africa from the Vandals, and checks the impulse of the Persians in Asia. Similarly, your majesty, you are yourself appointed to the task of emending the abuses and laws of the Christian religion, you have pacified Italy and freed it from war, have removed Africa from the hands of the Turk, have united the French by your friendship, and have corrected the Germanies, through reducing them to the true religion of the Catholic Church."

a connected series, and on account of their affinity, constitutes one action from many." One may distinguish, somewhat arbitrarily, several degrees of relatedness to the central taking of Jerusalem. Apart from the interpolated tale (or including it, if the episode of Olindo and Sophronia is such) every sort of digression may be found. Tangential episodes thrown off by the main plot may carry a major character off to an amour that does not noticeably advance the action. Some episodes compete with the main action: they have an elliptical effect, claiming enough attention to set up rival foci outside of Jerusalem. Armida's isle is the most notorious example. (It differs decisively from Achilles' tent in the *Iliad*, which is rather like a "little Troy," in that its siege-situation reflects that of Troy itself.) There are variational episodes, not essential to the nuclear story, but necessarily in orbit around it, such as the felling of the enchanted forest. There are centripetal episodes that principally illustrate the vocation of heroism, and are close to the nuclear area but are not truly indispensable, such as the duel of Tancredi and Argante, or the death of Sweno or of Latino's sons. Finally, if we try to describe an irreducible plot, as Aristotle did for the *Odyssey*, we find we cannot quite do it. The departure and return of Rinaldo is an obvious candidate. Rinaldo's movement resembles the movement of Achilles in the *Iliad*, but in Homer the effect of the champion's withdrawal from battle eventually produces the very occasion that causes him to rejoin it. In Tasso there is no such connection. Instead, there is a polarity: the truancy of an erotic pastoral, set against the recall to the martial and metropolitan.

Godfrey's difficulties with the enchanted forest are significant: the timber is needed for siege-engines, but the forest itself is a place where the private fantasies of the knights riot unchecked, preventing its being cut down. A distracting forest comes to Tasso as an immemorial symbol of romance, and he does not deny it its daemonological character; at the same time he sets himself the problem of how to bring it to bear on a central epic subject symbolized by a city.[40] Equally significant is Tasso's treatment of heroic death, which closely links *eros* and *thanatos*. Some of the poem's most compelling effects depend upon this tension of opposites. The *liebestod* of the virago Clorinda, who is slain by her lover Tancredi in nocturnal combat, is the most obvious example. Likewise Rinaldo, in the forest, must destroy, if not Armida herself, at least his love for her. The killing of the pagan champion Argante does not involve any love-interest, except that he is avenging the slain Clorinda; and yet something here impresses us as romantic, perhaps the apparent death of both of the noble combatants. Tancredi eventually revives under the kisses and tears of Erminia, something like an elegiac Adonis modulating into an erotic one. The

---

[40] For the felling of the sacred or daemonological grove, see Tasso's source in Lucan, *Pharsalia* III.373–453, and Ariosto, *Cinque Canti*, II.101ff.

early episode of Olindo and Sophronia seems designed to lead to an explicit emblem of this tension of love and death; within the heroic context, the lovers at the stake appear only slightly less iconographic than Shakespeare's emblem of married chastity, *The Phoenix and the Turtle*. The lovers are rescued by the virago Clorinda, who is party to both love and war. Tasso's reluctance to drop this piece, despite advice to do so, indicates that it may not be purely episodic after all.

In sum, the rivalries and dissension rife in Godfrey's army are driven through the poem as well.[41] The theme organizes itself in the reader's mind in terms of a cleavage between romantic self-indulgence and epic work, the aberrant and the conscientious. In Tasso's earthly paradise, the "natural" cannot, in good conscience, be enjoyed. It is enjoyed uneasily and surreptitiously, as in those darkened soft spots that wait for weakened spirits in the landscape beyond the Holy City. Before the city the soul is marshaled for honorable public service. In the retreats beyond, the unhealthy or morbid sensibility seeks its solace in the secrecy of a private amour. On the one hand, there is a flight into a tempting but illicit world of personal delectation and wish-fulfillment, where all the ladies are pagan; on the other, a focus on the ensigns of the army, where all the standards are standards of duty. Here is a poet who senses a moral flaw in the surrender to all earthly pleasure, but finds himself compelled to recur to its effects whenever he has occasion to treat a private life. Such surrender may well be counted for sin; good fame cannot allow it, and the soul that finds itself in this condition is in danger of being lost. And yet, how many souls are to be found precisely here, languishing in the soft Petrarchan toils of this malingering, unappeasable desiderium.

The Institution of the Hero

The laws governing Spenser's art are very unlike those governing Tasso's. In Spenser we find a multiplicity of coordinate units, separately articulated and given comparable importance; in Tasso we are nearer to the enforced unity of baroque structures, with their emphasis on the hegemony of a dominating motif. In terms of the styles of sixteenth-century painting, as Wölfflin described them, Spenser orders his material in parallel strata, and presents it "horizontally," in agreement with the picture plane. Tasso's poem is far more dramatized, with characters and events thrusting forward from the horizontal register of the picture plane into the foreground

[41] The following summation owes much to Giamatti, *Earthly Paradise*, pp. 179ff., and Graham Hough, *A Preface to "The Faerie Queene"* (New York, 1963), chap. iv, esp. p. 78.

of attention. Spenser is more like Botticelli, Tasso more like Tintoretto.[42] Both poets, however, seek an epic unification. Tasso determines to subordinate the recognized multiplicity of romance to a thesis of time, place, and purpose; Spenser is content to digest that multiplicity to a regular series. Tasso attempts to integrate the political and historical themes of epic with the a-historical and psychological themes of romance. Spenser typically relates the epic themes to his romance fictions by means of allegory. For example, national consecration is an epic theme; individual holiness is a romance theme. In Spenser holiness is conceived as a kind of spiritual chastity. The fictions of the legend of holiness are romantic, while the historical and ecclesiastical allegory attaching to them are epic. As another example, machines are epic, but automatons belong to romance. In Book V, Talus is a romance marvel, like all such *daedalia*; but in the allegory he has some of the functions and significance of an epic siege-engine.

To forge the Spenserian link between romance and epic, and especially the purposiveness of epic, one needs to know something about the defense of the Ariostan mode, a defense that took the form of discovering the unity of romances in a synoptic conception of either their action or their personnel. It is especially with the rhetorical ideal of the hero that we will be concerned here. This ideal emerges at the confluence of two streams of critical tradition: one concerns those educational intentions attributed to the epic; the other concerns the idea of the epic hero as an absolute or replete man. Repleteness was a formative notion in the characterization of Odysseus in the *Odyssey*, and the idea was abetted by the complementary nature of the Homeric epos as a whole.

Beginning from the educational idea, let us move toward the intermediate idea of creating "exemplary" characters; from thence we may extend our attention to the ideal of repleteness.

Horace said that the business of the poet is to delight and to instruct; Renaissance critics added that it is also to move.[43] Aristotle himself, in de-

---

[42] When I wrote this I was unaware that Wölfflin himself, applying the canons found in his *Principles of Art History*, draws the same comparison between Ariosto and Tasso, and Boiardo and Berni, in his *Renaissance und Barock* (1888), pp. 83–85. For the subsequent history of this application, see René Wellek, "The Concept of the Baroque in Literary Scholarship," in his *Concepts of Criticism* (New Haven, 1963), pp. 73ff.

[43] Scaliger, *Poetices libri septem . . . Editio quinta* (Heidelberg, 1617), III.xcvii; Minturno, *De Poeta* (Venice, 1559), pp. 102–106, 179f., and *L'Arte Poetica* (Naples, 1725), p. 76; Sidney, *Defense*, in Gilbert, *Literary Criticism*, secs. 26, 27, and 29. See the detailed discussion of Gilbert, *Literary Criticism*, pp. 459–461, with reference to Horace, *De Arte* 344, putting *movendo* for *monendo,* and Cicero, *Orator* 21. See also Cicero, *Brutus* 49 and *De optimo genere oratorum* I.3 ("docere, delectare, mouere"). Gilbert also cites Pontano, *Aegidius* (in *Opera*, Basil, 1556, pp. 1481f.). For the related idea that poetry should astonish or raise wonder, see the extract from Pontano's *Actius*, in Girolamo Frascatoro, *Naugerius*, ed. and trans. Ruth Kelso,

fining the *dianoia*, or intellectual element of poetry, had recourse to an oratorical conception. *Dianoia*, according to Gilbert's translation of the Gudemann text of *Poetics* vi,

> . . . is to be able to say what is possible and what befits the conditions, namely whatever in the speeches falls under the art of politics and rhetoric, for the older dramatists made their speakers talk like statesmen and those of the present like practised rhetoricians.[44]

The orator who moves our admiration on behalf of a client or cause and the Aristotelian poet who raises pity and fear in order to cast them out are typically likened to each other by Renaissance critical theorists. The poet is understood as a rhetor arousing commiseration for virtue and reprehension of vice.[45] This hortative function for the major poet is widely assumed. The poet is a public counselor, not very different in kind from Castiglione's courtier, who is concerned to educe his prince's best. Plato's poet, for example, "clothes all the great deeds accomplished by the men of old with glory, and thus educates those who come after" (*Phaedrus* 245a). When he is one of Spenser's "antique poets historicall," he records great deeds, as Puttenham says, "for example and good information of the posteritie."[46] Milton's nephew Edward Phillips writes that heroic poetry

> . . . ought to be the result of all that can be contrived of profit, delight, or ornament, . . . —it being but requisite that the same work which sets forth the highest acts of kings and heroes should be made fit to allure the inclinations of such like persons to a studious delight in reading of those things which they are desired to imitate.[47]

University of Illinois Studies in Language and Literature, vol. 9, no. 3 (Urbana, 1924), pp. 81–86. Also see Bundy's introduction here, pp. 16–20.

[44] Gilbert, *Literary Criticism*, p. 78. The sentence following reads, "Character is that which reveals an agent's moral habit, showing of what sort it is . . . ," in explanation of which Gilbert quotes *Rhetoric* II.21: "Speeches in which moral intention is revealed possess character."

[45] My authorities here are Marvin T. Herrick, *The Fusion of Horatian and Aristotelean Literary Criticism, 1531–1555*, Illinois Studies in Language and Literature, vol. 32, no. 1 (Urbana, 1946), pp. 41–47, 53–57; and Weinberg, *History of Criticism*, especially the text cited there from Robortelli in vol. 1, p. 395, where agreement of words, or consistent diction, has been substituted for verisimilar and probable action. See also the passage from Cinthio in Weinberg, *History of Criticism*, vol. 1, pp. 435ff., where similar rhetorical considerations prevail.

[46] George Puttenham, *Arte of English Poesie*, I.x, in G. Gregory Smith, ed., *Elizabethan Critical Essays*, vol. 2, p. 25. See also Puttenham's chapter xix, "Of Historicall Poesie," i.e., poetry that records "the good and exemplarie things and actions of the former ages" (Smith, *Elizabethan Critical Essays*, vol. 2, p. 41).

[47] Edward Phillips, preface to *Theatrum Poetarum*, in J. E. Spingarn, ed., *Critical*

Spenser implies the same educational purpose in the dedicatory sonnet to Cumberland:

> To you this humble present I prepare,
>   For love of vertue and of Martiall praise,
>   To which though nobly ye inclined are,
>   As goodlie well ye shew'd in late assaies,
> Yet brave ensample of long passed daies
>   In which trew honor yee may fashion'd see
>   To like desire of honor may ye raise,
>   And fill your mind with magnanimitee.

Likewise, Sir Thomas Elyot describes Homer as a fountain of "all eloquence and lernyng":

> For in his bokes be contained, and moste perfectly expressed, nat only the documentes marciall and discipline of armes, but also incomparable wisedomes, and instructions for politike governaunce of people: with the worthy commendation and laude of noble princis: where with the reders shall be so all inflamed, that they most feruently shall desire and coueite, by the imitation of their vertues, to acquire semblable glorie.[48]

In choosing his subject, the poet envisaged in each of the above formulations is an educator, determining what to praise. He chooses on the basis of what will be, in Milton's phrase, "doctrinal and exemplary to a nation."[49]

When a poem is conceived in these terms, as an instructive model that will inspire imitation, the probability and necessity constraining the characters' activity will not essentially differ from the adoption of conduct befitting the graveness of the given occasion. Characters in the Virgilian kind of epic, which offers a persuasive interpretation of the national or collective experience, tend to speak as if they were being overheard by posterity: their speeches form lessons in decorum, and their prayers teach

---

Essays of the Seventeenth Century (Oxford, 1908–1909), vol. 2, pp. 268f. Text modernized.

[48] Sir Thomas Elyot, *The Boke Named the Gouernour*, I.x, Everyman's Library (London, 1907), pp. 36f. Cf. Mazzoni, *Della difesa della Comedia di Dante* (1587), Introduction: "heroic poetry was chiefly directed to soldiers, since they may be encouraged to imitate the virtuous actions of the heroes presented in it as though by the sharp stimulus of glory." (Trans. Gilbert, *Literary Criticism*, p. 382.)

[49] Milton, *Complete Prose Works*, vol. 1, *Reason of Church Government*, II, prologue (New Haven, 1953), p. 815. According to Sidney's *Defense*, poetry is not "an art of lies, but of true doctrine" (Gilbert, *Literary Criticism*, p. 446). For the word "exemplary," which figures heavily in what follows, see Horace, *Epist.* I.2, 1.18: Homer "utile proposuit nobis exemplar Ulixen" (he proposes to us Ulysses as an exemplar)—of the capacity of "virtue" and sapience.

their larger audience how to pray. Such characters are likely to be dynamic, like the singers in an oratorio, when it is their turn to be dynamic.[50] The "occasional" appearances of Arthur in *The Faerie Queene* might be considered an extreme example of this tendency. As we shall see, Arthur's quest also involves the desire to acquire "semblable glorie," and there are good reasons for analogizing his animus to the indoctrination of the reader.

According to Badius, in his edition of Virgil's poem, Aeneas is a hortative imitation of Augustus, comparable to the Cyrus of Xenophon.[51] The *Cyropedia* is almost inevitably cited in these contexts, especially when the critic is talking about combining precept with example. Cicero says Xenophon's Cyrus is "not faithful to history, but to the image of a just ruler," and Sidney quotes him with approval in the *Defense of Poetry*.[52] Mulcaster's *Elementarie* (I.iii) mentions "the person of *Cyrus*," whom Xenophon "deuiseth so perfit, as the best boy for a patern to bring vp, & the best prince for a president to princes."[53] Likewise, Cicero's own orator is fashioned as one "from whom every blemish has been taken away."[54] In the Renaissance the purposes of literature in general and the epic poem in particular are understood to be continuous with this notable genre of intellectual prose, that is, the educational treatise, or "institution," which sets out to fashion an ideal vocational or social pattern and invites emulation by the elite to whom it is addressed. Thus E. K. speaks of Cicero's having "set forth the paterne of a perfect Oratour," in the preface to the *Calender*, and in the argument to the "October" eclogue he tells us that "In Cuddie is set out the perfecte paterne of a Poet." Scaliger's *Poetics* proposes itself the same end.[55] The proliferation of these institutions in the

---

[50] See Mario A. Di Cesare, *Vida's Christiad and Vergilian Epic* (New York, 1964), chap. v, "Dramatic vs. Oratorical Imagination," esp. pp. 187–191.

[51] Ioducus Badius Ascensius (Josse Bade of Assche), "in Aeneida argumenta," prefatory matter to his edition of the *Aeneid,* in *Opera Virgiliana* (Leiden, 1580), 2nd part, separate paging following p. XCV, Sig. A5ʳ–A6ʳ. Similar material is found in Christophoro Landino's prohemium to the edition of Virgil described by Don Cameron Allen in *Mysteriously Meant* (Baltimore, 1970), pp. 148f.: Cyrus provided the best possible example of a ruler, while Aeneas "represented the most perfect man and the unique exemplar able to instruct man in the proper conduct of life." So Badius, *loc. cit.*: "For even as they say that Xenophon described Cyrus, not such as that man was, but such as he ought to be, so I judge that Maro decided that it was allowable for Aeneas to be proposed to us as such, and as a mirror and exemplar of a perfect man."

[52] *Epist. ad Fratrem* I.i.8: "non ad historiae fidem, sed effigiem justi imperii"; Sidney, *Defense,* in Gilbert, *Literary Criticism,* p. 416. Erasmus, in *De Copia,* II.11, reflects on the unhistorical and exemplary character of Xenophon's treatment.

[53] *Mulcaster's Elementarie,* ed. E. T. Campagnac (London, 1925), p. 17.

[54] *De Oratore* I.xxvi.118, trans. Sutton, Loeb edn., vol. 1, p. 83.

[55] *Poetics,* III.xi, "Qvemadmodvm exactius omnia contemplemur" (Heidelberg edn. of 1617), p. 207: "Nunc vero quoniam perfectum Poetam instituimus. . . ."

Renaissance is closely related to the humanist ideal of learning, with its stress on the power of ethics and education to form the mind and character of man in its own image.[56] The ideal exerts its influence on the formation of literary characters as well, and indeed becomes a frequent literary theme. The shipment of books that Hythlodaeus brings to the Utopians on his last voyage, the letter of Gargantua to his son Pantagruel concerning his education in Paris, the catechizing of the young Malcolm by Mac-Duff in *Macbeth* before the battle for the Scottish throne, and the miniature *speculum principis* addressed by Don Quixote to Sancho Panza on the eve of Sancho's governorship—these texts exemplify an educational theme in works that might otherwise seem to have little in common.

The author of the institution, with Castiglione, is

> . . . content, to err with Plato, Xenophon, and M. Tullius; leaving apart the disputing of the intelligible world and of the Ideas or imagined fourmes: in which number, as (according to that opinion) the Idea or figure conceyved in imagination of a perfect commune weale, and of a perfect king, and of a perfect Oratour are conteined: so it is also of a perfect Courtier.[57]

The poet might well permit himself the same error, and hence the same three examples are cited in Robortelli's commentary on the *Poetics*, to illustrate Aristotle's recommendation that the dramatic poet enhance character traits.[58] Robortelli explains that the poet should look to type, aiming for a "perfect exemplar of the character traits which are to be described." Sidney also thinks of the poet as "liberal . . . of a perfect pattern" and cites

---

For the extension of the ideal to a well-rounded university education in Cardinal Newman's theory, see A. Dwight Culler, *The Imperial Intellect* (New Haven, 1955), chaps. ix–x.

[56] For similar remarks, see Thomas Greene, "The Flexibility of the Self in Renaissance Literature," in Peter Demetz, Thomas Greene, and Lowry Nelson, eds., *The Disciplines of Criticism* (New Haven, 1968), pp. 241–264. I did not know this essay when I wrote the present chapter.

[57] Text taken from Sir Thomas Hoby's translation of Castiglione, *The Courtier*, in Burton A. Milligan, ed., *Three Renaissance Classics* (New York, 1953), p. 249. The question of the courtier's ideality is raised again at Lib. IV, sec. 42: "I fear that he is like the Republic of Plato, and that we shall never see the like of him, unless in heaven perhaps" (Singleton trans., Garden City, N.Y., 1959, pp. 325f.). Castiglione is correct concerning Cicero's Platonic inspiration; see *Orator ad Brutum* ii.7 seq.: "in imagining the perfect orator I shall fashion him as perhaps no-one ever was. . . . so with our minds we conceive of the *speciem* of perfect eloquence, but with our ears only the effigy. These forms of things Plato . . . calls *ideas* . . . and says they always exist contained in our reason and intellect. . . ."

[58] *De Arte poetria explicationes* (1548), p. 87: in Hathaway, *Age of Criticism*, p. 145, from which the following quotation is taken, citing Robortelli, *De Arte*, p. 91.

the "doctrinable" Cyrus in the same breath with Aeneas and the *Utopia*.[59] Sidney's *Arcadia* is the pastoral romance its title promises, but it contains military, political, and legal intrigues; and in the *Defense* the fabulous *Aethiopica* is instanced with the edifying *Cyropedia* as proof that an "absolute heroicall poem" may be written in prose.[60] "In all these creatures of his making," Greville advises us, Sidney's "intent and scope was to turn the barren philosophy precepts into pregnant images of life"; elsewhere Greville speaks of his "excellent intended pattern," and Sidney's intention of creating "moral images and examples."[61] Spenser, in the letter to Raleigh, notes the preference of "commune sence" for Xenophon and "doctrine by ensample," as opposed to Plato's more impracticable ideal of "good discipline delivered plainly in way of precepts."[62] In the same vein one may also cite the translator's epistle introducing Pierre de La Primaudaye's *French Academy*—a Platonic dialogue that works through all the virtues and includes a great deal of apophthegm and anecdote:

> And least any man should have that opinion of these Morall precepts which all men have of *Platoes* commonwealth, or of Aristotles Felicities, of *Tullies* Orator, or of Moore's Utopia, that they containe in them rather the *Idea* of good life, than such a platforme as may be drawne from contemplation into action, he [the author] hath joined works with words, practise with precept, and the fruits of rare examples with the faire flowers of Philosophicall instructions.[63]

The language used in the Renaissance to describe the character of the epic hero also overlaps with the literary Platonism of the period. In the proem to his sixth legend, for example, Spenser says that he takes the virtue of courtesy from the queen, and asks "where shall I in all Antiquity / So faire a patterne find"—one thinks of "That wondrous Pa-

---

[59] In Gilbert, *Literary Criticism*, pp. 424, 423, 422.

[60] *Ibid.*, p. 416.

[61] *Sir Fulke Greville's Life of Sir Philip Sidney*, intro. by Nowell Smith (Oxford, 1907), chap. 1, pp. 12f.; chap. 18, p. 223.

[62] The superiority of Xenophon to Plato seems to have been an old chestnut: it is found in Aullus Gellius, *Noctes Atticae* xiv.3. In Plato, *Laws* III.xii (694a–695b), the education of Cyrus is roundly criticized. A somewhat similar contrast is drawn between the republics described by Plato and Cicero, in Macrobius, *Comm. in Somn. Scip.*, I.i. The criticism of Plato's impracticable ideal is frequent in the Renaissance. Examples in English are Thomas Starkey, *Dialogue Between Pole and Lupset*, ed. Kathleen M. Burton (London, 1948), pp. 38–40, and Milton, in *Areopagitica*.

[63] The translation is attributed to T(homas) B(owes) in the British Museum Catalogue. The quotation is from *The French Academie, wherein is discoursed the institution of maners* (London, 1586), Sigs. *2v–3r. At first it might be objected that La Primaudaye is here stated to have reversed the usual priority of exemplar over example; however, the text merely says that the author has *supplemented* his exposition of the ideal by examples.

terne" in the *Hymne in Honour of Beautie*, "Whether in earth layd up in secret store."[64] As a result of this Platonizing of the example, the literary subject is easily assimilated to the idea from which the poet worked, and hence it becomes an exemplar as well as an example. The following passage from Sidney's *Defense*, on the ideality of the hero, shows the whole process in a state of fusion: the poet, like the demiurge in the *Timaeus*, and perhaps a little like Spenser's Archimago, is assumed to copy or imitate an idea:

> . . . for every understanding knoweth the skill of each artificer standeth in that *idea* or fore-conceit of the work, and not in the work itself. And that the poet hath that *idea* is manifest, by delivering them forth in such excellency as he had imagined them; which delivering them forth also is not wholly imaginative, as we are wont to say that build castles in the air; but so far substantially worketh, not only to make a Cyrus, which had been but a particular excellency, as nature might have done, but to bestow a Cyrus upon the world to make many Cyruses, if they will learn aright why and how that maker made him.

The poem remains a kind of archetype or idea here, though a substantial one. Especially insofar as the reader's ethical life may be modeled on it, it retains precisely that characteristic that defines the original archetype: its usefulness as a model on which to base a creation—or its suitability for imitation, i.e., emulation by a readership.

It is perhaps impossible to overestimate the influence of the *Aeneid* in the formation of this notion. The *Aeneid* was generally regarded by the Renaissance as the representation of the whole man in all his parts. Speaking of the desirability of discovering the moral sense in Virgil, Petrarch writes that the poet's "end and subject seem to me to be a perfect man"; his perfection "was produced either solely or principally from virtue." Hence the investigation of Virgil's moral sense is most useful, because such a sense is an acceptable ornament of human life, and "because from the first it follows the writer's intention."[65] Virgil's glorification of Aeneas is permissible, because it is "as if he was not describing Aeneas, but the

---

[64] *F.Q.* VI, proem, 6; *Hymne*, ll. 36–37. Raleigh calls the queen "Th'Idea remayninge of thos golden ages" ("The 11th: and last booke of the Ocean to Scinthia," l. 348). In making the archetypal realm pre-lapsarian, Raleigh may also imply that Elizabeth is Astraea. Platonic Justice, as a Form, might well retreat to a realm of pure forms: see V, proem, 9 and V.i.11. For the development whereby the Platonic ideas or absolutes became identified with the preconceptions of the artist, see Erwin Panofsky, *Idea: A Concept in Art Theory*, trans. Joseph Peake (Columbia, S.C., 1968), pp. 11ff.

[65] *Epist. Rerum Senelium*, IV.iv, "De quibusdam fictionibus Virgili," in *Francisci Petrarcae . . . Opera quae extant omnia*, 4 vols. in 1 (Basel, 1581), 869.

brave and perfect man under the name of Aeneas."[66] Homer and Virgil describe the character and actions "of the perfect man whom they thought could not be formed if perpetually limited to a single place."[67] Similarly, Maphaeus Vegius, who provided the Renaissance *Aeneid* with its thirteenth book, declares that "Virgil means to show, under the guise of Aeneas, man endowed with every virtue."[68] The critic Minturno says in his *De Poeta* that whatever pertains to man, Virgil expressed "in uno Aenea, virtutis numeros confecerit, ut in uno Heroe absolutum perfectamque."[69] Scaliger speaks in this vein also, saying that the perfect poet will institute the perfect man, and the versatile Aeneas is such a man.[70] He concludes his remarks on Aeneas on the same note: "We therefore have in Aeneas alone a sort of Socratic idea of any person; his perfection seems to emulate Nature herself in genus, and in special and private instances even to surpass her."[71] The word "genus" here reminds us that however fantastic these interpretations might seem to us, they are not without some basis: Aeneas acts less as an individual than as the representative of his race— perhaps all typifications of this hero have that element of truth for their point of departure.

In view of this tradition, it is not surprising that the heroic poem, according to Renaissance authors, has as its end the "institution" of a praiseworthy man who may be a model to other men. The tradition moves easily between the ideality of the hero and the hero's perfection in virtue. Chapman says that Homer's object was "the information or fashion of an absolute man";[72] Thomas Nashe says that the *Odyssey* describes "a singular man of perfection."[73] Of Aeneas, Ben Jonson says, "Virgil makes throughout the most exquisite pattern of piety, justice, prudence and all other princely virtues."[74] To test the theory, we might apply it to Milton's Adam. Adam is a royal and majestic personage, a decidedly representative pattern of man, no inconsiderable orator, and his choices—albeit the wrong ones—involve a crucial theme of leadership.

---

[66] *Epist. De Rebus Familiares*, I.ii, paragraph 22, Fracassetti edn. (Florence, 1859), vol. 1, p. 34.

[67] *Epist. De Rebus Familiares*, XV.iv, Fracassetti edn., vol. 3, p. 319.

[68] *De educatione liberorum et eorum claris moribus libri sex*, II.28, as quoted in Ann Cox Brinton, *Maphaeus Vegius and His Thirteenth Book of the Aeneid* (Stanford, Calif., 1930), p. 27. See the text of *De educatione*, ed. Mary W. Fanning and Anne S. Sullivan (Washington, D.C., 1933 and 1936), pp. 83–90.

[69] *De Poeta* (Venice, 1559), p. 40.

[70] *Poetices Libri Septem* (Heidelberg edn. of 1617), III.xi (cap. x in other editions), p. 207.

[71] *Poetices, edn. cit.*, III.xi, p. 218, trans. in Gilbert, *Literary Criticism*, p. 464n.

[72] *Chapman's Homer*, ed. Allardyce Nicoll (Princeton, 1956), vol. 2, p. 11 (marginalia on *Od*. I.1).

[73] *Works*, ed. R. B. McKerrow (London, 1904–1910), vol. 1, p. 243.

[74] Note on l. 182 of *The Haddington Masque*, in *The Complete Masques*, ed. Stephen Orgel (New Haven, 1969), pp. 524f.

Milton's Adam is also the protagonist of a tragedy, and thus, according to Tasso, a royal person. But Adam is of mixed character, at least after he falls, and in this respect he falls away from the heroism of the heroic poem. Since the epic hero is idealized, characterization in the epic is dialectical:

> The epic, on the other hand, requires characters of supreme strength; in fact, it is this which gives them their name. In Aeneas, for example, we find the excellence of piety; in Achilles, of military strength; in Ulysses, of prudence; and, to speak of our own epics, we find the excellence of loyalty in Amadigi, and of constancy in Bradamante: indeed, in some of these characters, we can find combined all of these virtues. . . . In the epic, moreover, we find displayed not only the pinnacle of virtue, but as well the depth of vice—and this with much less danger than in tragic poems.[75]

Spenser confesses to having similar anxieties about a character whom he allows to go from bad to worse, in an indecorous Ariostan tale about a young and wayward wife:

> But never let th'ensample of the bad
>   Offend the good: for good by paragone
>   Of evill, may more notably be rad,
>   As white seemes fairer, macht with blacke attone;
>   Ne all are shamed by the fault of one:
>   For lo in heaven, whereas all goodnesse is,
>   Emongst the Angels, a whole legione
>   Of wicked Sprights did fall from happy bliss;
> What wonder then, if one of women all did miss?
>   (III.ix.2)

Hellenore's marriage, on the contrary, was no example of "happy bliss," and she seems to escape to something other than damnation: a pastoral night-world in which her abandonment to the satyrs turns into a kind of innocent self-realization on the level of nature. Such a conclusion is almost paradoxical with an author who ordinarily holds the mirror up to nature only to show virtue her own feature, and scorn her own image. What Spenser means, in fact, is that Hellenore is morally safer among the jolly satyrs than with either her jealous husband or her "learned louer." The comparison to the Fall of the angels is jocular and ironic, but the story remains an isolated instance in a poem where customarily "the persons are heroic, as their virtue is."[76]

[75] Trans. of the Second Discourse in Arturo Fallico and Herman Shapiro, eds., *Renaissance Philosophy: The Italian Philosophers* (New York, 1967), p. 292. Italian text in Tasso, *Prose*, ed. Mazzali, p. 360.
[76] *Discorsi del Poema Eroico*, Libro Secundo, in Tasso, *Prose*, ed. Mazzali, p. 545.

Tasso said that in some of the characters of the heroic poem—which "depends on supreme enterprizes of a warlike nature, on matters of courtesy, of generosity, of piety, of religion"—we can find combined all of the requisite virtues. Hence it seems to have been the intention of certain modern writers "to form the idea of a *perfect knight*."[77] In other words, the romance of chivalry, with its "verray, parfit gentil knyght," also educes an ideal analogous to that of the Virgilian hero. Sidney cites the palladin Orlando, the lover Theagenes, and the friend Pylades together with the just Cyrus and the replete Aeneas. Harington, following Gioseffo Bonome in Ruscelli's 1584 edition of Ariosto, says that the poet intends in Ruggiero "the verie Idea and perfect example of a true knight."[78] At this point, at least, it was possible to dissent: Cornelius Agrippa passes without interruption from a description of the falsifying of history for the sake of an "institution" to a condemnation of the romances. The passage contains more than a hint of *Don Quixote*:

> Many write histories not so much for truth's sake as to delight the reader, and to set forth some idea of a king which they have framed themselves. . . . They affirm, furthermore, that when they write for posterity, it does not matter whose name is used, or in what order of time the example of a good prince be exposed to the public view; thus Xenophon wrote the story of Cyrus, not as he was, but as he ought to have been, propounding him as a true pattern and example of a just and heroic prince. Hence it happens that many, prone by nature to sham, have, by applying themselves industriously, written those romances of Morgant and Morgalona, Amadis, Florian, Tyran, Conamor, Arthur, Lancelot and Tristram—works generally unlearned, worse than the mad dreams of poets, and more fabulous than comedies or fables themselves.[79]

[77] *Dell'Arte Poetica*, I, in *Prose*, ed. Mazzali, p. 365; and then again in *del Poema Eroico*, II, in *Prose*, p. 539, where Tasso commends Virgil's use of Aeneas: ". . . I do not know why anyone who wishes to form the idea of a perfect knight should deny him . . . this praise of piety and religion. That is why I put the persons of Charlemagne and Arthur far ahead those of Theseus and Jason." Similarly, in *del Poema Eroico*, III, in *Prose*, pp. 608f., Tasso cites the various virtues of the Homeric heroes and commends Virgil for placing in Aeneas "piety, religion, continence, fortitude, magnanimity, justice, and all the other virtues of the knight."

[78] *Lodovico Ariosto's Orlando Fvrioso in English Heroical Verse*, ed. Robert McNulty (Oxford, 1972), p. 567. For Bonome's contribution to Harington, see Townsend Rich, *A Study in Elizabethan Verse Translation* (New Haven, 1940), pp. 64–66, which collates Harington's indebtedness to Bonome's essay in the 1584 edn. of Ruscelli (Venice, Franceschi).

[79] *The Vanity of the Arts and Sciences*, chap. v, "Of History," trans. Arturo Fallico and Herman Shapiro, eds., *Renaissance Philosophy, Vol. II, The Transalpine Thinkers* (New York, 1970), p. 77.

The application of the institutional ideal to romance does not fare much better in Samuel Butler's *Hudibras*:

> Certes our Authors are to blame,
> For to make some well-sounding name
> A Pattern fit for modern Knights,
> To copy out in Frays and Fights,
> (Like those that a whole street do raze,
> To build a Palace in the place.)
> They kill, without regard of mothers,
> Or wives, or children, so they can
> Make up some fierce, dead-doing man . . .
>
> (I.ii.11–20)

The ideal of the complete knight is invoked in *Don Quixote*, whose hero declares himself more than the equal of the twelve peers of France.[80] The Don's initiative in self-institution and self-determination is treated as a spirited anachronism, and he leaves to posterity a memorable pattern of the aberrant, the idiosyncratic, and the factitious. More sympathetic is the canon's discourse in the same book. The canon belongs to Tasso's school, and moves easily from a description of the romances, perhaps "depicting a valiant captain with all the qualities requisite to such a character," to poets like Homer and Virgil, who take for their theme "all those attributes that go to make an illustrious man perfect, as shown sometimes in a single individual and other times as shared among many."[81] Minturno had expounded a similarly epic idea of the romance personnel:

> The heroic poem sets out to imitate a memorable action carried to its conclusion by one illustrious person. The romance, they say, has as its object a crowd of knights and ladies and affairs of war and peace, though in this group one knight is especially taken whom the author is to make glorious above all the others; he is to treat as many deeds by him and by the others as he thinks sufficient for the glory of those he is disposed to praise. . . .[82]

The terms of Minturno's and Cervantes' descriptions go back to Ariosto's biographer, the critic Pigna:

> The romances readily devote themselves to several deeds of several men, but . . . they concern especially one man who should be celebrated over all the others. And thus they agree with the epic poets in taking a single

---

[80] *Don Quixote*, Pt. I, chap. v.

[81] *Ibid.*, Pt. I, chap. xlvii; trans. Samuel Putnam (New York, 1968), p. 427.

[82] *L'Arte Poetica*, trans. Gilbert, *Literary Criticism*, p. 278 (from Naples edn. of 1725, p. 27a).

person, but not so in taking a single action; for they take as many of them as seems to be sufficient. The number is "sufficient" when they have put the heroes in all those honorable perils and in all those major actions which are sought in a perfect knight; in this way endless adventures are avoided. . . . And to finish the poem as soon as we have arrived at that goal which we have selected, the order of nature will help; for when all the attributes are present in matter, motion ceases.[83]

McMurphy's citation of Toscanella's *Beauties of Ariosto's Furioso* remains authoritative on this point; the poet

. . . placed several virtues in several individuals, one virtue in one character, and another in another character, in order to fashion out of all the characters a well-rounded and perfect man. A well-rounded and perfect man is one adorned with all the virtues.[84]

Toscanella's whole man is a hypothetical entity projected from the several heroes. Pigna's standard-bearer also emerges from a number of candidates, but he exists in his own right as well. A combination of these accounts leads us to Spenser's description of Arthur—a member of the heroic personnel, but one to whom the other knights will eventually be subsidiary; a participant in the poem, but also an ideal deduction from its composite parts:

I labour to pourtraict in Arthure, before he was king, the image of a brave knight, perfected in the twelve private morall vertues, as Aristotle hath devised, the which is the purpose of these first twelve bookes. . . . So in the person of Prince Arthure I sette forth magnificence in particular, which vertue for that (according to Aristotle and the rest) it is the perfection of all the rest, and conteineth in it them all, therefore in the whole course I mention the deedes of Arthure applyable to that vertue, which I write of in that booke. But of the xii. other vertues, I make xii. other knights the patrones, for the more variety of the history. . . .

The explanation is by now familiar, not only because it is Spenser's, but also because it expresses shared assumptions. The result is that Arthur functions not only as a character in *The Faerie Queene*, but also as a symbol for the theory of its genre.

[83] Pigna, *I romanzi* (1554), pp. 25f., trans. Weinberg, *History of Criticism*, vol. 1, pp. 445f.
[84] Oratio Toscanella, *Belleze del Fvrioso de M. Lodovico Ariosto, . . . con gli argomenti, et allegorie de i canti: con l'allegorie de nomi proprii principati . . .* (Venice, 1574), trans. Susannah Jane McMurphy, *Spenser's Use of Ariosto*, University of Washington Publications, Language and Literature, vol. 2 (1924), p. 15.

Arthurian Torso

A man, of many partes
(II.x.70)

[i]

The imitative epic, as we have said, can be an educator's interpretation of the primary epic; Spenser seems to be a similar interpreter of romance. His poem is like the work of a brilliant redactor who brings a canon and an interpretation out of a prolix and unclarified tradition. He begins by placing a nameless knight-errant in a distracting forest notable for its variety. Such a beginning can hardly help suggesting the issue of unity and multiplicity current in the critical debate over the nature of the romantic and heroic poem of Spenser's time.[85]

The structure of *The Faerie Queene* offers us a multiple unity. The full scheme of the poem seems to have been planned to accommodate both a deliberative Virgilian structure of twelve closed books and a rapid Ariostan structure of open-ended cantos. The same accommodation may also be observed at the level of the stanza, where Spenser's complex rhyme scheme and extra alexandrine purposively arrest the natural gallop of the *ottava rima*.[86] *The Faerie Queene* reads more slowly than the *romanzi*, partly because Spenser wants us to contemplate what a given marvel may mean rather than simply to hurry on to the next one.

The title page of *The Faerie Queene*, "Disposed into twelve books, Fashioning XII. Morall vertues," clearly came from the same hand as the title page of Spenser's *Calender*, "twelue Æglogues proportionable to the twelue months." The units of the larger poem might admit of a similar derivation. The letter to Raleigh refers to twelve quests being generated from the fairy queen's annual twelve-day feast, to which the poem would no doubt have recurred, had it been completed according to Spenser's announced plan. Minturno limits the epic action to a single year[87]—perhaps the whole cycle would have comprised such a period, each knight having his "moon" as well as his day.) Guyon reports that the yearly feast

[85] Cf. Tasso, in the second set of *Discorsi*, Lib. II: "No forest was ever so crowded with a great variety of trees as poetry is with a great diversity of subjects" (trans. Gilbert, *Literary Criticism*, p. 470).

[86] For "purposively arrest" one might almost put "madrigalize," especially in those places in Book II where Spenser dwells upon emotional states and harmonized landscapes.

[87] *L'Arte Poetica*, in Gilbert, *Literary Criticism*, p. 275 (from Naples edn. of 1725, p. 24).

was celebrated "The day that first doth lead the yeare around," in which case it may have coincided with the twelve days of Christmas. Being the patron of a classical virtue, Guyon may not be at liberty to confirm this; our information can be supplemented, however, by quoting E. K.'s argument to the *Calender*:

> . . . the incarnation of our mighty Saviour and eternall redeemer the L. Christ, who as then renewing the state of the decayed world, and returning the compasse of expired yeres to theyr former date and first commencement, left to us his heires a memoriall of his birth in the ende of the last yeere and beginning of the next.

A quest movement that renews "the state of the decayed world" is at least very close to the theme of Spenser's first book, and subsequent quests take their pattern from it.

A clockface has some advantages over a calendar for illustrating the mechanics of the whole design. Spenser planned to run through a twelve-part cycle twelve times, his cantos passing at the rate of the minute hand, his books at the rate of the hour hand. The two hands cross once an hour: the corresponding event in the poem is a given knight's meeting with Prince Arthur, a kind of "golden intersection" of each protagonist with his greater self. The clockface is divided into quintuple intervals, and Spenser's cantos—though they vary from thirty-five to eighty-seven stanzas —average about fifty-one; a "minute" of the poem would be ten stanzas. This last unit is not significant in *The Faerie Queene*, except perhaps once: the ninth canto of the fifth book looks as if it were regularly composed in five blocks of ten stanzas. Appropriately, a character here is named Order.

The multiple unity of *The Faerie Queene* has Arthur for its emblem. His resemblance to the other knights turns up often: his helmet is like the one worn by the hero of Book I; the name of the hero of Book II is once mistakenly used in place of his; the golden chain of concord, an important image in the legend of friendship, is first introduced when he allies himself with Redcrosse in Book I, and he forms friendships with most of the other knights in turn.[88] He and Artegall are introduced by a character

---

[88] The references are to I.ii.11, l. 6, with I.vii.32, l. 2; II.viii.48, where Guyon is used for Arthur before the 1609 edn.; and I.ix.1. See notes 97, 106, and 193 below. It follows from these resemblances that Arthur is a type-case—significantly a *stable* one—for the general phenomenon of the "dream-work" found throughout the poem: that is, a given figure resembles "A. in appearance, but is dressed like B., pursues the same occupation which recalls C., and yet all the time you know that it is really D." (Freud, *A General Introduction to Psychoanalysis*, reprint, New York, 1953, p. 183.) The most prominent example in Book I is the continuum represented by *Una : the false Una : Fidessa : Duessa : the whore of Babylon*.

whose name, Samient, derives from the root meaning "same," and Arte-gall's name may itself refer to their parity. As Spenser promised, the Prince regularly appears in each book engaged in behalf of the titular virtue, though in the legend of chastity he is no more effective than other male knights. His intervention typically allows Spenser to illustrate the limitations of some lesser knight or of that knight's virtue. Perfect holi-ness, for example, would be idolatrous if attributed to any other than the Deity—Redcrosse must depend on God's grace for salvation, and it is mediated to him through Arthur, Una, the penitential house of Celia, and the sacramental well and tree of life. Arthur is again associated with the specific intervention of heaven in his defense of the prostrate hero of temperance. In the subsequent battle with Maleger on Alma's behalf, Arthur's strength perhaps implies no more than a greater reserve of self-reliance or physical health; nonetheless, Maleger ultimately has his powers from a nature corrupted by sin and death, and these are enemies that temperance by itself cannot defeat.

If only because Arthur is greater than the other knights, his periodic intervention on their behalf carries a strong suggestion of a "descent from heaven" motif[89]—in Book I the descent of grace and the condescension of the Word, and in Book II the ministry of angels to fallen man. (Indeed, the Word of God comes down from heaven an armed warrior in Wis-dom 18:14ff., where it is identified with the destroying angel that passed over the houses of the Hebrews.) Thus the regular introduction of Arthur is readily referred to a supervisory view of the poem's action; Arthur's in-tervention not only aligns the poem with itself—if that expression can be allowed—but also with a divine milieu. This supervision is also suggested by allusions that synchronize the foreground narrative with the more leisurely movement of the heavens overhead. One evocative instance is the description—in Book III—of the moist daughters of huge Atlas moving into the ocean; there are parallels for the story-rhythms pertaining to both Florimell and Amoret. The first notable example of the alignment of the lower and upper worlds does not concern Atlas, but the Wagoner, other-wise known as Charles' Wain:

> By this the Northerne wagoner had set
>   His seuenfold teme behind the stedfast starre,
>   That was in Ocean waues yet neuer wet,
>   But firme is fixt, and sendeth light from farre
>   To all, that in the wide deepe wandring arre:
> (I.ii.1)

---

[89] For a complete study of this motif as a key to epic, see Thomas Greene, *The Descent from Heaven* (New Haven, 1963).

The constellation, Boötes, is also known as the Plow, and other team-drivers appear in Book I on the earth below. Saint George himself proves to be the adopted son of a plowman, who discovers the foundling while driving his toilsome team (I.x.66). Redcrosse is also discovered and raised up by Arthur, and it is very possible that the celestial prototype of the Wain has been chosen to intimate the Arthurian character of the heavens' watchful supervision. The errant Arthur turns up in Book III, canto iv, as the most rhetorically benighted character in the entire poem, and at first this occurrence seems to contradict any guiding role. Nonetheless, Arthur's sensitivity to the onset of darkness can suggest his affinity for its opposite, and therefore it is important that Arcturus (or Arthurus, according to a variant medieval spelling) is the name of the brightest star in Boötes, the "bear-guard" (*arktos* + *ouros*). Charles' Wain, it is proposed by the OED, comes by its name rather circuitously:

> The name appears to arise out of the verbal association of the star-name Arcturus with Arturus or Arthur, and the legendary association of Arthur with Charlemagne; so that what was originally the wain of Arcturus or Boötes ("Boötes' golden wain" *Pope* [*Thebais* 520]), became at length the wain of Carl or Charlemagne.[90]

Further, "the name *Carlewayne-sterre* occurs applied to the star Arcturus," and elsewhere it is said that "Arthurus is a signe made of vij sterres."[91] There are further reasons for postulating an astral Arthur, owing to his association with the number twelve.

It has more than once been suggested that Arthur was something of an afterthought on Spenser's part; he has been described as a device adopted late in the poem's composition to connect an otherwise disjointed Ariostan serial.[92] Such an explanation complicates as much as it simplifies. It does

---

[90] *OED, sub* "Charles' Wain." For the specific relevance of the wain image to the "georgic" subject of Book I, see Chap. II, "The Siege of Paradise," n. 219, and *ibid.*, sec. ii, nn. 235 and 236 with text, below. A. C. Hamilton, in a personal communication about this identification, directs me to the astronomy of Job, where the Geneva Bible glosses "Arcturus with his sonnes" (Job 38:32) as "The North Starre with those that are about him"; the gloss further explains the question in the second half of the following verse as asking, "Canst thou cause the heauenly bodies to haue anie power ouer the earthlie bodies?"

[91] *OED, sub* "Arturus," quoting John de Trevisa, *Bartholomeus* [*de Glanvilla*] *De Propretatibus Rerum*, VIII.xiii (W. de Worde, 1495), p. 334. Douglas' *Aeneis*, prologue to Book VIII, l. 151, mentions both "Charles wain" and "Arthur's House."

[92] See, e.g., Josephine Waters Bennett, *The Evolution of "The Faerie Queene"* (Chicago, 1942), pp. 61–79, and Graham Hough, *A Preface to "The Faerie Queene"* (New York, 1963), pp. 89–91. In proposing a variety of Arthurs that is nonetheless

not explain, for example, why Arthur himself behaves like an Ariostan knight in both those parts of the poem that seem to have been composed early and those that seem to have been composed late. Furthermore, the total rhythm of Arthur's activities in Spenser's first installment is rather closely duplicated by the second installment; whatever plan the poet may have once had, Arthur's place in the present poem was settled by the time the first three books were published.[93]

Some collective personage or corporate individual comparable to Arthur would be implied by any version of the poem we can now imagine. The allegory presumes the possibility of a mind embellished with all the virtues that the poem celebrates. Arthur comes to us as a kind of hypothesis, before we ever meet the knight. Thus the once and future king in Spenser is the duodecimal or "magnanimous" Arthur, in whose greater mind the virtues of all the other knights reside. The twelve knights of Spenser's declared plan are related to this Arthur in somewhat the way the Redcrosse knight is related to Christ: as members of a larger, unifying corporation. The twelve apostles are a prime symbol for that corporation, since the New Testament identifies them with the twelve tribes of Israel, and since the Church is also a new Israel. The Hebrew tribes themselves exhibit a twelvefold religious and political organization known as an *amphictyon*. An amphictyon is a federation of twelve clans that rotate, on a monthly basis among the members, the priestly functions of a common shrine.[94] Eventually these functions in Israel fell to a landless priestly class, but there are traces in the Bible of duodecimal orders for the Levites too (I Chron. 24:4, 25:7; cf. 27:1). Spenser's knights might be said to rotate the service of virtue from legend to legend, while the stationless and free-lance Arthur functions once in each of their legends in their stead—like an itinerant Levite. We may also mention here the metaphor of the "clock" of

---

answerable to a central conception, I have had the advantage of consulting Merritt Y. Hughes, "The Arthurs of *The Faerie Queene*," *Études anglaises*, 6 (1953), pp. 193–213.

[93] Arthur's constitutional inability to develop may be thought to keep him perpetually naive. See Frye, *Anatomy of Criticism*, p. 186, on romance, "at its most naive," being "an endless form in which a central character who never develops or ages goes through one adventure after another until the author himself collapses."

[94] Martin Noth, *Das System der zwölf Stämme Israels*, Beiträge zur Wissenschaft vom Alten (und Neuen) Testament (Stuttgart), IV:1 (1930), and *History of Israel*, rev. edn., trans. rev. by P. R. Ackroyd (New York, 1960), pp. 85–109. For other twelve-tribe groups, see Gen. 22:20–24 (sons of Nahor), Gen. 25:12–16 (sons of Ishmael), Gen. 36:10–14 (descendants of Esau). The ninth of Grimm's Folk Tales, "Die zwölf Brüder," when taken with its sacred equivalent, "Die zwölf Apostel" (the second of the *Kinderlegenden*), suggests such an amphictyon.

the Apostles, developed in early patristic authors; each Apostle constituted an hour in the "day" of the Lord.[95]

An obvious Arthurian symbol of completeness is the round table. In Malory we read that Merlin devised it as a symbol of the wholeness of the world, or the unity of the Arthurian order.[96] Spenser offers us no round table, but in starting his poem with St. George he serves notice that an analogous chivalric order is being instituted. The "knights of Maidenhead," sporadically referred to, manifest the same idea. Sir Satyrane, who is one of them, defends St. George's lady in Book I, and also Florimell, her counterpart in Book III. Using Florimell's girdle, he binds the beast that chases her, as the Saint in *The Golden Legend* bound the dragon with the lady's girdle. The girdle is of course identified with the emblem of the Knights of the Garter, who traditionally numbered twenty-four.

In *The Faerie Queene*, Arthur's number is twelve. He wears a jeweled "bauldrick" across his breastplate, "That shynd, like twinkling stars, with stones most pretious rare."[97] One thinks of Aaron's breastplate with its twelve stones symbolizing the sons of Jacob. Joseph dreams of his brothers as eleven stars bowing before him, so the identification (by Philo and Josephus) of the stones with the zodiac has a biblical basis.[98] Here the central stone seems to symbolize Arthur's lady, and the queen is elsewhere associated with the star-goddess Astraea, or Virgo, the sixth zodiacal sign. We may compare his service to Gloriana to Hercules' twelve labors for the "glory of Hera," for it is the service of glory that Spenser has "laboured to pourtraict." In his dedication the poet consecrates his "La-

[95] Examples are Augustine, *Tract. in Joan. Evang.*, Tract. XLIX.xi.8 (PL, XXXV, 1750–1751) and *Ennar. in Ps.*, LV.v (PL, XXXVI, 650) (trans. in NPNF, 1st Series, vol. 7, p. 272, and vol. 8, p. 220); Ambrose, *Expos. Evang. Sec. Lucam*, VII.222 (PL, XV, 1759); and *Clementine Recognitions*, IV.37. The remoter sources are described in Jean Daniélou, *Primitive Christian Symbols*, trans. Donald Attwater (Baltimore, 1963), pp. 124–135, "The Twelve Apostles and the Zodiac." An exactly comparable symbolism occurs in Dante's heaven of the sun, where the Church's intellectuals form two circles of twelve lights: the circle is a *horologe* (*Paradiso* X.139), and may also recall the twelvefold tree in Rev. 22:2 (*Paradiso* XII.96).

[96] *Morte d'Arthur*, Winchester ms. version, XIV.ii, in Malory, *Works*, ed. Eugene Vinaver, 2nd edn. (Oxford, 1967), vol. 2, p. 906: the table is described as a unity to which all the world repairs; it betokens the roundness of the world. (In the Caxton version, Everyman's Library, vol. 2, p. 193.) In Spenser the comparable Arthurian symbol is Merlin's crystal ball, which was "Like to the world it selfe, and seem'd a world of glass" (III.ii.19).

[97] I.vii.29f. For the use of *baudricke* to mean the zodiac, see V.i.11, and *Prothalamion*, l. 174. For the idea that the twelve cantos of Book V constitute an epyllionic *Heracleid*—a subject of Renaissance critical discussion deriving from *Poetics* viii (1451a)—carried out under the twelve zodiacal signs, see Chap. III, "The Course of Justice," sec. i. For Arthur and Artegall, see n. 106, below.

[98] Philo, *De Somnis*, II.xvi.111–113 (in Loeb *Philo*, vol. 5, p. 493); Josephus, *Jewish Antiquities*, II.xvi.

40

bovrs" to live with the eternity of his "Magnificent" and "Renowmed" queen's "Fame." Hercules' labors were often explained as a solar myth, but even without Spenser's frequent allusions to this classical type, Arthur has many of the qualities of the periegetic hero; and at least one long poem of the Renaissance, Palengenius' *Zodiac of Life*, was superficially organized by means of the twelve signs.

In light of these associations, it is significant that Arthur's link with the number twelve is pre-Spenserian. In his opening canto, Boiardo's Charlemagne sits with the Paladins at *the round table*,[99] and the peers of France were twelve in number. Arthur traditionally fought twelve battles and early in Malory there appears a memorial device which may be related: a twelvefold candlestick that represents eleven kings in attitudes of defeat before a twelfth candle representing Arthur. Merlin predicts that at the death of Arthur the candles will be extinguished, and then he prophesies the accomplishment of the Grail-quest elsewhere associated with the dissolution of the round table.[100]

The mutual attraction of symbols for the Christian and chivalric fellowships probably needs no special emphasis. It was easy to treat the Apostles as knights, "new cavaliers entered in the field against Pluto," as Boccaccio once calls them.[101] In the Spanish poem known as *The Celestial Chivalry*, reported by Ticknor, Christ is represented as a knight and the Apostles as the twelve knights of his round table.[102] The resonance of such

[99] *Orl. Inn.* I.i.13. (The two courts are again aligned in the celebrated stanzas on the deficiency of romantic interest in the traditional court of the French king —II.xviii.1–3.)

[100] *Morte d'Arthur*, Winchester ms. version, II.xi; Caxton version, Everyman's Library, vol. 1, p. 59. Cf. Joseph's dream in Gen. 37:9.

[101] *Filocolo*, Lib. I, in Boccaccio, *Opera*, vol. 1, ed. Salvatori Battaglia (Bari, 1938), p. 10. As the title "Pantheon" reminds us, the mythical counterpart for the legendary military leader and his elite comitatus would be a nuclear group of gods, such as the Olympian pantheon of the Homeric epic. For other such pantheons for military societies, see Toynbee, *A Study of History* (New York, 1963), vol. 5, *Disintegrations of Civilizations*, pp. 230–233. Beowulf, for example, takes twelve men with him when he goes to the dragon's barrow, and twelve warriors celebrate his funeral (ll. 2401, 3170). At the center of Dante's underworld, the buried Satan is ringed by a kind of comitatus of giants: one—Nimrod—is compared to the Peer Roland, and beyond him we meet both Gano and Judas. In *Le Tornoiement de L'Antechrist* of Huon de Mére, Arthur and his knights of the round table join with the virtues and St. Michael to conquer Antichrist and the vices (in P. Tarbé, ed., *Collection des poètes de Champagne*, Reims, 1851, vol. 12, pp. 59–61).

[102] Hierónimo de San Pedró, Pt. II of *The Celestial Chivalry*, "Leaves of the Celestial Rose" (Valencia, 1554), in George Ticknor, *History of Spanish Literature*, 6th edn. (Boston, 1888), vol. 1, pp. 256–260. Conversely, in the old *Pilgrimage of Charlemagne to Jerusalem*, sec. VIII, when the king enters the temple at Jerusalem with his twelve palladins, the rector exclaims to himself that the twelve Apostles have come, and that the thirteenth seems to be one like God. (Eduard Koschwitz

an analogy gives the Grail matter some of its portentous character. In *The Quest of the Holy Grail* the round table is derived from the table of the Last Supper, and the mystery is exhibited in the presence of twelve knights.[103] Malory carries this Christianization of the Grail knights almost as far when he has Christ himself allude to them as his Apostles. In a Latin eclogue called *Pantheon*, Boccaccio synthesizes an even more remarkable allegory:[104] one section of the poem treats twelve phases of Christ's life, each under an appropriate pagan or secular avatar: Christ harrows hell as Hercules, for example, recovering his herd from Cacus. The twelfth of these incarnations is none other than Arthur, sending forth the twelve knightly Apostles to preach the gospel.

[ii]

It may well be that Arthur is not fully developed in the present poem, because he is not allowed to emerge other than episodically. It would violate a decorum that Spenser's structure seems designed to enforce if Arthur were to gradually overshadow the knights in whose names he is being properly magnified. Therefore both the Arthur of the poem's fore-conceit and the Arthur that would have been fully fashioned upon the completion of the poet's greater design are posterior to the poem we now have. Arthur is merely "the *idea* of a perfect knight"—and likely to remain so. By the end of twelve books the Prince should have had his quota of twelve cantos, but until then the whole man can only be latent in the pattern, when compared to the self-realization allowed the other knights. Traditionally, of course, Arthur is asleep in Wales, and even in this poem he moves about like a man in a dream. Since he does not know who his parents are when he reads it, the point of the British chronicle history in Book II is rather lost on him, and it ends "without full point, or other Cesure right."[105] He has dreamed about the object of his quest, the fairy queen, but he is unsure what she looks like. In a certain sense, she cannot be revealed until the poem is.

Arthur's intimations of glory are paralleled by the less Quixotic vision that guides Britomart. Britomart is a British lady-knight who seeks her lover Artegall in fairyland on the basis of the vision she has had of him in

---

edn., Leipzig, 1900, trans. Margaret Schlauch, in *Medieval Narrative*, New York, 1928, p. 80.)

[103] *The Quest of the Holy Grail*, trans. P. M. Matarasso, Penguin Classics (Baltimore, 1969), pp. 97–99 (chap. vi), and p. 273 (chap. xv).

[104] *Opere Latine Minore* (*Opera*, vol. 9), ed. Aldo Francesco Massèra (Bari, 1928), pp. 49–55. The poem is described in W. Leonard Grant, *Neo-Latin Literature and the Pastoral* (Chapel Hill, 1965), pp. 102–104.

[105] II.x.68, quoted below as the epigraph for "The Testimony of Mutabilitie."

the looking-glass of Venus. The symbolism of the poem—especially the dynastic symbolism—partially relates these two pairs of royal lovers, as either alternates, or doublets, or surrogates. The British crown is destined to pass from Arthur's father, through Arthur, to the offspring of Britomart and Artegall. Arthur and Artegall are apparently half-brothers, although Spenser does not directly say so (Arthur's mother Igrayne is the wife of Artegall's father Gorlois.)[106] Artegall's quest is assigned him in the way prescribed in the letter to Raleigh, where prior to a given legend an aggrieved party seeks redress at the court of the fairy queen; Arthur is assigned a similar quest under similar circumstances in Artegall's legend proper. It has been remarked that the free-lance Arthur has the power of movement that belongs to the queen in chess, and the queen is the circumscribed figure here.[107] However, Britomart is like the same chess piece: she requires no assistance from Arthur, and she is able to rescue her own checkmated lover, as well as other stymied knights. The "Magnificke Virgin," in fact, is fully realized in a way the magnificent Prince is not. Like Alice, she is able to enter the looking-glass world and eventually encounter the knights she saw there. She crosses Arthur's path twice, but on both occasions the juncture is curiously muted. This is particularly noticeable in the legend of friendship when the two come into the same area, each accompanied by one half of a separated pair of lovers. Unaccountably, to generations of Spenserians, the two lovers are not reunited, though the epiphany of the "Great Venus Temple" canto follows just as surely as if they had been. Originally, in the 1590 edition, the lovers were joined by the questing Britomart; she was slightly envious of their prolonged embrace, mentally putting herself in the same situation.[108] Maybe this wishfulness would have been inappropriate after her actual meeting with her lover, and in the presence of Arthur.

In the historical allegory the inaccessibility of the queen in part refers to the reluctance of Elizabeth to marry, but there is more to it than that. One may compare the relation to that of Alice and the Red King. The problem in that story was who was dreaming whom, or, with respect to mental territory, who was inside whose. Arthur is an English prince inside fairyland; the Tudor queen seems to be a fay inside England—at least according to the elegant conceit of her courtliest poet. The fairy queen is not, at any rate, to be found in that part of fairyland actually presented in

---

[106] One concludes that Arthur is half-brother to Artegall by connecting the traditional story of Arthur's siring, alluded to in the letter to Raleigh, with *F.Q.* III.iii.27, where the husband of Arthur's mother Igrayne—namely Gorlois—is said to be Artegall's father. For the Arthur-Britomart exchange, see n. 193, below.

[107] Frye, *Anatomy of Criticism*, p. 195.

[108] III.xii.46, 1590 edn.; my description echoes Frye, "The Structure of Imagery," in *Fables of Identity*, p. 83.

the poem. Quests originate at her court and return to it; virtues are taken from her and referred back to her; but the "Presence" itself is always manifested indirectly, through hearsay or reflection or parody. Of the three knights whose quests are actually said to begin from her court, two are Britishers, rather than fays. Their quests involve historical allegories of the national church (Redcrosse) and British foreign policy (Artegall). Two negative versions of the court, the palace of Lucifera and the "Temple" of Philotime, treat worldly pride and corrupt ambition, and are intended to remind us of what the court of the fairy queen is not. A third version of the court is the palace of Mercilla. Its inclusion allows Arthur to receive a commission from a type of the British sovereign without entering British territory, just as he was enabled to read about British history, at the corresponding establishment in Book II, without seeing his own place in it. In short, the court is maintained as an English reality on the periphery of the poem. Its queen belongs to the poem's horizon, at the vanishing-point where the English and faerie parallels meet. Allegory, in its nature, requires just such an "otherness of parallels." Alice is told that if she were to awaken the Red King she would disappear, for she is what the Red King is dreaming. One supposes that a premature recognition of Arthur by Gloriana would have had a similar annihilating effect on *The Faerie Queene*.

It may be inevitable that the reader, as he progresses through the poem, will sense Arthur as more and more adventitious to its real establishment. The poem intends to build the structure of virtue in our minds, a structure for which Arthur on horseback becomes a somewhat out-of-touch factotum. What is needed is an appreciation of the different structures in the poem that correspond to different "ends." We have seen such a principle at work in Ariosto, where two knights in love seem to move against each other, in a kind of counterpoint of cross-purposes. One may compare the relation of the Arthur-Gloriana and the Artegall-Britomart strands in Spenser. The former gives the poem its framework and its title; the latter celebrates the ancestors of the poet's prince in the prominent foreground.

We also need to be able to entertain a plurality of Arthurs, beyond the "amphictyonic" Arthur just described. First there is a romantic Arthur, legendary for his chivalry and courtesy. He is a prince, but only first among equals, and therefore capable of forming sound friendships. He is famous for his largesse, and hence he is "magnificent"; his generosity also makes him capable of falling in love.[109] Perhaps there is a touch of the infatuated

---

[109] For Arthur's largesse, see *Romance of the Rose*, ll. 1063ff., 1264ff. For Arthur in the Chaucerian version, see F. N. Robinson's edn. of Chaucer, ll. 1197–1199. See also *The Chronicle of Iohn Hardyng*, ed. Henry Ellis (London, 1812), chap. lxxxv, p. 148, where Arthur's liberality is given notice.

Orlando about this character—as in his chase after Florimell—and even a hint of the fatuous Sir Thopas. There is something fantastic about his love for Gloriana, as there is about Don Quixote's for Dulcinea; the Don himself acknowledges that Dulcinea is a literary invention. Quixote especially modeled himself on Amadis de Gaula. Rather than an alienation similar to Orlando's, he elects Amadis' penitential rustication (for an imagined offense to his mistress) as the program for his own madness in the wilds. Spenser assigns this motif to Arthur's squire, Timias, who offends the private person of the queen, Belphoebe; nevertheless, Arthur's own rustication in fairyland is a larger version of the same romantic pattern. The long-lost love of Amadis was the famous British princess Oriana, and at least one fellow poet associated her directly with Spenser's fairy queen.[110]

A second Arthur is British and "historical," though as Spenser in the letter aptly remarks, "furthest . . . from suspicion of present time." (E. K. is rather less sympathetic: he speaks of "certain fine fablers and lowd lyers, such as were the Authors of King Arthure the great.") Arthur is patriotically introduced into the poem as a compliment to the Welsh ancestry of the Tudor dynasty. He is thus linked with a destiny, as are Ariosto's Ruggiero and Spenser's Artegall, and he may be said to represent the English imperial idea—here he is like the nautical Arthur cited at the opening of Hakluyt's *Voyages*.[111] He is the protagonist of a quest, and being the largest protagonist around, and a national savior, he takes on a decidedly messianic character.

The messianic Arthur appears in the eighth canto of the legend of holiness to rescue the Redcrosse knight from a giant, a harlot, and a dragon. Like St. Michael (who, in Tasso, carries a shield similar to Arthur's),[112] this Arthur throws down the dragon of the Apocalypse; like the Cyrus of Isaiah, he ends the Babylonian captivity of a chosen people; as with his British ancestor Constantine, there is a myth of his return (Constantine's latter-day appearance will be millennial, and Petrarch associates it with the purification of the church);[113] finally, like the "historical" Arthur of Geof-

[110] See *The Triumphs of Oriana*, ed. Thomas Morley (1601), reprinted in A. H. Bullen, *Shorter Elizabethan Poems* (Westminster, 1903; texts taken from Arber, *An English Garner*), pp. 153–164. The poem by Daniel Norcome on p. 155 identifies the nymph Oriana with "that maiden Queene of Fairy Land." A fairy with the name Gloriande is among the personnel of Berner's version of *Huon of Bordeaux*.

[111] *The Principal Navigations, Voyages* . . . (London, 1927–1928), vol. 1, pp. 53–55. E. K. on "Aprill," l. 120.

[112] *Ger. Lib.* VII.82, IX.53.

[113] Petrarch, Son. 108 (*Canz.* CXXXVIII). A preceding sonnet (*Canz.* CXXXVI) describes the judgment on the Papal Court at Avignon and the reunification of the Church under a new leader yet to come. A translation first attributed to Wyatt by Harington in *Nugae Antiquae* (London, 1769, 1775) reads: "thow filthie whore / Of Babilon . . . pallais of strompetts" (Son. 105). Son. 108 concludes: "Or Constantin non torna; / Ma tolga il mondo tristo che 'l sostene" (Constantine will not come, but let him take away the sad world that sustains it [hope of his return?]). Milton,

frey and Malory (who engages the emperor Lucius) he defeats the power of Rome.[114]

The patriotic celebration of Arthur is, in the language of the Italian critics, at least as close to the "end of the poet" as to the "end of the poem," which is the fashioning of a gentleman in virtuous and gentle discipline. Much has been written to explain Arthur's virtue of magnificence, since the inclusive virtue in Aristotle is high-mindedness, or magnanimity, rather than large-handedness. Aristotle groups these virtues together in the *Nicomachean Ethics* (II.vii and IV.i–iv), and also describes a nameless lesser virtue that is as closely related to magnanimity as generosity is to magnificence (II.iv.).[115] This virtue observes a mean between excessive and defective ambition, or *Philotimia*; Aquinas simply calls it by that name, and defines it as love of honor.[116] Vicious and virtuous personifica-

---

Of Reformation, translates: "Another *Constantine* comes not in haste." The translation attributed to Wyatt expands: "Loe! Constantine, that is turned into dust, / Shall not retourne for to maintaine thie lust; / For thei greate pryde shall teare thye seate asonder / And scourdge thee so that all the world shall wonder." For the celebration of Constantine as a Mosaic deliverer and a champion who wounded the beast of Revelation, see John Foxe, *Acts and Monuments*, ed. Cattley, vol. 1, Pt. II, pp. 289–304.

[114] Arthur's campaign against the Emperor Lucius is recounted in Book V of Caxton's version of the *Morte d'Arthur*.

[115] The virtues of magnificence and magnanimity are closely associated in Aquinas, *Summa Theol.*, Pt. II, 1st Pt., q.60, art.5, and Pt. II, 2nd Pt., q.128ff. They are also associated in Chaucer, *Parson's Tale*, ll. 727ff. Macrobius, *Comm. in Somn. Scip.*, I.viii, classifies both virtues among the seven subdivisions of fortitude (along with constancy); Cicero, *De Invent.* II.liv, classifies magnificence alone this way. Pierre de La Primaudaye, in *The French Academie* (London, 1586), p. 289, writes of magnanimity "as that which vndoubtedly is comprehended vnder the first part of *Fortitude*, which *Cicero* calleth magnificence." For the medieval tradition, see Michael F. Molony, "St. Thomas and Spenser's Virtue of Magnificence," *Journal of English and Germanic Philology*, 52 (1953), pp. 58–62; William O. Harris, *Skelton's Magnyfycence and the Cardinal Virtue Tradition* (Chapel Hill, 1965), pp. 62–69; and Rosemond Tuve, *Allegorical Imagery* (Princeton, 1968), pp. 57–63 and seq. See also below, Chap. III, "The Temper of Occasion," sec. ii, nn. 61ff. and text.

[116] *Summa Theol.*, Pt. II, 1st Pt., q.60, art.5. In *Summa Theol.*, Pt. II, 2nd Pt., q.134, art.1, magnificence is said to pertain to all the virtues, because the doing of great works does also. In *ibid.* q.132, art.2, the vice of vainglory is opposed to the magnanimity treated in q.129; in q.128, resp., and q.129, art.6, magnanimity is easily substituted for "confidence," one of the four Ciceronian parts of fortitude that also include magnificence; in q.130, art.1-2, the vice of presumption is opposed to magnanimity, and in q.131, art.2, ambition is said to be an extreme of this virtue. Philotimia, at q.129, art.2, is said to be the extreme of the virtue about ordinary honors. We may deduce from these texts that Spenser's Lucifera and Philotime are both opposed to magnanimity.

tions of this quality appear in the legend of temperance, in the persons of the proud Philotime and the high-minded Prays-desire—indeed, the latter name translates the former. Philotime, we have said, is a negative version of Arthur's aspiration, Gloriana. Desire-of-praise, on the other hand, is recognized as the proper animus of his quest, and he converses with her in the appropriate place, the parlor-heart of the Castle of Alma, or the soul. Arthur's hostess is herself a type of the virgin queen, and the scene turns on self-recognition, and even self-acceptance. In other words, Spenser conjugates Arthur with a virtue closely linked by Aristotle with magnanimity, and he distinguishes Gloriana from that virtue's degraded form.

To explain why Spenser identifies Arthur with magnificence, instead of magnanimity, we must turn to the "end of the poet." I mean the Renaissance epic poet, who inspires emulation in his patron or audience by praising his hero; one of his rhetorical aims is the celebration of what is praiseworthy. We remember that in Homer we find not only military and political instruction, but also "the worthy commendation and laude of noble princis":

> where with the reders shall be so all inflamed, that they most feruently shall desire and coueite, by the imitation of their vertues, to acquire sem blable glorie.[117]

In designating Arthur's animus as desire for praise or for glory, Spenser embodies in a character an "intention" of the hero that cannot be sharply distinguished from the intention of the poet toward the ideally responsive reader. A character in *The Faerie Queene* wishes Arthur good luck in his quest to aid Florimell in the appropriate terms:

> So may ye gaine to you full great renowme,
>   Of all good Ladies through the world so wide,
>   And haply in her hart find highest rowme,
>   Of whom ye seeke to be most magnifide:
>   At least eternall meede shall you abide.
>
> (III.v.11)

The heart in this stanza recalls the scene of Arthur's interview with Prays-desire in the Castle of Alma. But insofar as the poem's external audience also takes Arthur's example to heart, or accedes in his magnification, the receptivity in question passes from the internal characters of the poem and reappears in the reader. After all, Arthur's chosen audience, the fairy queen, shares her position with the poet's chosen audience, the queen who is her English counterpart. And yet the queen, external to the poem in this respect, remains internal to Arthur, in the form of his own "desire

[117] Elyot, *Gouernour*, I.x, Everyman's Library, pp. 36f.

of praise." Thus the reader, subjected to the same animus toward "praise-worthie deedes" (II.vii.2), might well anticipate a parallel Arthurianiza-tion. As Sidney would say, the poem bestows an Arthur upon the world to make many Arthurs.

Thus, in another version of the looking-glass situation, Arthur not only aspires to be praised—to be magnified by the fairy queen—but also attracts and deserves this magnification. In both cases the hero inspires emulation by being praiseworthy. Again, the *Aeneid* may offer a precedent. Behind Aeneas' image, according to Donatus, stands Augustus, "in whose honor this poem was written."[118] Servius says that Virgil intended to praise Augustus through his ancestors (*ad Aen., Praef.*). Boccaccio says that Virgil "desired to praise" the Julian gens in Aeneas' repudiation of Dido.[119] "In Aeneas' praise he praised Augustus also," writes the humanist Francesco Filelfo.[120] It was Virgil's intent, according to Gawain Douglas' prologue to his translation of the *Aeneid*, "Aenes for to loif and magnify" (l. 422). The connection between Aeneas and praiseworthiness seemed even closer to some. Fulgentius explained that the name Misenus means "hating praise,"[121] and perhaps with this as his clue, Landino reports that Aeneas' name means praise (*aenos*).[122] Scaliger takes up the same theme.

[118] *Interpretationes Vergilianae*, ed. H. George (Leipzig, 1905), Proemium, p. 2.

[119] *Genealogia Deorum Gentilium*, XIV.xiii, trans. Charles G. Osgood, *Boccaccio on Poetry*, The Library of Liberal Arts (reprint, Indianapolis, 1956), p. 69. (Hereafter referred to as *G.D.G.*)

[120] *Epistolae* (Hedmondi le Feuvre, Paris, 1520), Lib. I, fol. iii, 12: "Aeneae laudas Augustum quoque laudavit." Cf. Christoforo Landino, *Quaestiones . . . In P. Virgilii Maronis allegorias. Liber tertius . . . quartus* (Venice, n.d. [after 1500]), fol. fvi^v–gi^r: "maronis autem longe alia ratio est: qui cum Aeneae res in laudem Augusti exornandas: & librum ipsum omnibus poeticis luminibus illustrandum sibi sumpsisset: non iis quae ipse suo ingenio eligeret: sed iis quae historia porrigit hanc supremam ingenii sui laudem comparat. Mirus profecto vir qui non ex optatis sed ex datis ita opus intexat: ut cum historiam minime deserat: per eam tamen incredibile integuemento humanam foelicitatem exprimat. . . ." (With Virgil the reason is very different: when he took up the affairs of Aeneas to be elaborated for the praise of Augustus, and the book itself to be made illustrious by all the lights of poetry, then he prepared this high praise of his genius not out of those things which he himself chose by his own ingenuity, but from those which history offers. Indeed, what a wondrous man, who wove his work thus, not from what he wanted, but from what he was given: for he deserts history as little as possible. Yet through it he expresses human felicity incredibly, in his fiction.)

[121] *Virgiliana Continentia*, in R. Helm, ed., *Fvlgentivs. Opera* (Leipzig, 1898), p. 96: "misio enim Grece orreo dicitur, enos uero laus uocatur."

[122] *Quaestiones Camaldulenses* (Venice, after 1500), fol. gi^r: Aeneas follows Aphrodite, or divine love, ". . . qua matre quis ne sciat natum aeneam nomen ab eo quod est aenos id est a laude deductum. Virum enim ad omnia & excelsa natum: quis non summis laudibus prosequatur?" (. . . by which mother who does not know the name Aeneas to have been derived at his birth from what is *aenos*, i.e., from

He recounts the completeness of the capacities of Virgil's hero and maintains that such completeness was no accident, "for he was said to have been the most sapient of his times, dissuading from war, as a just man; fighting war, as a brave man," and so forth. Scaliger then adds that "therefore Homer is not to be heard, when he writes that Aeneas was called *ainon* by Venus on account of gloomy auspices: but because he was praised, as it is said, wholly by all—for this is *ainein*."[123]

Virgil intended to praise and magnify Aeneas; Spenser intends the same magnification for Arthur; thus, Arthur is magnificent. The probability that this reasoning is correct is increased by Scaliger's discussion of the three characters of style: low, middle, and high.[124] Aulus Gellius, Scaliger reports, calls the high style *uber*, others call it *magniloquum*, or *magnificum* or *altiloquum*. Still others call it *magnum*; some *plenum*. Scaliger himself will even call it "generous." Plutarch (i.e., the *Life of Homer*) defines it in terms of greatly emphatic reverberation, Hermogenes says it is vehement and inciting, and Gellius characterizes it in terms of dignity and magnitude. The styles may be applied to subject matter, and in another chapter, on grandiloquence, Scaliger remarks that the grand style has characteristic subjects:

> Therefore there is a kind of *Altiloquum* Poem, because it contains grave persons, excellent things: . . . Serious personae are Gods, Heroes, Kings, Generals, Unions of Citizens. . . . It is the nature of the king's office, to be superior to the rest, its end is to govern. And so a King: that nature falls to him, which excells in strength (*robor*) and wisdom (*sapientiam*). The condition of his nature is the application of his strength for protecting and his wisdom for ruling.[125]

The styles may also refer to persons, or rather orators. "Therefore, when he acknowledges *hathron* in Ulysses and Pascuius, he [Aulus Gellius]

---

praise. For [consider] a man born for all high things: who would not follow him with the highest praises?).

[123] *Poetices*, III.x (Heidelberg edn. of 1617), p. 207. Scaliger is rejecting the etymology of the Homeric *Hymn* to Aphrodite, ll. 198f.

[124] *Poetices*, IV.i, *edn. cit.*, p. 400; citing Aulus Gellius, *Att. Noct.* IV.xiv.7.

[125] *Poetices*, IV.ii, *edn. cit.*, p. 421. There is authority for this idea in Aristotle, who says (*Poetics* xxiv, 1459b): ". . . in Epic poetry, owing to the narrative form, many events simultaneously transacted can be presented; and these, if relevant to the subject, add mass (*ogkos*) to the poem. The Epic has here an advantage, and one that conduces to magnificence (*megaloprepeian*), to diverting the mind of the hearer, and relieving the story with varying episodes." (Trans. adapted from S. H. Butcher, *Aristotle's Theory of Poetry and Fine Art*, London, 1902, p. 93.) For *megaloprepia* as a quality of style, see also Dionysus Halicarnassus, *De compositione verborum* 16 and *De Thucydide* 23; and Demetrius Phalaris, *On Style* 37.

calls it magnificent. Plutarch assigns *hathron* to Thucydides. Truly, there are just as many vices as the contrary: for the elated and magnificent, Gellius substitutes the inflated and the tumid." Homer's Ulysses exemplifies the grand, rich, and *magnificum* style in speaking.[126] Tasso also calls the proper style for the heroic subject the "magnificent" style.

We may conclude that Arthur personifies the poet's own formal poetic ambition, which is to produce "twelue huge labours hight extold," or at least "a work of labour long, and endless prayse" (I.xi.27, I.xi.7). Arthur's appearance and reappearance thus come to symbolize rhetorical ideals. His "return" especially suggests the power of the poet to enlarge upon his subject—to amplify. And his "magnificence" stands for the power of the poet to magnify that subject—by means of the "haughtie" style, as Spenser calls it (I.x.7). Significantly, it is a magnificence that makes its first appearance in Spenser's high poem as the enemy of the inflated and tumid Orgoglio.

[iii]

"In that Faery Queene," Spenser advises Raleigh, "I meane glory in my general intention." We may therefore extend the above remarks to glorification. Gloriana reminds us a little of Juno or Hera, the offstage goddess who was ultimately responsible for the twelve labors of Heracles, "the glory of Hera." Arthur's Prays-desire holds the poplar branch sacred to that hero. Gloriana's capital is Cleopolis, the city to which her knights return, presumably in glory. We never visit Cleopolis, though we hear of its relation to the New Jerusalem in Book I. We do, however, enter the palace of Mercilla, which displays the golden roof and other signs of magnificence that also make their claims in the sinister environments of Lucifera and Philotime. We must reflect or speculate on glory, it appears, in Lucifera's mirror.[127]

---

[126] *Poetices*, IV.i; *edn. cit.*, p. 400: "Plutarch" again means the anonymous *Vita Homeri*, sec. 72 (text in Thomas Gale, ed., *Opuscula Mythologica, Physica et Ethica*, Amsterdam, 1688, p. 314). For Tasso on the magnificent style, see *Dell'Arte*, III, in *Prose*, ed. Mazzali, pp. 392–410: it is the sublime style proper to epic (p. 392); its vice is *il gonfio*, the swollen (p. 393); and the swollen "is similar to the *glorioso* who makes use of assets he does not have to make himself glorious and those he does have for a purpose" (p. 400). For the relation to Spenser's Braggadocchio here, see below, Chap. IV, "Perpetual Generations," sec. v, *ad fin*. The accepted doctrine is found in Castelvetro: "The fable of the two poetries, epic and tragic, ought to contain action not simply human, but magnificent as well, and royal" (*Poetica d'Aristotele*, Basel, 1576, p. 188); Dante's poem is "grande e magnifico" (p. 164); and the multiple plot conduces to "grandezza, & magnificenza" (p. 179).

[127] The references are to II.ix.39; I.x.58; I.iv.4, 8, II.vii.43–46; V.ix.21f., 27–29; I.iv.10. As shown elsewhere, Lucifera and Philotime are both Fortune figures; Fortune, in turn, is sister to Fame (according to Chaucer, *House of Fame*, III.1547).

Lucifera's gaudy pretense is subtly differentiated from Philotime's gloomy presumption, but in both cases their courts may be described as parodies of greatness. The deadly rivalry that characterizes the activity of Philotime's courtiers reflects her own rivalry with the gods. On her classical side, Philotime resembles the envious and ambitious Juno, whom Jove hung out of heaven by golden chains; on her biblical side, she rules a court that is closely related to all the satanic kingdoms of the world and the glory of them (Matt. 4:8). The enthronement and triumph of Lucifera even more directly suggest a parody of the biblical glory of God—both the glory that he is owed, and the "glory" that is the visible form of his presence, transcending any representation through idols and images.[128]

Given the ecclesiastical allegory of Book I in particular, we ought to remember that this semi-physical glory envelops Moses on Sinai, and that it settles on the tabernacle and temple when they have been properly sanctified. It then appears in the throne-visions of the prophets—the same visionary throne before which the saints in Revelation glorify God. Isaiah beholds this throne covered with the six-winged seraphim and the temple filled with their train. Ezekiel sees God moving on this throne, here a chariot borne by four sure-footed creatures with hooves that sparkle like burnished brass and wheels of beryl full of eyes. Spenser's imagery for Lucifera is based on sinister classical counterparts: Phaëthon, "rapt with whirling wheels," and Juno on her golden chair,

> . . . when she does ride
> To *Ioues* high house through heauens bras-paued way
> Drawne of faire Pecocks, that excell in pride
> And full of *Argus* eyes their tailes dispredden wide.
>
> (I.iv.17)

We may compare the triumphal chariot in Dante, drawn by the four creatures from Ezekiel:

> Each had six wings, their feathers
> were full of eyes; the eyes of Argus,
> if living, would be similar. . . .

> Africanus or even Augustus never delighted Rome
> with so beautiful a chariot;
> and that of the sun would seem poor beside it,

[128] The glory is partly a deduction from the pillars of cloud and fire of the exodus. It fills the newly raised tabernacle of Exodus 40:34f., and later the temple of Solomon (I Kings 8:10f.). Then on the eve of the destruction of Jerusalem, Ezekiel sees the glory lift from the temple and depart from the city (Ezek. 9:3; 10:4, 18f.; 11:22f.); later he sees it return to the new temple (43:1ff.). For the throne visions, see Isa. 6:14, Ezek. 1:4ff., Dan. 7:9ff., and Rev. 4.

> that of the sun which, going astray,
> was consumed at the prayer of the earth
> when Jove was mysteriously just.
> (*Purgatorio* XXIX.94–96, 115–120)[129]

"But this was drawne of six unequall beasts," and their processional does not bring down a cloud of glory; it raises a foggy mist.[130]

The cloth-of-state imagery from Lucifera's palace recurs at the palace of Mercilla, who represents the public person of the queen in the legend of justice:

> All ouer her a cloth of state was spred,
>> Not of rich tissew, nor of cloth of gold,
>> Nor of ought else, that may be richest red,
>> But like a cloud, as likest may be told,
>> That her brode spreading wings did wyde vnfold;
>> Whose skirts were bordred with bright sunny beams,
>> Glistring like gold, amongst the plights enrold,
>> And here and there shooting forth siluer streames,
> Mongst which crept little Angels through the glittering gleames.
> (V.ix.28)

One thinks here of the veil of the temple and the "cherubim of glory overshadowing the mercyseat."[131] Throne, cloud, shooting light, wings, angels, the garment of light, and the accompanying hymns are all paralleled in the descriptions of the glory in the Old Testament.[132] The curtains and the veil of the tabernacle specifically depict cherubim, the cherubs here. Elizabeth's very name seemed to consecrate her to God, or indicate an association with his house—singularly right for the reigning head of the renewed national church.[133] Spenser once says that he has "deified" the

---

[129] Trans. H. R. Huse, Rinehart edn. (New York, 1961), pp. 304f.

[130] I.iv.36. Vanity and mist are associated at II.xii.34f., where "vanity" is succeeded by "a grosse fog," a "wastfull mist." For the conjunction of the vain and vaporous, cf. James 4:14. "For what is your life? It is euen a vapour that appeareth for a little time, and afterwarde vanisheth away" (Geneva Bible). (Cf. also the cloud of Job 7:79 and the smoke of Ps. 102:3; at II.iii.5, Braggadocchio is "puffed vp with smoke of vanitie," and a peacock follows in the next stanza.)

[131] Heb. 9:5. Cf. Prov. 20:28: "Mercie and trueth preserue the King: for his throne shalbe established with mercie." The lion recalls those that decorated the throne of Solomon, I Kings 10:19f.

[132] Examples are: Isa. 6:1–4 (throne); Exod. 16:10, I Kings 8:10 (cloud); Ezek. 1:4 (shooting light); Ezek. 10:15 (wings); Ezek. 10:18–20 (angels); Pss. 104:1f., 105:39 (garment of light); Isa. 6:13 (hymns). For the cherubim decorating the veil of the tabernacle before the mercy-seat, see Exod. 26:31, 36:35; and cf. Exod. 28:18–22, 37:69, and I Kings 6:6f.

[133] See the dedicatory epistle to the Geneva Bible, where Elizabeth is compared to Zerubbabel as the builder of God's spiritual temple, and cf. Haggai's promise

queen with his "heavenly hymns";[134] certainly the description of Mercilla overlaps with his description of the divine Sapience in the *Hymne of Heavenly Beautie*. Sapience, the Old Testament Wisdom-personification, is also associated with the glory of the tabernacle, both in the New Testament and in the Apocrypha. All this seems vaguely idolatrous, but there was a feeling among Elizabethan Englishmen—to borrow the language of St. John—that something exceptional had tabernacled among them, and they beheld her glory.[135]

This impression was the calculated creation of Renaissance statecraft, of course: the queen's reign was conceived of as an extended *coup de théâtre*. But it is precisely the nearness of the theater to the other institutions of public life that insists upon attention here. We can think of the spectacular presentation of the queen upon the stage of the world as capitalizing upon an ideal moment in a general history of presence. The queen's absence from faerie tends to support the idea that presence is to be located primarily in the world, rather than in a sempiternal or transcendent sphere proper to divinity, or an immanent inner realm of timeless moments postulated by a reflection upon consciousness. Even if they were no more than parodies, the courts of Lucifera and Philotime could help make this clear. Both show that it is basically the *worldization* of presence —the transposition of its sphere from an eternal to a temporal context— that characterizes the typical Renaissance development.

The biblical "glory" is ordinarily intolerable to look upon, and both Moses and the Holy of Holies in the Old Testament are accordingly veiled. Paul takes Moses' veil to symbolize the revelation of God's glory concealed in the Hebrew Scriptures. A long tradition lies behind Spenser's

---

from the Lord to Zerubbabel (Hag. 2:7): "I will fill this house with glory." Elizabeth is compared to Solomon in Hakluyt's Epistle Dedicatory to the *Navigations*. Similarly the "Oration of John Hales" in Foxe, *Acts and Monuments*, ed. Cattely, vol. 8, pp. 678f., where allusion is made to the care over the house of God taken by David and Solomon. If Elizabeth will follow David's and Solomon's example, then all men will confess that she is "not only for proximity of blood preferred, but rather of God specially sent and ordained. And as the queen of Sheba came from far off, to see the glory of king Solomon, a woman to a man, even so shall the princes of our time come, men to a woman, and kings marvel at the virtue of queen Elizabeth."

[134] *Daphnaida*, l. 230. Cf. the laurel awarded Spenser by Francis Thynne, in *Emblemes and Epigrames*, ed. Furnivall, EETS, Old Series, no. 64 (1876), for "Crowning thy fayrie Queene with deitie."

[135] William Patten, *Calender of Scripture* (London, 1575), *sub* "Elizabeth." For "tabernacle" see John 1:14; also Ecclesiasticus 24:1-13 (Wisdom as the first-born of God, dwelling in Jacob, appointed a tabernacle, and enthroned in the pillar of cloud); and Baruch 3:33, 4:1-3 (the brightness of the Law).

description of allegory as good discipline "clowdily enwrapped in Allegorical devices," but the proem to Book II indicates that, like Jerome, Spenser identified allegorical technique with the mystical veil in the Bible.[136] He addresses the queen thus:

> And thou, O fairest Princesse vnder sky,
> In this faire mirrhour maist behold thy face,
> And thine owne realmes in lond of Faery,
> And in this antique Image thy great auncestry.
>
> The which O pardon me thus to enfold
> In couert vele, and wrap in shadowes light,
> That feeble eyes your glory may behold,
> Which else could not endure those beames bright,
> But would be dazled with exceeding light.
>
> (II, proem, 4–5)

Here Gloriana is explicitly described in terms taken from the third chapter of II Corinthians, which describes the veil over the face of Moses—transfigured by the glory of God—as the relation of the letter to the spirit:

> For if that which shulde be abolished, was glorious, much more shal that which remaineth, be glorious. . . .
>
> And we are not as Moses, which put a vaile vpon his face, that the children of Israel shulde not looke vnto the end of that which shulde be abolished.
>
> Therefore their mindes are hardened: for vntil this day remaineth the same couering vntaken away in the reading of the Olde testament, which vaile in Christ is put away.
>
> But euen vnto this day, when Moses is red, the vaile is layed ouer their hearts. . . .
>
> But we all beholde as in a mirrour the glories of the Lord with open face, and are changed into the same image, from glorie to glorie, as by the Spirit of the Lord.
>
> (Geneva Bible, II Cor. 3:11–18)

The Geneva gloss comments: "Moses shewed the Law as it was couered with shadowes, so that ye Iewes eyes were not lightened but blinded, and so colde not come to Christ who was the end thereof: againe the Gospel

---

[136] Jerome, *Epist.* LVIII, in PL, XXII, 585 (trans. in NPNF, 2nd Series, vol. 6, pp. 119–123). For the veiling of the New Covenant in the Old, see Augustine, *Civ. Dei*, XVI.xxvi, and Chap. II, n. 481, below. For the conception of veiled truth, see below, Chap. II, "Allegoria"; Osgood, *Boccaccio on Poetry*, p. 157, n. 8, and pp. 165f., and Ernst R. Curtius, *European Literature and the Latin Middle Ages*, trans. W. R. Trask (Princeton, 1957), pp. 203–219.

setteth forthe the glorie of God clearely, not couering our eyes, but driuing ye darkenes away from them."[137]

The tribute to Gloriana is no less hyperbolic than the one to Mercilla, and it makes a final point about the queen of the poem. It is much the same point we have made about the magnified but unfulfilled Arthur: the queen is allegorically concealed in the present poem, and allegorically revealed in it. Arthur and Gloriana belong to the poem's framework, and partly express the poem's theory. In a way, they "looke vnto the end of that which shulde be abolished," namely the poem itself. As symbols of its limits, the royal pair should be assimilated to not only the poem's "end," but also the poet's: to magnify, "But like a cloud, as likest may be told."

[iv]

We began by comparing Arthur and his knights to Christ and his apostles. One imagines that the Hostess of *Henry V* was not altogether wrong: British knights either go to hell with Duessa and the fair hot wench in flame-colored taffeta, or else they go to a greener place in Arthur's bosom. Even though the magnanimous Arthur awakens only fitfully in the present poem, he is a potential giant, like Blake's Albion or Joyce's bygmyster Finnegan. The cowardly Turpine of the sixth book was certainly right not to attack the Prince in his sleep; he should have known better than to approach him a second time—"he mote aread / Plaine signs in him of life and livelihead" (VI.vii.20). The power of Arthur to symbolize a nation, "rousing herself like a strong man after sleep," was an established fact of less eloquent Tudor propaganda, which proclaimed that "Arthur is come again."[138] The prince turns up regularly in the poem to aid the other knights when they are down, and thus comes to signalize their power of moral and physical recovery; he stands for the mysterious resurgence of heroism itself. Rhetorically speaking, then, we are again describing the Arthur of the poem's impetus.

It is particularly the legend of temperance that locates the life-forces of heroism in the Arthurian will. A somewhat technical analysis of the pertinent episodes in this legend supports the more general point.

[137] The text provides the gloss for Dante, *Inf.* IX.55–63, the confrontation with the Gorgon at the gates of Dis, where Virgil *covers the poet's eyes*, even while the reader is told to *look beneath the veil.* The sinner entering here puts the veil over his heart in hardening it, for as the Geneva gloss says, "The hardnes of mans heart before he be regenerat, is as a stonie table." Gloriana's veil is the reverse: it is that Pauline "mirror" in which we may behold "the glory of the Lord with open face."

[138] Sir George Buc, as cited in E. C. Wilson, *England's Eliza* (Cambridge, Mass., 1939), p. 66. The proverbial return of Arthur earns the scorn of Harington, in his remarks on Merlin's tomb, in his translation of *Orlando Furioso* (London, 1607), pp. 29f.

In the eighth canto of Book II, Arthur defends Guyon's corpse from despoliation by Pyrochles and Cymochles, and thus sympathetically effects Guyon's revival, "life hauing maistered her sencelesse foe" (II.viii.53). The inflammable Pyrochles and the lecherous Cymochles suggest the so-called irascible and concupiscent appetites. Arthur, in his victory over the pair, has the place of the rational appetite. In the Scholastic analysis of the soul, the rational appetite subjects the other two appetites to its will:[139] "The part of the soul which is obedient to reason is divided into concupiscence and anger [*ira*]."[140] An equally close analogy for Arthur's particular animus on this and other occasions is found in the Platonic "spirited element" in the soul, *thumos*, which is expressed in daring and in the ardor for victory and glory. Aristotle's description of the three species of appetite— wish, passion, and desire—gives the term *thumos* for the second appetite also. Thus the Platonic "spirited element" might easily be identified in the Aristotelian-Scholastic irascible appetite, as one can see from Albertus Magnus: "[Plato] moreover called the concupiscible power desirings of those things which affect one according to delectation. . . . However he called the power of the soul irascible that rises up to the difficulty [*ad arduum*] that belongs to daring and glory and victory and to everything that situates one in glory and a certain degree of sublimity and elevation. . . ."[141] The citation from John Damascene shows that Aquinas knew the Greek *thumos* as the Latin *ira*,[142] and his definition of the irascible appetite also recognizes in it the appetite for the arduous.[143] To apply this to Spenser's Arthur: the Prince is clearly characterized in terms of his susceptibility to challenge. But he is also contrasted to the excitable Pyrochles, whose evil *ira* is never incited by, or directed toward acquiring glory (even though he has grabbed Guyon's shield, which exhibits Gloriana). Arthur's defense of Guyon, on the other hand, recalls the positive kind of irascible appetite, which "regards the notion of good as something that wards off and repels what is hurtful";[144] the object of the irascible power "is to resist the onslaught of the unsuitable."[145] Guyon has just been exhaustively tempted by Mammon, i.e., tempted in his concupiscence. Therefore Arthur's protection of the fallen hero finds a distorted and sardonic reflection

---

[139] The three appetites derive from Aristotle, *De Anima* II.iii.

[140] John Damascene, *De Fide Orthodoxa*, ii.12, as cited by St. Thomas Aquinas, *Summa Theol.*, Pt. I, q.81, art.3, contra.

[141] Albertus Magnus, *De Anima*, III.IV.x–xi (in *Op. om.*, Leiden, 1651, vol. 3, pp. 181f.).

[142] According to W.H.V. Reade, *The Moral System of Dante's Inferno* (Oxford, 1909), p. 48.

[143] *Summa Theol.*, Pt. I, q.81, art.2, resp., and Pt. I, 2nd Pt., q.23, art.1, resp. and art.2, resp.

[144] *Summa Theol.*, Pt. I, q.82, art.5, resp.

[145] *Summa Theol.*, Pt. I, q.81, art.2, resp. ad obj.1.

in Pyrochles' last stand over the fallen Cymochles. The scene almost directly answers to the proposition that "the irascible is, as it were, the champion [*propugnax*] and defender of the concupiscible, when it rises up against what hinders the acquisition of the suitable things which the concupiscible desires, or against what inflicts harm, from which the concupiscible flies."[146] This seems to be the ghostly paradigm for the action of the episode. The soul of slain concupiscence flies from the scene of battle, while the outraged *propugnax* Pyrochles rises up against his indignant opposite, armed with Arthur's own sword. Arthur succeeds in preventing the greedy pair from acquiring the "unsuitable"—the heroic or glorious arms of Guyon.

Somewhat more broadly, the "appetitive" Arthur that we have been describing represents the will itself, especially the superior or rationally collected will, which does not exhibit that opposition otherwise found in the division of the soul into *"concupiscence and anger or desire and animus."*[147] In Arthur, desire for the fairy queen and desire for glory are the same. Within Book II, with its theme of self-preservation, Arthur also exhibits the simple will to live. This is particularly the case in the Maleger episode in the eleventh canto, which characterizes the Arthurian combination of "irascible ardor" and the general volitive faculty in terms of the virtues of fortitude and "sufferaunce" (II.viii.47). We need not extend this analysis here, except to note that, according to Aquinas, it is the part of fortitude to oppose weakness, especially weakness before the difficult or the arduous.[148]

Even more than the revival of Guyon in the eighth canto, the episode of Maleger associates Arthur with the resurrection of the body. This episode is one of two carefully placed occasions on which the Herculean Arthur comes into his own. The other is the Gerioneo episode in the eleventh canto of the legend of justice. Both show Spenser's control over a rather larger conception of Arthur than we may have elsewhere allowed. Perhaps there would have been two more such cardinal points in the poem had Spenser written his second six books. As they stand, they reveal a warrior equal to his fellow Worthy Judas Maccabaeus, who "put on a breastplate as a gyant," "grieved divers kings," harried cities, and cleansed the sanctuary (Geneva Bible, I Macc. 3:3–9). Perhaps something greater is here, however. Taking the two episodes together, we discover an Arthur who has the strength to rise from earth, besting sin and death, and the power to silence the riddling oracles of a sphinx, rending its temple. Milton once

---

[146] *Summa Theol.*, Pt. I, q.81, art.2, resp.

[147] *Summa Theol.*, Pt. I, q.82, art.5, contra, quoting Aristotle, *De Anima* III.ix.

[148] Also see below, Chap. III, "The Temper of Occasion," sec. ii, for Arthur's endurance under the blows of Fortune, and the virtue of fortitude that he opposes to wanhope.

considered writing an Arthurian poem, and in this connection he spoke of an otherwise unexplained Arthur "moving his wars beneath the earth."[149] One may hazard that if any traces of this plan remain, the comparisons for Christ's victory at the climax of *Paradise Regained* contain them. Milton compares the defeated Satan to both Antaeus, "Throttl'd at length in th'Air," and the sphinx, "that *Theban* Monster that propos'd / Her riddle."[150] As we shall see, Milton's oracle-silencing Christ also figures in Spenser's chivalric dragon-slaying myth; and the death of the sphinx monster in Book V resembles the death of Error at the opening of the poem. Likewise, the comparison of Christ's temptation to a threefold Herculean *agon* existed before Milton used it for his hero of sufferance or Spenser for his heroes of temperance.[151] "Truth shall rise from earth," the poets seem to say, "and righteousness look down from heaven."[152]

Epic Duplex

It is well known that *The Faerie Queene* is unfinished; Spenser tells us so himself in two *Amoretti* sonnets (XXXIII and LXXX). And yet in the later sonnet he calls the six-book remainder "that second worke," as if he were already talking about a sequel, such as the one he broached in the prospectus annexed to his first installment. The principle of amplification mentioned there is a treatment of the virtues proper to Arthur as king, rather than as crown prince. If Spenser was thinking of twenty-four books, the student can only murmur, "Hills peep o'er hills, and Alps on Alps arise!"[153]

Near the opening of *The Gouernour*, Sir Thomas Elyot anticipates two volumes, apparently to correspond to Aristotle's *Ethics* and *Politics*:

> In the fyrste shall be comprehended the beste fourme of education or bringing up of noble children from their natiuitie, in suche maner as they may be founde worthy, and also able to be gouernours of a publike weale. The seconde volume . . . shall conteine all the reminant . . . to the perfection of a iust publike weale. . . .[154]

Elyot did not write the second treatise, perhaps because as a theoretician he assumed that the moral virtue of the magistrate was his paramount acquisition: the force of his personal example would, of itself, make his

---

[149] *Mansus*, l. 81: "Artrumque etiam sub terris bella moventem."
[150] *Par. Reg.* IV.561–576.
[151] See below, Chap. III, "The Anatomy of Temperance," sec. iii, n. 25.
[152] Ps. 85:11.   [153] Pope, *Essay on Criticism*, II.232.
[154] Elyot, *Gouernour*, I.ii, Everyman's Library, p. 15.

a good government. One imagines that everything Elyot had to say is contained in his first volume, since for him it is the governor, not the form of government, from which the public weal "taketh his begynnynge."[155] Consequently his later *Image of Governaunce* is neither a treatise like *The Prince,* which deals with such virtues as cunning and expediency, nor one like the *Utopia,* which sets down a speculative order for society; it is a Xenophonic romance on the life of the emperor Alexander Severus. Shakespeare's *Henry V,* a "mirror to all Christian kings," also seems to be a sequel to a work treating the emergence of a prince, and it too takes the form of a romance. In his legend of justice Spenser begins, as Xenophon did, with the early training of his hero in savage sports, and treats justice as the effect of a person, rather than, as in Aristotle, the form of the body politic. In the *Vewe of the Present State of Ireland* Spenser seems hardly able to divorce questions of policy from the exemplary character of Lord Grey. Similarly, Elyot's theory of government is implicit in his choice to educate an elite. In this respect he is less like Aristotle and more like Isocrates, who seemingly paired orations to the private man *Demonicas* and the ruler *Nicocles.*[156] It is precisely in an analogy between the governor's self-conduct and his conduct of affairs that the limitation on Elyot's subject is to be located:

> It is to be noted that to hym that is a gouernoure of a publike weal belongeth a double gouernaunce, that is to saye, an interior or inwarde gouernaunce, and an exterior or outwarde gouernaunce. The firste is of his affectes and passions, which do inhabite within his soule, and be subiectes to reason. The seconde is of his children, his seruauntes, and other subiectes to his autoritie. To the one and the other is required the vertue morall called fortitude. . . .[157]

Thus when Spenser essays the virtue of justice in Book V, it is almost inevitable that the plan of the legend will become reflexive with respect to the legend of temperance in Book II. The overall result is a kind of closure, rather than a mere statute of poetic limitations. The very quality that allows Spenser to expand from Book I to Book II—and from Book III to Book IV—is the doubling power of analogy; but it will also determine the poem's size as a large number of analogies between the two installments complete themselves.

Epics, even epic romances, require turning-points if they are to sustain our interest in finishing them—if they turn on so wide a radius as to come round imperceptibly, they will be read selectively, rather than consecutively. Spenser hints that the bear baby in Book VI may grow up to be-

---

[155] *Ibid.,* III.xxii, *edn. cit.,* p. 262.
[156] *Ibid.,* I.xi, p. 42.
[157] *Ibid.,* III.viii, pp. 224f.

come the hero of a future legend,[158] but this would be a notable departure from the present poem, where all the heroes are contemporaries of Arthur. We shall try to show that the central part of Spenser's poem now exists, no matter what additions to it might have been planned. The letter to Raleigh already seems to contain a kind of minor critical Doppelgänger; and, since we cannot substantiate that "second worke," we must be content to exorcise it. We must learn to integrate our vision.

The letter to Raleigh twice speaks of "two persons." First, it distinguishes between the two persons of the epic hero. One kind of hero manifests the ethical virtues of the private person or prince, a warrior figure like Tasso's Rinaldo or a virtuous man like Odysseus; the other kind has the political virtues of the public magistrate or king, a governor like Agamemnon or Tasso's Godfredo. Spenser proposes, in his first twelve books, to treat only the private virtues. The letter was printed with the first installment, where the virtues are holiness, temperance, and chastity. "Two persons" are also said to obtain with reference to the allegorical presentation of Elizabeth Tudor and Elizabeth the First, the one a beautiful virgin, the other a royal "Empresse." Belphoebe does not appear in courtly society at all, but Gloriana is the political mistress of all the knights in the poem, and her court manifests the social order headed by the queen of England. Spenser's second installment goes on to treat the virtues of friendship, justice, and courtesy, which, unlike the first three, involve social loyalties rather than fidelity to a private ideal. Furthermore, Queen Mercilla appears as a version of the royal empress. The two distinctions, between the two persons of the hero and the two of the queen, have collapsed into one; perhaps the possible twenty-four books have similarly collapsed into the present six.[159]

The brief allegory with which Tasso supplied the *Gerusalemme Liberata* is similarly divided.[160] First Tasso makes a distinction between those epics that deal with a solitary contemplative man—such as the *Odyssey* and the *Commedia*—and those that treat a man of action in civil company—the *Iliad* and the *Aeneid*. Tasso adds that the *Aeneid* might be said to contain both types. The distinction, only slightly expanded, is between the private hero, the protagonist of a solitary or romantic quest, and the public leader, suited to the action of the metropolitan and military epic. Further on in the same text, Tasso contrasts Godfrey, the head and mind of his army,

---

[158] VI.iv.36. For further remarks, see the discussion of the "theme of realized faerie" in Chap. V, "The Quest for The Faerie Queene," sec. ii.

[159] My discussion is indebted to Frye, "Structure of Imagery," in *Fables of Identity*, pp. 75–77, and *Return of Eden*, pp. 11–15.

[160] Tasso's "Allegory" is translated in H. Morley's 1890 edn. of Fairfax's translation, pp. 436–443, the source of my subsequent quotations. For Tasso's division of the epic, see pp. 437f. of this edn.

with Rinaldo, the leader's spirited right-hand man; Tasso here is thinking of a contrast like that found between Agamemnon and Achilles, or Charlemagne and Rinaldo, to judge from his poem. In contrast to Spenser, Tasso of course believes he has written the more public poem, and he begins with the election of Godfrey to public office. The two distinctions disappear, however, for purposes of reading the poem. The *Gerusalemme Liberata*, as we have noted, is about equally preoccupied with the official campaign in Godfrey's charge and the personal adventures of the cavaliers in his service.

The currency of Tasso's and Spenser's divisions is well attested. The pseudo-Plutarchan *Life of Homer* explains that the *Iliad* expresses bodily strength and the *Odyssey* generosity of mind;[161] the division is frequently repeated in the Renaissance, for example in Porta's preface to his edition of Homer, in Cooper's *Dictionary* (s.v. Homer), and in Chapman's translation.[162] The Homeric allegorist "Heraclides Ponticus" describes the *Odyssey* as *ethicyn* and the *Iliad* as "military and bellicose."[163] Servius tells us that Virgil's first line refers to the subjects of the two halves of his poem, which are based on the *Odyssey* and the *Iliad*; Macrobius has this last also.[164] In the *Virgiliana Continentia* the Sibyl tells Fulgentius that "arms and the man" mean virtue and wisdom, "omnis enim perfectio in virtute constat corporis et sapientia ingenii."[165] This would seem to combine previous interpretations. Petrarch's phrase in *Canzionieri* CLXXXVI about "the ancient flower *di vertuti e d'arme*" reflects the reading of *virum* as *virtus*. Badius, in his argument for his Renaissance edition of Virgil, writes that Virgil's "man" is based on the *Odyssey* and the contemplative life,

---

[161] *Homeri Poeta Vita*, in Gale, *Opuscula Mythol.*, p. 284. Frequently, however, this "duplex" was located in Odysseus himself, as in Horace, who says that, in Ulysses, Homer propounded *quid virtus et quid sapientia possit* ("what strength and what wisdom can do," *Epist.* I.2, l. 17), and Statius, *Achilleis* I.472, where Odysseus is *consiliis armisque vigil* (alert in counsel and arms).

[162] Aemilius Portus, ed. and trans., *Homeri Ilias* [-*Odyssea* . . .]. *postremo editio . . . latine omnia ad verbum exposita* (Geneva, 1580), Sig. A5ʳ (the *Iliad* treats "robor corporis & fortitudo"; the *Odyssey*, "magnitudo animi ac tolerantia"); Cooper, *Dictionary* app. to *Thesavrvs* (London, 1565), *sub* "Homer"; *Chapman's Homer*, ed. Nicoll, vol. 2, p. 4 (the subject of the *Iliad* is the "Bodie's . . . fashion of outward Fortitude"; of the *Odyssey*, "the Mind's . . . Empire," etc.); for another example, see Weinberg, *History of Criticism*, vol. 1, pp. 268f., citing Antonio Maria de' Conti (Marcantonio Maioragio), *Orationes et praefationes* (1582), p. 157ᵛ, who refers to "Plutarch."

[163] *Allegoriae Homeri*, in Gale, *Opuscula Mythol.*, p. 485. The use of "ethical" may be a confused memory of Aristotle, *Poetics* xxiv, on Homer: "For each of the poems has a duplex (*hekateron*) character, the *Iliad* simple and pathetic, and the *Odyssey* complex—for recognitions run throughout—and *ethical*."

[164] Servius, *ad Aen.* I.1; VII.1. Macrobius, *Saturnalia*, V.ii.6.

[165] *Virgiliana Continentia*, in Helm, *Fvlgentivs: Opera*, p. 87.

his "arms" on the Trojan War and the active life, "as he has pictured each life for us (what is glorious) in a single man."[166] The same interpretation is found in a letter of Francisco Filelfo to which D. C. Allen draws our attention:[167] "What did Virgil—in one song, the *Aeneid*—imitate of honey-generated Homer's *Iliad* and Ulysses?" he asks, and answers by countering, "How else indeed would you describe the contemplative and active human condition?" Virgil "showed how it is possible to be prepared for the highest good through wisdom and virtue." In the proposal at the opening of his epic, Virgil "imitates not only Homer in his matter, but also in his order, though not in the work itself: thus the first six books of the *Aeneid* are largely occupied with contemplation and consultation. However, in the following books, the praise is of action."[168] Christophoro Landino treats the fourth and sixth books as dealing with the civil and contemplative life respectively.[169] Scaliger speaks of Aeneas as complete in both contemplation and action, "and that action is either in relation to himself, such as abstinence, or placed outside of himself, as in other virtues"; it may be placed in household or polis, and peace or war. Further, Virgil showed extraordinary skill "where he set out to unite in Aeneas alone the fortitude of Achilles and the prudence of Ulysses, and added to them piety—he took away the temerity of the one, the cunning of the other he placed in Sinon."[170]

Our quotations show the widespread application of the *sapientia et fortitudo* topos as an epic manifold. Isidore defined the hero as one made worthy for heaven by his wisdom and fortitude.[171] A similar pairing of characteristics was made in the *Iliad*; Hector and Poulydamous were born in the same night, but Hector was the greater in battle; Poulydamous, the greater in counsel (*Il.* XVIII.252). Curtius, who has drawn modern at-

---

[166] "In Aeneida argumenta," in *Opera Virgiliana* (Leiden, 1580), Sigs. A5ᵛ–A6ʳ.

[167] Allen, *Mysteriously Meant*, pp. 154f.

[168] *Familiares* . . . (Paris, 1520?), Lib. I, fol. iii, 12. Cf. Melanchthon, *in Aen.* I: "the argument in the *Aeneid* is duplex: the wars of Aeneas and the voyage. Through the voyage he shows an example of civil and private life. In the wars he shadows forth the Heroic life." (In C. G. Bretschneider and H. E. Bindseil, eds., *Philipi Melanchthonis Opera*, vol. 19, col. 437.)

[169] Landino's interpretation is offered in the course of allegorizing the first half of the *Aeneid* as a description of a process of psychological maturation and a preparation for philosophy: the poem illustrates the soul's progress from a Troy immersed in sensual preoccupations to an Italy comprehending the Platonic *summum bonum*. In common with the readings of Fulgentius and John of Salisbury (*Policraticus*, VIII.24), Landino reads the poem as the story of the soul's "coming of age." The distractions offered by Dido and her city are accordingly interpreted as "the lesser reason of civil life" (*Quaestiones Camuldulenses*, Sig. liʳ⁻ᵛ; for another typical summary, see Sig. miʳ).

[170] *Poetices*, III.xix; Gilbert, *Literary Criticism*, p. 245.

[171] Isidore of Seville, *Etymol.*, I.xxxix.9; Curtius, *European Literature*, pp. 170–178.

tention to the topos, suggests its antiquity in his comparison with the Indo-European division of the gods, founder-figures, and castes into a kingly or priestly function (Mitra) and a warrior function (Varuna).[172] As Tasso's allegory recognizes, the Mitra-Varuna division is found in Plato's distinction between the ruling and spirited elements in the soul: the one just, deliberative, and tribunary, and the other courageous, willful, militant, and irascible. There seems to be no reason to restrict this characterization of heroism to Indo-European culture, however. In the Bible, Moses divides his functions between an Aaron-levitical aspect and a Joshua-Caleb aspect. William Webbe saw Aeneas as combining both functions: "Under the person of *Æneas*" Virgil "expresseth the valoure of a worthy Captaine and valiaunt Governour, together with the perilous adventures of warre, and polliticke devises at all assayes."[173] But in the *Iliad*, in the Roland-Charlemagne epos (and the "rebel epics" of the Doon of Mayence branch of the chanson tradition), in the Lancelot-Arthur relation, and in Tasso's epic, the functions are clearly polarized—one may also compare Spenser's Talus and Artegall.

For explaining Spenser's letter to Raleigh, what is most important is the division of the *Aeneid* into an "odyssey" and an "iliad," as Tasso divided epics into "solitary" and "civil." Spenser conflates these two distinctions when he maintains that Aeneas is a combination of the two persons of the epic protagonist. He says the same of Orlando, though exactly what he means here is not clear. (He may have been referring to the *poem* rather than the man, in which case his reference to Tasso's Rinaldo and Godfredo might also have been to poems—Tasso did write a *Rinaldo*.)

Spenser and the tradition are correct about the *Aeneid*; Virgil's poem is clearly divided between six books treating the wanderings of the hero abroad and six books treating his mainland task of establishing a new homeland for Priam's household gods. Virgil's Sibyl calls the Turnus of the second part another Achilles[174]—which in this poem means another Pyrrhus, Achilles' son—and there are few who doubt that the Dido of the first part is intended as a civic Circe, like Cleopatra. Virgil takes this binary construction from the *Odyssey*, where the first twelve books de-

---

[172] Curtius, *European Literature*, pp. 171f., quoting Georges Dumézil, *Mitra-Varuna: Essai sur deux representations indo-européennes de la souveraineté*, Bibliothèque de L'Ecole des Hautes Etudes. Sciences religieuses (Paris, 1940), pp. 144f. For a summary of Dumézil, see C. S. Littleton, *The New Comparative Mythology* (Berkeley, 1966). For a parallel distinction, issuing from the conjunction of Plato with Dionysius of Syracuse, see Plato, *Epist.* II, 310e–311b, where Prometheus and Zeus would correspond to Varuna and Mitra respectively.

[173] *A Discourse of Englishe Poetrie* (1586), in Smith, *Elizabethan Critical Essays*, vol. 1, p. 237.

[174] *Aen.* VI.89, IX.742. For Pyrrhus, to whom Turnus is compared in the later case, as himself a second Achilles, see II.491, 540, 549.

scribe the hero's exile on the ocean, along with the parallel displacement of his son; and the second twelve books describe the reestablishment of the hero's proper authority in his own kingdom. The break between the twelfth and thirteenth books, which we owe to Homer's editors, is almost inevitable once we have it: the first section of the poem ends when Odysseus finishes his account of his adventures; a hundred lines later the sleeping traveler has been deposited at the cave of the nymphs, and he is home in Ithaca.

Thus the division of the *Odyssey*, within itself, duplicates the proportions of the Homeric epos as a whole, for it develops both the theme of wrath and the theme of a *nostos*. Virgil almost seems to acknowledge this principle of the successor-epic's repeating the ratios of the canon as a whole: he delegates to Aeneas the narration of the duplex formed by Books II and III, the fall of Troy in Book II being a "little Iliad" and the wanderings of the hero in Book III a "little Odyssey." The subdivision of *The Faerie Queene* into cantos obeys a similar epic rule of repeating the whole within the part.

We are told that the cave of the nymphs in the *Odyssey* has two entrances, one used by gods and the other by men. Only half fancifully, one may suggest that the two entrances correspond to the fabulous and the domestic emphases of the story. A comparable Homeric locus, the twin gates of sleep, is carefully introduced at the midpoint of the *Aeneid*. Armed with visions of Roman destiny, Aeneas emerges from the underworld through the ivory gate—the issue point for false dreams, as Virgil seems at pains to remind us. (A number of features suggest that Aeneas has visited the underworld only in a dream.)[175] The absent hero has been securing an oracle, and in the underworld he is shown both the founders of the Trojan *gens* and the unborn progeny of the Julian *gens* whose destiny he carries. In the *Gerusalemme Liberata* the epic midpoint is marked by the report that Rinaldo, apparently dead, is actually alive. The recall of this private hero, absent since the fifth book, is required for the success of the public quest of Godfrey, and the cavalier returns at the end of the sixteenth book. Peter the hermit, a kind of male sibyl, follows the discovery with his predictions of the accomplishments of Rinaldo's future offspring.[176] The return of Soliman offers a parallel in the pagan camp; he enters Jerusalem invisible by way of a secret underground passage, accompanied by Ismeno, Peter the hermit's pagan counterpart. A much more marvelous midpoint is found in *Beowulf*, where the return of the hero

---

[175] See the elm in the courtyard of Avernus, thronged with false dreams (VI.282–284); the presence of *Sopor* in the vestibule (278); Palinurus being told this is the realm of Sleep and drowsy Night (390); the vain attempt of Aeneas to embrace Anchises (700–703), "volucrique simillima somno"; and finally the identification of exit from the underworld with the ivory gate of sleep (893ff.). The death of Palinurus at V.835–861, who is deceived by Sleep, contributes to the theme.

[176] *Ger. Lib.* X.74ff. Ismeno's prophecy precedes, at X.19ff.

from the submarine lair of Grendel's dam is doubted by all. The midpoint roughly coincides with the slaying of the dam, and the hero then surfaces from the cleansed waters of the meer. An appropriate folklore motif, known as the "release of imprisoned waters," turns up with the dissolution of the fatal sword; it melts "most like to ice, when the Father releases the bonds of frost, unwinds the wave ropes, he who has the rule of times and seasons."[177]

Beowulf is also divided between overseas adventure in a foreign court and subsequent domestic duty on behalf of the hero's own people. The poet of the very old romance of *King Horn* is so fascinated by the possibilities in such a structure that he contrives to double it—more than double it, counting the coda at the end. This structure seems to be the most interesting feature of the poem, and it clearly illustrates the tendency of romance toward reiterative cyclic dilation. At the center of the tale is the story of a foundling who distinguishes himself at court by killing the king's enemies, is preferred, slandered, banished, preferred elsewhere, and, after seven years, repatriated. This inner cycle represents the exile-phase of a larger, outer cycle that includes the child's original separation from a fatherland at the mercy of invaders, who kill his father, and his eventual return to repossess this home, as its rightful king. Like Beowulf, Horn becomes the right hand man of a foreign king whose enemies he defeats; subsequently he engages a comparable enemy on his own soil. (The story of Joseph shows a similar organization, though Joseph is repatriated only by his bringing his family into Egypt; the greater cycle of return is not completed until the time of the Exodus, when Joseph's embalmed body is carried back to the patriarchal homeland.) There would be no reason to describe these more complicated story patterns if we were dealing solely with epic. We are not, and the long movement in *The Faerie Queene* that takes us through the third and fourth books seems to be a kind of inner cycle, marked off from the rest of the poem by two of the greatest water passages in English literature. An ivory gate (II.xii.44) and an underwater cave kept by a nymph (III.viii.37; IV.xii), turn up on the periphery of this movement.

Spenser's two installments also exhibit a version of the division into a first half focused on the quest or destiny of an individual, and a second half dealing with, in Northrop Frye's fine phrase, "the settling of a social order."[178] The preponderance of oracular caves and maternal grottoes in the central books is suggestive of the mysterious return of the hero or the transition between his two persons. Spenser's narrative radius is more

---

[177] *Beowulf*, ll. 1607–1611. The dragon of the Sigemund story also melts, from its own heat, at l. 897.

[178] *Return of Eden*, p. 13.

generous than that of the classical works, and the avatars of the quest movement are multiple. Both Britomart's visit to Merlin's cave and Agape's comparable descent to the Fates are concerned with the continuance of the heroic persona, through offspring in the case of Britomart and through a transfusion of souls in the case of Triamond. The twin-gated Garden of Adonis is concerned with natural continuance per se: it is the seminary for forms that are reborn into the world every thousand years. This period is presumably a detail borrowed from Virgil's account, in his sixth book, of the rebirth of souls from the underworld.[179] The Spenserian hero is not precisely absent from these books, but only a heroine is adequate for the quest in Book III. Even the title page seems confused about the name of the hero in Book IV; the parity of the candidates perhaps makes an allegorical point about friendship, but it also weakens one's sense of the hero as *protagonist* here.

In Book I the hero is restored by Arthur. When Arthur is hewing Orgoglio down to size, the flow of the giant's blood is compared to a "riven rock" (I.viii.10), and the reference to Moses' feat suggests the Spenserian association of the freeing of imprisoned waters with the return of the hero. The mysterious arrival of Arthur with Amoret, in Book IV, seems to prompt the description of the Temple of Venus, where we see Scudamour for the last time. He recounts the beginnings of his quest for Amoret, and his account closes his cycle. This ending seems to precipitate the stupendous descent of English rivers to the House of Proteus for the marriage of the Thames and the Medway; and this, in turn, provides the occasion for the uniting of the liberated Florimell and the revived Marinell. The next book begins with the *enfance* of the undoubted protagonist of the legend of justice.

The most interesting evidence of a disappearance and return pattern at the center of the poem is a circumstance of its publication in two installments. In the first edition Scudamour is reunited with Amoret at the end of Book III; in the second, he disappears from this position, and the passionate embrace of the lovers is displaced to the hermaphroditic Venus near the end of the following book. Other works issued in two installments show the same epic division; the absence and return of the heroic persona is simply determined by the circumstance of publication. This seems a fairly frivolous way of identifying an epic midpoint, and perhaps it really belongs to romance. One thinks of the "death" of Sherlock Holmes. Cervantes capitalizes on this division. The individual and private adventures of Quixote are the subject of Part One; in Part Two, the hero is a public figure—he even has a competitor. The second part begins with a discussion of government; later it sees the hero admitted to a court, just as his outline of romance had provided; it confers a governorship on Sancho, which Sancho

---

[179] *F.Q.* III.vi.33, *Aen.* VI.748; see *Republic* X, 615a, 621d.

undertakes armed with a prince's handbook authored by his mentor; and finally it sees Quixote enter a city for the first time, to behold not only an ocean, but also a printing press, the source of both his and his rival's notoriety. *The Pilgrim's Progress* is quixotic only at the outset, but the same pattern applies. Its first part is an allegory of the trials and salvation of a lonely Christian pilgrim on an exodus from a City of Destruction. Like Aeneas, he leaves his wife; he even has a burden like that of Aeneas—the burden from father Adam. The second part, the journey of his family, follows his death and treats the social aspect of the same quest. The tone is set by Christiana's remark that Giant Grim must make way, "now that I am risen a mother in Israel."[180] Christiana's family is also a young church: marriages mark the way, Vanity Fair has become more hospitable, and the imagery suggests not so much the years in the wilderness as the possessing of the promised land.

A very different example that belongs to Spenser's own period is Shakespeare's *Henry IV*. The emergence of a prince, rather than his education, is the theme, but the play still involves a division between chivalric and personal virtues in Part One, and civil virtues in Part Two. At the conclusion of the first part, by dinte of temperance and good timing, the Prince acquires the honors of his hot-headed rival; at the conclusion of the second part, the new king casts off the friend of Justices Silence and Shallow, and establishes the Lord Chief Justice in his place. The rebels of Part One are treated almost as rebellious humours; in Part Two they are more clearly a disease of an aging body politic, and it is the social order, rather than the Prince, that particularly wants reform. The epic midpoint is marked by the appearance of Rumour, who reports Hal's death instead of Percy's, in the prologue to Part Two; just as Ate, at the opening of Spenser's second installment, convinces Scudamour that all is lost regarding Amoret. (The reader will also recognize the function of Virgil's Allecto in initiating the second part of the *Aeneid*.) Of course the Shakespearean character we remember best in *Henry IV* is memorable for neither the chivalric virtues of Part One, nor the civil virtues of Part Two—neither is his less amusing but equally pretentious Spenserian counterpart, Braggadocchio.

The House of Wholeness

. . . they that have taught the art of memory have showed nothing so apt for it as a certain room divided into many places well and thoroughly

---

[180] Christiana is quoting the song of Deborah who marshaled Israel (Judg. 5:7). The transition from Part I to Part II, when taken with the death of Faithful at the middle of Part I, suggests the way in which the death of its prophet issues in the birth of his Church. The pattern is taken from Luke-Acts.

known. Now, that hath the verse in effect perfectly, every word having his natural seat, which seat must needs make the word remembered.

(Sir Philip Sidney, *The Defense of Poesie*)

. . . I was wont to seek the honey Bee
Working her formall rowmes in Wexen frame:
(Colin Clout in *The Shepheardes Calender*, "December," 68–69)

. . . Beauty is a kind of harmony and concord of all the parts to form a whole which is constructed according to a fixed number, and a certain relation and order, as symmetry, the highest and most perfect law of nature, demands.

(Alberti, *De re aedificatione*, iv.5, trans. Sir Antony Blunt, in *Artistic Theory in Italy 1450–1600*, Oxford, 1940, p. 15)

[i]

In his shorter poems, Spenser is preeminently an artist of completed formal designs; numerical completeness especially is important to his conceptions, in a way not true of any other English poet. A major theme of romance is magic, and Spenser has a magician's appreciation of ritual completeness, as though sheer enumeration could reestablish some lost rapport between human consciousness and natural cycles.[181] In *The Teares of the Mvses*, all nine Muses must go through their "equall plaints"— equally repetitious. (The fourth Muse gets one extra stanza, a deliberate irregularity marking the midway point of the six hundred line total.) *The Rvines of Time* insists on the preservative power of verse, in contrast to various other monuments and memorials; the poem consists of seventy stanzas of seven lines each, plus an addendum of two groups of seven "visions," each vision made up of two seven line stanzas. The seven-headed beast of Rome, the seven-years' siege of Roman Verulam, and the sevenfold gates of hell—the walls of which have all yielded to time—seem to be related to the formal design.

The eighty-nine *Amoretti* sonnets are vaguely coordinated with the calendar of the poet's courtship, and they were first printed with his marriage poem. A time scheme is implied, for example, by the appearance of "Love's mighty king"—i.e., Amor—in the two sonnets on the return of spring (19 and 70); the two sonnets enclose fifty-two sonnets. The sequence is followed by an irregular Anacreontic addenda, in which the mischievous Cupid and the concettist poet both seem to be just playing around. After the pause these trifles supply, the mistress of the sonnets returns in tri-

---

[181] I am synthesizing Frye's remarks on magic and ritual in *Anatomy of Criticism*, pp. 105–107, 119f., with his discussion of Spenser's habits in "Structure of Imagery," in *Fables of Identity*, p. 87.

umph as the bride of the greatest epithalamium in the language, "for short time an endlesse moniment." The *Epithalamion* takes full possession of the longest day of the year, the "day the sunne is in his chiefest hight / With Barnaby the bright." A solstitial feast day is particularly suggestive, and the poem has been successfully analyzed by A. Kent Hieatt as an elaborate timepiece consisting of twenty-four stanza-hours.[182] The bride, whom the imagery associates with the sun, is bedded precisely sixteen and a quarter stanzas through the poem, at the hour of nightfall on the longest day of the year. The whole shows an hourglass shape that is rhetorically "inverted" by the change of refrain in the sixteenth stanza. The year is aligned with the diurnal pattern as well, for the poem has 365 long lines.

A full reading of Spenser's *Amoretti* sequence is beyond our present scope, but a brief study of its regularities suggests that it too has a pattern.[183] One sonnet appears twice; other sonnets, though not repeated, are paired by theme. The Lent and Easter sonnets (22 and 48), the Spring-Amor sonnets (19 and 70), and the New Years sonnets (4 and 62) all deserve to be co-ordinated. To these one might add the two spider sonnets (23, on the poet's workmanship, and 71, on the lover's enmeshing of the beloved); the two sonnets on *The Faerie Queene* (33 and 80); the Angel sonnets (17 and 61); and the Idea sonnets (45 and 88).

The Spring-Amor sonnets are located the same distance from each end of the sequence of eighty-nine sonnets, as are the Lent and Easter sonnets —the latter are separated by an interval of forty-seven sonnets:

The first Spring sonnet begins fourteen sonnets after the first New Years sonnet. The second Spring sonnet begins only seven sonnets after the second New Years sonnet:

4	19		62	70
]---- 14 ----[			]-- 7 --[	

[182] A. Kent Hieatt, *Short Time's Endless Monument* (New York, 1960), *passim*.
[183] My analysis was conceived independently of Alexander Dunlop, "Calendar Symbolism in the 'Amoretti,'" in *Notes and Queries*, 214 (January, 1969), pp. 24–26, and the same author's "The Unity of Spenser's *Amoretti*," in Alastair Fowler, ed., *Silent Poetry* (London, 1970), pp. 153–169. I duplicate Dunlop in essentials, but he presses for the identification of Lent and Easter with the dates of a specific year (1594) in the earlier article; he also scants the evidence for a cycle that would make the sonnets approximate weeks as well as days. Dunlop's second study persuasively analyzes the first twenty-one sonnets as constituting a triple suite of resolved themes.

The Lent and Easter sonnets may be thought of as separated by forty-six "days," this being the Lenten interval; the two New Years sonnets may be thought of as separated by the interval between the first of January and the first of March, fifty-nine days (4–62), for both are new years. (Such a scheme cannot purport to explain why Spring should arrive twice in one year.) The duplicated sonnets (35 and 83) are separated by the same interval—forty-seven—that encloses the Spring-Amor sonnets, and their position seems to be determined by the larger pattern that begins with the Lent and Easter sonnets (22 and 35):

There are twenty-one sonnets before the Lent sonnet (22), and the duplicated sonnet (83) is seventh from last. The end of the sequence thus reads:

$$...62......68............83......89$$
$$[--\text{seven}--][--\text{fourteen}--][--\text{seven}--]$$

If the fourteenth sonnet were marked in some way, the beginning of the sequence would invert the proportions of this ending:

$$1............14......22............35...$$
$$[---\text{fourteen}---][--\text{seven}--][---\text{fourteen}---]$$

The fourteenth sonnet does seem to recognize its position in a scheme. Its first line, "Retourne agayne my forces late dismayd," implies a kind of second initiative, like that found in Shakespeare's fifty-sixth sonnet, "Sweet love, renew thy force," or the fifth and sixth lines of his hundredth, "Return, forgetful Muse, and straight redeem / In gentle numbers time so idly spent."

The two sonnets on *The Faerie Queene* also adhere to the pattern of the duplicated sonnets; the first is placed three sonnets in advance of the first of the duplicated sonnets, and the second is placed four sonnets in advance of the second of the duplicated sonnets (33–35, 80–83). The other pairs are separated by forty-three to forty-eight sonnets. If, as these observations suggest, Spenser has constructed a kind of double cycle for this collection, we might expect a decisive break to occur, perhaps between the forty-seventh and forty-eighth sonnets. It is the forty-eighth sonnet that reports a kind of nadir in the poet's courtship: the beloved has burned the poet's offerings.

The significance of such a pattern is easy to see. The pattern inculcates the delay and return motif of the poet's love. His love is reciprocated only gradually, and as earlier sonnets "return" a case is made for the poet's constancy. The Lent sonnet thus has a critical place in the pattern, because it is the first of the forty-six sonnets preceding the triumphant Easter sonnet, and thus suggests a Lenten period of discipline, trial, and abstinence —the "sad protract" preparatory to the sacrament of love. The Lenten number for this prolongation is hinted by the sonnet in which the poet says that "the spheare of Cupid fourty yeares contained," even though he has been in love for only a year. This sonnet announces, as clearly as any, that the sequence is being given a cyclical construction, for two sonnets later, and forty sonnets after the Lent sonnet, we meet the second or "spring" New Years sonnet (22–62). The pattern of closures also suggests the relenting of the mistress, if only because she is still suffering the poet's addresses.

The strictly formal properties of the pattern merit further comment. Why has the poet chosen fourteen, seven, forty-seven, and forty-nine (sonnets [35 . . . 83]) as significant intervals? The number seven suggests time, the number fourteen may be a tribute to the number of lines in a sonnet, and so forth. The point is that Spenser thinks formally: he arranges his sonnets in a line that may be subdivided twenty-one units from either end, leaving a Lenten interval between. He takes the seventh place from last to be significant, and he establishes another arch employing the larger interval. In short, he perceives a length to be tabulated in terms of duplicated intervals. Pause at such and such a point on this length, and the remaining length is charged with analogous proportions.[184] We might compare such a span to a fret board or a scale: imposing on it at any given point invites a complementary imposition over the remainder. A similar principle applies over the length of *The Faerie Queene*; once its division into private and public installments is admitted, a coordination of the subsidiary divisions will obtain a kind of incumbency also.

[ii]

Before considering the order of Spenser's virtues, one should recall Dr. Johnson's rebuke to overzealous exegetes of Pope's *Essay on Criticism*:

Almost every poem, consisting of precepts, is so far arbitrary and immethodical, that many of the paragraphs may change places with no apparent inconvenience; for two or more positions, depending on some

[184] My phrasing echoes the similar remarks in Rudolf Wittkower in *Architectural Principles in the Age of Humanism*, Studies of the Warburg Institute, vol. 19 (London, 1949), p. 100, on the generation of ratios in Renaissance architectural theory.

remote and general principle, there is seldom any cogent reason why one should precede the other. But for the order in which they stand, whatever it be, a little ingenuity may easily give the reason. "It is possible," says Hooker, "that by long circumduction, from any one truth all truth may be inferred." Of all homogeneous truths at least, of all truths respecting the same general end, in whatever series they may be produced, a concatenation by intermediate ideas may be formed, such as, when it is once shewn, shall appear natural; but if this order be reversed, another mode of connection equally specious may be found or made. Aristotle is praised for naming fortitude first of the cardinal virtues, as that without which no other virtue can be practised; but he might, with equal propriety, have placed prudence and justice before it, since without prudence fortitude is mad; without justice, it is mischievous.

As the end of method is perspicuity, that series is sufficiently regular that avoids obscurity; and where there is no obscurity it will not be difficult to discover method.[185]

Amply warned by this, we may court the very folly Johnson finds in those praisers of Aristotle, and ask whether there is in Spenser some virtue "without which no other virtue can be practised." All the heroes are heroic insofar as they are faithful to their "troth" or calling, all must exhibit steadfastness, loyalty, courage, and perseverance. The underlying prerequisite is most nearly constancy, literally "standing with." This virtue is said to be the subject of Spenser's seventh book, unwritten so far as we know, with the exception of a so-called fragment, the Mutabilitie cantos. Elyot mentions this virtue, contrasting the constant man with "that man whiche is mutable for euerye occasyon."[186] He advises us that in experience no virtue can survive or be certain without it, and he compares it to the mortar that holds together a fortress. Spenser's legends treat six varieties of constancy; Northrop Frye observes that the first three of these pertain to an ideal or steadfast self; and the second three, to a social ideal of concord. Frye goes on to say that both of Spenser's installments run in a Hegelian progression, with the third virtue of each triad reconciling the somewhat antithetical claims of the two preceding virtues.[187]

[185] *Johnson's Lives of the English Poets*, ed. G. Birbeck Hill (Oxford, 1905), vol. 3, p. 99 (text modernized). Johnson refers to Hooker, *Laws of Ecclesiastical Polity*, II.i.2, and Aristotle, *Nich. Eth.* III.vi–ix.

[186] *Gouernour*, III.xix, Everyman's Library, pp. 253–256.

[187] "The Structure of Imagery," in *Fables of Identity*, pp. 86f. Frye's analysis is anticipated by A.S.P. Woodhouse, "Nature and Grace in *The Faerie Queene*," *ELH*, 16 (1949), p. 225: "In broadest outline . . . Book I moves upon the level of grace and deals with a specifically Christian experience and virtue (call this Spenser's thesis); and the subsequent books which we possess move upon the level of nature and concern themselves with the natural virtues (call this the antithesis). Somehow, before the poem was completed, Spenser must achieve his synthesis. . . ." Frye has foreshortened this analysis.

Thus the faithful Redcrosse adheres to a spiritual ideal, and his quest anticipates a specifically human destiny in the heavenly Jerusalem. The shamefast Guyon adheres to a natural ideal—his is an earthly and physical excellence. The chastity of Britomart involves both the natural and spiritual ideals. Spenser indicates as much at the opening of her legend, where she meets both knights: she unhorses Guyon, and then comes to the rescue of Redcrosse. At one point the poet even confuses the knights' names (III.ii.4), as holiness modulates into temperance in the context of chastity. By virtue of the wound she receives from Gardante at the castle of Malecasta, Britomart becomes a white field stained with blood; Redcrosse's emblem is brought in at just this point (III.i.64). Britomart is also a radiant armed virgin, compared with Cynthia. According to the letter to Raleigh, Cynthia is another name for the private person of the fairy queen, and her image adorns the shield of the virginal Guyon.

The virtues of the second installment are similarly related. In the legend of friendship, the constancies are between friends and lovers. In the legend of justice, Artegall is loyal to a specifically human, but impersonal, political order, symbolized by the public person of the queen. The reconciling virtue, courtesy, is more personal, as evidenced by Calidore's special genius for striking up new friendships; it also contains an element of disinterest, for courtesy is extended to would-be foes and to the undeserving, as one can see in Calidore's unselfish treatment of his rival, the churl Corydon. Skilled in all the arts of the courtier, Calidore is·both a lover and a friend to lovers; he is also a friend of Artegall and is able to tame that knight's nemesis, the Blatant Beast.

A Renaissance equivalent of the progression appears in the Neo-Platonic dialectic of Proclus, where the three momenta are "abiding" (*monai*), "proceeding" (*proodos*), and "returning" (*epistrophe*).[188] This kind of

---

[188] *Elements of Platonic Theology*, prop. 35, ed. and trans. E. R. Dodds (1933), pp. 38f.; and *The Six Books of Platonic Theology*, IV.xvi., edn. and Latin trans. of Aemilius Portus (1618), p. 219. For summaries, E. Zeller, *Outline of the History of Greek Philosophy*, trans. L. Palmer, rev. W. Nestle, 13th edn. (New York, 1931), pp. 307–310; and W. Windelband, *A History of Philosophy*, trans. James H. Tufts (reprint New York, 1958), vol. I, p. 251: "The procession of the Many forth from the One involves, in the first place, that the particular remain like the universal, and thus that the effect abides or persists within the cause; in the second place, that this product is a now self-subsisting entity in contrast with that which has produced it, and that it proceeds forth from the same; and finally, that by virtue of just this antithetic relation the individual strives to return again to its ground. *Persistence, procession,* and *return,* . . . or identity, difference, and union of that which has been distinguished, are accordingly the three *momenta* of the dialectical process; and into this formula of emanistic development, by virtue of which every concept should be thought of as in itself—out of itself—returning to itself, Proclus pressed his entire scheme. . . ." For the resemblance to Fichte, Schelling, and Hegel, see W. Windelband, *History of Ancient Philosophy*, trans. H. Cuchman, 2nd edn. (New York, 1901), p. 318, and *Gesch. der neueren Philos.* (Leipzig, 1878–1880), vol. 2, pp. 306ff.

triad is communicated to the Renaissance by such texts as Ficino's commentary on Plotinus, near the head of which Ficino briefly indicates the analogous dialectic of "producing," "converting," and "perfecting."[189] As Edgar Wind explains, Ficino's scheme reads the second stage of Proclus back into the first;[190] we might say that Ficino has only advanced one step around a self-reverting circle, for Proclus' initial "abiding" and Ficino's terminal "perfecting" share an inherence that the other two steps do not exhibit. In his commentary on Plato's *Symposium*, Ficino, among his versions of this circle, offers *incipit, transit*, and *desinit* ("it originates," "it is converted," and "it makes an end").[191] Elsewhere the process is compared to the circle of the three Graces; curiously enough, we will discover the Graces in the terminal book of both of Spenser's installments.

The sequence of paradises in the first three books shows a pattern such as Proclus': the spiritual Eden, the antithetical and physical Bower of Bliss, and the metaphysical Garden of Adonis. The endings of the various books follow another progression. The first book in each triad ends in a major key of procession, epithalamium, betrothal, and imagery of rebirth and Isaiah's "married land"; music itself is heard. Books II and V end in more of a minor key: the hero is alienated from his environment, and disturbance and suppression hedge his conquest. The final book in each series ends with the hero separated from his beloved; she is in good hands, however, and we might expect her return in the next installment. Musically, perhaps the comparison is with a diminished seventh chord.

What is the evidence for this progression in Arthur's activity? Arthur's character in the eleventh cantos of Books II and V has already been mentioned. Some of the details of his services in the eighth canto of Book IV suggest comparison to a pattern found in the same canto of Book I: a captive victim (Redcrosse, Amyas); a relentless giant pagan (Orgoglio, Corflambo); a faithful companion who sues for Arthur's aid (Una, Placidas); a jailor who is himself in a kind of bondage (Ignaro with "the keyes of

---

[189] Commentary *In Plotinum* (on *Enn.* I, III), "De triplici reditu animae ad divinum, ad divinum praeludium, Argumentum," in *Op. om.*, II-2, p. 1559.

[190] Wind, *Pagan Mysteries*, p. 38, n. 9. Wind implies that Renaissance Neo-Platonists always misread the triads and Proclus. The evidence is not all on Wind's side, however, for in the fifty-five conclusions after Proclus, Pico mentions the trinities frequently, and the forty-ninth conclusion reads: "Prima Trinitas manet tantum; secunda manet, & procedit: tertia post processum convertit" (The first trinity abides only; the second abides and proceeds: the third turns back after having proceeded). (These conclusions are reprinted in Portus' edn. of the *Platonic Theology*, 1618, pp. 503–507.)

[191] The Latin is from *De Amore*, II.ii, which describes the cycle of Beauty, Love, and Pleasure created when Beauty attracts everything to itself. Although Ficino equates the Graces with Beauty at V.ii, it remained for the medal of Pico della Mirandola to complete the equation: see Wind, *Pagan Mysteries*, pp. 36–44, and below, Chap. IV, "Heroic Eros," sec. ii, and esp. the Ficino text cited in n. 189, above, where the Graces are among the paradigms for the Neo-Platonic trinitarian mode.

every door"; Paeana's captive dwarf with "the keyes of every prison door"), and the unveiling of Arthur's shield.[192] In each instance, of course, Arthur beheads the tyrant and enlarges the victim.

In the third book of each installment Arthur seems somewhat less than indispensable. In the legend of chastity he utters the apostrophe against the night, after chasing Florimell all day, and that is the extent of his contribution. In Book VI he sleeps rather often, and his rescue of Mirabella in the eighth canto is finally not much more successful than were his earlier efforts on behalf of Florimell. He went a different way from Britomart at the outset of Book III, and he fails to confer with the patron-knight of courtesy altogether. Britomart and Calidore are two of Spenser's most fully realized characters, as personalities, and no doubt there is a sense in which they are replacing Arthur.[193] This development is appropriate to the "synthetic" books, and to the theme of development itself.

Perhaps this explanation of the magnification and diminishment of Arthur can be carried further. The "succour" that Redcrosse receives from Arthur is also available at the House of Holiness. In fact, the hero of each book visits such a "house"—an Alma Mater devoted to the nurture and support of his virtue. This house functions to expound the symbolism of the virtue, and it therefore naturally occasions the hero's self-recognition in the first installment. In the second installment the recognition is social as well.[194] In the third and sixth books, however, the symbolic edifice is replaced by a *locus amoenus* that enjoys a continual spring and is a resort of Venus. In the legend of chastity the locus is the Garden of Adonis,

---

[192] "The keyes": I.viii.30, IV.viii.54. The exposure of Arthur's shield at IV.viii.42 is problematic, but apparently Corflambo's blow struck the shield and "did the couering reare," thereby rendering the Squire and the dwarf senseless, though not affecting Corflambo himself. If this ambiguous instance is *not* admitted, then it is possible to restrict the symbol of the revealed shield to triumphs of the Reformation alone; that is, to the defeat of Orgoglio and the beast (I.viii.19–21), the Soldan and the Armada (V.viii.37–41), and the idol of Gerioneo and its monster, or the Inquisition in the Netherlands (V.xi.21, 26).

[193] The text particularly insists upon the interchangeability of Arthur and Britomart. Like Arthur, Britomart is the "royall Infant" (III.ii.49). She is "Magnificke" (V.vii.21) like Gloriana, "th'idole of her Makers great magnificence" (II.iii.41), and like Mercilla's court, where the palace porch "most magnificke did appeare" (V.ix.22). Through her magnanimity to her enemies, Mercilla "her selfe the more doth magnify" (V.viii.17). Arthur seeks "full great renowme," and "to be most magnified" (III.v.11), while Britomart will become the ancestress of "Renowmed kings, and sacred Emperours" (III.iii.23). The alternate consort Artegall is "the prowest knight that euer was" (III.iii.24): Arthur is "the prowest knight aliue," or "the prowest man aliue" (II.viii.18, xi.30). Britomart rejoices to hear her future lover "so highly magnifide" (III.ii.11), i.e., elevated to Arthurian status, or Gloriana's favor. In the culminating episode of her own legend, Britomart is herself the Arthurian intervening figure, possessed of "huge heroicke magnanimity" (III.xi.19).

[194] The "house of recognition" is so described in Frye, "Structure of Imagery," in *Fables of Identity*, p. 77.

which symbolizes the order of nature. In the legend of courtesy the locus is Mount Acidale, which symbolizes that "second nature," the order of words. The heroine of chastity does not visit the Garden, though her psychological "little sister," Amoret, is reared there. Calidore, though he visits Mount Acidale, is only able to watch its activities; he does not, properly speaking, participate.

In each case, however, there is a significant figure inside the magic circle with whom one can communicate. In the Garden of Adonis the figure is called Genius; Spenser elsewhere explains his significance:

> That is our Selfe, whom though we do not see
> Yet each doth in him selfe it well perceive to bee.
>
> (II.xii.47)

In other words, the discipline of chastity particularly depends on our having a feeling for our own identity. On Mount Acidale the creative genius is our poet, and he is able to mediate his vision to the attentive Calidore. "Who knowes not Colin Clout?" the poem prompts,[195] and once again the act of recognition clearly devolves upon the audience.

At the conclusion of the Alice books, the heroine seems to become larger and larger in relation to her surroundings—she is not only waking up, but also growing up. The mysterious Red King is then free to disappear back into the emblematic world of the playing-card and the looking-glass, along with all the other parental imagos who haunt her dreams. In short, we too must replace Arthur.

The Testimony of Mutabilitie

> After him *Vther*, which *Pendragon* hight,
> Succeding There abruptly it did end,
> Without full point, or other Cesure right,
> As if the rest some wicked hand did rend,
> Or th'Authour selfe could not at least attend
> To finish it: that so vntimely breach
> The Prince him selfe halfe seemeth to offend . . .
>
> (II.x.68)

---

[195] For this rhetorical question, see Ovid, *Fasti* II.83: "Quod mare non novit, quae nescit Ariona tellus?" (What sea, what land knows not Arion?), where the subsequent verses describe Arion's Orphic powers of musicianship. I owe this citation to Dr. Fred Nichols. The reference to Arlo-hill is mixed in with references to Colin's celebration of the rivers Mole and Mulla (cf. VII.vi.36 and 40), and Mole recurs at VII.vii.11, followed by a reference to the poetry that celebrated the marriage of Peleus and Thetis. This would be Catullus, 64, I believe, and that poem is notable for its long digression retailing the story of Theseus and Ariadne: an allusion to this story climaxes the description of the rings or coronas on Mount Acidale (VI.x.13).

Despite the offense to Arthur, there are several signs that his author's poem has reached what Tasso would call its "natural and determinate magnitude." Book I, for example, promises a full-dress treatment of the victory of the fairy queen over the Armada; but when we come to the legend of justice, the subject has been abbreviated to an episode in the historical allegory (I.xi.7; V.viii). More important is the moral allegory, which Spenser, if anyone, could doubtless have expanded, though not without more and more redundancy in the giants, monsters, and foul-mouthed hags department. Many of the eligible virtues have already been appropriated for the supporting cast of the present six virtues. Prudence, for example, would have been a logical candidate for a title role, but much of its lore has found its way into the poem already: consider, in the legend of temperance, the heavy counselor, the theme of good timing, and the three sages at the Castle of Alma. The sages supply an analogue for the common allegory, derived from Cicero, of the three time-dimensions of prudence.[196]

In the dedicatory sonnets attached to his poem, Spenser promises the various noblemen to whom they are addressed that their virtues are or will be celebrated in his poem. The last sonnet is written "To all the gratious and beautifull Ladies in the Court" and perhaps they were meant to recognize themselves in the one hundred and four naked graces for whom Colin Clout pipes near the end of Book VI. As if he were thinking in terms of promise and performance, Spenser puts in this scene a number of "quotations" from the eclogues with which he officially opened his canon. We find Colin Clout celebrating his mistress, the conceit of the fourth Grace, the fairy ring, and the poet breaking his pipe. In the first eclogue Colin is frustrated as an unsuccessful lover; here, as an interrupted visionary. Because Spenser's poem ends shortly after, Colin's recreations have suggested a comparison with Prospero's revels; Colin's breaking his pipe thus anticipates the resolve of the greater illusionist to break his staff and drown his book.[197] Such a terminal symbol is not unprecedented in Spenser; the following are the final six lines of the sexagesimal *Teares of the Mvses*:

> Eftsoones such store of teares she forth did powre,
> As if shee all to water would have gone;
> And all her sisters seeing her sad stowre,
> Did weep and waile and made exceeding mone,
> And all their learned instruments did breake,
> The rest vntold, no liuing tongue can speake.

Another terminal symbol appeared in Spenser's *Calender*. Should Envy bark at the *Calender*, the envoi recommended the work to the protection

---

[196] See Chap. III, n. 67, below.
[197] Frye compares Colin to Prospero, "Structure of Imagery," *Fables of Identity*, pp. 86f.

of the chivalrous Sir Philip Sidney. The "hellish hound" that Orpheus tamed turns up in the "October" eclogue (l. 30), on the state of poetry, and Sidney is elsewhere compared to Orpheus (*Ruines of Time*, 607–609). In *The Faerie Queene* the equivalent monster is set at large by Envy at the end of Book V. The taming of the Blatant Beast, as he is now called, is the assignment of the chivalrous Sir Calidore, and Calidore is a visitor in a shepherd's Arcadia. In the last stanzas of the book the Beast escapes— no longer "furthest from the daunger of enuy, and suspition of present time," he fairly chases the poet out of his poem.

Prospero's vanishing revels are followed by his speech on the dissolving of the entire creation; Colin's recreations are followed by the Mutabilitie cantos. If the scene on Mount Acidale is a kind of poetic threshold, three "quotations" from it suggest that the two additional cantos are meant as a cosmic equivalent. First there is the parenthetical question concerning the location chosen for the lawsuit of Mutabilitie. "Who knowes not Arlo- hill?" Arlo-hill will remind us of Acidale, where it was asked, "Who knowes not Colin Clout?" Secondly, there is the theme of violated cyno- sure; in the subplot, Faunus spying on Diana corresponds to Calidore's in- terruption of Colin and his naked companions. Diana goes on to curse the surrounding countryside in the same way that the triumph of Muta- bilitie has cursed the whole sublunary creation; the thieves in Book VI had an analogous effect in wasting Calidore's Arcadia. Thirdly, Calidore's approach caused the Graces to vanish "which way he never knew"; Nature herself vanishes at the end of the Mutabilitie cantos, like the old earth in the Apocalypse, "whither no man wist."[198]

Like the letter to Raleigh then, the Mutabilitie cantos seem to have something to tell us about the six books of the poem, even though they purport to fit some unrealized scheme beyond the poem's present scope. The cantos are numbered six and seven, and they are said to belong to a legend of constancy for which we have no other evidence. If one can momentarily ignore this enumeration, an examination of the piece itself produces two important observations. First, in some important respects it differs from everything else in *The Faerie Queene*. No other passages of the same length are given over entirely to mythological characters, nor do any other episodes leave the sublunary world. There is no "knight" of constancy here (see VII.vi.37): he would seem to be *wholly* errant. But this piece does not treat constancy as a moral virtue in the first place, but rather as a metaphysical principle, analogous to Being. Neither is Muta- bilitie treated as a vice, nor even primarily as a quality characterizing the

[198] VI.x.16, VII.vii.59. For the word "dilate" in the two places, see below, Chap. V, "Fables of Green Fields," sec. ii.

state of sin; Mutabilitie is simply a condition of the fallen world, analogous to Becoming, which is understood to include entropy—for Mutabilitie is said to seek her own decay by desire (VII.vii.59).[199] Secondly, the Mutabilitie cantos may be read as a self-sufficient poem, exactly as they stand. Nothing in them is mysterious because of something we expect to be told elsewhere. They have the form of a fragment employing the symbolism of the larger poem, but they do not continue it. They are inevitably drawn into orbit around the larger body, like the moon that they describe, but only the state of *The Faerie Queene* itself—and the numbers—has suggested their incompleteness.

The two cantos are followed by two stanzas, said to belong to an "unperfite" eighth canto. Again, let us disregard the rubric. The two stanzas provide a conclusion that conforms the cantos to conventions of the dream-vision poem and the debate poem. Spenser reflects upon the argument the poem has presented, just as the awakened dream-vision poet puzzles over the meaning of his dream. (A noteworthy example is the debate over the pardon of Piers the Plowman.) If one thinks of the vanishing of Nature as signaling the end of such a dream-vision, one can also observe an analogy with the convention of a terminal event that abruptly brings the dream into alignment with an insistent reality outside the dream. Spenser cannot decide to abide by Nature's judgment of the speciousness of Mutabilitie's claim to sovereignty; he has already referred us to the *Parliament of Fowls*. Other debate poems also issue in conclusions in which nothing is concluded, and at least one debate in prose—Swift's *Battle of the Books* —breaks off with the pretense of a lost manuscript.

It is sometimes said that the Mutabilitie cantos would have become the "core" cantos of the legend of constancy.[200] Initially, this suggestion is attractive. First, the theme of order-in-change has a counterpart in the Garden of Adonis at the center of Book III: Adonis is "eterne in mutabilitie" (III.vi.47). Secondly, the symbolism of the locus of recognition is found here—the Alma Mater, the porter-guardian, the daughters of the sky-god, the potentially paradisiacal place, the sense of cynosure. That Mutabilitie should be allowed to loom up into the center of the pattern is more paradoxical, though Time with his scythe is at large in the Garden. There are two objections. One derives from the fact that the loci of recognition

---

[199] Mutabilitie's self-destructiveness contrasts with the natural intention of the creature, as expounded by Boethius: "Nature is diligent that all things may be propagated by the multiplication of seed. . . . They know to remain not only for a time but as if *in perpetuum permanendi*. For providence gave to her creatures this [the act of generation] that they naturally desire to continue so long as they may, wherefore there is no cause why one should any way doubt that all things which are desire naturally stability of remaining, and eschew corruption." (*De Cons. Phil.* III, prose xi, adapted from Loeb *Boethius*, p. 283.)

[200] C. S. Lewis, *The Allegory of Love* (London, 1953), p. 353.

THE ONE AND THE MANY

are prepared for; a series of adventures leads up to them, and they seem to be the episodic germ out of which such a series might have originally been generated.[201] The mortification of Redcrosse at the House of Holiness, for example, occurs throughout his legend. His penance leads to a vision of the New Jerusalem, just as his legend as a whole leads to the Garden of Eden. In contrast, the Mutabilitie cantos imply no knightly fiction for constancy, and they are fully equipped with a fiction of their own. The second objection is simpler: there are two cantos, not one, and the symbolism has been accordingly expanded. For such a doubling there is one slight precedent: the Garden of Adonis canto in Book III is followed by the Temple of Venus in Book IV. The goddess at the Temple is a veiled androgynous genetrix, as Nature is here, and it follows from this resemblance that the Mutabilitie cantos are reflexive to the present poem, rather than merely sequent to it.

The "legend" of constancy should have shown, to judge by Elyot's remarks, an unmoved will tempted to give way under pressure or persuasion; indeed, two of his examples involve Roman lawmakers, and one is an unmoved judge. Perhaps the best example in Spenser is Guyon in the Cave of Mammon, one of Milton's models for the unmoved Christ of *Paradise Regained*. One thinks of Milton's Job, "Whose constant perseverance overcame," whom Milton contrasts with military conquerors (*Par. Reg.* I.148, III.64–95). According to Milton, Job supplies the type for the "brief epic," which seems to correspond to *Paradise Regained*.[202] The Book of Job itself is mainly the argument on earth that follows on an upstart Satan's obtruding himself among the sons of the Hebrew sky-god. Mutabilitie initiates the action of her poem in a similar way, blocking out the upper heavenly world, the lower one being already subject to her curse— a curse that in fact would categorically include the catastrophes of Job. As with the Satan of Milton's second epic—and in contrast to the apocalyptic beasts of Book I or the Titans of classical legend—Jove's challenger is not disabled by local wounds of head or heel. Instead, we witness a colloquial conflict, and it is clear that Jove, unlike Redcrosse, would rather talk than fight. When the talk is sorted out, the lower nature represented by the Titaness has apparently been brought under the intellectual control of Nature as a whole.

[201] My terminology echoes Frye, *Anatomy of Criticism*, p. 56, where he speaks of germinal episodic forms characteristic of various literary modes, out of which encyclopedic forms are generated. My discussion is also indebted to pages 140, 204, and 299 of the same work.

[202] "That Epick form whereof the two poems of *Homer*, and those other two of *Virgil* and *Tasso* are a diffuse, and the book of *Job* a brief model. . . ." (*Complete Prose Works*, New Haven, 1953, vol. 1, p. 813.) For further generic considerations, see Chap. IV, n. 436, and Chap. VI, "The Triumph of Time."

Milton's brief epic reverses the tragic action of *Paradise Lost* by showing us one man who retains the vision of innocence and who does not fall. Perhaps the Mutabilitie cantos similarly qualify the romantic quest movement of *The Faerie Queene* by presenting, in satiric and philosophic form, the opposite tendencies manifested by ordinary experience. At the end of each legend Mutabilitie always gains a small victory that carries over into the next legend; something is either left unredeemed by the quest, or reverts to its former unredeemed state. In the Mutabilitie cantos, that qualification is enlarged to a veritable reconstruction. Mutabilitie, rather than a knight, is the protagonist of the quest, and she has the subversive and libidinous character of the hero's usual adversary. She has been allowed to penetrate just such an area as the other loci of recognition seal off. The Garden of Adonis, for example, treats the natural cycle in terms of its high points; low points, represented by the wounding of Marinell and the imprisoning of Florimell, are found outside it. Hence the form of the sequel turns the larger legends inside out: it draws the serial circumference into the central cynosure and expands the latter to include all of nature.

Has Spenser's reversal of procedure anything to tell us about the "accomplishment" of *The Faerie Queene*? The thirty-third *Amoretti* sonnet, published a year before the second installment, contains ambiguities:

> Great wrong I doe, I can it not deny,
>> to that most sacred Empresse my dear dred,
>> not finishing her Queene of faëry,
>> that mote enlarge her living prayses dead:
> But lodwick, this of grace to me aread:
>> doe ye not thinck th'accomplishment of it,
>> sufficient worke for one mans simple head,
>> all were it as the rest but rudely writ.
> How then should I without another wit,
>> thinck euer to endure so taedious toyle,
>> sins that this one is tost with troublous fit,
>> of a proud loue that doth my spirite spoyle.
> Ceasse then, till she vouchsafe to grawnt me rest,
>> Or lend you me another liuing brest.

On the basis of this text there is no deciding how large a poem the speaker has in mind, or what proportions of it are potential and what actual. My own interpretation (based on the fact that the same language about the poet's inspiration is found in the eightieth sonnet, where six books are said to be complete) is that the speaker feels that the presently drafted six books are enough for one poet to have accomplished, even though the second three, when published, will be no more polished than the first three. One is inclined to agree.

There is more in this sonnet. Both the poet's political mistress and his personal one keep him from rest. The word *rest* has two meanings: some portion of the poet's work, and the poet's repose. Curiously, this unsuspicious homonym turns up in another poem that celebrates the poet's two mistresses. *Colin Clouts Come Home Againe* ends on a rich rhyme of the two meanings:

> So hauing ended, he from ground did rise,
> And after him vprose eke all the rest:
> All loth to part, but that the glooming skies
> Warnd them to draw their bleating flocks to rest.
>
> (952-955)

The last line of *The Teares of the Mvses*, quoted previously, contains this word also, a repetition that aligns the ending with the last line of the prologue. And the *Hymn of Heauenlie Beautie* ends on an upturned gaze and an eternal rest. The Sapience of this poem is a sacred counterpart of "the God of Nature" to whom Mutabilitie says she will appeal (VII.vi.35). Spenser says of Sapience:

> Both heauen and earth obey vnto her vill,
> And all the creatures which they both containe:
> For of her fulnesse which the world doth fill,
> They all partake, and do in state remaine,
> As their great Maker did at first ordaine,
> Through obseruation of her high beheast,
> By which they first were made and still increast.
>
> (197-213)

"By me kings rule," says the Wisdom of Proverbs 8:15; Mutabilitie makes much the same claim when she attempts to abrogate the "imperiall see" of Jove to herself. Nature does not take quite so unqualified a view at the end of the Mutabilitie cantos, but she does assert that all things "are not changed from their first estate; . . . But their raigne ouer change, and doe their states maintaine."[203] Beyond motion, time, and change, however, will

---

[203] Nature's argument is a loose paraphrase of *De Cons. Phil.* III, metre ii: "Each thing seeks again its proper course, and returning to its own rejoices, nor does any settled order abide, except that which joins the beginning to the end and makes of itself a stable round." That Fate governs this process appears from *De Cons. Phil.* IV, prose vi: "Fate moves the heavens and the stars, governs the elements in their mixture, and transforms them by mutual changes; it renews all things that are born and die by the reproduction of similar offspring and seeds. . . . This order, by its own unchanging nature, controls mutable things which otherwise would be disordered and confused." For the principle whereby Nature is "Still mouing, yet

be Boethius' "whole plenitude of endless life together";[204] and the word *rest* occurs twice in the last stanza, where again there is an upward turn to the contemplation of God. The terminal word-play has been shifted to the Hebrew words "Sabbaoth," hosts, and "Sabbath," rest. The original end of the first installment read, "Now cease your worke; to morrow is an holy day," and of course the Lord of Hosts is also the Lord of the Sabbath. The other word, "Sabbaoth," is used twice in the New Testament, and both places are eschatological in character. Romans 9:29 quotes Isaiah regarding God's salvation of a chosen remnant; the preceding verse reads, "For he finisheth the word, and maketh it short in righteousnesse; for a short word will the Lord make on earth" (Bishops' Bible; Rheims, "a word abbridged"). James 5:4 is concerned with defrauded reapers: their rich masters have hoarded treasure against the last day, and "the cries of them which have reaped are entred into the eares of the Lord of sabbaoth" (Bishops' Bible). With these texts in mind we may read the poet's final petition as a dramatic foreshortening or abridgement of the poem:

> Then gin I thinke on that which Nature sayde
>   Of that same time when no more *Change* shall be,
>   But stedfast rest of all things firmely stayd
>   Vpon the pillours of Eternity,
>   That is contrayr to *Mutabilitie*:
>   For, all that moueth doth in *Change* delight;
>   But thence-forth all shall rest eternally
>   With him that is the God of Sabbaoth hight:
> O that great Sabbaoth God, graunt me that
>   Sabaoths sight.
>
>   (VIII.viii.2)

These lines leave little doubt as to the completeness of the Mutabilitie cantos. Further, it is hard to believe that they do not also make a final gesture toward that longer poem dedicated to Elizabeth, whose name in Hebrew—Eli-sabbath—can mean Sabbath God.[205] It is the finishing of her poem that will grant her poet rest.

---

vnmoued" (VII.vii.13), see Emerson, "Nature" (*Essays: Second Series*): "The uneasiness which the thought of our helplessness in the chain of causes occasions in us, results from looking too much at one condition of nature, namely, Motion. But the drag is never taken from the wheel. Wherever the impulse exceeds, the Rest or Identity insinuates its compensation."

[204] *De Cons. Phil.* V, prose vi.

[205] William Patten, in his *A Calender of Scripture, sub* "Elizabeth," devotes several pages to an exposition of the queen as the "seventh of God," deriving her name from Heb. *Eli-sheba*. But the forms *shabua*, week; *sheba, shibah*, seven; and *shabbath*, cessation, sabbath; are all related. Jerome, *Liber de Nom. Hebr.*, in PL, XXIII, 843, *sub* "Elisabe," reads: "Dei mei saturitas, vel Dei mei juramentum, aut septimus"; but see *vol. cit.*, col. 1221, *Origenianum Lexicon Graecum Nom. Hebr., sub*

The Mutabilitie cantos clearly issue in a conclusion that suggests the rhetorical determination of the poem. Less obviously, the cantos supply a last term in that seriatim multiplication of the hero, which we have described in preceding essays. As the quotation from Boethius might remind us, Neo-Platonic thought considers temporality to be a circumstance attendant upon the pluralization or dissemination of the One. Spenser's serialization of the quest creates a kind of temporal dimension too, a protraction of Being over time that might lead to an apotheosis or triumph of time itself. Thus the Mutabilitie cantos follow logically upon the ending of Book VI, where the ultimately unsuccessful pursuit of the Blatant Beast seems to take place over successive generations of heroes. Mutabilitie would appear, then, upon the passing of the heroic animus, not from one hero to the next, but out of the poem altogether; so ends the extenuation of the hero that has taken place over the several legends of the poem. The Mutabilitie cantos themselves, however, conclude with an eschatological reversal upon this very process that seems to have brought them into existence. Time takes survey of all the world, in the words of another defeated hero, but time must have a stop.

The relation between the Mutabilitie cantos and *The Fairie Queene* almost necessarily entails a comparison with Ovid. It is well known that Spenser has borrowed much of Mutabilitie's discourse on the topic of change from the Pythagorean oration that occupies the terminal book of the *Metamorphoses*.[206] Ovid brilliantly culminates his poem with one further change; he elevates his subject matter to a philosophical plane, and reincarnates the doctrine of the dead Pythagoras in the text of a latter-day exponent, Ovid himself, whom in the meantime he pronounces immortal. However, the soul of Pythagoras passes from Ovid into, not Spenser, but Mutabilitie. It is somewhat ironic that Mutabilitie is unaware that the

---

"Elisabet," which compares the Old Latin interpretation, "domini requies." For this identification, cf. A. C. Hamilton, "Our new poet: Spenser, 'well of English undefyld,'" in *A theatre for Spenserians*, ed. Judith Kennedy and James Reither (Toronto, 1973), p. 110. When the poet anticipates that his mistress will "grant" him "rest" in *Amoretti* XXXIII, the reference seems to be to Elizabeth Boyle, rather than Elizabeth the queen, but in either case the name implies the mistress' particular capacity to make the grant in question. This exaltation of Elizabeth's name might be compared to the apotheosis of Julius Caesar at the end of Ovid's *Metamorphoses*, though of course it is necessarily more oblique, given the transcendent otherness of Spenser's God. The double meaning inherent in *rest* also lurks in the quietus to Shakespeare's most elongate and abiding dramatic action: flights of angels sing the hero to his rest, but of his story, the rest is silence.

[206] See the summaries of the papers of William Cumming, "The Influence of Ovid's *Metamorphoses* on Spenser's Mutabilitie Cantos," and Brents Stirling, "Two Notes on the Philosophy of *Mutabilitie*," in the Variorum *Works*, ed. Greenlaw, et al. (Baltimore, 1939–1949), *Books VI and VII*, pp. 408–410, 421f.

source of her argument is another poet's triumph over time and change with the completion of his magnum opus. One can compare the ignorance of Spenser's Arthur, who does not know that the unfinished history he reads in Book II (x.68) culminates in him: he is himself the final term of the book that he reluctantly abandons.[207]

Professor Michael Holahan has recently pointed out[208] that it is not Ovid's *Metamorphoses* but his *Fasti* that remain unfinished, breaking off six-twelfths of the way through the calendar of the festal year that they commemorate. The counterbalancing is extensive here, for in contrast to the *Fasti*, Spenser's *Calender* is complete. Thus, in a complex reversal upon his predecessor, Spenser co-opts the ending of the *Metamorphoses* for his own unfinished work, even while making the piece serve as part of yet another completed calendar poem.

The exchange between Spenser and Ovid is what we might call "a stressed analogy": it is stressed, because something very like it obtains within the Spenserian oeuvre itself. Spenser tells us that the material of the Mutabilitie cantos is taken from the records of fairyland; thus the pendant belongs to the fairyland subject, and has its canto and stanza format. It treats a complete cycle of the months, along with the twelve zodiacal signs, after what appears to be an eclipse of the moon. It includes such characters as the Hours, Order, and Time, with his hour-glass. It ends with a judgment that, "rightly waid," shows that all things work their own perfection by dilation, and yet it ends "unperfite." It presents what seem to be very carefully balanced claims of Mutabilitie and her opposites. Even the sabbatical numbers six and seven begin to look as though they were deliberately chosen. The sixth sign is Virgo, who retreated to the stars at the triumph of Mutabilitie, as Diana abandoned Arlo-hill. The seventh sign is Libra, the scales of justice, in which are weighed the merits of doubtful cases (cf. VII.vii.38, 57–58). There is something familiar in all these numbers, except that Spenser has reduced his scale from the hour hand to the minute hand. Even the two concluding stanzas are only "unperfite" with respect to an "eighth" canto; otherwise they are not. They provide for the Mutabilitie cantos what the cantos themselves provide for *The Faerie Queene*, an abbreviated contemplative sequel. Thus the Mutabilitie cantos are not a fragment, but a fraction. And they seem to be offered in lieu of any continuation of *The Faerie Queene*.

---

[207] In passing one may compare the ignorance of Aeneas concerning the future history of Rome portrayed upon the shield he bears, at *Aen.* VIII.730f.

[208] In his paper, *"Iamque opus exegi*: Ovid's Changes and Spenser's Brief Epic of Mutability," delivered to the MLA, Comp. Lit. 4, New York, December, 1972. I owe the whole idea of an extended ratio between Spenser and Ovid to this paper, though I by no means do justice to Professor Holahan's complete argument, which especially turns on a contrast between Ovid's and Spenser's personal claims: Ovid's self-assertion vs. Spenser's self-abnegation, and Ovid's triumph over history, vs. Spenser's admission of defeat before it.

We said that, as a seventh legend, the cantos turn the preceding six legends inside out. Perhaps they also get their proportions by inverting the whole numbers of the larger poem. If we talk about *The Faerie Queene* of the letter to Raleigh, we talk in fractions: we say we have half the poem plus one-sixth of a book; but if we look at what we actually have before us, we see six books in two halves, plus a pendant, also in two parts. Thus the form of the Mutabilitie cantos expresses their theme: in apparently mutable things, a case may be made for an ordered whole. Each of Spenser's books forms a completed rhetorical period; subsequent installments reveal the membership of a prior book in a more inclusive pattern. The coherence of a given unit is not obscured by the addition of a counterpart, but clarified by the analogy between them. On this basis, I should like to argue that the present poem also forms such a coherent period. As for that "seconde worke," and the second wind required to write it—they are lost with Orlando's wits. These last flew to the moon, at the precise midpoint of the model Spenser knew so well. Ariosto's moon is the final resting-place of fond intentions, unkept promises, and lost time, and this is where the lawsuit of Mutabilitie properly begins. Spenser's poem itself has ended in a kind of hung jury, six books for its completion, and six against:

> Meane while, all creatures, looking in her face,
> Expecting th'end of this so doubtfull case,
> Did hang in long suspence that would ensew,
> To whether side should fall the soueraigne place:
> At length, she looking vp with chearfull view,
> The silence brake, and gaue her doome in speeches few.
>
> (VIII.vii.57)

Then, even Nature vanishes; one thinks of Colin's missing emblem in "December." E. K. tells us that its purport was, "all thinges perish and come to theyr last end, but workes of learned wits and monuments of Poetry abide for ever." It is time to put away expectations of some noisier or more tangible apocalypse. Almost without allowing us to know it, Spenser has his vision, and its crisis is closed.

The argument of the Mutabilitie cantos will allow of nothing more definitive, and neither will *The Faerie Queene*. That self-balancing progression of becoming and decline and replenishment, through which all of Being is regularly perpetuated throughout Spenser's long poem, rightly issues, not in an apocalyptic cataclysm, but in an apocalyptic homeostasis. The kind of equilibrium reached by the Mutabilitie cantos also obtains over the various parts of Spenser's poem considered as a whole. In words like those of Nature, we must turn at length again, to dilate upon the large evidence already put before us.

II

THE BOOK OF LIFE

A foe deprived me of life, took away my bodily strength; afterwards wet me, dipped me in water, took me out again, set me in the sun where I quickly lost the hairs I had. Afterwards the hard edge of the knife cut me, with all impurities ground off; fingers folded me, and the bird's delight sprinkled me over with useful drops; it made frequent tracks across the dark brim, swallowed the tree-dye, part of the stream, again moved on me, journeyed on leaving a dark track. Afterwards a man covered me with binding, stretched skin over me, adorned me with gold; and so the splendid work of smiths, circled with wire, decked me. Now the ornaments and the red dye and the glorious possessions make renowned far and wide the Protector of multitudes, in no wise the torments of hell. If the sons of men will use me they will be the safer and the more victorious, the bolder in heart and blither in thought, the wiser in mind; they will have the more friends, dear ones and kinsfolk, true and good, worthy and trusty, who will gladly increase their honour and happiness, and lay upon them benefits and mercies and hold them firm in the embraces of love. Ask what is my name, useful to men; my name is famous, of service to men, sacred in myself.

(Anglo-saxon riddle, from the *Exeter Book*, trans. R. K. Gordon)

Allegoria; or, The Figure of False Semblant

LITERARY surveys often describe a given work as "an allegory" in the same way that one might classify a play as a comedy. This usage is misleading where it implies that allegory is a genre in its own right—we only have to glance at Spenser to discover that allegory may be found in pastoral, elegy, satire, dream-vision, romance, and in sacred and profane mythology.[1] We are not dealing with a genre, but a theory of poetry.

The theory is expounded in Boccaccio's seminal defense of poetry. The poet composes stories, or fictions: "Fiction is a form of discourse, which, under guise of invention, illustrates or proves an idea; and, as its superficial aspect is removed, the meaning of the author is clear. If, then, sense is revealed under the veil of fiction, the composition of fiction is not idle nonsense."[2] Boccaccio goes on to argue that the fictions of poetry veil truths, or truth, just as the Old Testament prefigures the New, and just as the figurative language of both contains the Word of God. Boccaccio maintains that biblical exegesis and the exposition of meaning in poetry almost comprise a common activity, because in both Scripture and literature the "outward literary semblance"[3]—whether one calls it a fiction or a figure— intends or veils the esoteric sense, or truth.

> Yet if they will insist that whatever is not literally true is, however uttered, a lie, I accept it for purposes of argument; . . . Rather I will ask them to tell me what name should be applied to those parts of the Revelation of John the Evangelist—expressed with amazing majesty of inner sense, though often at first glance quite contrary to the truth—in which he has veiled the great mysteries of God.[4]

Boccaccio is invoking a hermeneutical tradition of some antiquity, found, for example, in Clement of Alexandria:

> . . . all things that shine through a veil show the truth grander and more imposing; as . . . figures through veils, which give added reflections to them . . . we may draw several meanings, as we do from what is expressed in veiled form. . . . Further, those who instituted the mysteries, being philosophers, buried their doctrines in myths, so as not to be obvious to all. Did they then, by veiling human opinions, prevent the ignorant from handling them; and was it not more beneficial for the holy and blessed contemplation of realities to be concealed? . . .

[1] For my argument, see Northrop Frye, "Allegory," in Alex Preminger, ed., and Frank J. Warnke and O. B. Hardison, assoc. eds., *Encyclopedia of Poetry and Poetics* (Princeton, 1966), and *Anatomy of Criticism* (Princeton, 1957), pp. 86–92.

[2] *G.D.G.*, XIV.ix, in Osgood, *Boccaccio on Poetry*, p. 48.

[3] *Ibid.*, p. 49.

[4] *G.D.G.*, XIV.xiii; in Osgood, *Boccaccio on Poetry*, p. 64.

But even those myths in Plato . . . are to be expounded allegorically, not absolutely in all their expressions, but in those which express the general sense. And these we shall find indicated by symbols under the veil of allegory.[5]

The same associations are found in "Demetrius" (*On Style* II.99f.): "In the phrase actually used the speaker has shrouded his words, as it were, in allegory. . . . Hence the Mysteries are revealed in an allegorical form in order to inspire such shuddering and awe as are associated with darkness and night. Allegory also is not unlike darkness and night." Spenser's Night has "couered her vncomely face / With a blacke veile" (VII.vii.44), a usage that might be insignificant in the present context, if it did not occur in the Mutabilitie cantos, where Nature herself—presented as a mystery par excellence—also wears a veil. There is every reason to classify this example with the mediatory veils that belong to Moses and the sanctuary.[6] Nature is a veiled Wisdom.

[5] *Stromata*, V.ix, in ANF, vol. 2, pp. 457f. The citation of this author and his importance for the tradition has been suggested by Michael Murrin, *The Veil of Allegory* (Chicago, 1969), pp. 34f., 44.

[6] For the sum of the above, compare Erasmus, *Enchiridion*, xiv: ". . . you should observe in all your reading those things consisting of both a surface meaning and a hidden one—comparable to body and spirit—so that, indifferent to the merely literal sense, you may examine most keenly the hidden. . . . In unveiling the hidden sense, however, one ought not to follow the conjectures of his own mind but acquire a method. . . . Augustine prefers [the Platonists and Pythagoreans] . . . because their very manner of using a language figurative and, as I have said, appropriate to allegory, comes closer to the style of Holy Scriptures. So it is not to be wondered at that . . . any subject . . . could be enriched . . . by those who . . . had already practised on the books of Plato and the poets the skill which they were to exercise later on in the interpretation of holy mysteries. . . ." Further, the hidden sense ought to be the reader's provocation: "This is true not only of the Old Testament but also of the New. . . . Even if the veil has been drawn from the face of Moses, Paul is as yet seen through a glass darkly." (Trans. Raymond Himelick, in *The Enchiridion of Erasmus*, Bloomington, 1963, pp. 105, 107f.) Similarly Pico della Mirandola, *Heptaplus*, First Proem: "Plato himself concealed his doctrines beneath the coverings of allegory, veils of myth, mathematical images, and unintelligible signs of fugitive meaning." "On the summit of the mountain, that very mountain on which the Lord also addressed his disciples, the face of Moses used to become wonderously bright, illuminated by the light of the divine sun; but since the people with their owl-like and unseeing eyes could not endure the light, he used to speak to them with his face veiled." (Trans. Douglas Carmichael, in *Pico della Mirandola: On the Dignity of Man* . . . , Library of Liberal Arts, Indianapolis and New York, 1965, pp. 69f.) Cf. the Proem to the Second Book: "But why do we longer delay the Prophet's coming forward with unveiled face to speak to us of heavenly mysteries?" (p. 95, trans. cited). Cf. also Macrobius, *Comm. in Somnium Scipionis*, I.ii, secs. 11 and 18, for the "veil of allegory." At sec. 19 it is implied that to reveal the mysteries of the Eleusinian goddess is to expose her to harlotry: one may compare the slandered honesty of Una at I.iii.25. See also Weinberg, *History of Literary*

Poetry is the faithful guardian of the Philosophy that investigates truth, "protecting it as she does beneath the veil of her art"; poets "never veil with their inventions anything which is not wholly consonant with philosophy"; and "The poet conceives his thought by contemplation, and, wholly without the help of syllogism, veils it as subtly and skillfully as he can under the outward semblance of his invention." So Boccaccio.[7] Petrarch asserts that history, morals and the study of nature may all be found in poetry, "but with the condition that these things elsewhere revealed, are concealed under a veil of mystery, that they elude our eyes because of this light veil, and that sometimes they are made clear and that sometimes they are hidden" (*Africa*, IX.101–102).

In particular, the epics of Homer and Virgil were supposed to contain vast reservoirs of humane learning—from the arts, sciences, and the ethical and political disciplines—covertly expressed. The pseudo-Plutarchan *Life of Homer* found in the epics a handbook of practical rhetoric, speculative natural philosophy, and military science. Plato contests this opinion in the *Ion* and the tenth book of *The Republic*, but the following passage from Bruni belongs to Ion's school and is representative:

I adjudge that one who does not hallow the poets is deficient in letters generally. For in them are found the principles and causes and, as it were, the seeds of all doctrines concerning life and mores, and much spoken fittingly and wisely about them; and great authority accrues to them owing to the opinions of the wise and owing to their antiquity, and also owing to their beauty by way of elegance. They have a certain genius worthy of a free man, such that, when one does not have it, he seems almost *sub-rusticus*. What does Homer lack, that he cannot be judged the wisest in all wisdom? Indeed, we are told that all his poetry is teaching for living, in times of war and intervals of peace; and indeed, what provision for the

---

Criticism in the Italian Renaissance (Chicago, 1961), vol. 1, pp. 257–259, where the veil of fiction, in the passage cited from Lodovico Ricchierri, is specifically the veil of the sanctuary. For the veil-relation of the two testaments, see Augustine, *Civ. Dei*, XVI.xxvi, *De Trinitate*, XV.xi.20, and *On the Spirit and the Letter*, xxx and xli. Cf. Thomas Aquinas, *Summa Theol.*, Pt. I, q.1, art.9, resp.: "In Holy Scripture spiritual truths are fittingly taught under the likeness of material things. This is what Dionysus says: *We cannot be enlightened by the divine rays except they be hidden within the covering of many sacred veils* [*De Cael. Hier.*, I.2; PG, III, 121]."

[7] G.D.G., XIV.xviii, xvii, in Osgood, *Boccaccio on Poetry*, pp. 84, 79. Cf. Lactantius, *Epitome of the Divine Institutes*, xi, on pagan fables: "But some one will say that these things are feigned by the poets. This is not the usage of the poets, to feign in such a manner that you fabricate the whole, but so that you cover the actions themselves with a figure, and, as it were, with a variegated veil. Poetic license has this limit, not that it may invent the whole, which is the part of one who is false and senseless, but that it may change something consistently with reason." (Trans. in ANF, vol. 7, p. 227.)

general in war, what cunning or fortitude of the soldiery, what trap or caution, what action, what warning, what deliberation is missing from him?
. . . In this poet examples of this kind are contained in thousands; and
moreover, on the other hand, there are not less with respect to peace, nor
are they any less excellent.[8]

For Spenser also the writing of major poetry requires the establishment
of a more or less uncontestable and exemplary relation with the other institutions of civilization: religion, law, marriage, and private and public
education. Thus his poem is, among other things, an entry on the side of
the defense of poetry, as it is found in such contemporary apologists as
Golding, Nashe, Lodge, and Harington, going back to Boccaccio. Allegory,
for this school, is no more than a formal version of what is asserted to be
the technique of poetry as a rule: "whatever is composed as under a veil,
and thus exquisitely wrought, is poetry and poetry alone."[9]
    In these circumstances, the Elizabethan did not always sharply differ-
entiate allegory from the meaning, or "intention," of literary works of any
kind. The poet's detractors, according to Sidney's *Apology*, "will never
give the lie to things not affirmatively but allegorically written." Puttenham, to take a very different example, acknowledges the generality of the
term *allegory* even when it describes a figure: "The vse of this figure is so
large, and his vertue of so great efficacie as it supposed no man can pleasantly vtter and perswade without it. . . . Of this figure therefor . . . we
will speak first as the chief ringleader and captaine of all other figures,
either in the Poeticall or oratorie science."[10] There is nothing implausible
in the suggestion that allegory is potentially the type-case for literary meaning in general. The idea is suggested by allegory itself: an allegory has a
design upon the critical faculty of the reader from the start, and a discov-
erable foreknowledge of "intention" is designed into any allegory at the
outset. The word *meaning* alone suggests that division—so marked in allegory—between what is said and what is intended, or meant. And if interpretation may be defined, as it is by Paul de Man, as "a generalization that

[8] Leonardo Bruni, *De Studiis et Litteris Liber*, ed. H. Baron, printed and trans.
in E. Garin, ed., *L'Umanesimo italiano* (Bari, 1952), pp. 158–161. Cf. Sidney, *Defense*,
". . . it pleased the heavenly Deity, by Hesiod and Homer, under the veil of fables,
to give us all knowledge, logic, rhetoric, philosophy, natural and moral . . . ," citing
"Clauserus, the translator of Cornutus."
    [9] Boccaccio, *G.D.G.*, XIV.vii, in Osgood, *Boccaccio on Poetry*, p. 42. See Golding,
in the translation of the *Metamorphoses*, Epistle, ll. 63–66, 298–341, 528–542, 581–
585; Preface, ll. 80–85, 123–154, 185–188. Nashe, in Smith, *Elizabethan Critical Essays*, vol. 1, pp. 307–337, esp. pp. 328f. Lodge, *Defence*, in Smith, vol. 1, pp. 63–88,
esp. p. 73. Harington, *Apology*, in Smith, vol. 2, pp. 194–222, esp. pp. 201–206.
    [10] George Puttenham, *The Arte of English Poesie*, ed. Jos. Haselwood (London,
1811), III.xviii, p. 155.

expands the range of applicability of a statement to a wider area,"[11] then all interpretation involves the construing of a "general intention," or the realization of an allegorical sense: it is the allegorical sense that requires a shift in meaning "from the proper signification to another not proper, but yet nigh and like."[12] In Boccaccio the "outward literary semblance" was not literally true; it disguised the author's meaning. Puttenham thinks of allegory as a kind of second intention, one dissembled by the more obvious or ostensible one, and therefore he calls allegory the figure of False semblant.[13]

These larger considerations, however, need not prevent us from introducing the narrower and more technical conception of allegory, without which the adduced comparison would become merely tautologous.

Allegory is a technique of controlled or stipulated meaning, and it occurs whenever the allegorist formalizes an interpretation for a fiction or some comparable literary pattern. As the handbooks often note, it is especially the "continuous" or point-for-point interpretation that is allegorical.[14] When it is present in a fiction, the allegory is introduced by allusion,

[11] *Blindness and Insight* (Oxford, 1971), p. 29.

[12] Henry Peacham, *The Garden of Eloquence* (1593), intro. William G. Crane, Scholars Facsimiles and Reprints (Gainesville, Florida), p. 3. Cf. the German word for allegory, *Gleichnis*, "likeness." Cf. Democritus, Frg. 11, on Delphic style.

[13] *Arte*, III.xviii, p. 155. Cf. *F.Q.* V.xii.36: "misconstrue of a mans intent, / And turne to ill the thing that well was ment." In passing we may note that all translation constitutes a low-level construction or allegorizing of a text, in respect of its realizing the "intention" of a text—what is meant—as opposed to what is said.

[14] Quintillian calls allegory a *continua metaphora* (*Inst. Orat.* IX.ii.46), and says "prius fit genus plerumque continuatis translationibus" (VIII.vi.44). Cicero has this last also, in *Orator* 94. English definitions from Peacham, Angel Day, and Puttenham are cited in Hough, *A Preface to "The Faerie Queene"* (New York, 1963): Peacham, "a continued Metaphore"; Puttenham, "a long and perpetuall Metaphore." Cf. Dudley Fenner, *The Artes of Logike and Rhetorick* (Middelburg, 1594), sig. Di^v: "The continuance of Tropes called an Allegorie, is when one kind of Trope is so continued: as, Looke with what kind of matter it be begunne, with the same it be ended." (Quoted in Sister Miriam Joseph, *Shakespeare's Use of the Arts of Language*, New York, 1947, p. 328.) For the definition of Susenbrotus (cited from *Epitome Troporum ac Schematum*, 1563, p. 13), see Herbert David Rix, *Rhetoric in Spenser's Poetry*, Pennsylvania State College Bulletin, vol. 34, no. 35 (1940), p. 34: in part, "Continet illa plures translationes et continuas, ob idque perpetual etiam Metaphora dicta." Cf. Erasmus, *De Copia*, I.xviii: "Allegory has the same force as metaphor. For allegory is nothing but a continuous metaphor." (Trans. Donald B. King and H. D. Rix, in *On Copia of Words and Ideas*, Medieval Philosophical Texts in Translation, no. 12, Milwaukee: Marquette University Press, 1963, p. 30.) Also see the *Rhetorica ad Herennium* IV.xxxiv.46: "Allegory is a manner of speech denoting one thing by the letter of the words, but another by their meaning (*aliud verbis aliud sententia*). It assumes three aspects: comparison, argument, contrast. It operates

or by some reference extrinsic to the ostensible fictional framework. The pattern of such allusions forms the allegory. This informing pattern may be a second narrative, or a pattern of ideas—an argument, or any program of alternate significances with some topological similarity to the original literary pattern. Insofar as the literary pattern can be aptly rendered into the second pattern, it is allegoric. Fully developed allegory is thus a technique of extended symbolic correspondence or adequation, partly analogous to such structural principles as parallel plots and underlying myths. The correspondence appears in the interpenetration, regulation, rationalization, or displacement of the one pattern by the other.[15] To give a simple example of such allegorical interpolation: a medieval painting of the Last Supper might flank the central subject with panels depicting the meeting of Melchizedek and Abraham, and the feeding of the Israelites in the wilderness. To indicate the relation, Melchizedek will offer Abraham a cup exactly resembling the chalice of the central panel, and the manna will fall in the form of sacramental wafers.[16]

Depending on which pattern takes precedence in our minds—the manifest fictional one, or the latent, supervisory, or interpretative one—allegories may be classified on a sliding scale of explicitness, from the most problematic or subliminal, to the most didactic or insistent. A somewhat different classification would range allegorical significance according to our sense of its importance in determining the fiction, for the allegory may be somewhat problematic and yet essential, as in the case of parables that depend either on some kind of *gnosis* or prior knowledge, or intimate such a dependence (cf. Mark 4:10–12). Strictly educational allegories, however, when explicit, may well slight the fiction. The *Table of Cebes* would be meaningless without its labels, and its fiction is essentially

---

through a comparison when a number of metaphors originating in a similarity in the mode of expression are set together. . . ." (Trans. H. Caplan, Loeb edn., pp. 345–347.) By "argument" the text means allusion; and by "contrary," the subversive or facetious relation mentioned hereafter.

[15] Cf. Augustine, *De Trinitate*, XV.ix.15 (NPNF, 1st Series, vol. 3, p. 207): "some Latin translators, through unwillingness to employ a Greek word, when the apostle says, 'Which things are an allegory' [Gal. 4:24], have rendered it by a circumlocution —Which things signify one thing by another." Augustine is explaining the *enigma* of I Cor. 13:12. "Every enigma is an allegory, but every allegory is not an enigma. What then is allegory, but a trope wherein one thing is understood from another?" Cf. also *On the Spirit and the Letter*, xli: because of human ignorance, "there is use for tongues, the variety of meanings whereby one thing is conveyed by another in allegory to the mind that cannot contemplate in purity the eternal light of transparent truth."

[16] Unknown Antwerp Mannerist, first quarter of the sixteenth century, "The Last Supper Triptych," in Harry B. Wehles and Margaretta Salinger, for the Metropolitan Museum of Art, New York, *Catalogue of Early Flemish, Dutch and German Paintings* (New York, 1947), pp. 129f.

tabular. Simple linking schemes such as processions and genealogies are of this kind, though even genealogies are a tabulation based on the prior idea of a generalization as a statement of a kinship group.

Aristotle names six parts of poetry: *dianoia* (thought), *ethos* (character), *mythos* (plot or story), *phanos* (spectacle), *lexis* (diction), and *melos* (music).[17] Allegory would seem to be a special way of treating *dianoia* in relation to the other five. In allegory proper, *dianoia* takes the form of an internalized commentary on the *mythos*, compounding the fiction with the theme, as we have just described it. The allegorical *ethos* is the personification, though the agent need not be a person, or even a whole personality. The allegorical *phanos* is imagery with a formalized meaning attached to it: iconography, emblems, conventional or allusive symbols.[18] The *lexis* of allegory is simply the rhetorical figure known as the "allegory," or detailed similitude, as described in Renaissance rhetorical handbooks. The figure of the house for the body in Ecclesiastes (12:3–4) is a haunting biblical example.[19] A slightly larger figure of the same kind is Spenser's smithy of heart-fretting Care, with his throbbing hammers of jealousy, and bellows of sighs moved by Pensiveness (IV.v).[20] The al-

[17] *Poetices* vi (1450a). My subsequent use of the term *dianoia* in this context will remind some readers that the older word for allegory in Greek is *huponoia*, "deeper meaning" (lit. "under-mind"), otherwise meaning "conjecture," or "suggestion." See Plutarch, *Aud. Poet.* 4, *Moralia* 19E–F.

[18] For a study of the Renaissance theory of the emblem, see Robert Klein, "La théorie de l'expression figurée dans les traités italiens sur les imprese, 1555–1612," *Bibliothèque d'Humanisme et Renaissance* (Geneva), 19 (1957), pp. 320–342, esp. p. 335 on the interaction of motto and design, and the inadequacy of either by itself. For the emblem as "tableau," see Rosemary Freeman, *English Emblem Books* (London, 1948), p. 11. Since an emblem is a combination of verbal and design elements, the verbal element may well be an epigram, in the original sense of a wording imposed on an image. Hence some of Alciati's emblems are adaptations from the statuary inscriptions of the *Greek Anthology*. The inherent *stillness* of sculpture, in particular, makes a labeled statue seem to be an image fixed or arrested by the specification of its meaning, or the drawing of its moral. Cf. Guyon's apt commemoration of the death of Mordant: "Behold the image of mortalitie" (II.i.57)—this evaluation is decidedly a "post-mortem" or retrospective one, as is Guyon's nearby commemoration of the sanctification of Redcrosse (Redcrosse's "race" is now "runne").

[19] Taking the allegorical householders as its clue, the Geneva Bible solves the meaning of the other figures systematically (the voice of the bird, insomnia; the daughters of singing, the windpipes; the almond tree, white hair; the silver cord, the spinal cord; the pitcher, the veins; the well, the liver; the cistern, the heart, "out of which ye head draweth the powers of life").

[20] The relation of Spenser's figure to the emblematic mode is insisted upon by its origins in the emblem poem of Bruno's *Heroic Frenzies*, V.x, which is based on the conceit of the *hammer* of jealousy, as discovered by John Steadman, "Spenser's House of Care: A Reinterpretation," *Studies in the Renaissance* 7 (1960), pp. 207–223. Regarding the lover, Bruno's Vulcan says, "A better forger of Aetna, a

legorical *melos*, if there is one, is portentous-sounding speech, or oracular speech, "where more is meant than meets the ear." It is present whenever a distinction is drawn between what is said and what is meant. Portentous, cryptic, or sarcastic speech may have such a tone, especially when what is heard does not "make sense," as in a riddle: "here is wisdom. Let him that hath understanding count the number of the beast, for it is the number of a man" (Rev. 13:18). Here we meet the "twofold intercourse" of the associates of Pythagoras, described by Clement in the passage already quoted; this discourse "designates the majority, hearers, and the others that have a genuine attachment to philosophy, disciples, yet signified that something was spoken to the multitude, and something concealed from them."[21]

Aristotle's last three elements are best illustrated in isolated or abbreviated forms, such as the emblem (*phanos*), the oracle or riddle (*melos*), and the proverb (*lexis*). The abbreviated form of the allegorical *mythos* comparable to the emblem and the oracle, addressed respectively to the eye and to the ear, is the parable, addressed to the mind. The corresponding allegorical *ethos* would be some sort of gnomic personification, like the characters of the beast fable. Presumably such fables originate in the imaginative animism that discovers human characteristics in the animal kingdom. Aside from animal personifications, one may cite the somewhat uncanny objects of Anglo-Saxon riddle and the speaking tree of *The Dream of the Rood*—they seem to be possessed by demons.

---

better smith, anvil and hammer do I find / here in this breast which exhales sighs and whose bellows vivify the furnace, where the soul lies prostrate from so many assaults / of such long tortures and great martyrdoms, and brings a concert which divulges so bitter and cruel a torment." The poet explains that "there is no love without fear, zeal, jealousy, rancor" and that the Smith is Penury, in Plato's myth of the birth of Love: "the spirit affected by this frenzy is distracted by profound thoughts, tortured by pressing cares, burned by fervent longings, and solicited on occasions without number," with the consequent negligence of self exhibited in the condition of Spenser's Care. (Cf. *Symposium* 203c–d.) The tormentors of the lover are represented by "the bellowings, coals, anvils, hammers, pincers and the other tools found in the work shop of this sordid and squalid spouse of Venus." (Trans. by Paul Eugene Memno, *The Heroic Frenzies*, Chapel Hill, 1964, pp. 165–167.) For *martello* as jealousy, add to Steadman's citations, Berni, *Orl. Inn.* V.5 ("In tutti questi gradi poi l'ardore, / La gelosia, il furore, il martell / Si mostra estreamemnto") and XVIII.58. For Care's blackness, see the *atra cura* of Horace, *Odes* III.1 and IV.11. The discord of the smiths ironically recalls the discovery of harmonics in a smithy by Pythagoras, or else by Jubal, brother of Tubal-Cain; the latter is illustrated on the title page of F. Gafurio's *Theorica Musica* (1492), where Jubal presides over six smiths with their sledges.

[21] *Stromata*, V.ix, trans. in ANF, vol. 2, p. 458. Cf. Petrarch, *Ad Familiares*, X.4: "What indeed are the parables of our Saviour in the Gospels, but words whose sound is foreign to their sense, or allegories?" (Quoted in Osgood, *Boccaccio on Poetry*, p. 166, n. 20.)

Emblematic beasts often lead us into allegorical worlds: Alice follows the white rabbit into Wonderland; a strayed whelp brings the narrator of *The Boke of the Duchesse* into the area of the allegorical chess game. A beast fable appears in the prologue to *Piers Plowman*; on the threshold of his journey Dante is confronted by three emblematic beasts from Jeremiah. Perhaps Una's lamb, mentioned at the outset, has a similar function in *The Faerie Queene*. The lamb itself never reappears, but the imagery of lost or slaughtered sheep turns up at the appropriate crises later in the legend. The imagery is used at comparable crises in the sixth book, but real lambs do not reenter the poem until Calidore's adventures among the shepherds. The final episode in the shepherd's world shows Calidore emerging from a dangerous underworld, leading a potential bride and her sheep into the ordinary light of day. The sheep have become sheep again. Shortly thereafter, the poem is over.

The parable tends to become an allegory where it is enigmatic or incomplete enough to suggest our adducing a scheme of significances, though the same qualities may discourage our actually doing so.[22] The parables of Hawthorne and Kafka have this quasi-allegorical suggestiveness, and Hawthorne shows a strong interest in emblems that focus the attention of the interpreter. The typical parable is either commended to us ("Go thou and do likewise") or presented as a caution ("Those who have ears, let them hear"). In the Aesopian fable, this terminal indication takes the form of a moral, and the moral is really a proverb or maxim or gnome, a net yield of wisdom that detaches the *dianoia* from the fiction, in the way that the solution to a riddle does.[23] Patristic interpretation of the parables of Jesus shows a somewhat similar process, and indeed such allegorization can be seen to have taken place in the formulation of the gospel versions themselves.[24] The entering wedge for such interpretations is often a titled person, who may become a personification, such as the king's son, the owner of the vineyard, or the bridegroom. The Levite functions in this way in the parable of the Good Samaritan: he becomes the

[22] Cf. Augustine, *De Trinitate*, XV.ix: "an enigma is, to explain it briefly, an obscure allegory"—referring to I Cor. 13:12, "through a glass *en ainigmati*."

[23] I owe this point directly to Frye, *Anatomy of Criticism*, p. 300. Complementary remarks may be found in Murrin, *Veil of Allegory*, pp. 61f. A proverb or adage is the more shrunken form of the *lexis* of allegory not only because the moral in which the fable issues may take a quasi-proverbial form, but also because the exposition of adages often consists in the recovery of the context of an allusion. See also below, n. 145, and text.

[24] This point is thoroughly demonstrated in Joachim Jeremias, *The Parables of Jesus*, trans. S. H. Hooke (New York, 1963). Cf. also Ian T. Ramsey, *Christian Discourse: Some Logical Explorations* (London and New York, 1965), pp. 6-13, for the distinction between parable as leading up to a "disclosure-point," and allegory as the correlation of two discourses.

Law that could not help the man who left Jerusalem and fell among enemies, and who was saved by the sacramental ministrations of the merciful
stranger.[25] Spenser's *Mviopotmos* tells the story of a carefree butterfly in
a pleasure garden, "Lord of all the workes of Nature," who ends up the
victim of the nets of a vengeful spider descended from envious Arachne:
the possibility that the mythopoeia is parabolic is suggested by the butterfly's descent from a transformed nymph associated with Psyche—the Greek
word for both soul and butterfly.[26]

At this point we can see how clearly the *Calender* introduces an allegorical canon. With its good shepherds, its beast and plant fables, contemporary allusions, stylized illustrations, "emblems" (which are actually
mottoes, with the exception of hope's anchor), and attached arguments
and commentaries, it seems deliberately propaedeutic. However, the *Calender* can hardly rival the opening cantos of Book I in this respect.

Personification is sometimes thought to be the irreducible minimum for
allegory; it is natural to think of allegory as starting from an abstraction
and embodying it in an image. Some allegory is originated in this way,
but without the adoption of a fictional scheme it cannot go much beyond
sculptural programs, pageantry, and tableaux. The morality play, for example, personifies the conflict of such psychological principles as Reason and
Sensuality, but without stories of temptation and prodigal sons nothing
really dramatic can come of it.[27] Taken as a whole, the morality play
seems to be the story of a dissociated personality. The final dispersal or
ascesis of the continuous elements of such a personality is the subject of
Everyman. We have already mentioned the story of Hellenore because of
its quizzical ending. The fate of her cuckolded husband Malbecco (Italian,
"evil horn") is more orthodox: he "Forgot he was a man, and *Gelousie*
is hight" (III.x.60); with the change from the Italian to the italics, he

[25] The patristic allegory is developed in *Piers Plowman*, B-Text, Passus XVII.48–
123, where the Good Samaritan has become Charity and Christ; the priest, Faith
and Abraham; and the Levite, Moses and the Hope to be found in the Law. For
the tradition, see *Glossa ordinaria* on Luke 10:30ff. (PL, CXIV, 286f.); Honorius of
Autun, *Speculum Ecclesiae*, Dom. xiii, post Pentecosten (PL, CLXXII, 1059f.); Hugh
of St. Victor, *Allegoria in Nov. Test.*, IV.xii (PL, CLXXV, 814f.); and esp. Ambrose, *Expos. Evang. Sec. Lucam,* VII.73ff. (PL, XV, 1718f.).

[26] The possibility is explored at length in the study of Don Cameron Allen, "Mui-
opotmos, or the Fate of the Butterflie," in *Image and Meaning: Metaphoric Traditions in Renaissance Poetry* (Baltimore, 1960), pp. 21–44.

[27] The point has been variously made, with respect to Shakespeare especially; see
S. L. Bethell, *Shakespeare and the Popular Dramatic Tradition* (Durham, N.C.,
1944); John Dover Wilson, *The Fortunes of Falstaff* (Cambridge, 1943); Bernard
Spivack, *Shakespeare and the Allegory of Evil* (New York and London, 1958); and
David Bevington, *From Mankind to Marlowe* (Cambridge, Mass., 1962).

promptly drops out of the human fiction. The "moral" thus coincides with the exhaustion of the fictional impulse in the creation of a pure abstraction. Spenser's Despair embodies the death-in-life condition of a completely abstracted personality. He cannot surrender to an appropriate end for the paradoxical reason that he must despair even of his own suicide. In hanging himself, however, he moves in the opposite direction from Malbecco, that is, from human Despair to a despairing man. He no doubt will hang himself again on some future occasion, but because he would cease to despair if he succeeded, he is dismissed by the poet until the second death of Revelation, "Till he should die his last, that is eternally" (I.ix.54).

Our examples show that the imaginative allegorist draws out the effects of abstractions upon their human patrons and upon the fictional pattern in which they appear, in something like the way a dramatist extends and exploits a "humour" for the length of a play. The analogy can be seen in a character like Bunyan's Talkative; from the moment that he opens his mouth, Talkative is as glib and voluble a fop as ever stole a scene upon the Restoration stage. A parody of the very Word he so much loves to talk about, he is a veritable Talk-made-flesh. But in the same momentum, he is a persona soon overtaken by his own loquacity; his compulsion is a kind of incipient possession.

A somewhat more obscure point is also suggested by these examples, namely that the personification survives the person. In this it surely resembles the species-type, or *genos*, "race," rather than the individual. That is why the animal species proves so useful for the purposes of personification. There is also the implication here that we have got it the wrong way round: the first allegorist did not animate an abstraction, he conceptualized something originally felt to be animate. Malbecco forgot he was a man, but he did not so much become an abstraction, as a *demon*, the evil spirit that possesses a jealous man. This point bulks large in any consideration of allegory as a *fonction mentale*.

The allegorical *mythos* is not properly the fable. Rather, it is similar to what Spenser calls a "legend," that is, a fiction that is provocative because of its apparent improbability or absurdity, or its aptness for other than a literal construction.[28] Spenser begins his letter to Raleigh worrying

---

[28] More technically, a legend is a "reading" or recounting of a singular life, which promotes in the audience for which it is designed an appreciation for the calling that the life in question exhibits: the legend of Elisha is intended for the schools of the prophets; the legend of St. George, for a class of knights; the legend of St. Francis, for Franciscans; the legend of Paul Bunyan, for the American lumber-industry; etc. It is the illustration and idealization of the virtues or strengths re-

about "misconstructions" and "how doubtfully all Allegories may be construed." As we have seen, some traditional thinking about allegory postulates a quasi-sacramental relation between the fiction and the allusion, making allegories "mysteries" in the New Testament sense. The typological explanation of the Old Testament and the Stoic allegoresis of the Homeric gods and fables share this character.

The *protagonist* of the allegorical mythos is somewhere between numen and nomen, being, as it were, a daemon with a name. We may call him an "avatar," this term suggesting the incarnational character of the relation just described.

Nevertheless, the relation between what is said and what is meant may be subversive, mocking, or facetious, as in irony and satire written allegorically. As the *Life of Homer* says, "Sarcasm is a certain species of Irony, when taunting provokes laughter by means of the contrary to something. . . . This is not at all dissimilar to allegory, which presents one thing by means of another."[29] The relation between what is said and what is meant may also change, along our scale of explicitness, starting from the purely fictional and becoming more and more obviously otherwise. This gives us the allegorical equivalent for the Aristotelian *anagnorisis*, or recognition, which ends the fiction—as might an anxiety dream that has failed to protect the dreamer. We may compare the technique of initiating a satire by means of a fantastic hypothesis that begins to develop sug-

---

quisite to the fulfilling of the vocational ideal that allows the legend to develop improbably. The word *myth* is defined in the way we are using *legend* here by Theon, *Progymnasmata* III: "A myth is a *logos pseudēs* imaging (*eikonidzon*) truth." (*Rhetores Graeci*, ed. Walz, 1832, vol. 1, p. 172.) Edgar Wind, *Pagan Mysteries in the Renaissance*, rev. edn. (reprint, New York, 1968), p. 237, compares Macrobius on "fable," *Comm. in Somm. Scip.*, I.ii.9: "a mode for referring to the true through figments." The theory is little changed in Edward Phillips, who says that the poet chooses a traditional story in which "in proper Allegorie, Invention . . . principally consisteth, and wherein there is a kind of truth even in the midst of fiction; for what ever is pertinently said by way of Allegorie is Morally though not Historically true." (Preface to *Theatrum Poetarum*, in Spingarn, *Critical Essays*, vol. 2, pp. 267f.)

[29] *Homeri Poetae Vita*, in Gale, *Opuscula Mythologica, Physica et Ethica* (Amsterdam, 1688), p. 313. Likewise Trissino, *De La Poetica*, sixth division (in *Opere*, Verona, 1729, 2nd Pt., p. 136): "Sarcasm is a species of Irony, but much more mordant. . . . Similar to this is Allegory, which speaking of one thing, wishes that it be intended as another, with which the poem of Dante is most full, as here, 'Nel mezo . . . ,' which intends by the wood, allegorically, the evil and vicious life." Cf. also Scaliger, *Poetices* (Heidelberg, 1617), III.lxxiv, "Last Class of Figures that say things to the contrary. Irony"; p. 322: irony "differs from allegory in that allegory points out what things have in common and brings them together, whereas irony brings together things which are contraries, pointing out the basis of their separation." I.e., irony says one thing and means the contrary, allegory says one thing, and "also" means something "else."

gestively—i.e., allegorically—as soon as its incongruities are allowed to betray an analogy with an equally ridiculous pattern back home. For example, Karel Capek's *War with the Newts* is cast in the form of science fiction. It begins, improbably enough, with the discovery of a South Seas species of humanoid amphibian. First we have the employment of the newts as convenient labor-saving devices, like the Capeks' robots; then there is a burgeoning conflict in which the aliens have the place of invaders from outer space. We recognize the science fiction motifs of the sorcerer's apprentice and the apocalyptic beast from the sea. When the rebellious newts attempt to impose their will on mankind through a series of suspiciously unnatural catastrophes, the hypothetical fiction increasingly suggests Flood, Nile, and Red Sea archetypes. However, long before the Grand Salamander broadcasts his people's demands for more coastline and more living room and more steel for the newt-idol Moloch (German *Molch,* "newt"), we are aware that this is not a story solely about newts. The fiction ends when the aliens turn up in the supposedly landlocked waters of Czechoslovakia.

It is this pre-allegorical character of a deepening *double entendre* that makes the dream-vision a useful starting-point for the allegorist. The dream provokes psychoanalytic discussion in the way quizzical patterns of imagery provoke allegorical commentary, and many allegories, including Revelation, are cast in the form of interpreted visions. Spenser's first surviving works are translations of emblematic visions of Petrarch and DuBellay, which are based on Revelation. Spenser's early productions also seem to have included his *Dreames,* a lost work that was equipped with another of E. K.'s commentaries.

Allegorical interpretation, we have said, is based on the felt presence of the secondary pattern. Spenser begins *The Faerie Queene* with a monster that has been eating raw flesh, like Hesiod's snake goddess, and also frogs, like the beast in Revelation. The frogs are identified with error in John Bale's commentary on the biblical place,[30] but Spenser's inclusion of books and papers in the monster's diet is the telling interpolation for the reader. Like the bookworm in the Old English riddle, "the thievish visitant was no whit the wiser for swallowing the words."[31] One can see from this example that the two patterns must be appropriable to each other—through some natural congruity or established association—if they are to produce a recognition of "intendment" or aptness. And yet they must be alien enough

---

[30] Hesiod, *Theogony* 299f.; Rev. 16:13. John Bale, *The Image of Both Churches,* in Parker Society *Select Works,* ed. Rev. Henry Christmas (Cambridge, 1849), p. 486.

[31] Exeter Book, trans. R. K. Gordon, in *Anglo-Saxon Poetry* (London, 1954), p. 303. Cf. Wormius in Pope, *Dunciad* (1743 edn.), III.185–190, for the prosopopoeia in question, and *F.Q.* IV.ii.33.

to produce an allegory. Where there is no differentiation between the figure and its significance, and where the significance is unrecognizable except in the figure, we relapse into the portentous yet inexplicable world of the unawakened dreamer and the uncritical religionist. The mental processes belonging to such a state are neurotic or superstitious, or characterized by archaic or atavistic identifications: in terms of the opening of Spenser's first book, an overcharged realm of shrouded females, terrible mothers, treacherous succubae, and bleeding trees—which are nothing else.

The Pledging of Faith

What, brethren, does He promise believers? "And ye shall know the truth." Why so? Had they come to such knowledge when the Lord was speaking? If they had not, how did they believe? They believed, not because they knew, but that they might come to know. For we believe in order that we may know, we do not know in order that we may believe. For what we shall yet know, neither eye hath seen, nor ear heard, nor hath it entered into the heart of man. . . . Faith then is to believe what you see not; truth, to see what you have believed. . . . The Lord then walked on earth, first of all, for the creation of faith. He was man, He was made in a low condition. He was seen by all, but not by all was He known. . . . Even by those who mourned Him, His true being was still unrecognized. All this is the beginning as it were of faith's lineaments and future upbuilding.

(St. Augustine, *Tract. in Joan.*, XL.9)

Peter said: "By the word of truth He certainly divides the kingdom of the world, which is founded in error, and every house in it, that error may fall, and truth may reign. But if it happen to any house, that error, being introduced by any one, divides the truth, then, where error has gained a footing, it is certain that truth cannot stand." Then Simon said, "But it is uncertain whether your master divides error or truth."

(*Clementine Recognitions*, II.xxxv)

[i]

In his opening cantos Spenser lays down many of the presuppositions of his art, and in some uncanny way they are almost an allegory about the emergence of allegory. One can hardly miss the theme of interpretation in episodes dealing with Hypocrisy and Error, and all the allegorical apparatus previously named turns up as well: veiled truth, riddling speech and *double entendre*, dreams requiring interpretation, personification (in the form of demonic imposture), and, finally, a talking tree. Perhaps the most important character here is Archimago.

Archimago's name is similar to that of the evil sorcerer, Archelaus, in the *Amadis de Gaula*. His other romance affinities are with Ariosto's hermit, who summons up a spright to possess Angelica's horse, and Tasso's Ismeno, who makes himself invisible and cooperates with the enchantress Armida. Archimago is a *mage*, and hence potentially a sorcerer: Paracelsus warns us against regarding the Three Wise Men of the East as "arch-sorcerers,"[32] and Bodin speaks of Cornelius Agrippa as both "magorum magistrum" and "le Maistre Sorcier." The Spanish demonologist Del Rio, writing after Spenser, calls Agrippa the Archimagus,[33] and so in England does John Heywood.[34]

For the Renaissance the *mage* was a symbol for the human arts in general,[35] even though some Renaissance magic, following the Hermetic literature, involved the attraction of demons into idols.[36] According to a common distinction found in Pico's *Oration on the Dignity of Man*, there are two kinds of magic. One kind compels demons, and the other, whose practitioner is an "interpreter" and a "worshipper of the divine," works through nature:

> The former is the most deceitful of arts; the latter a higher and more holy philosophy. The former is vain and empty; the latter, sure, trustworthy, and sound. Whoso has cherished the former has ever dissembled, because

[32] *De occulta philosophia*, in *Sämtliche Werke*, ed. Darl Sudhoff and Wilhelm Matthiessen (Munich and Berlin, 1928–1933), Pt. I, vol. 14, p. 521. The passage is taken from Jolande Jacobi, *Selected Writings*, trans. Norbert Guterman (New York, 1951), pp. 212f.

[33] Jean Bodin, *De la Demonamie* (Paris, 1582), fol. 38ʳ, fols. 219ᵛ–220ʳ, and *De Magorum daemomania libri IV* (Basel, 1581), p. 72. Martin Del Rio, *Disqvisitionvm magicarvm*, I.iv, qvaest. iii (edn. of Venice, 1652), p. 39; so also I.iv, q. iii, p. 43, and II, Q. iii, p. 70.

[34] In Sozomus, *Eccles. Hist.*, II.xiii, the word *Archimagos* is the name of a torturer of Christians in Persia, in the king's service. From thence it comes into Foxe's *Acts and Monuments*, as in the 4th edn. of 1583, p. 98, col. 2, where we find "Arch-magitians," "Archimagus," and "the master Magus." Cf. also John Heywood, *The Hierarchie of the blessed Angells: Their Names Orders and Offices* (London, 1635), p. 506: "Archimage Zoraster"—"(Who of art Magicke was the first Art-master)." For Heywood on Agrippa, see *ibid.*, p. 615.

[35] For a rhetorical summary on this point, see E. Garin, "Magic and Astrology in the Civilisation of the Renaissance," in his *Science and Civic Life in the Italian Renaissance*, trans. Peter Munz (New York, 1969), pp. 145–165. (Originally an essay in his *Medioevo e Rinascimento*, Editori Laterza, 1966.)

[36] See the discussion of *Asclepius*, xiii, in Frances Yates, *Giordano Bruno and the Hermetic Tradition* (Chicago, 1964), esp. chaps. ii–iv, and D. P. Walker, *Spiritual and Demonic Magic from Ficino to Campanella* (London, 1958), pp. 36–41, 162f.

it is a shame and a reproach to an author; but from the latter the highest renown and glory of letters was derived in ancient days, and almost always has been.[37]

The assumption, in either case, seems to be that magical production entails a concomitant literary production. Archimago resorts to the "Magick bookes and artes" that lost Prospero his kingdom, and, more relevant here, Faustus his soul. Like Faustus, who swears by Demogorgon, Archimago swears by "Great Gorgon, Prince of darkness and dead night"; and he himself appears, as Faustus commanded Mephistopheles to appear, in the shape of an old "religious." The scene in Spenser reminds us of one in Tasso in which Ismeno raises spirits to enchant the forest (*Ger. Lib.* XIII. 7–11); but, unlike Ismeno and his classical antecedents, Archimago does not forbear to name the forbidden name.[38]

[37] *Oration on the Dignity of Man*, sec. 32, trans. Elizabeth Forbes, in Ernst Cassirer, Paul Kristeller, and John Randall, Jr., eds., *The Renaissance Philosophy of Man* (Chicago, 1948), pp. 246f. For the two magics, see also Pico's *Apologia*, in *Opera omnia* (Basel, 1587), pp. 120–122, and the twenty-six "Conclusiones Magicae." Further texts are cited in Ernst Cassirer, *The Individual and Cosmos in Renaissance Philosophy*, trans. Mario Domandi (reprint, of Philadelphia, 1972), p. 151, n. 29. See also Giambattista Porta, *Magiae naturalis*, I.ii (Naples, 1589; 1st 4 books, 1558); Tommaso Campanella, *De Sensu rerum et magia*, V.i (Frankfurt, 1620); and Francesco Maria Guazzo, *Compendium Maleficarum* (Milan, 1608), I.ii.

[38] Spenser is also broaching the forbidden names, as in his use of the word "terrible" (I.i.37), which is one of the meanings Boccaccio gives for the name of Demogorgon (Gr. *gorgos*, "terrible"). The crucial classical text here is the conjuration of Erichtho in Lucan, *Pharsalia* VI.695–697: "I invoke . . . Chaos; I invoke the Ruler of the Earth, who suffers endless agony below"; and 744–749: "must I appeal to that one, at the sound of whose name the earth ever trembles and quakes, who looks on Gorgon openly . . . who breaks oaths [sworn] by the Stygian waves?" Cf. Archimago's cautionless invocation of Gorgon, "At which Cocytus quakes, and Styx is put to flight." The scholiast on Lucan identifies the unnamed deity as the demiurge, and the contamination of this identification by the nearby word *Gorgon* is suggested by Arnulfus of Orleans' twelfth-century commentary on the *Pharsalia*: "ILLE Demogorgon, qui fuit pater Omagionis, Omagion Celii, Celius Saturni, Saturni Iovis. QUI GORGONA CERNIT APERTAM id est aperte, nec mutatur in lapidem, sed aperte dicit pro Perseo qui eam vidit nec mutatus fuit, sed non aperte vidit immo per [a]egidem." (*Glosule super Lucanum*, ed. Berthe M. Marti, *Papers and Monographs of the American Academy in Rome*, vol. 18, 1958, p. 350: I owe notice of this pre-Boccaccian Demogorgon to David Quint, "Epic Tradition and *Inferno* IX," a forthcoming paper in which he comments on the Gorgon at *Inf.* IX.56 and Erichtho at IX.23.) The same interchangeability of Gorgon and Demogorgon is found in Mazzoni, *Della difesa della Commedia di Dante* (Cesena, 1587), I.lxxiii, p. 188: "Gorgone, o Demogorgone, del quale hà parlato Statio nella Thebiade [IV.514–516]." Cf. Robin's conjuration in *Dr. Faustus*, scene viii, l. 7: "*deny orgon, gorgon.*" The vaporous realm of Morpheus may owe something to the tenebrous and humid subterranean mansion of Demogorgon in Boccaccio, *G.D.G.*, I, preface to cap. l, Romano edn., vol. 1, p. 12. For further on the theme, see below, Chap. VI, "The Triumph of Time," sec. i.

Archimago is a man of words, "For pleasing words are like to Magick art" (III.ii.15). This "artmagick" lays the "charmed Snake in slomber"; Archimago's similarly "pleasing wordes" (I.ii.25) induce the lady and the knight to become his guests; so it seems these words also charm them to sleep. Thereupon, he consults his texts, "Then choosing out few words most horrible, / (Let none them read) thereof did verses frame"; he conjures up "Legions of Sprights" and goes on to feign, in Sidney's language about the poet, notable images of virtues and vices.

Since the magician may be a man of letters—Hermes is the patron of both magic and the art of writing—the man of letters may also be a magician. Such an analogy offers to equate Archimago's activity with the imagination concurrently shaping Spenser's poem. This seems unlikely at first, but in the penultimate movement of the poem we meet the poet's persona Colin Clout, who has surrounded himself with a hundred naked maidens, dancing to the tune of his pipe. As the breaking of the spell by Calidore hints, Colin has also been doing magic. His may not be the Faustian magic of Spenser's opening canto, and the shepherd may well be one of those poets, mentioned by Sidney, who "never maketh any circles about your imagination, to conjure you to believe for true what he writes."[39] And yet this humbler magic draws on the same verbal resources as does that of the character Robin in *Doctor Faustus*:

> O, this is admirable! Here I ha' stolen one of Doctor Faustus' conjuring books, and i' faith I mean to search some circles for my own use. Now will I make all the maidens in our parish dance at my pleasure, stark naked before me; and so by that means I shall see more than e'er I felt or saw yet.
>
> (scene viii)

There is, then, a touch of the artist about Archimago. He is an "Architect of cancred guile" (II.i.1), a contriver of plots, and a stager of shows.

It was the Word of God that exorcised the demons who were "Legion," and all good words are an analogy for this Word; all bad words, raising the demons that Christ casts out, are a kind of parody of this Word. The Word has been entrusted to the keeping of the Church, and the art of words is similarly entrusted to the poets. Given this analogy, it is not unlikely that all the criticisms that Plato makes of poets, rhapsodes, and sophists might be leveled against the verbal arts of Archimago; he is only a creator manqué, and converse with him can only bring one to a virtual knowledge of the truth.

[39] *Defense*, in Gilbert, *Literary Criticism*, p. 439.

The sophist in Plato's dialogue closely resembles Archimago. The sophist angles with a baited hook, as Duessa does (I.i.49); he is a wizard, an illusionist; he lurks in inaccessible places and is elusive; he is a flatterer, an impersonator, allied with appearance and opinion; and he produces fantastic and deceptive, rather than accurate and "eikastic," imitations.[40] In short, what sophistry is to dialectic, and what lying fables are to poetry, Archimago is to the word in general. Poetry's detractors say that the poet is a father of lies, a slanderer of the truth, a seducer of the mind, and an inciter of corrupt passions.[41]

The tenth book of *The Republic* makes the same charges against the poet as those just cited from *The Sophist*. The Italian critic Mazzoni, in a theory with which Scaliger, Sidney, and Tasso take issue, adopts Plato's distinction between the fantastic and eikastic to explain the varieties of poetic imitation. Basing his usage on Suidas' lexicon, Mazzoni maintains that "the object of icastic poetry is the true insofar as it is the marvelous credible and that the object of fantastic poetry is the false insofar as it is the marvelous credible."[42] Mazzoni says that "every species of poetry makes idols and images," either verisimilar or purely inventive; it is the phantasy or the imagination which obtains the "true power over poetic fables." The same power causes dreams, and poetry "is founded on phantasy." Yet at the same time, poetry is "a subdivision of the rational faculty, called by the ancients sophistic," an art that is "the maker of images."[43]

> Now I say phantastic poetry regulated by the proper laws is part of this ancient sophistic, since it also propounds feigned things to our intellect in order to regulate the appetite, and many times contains beneath the husk of the fiction the truth of many noble conceptions.[44]

[40] In order, the references are *Sophist* 221c–d; 235a–b; 226a; 231c; 233a; 231–232a; 233c; 241b; 231b; 235.

[41] Boccaccio, *G.D.G.*, XIV.xiv–xv; Giovanni Francesco Pico, whose Platonic position is described in Weinberg, *History of Criticism*, vol. 1, pp. 255–257; Sidney, *Defense*, in Gilbert, *Literary Criticism*, pp. 438–441.

[42] Mazzoni, according to Baxter Hathaway, *Marvels and Commonplaces: Renaissance Literary Criticism* (New York, 1968), p. 74, quoting *Della difesa della Comedia di Dante* (Cesena, 1688), vol. 1, pp. 574f. (1587 edn., p. 404): "Idols are the effigies of things not subsistent, as are Tritons, Sphinxes, Centaurs. But the similitudes are the images of things subsistent, such as beasts and men." The reference is to Suidas, *Lexicon, sub eidolon*. Mazzoni quarrels with the distinction, but later adopts it after assimilating it to Plato. Cf. the introduction to the 1587 edn., pp. 15f.

[43] Quotes taken from the introduction to the *Difesa*, trans. Gilbert, *Literary Criticism*, p. 364; and *Difesa*, I.lxvii, in Gilbert, p. 387; and again the introduction, in Gilbert, pp. 367f. For the disagreement with Mazzoni, see Scaliger, *Poetices* VII.ii; Sidney, *Defense*, in Gilbert, *Literary Criticism*, p. 440; Tasso, second series of *Discourses on the Heroic Poem*, II, in Gilbert, pp. 473–478 (in *Prose*, ed. Mazzali, p. 528).

[44] *Difesa*, introduction, in Gilbert, *Literary Criticism*, p. 370.

Allegorical poetry, moreover, is eikastic, or verisimilar in its mode of imitation: despite the superficial fancifulness of its literal sense, its allegorical sense alleges truths.[45] Dramatic imitations also raise problems in the combining of the two modes:

> The first and most important [of four possible species of imitation] is the dramatic-phantastic, which is an imitation because it necessarily contains two sorts of idols and images. The first image is that of the person represented. The other is the false but verisimilar image which the actor presents; since he does not represent the true but the verisimilar, he consequently represents the image and the simulacrum of truth.[46]

The demon through whom Archimago represents Una, however, misrepresents himself (he is *not* a person), though he also presents her "false but verisimilar image," or "the image and similacrum of the truth": Una *is* Truth, at least when "in her selfe-resemblance well beseene" (I.xii.8).

Contrary to Mazzoni, Tasso argues that the poet is not a maker of images like the sophist, but one like the divine theologian, "who forms the ideas of things and commands that they be realized." He is comparable to both the painter and the dialectician, and he makes images of subsisting things.[47] A theologian who commissions images and who is "like a speaking painter" might not recommend himself to a Reform Churchman, however. It is a wicked opinion, according to the gloss on the Geneva Bible (Hab. 2:18), that images "are the bokes of the laye people." John Jewel, starting from the comparison between religious imagery and the imagery that makes poetry a "speaking picture," writes as follows:

> But the comparison that M. Harding useth between imagery [in churches] and poetry seemeth nearest to express the truth. For painters and poets, for liberty of lying, have of a long time been coupled both together. . . . And therefore, like as Plato commanded all poets for their lying to be banished out of his commonwealth; so likewise Almighty God, for like liberty, banished all painters out of Israel.[48]

[45] Hathaway, *Marvels and Commonplaces*, p. 75, citing Mazzoni, *Difesa*, III.vi (1587 edn., pp. 409ff.).

[46] Gilbert, *Literary Criticism*, p. 361.

[47] Tasso, *Del Poema Eroico*, II, in *Prose*, ed. Mazzali, p. 528.

[48] *The Works of John Jewel*, ed. Rev. John Ayre, Parker Society (Cambridge, 1845–1850), vol. 2, *A Reply to Harding's Answer*, Article XIV, Tenth Division, pp. 659–661. Note Jewel's citations in his exposition of II Thessalonians, in the same volume, p. 918: "As Hierome, upon the words of the prophet, 'O pastor et idolum' etc., 'O idol shepherd, that,' etc., saith: '. . . I doubt nothing but that this foolish and unskilful shepherd is antichrist, which should come towards the end of the world.' And further saith: '. . . This shepherd is so wicked that he is not called a worshipper of idols, but an idol itself; because he calleth himself God, and will be worshipped of all men.' "

Archimago's name makes him a "beginning of imagery," and perhaps he is himself an image. Jewel writes of the Romanists: "Of their priests they have made images, and of their images they have made priests. For their priests for the more part have eyes, and see not. . . . Their images have no eyes, and yet are made to see. . . . Thus they bar the people from the hearing of God's holy word, and bid them go and look upon their images."[49] Here, however, we will explore the natural idolatry of the imagination, and reserve the more specific object of the prophetic and Reform diatribe for later consideration.

The dramatic-phantastic form of imitation, in the passage quoted above from Mazzoni, consists in a kind of impersonation. Two episodes involving Una and Archimago deserve mention here. In the first, the enchanter adopts the semblance of the true but deluded knight, and so insinuates himself into the company of Una, or Truth. Archimago is then attacked by Sansloi, and the fanaticism of the younger is sufficient to expose the hypocrisy of the elder. In the second episode, Archimago gets revenge by leading Sir Satyrane to attack Sansloi, whom Archimago accuses of Redcrosse's death (as earlier Sansloi accused the pretender of Sansfoy's death). All these reversals are standard romance idiom. In the *Amadis de Gaula* the evil enchanter appears at court and falsely reports the death of the enchanted Amadis, whose arms he wears—the enchanter is mistaken for Amadis, at a distance, by the father of the knight's inamorata.[50] The motif of the true knight bedeviled by impostors who act on his behalf only in order to misrepresent him is taken much further in *Don Quixote*. The Don fights a Knight of the Mirrors, a rival who claims to have already defeated him; although Quixote's subsequent triumph vindicates his own authenticity and gives his challenger the lie, it also reveals that the rival is not a knight at all. The Don blames the transformation of his antagonist into a local townsman on his persecutor, an enchanter elsewhere compared to Arcelaus of the *Amadis*.[51]

Boccaccio explains that the word *allegory* means either *alien* or *diverse*.[52] Archimago produces a "diuerse dreame" (I.i.44) that "divorces" the Redcrosse knight from Truth. The divorce makes the truth of the knight's holiness somewhat factitious; Redcrosse himself becomes a

[49] *Ibid.*

[50] *Amadis de Gaula*, I.xix and xxi, attributed to Vasco Lobeira; in Southey's trans. (London, 1803), vol. 1, pp. 181, 189–191.

[51] Pt. II, chap. xvi. Arcelaus is cited in Pt. I, chap. xv.

[52] *G.D.G.*, I.iii, Romano edn., vol. 1, p. 19. Boccaccio's source here is Dante's Tenth Letter, to Can Grande, paragraph 7.

THE PLEDGING OF FAITH

hypocrite, while the hypocrite appears in the "semblaunt" of Saint George. Truth in poetry is veiled, and both Duessa, at work under Night's "cole-black curtein" (I.iv.44), and Morpheus, the figure maker under Night's "mantle black" (I.i.39), parody the allegorical faculty that operates "vnder couert and darke termes."[53]

Thus a dual anxiety hangs over Spenser's first canto: the image maker may be either a hypocrite in religion, or an abuser of the truth that allegorical poetry veils. The same identification is present in Puttenham, in the passage referred to in the preceding essay. Puttenham introduces those figures that alter and affect the mind by means of "alteration of sence or intendements in whole clauses or speaches." Allegory, the first of these figures, is a form of dissimulation:

> And ye shall know that we may dissemble, I meane speake otherwise then we thinke, in earnest aswell as in sport, vnder couert and darke termes, and in learned and apparent speaches, . . . and finally aswell when we lye as when we tell truth. To be short euery speach wrested from his owne naturall signification to another not altogether so naturall is a kind of dissimulation, because the wordes beare contrary countenaunce to th'intent.[54]

As we noted, Puttenham's English name for this figure is "False semblant."

In the *Romance of the Rose*, the monologue of the mendacious and versatile character of Fals-Semblant provides a rough sketch for Archimago's activity:

> Now am I knight, now chastelyn,
> Now prest, now clerk, and now forster;
> Now am I maister, now scoler,
> Now monk, now chanoun, now baily;
> Whatever myster man am I.
> Now am I prince, now am I page,
> And kan by herte every language.[55]

---

[53] For the phrase, see the following quotation from Puttenham. For the night as a covering, mantle, or veil, see Ignaz Goldziher, *Mythology Among the Hebrews*, trans. Russell Martineau (London, 1877), pp. 190–194.

[54] Puttenham, *Arte* (London, 1811), p. 155. For dissimulation and Fals-Semblant, cf. Gower, *Confessio Amantis*, II.1890–1892: "For Falssemblant hath everem / Of his conseil in compaignie / The derke untrewe ypocrisie," with the Latin gloss, which says that the Confessor treats the fourth kind of envy, "que dissimilacio dicitur, cuius vultus quanto maioris amicicie apparenciam ostendit, tanto subtilioris doli fallacias ad decipiendum mens ymaginatur." Text from *The English Works of John Gower*, ed. G. C. Macaulay, EETS, Extra Series, nos. 81–82 (London, 1901–1902), vol. 1, p. 181.

[55] I quote the Chaucerian translation, ll. 6327–6334, in Chaucer, *Works*, ed. F. N. Robinson (2nd edn., Cambridge, Mass., 1957), p. 624. For Proteus himself, see ll. 6319–6326. My citation is suggested by A. Bartlett Giamatti's article, "Proteus Un-

And so forth. Similarly, Archimago impersonates the knight, the religious, and the page, in order to abuse the truth. Fals-Semblant brags that in his guile he outdoes Proteus; Spenser also compares his master of transformations to Proteus. Both characters are adept with words, and elsewhere in Spenser we meet a Proteus who is a prophet, "full of subtile sophismes, which do play / With double senses" (III.iv.28). All allegory is such a Duessan enterprise, but this particular comparison will merit further attention.

[ii]

As a classical type for Archimago, the poet chooses Proteus, the patron of evasion through shape-changing who is introduced into the *Odyssey* as a source of intelligence about Odysseus. Impersonation figures prominently in the lies and ruses of the hero himself, and doubtless the person of Proteus tells the truth about the man of many turns in more ways than one. It will be useful to have at hand a brief account of the allegorical traditions attaching to the sea god.[56]

Plato refers to Proteus four times, each of them in connection with an art of words or argument. At the end of the *Euthyphro* (15d) Socrates calls Euthyphro a Proteus; according to Giamatti, Socrates does so because Euthyphro has left him with a circular argument about the nature of holiness.[57] Similarly, at the end of the *Ion* (541e), Socrates calls the rhapsode Ion a Proteus, because as a Homerist Ion claims to be able to take on any of the roles described by the poet, even though he avoids

---

bound: Some Versions of the Sea God in the Renaissance," in Peter Demetz, Thomas Greene, and Lowry Nelson, Jr., eds., *The Disciplines of Criticism* (New Haven and London, 1968), pp. 437–475.

[56] In many places the following section duplicates the study of Giamatti, cited in the preceding note. I especially owe to his article the discussion of the *Euthydemus* and *Euthyphro*. I had come to Giamatti's general conclusions on the basis of the other citations here, and those in "Perpetual Generations," section ii, below. Giamatti offers Proteus as a type of the poet, being a *vates*, and a magician, since Virgil speaks of Proteus' "arts" (*Georg.* IV.440). In Lucian, Proteus is an illusionist (*Dialogues of the Sea Gods* IV, "Menelaus and Proteus"), and Eustathius, p. 1506, in *Od.* IV.456, states the opinion that Proteus is a magus. In Sannazaro's *Arcadia*, as Giamatti points out, the sixth eclogue, ll. 46–54, compares an artful shepherd-thief, equipped with herbs and "magic verses very strong," to Proteus. Natalis Comes (Conti), in his *Mythologiae*, VIII.viii (edn. of Geneva, 1641), p. 845, suggests that Proteus changes shape *by magic arts*; and further, "others say that he was a man skilled in speaking, who can easily impell men into any emotion of souls, and therefore was said to assume predictable forms." This last Proteus owes something to the dancer-mime of Lucian's *On the Dance* 19, also cited by Comes, *Mythologiae*, p. 843.

[57] Giamatti, "Proteus Unbound," p. 453.

any detailed account of Homer's supposed lore. The Homeric allegorist known as Heraclides offers a good example of just such lore as Ion fails to divulge. Plato specifically finds the poets' reports about Proteus offensive (*Republic* 381d), and when Heraclides comes to Menelaus' report in the *Odyssey*, he begins by stating how fantastic it apparently is ("figmenti phantasiam . . . ceu plane fabulosus"). He recounts the tale; "quae omnia poeticae et monstrosae fabulae videntur"—"unless one treats the divine Homeric mysteries, as if holy, in relation to the celestial mind."[58] In the *Euthydemus* Socrates confronts two punning "eristics" or fighters with words, who claim to be able to impart a great variety of knowledge. Socrates says that they are merely "doing conjuring tricks with us like Proteus, the Egyptian Sophist" (288b). Hence Abraham Fraunce reports that Plato compares Proteus to "the wrangling of brabling sophisters."[59]

If Proteus is deceptive, and his shapes are "lying," then the capture of Proteus, whom Homer calls "truthful," is naturally a type of truth-seeking. Heraclides, who gives an important physical allegory, commends the Homeric epithet: for what greater source of truth is there than the original substance?[60] In Fraunce's mythography Proteus is also a type of nature, and thus a type of truth, "obscured by so many deceauble appearances."[61] As the oldest of gods (Orphic *Hymn* XXV), or first in existence (*to protonon*), Proteus, according to Comes, preexists "in intellect."[62] In his *Dictionary* Charles Stephanus cites the Platonic reference to sophistry and asserts that some authors "accommodate him to truth itself"; Stephanus then refers us to Achilles Bocchius.[63]

We may first look at the tradition to which Bocchius belongs, which presents Proteus as a type of truth reached through intellection. It is through its Protean adaptability, according to Melanchthon, that the mind can know truth:

> The poets depict Proteus as various, taking on the appearances and forms
> of all things. By this fiction they clearly mean that metamorphosis of our

---

[58] I quote the Latin translation of Conrad Gesner, *Allegoriae Homeri*, reprinted with the Greek in Gale, *Opuscula Mythologica*, pp. 488f.

[59] Abraham Fraunce, *Third Part of the Countess of Pembrokes Ivychurch: Enituled, Amintas Dale* (London, 1592), fol. 22ᵛ.

[60] *Allegoriae Homeri*, loc. cit.

[61] *Loc. cit.*, n. 59.

[62] *Mythologiae*, VIII.viii (Geneva, 1641), p. 842; hereafter *Mythol.*, edn. cit. (Natalis Comes is otherwise Natale Conti.)

[63] Carolo Stephanus, *Dictionarium historicum, geographicum, poeticum: gentium, hominum, deorum gentilium, regionem . . .* (Leiden, 1686), *sub* "Proteus." Cf. Lilius Gregorius Giraldus, *Historiam de Deis Gentivm*, Syntag. V (in *Op.om.*, Leiden, 1646, I, col. 168F): "Others saying him [Proteus] to be truth, which does not show itself to all indiscriminately, but only to the few, those who know how to grasp it thoroughly." Giraldus' compendium is hereafter cited as *Hist. Deorum.*

intelligence into all the species of things. But it distinguishes the species of things by means of dialectic, the constant and unshakeable science of the true.[64]

It may be that we owe this allegory to Alypius, the friend addressed by Augustine in *Contra Academicos*:

"But, Alypius, you have told us who it is that is able to show us truth, and I must sedulously endeavour not to disagree with you. Alike with brevity and piety, you have said that only some kind of deity is able to show a man what truth is. Wherefore, in this discussion of ours, I have heard . . . nothing more true. For with what depth of understanding . . . has the famous Proteus been mentioned by you! That Proteus . . . is portrayed after the image of truth. In poems, I say, Proteus portrays and personates truth, which no one can lay hold on, if he is deceived by false images, and loosens or loses his holds on the nodes of understanding."[65]

This interpretation of Proteus comes close to Spenser, but it says nothing about the sleep situation common to Homer and the house of Archimago.

It is Bocchius' sixtieth emblem that explains the meaning of the capture of the *sleeping* Proteus: "With opinions put to sleep, captive truth is to be grasped," or "truth, once grasped, must be held firmly by putting false ideas to sleep." The poem explaining the emblem reads:

By what figure are you depicted, wonderful Proteus, if you are transformed into all kinds of shapes, and though you are the same, still can scarcely seem the same? Neither rock, nor liquid wave, nor flashing flame, nor leafy tree, nor the faces of various beasts are satisfactory. But such as you were when the shepherd Aristaeus spread the chains—be present now in that form to me. Do not refuse the oracle I seek in this ambiguous matter [see *Georgics* IV.449]. For what else is Proteus but the image of Truth itself, turning itself into all the wonderful variety of things? The divine form of the inner man is the same: the shifting face of things and false opinion abuse it. Here is that vast cave of error, where blind appetite distracts the diseased senses into wanting what is bad for them. Wherefore it takes the utmost exertion of the mind to grasp the truth zealously and hold on to it wisely. As soon as the chance is offered by sleep [*somnum*], and the seals of concupiscence are stretched out on the shore, and the old man composes his tired limbs to rest, then throw the chains of sincere faith on the captured one until no trick can find him a way out, and the truest form of the man can at last return to itself.[66]

---

[64] *Declamationes*, "De Artibus Liberalibus," in *Werke*, ed. R. Stupperich (Gutersloher, 1961), vol. 3, *Humanistische Schriften*, ed. R. Nürnberger, p. 22.

[65] *Contra Academicos*, iv.13, trans. Robert P. Russell, in *Writings*, Fathers of the Church (New York, 1948), vol. 6, p. 181.

[66] *Symbolicarvm Qvaestionvm* (Bologna, 1574), symb. lxi, pp. CXXX-CXXXI. I am indebted for this translation to the kindness of a colleague, Professor Traugott

At the house of Archimago, of course, "Proteus" is very much awake, and the situation is reversed: truth having been put to sleep, elusive appearances—dreams, phantasms, and "true-seeming lyes" (I.i.38)—are enlarged to wander at will. In the same vein, Milton says that Hypocrisy makes its way by prevailing over Simplicity, to whom Suspicion resigns her charge while sleeping at Wisdom's gate (*Par. Lost* III.382ff.).

Proteus is deceptively plural, but actually a single being. Thus the other title for Bocchius' emblem is "One truth to be seen in all things." Since Spenser gives his Truth the same number (cf. V.xi.56, "Truth is one in all"), we may wonder if this number is that universal key, answering to the numerical proportioning of the world, inquired into by the Pythagoreans. Reason, according to Augustine,

> ... began to suspect that it itself was perhaps the very number by which all things are numbered, or if not, that this number was there whither it was striving to arrive. And he of whom Alypius made mention when

Lawler. With Bocchius, cf. Melanchthon's commentary on Ovid, *Metam.* VIII.731: "Now there is a learned allegory of Proteus, which is conspicuous in Caelius Calcaginus; he understands in Proteus truth, which is not easily apprehended since it lies hidden, and he has it that this one is for this reason imagined as falling asleep in a cave, and as speaking true things when grasped; however, he changes into various forms because when the mind is led to the truth, tracking it down through reason, various forms arise, which have the appearance of truth, that is, false opinions, by which we are deluded; for we think many things true which are not. By what are these opinions indicated? Surely, by many simulacra or fictions, until Proteus returns to his own form, that is, until the truth dawns." (*Ennaratio Metamorphoseon*, in *Opera*, ed. G. Bretschneider and H. E. Bindseil, vol. 19, Brunswig, 1853, col. 587f.) For the whole allegory and its biblical equivalent, as developed below, cf. Milton, *Areopagitica*: truth "needs no policies, nor stratagems, nor licensings to make her victorious—these are the shifts and the defenses that error uses against her power. Give her but room, and do not bind her when she sleeps, for then she speaks not true, as the old Proteus did, who spake oracles only when he was caught and bound, but then rather she turns herself into all shapes except her own, and perhaps tunes her voice according to the time, as Micaiah did before Ahab, until she be abjured into her own likeness." In Alciati's *Emblems* Proteus stands for "Antiquissima quaeque commentitia." The actor-like god is asked why he adopts such a variety of forms, and he answers that he signifies the character of antiquities, "about which everyone dreams according to his own will." Alciati's commentator Claude Mignault explains that the poet "has accommodated the fable of the polymorphous Proteus to certain writers of rhapsodies and of very old things." Mignault goes on to give the physical allegory of Heraclides, Plato's comparison of the sophists, and classical references that make Proteus a remarkable Egyptian ruler. It is asked whether Proteus is an adaptable and wise man, or an unreliable imposter, contrasting Julian's letter to Iamblichus (*Epist.* LXXIX, 405B–C, in Loeb *Julian*, vol. 3, pp. 264f.) with Basil's oration *Pros Neos* (PG, XXXI, 585–588; also XXXII, 1127–1130). In Basil the *Egyptian sophist* represents the inconstant person. (My text is *Omnia Andrea Alciati v. c. Emblemata . . . Comm. . . . per Claudium Minoem*, Antwerp, 1581, pp. 629–634.)

we were treating of the Skeptics, grasped with all his might—as if Proteus were in his hands—this number which would be the discloser of universal truth.[67]

The relation between Archimago and Proteus is sealed in the final developments of Book I. When Una exposes his last disguise, Archimago is fettered like Virgil's Proteus, even though he "often semblaunce made to scape out of their hand" (I.xii.35). And at the opening of Book II,

> His artes he moues, and out of caytiues hand
> Himself he frees by secret meanes vnseene;
> His shackles emptie left, him selfe escaped cleene.
>
> (II.i.1)[68]

In other words, Proteus is also a type for mutability, that which the quest cannot redeem: "So tickle be the termes of mortall state, / And full of subtile sophismes" (III.iv.28; cf. VII.viii.1).

The analogy between Archimago and the classical shape-changer is useful because it helps to unify the poem. For Spenser has another Proteus, in Books III and IV, who abuses Florimell in the same way that the multiform Archimago works against Una. He too changes himself into a knight to supplant the lady's proper lover, and in fact the whole parallel is so complete that we cannot avoid concluding that it belongs to the poem's manifold design. The part of this second Proteus—who imprisons Florimell—is derived from an alternate story of Helen, which states that she did not go to Troy. Her chastity and reputation, as well as her beauty, were preserved by this invention; the battle was fought over an image of Helen, while the lady herself was retained in Egypt by a king named Proteus. Blown off-course in his return from Sparta, Paris visited Egypt, like Menelaus later, and according to some versions of the story Proteus himself formed the surrogate image that accompanied the Trojan home. The comparable impersonations in Spenser are the False Florimell and Duessa; both are condensed by sorcerers for the delectation of concupiscent and dishonest appetites, even though they are taken for chaste patterns of truth and beauty. In the "ydle dream" Una appears as a pagan goddess, decorated like Flora; Flora's worship in Spenser's "Maye" is a type of frivolous ceremonial religion, and the False Florimell is also an "Idole."

---

[67] *Divine Providence and the Problem of Evil*, xv.43, trans. Robert P. Russell, in *Writings*, p. 319. The passage adds: "But, false images of things which we number drift away from that most hidden something by which we enumerate, . . . and frequently make that hidden something slip away even when it has been already in our grasp." Cf. also Plato, *Epist.* II, 313b–c.

[68] Ariosto's enchanter Atlante also escapes his chain (*O.F.* IV.39), though otherwise he more nearly resembles Busirane: both of Spenser's enchanters abuse the fancy of their victims.

Each meretrix is an indictment of our capacity to discriminate between the true and the false, the ideal and the idol. The following stanza from another such indictment, Greville's noble but melancholy *Treatise of Human Learning* (25), adumbrates a comparable idolatry:

> Who those characteristical ideas
> Conceives, which science of the Godhead be?
> But in their stead we raise and mold tropheas,
> Forms of opinion, wit, and vanity,
> Which we call arts, and fall in love with these,
> As did Pygmalion with his carved tree;
> > For which men, all the life they here enjoy,
> > Still fight, as for Helens of their Troy.

Greville's comparison might remind us that the original Angelica, standing on the walls of the besieged Albracca, had something of the illusory Helen about her in the first place.

As every Spenserian knows, Angelica appears in Spenser as the two Florimells. Spenser has divided Angelica into double parts, very much on the analogy of the Helen in Stesichorus' widely reported palinode. E. K. compares Spenser's Colin Clout to Stesichorus because of the shepherd's idolatry of Rosalind, and Spenser cheerfully adopts the comparison at *Colin Clout*, 919–926.[69] Una and Duessa are similarly opposed, and the difficulties Marinell has distinguishing between the two Florimells (V.iii) are like those Fraudubio reports regarding his betrothed and Duessa (I.ii). Thus Ariosto's descriptions of Angelica might also prepare us for the debut of Spenser's Duessa. Looking at Angelica one might doubt whether she was "sensitiva e vera," or a rock colored in some manner (*O.F.* VIII.38). Orlando pursues a phantom of her at the opening of the twelfth canto and later she disappears from him, "come fantasma al dipartir del sonno," as a phantasm at the parting of sleep, or "come sparir *notturne larve*" (*O.F.* XII.59–60)—a "nocturnal larva."

A larva is both a mask, a phantasm, and a malignant night-walking spirit or demon (as in Tasso, *Gers. Lib.* XI.15), ultimately from the Roman *lar*, and akin to lemure, lamia, and *strix*. Affinities with the false Una are clear enough. The erotic dream that Archimago's demon applies to Redcrosse seems to be a nightmare in the older sense of a demon, "That nigh his manly heart did melt away, / Bathed in wanton blis and wicked

---

[69] E. K. on "Aprill," l. 26. Cf. Horace, *Epodes* XVII.40ff, where it is implied that Horace, with Stesichorus, is willing to lie to preserve the reputation of the beloved for chastity. For the Helen story in relation to Stesichorus, a crucial gathering of witnesses is to be found in Fulvius Ursinus, ed., *Carmina novem illustrivm feminarvm, . . . Et Lyricorvm . . . Stesichori . . .* (Antwerp, 1568), pp. 304–307, citing many of the more recondite sources.

joy" (I.i.47). The symbolism of the succuba, or female sexual demon seeking nocturnal congress, is amplified by the bedside presence of the false Una herself.

Duessa, it follows from the above, first appears as a kind of Doppelgänger for truth. As Redcrosse separates from Una, Duessa also takes on an independent existence, returning in the second canto as another man's idol. Like the incipience of allegory, the first approaches of Duessa may only be "doubtfully construed," and her later association with the Roman Church is not properly an issue here at all. Rather it is a question of an increasingly wrong opinion. Opinion, of course, may go either way: it may gradually become identical with truth, and disappear into it; or it may become more and more misleading, an institutionalization of Error, and thus ripe for exposure as a monstrosity. Spenser has both allegories, attached respectively to the False Florimell, who evaporates, and Duessa, who is cast out. Duessa *begins* by being covered by a veil (I.i.45); the False Florimell *ends* with her veil being removed (V.iii.17). Thus the poet thematizes the two termini of allegorical accommodation.

There may be a further step to be taken here. Since Archimago does what the poet does, in making two out of one (as Stesichorus distinguished a false from a true Helen), he may also be a rival for the poet, especially for the poet who wrote the Hymns to the two Beauties, the second of which is introduced as a palinode for the first. The two Florimells, in fact, attract allegories rather like those attaching to the two Helens. An example would be Plato's reference to Stesichorus' story in the *Republic* (586c), where the false Helen is compared to phantoms of true pleasure. With reference to this Platonic interpretation, Proclus writes in his defense of poetic theology:

> I think it [the Trojan War] all that lingers about at the generation of beauty, from the making of anything. And on this account it needs be, that the fable of Helen signifies, that about which there is always the war of souls, until the more intellectual having conquered the life of the more sensual, pass over hence to that place, from which they parted at first. Thus this period, which, it is said, was ten years, that is to say, ten thousand years. For there is not any difference in saying it either in this way, or in that, since a millennium is a period which the soul crosses anew from generation into generation; and when the soul has fluctuated about the earth nine thousand years, it is given peace in the tenth millennium. And so, when the war about generation has lasted the space of nine years, the barbarian flood conquers in the tenth, and it is said that they are taken back into their proper home.[70]

[70] Translated from Mazzoni's citation, as it appears below, in note 72. For the text, *In Plat. Rem Pub.*, ed. William Kroll (Leipzig, 1901), vol. 1, p. 175 (15-21).

The allegory of the scholiast Hermeas Alexandrini—on Plato's other reference to the two Helens (*Phaedrus* 243a)—is even more explicit about the object of the war:

> By *Ilion* we must understand the generated and material place, which is so denominated from *mud* and *matter*, and in which there is war and sedition. But the Trojans are material forms, and all the lives which subsist about material bodies. . . . On the contrary, the Greeks are rational souls, coming from Greece, *i.e.* from intelligible into matter. . . . But they fight with each other about the image of Helen, as the poet says: "Around the phantom the Greeks and Trojans fight" [*Iliad* V.451], Helen signifying intelligible beauty, being a certain vessel attracting to itself intellect. An efflux, therefore, of this intelligible beauty is imparted to matter through Venus; and about this efflux of beauty the Greeks fight with the Trojans. And those, indeed, that oppose and vanquish matter, return to their true country; but those who do not, as is the case with the multitude, are bound to matter.[71]

No one is likely to miss the possible relevance of these passages to the strife over the False Florimell.

Mazzoni, the reader will recall, gives as the product of the imitative poet either the phantastic idol, or the eikastic and verisimilar one, the image and simulacrum of the truth. After an important summary of his theory of the kinds of falsification allowed to poetry, he digresses into a twenty-four chapter disquisition on the "credible marvellous" in poetry, which is the effect of the phantastic kind of imitation. He begins with a collection of examples of alterations in histories, made by poets for the sake of this effect. His first example is Stesichorus' account of Helen; the terms inevitably echo those for the two kinds of imitation:

> Beginning from the supportable then, I say that an example of the alteration of the subject towards greater wonder in the reader, is the account Stesichorus has left in the Encomium of Helen, in that place where it is

---

Cf. the translation of Thomas Taylor, in *Works of Plato* (London, 1804), vol. 3, pp. 312f., where Helen signifies "all the beauty subsisting about generation, from the fabrication of things."

[71] *In Plat. Phaedrum Scholia*, 98–101, ed. P. Couvreur (Paris, 1901), pp. 77f., and trans. Taylor, in the appendix to *Select Works of Porphyry* (London, 1823), pp. 441–443. The deceptive image of Aeneas, to which Hermeas refers, is more fully developed in *Aen.* X.636–644: "Then the goddess [Juno] out of hollow mist fashions a thin, strengthless phantom in the likeness of Aeneas, a monstrous marvel to behold, decks it with Dardan weapons, and counterfeits the shield and plumes his godlike head, gives it unreal words, gives a voice without thought, and mimicks his gait as he moves; even like shapes that flit, 'tis said, when death is past, or like dreams that mock the slumbering senses." (Trans. H. R. Fairclough, in the Loeb edn.)

said that the true Helen was not transferred to Troy, as was believed up until then, and as was stated first in the writing of Homer: but an Idol, and a Simulacrum of her. In this he was followed a little afterwards by Euripides in the Tragedy of Helen. Dio of Prusa [in his oration on the falsehoods of Homer, the eleventh or Trojan discourse] has reasoned thusly about this alteration: *But then as ridiculous* [as Homer's story] *is attested (he says)—that another poet, who gave credence to Homer, and said the same things about Helen, (I think it was Stesichorus), and said that he was made blind by Helen for having declared these lies, and that sight was restored to him, when he wrote the contrary. And* [you Greeks] *confessing nevertheless this, as I said* [an Egyptian is speaking], *that the Poetry of Homer is true. And Stesichorus even said in the last hymn, that Helen did not even voyage, and some others say, that Alexander did carry her off, and that she reached us in Egypt.*[72]

Mazzoni also quotes Aristides' oration about rhetoric, and the relevant lines of Lychophron's *Alexandra* (113-114) ("The vain embrace, and with the empty / Arms touching the bed after the dream"), along with Tzetes' exposition ("Wherefore it is said, Alexander being come into Egypt, Proteus took Helen from him and, in her place, gave him the Idol of Helen, as Stesichorus says"). Then Mazzoni expounds:

> Now who does not see that this *tropasso* that the poet made from the true Helen to the Simulachrum of her was made to produce the greater wonder in the reader, and in observers of his poem? Certainly no one. Then it follows from this marvel that the poet has believed that it would be licit to change, and to falsify an ancient history already recounted in another mode: although in that which pertains to the Simulachrum there is seen some semblance to the possible through the absolute power of God [a secondary category of the sources of the credible in poetry—with God all things are possible].[73]

In treating allegory—that variety of the credible marvellous in which the literal sense is incredible, while the philosophcal or allegorical sense is credible—Mazzoni again reverts to the story of Stesichorus:

> Proclus, in the observations which he has left on the Republic of Plato, discussing Stesichorus, says, that he was considered blind because of his having recounted the fable of Helen as true, not having penetrated into the truth of the allegorical sense which comes from that philosophical explanation in the words written below. [Mazzoni then gives the passage from Proclus that we have quoted.] Thus Proclus values the allegory in the poem so much that he denominates those who do not understand it

[72] *Difesa* (Cesena, 1587), III.vii, pp. 417f.
[73] *Difesa, loc. cit.* (The reference to Aristides is *Orat.* XIII.131, with scholia: Proteus sent a *picture* of the phantom to Troy. Cf. the word "picture" at V.iii.25.)

as blind, as if he wants to say, that this is the object and the scope wherein all good Poets aim, and wherein every one who reads the Poem ought to aim. But our Adversaries will say that even if this is true, it is not thereby proved that the literal sense is ever omitted in making the account solely about the Allegorical. To which I respond that it is true that in the Poets the sense many times is literal, and the allegorical must attend to itself. But yet when in some passages the literal is left, then the Poet passes beyond a certain great inconvenience, and the allegorical is understood.[74]

These texts raise as many questions as they answer, but they agree in assimilating Stesichorus' insight into Homer to his alteration of the Homeric fable: Stesichorus revised the poet by way of allegory. Thus Archimago is not only a Proteus who doubles the bride figure; he is also a Stesichorus who substitutes an "allegorical" bride for a literal one. Una, however, is not altogether literal to begin with. Stesichorus discovered the literal Helen to be a mere simulacrum of a true bride, or of troth: the ideal or "troth-ful" bride would have been chaste. Archimago, however, makes the true bride into a simulacrum of the untrue Helen. His allegorical reading of Una is allegorical sarcasm. Archimago thus denies the inner sense properly found beneath the veil of a fiction. Rather than divine this sense, he complicates the fiction with a further one of his own. His slanderous fabrication multiplies appearances, and thereby divides the unity of truth.

An honored tradition—one that apologists felt included Scripture—recommended the obscuring of the truth in recondite forms to safeguard it against vulgarization or abuse by inferior understandings, and to provoke investigation of it by devotees. One may argue that Archimago, as archpoet, has unwittingly abetted the purposes of that other archpoet who is writing Book I of *The Faerie Queene*. At the same time, the mage is also to be numbered among those pseudopoets, mentioned by Henry Reynolds, who create counterfeits out of the clouds;[75] or one of those mongerers of opinion, mentioned by Greville, who "entangle clouds to posterity." The example of Greville brings us to our next subject: the false Una attracts to her the whole Renaissance diatribe against the deceptions foisted on us not by poets, with their notorious susceptibility to Report, but by Opinion itself.

[iii]

If, as we said, Archimago raises the devils that Christ casts out, the devils are primarily those of the human imagination. The imagination,

---

[74] *Ibid.*, III.xxxviii, p. 565.

[75] *Mythomystes*, in Spingarn, *Critical Essays*, vol. 1, p. 148, in the course of a diatribe against the affected learning of some poets.

in Spenser's first canto, is a kind of bedeviled conjurer. According to the dream-theorist Synesius, man shares this imagination with animals, and —one might add on the basis of the following—with a creature like Shakespeare's Tom O'Bedlam:

> Whole races of demons also have their existence in such a life as this. For whereas these throughout all their being are phantasmic, making their appearance as images in things that are coming into being, in the case of man most things come by imagination and that alone, though in truth a good many in company with another, for we do not form thought-concepts without imagination, unless it so be that some man in a rare moment of time grasps even an immaterial form.[76]

Man realizes his thoughts through images, rather than demons, the text seems to say, but the distinction seems almost to be one without a difference. The same author observes that these images are parasitic when they portend things not yet in existence:

> Now the imaginative pneuma is a powerful reflecting mirror of all the images that flow off in this way. For, wandering in vain and slipping from their base, on account of the indefiniteness of their nature, and because they are recognised by no being of real existence, whenever these fall in with psychical pneumata, the which are images indeed, and have a seat fixed in nature, then they lean upon them and take their rest as though at their own hearthstone.[77]

That is, undreamed images of preexistent occurrences are like waifs, or like the demons in the Gospel looking for a swept and garnished house to possess (Luke 11:24-26).

Man cannot think without images; but, being likenesses, images can be defective, and hence the occasion for false opinions. Aquinas makes the point that "Now falsity is attributed to imagination, because it presents the likeness even of absent things; so that when a person turns to the likeness of the thing, this apprehension gives rise to falsity. Hence too

---

[76] *Concerning Dreams*, trans. Augustine Fitzgerald, in *The Essays and Hymns of Synesius of Cyrene* (London, 1930), vol. 2, p. 335. Ficino's Latin version of this passage may be found in *Opera omnia* (rprnt. Torino, 1959), II-2, p. 1971. For the penetration of the human fantasy by the demons who take on aerial bodies, see Ficino, *Theologia Platonica*, XIV.vii, in *Op. om.*, I-1, pp. 379-381, with the Platonic *Epinomis* 984e-985d, and Origen, *Contra Celsus*, V.5 and *De Principis*, III.ii.1-2. Cf. Augustine, *Civ. Dei*, IX.viii seq. For the evils and unreliability of the imagination, and the use of the phantasms by the evil angels—especially in the making of a false prophet—see Gianfrancesco Pico, *On the Imagination*, trans. Harry Caplan, Cornell Studies in English, 16 (New Haven, 1930), cap. vii, pp. 42-49, cap. viii, pp. 56-59, and cap. xii, pp. 84f.

[77] Fitzgerald trans., p. 350; in Ficino, *Op. om.*, II-2, p. 1976.

Aristotle says that shadows and pictures and dreams are said to be false as being insubstantial likenesses."[78] Idols comprise an especially definitive example of such a falsehood of likeness. They imply a false opinion about God merely by being differentiated from God, who is a unity: "A false opinion about him is the contrary of a true opinion. In this sense idols are called 'falsehoods,' opposite to the divine truth, because false opinion concerning idols is the contrary of true opinion concerning the unity of God."[79] Idolatry is thus defined as the holding of an untrue opinion on the basis of an imperfect likeness; it is scarcely possible *not* to have a false opinion about God, under the circumstances. In the poem earlier quoted, Greville allowed the entertainment of true ideas to the godhead alone—the human mind always wanders into idolatry, like Jove deceived into begetting the fantastic centaurs on the clouds. "Books be of men, men but in clouds do see, / Of whose embracements centaurs gotten be":

> What then need half-fast helps of erring wit,
> Methods, or books of vain humanity
> Which dazzle truth, by representing it,
> And so entangle clouds to posterity,
> > Since outward wisdom springs from truth within
> > Which all men feel, or hear before they sin.[80]

The truth that is falsified in representing it is much like Redcrosse's "bad faith" in deserting Una and entrusting himself to Duessa. The supplanting of the one faith by the other is among Spenser's most carefully detailed allegories.

---

[78] *De Veritate*, q.17, art.2, resp.2, trans. Robert Mulligan, S.J., *Truth* (Chicago, 1952), vol. 1, p. 107. See also art.1, resp.4, of the same text.

[79] *Ibid.*, q.17, art.4, resp.3; *edn. cit.*, p. 113.

[80] *Caelica*, 66. For the story, see marg. on Pindar, *Pyth.* II.33ff.; Ovid, *Metam.* XI.123, XII.504; Servius, *ad Aen.* VIII.294; Hyginus, *Fab.* XXXIII, LXII; Lucian, *Dial. Deorum* 6, "Hera and Zeus"; Boccaccio, *G.D.G.*, IX.xxv, xxxiii. For the *nubigenes* Centaurs as a figure of the deceptions wrought by intellect, cf. Milton, *Paradise Regained* IV.321ff.: the one who seeks true wisdom in the classical schools "finds her not, or by delusion / Far worse, her false resemblance only meets, / An empty cloud." (Cf. also *Tetrachordon*, Columbia edn. of Milton's *Works*, vol. 4, pp. 86f. and the last line of *The Passion*.) For truth, cf. Augustine, *De Trinitate*, VIII.ii.3: "Ask not what is truth; for immediately the darkness of corporeal images and the clouds of phantasms will put themselves in the way, and will disturb that calm which at first twinkling shone forth to thee, when I said truth. See that thou remainest, if thou canst, in the first twinkling with which thou art dazzled, as it were, by a flash, when it is said to thee, Truth. But thou canst not; thou wilt glide back into those usual and earthly things. And what weight, pray, is it that will cause thee so to glide back, unless it be the birdlime of the stains of appetite thou hast contracted, and the errors of thy wandering from the right path?" (Trans. Haddon, NPNF, 1st Series, vol. 3, p. 117.)

Archimago begins the process with a troublesome dream; like Eve's dream in Book IV of *Paradise Lost*, it is a demonic suggestion appealing to a carnal appetite, or to the mind of the flesh. The domain of Morpheus, from whence the dream hails, is represented as a vaporous, amorphic, and self-drowned realm, which generally keeps the sleeping state oblivious to "troubled sights and fancies weake" (I.i.42). And yet the sleeping Morpheus mumbles. In Ovid, one finds that Morpheus is not Somnus, but rather *Phantasos* (*Metam*. XI.642), a maker of images of men and a clever imitator of figures. Boccaccio says that Morpheus' name means *formatio* or *simulachrum*, and that it is Morpheus' office "to feign at the command of his lord the faces, words, manners, voices, and idioms of men." These phantasms include the *ephialtes*, "whom common persuasion takes to invade the sleeping and to weigh down on them, pressing and oppressing the senses."[81] Under such a burden, Spenser's knight awakes—"as seeming to mistrust" (I.i.49)—but his dream will not go away. It has apparently come true. Redcrosse, the contemplative subject, has crossed the threshold into an allegory of the self, a place in which imaginative projections—anxieties and opinions—are part of the external world, and objective only in the sense of being the *ob-jectum* of the perceiving ego. Redcrosse's impulse is to slay the amorous spright, but he can hardly trust his senses. He is still asleep, in a way, and he does not fully awaken until the third morning of the dragon fight.

The unreliability of a thought-work dominated by our fantasy and our preoccupations is the subject of a poem by Greville that describes how the eye, with nothing to see in the night, combines with anxieties to "forge and raise impossibility":

> Such, as in thick depriving darknesses,
> Proper reflections of the error be,
> And images of self-confusednesses,
> Which hurt imaginations only see,
>   And from this nothing seen tells news of devils,
>   Which but expressions be of inward evils.[82]

We have already mentioned Tasso's forest, enchanted by Ismeno, where Rinaldo must slay the apparition of the enchantress Armida.[83] Here Tas-

---

[81] *G.D.G.*, I.xxxi, Romano edn. (Bari, 1951), vol. 1, pp. 60, 58. For Morpheus as a prophet and poet, cf. Sidney, *Astrophel and Stella*, Son. 32: "A poet eke, as humours fly or creep," whose father Sleep charms the dreamer while Morpheus himself steals the image of the beloved from the lover's heart, and exhibits it by means of "ivory, rubies, pearls and gold" (i.e., through Petrarchan comparisons).

[82] *Caelica*, 100.

[83] *Ger. Lib.* XIII.1–51, XVII.25–38; for Tasso's allegory, see Morley's edn. of Fairfax's translation (1890), p. 437.

so's allegory is not, as Coleridge maintained,[84] impossible to remember—
at least when we are comparing Spenser. Ismeno, Tasso tells us, stands
for "that temptation which seeks to deceive with false belief the virtue
. . . opinionative," while Armida is "that temptation which layeth siege
to the power of our desires: so from that proceed the Errors of Opinion;
from this, those of appetite." And further: "The enchantments of Ismen
. . . , deceiving with illusions, signify no other thing than the falsity of
the reasons and persuasions which are engendered in the wood; that is,
in the variety and multitude of opinions and discourses of men." In Jonson's masque *Hymenia*, Truth and Opinion emerge from a mist as look-
alikes, arguing opposite sides of a question; Truth calls Opinion an "il-
lusive sprite" (l. 633) created out of empty fumes by the sorceress Night.

These parallels help explain the bedroom scene in Spenser as depending
upon Redcrosse's susceptibility to opinion. In the absence of the true
Una, Redcrosse imagines that Una may be false. The knight of faith
himself is reduced to two minds—opinion is seldom unanimous. The
suddenly heavy wordplay shows this division of opinion undermining the
knight's strength of conviction:

> Her doubtfull words made that redoubted knight
> Suspect her truth: yet since no 'vntruth he knew, . . .
>
> (I.i.53)

The naive knight, incapable of "untruth," cannot *re*-cognize that the false
Una is an unfaithful representation of the true one, because he is cog-
nizing this unfaithfulness for the first time. And yet he does not know
Una herself well enough to be confident of her fidelity, or truth.

Further interpretations of Spenser's opening scenes are suggested by
Cebes' *Tabula*, a textbook allegory about the education one gets in life.[85]
Just beyond the threshold of an enclosure that comprehends human ex-
istence, one meets a bevy of harlots: Opinions and Desires. Upon the
same threshold, a character whose name is translated "phantom of truth,"
or "Imposture," proffers a cup from which the initiates drink Error and
Ignorance. This Lethean soul-drink is also Circean (as analogies from
Spenser's second book insist), and hence Duessan. But what Cebes espe-

---

[84] *Coleridge's Miscellaneous Criticism*, ed. T. M. Raysor (Cambridge, Mass., 1936),
p. 31. Coleridge echoes John Hughes, *An Essay on Allegorical Poetry*, in Spenser's
Works (1715), vol. 1, pp. lii–liii.

[85] Spenser's enchanters form the specious double from a cloud-stuff because opinion clouds or obscures truth; conversely, God's truth penetrates to the clouds ("For
thy mercie is great above the heavens, and *thy trueth vnto the cloudes*" [Genevan
Psalm 108:4—the source of the motto of the book-emblem on the title page of the
Epithalamion, which comes from Whitney's *Emblemes*, p. 166a, "Veritas inuicta,"
or Georgette de Montenay, *Emblèmes* (1571), no. 72]). Cf. Merlin's begetting, "By
false illusion of a guilefull Spright, / On a faire Ladie Nonne" (III.iii.12).

cially shares with Spenser is the educator's idea of a convertible analogy between the thresholds crossed by the internal characters and those crossed by the reader. In Cebes, the prolegomena to the allegory proper reports that the learned table is kept within a temple guarded by a sphinx. The priest who introduces his visitors into the temple to study the table tells them that figuratively ignorance is a sphinx: the person understanding the table will slay the sphinx. Thus the occasion for error upon the threshold of the allegorical world of the table is ultimately redeemable—by the conscientious reader.

The guardian sphinx was often interpreted as the obstructions or obscurities placed in the way of those who did not understand a mystery. This barrier between the ignorant and the initiated appears frequently in the hermeneutic tradition adopted by the Renaissance, and in Spenser its preliminary position is occupied by Error, who proves a very Delphic sort of hybrid.[86] Spenser repeats the idea of a double threshold from Cebes, and the prolegomena material again comprises a reversible perspective upon the interior allegory: Redcrosse has slain Error, but understood nothing. The ostensible success of the knight's opening campaign yields to the perception that there are kinds of error that can only be destroyed through hindsight, and from within.

Error was easily recognized as a monstrosity, or, more precisely, as the deformity of truth. (The definition is Scholastic: "Just as a thing has being through its own form, so a power of knowing has its act of knowing through a likeness of the thing known."[87] To say that a thing is true may only predicate the conformity of the thing known to the intellect,

[86] For the Sphinx before the temple, besides *Cebes' Table*, see Plutarch, *De Iside* 9; Clement, *Stromata*, V.v; Pico, *Heptaplus*, first proem, and *Oration on the Dignity of Man*, 34. Compare also the sphinx of Alciati, Emb. CLXXXVII, "Svmomendam Ignorantiam" (Mignault cites both Cebes and Clement), and Comes, *Mythol.*, IX.xviii, *edn. cit.*, p. 1009, on the concealment of philosophical precepts. Comes departs from the Oedipus story to remark: "I do not believe that historical narrations are the only thing contained under these fables. For it would be ridiculous to hide simple exploits thusly, lest they be understood by just anybody—and they always do find some Oedipus. But this was done, as is often said, because fabulous narrations are imbibed with pleasure by those who abhor living rightly by hearing naked precepts. For at first perhaps the explications of the fabulous precepts were allowed with no less pleasure than the perceptive fables themselves. Because—if I am asked what I mean—I think there was no easier way to teach philosophy to youth than by the diligent learning of fables, followed by the revelation of the precepts hidden beneath them." The association of *Cebes' Table* and the thresholds of a text is reinforced by the use of the table as a border design for the frontispiece of several Renaissance books. By far the most important of these was the New Testament translated into Latin by Erasmus (Basel, 1522). (Others were Strabo, *Geographie*, Basel, 1523; *Dictionarium graecum*, Venice, 1525; *Lexicon Graeco Latinum*, Basel, 1545.) The design was by Hans Holbein the Younger.
[87] Aquinas, *Summa Theol.*, Pt. I, q.17, art.3. See also *ibid.*, q.16, art. 2.

but even so, "deformities and other defects do not possess truth in the same way other things do.")[88] Opinion, on the other hand, though it may be misinformed nonetheless offers itself as a kind of provisional approximation of the truth. It proceeds by the educated guess, substituting known values for unknown ones, and vice versa. Commitment to such an approximation bears an unfortunate resemblance to an act of faith. As Truth itself hath said, faith is the evidence of things unseen.

Redcrosse is committed to Truth from the time he adopts the shield of her faith, but he has not seen her. She has worn a veil since the usurpation of her father's lands in Eden, truth for the fallen mind being almost by definition numinous. The basic weakness in Redcrosse's faith is that his faith is more ignorant than innocent; his commitment easily degenerates into an anxious tension between doubt and credulity, or scepticism and superstition. This credulity is the theme of an ambiguous passage from the magic book of that Archimage Cornelius Agrippa, who begins by implying that superstition imitates faith, but ends by saying almost the reverse:

> . . . superstition requireth credulity, as Religion saith, seeing constant credulity can do so great things, even as to work miracles in opinions and false operations; whosoever therefore in his Religion, though false, yet beleeveth most strongly that it is true, and elevates his spirit by reason of this his credulity, untill it be assimilated to those spirits who are the chief leaders of that Religion, may work those things which nature and reason discern not; but incredulity and diffidence doth weaken every work not only in superstition, but also in true Religion, and enervates the desired effect even of the most strong experiments. But how superstition imitateth Religion, these examples declare; namely when worms and locusts are excommunicated, that they hurt not the fruits; when bels and Images are baptised and such like; but because the old Magicians and those who were the authors of this art amongst the ancients, have been Caldeans, Egyptians, Assyrians, Persians and Arabians, all whose Religion was perverse and polluted idolatry, we must very much take heed, least we should permit their errors to war against the grounds of the Catholick Religion; . . .[89]

---

[88] Aquinas, *Veritas*, q.1, art.8, resp.

[89] *Three Books of Occult Philosophy*, III.iv, trans. J[ohn] F[rench] (London, 1651), pp. 354f. See also *Henry Cornelius Agrippa's Fourth Book of Occult Philosophy and Geomancy* . . . , First translated into English by Robert Turner, Philomathees (reprint, 1783), Fol. A3^{r-v}: Witches and Necromancers, otherwise called sorcerers "make pictures of wax, or clay; or otherwise (as it were *sacramentaliter*) to effect those things which the Devil by other means bringeth to pass." For further remarks

The passage anticipates more of Spenser's theme than we can readily take in here, but it is easy to forecast from it which kind of religion will benefit from this credulity: the magical kind.

According to Bullinger, we are prey to superstition as a result of the Fall:

> All our understanding is dull, blunt, gross, and altogether blind in heavenly things. Our judgment in divine matters is perverse and frivolous. For there arise in us most horrible and absurd thoughts, and opinions touching God, his judgments, and wonderful works. Yea, our whole mind is apt and ready to errors, to fables, and our own destruction: and when as our judgments are nothing but mere folly, yet do we prefer them far above God's wisdom, which we esteem but foolishness in comparison of our own conceits and corrupt imaginations; . . .[90]

As we have seen, Greville in particular shares this theme with Spenser. In the following example the relation between truth and opinion is assimilated to a conception of two Churches:

> Man's superstition hath Thy truths entombed,
> His atheism again her pomps defaceth;
> That sensual unsatiable vast womb
> Of Thy seen church Thy unseen church disgraceth.
>   There lives not truth with them that seem Thine own
>   Which makes Thee, living Lord, a God unknown.[91]

For a final summary, one may compare Archimago's legions and the cave of Morpheus to a passage from Calvin's *Institutes*, denouncing the workings of the fallen mind:

> But if at any time we be by the guiding & direction of these things driuen to the consideration of God (as all men must needes be) yet so soone as we haue without aduisement conceiued a feeling of some Godhead, we by and by slide away to the dotages or erroneous inuentions of our flesh, and with our vanity we corrupt the pure verity of God. So heerein in

---

of the magical power of the imagination, see Ficino, *Theologica Platonica*, XIII.i, in *Op. om.*, I-1, pp. 284–286. D. P. Walker, in his *Spiritual and Demonic Magic from Ficino to Campanella*, p. 107, cites Pomponazzi's *De Incantionibus*, to the effect that the imagination of operators is so violently affected by words and images that their spirits are suddenly and greatly altered—operators change themselves. So Archimago at *F.Q.* I.ii.10. See also Del Rio *Disqvistionvm Magicarvm*, I.iii, qvaest. iii, *edn. cit.*, pp. 14–61.

[90] *The Decades of Henry Bullinger*, 4 vols., ed. Rev. Thomas Harding, Parker Society (Cambridge, 1849–1852), vol. 2, *The Third Decade*, Sermon X, trans. "H.L.," p. 393. All references hereafter are to this edn.

[91] *Caelica*, 109.

deede we differ one from another, that euery man priuately by himselfe procureth to himselfe some peculiar error: but in this point we are most like together, that we all, not one excepted, doe depart from the one true God to mostruous trifles. To which disease not onely common and grosse wits are subiect: but also the most excellent and those that otherwise are endued with singular sharpness of vnderstanding, are entangled with it. . . . Heereof proceedeth that vnmeasurable sink of errors wherewith the whole world hath bin filled and ouerflowne. For ech mannes wit is to himselfe as a maze, so that it is no maruell that euery seuerall nation was diuersly drawen into seuerall deuises, and not that onely, but also that ech seuerall man had his seuerall gods by himselfe. For since that rash presumption and wantonnes was ioned to ignorance & darkenesse, ther hath bin scarcely at any time any one man found, that did not forge to himselfe an idole or fansie in steede of God. Truely euen as out of a wide and large spring do issue waters, so the infinite number of Gods hath flowed out of the wit of man, while euery man ouer licenciously straying, erroneously deuiseth this or that concerning God himselfe.[92]

Thus Archimago has unbottled the same troubled world that, in Milton's *Nativity Ode*, the coming of Christ "in straiter limits bound." "To purge the world of idolatry and superstition," Burton writes at the head of his section on the cure of religious melancholy, "will require some monster-taming Hercules, a divine Aesculapius, or Christ himself to come in his own person."[93] Out of the mass of evidence accumulated in the "Digression of Spirits," as in Milton, emerges a picture of a universally abused credulity, a world-wide faith in something half-real and half-illusory, doleful, and finally a heavy burden to the spirit.

[iv]

Broadly speaking, the theme of Book I is the establishment of faith: faith in one's self, faith in an ideal, and faith in the Word of God. These faith-relations are symbolized by the "troth" of Redcrosse and Una, the faithful knight and the true bride of Revelation. "Sanctify them through thy truth," Christ prays for his disciples, "thy word is truth."[94] Sanctifica-

---

[92] *The Institution of the Christian Religion*, I.v.10f., trans. Thomas Norton (London, 1587), pp. 11f. I owe the idea of citing this passage to Harry Berger, Jr., "Spenser's *Faerie Queene*, Book I, Prelude to Interpretation," *Southern Review* (Australia), 2 (1966), pp. 18–49.

[93] *Anatomy of Melancholy*, Pt. III, Sect. iv, Member 1, subsec. 5.

[94] John 17:17. Cf. I Peter 1:22: "Seing your soules are purified in obeing the trueth through the spirit, to love brotherly without faining . . ." (Geneva Bible). It is also this mutualizing of dedication and sincerity that relates Books I and IV: the Church is a *fellowship*; see I.x.56 and IV.ii.53, x.26.

tion through truth is the goal of Book I, and together Una and Redcrosse manifest the "one faith"—Unam Sanctam[95]—of Ephesians 4:5; "Knights ought to be true, and truth is one in all" (V.xi.56, on the defection of Burbon from the Protestant faith). Redcrosse is one of the elect of II Thessalonians 2:13, chosen "to salvation through sanctifying of the spirit and the faith of the truth." Indeed, the Christian is said to be "begotten" by the word of truth (James 1:18), and this in part accounts for Una's somewhat maternal character in relation to her knight. But what is truth? as Pilate asks. Una is veiled, like the ark and temple of the old covenant, and Redcrosse has not yet entered behind the veil (Heb. 9:3).

Pilate's question is particularly pertinent where Archimago is concerned, for Archimago is a father of lies, and one of the unrighteous idolators of Romans 1:25 "who changed the truth of God into a lie, and worshipped and served the creature more than the Creator." As such, he belongs to the Antichrist complex of the New Testament:

> Euen him whose comming is by the working of Satan, with all power and signes, and lying wonders,
> And in all deceiueablenes of vnrighteousnes, among them that perish, because thei receiued not the loue of the trueth, that they might be saued.
> And therefore God shal send them strong delusion, that they shulde beleue lyes,
> That all they might be damned which beleued not the trueth, but had pleasure in vnrighteousnes.
>
> (Geneva Bible, II Thess. 2:9–12)

This text was linked with one in II Timothy 4, concerning the success of the false teacher. The Protestant demonologist Lavater writes that there comes a time when the church will not hear "holsome doctrine." He alleges examples that include Pharaoh's Magi and Ahab's false prophets, and then goes on:

> The very same happened vnto the Christians after the Apostles tyme. For when the word of God began to be lesse esteemed than it shoulde haue bin, and men preferred their owne affections before the hearing thereof: and whenas they woulde incurre no manner of daunger, for the defence of their faith, and of the truth, but accounted all religions alike, God

---

[95] The name of the papal bull (November, 1302), which begins by affirming that "there is *one holy*, Catholic and apostolic church," outside of which there is no salvation, citing Song 6:8: "*Una* is my dove, my perfect *una*. She is the only *una* of her mother, the chosen of her that bore her." So also the *Glossa ordinaria* on this verse (PL, CXIII, 1159). Cf. Una, "th'onely daughter of a King and Queene," at I.vii.43. The phrase "one, holy, catholic and apostolic Church," of course, comes from the Constantinopolitan Creed of 381 (the Nicene Creed). See also n. 273, below.

so punished them, that nowe they began to giue eare vnto false teachers, whiche framed themselues vnto theyr vaine affections, they learned of images, whom they called lay mennes bookes, they kissed these mens boanes, and shrined them in golde . . . whose doctrine before they disdayned to receyue: the gaue credite vnto false apparitions and diuelishe visions: . . . they fell dayly more and more from the word of God, in so much that when they had once lost the truth, some ranne one waye, and some an other to fynde a meanes for the remission of their sins: and one man beleued this spirite, an other that, which no man can deny.[96]

The most important instance of the false prophet in the Old Testament, apart from the enemies of Jeremiah, is found in the story of Michaiah. Michaiah, by means of a parable, ridicules King Ahab's other prophets for their comforting "doctrine" (Geneva gloss, I Kings 12:11). The prophet, the parable presumes, is privy to a heavenly council, like the one that introduces Job, because the prophet shares an intimate fellowship with God.[97] A spirit comes before the Lord and volunteers to be a lying spirit in the mouths of Ahab's uncritical supporters. The Geneva gloss on the version of the story in II Chronicles 18 quotes the passage from II Thessalonians to explain Ahab's deception: "God shall send them a strong delusion, that they should believe lies." Jeremiah, on the other hand, prophesies that God will repudiate the dreamers of lies who come in the Lord's name: "Behold, I wil come against them that prophecie false dreams, saith the Lord, & do tel them, and cause my people to erre by their lies, and by their flatteries, and I send them not, nor commanded them" (23:32). The Geneva Bible comments on those who declare their dreams in God's name: "Let the false prophet declare that it is his owne fantasie, & not sclander my worde as thogh it were a cloke to couer his lies" (on v. 28). "Nether giue eare to your dreames, which you dream," says the Lord, "For they prophecie you a lye in my Name: I haue not sent them" (Jer. 29:8–9). We find the sorcerer of II Thessalonians again in Revelation; he is the "false prophet," doing wonders, animating images, and deceiving the whole world.

The imagination, as a maker of images or idols, does the devil's work. "What is you Masse els," asks Bale, "but a gawkishe fopperye or a toye of your owne ymaginacyon?"[98] And, conversely, the devil has exploited the susceptibility of the imagination. Lavater cites Lactantius to the effect that "euill angels lurking vnder the names of the dead, did wound and

[96] Lewes Lavater, *Of Ghostes and Spirites Walking by Night* (1572), ed. J. Dover Wilson and May Yardley (Oxford, 1929), p. 182.

[97] Amos 3:7, Jer. 23:18–22, Zech. 3. Cf. Num. 12:6–8, Isa. 6:8, and I Kings 18:15. In Deut. 13:1ff. (with 18:20, 32:16f.), the prophet or dreamer of dreams counsels the people to go after strange gods.

[98] John Bale, *A Mysterye of inyquyte* (Geneva, 1545), fol. 44ᵛ.

hurt the liuing, that is, they tooke vnto themselues the names of *Iupiter* and *Iuno*, whom the heathens tokke to be gods, or as we now say, tooke vnto them the names of S. Sebastian, Barbara, and others."[99] Thus the demon-drawing religious imagination finds its personification in the figure of the magician who asserts his power over images and demons alike. A passage from Burton shows this confluence: "For the Gentiles' gods were devils (as Trismegistus confesseth in his *Aesculapius*), and he himself could make them come to their images by magic spells: and are now as much 'respected by our papists,' saith Pictorius) 'under the name of Saints.' "[100] In animating the false Una, Archimago acts not only the part of the false prophet and the fallen imagination, but also the part of a papal Trismegistus. Duessa, in seeking to revive Sansjoy, may well have recourse to the same Roman authority, namely a healer called Aesculapius.

The other major factor in the Archimago episode, apart from Archimago himself, is the division of Redcrosse from Una. The connection between the desertion of the lady by the knight and Archimago's conjuration of the false Una may be illustrated by a passage from John Bale's commentary on Revelation in which he denounces papistry in terms from Calvin's discussion of the idolatry of the natural imagination. Bale expounds God's rebuke to the Church of the Ephesians, and addresses himself specifically to the consequences of the Church's *leaving the love it had at first* (Rev. 2:4-5):

> ... I will remove thy candlestick out of her place. I shall take away from
> thee the sincere doctrine and pure preaching of my word, and suffer men's
> fantastical traditions, old women's dreams, the spirits of error, the doctrine
> of devils, the lies of hypocrites, with all blindness, darkness, abomination,
> and idolatry, there to remain. For where as my word is not sincerely
> taught, believed, and observed, but uncharitably despised, hated, and per-
> secuted, there shall not my church remain, but in her place shall stand
> up the synagogue of Satan, with blindness and induration. For that con-

---

[99] *Of Ghostes and Spirites*, p. 142.

[100] *Anatomy of Melancholy*, Pt. I, Sect. ii, Member 1, subsec. 2. Burton cites the opinion that the aerial demons in question served magicians like James and Jambres and Simon Magus. According to the polemic of the earlier church fathers, the demons were a fertile source of error. With Archimago's activity, one may compare Minucius Felix, *Octavius*, xxvi: "The Magi, also, not only know that there are demons, but, moreover, whatever miracle they affect to perform, do it by means of demons; by their aspirations and communications they show their wondrous tricks, making either those things appear which are not, or those things not to appear which are." The same who lurk under consecrated statues and images, we learn in the next chapter, also "render slumber unquiet; creeping also secretly into human bodies," they "alarm the minds" of the ignorant. (Trans. in ANF, vol. 4, pp. 189f.) For manifestly the same opinion concerning devil-worship, see Hooker, *Laws of Ecclesiastical Polity*, I.iv.

gregation is not mine, which hath not my words. No longer is it my church, than it hath my verity.[101]

I have more or less identified the creation of the false Una by Archimago—"that new creature borne without her dew" (I.i.46; cf. "due" at I.iii.2)—with the origin of Duessa. This is precisely what Spenser refrains from doing, and what the novice Redcrosse, lacking a structure of analogy, cannot do. A comparison of Fradubio's account of Duessa's dealings with his love Fraelissa supports our inference, however, for Fradubio describes an analogous process of doubts, falsified appearances, confusing comparisons, slander, and magic arts. Once Redcrosse is of two minds about Una, Duessa is brought into existence; to doubt is literally to go two ways—*dubitare*.

The double first appears in Redcrosse's "diverse dream," and Archimago's intention is to divide his guests into "double parts," two ladies and two knights, he himself taking the part of the facsimilar, imaginary Redcrosse. Thus when the spright explains her subjection to Cupid, her double-talk almost declares her name as well as her nature:

> Yet thus perforce he bids me do, or die.
> Die is my dew: yet rew my wretched state
> You, . . .[102]
>
> (I.i.51)

The counterfeit's accents are smoother, but still ambiguous, when she makes her profession of faith in the following canto:

> Now miserable I *Fidessa* dwell,
> Crauing of you in pitty of my state,
> To do none ill, if please ye not do well.
>
> (I.ii.26)

She sings a similar tune for Sansjoy:

> Ah deare *Sans ioy*, next dearest to *Sans foy*,
> Cause of my new griefe, cause of my new ioy,
> Ioyous to see his ymage in mine eye,
> And greeu'd to thinke how foe did him destroy,
>
> . . . .
>
> Lo his *Fidessa* to thy secret faith I flye.
>
> (I.iv.45)

---

[101] *The Image of Both Churches*, in Parker Society *Select Works*, pp. 274f. George Joye, in *The Unite and Schisme of the Olde Chirche* (STC 14380; 1543), fol. iii[v], likewise speaks of the unity of the faith being divided by "mens dreamed rites / superstitious ceremonies / troublous tradicions."

[102] These lines are quoted to approximately the same effect in Frye, *Anatomy of Criticism*, p. 261.

Always there are the puns on her name, and the ambiguities of *I* and *you*: Sansjoy pledges her that he will "with *Sans-foyes* dead dowry you endew":

> Ay me, that is double death (she said)
> With proud foes sight my sorrow to renew:
> Where euer yet I be, my secrete aid
> Shall follow you. . . .

(I.iv.51)

Finally there is her revelation—if that is possible—to her grandmother Night (for she was created in the night, like the *pseudes logous* of Hesiod's *Theogony* 228):

> I that do seeme not I, *Duessa* am,
> (Quoth she) how euer now in garments gilt,
> And gorgeous gold, arrayd I to thee came:
> *Duessa* I, . . .

(I.v.26)

With the siren in the second dream of the *Purgatorio* (XIX.1–36), Duessa stammers at the start, but then she seems to sing.

If our reading of the first canto is correct, Duessa originates in a hiatus analogous to the "phantasma" or "hideous dream" that, in the mind of Shakespeare's Brutus, intervenes between first motions and their ultimate issue (*J. C.*, II.i.61–69). Considered overall, there is also much in *The Faerie Queene* to connect Duessa with the processes of fiction, and especially the secondariness of an imitative production; we note her return at the opening of Book II, for example. Redcrosse, in biblical parlance, ought to "cleave" unto the truth, and hold fast to that which is good. But in fact his dream saddles him with a fiction, especially if, following the rhetorician Theon's explanation of myth or fable, we define fiction as a *pseudo-logos* imaging the truth. In the context of truth, such a fiction is also faction, and Duessa eventually shows the "uneven paw," or unevenly cloven hoof, which belongs to an unholy or divisive nature (cf. Deut. 14:6).

From the dream onwards, the knight's grasp on truth becomes like ours, fitful and proximate. He shortly meets Fradubio, who knows better only by having known worse. With Fradubio, he has fallen into the conditions of ordinary experience, where subject is divided from object, "I" from "you," and where knowing good and evil means knowing good lost and evil got. As Blake might say, commenting on the relation of Eve and Lilith, Duessa is a *cloven* fiction.

Una has gone about her father's business, and sought a champion. The false Una gets this backwards; she tells Redcrosse, "Your owne deare sake forst me at first to leave / My Fathers kingdome" (I.i.52). Such flattery—the kind that Milton's Eve will use with Adam—confuses the quest, and also the quester,

> Much grieu'd to thinke that gentle Dame so light,
> For whose defence he was to shed his blood.
>
> (I.i.55)

Redcrosse's mind is now prepared to abandon so apparently dishonest a love, and after a final nocturnal vision of Una's infidelity, they are "divorced," like God and Israel (I.iii.2, Jer. 3:1–10, Hos. 2:2), or Joseph and Mary (Mt. 1:19; cf. Isa. 50:1).

Our trust in ourselves is originally based on our trust in those who have cared for us, but for the moment the faithful knight is on his own. He is even a little beside himself, "Still flying from his thoughts and jealous fear" (I.ii.12). Although his flight may seem to get his quest started, it really reverses its proper direction, and signals a desertion of his true calling. An act of bad faith is involved. The knight wills not to know the truth: that he can entertain unworthy thoughts about the fidelity of Una. The falling Adam also retreated from self-knowledge: "he fell of his own accord into the darkness of sin, because he deserted the light of truth, he concealed himself as it were in the night of error."[103] God asked where Adam was, not because he did not know, but because Adam himself did not want to know. God's question was rhetorical:

> For Divine Power was not ignorant to what hiding place His servant had fled after his offence, but for that He saw that he, having fallen in his sin, was now as it were hidden under sin from the eyes of Truth, in that He approves not the darkness of his error. . . .

It is not unlikely that Redcrosse, in this state of mind, should suddenly have to do battle with the Saracen Sansfoy, for his own faith is alienated and threatened. Such intrusive characters may be understood as providing a critique of that self-ignorance whereby we encounter in the objective world a part of ourselves that we do not properly know, or will not willingly face.

Nonetheless, Redcrosse's victory over the challenger indicates that something in the knight has survived whole enough to be called "self-confidence." And yet his trust is immediately reposed in a treacherous caretaker. Redcrosse has been willful, and willfulness is a self-imposed narrowness, an assumed self-confidence that becomes joyless, blind, and exaggerated. Out of his willfulness develop the episodes of the House of Pride and Orgoglio's dungeon.

---

[103] Gregory the Great, *Morals on the Book of Job*, XXXV.xvi.43, in the trans. of The Library of the Fathers, vols. 18, 21, 23, and 31 (Oxford, 1844–1850), vol. 3 (in 2 parts), p. 693.

With this background in the opening cantos, we are in a position to broach the psychological archetypes for the legend of faith. Redcrosse's quest is ultimately directed toward communion with an innocent paradise, which is also a promised land flowing with milk and honey. Parental archetypes, in the form of Adam and Eve, are near at hand. More important are a comforting Mother Church and a providential Father God, and of course the Church is typologically a second Eve.[104] The House of Holiness has this parental function, and so does the rescue provided by Una and Arthur. Redcrosse is frequently in the care of loving females— Una, Fidelia, and the supposedly devoted Fidessa—and his dependency on sacramental ministrations is stressed. The threats to these relations of trust and promise are the delusion and betrayal we have been discussing; Archimago's words and Duessa's paralyzing potions are apt representations of its oral character. Significant and reliable speech belongs to the analogy. The untrustworthy speech of Despair is another such threat; Sansjoy, representing the loss of Christan cheer or the long-facedness of the Pharisee (see Mark 6:50, etc.), is a related danger. (Sansjoy is not so much a sibling, as a sibling *rival*—for the nocturnal attentions of the widowed mother-figure.) The knight's first encounter is with Error, a monstrous dam with a demonic brood at her dugs. Her disgorging of books and papers suggests a bad case of indigestion, and her loathed embrace may be contrasted with the part taken by Charissa. The latter is a Protestant madonna figure at the House of Holiness; she nurses infant souls, presumably on the sincere milk of the Word (I Peter 2:2; see I Cor. 3:1–3; also Bar. 4:8 and Rev. 12:1f.). Charissa's relation to Mercy may be

---

[104] I am applying Erik Erikson, *Childhood and Society*, 2nd edn. (New York, 1963), pp. 247–251. For the first notice of the Church as Eve, apart from the deductions to be made from Eph. 5:23–32, I Cor. 6:15f. and Gen. 2:4, and II Cor. 11:3, see the Second Epistle of Clement 14, which is cited for this identification in Peter Martyr, *Comm. In Primum Librum Mosis*, cap. ii (Heidelberg, 1606), p. 12ʳ. See nn. 250f., below. For a summary of the parental archetypes suggested here, cf. John Bradford, "Conferance with Harpsfield," in *The Writings*, ed. Aubrey Townsend, Parker Society (Cambridge, 1848), vol. 1, p. 503: " 'We agree that by baptism then we are brought, and, as one would say, begotten of Christ; for Christ is our Father, and the church his spouse is our mother. As all men naturally have Adam for their father and Eve for their mother, so all spiritual men have Christ for their father and the Church for their mother; which church, as Eve was taken out of Adam's side, so was she out of Christ's side. . . .' " For the link of "trust" and "nurture," see *F.Q.* V.v.53. For the "Church maternal," see Bullinger, *Decades*, III, Sermon VIII, *edn. cit.*, vol. 2, p. 297: ". . . our mother Sara gendereth us unto liberty. She is the mother of us all. Of that mother (which is also called the holy mother church) we have the seed of life: she hath fashioned us, and brought us forth into the light; she calleth us in her bosom, wherein she carrieth both milk and meat, (I mean the word of God,) to nourish, save, and bring us up."

compared to Ruth's relation to Naomi, who takes over the nursing of Ruth's child; the stepdame to whose care Redcrosse is entrusted is described as a "carefull Nourse" (I.x.35). The Hebrew word for fidelity and truth (*'em*) anciently meant the carrying or support of a suckling child (cf. Ruth 4:16). Being untruthful, Duessa possesses breasts as "rough as maple rind": the detail is not gratuitous. Spenser's other maple, in the wood of Error, is "seeldom inward sound" (I.viii.47, i.9).

The Advent of the Word

So for the first thing, the knight will have power to concentrate the whole content of life and the whole significance of reality into one single wish. If a man lacks this concentration, this intensity, if his soul from the beginning is dispersed in the multifarious, he never comes to the point of making the movement; . . . In the next place the knight will have the power to concentrate the whole result of the operations of thought into one act of consciousness. If he lacks this intensity, if his soul from the beginning is dispersed in the multifarious, he will never get time to make the movements, he will be constantly running errands in life, never into eternity, for even at the instant when he is closest to it he will suddenly discover that he has forgotten something for which he must go back.
(Søren Kierkegaard in *Fear and Trembling*, on the Knight of Faith; trans. Walter Lowrie)

[i]

Let us put ourselves on the threshold of fairyland. Like Alice passing through the looking-glass, we enter a speculative world where the vegetation speaks and an elaborate heraldic symbolism of red and white hovers over the action. A champion appears, precipitously engages a monster, and is suddenly swamped with its disgorge of unintelligible books and papers. When we first come to this poem, we may not have had much training in the looking-glass language of allegory; but with a little reflection we probably know what Alice did when she held the Jabberwocky poem up to the mirror: *somebody* killed *something*. The accompanying drawing of the battle in the tulgey wood allows us to form at least a picture; a study of Spenser's imagery illustrates his primal dragon-slaying too.

The critic Vida, in his *Art of Poetry*, advises the poet to begin with something that contains the poem in little: "Before the entrance-court itself, and on the threshold, the prudent make an offering of the principle elements of things and touch lightly, in economical verses, the things which it has been decided to sing."[105] The advice differs somewhat from that of Vida's mentor Horace, even if it does not mean, as Pitt's translation seems to suggest, that the opening of the poem should contain the entire action in miniature.[106] Spenser does employ the symbol of the threshold, a threshold peculiar to the theme of knight errantry. When, after becoming the Knight of the Lion, Don Quixote describes his vocation, he begins his summary, "The knight-errant searches all the corners of the world; he enters upon the most intricate labyrinths. . . ." (Pt. II, chap. xvii). Following Vida and Pitt, one may also say that the episode of Error contains, *in ovo*, the whole theme of the emergence of a dragon-slayer—a Theseus who penetrates the labyrinth and kills a monster, a Perseus armed with shining armor, and an Apollo who signalizes his advent by killing Python.[107]

The metaphors of the wood of Error—the wilderness and the way—hardly require illustration. It is scarcely possible to imagine even the most restricted vocabulary of figurative speech without them. In his *Vewe* (2661f.) Spenser says that the Irish priests and their people "shall all dye in their sinnes for they haue erred and gone out of the waye togeather," a fairly close echo of Romans 3:12 (cf. Exodus 32:8); like Redcrosse and Una,

> They cannot finde that path, which first was showne
> But wander too and fro in wayes vnknowne,
>
> (I.i.10)

Wisdom 5:6–7 has a good example:

> Therefore we haue erred from the waye of trueth, and the light of righteousnes hathe not shined vnto us, and the sunne of vnderstanding rose not vpon us.
> We haue wearied our selues in the waye of wickednes and destruction,

---

[105] *Vida's Art of Poetry*, II.17–20, in A. S. Cook, ed., *The Art of Poetry* (New York, 1926), p. 78.

[106] Horace, *De Arte Poetica* (*Epist.* II.iii, ad Pisones) 143–152. Compare the advice of Scaliger, *Poetices*, III.xcv (edn. of Heidelberg, 1617), p. 331: the poet should begin with something grand, cognate with the theme and intimately related to it.

[107] With what follows, compare William Dunbar, *On the Resurrection of Christ* ("Done is a battell on the dragon black"):

> On loft is gone the glorious Appollo,
> The blisfull day depairtit fro the nycht: . . .
> The grit victour agane is rissin on hicht,
> That for our querrell to the deth was woundit;
> The sone that wox all paill now schynis bricht,
> And dirknes clerit, our fayth is now refoundit; . . .
> The Jowis and their errour ar confoundit: . . .

and we haue gone through dangerous waies: but we haue not knowen
the way of the Lord.

(Geneva Bible)

The most terrible vision of this kind is perhaps in Bunyan, and is based
on Proverbs 21:16 ("The man that wandereth out of the way of understanding shall remain in the congregation of the dead"). Bunyan's pilgrims are shown the blinded victims of giant Despair, wandering and
stumbling among the tombs at the foot of the hill called Error. The messianic hope is associated with the building of a highway through the
wilderness (Isa. 35:7-8, etc.), and the fulfilling of this prophecy is announced by John, who makes straight the way of the Lord in the wilderness (John 1:23). Redcrosse's armour makes only "A little glooming light"
as he enters the cave; the Precursor is also a lesser light (John 5:35), a candle or lamp. (The light is "vncouth," however, because "the world knew
him not"; John 1:10; I.i.15.)

Spenser specifically calls his wood a "labyrinth" (I.i.11), signifying, according to Comes, "the life of man to be full of perplexity, *multisque diffi-
cultatibus implicatam*, and from which no man can extricate himself except through singular prudence and fortitude."[108] Virgil describes the
labyrinth as having "a path woven with blind walks," and as "a bewildering work of craft with a thousand ways where the tokens of the
course were confused by the indiscoverable and irretraceable maze"—
"inremeabilis error" (*Aen.* V.589-591). The entrance to the Sibyl's cave
also portrays the "dolos . . . ambagesque" of the labyrinth—"inextricabilis
error" (VI.27). The possibility of a threshold symbol here is hard to miss,
and the Sibyl herself "horrendas canit *ambages* . . . obscuris vera involens"

---

[108] Comes, *Mythol.* VII.ix; *edn. cit.*, p. 734. A labyrinth may be usefully defined
here as a wandering in a fixed pattern or place. The "perplexed circle" of Henry
King's "The Labyrinth" appears in marine form in the "circled waters" which enter
into the "wide *Labyrinth*" of Spenser's Whirlepoole of decay (II.xii.20). For another
labyrinth of error, see Guillaume de Deguilleville, *Pilgrimage of the Life of Man*,
as Englished by John Lydgate, ed. F. J. Furnivall, EETS, 2 parts in 2 vols. (London,
1899-1904), vol. 2, p. 459. For an exposition to which my essay is partly indebted,
see John Steadman, "Spenser's Errour and the Renaissance Allegorical Tradition,"
Neuphilogische Mitteilungen, 62 (1961), pp. 22-38. The interpretation of life's journey as a labyrinth may have been at least twice monumentalized, according to the
evidence in W. H. Matthews' chapter on church labyrinths, in his *Mazes and
Labyrinths* (London, 1922): p. 57, Sans Savino at Piacenza; p. 68, inscription at
Lyons Museum. The first describes the labyrinth as broad at the entrance, but narrow
at the exit, when the doctrine of life can be regained only with difficulty. One name
for a labyrinth, "chemin de Jérusalem," has given rise to the speculation that the
goal of the possibly penetential journey through the maze was the heavenly city
(Matthews, *Mazes and Labyrinths*, pp. 60, 66-68). The cover design for Angus
Fletcher's *Prophetic Moment* (Chicago, 1971) implies as much. See the same book,
pp. 24 and 32n, for the life-labyrinth trope in King and Seldon's notes to Drayton.

(sings dread enigmas . . . wrapping truth in darkness [VI.99-100]). Servius refers to the phrase "inextricabilis error" (*ad Aen.* II.48) to explain the meaning of *dolon* in the warning speech of Laocoön. The Laocoön posture is Redcrosse's at I.i.18; he is the struggling victim of a "serpens amplexus," almost strangled, and engulfed in a black poison. The posture is also implied for Zeus in a battle with Typhon described in Apollodorus, where the monster coils around Zeus before dragging him into a cave. The story insists upon a connection with Delphos, and hence with the Python.[109] The Python-Typhon link proves crucial in connecting Spenser's imagery to Spenser's myth.

That Error is specifically a "wandering *wood*" the poet probably has on good authority. In his commentary on Ariosto's fourth canto, Harington is aware of "that wandering wood" of Dante and Petrarch. We might refer here to Petrarch's fifty-fourth sonnet ("How many steps lost in the wood alas"), as it is cited in a Renaissance commentary on Dante's first canto. (*Canzonieri* CCIV describes love as "an endless erring through a blind labyrinth," and wilderness imagery figures prominently in CCCLX, stanza 4.) The commentary, Vellutello's, describes Dante's wood as the "selva erronea di quest vita," "una selva di spessi error," and "selva di errori."[110] The wood is also "materia corporea"—"this wood is dark because all error always proceeds from ignorance and blindness of mind."[111] These Platonizing allegories are also found in Fornari's commentary on the various forests of Ariosto. Fornari refers to Dante's wood of life as a place where Diana hunts for moral virtue, as the dark cavern of our mortal body, and as the darkness of ignorance and the obfuscation of corrupt appetites.[112] Most of these interpretations stem from Servius' comment on Virgil's *silva* in *Aeneid* I.314, an allegory that, as William Nelson shows, appears in Renaissance Virgils.[113] At the juncture between medieval and Renaissance, Petrarch, in the letter earlier cited, writes of the opening of the *Aeneid*:

> The wood is truly this life, full of shadows and errors, tangled and uncertain paths, and inhabited by beasts; that is, difficulties and many secret dangers—sterile and inhospitable—and yet there is beautiful vegetation

[109] Apollodorus, *Bibl.* I.vi.3. For the ancient Python-Typhon links, see Joseph Fontenrose, *Python* (Berkeley, 1959), pp. 70-93. In the Homeric *Hymn to Apollo*, 354ff., Typhaon is said to have been raised by the Delphic dragoness; in Statius, *Thebiad* I.563, Python ringed Delphi with his coils.

[110] *Dante con l'espositione di Christoforo Landino et di Allesandro Vellvtello* (Venice, 1964), Sig. A2ᵛ. "Selva erronea" is taken from Dante's *Convivio*, IV.24. For Ariosto and Horace, see Chap. I, n. 32 and text.

[111] *Dante con l'espositione, loc. cit.*

[112] *La Spositione di M. Simon Fornari . . . sopra l'Orlando fvrioso* (Florence, 1549-1550), 2 vols. in one, vol. 1, pp. 94, 182; vol. 2, p. 256.

[113] William Nelson, *The Poetry of Edmund Spenser* (New York, 1963), pp. 158-160.

and birdsong and murmuring of waters; that is, brief and transitory appearances, and empty charms of things for the eyes and ears of the traveler and the dwellers nearby. By day it is assuaging and caressing, at nightfall dreadful and frightening; and with the advent of winter, a foul mud, a covered sun, a horrid trunk, and stripped branches.[114]

Spenser's catalogue of trees can also be taken to represent the ambiguous variety of the world, as yet a world of only potential moral significances. Thus "The Mirrhe sweete bleeding in the bitter wound" might be retrospectively connected with the sacrifice of the dying god: Fradubio, or Adonis, or Redcrosse himself, who lies beneath the balm-dripping tree of the eleventh canto. Inscrutably, the "obedient" yew contrasts with the maple, "seeldom inward sound" (I.i.9).

The romantic Redcrosse, unlike the epic woodsmen in the *Aeneid* (VI.179f.) and *Gerusalemme Liberata* (III.75) is not here to fell trees, but rather dragons.[115] This of course was a highly allegorized occupation. The *Variorum* cites Lydgate's Christological treatment of St. George;[116] there is also the *Prayer* of Richard Vennar for her majesty's forces, where the princess is the Church.[117] Stephanus' *Dictionary*, s.v. *Georgius*, states that "some theologians adjudge the name to be a fiction, under which the elders set forth the image of Christ delivering the Church from Satan, and the service (*meritum*) of the Passion." If we don't believe the story, says Raleigh in his *History* (II.vii.5), we may treat it as allegorical of Christ. The same observation extends to pagan dragon-slaying myths. Drayton, in his notes to the fourth Song of *Poly-Olbion*, explains that St. George saved the king's daughter "as Hesione and Andromeda were delivered from whales by Hercules and Perseus":

> Your more neat judgments, finding no such matter in true antiquity, rather make it symbolical that truly proper. So that some account him an allegory of our Saviour Christ; and our admired Spenser hath made him

[114] *Francisci Petrarcae . . . Opera quas extant omnia . . .* (Basel, 1581), p. 869. See Chap. I, n. 65, above.

[115] Cf. Chap. I, n. 40, above.

[116] *The Works of Edmund Spenser: A Variorum Edition*, ed. Edwin Greenlaw, Charles Osgood, Frederick Padelford, and Ray Heffner (Baltimore, 1932–1949), *Book I*, pp. 386–389, where Lydgate's poem is discussed by Padelford and Matthew O'Connor. For the poem, see *Minor Poems of John Lydgate*, ed. Henry MacCracken, EETS, Extra Series, no. 107 (London, 1911), pp. 145–154: George's name means knight and holiness, he vanquishes the world and the flesh, he ventures out to magnify the faith, he kills the dragon, and builds the church.

[117] For Vennar's poem, see Elkin Calhoun Wilson, *England's Eliza* (Cambridge, Mass., 1939), p. 186 (cited from Nichols, *Pageants and Progresses*, vol. 3, pp. 541f.), "A Prayer for the prosperous success of her Majestie's Forces in Ireland." Vennar's knight departs bearing his Saviour's badge within his breast.

an emblem of religion. . . . Others interpret that picture of him as some country or city (signified by the virgin) imploring his aid against the devil, charactered in the dragon.[118]

Madeleine Doran, describing the method of the *Bible of the Poets*, mentions that Cadmus may be either a wise philosopher who conquers the dragon of study to win the fountain of philosophy, or the son of God in the armor of our fragility, fighting the serpent and freeing his fellows; the fountain may be the water of life sought by the patriarchs and prophets through the forest of the world.[119] As late as Ross's handbook, *Mystagogus Poeticus* (1647), Cadmus' well is the clear fountain of God's word polluted by the dragon.[120] The prose *Ovid Moralisé* explains Perseus as Christ, Andromeda as Eve, the sea-monster as the gulf of hell, the espoused bride as Holy Church, and the marriage feast as paradise.[121] This is naturally rather close to the allegory of Spenser's Saint George, since St. George is the Christian Perseus.

The Messiah will tread on the serpent's head, as a second Adam, conformable to Psalm 91:13, "Conculcabis leonem et draconem," which is the motto for Vennar's poem. In the messianic age the sucking child will be able to play on the hole of the asp, and the weaned child shall put his hand on the adder's den. Redcrosse, the "youthfull knight," advances intrepidly to the "darksome hole" of the monster, and although the anxious mother of the final canto is unwilling to let her babe go quite so far, the purport is essentially the same (I.i.14, xii.11).

In Mantuan's Latin *Life of St. George*, the dragon is compared to Python, and also to the Hydra;[122] Spenser's dragon is also a water-monster

---

[118] Text taken from Alexander Chalmers, ed., *The Works of the English Poets* (London, 1810), *vol. IV: Drayton, Warner*, p. 204. Cf. Bale, *The first two partes of the Actes . . . of the Englysh Votaryes* (1551), fol. 77ᵛ, where Bale urges Edward VI to be a Josias: "As great honour wyl it now be to you (yea, rather much greater) to flee the sede of the Serpent by the worde of God, as euer it was Saynt George the noble captayne, to slee ye great hydre or Dragon at Silena, as Baptists Mantuanus specifieth. I speake not thys for that I wold ye to fal upon that forte with materiall weapon, but with the myghtye stronge word of the Lorde."

[119] "Some Renaissance 'Ovids,' " in Bernice Slate, ed., *Literature and Society*.

[120] Alexander Ross, *Mystagogus Poeticus or The Muses Interpreter*, 2nd edn. (London, 1648), *sub* "Cadmus."

[121] *Ovid moralisé en prose (texte du quinzième siècle)*, ed. C. de Boer, Verhandelingen de Koninklijke Nederlandse Academie, 61 (Amsterdam, 1955), p. 168.

[122] The dragon fight from Mantuan's Latin *Life* is translated in the Spenser Variorum, *Book I*, pp. 381–385. The Latin may be found in the marginal apparatus of William Nelson's edn. of Alexander Barclay's *The Life of St. George*, EETS, no. 230 (Oxford, 1960); see p. 30 (*hydra*; "deedly monster of Lerna," l. 520), p. 36 (*pythone*), and p. 32 for the analogy with the Minotaur slain by Theseus (ll. 575–578).

(I.vii.44); Duessa's beast is Hydra-like (I.vii.17) as well as leviathanic. The Hebrew word for *draconem* (and for the adder in Isaiah 11:8) is *pethen*, and Stephanus' *Dictionary*, under Python, says that the name of Apollo's enemy seems to be derived from the Hebrew word. Stephanus then goes on to say that the Hebrew word has a cognate, *patha*, "i.e., persuasit, illexit, decepit": "however, when the Sun with his rays . . . removes the dark cloud, Apollo is said to have killed Python with arrows." The various physical effects of the sun provide the usual explanation for the death of the Python, and there is some basis for this idea in both the Homeric *Hymn to Apollo* and Ovid's version of the story in the first book of the *Metamorphoses*. Like the Hebrew word, however, the Greek word is linked to a word meaning "induce" or "persuade," *peitho*. The *Mytologiarum* of sage Fulgentius would seem to be the source of this idea. There the name of the dragon is explained as "credulitas": ". . . the manifestation of his [Apollo's] rays breaks through all the darkness of doubt. . . . And because all false belief, as serpents, is put down by manifest light, they say he killed Python."[123] The identification of the most intellectual of the Greek gods with truth is not uncommon in medieval treatments; it can be found, for example, in St. Augustine.[124] Boccaccio explains that augury pertains to Apollo, and that Albericus (or the Third Vatican Mythographer) says that Apollo killed Python, "because Python is interpreted *fidem auferens*, which infliction on faith is done away with, since he is reckoned the clarity of truth, because it is brought about through the light of the sun."[125] Comes asks, "Quid enim veritatem magis aperit quam Sol, & omnem tenebrarum caliginem ex humanis rebus dispescit?"[126] The commentary of Lavinius on the first book of a standard Renaissance Ovid is also in this vein:

[123] *Mitologiarum*, I.xvii, in R. Helm, ed., *Fvlgentivs. Opera* (Leipzig, 1898), p. 28.

[124] For a tabulation of the medieval tradition embodied in versions of the *Fulgentius metaforalis*, see Hans Liebeschütz, intro. to his edn. of *De deorum imaginibus libellus: Fulgentius Metaforalis, ein beitrag zur geschichte der antiken mythologie im mittelalter*, Studien der Bibliothek Warburg, no. 4 (Leipzig, 1926), pp. 56f.: the standard entry for Apollo is *veritas*. (In the version of Ridewall, printed here, an article on idolatry has been substituted; Robert Holcot's *Moralitates* are reported to conform to the Apollo-veritas tradition.) Augustine, *De Ordine*, I.iv.10 (PL, XXXII, 982f.), identifies the "other" of the Apollo of *Aen.* X.875 as "Truth itself, whose prophets are all those who can be wise." Erasmus invokes Christ as the Apollo or Pytho who makes truth manifest, at the conclusion to his preface to his translation of the New Testament, *Paraclesis*.

[125] Boccaccio, *G.D.G.*, V.iii, Romano edn., vol. 1, p. 238, referring to Mythographus III, George H. Bode, ed., *Scriptores rerum mythicarum latini* (Cellis, 1834), III.8.1, p. 200.

[126] *Mythol.*, IV.x; *edn. cit.*, p. 361. (Comes reports the oracle-giving function of the Delphic serpent at pp. 348f.)

. . . Python is interpreted *fidem auferens*, which deprivation of faith is now abolished. To which clearness of distinctions is referred, because it is effected by the light of the Sun. And the Sun of wisdom is God: because he illuminates by means of his living light and even represents it for the wise. In an allegorical sense Apollo signifies Christ the Sun of justice. . . .[127]

Sandy's Ovid, in the seventeenth century, recognizes this tradition, and in the essays of the 1632 edition, which follow each book, the physical allegory is followed by: "so serpentine Error by the light of truth is confounded. The Spirit which inspired the Priests of *Apollo* was called Pytho, as they themselves Pythonists."[128]

The Protestant reading of the twenty-fourth chapter of Matthew maintains that the chosen will be brought into error.[129] In the wood of Error, Redcrosse is tested and blooded. A. C. Hamilton gives an apt parallel from Ecclesiasticus (4:17-19), describing Wisdom trying her devotee in "crooked ways," and then, having proved him, returning him to the straight way with comforting knowledge.[130] Una herself seems to cite Ecclesiasticus 21:22-23: "The foot of a fool is quick to enter a house, But an experienced man waits respectfully before it":

> Yet wisedom warnes, whilst foot is in the gate,
> To stay the steppe, ere forced to retrate.
>
> (I.i.13)

[127] *P. Ovidij Nasonis . . . Metamorphoseos . . . Petri Lauinii Commentarii*, ed. Raphael Regius (Venice, 1540), pp. XXᵛ–XXIᵛ (Sigs. C4ᵛ–C5ᵛ). Similarly in "Walleys," *Metamorphoses Ovidiana Moraliter* (Paris, 1515), fol. VIᵛ and VIIᵛ. (This text is the fifteenth book of Pierre Bersuire's *Reductorium Morale*.) See also the 2nd Vatican Mythographer, in Bode, *Scriptores rerum mythicarum latini*, II.20, p. 81. Luther objected to monks who turned Christ into Apollo (in *Commentary on Genesis* 30:9), but Jean De Sponde, in the "Prolegomena" to his edition of *Homeri qvae extant omnia* (Basel, 1583), I, prol., p. 28, says that the killing of Python by Apollo with arrows describes the future combat of the second person of the Trinity with the prince of the world, since the sun is allegorically accepted for the Son of God.
[128] *Edn. cit.*, p. 34. For the same Apollo-myth, without any actual mention of the pagan god, cf. Gregory, *Moralia*, XXXIII.xxix.51, on the invulnerability of Job's Leviathan: "In like manner the whole body of the devil, that is, the multitude of the reprobates, when reproved for its iniquity, endeavours to excuse itself with whatever evasions it can, and opposes, as it were some scales of defence, that it may not be transfixed with the arrow of truth. For whoever, when reproved, seeks to excuse rather than lament his sin, is covered, as it were, with scales, when assailed by holy preachers with the sword of the word." (Library of the Fathers trans., vol. 3, p. 604.)
[129] For this theme at length, see below, "Errant Damozell: The Church in the Wilderness," sec. iv. Babylon, or Avignon, is the "mother of Error" in Petrarch's Son. 91, and Rome is now the "school of error" in his Son. 107.
[130] *The Structure of Allegory in "The Fairie Queene"* (Oxford, 1961), p. 35.

Of man's search for wisdom through history, Hooker translates Lactantius to the following effect:

> . . . God did not suffer him being desirous of the light of wisdom to stray any longer up and down, and with bootless expense of travel to wander in the darkness that had no passage to get out by. His eyes at length God did open, and bestow upon him the knowledge of the truth by way of Donative, to the end that man might both be clearly convicted of folly, and being through error out of the way, have the path that leadeth unto immortality laid plain before him.[131]

We may conclude that in his descent into the dark Redcrosse is accompanied by Wisdom, like the dreamer Joseph in Wisdom 10:13-14; the text anticipates future developments:

> When the righteous was solde she forsoke him not, but delieuered him from sinne; she went down with him into the dongeon,
> And failed him not in the bandes, til she had broght him the sceptre of the realme, and power against those who had oppressed him, and them that had accused him, she declared to be liers, and gaue him perpetual glorie.
>
> (Geneva Bible)

Una accomplishes no less.

We are now in a position to see the whole pattern. Redcrosse is one of the "sonnes of Day" (I.v.25), and his victories are associated with the rising sun. His "sun-bright arms" are also linked with the bridegroom-sun of Psalm 19:5 (I.v.2), a passage traditionally applied to the coming of the "dayspring" of Luke 1:58. "Ruddy Phoebus" is only lightly mentioned in the opening episode (I.i.23), and initially Redcrosse's "Armorie" makes only "A little glooming light," at least while Error is alive. The connections of the monster with Python seem more distinct. One may compare Ovid's passage on the receding of the flood from which Python is engendered, particularly the stanza about the Nile mud (I.i.21, cf. *Metam.* I.416-36). In an account of a Renaissance masque, published a year before the opening installment of Spenser's poem, a description of the slaying of Python has a descending Apollo attack her lair in the middle of dark wood: "a great quantity of blood poured out, filthy and black, which appears besmudged with ink [*inchiostra*]."[132] We are not likely to come much closer to the effusions of Error, "a floud of poyson

---

[131] *Laws of Ecclesiastical Polity*, I.xi.5, Everyman's Library, vol. 1, p. 207, quoting Lactantius, *Div. Instit.*, I.1; the relevant phrases in the Latin are: "aberrare . . . vagari per tenebras inextricabiles. . . . erranti ac vago viam."

[132] Bastiano De'Rossi, *Descrizione dell'Alparato e degl'Intermedi* . . . (Florence, 1589), p. 42.

horrible and blacke," "spawne . . . blacke as inke," "A streame of cole black bloud" (I.i.20, 22, 24). Most important is Python's association with Apollo's oracle at Delphi, where the priestess was of course the pythoness. According to the usual account, Apollo's first act—on behalf of his mother, whom Python was sent to oppress—is the establishment of this oracle. In one account the intrepid hero dares to follow the monster into the shrine, and dispatches it beside the holy chasm.[133] Thus the death of Python is attached to the advent-myth of Apollo, as the ceasing of the pagan oracles is attached to the birth of Christ.

Such a comparison might have been quickly understood in the Renaissance. Ficino's version of the myth, with the appropriate Christianizing overtones, is from *De Sole*:

> In the same way divine light shines even in the darkness of the soul, although the darkness does not understand it. . . .
>
> Thus the Sun illuminates instantaneously those natures which are already pure, harmonious, and celestial; whereas those that are opaque and material, it warms first with light, enlightening and purifying them so that they can be illuminated. Having been made light and transparent by warmth and illumination, they are then lifted by the Sun and made sublime. It is in this manner that Apollo pierces, purifies, and breaks up the mass of Python with his arrows the rays.[134]

Without actually naming Apollo, Raleigh seems to fall into the same metaphors; he is writing about the destruction of Dagon, the Philistine fish-god, in the presence of the ark:

> And if this idol could not endure the representation of the true God, it is not to be marvelled, that at such time as it pleased him to cover his only begotten with flesh, and sent him into the world, that all the oracles wherein the devil derided and betrayed mortal men, lost power, speech, and operation at the instant. For, when that true light, which never had

---

[133] *Mythol.*, IV.x; *edn. cit.*, p. 348, citing Apollodorus, *Bibl.* I.iv.1.

[134] *De Sole*, ix, A. Fallico and H. Shapiro, eds. and trans., *Renaissance Philosophy: The Italians*, p. 131. See p. 130: "this light is that which Plato calls truth with respect to comprehensible things, and science with respect to the mind." Cf. Plutarch, *De defectu orac.* 42: "But I incline most to the opinion that the [prophet's] soul acquires toward the prophetic spirit a close and intimate connexion of the sort that vision has towards light, which possesses similar properties. For, although the eye has the power of vision, there is no function for it to perform without light; and so the prophetic power of the soul, like an eye, has need of something kindred to help kindle it and stimulate it further. Hence many among earlier generations regarded Apollo and the Sun as one and the same god; but those who understood and respected fair and wise analogy conjectured that as body is to soul, vision to intellect, and light to truth, so is the power of the sun to the nature of Apollo." (Trans. Frank Babbitt in Loeb *Moralia*, vol. 5, p. 475.)

beginning of brightness, brake through the clouds of a virgin's body, shining upon the earth, which had long been obscured by idolatry, all these foul and stinking vapours vanished.[135]

He goes on to cite Plutarch's story of the death of Pan. E. K. recounts that famous story from Lavater: "Yet I think it more properly meant of the death of Christ, the onely and very Pan, then suffering for his flock" (on l. 54 of "Maye").

Milton's famous invocation of the English dragon-slayer tends to support our reading. Near the end of *The Reason of Church Government*, he describes St. George's adventure against "that huge dragon of Egypt breathing out waste and desolation to the land." Milton's dragon is female; we are asked to consider "from what a mass of slime and mud, the slothful, the covetous, and ambitious hopes of church promotions and fat bishoprics, she is bred up and nuzzled in like a great Python from her youth, to prove the general poison both of doctrine and good discipline in the land":

> For certainly such hopes and such principles of earth as these wherein she welters from a young one, are the immediate generation both of a slavish and tyrannous life to follow and a pestiferous contagion to the whole kingdom, till like that fen-born serpent she be shot to death with the darts of the sun, the pure and powerful beams of God's word.

---

[135] *History*, II.xv.2. Text from Edinburgh edn. of 1820. That similar terms apply to the triumph of the English Reformation, quite humble poetic effusions can show us. For example, the victory of Elizabeth over the designs of Popery is the burden of James Aske's *Elizabetha triumphans* (London, 1588), where we read, on p. 3:

> The *Night* is gone, and now the Day appeares:
> The God of heaven, who knoweth euery thought, . . .
> The God of Gods, who is the morning *Starre*,
> Which giueth light in euery creatures heart,
> That God (I say) did see his [the Pope's] wickednesse,
> And seeing, would not let it longer last,
> For by the *Sunne, Elizabeth* our Queene,
> Whose vertues shine as bright as *Sol* it selfe,
> By that same *Sunne* the *Wolfe* is put to flight,
> And by that *Sunne* Gods flock doth liue in rest.
> From that bright *Sunne, Religion* hath her beames,
> Which lightens those who did in darkenesse sit:
> By that same *Sunne, Sinceritie* is plast,
> Where heeretofore *false Error* ruled Lord,
> Through that same *Sunne* Gods word is truly preacht,
> And by that *Sunne* all Popish reliques burnt.

The solar Elizabeth also appears in Sylvester's translation of DuBartas, where she emerges triumphant over *"the* Deluge *that* Rome's *Dragon spet"* (*Divine Weeks*, I.III, l. 653).

Redcrosse's mission in this opening canto resembles an attempt both to secure an oracle and to supplant one. Cicero associates the pythoness with the Sibyl (De Divinatione, I.xxxvi); the quest for the golden bough in Virgil's wood was proverbially a search for wisdom.[136] Cicero notes the decadence of the oracle, and the departure of Apollo's truth. One may compare the nether parts of Spenser's Error with the usual account of the Delphic priestess' inspiration, a subterraneous exhalation that entered her from beneath. Error's destruction may recall the solar allegory that derives Python from the word for putrefaction—Plutarch even offers a related physical allegory for the frogs, snakes, and water that he reports are to be found around her shrine.[137] The celebrated ambiguity of Apollo's oracles led Cornutus to derive the epithet Loxias ("spokesman of his father Zeus," as Aeschylus explains) from the word for crooked;[138] Spenser's wood is characterized by "diverse doubt" and "turnings," including the turning of the uncomprehending monster. Hence the redeemed counterpart for Error's books, steeped in ink, is Fidelia's sacred book, "with bloud ywrit, / That none could read, except she did them teach" (I.x.19). It follows that the choking of Error, and her disgorging, parody an oracular delivery of the Word.

Spenser intends the dragoness to remind us of his other dragons. The words of Una's "fearfull" dwarf—"Fly fly"—originally belonged to the fearful princess of the St. George legend, who warns the hero away from the vicinity of the dragon.[139] Spenser's dragons are otherwise referred to biblical apocalyptic, and the imagery of vomiting and bursting here may have a similar biblical basis. Typologically, Error anticipates the seven-

[136] For the mystery of the golden bough, see Servius, ad Aen. VI.137, where it represents the quest for virtue in a confused world. It represents wisdom, in Erasmus, De Copia, II, on fabulous examples (Op. om., Leiden, 1703-1706, Tomus I, p. 91D), and is so employed in the discourse of Erasmus' Folly. Nelson, Poetry of Edmund Spenser, p. 179, cites Palingenius' Zodiac of Life, in the facsimile edn. of 1576 edn. of Googe's trans. (New York, 1947), p. 87, for the same meaning.

[137] For the frogs, De Pythiae oraculis 12, Moralia 399F-400D (Loeb edn., vol. 5, pp. 288-293). For other examples of the physical allegory—Python's death as the sun's power over humidity—see Macrobius, Saturnalia, I.xvii.36, 57; Cartari, Imagini de gli Dei (Venice, 1625), p. 42; Giraldus, Hist. Deorum, Synt. VII, in Op. om., I, col. 230C-G. The epithet "Pythian" is also connected with "to inquire" (punthanesthai). For examples, see Plutarch De E 2, Moralia 385B; Macrobius, Saturnalia, I.xvii.50; Cornutus, De Natura Deorum 32 (in Gale, Opuscula Mythologica, p. 226); and Giraldus, Hist. Deorum, Synt. VII in Op. om., I, col. 230C-G. In the light of what has been said, we are not surprised to learn that the final portion of the road to Delphi was posted with statues of the sphinx.

[138] Cornutus, De Natura Deorum, "De Apolline et Diana," in Gale, Opuscula Mythologica, p. 226. Aeschylus, Eumen. 19.

[139] A useful account is still S. Baring-Gould, Curious Myths of the Middle Ages (Boston, 1880), "St. George," pp. 478ff. The poem of Lydgate has most of these details. The fearful dwarf is a notable feature of the Amadis de Gaula.

mouthed Nile monster of Book I (v.18), for at the time of the plagues the earth bred flies, and the river "vomited up [Vulgate *eructavit*] the multitude of frogs" (Wisdom 19:10; cf. the cycle in Exod. 8:5–14). In the story of Bel and the dragon, appended to Daniel, the Lord fulfills a prophecy made in Jeremiah 51:44: "I will also visite Bel in Babel and I will bring out of his mouth, that which he hathe swallowed vp." Fed lumps of hair, fat, and pitch by Daniel, the dragon of the Babylonian shrine explodes. In Revelation, the dragon of the thirteenth chapter sends a flood of water after the newly delivered mother, who corresponds to Leto in the Apollo-Python myth. Bale's commentary identifies this water as a poisonous outpouring of "a doctrine of hypocrisy, errors and lies." Bale adds that the carnal multitude drink up this filthy water—"erroneous doctrine."[140] C. S. Lewis mentions the vomiting of Philologia in the allegory of Martianus Capella, who disgorges an amazing variety of reading matter to prove her worthiness for a drink of immortality.[141] One may also cite the initiates of the *Table of Cebes*, who take, as it were, an antidote for their first drink, this time a potion called "error's purgation"; they must "vomit up all the evils that offended their minds."[142]

The death of Error is the birth of Truth, and Spenser's monster seems to perish like the emblematic "dying pelican," a sacrifice to her young.[143] If we regard the episode as an advent-myth, we might also expect links with the Apostolic Age and the preaching of the Gospel. The Protestant

---

[140] Bale, *Image of Both Churches*, in Parker Society *Select Works*, pp. 417f. Cf. George Joye, *The Unite and Schisme of the Olde Chirche* fol. viii^v–ix^r, on the generation of *echidna* in Matt. 12:34 and 23:33: "By these edders spirituall spume the way of trwthe and unite is blasphemed: nether ar ther liuing more pernicious pestilent enymes to the unite of the chirche and to the chrysten doctryne then this serpentyne sead out of whose mouthes continuallye the spightfull lothely names of heretiks and heresyes and new lerning ar forth vomited and out spewed into euery disshe upon their tables." For the bursting dragon, see also n. 217 and text.

[141] Martianus Capella, *De Nuptis*, II.136 (in the Dick edn., p. 59[5]ff.); C. S. Lewis, *Allegory of Love*, p. 80.

[142] Quotes taken from *Epictetus Manuall. Cebes Table . . .* , trans. Io. Healey (London, 1616), pp. 134f. I have also consulted *The table of Cebes the philosopher*, trans. by Sir F. Poyntz (London, 1530?). For the idea, compare Cornelius Agrippa, *On the Vanity of the Arts and Sciences*, sec. 102: "He created our souls, which are like rational trees, full of forms and ideas, though, through the sin of our parents, all things were concealed, and there ensued oblivion, the mother of ignorance. ¶ But you, wrapped up in the darkness of ignorance, can remove the veil from your understandings. Vomit up that Lethan drench which has made you drunk with forgetfulness! Awake in the true light, you that are drowned in the sleep of irrationality, and then, forthwith, with an open countenance, you shall pass from light to light." (Trans. A. Fallico and H. Shapiro, in *Renaissance Philosophy: Vol. II, The Transalpine Thinkers*, New York, 1970, p. 92.)

[143] Hence Error might well say of her books, "this is my blood of the Newe testament, that is shed for manie" (Matt. 26:28, Geneva Bible).

demonologist Lavater regularly links his subject with current manifestations in religion; the passage cited above on the degeneration of truth in the early church continues as follows:

> The like chaunced vnto the Gentiles in times past, as it appereth by the first chap. to the Romans, & also by their own writings. They worchipped many gods, many miracles were shewed amongst them; they had many visions of gods, and many oracles: which when ye Apostles began to preach, al cessed. S. Anasthasius in his booke "De Humanitate verbi" Fol. 55 & 64 writeth, that in auncient time ther were oracles at Delphos in Baeotia, Lycia, & other places whiche he nameth: but nowe since Chryste is preached euery where vnto all men, this madnesse hath ceassed &c. In the like manner writeth Lactantius and others. But in these our daies, since we haue refused mens traditions and willingly imbraced the doctrine of the Gospell, all appearings of Soules and Spirites haue vanished away.[144]

The power over pagan oracles is an apt symbol for the triumph of the Word, and in Acts 16:16–18 Paul in fact purges a possessed prophetess—in the Vulgate, "puellam . . . habentum spiritum pythonem." Spenser's episode ends with what appears to be an echo of Acts 1:18, suggesting that, here also, we are to understand a renewed infancy of the Church:

> Their bellies sowlne he saw with fulnesse burst,
> And bowels gushing forth: well worthy end
> Of such as drunke her life, the which them nurst;
>
> (I.i.26)

"His foes haue slaine themselues." All of the English translations agree in their rendering of the fate of Judas Iscariot, which explains the name of the Field of Blood: "he brast a sondre in the middes, and all his bowels gushed out." Of course, Redcrosse has yet to meet Archimago; but, as we have seen, the early church also had false prophets. One of these may be identified with the magician in Acts 8, Simon Magus.

The reader who is willing to accept that the mythographic tradition adduced here does indeed lie behind the episode of Error may still ask how the poem enlists this tradition. Being allegorical in mode, the poem can engage such materials rather disjunctively on occasion, but the relation in this case is particularly problematic. If the reader is surprised to learn that Redcrosse is an Apollo-figure at the very outset of his legend, he may reflect that Redcrosse would probably be no less surprised; we see the episode through the knight's eyes, and he is not very aware of who he is. One might compare his ignorance of his proper iconography with that

---

[144] *Of Ghostes*, ed. J. D. Wilson and May Sarton, pp. 182f.

148

of the speaker in Robert Frost's "The Road Not Taken." There the traveler stands in the place of Hercules at the Samian Y, making his momentous choice between the broad and narrow roads, which are traditionally the roads of Pleasure and Virtue. In explaining the material wood of *Aeneid* VI.136, Servius cites this Pythagorean Y, commending those "who have held the way after the *errorem sylvarum*, which leads to either vices or virtues" (*ad Aen.* VI.295). Redcrosse similarly makes the choices which the "wandering of the woods" compels. But in Frost's poem the choice is disguised; both roads are covered with leaves. And although the choice of "the road less traveled by" has made all the difference, it is not a difference that can be moralized—it may only entail a rueful sense of loss. Further, Frost implies that all roads diverge from themselves, and so the speaker, far from following truth wherever it may lead, might never really leave his latter-day wood of error.

If the mythography of Spenser's episode is also rather disguised, Spenser may be making a similar point. The path that led to Error—"that beaten seemd most bare"—is hard to distinguish from the path that leads away from it—"That path he kept, which beaten was most plaine" (I.i.11, 28). Either path might recall the broad way that leads into a labyrinth, and thence to destruction (Matt. 7:13); however, since Redcrosse will ultimately arrive in Eden, he must also be recovering the broad way that once led to immortality (II Esdras 7:11–14). The addition, that the knight "Ne euer would to any by-way bend," also indicates that he has "chosen the way of trueth" (Ps. 119:30), not deviating from that path lightened by the lantern of God's word, "which shineth in this darke world, which is full of errours" (so Lavater, *Of Ghostes, edn. cit.*, p. 198, on Ps. 119:105). And yet the likeness to that other way surely hints that Redcrosse will be led through many of these same errors. Not too differently, Redcrosse's identity is kept ambiguous here; it may only be "doubtfully construed," and in our interpretations of it, we must allow a margin for error.

By way of conclusion, the episode of Error can be reviewed under the aspects of our formal theory of allegory, in terms of Aristotle's six parts of poetry. The *mythos* of the episode is a story about the slaying of a dragon, the hero's legend being that of St. George, with mythical overtones of Perseus, Theseus, and Apollo. Error disgorges books, and the larger mythical outline shows something similar: the champion of the Word enters and emerges from the wood, its labyrinthine interior corresponding to the viscera of the monster, and its darkness failing to comprehend him. The *ethos* for the episode is the personification of Error as only half a person; the effect of an abstraction upon a character is suggested by Error's half-transformed form. The more condensed or "gnomic" personification of the beast and plant fable appears in the vestigial animation of the wandering wood (woods do not literally wander), and in the wary dwarf, who seconds Spenser's personification of Wisdom. (We have already mentioned the gnomic form of a book-eating dragon in the idea of a bookworm.) The *dianoia* for allegory is represented in this episode by the figure of "veiled Truth," which is the *dianoia* for the poem as a whole. The dwarf's prudential and proverbial kind of deduction is the shrunken counterpart for this wisdom: "Fly, fly (quothe then / The feare-full Dwarf:) this is no place for liuing men." This exclamation corresponds to the disclosure point of the parable or the moral of the fable. The allegorical *melos* is suggested by the oracular character of the monster, and especially by the allusion to the Delphic pythoness. The riddle form of this *melos* turns up in the possibility of an allusion to the Sphinx, a symbol of the Inquisition in Book V (cf. I.i.22, V.xi.31). Redcrosse is "amazde" (I.i.26) in a labyrinth, an image of puzzlement. The *lexis*, or basis for the figurative rhetoric of the episode, may be found in the etymology of the word *error* itself, in language about apostasy as a divergence from the "ways" of God, and in the description of error as a deformity of truth. The abbreviated form of this *lexis* is the *paroemia*, which Bede lists as one of the seven prominent types of *allegoria*, in his classification of schemes and tropes. If we were to try to condense a proverb out of Spenser's episode, in fact, we could hardly improve upon Bede's own example of *paroemia*, which he takes from II Peter 2:22; the passage describes those who have heard the word and still departed from the way of truth: "the dog is returned to its own vomit."[145] A line like Spenser's "His foes haue slaine themselues" shows this deductive tendency also; it is *potentially* a proverb. Finally, there is the more obvious or explicit deduction attached to Redcrosse's struggle: "God helpe the man so wrapt in Errours endlesse traine" (I.i.8). The drawing of this moral might well have supplied an epigrammist with the motto for an emblem based on the Laocoön; a statue with an inscription on it is an earlier form of allegorical *phanos*.

Regarding the episode overall, one notes that allegory, as a general rule, requires the perpetration of a kind of "error." The error is very much like the one that Panofsky thinks of medieval artists as making in the depiction of classical subjects: on the one hand, the gods of the pagans lost their traditional configurations; but, on the other, many of these configurations survived, having migrated from classical to Christian subjects. Without some such error Christ could not be conceived of as Phoebus-Apollo-Veritas, and there would be no allegory of the divinely illuminating Word as specifically solar in character. Conversely, there would be no representation of the sun-god as a medieval knight, at large in the wood

---

[145] *De Schematis et Tropis*, II.12 (PL XC, 184). Perhaps the other proverb basic to the episode is *Errare humanum est*, for which Erasmus cites the classical sources with Proverbs 28, in *Adagia* (Antwerp, 1648), p. 518.

of knight errantry. Similarly, it is the decomposition of the Laocoön image into a man wrestling with snakes and a mind struggling to free itself from error that makes the allegory possible. Thus, there is an analogy between the disintegration and reintegration of classical form and content—as part of the larger history of the development of allegorical techniques—and the termini in the development of any particular allegory. All allegories "deform" or alter a story to conform it to the requirements of a secondary pattern of discourse or an "ulterior" meaning or intention. At the outset, allegory misleads us by allowing us to entertain an error about the literalness of a fiction. In the dénouement, it tends toward an exposure of that error. The "adventure" of Spenser's opening episode traces the path of his legend as a whole, which ends with the unveiling of Truth.

[ii]

The Bible insists that God is known through his Word, and the patronage of major biblical heroes extends to large portions of that Word. Thus Una's frequent quotation of Scripture and the veil that in part identifies her with the ark of the testimony make her, among other things, the Word of God that Redcrosse properly champions. It is of some significance for this theme that in each of the low points of the knight's passage Spenser includes a sinister version of the Word; we have already met Error's books, like the Bible, "hard to be vnderstood" (I.x.13, II Peter 3:16), and Archimago's "Magick bookes" and saints' legends (I.i.35). At the House of Pride the first of Lucifera's six "Wizards," Idleness, is a monk who guides Lucifera's way. He rides an ass, is "Arayd in habit blacke, and amis thin" (I.iv.18), and carries a "portesse" or breviary; Una is similarly mounted. The ass has an association with the bearing of the Word of God of some antiquity; Christ's beast is sometimes a figure for those who teach the Word, faithful and humble preachers.[146] In Orgoglio's realm

---

[146] This allegory is pointed out by John Steadman, "Una and the Clergy: The Ass Symbol in *The Faerie Queene,*" *Journal of the Warburg and Courtauld Institutes,* 21 (1958), pp. 134-137. An example may be found as early as Origen, *Comm. on John,* 18 (trans. ANF, vol. 9, pp. 396-398): the ass freed from bonds is the simple language of the Old Testament, interpreted by the disciples who loose it; the colt is the New Testament. In Jerome's *Comm. on Matt.,* III.xxi (PL, XXVI, 147f.), the ass is the synagogue—and this becomes the more typical interpretation. Jerome himself, however, allegorizes the vestments the apostles put over the ass as the understanding of the Scriptures, or the doctrines taught by the Church. Bale's commentary on the white horse of Rev. 6:4 and 19:11 makes it stand for the evangelists who "carry the glorious verity of the Lord the world over" (Parker Society *Select Works,* pp. 312, 546f.). Thomas Nashe has occasion to refer to Cornelius Agrippa (*De Incert.,* cap. 102), on the significance of asses as philosophers, orators, and poets —a company in which Agrippa includes the apostles (Nashe, in *Fovre Letters Confuted,* in *Works,* ed. McKerrow, Vol. 1, p. 328). The mule in *Mother Hvbberds Tale*

the custodian is the foster-father Ignaro, with his "sencelesse speach" (I.viii.34). He has been entrusted with the keys to the kingdom, keys that Jewel in his *Apology* identifies as the Word of God or knowledge of the Scriptures; a large number of authorities are cited for this interpretation.[147] The allegory develops from Luke 11:52, "Wo be to you interpreters of the law: for ye have taken away the key of knowledge: ye entered not in your selues, and them that came in ye forbade [hindered]." The Geneva gloss adds, "They hid & toke away the pure doctrine & true vnderstanding of the Scriptures." Ignaro is a "blind guide" who has lost the meaning of the apostleship given to Peter (Matt. 23:13, 24; 16:19).

Despair is also an interpreter of the Law, and a manipulator of words unmatched anywhere else in the poem. Like the old man at the House of Holiness, he is a contemplative with great powers of concentration; what he contemplates is the old covenant to the exclusion of the new one. A prophet of doom in the biblical sense, he proves to be a great searcher of hearts, like God himself; and, a little like Satan tempting Christ to throw himself from the temple, he tries Redcrosse for his own death-wish. He is a spellbinding preacher of the "accurst hand-writing" (I.ix.53), which Christ has nailed to the cross (II Cor. 3:7). Redcrosse was disarmed in the preceding episode, and it is significant that Sir Treuisan arrives here "barehead" (I.ix.34), that is, without the Pauline helmet of the hope of salvation (I Thess. 5:8). Redcrosse may be missing the shield of faith (to "quench the fiery darts of the wicked," Ephesians 6:16; "quench the brond of hellish smart," I.ix.53). Essentially, Despair urges that Redcrosse cut

---

represents worldly prelates; perhaps, in that case, the sheep and the ass of the same poem—who are said to be endangered by the new lion (l. 1068)—are the congregation and its preachers. (The wise ass who becomes a fool for Christ has something to do with the peroration of Erasmus' *Praise of Folly*; Folly's commendation concludes by citing I Cor. 2:9f., on the "botome of Goddes Secretes" revealed to those granted a wisdom not of this world—the same text garbled by the ass-headed Bottom in *Midsummer Night's Dream*, IV.i.216.) The crucial text for Spenser is Alciati's sixth emblem, to which Steadman draws attention. See nn. 300 and 458, below. The ass as a type of Christian vocation appears in Henry Vaughan's poem, "The Ass." The important features of Spenser's treatment would be the ass's loyalty when apparently given his liberty, a good kind of stubbornness, and the appeal Una makes to a beast that is traditionally an outlaw (I.iii.44; vi.19); the ass is thus opposed to Sansloi, who has "dull eares" (I.iii.44).

[147] Jewel, *Apology*, II.vii: "And touching the keys, wherewith they [Christ's ministers] may either shut or open the kingdom of heaven, we with Chrysostom say they be 'the knowledge of the scriptures:' with Tertullian we say they be 'the interpretation of the law;' and with Eusebius we call them 'the word of God.' . . . Seeing then the key, whereby the way and entry to the kingdom of God is opened unto us, is the word of the gospel and the expounding of the law and scriptures, we say plainly, where the same word is not, there is not the key." (*The Works of John Jewel*, ed. John Ayre, Parker Society, Cambridge, 1845-1850, vol. 3, p. 61.)

his losses to the Law, and Una must intervene with the promises of the New Testament.

In Thomas Becon's homilectic dialogue *The Christian Knight*, Satan similarly tempts his victim: "Wherefore dost thou not despair? For doubtles thou art cast away for ever and ever." Becon's Satan urges the damnation of sinners under the Law, and threatens the knight that he will so vex him with misfortune and calamity "that thou shal be weary of thy life, and wish rather to die than to live," probably echoing Job 10:1 (cf. Job 3:20–22, 6:8–9, Jonah 4:8, Tobit 3:6). A man's death pains include Satan's accusation; the tempter argues from the knight's failure in good works, and the knight, in turn, cites Galatians on Christ's assumption of the curse of the Law.[148]

In Spenser, "the day of wrath" awaiting the sinner whose "measure" is "High heaped vp with huge iniquitie" (I.ix.46) is the Pauline *dies irae* of Zephaniah 1:15, as it is invoked in Romans 2:5f. ("But thou, after thine hardnes and heart that can not repent, heapest vnto thy self wrath against the day of wrath and of the declaration of the iuste iudgement of God, Who wil reward euerie man according to his workes."). Spenser's sinner "that once hath missed the right way" (I.ix.43) shares in the general condemnation: "They haue all gone out of the way . . . there is none that doeth good, no not one" (Rom. 3:12, Ps. 14:3). The "righteous *sentence* of th'Almighties law" (I.ix.50), under which Redcrosse is prepared to die, is Pauline too, for Paul at one point "all to gether douted [Great Bible, *despayred*], euen of life": "Yea, we receuied the sentence of death in our selues, because we shulde not trust in our selues, but in God, which raiseth the dead. Who deliuered vs from so great a death, and doeth deliuer us: in whome we trust, that yet here after he wil deliuer vs" (II Cor. 1:8–10). According to the Geneva gloss on this place, Paul, in his "infirmity" (cf. I.ix.30), was utterly resolved to die; he exposes himself so that "it might appeare how wonderfully Gods graces wrought in him," and Spenser draws the same conclusion in the opening stanza of the following canto.

The speech of Despair—who offers Sir Terwin a knife—resembles the sword of God's word in Hebrews 4:12–13, which sunders soul and spirit, and discerns the thoughts of the heart:

> That as a swords point through his hart did perse,
> And in his conscience made a secret breach,
> Well knowing true all, that he did reherse
>
> (I.ix.48)

---

[148] *The Catechism of Thomas Becon . . . with Other Pieces*, ed. John Ayre, Parker Society (Cambridge, 1844), pp. 629ff. The accursed handwriting duplicates the painted "table" of I.ix.49.

The condemnation that Redcrosse feels is also the Pauline "effect of the Law written in their [Gentile] hearts, their conscience also bearing witnes, & their thoghts accusing one another, or excusing" (Rom. 2:15). Despair's argument perverts a maxim from Romans 6:7: "For he that is dead, is freed from sinne"; the context shows Paul to mean metaphorically dead: dead in Christ and dead unto the Law. Despair's unarmed head, with "curld vncombed heares / Vpstaring stiffe, dismayd with vncouth dread," recalls the vision of Eliphaz in Job:

> In the thoghts of the visions of the night, when slepe falleth on men,
> Feare came vpon me, and dread which made all my bones to tremble
> And the winde passed before me, & made the heeres of my flesh to stand
> vp
>
> (Job 4:13–15, Geneva Bible)

Despair tries to bring Redcrosse around to Job's conclusion that oblivion and the grave are his only hope, and thus he resembles Job's counselors, who "mainteine with manie goodlie arguments, that God punisheth continually according to the trespas, grounding vpone Gods prouidence, his iustice, and mans sinnes"; "yet," the Geneva Bible continues, "their intention is euil: for they labour to bring Iob into dispaire, and so they mainteine an euil cause." As the imagery makes clear, the "cursed place" occupied by Despair is also that grave or pit or Sheol unto which the soul is brought in its extremity in the Old Testament.

More complicated biblical overtones anticipate the reversal at the end of the canto. "Christ cannot save thy soul," Lucifer will tell the distraught Doctor Faustus, "for Christ is iust"[149] ("Is not he iust," Despair asks [I.ix.47]). The argument of the Adversary inverts that of I John 2:1ff., where his righteousness is precisely the reason that Christ *can* save. Despair asks:

> Shall he thy sins vp in his knowledge fold,
> And guiltie be of thine impietie?
>
> (I.ix.47)

The answer on both counts is yes, for God will remember man's sin no more (Jer. 31:34; Heb. 8:12, 10:17; Ps. 103:3; Isa. 38:17); he has made Christ sin for us, even as he has made us righteous in Christ (II Cor. 5:21). A somewhat similar solution is reached in Job, in the speech in which Elihu speaks of a "messenger" who will be a reconciliation between God and man (Job 33:23–24). "That is, the minister shal by the preaching of the word pronounce vnto him ye forgiuenes of his sinnes," the Geneva gloss explains. More specifically, Christ was made a curse for us, according to the chapter in which Paul addresses the "bewitched"

---

[149] Scene vi, l. 90.

Galatians (cf. I.ix.53, "Ne let vaine words bewitch thy manly hart"). Paul is explaining the doctrine of justification by faith, and the adoption of Christians into the promises made to Abraham, and to his "one" seed, which Paul identifies as Christ (Gal. 3:16). In the Old Testament this promise is brought to the edge of annulment in its very inception, when Abraham is summoned to sacrifice his only son: "Herein stode ye chiefest point of his temptation, seing he was commanded to offre vp him in whome God had promised to blesse all the nations of the worlde" (Geneva gloss on Gen. 22:2). Despair proffers a "cursed knife" to Redcrosse: "He to him raught a dagger sharpe and keene, / And gaue it him in hand. . . . He lifted vp his hand" (I.ix.51). With this we may compare Genesis 22:10: "And Abraham stretching forthe his hand, toke the knife to kil his sonne." It is an angel or messenger that interrupts the sacrifice, and reasserts the promise. Spenser seems to have this interruption too, for Redcrosse's blood is seen "To come, and goe with tydings from the hart, / As it a running messenger had beene" (I.ix.51), and the knight's hesitation is followed by Una's snatching of the knife and asserting Redcrosse's election.

One further relation to Galatians 3 may be adduced. Despair, in his death, becomes an ironic substitute for the "faeries sonne" he has implored to die (I.ix.47). There is a special appropriateness in Despair's choosing to hang himself in a "cursed place," among "old stockes and stubs of trees" (I.ix.52, 34). The "accurst hand-writing" includes the "curse of the Law" that Christ in his death assumes; in the Law it is written, "Cursed is euerie one that hangeth on tre" (Gal. 3:13). In other words, Despair is cursed in the very form of the death through which the sinner is redeemed.

At the House of Holiness, in the next canto, Fidelia also appears to wield "the dart of sinfull guilt" (I.x.21) because "she was able, with her words to kill, / And raise againe to life the hart, that she did thrill." Hers are the words of which the letter killeth, but the spirit giveth life (II Cor. 3:6); the beams radiating from her "Christall face, / That could haue dazed the rash beholders sight"(I.x.12), are the Old Testament glory from the same Pauline text, the glory that transfigured the face of Moses. Being "Christall," Fidelia's faith is also a glass or mirror, that glass in which the face of Christ is beheld typically in the Old Testament, and interiorly in the New: "But we all behold as in a mirrour the glorie of the Lord with open face, and are changed into the same image, from glorie to glorie, as by the Spirit of the Lord" (II Cor. 3:8). On Sinai, according to Spenser's "Iulye" (ll. 157ff.), "Moses . . . sawe hys makers face . . . more cleare, then Christall glasse."[150]

[150] The allusion to Moses (I.x.53) perhaps helps explain why it is Fidelia who has given Contemplation the "keyes" to the attainment of high heaven (I.x.50). For Moses' absorption in the Sinai theophany cf. notes 6 and 15 above. Moses died with

The Old Testament ends with the threat of a curse (Mal. 4:6), but also with the promise of an Elijah figure whose office will consist "in the turning of men to God and ioyning the father & children in one vnitie of faith: so that the father shal turne to that religion of his sonne which is conuerted to Christ, and the sonne shal imbrace the faith of the true fathers, Abraham, Izhák and Iaakób" (Geneva gloss). The New Testament, the book that Fidelia carries, ends with a vision of the New Jerusalem. Redcrosse's recuperation ends with the same vision. It is mediated by the mountaintop visionary named Contemplation, who in the geography of the poem corresponds to Ariosto's St. John.

> Great grace that old man to him giuen had;
> For God he often saw from heauens hight,
> All were his earthly eyen both blunt and bad,
> And through great age had lost their kindly sight,
> Yet wondrous quick and persant was his spright,
> As Eagles eye, that can behold the Sunne:
>
> (I.x.47)

The allusion to the absorption of Moses in the glory-cloud on Sinai (Exod. 24:15–18, 34:29–35), and a more or less conventional phrasing, do not rule out a particular reference to the author of the Fourth Gospel and Revelation. John is traditionally believed to have written Revelation late in life; he is shown Jerusalem from a high mountain (Rev. 21:10); as the beloved apostle he may have received special grace (his name means "God is gracious"); he may have been granted an exceptionally long life; and the traditional symbol of his Gospel is the eagle. These associations meet in Rupert of Deutz's introduction to his commentary on John's Gospel, where he is discussing the purity required of those who would study "the venerable writings in the school of Christ":

---

his eyes undimmed (Deut. 34:7), and Contemplation, having lost much of his physical sight, often sees God, owing to his "persant" spiritual sight (I.x.47): cf. Hebrews 12:27, on the capacity of Moses' faith: "By faith he forsoke Egypt, . . . for he endured, as he that saw him which is inuisible" (Geneva Bible). The link between Moses and John, established in the reading of Contemplation given below, is pre-Spenserian. In the pageant of the Church in Dante, the old man who brings up the rear, "sleeping, with a keen visage" (*Purg.* XXIX.144), is the author of Revelation; like Dante, this author is asleep in a vision of the Church. But as Cary writes in his note, "in the poem attributed to Giacopo, the son of our Poet, which in some MSS. and in one of the earliest editions, accompanies the original of this work, and is descriptive of its plan, this old man is said to be Moses. 'E' vecchio, ch'era dietro a tutti loro, / Fu Moyse.'" (Cary cites "No. 3459 of the Harl. MSS. in the British Museum.") Moses, like Elijah, is a prophet in a mountain, but the evil shepherds of "Iulye," who are addicted to lofty places—the Vatican Hill is implied—"heapen hylles of wrath" (l. 202).

Thus only may they be able in some measure to follow that eagle who delights in purity of heart; thus only may they dare with undazzled sharpness of mind to contemplate longer than other creatures the splendor of the everlasting sun, the vision of God himself.

Of him who by the path of purity attains true wisdom, the Lord speaks through Isaiah, "He will dwell on the heights; his eyrie will be the fastnesses of the rocks; bread has been given to him, and his waters are unfailing. His eyes will see the king in his comeliness; they will behold a land of far frontiers." Indeed, what pertains even more clearly to the present matter has been said here as to blessed Job, with different words but with the same meaning: "At the command of the Lord the eagle soars upward and makes its nest on high places; it stays on the rocks and dwells among the steep crags and inaccessible fastnesses. Thence it spies out the prey; its eyes behold it afar off." All these things John, the sublime observer of that Word and His eternal beginnings, has so eloquently pursued, soaring upward as the eagle, gazing with eyes wide open at the rays of the Godhead. On the heights he made his nest, that is, the fortress of his everlasting Gospel.[151]

These remarks on the Gospel of John are typical, and they stem from St. Augustine's *Harmony of the Four Gospels*. Augustine contrasts the writers of the other Gospels, which are more earthbound, with John, who "soars like an eagle above the clouds of human infirmity, and gazes upon the light of the unchangeable truth with those keenest and steadiest eyes of the heart." St. Thomas Aquinas, in the prologue to his commentary on John, expounds the highness, fullness, and perfection that define the modes of contemplation found in this Gospel, and he cites both Job's eagle and Augustine's remark that the other Gospels inform as to the active life, but John as to the contemplative one. Augustine had written that "the former finds its sphere in the purging of sins, the latter moves in the light of the purged . . . [it] subsists on faith, and is seen . . . only in part in a kind of vision of the unchangeable truth."[152] This is surely Redcrosse's movement also, and it is a movement towards clarification of the Word. The other Gospels "describe, as it were, the bodie, and Iohn setteth before our eyes the soule," the commentator quoted at the head of the Geneva Gospel of John says: "Wherefore the same aptly termeth the Gospel writ by Iohn, the key which openeth the dore to the vnderstanding of the others." Like Ignaro, whose keys Arthur made free use of, Spenser's Contemplation is characterized in terms of his eyesight, and he too possesses

[151] *In Evang. S. Joan Comm. libri XIV*, "Prologus Ruperti," PL, CLXIX, 203–206, trans. George McCracken and Allen Cabaniss in *Early Medieval Theology*, Library of Christian Classics, vol. 9 (Philadelphia, 1957), p. 259.

[152] Augustine, *Harmony of the Gospels*, I.iv–vi, trans. in NPNF, 1st Series, vol. 6, pp. 80, 81, 79.

the keys (I.x.50)—the keys to the kingdom that he reveals to the knight. We conclude that Contemplation is Johanine, because John exemplifies heavenly contemplation:

> . . . he is borne to loftier heights, in which he leaves the other three [evangelists] far behind him; so that, while in them you see men who have their conversation in a certain manner with the Christ on earth, in him you perceive one who has passed beyond the cloud in which the whole earth is wrapped, and who has reached the liquid heaven from which, with clearest and steadiest mental eye, he is able to look upon God the Word, who was in the beginning with God, and by whom all things were made.[153]

Like Despair, then, Contemplation not only retails a part of Scripture, but implies the taking of a particular view of it, in this case from the summit of the New Testament.

Thus the two cantos in question form a biblical diptych, hinging on Romans 5:2: "Moreouer the Law entered thereupon that the offence shulde abunde: neuertheles, where sinne abunded, there grace abunded muche more" (cf. I.ix.53). The diptych reproduces the Christian conception of the argument of the Bible as a whole.

The implication of the foregoing is clear: Book I is a deduction from the Bible—the Bible supplies its "type." Spenser's allusion to virtually the last "book" referred to within the Bible supports this implication. After Book I ends—"happily ever after"—Guyon salutes its sanctified hero, saying that his name is "enrolled . . . in heauenly registers aboue the Sunne" (II.i.32). The Saint has indeed won a seat among the saints, but Guyon is not referring to a place in Archimago's copy of *The Golden Legend*. Rather, he reveals Redcrosse's election, which is recorded in the eschatological "book of life" (Ps. 69:28, Dan. 12:1, Phil. 4:3, Rev. 3:5, 13:8, 20:12, 21:27).

The Tree of Life

As the apple-tree among the trees of the woods, so is my beloved among the sons. It is customary for Scripture to call the wilds of human life a wood, where the various kinds of perturbations of soul flourish, and where destructive beasts dwell and—as if in a cave—lie hid: their nature is slug-

---

[153] Thomas Aquinas, *Prologue to John*, in *Op. om.* (New York, 1949), Tomus X, pp. 279–281. In *The Golden Legend*, St. John tells a questioner that the human spirit requires respite from the contemplation of heavenly things, just as the sun-gazing eagle must upon occasion return to earth.

gish, lacking effective power, in the light and the sun, but it has powers in darkness. For after the sun is eclipsed, night having fallen, the Prophet says *the beasts of the wood emerge from their caves.* Therefore, since that "singular beast" feeds in the wood, which most gravely brought the curse upon the beautiful vine of human nature, the Prophet says, *the boar from the wood lays waste to it, and a singular beast feeds on it.* Afterwards, the apple-tree was planted in the wood, which, in that it is a tree, is of like nature with the wood of our humanity, for it was tried in our similitude without sin. . . . Therefore the purified soul beholds her Bridegroom made the apple-tree in the wood, that grafting into Himself all the wild boughs of the wood, He may cause them to bring forth fruit like His own.

(St. Gregory of Nyssa, *Comm. in Cant. Cant.* 2:3, Hom. IV, in PG, XLIV, 842D–843C)

> And as Adam and alle . thorw a tre deyden,
> Adam and all thorwe a tree . shal torne aȝeine to lyue
> (*Piers Plowman*, B-Text, Passus XVIII.356–357)

[i]

Out of the opening episodes of Book I emerges a figure who would willingly serve truth, and yet cannot be trusted to distinguish it from imitations. If Redcrosse is to be a second Adam, the emphasis seems to fall on Adam. He will not cast "that old Dragon" (I.xi, rubric) out of heaven; he can only engage him on the earth to which he fell. He adores his "dying Lord," but he adores him "dead as liuing," a phrase that weakens Revelation 1:18 ("I am alive, and was dead: and behold, I am alive for evermore").[154] There is a sense in which Adam is still in Limbo; even though Christ is risen, the Christian is still on the road to Emmaus. When Redcrosse sets out from the house of Archimago he is alone, a little like Abraham, who left the land of his fathers to become a stranger in the land of promise. And yet, like the church of Ephesus in Revelation 2:4, he has "abandoned the love he had at first." He shores up his confidence with the defeat of Sansfoy; at the same time he takes on the pagan's consort Duessa. The last error seems to be worse than the first.

In taking on Duessa, Redcrosse makes a bad mistake, and to explain how this happens Spenser introduces the parallel story of Fradubio ("from doubt" or Brother Doubt) and Fraelissa (that human infirmity,

---

[154] Cf. I.vi.36, "These eyes did see that knight both liuing and eke ded," and I.vi.39, "how might I see / The thing, that might not be, and yet was donne?" where Archimago is "building the sepulchres of the prophets," as the hypocritical Pharisee is wont to do (Luke 11:47); we are to contrast Una, at I.vii.28, who "vp arose, resoluing him to find / Aliue or dead." Cf. also I.xii.28.

"the fraylty of man, wych seyng the best folowyth the worst";[155] the "frelnes of oure flesshe";[156] the weakness of Adam and Eve, "which by theyre fragylte brake goddes commaundment";[157] that "humayne fragilyte or freyltee" that leads one to "trespas agenst the commaundment of almyghty god").[158] Being a woman, Fraelissa is also that frailty whose name is said to be woman, especially since the woman's first name in Scripture is not Eve, but, according to a medieval reading of Scripture, Issa, or Isha, the "female" of Genesis 2:23.[159] In his commentary on Genesis (1589), Pererius gives various examples of attempts to translate the Hebrew wordplay on Is and Issa, and reproves Paginus' choice of Vir and Virissa.[160]

In Tasso the comparable trees were the externalized forms of the hero's anxieties, and here also they seem to correspond to transactions in the mind of the hero. Thus Redcrosse is making a garland for his new idol when he discovers Fradubio, just as the doubtful Fradubio was offering a garland in the contest between Duessa and Fraelissa. The trees shadow forth the condition of fallen man, and man fell, according to Calvin, not through the more traditional pride or rebellion or ambition, but through the infidelity that must have preceded them:

[155] *OED*, citing Thomas Starkey, *Dialogue between Pole and Lupset*, ed. J. M. Cowper, EETS, Extra Series, no. 12 (London, 1871), I.i.8.

[156] *OED*, citing *Cursor Mundi*, l. 25337 (Fairfax ms.), ed. Richard Morris, EETS, in 5 vols. (London, 1874–1893). Cf. Frailissa's counterpart Amavia, in Book II, who declares that "All flesh doth frailtie breed" (II.i.52), and Mutabilitie, who is part of the Fall and is addressed as "fraile woman" (VII.vi.25).

[157] *OED*, citing Lord Berners' trans. of *Huon of Bordeaux*, l. 167, ed. S. L. Lee, EETS, Extra Series, 2 vols. (London, 1882–1887).

[158] *OED*, citing John de Trevisa, *Bartholomeus De Proprietatibus Rerum*, I (W. de Worde, 1495), p. 8. For a "frail tree" in Scripture, an idol, see the *fragilum ligna* of the Vulgate Wisdom 14:1, and cf. the "fraile legno" on which the speaker of Petrarch's *Canz.* LXXX depends.

[159] *The Story of Genesis and Exodus*, ed. Richard Morris, EETS, Original Series, no. 7 (London, 1865), p. 7, l. 233: "Issa was hire firste name." Cf. Juan Luis Vives, *Instruction of A Christian Woman*, trans. Richard Hyrde: "a frail thing, and of weak discretion, and that may lightly be deceived, which thing our first mother Eve showeth, whom the devil caught with a light argument." (Text from Foster Watson, ed., *Vives and the Renaissance Education of Women*, New York, 1912, p. 65.) Cf. Romans 15:1: "Wee which are strong, ought to beare the frailenesse of the weake" (Bishops' Bible), and I Peter 3:7, "giving honour unto the woman, as unto the weaker vessel" (Geneva Bible). (Spenser indicates his knowledge of the Hebrew at III.xi.39: "He loued *Isse* for his dearest Dame.")

[160] Benedictus Pererius, *Commentarivm et Dispvtationum in Genesim* (Cologne, 1601; first publ., 1589), Vol. 1, Tom. I, Lib. IV, "De creatio. Hominis," p. 214, para. 218. The name is "Virissa," in the citation in Peter Martyr's *Commentary* (Zurich, 1569) on this place.

... we must consider the very fourme of the same [negligence] in the fall of Adam. . . . It is a childish opinion that hath commonly bin receiued, concerning the intemperaunce of glottonie, as though the summe and head of all vertues consisted in the forebearing of one only frute. . . . Therefore we must looke further bicause the forbidding him from the tree of knowledge of good and euill, was the triall of obedience, that Adam in obeying might proue that he was willingly subiect to the gouernement of God. . . . But the promise whereby he was bidden to hope for eternall life, so long as he did not eate of the tree of life, and again the horrible threatening of death so sone as he shoulde taste of the tree of knowledge of good and euill, serued to proue and exercise his faith. . . . For sith the woman was with the deceit of the Serpent lead away by infidelitie, now it appeareth that disobedience was the beginning of the fall. . . . But it is withall to be noticed, that the first man fell from the subiection of God, for that he was taken with the entisements of Satan, but also despising the trueth, did turne out of the waie to lying. . . . Therefore infidelitie was the roote of that falling away. . . . Albeit it was no simple Apostasie, but ioyned with shameful reproches against God, while they assented to the sclaunders of Satan, wherein he accused God of lying, enuie, and niggardly grudging. Finally, infidelitie opened the gate to ambition, ambition was the mother of obstinate rebellion, to make men cast away the feare of God, and throw themselues whether their lust carried them. . . . For Adam woulde neuer haue bin so bolde, as to do against the commaundement of God, but for this that he did not beleue his word.[161]

This passage is quoted at length because the progression out of incredulity that Calvin describes corresponds to the unfolding history of Spenser's protagonist.

Like Ask and Embla in the Norse mythology, or Gaya and Gayomart in the Persian, Spenser's two trees are the archetypal parents of the race. Leaving for later discussion Duessa's relation to the Adamic pair, we may now turn to Spenser's first and second Adams, here and in the garden of Eden. They also manifest a theme of "two trees."

Fradubio is clearly Adam's ironic aspect. As a bleeding tree who was once a man, he conforms to a type known to folklore, namely the soul cut off in the midst of life—and thus cut off unjustly—whose existence is continued thereafter in the compensatory form of vegetation.[162] The

[161] *Institutes*, II.i.4; trans. Thomas Norton, p. 88. According to Ecclesiasticus 10:14, "pride is the original of sinne," but at 10:13 "The beginning of mans pride, is to fall away from God, & to turne away from his maker."

[162] See Mircea Eliade, *Patterns in Comparative Religion*, trans. Rosemary Sheed (reprint, Cleveland, Ohio, 1968), chap. VIII, sec. 113, p. 301.

treacherously slain Polydarus in Virgil's third book and Dante's suicide Piero della Vigna—to himself unjust[163]—are literary examples. Adam is properly included in this company because he is cut off from that paradise containing the tree of life (the eternal life that was intended for him), and because his life is extended, not in himself, but in his "stock." So in the C-Text of *Piers Plowman*, in a passage treating the Fall: "Adam was as tree . and we aren hus apples" (XIX.68). The metaphor is a frequent occasion for homily: "There was in our father Adam before his fall the very image and likeness of God . . . corrupted . . . so hath he begotten us his sons corrupt. . . . For of a rotten root do spring as rotten branches, which in like manner put over their rottenness into the little twigs that shoot out and grow upon them."[164] Adam is probably a tree for Spenser, as Nelson has shown, because at his fall he hid himself *in medio ligni paradisi* (literally, "in the middle of the tree of paradise"),[165] where according to Revelation the tree of life ought to have been. We have already quoted Gregory on the meaning of Adam's retreat from God—a retreat that Gregory specifically links to Adam's hiding in the tree:

> Hence now also the branches of the human race derive bitterness still from this root, so that when a man is charged home for the evil in him, he hides himself under words of self-defense, as under a kind of leaves of trees, and as it were flies the face of the Creator to the darkened retreats of self-exculpation, whereas he has not the mind to have that known that he has been guilty of. By which concealment he has not hidden himself from the Lord, but the Lord from himself. For he manages that he should not see Him Who sees all things, not that he himself should not be seen.[166]

An allegory of a royal tree—whom Jerome identifies with Adam[167]— banished from Eden, may be found in Ezekiel 31: once it was in the garden of God, now its shadow is avoided by men; and yet it "shall be com-

[163] *Inf.* XIII.70: my soul *ingiusto fece me contra me giusto* ("made me unjust to myself who was just").

[164] Bullinger, *Decades*, III, Sermon X, in Parker Society edn., vol. 3, p. 394. Cf. Gregory, *Moralia*, XVII.xv.21: "the frailty of the first guilt is inherited in the offspring; and because the branch of the human race was made rotten in the root, it does not hold up in the greenness of its creation" (Library of the Fathers trans., vol. 2, p. 293).

[165] Nelson, *Poetry of Edmund Spenser*, pp. 163f. (For the central location of the tree, see Rev. 22:2 and 2:7, "the tree of life which is in the middes of the Paradise of God"—this is where the tree of knowledge is in Gen. 3:3.)

[166] *Moral.* XXII.xv.31, Library of the Fathers trans., vol. 2, pp. 572f. (Latin in PL, LXXVI, 231.)

[167] *Comm. in Ezech.*, X.xxxi (PL, XXV, 302D), citing Romans 5:12, on the tree as symbolizing a universal sinner.

THE TREE OF LIFE

forted in the nether parts of the earth," a little like Adam in Limbo. Fradubio's voice, at any rate, sounds like that "of damned Ghost from *Limbo* lake" (I.ii.32).

Adam's kingly aspect is represented by the venerable patriarch in the Eden of the twelfth canto; this Adam, like his own son Seth, is the image of his Father.[168] And yet the analogies with Fradubio are there. Fradubio is "enclosed in wooden wals full fast," and the kingly Adam is "fast imprisoned in sieged fort" (I.ii.42; xii.4). The prison of the latter is a "brasen towre" with a "brazen gate" and an eager watchman (I.xi.2; xii.3).[169] These details conform to two texts normally cited for the doctrine of Limbo and the harrowing of hell: "For he hath broken the gates of brasse, and brast the barres of yron a sundre" (Ps. 107:16, Geneva Bible), and "he went and preached to the spirits that were in prison"—"or rather a *watch-tower*" (or "dongeon"), as Calvin explains I Peter 3:19 (*phulakē*, a "watch").[170]

The paralyzed tree will not be disenchanted until he is "bathed in a liuing well" (I.ii.43), and the well in question turns up, along with the tree of life, in the eleventh canto. Redcrosse rises from the well on the second morning of his dragon fight with "baptised hands" (I.ix.36). Tree and well presume on associations like these:

> Knowe ye not, that all we which have bene baptized in Jesus Christ, have been baptized into his death, that like as Christ was raised up from the dead . . . , so we also shulde walk in newnes of life. For if we be grafted [*sumphutos*] *with him to the similitude of his death*, even so shal we be to the similitude of his resurrection. Knowing this, that our olde man is crucified with him, that the bodie of sinne might be destroyed, that henceforthe we shulde not serve sinne. For he that is dead is freed from sinne. (Romans 6:3-7, Geneva Bible)

For "grafted" the Rheims Bible translates "complanted" (*complantati facti sumus*). Showing that a figure might be understood here, the Geneva gloss reads: "The greke worde meneth, that we growe up to gether with Christe, as we se, mosse, yvie misteltowe, or such like, growe up by a tre and are nourished with the ioyse therof"—Spenser's tree is also overcast with moss (I.ii.28). The commentary of Peter Martyr on this text immediately suggests a comparison of Christ and Adam to two trees,

---

[168] Gen. 1:27, 5:3; Luke 3:38, "Adam, the son of God."

[169] For the watchman, cf. Isa. 21:8, Hab. 2:1, Neh. 4:9.

[170] *Institutes*, II.xvi.9. (Cf. Norton trans., p. 204: "I do in deede willingly confesse, that Christ shined to them by the power of his spirit. . . . And to this purpose may the place of Peter be probably applied, where he sayeth, that Christ came and preached to the spirites that were in a dongeon or prison, as it is commonly translated.") The *castello* that domiciles the virtuous pagans in Dante's Limbo belongs to the same tradition (*Inf.* IV.106).

"For whatsoever good fruit is in us, the same commeth wholy from Christ, as from the liuely root."[171] Man can only attain salvation by passing from the kindred of the condemned first Adam to the kindred of the redeeming second one:

And this passage Paul aptly compareth with ye grafting of trees. For euen as a grafte is plucked away from his naturall plant, and graften into another straunge plant, and thereout draweth both lyfe and sappe. So ought we to be remoued from the vitiate and corrupt nature, which we haue drawen of Adam, and to be grafted into Christ, as into the most holy stock. But this spirituall grafting differeth not a little from natural grafting. For husbandmen are accustomed to breake of the slip which they will graft, from a good and excellent tree, and to fasten it into an other which is barren and wilde, that the grafte may liue in it, but yet retaine the nature and properties of the old tree, from whence it was cut of. But we far otherwise being cut of from the wilde oliue tree, and unfruitful plant that it is, from the corrupt nature of *Adam*, are grafted in Christ, that from him we should not only take lyfe and spirite, but also leuing our olde affections, should put on his nature and properties.[172]

Fradubio is, as it were, grafted into Redcrosse; and Redcrosse, under the tree of life, is grafted into Christ in the similitude of his death.

A further hint of Adam's presence in canto ii occurs at the end of the scene, when Redcrosse puts the bleeding bough into the ground and closes the wound with fresh clay. The parallel scene in Book II is the burial of Mordant. In Book I there would seem to be an allusion to the red clay from which man was created, and the dust to which he is destined to return. There may also be a faint recall of the closing of Adam's side at Genesis 2:21—the "earth" (*adamah*) out of which Eve is taken.

The seemingly abstruse allegory whereby the tree, to be regenerated, must be bathed in a living well, belongs to the idea that an unfallen man is like a watered tree, especially the one found in Psalm 1:3.[173] The Geneva

---

[171] P. M. Vermigli, *Most learned and fruitful commentaries . . . vpon the Epistle . . . to the Romanes* (London, 1586), trans. H. B., p. 144

[172] *Ibid.*, p. 145. Cf. the word "transplanted" in *Par. Lost* III.285–294, where Christ is a "second root." With Spenser, compare Thomas Becon, *Another Book of Demands of Holy Scripture*, in *Prayers and Other Pieces*, ed., John Ayre, Parker Society (Cambridge, 1844), pp. 621f.: "What is the old man that we must put off? The naughty, corrupt, and rotten nature which sithence the fall of Adam we have lineally at our first generation received of our parents through the corruption of the first root Adam."

[173] Patristic texts are cited in Jean Daniélou, "Catéchèse Pascale et Retour au Paradise," *La Maison-Dieu*, 45 (Centre de Pastorale Liturgique, Les Editions Du Cerf, Paris, 1956). The most important is Eusebius, *Comm. in Ps.* 1:3 (PG, XXIII, 77B–C), where the watered tree is interpreted as the Christian planted in Paradise,

Bible comments that "God's children are so moystened euer with his grace." The Epistle known as *Barnabas* (11:1-11) compares the same tree to the watered trees of Ezekiel's New Jerusalem, which give eternal life: "That is to say we go down into the water full of sin and defilement, but we come up out of it bearing fruit." Similarly, Gregory of Nyssa, on the subject of the baptism of Christ, says the Jordan is "glorified by regenerating men and planting them in the Paradise of God."[174] One could also compare the waters of Marah, which Moses sweetened for the thirsty Israelites when he cast a tree into them (Ex. 15:25). As we can see, the symbolism of Spenser's first tree inevitably attracts that of his second tree. A large number of texts can be cited that understand the trees planted in paradise to be redeemed men, or Christian neophytes, installed in the Church. Conversely, the trees may be the virtues implanted in the redeemed man.[175] It is axiomatic in the catechistical literature (as in a book like Herbert's *Temple*), that the ecclesiastical and soteriological themes be mutually entailed: Church and Christian are born and edified together.

---

and at the same time is assimilated to the tree of life which is Christ. We may compare Jerome on the same place: "We however comparing spiritual things with spiritual things, and reading the tree of life to have been planted in paradise, and the tree of the knowledge of good and evil," may consider that the just and blessed man "will be planted as if he were a tree which is planted by the passage of waters, that is, he will be like Christ; since 'he made us to sit in the heavens, and to reign with him.' . . . You see because this tree is planted in paradise, and we all are planted with him (*complantati sumus*)." (Jerome, *Tractatus sive Homiliae in Psalmos*, ed. D. Germanus Morin, Corpus Christianorum Serie Latina LXXVIII, Turnholti, 1957, pp. 6f.) For the watering of the tree, cf. Fornari, *Spositione*, vol. 2, p. 235, on *O.F.* XXXIV.47, the bathing of Astolfo before mounting to Paradise: "Then Astolfo, as a true Theologian, and learned in the holy faith, seeks no other fount than this, which goes out from a rock, and takes its course through the forest, which denotes the world or dwelling of men, as trees in a wood. . . ."

[174] PG, XLVI, 92f. (trans. in NPNF, 2nd Series, vol. 5, pp. 522f.).

[175] *Neophutos* (new plant) is the term of I Tim. 3:6. Daniélou, "Catéchèse Pascale," gives many examples: Ephraim, *Hymn. Par.*, VI, 7-9; Irenaeus, *Adv. Haer.*, V.x.1 (ANF, vol. 1, p. 536): "The men who have progressed in the faith and have received the spirit of god are spiritual, as planted in Paradise"; they are "grafted into the good olive tree"; Cyprian, *Epist.* LXXII.10 (ANF, vol. 5, p. 382); Hippolytus of Rome, *Comm. Dan.* 1:17: "Eden is the name of the new garden of delights planted in the Orient, ornamented with good trees, in which it is necessary to understand the reunion of the just. For what else is this—other than the Church—but the reunion of the just? The concord there, which is the passage of the saints to communion, is what the Church is, spiritual garden of God, planted in Christ as in the East, where one sees all varieties of trees, the wood of the patriarchs and prophets, the choir of the Apostles, the file of Virgins, and ranks of bishops, priests, and levites" (quoted by Daniélou, "Catéchèse Pascale," pp. 101f., from *Comm. sur Dan.*, trans. M. Lefèvre, Sources Chrétien 14, Paris, 1947).

There is a hint of the tree's presence in the "holy water" of the well of life too. When Redcrosse rises from the well, he is thrice-renewed, like an eagle with "newly budded" plumes: "So new this new-borne knight to battle new did rise" (I.xi.34). Cary, in his translation of Dante, compares this line to *Purgatorio* XXXIII.142ff., where the image of the baptised catechumen as a watered tree is somewhat more noticeable: "From the most holy waters," the pilgrim says, "I came forth again remade, even as new plants renewed with new fronds."

Spenser's other tree, in the Garden of Eden rather than banished to a "desert waste" (I.ii.42), is also associated with anointment and appointment. Its circle makes it a sacred place, as Fradubio's circle makes a cursed one. Redcrosse is preserved within its sanctuary, and though at the outset there is a sense in which the dragon comes between Redcrosse and the tree, eventually the tree intervenes between Redcrosse and the dragon. The dragon avoids the tree, "for he was deadly made, / And all that life preserued, did detest" (I.xi.49). The reciprocity of the dragon-haunted tree and the tree-haunted dragon is found in Christian allegory as early as the *Physiologus*, which describes the tree Peridexion. The shadow of that tree protects certain doves—which are accustomed to feed on its fruit—from the depredations of a hostile snake:

> The snake is afraid of this tree, even of its shadow, and dare not approach the Doves or come under the shadow of the tree. But, when the shadow goes to the Western side of the tree, the snake flies to the East, and goes around it and comes back when the shadow turns. But should a Dove leave the tree in darkness, then the snake finds it and kills it.

The tree is the Father, its wood Christ, and its shadow the Holy Ghost.

> But, when we wander away into the darkness then the Devil finds us, since we do not stay near the wood of life, and catches us easily. And thus said holy Paul because he knew this, "Far be it from me to glory save in the Cross of my Lord, by which the world is crucified to me and I to the world." (Gal. 6:14).[176]

The counterpart for the tree of life in Revelation, along with the apple tree in the Song of Songs (2:3), was often referred to Christ. When Redcrosse is saved by this tree, the reader is expected to think in terms of Song 8:5: "... I raised thee vp vnder an apple tre: there thy mother conceiued thee: there she conceiued that bore thee." The Vulgate says that it was there that thy mother was corrupted and deflowered, for which the

---

[176] *The Epic of the Beast. Physiologus*, trans. James Carrill (Broadway Translations, London, n.d.), p. 243.

allegorical paraphrase might be, "Christ redeemed mankind at the foot of the Cross, where the Synagogue, denying him, was corrupted, as once Eve, the general mother, was corrupted by the serpent and denied God at the foot of the tree of knowledge."[177] Thus the apple tree, standing guard over the hero in silent efficacy, conceals a life-giving spirit. A somewhat similar image is found in Dante's earthly paradise, where the forbidden tree—from which the cross was taken—is made barren at the naming of Adam, and turns purple and bears fruit at the crucifixion (*Purg.* XXXII. 37–87). Adam's son Seth, in his legendary journey to paradise, beholds both the faded Adamic tree and the tree from which man's redemption will ultimately come, according to the version of the story in the *Cursor Mundi* (ll. 1320ff.).

A peculiar property of Spenser's tree is its shedding of ointment or balm. Both tree and well are associated with dew, especially with morning dew. One may feel a rapprochement with the imagery of the first canto, which seems to be steeped in evening dew.[178] There is the "Sweet slumbring

[177] My paraphrase is synthetic. Bishop Challoner, whose explanation is adopted for the notes to the Song in the Douay Bible, explains at Song 8:5, "*under the apple tree I raised thee up*: that is, that Christ redeemed the Gentiles at the foot of the cross where the synagogue of the Jews (the mother Church) *was corrupted* by their denying him, and crucifying him." Challoner's explanation may be readily synthesized from *Glossa ordinaria* on Song 8:5 (PL, CXIII, 1164f.); Bede, *in Cant. Cant.*, VI.xxxv (PL, XCI, 1210f.); Rabanus Maurus, *Alleg. in Sac. Script., sub* "Mater" (PL, CXII, 996); and Alanus de Insulis, *Elucid. in Cant. Cant.*, viii (PL, CCX, 105C). As Spenser suggests that it was at this tree that our first father was corrupted (I.xi.46), he would read the "mother" as Eve, the more typical reading. So St. John of the Cross, *Spiritual Canticle*, comm. on stanza 28 (1st redaction): "He speaks with her and tells her how by the means of the Tree of the Cross she was betrothed to Him; . . . . He restored and redeemed her [the spouse-figure] by the same means whereby human nature had been ruined, namely, by means of the tree of Paradise, in our first mother who was Eve. Thus the Spouse says: 'Beneath the apple-tree,' meaning by the apple-tree the Tree of the Cross. . . . 'And thou wert redeemed where thy mother had been corrupted.' For thy mother, human nature, was corrupted, in thy first parents, beneath the tree. . . . So that, if thy mother caused thy death beneath the tree, I gave thee life beneath the Tree of the Cross." (Trans. E. Allison Peers, Garden City, New York, 1961, pp. 179f.) Duessa has some of the attributes of the deflowered and denying Synagogue-figure. An early example of our allegory is Cassiodorus, *Expos. in Cant. Cant.* VIII.5 (PL, LXX, 1101): the *mater* is the Synagogue, guilty of original sin in betraying Christ; the tree is the cross under which the Synagogue is raised up, redeemed from the power of the devil.

[178] Because of its mediate character in both space and time, dew becomes a natural symbol for the impingement of two orders (dawn, dusk; awakening, retirement; sky, earth), or of the convertibility of the materialization of spirit (descent and condensation) and the spiritualization of matter (ascent and sublimation). Consequently dew also mediates between purity and fecundity, as in the immaculate conception described in Book III. For Christ as the sweetness of the dew, see Augustine,

deaw" that weighs down the eyelids of Archimago's guests; near the house of Morpheus the moon steeps the head of Tethys "In siluer deaw" (I.i.39); the house itself contains a "trickling streame . . . And euer-drizling raine" (I.i.41). With this last may be compared the "trickling streame of Balm" with which the tree waters Eden, "As it had deawed bene with timely raine" (I.xi.48). Redcrosse rises with the sun—the second morn in Eden we have "Titans deawy face" (I.xi.33), and, on the third, Aurora's "deawy bed" (I.xi.51). The knight's "bright deaw-burning blade" is annealed in the "holy water dew" of the fountain (I.xi.36). The slight pun on due and dew—the rain fell in due time, for example—reminds us that the false Una is described as "that new creature borne without her dew" (I.i.46);[179] in other words, she lacked that sanctification or supernatural endowment with which a regenerate nature is blessed. In the first canto this seems merely to be the blessing of "innocent sleep":

> The death of each day's life, sore labor's bath,
> Balm of hurt minds, great nature's second course,
> *(Macbeth*, II.ii.37–39)

In the penultimate canto, however, the tree drips with the healing dew of the resurrection (Isa. 26:19):

Ennar. in Ps. CXXXVII.9 (PL, XXXVII, 1779); for the Virgin as impregnated by the refined dew of Judges 6:36ff., see Honorius of Autun, *Speculum Ecclesiae*, "In Annuntiatione" (PL, CLXXII, 904C): the incarnational and fecundating nature of the divine dew turns up in the Middle English poem "I sing of a maiden." I owe to Stephen Barney the insistence that the dew in the first canto require interpretation, and to David Quint the suggestion that this dew is symmetrical with the "chrisms" (as it were) of canto xi.

[179] This line is not an idle pun, but a telling one. It owes something to the discussion, like that of Aquinas in *Summa Contra Gentiles*, Lib. II, cap. 28f., concerning the "dueness" entailed in the production of things: "there is something conditionally due in each creature as regards its parts, properties, and accidents, upon which the creature depends either for its being or for some perfection proper to it. For example, given that God willed to make man, it was man's due, on the supposition, that God should unite in him soul and body, and furnish him with sense, both intrinsic and extrinsic." (Trans. James Anderson, *On the Truth of the Catholic Faith*, vol. 2, New York, 1956, p. 83.) Aquinas in the same place treats the dueness in the time and nature of a production subsequent to a creature prior in time or nature. We may compare the priority of Una: historically hers is the priority of the Church of the Apostles; metaphysically, it is the priority of the One to the Many. The critical term echoes in the de-creation of Redcrosse, whose empty sides at I.viii.41 are "deceiued of their dew," and in Sansjoy's promise at I.iv.51 to "endew" Duessa. For the connection between Redcrosse's baptised hands and the annealing of his sword, cf. Clement of Alexandria, *Exhortation to the Heathen*, xi, on the Christian armament: " 'the fiery darts of the evil one' let us quench with the sword-points dipped in water, that have been baptized by the Word."

> From that first tree flowd, as from a well,
> 　A trickling streame of Balme, most soueraine
> And daintie deare, which on the ground still fell,
> And oerflowed all the fertill plaine,
> 　As it had deawed bene with timely raine:
> Life and long health that gratious ointment gaue,
> And deadly woundes could heale, and reare againe
> The senselesse corse appointed for the graue.
>
> (I.xi.48)

There is a sense then, in which one may say of the reborn Redcrosse, with the messianic Psalm, his "berth was of the wombe of Morning dew" (Ps. 110:3; III.vi.3).

The ointment is an attribute of the tree of life at II Esdras 2:13: the Lord's people "shal haue at will the tre of life, smelling of ointment." However, Spenser's description also implies a comparison to the providential manna shed on the Israelites in the wilderness (Exod. 16:13: "in the morning ye dewe laye rounde about the hoste"; Num. 11:6, 8-9: "But now our soule is dried way, we can se nothing but this MAN. . . . the taste of it was like vnto the taste of fresh oyle. And when the dewe fel downe vpon the hoste in the night, the MAN fel with it"; Ps. 78:24: God "rained downe MAN vpon them for to eat, and had giuen them of the wheat of heaune"). The manna, being supernatural, is not merely food; it is in some sense sacramental, and it belongs to the complex of biblical ideas about what God puts in man's mouth. The Gospel of John identifies manna as the "bread of life" (John 6:31-35), and the edible tree in Genesis, on the basis of the commentary of St. Augustine, was generally taken to be a "sacrament" or sign of some sort also.[180]

Given the association of the well of life with baptism, we ought to be able to make the tree correspond to the Eucharist, the other sacrament accepted by the reform church. The apples conform to its sacrificial symbolism: "apples rosie red, / As they in pure vermillion had beene dide" (I.xi.46). (The image is faintly Ovidian, with Redcrosse beneath the tree

---

[180] Augustine, *De Genesi ad Litterarum*, VIII.iv-v (PL, XXXIV, 375f.), where the tree is compared to the rock which was Christ of I Cor. 10:4, and also to the paschal lamb. Aquinas, *Summa Theol.*, Pt. I, q.102, art.1, resp. ad. obj.4, repeats the first example. Calvin, *Institutes*, IV.xiv.18, asserts the tree to be a "sacrament" in the wider sense. In Sylvester's translation of DuBartas, the tree of knowledge is called a sacrament (II.I.i, l. 465) and "a sure pledge, a sacred signe, a seal" (*ibid.*, l. 264); both trees are said to have been "seals" provided to sustain the mind (*ibid.*, ll. 214f.). Sylvester's marginalia call both trees sacraments. According to Arnold Williams, *The Common Expositor* (Chapel Hill, 1948), p. 103, Renaissance commentaries on Genesis often follow Augustine in this matter.

having the place of Pyramus beneath the mulberry. Following St. Augustine, the mulberry of Luke 17:6 in the Vulgate was traditionally glossed as an allusion to the cross, "on account of its bloody fruit.")[181] A certain density seems to have been sought in these symbols: the tree itself is compared to a well, and the waters of the well are said to have become mingled with blood. In either case we are reminded of the sacramental flow from Christ's side. With regard to the tree, Spenser has also left room in the symbolism for the sacrament of extreme unction—we will see why presently. As it stands, Redcrosse receives the sacrament as a kind of *viaticum*, the provision for his journey given a dying man.

The red apples and the "siluer flood" repeat the colors on the knight's shield, "the deare remembrance of his dying Lord" (I.i.2: cf. Luke 22:19: "Do this in remembrance of me"). Redcrosse's shield, then, is the chivalric form of the same life-giving tree, and it protects the knight on other occasions as the tree does here. In Malory's Sangreal a redcross shield is painted by the dying Joseph of Arimathaea with his blood; it is claimed by his descendant Sir Galahad, preliminary to his achieving the grail quest.[182]

Since Redcrosse specifically imitates Christ, and especially the Christ who conquers sin and death, it is not insignificant that Christ himself carries a redcross pennon, attached to a long but light cross, when he enters into death and rises from the tomb. This symbol is a commonplace of the medieval iconography of the resurrection; it was a property of the miracle play on the same subject.[183] The transition from Christ's banner to St.

---

[181] "Per poma sanguinea": *Il Quaest. Evangelior*, q.39, no.2, which is cited in the *Glossa ordinaria*, PL, CXIV, 318B. The word "dide" implies a metamorphosis analogous to the color-change cited from Dante (*Purg.* XXXII.37ff.); this change is anticipated by *Purg.* XXVII.39, where the pilgrim responds to the name of Beatrice like Pyramus to Thisbe's, "at the time when the mulberry became red." The idea is repeated at *Purg.* XXXIII.69, where the mind of the pilgrim is "a Pyramus to the mulberry." For more on this symbolism, see John Freccero, "The Sign of Satan," *MLN*, 80, no. 1 (1965), pp. 11–26, to which I owe the Augustine reference. For Spenser's blood-stained well, cf. John Jewel, *A Treatise of the Sacraments*, "Of Baptism," in Parker Society *Works*, vol. 2, p. 1106, on an analogous change made in that sacrament: "Through the power of God's working the water is turned into blood. They that be washed in it receive the remission of sins: their robes are made clean in the blood of the Lamb."

[182] *Morte d'Arthur*, Sangreal, ii; Caxton version in Everyman's Library, vol. 2, pp. 176ff. (In the Winchester ms. version, ed. Vinaver, *Works*, vol. 2, pp. 879–881.) In Hardyng's *Chronicle*, ed. H. Ellis (London, 1812), cap. xlviii, pp. 84f., Joseph's shield is said to bear what are called St. George's arms. The same is also said of the shield of Constantine, which is a gold cross on a white ground (*ibid.*, cap. lxii, p. 99).

[183] Cf. *Howlegas*: "at Easter they should play the resurrection of our Lord; . . . and the parson plaied Christe, with a baner in his hand." Text in John Ashton, ed.,

George's shield can be found in those paintings of St. George that show the knight's lance wrapped in red and white streamers; even more striking is the representation by the painter called Sodoma, where the banner or standard of the cross specifically adorns the knight's lance.[184] St. Michael, a figure with analogies to both Christ and St. George, is shown with the crucifer standard in a painting by Mabuse,[185] and a fourteenth-century illumination pairs St. George's shield with the flag.[186] The flag itself belongs to the ancient Christian symbol of the sacrificial lamb, where the colors are repeated by the flow from the lamb's side.

When Redcrosse unites with Una, the bride "withoutten spot" (I.xii.22, echoing Song 4:7 and Ephesians 5:27), he also reproduces the union of colors found in the Tudor sovereign, who is the head of the English Church—"The red and white rose quartered in her face," Greville writes in an emblematic poem.[187] Frye notes the proximity of the two symbols in *Richard III*, at the end of which the Tudor dynasty is created: "And then, as we have ta'en the sacrament, / We will unite the White Rose and the Red" (V.v.18–19).[188]

In sum, one may say of Spenser's bridegroom, with the bride of Song 5:10, "My beloved is white and ruddy."

Romances of Chivalry (London, 1887), p. 331. For the interaction of the Roman military tradition with the Christian one, cf. Tertullian, *Apology*, xvi: "All those hangings of your standards are robes of crosses," and Venantius Fortunatus' hymn, *Vexilla Regis*, echoed in *Inf.* XXXIV.1, as the exordium to the canto in which Dante will emerge alive from hell.

[184] National Gallery of Art, Washington, D.C. (Reproduced in George Ferguson, *Signs and Symbols in Christian Art*, Oxford, 1954, Plate II.) St George's lance has this banner in the representation of him in the high-altar of the Mary-church in Gelnhausen, as illustrated in Walter Hotz, "Der Hausbuchmeister Nikolaus Nievergalt und Sein Kreis," *Der Wormsgau* (Zeitschrift der Kulturinstitute der Stadt Worms und Altertumsvereins Worms), vol. 3 (1953), fig. 21, p. 111. So also in the Ghent Altarpiece of the Van Eycks, Cathedral of St. Bavon.

[185] Reproduced in Anna B. Jameson, *Sacred and Legendary Art* (1874; reprint, New York, 1970), vol. 1, p. 109, fig. 38. For Michael as bannerer, one may compare *Par. Lost* VI.762f., 775-779.

[186] "St. George Codex," fol. 85^r, Rome, Vatican Library; reproduced in *The Encyclopedia of World Art*, vol. 6, p. 351 (New York, 1959). For the red and white striped pole-lance, see Bellini's painting in the Museo Civico, Pesaro, Italy, reproduced in vol. 2, p. 254. Vol. 12, p. 42, reproduces Crivelli's St. George, which is an étude in red and white.

[187] *Caelica*, 82. Cf. Spenser's hero at II.i.18: "He bore a bloudie Crosse, that quartered all the field."

[188] *Anatomy of Criticism*, pp. 284, 363. The Roman *sacramentum* was the soldier's loyalty oath to the Emperor. The use of the sacrament as a binding ceremony in coronations, weddings, and convocations of the Grail fraternity, all suggest this earlier pledge of allegiance.

We may take this opportunity to fill in some related symbolism. The evil counterpart for the well of life, corresponding to the paralyzed tree, is the knight's enervating drink from the fountain of a lax nymph. A dalliance with Duessa is of course in the offing at the time, and a related symbol is Duessa's magic cup. This is the golden cup borne by the whore of Babylon in Revelation, filled with the blood of the saints and sometimes identified with the abuses of the chalice in Protestant commentary.[189] It has the same incapacitating effect as Duessa's ointments. Duessa calls herself Fidessa, and the contrasting vessel, filled with wine and water, is borne by a character at the House of Holiness named Fidelia. Fidelia is a white witch, said to be able to raise to life (I.x.13, 19). Her cup also contains a snake—a symbol of poison, as in paintings of Saint John, who traditionally did not taste of death (John 21:23).[190] (Cf. Mark 16:18: "They shall drive away serpents, and if they drink any deadly thing, it shall in no wise hurt them.") Fidelia's snake "horrour made to all," but her book would explain it as the brazen serpent that cured the Israelites from the fiery serpents: "So must the Sonne of man be lift up, / That whosoever beleveth in him, should not perish" (John 3:14–15). Luther says that Christ was hung from the cross like a poisonous thing—"Yes, he even appears like the snake which has brought us, in paradise, into labour: that is, the Devil."[191]

The comparable pagan symbolism is attached to the healer Aesculapius. Spenser does not directly mention Aesculapius' emblem the snake, or his ophidian incarnation ("dyabolo operante," as Boccaccio explains it),[192] but the chaining of the malefactor alive in hell is perhaps enough to recall the imprisonment of the satanic serpent in Revelation 20. Medieval moralization of Ovid associates Aesculapius' symbol with Moses and the sacraments, and compares the healer, condemned to hell for curing Hippolytus-Virbius, to Christ, condemned to death because he raised Lazarus (see John 11:45–53).[193] The Hippolytus-Virbius story itself reminds one

[189] For example, in Bale, Parker Society *Select Works*, pp. 496f.; Jan van der Noot, *Theatre for Voluptuous Worldings*, Scholars Facsimiles and Reprints (New York, 1937?), fol. 45ᵛ; and Calvin, *Institutes*, IV.xviii.18, cited below.

[190] For John's immunity to poison, see *Acts of John*, xx, in M. R. James, ed., *The Apocryphal New Testament* (cor. edn., Oxford, 1953), pp. 262f. As Nelson notes (*Poetry*, p. 149), a very similar story is told of St. George in *The Golden Legend*, Caxton trans. (London, 1900), vol. 3, p. 130.

[191] *Auslegung des dritten und vierten Kapitals Johannis*, in Luther, *Werke* (Weimar, 1912), vol. 47, pp. 67f.

[192] *G.D.G.*, V.xix, Romano edn., vol. 1, p. 253.

[193] Emile Mâle, *Religious Art in France in the Thirteenth Century*, trans. Dora Nussey as *The Gothic Image* (New York, 1958), p. 339, citing a ms. of Legouais' *Bible of the Poets*. I am assuming a recognition that Aesculapius and Christ belong to the general type of the Good Physician. For an example, see Justin Martyr, *Apol. Prima*, xxi–xxii (ANF, vol. 1, p. 170). Cf. also Augustine, *De Doctrina Christiana*, I.xiv.13: "the medicine of Wisdom by taking on humanity is accommodated to our wounds,

of the resurrection, and this must be the key to explaining its attachment to Redcrosse's evil counterpart at the House of Pride, where Spenser reproduces a detail from Ovid's version, the mistress' secreting of the body by means of a cloud (*Metam.* XV.434–441). Duessa's intervention for Sansjoy corresponds to Diana's for Hippolytus. To expand the comparison we will need to study Duessa's own relation to the resurrection.

In her first profession, Duessa gives Redcrosse an account of the mysterious theft of her lord's body; thus she puts abroad a story like the one circulated among the Jews in Matthew 28:13–15: the story that the disciples had come in the night and stolen the body of Christ from the tomb. Duessa describes her lord as a kind of fallen and disgraced courtier, rather than as the Christ who humbled himself to death and is now highly exalted (Philippians 2:8). Duessa, in a way, commits the error, mentioned in II Timothy 2:3, of believing that the resurrection is over. For her, Redcrosse's dying god is a dead one. What is doubt in the mind of the knight is more like apostasy in the lady. Her supposed search for her lord's remains is a pretentious parallel for Una's sincere search for Redcrosse. Una may be compared to Mary Magdalene seeking Jesus at the tomb; Duessa, to pilgrims seeking the true cross, or, better, to the Crusaders attempting to recover the holy sepulchre. Later we will note Una's resemblance to Isis searching for Osiris; Duessa acts the parallel part of Diana, preserving the "relicks" of her Hippolytus-Virbius, whose body she conveys and hides. "They have taken away my Lord, and I know not where they have laid him," laments Mary Magdalene (John 20:13). "Where have you left your Lord?" begs Una of Redcrosse's "reliques," his sword and spear (I.vii.48; cf. v.39). Thus Duessa's conveyance of Sansjoy not only recalls but also seems to repeat her earlier story about her lord; ceremonial religion, Spenser implies, recreates that story whenever it substitutes *corpus Christi* for the Christ who is in heaven. Her descent into hell, for the reanimation of Sansjoy by Aesculapius, brings Duessa close to the kind of ghoulish *strix* who traffics in corpses, in contrast to the women ministering to Redcrosse—they rather recall the women preparing Christ's body for the tomb.

[ii]

The sinister overtones of the imagery just catalogued are apparent enough, but what is being characterized as sinister remains elusive. In the

---

healing some by contraries. . . . Thus the Wisdom of God, setting out to cure men, applied Himself to cure them, being at once the Physician and the Medicine. Because man fell through pride, He applied humility as a cure. We were trapped by the wisdom of the serpent; we are freed by the foolishness of God. . . . Christ used his mortality well to restore us." (Trans. D. W. Robertson, Jr., *On Christian Doctrine*, Library of the Liberal Arts, Indianapolis, 1958, pp. 14f.)

interpretation of this imagery, a point of some importance is the Protestant understanding of the sacraments. "The Word comes to the element," Augustine wrote, "and it becomes a sacrament."[194] A reform theologian, advancing on this description, would say that the tree in Genesis, as a "sacrament," derived its efficacy from the word annexed to it.[195] This semiotic approach might be taken for the theme of the standard Protestant position on the nature of the sacraments. The sacraments signify grace and salvation, but only faith in the associated Word confers these things. "The body of Christ is given, taken, and eaten, in the Supper, only after a heavenly and spiritual manner," according to the twenty-eighth Article: "And the means whereby the Body of Christ is received and eaten in the Supper, is faith."

The Protestant position is anticipated in Scripture itself, in the Deuteronomistic interpretation of the manna, which abrogates the physical miracle in favor of sustenance, not by bread alone, but by every word that proceeds out of the mouth of God. Besides sustaining power, however, Spenser's manna tree has healing power; it is of some interest, then, that what Deuteronomy says about the manna, Wisdom repeats with respect to the brazen serpent. It considers the serpent a "sign of salvation":

> For nether herbe nor plaster healed them, but thy word, o Lord, which healeth all things.
> For thou hast the power of life & death, and leadest downe vnto the gates of hel, and bringest vp againe.
>
> (Geneva Bible, Wisdom 16:12–13)

---

[194] *Tract. in Ioan.*, LXXX (trans. in NPNF, 1st Series, vol. 7, p. 344), as quoted with emphatic approval by Luther, in his *Sermons on the Catechism* (trans. in *Martin Luther: Selections*, ed. John Dillenberger, pp. 233, 235). Luther's doctrine, in the *Pagan Servitude*, that a sacrament is a sign accompanied by a word of promise demanding faith, makes the sacraments something like the visible word of God (see *Selections*, p. 299).

[195] The catechism in the edition of the Geneva Bible printed for Christopher Barker in 1586, called "Questions and Answers," and placed between the two Testaments, defines a sacrament in just this way. So also did the Calvinist theologian David Pareus, according to Williams, *Common Expositor*, p. 103, citing *In Genesin Mosis commentarius* (1609), cols. 320–322. The association of *verbum* and *sacramentum* is at the very heart of the Calvinist doctrine, in *Institutes*, IV.xvii.39: "the right administering of the Sacrament cannot stand apart from the Word. For whatever benefit may come to us from the Supper requires the Word: . . . . Here we should not imagine some magic incantation, supposing it enough to have mumbled the words, as if they were to be heard by the elements: but let us understand that these words are living preaching which edifies its hearers." (Trans. Ford Lewis Battles, in the edn. of John T. McNeill, Philadelphia, 1960, vol. 2, p. 1416.) Thus when the Geneva Bible glosses the words of promise that accompany the rainbow of Gen. 9:13, we read: "Hereby we se that signes or sacraments oght not to be separate from the worde." For another example of a "healing word," see Ps. 107:20.

To believe otherwise would be to make of the brazen serpent an idol; the physical brazen serpent kept in the temple was destroyed in the reform of Hezekiah for just this reason (II Kings 18:4). Spenser's Aesculapius may stand for a similar kind of unreformed religion.

In the Latin poem of Boccaccio on the poetic avatars of Christ, Christ is resurrected as Hippolytus-Virbius.[196] Boccaccio's poem, along with the following passage from Erasmus' *Folly*, suggests the direction that commentary on the traffic of Duessa should take. Folly is discussing those who enjoy macabre stories; very similar are those who adhere to superstitious beliefs in the powers of the saints:

> In St. George they have found another Hercules or Hippolytus. They all but adore his horse, which is piously adorned with ornaments and jewels; and they offer little gifts to obtain favors. It is even the custom of kings to swear by St. George's brass helmet. Then what shall I say about those who happily delude themselves with false pardons for their sins? They calculate the time to be spent in Purgatory down to the year, month, day, and hour as if it were a container that could be measured accurately with a mathematical formula. There are also those who think there is nothing they cannot obtain by relying on the magical prayers and charms thought up by some charlatan for the sake of his soul or profit. Among the things they want are: . . . a place next to Christ in heaven.[197]

In the Protestant mind this kind of magical religion includes the intercession of the saints, propitiatory masses for the dead, the doctrine of purgatory, the doctrine of indulgences, the worship of Corpus Christi, the worship of the saints and the belief in their power over various departments of nature, and the veneration of relics. The nexus of meanings for which I am here arguing is nicely summed up by Bale, who says that the Roman Antichrist ministers to the world "ydolatrie and necrolatrie."[198]

Duessa's recourse to Aesculapius, in such a reading, stands for the intercession of the saints. Lavater, for example, mentions Aesculapius as an idol through whom Satan worked healing miracles: "Wherefore there is no cause," he adds, "why the Papists at thys daye, should so insolently

---

[196] *Pantheon*, ll. 209–211, in *Opera Latine Minore*, ed. Aldo F. Massèra (Bari, 1928), pp. 54f.

[197] Trans. taken from John P. Dolan, ed., *The Essential Erasmus* (New York, 1964), p. 129.

[198] *A mysterye of inyquyte* (Geneva, 1545), fol. 54ᵛ. See Bale, *Pageant of Popes*, trans. Studley (London, 1574), fols. 73ᵛ–74ʳ: "all the Popes wer famous enchaunters: by theyr charming they sturred up walking spirits. . . . And those spirites being coniured up by priests, deluded men, dessemblinge that they were the soules of the dead, complayning theyr untolerable paynes in Purgatorye fyre, and craued to be released by the meritorious deedes of theyr frendes & kindred, bestowinge dirges, masses, and trentalles on them."

glorie of the lyke miracles, by the which the go about to proue their intercession of Saints, and such like trumperie."[199] Even more central to the
imagery of the episode is the idolatry of Corpus Christi, along with the
magical belief that the crucifixion is renewed in every mass, rather than
memorialized there. The Protestant objected that in this kind of offering
the sacrifice is never done and Christ is kept bleeding on the cross. In
such a religion one might almost speak of an unexorcised spirit of vengeance, one that takes the form of obsession and morbidity; here one thinks
of the return of Sansjoy to avenge Sansfoy. It may be argued that such
a faith turns Christ's sacrifice into a worldly sideshow; Lucifera does
this when she makes Sansjoy's grievance an occasion for a tournament,
that is, a courtly entertainment. The procession through the fields looks
like a sardonic parody of the chariot that carries Beatrice in Dante—the
"triumph" of the earlier poet has been suggestively compared to Corpus
Christi celebrations.[200] The honoring of the host also took the form of a
triumph, as it is described by Thomas Becon: "that sacramental bread is
carried about with great pomp like a puppet of that thrasonical, boasting,
and glorious knight. Verily Christ did give the mystery of his body to be
eaten, and not to be shewed, not to be heaved up, not to be honoured and
worshipped as a god, not to be carried about in processions. . . ." And he
cites the strictures of Erasmus, who says that the sacrament was not given
"that it should be shewed abroad, or carried about in plays and common
pomps or pastimes, or yet borne about the fields on horseback."[201]

More support for this reading comes from the Protestant objection to
the doctrine of the Real Presence. A difficult typology in Romans 10:6-7
came to be used: "But the righteousness which is of faith speaketh on
this wise, Say not in thine heart, Who shal ascende into heauen? (that is
to bring Christ from aboue) Or, Who shal descend into the depe? (that is
to bring Christ againe from the dead)" (cf. Deut. 30:12-14 for the source).
In his discussion of the immateriality of Christ's presence in the elements,
Calvin alludes to this passage: "we feed our faith by this participation of
the body of Christ which we have mentioned as fully as they do who
bring him down from heaven" (*Institutes*, IV.xvii.32). Bale rebukes the
Romanists in the same terms:

> . . . youre uncommaunded exorcysmes and blessynes are non other than
> the playne practyses of Necromancye. By the vertu werof though ye

[199] *Of Ghostes, edn. cit.*, pp. 163f.
[200] See Charles H. Grandgent, ed., *La Divina Comedia* (rev. edn., Boston, 1933),
p. 591.
[201] *A Comparison Between the Lord's Supper and the Pope's Mass*, sec. 35, in
Prayers and Other Pieces of Thomas Becon, ed. John Ayre, pp. 374f., citing Erasmus
De Amab. Eccles. Conc. Enarr. Ps. lxxxiii.

maye with your Pope fatche the deuyll from hell (for youre sacrifices are all one) yet can ye not drawe the sonne of God out of heaune. . . .[202]

For Christ remains in heaven in his glorious body. We also remember that while Duessa is trying to procure the raising of Sansjoy, Redcrosse is administered to in his bed with sacramental wine and oil. We may note that the idolatrous "bed" of the harlot-allegory in Ezekiel 23 is otherwise an altar.[203] In arguing that the mass is indeed a propitiatory sacrifice, the English Catholic apologist Harding refers to a sermon attributed to St. Augustine, where it is said that it is appropriate that martyrs receive burial under the altar, "to rest where Christ is both the host and the priest . . . to the intent that they might attain propitiation by the oblation of the host." Harding's Protestant opponent Jewel notes that the reference to earthly altars is mixed in with a citation of the heavenly altar in Revelation 6, and he accuses the Catholic apologist of having confused the two. "Hereby it is plain that St. Augustine speaketh of heaven, and not of earth, nor of purgatory; of the souls received above, and not of the bodies buried beneath; . . . But M. Harding, to serve his turn, is fain of souls to make bodies; of joy to make pain; and of heaven to make purgatory: . . ."[204] Thus, on the human level, the idea of a continuous crucifixion finds its equivalent in the joyless doctrine of a purgatory to be met with in the afterlife, a place that the virtues of the mass—or Duessa with her golden cup—can reach. Purgatory is customarily thought of as being fiery (see I Cor. 3:13–15), as is the disease that afflicts Aesculapius himself, in his "endless penance" (I.v.40, 42). The contrasting satisfactions are made in this life by Redcrosse at the House of Holiness, where the house physician, Patience, is assisted by Penance. To Patience we might offer the advice of Canon XXI of the Fourth Lateran Council, which binds the Christian to receive the Eucharist at least once a year, at Easter, and to confess once a year to the parish priest:

[202] *Mysterye of inyquyte*, fol. 47ʳ. So also Zwingli, *An Exposition of the Faith*, in *Zwingli and Bullinger*, ed. and trans. G. W. Bromily, Library of Christian Classics, 22 (Philadelphia, 1953), p. 256.

[203] See below, "The Beginning of Idolatry," sec. i.

[204] Harding's work and Jewel's reply—*A Reply to M. Harding's Answer*—are printed in Parker Society *Works*, ed. John Ayre, vols. 1–2. The quotations are from vol. 2, pp. 755ff. Cf. Becon, *A Comparison*, sec. 43, on the application by the Mass-monger of the elements "unto the dead, while in his Masses he goeth about to pluck them out, and to save them . . . from the pains of purgatory." Becon warns that one is not cleansed by another man's participation in the Lord's supper: "Neither is the place, state, and condition of the dead such that they have need of our help, which are either in continual torment, or else in everlasting joy: there is no third place. . . ." (*Prayers and Other Pieces*, p. 379.)

Let the priest be discreet and cautious, *so that he may pour wine and oil into the wounds of the injured person* like a skilled physician, diligently inquiring into the circumstances both of the sinner and of the sin, so that he may wisely understand what advice he should give him and what remedy he should apply, trying different tests to heal the patient.[205]

Without insisting on all the interpretations just offered, one can say that they form a unity that conforms to the logic of the symbolism.[206] In an ecclesiastical allegory, any edifice is potentially a church. The House of Pride, if it were a church, would be a church full of images—and parasitic churchmen. The activities under these auspices, it follows, would tend to illustrate the futility of ceremonial religion: it cannot confer "life."

The Siege of Paradise

ergo ex futuris prisca coepit fabula
factoque primo res notata est ultima

so from the future the story took its beginning
and the ultimate deed was indicated by the first
(Prudentius, *Hamartigenia*, 25–26)

This is he of whom I said, After me cometh a man who
is become before me: for he was before me.
(John 1:30, Authorized Standard Version of 1901)

[i]

Starting from the contrast between the disgraced tree and the gracious one, we see that Spenser's legend extends from the paradise lost by Adam to the paradise regained by the Messiah, who is a second Adam.[207] Adam falls in the garden he was set to dress, and Christ rises in another garden, where Mary Magdalene mistakes him for the gardener (John 20:15): Aquinas allows the relation between these two gardens to be typological.[208]

[205] Canon XXI; Rev. H. J. Schroeder, O.P., *Disciplinary Decrees of the General Councils, Text, Translation and Commentary* (St. Louis, Mo., 1937), p. 260 (cf. p. 570). Both obligations are relevant to Redcrosse's religio in this episode.

[206] Much support for this assertion is found in the recent study of Douglas Waters, *Duessa as Theological Satire* (Missouri, 1970). My conclusions were reached quite independently of this study, and they are in close agreement with it.

[207] I owe my title to Stephen Barney's chapter title for an essay on Prudentius in a forthcoming study of allegory. He has graciously allowed me to borrow it here.

[208] *Summa Theol.*, Pt. III, q.51, art.2, resp. ad obj.4. Cf. Cyril of Jerusalem, *Catech. Lect.*, XIII, trans. in NPNF, 2nd Series, vol. 7, p. 87: "In Paradise was the Fall, and

Ambrose compares Eden to the garden of Gethsemane where the Lord explained the words of eternal life and allowed himself to be seized, this "signifying that our soul, or rather human nature, after the bonds of error are loosed, returns to the place from which in Adam she was exiled."[209] These associations form a natural part of the standard expositions of the antithetical conformity of the first and second Adam:

> It is comfortable to consider, and wonderful to behold, how the wisdom of God hath made the circumstances of our destruction by Adam, and salvation by Christ Jesus, to agree. Adam in paradise, a garden of pleasure, offended God, and was cast out for his disobedience, and we all his posterity: Christ Jesus was buried in a garden, and hath by his death restored us to life again. . . . In that garden had Adam all pleasant things freely given to him: and in this garden without the city had Christ our Lord all spiteful torments that could be devised.[210]

Between the two gardens stretches the wilderness of history and the moral law; the latter, in the New Testament mind, is closely identified with sin and death.

Parallel to the myth of a paradise regained, and almost coextensive with it, is the history of the national redemption of Israel. Here the types for deliverance are the recovery and fertilization of the promised land, and the building and restoration of the temple at its capital Jerusalem. The

---

in a Garden was our salvation. From the tree came sin, and until the Tree sin lasted. *In the evening, when the Lord walked in the Garden, they hid themselves*; and in the evening the robber is brought by the Lord into Paradise." Hippolytus of Rome must be among the first to draw a parallel between Eve driven from the tree of life in Paradise, and Mary Magdalene laying hold of Jesus in the garden; see the surviving part of his commentary on the Songs of Songs, *Comm. Cant.* 15, in *Hippolyts Kommentar zum Hohenlied*, ed. and trans. Nathanael Bonwetsch (Leipzig, 1902), pp. 351f.

[209] Epist. LXXI, ad Horontianum, trans. Sister Mary Melcher Beyenka, in *Letters*, Fathers of the Church, vol. 46 (New York), p. 241. Cf. Ambrose's *Expositio Evangelii Secundam Lucam*, IV.7 (on Lk. 4:1) (PL, XV, 1614): "It is fitting to be recorded that as the first Adam was ejected from Paradise into the desert, so the second Adam returned from the desert into Paradise. . . . Adam in the wilderness, Christ in the wilderness; for he knew where he could find damnation, towards the Paradise he would regain by dispelling the error. But because he could not be dressed in unholy clothes, nor be resident in Paradise unless naked with respect to sin, he put off the old man; so that, because men could not fulfill the divine decree, by that much greater a person the sentence should be changed."

[210] James Pilkington, *Exposition upon certain chapters of Nehemiah* (1585), in Parker Society *Works*, ed. Rev. James Scholefield (Cambridge, 1852), p. 374. For other examples, see Jacob of Voraigne's account of "The Passion" in the Caxton version of *The Golden Legend* (London, 1900), vol. 1; Bullinger, *Decades*, I, *edn. cit.*, vol. 1, p. 113; and John Foxe, *Of Justification*, sec. 22, in *British Reformers*, ed. W. M. Engles (1st American edn., Philadelphia, n.d.), vol. 12, pp. 193-200.

prophets compare the restored Israel to Eden (Isa. 51:3; Ezek. 36:35); and Spenser's Eden, like the one in Revelation, is metropolitan. From this develops the analogy between the fallen world and the tyrannies of Egypt and Babylon. Israel is also a land blocked off by giants like Og; or usurped by Philistines, who include Goliath; or threatened by invaders like Ezekiel's Gog and Magog. The possessing of Britain by Brute also traditionally required the subduing of giants, including Goemagot (II.x.10). Spenser's Orgoglio surely belongs in this company.

The name *Jesus*, the Greek form of *Joshua*, indicates that he too may be a conqueror of the promised land, and the Matthew conception of a new exodus is indicated frequently in the gospel, starting from the genealogy that makes Jacob the father of Joseph (Mt. 1:15-16). The parallel may be developed, with occasional help from the other Gospels, as follows.[211] Israel is brought into Egypt by Joseph, and falls under the wrath of a tyrant who seeks the life of the Israelite newborn; Christ goes with Joseph into Egypt to escape the wrath of the child-killing Herod. Israel passes over the Red Sea and wanders in the wilderness forty years, tempting God and tempted to apostasy; Christ enters the Jordan to be baptised, retires into the wilderness for forty days, and is tempted by Satan. God delivers the law at Sinai, a priesthood is appointed, and the promised land is divided among the twelve tribes; Christ delivers an interpretation of the law from "the Mount" and appoints the twelve apostles to go unto all nations. Moses also is aided by seventy elders; Luke (10:1-16) records the mission of the seventy to preach the gospel. Moses ascends Pisgah to view the promised land and then disappears, perhaps to be conveyed, like Elijah, directly to paradise; Christ is transfigured before the inner circle of his apostles on Mt. Tabor, where he is shown with Moses and Elijah. Israel passes over the Jordan's divided waters and begins the conquest of the promised land; Jesus goes up to Jerusalem for the Passover—the antagonist is, in E. K.'s words, "the great Satanas, whose kingdome at that time was by Christ conquered, the gates of hell broken vp, and death by death deliuered to eternall death."[212]

To take an example: the mountain at the end of the House of Holiness canto, from which Redcrosse is able to see the New Jerusalem, is compared to Sinai and Olivet (I.x.53-54). God spoke from Sinai, and Christ taught from Olivet, but the allusion probably goes deeper. Moses in the mountain was shown the pattern for the tabernacle, and hence a prototype for the New Jerusalem. Christ wept over the old Jerusalem, visible from Gesthemane on Olivet, just before his passion. With respect to the struc-

[211] The following synthesis is taken largely from Northrop Frye, "The Typology of Paradise Regained," *Modern Philology*, 53 (1956), pp. 227-238.

[212] E. K. on "Maye," l. 54.

ture of the narrative, the mountain also corresponds to Pisgah, from which Moses viewed the promised land that Joshua went over to possess. There is also an allusion to the Mount of Transfiguration,[213] for Redcrosse's desire to go no further recalls Peter's feeling on Mount Tabor that "it is good being here" (Matt. 17:4). The Geneva Bible explains that "After Moses and Elias departure Peter fearing he shuld lose that ioyful sight, speaketh as a man distract & wold haue lodged them in earthely houses, which were receyued in glorie." Peter wished to build three temples here; on Spenser's mountain there is a chapel and a hermitage. The link between Olivet and Tabor also becomes more apparent when we know that Christian tradition (owing to Acts 1:12) regards Olivet as the scene of the Ascension; pilgrims in the sixteenth century were shown on Olivet the scene of the Transfiguration.[214]

After his symbolic elevation, Redcrosse is brought to Eden, where he is immersed in the well of life. Spenser compares the well to a variety of healing waters, including the Jordan. In this case he is thinking in the vein of the liturgy for Easter eve, which is taken from Deuteronomy 31:22-30 and invokes Moses at the borders of the promised land. The liturgy cites a deluge of baptismal types, for this is the point in the Church year where the catechumen enters the paradise of the Church. We may compare the tradition of the Paschal catechism as it is represented by such authors as Gregory of Nyssa and Cyril of Jerusalem: "You are this day in Paradise, O catechumen, you part from the exile of Adam, our first father. Now the port is opened. Return to the place you went out from."[215] As in Spenser, the way lies by a dragon:

> Great is the baptism to which you are coming: . . . It is . . . the delights of paradise, the pledge of the kingdom. . . . But a dragon is keeping watch beside the road you are walking. Take care lest he bite you with unbelief. He sees so many on the way to being saved, and seeks whom he may de-

---

[213] As noted by John E. Hankins, *Source and Meaning in Spenser's Allegory* (Oxford, 1971), p. 116. For the Pisgah vision in a saint's life, cf. Gregory, *Vita S. Benedicti*, in *Dialogues*, II.37 (PL, LXVI, 202B): at the death of St. Benedict, two monks at separate places saw the same vision of a magnificent road glittering with innumerable lights: from Benedict's monastery it stretched eastward in a straight line until it reached up to heaven. The monks are told by an interpreter that this is the road taken by Benedict, "the Lord's beloved." Spenser's Contemplation is thus not only Johannine, but also Benedictine.

[214] *Encyclopedia Biblica*, ed. Cheyne and Black (New York, 1903), *sub* "Olivet," where the name of Tabor, Jebel et-Tor, is compared to that of Olivet, Jebel et-Tur. Karl Baedeker, *Palestine and Syria*, 4th edn. (Leipzig, 1906), p. 77f.: "The scene of the Ascension was located on the Mt. of Olives as early as 315"; Baedeker adds a description of the buildings there.

[215] Gregory of Nyssa, *De Baptismo*, PG, XLVI, 418C-D.

vour. The end of your journey is the Father of Spirits, but the way lies past that dragon. . . . If you meet someone who says "Are you getting ready to plunge in the water? Are there no city baths any more?" then know that the dragon of the sea got ready these temptations for you.[216]

The regaining of a promised land implies the destruction of the un-promising one. If we imagine the deathly place as having the form of the dragons or tyrants who occupy it, we are on the way to the Molech-like iconography for the mouth of hell. The harrowing of hell is not in the New Testament, except in unassembled bits and pieces, but God's power over Leviathan and his human representatives easily makes him something of a dragon-killer. This power is more than once expressed in the Bible in terms of fishing—like Ariosto's Orlando in his mission against the Orco, God is able to put hooks in the water-monster's jaws.[217] Christ's choice of the sign of Jonah might make him a dragon-killer as well; he has gone "in medium oris" (Job 41:14), by entering what Paul, in a telling phrase, calls "the body of this death" (Rom. 8:24). Spenser's dragon has his brazen scales from Job's Leviathan,[218] and a description like the following brings the dragon fairly close to the chaos-monster of the Old Testament:

> He cryde, as raging seas are wont to rore,
>   When wintry storme his wrathfull wreck does threat,
> The rolling billowes beat the ragged shore,
> As they the earth would shoulder from her seat,
> And greedie gulfe does gape, as he would eat
> His neighbour element in his reuenge:
> Then gin the blustring brethren boldly threat,
> To moue the world from off his stedfast henge,
> And boystrous battle make, each other to auenge.
>
> (I.xi.21)

This dragon is obviously about ready to be swallowed up in victory. Death and hell and the sea itself give up their dead in the Apocalypse (Rev. 20:13), when there will be no more sea.

Spenser's dragon is of a notable immensity, and the territories ruled by Adam and Eve were also large. The dragon occupies what they lost, for he shares an identity with the fallen world. Even small details express this

[216] Cyril of Jerusalem, *Catech. Lect.*, Protocat., 16; trans. from Library of Christian Classics (Philadelphia, 1955), vol. 4, pp. 75f.

[217] Ezek. 29:34, 38:4; Job 40:25f. See Job 26:13, Isa. 27:1.

[218] Job 41:6: "The maiestie of his scales is like strong shields, and are sure sealed"; vs. 18: "He estemeth yron as strawe, and brasse as rotten wood"; Behemoth's bones, at 40:13, "are like staues of brasse" (all quotations from Geneva Bible). For a brass-shielded dragon whose bowels are made to burst, see *Visions of the worlds vanitie*, 6.

identity. The dragon both flies and walks on all fours, like an insect, which makes him an unclean beast (Leviticus 11:20, "euerie foule that crepeth and goeth vpon all foure").[219] The whole creation groans to be delivered in Romans 8:22, and Spenser's earth groans under the weight of the dragon —and also under the weight of Orgoglio (I.vii.8, viii.8; xi.54). At least one passage in the Bible—Job 26:7–13—equates the act of creation with the slaying of a water-monster, and Spenser, as we have noted, echoes Ovid's account of the classical deluge in the dragon-slaying at the opening of his legend. In a quadruple refrain that perhaps imitates the fall of Sisera at Judges 5:27, the last dragon collapses, also in an imagery of natural cataclysm:

> So downe he fell, as an huge rockie clift,
> Whose false foundation waues haue washt away,
> With dreadfull poyse is from the mayneland rift,
> And rolling downe, great *Neptune* doth dismay:
> So downe he fell, and like an heaped mountaine lay.
>
> (I.xi.54)

As Micah 7:19 has it: "he wil subdue our iniquities, & cast all their sinnes into the bottome of the sea."

It follows that so long as the dragon is alive, Redcrosse's adventure is in some sense an adventure inside a monster. Infernal basements, caves, and graveyards mark this aspect of his passage. It also follows that man, as well as Israel, has an exodus myth, one represented in paintings of Christ leading Adam and Eve and all their children out of the monster or cave of hell. Satan, "who has the empire over death" (Heb. 2:14), is chained in the Apocalypse; some such imagery also lies behind St. Paul's use of the phrase in the psalm about leading captivity captive, as an allusion to the descent and ascension of Christ (Eph. 4:8, Ps. 86:18, Judg. 5:12). Spenser applies the passage in his Easter sonnet:

> Most glorious Lord of lyfe, that on this day,
> Didst make thy triumph ouer death and sin:
> And hauing harrowd hell, didst bring away
> captiuity thence captiue vs to win:
>
> (*Amoretti* LXVIII)

---

[219] Duessa's "beares vneven paw" (I.viii.48) is also technically unclean (Lev. 11:26f.). Similarly, Lucifera's "unequal beasts" violate Old Testament legislation against the mixing together of divers kinds; this includes plowing with a mixed yoke (Deut. 22:10). We may contrast the six wild beasts constrained by Sir Satyrane at I.vi.26: he compels them "in equall teme to draw." Paul warns the Corinthians against being "unequally yoked" with the unrighteous (II Cor. 6:14). For the unholiness in question, see Mary Douglas, *Purity and Danger* (Harmondsworth, England, 1970), chap. 3.

Spenser's comic allusion to extracting a bone from the jaws of Cerberus, the beast Hercules chained and dragged back from hell, belongs to the same pattern of imagery (I.xi.41).[220] The comparison with the concluding events of Book VI, found later in this study, makes this clear.

The relation of the harrowing of hell to the story of St. George is clearly explained by Spenser, though he does not give all the details.[221] Traditionally, a water-monster is devouring the substance of the kingdom—alternatively, a castle is represented in which the besieged inhabitants are perishing for want of water. The supply of sheep having been exhausted, the monster can only be propitiated with human sacrifice, and the choice eventually settles on the king's daughter. A champion from abroad appears on her behalf, dispatches the monster, and thus wins her hand. In many such stories the hero's marriage also secures his title to the kingdom; in the case of St. George the hero converts the kingdom to Christianity. He builds a church that is sanctified by the rising of a healing spring. In biblical terms, the symbolism passes from Zechariah's harrowing of hell text, "I have sent forth the prisoners out of the pit where there was no water" (9:11) to the life-giving stream that flows from the temple of the New Jerusalem—and from the temple of Christ's body, which is also the Church.

As Frye explains, the wasteland myth of the sick king who is made whole by the grail quester shows the same pattern.[222] The king's incurable wound doubles for his inability to cure the wasteland. In seasonal ritual, this powerlessness belongs to a dying fertility spirit, one like Adonis, or Thammuz with his "annual wound"; the relation of Spenser's Eden to his Garden of Adonis is quite clear. Redcrosse, exhausted and prostrate, like one "appointed for the graue," corresponds to the elegiac Adonis. And yet Redcrosse is within the sanctuary of the tree of life, as Adonis has been secreted in a dew-dropping myrtle grove, "Lapped in flowers and pretious spycery" (III.vi.46). Time, "with his flaggy wings," is at large in Adonis' garden, as the dragon is in Adam's (III.vi.39; cf. I.xi.10). And the dragon will be defeated, as the boar has been confined.

Since Redcrosse is St. George, one may compare his prostration to that of the protagonist of the mummers' play, where the knight dies with the

---

[220] Cf. the Cerberus reference in a harrowing of hell scene in Dante, *Inf.* IX.98f.

[221] The following account depends upon a synthesis of Frye, *Anatomy of Criticism*, pp. 186–195; Baring-Gould, *Curious Myths of the Middle Ages*, pp. 278ff.; Lydgate's poem (see n. 116, above); and Caxton's version of *The Golden Legend* (London, 1900), vol. 3, pp. 125–134.

[222] Galahad(t) is the healer-balm of Vlg. Jer. 22:8: so Craig Davis.

dragon, to be afterwards revived by a doctor with an elixir—the elixir corresponding to the well of life. There is such a motif for Adam too, not only in those typologies that make Christ an anti-venom for the affliction of the serpent, but also in the legend of Seth's journey to the gates of paradise. Seth seeks to secure from St. Michael the oil of mercy from the tree of life for the relief of his dying father. In the cycle of Israel the place of the stymied king, dying, as it were, offstage, is taken by Moses. For mysterious reasons Moses is condemned to perish outside the promised land, and he easily becomes a type representing the inability of the law to redeem from the wilderness of sin. His office is inherited by Jesus' namesake (Acts 7:44f.); so Galahad succeeds his morally sick father.

In accomplishing his quest, Redcrosse in some measure displaces his father-in-law. Psychologically, the father-figure occupies a place analogous to that of the dragon, as does the monster in the story of Oedipus. In slaying the dragon and redeeming the kingdom, Redcrosse puts to death the Old Adam. This potentially parricidal motif turns up in Shakespeare's Henry plays, for Hal's assumption of the throne entails both the burial of his father and the repudiation of the old man Falstaff. The clergy of *Henry V* seem sensitive to this comparison:

> *Canterbury*: The King is full of grace and fair regard.
> *Ely*: And a true lover of the holy Church.
> *Canterbury*: The courses of his youth promised it not.
> The breath no sooner left his father's body
> But that his wildness, mortified in him,
> Seemed to die too; yea, at that very moment
> Consideration like an angel came
> And whipped th'offending Adam out of him,
> Leaving his body as a paradise
> T' envelop and contain celestial spirits.
>
> . . . .
>
> Never came reformation in a flood
> With such a heady currance scouring faults;
> Nor never Hydra-headed willfulness
> So soon did lose his seat—and all at once—
> As in this king.
>
> *(Henry V,* I.i.22-31, 33-37)

This passage also provides a convenient summary of the concluding cantos of Book I, including the cleansed dwelling place of the spirit, whipped and scoured; the strong hint of baptismal typologies; the comparison of the purified and regenerate Christian body to a harrowed paradise; and, finally, the expulsion of a water-monster from the domain of a king.

[ii]

We may distinguish at least four prototypes for the Redcrosse of the last adventure, each corresponding to a historical layer in Spenser's conception. First would come the messianic figure who repossesses paradise. One of the best descriptions of his role comes from the Old Testament pseudepigrapha, the *Testament of the Twelve Patriarchs*, known in England from the time of Robert Grosseteste, its Latin translator. God will "raise up a new priest, unto whom all the Lord's word shall be opened":

> In his priesthood all sin shall come to an end, and the unrighteous shall cease from their naughtiness: but the righteous shall rest in him, and hee shall open the gates of Paradise, and stay the threatening sword against *Adam*, and feede the Lambes with the fruit of life, and the spirit of holinesse shall bee in them. He shall bind up *Belial*, and give his own children power to tread down hurtfull spirits, and the Lord shall rejoyce in his children, and accept them as his beloved evermore.
>
> (*Testament of Levi*, 18:9–13)[223]

This text supplies a redemptive counterpart for the "covering cherub" of Ezekiel 28, where we read of a degraded guardian angel (he seems to wear a priestly garment—it has all twelve stones in the Septuagint). This angel is thrown out of Eden, the blazing and bejeweled garden of God, in a myth that combines the exile of Adam with that of some greater blocking spirit. He is traditionally taken for Satan, partly by way of his similarities to the fallen Lucifer of the analogous taunt song in Isaiah 14; he occupies the same impasse mediated in Spenser by the dragon.

The imagery that makes Christ's triumph over death a return to paradise originates in the promise to the good thief in Luke. Cyril of Jerusalem encouraged the catechumen by his example, asserting that the convert was pardoned as speedily as Adam was sentenced: "Adam by the Tree fell away; thou by the Tree art brought into Paradise. Fear not the serpent; he shall not cast thee out; for he is fallen from heaven. . . . Be of good courage: thou shalt not be cast out. Fear not the flaming sword; it shrinks from its Lord."[224] This is also the import of the so-called narrative of Joseph, a part of the harrowing of hell legend found in *The Golden*

[223] Trans. Anthony Gilby (London, 1576); several times reprinted while Spenser was writing his poem. The translation depends on the Latin of Robert Grosseteste.

[224] *Catech. Lect.*, XIII.31, trans. in NPNF, 2nd Series, vol. 7, p. 90. That the usurping Prince of Tyre is to be understood as a type of the devil perhaps requires no annotation. Examples are Origen, *De Principis*, III.ii.15; Jerome, *Epist.* XXII.4, and *Comm. in Ezech.*, IX.xxviii (PL. XXV, 273); Gregory, *Moralia*, XXXII.xii.17, xxiii. 47f.; Augustine, *Civ. Dei*, XI.xv.

Legend and Vincent of Beauvais.[225] According to this story, in the aftermath of the harrowing the Lord commissions Michael to lead Adam into paradise, where they meet Enoch and Elijah and the crucified thief. The thief has been admitted into the garden by the angel that keeps it, on the cognizance of the sign of the cross. In the version of the story in M. R. James' edition of the New Testament Apocrypha, the angel is not only satisfied, but the barrier of fire is extinguished.[226] In Dante the fire forms the last purgatorial ordeal before entry upon Eden, in accordance with an interpretation one finds in Ambrose: "All who desire to return to Paradise must be tried by fire: for not in vain the Scripture says, that when Adam and Eve were driven out of their abode in Paradise, God placed at the gate of Eden a flaming sword which turned every which way."[227] Adam is also led back to Eden in II Esdras 3:6.

The contest for Eden is represented as a three-day fight in forty stanzas. Christ was traditionally in the tomb for forty hours, and thus Spenser's number is probably no accident.[228] The comparable underworld conquest in Book II, Guyon's temptation by Mammon, is partly based on the temptation of Christ, and Guyon is in Mammon's realm for three days and forty stanzas also. Sinister underworld versions of the baptising water and the precious fruit tree enforce the parallel. The Church calendar, of course, equates the forty days of Lent with the forty days in the wilderness. As Satan hopes to find Christ pervious to sin, so the dragon is distressed to find on the third morning that Redcrosse is not "damnifyde" (I.xi.52). In the older theory of the atonement, Satan is defeated partly by virtue of Christ's ineligibility for a sinner's legal death.[229]

[225] Jacob of Voraigne, *Golden Legend*, vol. i, "The Resurrection," pp. 100f. Vincent of Beauvais, *Bibliotheca mvndi*, vol. 4, *Speculvm Historiale*, Lib. VII, cap. lvii seq. (1624; reprint, Graz: Akademisch Druck-u. Verlagsanstalt, 1964–1965), esp. cap. lxii, p. 244. See also the passage from Cyril of Jerusalem in n. 208 above.

[226] *The Apocryphal New Testament*, p. 164.

[227] *In Psalmum CXVIII Expositio*, Sermo Vigesimus, 12 (in vers. 153), PL, XV, 1487B.

[228] Vincent, *Speculvm Historiale*, Lib. VII, cap. liii, *edn. cit.*, p. 240, quoting Peter Comestor, *Historia Scholastica*, Historia Evangelica, cap. 185: "*Augustinus* autem dicit, quod diluculo, cui consentiunt, qui dicunt Dominum 40. horis mortuum fuisse, scilicet quatour horis vespertinus parasceues, & 36. duarum noctium, & vnius diei. Ecclesia quoque assentire videtur, quae matutinas laudes, pro Christi resurrectione celebrat." (So Comestor, in PL, CXCVIII, 1636–1637, referring to Augustine, *Harmony of the Gospels*, III.xxiv.66.)

[229] Harnack, *History of Dogma*, trans. James Miller (London, 1897), vol. 3, appendix to chap. VI, pp. 305–315; for Anselm's theory, vol. 6, pp. 54–83. For a recent study, see Gustav Aulén, *Christus Victor*, trans. A. G. Hebert (London, 1965), pp. 47–55.

A second prototype for Redcrosse is the Christ who specifically conquers hell. This Christ appears in the New Testament apocrypha, most importantly in the *Gospel of Nicodemus*. There are scriptural touches in this; for example, the magnificent liturgical use made of Psalm 148. Nonetheless, the "gospel" is partly a Christian romance—a recurrent feature of the Greek romances contemporary with it is the heroine's underground captivity among brigands. Another "legendary" feature of the *Gospel of Nicodemus* is the "quest of Seth," told in response to John's account of Jesus' baptism.[230] These two accounts fit just inside the Fall and Atonement themselves, Seth having a relation to the dying Adam something like the converse of John's relation to the manifested Christ. The story Seth tells is found in *The Golden Legend*, the *Cursor Mundi*, and *Mandeville's Travels* (I.2), as well as the Latin *Life of Adam and Eve*.[231] It may well go back to the Assyrian myth of Adapa (possibly Adam), who is offered the food of immortality at the gates of heaven.[232] From the angel Michael, Seth generally succeeds in obtaining, not the oil of mercy itself, but the promise of a redeemer, who will annoint Adam in the fullness of time.

The importance of Seth as a prototype for Redcrosse should not be missed. Begotten in the image of his father (Gen. 5:3), Seth is the first Second Adam, so to speak, even as Adam, made in the image of God, is the first "son of God" (Luke 3:38). When Redcrosse becomes Adam's son-in-law, he too will be a second Adam. Seth partly succeeds where his father has failed, and he brings back from Eden, in the full version of the story, the branch or seeds that eventually become the holy rood. In the grail legends themselves, the same wood has become a bleeding tree, though its origins have been forgotten. One version of the grail story, in fact, has Eve take the plant in question from paradise herself.[233] We meet the image of the bleeding tree in the suffering Adam figure of Fradubio; the

[230] The legend is fully studied by Esther Quinn, in *The Quest of Seth for the Oil of Life* (Chicago, 1962). In Paradise Adam had the tree of life "to banish the dissolution of old age," according to Augustine, *Civ. Dei*, XIV.xxvi, and "the tree of life, like a drug warded off all bodily corruption"—so Thomas Aquinas, *Summa Theol.*, Pt. I, q.97, art.4, resp. (quoting Abrosiaster, *De Quast. in Vet. et Nov. Test.*, I, q.19; PL, XXXV, 2228).

[231] *The Golden Legend*, "The Life of Adam," in the Caxton version, vol. 1, pp. 169–181; *Cursor Mundi*, ll. 1237–1448 (EETS, no. 57, pp. 79–91); *Mandeville's Travels*, chap. 2; the Latin *Life of Adam and Eve* in R. H. Charles, gen. ed., *Apocrypha and Pseudepigrapha of the Old Testament* (Oxford, 1913), vol. 2, pp. 144f.

[232] See the translation by E. Speiser, "Adapa," in James B. Pritchard, ed., *Near Eastern Texts*, 2nd edn. (Princeton, 1966), pp. 101–103.

[233] For the legend of the cross in the Grail literature, see *Le Saint-Graal*, ed. E.F.F. Hucher (Au Mans, 1875–1878), vol. 1, pp. 452–479; *Grand saint graal*, in *The Vulgate Version of the Arthurian Romances*, ed. H. Oskar Sommer (Washington, D.C., 1908–1916), vol. 1. For Eve, see *Queste del Saint Graal*, xi, trans. as *The Quest of the Holy Grail* by P. M. Matarasso (Baltimore, 1969), pp. 222ff.

place of the original tree of mercy is taken by the oil-producing tree at the end of the legend.

Seth, whose name means "plant," accomplishes a messianic quest in ultimately reclaiming the tree of life. The following text from *The City of God* seems prophetic; Augustine plays on the other meaning of Seth's name, "resurrection":

> But as for the son of Seth, the son of the resurrection, let him hope to call on the name of the Lord God. For he prefigures that society of men which says, "But I am like a green olive-tree in the House of God: I have trusted in the mercy of God."[234]

(Ps. 73:20)

Redcrosse, being a descendant of those who will ultimately have an inheritance in the heavenly city, is also a kind of "son of Seth." And yet for our hero, as for his forebearer in the legend, the redeemer is still to come, and his sacrifice still to be made. Or else the healing sacramental death has already taken place, but it remains to be put into effect. Thus the knight's sacrificial colors are both prior and posterior to this death. In words like those that Paul uses for the Eucharist (I Cor. 11:26), these colors "declare the Lord's death till he come."

Particularly in the Error episode, Redcrosse acts the part of his own precursor. As John the Baptist himself says, in what was originally probably a reference to the promise of a second Elijah: "One comes after me who is become before me, because he was ahead of me." The gospel interposes this witness between the two testaments, so to speak, in a way that reverses their priority: "Before Abraham was," Christ says, "I am" (John 8:58). Herein lies the secret of biblical typology, and an answer to the question of John's disciples, which comes to mind after every failure of the Redcrosse knight: "Art thou he who is to come, or are we to wait for another?" (Matt. 11:3). Herein also lies the secret of our Sethite hero's ultimate improvement upon himself.

A third prototype for Redcrosse is the chivalric Christ. He is already on horseback in Revelation, and even before that the Word of God in Wisdom is armed as a fierce man of war who wreaks vengeance on the Egyptians. The imagery of the shield of his body, the beloved in a castle, and the heraldic "colors" of human nature, are more specifically feudal.[235]

[234] *Civ. Dei*, XV.xxi, trans. M. Dods (New York, 1950), p. 509. Seth signifies "resurrection" at *Civ. Dei*, XV.xviii.

[235] Cf. *Ancrene Wisse*, Pt. VI, in the text ed. by Geoffrey Shepherd, Nelson's Medieval and Renaissance Library (London and Edinburgh, 1959), p. 22. Another example is Dante, *Parad.* XXXII.128f. Cf. the following story from the *Gesta Ro-*

Though by no means a fully developed motif in Langland, the identification of Piers the Plowman, who harrows hell, with Jesus the Jouster, who undertakes the tournament, provides a remarkable instance. On Easter morning, after writing his vision of the harrowing, the poet went to mass:

> Thus I awaked and wrote . what I had dremed,
> And diȝte me derely, . and dede me to cherche,
> To here holy the masse . and to be houseled after.
> In myddes of the masse . and men ȝete to offrynge,
> I fel eftsones a-slep . and sodeynly me mette,
> That Pieres the Plowman . was paynted al blody,
> And come in with a crosse . bifor the comune peple,
> And riȝte lyke in alle lymes . to owre lorde Iesu;
> And thanne called I Conscience . to kenne me the sothe.
> "Is this Iesus the Iuster?" quot I . "that Iuwes did to deth?
> Or it is Pieres the Plowman! . who paynted hum so rede?"
> Quode Conscience, and kneled tho . "thise aren Pieres armes,
> His coloures and his cote-armure . ac he that cometh so blody
> Is Cryst with his crosse . conqueroure of Crystene."
>
> (B-Text, Passus XIX.1–14)

Langland's bloody crucifer goes back to an even more traditional country-man in Isaiah 63, the treader of the winepress in Edom. The agricultural figure and the military figure are brought together again in the Apocalypse: the reddened vesture is worn by the horseman called Faithful and True, whose other name is "the Word of God" (Rev. 19:11–13).

The association between the plowman and moral vision is well established in the English imagination. Chaucer's preacher has a plowman for a brother; the poet's descriptions of the two occupations show the parallel. That plowing is a type for preaching appears in Langland, and both the

---

manorum (no. lxvi in the Oesterly edn.): a beautiful daughter of a king who has died is seduced by a baron who wins his way by false promises; the tyrant then expels her from the throne, and she is reduced to begging. "It happened that as she sat weeping by the wayside, a certain knight passed by, and observing her great beauty, became enamored of her. 'Fair lady,' said he, 'what are you?' 'I am,' replied the weeping girl, 'the only daughter of a king.'" (Cf. *F.Q.* I.vii.43.) The knight engages the tyrant, whom he defeats, but on the third day after the battle he dies of his wounds. The lady retains his bloody arms, devoting herself to the relics and remaining single the rest of her life. In the moralization of the fable, it is explained that the king is the Father, the daughter is the soul, the tyrant the devil, the wayside the world, the knight Christ, and the armor the cross. For other examples, see Wilbur Gaffney, "The Allegory of the Christ-Knight in Piers Plowman," *PMLA*, 46 (1931), pp. 155–169, citing *Townely Plays*, ed. G. England and A. W. Pollard, EETS, Extra Series, no. 71, p. 261, and *Religious Lyrics of the XIV Century*, ed. Carleton Brown, pp. 63f., 67.

unmuzzled ox of I Timothy 5:17-18 and the apostle who puts his hand to the plow in Luke 9:61-62 contribute to the patristic trope. In the House of Holiness canto, when Redcrosse is sufficiently himself for Contemplation to reveal the knight's name and future sainthood, Spenser refers us to the etymology of George, "working the earth": a fairy conveyed the infant to Fairyland,

> And in a heaped furrow did thee hyde
> Where thee a Ploughman all vnweeting fond
> As he his toylesome teme that way did guyde,
> And brought thee vp in ploughmans state to byde
> Whereof *Georgos* he thee gaue to name;
>
> (I.x.66)

One notes that a French proverb cited by Mâle makes St. George's Day a date of some significance in the agricultural calendar: *A la Saint-George / Seme ton orge* (On St. George's sow your seed).[236] God the Father is a husbandman (*georgos*) in St. John's comparison of Christ to the vine, and St. Paul tells the Corinthians that they are God's husbandry (*georgion*, I Cor. 3:9). Gregory of Nyssa, starting from such a usage, develops an image that brings us back to the Johanine motif of Christ the gardener:

> The [true husbandman] is he who at the beginning in Paradise cultivated human nature, which the heavenly Father planted. But the wild boar [Ps. 80:13; "from the forest"] has ravaged our garden and spoiled the planting of God. That is why he [the husbandman] has descended a second time to transform the desert into a garden, ornamenting it by planting virtues and making it flourish with the pure and divine stream of solicitous instruction by means of the Word.[237]

[236] *Gothic Image*, trans. Nussey, p. 271. For the ministry of the plowman in the Fathers and Langland, see Stephen Barney, "The Plowshare of the Tongue: The Progress of a Symbol from the Bible To *Piers Plowman*," *Mediaeval Studies*, 35 (1973), pp. 260-293, and cf. Hos. 10:12, and Gregory, *In Primum Regum Expositiones*, V.iv.18, in PL, LXXIX, 370. Oxen signify preachers who plow the field of the church. Compare *Piers Plowman*, B-Text, Passus XV.122, on the priest's breviary, "a portous that shulde be his plow," with Idleness and his "Portesse" at the head of Lucifera's "wayne" (I.iv.19); see n. 219, above, for this wain as a team. For another well developed allegorical wain, drawn by the four evangelists (Matthew = tilling; Mark = sowing; Luke = harrowing; John = watering), see *Cursor Mundi, edn. cit.*, ll. 21263ff., esp. 21301-21305. The most important Tudor plow of the ministry is in Hugh Latimer, Parker Society *Sermons*, ed. G. E. Corrie (Cambridge, 1844), "Sermon on the Plough."

[237] Homilia XV, *In Cant. cant.*, PG, XLIV, 1091D. A very similar mission is implied for St. Dominic in Dante, *Parad.* XII.72, 86f., 104-106. (Dominic is also part of a wain image, being placed in one of the two wheels in the heaven of the sun, and the Dominicans being allegorized as one of the two wheels of the chariot of the triumphant church in *Purg.* XXIX.107—see *Parad.* XII.106ff.) Gregory is

A fourth prototype has also been discussed, the kind of traveling adventurer represented by Huon of Bordeaux, who conquers a dragon guarding the elixir of immortality. The weary hero is afterwards revived in the waters of the fountain. On the same adventure he gathers the nearby apples of immortality and later uses them to rejuvenate an old sultan, whom he also converts to Christianity.[238] Rather likelier to have influenced Spenser is the story of Astolfo in the *Orlando Furioso*. The knightly braggart would commend himself to Spenser's attention because he is specifically English (he may even be related to Falstaff, or Fastolf as he is first called).[239] Astolfo, like Fradubio, is introduced as a tree-victim of an enchantress. The climax of his adventures is his visit to the Ethiopian kingdom of Senapo, an aged king identified with Prester John. In Homer the "blameless" Ethiopians are visited by the gods, who feast and holiday among them;[240] their kingdom is also idealized in Heliodorus. Finally, there is the legend of a mountain-guarded paradise at the source of the Nile, and traditionally the Nile rises in Eden. Prester John is usually an Asian, rather than an African, monarch; his far-eastern kingdom was distinguished by its wealth, and also by an original Christianity early separated from the mainstream of belief and practice. And because it was in the east, paradise was within its borders. One guesses that Ariosto is at least vaguely aware of the identification of Prester John with Presbyterian John, the seer in Patmos who was elevated to a vision of the New Jerusalem. The association of these traditions in Ariosto, then, would potentially suggest a state of happy innocence somewhat shielded from the outside world.

> Senapo Imperator de la Etiopia
> Ch'in loco tien di scettro in man la Croce
> De gente, di cittadi e d'oro ha copia

quoted from George H. Williams, *Wilderness and Paradise in Christian Thought* (New York, 1962), p. 40.

[238] *The Boke of Duke Huon of Bordeaux*, ed. S. L. Lee, EETS, Extra Series, nos. 40, 41, 43, 50 (London, 1882–1887), chap. cxxi, cxxvii, pp. 432ff., 465ff. (See also pp. 552–555, 568, for further instances of the apples' rejuvenating powers.) DuBartas compares the apples of the tree of life to those of the Hesperides and with the restorative that Medea applied to the father of Jason (*Weeks*, Sylvester trans., II.I.1, ll. 240–249). We may compare Wolfram von Eschenbach's *Parzifal*, IX.481, where messengers try to procure herbs for the salving of the Fisher King's wounds from the four rivers flowing down from paradise. (They also try the golden bough, on the reasoning that the spear that wounded the King may well come from the same infernal place as the bough: here the bough would have the place of Longinus' lance in the Grail symbolism.)

[239] The suggestion is Antonio Panizzi's, in his edn. of Boiardo's and Ariosto's romanzi (London, 1830–1834), vol. 2, pp. 184–186.

[240] *Iliad* I.423, *Od.* I.22–25; see Ariosto, *O.F.* XI.44.

Quindi fin là dove il mar Rosso ha foce
E serva quasi nostra fede propria,
Che può salvarlo da l'esilio atroce,
Gli è (s'io non piglio errore) in questo loco
Ove al battesmo loro usano il fuoco.

(XXXIII, 102)

Senapo King of Ethiopia here holds power with the scepter of the Cross; of peoples, cities, and of gold he has an abundance, as far as the shore where the Red Sea debouches; he serves a faith nearly like ours, which could save [man] from the Awful Exile; here it is (if I'm not mistaken) they use, for baptism, fire.

But of course the king has spoiled his good fortune by attempting to take the mountain of paradise by force, and he is compared to Lucifer—no doubt the figure in Isaiah 14:13-14 who would ascend to heaven and set his throne "on the mount of assembly." Ariosto's jewel and fire imagery also suggest the mountain of Eden in Ezekiel's oracle prophesying the expulsion of the prince of Tyre. Punishing his presumption, a destroying angel has blinded the king and unleashed a flock of harpies from hell who regularly pollute his table. Astolfo comes on the scene, and by blasting on his magic horn drives the harpies back to their smoky abode. Somewhat incidentally, he hears the confession of the shade of the feckless Lydia—an interpolated tale. After a bath in a spring flowing from a "living rock" (XXXIV.47), he ascends to paradise, where he meets St. John. From thence, under the guidance of the saint, he goes to the moon to retrieve Orlando's wits, and he also secures an herb to cure Senapo's blindness.

It is not surprising that Senapo wants to call Astolfo a "new Messiah" (XXXIII.114), and such a story is unlikely to be lost on a commentator like Fornari, who could explain the baptism of Ruggiero as the election of the Gentiles. For Fornari, the mountain represents the heights of contemplation; Astolfo's conquering horn, apostolic eloquence; his magic book with its invaluable index, the Old Testament interpreted through the New, written in red ("by means of which one discovers what the brazen serpent and the swallowed Jonah signify"); the bath, sacramental immersion, with a reference to Paul's explanation of Moses' rock (see I Cor. 10:4); the actual ascent to paradise, the entry into a state of grace (for John's name refers to God's grace); John's red and white garment, charity and purity; the jewelled edifice in Eden, the spouse of the redeemer; the precious stones, the graces and sacraments and gifts bestowed on the Church.[241] Dante is cited as the authority for the mountaintop locale. Allegorically this is "the mountain of contemplation, which is the

[241] *La Spositione di M. Simon Fornari . . . sopra l'Orlando furioso . . .* , vol. 2, p. 243.

highest consciousness, taking no thought of earthly things, but only of celestial."[242] Most importantly, the whole episode is treated as an allegory of regeneration, the restoration of the senses through grace. About the same interpretation is found in the encapsulations in Porcacchi's edition of Ariosto:

> Senapo, delivered from the cruelties of the harpies by Astolfo, shows that the man who, as a sinner, has immediate recourse to God is not abandoned —rather he is recommended to Him by his good heart. As for Astolfo, who enters the infernal depth, and who washes himself head to foot in a fountain before he is raised to the summit of the mountain—the same advises that no Christian is lifted from this center full of sins and vices to this summit of eternal beatitude before the soul is washed of all earthly concupiscence with the sacraments of the Church, confessed and houseled and cleansed from all stain, and soilure, which infects and contaminates everyone in this vale of misery.[243]

This might be taken to illustrate the passage from the purgatorial House of Holiness to the mountain of Contemplation, and the Garden of Eden.

There is one further link between Astolfo and Redcrosse. Astolfo is an English knight, and earlier (XV, 98) he exchanged gifts with the Christian king of Jerusalem. For his part, Astolfo receives prizes taken from Joppa; his prizes turn out to be the girdle and spurs worn by the warrior "who freed the damsel from the dragon," i.e., St. George.

There is a classical counterpart for St. George in the hero Perseus. Fornari notes that Joppa preserved the relics of the Orco slain by Perseus,[244] and Ariosto's story of the Orco adopts Perseus' legend for chivalric romance. Perseus is the original "knight in shining armour"; he reminds us

---

[242] *Ibid.*, vol. 2, pp. 236f.; and also vol. 1, p. 574.

[243] *Orlando Furioso . . . con nuoui argomenti di M. Ludovico Dolce . . . le nuoue allegorie, 8 annotationi di M. Tomaso Porcacchi . . .* (Venegia, 1583). I have taken the considerable liberty of printing the two allegories for cantos 33 and 34 without interruption: their argument seems continuous. Also cf. the "Allegorie" of Harington: "First, whereas *Astolfo* washeth himselfe in a Christall well of clear water before he can fly up to Paradise, it signifieth that a man shall by remorse and devout consideration weigh and behold the filthines of his sinne he must then washe himselfe with the cleare spring water of prayer and repentance, and then and not before, he may mount to Paradise, which may here be understood the comfortable peace of conscience, the only true Paradise of this world." Only St. John, "whose name signifieth grace," can restore those wits lost "with following the vanities and pleasures of this world." (*Ludovico Ariosto's Orlando Fvrioso*, ed. Robert McNulty, Oxford, 1972, pp. 398f.)

[244] *Spositione*, vol. 1, p. 339, citing the authority of St. Jerome, i.e., *Comm. in Jonam*, I (in PL, XXV, 1123).

especially of Arthur, for like Ruggiero in the Orco story, Arthur conquers the monster with the unveiling of his radiant shield. The Renaissance allegorization of Perseus' victory sounds rather like an exposition of Arthur's defeat of Orgoglio:

> . . . the mind of man being gotten by God, and so the childe of God killing and vanquishing the earthlinesse of the Gorgonicall nature, ascendeth vp to the vnderstanding of heauenly things, of high things, of eternal things, in which contemplacion consisteth the perfection of man.[245]

A last prototype for St. George is the archangel Michael, to whom Arthur is also related. It is Michael, according to Dante, who "avenged the proud adultery,"[246] and of course he fought the dragon in paradise. He too is portrayed with a redcross shield, or with the banner of Christ's victory.

> He received the souls of saints and brought them into the paradise of exultation and joy. He was the prince of the synagoge of the Jews, but now he is established of our Lord, prince of the church of Jesu Christ. And as it is said, he made the plagues of Egypt, he departed and divided the Red Sea, he led the people of Israel by the desert and set them in the land of promission, he is had among the company of holy angels as bannerer, and bearing the sign of our Lord, he shall slay by the commandment of God, right puissantly, Antichrist that shall be in the Mount of Olivet.[247]

[245] Sir John Harington, in his *Apology*, in Smith, *Elizabethan Critical Essays*, vol. 2, p. 202. Cf. Boccaccio, *G.D.G.*, I.iii: "Allegorically [the victorious Perseus] figures the pious man who scorns worldly delight and lifts his mind to heavenly things." So Leone Hebraeo, *Dialoghi d'Amore*, ed. Santino Caramella (Bari, 1929), p. 99: "Perseus . . . son of Jove . . . signifies the prudent man, endowed with every virtue, who, destroying the base and earthly vice signified by the Gorgon, ascended into the heaven of virtue. Again, [the story] signifies allegorically how the human mind, offspring of Jove, destroying and overcoming the earthiness of the gorgonic nature, is raised to understand heavenly things high and eternal, in which speculation human perfection consists."

[246] Sinclair trans., *Inf.* VII.12. "Strupo" also means revolt: cf. *stupro*, violence, rape. (At *Inf.* XIX.57, *strazio*, destruction, is used with reference to the fraud and violence committed against "the Lady Beautiful" by the Papacy.) The meaning given here is attested in three ages: the anonymous Florentine—"stupro, because some force a virgin this sin is called stupro: as Lucifer wanted to force the deity from heaven" (*La Divina Commedia . . . con commenti secundo la Scolastica*, ed. P. Gioarchino Berthier, Friburg, 1892, p. 108). So also Castelvetro, *Sposizione* (Modena, 1886), p. 94; and Tommaseo, *Commedia* (Milan, 1865), vol. 1, pp. 93f., quoting Hosea 1:2, on the fornication of the lords of the earth, and Wisdom 14:12, on fornication the beginning of idolatry. Tommaseo adds: "In the Book of Enoch the evil angels ravish (*stuprano*) the women and Michael binds them."

[247] *Golden Legend*, Caxton trans., vol. 5, p. 181. See also Honorius of Autun, *Speculum Ecclesiae*, "De Sancto Michaele," in PL, CLXXII, 1012, for the same lore.

God says that he will send his angel to the church in the wilderness (Acts 7:38; see Exodus 32:34), and in Spenser it is Arthur who adopts Una's cause when she is in the same place.

[iii]

To conclude, let us return to the paradise-regained motif in Spenser. The tone of the dragon fight will not strike many readers as doing anything like justice to the Crucifixion—it certainly is not the *St. Matthew Passion*. The fun-loving dragon exhibits a naive exuberance that reminds one a little of Orlick in *Great Expectations*, with his childlike gloat, "O you enemy!" (chap. 53). Redcrosse, far from undergoing the agony in the garden, lies beneath the tree of life, "as in a dreame of deepe delight" (I.xi.50). There are also the mock-heroic comparisons, such as the one for the knight's difficulty in recovering his shield: "Nor harder was from Cerberus greedie iaw / To plucke a bone" (I.xi.41).[248] The joco-serious undertone pretty much gets the better of the narrative here, once the dragon is dead. The "raskall many" come upon his remains:

> Some feard, and fled; some feard and well it faynd;
> One that would wiser seeme, then all the rest,
> Warnd him not touch, for yet perhaps remaynd
> Some lingring life within his hollow brest,
> Or in his wombe might lurke some hidden nest
> Of many Dragonets, his fruitfull seed;
> Another said, that in his eyes did rest
> Yet sparckling fire, and bad thereof take heed;
> Another said, he saw him moue his eyes indeed.

Antichrist's appearance on Olivet may well help explain "Iulye," ll. 49–52, where Morrell cites the great God Pan feeding the blessed flock of *Dan* on the same mount. E. K. says Pan is Christ, but at l. 179 he is the Pope, who has sold his flocks to shepherds (i.e., trafficked in the pastoral office). Since Morrell is defending the exalted position of the vicar of Christ, we may well question E. K.'s idea that Dan is "put for the whole nation per Synechdochen." On the contrary, Dan was notorious as a seat of idolatry, it was eliminated from the list of tribes in Revelation, and it was widely supposed to be going to beget Antichrist. Morrell's *teribinth* may be an herb, but the same tree is the occasion of idolatry in the LXX trans. of Hos. 4:13, Ezk. 6:13, Isa. 6:13 and 57:5.

[248] For the allegory, cf. *Areopagitica*, where Milton speaks of the eagerness of the English people—who "care not to keep truth separated from truth, which is the fiercest rent and disunion of all"—"to recover any enthralled piece of truth out of the gripe of custom." With the torn and abandoned shield of Sir Burbon at V.xi.46 this allegory becomes more necessary. Redcrosse may also be retrieving his standard, on the analogy of Christ who took from hell (death) its victory, or *standard*. For such an interpretation of I Cor. 15:55, see Lancelot Andrewes, *Ninety-six Sermons* (Oxford, 1841–1843), vol. 3, p. 66.

196

One mother, when as her foolehardie chyld
  Did come too neare, and with his talants play,
  Halfe dead through feare, her litle babe reuyld,
  And to her gossips gan in counsell say;
  How can I tell, but that his talants may
  Yet scratch my sonne, or rend his tender hand?
  So diuersly themselues in vaine they fray;
  Whiles some more bold, to measure him nigh stand,
  To proue how many acres he did spread of land.
                                        (I.xii.10–11)

In the "one that would wiser seeme," the reader will recognize the comic aspect of the dwarf at the mouth of Error's den.

The overall point these various indications of light-heartedness make is twofold. First, in regaining paradise, Redcrosse is regaining his own generic childhood; hence the emergence of actual children here. And secondly, inasmuch as death is slain by the crucifixion, it causes no suffering to Christians. This is the consolation theme of an ancient homily on the Syrian martyrs Guria and Shamuna, written by Mar Jacob of Serug (d. 521 A.D.):

With a wounded serpent one playeth without fear;
  A slain lion even a coward will drag along:
The great serpent our Lord crushed by His crucifixion;
  The dread lion did the Son of God slay by His sufferings.
Death bound He fast, and laid him prostrate and trampled on him
      at the gate of Hades;
  And *now* whosoever will draweth near and mock at him, because he
    is slain.
These old men, Shamuna and Guria, mocked at death
  As at that lion which by the Son of God was slain.
The great serpent, which slew Adam among the trees,
  Who could seize, so long as he drank not of the blood of the cross?
The Son of God crushed the dragon by His crucifixion,
  And lo! boys and old men mock at the wounded serpent.[249]

We may add that Redcrosse's happy sleep represents a heartening improvement on his sad and anxious condition in the first canto.

Redcrosse, however, does not merely sleep. He appears to dream, and it is possible to guess what he is dreaming about. Redcrosse has already proved to be a prophetic dreamer, as has his fellow prisoner Joseph, but the more relevant type is again Adam, whom tradition also makes a dreamer. The notion stems from the creation of Eve, for the Septuagint

[249] ANF, vol. 8, p. 719.

translates the deep sleep of Genesis 2:21 as an *ecstasis*.[250] Because Adam was taken up into such a state he was able to divine, upon awakening, Eve's origins. The tradition survives in *Paradise Lost*, but Dante's swoon in the earthly paradise may supply the more illuminating parallel. Dante faints after the symbolic tree blooms and reddens with the Crucifixion; he awakens to behold Beatrice alone, and there follows a pageant of the history of the Church. The connection between these events becomes clearer when we know that it was believed that Adam's awakening words prophesied the Church, and that the taking of Eve out of Adam's side typified the taking of Church out of the side of Christ.[251] The Church, it follows, is a second Eve. In Spenser the Church as a bride is represented by Una. She too is a second Eve, being Eve's daughter. Thus in the first canto Redcrosse dreams about Una, whom Archimago, in a marked parody, separates from the mind of the sleeping knight. At the other end of the legend the "hoarie king" (I.xii.12) presents Una to Redcrosse in a scene that repeats the traditional presentation, by God the Father, of Eve to Adam. In short, the Adamic Redcrosse must once again be dreaming about his marriage.

Errant Damozell: The Church in the Wilderness

A right good knight, and true of word ywis:
I present was, and can it witness well,
When armes he swore, and streight did enterpris
Th'aduenture of the *Errant damozell*

(II.i.19)

[250] See Augustine, *De Genesi ad Litterarum*, IX.xix.36: "his mind understood on account of *ecstasis* just as if both participating in the angelical congress and entering into the sanctuary of God. Thus when awake, as if full of prophecy, he saw his woman, since she was drawn from his side, and he immediately exclaimed that great sacrament commanded by the Apostle." Similarly, Peter Comester, *Historia Scholastica*, Lib. Gen., cap. xvi (PL, CXCVIII, 1070B). For Milton, see J. M. Evans, *Paradise Lost and the Genesis Tradition* (Oxford, 1968), pp. 169, 262.

[251] Tertullian, *De Anima*, xliii, *De Jejune*, 3; anonymous, *Five Books in Reply to Marcion*, II.237–257 (ANF, vol. 4, p. 149); Methodius of Olympia, *Convivio Decem Virgin.*, iii.8; John Chrysostom, *Comm. Colos.*, ii.6; Augustine, *Tract. in Joan.*, IX.10, *Contra Faust.*, xii.8, *Comm. in Gen. Contra Manich.*, II.xii.16–xiii.19 (PL, XXXIV, 205f.), *Ennar. in Ps.* XL.10 (PL, XXXVI, 461); Avitus, *De spirit. hist. gestis*, I.60; Gregory, *Hom. in Ezch.*, Lib. I, Hom. vi.15 (PL., LXXVI, 835); Aquinas, *Summa Theol.*, Pt. I, q.92, art.3, resp.; Vincent of Beauvais, *Speculvm historiale*, VII.xlvi. For the "building" or *aedificatio* of Eve as an ecclesiastical foundation, see Peter Martyr, *In Primum Librum Mosis*, cap. ii (Heidelberg, 1606), p. 11ᵛ.

. . . O Lord, Lord: of euerie forest of the earth, and of all the trees thereof thou hast chosen thee one onely vineyarde. . . .

And of all the depth of the sea thou hast filled thee one riuer, and of all buylded cities thou hast sanctified Sion vnto thy self.

And of all the soules that are created, thou hast named thee one doue, and of all the cattel that are made, thou hast appointed thee one shepe.

And among all the multitude of people thou hast gotten thee one people, and vnto this people whome thou louedst, thou gauest a Law, that is proued of all.

And now, o Lord, why hast thou giuen this one *people* ouer vnto many? and vpon one roote thou hast set others, & hast scattred thine onelie *people* among many.

(II Esdras 5:23, 25–28, Geneva Bible)

[i]

With terminal points for the symbolism of Book I established in the Fall and reconquest of Eden, we may now fill in the intervening passage. We have already discussed Spenser's advent imagery, with a view toward showing that in Book I, as in the Gospel, "In the beginning was the Word."[252] After the loss of paradise through the subtlety of the serpent, and the consequent separation from the presence of God, human history as we know it begins. Out of this history, a particular people is chosen to understand God's will. A characteristic exodus movement is established with the departure of Abraham from the chaos of the nations, and Abraham and Lot from the cities of the plain, which almost seem to become the Dead Sea. There follows the descent into Egypt and the Exodus proper. After the giving of the law in the wilderness, the promised land is entered, but its occupation proves problematic in the Judges period. With the establishment of the kingship in Judah, the defeat of the Philistines, the bringing of the Sinaitic ark into Jerusalem, and the building of the Jerusalem temple, the whole pattern of God's will for this people is established. The united monarchy, which was preceded by the anarchy of the Judges period, is followed by the schism of the Kings period. The divided kingdom falls by halves, and with the deportation of Judah to Babylon another low point is reached. The exodus movement recurs in the return of a remnant to rebuild the walls of Jerusalem under Nehemiah and Zerub-

---

[252] For the typology of Christ's advent or revelation as the genesis of light, see esp. John 1:4f., 9, 3:19, 8:12, with II Cor. 4:6: "For God that commanded the light to shine out of darkenes, is he which hathe shined in our hearts, to giue the light of the knowledge of the glorie of God in the face of Iesus Christ." (Here the Geneva gloss cites Matt. 5:14, where Christ calls his apostles the light of the world.)

199

babel—in Isaiah the messianic role in this cycle is divided between Cyrus, who fulfills the oracles against Babylon and frees her captives, and the Suffering Servant, who accomplishes what no one would have believed possible.

The pattern of Israel's history is extended through the intertestamental period, where the Syro-Hellenic occupation is successfully contested by Judas Maccabaeus, who cleanses the Temple. Finally, there is the Roman occupation, and the physical temple is destroyed. In the meantime the last of the prophets has proclaimed a kingdom "not of this world," and the Apocalypse takes up the burden of the doom-song over its fallen prince.

This is perhaps not the place to develop a full theory of biblical romance, but some indications can show us the relation of the pattern just discussed to Spenser's first legend. The reader has already met the form of this narrative, namely, the redundant quest. Romance quests are teleological: they have in view an end in some sort of fulfillment, a fulfillment that provides the determination of the fiction. The four cardinal points of such a quest may be described in chivalric terms. The first phase shows the knight errant setting out upon the proposed adventure. We may call this venturing forth or point of departure "initiative," to suggest that—in the words of a colleague—the quest is the allegory of purpose. As the knight diverges from his errand, he enters upon errantry proper, where adventure is pursued for its own sake. He may then be shown losing his way, or becoming an exile from a chivalric fellowship, or succumbing to a temptation implicit in errantry—contributing factors may be the knight's failure to ask the right questions, or a former misdeed that it was the knight's quest to redeem. As his error deepens into trespass, and his trespass into impasse, the quest becomes stymied altogether. This negative threshold is cleared whenever it modulates into a mere suspension of the quest upon enchanted ground—some period of intermission or delay during which the knight avoids further temptation or error. The final phase of the quest takes its beginning from an invitation to the knight to rejoin the chivalric fellowship, or to behold a wonderful vision with which he may hope to be united. The knight successfully passes through tests or ordeals or examinations, the *gradi* of initiation, and comprehends symbols for the completion or determination of the quest.

Analogies for these four phases of the quest may be discovered in the Deuteronomistic superstructure for the scheme of the stories told in Judges, where apostasy is followed by oppression, and the resulting impasse is followed by repentence and a "man raised up" who effects deliverance. There is a sense in which the deliverer, following Joshua, reinstalls the people in the promised land. Since the peace that follows is said to be forty years, the cycle is repeated in every generation.[253] We may diagram this quest cycle as follows:

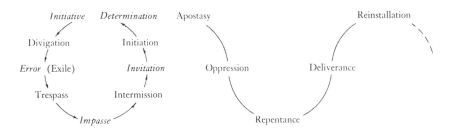

Dr. Frye, to whom I owe the following schemata, has suggested that the whole history of Israel be constructed along similar lines:

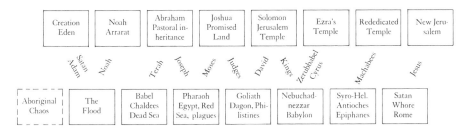

[253] See Gerhard von Rad, *Old Testament Theology*, vol. 1, trans. D.M.G. Stalker (New York and Evanston, 1962), pp. 330–332, 347.

Redcrosse's pattern shows the same cyclic alteration as that of Israel. Like Israel, the knight is chosen before he sets out. (A minor proof of his election is his dipping his head to drink from the stream at the opening of the Orgoglio episode; this gesture includes him in the select inner group of Gideon's warriors [I.vii.6, Judges 7:5–7].) Redcrosse's pre-election, described in the letter to Raleigh, is followed by a succession of triumphs and reverses deliberately reiterative in character; the pattern has been framed with some appreciation for the falling of the just man seven times (Prov. 24:16):

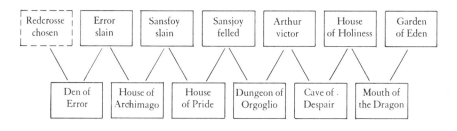

This schema somewhat belies the gradual nature of the process in Book I, in which the victories improve and the defeats deepen with each successive episode. Further, the separation of good from evil, or the wheat from the tares, is not absolute in any given instance; if it were, the cycle would be replaced by the final confrontation of the sons of day with their opposites. As it stands, a subversive element implicit in each "daytime" victory reveals itself as the dominant element in the "nighttime" aftermath in which the victory is undone. The victory itself determines that when the evil returns, it returns in a compounded or aggravated form. Thus the elimination of an explicit Error seems to blind Redcrosse to more cryptic and subtle kinds of error. The defeat of Sansfoy leaves the way open for the ready adoption of Fidessa. The escape from the joyless House of Pride issues in a vain and shallow optimism, and the void left by the rejected trappings of external pride is suddenly filled by an overwhelming interior pride. The hero's "postmortem" contemplation of his humiliation by this pride, after its alleviation, is so dismaying that it leads to Despair: the humiliation of the earlier episode is retroactivated, as it were, upon the withdrawal of Arthur's support.

The setting apart of the holy from the unholy, which the schema also implies, is far more explicit after the *krisis* of the legend has been precipitated in the eighth canto. And yet another near defeat follows. The separation itself gives the new evil its power, for the recognition of all the earlier defeats feeds into the argument for despair:

> Is not the measure of thy sinfull hire
> High heaped vp with huge iniquitie,
> Against the day of wrath, to burden thee?
>
> (I.xi.46)

Thus the *krisis* in the Despair episode is the imminence of Judgment itself; and it is accompanied by the other three of the Four Last Things, namely the hope of Heaven, the threat of Hell, and the fear of Death. Despair's attempt upon the hero falls into place as an attempt upon the very nature of the quest—upon its continuous and prospective orientation. Such an attempt, finally directed by the impatient "man of sin" (I.ix.46, II Thess. 2:3) against himself, raises the question of whether Redcrosse will be able to make the "good end" traditionally expected of Christians (the death exhibiting a healthy conscience, a calm and patient trust in one's author, and a resigning to Him of the ultimate issues of life and death). Despair raises the spectres he does, not to prepare the sinner, but to incapacitate him, and fatally pre-judge the answer to the question. This prejudicial determination of the quest might well issue from Spenser's "man of hell" (I.ix.28), for Paul's man of sin is also "the son of perdition." The juncture between cantos ten and eleven also suggests the point of *krisis*, and here one could say that the armies of good and evil have achieved the fullness of their numbers, and the time is at hand. After the "interior" discipline of the House of Holiness, the dragon is a visible, external, "daytime" evil, and Redcrosse is no longer beside himself in a way that cooperates with his enemies. We might seem to have returned to the monster of the first episode, but the exposure of Archimago in the aftermath argues that Redcrosse has finally reversed the prevailing pattern of subversion and defeated the evil as well as the monster. The quest for sanctification can now be seen to have polarized experience into the two registers. The upper register is a record of dedication, enlightenment, self-confidence, self-reliance, messianic hope, regeneration, and rejoicing; the lower register is a record of ignorance, distrust and doubt, depression, disgrace, despair, and death.

[ii]

For an example of the biblism of one of the loci, we may take the House of Pride, from the lower register, where we would expect to find symbols of the various biblical tyrannies, from Nimrod on. Like the Tower of Babel, the brick pile "spake the praises of the workmans wit" (I.iv.5). In Spenser's *Rvines of Time*, the Tower of Babel is built on sand (l. 508), and so is the House of Pride. The sand ought to be in the mortar it lacks. The walls are "painted cunningly" and shaken by the breath of heaven—Hamilton compares the whitewashed wall of Ezekiel 13:10f., by which the prophet represents an unsound and self-deceiving confidence before the impending wrath.[254] Both Pharaoh and Nebuchadnezzar, the king of Babylon, are compared to dragons.[255] Ezekiel calls Pharaoh the "great dragon of his rivers" (Ezk. 29:3), and Nahum, who describes Ninevah as "the harlot that was beautiful and agreable, and that made use of witch-craft," compares that city to Alexandria, "that dwelleth among the rivers" (Nah. 3:4,8, Douay Bible). At the House of Pride a dragon lurks beneath the queen's throne, and Duessa is compared to a deceptive Egyptian crocodile (I.v.18). Elsewhere Spenser takes the crocodile to be emblematic of the gates of hell (*Visions of the worlds vanitie*, 3), and both Spenser's Nile and Duessa's beast have seven mouths. Given Duessa's association with the Rome of Revelation, the Nile is a symbolical double for the Tiber with its city on seven hills. A similar Tiber and Babel symbolism is found in John Studley's preface to his translation of Bale's *Pageant of Popes*. Studley is answering the Catholic objection to a point of Reform theology concerning the Church as the community of the regenerate, and he takes the occasion to warn the reader against the encroachments of the rival edifice:

> Deceitfull therefore is theyr dealing, who to withdraw men from our Church, do uniustlye saye that when we fall, our foundation falleth also:

[254] A. C. Hamilton, *Structure of Allegory in "The Faerie Queene"* (Oxford, 1961), p. 67. Cf. Lamentations 2:14 and Acts 23:3 for the figure. The gold foil on the surfaces of the building makes its façade a hypocritical one, according to an old pseudo-etymology, *hypo-chruses*, "gold-over," used to explain the cloaks of the hypocrites in Dante, *Inf.* XXIII; see Grandgent, ed., *La Divina Commedia*, p. 204. Similarly Abraham Fraunce, *Lawier's Logike* (London, 1588), I.xii, p. 57, "Hypo-crisis, of *hypo*, which is over, and *chrysos*, gold, because hypocrites bee cloaked with a golden shew overcast." (Quoted by Martha Craig, "The Secret Wit of Spenser's Language," in Paul Alpers, ed., *Elizabethan Poetry: Modern Essays in Criticism*, New York, 1967, p. 471.) Cf. the German for hypocritical, *gleissneisch*, "shining," and *scheinheilig*, "shine-holy."

[255] Jer. 57:34 (Geneva Bible): "Nebuchad-nezzar ye King of Babel hathe deuoured me . . . he swalowed me vp like a dragon, and filled his belie with my delicates, & hathe cast me out."

but most iustley may wee assure men that theyr Babilonicall building must needes come to decaye, being founded on the sand of Tiber banckes, which is dayleye washed and eaten awaye.[256]

Anticipating the symbolism of Orgoglio's palace, Studley adds that "This foundation will not last to uphold their Babylonicall buildinges against the assaultes of Gospell."[257]

The "donghill of dead carkases" (I.v.53) dumped outside of Lucifera's walls is also scriptural. Corpses without decent funeral, left unburied "as dongue vpon the earth" (Jer. 16:4), are found in biblical contexts of judgment; they are the bodies of those who, like Antiochus here (I.v.47), have put their abominations in the Temple (Jer. 7:30–8:2). Thus the "privie Posterne," through which Redcrosse leaves, is another "Port Esquiline," the Roman dump that Spenser compares to the exit from the body (II. ix.32). Jerusalem also had a "Dung gate" (Neh. 2:13). Lucifera's name comes from the doom-song in Isaiah over the king of Babylon, whose golden city—it is prophesied—will fall. Lucifera's basement, "A great Lay-stall / Of murdred men" (I.v.53), probably owes something to the pit prepared for the proud in the same text:

> Hell from beneath is moved for thee to meet thee at thy coming: it stirreth up the dead for thee, even all the chief ones of the earth; it hath raised up from their thrones all the kings of the nations.
>
> All they shall speak and say unto thee, Art thou also become weak as we? art thou become like unto us?
>
> Thy pomp is brought down to the grave. . . .
>
> But thou art cast out of thy grave like an abominable branch, and as the raiment of those that are slain, thrust through with a sword, that go down to the stones of the pit; as a carcase trodden under feet.
>
> (Isa. 14:9–11, 19, Geneva Bible)

As the imagery might also suggest, the House of Pride is one of those whited sepulchres, or painted tombs, "which indeed appeare beautiful outward, but are within ful of dead mens bones, and of all filthinesse" (Matt. 23:27, Bishops' Bible). As part of the "idolatry and necrolatrie" of the Roman Church, Studley would ask, "How can it stand . . . being made of earth, clay, relics, Limbo of the fathers Purgatory?" It will "putrifye rotte and consume to nothing."[258]

The fall-of-princes theme at the House of Pride also makes it a symbol of Fortune. Its clock does duty for Fortune's wheel, and represents time-serving. A classical example of such an establishment is found in Lucian's *On Salaried Posts in Great Houses* (42), with its golden entrance to high

---

[256] *Pageant of Popes*, trans. John Studley (London, 1574), Sig. *biii^v–biiij^r.
[257] *Ibid.*, Sig. *biiij^r.   [258] *Loc. cit.*, n. 257.

hopes, and its much less prepossessing secret postern, symbolizing old age and repentance. Similar ambivalent loci of fortune are found in Alanus' *Anticlaudianus* and the *Romance of the Rose*.[259]

The entertainments at the House are the stuff of Vanity Fair, or of a "Theatre for voluptuous Worldlings." Redcrosse, a stranger and estranged, feels and resents the spite of the place; one suspects that he must fight Sansjoy because he is depressed. Pride is closely linked to shame, especially the fear of being shamed, and Sansjoy threatens in this way as well. Duessa, who has brought her knight here, exercises the joyless and confused attractions of the coy mistress in a poem by Greville:

> And as hell fire, not wanting heat, want light
> So these strange witchcrafts, which like pleasure be,
> Not wanting fare enticements, want delight,
> Inward being nothing but deformity,
>   And do at open doors let frail powers in
>   To that straight building, little-ease of sin.[260]

Though Duessa is not quite yet the whore of Babylon, she is already deeply involved in the harlot's "faire speache and pleasant doctrine to deceaue the world" (Geneva Bible, argument to Revelation). As a crocodile, she weeps what Shakespeare calls "Siren tears, distilled from limbecks foul as hell within" (*Son.* 119):

> What wretched errors hath my heart committed
> Whilst it hath thought itself so blessed never!

And as an enticing female, she may be compared to the harlot in Proverbs, the Dame Folly whose house takes hold on hell (Prov. 7:27, 9:18). The fool who enters this house "does not know *the dead* are there." Pope aptly compares the same seductive woman to Homer's sirens,[261] correctly perceiving that their sepulchral isle amounts to a marine version of Sheol.

Her victims are bewildered fools, but Folly herself is cunning, according to a kind of allegorical law whereby she usurps the defenses that fools have abandoned. It is therefore significant that Lucifera actually exhibits a parody of Prudence, iconographically the queen of the virtues, equipped with Prudence's mirror of counsel and her serpent of wisdom. In the face of the danger that Lucifera's house presents, Una's wary dwarf—all the wisdom remaining to the knight—speaks for a rationality based on fear. Redcrosse will leave this place, not because it is unholy, but because it is unsafe. The dwarf warns him away on purely prudential grounds.

---

[259] *Anticlaudianus*, VIII, ll. 1–62; *Romance of the Rose*, ll. 5921ff., esp. 6043–6073.
[260] *Caelica*, 102.
[261] Twickenham edn. of Pope's *Poems*, vol. 9, *The Odyssey of Homer*, Books I-XII, ed. Maynard Mack (London, 1967), p. 432.

[iii]

A succession of covenants or revelations accompanies the biblical quest pattern, for which the most important symbol is the ark borne through the wilderness. The faith of Abraham, the law of Moses, and the oracles of the prophets form this succession; the temple at Jerusalem, which is veiled like the ark, also belongs to the symbolism. Una's veil was adopted at the Fall, and it is black. The reference is to the bride of the Song of Songs, who is black but comely, "as the *curtines* of Salomon" (1:4). For the significance of the color we may cite van der Noot's *Theatre*: "Although I am blacke (sayth the true Church) yet am I nevertheless faire and cleane." He goes on to explain, "Albeit our outward man (saith S. Paule) perish, therefore doe we not goe forward, or are any thing weary, for the inward man renuweth and augmenteth every day."[262] The bride says that the sun has looked upon her, and the Geneva Bible explains: "The corruption of nature through sinne, and afflictions." The ark is a palladium in war; this aspect of it is symbolized by Arthur's veiled shield. The dropping of this veil blinds Orgoglio, and is a powerful symbol for the manifestation of God's Word, meant to remind us of both the rending of the veil of the temple, or the end of the Law, and the blinding of those who persecute God's Church. Orgoglio is reduced by Arthur to a "trunked stocke," and this description may echo the humiliation of the idol of the Philistine god Dagon in the presence of the ark: it was reduced to a "stump" (I Sam. 5:4).

The theophanic overtones are also present in Sansloi's attack on Una. When he seizes her veil, her light "burnt his beastly hart t'enforce her chastitye" (I.iv.4). The forsaken bride of the Song is similarly abused by

---

[262] Van der Noot, *Theatre, edn. cit.*, fol. 85ʳ. For the identification of the bride's blackness with sin, see Jerome, *Epist.* XXII.1 (NPNF, 2nd Series, vol. 6, p. 22). In Origen's *Comm. in Cant. Cant.*, II.1f. (Lawson trans., Ancient Christian Writers, 26, London, 1957, pp. 91–110), the curtains of Solomon are said to be the curtains of the tabernacle, and the Bride's blackness the stigma of sin. Cf. the gloss of Bishop Challoner in the Douay Bible: "That is, the Church of Christ, founded in humility, appearing outwardly afflicted and as it were black and contemptible; but inwardly, that is, in its doctrine and morality, fair and beautiful" (*The Holy Bible*, Dublin, 1857). So the *Glossa ordinaria*, in PL, CXIII, 1130: "I appear mean in the eyes of persecutors, but before God I shine gloriously on account of my confession of truth." With Una's mourning garb also compare John Foxe, on the decay of the true Church, ca. A.D. 1080: "Then began the sincere faith of the English Church, which held out so long, to quail. Then was the clear sunshine of God's word overshadowed with mists and darkness, appearing like sackcloth to the people, who neither could understand what they read, nor yet were permitted to read what they could understand." (*Acts*, Cattley edn., London, 1837, vol. 1, Pt. I, xxi, "Epistle To the True and Faithful Congregation.")

the watchman (5:4–6).[263] Sansloi himself may be linked to the Antichrist complex, for the Antichrist of Matthew 24:12 is accompanied by *a-nomia*, lawlessness. The Law, according to Paul in I Timothy 1:8ff., is given "vnto the lawles and disobedient," including "men stealers" and all the criminality "that is contrarie to wholsome doctrine." Paul goes on to say that this law is according to the gospel, "whiche is committed vnto me. . . . for he put me in (his) service: When before I was a blaspheme; and a persecuter, and an oppresser. . . ." One might also compare the smiting of the men of Beth-shemesh, "because they had loked in the Arke of the Lord" (I Sam. 6:19). Sansloi's attack thus falls into place as any act of sacrilege offered against the Holy of Holies: included here would be the violations of Nebuchadnessar, Heliodorus, Antiochus, Ptolemy, and Titus. Cyril of Jerusalem specifically says that Nebuchadnessar violated the temple veil.[264] The mention of Una's "Ransackt chastitie" (I.vi.5) suggests the plundering of the Temple. The moral allegory implies that fanaticism, like the attempt to seize the ark or penetrate the Temple, is a kind of rape of the truth, as opposed to hypocrisy, which is a seduction of it. Thus the story opposes Sansloi, or zeal without knowledge, to Archimago, or subtlety without sincerity. As the story shows, the integrity of truth is not well served by either.

Una, like the ark (II Sam. 6), is separated from those who depend on her; she sojourns among strangers and is only latterly brought into the royal presence with rejoicing. David's celebration (I Chron. 15:28) is one of those that seems to be echoed in the festivities. Another Davidic theme is introduced with the comparison of Kirkrapine to the corrupt sons of Eli (I.iii.18 I Sam. 3). The sons of Eli are also the priests of Nob, who harbor the fugitive David, as Kirkrapine's paramour ends up harboring Una. The priests are slaughtered for their pains, and a like end awaits Kirkrapine (I Sam. 21–22). Behind both the biblical story and the Spenser episode lies the theme of the preferment of a new priesthood.

[263] As noted in Hankins, *Source and Meaning*, pp. 107f. For the interpretations below, cf. Hankins, p. 124. For the furnishing of the temple or ark as the adornment of a woman, see the allegory of Ezk. 16:9–13. For the allegory, cf. Bishop Challoner on Song 5:8: "signifying the violent and cruel persecutors of the Church taking her veil, despoiling the Church of its places of worship and ornaments for the divine service." (Cf. *Glossa ordinaria* on Song 1:5, in Pl. CXIII, 1131, explaining that the "sons of the mother that have turned against" the bride refers to Paul turning against the Synagogue.)

[264] *Catech. Lect.*, II.17 (trans. in NPNF, 2nd Series, vol. 7, p. 12). Cf. I Macc. 1:22: "Antiochus . . . entred proudly into the sanctuarie, and tooke away . . . the vaile." At I.v.48 Spenser says that Anitochus *danced* upon the altar: the contrast is with David, who danced before the ark (II Sam. 6:14–16). See also Jerome, *Epist.* CVII.7: "Don't let Paula go abroad lest the watchmen find her . . . and smite . . . her . . . and take away from her the veil of her chastity." (Trans. in NPNF, 2nd Series, vol. 6, p. 192.)

When Una awakens and rises from her bower to look for her knight (I.ii.7), she resembles the seeking and forsaken bride of the Song of Songs. According to various interpretations of the Song, she may be either Israel, or the soul inquiring after God, or the Church seeking her redeemer.[265] Quarles' emblem on this theme makes her the soul seeking Jesus. The *Glossa* quotes Jerome(?), who says that the soul has an appetite to see God; Bernard of Clarvieux says that it asks after the Word.[266] Alanus understands in the bride's quest Mary Magdalene's visit to Christ's tomb, an interpretation rather older than its appearance in Cyril of Jerusalem. The bride's accents are accordingly heard in the medieval homily on Mary Magdalene attributed to Origen and translated into English in 1565.[267] Gregory explains that "in Holy Writ a 'bed,' a 'couch,' a 'litter,' is usually taken for the secret depth of the heart":

> For it is hence that under the likeness of each separate soul, the Spouse, urged by the piercing darts of holy love, says in the Song of Songs, By night on my bed I sought him, whom my soul loveth. For "by night and on the bed is the beloved sought," in that the appearance of the Invisible Creatour, apart from every image of a bodily appearing, is found in the chamber of the heart.

Gregory also allegorizes the watchmen as the prophets, whom the Church passes by in seeking her redeemer (Song 3:3-4).[268]

[265] For the interpretations of the Song of Songs, see the study of H. H. Rowley, in *The Song of the Servant* (London, 1952), pp. 189–234. For the bride as Israel, Rowley cites Rashi on Song 3:1 (trans. in 1714 by J. F. Breithaupt in *R. Salomonis Jarchi commentarius hebraicus in librr. Josuae . . . et Canticum Canticorum . . .*); as the Church, see n. 268; as the *ecclesia* of both testaments, but as Israel in the wilderness at Song 3:1, Nicholas Lyra, in *Biblia sacra cum glossa interlineari, ordinaria, et Nicolai Lyrani postilla* (Basel, 1498), Tertius pars, fols. ffi^r and ee5^{r-v}. The *Glossa ordinaria* reads the tribulation of both Israel and the Church into many places in the Song.

[266] Jerome on Song 3:1, in *Glossa ordinaria*, PL, CXIII, 1142D; Bernard, *Sermones in Cant.*, Sermo LXXXIV.3, PL, CLXXXIII, 1185D.

[267] Alanus, *Elucidatio in Cant. Cant.*, III, PL, CCX, 72; Cyril of Jerusalem, *Catech. Lect.*, XIV.11f. (trans. in NPNF, 2nd Series, vol. 7, p. 97), with which compare *Homilia in Paralyticum*, x–xi, in PG, XXXIII, 1141–1146, and Hippolytus of Rome, *Comm. Cant.* 15, as cited in n. 208, above; *Opera Origenes* (Paris, 1572), vol. 2, pp. 291–294; *An Homilie of Marye Magdalene declaring her fervent love and zele towards Christ*, trans. R. Wolfe (STC 18847, London, 1565). For the history of this homily, see John P. McCall, "Chaucer and the Pseudo Origen *De Maria Magdalene*," in *Speculum*, 46, no. 3 (1971), pp. 491–509. For Spenser's Magdalen motif, see "The Tree of Life," sec. i, *ad fin.*

[268] *Moralia*, VIII.xxiv.41, in the Library of the Fathers trans., vol. 1, p. 447; *ibid.*, XVIII.xlix.80, vol. 2, p. 380. Cf. also St. Bernard's *Jubilus Rhythmicus, De Nomine Jesu*: "I ask for Jesus on my bed, in the closed room of my heart: privately and in public I ask for my love assiduously; with Mary at dawn I ask for Jesus at the tomb;

Una is the seeking bride, but as the removal of the bride's veil indicates, she is also the thing sought, or veiled truth.[269] When the search is abandoned, or truth is resisted, she becomes "forsaken truth." At the outset of his *Apology*, Tertullian describes such a Truth: "She knows that she is but a sojourner on the earth, and that among strangers she naturally finds foes; and more than this, that her origin, her dwelling place, her hope, her recompense, her honours, are above." Tertullian also describes Truth as making her case before the bar of public opinion. Duessa is still appropriating such commonplaces at the close of Spenser's legend: "truth is strong, her rightfull cause to plead, / And shall find friends" (I.xii.28). There is some evidence for a type that Raffaello Piccoli denominated *Veritas Derelicta*, and asserted to be the subject of a Botticelli panel called "La Derelitta," a painting of a solitary weeping figure before a closed door in a wall. He paired this picture with one by Mantegna whose subject was the "triumph of ignorance," which appears to have shown the activities on the other side of the door.[270] In a Christian context, such a Derelict Truth would also be the Church in the wilderness (Acts 7:38), or a figure like that of the female Jerusalem in II Esdras who mourns in tatters. A strong example for our purposes is found in the dedication of Philpot's translation of Curio. Philpot compares a dragon-haunted Philosophy, whose garments are rent, to the Church forced into the wilderness, and brought out from thence in his own times by a Davidic Henry VIII;[271] the tabernacle of Psalm 132:6 also was found in the fields of the wood (cf. I Chron. 13).

with querulous clamor in my heart, I ask with my mind, not my eye" (PL, CLXXXIV, 1317).

[269] In this case the watchmen (Song 5:7) are preachers: so *Glossa ordinaria*, PL, CXIII, 1154, citing Gregory: "preachers take away the mantle when, if anything of secular pomp remains, they remove it from the soul, or, if some sin is in it through ignorance, they lay it bare."

[270] "Veritas Derelicta," in *The Burlington Magazine*, 56 (1930), pp. 244ff. The subject, as Piccoli notes, has connections with paintings based on Lucian's description of the *Calumny* of Apelles, in which Truth is *delayed*, rather than excluded. Piccoli cites another painting, the Calumny of Girolamo Siciolante (Nimes Museum), in which excluded Truth—as he believes "the Mother of the Virtues" to be—hangs her banner into the room where Ignorance prevails, through a barred window. A third painting on the theme, *Allegoria della Fortuna*, by Lorenzo Leonbruno (reproduced in H. R. Patch, *The Goddess Fortuna in Medieval Literature*, Cambridge, Mass., 1927, at the end of the text) shows the Calumny subject, with Fortune presiding: the same barred window and excluded lady with her banner are found there.

[271] Dedication of *A Defence of the True and Old Authority of Christ's Church*, trans. from Coelio Secundo Curione, in *The Examinations and Writings of John Philpot, B.C.L.*, ed. Rev. Robert Eden, Parker Society (Cambridge, 1842), pp. 321f. Hankins, in *Source and Meaning*, p. 70, cites the perfect text for putting the ecclesiastical symbol among the satyrs: Alanus de Insulis on Ps. 132:6, in his *Distinctiones, sub campus* (PL, CCX, 727), on finding "her"—the tabernacle—"in the fields of the *silva*": "We found the Church among the Gentiles; i.e. among rude and forest-dwelling men [*silvestribus hominibus*]." See sec. v, below.

[iv]

There is also implicit in Una's fortunes a theme of "divided truth," or even errant truth. Una, as the truth, can err, insofar as the Church itself, the pillar of truth, "erreth and strayethe farre from the waye of trwthe." On II Thessalonians 2:1, Jewel writes that "even among that nation which God hath chosen unto himself the apostacy was so great, the departure from true holiness was so universal, that not only every city, but every street was defiled with their idolatry." In the *Apology* Jewel cites not only II Thessalonians but also II Timothy 4:3-4 (men will be "turned back unto fables and lies"); Daniel 8:12 ("Truth . . . in that season shall be thrown under foot, and trodden upon in the world"); and Matthew 24:24 ("even the chosen, if it were possible, shall be brought into error").[272] Thus it is Abessa's and Corceca's wish for Una "that in endlesse error she might euer stray" (I.iii.23). Bullinger may be quoted at greater length on the theme:

In this place it seemeth unto to me not unfitly may the famous question be handled or briefly expounded, Whether the church of God may err? . . . Now, therefore, if we understand by the church the blessed spirits in heaven, the church can never err. But if we understand the wicked or hypocrites joined and mingled with the good, and the wicked alone by themselves, they do nothing else but err; but as they are joined unto the good and faithful, and follow them, they either err, or they err not. . . . As concerning the manners and life of the church, it cannot wholly and clearly acquit itself of errors; that is to say, from sin. . . . it is said that the church is without spot, because of the continual study of the church, whereby she laboureth and travaileth by all means, that as far as it is possible she may have as few spots as may be. And by that means, and chiefly by the benefit of imputation, the church erreth not, but is most pure and without sin. . . . the church is the pillar and ground of truth [I Tim. 3:15]. . . . For the truth of God is in the Church. . . . the same church doth err in doctrine and faith, as often as she, turning from Christ and his word, goeth after men. . . . I think no man will deny that the great congregation of the people of Israel in the desert was an excellent church of God. . . . And yet how shamefully she erred whilst neglecting God's word, and . . . she both made a molten calf, and worshipped it as a god. . . . The church therefore is said

---

[272] For the "waye of trwthe," see George Joye, *The Unite and Schisme of the olde Chirche*, fol. xii[v]. Jewel is cited from Parker Society *Works*, vol. 2, p. 892, and vol. 3, p. 80 (*Apology*, IV.xiii). See also Foxe, *Acts and Monuments*, ed. S. Cattley (London, 1837), vol. 2, pp. 413, 418f.; Lavater, *Of Ghostes, edn. cit.*, p. 153; and Milton, *Reason of Church Government*, on "the general apostasy that was foretold and the Church's flight into the wilderness," in explanation of how "sixteen ages should be taxed with an error."

to err, when a part of it, having lost God's word, doth err: and the same
erreth not wholly and altogether; forasmuch as certain remnants (through
the grace of God) are reserved, by whom the truth may flourish again and
may again be spread abroad in every place.[273]

On the same text in II Thessalonians, Calvin explains that "a certain
vniuersall departing shall possesse the Church: Howsoeuer many mem-
bres of the Church here and there continue in the true vnitie of faith."[274]

This paradox of the errant unity of the faith lies behind Donne's *Holy
Sonnet:*

> Show me, dear Christ, thy spouse so bright and clear
> What! is it she which on the other shore
> Goes richly painted? or which, robbed and tore,
> Laments in Germany and here?
> Sleeps she a thousand, then peeps one year?
> Is she self-truth, and errs? now new, now outwore?
> Doth she, and did she, and shall she evermore
> On one, on seven, or on no hill appeare?
> Dwells she with us, or like adventuring knights
> First travel we to seek, and then make love:
> Betray, kind husband, thy spouse to our sights,
> And let mine amorous soul court thy mild dove,
> Who is most true and pleasing to thee then
> When she'is embraced and open to most men.

Donne threatens the Bride with the commonness of Duessa, and doubtless
he would say that Redcrosse has not yet "known" Una. In the meantime,
like the errant Israel, Una is likened to a harlot (I.ii.23, 25).

Since the true church is the only and universal church, the separation
of Redcrosse from Una makes them both potentially Duessan. Their
separation may be said to represent the dissociated church, of whatever
age. The most prominent biblical examples begin with the schismatic ten

---

[273] *Decades*, V, Sermon i, "Of the Holy Catholic Church," *edn. cit.*, vol. 4, pp.
35–38. For the diffused unity and adulterated purity of the Church, cf. Cassiodorus
on the proof-text of Song 6:8: "*One is my dove. . . .* That is, there is one catholic
Church diffused throughout the whole world. It is constituted of queens and virgins; or rather, though constituted by virgins, it yet contains concubines: that is,
those who are Christians in name only. *Una est*: the Church, of course, which admits
of no rent or schism. So even as *unus est Deus, una fides, unum baptisma,* so there is
one general Church. . . ." (*Expos. in Cant. Cant.,* VI.8, in PL, LXX, 1091). See n. 95,
above. See Clement of Alexandria, *Stromata,* VII.17, for the unity of the church
as Monad.

[274] *Institutes,* IV.vii.25, trans. Norton, pp. 475f.

tribes, who break union, and go off to worship the golden calf. This worship is blamed for their Assyrian captivity. Then there is the Samaritan schism; and, finally, the division between the Jerusalem Church and the Gentile Church. Outside the Bible, there is the separation of the Eastern and Western Church (a division that Protestant polemic, deriving the Reform patrimony from the East, laid at the door of Rome);[275] the Babylonian captivity of the Avignon Papacy; and the Reformation itself.

The evidence for this theme in Spenser is clear: Una has Eastern parents; Redcrosse adopts an infidel's idol; and Una is gracelessly received by the unknowing Abessa. This last episode contains, I believe, allusions to the Samaritan schism, by way of Christ's colloquy with the Samaritan woman at the well: "The woman then left her waterpot, and went her way into the city" (John 4:28), with which we may compare Spenser's Abessa, who "on her shoulders sad a pot of water bore. . . . her pitcher downe she threw / And fled away" (I.iii.11). The Geneva gloss on the story in John refers us to II Kings 17, where the idolatrous worship of the future Samaritans is divinely rebuked: "And at the beginning of their dwelling there, thei feared not the Lord: therefore the Lord sent lyons among them, which slewe them" (II Kings 17:25). It is a descendant of these lions that slays Abessa's lover Kirkrapine. The dwellers in Samaria were not much better off for having imported an Israelite priest to teach them the fear of the Lord, for they put the gods of the nations in the high places at the same time: "So these nacions feared the Lord, and serued their images also . . . so do they vnto this day" (II Kings 17:41). The Geneva gloss draws the modern parallel:

> . . . thei had a certain knowledge of God & feared him because of the punishment, but thei continued stil idolaters, as do ye Papists, which worship bothe God & idoles: but this not to feare God. . . .

Duessa's letter of accusation at the return of Redcrosse to Una's kingdom brings the same schism down to the time of the Second Temple; it recalls Ezra 4, where the adversaries of Judah write a letter of accusation to the king of Persia, against the building of Jerusalem. The adversaries claim that they themselves should build the temple: "to erect idolatrie," says the Geneva gloss, "in steade of true religion."

The mournful Una, one might well conclude from this history, partly mourns the rending of the seamless garment of Christendom.

---

[275] For this theme, see now Hankins, *Source and Meaning*, pp. 211f. Hankins points out that the Emperor of the West (I.ii.22, xii.26) was the title of the murdered son of Constantine—Constantine divided the empire between his two sons and allegedly gave the empire to the Pope. Cf. Milton, *Of Reformation*: "through *Constantines* lavish superstition they forsook their *first love* [Rev. 2:4]."

Edgar Wind also undertook to identify the subject of the Botticelli *Derelitta*, and he placed the picture in a sequence of panels that tell the story of Esther.[276] It is not impossible that the woman is both Truth and Esther. Certainly this is likely to be the case with Una, since the true Church in disgrace, or stigmatized, takes as its type the figures for the imperiled Israel. The last of these in the Bible, the *ecclesia* figure who gives birth in Revelation 12, has been compared to Rachel mourning for her children, the mother of Moses, and Eve in her travail.[277] It is in the dénouement of the Book of Esther, however, that we find the romance of the vindication of Israel in its more romantic form.

Jerome's appendix to Esther translates the expanded version of the story, as it appears in the Septuagint. To summarize: Mordecai has dreamed of the rising of the light and the sun, and the exaltation of the humble, his people of Israel. With the contrary success of Haman's plot against the Jews, the king's new bride, Esther, goes into mourning, for the Jews are her people also:

> And when she laid away her royal apparel, she put on garments suitable for weeping and mourning, instead of divers precious ointments, she covered her head with ashes . . . , and all the places in which before she was accustomed to rejoice, she filled with her torn hair.[278]

She prays to God for presence of mind before her sovereign,

> And on the third day she laid away the garments she wore, and put on her glorious apparel.
> And glittering in royal robes. . . .
> But she with a rosy colour in her face, and gracious and bright eyes, hid a mind full of anguish, and exceeding great fear.
> So going in she passed through all the doors in order, and stood before the king, where he sat upon his royal throne, clothed with his royal robes, and glittering with gold. . . .[279]

The queen sinks down, and her color turns pale; the king takes her in his arms and kisses her. The king is moved, and Esther asks his leave to

---

[276] "The Subject of Botticelli's Derelitta," *Journal of Warburg and Courtauld Institute*, vol. 4 (1940–1941), pp. 114–117.

[277] In Austin Farrer, *A Rebirth of Images* (London, 1949), pp. 47, 139–145, 204. Like Moses, the child is rescued from the river-dragon (Pharaoh); like Joseph, his mother is associated with the moon (Gen. 37:9f.), and with the persecution of innocents (in the Nativity story, Matt. 2:18, comparing Gen. 37:30 and 42:13, 36); and like the children of Eve, the mother's offspring will be at enmity with the serpent (cf. the inversion of this enmity at *F.Q.* I.ii.9).

[278] Douay trans. of the Vulgate of Esther 14:2. Cf. Esther 4:16.

[279] Vulgate Esther 15:4f., 8f. Cf. Esther 5:1–3. The LXX passages are included in the Apocrypha in the Geneva Bible.

expose her enemy. Then the king orders that the letters condemning the
Jews be recalled, and new letters written; he restores Mordecai to favor,
and sends Haman to his death: "But to the Jews a new light seemed to
rise, joy, honour, and dancing . . . there was wonderful rejoicing, feasts
and banquets, and keeping holy-day."[280] Una also is kissed by the king,
and she too enters into the royal presence "with sad sober cheare"; she
bows low in humble reverence, and after the false messenger has delivered
himself (and after Redcrosse has explained his dereliction), she steps
forth again:

> And on the ground her selfe prostrating low
> With sober countenaunce thus to him sayd;
> O pardon me, my soueraigne Lord, to show
> The secret treasons. . . .
>
> (I.xii.33)

The malefactor is denounced and attached, and the new dispensation is
published and celebrated with festivities. Una finally appears without her
veil, for at the messianic banquet, we are told at Isaiah 25:6–8, the stigma
on Israel will be taken away, and the veil of mourning removed. So ends
the reproach upon Israel.

[v]

The idea of the Church in the Bible develops out of the fusion of three
prophetic themes: the preservation and sanctification of the "remnant" of
Israel; the election of a new or spiritual or priestly Israel; and the mission
of Israel unto the Gentiles (cf. Rom. 11:5), Thus the pattern of the history
of Israel is repeated in the cycle of the Church, for the church also will be
driven into the wilderness and will suffer from false prophets and world-
tyrants. We may begin this history from Archimago, whose lies correspond
to the heresies sent abroad by the false prophet.[281] George Joye, in his
Unite and Schisme of the olde Churche, gives a pre-history of the corruption of the faith, and division of its unity, by "mens dreamed rites / super-
sticious ceremonies / troublous tradicion."[282] He starts from Jereboam, who

---

[280] Vulgate Esther 8:16f. Cf. Vulgate Esther 16:21: "God hath turned this day of
sadness and mourning into joy to them"; see Esther 9:17–19 for the institution of
the joyful feast of Purim.

[281] For False-Seeming as a pseudo-prophet, see *Romance of the Rose*, ll. 19344:
". . . False Seeming, who associates / With hypocrites most dangerous and vain /
And felons whom the Scriptures designate / As pseudo-prophets." (Trans. Harry W.
Robbins, New York, 1962, p. 410). Hankins also emphasizes the identity of
Archimago with the false prophet, *Source and Meaning*, pp. 105f., with reference to
the beast from the land (Rev. 13 and 19:20). See n. 406, below.

[282] Fol. iii[v].

"broke this auncient intire unite of that chirch."[283] After Babylon the Jews preserved "the unitie of the trew doctrine," "but then evil men were sprongen up / which yet for their shyning hipocrysye semed somwhat pope holy."[284] A *locus classicus* for "the doctryne of the trwthe and unitie of the church," as Joye calls it,[285] is the first treatise of Cyprian. Cyprian makes Christian unanimity an article of faith, and defines it in terms of unity of doctrine. His account of Satan's recourse after the advent of the truth should be compared to the machinations of Archimago after the defeat of Error:

> And what can be more crafty, or what more subtle, than for this enemy, detected and cast down by the advent of Christ . . . —seeing his idols forsaken, and his fanes and his temples deserted . . . —to devise a new fraud, and under the very title of the Christian name to deceive the incautious? He has invented heresies and schisms, whereby he might subvert faith, might corrupt the truth, might divide the unity. Those whom he cannot keep in the darkness of the old way, he circumvents and deceives by the error of a new way. He snatches men from the Church itself; and while they seem to themselves to have already approached to the light, and to have escaped the night of the world, he pours over them again, in their unconsciousness, new darkness; so that . . . they still call themselves Christians, and, walking in darkness, they think that they have the light, while the adversary is flattering and deceiving, who, according to the apostle's word, transforms himself into an angel of light, and equips his ministers as if they were the ministers of righteousness . . . ; so that while they feign things like the truth, they make void the truth by their subtlety.[286]

The next phase of Redcrosse's history, the defeat of the pagan Sansfoy, corresponds to the victory of Constantine, who conquers, as Redcrosse does, in the sign of the cross. At this point the faith acquires its connection with the Roman Empire through the donation of Constantine; Duessa-Fidessa's mitre suggests the pre-eminence accorded to the see of Rome. The worldly or imperial church develops from this beginning, while truth

---

[283] *Ibid.*, fol. ii^r.   [284] *Ibid.*, fol. ii^v.   [285] *Ibid.*, fol. iii^v.

[286] Treatise I, *On the Unity of the Church*, sec. 3, trans. in ANF, vol. 5, p. 422. Cf. the following from the memoirs of Hegisippus, as quoted in Eusebius, *Ecclesiastical History*, IV.xxii.4–5, on the corruption of the unity of the word of truth: ". . . they called the Church a virgin, for it was not yet corrupted by vain discourses. But Thebuthis, because he was not made bishop, began to corrupt it. He also was sprung from the seven sects among the people, like Simon, from whom came the Simonians. . . . Each [heretic] introduced privately and separately his own peculiar opinion. From them came false Christs, false prophets, false apostles, who divided the unity of the Church by corrupt doctrines. . . ." (Trans. in NPNF, 2nd Series, vol. 1, p. 199.)

passes through the desert fathers, the monasteries, and into the hands of sects like the Albigenses. We might also compare the "eremite" Francis in Milton's poem, who "bore the pious word of salvation to the woodland folk, and tamed the wolves and Libyan lions."[287] In the meantime the Church of Rome becomes a European power through alliances with foreign rulers. Finally, with the Reformation, under the sponsorship of enlightened secular princes, this power is broken, and the purification of the Church begins. The reader will have followed us up to the defeat of Orgoglio by Arthur and the casting out of Duessa.

From this point the pattern is a more personal one of individual conviction of sin and spiritual discipline to mortify it. In the cycle of Irsael, the episode of Despair has the place of the Israelites' inability to enter the promised land under Moses, and their willingness to return to Egypt. In entering the House of Holiness, Redcrosse is a Solomon, a prototype of edification. The temple could not have been built by David, a man of war who "shed muche blood" and "made great battels" (I Chron. 22:8, Geneva Bible). Redcrosse's "great battels" won by "strife, and bloudshed" (I.ix.43) similarly debar him in the preceding Despair canto. There is also the despair of the oracles of doom leading up to Babylon, where the psalmist wept. The prototype for Redcrosse's regeneration at the House of Holiness would then be the return of the remnant to rebuild Jerusalem, as an echo from Nehemiah's description might indicate (I.x.5, "It was warely watched night and day"; cf. Neh. 4:9).[288] Perhaps the uncertain establishment of the new churches is signified. In the calendar of the Church, the House of Holiness corresponds to Lent, and Redcrosse is arrayed in sackcloth and ashes here.

The cycle of the English Reformation may also be mentioned, though it has been explained often enough. Una is the protagonist of this history, more than Redcrosse. Protestant Englishmen would have seen Queen Elizabeth in her, the builder of God's spiritual temple and the leader of a new Israel. Two common types for Elizabeth were Judith[289] and Deborah,[290] and the victory over Orgoglio belongs to Una in a way that

---

[287] *In Quintem Novembris,* l. 86.

[288] As noted in Hankins, *Source and Meaning,* p. 116. See Augustine, *Ennar. in Ps.* CI, Sermo II.4 (PL, XXXVII, 1307) for the Church as a "Zion," of which the "shadow" was "that Zion signified watchtower [*speculata*]," from which the watchers look into the future (as Contemplation foresees Redcrosse's entry into the New Jerusalem).

[289] See E. C. Wilkins, *England's Eliza,* Index, *sub* "Judith."

[290] *England's Eliza,* Index, *sub* "Deborah," and esp. p. 218. So the Epistle in van der Noot's *Theatre* (Elizabeth, like Deborah the prophetess, is "God's champion to defend his beloved church"); the "Oration of John Hales to the Queen's majesty," in Foxe, *Acts,* ed. Cattley, vol. 8, p. 678 ("it hath pleased his divine providence to constitute your highness to be our Deborah"); and John Bale, *The Pageant of Popes,* trans. Studley, fol. 198r.

it cannot belong to Redcrosse. (In the song of Deborah there is mention of "ye that ride on white asses, ye that sit in judgment;" "magistrates," the Geneva gloss says.) Elizabeth was also compared to Daniel in the lions' den, for she was imprisoned in the Tower of London during the reign of Mary.[291] Influential in this reading might be the identification of Pope Sylvester II's reign with the releasing of Satan at the end of the thousand years of the Church's peace. Protestant commentators treated later Popes not only as Antichrist, but also as notable necromancers.[292] Truth is eventually defended by the royal lion, Henry VIII; together Una and the lion mar "blind Devotions mart," though Kirkrapine's offense, as has been pointed out, could just as well refer to the "plural livings" of reform churchmen.[293] Truth is then rejoined by Hypocrisy, or Archimago, now a look-alike for the faith (covert sympathizers with Rome). He is challenged by Sansloi, and in the ensuing fray the lion is killed. Henry's reign also broke down in a kind of anarchy, as Protestants were executed indiscriminately with Catholics.

In the meantime the Bible has been given to the people, and the English plowman has begun to read the "Trew sacred lore" (I.vi.30) that Una teaches the satyrs. The satyrs have a tendency toward natural religion;

[291] Wilson, *England's Eliza*, p. 65: Elizabeth is a Daniel owing to her providential preservation amidst enemies.

[292] For the necromancy of the popes, cf. John Bale, *Pageant of Popes*, fols. 72ʳ–76ᵛ, 82ʳ–86ʳ, and *Image of Both Churches*, in Parker Society *Select Works*, pp. 561ff., on Rev. 20:12; Lavater, *Of Ghostes, edn. cit.*, p. 247; Foxe, *Acts, edn. cit.*, vol. 2, pp. 93–95, 115–134; *Sermons of Archbishop Sandys*, ed. Rev. John Ayre, Parker Society (Cambridge, 1842), pp. 66f. (on the sorcery of Silvester). See n. 198, above.

[293] See the article of Mother Mary Robert Falls, "Spenser's Kirkrapine and the Elizabethans," *Studies in Philology*, 50 (1953), pp. 457–475. Since Kirkrapine stands for "church-robbing," his sacrilege may consist in that diversion of the Church's goods to personal use entailed in the practice of absenteeism: this would be the meaning of the concubinage of Abessa and Kirkrapine. Una's hostess slanders her for harlotry, conceivably with reference to the marriages allowed to the clergy of the reform Church—Elizabeth herself did not approve of marriage for her prelates. It was argued that the "one wife" allowed to the bishop in I Tim. 3:2 meant one *living*, or one parish. One may compare the *good* church-robbing of Paul, who preached to many churches on the wages of one (II Cor. 11:8). Also note that while Una is absent with Ab-esse, Redcrosse is divided with Du-esse. The dissolution of the monasteries still belongs to the allegory, *pace* the rubric for this canto, for that too was an alienation of Church property. Una is wimpled like a nun at the opening of the poem, and she may in part mourn this violation, which is also found on the poem's closing pages. Therefore the lion also is guilty of sacrilege or church-robbing (equated at IV.x.53), though he is marring blind Devotion's *market* (I.iii, rubric; cf. the house of merchandise that the money-changers have made of the temple, at John 2:16; a den of thieves, at Matt. 21:13). The lion thus duplicates the Blatant Beast's violation of monastic houses in Book VI: "into the sacred Church he broke / And robd the Chancell" (VI.xii.25).

they violate Old Testament prohibitions on satyr worship.[294] There is also a famous story of St. Anthony encountering a satyr in the wilderness; the satyr warned the saint against such worship.[295] The satyrs worship Sylvanus, who may be identified with the god Pan; and, if Pan can be the God of Nature,[296] he can also be almost anything else. We may pause to

[294] II Chron. 11:15; Lev. 17:7. In Golding's "Epistle" for his translation, ll. 75f., we are told that we are to understand *"Satyres, Silvanes, Nymphes* and *Faunes"* in Ovid's *Metamorphoses* as "The playne and simple country folke that every where abyde" (Rouse edn., reprint, New York, 1966, p. 16). For the fauns and satyrs as the populace of gods, see *Metam.* VI.392, *illum ruricolae* (the country people), and *Metam.* I.193ff., the *"semidei . . . rustica numina, nymphae faunique satyrique et monticolae silvani"* (demigods, rustic divinities, fauns and satyrs, and sylvan mountain-dwellers) who are alloted lands beneath the heavens.

[295] The story of St. Anthony and the satyr is told in Jerome's *Life of Paulus the Hermit*, 7f., and comes from thence into Isidore, *Etymol.*, XI.iii.21, and such a text as *Battman vpon Bartholeme . . . De Proprietatibus Rerum* (London, 1586), XI.x. In Jerome we read that Anthony, meeting this satyr, asks his identity: " 'I am a mortal being,' " the satyr answers " 'and one of those inhabitants of the desert whom the gentiles deluded by various forms of error worship under the names of Fauns, Satyrs, and Incubi. I am sent to represent my tribe. We pray you in our behalf to entreat the favour of your Lord and ours, who, we have learnt, came once to save the world, and "whose sound has gone forth into all the earth." ' As he uttered such words as these, the aged traveler's cheeks streamed with tears, the marks of deep feeling, which he shed in the fullness of his joy. He rejoiced over the Glory of Christ and the destruction of Satan, and marveling all the while that he could understand the satyr's language, and striking the ground with his staff, he said, 'Woe to thee, Alexandria, who instead of God worshipest monsters! Woe to thee, harlot city, in which have flowed together the demons of the whole world! What will you say now? Beasts speak of Christ, and you instead worship monsters.' " (Trans. in NPNF, 2nd Series, vol. 6, p. 300.) For the same lament as Anthony's, see Sulpitius Severus, *Dialogues*, xiv (trans. in NPNF, 2nd Series, vol. 11, p. 31). The association of Hebrew satyr-worship, devil-worship, and the story of Anthony can be found in Jean Bodin, *De La Demonomanie* (Antwerp, 1586), II.vi, pp. 161ff. It may be appropriate to note here that early Christians were accused of worshipping the ass: see Tertullian, *Ad Nationes*, I.xi, and *Apolog.*, xvi, citing Tacitus, *Hist.* V.3; and Minucius Felix, *Octavius*, ix.

[296] See Isidore, *Etym.*, VIII.xi.81: "Pan is a Greek name; the Latin is Sylvanus, the god of country people whom they invented to represent nature; whence he is called Pan, that is, *all*." Boccaccio, *G.D.G.*, I.iv (Romano edn., vol. 1, p. 22), cites the evidence from Virgil that contravenes the same identification in Rabanus Maurus. Virgil pairs Pan and Silvanus at *Ecl.* X.24–26; Milton makes them alternatives at *Comus*, l. 268, *"Pan or Silvan,"* and describes Sylvanus as a Pan, "semicaperque Deus, semideusque caper," in *Elegy* V, ll. 121f., following Sannazaro, *Eleg.* II.vi.15, l. 28 (in *Opera*, Amsterdam, 1728). In the emblem "Natura," Alciati calls Pan "semicaprumque hominem, semivirumque Deum." This poem begins, "The people worshipped Pan (that is to say, the nature of things)," and Mignault says that Servius, on the *Eclogues*, "writes that Pan is a rustic God made in the likeness of nature" (Emb. XCVII, Antwerp edn. of 1586, pp. 342–344). See below, Chap. VI, n. 65, and Bode, *Scriptores rerum mythicarum latini*, III.8.2, for the equation Pan:Silvanus:*silva:ulē.*

expand on this theme, though it takes us apart from the historical allegory momentarily.

Worship of Pan represents just such truth as natural reverence can arrive at on its own, the kind of truth, for example, found in the Hermetic *Asclepius:*

> It is impossible that the creator of the majesy of the All, the father and lord of all beings, should be designated by one or even by a multitude of names. God has no name, or rather he has all names, since he is at once One and All, so that one must either designate all things by his name, or give him the names of all things.[297]

As Frances Yates points out in her discussion of this passage, the wisest of More's Utopians, having gone beyond star and hero worship, arrived at a not dissimilar religious opinion:[298]

> . . . the moste and wysest parte . . . beleve that there is a certayne Godlie powre unknowen, everlastinge, incomprehensible, inexplicable, farre above the capacities and retche of mans witte, dispersed throughout all the worlde, not in bignes, but in vertue and power. Him they call the father of al. To him alone they attribute the beginnings, and encreasinges, the procedinges, the chaunges, and the endes of al things. Neither they geve any divine honours to any other then to him.

This is the best expression of what reason might aspire to accomplish without revelation; from the point of view of the latter, however, it appears as a state of arrested development, not far removed from a confession of ignorance.

In Macrobius, *Saturnalia,* I.xxii.3, Pan is the Lord of the *ulē,* meaning not of the forest, but of all material substance. See also his *Comm. in Somn. Scip.,* I.xvii.5, on *to pan.* The Renaissance Latin version of the Orphic Hymn to Pan (X, l. 1) calls him *Faunus* and *mundi substantia totus.*

[297] *Asclepius,* xxx, in *Corpus Hermeticum,* ed. A. D. Knock, trans. A.-J. Festugière, vol. 2, p. 321. A very similar kind of religiosity, deriving from the same premises, is given voice in Cicero, *De Nat. Deorum* II.xi. seq.: there is nothing in the cosmos which is not part of the whole, and the evidence of a wise, governing principle there means that the cosmos is god. This is a step down from the "natural theology" of the Stoa. Cf. *Shepherd of Hermas,* mand. 1: "First of all believe that God is one, who made all things and perfected them. . . ."; and Lactantius, *Divine Inst.,* I.iii. Cf. also Boethius, *De Cons. Phil.* III, prose xii, on the One that unites and disposes nature. The oneness of the All is also a theme of Agrippa, *De Occulta Philosophia,* II.iii. For the oneness of the Christian god, see I Cor. 8:5f. (there is no god but the One), I Tim. 2:5 (only [*monos*] one God), and Eph. 4:6 (there is one God who is Father of all, over all, through all, and within all).

[298] *Giordano Bruno and the Hermetic Tradition* (Chicago, 1964; rprnt. of New York, 1969), pp. 185f., quoting the Everyman's Library edn. of the Robinson trans., p. 100. With More, compare Eph. 4:6, quoted in preceding note.

The satyrs prove unable to long entertain the conception of a Wisdom that transcends the allness of nature, and on which the unity of nature depends. They go off to pay their service to Silvanus old (I.vi.33), and we feel they will never advance beyond that point spoken of by Sidney's Pamela, in her argument with Cecropia, namely the subscription to a belief that "one universall Nature (wich hath bene for ever) is the knitting togethr of these many partes to such an excellent unitie." Pamela argues against confusing this universal nature with God: "For this worde, one, being attributed to that which is All, is but one mingling of many, and many ones." The parts do not join "from a conspired unitie"; rather, "a right heavenly Nature indeed, as it were unnaturing them, doth so bridle them":

> This worlde therefore cannot otherwise consist but by a mind of Wisedome, which governes it, which whether you wil allow to be the Creator thereof, as undoubtedly he is, or the soule and governour thereof, most certaine it is that whether he governe all, or make all, his power is above either the creatures or his governement.[299]

Unable to make this distinction, the woodlanders easily slip from the worship of Una to the worship of her beast, and thence back to the wood-god Sylvanus, or mere matter (*silva*). Their goddess is essentially the decorated image of Redcrosse's prophetic dream. And yet, even in the worship of the ass, they may achieve some faint approximation of the worship of the one god, the word for ass in Greek being *onos* (vocative *one*). The demons also believe in the one god (James 2:19), and he is the god of the pagans too (Rom. 3:29f.).

In the idealizing context of romance, the satyrs represent nature without nurture: the world of the naif, the primitive, and the childlike. Its natives are only fitfully accessible to adult civilization. In idolizing Una's ass, they repeat their error in worshiping Una, that is, the vehicle of the Word of God (see Rev. 22:8–9).[300] More important than merely delivering the

[299] *Arcadia*, III.x, in *Works*, ed. A. Feullerat (Cambridge, 1964), p. 409. Preceding quotes from pp. 407f. D. P. Walker, in a thorough study reprinted as chap. 4 of *The Ancient Theology* (London, 1972), pp. 132–165, also suggests Sidney echoes the Hermetic philosophy. See also *ibid.*, pp. 35–39.

[300] So in the emblem cited above, n. 146, and below, n. 458. Alciati's commentator Mignault refers his reader to the proverb *onos agōn mysteria*, an ass bearing mysteries —these mysteries are only minimally entrusted to the vulgar, and the faithful ought to keep silent about them (Emb. VII, "Non tibi, sed religione," p. 50 of edn. cited). For the pun, note the use of the word "own" in the line describing the diversion of the satyrs' religious zeal from Una: "From her *own* worship, they her *Asse* would worship faine" (I.vi.19). Compare the question of the owner of the ass in the Aesopic fable: "Do you suppose that it is come to this, that men pay worship to an ass?" For the proverb, see Aristophanes, *Frogs* 159, and Erasmus, *Adagia* (Geneva, 1606), cols. 445f., *asinus portans mysteria*.

Bible to this society, as early English reformers like Latimer insisted, was the training of a better organized class that could be relied upon to defend the Word doctrinally. To preserve the gains the Reformation, Jewel says in a sermon on the defeat of Jericho, the first consideration is "maintenance of schools and learning":

> In the time of Moses' law, Aaron the great bishop and high priest had written in a tablet before his breast "doctrine" and "truth"; not only learning, but also truth: whereby was meant, that neither might be without other. For, as learning is dangerous and hurtful without religion, so is religion unable to defend itself, and to convince the gainsayers, without learning.[301]

This is the significance of Sir Satyrane's education in Una's "discipline of faith and veritie" (I.vi.31). It is Sir Satyrane—his anagrammatical name indicating that he possesses "nature," and his rank implying formal training—who is able to bring Una out of the woods.

Redcrosse, in the last phase of this history, falls under the power of Duessa and her new ally Orgoglio; here we may be confident that Queen Mary, her husband the king of Spain, and the Catholic restoration were understood. The defeat of Orgoglio and the rest of the legend suggest the consolidation of the reform Church under Elizabeth. This again implies a comparison of the sanctified or purified Church to Eden—God's "moste pleasaunt garden."[302] England as well is compared to Eden, at the end of Greene's *Friar Bacon and Friar Bungay*, in John of Gaunt's speech in *Richard II*, and in Sylvester's patriotic embellishment of his translation of DuBartas.[303] The last two examples come too late for Spenser; perhaps he did something to make the notion current.

The Beginning of Idolatry

[i]

Una's rival, Duessa, might conveniently have been studied rather earlier. Much of the treatment here supplies a logical sequel to the themes of

[301] *Sermon I* on Joshua VI, in Parker Society *Works*, vol. 2, p. 980. Satyrane, like Redcrosse, is "faithfull, true" (I.vi.20; cf. I.i.2).

[302] Van der Noot, *Theatre*, fol. 89ʳ.

[303] Greene, *Friar Bacon and Friar Bungay*, xvi, 65f.; *Richard II*, II.i.42; Sylvester's trans. of DuBartas' *Weeks*, II.II.iii, l. 777 (England is "The World's rich Garden, Earth's rare Paradise"). Similarly Marvell, *Upon Appleton House*, xli, where pre-Civil War England is "The Garden of the World," guarded by "watry if not flaming Sword." See also Josephine Waters Bennett, "England Among the Fortunate Ïsles," *Studies in Philology*, 53 (1956), pp. 114-140.

"The Pledging of Faith" above. However, it is helpful to have some command over Spenser's symbolism for the *ecclesia* theme, the subject we have just been over, before taking up the topic of the present section, *ficta religio*.

From the biblical point of view, all false gods are idols, and all false faith is idolatry. The devotions that Duessa secures are idolatrous in this sense, according to that biblical usage whereby to commit idolatry is to commit adultery.[304] The apostate "play the harlot," and "the inventing of idols was the beginning of whoredome."[305] Duessa, as Duessa, first appears decked with ornaments, and the link between this particular meretriciousness and idolatry is biblical also, for a number of biblical idols are smelted from jewelry.[306] As a result, idols are "molten images," and the framing of the false Una is in part the creation of such an image. The sight of the false Una ravishes the beholder, and also her maker (I.i.45), precisely as the Bible says the idol does (Isa. 44:9, 17, 20). The idol "stirreth vp the desire of the ignorant: so that he coueteth the forme that hathe no life, of a dead image" (Wisd. 15:5). Thus the infatuated Redcrosse, in trying to revive the faint Duessa, is as one addicting himself vnto idols (Wisd. 14:29). He suggests the solicitude of the idol maker for the idol: "for the maker thereof hath made it an image, and a teacher of lies, though he that made it, trust therein, when he maketh dumme idoles. Wo vnto him that saith to

---

[304] Geneva gloss on Isa. 1:29 with *F.Q.* III.xi.29. See Jer. 3:1ff., Ezek. 16:15, 23:5; Hosea 1:2, 2:5, 3:12–15, 4:12–14, 9:1. For the usage, Exod. 34:15f.; Deut. 23:18, 31:16; Judg. 2:17, 8:27–33; II Kings 9:22, 34ff.; Ps. 73:27; Isa. 1:21; Lev. 17:7, 20:5f.; Num. 25:1f.; I Cor. 6:15 ("Knowe ye not, that your bodies are the members of Christ? shal I then take the members of Christ, and make them members of an harlot?"). Cf. Bishop Otto of Freising, *The Two Cities*, VIII.20: "When they [the foolish] have been lured on by false promises she [Babylon] entices them to drink and, when they have been enticed, she leads them to the brink of the precipice in their drunkenness; and lures them—not only by her clamorousness but also by her harlot's attire and her bearing—to her unlawful embraces, as to fornication, and casts them down to destruction. For there is a spiritual fornication, whereby every soul that departs from the love of its Creator and embraces the various delusions wrought by demons plays the harlot, departing from his God, even as it is written, 'Thou hast destroyed all them that play the harlot, departing from thee' [Ps. 73:27]." (Trans. C. C. Mierow, Columbia Records of Civilization, New York, 1928.)

[305] Wisdom 14:11, Geneva Bible.

[306] Gen. 35:4 (the burial of earrings with the putting away of strange gods—the Geneva gloss compares "Agnus deis," inferring the ornaments to have been superstitious); Exod. 32:3f. (the golden calf); Judg. 8:24–27 (ephod of Gideon); Ezek. 16:16f., with Geneva gloss; Hos. 2:13, with Geneva gloss ("By shewing how harlotes trimme themselues to please others, he declareth how the superstitious idolaters set a great parte of their religion in decking them selues on their holie dayes"). Cf. the "gold and rings" offered Corcecca by Kirkrapine (I.iii.18), and the booty of jewels of gold, chains, and bracelets offered to the priest Eleazar for the decoration of the tabernacle at Num. 31.50ff. For the moltenness of idols, see Isa. 40:19, Hos. 13:2, II Kings 19:17f., Neh. 9:18, Ps. 106:19f.

the wood, Awake, and to the dumme stone, Rise vp, it shal teach thee"
(Hab. 2:18b-19, Geneva Bible). "Too simple and too trew," says the poet
(I.ii.45), putting the best possible interpretation on the matter. But we
will say, a "seduced heart hathe deceiued him, that he cannot deliuer his
soule, nor say, Is their not a lye in my right hand?" (Isa. 44:20).

The symbolism of the molten image is also found in the creation of
Duessa's counterpart in Book III; the False Florimell is the "purest snow
in massy mould congeald" (III.viii.6), and she is colored with "vermily"
as the idol is daubed with vermillion (Wisd. 13:14, Ezek. 23:14). The
idol is made, according to Wisdom (14:17–20), to flatter the absent one,
and the artist secures devotion to it by augmenting the subject's beauty. The
idol is "molten" because it is cast, and it is a cardinal point of the biblical
diatribe that the idol is perishable; it will be melted again, when the idols
shall pass away (Isa. 2:18, Jer. 10:15). The same doom overtakes the False
Florimell in the third canto of the legend of justice: "her snowy substance
melted as with heat" (V.ii.24). This judgment is anticipated in the canto
immediately preceding, where Lady Munera, a descendent of Langland's
harlot, Lady Meed, is liquidated by the Mosaic Talus in the manner of
the golden calf.[307] Both "Beautie, and money" (II.xi.9) forge idols.

The razing of Munera's castle is also conceived in Old Testament terms:

> And lastly all that Castle quite he raced,
> Euen from the sole of his foundation
> And all the hewen stones thereof defaced,
> That there mote be no hope of reparation,
> Nor memory thereof to any nation.
>
> (V.ii.28)

We may compare Micah's prophecy of the destruction of Samaria:

> Therefore I will make Samaria as an heape of the field, & for the planting
> of the vineyarde, and I wil cause the stones thereof to tumble downe into
> the valley, & I wil discouer the fundacions thereof.
> And all the grauen images thereof shalbe broken, and all the gifts
> thereof shalbe burnt with the fyre, and all the idoles thereof wil I destroye:
> for she gathered it of the hyre of an harlot, and they shal returne to the
> wages of an harlot.
>
> (Mic. 1:6–7; Geneva Bible)

The exposure of Samaria's foundations and the exposure of the harlot
are essentially the same action if we take the foundations to be the city's
skirts: "Her filthiness is in her skirtes: she remembered not her last end,

---

[307] Exod. 32:20, Deut. 9:12. Cf. Deut. 7:25: "The grauen images . . . shal ye burne
with fire, and couet not the silver and golde, that is on them, nor take it vnto
thee."

there she came down wonderfully. . . . she hathe sene the heathen entre into her Sanctuarie . . ." (Lamentations 1:9a, 10b). The character of this defilement in the Orgoglio episode, where we find such a symbolism, is bloodshed: "Also in thy wings [King James Version, "skirts"] is founde the blood of the soules of the poore innocents" (Jer. 2:34, Douay Bible):

> For the multitude of thine inquities are thy skirts discouered and thy heles made bare. . . .
> I haue sene thine adulteries . . . ye filthiness of thy whoredome. . . .
> (Jer. 13:22, 27, Geneva Bible)

Duessa's shameful parts, then, are filthy in the same way that Orgoglio's floor is filthy, with the blood of persecution. In the fifth book Duessa is brought to justice, and her trial forms a kind of lesson for Arthur, who follows it up with the destruction of a golden idol at an altar much like the one maintained by Orgoglio.

In Hosea the metaphor of spiritual adultery has become the subject for parable and parabolic autobiography, and in Ezekiel the parable has become an allegory. Israel and Judah, personified as Aholah and Aholibah, "haue played the whore . . . and with their idoles haue they comitted adulterie" (Ezk. 23:37). The harlot Israel has decked herself with ornaments and sent messengers inviting men from afar: "And satest vpon a costlie bed, and a table prepared befor it, whereupon thou hast set mine incense and mine oyle" (Ezk. 23:41, Geneva Bible). The Geneva gloss accurately explains that by the bed the prophet "meaneth the altar, that was prepared for the idoles." This is the bed on which Duessa perches in Spenser's first canto, and it is analogous to the beds Duessa visits in the Sansjoy episode. The prophets also condemned foreign alliances as idolatrous, and from the time of the wives of Solomon it was natural to express this condemnation in the imagery of political promiscuity: Israel is told that she "didst enlarge thy bed, & make a couenant betwene thee and them, and louedst their bed in euerie place where thou sawest it" (Isa. 58:9). Duessa goes to Sansjoy's bed to renew her relation with Sansfoy, and she carries him to hell while Redcrosse is administered to with wine and oil: "Thou wentest to the Kings with oyle, & didst increase thine oyntments & send thy messengers farre of, and dist humble thyself vnto hel" (Isa. 57:8). Thus Duessa easily becomes the whore of Babylon, who has consorted with the kings of the earth.

The same text from Isaiah, in fact, takes us up to the congress of Duessa and Redcrosse under the green tree, where the garland with which the hero honors his paramour represents the decoration for an idol. Isaiah addresses the "witches children . . . the seed of the adulterer and of yee whore" who are "inflamed with idoles vnder eurie grene tree." (The idols include the smooth stones of the river, to which the idolator has poured a drink offering.)[308] And it is according to biblical precedent that Redcrosse proves helpless before Orgoglio: "All they shalbe ashamed and also confounded: they shal go to confusion together, that are the makers of images" (Isa. 44:9).

Una and Duessa are contrasted as the veiled Moses and the Egyptian golden calf (cf. Jer. 46:20). Redcrosse, like Israel, deserts the one for the other. The comparison gains significance in the context of Hosea, where calf worship is pointedly allegorized as harlotry.[309] More important, it is the worship of the golden calf that divides the union of Israel into a faithful church and a specious one (I Kings 12:28). Thus Luther urges that priests who fail to preach the word "are the priests of the Hours and the Missals, merely a kind of living idols which bear the name of the priesthood; they are exactly the kind of priests whom Jeroboam ordained at Bethaven, and whom he had taken from the lowest dregs of the people, and not from the tribe of Levi."[310] Specifying things adverse to the true worship of God, Luther names "pilgrimages, the perverse worship of saints, . . . various beliefs in works and in the practice of ceremonies; by all of which, faith in God is lessened, while idolatry is fostered. . . . The result is that now, all our pontiffs are of the kind that Jeroboam formerly instituted in Dan and Beersheba. They were to serve golden calves."[311] Similarly, Bullinger says that Jeroboam and the kings of Israel "did sin most grievously, when they forsook the temple to make sacrifices in the high places, in their cathedral churches at Bethel and at Dan, and in other high and pleasant places."[312] And John Bradford, in his "Hurt of Hearing Mass," says that the ceremonies at Jerusalem were not like the mass; rather, the mass is "like to those sacrifices which were at Bethel and Dan, and in their orchards, groves, woods, hills, &c."[313] They were without God's word, or "verity."[314]

Because idols are "untrue," the nexus of idolatry with false prophecy is as much a consequence of the biblical diatribe as is the nexus of idolatry

---

[308] Cf. *F.Q.* I.vii.6, "the sandie graile."

[309] Hos. 1:2, with Geneva gloss (the prophet's taking a wife of fornications is a parable of the idolatry of the synagogue); 3:12–16; 6:10 with 7:5f., 7:11; 9:3, 9:10; 10:5, 10:11; 13:2.

[310] *Pagan Servitude of the Church*, in *Martin Luther: Selections*, ed. J. Dillenberger, p. 346.

[311] *Ibid.*, p. 320.

[312] *Decades*, III, Sermon V, *edn. cit.*, vol. 2, p. 151.

[313] Parker Society *Writings, Containing Letters* . . . , ed. Aubrey Townsend (Cambridge, 1853), p. 337.

[314] *Ibid.*, p. 335.

with apostasy. In Hosea, God says that the people ask counsel at their stocks, "for the spirit of fornications hathe caused them to erre" (Hos. 3:12). The same ideas combine in Jeremiah, where God says that the people "hast forgotten me and trusted in lies." These lies are alternately idols and the flattering predictions of Jeremiah's *bête noire*, the false prophet: "Then the Lord said vnto me, The Prophetes prophecie lies in my Name ... they prophecie vnto you a false vision ... and deceitfulnes of their owne heart" (Jer. 14:14). "The stocke is a doctrine of vanitie" (Jer. 10:8). To worship abominations is to trust in lies; thus, the Lord has discovered Israel's skirts upon her face—that her shame may appear (Jer. 13:25–26). St. Thomas, referring to Jeremiah 8:5, writes, "*They took hold of a lie,* on which the Gloss says, *idols.*"[315] The image-maker makes a "teacher of lies" (Hab. 2:18); enchanters and soothsayers are patronized by the same people who patronize the idols and groves (Mic. 5:12–14); Jerusalem's prophets commit adultery, and walk in lies (Jer. 23:14); and in the New Testament the worship of the creature and the idol changes the truth of God into a lie (Rom. 1:25). Thus the dream of the false Una that Archimago brings to Redcrosse expresses the same unity of ideas that we find in Zechariah 10:2: "Surely the idoles haue spoken vanitie, and the sothsayers haue sene a lie, and the dreamers haue tolde a vaine thing: they comfort in vaine: therefore thei went away as shepe: thei were troubled, because there was no shepherd" (Geneva Bible). Comparably, the false Una seems to be an idol, a dream image, and a divisive quality in the faith. And the false Una is the bigamous Duessa.

The false Una is Duessa because she is not Una. The evil nature of the duad goes back to Pythagoras' doctrine that "the monad is god: the good, which is the nature of the One, is the mind itself. But the unlimited duad is a daemon and the evil, and it is surrounded by the multitude of matter and the visible world."[316] Vincent of Beauvais reports that the Hebrews treat two as evil because the angel made on the second day is the devil (*Speculum Naturalum*, II.24). The doctrine was also to be found in Homer, according to the *Life of Homer*: ". . . Homer seems to place the nature of unity in the condition of goodness and duality in that of evil, when he often calls a good man courteous and gentle from unity, while on account of duality with respect to conflict he says, 'It is not at all fitting

---

[315] *Summa Theol.*, Pt. I, q.17, art.4, obj.3, citing the interlinear gloss.

[316] Plutarch, in *De Placitis Philosophorum*, as quoted in Eusebius, *Praep. Evang.*, XIV.xvi (p. 754d), trans. H. Gifford (Oxford, 1903), Tom. III, Pt. 2, p. 812. For other texts on the evil nature of two, with reference to God's failure to bless the second day of the creation, see Remigius, *in Gen.* (PL, CXXXI, 56B); Peter Lombard, *Libri Sent. IV*, II.xiv.4 (PL, CXCII, 680); Peter Comestor, *Hist. Schol.*, Lib. Gen., cap. iii (PL, CXCVIII, 1058D–1059A). Cf. "the falsest twoo" at I.i.38, which is doubled in the rime-word "too" (meaning also). "Me too," the copy might say.

for many to rule, but one will be king.' "[317] "For all evil is born from discord and division." Therefore Duessa accompanies Ate at the opening of the second installment of the poem. The most important text on the untowardness of the dyad for our purposes is a pasage from Cornelius Agrippa:

> It is also reported, that the number of two doth cause apparitions of Ghosts, and fearfull Goblins, and bring mischiefs of evill spirits to them that travell by night. *Pythagoras* (as *Eusebius* reports) said, that Unity was God, and a good intellect; and that Duality was a Divell, and an evill intellect, in which is a material multitude: wherefore the *Pythagorians* say, that two is not a number, but a certain confusion of unities.[318]

It would be hard to improve upon "a certain confusion of unities" as a definition of Duessa. We have yet to explain why she is also an evil night spirit.

[ii]

"Surely the idoles haue spoken vanitie, and the sothsayers haue sene a lie"—so we may say of Duessa and Archimago in the cycle of Israel or the "old church." But the old Church typifies the new Church, and the new Church, it is logically deduced from Paul's Adamic Christology, is a second Eve. If Una is an Eve, then to whom does Duessa answer? She must be the wife of Adam too, that is, Adam's other wife, or Lilith.

The poem tells us that Duessa, as the false Una, is created from "liquid air," and yet there is a sense in which she is taken out of the psyche of the sleeping Redcrosse. She is a fantasy. Duessa proper, in the second canto, is an interloping rival for both Una and Fraelissa, who is Spenser's "first Eve." She consorts with Redcrosse in a period that follows on his pledgement to Una, and yet is prior to his actually beholding her. Duessa is increasingly absorbed into a demonic context that makes her a succuba, a granddaughter of Night, and the mistress of a beast that feeds on innocent blood. When she is exposed, there is an especial emphasis on her breasts—"filthy matter from them weld" (I.viii.47). She is allowed to "fly," and when she departs from Redcrosse as a hag she enters the wilderness. She returns to Redcrosse in Eden, at the end of Book I, in the form of a letter, asserting a claim on his loyalties prior to that of Una.

To all this we may compare the general outline of the Lilith legend,

---

[317] Text from Gale, *Opuscula Mythologica*, p. 358.
[318] *Three Books of Occult Philosophy* (London, 1645), II.v, trans. J[ohn] F[rench], p. 178. If the reader still doubts Duessa to be present in canto i, though in a covert way, it may be mentioned that she appears by name in the first canto of the next three books: see II.i.21; III.i, rubric; IV.i.18.

which in its fully developed form makes Lilith both a night-hag and Adam's other spouse. Lilith seduces dreaming men, or causes sexual dreams, as the Talmud and the Zohar (or Cabbala) report.[319] As Adam's wife, Lilith's tradition stems from differences in the Priestly and Jehovist accounts of the creation of the sexes. We have mentioned the Middle English Genesis poem that explains Adam's wife's first being called Isha;[320] the medieval commentator Peter Comestor's digest on Genesis notes the rabbinic tradition of a different first wife for Adam.[321] In the Lilith myth proper, she was created separately from Adam, and either preceded Eve, or else consorted with Adam during an assumed period of separation from Eve, after the expulsion from Eden. (The latter hypothesis is part of a legend that has Adam beget on Lilith hosts of demons.) At Lilith's and Adam's eventual falling out, Lilith is said to fly off to Egypt as a demon herself, vowing vengeance. She seeks the death of infants and is the enemy of nursing mothers, as the blood-drinking lamia and the child-stealing witch, to this day. Though this description is somewhat synthetic, its various elements are attested in places that often are commended to our attention on other grounds than their merely containing material on Lilith.

In his digression on spirits, Richard Burton devotes a section to aerial spirits, and notes that "Concerning the first beginning of them, the Talmudists say that Adam had a wife called Lilis, before he married Eve, and of her he begat nothing but devils."[322] He cites the Genesis commentary of Pererius (1589), where we may read about the "most absurd interpretation of the Talmudists" to be found in one Tostatus, whose commentary was first published in 1559. Pererius writes:

These say that Adam had another wife before Eve, for whom the name was Lilis, and he was with her 130 years, and in that time he begat no men by her, but rather he begat demons. Who will not laugh at these trifles [*nugas*] of the Jews—imaginary and delusory, or rather blasphemies against Holy Writ? For Moses' narration makes it clear that there was no woman with Adam before the procreation of Eve, and indicates that it was necessary that Eve be generated because there was no one like himself

---

[319] Talmud: Shab. 151b (in the 18 vol. Socino Press trans., London, 1961, *Mó ed*, vol. 1, p. 773); Zohar: I.55a, III.19a, and Naamah at I.19b (Socino Press trans., London, 1931, vol. 1, p. 175; vol. 4, p. 359; vol. 1, p. 83).

[320] N. 159, above.

[321] *Hist. Schol.*, Lib. Gen., cap. xvii (PL, CXCVIII, 1070C).

[322] *Anatomy of Melancholy*, Pt. I, Sect. ii, Member 1, subsec. 2. For the comparable spirit in Muslim lore, the jinn-like Qarina or Iblis who was unable to lead Muhammed astray as Eve did Adam, see Samuel M. Zwemer, *The Influence of Animism on Islam: An Account of Popular Superstitions* (New York, 1920), pp. 107–124.

for Adam: moreover, there was no accomplishment in the generation of Eve, if Adam had another prior wife. Then as soon as Adam was ejected from Paradise, he knew his wife Eve, and thenceforward; he begat two children. . . . Therefore it is false that Adam for 130 years did not touch Eve. And besides, who is mad enough to believe that demons were generated from Adam and that prior wife? For it is not possible for a man and a woman to generate a demon, since it is incorporeal. . . .[323]

Peter Martyr's notice in his Genesis commentary is much shorter—"The Jews rave of their Lilith previously produced from Adam"—but it occurs in a significant context, namely, in the midst of references to the founding of the Church in the creation of Eve.[324] Eve, as Maurice Evans reminds us, is the woman, *mulier*, for which one supposed etymology was *mollis aeris*, or "yielding air."[325] Pererius quotes Tostatus elsewhere in his commentary, on Genesis 6:2, to the effect that "when men are polluted by nocturnal seed, a succubus-demon is there, *corpore ex aere in speciem muliebrem*" (through a body from the air in the appearance of a woman).[326] The same stories found in Pererius are found in Tostatus, including the confusion over whether Adam knew Lilith before Eve or in the period after his excommunication from the tree of life, during which he begat demons.

What amounts to a Lilith motif appears in the Christian iconography of the tree of the knowledge of good and evil, for the snake that coils

[323] Benedictus Pererius, *Commentarivm et Disputationum in Gen.* (Cologne, 1601), Vol. 1, Tom. I (1st publ. Rome, 1589), p. 214, col. a, para. 215, following Alphonsus Tostatus, *Opera omnia* (Cologne, 1613), Tom. I, *Super Genesim liber unus* (1436), p. 318, col. E, quaest. 404 (on Gen. 13), and similarly at p. 19, quaest. 28 (on Gen. 2): "Habetur etiam in Talmud Iudaeorum quòd ante creationem Euae Adam habuit aliam vxorem nomine Lilis primum; & istam habuit centum, & triginta annis, quibus fuit excommunicatus pro comestione ligni vetiti; & in toto illo tempore genuit ex ea daemones." I am greatly indebted to Stephen Barney for locating this passage for me in the edn. of Tostatus in the British Museum, and for the references to Evans, and Zohar I.55a and I.19b.

[324] D. Petri Martyris Vermilii Florenti, *In primum librum Mosis, qui vulgo genesis dicitur commentarii* (Zurich, 1569), cap. iii, on *Et erunt in carnem unam.* Cf. Zohar, I.34b: " 'And he took one of his sides and closed up the place with flesh' (Gen. 2:21). I have found it stated in an old book that the word 'one' here means 'one woman,' to wit, the original Lilith, who was with him and who conceived from him." (Socino Press trans.)

[325] *Spenser's Anatomy of Heroism* (Cambridge, 1970), pp. 30f.; cf. Shakespeare, *Cymbeline*, V.v.446ff.: "The piece of tender air . . . Which we call 'mollis aer' . . . We term it 'mulier.' "

[326] *Commentarivm et Disputationum in Gen.*, Vol. 1, Tom. I, p. 387, col. b, para. 64, on Gen. 6:2. Dr. Barney located this passage and pointed out its relevance to the Lilith material here adduced. Pererius cites the story of Merlin's begetting, which is inherently Archimagesque (see n. 85, above).

around the tree is often shown as coming between Adam and Eve and as presenting the face of an attractive woman.[327] This analogy may help us to appreciate the implications of Fradubio's choice between his two mates. The story of Lilith's falling out with Adam (which may be an interpretation of Adam's saying that *now*, with Eve, he has a satisfactory wife [Gen. 2:23]), is first told in the tenth century (?) *Alphabet of Ben Sira*, a text cited by Rivetus in his 1633 commentary on Genesis. Spenser is unlikely to have known other medieval Jewish texts that say that Lilith is a serpent and a prostitute, and that "Wherever there are scoffers, there is Lilith, in the multitude, making her place filthy like the ritually impure"; but the bathing-scene and the exposure scene obviously develop similar motifs for Duessa.[328]

More important is the Lilith who causes sexual dreams, and the Lilith who is a lamia, or *strix*. In fact, the Lilith who is a succuba and the one who is Adam's wife must both be deductions from the tradition of Adam's visited sleep, though no text known to me is quite so explicit. The following, however, comes close:

> Now in the depth of the great abyss there is a certain hot fiery female spirit named Lilith, who at first cohabited with man. For when man was created and his body completed, a thousand spirits from the left side assembled round that body, each endeavouring to enter, until at last a cloud descended and drove them away and God said, "Let the earth bring forth a living

---

[327] For the face of the serpent, see Peter Comestor, *Hist. Schol.*, Lib. Gen., cap. xxi (PL, CXCVIII, 1072B). I owe this point to Dr. Frye. Frye was glossing Blake's Laocoön engraving, but the glosses on the Zohar quoted in Reuben Margulies, *Malakhe elyon . . .* , 2nd edn. (Jerusalem, 1964), pp. 235–241, also show that Lilith is ophidian (*Tiqunei Zohar* 469: the serpent that "took" Eve is Lilith; *ibid.* 431:53:2: the great fish is Samael, the female fish is serpent-Lilith). The notion of an ophidian rival for Eve, or Heva, must owe something to Clement of Alexandria's assertion, that the Hebrew term Hevia, aspirated, signifies a female serpent (*Exhortation to the Heathen*, i.2, trans. in ANF, vol. 2, p. 175).

[328] *Alphabetum Siracidis*, ed. Steinschneider (Berlin, 1858), fol. 23a, and *Otzar Midrashim*, ed. J. D. Eisenstein (New York, 1915), vol. i, p. 47, where Adam claims to have been deserted by Lilith and where three angels attempt to recover her from the Red Sea in which God will one day drown the Egyptians. Though similarly threatened, she remains there, and loses one hundred of her demon children a day, the implication being that she cohabits with lascivious demons. Andreas Rivetus, in *Theologicae . . . excertationes in Genesin* (Leyden, 1633), reprint, as *Excercitationes . . . In primum Librum Mosis*, in *Operum* (Rotterdam, 1651–1660), Vol. i, Tom. I, Exc. xxv, p. 102, cites intermediary sources apart from Tostatus and the *Alphabetum Siracidis*. Lilith consents to not molesting children protected by the charm consisting of the angels' three names; see Moses Gaster, "Two Thousand Years of a Charm Against the Child-stealing Witch," *Folklore*, 11 (1900), pp. 129–169. The following quotes are taken from Margulies' *Malakhe elyon*, pp. 235–241; he is citing Zohar, Mishpatim I.15.1, and the glosses, *Tiqunei* 413:27:272. For the menstrual uncleanness in question, see Lev. 12:1–5, 15:19–33.

soul" (Gen. 1:24). . . . When man arose, his female was affixed to his side.
. . . Afterwards God sawed the man in two and fashioned his female and
brought her to him like a bride to the canopy. When Lilith saw this she
fled. . . .[329]

The text goes on to provide a charm as a remedy against Lilith's wiles,
to be employed before intercourse. Elsewhere in the same text we read
that from the time that Cain killed Abel "Adam separated from his wife.
Two female spirits [unnamed] then used to come and have intercourse
with him, and he bore from them spirits and demons that flit about the
world." But this demonic visitation of Adam need cause us no surprise
"because now also when a man dreams in his sleep, female spirits often
come and disport with him. . . ."[330] Lilith is a succuba in her association
with the spirit Naamah (Zohar I.55a), and "Adam for a hundred and
thirty years had intercourse with female spirits until Naamah was born"
(I.19b). Naamah "wanders about at night time, vexing the sons of men
and causing them to defile themselves." We also read in the Zohar (I.34b)
that God may have taken Lilith from the sleeping Adam, rather than the
rib, and replaced her with flesh, that is, replaced the guilty pleasure that
Adam had previously enjoyed in his cohabitation with Lilith with the
pleasure of the flesh; thus God "created man here below with all that was
necessary to replace that with which the demons dazzled his eyes."

The false Una is also the cause of a sexual dream; Redcrosse is "Bathed
in wanton blis and wicked ioy," "That nigh his manly hart did melt away"
(I.i.47). His dream is interrupted, either by a censor-principle or the imminence of realization ("this great passion of vnwonted lust, / Or wonted
fere of doing ought amis" [I.i.49]). The false Una is also a demon, and
demons are given the power to cause nocturnal emissions.[331] The same
power is attributed to witches; the witch that discharges upon the sleeper
in Apuleius' *Golden Ass* (I.6) is a related conception. There may also be
an indication of this character in Duessa's name, if the reader will allow
yet another explanation of it. In a chapter on the substance of the angels
who were supposed to have fallen in love with mortal women, Augustine
reports that the phenomenon of the incubus is not easily dismissed, it
being widely affirmed that

> . . . sylvans and fauns, who are commonly called "incubi," had often made
> wicked assaults upon women, and satisfied their lust upon them; and that

[329] Vayikra 19a, on "And if the whole congregation should err," in Zohar (Socino
Press: London, 1931), vol. 4, p. 359.
[330] Zohar, 54b, trans. cited, vol. 1, p. 173. The following quotes are from pp. 175,
83, and 130 of the same volume.
[331] Scholia on Aristophanes, *Clouds* 16, and Sprenger, *Malleus Malificarum* (edn.
of 1578), pp. 201–204, on incubus and semen.

certain devils, called Duses [*Dusi*] by the Gauls, are constantly attempting and effecting this impurity is so generally affirmed, that it were impudent to deny it. From these assertions, indeed, I dare not determine whether there be some spirits embodied in an aerial substance (for this element, even when agitated by a fan, is sensibly felt by the body), and who are capable of lust and of mingling sensibly with women;[332]

Duessa, like the Dusii, is "embodied in an aerial substance."

It remains to connect Redcrosse to such a spirit. In Scot's *Discovery of Witchcraft* a charm is given for the cure of a sleeper groaning under the incubus:

> S. George, S. George, our ladies knight
> He walkt by daie, so did he by night:
> Untill such time as he hir found,
> He hir beat and he hir bound,
> Untill hir troth she to him plight
> She would not come to hir [him?] that night.[333]

The episode to which the charm refers is unclear, but the charm itself tells us that St. George, a little like St. Swithin, conquered a nightmare that may have been annoying his lady or himself, and that he exacted troth-plight from her.

The Lilith who visits men in their sleep is also recognized in Renaissance demonology. Weir, for example, explains that *strix* is a name for a sorceress, or an evil bird, with an enmity to infants:

> The Hebrew Rabbis call this bird-like enemy of the sleeping Lilith, a word derived from another which means night, because this bird flies at night: they even write two Hebrew words in the four corners of the bedroom, meaning, Go away, unhappy bird—stupidly thinking that one can chase away this diabolical phantom with such a charm. There are other Rabbis who babel foolishly about this bird in their books.[334]

Scarcely less interesting is the notice in the compendium of Del Rio, where a listing of nocturnal spirits includes "the prince of demonic Succubae, whom in Hebrew they call Lilith, that is, a nocturnal apparition from Laila (which is night): because such demons are accustomed to be aggressive towards men only at night. Hence the Church prays against them with Ambrose, 'Procul recedant somnia / Et noctium phantasmata / Hostemque nostrum comprime / Ne polluantur corpore' (May dreams

---

[332] *Civ. Dei*, XV.23, trans. M. Dods, *edn. cit.*, pp. 511f.

[333] *Discovery*, IV.xi; in Montague Summers' edn. (London, 1930), p. 49.

[334] Johan Weir (Weyer), *Histoires . . . en six liures*, II.i, trans. from *De Praestigiis Daemonum*, by Jacques Grévin (1569) (reprint, Paris, 1885; in 2 vols.), vol. 1, p. 275.

and phantoms of the nighttime retreat far away; and restrain our enemy
—lest they defile us in our body)."[335] Redcrosse, who has "defilde" himself
with Duessa (I.ix.46), might well pray such a prayer, for it is the ancient
evening hymn, *Te lucis ante*. It is sung in the valley of the princes in
Dante's *Purgatorio*, and its protection specifically extends to the sleep of
Adam at *Purgatorio* IX.10f., where Dante falls asleep and dreams prophetic dreams. Spenser, then, would be remarkable for having seen the
connection between the two matters pertaining to Lilith that these texts
illustrate: the one matter of Lilith's differentiation from Adam as his wife;
and the other of her approaching Adam's sons in their sleep.

The Lilith demon belongs to the same type as the classical lamiae, which
are variously explained as "certain shapes of divels, which taking on them
the shew of beautifull women, devoured children and yong men, allured
vnto them with sweete inticements," and "extremely cruel animals, who
have the face and torso of women, and those so beautiful that no one
could depict them, even their gaze and eyes have so much grace, and give
so much pleasure, that he who looks at them, thinks them very pleasing.
. . . The rest of the body is covered in very hard scales, changing them into
snakes."[336] Lavater classifies the lamiae with the "heg" and the *striges*, and
translates Lilith as the night-hag.[337] Erastus and Cartari note the attempt
to link the lamia and the *strix*, though Cartari thinks Pliny has reason to
say that "it is a poetic fiction to say that it suckles little children on its
breast."[338] Cartari and Lavater mention the exposure of the lamia's breasts
as alluring; so does Peter Martyr:

> Ieremie in the fourth chapter of his lamentations saith, that the Lamiae
> discoured their breasts, for they haue uerie faire breasts. Albeit in the
> Hebrue it is written Lilith, about which word the Rabbins doo verie much
> trifle.[339]

[335] *Disqvistionvm Magicarvm*, Lib. II, Qvaest. xvii, sec. ii, *edn. cit.*, p. 222. Aquinas
quotes the same hymn to the same effect, in his article on nocturnal pollution,
Summa Theol., Pt. II, 2nd Pt. q.154, art.5, resp., on the spiritual and external
cause, "when by the work of a devil the sleeper's phantasms are disturbed so as to
induce the aforesaid result."

[336] Lavater, *Of Ghostes, edn. cit.*, p. 5; Vincenzo Cartari, *Le Imagini de gli Dei
de gli Antichi* (Venice, 1625), p. 218 (in Antoine du Verdier's translation, *Les
Images*, Lyon, 1581, pp. 355ff.).

[337] *Of Ghostes*, pp. 5f., 90.

[338] Erastus, *Second Dialogue against the Sorcerers*, trans. by Jacques Grévin, in
Weir, *Histoires, edn. cit.*, vol. 2, pp. 466f.; Cartari, *Imagini*, p. 218 (in Verdier, *Les
Images*, pp. 355ff.). Erastus describes the lamia—she appears in the form of a beau-
tifully adorned woman and is amorous toward young men, whom she destroys—as
the same phantasm as the striges.

[339] *The Common Places of . . . Martyr*, trans. Anthonie Marten (London, 1583),
I.x.29, p. 89. Martyr suggests that the "Empusae, Lamiae, Mormolyciae, Striges" are
of a kind. The same is found in Giovanfrancesco Pico, *Libro detta Strega*, trans.
Leandro delli Alberti (Bologna, 1524), fol. 15ʳ: "demons . . . called by Philostratus

Martyr is wrong about the Hebrew in this instance, but the lamia's connections with the Lilith are biblical nonetheless, for the Vulgate translates both the *lilith* of Isaiah 34:14 and the *tannin* of Lamentations 3:4 as *lamia*.

Once we know Lilith's mythology, we will want to know what commentary made of it. Luther's commentary on the lilith of Isaiah brings out the importance of Martyr's maternal Lilith for the student of Spenser:

> There shall the night hag alight. . . . They are witches and night hags who at night give suck to children and inflict injury on babies, as the prophet says, "Even the night hags give the breast." By allegory: All ungodly teachers are witches and night hags, goblins, who perplex us with false milk and teaching. They are male and female demons who cause nightmares; goblins, devils of all kinds that lie in wait for us during the night.[340]

Similarly, Jerome had allegorized the dry breasts deprecated in Hosea's condemnation of Ephraim's pride in its numbers:

> They do not have cause for pride, considering that they are confounded in what they ought to pride themselves. It is apparent that this can be understood of both teachers of adverse dogmas who are glorified among the multitudes of the people, and those books which they have suckled unto death, as they lead them away from the church and draw them into the murderer. For as many as the devil kills, just so many sons the heretics have begotten unto error.[341]

We begin to see the connection between Duessa's speech and her "false milk."

Even if we were to dismiss the connection of Duessa and Lilith ultimately, we will be impressed by the comparable morphology of their legends. It is time to turn to the one specifically biblical Lilith, to put Luther's comment into its original context. As it turns out, that context is ruins poetry.

Empusae, Lamiae, and Mormolichiae. . . . But regarding the Lamia that we meet in the prophet Isaiah, the dwelling-place of the lamiae, where he makes mention of the congregation of the incubus-Demons, namely of those that otherwise manifest themselves to men in the figure of a female, and thereby give lascivious pleasure to men, I take them to be those Lamiae that are made in the human figure to the waist, and from there down are said to represent a certain bestial form." Martyr's information on the Lamentations lamia might have been from the Bible cited in note 265 above, which records the *Glossa ordinaria* as saying "Lamia hebraice lilit nominatur: quas quidam hebreorum unam de furiis infernalibus suspicantur quae parce dicuntur: eo qu- nulli parcant quibus similes . . . quasi strutio" (*op. cit.*, vol. 4, fol. E6ʳ).

[340] *Lectures on Isaiah 1–39*, trans. H.J.A. Bowman, in Luther, *Works*, ed. Jaroslav Pelikan (St. Louis, 1969), vol. 16, p. 267.

[341] *Comm. in Ossee*, II.ix, in PL, XXV, 899.

Lilith is mentioned only once in the Bible: in Isaiah 34:14, in connection with the destruction of Edom. Its land will be possessed by the satyr, and the *lilith* will make her dwelling there. The demon's name tells us very little. The Geneva Bible translates the word as *scricheowle*; all other English translations gave *lamia*, with or without the owl, following the Vulgate. This passage is always associated with Isaiah 13:21–22, where the same imagery is used for the desolation of Babylon. (In the deutero-canonical book of Baruch, 4:35, "lillim" are said to be going to possess the burnt-out city of the enemy, presumably Babylon.) There is no lamia at Isaiah 13, but for the word now translated *jackals* the Septuagint translates *seirenes* (sirens). The Vulgate retains this reading, and in fact the Septuagint regularly uses sirens where the English translations use "dragon," and occasionally "lamia" (see *lamia* at Jer. 50:39, Bishops' Bible; and Lam. 4:3, Coverdale Bible—"The Lamyes give their yoge [young] ones sucke with Bare Brestes"). Lilith's association with dragons is suggested by Isaiah 34:13, the verse preceding hers: "it shalbe a habitation for dragons" (Septuagint, "sirens").

Both of the Isaiah passages would impress a poet on literary grounds alone; they are supreme in their kind, which is the elegy over fallen buildings, *letterature delle rovine*:

> But the pelicane and the hedgehog shall possesse it, and the great owle, and the raven shal dwel in it, and he shal stretch out upon it the line of vanitie and the stones of emptinesse.
>
> The nobles thereof shal call to the kingdome, and there shalbe none, and all the princes thereof shalbe as nothing.
>
> And it shall bring forth thornes in the palaces thereof, nettles and thistles in the strong holdes thereof, and it shalbe an habitation for dragons and a court for ostriches.
>
> There shal meet Ziim and Iim, and the Satyre shal crye to his felowe, and the scricheowle shal rest there, and shal find for her selfe a quiet dwelling.
>
> There shall the owle make her nest, and lay, and hatche, and gather them under the shadowe: there shall the vultures also be gathered, every one with her make.
>
> (Isa. 34:11–15, Geneva Bible)

Ziim and Iim are variously rendered "wild beasts of the desert" and "of the island" in the AV. Ohim, Isa. 13:21, are "doleful creatures" in the Authorized Version. The Geneva gloss explains: "Which were either wilde beasts, or foules, or wicked spirits, whereby Satan deluded man, as by the fairies, gobblins, and such like fantasies." Calvin translates *lilith* as *fairy*, and on the wild beasts and the satyr he writes similarly:

These animals are thought by some to mean fauns, by others screech-owls or goblins, and by others satyrs: . . . Though we cannot absolutely determine whether the Prophet means witches, or goblins, or satyrs and fauns, yet it is universally agreed that these words denote animals which have the shape of men. We see also what various delusions are practiced by Satan, what phantoms and hideous monsters are seen, and what sounds and noises are heard.[342]

That Spenser knew the Isaiah imagery is suggested by the following from *The Rvines of Time*, on the desolation of Verulam:

> Wasted it is, as if it neuer were,
> And all the rest that me so honord made,
> And of the world admired eu'rie where,
> Is *turnd to smoake*, that doth to nothing fade;
> And of that brightness now appears no shade,
> But greislie shades, such as doo haunt in hell
> With fearfull fiends, that in deep darknes dwell.
>
> Where my high steeples whilom used to stand,
> On which the lordly Faulcon wont to towre,
> There now is but an heap of lyme and sand,
> *For the Shriche-owle to build her balefull bowre*:
> And where the Nightingale wont forth to powre
> Her restles plaints, to comfort wakefull Louers,
> There now haunt yelling Mewes and whining Plouers.
>
> (120–133, my italics)

"The smoke thereof shal go vp euermore," reads the verse preceding the ones quoted from Isaiah; "it shal be desolate from generation to generation." Euterpe's lament in the *Teares of the Muses* (ll. 235ff.), gives an even fuller version of this imagery: "Darknesse more than *Cymerians* daylie night . . . monstrous error flying in the eyre. . . . Ignorance / Borne in the bosome of the black *Abysse*." "A ragged rout / Of *Faunes* and *Satyres*, hath our dwellings raced," the pastoral Muse complains:

> In stead of them fowle Goblins and Shriekowles,
> With fearfull howling do all places fill
> And feeble *Eccho* now laments and howles,
> The dreadfull accents of their outcries shrill.
> So all is turned into wildernesse, . . .
>
> (282–288)

---

[342] *Comm. on Isaiah*, trans. William Pringle, in 4 vols., for the Calvin Translation Society (Edinburgh, 1850–1852), vol. 3, p. 55. Cf. Calvin on Isa. 13, in vol. 1, p. 429. For Calvin's trans., see vol. 3, p. 496.

We may compare with this a text from Zephaniah (2:14–15) on the desolation of Ninevah, which shall be "waste like a wildernes":

> And flockes shal lie in the middes of her, and all the beastes of the nacions, and the pellicane, and the owle shal abide in the vpper postes of it: the voyce of birdes shal sing in the windowes, and desolations shalbe vpon the postes: . . .
>
> This is the reioycing citie that dwelt carelesse, that said in her heart, I am, and there is none besides me: how is she made waste, and the lodging of the beastes euerie one that passeth by her, shal hisse and wagge his hand.

What is said here of Verulam and the state of learning is said of Babylon in Isaiah 13 and Jeremiah 50:39, and these biblical texts were traditionally adduced in explaining Revelation 18:2: "It is fallen, it is fallen, the great Babylon, and is become the habitation of deuyls, and the holde of all fowle spirites, and a cage of euery vncleane & hateful byrde" (Geneva Bible). Thus a whole class of Spenser's earlier poetry—the Roman ruins poetry, the emblems of collapse, and the emblems from Revelation—has a unity of imagery with a biblical analogy.

It follows from the Protestant interpretation of Revelation that Edom and Babylon in Isaiah would be compared to the Roman Church. This is found in the Geneva Bible on Isaiah 34:5 ("Papists"), and in Bullinger,[343] Bale, and van der Noot. Here is Luther on the text in Isaiah 13:

> Rome is the true Babylon, and these things are said of Rome at least in a general way, if not in specific detail. For in general all the ungodly will perish. The defenders of the pope are struck with fear, they do not know how to interpret Scripture. They howl and hiss for the pope, they have become hairy satyrs, ostriches, owls, dragons, etc.[344]

The older interpretation of Jerome is not all that different:

> These follow a certain trope who affirm that in the people of the Jews, expelled under the names of beasts and portents, are the idolatries and various servile superstitions making their residence in Jerusalem: and these are the *onocrotalos* and hedgehogs, *ibin* and *corvum*, dragons and ostriches, and ass-centaurs, and demons, and satyrs, and the lamia, which in Hebrew is said LILITH; and by Symmachus alone it is translated as *lamia*, which indeed is suspected to be the Erinny—that is, the Fury—of the Hebrews.[345]

[343] *A Hundred Sermons Vpon the Apocalips* (London, 1561), xviii, fol. 244ᵛ.
[344] *Works, edn. cit.*, vol. 16, p. 137.
[345] *Comm. in Isa.*, X.xxxiv, in PL, XXIV, 373.

Thus both the nursing lamia and the ruin-occupying Lilith seem to symbolize what Duessa symbolizes, Luther's "night-hags who perplex us with false milk and teachings," Jerome's "idolatries and various servile superstitions making their residence in Jerusalem." Rather more curious is the following passage from the text in the Zohar that we have already cited for the creation of Lilith. When Lilith saw God bring man to his female, she fled:

> . . . and she still cries in the cities of the sea coast trying to snare mankind. And when the Almighty will destroy the wicked Rome, He will settle Lilith among the ruins, since she is the ruin of the world, as it is written: "For there Lilith shall settle and find her place of rest."[346]

It would appear that Jewish commentary had at least once arrived at a prophetic interpretation of the text in question not dissimilar to the one that eventually emerges in the literature of Christian protest.

To conclude: Lilith is both screech-owl and witch, with a name traditionally derived from *laylil*, night, and with her resting-place established in the desolation of Israel's enemies. Duessa is a hag who comes in the night, flies with the night—to the sound of shrieking owls in I.v.30—and, with the fall of the Babylonical realm of Orgoglio, returns to the darkness and the wastes. "She flying fast from heauens hated face," with the beasts in Isaiah, "Fled to the wastfull wilderness. . . And lurkt in rocks and caues long vnespied" (I.viii.50). This too is biblical:

> And the idoles will he vtterly destroye.
> Then they shal go into the holes of the rockes, and into the caues of the earth, from before the feare of the Lord, & from the glorie of his maiestie, when he shal arise to destroye the earth.
> At that day shal man cast away his siluer idoles, and his golden idoles (which they had made them selues to worship them) to the mowles and to the backes,
> To go into the holes of the rockes, and into the toppes of the ragged rockes. . . .
>
> (Isa. 2:18–21, Geneva Bible)

Spenser's conception—of a rival for Eve who is also the occasion for apostasy—forms a mysterious whole. We read in the Talmud that the generation that built the Tower of Babel also fashioned idols; somehow we are not surprised to learn that these idols were animated by the demon Lilith.[347]

---

[346] Vayikra 19a, Socino Press trans., vol. 5, p. 359.

[347] Ra'ya Mehemna, III.277b. The fall of Babylon at Rev. 18:2 entails the breaking of the graven images of her gods unto the ground, and Baruch 6:21 describes the alighting of bats, birds, and wild cats on her idols.

[iii]

Bale writes on the ruins verse in Revelation:

Now is she the corrupt cage of all unclean fowls and hateful birds. For in her dwelleth the adulterous cardinals, the filthy bishops, the prostibulous prelates and priests the Gomorre and monks, canons, friars, and nuns, an innumerable swarm of Sodomites. These doth Esay in similtude compare unto wild beasts, dragons, ostriches, dancing apes, owlets, mermaids, and other odible monsters. For there is mocking and mowing, crying and yelling, . . .[348]

So also van der Noot: the wild beasts are prelates, "namely Dragons, Ostriches, Eagles, Monkeis, Owles, Mermaides, and other ravenous and greadie birdes, and monsterous and straunge beasts."[349]

The mermaids in these passages must go back to the sirens of the Septuagint. In fact, the whole Judaeo-Hellenic siren complex affords a parallel for Lilith, once we understand the assimilation of the siren to ruin-haunting demons of a desert cast.[350] Hence a summary of the siren's characteristics will also show an analogy with Duessa. Sirens have erotic designs on men; they are compared to harlots;[351] they paralyze the

---

[348] *Image of Both Churches*, in Parker Society *Select Works*, pp. 517f.

[349] *Theatre*, fol. 52[r].

[350] My attention was first drawn to the biblical and patristic siren by the chapter on it in Hugo Rahner, *Greek Myths and Christian Mystery*, trans. Brian Battershaw (New York, 1963), pp. 353–371; to Rahner I particularly owe my references to Ambrose, Jerome on Micah, and the *Physiologus*.

[351] Sirens may have been conceived of as mounting men during their noontide sleep, according to Otto Crusius, "Die Epiphanie der Sirene," *Philologus*, New Series, 50 (1891), pp. 93–107, instancing the relief of a winged female mounting a slumbering harvester, and recalling the siren Parthenope, who resisted falling in love with one Metiochus (Eustathius on Dionysus Periegetes 358, p. 180M, in *Geographi Graeci Minore*, ed. Charles Muller, Paris, 1882, vol. 2, p. 280). Sirens look like the woman-faced birds of a mosaic, ca. A.D. 500, labeled *lamiae* (cited in Georg Weicker, *Der Seelenvogel*, Leipzig, 1902, pp. 32f.). Hesychius, *sub* "Seirenes"; Heraclitus, *De incred.*, xiv; scholia on *Od.* XII.39 (the sirens were changed into birds as a punishment from Aphrodite for their denial of their sexuality, or because they wished to remain virgins; see Aelian, *Hist. anim.* XVII.23; Apollonius Rhod., IV.896; Eustathius on *Od.* XII.47, p. 1709). Servius, *ad Aen.* V.864: "To tell the truth, they were *meretrices* because they seduced those passing by for their purpose; they were feigned to cause shipwreck on this account." Isidore, *Etym.*, XI.iii.31f., says they have wings and claws because love both flies and wounds, and they dwell in the waves, because the waves created Venus. In Jerome, *Epist.* XXXIV.13, they are singing courtesans that exhibit the devil's wiles. In Lucian, *Ver. Hist.* II.46, they are courtesans dwelling on an island where witchcraft prevails. In Clement of Alexandria, *Exhortation to the Heathen*, xii, they personify pleasure. In Justin Martyr, *Ad gent.*, i, they are harlots. See *F.Q.* II.xii.30–32.

waves;[352] they induce sleep in men at midday with their song;[353] they are spirits of lament;[354] they are monstrous;[355] they are owls, or daughters of the screech-owl.[356] They are under the spell of Hades;[357] they mourn at graves, they convey the dead.[358] They are certain demons nourished in the desolation of a city under God's wrath.[359] In short, they are both *femme fatale* and "doleful creature," and they visit men in their sleep, or induce that sleep.

The reader can match many of the characteristics of the sirens and Duessa. Duessa mourns over Sansjoy and conveys him to Hades, and she may be identified with a "ruins of Rome" motif in the ecclesiastical allegory. She is also the torpor-inducing siren of the noonday, for she arrests

[352] Hesiod, *Theog.* 275, and *Frg.* 197. They are singers at whose song "the oars can move no more," in Claudian, *De Raptu* III.204, 254. In *Od.* XII they are announced by an uncanny sea-calm and exceptional noontide heat.

[353] Pindar, *Frg.* 53: they spellbind their victims; Pliny, *Nat. Hist.* X.136: they charm men to sleep before destroying them. Plato, *Phaedrus* 259a: they induce sleep in men at midday with their song. Hence the Siren Idleness (*Desidia*) in Horace, *Sat.* II.3, l. 14.

[354] Sophocles, *Frg.* 777; Euripides, *Helen* 168; Plato, *Cratylus* 403d-e; Seneca, *Her. Oet.* 188; *Sybylline Oracles* V.457; LXX Job 30:30 and LXX Micah 1:8.

[355] Jerome says they are called *Thennim* in Hebrew (*tannim*, dragons or jackals in Job 30:29; Isa. 13:22, 23:13, 35:7; Jer. 9:11, 10:22, 49:33, 51:37, Mic. 1:8): "which are interpreted for us either as demons, or certain monsters, or rather great dragons" (*Comm. in Isa.* 13:22). Isidore says they are winged serpents (*Origins*, XII.iv.29). Lucian gives them donkey legs (*Ver. Hist.* II.46). In this last respect they would resemble the Empusa (Suidas, *sub* "Empusa"; Aristophanes, *Frogs* 288ff.; Philostratus, *Vit. Apol.* iv.25). Erasmus notes that Aristophanes' Empusa is mutable, in that she can turn herself into many forms—these include that of a most beautiful woman: "Some believe her to appear at the hour of noon alone to those who mourn for the dead. Which indeed—I certainly do not know whether rightly or not—can be referred to that which appears in the psalm of the Hebrews . . . 'From attack and the noonday demon'" (*Adagia*, *sub* "Proteo mutabilior"). Duessa is also *chameleonte mutabilior*, mentioned in the same place in Erasmus: "she could d'on so manie shapes in sight, / As euer could Cameleon colours new; / So could she forge all colours, saue the trew" (IV.i.18).

[356] Birds: Pliny, *Nat. Hist.* X.136; paired with owls: Vulgate Isa. 13:22; called owls: Chrysostomon Job 30:29, as cited in Stephanus, *Thesaurus Graecae Linguae,* ed. Hase, *et al.* (Paris, 1831-1865), *sub* Seirenes; called *filiae ululae* (*bənoth yatsanah*) in Scripture: (see Basil, *Comm. in Isa.,* xiii, PG, XXX, 599-605); paired with *struthioi* (ostriches): LXX Job 30:30, Mic. 1:8, Isa. 34:13, Suidas, *s. v.,* identifies the sirens with ostriches on the basis of the Job text, but also says they have the feet and neck of the ass. Lilith and siren are parallel members in a text discovered in modern times, II Baruch 10:8, trans. in R. H. Charles, *Apocrypha and Pseudepigrapha,* vol. 2, p. 485.

[357] Plato, *Cratylus* 403d.

[358] *Cratylus,* 403d; Sophocles, *Frg.* 777; Plutarch, *Conviv. Quaest.* IX.xiv.6; and the grave-siren texts cited in Weicker, *Der Seelenvogel,* p. 78, n. 1.

[359] Suidas, *sub* Seirenes.

Redcrosse—one of the sons of day—"in middest of the race" (I.vii.5). Here it helps to know that an old patristic tradition, originating with the Desert Fathers, associates the noonday demon of Psalm 91:6 with the sin of sloth and incapacitation of the will.[360] The siren's counterpart in Book II, namely Phedria, appears at the corresponding point in Guyon's race, and Phedria stands, not only for idleness and indolence, but also for the restlessness, vagrancy, and carelessness, which the sin of sloth also includes: the wayward monk Idleness shakes with fever (I.iv.20).

The example of Phedria reminds us that sirens are also marine creatures, with a seductive song "that leads the auditor to death," as the interlinear *Glossa* on Isaiah 13:22 explains.[361] In this category is the Babylonian siren of St. Ambrose:

> Jeremiah also hath prophesied concerning Babylon, that the daughters of sirens shall dwell therein, in order to show that the snares of Babylon, that is, of the tumult of the world, are to be likened to stories of old-time lust, that seemed upon this life's rocky shore to sing some tuneful song, but deadly withal, to catch the souls of youth. . . .[362]

Ambrose then cites Ulysses' restraint before their "deceitful shows and allurements of pleasure," and refers to I Corinthians 9:27, on Paul's need for self-discipline, lest he become a castaway. In the *Physiologus* the sirens represent hypocrisy,[363] and Jerome echoes this interpretation in his com-

---

[360] See Siegfried Wenzel, *The Sin of Sloth: Acedia in Medieval Thought and Literature* (Chapel Hill, 1960), pp. 4–7 and *passim*; Wenzel cites the Desert Father Evagrius to the effect that the period of the fourth to the eighth hour slows the progress of the sun, and tempts monks to wander forth from their cells. For the link between the noonday demon and the sirens, see R. Caillois, "Le démon de midi," in *Revue de l'Histoire de Religion*, 115 (1937), pp. 142–173, and *ibid.*, 116 (1937), pp. 54–83, 143–186. For Phedria and the subsequent idleness and repose tradition, see Patricia Parker, "The Progress of Phaedria's Bower: Spenser to Coleridge," in *ELH*, 40 (1973), pp. 372–397. Mrs. Parker has suggested the above references to me. On the fourth cornice of Dante's Purgatory, where the sin of sloth is purged, "the slackened oars are plied again" (*Purg.* XVII.87), and Dante dreams of a Siren who thus delays his wakening.

[361] *Biblia sacra* (Basel, 1498), Quarta pars, fol. e3ᵛ.

[362] *On the Christian Faith*, III.i.4, trans. in NPNF, 2nd Series, vol. 10, pp. 242f.

[363] *Physiologus*, "The Sirens and the Centaurs," in the Carlill trans., p. 207. The *Glossa ordinaria* on Isa. 13:22 also treats the sirens as hypocrites; the interlinear gloss on the lamia of Lam. 4:3 reads *heretici et hypocrite*. Cf. Gregory on the lamia of Isa. 34:14: "by the 'lamia' are designated hypocrites. . . . For the 'lamia' is said to have the face of a man, but the body of a beast. Thus also, in the first appearance which all hypocrites present, there is a kind of fashion of sanctity; but that which follows is the body of a beast, because the deeds which they attempt under show of goodness are very wicked" (*Moralia*, XXXIII.xxix.53, Library of the Fathers trans., vol. 3, p. 605). The biform *onocentaur* is an analogy for the hypocritical siren because of the LXX trans. for Isa. 13:22, 34:11, 14. The Vulgate retains from LXX the onocentaur for the *iyyīm* of Isa. 34:14, "wild beasts of the island" (AV). Where

ment on Micah 1:8, where the Septuagint says that Samaria "will intone a song of mourning like the daughters of the Sirens": "for," Jerome explains, "the song of heretics can be sweet indeed and they deceive the peoples with pleasant sounds."[364] All these traditions take us toward Dante's second dream in the *Purgatorio* (XIX.7–60), where a kind of synthesis is achieved. We are on the cornice of Sloth, and the pilgrim is asleep. Just before dawn a bald "old witch" (as she is afterwards called) comes to the dreamer; under his gaze she seems to become seductively beautiful, and she sings of having allured Ulysses. Then a holy and alert lady appears to "confuse" her. At the direction of the "honest one," Virgil intervenes. "Tearing her clothes," Virgil "laid bare her breast and showed her belly / the stench of which awakened me." Duessa is similarly stripped by Arthur at the behest of Una.[365]

The exposure of a witch is a romance motif in its own right. The celebrated classical instance is the story of the lamia-wife in Philostratus.[366] Another such story is that of Melusine, a story that bears a close resemblance to that of Fradubio's discovery of Duessa's secret ablutions: Melusine's husband made the same discovery.[367] Cornelius Agrippa speculates that Melusine was a succuba.[368] Rather closer to Spenser is Paracelsus' comment in *De Nymphis*, where he takes Melusine to have been a nymph possessed of an evil spirit:

> But then, as *superstitio* seduces and vexes all beings, she [Melusine] went away from her people in her superstitious belief, to places where the seduced people come who are bewitched in *superstitiones* and spellbound. . . . Yet there are more *superstitions* in the Roman Church than in all these women and witches. And so it may be a warning that if a *superstitio* turns

---

Symmachus and the Vulgate have *lamia* in the same text, for *lilit*, the LXX has *onocentaur*. The Greek term brings one closer to the satyrs or goat-demons of the same texts. See Aelian, *Nat. Hist.* XVII.9.

[364] *Comm. in Michaeam*, I.i (PL, XXV, 1158C), trans. in Rahner, *Greek Myths*, p. 364.

[365] Falsehood is old and bald in Alanus de Insulis, *De Planctu Naturae*, prose ix. Boccaccio describes the classical sirens at some length (*G.D.G.*, VII.xx, Romano edn., vol. 1, p. 355): they are pleasure-stimulating, flattering, and sleep-inducing. He ends: "Indeed, the inspired Isaiah speaks of these sirens: Sirens and demons will dance in Babylon: perhaps because we seem to have touched upon a new Babylon in our age" (Romano edn., vol. 1, p. 357). Boccaccio's later commendation of Petrarch's scorn for the "western Babylon" (*G.D.G.*, XIV.xxiv) fixes the reference as the papal see at Avignon.

[366] *Vita Apol.* iv.25.

[367] The story of Melusine was widely retailed: the Early English Text Society prints two Middle English examples. John Ashton, ed., *Romances of Chivalry*, excerpts and paraphrases an early Renaissance prose version that Spenser could have known. Cf. also the story of Manto, in Ariosto, *O.F.* XLIII.97–105.

[368] *Three Books of Occult Philosophy*, III.xix; trans. cited, p. 404.

a man into a serpent, it also turns him into a devil. That is, if it happens to nymphs, it also happens to you in the Roman Church. That is, you too will be transformed into such serpents, you who are now pretty and hand-some, adorned with large diamonds and jewels. In the end you will be a serpent and a dragon, like Melusine and others of her kind.[369]

Paracelsus seems to pass easily from the transformation of Melusine to the Protestant interpretation of the fall of the whore of Babylon.

Duessa's next of kin, however, are Ariosto's Circean fay, Alcina, and Trissino's Acratia.[370] The enchanting Alcina, like Spenser's Phedria, is also something of a siren; at least she promises Astolfo that she will show him one (*O.F.*VI.40), and she allures him aboard a whale. Later, Ruggiero (armed with Melissa's spell-breaking ring) will see her for what she is: like Dante's siren, balding, toothless, and a hag (*Purg.* VII.72f.). Tris-sino's sorceress—whom we will meet again in our discussion of the Bower of Bliss—merits particular notice. Like Archimago, she is a protean shape-changer, under compulsion; and, like Duessa, she is exposed as a lamia. In order to bring the bewitched knight Corsamonte to his senses,

> ... the good Trajano—
> Who held Acratia in his arms, lifted her gown,
> Showing the secret parts.
> He saw what shame the dress covered
> And he saw the thighs to be two watersnakes
> Of fierce aspect; and there went out from there a stench [*puzzo*]
> That exceeded all other horrible smells.
> Then, as if awakening from a lethargy,
> Hearing again—and the veil
> Which stood within his ears and covered his eyes unloosed—
> Suddenly the one knew the other.[371]

As this passage helps make clear, the lifting of the veil and the lifting of the skirts are in some sense the same action.

Spenser's analogy between the witchcraft of Circe and the works of the whore of Babylon is well established in Protestant polemic. Bale calls the pope "ye witch and *Circes* of the whole worlde";[372] Calfhill speaks of be-

---

[369] *De Nymphis*, Tract IV, trans. by Henry E. Sigerist, in *Four Treatises of . . . Paracelsus*, Publications of the Institute of the History of Medecine, The Johns Hopkins University, 2nd Series, Texts and Documents, vol. 1 (Baltimore, 1941), p. 246.

[370] See below, Chap. IV, "Gardens of Pleasure," sec. i.

[371] Book V, ll. 367ff., in Trissino, *Opere* (Verona, 1729), p. 47.

[372] "Epistle Dedicatorie," *Pageant of Popes* (London, 1574), fol. *di^v. So also Curio, in his *Defence*, on the whoredom of the papistry: "After this followeth the golden cup, the which what shall we say else to be, but a cup of love full of poisonous

lievers "bewitched with the sorcery of Romish Circe";[373] Fulke uses the phrase "Babylonical Circe."[374] As Waters' study has recently shown, Duessa shares this character with Mistress Missa, "Madame Mass," a personification who in Coverdale is the daughter of Idolatry.[375] She is not so much a Circe figure as a Circe *in potentia*, like Phedria, whom the 1590 edition of Spenser's poem made "as merry as Pope Ione" (II.vi.3):

> ... horribly abused to be a mermaid to amuse and bewitch men, sailing in the seas of this life to be enamoured on her. And therefore besides her aforesaid goodly apparel, she hath all kinds of sweet tunes, ditties, melodies, singing, playing. ... And lest men should think her too coy a dame, lo, sir, she offereth herself most gently to all that will come, be they never so poor and stinking and foul, to have their pleasure on her. Come who will, she is "Hail, good fellow"; and that not only to make herself common to them that will, but also to ply them plentifully with most pleasant promises falsely, and giving most licentious liberties to all her lovers. ... .[376]

The idea that imagery like Alcina's and Acratia's belonged, not to Pleasure, but to Apostasy, the Reformers had on biblical authority, as Hankins indicated in his pioneering article. It is specifically Babylon that will be exposed in Isaiah 47:3: "Thy filthines shalbe discouered, and thy shame shalbe sene." This example is important because the "ladie of kingdomes," the "mayden of Chaldea," is said to have wearied herself from her youth with enchanters and practitioners of superstitious arts. The same retribution is promised to an idolatrous Jerusalem:

> Beholde, therefore I wil gather all thy louers, with whome thou hast taken pleasure, and all them that thou hast loued, with all them that thou hast hated: I wil euen gather them rounde about against thee, & wil discouer thy filthines vnto them that thei may se all thy filthines.
>
> And I wil iudge the after the maner of them that are harlots, and of them that shead blood, & I wil giue thee the blood of wrath and ielousie.

---

enticements and whorish drinks, by the which she allureth unware folk unto her filthy delights and outrageous love, and turneth them as it were another Circe, which was a witch or a charmer, into divers kinds of beasts and monsters?" (Trans. John Philpot, in Parker Society *Writings*, p. 428.)

[373] *Answer to Martiall*, in Parker Society edn., ed. R. Gibbings (Cambridge, 1846), p. 248, with Gryllus.

[374] "A Sermon Preached at Hampton Court," 12 Nov. 1570: "Wherein is plainly proued Babylon to be Rome" (London, 1572), Sig. G4v.r, as cited in Waters, *Duessa as Theological Satire*, pp. 9f.

[375] *Duessa as Theological Satire, passim.*

[376] Coverdale, *An Exhortation to the Carrying of Christ's Cross*, in Parker Society *Remains*, ed. Rev. George Pearson (Cambridge, 1846), pp. 266f. Waters has quoted the same passage from John Bradford, Parker Society *Writings*, vol. 2, pp. 287–289.

I wil also giue thee into their hands, and they shal destroy thine hie
place, and shal breake downe thine hie places: they shall strippe thee also
out of thy clothes, & shal take thy faire iewels, and leaue thee naked and
bare.

(Ezek. 16:37–39, Geneva Bible)

At Isaiah 3:16–24 the mincing and adorned daughters of Zion are threatened with a desecration that includes the headscabs, baldness, and stench
found in Spenser.[377]

Bale accumulates the whole sequence of biblical texts on this theme:

The same God hath dyscouered the shame of Babylon (whych now is the
Romysh churche) and shewed fourth her concomely preuytees, accordynge
to promyse, Esay. xlvii. Beholde (sayth the lorde of hostes) I wyll brynge
thyne owne ways upon thyne heade, Ezech. xvi. I wyll upon the, thou
bewtyfull harlot and maistres of witchcraft (sayth God) and wyll pull
thy clothes ouer thy heade, that I maye shewe thy nakednesse among the
heathen, and thy shame amonge the kyndedomes. I wyll caste durte upon
the, to make the be abhorred and a gasynge stocke, Nahum iii, for he that
comytteth adoutry, getteth hym selve shame and dyshonour, such as neuer
shall be put out of memory. Prover. vi.[378]

Bale urges the princes of his time to "thorow fourth that wretched bonde
woman with her doughter, that Rome churche with her whorishnesse."[379]
He is thinking of the allegory of the two churches in Galatians 4; and, like
Hagar, Duessa is also exiled into the wilderness. The biblical motif culminates in the judgment upon the whore of Babylon in Revelation, where
retribution is urged: "Render to her as she also hath rendred to you: and
double ye double according to her workes: In the cuppe wherein she hath
mingled, mingle ye double unto her" (Rev. 18:6, Rheims Bible). *Duplicate
duplicia*, Duessa's name, like that of the whore, has been a Mystery, and
yet one may suspect that at last she has been given something like her
"due."

[iv]

If Archimago and Duessa correspond to Satan and Lilith in the cycle
of Adam, to Babylon and the false prophets in the later cycle of Israel, and
to the Antichrist and Rome in the cycle of Revelation, then to whom do
they correspond in the cycle of the Church? Duessa is discovered to have

[377] Hankins, *Source and Meaning*, pp. 101f., 107.
[378] "John Bale to the Reader," at the head of Part II of *The first two partes of the
Actes or unchaste examples of the Englysh votaryes* (London, 1551), fol. vii^r.
[379] *Pageant of Popes*, Preface, Sig. Avi^v.

a fox's tail; this comes from the false prophets of Ezekiel 13:4, who resemble jackals in a ruin and are traditionally linked to the foxes who spoil the vineyards in the Song of Songs (2:15). The foxes were thus recognized as a type of heresy,[380] and in the cycle of the Church the false Una must in part represent early errors. One thinks especially of Gnostic dualism and the Docetist doctrine that Christ's mortal body was only a seeming body. Christian Gnosticism, as we know it, dates from the second century, but early heresiologists identified its founder as Simon Magus, the magician of Acts. How this came about is less important to us than early expansions on the report in Acts that form a legend of Simon.[381]

The legend of Simon depends on three different traditions: that of the Church heresiologists and historians; that of the Apocrypha concerning the Apostle Peter; and that of the "Clementine" literature, which takes its title from Peter's successor, the first pope.

According to the heresiologists, Simon Magus is the demogorgon figure of all Christian heresy, and he stands at the head of its history. As Nicephorus puts it, in his *Ecclesiastical History*, he is held to be the leader and prince (*archagos kai protos*) of all heresies.[382] So also Philaster of Brescia, Epiphanius of Cyprus, Theodoret of Cyprus,[383] and Cyril of Jerusalem; Cyril says that in Simon the dragon of malice first appeared.[384] Ireneaus says that Simon impelled many into bewilderment, and all who adulterate

---

[380] So the *Glossa ordinaria* on Song 2:15 (PL, CXIII, 1141), and at great length, Origen, *Comm. in Cant. Cant.*, IV.2 (or III.15 in the trans. by J. P. Lawson, London, 1957). The same allegory is found in the Genevan gloss on this place. Cf. the *volpe* of Dante, *Purg.* XXXII.119, and Augustine, *Ennar. in Ps.* LXXX.14 (PL, XXXVII, 1040).

[381] The following have been consulted usefully: James M. Hastings, ed., *Encyclopedia of Religion and Ethics*, vol. 8, *sub* "Simon Magus"; Smith and Wace, eds., *Dictionary of Christian Biography*, *sub* "Helena"; *Encyclopedia Britannica*, 11th edn., *sub* "Simon Magus" and "Clementine Literature"; *Encyclopedia Biblica*, ed. Cheyne and Black, *sub* "Simon Magus"; and James Shotwell and Louise Loomis, *The See of Peter*, Columbia Records of Civilization (New York, 1927), in which many of the adduced texts are classified and translated. At the outset, it should be noted that the Simon of the apocryphal tradition often claims to be Christ.

[382] Nicephorus Callisti (d. A.D. 1327), *Ecclesiasticae Historiae*, Tom. I (Paris, 1630, reprinting the Latin version of Jo. Langi Erphurdiensis, Basel, 1553, or Antwerp, 1560), II.xiv, p. 154. A French trans. of the Latin by Jo. Gittoto was published at Paris in 1562 and 1573. (For the Greek, see PG, CXLV, 787–792.) Nicephorus gives very full accounts of Simon, and later writers often rely upon him. For the docetism of Simon, see *Acts of Paul*, vii, in James, *Apocryphal New Testament*, pp. 288f.

[383] Philaster of Brescia, *Liber de Haeresibus*, in PL, XII, 1139–1142; Epiphanius of Cyprus, *Adv. Haereses*, XXI.1, 5, in PG, XLI, 285f., 291–294; Theodoret of Cyprus, *Haereticarum Fabularum Compendium*, I, in PG, LXXXIII, 341–344. So also the *Apostolic Constitutions*, VI.vii–ix (trans. in ANF, vol. 7, pp. 452f.).

[384] *Catech. Lect.* VI.14f. (NPNF, 2nd Series, vol. 7, pp. 37f.).

truth are his successors.[385] Simon was also the cause of idolatry, and the object of it; Tertullian reports him to have been among the pagan deities installed in the Pantheon, and says his doctrines inculcated the worship of angels and were reckoned among the idolatries.[386] Eusebius also names Simon as the first leader of all heresy, and synthesizes a long report of the idolatry in which Simon's followers have become ensnared—the idols are those of Simon and his companion, a woman named Helena. At Rome, Eusebius says, "the inhabitants gave him divine honors by erecting his statue."[387] Depending on reports going back to Justin Martyr, who said Simon was worshiped as a god, St. Augustine reports that Simon

> . . . asserted that he was Christ and likewise desired to be considered Jupiter, while a certain harlot, Helen, whom he had made an accomplice in his crimes, was to be considered Minerva. Images of himself and of this harlot he offered to his disciples for adoration. Even at Rome, with public authorization, he set up these images as likenesses of gods.[388]

This Helena is conceivably Spenser's false Una.

Another feature of the legend of Simon is his command of demons. Simon, according to Justin, "did mighty acts of magic by virtue of the craft of demons operating through him";[389] the demons enabled Simon to fly before Nero, and *Il Mago* is still flying as late as the opening of Ariosto's *Cinque Canti* (I.7). Remembering what Archimago is able to accomplish with demons in Spenser's opening canto, we are reminded of the report of Hippolytus. The disciples of Simon, he says, "celebrate magical rites, and resort to incantations. And (they profess to) transmit both love-spells and charms, and the demons said to be senders of dreams, for the purpose of distracting whomsoever they please."[390]

The second branch of the Simon literature, the apostolic Apocrypha,

---

[385] *Adv. Haer.*, I.23 (ANF, vol. 1, pp. 347f.).

[386] *Apolog. adv. Gentes*, xiii (ANF, vol. 3, p. 29).

[387] *Eccles. Hist.*, II.xiii.1–8, xiv.1–6 (NPNF, 2nd Series, vol. 1, pp. 113–115). Cf. *The Avncient Ecclesiastical Histories of the First Six Hvndred Yeares After Christ*, trans. Meredith Hanmer (1st edn., London, 1577), which titles Eusebius' chapter "Of Simon Magus, and Helena a certain witch his yoke-fellow": "This Simon wee learne to have bene the first author of all heresies, and they that of him hold this heresie unto this day, faining through puritie of life the chast philosophie of Christians renoumed among all men, put in use against the pestilent superstition of pictures, from the which they seemed once to be free, falling prostrate before the pictures and carued Images of *Simon* and his gill *Helena* (mentioned before) worshipping them with incense, and sacrifices, and sweete odours." (Text from edn. of London, 1607, p. 26.)

[388] *De Haer.*, i, trans. Rev. Liguori G. Muller, Catholic University of America Patristic Studies, vol. 90 (Washington, D.C., 1956), p. 171.

[389] *Apolog. Prima*, xxvi (ANF, vol. 1, p. 171).

[390] *Refutation of All Heresies*, VI.xv (ANF, vol. 5, pp. 8of.).

makes Simon Magus a great rival for Simon Peter; this antagonism forms the basis for the twenty-third canto of Dante's *Inferno*.[391] The Apostle and the Magician are seen as engaged in a mighty contest in which Peter eventually prevails. As Theodoret has it, Peter breaks through cloud and darkness, and displays the rays of the light of truth.[392] (Eusebius adopts the same rhetoric: "All were overcome or overwhelmed by the light of truth and by the Word of God, Who had lately shone, a beacon to men from God, growing brilliant on earth and dwelling with His apostles.")[393] The contest of the two wonder-workers before Nero is variously reported. It should be noted, however, that Simon's aerial feats on this occasion (which end in his death or his demise) are not his only ones: he causes statues to move and he changes shapes.[394] Nicephorus tells us that Simon induced in himself the form of a dragon, and was changed into various species of animals; on other occasions his face was perceived as having assumed two parts, he transformed himself entirely into gold, he exhibited likenesses of fare of all kinds at a banquet (having commanded the doors to be shut with bars and the company thoroughly closed in), and he changed not only himself but whom he pleased into the forms of various animals.[395] We also read that Nero honored Simon with a statue with two faces.[396]

[391] As texts in Shotwell make clear, holes made in the rock where Simon Magus landed were exhibited in Rome. The rock in the *Inferno* is *pietra livida* (XIX.13), whereas Peter in his epistle says the church is made up of *living stones* (II Peter 2:4f.). Peter turns red with anger (*Parad.* XXVII.54), here the Pope's feet turn red. Peter was crucified upside down according to the *Martyrdom of Peter*, in *Acts of Peter*, xxxviii (James, *Apocryphal New Testament*, pp. 334f.), in order to right the sinister effects of the Fall, whereby man is born unconverted and upside down. Dante is similarly inverted as he passes by the fallen Satan, who is fixed in a parody of the Crucifixion. On these themes see Charles Singleton, "*Inferno* XIX: 'O Simon Mago'," in *MLN*, 80 (1965), pp. 92–99, and John Freccero, "Infernal Inversion and Christian Conversion (*Inferno* XXXIV)," *Italica*, 42 (1965), pp. 35–41.

[392] *Haer. Fab.*, I, PG, LXXXIII, 343.

[393] *Eccles. Hist.*, II.xvi (NPNF, 2nd Series, vol. 1, p. 115).

[394] *Acts of Peter and Paul*, in ANF, vol. 8, pp. 480ff. (corresponds to Lipsius, *Acta Apostolorum Apocrypha*, vol. 1, pp. 178ff.); Vincent of Beauvais, *Speculvm Historiale*, Lib. IV.xii, "De conflictu Petri cum Simone Mago, & morte illius"; and very similarly, Hegesippus, *Historia de Bello Iudaico*, trans. Ambrose as *De excidio Hierosolym* (Paris, 1510), III.ii (quoted in part in Foxe, *Acts*, Cattley edn., vol. 1, p. 101).

[395] *Ecclesiasticae Historiae*, II.xxvii; *edn. cit.*, pp. 178f. In the *Martyrdom of the Holy Apostles Peter and Paul*, xii–xv, Simon changes shape before Nero; in *Acta Apostolorum Apocrypha*, ed. R. A. Lipsius and M. Bonnet (1891), vol. 1, pp. 118ff. (Simon also changes shape in the longer Greek *Acts of Peter and Paul*, in Lipsius, vol. 1, pp. 178ff.—for a translation from the text of Tischendorf, see ANF, vol. 8, pp. 477ff.) Simon's shape-changing may also be implied in the older Vercelli *Acts of Peter*, iv. xvii, xxxi, xxxii, in James, ed., *Apoc. New Testament*, pp. 306–332; *The Acts of Peter and Paul* was translated in part by Constantine Lascaris in 1490. Other reports of Simon's acts—his use of demons, animation of a bronze serpent,

The contest between the Mage and the Apostle is not strictly our theme, except insofar as it points to something at the heart of the romance subject, namely, the contest between two magics, or magicians, the one pure, the other not. In a Christian romance the good or beneficent magic can be largely understood, for as Paracelsus claims, "magic is an art which reveals its highest power and strength through faith":

> As God awakens the dead to life, so the "natural saints," who are called magi, are given power over the energies and faculties of nature. For there are holy men in God who serve the beatific life; they are called saints. But there are also holy men in God who serve the forces of nature, and they are called magi. God shows his miracles through his holy men, both through those of beatific life and through those of nature; what others are incapable of doing, they can do, because it has been conferred upon them as a special gift.[397]

If the saints are natural magicians, the emphasis on the characterization will be thrown on the evil magician. Where a Christian society is assumed, good magicians, like Prospero or Mozart's archimagus Zorastre, are likely to look rather like stand-ins for Providence.

The third branch of the Simon material, found in the Clementina, adopts the Simon of the Petrine tradition into the literature of Christian romance proper. The story told in the *Clementine Recognitions* is thought to have some bearing on the Faust legend, for the evil necromancer is not only opposed to Peter, but also involved in untoward designs against the family of Clement, whose father and brothers (or sons) bear varieties of the name Faustus.[398]

---

making stone statues to laugh and run, and himself to fly and be seen suddenly in the air—are found in Vincent of Beauvais, *Speculvm Historiale*, Lib. IX.xii, *edn. cit.*, p. 326 ("Ex passione sancti Petri Apostoli qua habetur in tomo 10. Bibliotheca veterum Patrum Authore S. Lino," in Lipsius, *Martyrdum beati Petri . . . a Lino*, vol. 1, pp. 1–22; and "Ex Passione Pauli ibidem ex S. Lino.") These acts agree with the *Martyrdom*, cap. xi, in Lipsius also.

[396] *Passio Apostolarum Petri et Pauli*, ms. in the Laurentian Library at Florence, in Lipsius, *Acta Apostolorum Apocrypha*, vol. 1, pp. 223–234. In the Vercelli *Acts of Peter*, x (in James, *Apocryphal New Testament*, pp. 313f.), Marcellus confesses to having set up a statue to Simon.

[397] Quoted and translated in Jolande Jacobi, ed., *Paracelsus: Selected Writings*, trans. Norbert Guterman, pp. 213f. Taken from *Astronomia magna*, in *Sam. Werk*, ed. Sudhoff and Matthiessen, Pt. I, vol. 12, p. 130.

[398] See *Sources of the Faust Tradition*, ed. P. M. Palmer and R. M. More (New York, 1936). So also E. M. Butler, *The Myth of the Magus* (Cambridge, 1948) and *The Fortunes of Faust* (Cambridge, 1952).

Here we meet a Simon who "is a most vehement orator, trained in the dialectic art, and in the meshes of syllogisms; and what is worse than all, he is greatly skilled in the magic art. And therefore, being so strongly fortified on every side, he shall be thought to be defending the truth while he is alleging falsehoods in the presence of those who do not know him."[399] This Simon brags:

> ... I am able to render myself invisible to those who wish to lay hold of me, and again to be visible when I am willing to be seen. If I wish to flee, I can dig through mountains, and pass through rocks as if they were clay. If I should throw myself headlong from a lofty mountain, I should be borne unhurt to the earth, as if I were held up; when bound, I can loose myself, and bind those who had bound me; being shut up in prison, I can make the barriers open of their own accord; I can render statues animated, so that those who see suppose that they are men. . . . I can throw myself into the fire, and not be burnt; I can change my countenance, so that I cannot be recognized; but I can show people that I have two faces. . . . I shall ascend by flight into the air; I shall exhibit abundance of gold, and shall make and unmake kings. I shall be worshipped as God; I shall have divine honors publicly assigned to me, so that an image of me shall be set up, and I shall be worshipped and adored as God.[400]

"I am first truth and may fly by air," Simon boasts in the legend of Peter in *The Golden Legend*.[401] The same powers are assigned to Simon by Anastasius Sinaitica, including the power to loose iron chains.[402] Epiphanius also makes him a shape-changer, for in his descent into our world, Simon says, "in each heaven I changed my form in accordance with the form of those who were in each heaven, that I might escape the notice of my angelic powers and come down to the Thought, who is none other than her who is also called Prounikos and Holy Ghost, through whom I created the angels. . . ."[403] In the Clementine literature Simon not only

[399] *Clem. Recog.*, II.v, trans. in ANF, vol. 8, p. 98.

[400] *Ibid.*, II.ix, p. 99. Similar lists of Simon's feats are found at III.xlvii (p. 126) and III.lx (p. 130); he can make himself big or small at II.xiv (p. 101). Simon's face-changes are the subject of Vincent of Beauvais, *Speculvm Historiale*, Lib. IX.xxxv, "De mutatione vultus eius dolo Simonis Magi"—the Renaissance edn. corrects Vincent's text from the Basel edn., 1536, of the *Recognitions*. See also "Life of St. Clement," in Caxton's trans. of *The Golden Legend* (London, 1900), vol. 6, pp. 261–263, for Simon's changes.

[401] "Life of St. Peter," Caxton trans., vol. 4, p. 15. Archimago flies at II.iii.19, where he vanishes in "aerie flight": "The Northerne wind his wings did broad display / At his commaund, and reared him vp light / From off the earth." The devil is the prince of the power of the air (Eph. 2:2), and Lucifer retreats to the heights of the North (Isa. 14:13f.).

[402] *Questiones*, XX, in PG, LXXXIX, 523.

[403] *Haer.*, XXI.ii.4, trans. in Hans Jonas, *The Gnostic Religion*, 2nd edn. (Boston, 1963), p. 108.

THE BOOK OF LIFE

can change his face, but also exchange it with others' faces: he is able to make Faustinianus, the father of Peter's converts, appear to have his (Simon's) face. (Peter, penetrating the transformation, thereafter works a similar fraud against Simon himself.)[404] Simon also creates a body from air, a process he describes in a long and interesting boast:

> "But I would not have you doubt that this is truly to be God, when one is able to become small or great as he pleases; for I am able to appear to man in whatever manner I please. Now, then, I shall begin to unfold to you what is true. Once upon a time, I, by my power, turning air into water, and water again into blood and solidifying it into flesh, formed a new human creature—a boy—and produced a much nobler work than God the Creator. For He created a man from the earth, but I from air—a far more difficult matter; and again I unmade him and restored him to air, but not until I had placed his picture and image in my bedchamber, as a proof and memorial of my work." Then we understood that he spake concerning that boy whose soul, after he had been slain by violence, he made use of for those services which he required.[405]

Simon Magus thus presents us with a near relative of Archimago: the original enemy of the new faith, an animator of idols and a maker of images, a shape-changer and a master of imposture, and an adept in the demonic arts.

Behind Simon's legend, one suspects, there lies the New Testament complex that includes the false prophet, the Antichrist, and the magician.[406] The last times, according to II Timothy 2:6–8, will include men

---

[404] At *Clem. Recognit.*, X.liii (= *Clem. Homilies*, XX.xii–xiv), ANF, vol. 8, pp. 806f., the father Faustianus is transformed to look like Simon.

[405] *Clem. Recog.*, II.xv, trans. cited, p. 99. See also *ibid.*, III.xliv, p. 126.

[406] *False prophets and false Christs*: Matt. 24:24, Mark 13:22 (cf. Mt. 24:5, 23); *false apostles* transforming themselves into apostles of Christ: II Cor. 11:13 (Lavater, *Of Ghostes, edn. cit.*, pp. 167f., compares Simon's arts to Satan's shape-changing); *false prophets*: Matt. 5:15; Acts 13:6 (a false prophet named Bar-Jesus, who was a Jewish magician; identified with Elymas Magos in the following verse); II Peter 2:1; Rev. 16:13, 19:20, 20:10; *Antichrist*: I John 2:22, 4:3; *a deceiver and an antichrist*, II John 4:7; *the lost apostate*: II Thess. 2:3 (he claims to be greater than all that men call god, somewhat like Simon Magus in Acts 8:9f.). See William Bousset, *The Antichrist Legend*, trans. A. H. Keane (London, 1896), and Brother Linus Urban Lucken, *Antichrist and the Prophets of Antichrist in the Chester Cycle* (Washington, D.C., 1940). (Simon Magus is identified as both the first heretic and the beginning of the false prophet and false apostle in *Clem. Hom.*, XVI.xxi; see also XI.xxxv.) I have not emphasized the Antichrist figure, but the following quotation suggests the relevance of his character: "And when he begins to trust every person, and to reveal a little the latent hypocrisy from within, the savage executioner will

"having the form of godliness, but denying the power thereof . . . ever learning, and never able to come to the knowledge of the truth. Now as Jannes and Jambres withstood Moses, so do these also resist the truth." Weirius, an authority on magic, writes in the Renaissance that "There is still an infinity of heretics, who left the college of Magicians and entered into the Church and who are opposed to the Apostolic truth: thus it is that 'Jannes' and 'Mambres' resist Moses. The first and greatest of them was Simon the Samaritan, to whom a statue in Rome was raised."[407] The Church had to deal with Elymas the sorcerer and Bar-Jesus, "a certain *mage*, a false prophet" (Acts 3:6-10). II Peter 2:1-3 identifies heterodox teachers with "false prophets in the past history of our people." It is by their successors that "the way of trueth shalbe euil spoken of, and through couetousnes shal they with fained words make merchandise of you" (Geneva Bible). Bullinger thought that Peter here foresaw Simon Magus' attempt to buy the Holy Ghost,[408] and the Geneva gloss reflects, "This euidently sene in the Pope and Priests who by lies and flatteries sel mens soules, so that it is certeine that he is not the successour of Simon Peter, but of Simon Magus."

Nor do the presumptuous claims of Simon, who had bewitched the Samaritans with his sorceries (Acts 8:8-11), at all disagree with those of the Antichrist of II Thessalonians. Jewel merely compares Paul's "lawless one" to the false Christ of Mark 13:22, who would deceive, if it were possible, the very elect;[409] but Hugo Grotius, as cited in the 1686 edition of Stephanus' *Historical, Geographical and Poetical Dictionary, sub* "Simon," observes that the description fits Simon best. Lavater explains the abusing of the fantasy of the early Church by the Antichrist of II Thessalonians on the analogy of the tricks of Pharaoh's Magi, whom he elsewhere compares to Simon.[410] And Tertullian, concerning the appearance of the serpents to Pharaoh, writes: "It is true that the verity of Moses

---

first slaughter Enoch and Elijah: and laying aside pretense, assume in addition the wrath of furies, cruel, inexorable, arrogant, persecuting, impudent, enraged, bold, possessing no part of a good man, entirely of divers wickedness, a mind-terrifying thing, a spectre, an imposture, showing himself as something great, as a tyrant, one possessed, an artifex of empty visions, fictions, and astounding changes of both figures and colors, from one to another, approaching Proteus. Flying on the heights as an angel (rather as a demon), and by deception effecting terror and prodigies, so that he seems to transport mountains by the merest thoughts." So Philip the Solitary, *Dioptra*, III.10, in PG, CXXVII, 816. It is easy to see why Sansloi addresses Archimago as "syre" (I.iii.39).

[407] *Histoires, edn. cit.*, vol. 1, p. 176.

[408] Parker Society *Decades*, IV, Sermon ii, vol. 4, pp. 96f.

[409] *An Exposition upon the Two Epistles of St. Paul to the Thessalonians*, in Parker Society *Works*, vol. 2, p. 921.

[410] *Of Ghostes, edn. cit.*, pp. 178f., 167f.

swallowed up their lying deceit. Many attempts were also wrought against the apostles by the sorcerers Simon and Elymas. . . . What novelty is there in the effort of an unclean spirit to counterfeit truth?"[411] Jerome, on Matthew 24:5 (cf. Matt. 24:11, 24), cites Simon as an example of the false Christs and false prophets who will seduce many,[412] and Ambrose identifies the miracle-worker of Revelation 13:14 with the Simon who claimed to be able to die and resurrect himself.[413] Adso, a redoubtable authority on the Antichrist, notes his similarity to Simon also, and in fact they share peculiar common features. Both are reputed to have been begotten upon a woman with the name Rachel, and both cause the martyrdom of the witnesses who expose their divine pretentions—Enoch and Elijah in the case of the Antichrist, and Peter and Paul in the case of Simon.[414]

Once we have identified the false prophet with Simon, we will think of Simon when we think of Archimago. When we consider the shadow cast on Redcrosse by the magician's hypocrisy, we will be reminded of Calvin's remarks on Simon: "The human heart has so many places for falsehood, is so shrouded by fraud and hypocrisy, that it often deceives itself." Originally men such as Simon do not intend "to impose on men by a false semblance of faith; but even to impose on themselves. They imagine that the reverence which they give to the word is genuine piety. . . ."[415] When we consider Archimago as the imagination, we will remember that the Simon

[411] *De Anima*, lvii, trans. in ANF, vol. 3, pp. 233f.

[412] *Comm. in Evang. Matt.*, IV.xxiv (on Matt. 24:5), in PL, XXVI 176: "Of these [many false Christs] one is Simon the Samaritan, about whom we read in the Acts of the Apostles, who is said to give himself out to be the power of God, this among other things in his voluminous writings: I am the word of God, I am beautiful, I am the Paraclete, I am almighty, I am wholly of God. But John the apostle in his epistle writes: *you hear that Antichrist is come, now however there are many antichrists* [I John 2:18]. I presume all heresiarchs to be Antichrist, and under Christ's name to teach things contrary to Christ. No wonder we see some led astray by these, since the Lord has said: *and he will seduce many*." (Similarly Bede, *In Matt.*, VI.xxiv, in PL, XCII, 101f.) In Dunbar's poem *The Birth of Antichrist* (no. 37, Mackenzie edn.)—which alludes to the Feigning Friar of Tungland, a court retainer who undertook to fly to France—the abbot flies up in the air as a gryphon, couples with a dragon, begets the Antichrist, is met by Simon Magus and Mahomet in Saturn, and Merlin and the widow Joan in the moon, and returns with them to earth to preach the advent of Antichrist's kingdom. The text in I John is important: it opposes the knowledge of the truth belonging to those annointed by the Holy One, to the plurality of the antichrists. Conformably, Archimago, Sansloi, and Orgoglio are all "antichrist."

[413] *In Apoc.* 13:14, in PL, XVII, 886.

[414] *De Antichristo*, in PL, CI, 1293D–1294A. The Two Witnesses of Rev. 11:4ff. are traditionally identified with both pairs.

[415] *Institutes*, III.ii.10, trans. H. Beveridge (Grand Rapids, Mich., 1964), vol. 2, p. 107.

of the *Clementine Recognitions* champions the reality of any fantastic images that the mind might entertain: "It is impossible," he says, "that anything which comes into a man's thoughts should not also subsist in truth and reality. For things that do not subsist, have no appearances; but things that have no appearances, cannot present themselves to our thoughts." Peter replies that if Simon were correct, the imagining of contradictory attributes for a given entity would necessitate an intolerable veracity for both opinions. Elsewhere Peter accepts rebuke for daydreaming: "Give over," says his advisor,

> For those who are beginning to be possessed with a demon, or to be disturbed in their minds, begin in this way. They are first carried away by fancies to some pleasant and delightful things, then they are poured out in vain and fond motions towards things which have no existence. Now this happens from a certain disease of mind, by reason of which they see not the things which are, but long to bring to their sight those which are not. But thus it happens also to those who are suffering phrenzy, and seem to themselves to see many images. . . .[416]

When we think of Archimago's shapes, we may recall with Lavater that "it is no difficult matter for the deuill to appear in divers shapes. . . . he may easily deceyue the eye sight. . . . Did not Simon Magus so bewitch the Samaritanes wyth his vnlawfull Artes, that he would say he was the great vertue of God?"[417] And when we think of Archimago's dividing Redcrosse from Una, we should recall with the author of *The Pedegrewe of Heretiques* that all heresies that divide the unity of the faith are grounded on Simon:

> Before the dayes of their father the Sorcerer, the Church as a people not of one lippe, but heart, as S. Luke testifieth, abyding in the sincere truth and obedience of Christes gospell onely. Then factions were not knowen, scismes not practiced, lies and Heresies not embraced, defended or outfaced. Then the will of man not esteemed, and Gods neglected. This unhappy man hath begonne all.[418]

Archimago is a Renaissance magician like Agrippa, but Agrippa, accompanied by his famous dog, was a magician like Simon.[419] Thus the later John Heywood, in his *Hierarchie of the blessed Angells* (1635),

[416] *Clem. Recog.*, II.lxvi, ANF, vol. 8, p. 115; II.lxiv, p. 115.

[417] *Of Ghostes, edn. cit.*, pp. 167f.

[418] John Barthlet, *The Pedegrewe of Heretiques Wherein is truly and plainly set out, the first roote of Heretiques begon in the Church, since the time and passage of the gospell* (London, 1566), p. 7.

[419] Simon's dogs: *Acts of Peter and Paul* (trans. ANF, vol. 8, p. 481); Pseudo-Marcellus, *The Passion of Peter and Paul*; Glycas, *Annalium*, III (in PG, CLVIII, 443–446). Agrippa's dog: Weir, *De Praestigiis Daemonum* (1583), II.5; Bodin, *De la Demonomanie* (1580), fols. 219ᵛ–220ʳ.

begins his account of infamous magicians with Simon, and ends with Agrippa: "I will conclude," his summary paragraph begins, "with the great Arch-mage of these our late times, *Cornelius Agrippa*," and he ends by warning that those who practice magical arts "are fore-doomed to be tormented in eternall fire, with *Iamnes, Mambre,* and *Simon Magus*."[420] Archimago is a figure for papistry, but papistry was accused of Simony; we may quote the comparison of the pope to Simon in Curio's *Defence*:

> Alder first, who with Simon maketh himself God and Christ upon the earth? the pope. Who hath deceived the world with magical crafts, that is to say (as Paul speaketh), with false miracles and wonders? the pope. Who do chop and change for present money the gifts of the Holy Ghost, the sacraments and divine affairs? whether not the pope and all his generation of papists? But subtly Florebell [Curio's opponent] omitted the fault of ambition, and the most sacrilege of all, when yet he touched the other errors of Simon. . . . —With the Gnosticks, doth not the papists entangle the weak souls of men, with terrible names, either of princes or else of angels, and teach a doctrine full of fables and lies?[421]

Finally, if we want to compare Archimago to Antichrist, we may consider a sequence like the following from Reginald Scot's *Discoverie of Witchcraft*:

> It will be said, the people had reason to beleeve him [Simon], because it is written, that he of long time had bewitched them with sorceries. But let the bewitched *Galatians* be a warning both to the bewitched *Samaritans,* and to all other that are cousened or bewitched throgh false doctrine, or legierdemaine; least while they attend to such fables and lies, they be brought into ignorance, and so in time be led with them awaie from God. And finallie, let us all abandon such witches and couseners, as with *Simon Magus* set themselves in the place of God, boasting that they can doo miracles, expound dreames, foretell things to come, raise the dead, &c: . . . . It is written, that in the latter daies there shalbe showed strange illusions, &c: in so much (if it were possible) the verie elect shal be deceiued: howbeit, S. *Paul* saith, they shalbe leing and false wonders. . . . Howbeit, by the waie I must confesse that I take that sentence to be spoken of Anti-Christ, to wit: the pope, who miraculously, contrarie to nature, philosophie, and all divinitie, . . . hath placed himself in the most loftie and delicate seate. . . .[422]

---

[420] *Edn. cit.,* p. 615.

[421] Trans. of John Philpot, in Parker Society *Examination . . . Writings,* p. 417.

[422] VI.i; in Summers' edn., pp. 64f. Cf. also the first page of Robert Turner's Preface to his translation of the spurious *Henry Cornelius Agrippa's Fourth Book of Occult Philosophy and Geomancy* (1555, reprint 1783): "Many men there are, that abhor the very name and word *Magus,* because of Simon Magus, who being indeed not *Magus,* but *Goes,* that is, familiar with evil spirits, usurped that title."

This takes us through almost the whole repertoire of comparisons that logically attach themselves to Archimago.

The reader will have noticed suggestive traces of one further tradition concerning Simon, namely the character of his heresy. The Simonians, according to Epiphanius, were the first Gnostics.[423] Justin Martyr reports Simon to have had as his companion a woman named Helen who "had previously had a stand in a brothel," whom his followers called "the First Thought conveived by him."[424] Origen mentions that some of Simon's sect were called Heleniani.[425] Simon's attaching Helen to him is reported by Cyril of Jerusalem, Philaster, Theodoret, Eusebius, and the author ("pseudo-Tertullian") of *Against All Heresies*, who calls her Sapientia;[426] Simon called her, according to Theodoret, the first understanding of his mind and the mother of all.[427] Irenaeus tells us that Simon purchased Helena as a slave at Tyre and claimed she was the first conception of his mind; she created the angels through whom the world was made. The angels, in turn, detained her through jealousy, and compelled her to assume a human body, from which she passed down to Simon's own time by transmigration. She was Helen of Troy, on whose account the Trojan War was fought; for reviling her, Stesichorus was struck blind, and with his palinode, his sight was restored; and at last she became a public prostitute. Simon had come to reclaim her and free her from her bondage.[428] (Hippolytus also recognizes the relation of this story to the Stesichorus legend.[429] He further mentions a Simonian allegory for the wooden horse at Troy: Epiphanius and Philaster state that Simon allegorized the horse as the ignorance of the nations.) Both Irenaeus and Hippolytus report that the idols of Jupiter and Minerva represented Simon and Helen to their followers. The *Clementine Recognitions*, where Helena is called Luna (going back to a Greek doublet of "Selene" for Helen), do not develop this story, though they have Simon say that

[423] *Adv. Haer.*, XXI.4, in PG, XLI, 291ff. For Helen and the Trojan Horse, 2–3 (cols. 287–290).

[424] *Apolog. Prima*, xxvi (also lvi, and *Dial. with Trypho*, cxx).

[425] *Contra Celsus*, V.62 (trans. in ANF, vol. 4, p. 570).

[426] Cyril, *Catech. Lect.*, VI.14–15 (NPNF, 2nd Series, vol. 7, pp. 37f.); Philaster, *Liber de Haeresibus*, xxix (PL, XII, 1140f.); Theodoret, *Haeret. Fab.*, I (PG, LXXXIII, 343B); Eusebius, *Hist. Eccles.*, II.xiii.1–8; pseudo-Tertullian, *Against All Heresies* (trans. in ANF, vol. 3, app., p. 649).

[427] *Haeret. Fab.*, I (PG, LXXXIII, 343B).

[428] *Adv. Haer.*, I.xxiii.1 (trans. in ANF, vol. 1, pp. 347f.).

[429] *Philosophumena; or The Refutation of all heresies*, VI.xiv–xv (trans. in ANF, vol. 5, pp. 8of.). The Renaissance cannot have known this text, discovered in 1842, and it is adduced only as testimony to the unity of a tradition.

Luna . . . has been brought down from the higher heavens, and that she is Wisdom, the mother of all things, for whom, says he, the Greeks and barbarians contending, were able in some measure to see an image of her, but of herself, as she is, as a dweller with the first and only God, they were wholly ignorant.[430]

The single reference of a related text, not published in the Renaissance, is more explicit here. The *Clementine Homilies* say that it was Helena, "for whose sake the Greeks and barbarians fought, having before their eyes but an image of the truth, for she, who really is the truth, was then with the chiefest god."[431] Helena, then, is degraded *ennoea* or an image of the Gnostic Sophia, related to Simon Magus as Spenser's Sapience is to the Creator. One also gathers that the meretricious Simonian Helen has a relation to truth analogous to the relation of the adulterous Homeric Helen to honest beauty.

On the one hand we have a magician who fashions agents from air, and on the other the father of heresy claiming divine powers and attaching the personification of his doctrines to the Helen-myth of Stesichorus. There is then, overall, some resemblance to Archimago's fabrication of the false Una, who is also Duessa. She is the first conception of Archimago's mind, though Redcrosse's mind is required for her perpetration. Duessa divides Redcrosse from Una; in Epiphanius, Helena is *sent* spirit of division, and battle is also fought over Duessa. Finally, Spenser's mage "redeems" the harlot. At the end of Book I Archimago takes the part of her messenger, and at the opening of Book II the part of her squire:

> Her late forlorne and naked he had found,
> Where she did wander in waste wildernesse,
> Lurking in rockes and caues farre vnder ground,
> And with greene mosse cou'ring her nakednesse,
> To hide her shame and loathly filthinesse;
> Sith her Prince *Arthur* of proud ornaments
> And borrow'd beautie spoyld. Her nathelesse
> Th' enchaunter finding fit for his intends,
> Did thus reuest, and deckt with due habiliments.
>
> (II.i.22)

This is how authors like Eusebius and Tertullian saw Simon's redemption of the harlot from the brothel. Tertullian, in particular, posed the issue in terms that we can appreciate: "O hapless Helena," he exclaims, "what

---

[430] II.xii; trans. from ANF, vol. 8, p. 100.

[431] II.xxv; trans. in ANF, vol. 8, p. 233. Nicephorus, *Eccles. Hist.*, II.xiv, describes the statues of Simon and Helen as *eidola kai eikonas* (Lat. *simulachre et imagines*). (In the *Epitome De Gestis S. Petri*, xxvii, in PG, II, 491, Helen is *eikona phantasthentes alētheias*, or as the Latin trans. says, *imaginati speciem veritatis*.)

258

a hard fate is yours between the poets and the heretics, who have blackened your fame sometimes with adultery, sometimes with prostitution!"[432]

In conclusion, we need to connect the heterodox Helena with Helen of Troy. A passage in Calvin combines the classical and biblical harlot symbols to describe the abomination of the mass,

> which being offred in a golden cup, hath made dronke the kings and peoples of the earth, from the hiest to the lowest, hath so striken them with drowsinesse and giddinesse, that being become more senslesse than brute beastes, they haue set the whole ship of their safetie onely in this deadly deuouring gulf. Truely Satan neuer did bende himselfe with a stronger engine than this to assaile and vanquish the kingdome of Christ. This is the Helene, for whom the enemies of the trueth fight at this day with so great rage, so great furiousnesse, so great crueltie: & a Helene in deede, with whom they so defile themselues with spiritual whordome, which is the most cursed of all.[433]

Over such a Helena one might exclaim—in the words of Hecuba imposing on her destroyer the humiliation reserved for the remnant of defeated peoples—"O you abomination! You should have come crawling out in rags and tatters, in fear and trembling, your hair cropped to the scalp; modesty would become your guilty past better than impudence."[434] The bedizened Menelaus, despite this advice, does not quite manage to put the traitoress to death, however; and Duessa does not die either.

Calvin does not say that the harlot is specious, though he clearly describes her as an "engine" and a delusion (like the Trojan horse), and as a cause of division between the enemies and the friends of truth. But as we know from the Faust legend, it is in the nature of necromancers to conjure up Helen,[435] and classical fable tells us that she may be a counterfeit. Hence this link in Spenser's symbolism is better glossed by a passage in Milton's *Reason of Church Government*, which attacks the sale of spiritual goods:

[432] *De Anima*, xxxiv; trans. from ANF, vol. 3, p. 215.

[433] *Institutes*, IV.xviii.18; Norton trans., *edn. cit.*, pp. 603f.

[434] Euripides, *Trojan Women* 1024ff. For the shaved head, cf. Jer. 2:16; Isa. 3:17, 7:20.

[435] Besides the *Faustbook*, see John Lyly, *Euphues His England*: "As the ladies in this blessed island are devout and brave, so are they chaste and beautiful; insomuch that when I first beheld them I could not tell whether some mist had bleared mine eyes or some strange enchantment altered my mind. 'For it may be,' thought I, 'that some Artimidorus or Lismandro or some odd necromancer did inhabit, who would show me fairies, or the body of Helen, or the new shape of Venus.'" (Text in Croll and Clemons, eds., *Euphues*, London, 1916, p. 456.) The magicians Vandermast and Bacon also contest in the revival of Trojan subjects, in *Friar Bacon*, though Helen is not among them (William Thomas, ed., *Early English Prose Romances*, vol. 1, London, 1858, pp. 242f.).

That undeflowered and unblemishable simplicity of the gospel, not she herself, for that could never be, but a false-whited, a lawny resemblance of her, like that air-borne Helena in the fables, made by the sorcery of prelates, instead of calling her disciples from the receipt of custom, is now turned publican herself; and gives up her body to a mercenary whoredom under those fornicated arches which she calls God's house, and in the sight of those her altars, which she hath set up to be adored, makes merchandise of the bodies and souls of men.[436]

What James Russell Lowell says of Una, in his famous essay on Spenser, might be more properly applied to Una's rival—"who, like the visionary Helen of Dr. Faustus, has every charm of womanhood except that of being alive."

The Man Who Would Not Live

Therefore my people is gone into captiuitie, because they had no knowledge, and the glorie therof are men famished, & the multitude thereof is dryed vp with thirst.

Therefore hel hathe inlarged itself, and hathe opened his mouth, without measure, and their glorie, and their multitude, and their pompe, and he that reioyceth among them, shal descende into it.

And man shalbe broght downe, and man shalbe humbled, euen the eyes of the proude shalbe humbled.

(Isa. 5:13–15, Geneva Bible)

That Hiericho of which we have now to consider is a spiritual power of darkness, that resteth only in flesh and in worldly promises, that withstandeth God's people, and exalted itself against God. For even in this life, as there is a Jerusalem, so is there a Hiericho: as truth hath her house, so is there also a house wherein falsehood and error dwelleth. As there is a glory of the light, so there is a power of darkness. This Hiericho of falsehood and darkness God overthroweth when it seemed good in his sight: with the breath of his mouth and the blast of his holy word he doth overthrow it. . . .

(John Jewel, Sermon on Joshua 6, in Parker Society *Works*, vol. 2, p. 970)

O what a *Giant* is *Man*, when he fights against himselfe, and what a Dwarfe when hee *needs*, or *exercises* his owne assistance for himselfe!

(John Donne, *Devotions upon Emergent Occasions*, XXI)

[436] Text from Hughes, ed., *Complete Poems and Major Prose*, p. 683. In *Complete Prose Works*, vol. 1 (New Haven, 1956), p. 849.

In what follows we will be considering the Orgoglio episode, the episode that most typifies Redcrosse in many ways, even though he is absent from the better part of it. Such a paradox has something to tell us about our hero generally, and helps to define his provisory relation to the larger initiative of the legend, which we may take to be the quest on behalf of God's word.

It is not uncommonly asserted that Redcrosse is an everyman, and indeed his links to Adam have been shown. More specifically, he is a Christian everyman, for Una, or the biblical revelation, will not desert him in the way Knowledge will desert the hero of the morality play. But the knight is not, in fact, generalized in quite this manner. Neither do the types of the missionary Redcrosse—Christ, St. Michael, St. George, Perseus, Seth, and the allegorized Astolfo—establish Redcrosse's personal character. Spenser contrives to be somewhat cagey about the link to St. George, and for the most part the knight is known by his emblem rather than his name. The young man inside the old arms remains to be characterized, which is very much the point—that is, it is the point about the education of a type we may call the "high fool."

Redcrosse is described in the letter to Raleigh as a "tall clownishe young man," and his naiveté, his susceptibility to deception, his stumbling and humiliation, all suggest his type. Percival is the best known example. Don Quixote is related ironically, as he is to those saints, invoked in the peroration to Erasmus' *Praise of Folly*, who make themselves fools for the Gospel.[437] The corresponding low fool, or comic squire, represented in Don Quixote by Sancho Panza, need not appear in the heroic characterization of chivalric romance at all, though Glauce and the nameless Squire of Dames in Book III are there to remind us that romance will not always be taken seriously. A more representative vestige of the low fool type survives in Una's dwarf. The dwarf is a retainer figure, carrying a bag of needments, and remaining loyal through adversity, like Una's ass. As the ingenuous high fool descends from the innocent saint, so the wittier or more commonsensical low fool may descend to become the clever rogue or witty knave. The link between the low fool and the knave also appears in Book I, in the character of Archimago. Like the dwarf, Archimago carries a bag of needments (I.vi.35), acts the part of messenger for the knight's lady, and attaches himself to the heroine as her retainer. In a more sinister context, the delaying or reluctant figure hanging behind the

[437] In John P. Dolan, ed. and trans., *The Essential Erasmus* (New York, 1964), pp. 167-173.

hero's entourage would be a traitor (Judas carried the bag). These are the links that make Archimago, for all his evil designs, slightly comic, and the dwarf, for all his demonstrated reliability, somewhat inscrutable.

The high fool, or saintly *simplicissimus*, is a character on whom much depends, who nevertheless does not know well what he is about or who he is. His adventures take the form of misadventures, and there is always an element of backwardness in his forwardness. Still, no matter how bemused or unaware, the *dummling* type will become the hope of others whenever in his blundering way he seems to have gotten himself adopted by an unseen order perceived by faith. Although our hero often seems to be engaged upon a fool's errand, the student of Book I learns with St. Paul that not all fools are condemned ultimately to err. And yet we often despair of Redcrosse's success because he fails to ask the right questions. There is a sense in which Adam is the prototype for such a high fool, for he is in this world, but not of it, and he has failed to ask the questions on which all has depended:

> O Adam, what hast thou done? for in that that thou hast sinned, thou art not fallen alone, but the fall also redundeth vnto vs that come of thee.
> For what profit is it vnto vs, if there be promised an immortal life, when we do the workes that bring death? . . .
> And that an eternal Paradise shulde be shewed, whose fruite remaineth incorruptible, wherein is safetie and health, if we wil not enter into it?
> (II Esdras 7:48–49, 53, Geneva Bible)

We have derived vicissitudes in Redcrosse's "force" from fluctuations in his "faith": faith has meant both self-confidence and confidence in Another. When the knight's trust is misplaced—either lost or betrayed—he becomes weak and "faint." Trust is, in its nature, a kind of partnership between a trusting subject and the object of trust. The trustee, in whom confidence is reposed, is symbolized by Una and "Fidessa." Thus Una cries, "Add faith vnto your force" (I.i.19), as Redcrosse struggles with Error. In the duel with Sansjoy, Fidessa-Duessa also shouts her encouragements. "Thine the shield, and I, and all" (I.v.11):

> Soone as the Faerie heard his Ladie speake,
>> Out of his swowning dreame he gan awake,
>> And quickning faith, that earst was woxen weake,
>> The creeping deadly cold away did shake:
>> (I.v.12)

This is another example of Duessa's divided speech, and of course the knight is mistaken in believing the encouragement was meant for him. The effect of Una's infusion is also carefully described:

> . . . in great perplexitie,
> His gall did grate for griefe and high disdaine,
> And knitting all his force got one hand free,
>
> (I.i.19)

The knight's emotions, we are meant to notice, are based on a fear of disgrace; they suggest the whole tangle in the human mind between self-respect and self-doubt, and between pride and shame.

When Redcrosse leaves the House of Pride he forsakes Fidessa, but he takes Una's prudent dwarf with him. In other words, he starts out on a fairly even keel of skepticism—a good look at Sheol and he has put aside vanity. On the other hand, Redcrosse was not popular at court in the first place, and his pride was hurt. It is not obvious why Redcrosse is so "prone" to pride after escaping its House; the triumph of Orgoglio seems to follow on no great overweeningness, but merely on the return of Duessa. The man who makes an idol "chuseth his own deuises," says the Geneva gloss in Isaiah 41:24, and perhaps this reliance is a form of pride. It seems, at any rate, that Redcrosse, like Israel, must go back to Egypt (Hosea 8:13, 11:5).

The suggestion is that pride is always looking for an occasion; after the Fall it is something of an independent reflex. The disarmed Redcrosse has been relying mainly on himself for some time now, and in the context of holiness self-reliance is really a choice of the wrong trustee. It is also a failure of self-knowledge; the ideal of holiness is based on an impossible model, and pride is partly the unwillingness to make the damning comparison.[438] The scene at the fountain certainly implies this failure of vigilance. Redcrosse seems to be in a self-congratulatory mood, and a collapse into frailty is not illogical here. The enervate spring itself, like other sluggish waters in the poem and outside it, manifests an effeminate slackness, or sensuality. It reminds us, naturally, of Fradubio: it too is a disgraced being, and consequently disabled. The allegories usually attaching to metamorphosed beasts and trees more properly belong to it ("For it is not the bark that makes the plant but its senseless and insentient nature; . . . For if you see one abandoned to his appetites crawling on the ground, it is a plant and not a man you see").[439]

The enchanted waters of the spring are soon circulating in the suscepti-

---

[438] Echoing Erasmus, *Enchiridion*, xxi, "Trust not Yourself but Christ," and xxxviii, "Against Pride and Swelling of the Spirit": titles from the trans. of Raymond Himelick (Bloomington, Ind., 1963), pp. 165, 191f.

[439] Pico, *Oration*, 5, trans. Elizabeth Forbes in Cassirer, *et al.*, eds., *Renaissance Philosophy of Man*, p. 226. Cf. Plato, *Timaeus* 91e–92c, for the same moralization of the doctrine of metempsychosis. For the relation of the "dull and slow" waters to sloth, see n. 360, above.

ble Redcrosse. Almost before we know it the Philistines are upon him (Judges 16:20) and the knight has disappeared into Orgoglio's dungeon. In effect Orgoglio replaces Redcrosse, becoming Duessa's new master. And yet Redcrosse survives at the bottom of the palace, Orgoglio's "eternall bondeslaue" (I.viii.14). Interpreting the allegory, we may say that beneath any haughty exterior there is the fearful victim of a humiliation. He is kept by Ignaro, of course, since we do not usually acknowledge the poor creature's existence.

It is Arthur who rescues Redcrosse. Whereas Redcrosse is a dragon-slayer, Arthur is a giant-killer. Again the Elizabethan reader might see Spenser going about his reconstruction of romance. The name Orgoglio (Italian, "pride") could recall the giant-oppressor called l'Orgueilleux in the French *Huon of Bordeaux*; Arthur slays an evil Duke of Orgoule in Lord Berners' translation of *Arthur of Little Britain*.[440] (In Malory there is a sinister Castle Orgulus, in the *Boke of Sir Tristram*.) A giant is the natural symbol for the tyranny of grandiose self-conceptions. At least that other great reconstructor of romance, Don Quixote, thought so. He says of his chivalrous class: "in confronting giants, it is the sin of pride we slay."[441]

As a club-wielding Polyphemus who is eventually blinded, Orgoglio is the kind of giant who reduces his victims, almost by comparison, to being "no man." The victim of Orgoglio is "berobbed" of himself, as Una says (I.viii.42). The subsequent shrinkage of Orgoglio, where the comparison is with the more genuine greatness of Arthur, obeys a similar principle. All giants are subject to this critique of size, since their bulk makes them naturally liable to a reduction or mortification or fall. It is this potential for diminution that draws them into a hubris myth in the first place. Orgoglio's overweeningness cannot be dissociated from his vulnerability: pride, in the sense of loftiness or hauteur (Latin, *altus*), always goes before a fall.[442]

---

[440] The name of the giant who keeps the castle of Dunostre in *Huon* has been lost in Lord Berners' version. For the French, see the edn. of Guessard and Grandmaison (Paris, 1860), ll. 4550ff., pp. 136ff. For the Duke of Orgoule, see Berners' translation of *The hystory of Arthur of lytell brytayne* (London, 1555), cap. xxxiii (Fol. 33ʳ) through cap. xxxix: Arthur defeats the proud Duke and wins the royal daughter (whom the importunate Orgoule sought) for his man Hector; Arthur is given the keys to the city.

[441] Pt. II, chap. viii: "Hemos de matar en los gigantes a la soberbia," and so forth through *envidia, ira, gula, lujuria* and *peroza*.

[442] Prov. 16:18: "Pride goeth before destruction, and an high minde before the fall"; Prov. 21:4: "A hautie loke and a proude heart . . . is sinne"; Prov. 29:23: "The pride of a man shal bring him lowe: but the humble in spirit shal enjoye glorie"; Prov. 21:24: "Proud haughtie & scorneful is his name that worketh in his arrogancie wrath"; Jer. 48:29: "We haue heard the pride of Moab (he is exceding proude) his stoutnes, and his arrogancie, and his pride, and the hautenes of his heart"; Isa. 2:11: "The hie loke of man shalbe humbled, and the loftines of man shalbe abased, &

Apart from this loftiness, Orgoglio has little identity to offer. In its exclusiveness and rebuff of other natures, pride never does. Its morose attachment to the idol of self—Orgoglio's altar corresponds to Lucifera's throne and mirror—starves the whole man. An all-consuming self-importance deprives him of his true manhood. Presently we will be comparing the missing hero to the embalmed Osiris: there is a sense in which Orgoglio retains the god's missing organ, since Orgoglio is the tumescence of the proud man to the exclusion of any other characterization.[443]

The proud man becomes human Pride, and the man himself is correspondingly emasculated. This reciprocity is at the heart of the humiliation-exaltation theme of the New Testament. St. Augustine treats the topic:

> For it is good to have the heart lifted up, yet not to one's self, for this is proud, but to the Lord, for this is obedient, and can be the act only of the humble. There is, therefore, something in humility which, strangely enough, exalts the heart, and something in pride which debases it. This seems, indeed, to be contradictory, that loftiness should debase and lowliness exalt.[444]

---

ye Lord onely shalbe exalted in that day"; Isa. 2:17: "And the hautenes of men shalbe broght lower, and the loftiness of men shalbe abased," etc.; Isa. 5:15: cf. epigraph, above.

[443] Cf. Jacques Lacan on the phallus: "Si le désir de la mère est le phallus, l'enfant veut être le phallus pour le satisfaire. Ainsi la division immanente au désir se fait déjà sentir d'être éprouveé dans le désir se fait déjà à ce que le sujet se satisfasse de présenter à l'Autre ce qu'il peut avoir de reél qui réponde à ce phallus. . . ." ("Le Signification du Phallus," in *Ecrits 2*, Paris, 1971, p. 112.) Lacan says that the desire of the subject is divided between presenting himself as having the phallus, and as *being* the phallus. Cf. also the same author on circumcision: "Ce moment de coupre est hanté par la forme d'un lambeau sanglant: la livre de chair que paie la vie pour en faire le signifiant des signifiants, comme telle impossible à restituer au corps imaginaire; c'est le phallus d'Osiris embaumé." ("La Direction de la cure," in *Ecrits*, Paris, 1966, pp. 626f.) Cf. nn. 459–461 below, and Spenser's Hippolytus, "quite dismembred, and his members chast / Scattered on euery mountaine" (I.v.38); for the sexual overtone of "member" here, see III.i.60. The phallic character of the giant is the burden of J. W. Schroeder, "Spenser's Erotic Drama: The Orgoglio episode," *ELH* 29 (1962), pp. 140–159. As noted below, Orgoglio's seventh canto counterpart in Book IV is an ogre of greedy lust, whose Priapan features identify him as phallic also—Priapus is that deity in whom the normal ratio of body and appendage is symbolically reversed: a good example of what is meant by the tail wagging the dog.

[444] *Civ. Dei*, XIV.xiii, trans. M. Dods, *edn. cit.*, pp. 460f. Cf. also *De Trinitate*, IV.x: "For as the devil through pride led man through pride to death; so Christ through lowliness led man back through obedience to life. Since, as the one fell through being lifted up, and cast down [man] also who consented to him; so the other was raised up through being abased, and lifted up [man] also who believed in Him." (Trans. A. W. Haddon, rev. W.G.T. Shedd, in NPNF, 1st Series, vol. 3, p. 76.)

At the House of Holiness Redcrosse undertakes a regimen "proud humours to abate" (I.x.28), but the suggestion of the earlier episode is that pride exacts its own penance. Orgoglio is above all overbearing; as a part of Redcrosse, he suggests the victimization of the proud man by himself.

Orgoglio's parents, Aeolus (or blustering) and Earth (or fallen nature), also relate him to pride. Aether and Earth bore the presumptuous Titans, and also Pride, in Hyginus' version of the Hesiodic theogony (*Fabulae*, preface). We have mentioned the biblical giants, all assumed to be as proud as the insulting Goliath. Isidore refers Nimrod's tower to the attempt of the classical giants to displace Jove: "Gigas diaboli typum expressit, qui superbo appetitu culmen divinae celesitudinis appetivit."[445] The *Glossa ordinaria* explains the territory of Og in Deuteronomy 3:4: "Argob . . . , id est maledicta sublimitas, terrenam superbiam significat, quae in filiis irae regnat."[446] "An accursed loftynes," translates William Patten's *Calendar of Scripture*, which gives as one of the meanings for Og, *substannatio*, or "scorning."[447] On the giants of Genesis 6, Calvin writes: "their first fault was pride; because relying on their own strength, they arrogated to themselves more than was due. Pride produced contempt of God, because being inflated by arrogance, they began to shake off every yoke."[448] The Geneva Bible simply says, "All were giuen to the contempt of God, & oppression of their neighbors."

Nimrod, "That first the world with sword and fire warrayed" (I.v.48), belongs in this company. One may note that Orgoglio's knock-down blow provokes the poet to record his version of the evil gunpowder *topos* of Renaissance epic.[449] Nimrod is traditionally the first tyrant, as well as a giant.[450] The idea that the classical Titans were a reminiscence of Nimrod gave him an association with the imperial beasts of the Apocalypse, by way of an interpretation of the number 666. Irenaeus proposed the solution *teitan*, and it became part of traditional commentary.[451] Bullinger

---

[445] *Allegoriae Quaedem*, xvii (PL, LXXXIII, 103). Nimrod is an illustration of pride in Dante, at *Purg.* XII.34–36, and a giant at *Inf.* XXI.77.

[446] PL, CXIII, 456C.

[447] London (1575), fol. 148ᵛ.

[448] *Commentary on Genesis*, trans. John King, Calvin Translation Society (Edinburgh, 1847, 1850), vol. 1, p. 246.

[449] *F.Q.* I.vii.13; Ariosto, *O.F.* XI.21–27 (firearms are the devil's instrument); Tasso, *Ger. Lib.* XVIII.42–48 (Ismeno makes gunpowder from the bitumin of the Dead Sea where Sodom sank, and the stuff of hell's rivers—Ariosto predicted that the devil would guide a necromancer to the discovery of Cymoscoe's weapon); Camoëns, *Os Lusiadas*, VII.12; Milton, *Par. Lost* VI.469ff. (Satan invents the firearms that man will rediscover).

[450] Nimrod is a giant because of the LXX trans. of "mighty man" in Gen. 10:8.

[451] Irenaeus, *Cont. Haer.*, V.xxx.3 (ANF, vol. 1, p. 559); Victorinus (d. 304 A.D.), *Commentary on the Apocalypse*, xiii.18 (ANF, vol. 7, p. 356); Hippolytus, *Treatise on Christ and Antichrist*, 50 (ANF, vol. 5, p. 215); Bede, *Explanatio Apoc.*, II.xiii

mentions it ("the royall or tyrannicall name of *Nimrod*"), and so does van der Noot ("Titan that is the sonne or the name of Nemroth the tirant").⁴⁵² Thus the introduction of a Titan into the Apocalypse seems to be established rather earlier than Spenser. In the allegory of the Church in the *Purgatorio* the harlot on the seven-headed chariot consorts with a tyrannical giant.⁴⁵³ He represents a great secular power and its sovereign, Philip the Fair of France. Comparably, Spenser's first readers would have connected Duessa with the papacy and Orgoglio with Philip of Spain, and they might have said, "Et gigas non saluabitur propter multitudinem virtutes suae" (And a giant will not be delivered by his great strength [Vulgate, Ps. 33:16]). "The proud gyants perished" (Wisdom 14:6); they perished, we are told, from want of wisdom (Baruch 3:26-28).

[ii]

Proverbs 9:18 speaks of the fool entering the dwelling of the seductive woman: "he does not know that the *dead* are there." The Hebrew word for "dead" here may also be interpreted "giant," and the Vulgate reads: "he does not know that there are *giants*." During Guyon's underworld trial, corresponding to Redcrosse's defeat by Orgoglio, a Titan named Disdain threatens the hero. Guyon is ready to strike out at him, but is told that Disdain is invulnerable. The scene recalls a similar incident in the underworld of the *Aeneid* (VI.290–294) where the Titans and monsters cannot be hurt because they are imaginary. Orgoglio too has a bogey-like quality. Deflated, he is "like an emptie bladder" (I.vii.24). It is only the "wind" of his blow that overcomes Redcrosse (I.vii.12).

Pride is "puffed up," in contrast to Charity. Orgoglio's Mother Earth was "Pvft vp with emptie wind" (I.vii.9). Upton compares Orgoglio's name to the Greek *orgaō*, meaning "to swell," with ripeness or excite-

---

(PL, XCIII, 172B-D): "Et hoc sibi nomen Antichristus, quasi omnibus potentia antecellat, usurpatum ire putatur, et ipsum se esse jactans de quo scriptum est: *Exsultavit ut gigas ad currendam viam, o summo coelo egressio ejus,* etc. (Psal. xviii)." Not dissimilarly, the *Glossa ordinaria* (PL, CXIV, 734C): "Vel Tei[t]an, id est sol gigas, quod vero Christo, usurpative convenit Antichristo." The point of this link between the Titanic Antichrist and the sun-giant Christ will meet us presently.

⁴⁵² Bullinger, *Hundred Sermons Vpon the Apocalips* (London, 1561), chap. 18, fol. 244ᵛ. Van der Noot, *Theatre*, fol. 52ʳ.

⁴⁵³ *Purg.* XXXII.148–160, XXXIII.33–45. See R. E. Kaske, "Dante's DXV," in John Freccero, ed., *Dante: A Collection of Critical Essays* (Englewood Cliffs, N.J., 1965), pp. 122–140 (article adopted from *Traditio*, XVII [Fordham University Press, 1961], pp. 185–254). In suggesting that 515 is a counterpart for 666 (or 616), Professor Kaske does not mention that the letters DICLUX are often offered for the number of the Beast.

ment.[454] The pregnant Charissa, in contrast, is "Full of great loue" (I.x.30). The doves attending her of course represent another *pneuma*, the impregnating Holy Spirit. Her nursing contrasts with the "dried dugs" of Duessa, which at the end are "like bladders lacking wind" (I.viii.47).

Orgoglio's association with wind may have a further significance. His triumph and fall are both expressed by an imagery of natural cataclysm.[455] In this he resembles the classical wind-monster Typhon. Rather like Orgoglio, Typhon approaches with "the noise of a bull loud bellowing" in Hesiod; he shakes the earth with his stride and the earth groans beneath him.[456] Typhon is specifically said to be puffed up with pride in Plato's *Phaedrus* (230a). For Comes he represents ambition, and Comes notes his association with subterraneous winds.[457] The Geneva gloss compares the "puffed up" bishop of I Timothy 3:6 to the devil with his pride—the word for puffed up here is *tuphuō*.

Orgoglio thus has the place in the *ascesis* of Redcrosse that Set-Typhon has in the *sparagmos* of Osiris. This would make Una an Isis, in search of her lover's "reliques" (I.vii.24) and remains. Wearing a black stole and mounted on an ass, Una already has some resemblance to Isis, and an emblem of Alciati's referring to an Aesopic fable brings her even closer. In the fable the ass bearing the image of Isis makes the mistake of thinking *he* is the object of adoration; the emblem applies the lesson to churchmen.[458] With our three characters related to the myth, we might proceed to educe the allegory of the search for truth, but the work has been done for us by Plutarch in *De Iside*. In Amyot's French translation, Plutarch says the goddess

> . . . is very wise and very knowing, even as the very derivation of her name gives us to understand, that knowingness and knowledgeability

[454] *The Faerie Queene* (London, 1757), vol. 2, p. 385: ". . . the etymology of which, according to Menage is, *orgaō*, tumeo." The beast, likewise, is "swolne" at I.viii.12.

[455] See S. K. Henniger, Jr., "The Orgoglio Episode in *The Faerie Queene*," *ELH*, 26 (1959), pp. 171–187. Calvin associates the giants of Genesis with a violent tempest in his *Commentary on Genesis*, trans. cited, vol. 1, p. 244.

[456] *Theogony* 831f., 842f. Cf. the bull-like bellowing of the wounded Orgoglio at I.viii.11. For the link between bellowing and pride, note Braggadocchio's servant Trompart, who volunteers to "blow the bellowes to his swelling vanity" (II.iii.9). The Typhonic character of the giant is noted by Henniger, in the article cited in the preceding note. Typhon also means "swelling" according to Bacon's *Wisdom of the Ancients*, preface.

[457] *Mythol.*, VI.xxii; *edn. cit.*, pp. 651–653.

[458] Henry Green, ed., *Whitney's Choice of Emblemes* (London, 1866), no. 8, based on Alciati, Emb. VII, "Non tibi, sed religione." Aesop's fable is number 267, "onos bastadzōn agalma," in Chambry, ed., *Èsope* (Paris, 1927), pp. 118f.; in Halm, (Tuebner edn.), number 324. A reference is Samuel Daniel, *Musophilus*, ll. 629–631, which also mentions the key of knowledge.

pertain to her more than to any other, for Isis is a Greek word; and Typhon as well, the enemy and adversary of the Goddess, puffed up and swollen by his ignorance and error [*enfle & enorgueilly par son ignorance & erreur*], dissipating and effacing the holy word, which the Goddess re-assembles, composes and delivers to those who aspire to deify themselves by a continual observance of a life sober and holy. . . .[459]

One might translate the Greek, however, "he tears in pieces and buries the holy word out of sight, which the goddess gathers up again and puts together, and gives into the care of those who are initiated." That the myth had something to do with the integrity of truth the Renaissance seems to bear witness. For Pico the story contained a metaphor—naturally Neo-Platonic in character—for the life of the mind, or discourse of reason:

> We shall at one instant descend, sundering the unity of the many, like the limbs of Osiris, with *Titanic* powers; at another instant, we shall ascend, collecting by the powers of Phoebus those same limbs into their original unity. At the last, in the bosom of the Father who reigns above the ladder, we shall find perfection and peace through the felicity of theology.[460]

Pico would seem to have combined the myth with another Plutarchan allegory (from *De E, Moralia* 388F–389C), in which the dismemberment of Dionysus by the Titans stands for the separation of the One into the Many, in contrast to the unity of Apollo. Milton's fable in *Areopagitica*, of Truth sundered at the departure of her Master from earth, belongs to the same tradition: "From that time ever since, the sad friends of Truth, such as durst appear, imitating the careful search that Isis made for the mangled body of Osiris, went up and down gathering up limb by limb,

[459] *De Iside* 2 (*Moralia* 351F); Jacques Amyot, *Les Oeuvres Morales . . . de Plutarch* (Basel, 1573); trans. of Amyot based on Philemon Holland, *The Philosophy Commonly called the Morals* (London, 1657), p. 1048.

[460] *Oration on the Dignity of Man*, 11; trans. Elizabeth Forbes, in Cassirer, *et al.*, eds., *Renaissance Philosophy of Man*, p. 230. (For the Neo-Platonic Dionysus myth, see Macrobius, *Comm. In Somn. Scip.*, I.xii, and Olympiodorus on *Phaedo* 67c.) With Plutarch and Pico, cf. Clement of Alexandria, *Stromata*, I.xiii: "For we shall find that very many of the dogmas that are held by such sects have not become utterly senseless . . . correspond in their origin and with the truth as a whole. For they coincide in one. . . . In the whole universe, all the parts, though differing one from another, preserve their relation to the whole. So, then, the barbarian and Hellenic philosophy has torn off a fragment of eternal truth not from the mythology of Dionysus, but from the theology of the ever-living Word. And He who brings again together the separate fragments, and makes them one, will without peril, be assured, contemplate the perfect Word, the truth." (Trans. in ANF, vol. 2, p. 313.) Ralph Cudworth, in his *True Intellectual System of the Universe* (Cambridge, 1678), p. 355, interprets Plutarch's myth to similar effect. For the philosophical and theological problem of "the unity of truth" in the Renaissance, see Paul O. Kristeller, *Renaissance Concepts of Man* (New York, 1972), pp. 43–63.

still as they could find them." Only with the Master's second coming will Truth be made whole.[461]

Orgoglio's victory in the seventh canto sets a pattern for subsequent legends. We have mentioned Disdain in Book II. A sibling of Orgoglio's of the same name is vaunting over a victim in the same canto of Book VI. Orgoglio's "pride" may also be sexual pride or tumescence, given the preliminary dalliance of the hero with Duessa (cf. III.xi.32). In the seventh canto of the legend of friendship, an ogre representing "greedie lust" is armed with a club like Orgoglio's (I.vii.10; IV.vii.7); and the monster's physiognomy is an allegory of the male sexual organs. The seventh canto of the legend of justice shows Britomart seeking her imprisoned lover Artegall, and that canto begins with an allegory of Isis and Osiris.

[iii]

The interment of Sansjoy, if our interpretation of the House of Pride episode is correct, might be described as an ironic deposition of the body of Christ. Duessa's disposal of Redcrosse in the Orgoglio episode invites a similar interpretation, since Arthur's lifting of Redcrosse's "pined corse" (I.viii.40) decidedly suggests a pictorial "quotation" from the deposition subject. But why does Duessa preserve Redcrosse at all? And what is meant by the conditions in which the knight survives? A passage from Calvin, once again, might answer here: Calvin says that the Bishop of Rome has placed his seat in the temple of God, like Antichrist, and that his kingdom maintains the name of Christ:

> . . . we do not deny but that euen vnder his tyrannie remain Churches: but such as he hath prophaned with vngodlinesse full of sacrilege, such as he hath afflicted with outragious dominion, such as he hath corrupted and in maner killed with euill & damnable doctrines, as with poisoned drinkes: such wherein Christe lieth halfe buried, the Gospell ouerwhelmed, godlinesse banished, the worshipping of God in a maner abolished; such finally wherin all things are so troubled, that therin rather appereth the face of Babylon then of the holy citie of God. In a summe, I say that they be Churches, in respect that the Lorde there maruelously preserueth the remnauntes of his people howesoeuer they were dispersed and scattered

---

[461] Since Redcrosse's unconverted counterpart Sansjoy is something of an unhealed Hippolytus, we may compare Boccaccio in his Preface to the *Genealogia*: "I can quite realize this labor to which I am committed—this vast system of gentile gods and their progeny, torn limb from limb and scattered among the rough and desert places of antiquity and the thorns of hate, wasted away, sunk almost to ashes; and here I am setting forth to collect these fragments, hither and yon, and fit them together, like another Aesculapius restoring Hippolytus." (Trans. Osgood, *Boccaccio on Poetry*, p. 13.)

abroade, in respecte that there remaine some tokens of the Church, specially these tokens, the effectualnesse whereof neither the craft of the Deuill, nor the maliciousnesse of man can destroy.[462]

To repeat: in such churches Christ lies half-buried, the church itself being half-dead from poisoned drinks and under the domination of its Babylonian aspect; meanwhile the true church, a saving remnant, is obscured and dispersed, though not completely destroyed.

Orgoglio, if the above is any guide, belongs to the Antichrist complex we have elsewhere indicated for Archimago. If so, he ought to be defeated as Antichrist will be, that is, with "the spirit of the Lord's mouth" (II Thess. 2:8). Jewel reports that these words are diversely taken: "Some expound them thus: God shall appoint the great angel Michael to set upon antichrist; and he shall destroy him. . . . But the apostle speaketh of the preaching of the gospel. That God by his word, which is mighty to do all that whereunto he appointeth it, shall make his doings manifest. . . . This overthrow is already begun, as our eyes may behold this day."[463] Keeping this in mind, we may turn from Redcrosse's defeat to his salvation, which does not begin with Redcrosse at all, but with Una.

At her separation from Redcrosse, Una reminds us of an abandoned Ariadne: her knight defeats the monster in the labyrinth; for mysterious reasons she is thereafter forsaken (sometimes in connection with a dream or spell from Bacchus); and she laments that the beasts are kinder than her lover.[464]

---

[462] *Institutes*, IV.ii.12; Norton trans., *edn. cit.*, pp. 437f.

[463] *Exposition upon . . . Thessalonians*, in Parker Society *Works*, vol. 2, p. 927. "This sword hath hewn down in many places . . . the errors, ignorance, darkness, vanities, hypocrisy, superstition, and idolatry which have been brought into the church and used by antichrist." *Ibid.*, p. 930: "So we see the breath of the mouth of Christ is a sword. This sword shall overthrow Antichrist. Remember how Dagon fell on his face upon the ground before the ark. . . . So shall antichrist fall at the presence of Christ." That Michael may be going to slay Antichrist appears in Bede, *De Temporum Ratione*, lxix, "De temporibus Antichrist" (in PL, XC, 574). In Huon de Mére's *Tornoiement de l'Antechrist, edn. cit.* (Chap. I, n. 101, above), pp. 87–89, St. Michael captures Antichrist, who escapes during the subsequent festivities (p. 101). Arthur has fought on Michael's side in the preceding battle.

[464] Catullus, 64; Ovid, *Heroides* X; *Ars Amat.* I.525–564. For the dream of Theseus, or the spell cast on him, see *Diod. Sic.*, V.li.4; Pausanius, X.xxix; Plutarch, *Theseus* 29; Hyginus, *Fab.* XLIII. The story is told in Comes, *Mythol.*, VII.ix, *edn. cit.*, p. 731: Theseus, "on account of his reverence for the divine fear, seemed immersed in a most deep sleep, as the ancients explain, and he fled from the island." See Gower, *Confessio Amantis*, V, ll. 5424ff.: "For more than the beste unkinde / Theseus, which no trouthe kept / While that this yonge lady slept"; Chaucer, *Legend of Good Women*, l. 2198: "meker than ye," Ariadne says, "Fynde I the

Subsequently Ariadne was espoused by Bacchus, who descends on her in Catullus' poem with his band of satyrs; the scene is reminiscent of that in which the satyrs rescue Una, though she remains "sober" (I.vi.16). Thus the Church in the wilderness secures the loyalty of a succession of champions, each more human than the last, until, with the coming of Arthur, she is ready to reclaim the bridegroom—here the English people.

Most of the messianic types we have discussed are brought to bear on Arthur's victory. Joshua's trumpets brought down the walls of Jericho, and Arthur's squire has an irresistible horn that reminds us of Astolfo's (Fornari does not hesitate to make the biblical connection).[465] David defeats the overweening Goliath; and "the key of David," which opens the kingdom of heaven, is given to the Messiah. Perhaps there is some slight allusion to this in Ignaro's keys. (In the structure of the legend, Arthur's victory lays down the type for Redcrosse's, as David's reign establishes the type for the Davidic messiah.) Next is Cyrus, who ends the Babylonian captivity and restores the sacred objects to the Temple. At the advance of Cyrus the Lord "will break in pieces the gates of brass, and cut in sunder the bars of iron" (Isa. 45:2; cf. I.vii.4, 39). Judas Maccabaeus has been cited already: Orgoglio's altar has the place of what Daniel and Jesus call the "abomination of desolation" (Daniel 9:27, 10:31, 12:11; Matt. 24:15; Mark 13:14) set up in the temple. Like Antiochus Epiphanes, Orgoglio's beast has trod down "The sacred things, and holy heasts foretaught" (I.vii.18; I Macc. 1:21–24, 44–50). The altar has been defiled with "sacred ashes" and "bloud of guiltlesse babes and innocents trew" (I.vii.35); the ashes and blood relate it to the impious altars of Jereboam and Antiochus respectively (I Kings 13:2–3; I Macc. 2:37, 54–61). Antiochus' altar prefigures the altar of martyrdom that Spenser takes from Revelation 6:9.

Another millennial figure, extra-biblical, is the legendary "King of the Last Days." In the *Cursor Mundi*, he is the returning Constantine.[466] It was the business of this personage to conquer Gog and Magog, and to

bestes wilde!"; Politian, *Stanze per la Giostra*, I.110: "Any beast is less cruel than you, any beast would be more faithful." Cf. *F.Q.* I.iii.44, where it is the ass that proves "More mild in beastly kind, than that her beastly foe"; the same may be said of the lion (I.iii.7), and the satyrs. For the biblical equivalent of Redcrosse's dream, see Isa. 29:10: "For the Lord hathe couered you with a spirit of slomber, and hathe shut vp your eyes: the Prophetes, and your chief Seers hathe he couered."

[465] *Spositione, edn. cit.*, vol. 2, p. 207, where the horn is also linked to the gift of tongues and the trumpet of the prophet's voice in Isaiah (see Isa. 58:1).

[466] *Cursor Mundi*, ed. Richard Morris, EETS, nos. 57, 59, 62, 66, 68, 90, 101 (London, 1874–1893), vol. 4, pp. 1272–1279 (ll. 19267–23790). The King of the Last Days is a character in the medieval Antichrist play. As Constantine, he appears in Petrarch, *Canz.* CXXXVIII (Son. 108). Elizabeth is celebrated as a new Constantine in Foxe's Dedication, *Acts, edn. cit.*, vol. 1, Pt. I, pp. vi*–ix*.

expose the pretensions of his opposite, the imperial Antichrist. It has been suggested that Arthur belongs to such a conception.[467] Rather nearer to Spenser's actual pattern of allusion is St. Michael, who makes war on the dragon in Revelation. Michael also disputes the body of Moses with Satan at Jude 9, and we may think of Redcrosse as a similar battleground—he may either be damned by Orgoglio's pride or saved by Arthur's grace. Arthur's shield, being of diamond, may remind us of Michael's shield in Tasso; Tasso's allegory identifies it as "the special safeguard of the Lord God,"[468] a protection extended to the otherwise unequal Raymond. The Geneva Bible explains the subject of the twelfth chapter of Daniel as "the deliuerance of the Church by Christ," and at Daniel 10:13, where Michael is first introduced, the Geneva gloss says, "This Angel was appointed for the defence of the Church under Christ." Michael is the patron saint of Israel as St. George is the patron saint of England, and a treatment of the English Church as a spiritual Israel will show the lesser and the greater patrons in analogous parts.

Like Redcrosse's, Arthur's triumph in this legend ought to be on the analogy of the harrowing of hell. Once again, in the background, will be the Passion itself, Christ as victor corresponding to Arthur, and, as victim, to Redcrosse. Orgoglio is a victim, too, like the Adamic dragon in the eleventh canto, and after Redcrosse has disappeared into the dungeon Orgoglio remains to symbolize the death that dies on the cross. This transference is easily established: Redcrosse is "dismayd" at the onset of Orgoglio, and Orgoglio is in turn "dismaid" with the coming of Arthur (I.vii.11, viii.5). However, the motif of the *crucifixion* of Orgoglio is not one that the moral allegory of the two mortifications—*by* pride and *of* pride—really prepares us to discern. A rather different series of deductions is required to elicit the symbolism.

Here one needs to know a somewhat complex patristic trope, which derives from the bridegroom-sun of Psalm 19:5, who "has rejoiced as a giant to run the way." It was widely agreed that this giant represented Christ. Langland speaks of "Gygas the geaunt" in the B-Text of his poem, which becomes "Iesus as a gyaunt" in the C-Text.[469] It was especially the

---

[467] J. Frank Kermode, "The Faerie Queene: I and V," *Bulletin of the John Rylands Library*, vol. 47, no. 1 (Sept., 1964), pp. 123–150, and the same author's 1962 Warton Lecture, "Spenser and the Allegorists," in *Proceedings of the British Academy*, 48 (1962, publ. 1963), pp. 261–279.

[468] Trans. Fairfax, in Morley's edn. of *Jerusalem Delivered*, p. 440.

[469] B-Text, Passus XVIII.250; C-Text, Passus XXI.263. For the giant as Christ, see Augustine, *Ennar. in Ps.*, XVIII.6, PL, XXXVI, 155, 161, and also PL, XXXVII, 1116; Alanus de Insulis, *Liber in distinctionibus, sub Gigas*, in PL, CCX, 803. In Alanus and Ambrose, *De Incarnationis Dominicae*, I.v.35 (*PL*, XVI, 827), the giant's double nature, as the offspring of the sons of God and daughters of men (Gen. 6:2–4), is thought to betoken the biform nature of the god-man. That Spenser's *Geant* rep-

Christ who suffered the crucifixion that the giant came to personify. In Dante, for example, the giant Nimrod cries out in an unintelligible parody of the words from the cross.[470] Writing on the subject of Christian mortification in Romans, Luther speaks of those who "die" willingly: "Their prototype is Christ—Christ who died crying with a loud voice like the bravest giant."[471] Thus the comparison of Redcrosse to the bridegroom-sun of the psalm, preceding his contest with Sansjoy (I.v.2), has a specifically Christological overtone, and a special aptness in its place. Orgoglio, since he is both a giant and a "Titan," might also share in this complex of images. Because the sun was a giant in the psalm, and Titan, in pagan fable, the *teitan* of the Apocalypse came to be thought of as borrowing his title from the Messiah. Bede, for example, explains the name Titan: "And this name Antichrist thinks to usurp for himself, as if he excelled all in power, and he boasts himself to be the one of whom it is written: 'He rejoiced as a giant running the way. . . .'" The *Glossa ordinaria* similarly explains Titan: "that is, the *sol gigas*, which, with a glance at the true Christ, he [the author] appropriates by usurpation for the Antichrist."[472] Thus Orgoglio dies as a suffering giant of a special kind; his blood, for example, "Forth gushed, like fresh water streame from riuen rocke" (I.viii.10), the image suggesting the rock that was Christ and the sacramental release from Christ's side (I Cor. 10:3f.; John 19:34; I John 5:6). Other allusions to the events of the crucifixion are more readily perceived: the earthquake,[473] the rending of the veil of Arthur's shield, and the blinding of the beast (I.viii.19f.). The angels at the tomb who transfix the guards are dazzling to look upon, and in the harrowing of hell legend Satan is blinded by the "great light" of Isaiah 9:2.[474] Arthur likewise

resents man's earthly nature is clear enough from I.vii.5, which makes Gea his mother.

[470] *Inf.* XXXI.67; *Raphèl mày amèch zabì almì*, which is rimed with *salmi*, is a distorted version of Ps. 22:1, as it appears in Matt. 27:46, *Eli, Eli, lamma sabatchthani*: Nimrod is praying to Raphèl, or "giant-god." See *De Vulgaria Eloqventia*, I.vi.49–61 and I.iv.26–31, and *Parad.* XXVL.123–137; and cf. Ps. 22:2 with *Inf.* XXXIII.69.

[471] *Lectures on Romans*, ed. and trans. Wilhelm Pauck, Library of Christian Classics, 15 (Philadelphia, 1961), p. 182.

[472] *Glossa ordinaria*, PL, CXIV, 734C; see n. 451, above, for Latin text.

[473] I.vii.7–9, viii.4f., 8. For the link to the harrowing of hell, cf. Dante, *Inf.* III.130–132, V.34, XII.4–11, 32–45, XXI.112–114, *Purg.* XXI.55–72 (and cf. *Parad.* XXI.139–142, XXVII.35f.).

[474] So in *Piers Plowman*, B-Text, Passus XVIII.323: "Lucyfer loke ne myȝt . so lyȝt hym ableynte." In the Gospel of Nicodemus, Christ is the King of Glory, and hence a light-bringer, as in the Latin versions trans. in James, *Apocryphal New Testament*, pp. 135f., where it is the King's brightness that routs the demons. (For a brief notice of a black letter version of this Gospel in English, ca. 1525, see W. H. Hulm's edn. of Middle English pieces, *The Harrowing of Hell*, EETS, Extra Series, no. 100, pp. lvii–lx.)

fulfills the messianic injunction of Isaiah 42:6–7: "bring . . . them that sit in darknes, out of the prison house."

As these last details suggest, the imprisoned Redcrosse occupies that Limbo or "Dongeon" (I.vii.15) elsewhere endured in this legend by the Adam figures.[475] Arthur, in taking the part of the biblical redeemer may be compared to the Lord of the Exodus, the Cyrus of Second Isaiah, and the descending angel who breaks the bond on Christ's tomb in the Gospel of Matthew.[476] Redcrosse's prison thus stands in the place of death itself, and its stench becomes that of the tomb of Lazarus (John 11:39). The unbinding of Lazarus also entails the motif of the emancipation of a "Prisoner" (I.viii.40). Indeed, the Johanine pericope employs the resurrection images of the stone and grave clothes, and the lapse of time that otherwise belong to the Easter story itself.[477] John's theme of Mary grieving at the tomb is also found in the Lazarus narrative, and the well of tears that Una expends upon Redcrosse makes her a Magdalen too (John 11:33, 20:11; I.vi.27, 52; viii.42).

By this point in the evolution of the symbolism and our exposition of it, Orgoglio as pride has been more or less superseded—Orgoglio himself, in fact, is out of the way considerably before Redcrosse is raised up. The dominion the giant has enjoyed over his victim remains before us. The emerging metaphor of spiritual bondage to the prince of this world deserves the description of it found in Bullinger:

> The spiritual bondage hath a certain likeness to the bodily servitude. For Adam by his own fault became a bondman; and we of him are all born bondmen. He was once at liberty and had the Lord to be his friend and favourer; but he did disloyally revolt from God, and got himself another master, the devil, a tyrant as cruel as may be, who for his sin having gotten power over him did, like a merciless lord, miserably handle him like a bond-servant.[478]

Duessa has promised Orgoglio that he can make of Redcrosse his "eternall bondslaue" (I.vii.14). Conversely, Arthur "aquits," or ransoms, his fellow

---

[475] The prison is a Limbo because it is the waterless place of Zech. 2:9 (compare the "withered" Redcrosse who lacks his "dew" at I.viii.41f.). Cf. Deut. 8:15f. for drought, manna, and the release of water.

[476] Arthur's calling through the house, which "no man car'd to answere" (I.viii.29), recalls the redeemer-Lord of Isa. 50:1–4: "wherefore came I, & there was no man? I called, and none answered: is mine hand so shortened, that it can not helpe? or haue I no power to deliuer? . . . he will raise me vp in the morning: in the morning he will waken mine eare to heare as the learned." (The same accents are found at IV.x.11: "I knockt, but no man aunswred me by name; / I cald, but no man answerd to my clame.")

[477] The "filthy bands" which affection does not eschew at I.viii.40 may glance at the bandages which Lazarus' friends are told to remove, at John 11:44.

[478] *Decades*, III, Sermon IX, Parker Society edn., vol. 2, p. 304.

knight (I.vi.52f.). Ransom is specifically one of the seven corporal works of mercy, and Spenser compares it with the harrowing of hell (I.x.40), this being one more indication of the theme of spiritual deliverance here.

The meaning of Arthur's triumph in this episode remains to be stated in terms the reader will recognize from Spenser's initial premise in the defeat of Error. For the Christian who needs help, the meaning is the ready extension of God's grace to the sinner, as the opening stanza of the eighth canto tells us. But "heauenly grace" is brought by "stedfast truth" in this instance; the episode clearly develops toward an analogy for the revelation or unveiling of the truth—that truth addressed to the bond-slaves of sin whom it is said the truth will set free (John 8:30–36). The evangelistical trumpet, the blinding light, the keys of knowledge taken away from ignorance, the exposure of the "counterfesaunce" of Duessa, and the vindication of Una all support this interpretation.

In the sermon of Jewel quoted as an epigraph for this essay, the preacher describes the induration and resistance of the spiritual Jericho to the knowledge of the truth. Jewel takes the city shut up against the Israelites to signify the willful blindness of those not reached by the Gospel.[479] We have earlier cited the Antichrist passage from II Thessalonians on the sending of a strong delusion to those who "received not the love of the truth." The preceding verse reads: "And then shall that wicked bee revealed whom the Lord shall consume with the spirit of his mouth, and shall destroy with the brightnesse of his coming" (II Thess. 2:8, Bishops' Bible). "The apostle," Jewel explains, "speaketh of the preaching of the gospel."[480]

Redcrosse, amazed by the denuded Duessa, and the beast, amazed by the exposed shield, are really subject to the same revelation (I.viii.20, 40). The disarming of the beast in particular recalls the blinding of Paul on the road to Damascus. Here Spenser compounds the sundered veil and the "starke blind" persecutor to form a single symbol, making the Easter and Damascus theophanies the recto and verso of essentially one divine incursion into the world. Paul went on to proclaim the breaching of the wall dividing Jew from Gentile and so became the apostle of the unity of the Church. The Christ of Ephesians 2:14, who has "broken the stoppe of the particion wall," is easily linked to the Christ who entered the veil (Heb. 9:8, 12, 28, 10:20); the abrogation of Israel's peculiar election thus coincides with the violation of her exclusive sanctuary. In this symbolism Arthur would have the place of the high priest or mediator of the New Testament who enters the old tabernacle "wherein were offred giftes and sacrifices that colde not make holie"—sacrifices that the priest "offered

---

[479] *Sermons on Joshua VI*, Parker Society *Works*, vol. 2, pp. 970–972.
[480] *Upon . . . Thessalonians*, in *Works*, vol. 2, p. 927.

for the ignorances of the people" (Heb. 9:9, 7). At the same time this mediation destroys the old temple as a shibboleth. Thus when Redcrosse is rejoined to Una, or Holy Church, Spenser's Synagogue figure is correspondingly profaned. So Ambrose, on the veil in Luke 23:45:

> . . . And then the veil is torn, which proclaims the separation of the two peoples, and the profanation of the mysteries of the Synagogue. The ancient veil is thus torn, so that the new Church may hang its cloth; the veil of the Synagogue is raised, to let the secret mysteries of religion be revealed to our soul's sight.[481]

On the cursing of the daughters of Jerusalem (Isa. 3:17)—which we have seen to be a type for this profanation—the *Glossa ordinaria* simply reads: "What is secret will be exposed, and a foul baldness will appear. For nothing is covered which is not revealed."[482] This is Christ's promise when he sends forth his Apostles (Matt. 10:26, Greek *apokalupsthāsetai*, revealed).

In the following canto Arthur extends to Redcrosse the Pauline right hand of friendship (I.ix.1, 18), and the friendship is sealed by an exchange of gifts. Arthur gives Redcrosse a magical liquor, which might remind one a little of the golden pot of manna kept within the Holy of Holies (Heb. 9:4, Exod. 16:32), and which should symbolize either the administration of the sacrament or the preservation of Christ's body against the day of his burial. However, it is not salves but God's word that saves, and in Spenser such a *sacramentum*, or preservative, ought to be paired with a *verbum*, or healing word. Therefore Redcrosse, in return, offers Arthur "his Saueours testament . . . A worke of wondrous grace, and able soules to saue" (I.ix.19). In other words, at the end of the Orgoglio episode, the Word of God has once again been released into the world.

[iv]

If Redcrosse had received Orgoglio's blow directly, "He had been pouldred all, as thin as flowre" (I.vii.12). "Heauenly grace" prevents this,

---

[481] *Expos. Evang. Sec. Lukam*, X.128 (PL, XV, 1836). Una being Ecclesia, Duessa may be a Synagogue-figure, but she is not the only such one here. Ignaro is another, his blindness corresponding to that of the veiled or blindfolded Synagogue of iconography, whose attributes derive from Lamentations 5:16f. ("the crown has fallen from our head . . . our eyes are become dim"). Since he is a backward Peter and a backward Contemplation, Ignaro is also a backward St. John, who arrived at Christ's tomb before Peter, but hesitated to enter in, letting Peter pass before him. In this instance, John was interpreted as a Synagogue-figure: see *Glossa ordinaria*, on John 20:4 (PL, CXIV, 422). In Spenser the contrast is between Ignaro and Arthur, the latter inquiring where Redcrosse is "layd" (I.viii.32; for the question cf. John 11:34, and John 20:2, 13, 15). The whole schemata of the veiled or blindfolded Synagogue-figures vs. the enlightened Ecclesia-figures converging upon the Crucifixion is explained in Emile Mâle, *The Gothic Image*, trans. Nussey, pp. 188–193.

[482] PL, CXIII, 1240A.

but the fleeting metaphor of John Barleycorn is appropriate nevertheless. A medieval altarpiece is reported that shows Christ being thrown by the soldiers into the hopper of a wheat mill, because Christ is made into bread.[483] Protestant commentary, of course, condemns the adoration of the host as idolatrous. Foxe writes:

> That which was threshed out of a wheaten sheaf they set up in the church, and worship for a Savior: and when they have worshipped him, then they offer him to his Father: and when they have offered him, then they eat him up, or else close him fast in a pix, where, if he corrupt and putrefy, before he be eaten, then they burn him to powder and ashes. And notwithstanding they know well . . . that the body of Christ can never corrupt and putrefy.[484]

This passage describes the sort of thing that *can* happen to the "dismaid" Redcrosse, who does corrupt and putrefy. Many such passages would show the way in which Protestant commentary lets the mortified old Adam invade the imagery of the host, and insofar as Redcrosse merely imitates Christ, he approximates the inadequacy of other imitations.

It is at the House of Holiness that Redcrosse is made whole. His spiritual mortification here consists in torments like those that are said to have made George a saint in the first place. *The Golden Legend* derives his name from the Greek words *geos* and *orge*, tilling the earth: "that is, [harrowing] his flesh." His defeat by Orgoglio, the son of Earth, anticipates the theme, ironically burying or sowing the knight, but forgetting to raise him up.[485] At the House of Holiness, while Fidelia and Speranza teach Redcrosse the promises, Charissa is kept off-stage. This is explained as due to her being in labor, and there can be little doubt that the child to whom she is giving birth is the regenerate Redcrosse, the same Redcrosse whom the plowman found in the furrow.

The idea of wholeness here is naturally associated with the idea of perfection, and we need to appreciate the scriptural basis for this connection. The Geneva Bible glosses the wholeness or integrity required of Abraham (Gen. 17:1) and of Israel (Deut. 18:13) as meaning "without hypocrisy." The priests who make the offering before the Lord must be "without blemish," and the acceptable sacrificial lamb must also be without blemish (Lev. 21:17, 23:12; Num. 28:8—"without spot"). The Septuagint uses the

---

[483] A Worms altarpiece, cited in Jack Lindsay, *A Short History of Culture* (1962; reprint, New York, 1966), p. 439. For the body of Christ as "one loaf" of which the partakers are members, see I Cor. 1:16f. Orgoglio is the folktale ogre who grinds the bones of Englishmen to make his bread.

[484] *Acts, edn. cit.*, vol. 1, Part II, p. 83.

[485] Note the "furrow" Orgoglio digs (I.viii.8), and cf. French *orge*, barley.

New Testament word for "perfect," *telion*, for whole, or unblemished, in its translation of the unblemished lamb and the spotless bride of Song 5:2 and 6:9. Likewise, the Lamb of God in I Peter 1:19 is "vndefiled & without spot" (Geneva Bible). In the New Testament it is Christ who "makes whole" (Mark 5:34) and "perfect" (I Peter 5:10), and the Christian is enjoined to "be perfect" (Matt. 5:48, II Cor. 13:11), as Israel is commanded, "Be ye holy," and "let your heart be perfect with God."[486] What is made perfect is "consecrated," in the Geneva translation of Hebrews 5:9, and in this epistle the notion of the unblemished state is closely linked to sanctification. In Ephesians 5:27 it is said that the Church espoused by Christ is to be sanctified and cleansed and made unto him "a glorious Church not hauing spot . . . that it shulde be holie and without blame." According to the Geneva Bible the likeness of man to God in Genesis 1:26 "is expounded [at] Ephes 4, 24: where it is written, that man was created after God in righteousness & true holines, meaning by these two words all perfection, as wisdome, trueth, innocencie, power, &c."

Thus Spenser's knight of holiness is often presented to us in terms of his health, or his wholeness: etymologically, *holiness* in Hebrew is *set-apartness,* but in English it is *wholeness.* The sins at the House of Pride are all unwholesome, running a gamut from narcolepsy to leprosy. Despair, with his imputation of sin, causes a man "to spoyle the Castle of his health" (I.ix.31). Aesculapius, if his allegorical function is priestly, must be one who tries to make holy: the healer of the dismembered Hippolytus "joined euery part" (I.v.39). In contrast to the reprieve for Sansjoy sought from this healer, Una conducts her despairing knight "where he chearen might" (I.x.3), the House of Holiness—Despair tempted him to "spoyle the Castle of his health" (I.ix.31). The House is well glossed by the following typology from Cyprian, which starts from the rule concerning the "unity" of the Passover lamb:

> God speaks, saying, "In one house shall ye eat it; ye shall not send its flesh abroad from the house." The flesh of Christ, and the holy of the Lord, cannot be sent abroad, nor is there any other home to believers but the one church. This home, this household [*hospitium*] of unanimity, the Holy Spirit designates and points out in the Psalms, saying, "God, who maketh men to dwell with one mind in a house." In the house of God, in the Church of Christ, men dwell with one mind, and continue in concord and simplicity.[487]

---

[486] Lev. 11:45; 19:2; 20:7, 26; and I Kings 8:61. Cf. Martin Buber, *Two Types of Faith,* trans. Norman Goldhawk (reprint New York, 1961), pp. 59–61, for this point.

[487] *Treatise,* I.8, trans. in ANF, vol. 5, p. 424. Cf. Irenaeus, *Cont. Haer.,* I.x.1f. (ANF, vol. 1, pp. 330f.), for the same doctrine.

It is in such a place that Redcrosse is restored to health and wholeness, though Duessa has dropped out of the symbolism a canto earlier. The knight grows to a "perfection of all heauenly grace" (I.x.21); his "filthy blots of sinn" are washed from him (I.x.27); he becomes "perfect" in charity (I.x.45). His regeneration parallels his steady exposure to what the New Testament calls "wholesom doctrine" (I Timothy 1:10, II Tim. 4:3), "wherewith our soules are fed & mainteined in helth" (Geneva gloss on Titus 2:9). He is healed by Patience; the Christian is enjoined to "let Patience haue her perfite worke, that ye may be perfite and entire, lackyng nothing" (James 1:4).

On the other side of the chief equation of Spenser's legend is the oneness of Una. Earlier in this chapter we studied Duessa's characteristically divisive mode of expression. We may contrast Una, who asserts that Redcrosse "is one the truest knight aliue" (I.iii.37); her singular usage does not really recognize the existence of any other knight.[488] The ideal faith is monogamous, as it were, and Christ prays for the oneness of his Church. In the ideal Age to Come, Israel will be a united kingdom;[489] there will be one sanctuary and one priesthood for the worship of the one God, who is defined by his solity.[490] And just as there is only one true faith, so the Word of God is also one: it is *the* Word, and the unicity of its revelation has taken the form of one Book.[491]

We are now in a position to sum up the implications of the union of Redcrosse and Una. Psalm 106:39–40 uses a metaphor with which we have become quite familiar:

> Thus were they stained with their owne workes, and went a whoring with their owne inuentions.
> Therefore was the wrath of the Lord kindled against his people, and he abhorred his owne inheritance.[492]

---

[488] Note also Una's single-double description of Duessa: "Mine onely foe, mine onely deadly dread" (I.vii.50).

[489] The reunification of the two houses of Israel is a prophetic restoration-theme, often Davidic in character: Jer. 3:18, Ezek. 37:15–22; Isa. 11:13; cf. Zech. 11:7–14.

[490] Deut. 6:4, 12:4; Zech. 14:9: "In that day shal there be one Lord, and his Name shalbe one" (Geneva gloss: "All idolatrie and superstition shalbe abolished, and there shalbe one God, one faith, and one religion"). Una is the woman clothed with the sun, so there may be an unspoken Latin pun on *sol*, sun, and *solus*, only. (Spenser knows such a pun, at VII.vii.51: "Phoebus self, who lightsome is alone"; God's solity and the sun of justice are equated in Augustine, *Ennar. in Ps.* LXXX.14 [PL, XXXVII, 1041], for example.)

[491] For this point, with reference to the prophet's announcing *the* word of God, see L. Köhler, *Old Testament Theology*, trans. A. S. Todd (London, 1957), p. 106. For the extension of the prophetic term to the canon as a whole, cf. Th. C. Vriezen, *An Outline of Old Testament Theology*, English edn., Oxford, 1958, pp. 94–96.

[492] Una is likewise "abhord" by her "Lord," at I.ii.7. Cf. Ps. 42:8 for her phrase,

Here the Geneva Bible succinctly extrapolates, "Then true chastitie is to cleaue wholly & onely vnto God."[493] "Wholly & onely"—by the end of Book I this ought to strike us as an exact choice of words. On the one hand, there is the dedicated Redcrosse, "Right faithfull true" (I.i.2); on the other, there is Una, "th'only daughter of a King," with her "trew sacred lore" (I.vii.43, I.vi.30). Without Una, Redcrosse's dedication can be neither wholly one, nor wholly true—it is a peculiar property of Spenser's symbolism that Redcrosse, in losing Una, achieves a spurious autonomy at the expense of his actual integrity. And without the single-minded Redcrosse, Una herself cannot be wholly one, for she is soon dispersed among the many; nor can she be wholly true, for truth is not itself when it is unknown and unappreciated, nor when it is adulterated and vulgarized. Using alternative translations of the same words in Ephesians 4:24, we might say that Redcrosse stands for "true holines," while Una represents the "holinesse of trueth" (Geneva and Bishops' Bibles). Together they symbolize the edification of that Church in which "we all mete together in the vnitie of faith & knowledge of the Sonne of God, vnto a perfite man" (Eph. 4:13, Geneva Bible). This perfected man, we are told, "hath made both one," reconciling those "alienated from the conversation of Israel": "that he may create the two in himself into one new man" (Eph. 2:14, 12, 15, Rheims Bible).

The end of Spenser's legend is the uniting of the faithful and the true. Truth, if she is going to prevail, needs a champion. And the champion, if he is going to prevail, needs to know what he is doing. Spenser's theme, though, is the establishment of faith, and to be a legend of faith the story must not end in marriage, but in trothplight, or betrothal: that is, in a renewed pledging of faith. Near the end of the Apocalypse, John says that his words are "faithful and true." This serves to identify his "moste wonderful Propheticall or Poetical Vision," as Harvey called it, with the messianic horseman whose ride to victory the vision has announced and whose name—Faithful and True—the vision has revealed. Such an alignment of word and person makes the point that the New Testament in Christ's blood is not only a sacrifice, but also a sign, a disclosure of "the word of truth," which requires faith. At the House of Holiness, Fidelia carries not only a cup, but also a book. Spenser's first legend, we have

---

"God of my life," and for abhorred, see also Ps. 78:59, 89:38, Jer. 14:21, Prov. 22:14, and Lam. 2:7. For the link of abhorrence and whoredom, see also Ezk. 16:25. Kirkrapine uses "whoredom" with Abessa (I.iii.18), and Una is accused of "dishonesty" (I.iii.23), slandered as a "harlot" (25), and fears "to haue bene quite abhord" (27).

[493] Cf. Zech. 8:3, on the Lord's return to Zion, when Jerusalem "shalbe called a citie of trueth": "Because," the Geneva gloss says, "she shalbe faithful, and loyal towarde me her housband."

endeavored to show, has as many analogies with Fidelia's book as with her cup. Indeed, the pages of such a book, "with bloud ywrit," must manifest the sacramental color pattern in yet one more place. The legend of the Redcrosse knight, in its loving elaboration of this pattern, has many of the qualities of the Church's principal ceremony, but it is no idol. As the reformers said of the cup, its efficacy derives from the Word annexed to it.

III

BOOKS OF THE GOVERNORS

[i]

THE preceding essay has described Spenser's first legend as an analogy for the Word itself. Subsequent legends develop their own analogies, internal to the poem. For purposes of organizing the ensuing commentary, I will indicate three such analogies, based on the more or less inevitable comparison of the two parts of the poem we have. Occasionally Spenser is rather pointed about these analogies and it seems clear that he drew on his first installment for inspiration in the composition of the second. Starting from the center of the poem and working outward—and this may be how the second installment was composed—we find an analogy between sexual and social love. The legend of friendship is conceived as both a sequel to, and a partner book for, the legend of chastity; thus some basis for this analogy, at least, is given. Next there is an analogy of private and public order, in the legends of temperance and justice, which we shall treat in the present chapter. Last is an analogy of grace, especially gracious speech, in the legends of holiness and courtesy. Suggestive correspondences are the donnée for this scheme of commentary. One can err in letting one suggestion crowd out others equally valid, and Spenser did have other analogies in mind. These three, however, are far-reaching, and, once observed, not easily laid aside. This, of course, reports my own experience; perhaps the established commentaries of other Spenserians can be counted upon to remind us of other unifying schemes.

The change from Book I to Book II corresponds to a historical shift in emphasis, in martyrology, from the retailing of the martyr's passion, to the description of the spiritual and interior martyrdom of ascesis and Lenten self-denial: St. George is followed by St. Anthony. The pattern of redefinition established by the movement from Book I to Book II also obtains in successive paired books—III–IV and V–VI. The odd-numbered books treat a specifically human hero whose virtue comes into existence with a "fall": the fall into sin (Book I), the fall into sexual consciousness (Book III), and the fall into history (Book V). The high-minded and righteous virtues of these books are tempered, naturalized, and domesticated by their humbler sequelae in the even-numbered books, where the protagonists are faerie, and hence do not fall in the way the human heroes do. As a result of this distinction between odd and even books, each hero in the symmetrical conjugation of the poem (I–VI, II–V, III–IV) has a human or faerie counterpart in the "other" installment. Guyon, in the first installment, is "faerie" to the human Artegall, in the second.

The comparison of the two installments is based on the analogy of self-realization and social realization. A person who has faith in himself will normally have faith in others; a person who has self-control will be responsive to the controls of society; a person who has self-respect will be respectful of others. The relation is almost tautologous, since, for example, we learn to have faith in ourselves through experiencing the faithfulness of others toward us.

Our "virtues" are really early character strengths that have been educationally interpreted, especially through the institutions of society.[1] The institution of religion, Book I implies, is partly elaborated from the securing of hope and trust, and Spenser manages to get the words "faithfull," "hope," and "cheere"—as well as "helpe," "sad," "dread," and "ydrad"—into his second stanza alone. One must enter heaven as a little child, and that there is something childlike about Redcrosse can scarcely be denied. Children do not kill giants or dragons, of course, but they are certainly faced with towering fathers, nursing mothers, and occasionally a very rambunctious puppy. The dragon is described as such a beast:

> So dreadfully he towards him did pas,
>   Forelifting vp aloft his speckled brest,
>   And often bounding on the brused gras,
>   Eftsoones he gan aduance his haughtie crest, . . .
>   (I.xi.15)

Romance is often childlike because it often presumes a solemn-eyed willingness to accept wonders as probabilities, and vice versa. An element of play in Spenser's poem is hardly to be missed; like Ariosto, Spenser shows an appreciation for romance as an enlightening form of recreation, or imaginative exercise. But unlike the Orlando poets, Spenser never requires the good Bishop Turpin to confirm the proliferation of marvels, because they are supported by the steady allusion to the issues—"too solemne sad"—of ordinary adult experience.

---

[1] The origins of "ego strengths"—or virtues—in given psychological stages is the subject of Erik Erikson, *Childhood and Society*, 2nd edn., chap. 7, where "eight ages of man" are described as a succession of "nuclear conflicts" of characteristic strengths and weaknesses. The basis for the first three of these stages is discussed in Erikson's second chapter, on infantile sexuality. The first stage is oral-sensory: its polarity is trust vs. mistrust. The second stage is anal-muscular: its polarity is autonomy vs. shame. The third stage is genital-locomotor: here the polarity is initiative vs. guilt. The three virtues pertaining to the respective stages are *drive* (based on hope); *control* (based on willpower); and *direction* (based on purpose). I apply these to Spenser's first three protagonists. The "bases" are supplied from Erikson's essay, "The Roots of Virtue," in Julian Huxley, ed., *The Humanist Frame* (New York, 1960). I have also consulted Erikson's *Identity and the Life Cycle*, monograph 1 (International Universities Press, New York, 1959).

Before proceeding to discuss the character strengths belonging particularly to temperance, I wish to treat the analogies for the Fall near the opening of Book II; it will be convenient to show the relation to the opening of Book V, as well, though fuller discussion of the parallel is deferred to a later section.

Temperance and justice are virtues of experience, and involve the expertise needed to cope with experience. They are associated with safeguards, like the Palmer and Talus, and they react against the physical and social disintegration of a "fallen" world. In the unfallen world there was only one prohibition; experience, on the other hand, abounds in natural limits and legal codes, and consequently in the exacerbation of transgression. Both books open with an extended allusion to the triumph of Mutabilitie. Spenser's account of the outlaw, from her own legend, emphasizes her corruption of reliable limits:

> Ne she the lawes of Nature onely brake,
>   But eke of Iustice, and of Policie;
>   And wrong of right, and bad of good did make,
>   And death for life exchanged foolishlie:
>   Since which, all liuing wights haue learn'd to die,
>   And all this world is woxen daily worse.
>   O pittious worke of MUTABILITIE!
>   By which, we all are subject to that curse
> And death in stead of life haue sucked from our
>   Nurse.
>
> (VII.vi.6)

Nature and Justice, according to the first book of Cicero's *Legges*, are equally determined by Law (cf. I.xv-xvi).

The first sign of mutability in Book II is the escape of Archimago, who is now working against the knight of temperance. He tempts knights "To slug in slouth and sensuall delight" (II.i.23); the Bower of Bliss, with its ivory gate, will show the image-making power in just such a context. Archimago is also still the spirit of division and calumny, and he slanders Redcrosse to Guyon. The impending battle is a stand-off: holiness and temperance only *seem* to be opposed, and the knights reach an accord implying their equivalence.

In Book I the Archimago episode was followed by the episode of Fradubio, whom we identified with the Pauline Adam. In Book II the corresponding character is Mordant, "the image of mortalitie" (II.i.57).[2]

---

[2] Similar interpretations are made by Alastair Fowler, "Emblems of Temperance in *The Faerie Queene*," *Review of English Studies*, New Series, vol. 11, no. 42 (May, 1960), pp. 143-149; see esp. pp. 144f. Drunkenness can be a *mortal* sin, according

Mordant falls victim to Acrasia's charmed cup, but only after he has left the enchantress' realm; he dies, not from intemperance itself, but on the moral rebound from it, when he is taking his drinks tempered with water. The legend on the cup reads, "giue death to him that death does giue," which must refer to the mortification of the old Adam in baptism. (The mixture of "Bacchus with the Nymphe" probably alludes to the water and the Spirit of John 3, as did the wine and water in Fidelia's cup.) The drink proves fatal to the apparently heedful Mordant: "For I once was aliue, without the Law: but when the commandement came, sinne revived. But I dyed: and the same commaundement which was ordeined unto life, was founde to be unto me unto death" (Romans 7:9–10, Geneva Bible; Bishops' Bible, "unto me an occasion of death"; Rheims version, "For sinne taking occasion by the commaundement, *seduced me*, and by it killed me"—this is especially close to Spenser's allegory).

The allusion to baptism is supported by the evidence of Mordant's sole survivor, the child Ruddymane. Like the uncovenanted Israel in a notable similitude of Ezekiel, Ruddymane is born in corruption:

> And as for thy nativity, in the day thou wast born thy navel was not cut, neither wast thou washed in water to supple thee; thou wast not salted at all, nor swaddled at all.
>
> None eye pitied thee, to do any of these unto thee, to have compassion upon thee; but thou wast cast out in the open field, to the lothing of thy person, in the day that thou wast born.
>
> And when I passed by thee, and saw thee polluted in thine own blood, I said unto thee when thou wast in thy blood, Live; . . .
>
> (Ezek. 16:4–6)

His bloody hands cannot be cleansed in the stainless waters of Diana's well. The stain betokens the persistence of "birth sin"—as the ninth Article calls it—"whereby man is very far gone from original righteousness," which "deserveth God's wrath and damnation" (cf. II.ii.4). This sin is found even "in them that are regenerated"; Guyon's kind of moral virtue is especially insufficient to recover generic innocence. The well itself, we learn, is the tearful and stony metamorphosis of a besieged nymph of Diana. The nymph was retreating from a lustful Faunus, and concupiscence is a particular evidence of our "infection of nature." The rustic subplot of the Mutabilitie cantos features the corruption of a nymph of the same goddess by another irrepressible Faunus; Diana consequently stones the brook identified with the nymph. As Frye remarks, Diana is

---

to Thomas, *Summa Theol.*, Pt. II, 1st Pt., q.88, art.5, obj.1 and resp. ad obj.1, 3rd para.: significantly, it is a mortal sin by reason of its genus, that is, because it entails the rejection of reason.

like the Old Law: she cannot absolve sin, precisely because she is still resisting adulteration by it.[3] The water in the well is "cold through fear, and old conceiued dreads" (II.ii.9).

The plight of Astraea at the opening of the legend of justice is similar. When corruption comes into the world, she retreats to the fixed stars, and the Golden Age goes with her. Diana retreats from Arlo Hill leaving stones in her wake, and with the departure of Astraea men have become like the stones Deucalion threw—"so backward bred" (V, proem, 2). Like Diana, Astraea cannot reverse what Mutabilitie has begun; she can only resist its effects in the jurisdiction remaining to her. The organization of this resistance is the essential subject of Books II and V.

Astraea's legacy, Talus, also suggests life under the law, for he is a policeman. The goddess has trained her instrument Artegall to tame wild beasts; his control of Talus is a related skill. Artegall's training is our first indication that Spenser conceives of justice as the control of brute force, and the use of physical power: "For powre is the right hand of Iustice truely hight" (V.iv.1). The analogy with temperance is obvious, unconditioned impulse in Book II having the place of power without law in Book V. The individual's goal of achieving a temperate existence in the physical world corresponds to the justiciar's goal of securing of an orderly basis for life in society. Initially, the one requires willpower; the other, as Spenser conceives it, the will-to-power.

[ii]

A prominent function of the House of Holiness was the provision of loving care. Its affiliated institution, the Holy Hospital, especially had charge of the care and protection of the helpless and dependent. The conviction that the theological equivalent of such care is available to Redcrosse is crucial to the strengthening of the knight's faith. Una takes him to the House "to cherish him with diets daint, . . . where he chearen might" (I.x.2), and later she urges him, "Himselfe to chearish." We learn then that Charissa "late in child-bed brought / Was woxen strong" (I.x.29). We are told that Charissa eventually weans her nurslings ("But thrust them forth still, as they wexed old," I.x.31), but Spenser does not indicate who takes charge of them thereafter. Or perhaps he does.

---

[3] Frye, "Structure of Imagery," in *Fables of Identity*, p. 80, comparing *Par. Lost* XII.28off. (see l. 290, "Law can discover sin, but not remove"). Cf. Augustine, *Enchiridion*, cxvii: "the law can command, but it cannot assist; and moreover, it makes a man a transgressor, for he can no longer excuse himself on the plea of ignorance." Ruddymane is "born of woman, born under the law" (Gal. 4:4). My theological citations are corroborated by a second article of Alastair Fowler's, "The Image of Mortality: *The Faerie Queene*, II i–ii," *Huntington Library Quarterly*, 24 (1961), pp. 91–110; my text is independent of this article.

The next child we meet in the poem is the orphaned Ruddymane, whom the Palmer conveys to the care of Medina, the "golden Meane." This temperate householder stands for a measure between too much and too little; her "gouernaunce" especially appears at table. (An orphan, according to E. K., is "A youngling or pupill, that needeth a Tutour and gouernour.")[4] Students of child development explain that after a sense of security has been established, the will can be trained. If we were to put this relation in the terms of Spenser's first two books, we might say that prevenient grace precedes individual moral achievement.[5] Parental figures in this book are not so much trustworthy ministers who inspire love and reverence as judicious guides who help the hero mark out a course of action, like the Palmer; or monitory figures concerned with law and order, like the central sage in the advisory council at the Castle of Alma. The assistance that the Palmer renders with his staff differs from that rendered by the tree of life. The latter suggests sacramental ministration and the infusion of grace; the Palmer's powers derive from his wisdom, the kind of developed foresight and expertise that a pupil finds in a preceptor or mentor.

In contrast to Book I, where the hero's drive to victory is an essential aspect of that victory, there is a premium in Book II on resistance and restraint. In the sequel, in other words, the emphasis falls on consolidating or defending an achieved innocence. As Frye points out in this connection, the archetype is the installation of the divine victor in a dwelling-place—here, the human body, symbolized by the Castle of Alma.[6] The entry of the victorious virtues into the New Jerusalem at the end of the *Psychomachia* of Prudentius establishes this archetype for Christian allegory; a later example would be the lodgment of Christendom in the house called Unitas after the victory of Piers the Plowman. Similarly, in Guyon's own legend, the hero enters the Castle of Alma, or the temperate body, after the triumph of his continence over Mammon. We assume that it is continence, since he faints afterwards, implying a trial of the will, and the will's exhaustion; temperance proper would have had no occasion to faint.[7]

---

[4] E. K. on "Maye," l. 191.

[5] Not very different is found in Hough, *Preface to "The Faerie Queene,"* p. 234.

[6] Frye, *Anatomy of Criticism*, p. 101, and note on p. 361.

[7] *Nich. Ethics* VII.ix, 1152a. Cf. *The Courtier*, IV, sec. 17: "Continencie may be compared to a Captaine that fighteth many, and though his enimies bee strong and well appointed, yet giveth he them the overthrow, but for all that not without much ado and danger. But temperance free from all disquieting, is like the Captaine that without resistance overcommeth and raigneth. And having the mind where she is, not onely aswaged, but cleane quenched the fire of greedy desire, even as a good prince in civil warre dispatcheth the seditious inward enimies, and giveth the scepter and whole rule to reason." (Hoby trans., in *Three Renaissance Classics*, ed. Burton Milligan, New York, 1953, p. 554.) For the soul-battle in Book II, cf. Augustine, *Civ. Dei*, XIX.iv, on the part of virtue: "What is its occupation save to wage perpetual war with vices—not those that are outside of us, but within; not other men's, but

The psychological archetypes for the legend of temperance belong to the second Freudian phase, which is dominated by the mastering of bodily functions. The control of these functions bulks large as a model for the training of the will, especially as a model for "holding on" and "letting go."[8] The two foci for this larger polarity are the cave of Mammon and the Bower of Bliss. Each is presented as a temptation, representing the extremes of greed and prodigality, hoarding and "looseness" (or dissipation): an avarice of the spirit and the expense or squandering of it. Spenser indicates that we are to make this comparison by a number of symmetries. Each episode takes three days, and Vulcan, the Harpies, and Arachne lurk in the symbolism of both places.

In the antithesis between the cave and the Bower we meet one of the many versions of the myth of Scylla and Charybdis in this legend. The Virgilian allegorizer Landino explains Scylla as a delectable *luxuria* and Charybdis as an anxious avarice.[9] The Virgilian *Ciris* says that Scylla portrays "the sin of lustfulness and the incontinence of Venus" (ll. 69f.). Dante associates Charybdis with hoarding, and opposes hoarding to spending (*Inf.* VII.22–45). Spenser's own symbols include the Charybdis-like "Gulfe of Greedinesse," into which the "worldes prey" pours, in the way

---

our own—a war which is waged especially by that virtue which the Greeks call *sophrosunē*, and we temperance, and which bridles carnal lusts and prevents them from winning the consent of the spirit to wicked deeds?"

[8] Borrowing directly from Erikson, *Childhood and Society*, 2nd edn., p. 254.

[9] Landino, *Camuldulenses Quaestiones* (Venice, before 1500), fol. hi^v: Scylla and Charybdis are "two kinds of cupidity, the principal of which no one doubts to be *luxuria* and avarice," and so forth. So Baldwin, *Treatise of Moral Philosophy*, Vi.vii: "Abstinency and Continency are two forcible vertues against Avarice and Lechery, two capitall vices" (edn. of London, 1620, fol. 115^v), and likewise Elyot, *Gouernour*, III.xvii (Everyman's Library, p. 246). In Comes, *Mythol.*, VIII.xi, *edn. cit.*, pp. 870f., Scylla signifies voluptuousness: "Others suppose that this fable applies to moderation in expenditure." In the sequence of the capital sins at the House of Pride, Lechery and Avarice are paired at the center (I.iv.24ff.). The Gulf of Greediness and the covetous Whirlpool of decay are respectively paired with Rock of Reproach ("lustfull luxurie and thriftlesse wast," II.xii.9) and the quicksand of Unthriftyhead. The rock is otherwise the *scopulum* of a notable passage in Cicero, *De Oratore* III.xli.163, warning against far-fetched resemblances; in this case, figures for spendthrifts: "I might more readily have said, for 'the Syrtis of a patrimony,' *scopulum* [a rock in the sea], and for a 'Charybdis of goods,' *voraginem* [whirlpool]." Spenser also prefers the less express names. The Geneva Bible glosses the "fallen into Syrtes" of Acts 27:17, as "the goulf Syrtes, which were certeine boiling sandes that swallowed vp all that thei caught." The attempt of Spenser's sailors to save their rich ship (II.xii.19) may remind us of the same passage in the description of Paul's voyage. Otherwise a Syrtis is a sandbank, after those of that name off Northern Africa. In DuBartas' personification of the Furies assaulting human life, Avarice is described as venturing without a bridge "Through fell *Charybdis*, and false *Sertes* Nesse" (*Second Week*, Third Part of the First Day; Sylvester trans., l. 710): i.e., he is safe from extravagant expenditure.

that Mammon's wealth is poured down his hole. In the light of this theme it is structurally significant that at the center of his course Guyon passes from a "Scylla" of carelessness—namely Phedria—to a "Charybdis" of anxiousness for the morrow—namely the service of Mammon; the contrast goes back to linked verses in the Sermon on the Mount (Matt. 6:24ff.). Phedria counsels Guyon to consider the beauty of the lilies, and Mammon suggests that Guyon make the money-god his one master: "wage / Thy workes for wealth, and life for gold engage" (II.vii.18).[10] The two major temptations of the legend are also placed as Scylla and Charybdis in the canto scheme; midway between them Guyon visits the Castle of Alma, which maintains a mean position between cantos seven and twelve. Conformably, the Castle is assaulted by the engines of beauty and money (II.xi.9), each an appeal to the lust of the eyes.[11]

The familiar Freudian symbol of this phase is the child's training in cleanliness, an early model for orderliness in general.[12] In its broadest sense,

[10] For the observation of the Scriptural link between the two episodes, see Paul Alpers, *The Poetry of "The Faerie Queene"* (Princeton, 1968), pp. 254f.

[11] Mammon counts his money in order to "feede his eye / And couetous desire" (II.vii.4), as does Claudian's greedy Rufinus, who is drawn into temptation by a demonic show of gold: "Inlecebris capitur nimiumque elatus avaro / *pascitur* aspectu" (he is captivated by his senses, and thrilled beyond measure he feasts his greedy eye [*In Rufinum* I.165]). This feeding of appetite recurs in the Bower of Bliss: there Cymochles "his fraile eye with spoile of beautie feedes" (II.v.34); Acrasia's breast is exposed "to ready spoyle of hungry eies" (II.xii.78); and her "false eyes" are "fast fixed in his [Verdant's] sight . . . As . . . greedily *depasturing* delight" (II.xii.73). For lust-of-the-eyes in Mammon's realm, see below, "Journey Into the Interior," sec. i, on curiosity; for Acrasia, see Chap. IV, "Gardens of Pleasure," sec. iii. with n. 198.

[12] The metaphor of unwashed or unpurged soilure is found throughout the legend: the blood of Ruddymane's parents may be infected with "secret filth" (II.ii.4); Occasion is in "ragged robes and filthy disaray" (II.iv.4); Phedon is "all soild with bloud and mire" (II.iv.16); Love is a monster that breeds a filth that in turn is wiped away (II.iv.35); the "dull billowes" of the Idle Lake are "thicke as troubled mire" (II.vi.20); Pyrochles is unable to quench the flames that consume his "secret bowels" in this same "lake of mire" (II.vi.49, 44); Mammon's head and beard are covered with soot (II.vii.3); untroubled Nature is pure, but the branches beyond the source are annoyed by "mucky filth" (II.vii.15); Pilate's hands are "filthy feculent" and his soul "soyld with foul iniquitie" (II.vii.61f.); the Lord was enwombed "in fleshly slime . . . to purge away the guilt of sinfull crime" (II.x.50); the Castle of Alma is made of "Ægyptian slime" (II.ix.21); the unregenerate Grylle "delights in filth" (II.xii.139). For a comparison of Pilate and Grylle a basis may be found in Plotinus on the subject of purificatory initiation: "in the mysteries it is suggested that the unpurified soul, even in Hades, will still be immersed in filth because the unpurified loves filth for filth's sake quite as swine, foul of body, find their joy in foulness. For what is temperance, rightly so called, but to abstain from the pleasures of the body, to reject them as unclean and unworthy of the clean?" (Trans. Elmer O'Brien, *The Essential Plotinus*, New York, 1964, pp. 39f.) See n. 86, below, for further on this text, *Enn.* I, VI.6.

cleanliness is the discipline of distinguishing the virginal body from its polluting natural environment; cleanliness is thus an obvious symbol for moral purity or integrity, if in fact it is not an essential prototype for the idea.[13] We have mentioned the stainless character adopted by Diana's fountain-nymph; the washing of Ruddymane's hands, albeit unsuccessful, is part of the same complex. An ironic version of the nymph's well, where abandonment rather than resistance is celebrated, is the fountain at the Bower of Bliss, where we meet two salacious bathing beauties. The Ruddymane symbol is repeated in the underworld, where Pilate compulsively washes his "feculent" hands above the river Cocytus. Port Esquiline, the Roman dump, offers an apt analogy for this discipline with respect to the body politic.

These last examples correctly suggest that the *internal* environment may also become polluted. As we will learn in our discussion of the Cave of Mammon, temperance is traditionally classified as one of the "purgatorial" virtues; it is therefore an eliminative virtue too, and contrasts with the mud accumulating in the Idle Lake. The Freudian association of waste and lucre reminds us that this is the legend in which the money-god appears. One supposes that there is no possibility of a pun on Mammon's "silver stool," though the seat in question is a "stool of ease" in a general way, and Pilate is purging himself amid the stench of Cocytus nearby. Sitting is also related to thinking; as Swift writes in *Gulliver's Travels* (III.vi), "Men are never so serious, thoughtful, and intent, as when they are at stool." At any rate, one cannot avoid the comparison of the seat in Mammon's underworld with the seat to which the restless, preoccupied, and retentive Eumnestes is found attached.

Guyon leaves the Castle by an otherwise unmentioned waterway. Water is an important image of the relation of the person to the environment throughout this book, an environment that includes the interior conditions of the body. The surges of the deep over which Guyon voyages to the Bower seem to contain the trapped energies of dehumanized men. The four bodily humours are fluid in nature, and one of them is suggested in Guyon's enemy Cymochles ("disturbance of the wave"), a turbulent and dissolute character—phlegmatic types are sometimes reported as given to bodily pleasures.[14] The Idle Lake in which Cymochles becomes becalmed

[13] For the comparison of moral discipline and toilet training, see Robert Fliess, *Erogeneity and Libido* (New York, 1967), pp. 121–130, on the sphincter and morality.

[14] By Levinus Lemnius, for example, in his *Touchstone of Complexions*, trans. T. Newton, in the selection in James Winny, ed., *The Frame of Order* (New York, 1957), p. 41. According to Cicero, *Tusc. Disp.* IV.xxi.47f., *all* perturbations are violent: "perturbatio sit appetitus vehementior, vehementior autem intelligatur is, qui procul absit a naturae constantia." For further on the perturbations, see Cicero, *De Finibus* III.x.35, and Seneca, *De Ira* III.xiii.1. See note 142, *infra*.

is a kind of Dead Sea of sloth. Its sluggish humour is apparently in marked contrast to Phedria's little "skippet," which skims its surface. But as the mistress of this shallow craft becomes increasingly ribald, her buoyant hilarity exhibits the same passivity before the welter of experience as is found in the supine Cymochles. An earlier *bateau ivre*, the fantastical and euphoric boat of Spenser's pre-Atlantean witch seems to run with a with a will of its own, under no visible or conscious control.[15] One is meant to compare this skippet without a skipper to the craft piloted by the Palmer, where the steersman or helmsman is surely to be understood as reason. The boatman's oars methodically "sweepe the watery wilderness" (II.xii.23), and the steady and unrelenting tempo carries Guyon past a notably schematic series of distractions to his assignation.[16] The second journey seems to symbolize a will to organize physical energy, rather than merely yield to it. The perils and distractions are orderly because the mind that scans and reviews them is now orderly also.

The physical basis for the practice of temperance by no means exhausts the psychogenic data offered by Book II, especially since physical control is closely related to emotional control in this phase of development. It is not only the presence of a character like Pyrochles in this legend that causes one to remark its emotionality; the age of the overall persona might

---

[15] For the lineage of Shelley's wizard maid, cf. *Witch of Atlas*, l. 453, with *L'Allegro*, ll. 26–28, and *F.Q.* II.vi.6f., 21. (I assume that an "Inland" or Mediterranean Sea may also be Atlantic; sunken Atlantis, according to Plato, *Critias* 108e, "is the source of the impassable mud which prevents navigators from this quarter from advancing through the straits into the open ocean.")

[16] Cf. Bruno's conceit in *Heroic Frenzies*, I.i: the captain Will, using the rudder of Reason at the stern of the soul, governs "the affections of the interior potencies against the surges of their natural violence." For the Palmer as Hermes, and therefore Reason, see n. 72, below. Hermes appears as a soul-guide to the otherworld at the end of both Homeric poems; note also the vaguely Charonic overtone of Spenser's nameless Ferryman. The rationalization of *travel* is important here. By definition the Palmer is one who has traveled before, and Guyon's voyages themselves evince a quasi-generic relation to the literature of travel and travelers' tales. They also suggest that Italianation of the Englishman in the Circean settings deplored by Ascham at the end of the first book of *The Scholemaster*. In the same place Ascham complains about the invasion of England by Italian books, which would be likely to include the Boccaccian "merry tales" favored by the ribald Phedria. Her "Gondolay" riding on the inland sea recalls Venice, and the arts of her mistress Acrasia suggest that "*Italy* the Paradice of the earth, and the Epicures heaven," which "maketh a man an excellent Courtier, a curious carpet knight: which is, by interpretation, a fine close lecher" (so Thomas Nashe, in *The Unfortunate Traveller*, chap. ix). For the theme, see Martha Craig, "The Secret Wit of Spenser's Language," in Paul Alpers, ed., *Elizabethan Poetry: Modern Essays in Criticism* (New York, 1967), pp. 464f.

seem to be about two-and-a-half. A child of this age is notably inflexible, and seems to love to resist. Ruddymane's stain—orneriness—exhibits this stubborn streak, and Guyon's legend repeatedly illustrates the maxim that all growth takes place in a resisting medium. Muscles are hardened by exercise and strain, movement entails conflict and friction, and intellectual growth results from the effort of study. Accomplishment is proportional to such effort; drifting ends in stultification, inanition, and flaccidity.

The temperament of the two-and-a-half year old offers other clues to the theme of Book II. This child insists on having things in their proper places, a need reflected in the frequent motif of orientation in this legend. The same child becomes addicted to rigid sequences of events, from which he does not easily tolerate deviation; repetition is a marked feature of the Maleger and Mammon episodes, and compulsive reiteration especially appears in Pilate. The child's decision to do something himself, once made, seems irreversible, no matter how much beyond him a given task may prove; the Mammon and Pyrochles episodes supply two very different examples of willful perseveration—the child wants to go on and on with whatever he is doing, we are told. It may be added that the child of this age cannot wait; two characters in this legend are Impatience and Maleger, or Evil Eagerness.

Perhaps the chief feature of the emotional life of the two-and-a-half year old is its lack of modulation, reflected in Book II by the number of extremes that so badly want a mean: "it is an age of opposite extremes. With no ability to choose between alternatives, the child of this age shuttles back and forth endlessly between any two extremes, seeming to be trying to include both in his decision."[17] The part of the parent is clear: to get the child past such choices, to avoid their arising, to distract the child's attention from things he cannot presently have or do, and to provide transitions. And the parent must frequently humor the child, substituting his own affect for the "moods" or modulations that the child himself is unable to generate; in the following legend such self-generated moods will figure prominently as emotional buffers. In Book II the banter of Phedria and the reasoning of Medina mediate such transitions.

Naturally the most important modulation of extremes centers on the symbolism of the golden mean. Observing it is a matter of balance, equanimity, and keeping on an even keel. The association of this mean with sailing is both Aristotelean (*Nich. Ethics* II.ix), and Horatian:

---

[17] This description of the two-and-a-half year old may require little authority beyond a parent's experience; however, my quotations are taken from Francis L. Ilg and Louise Bates Ames, *Child Psychology* (New York, 1966), p. 26. I owe the homily on resistance to Ernest A. Fitzgerald, in an article, "Chased by Your Own Heartbeat," in *Pace: The Inflight Magazine of Piedmont Airlines*, vol. 2, no. 3 (1975), p. 26.

Rectius vives, Licini, neque altum
semper urgendo neque, dum procellas
cautus horrescis, nimium premendo
    litus iniquum.

Auream quisquis mediocritatem
diligit tutus, caret obsoleti
sordibus tecti, caret invidenda
    sobrius aula.

You shall live better, Licinius, by neither always tempting the deep; nor, while you cautiously dread the storms, by too much pressing on the dangerous shore.

Whoever chooses the golden mean, being safe, he is free from the sordidness of a poor house; being sober-minded, he is free from a mansion which is envied.

(*Odes* II.10)[18]

With its potential for symmetry, the theme of Scylla and Charybdis proves a natural one for Spenser, and he handles it with the requisite poise and address. Extremes of carelessness and care are represented in Mordant and Amavia. The manic and morose are contrasted in Sansloi and Huddibras: the unruly Sansloi is the outrageous "wild boy," or rakehell; the brassbound Huddibras is the "tough hombre," an overbearing and inhibited sourpuss, in contrast to his anarchically disposed opposite. Shakespeare characterizes Hotspur and Glendower as two such humours, in a memorable confrontation,[19] and Samuel Butler denominates the Roundheads of his time as Sir Hudibras—one wonders if we are also to understand the unconstrained Cavaliers as Sansloi. The profligate and the penurious are opposed in Perissa and Elissa; and also, in the same pair, the promiscuous and the jealous. As this last suggests, the division extends to extroversion and introversion, self-abandon and self-torment, and slavish concupiscence and tyrannic irascibility. Sansloi and Huddibras are also choleric and melancholic, respectively, and they therefore introduce the theme of the balancing of the four humours in the well-tempered man.

Two of the humours are easily found in two of Guyon's enemies already mentioned, the choleric Pyrochles and the phlegmatic Cymochles, asso-

---

[18] There is a translation of this part of Horace's poem by Henry Howard, Earl of Surrey, in "Of thy life Thomas, this compass well mark" (in Gerald Bullet, ed., *Silver Poets of the Sixteenth Century*, p. 139). For the image of the steady ship in Book II, see esp. II.ii.24 and II.xii.3.

[19] *The First Part of Henry IV*, III.i.5-138.

ciated respectively with fire and water. The ashen Maleger, Arthur's antagonist, is a son of the earth, and so he must be the corresponding spirit of melancholy; more technically, "melancholy adust." The melancholy complexion is cold and dry:

> As pale and wan as ashes was his looke,
>   His bodie leane and meagre as a rake,
>   And skin all withered like a dryed rooke,
>   Thereto as cold and drery as a Snake
>   That seem'd to tremble euermore, and quake:
>   (II.xi.22)

The earthbound snake is an apt image for Maleger, as subsequent events bear out. A somewhat complicated piece of evidence for the identification of Maleger with melancholy is furnished by the nature of Phantastes. Outside the Castle of Alma, Maleger's besieging hosts make up a fantastic array; they seem, however, to be the reified forms of a somewhat overlapping collection of hybrids inside the forechamber of the brain, which is the study of Phantastes. There is a suggestion that Phantastes suffers from the hallucinations produced by the melancholic humour. The sage is "Of swarth complexion," "full of melancholy," and was born "When oblique *Saturne* sate in the house of agonyes" (II.ix.52). Perhaps the "agonyes" include the struggle with Maleger, who is certainly saturnine in some respects.

Guyon himself remains relatively sanguine in the face of these enemies; it may be that his blushing in the heart of the Castle is meant to indicate as much. The heart is the seat of the sanguine humour, and the scene of Guyon's self-recognition is set there. Guyon's susceptibility to the charms of the Bower also conforms to the lore of the sanguine complexion. Its element is air—temperate weather and fresh air are congenial to Guyon also (II.xii.51; see II.vii.66). His inner self, Shamefastness, blushes in the heart as well, and her flushed complexion, we are told, "became" her (II.ix.41).

While on the subject of the temperaments, we may add that Guyon's disposition is active. He is paired with the Palmer, who is dressed in black, "staid wisdom's hue";[20] contemplative natures tend to be pensive, melancholy or black bile being a possible pathological development of this tendency. We are not surprised to discover that Arthur's "other," Praysdesire, is also "Pensive," a point of some importance in what follows. Being "sad," the Palmer is opposed to the jocose Phedria, who is the contrasting *allegro* figure. Phedria's merrymaking and gamesomeness are intended to drive away the dullness over which she skims; she likes a

---

[20] *Il Penseroso*, l. 16.

good time, and this makes her a kind of Erasmian Folly, both heedless and hedonistic. Folly was a great humorist, and Phedria is humorous in a variety of senses too. Folly is a malapert wisdom; brazen Phedria is "brilliant" in the same saucy and impudent way.

The well-balanced temperament includes all the humours. There is some reason to believe that Spenser expects us to observe that the various corrupted humours and ruling passions are mortified by their contraries. Pyrochles dies distraught and even fearful, torn by "sad melancholy," hardly his usual state of mind (II.viii.50). Cymochles, on the other hand, dies in a manner more suited to the violent Pyrochles than to himself, though in fact his volatility is not especially new. Maleger, clearly out of his element, dies in the air, and his corpse is cast into a "standing lake," a symbol elsewhere associated with the sluggish phlegmatic humour (II.xi.46). The whole question of what constitutes an allegorical agent's "death" is raised here, and this legend throughout seems to raise questions about the phenomenology of allegory, and the effects of observing a phenomenon to be allegorical.

Maleger is not only a diseased humour—even if he began as that. He is also disease—the "evil of sickness"—itself. He specifically puts us in mind of Hercules' antagonist Antaeus; indeed, he cannot be defeated until Arthur himself has remembered Maleger's Antaeus-like origins. The older explanation of Antaeus makes him represent our contrary libido, and Maleger's twelve bands reflect this tradition. Comes' explanation gives the "physical" explanation that we should also expect of the Renaissance:

> [The fable] signifies, I believe, nothing other than the medical doctrine that it is necessary that contraries be cured by contraries, as the name Antaeus would seem to signify. . . . For when Hercules the sun comes up, the cold earth, which had been exhausted by the excessive heat, revives at the contact, wherefore [it is said] he calls back Antaeus to life itself. And so, therefore, we learn that a cooling medication is to be employed for a warm sickness [*callidis aegritudinibus*], but nonetheless not a violent one, lest it create an apostem on account of an antiperistasis [i.e., a suppurating abcess due to a resistance or reaction aroused by opposition or by the action of an opposite principle]. . . . For this is signified because this nearly extinct heat of the sun, touching the earth so much, revives: for by contraries the force of nature is vivified and stimulated. But not by the crushing weight of contraries.[21]

This physico-medical allegory may be original with Comes; it certainly fits Spenser's subject, though Spenser treats the earthborn giant as the

---

[21] *Mythol.*, VII.i, "De Hercule"; *edn. cit.*, p. 682.

disease, rather than the patient. The danger Comes warns of—an adverse reaction to a too violent application of a contrary—is perhaps exemplified in the various upsets mentioned below. The best example is the "fit" of Guyon, brought on by too sudden an exposure to fresh air after his three days in the earth.

[iii]

At the typical locus of recognition, Spenser's knight meets an analogy for the lady he serves, and she symbolizes the animus—or rather the *anima*—for the quest he follows. Guyon is fairly unique among his peers in not having a lady; his virtue is almost too "private" for that. Nonetheless, at the Castle of Alma Guyon pays court to his "interior paramour."[22] She is Shamefastness by name, and we could characterize her as self-consciousness itself.

And what, one may ask, is threatened with "shame"? In the context of temperance, the answer seems to be personal autonomy. This answer puts the theme of self-mastery in what must have been its original context, motor and muscular control. Guyon is said to possess a pedestrian virtue,[23] and hence he goes on foot (at least between cantos three and eight). A more pedestrian explanation is that temperance, understood as the whole discipline of self-reliance, means learning to stand on one's own two feet. Some support for this explanation comes from Guyon's endurance test in the underworld, where he is on his feet for three days. At the end of this time Guyon faints, and Spenser mentions "food, and sleepe" as the two pillars that bear up man's life (II.vii.65); Belphoebe is also supported by "two faire marble pillours" (II.iii.28). Like Virgil's Venus, Belphoebe is identified by her "stately portance" (II.iii.21). The fear of being "overthrown" by the various enemies of temperance might also be adduced here (see II.iv.8, v.15, xi.29, 35). Guyon, unhorsed by Britomart at the opening of Book III, wants to fight on foot (III.i.9). A fiend follows the hero through the underworld, while Mammon attempts "to doe him deadly fall"; the fiend's counterpart at the Bower of Bliss is an evil genius "That secretly doth vs procure to fall" (II.vii.64; xii.48). "Fall" is a technical term in wrestling, and the echoes of the Antaeus myth in the Maleger episode make Arthur's antagonist another character who seeks the fall of the heroic persona, through his own fall. Even the bathing beauties wrestle (II.xii.63).

[22] See the title of a poem by Wallace Stevens, "Final Soliloquy of the Interior Paramour," in *Collected Poems* (New York, 1954), p. 524.

[23] That Guyon's virtue is pedestrian appears in C. S. Lewis, *Allegory of Love*, p. 338, and Frye, "Structure of Imagery," in *Fables of Identity*, p. 75. My own interpretation derives from Erikson, *Childhood and Society*, 2nd edn., p. 85.

The analogy between Guyon's fall and Arthur's is indicated by a feature of the Antaeus story that appears to have been displaced from Arthur to Guyon. After conquering Antaeus, Hercules lay down exhausted; then, as we may learn from the sequel in Philostratus' *Imagines*, the hero was set upon by the Pygmies, who wanted to avenge the dead and withered Antaeus. To this curious anticipation of the scene at the opening of *Gulliver's Travels*, Philostratus adds that "Sleep himself stands over him in visible form, making much, I think, of his own part in the fall of Hercules."[24] Somewhat similarly, Pyrochles and Cymochles attack the body of the prostrate Guyon. The allusion to the Antaeus myth, then, obtains for more than the Maleger episode. Its evocation at the end of Guyon's temptation shows that Spenser probably knew the comparison, traditional long before Milton took it up in *Paradise Regained*, of the three temptations to the three falls of a Herculean wrestling match.[25]

Temperance, in observing the mean, requires steadiness: "goodly carriage" and an "euen hand" (II.ii.38, xii.18), or motor skills. The animal body, like the "nimble" boats with their "gate" (II.vi.20, xii.38; xii.17), is a vehicle in its own right. Indeed, the psychogenic basis for the very broad reflection upon human freedom contained in Book II must be found in Guyon's ambulatory mode, freedom and independence being first experienced in learning how to stand and walk. The theme is greatly extended by the motifs of travel and vagabondage in this legend.

The examples of orientation and disorientation in physical space go much beyond a character's occasionally losing his footing or balance. The defiance or unreliability of normal physical laws is repeatedly suggested by images like the wandering islands, the quicksand of unthriftihood, the water of the Idle Lake in which things do not sink, the compulsion exerted

---

[24] *Imagines* II.22; cf. Alciati, Emb. LVIII (Antwerp edn., 1581), pp. 232ff., "In eos qui supra vires quicquam audent." (Alciati places the scene after the labor of the Nemean lion.) Although Spenser does not draw attention to it, Arthur and Guyon are lilliputian in relation to the Castle of Alma.

[25] For the three temptations as three falls inflicted on Satan by Christ the wrestler, see Chrysostom, *Hom.* XIII, on Matt. 4:1 ("Just so do wrestlers . . . they voluntarily in the lists engage with others, to afford these in the persons of their antagonists the means of seeing and learning the mode of conquest. . . . So He dashed him to earth, once, twice, three times"); Sedulius, *Carmen Paschale*, II.198–200 ("Defeated [Satan] dares to wage war with fragile man, rising three times to be thrown"); Aquinas, *Catena Aurea, Comm. on the Four Gospels, St. Luke* (Oxford, 1843) Pt. I (= vol. 3), p. 151, citing Gregory of Nyssa ("In lawful contests the battle is terminated when the adversary . . . is defeated in three falls, according to the rules of the art of fighting"—explaining why the temptations in Luke 4:13 are *completed*). I have not found such a place in Gregory. On Luke 4:9 (*Catena Aurea*, p. 150), Aquinas quotes Origen: "He followed evidently as a wrestler, gladly setting out to meet the temptation." For the arts of argument as involving three falls, see Plato, *Euthydemus* 277d, with *Theaetetus* 169b (where Antaeus is instanced).

by Magnes' stone, the fruit and drink that elude the grasp of Tantalus, and the non-engagement of Arthur with the vacuous Maleger. The allegory of Phedria's boat implies a fit of the giggles, or some such prelude to illecebrous behaviour that a distracting hilarity might invite; but there is also simply the threat here of a loss of physical coordinates, of warping perimeters and drifting parameters—the kind of thing we suspend in the fun-house or on the rides in an amusement park. There is also the implication of drunkenness in the collapse of Mordant. The affluence of Acrasia's garden, the various images of excess as physical superfluity, of idleness as a spreading stagnation, of distress as an experience of voidness, and the number of characters dissolved in grief or pleasure, or consumed with wrath—all express the sense of the person proper as occupying a narrow margin between two physical environments in which his own identity might easily be lost.

One form of autonomy that can be shamed in this legend is emotional integration. Spenser's Pyrochles-Furor complex is a minor masterpiece describing its deterioration. Pyrochles—who enlarges Furor and only seeks Occasion—is a kind of tantrum going somewhere to happen. He represents the choleric or fiery man, and Furor also has a choleric complexion. But as in Maleger, there is something larger in Pyrochles—as if he were a Senecan treatment of one of the four horsemen of the Apocalypse: "And there went out another horse that was red: and power was given to him that sate thereon, to take peace from the earth and that they shulde kill one another, and there was given unto him a great sworde" (Rev. 6:4, Geneva Bible). Pyrochles also gets hold of a great sword, to which we will recur. As the *Aeneid* says, "furor arma ministrat" (I.50).

Temperance is a classical virtue, and the classical ideal of restraint is surely to be understood in relation to the classical epics, which are—as Milton's criticism implies—so much under the wrath.[26] Some of the classical material may be brought to bear on the episodes in question. Anger was traditionally described as a short madness, *furor brevis*:[27] Furor, "A mad man, or that feigned mad to bee" (II.iv.3), drags his victims through the dirt, as the possessed Achilles outraged the corpse of Hector. Pyrochles' possible link with Achilles has been suggested by Hamilton, and the idea is worth pursuing.[28] There is a good deal to connect Achilles with

[26] My account is heavily influenced by Hamilton, *Structure of Allegory*, pp. 116–120, who cites the invocation of Book IX of *Paradise Lost*.

[27] Horace, *Epist.* I.ii.62: *Ira est furor brevis*; Petrarch, *Canz.* CCXXXII: "Ira è breve furore e, chi no 'l frena, / È furor lungo" (Wrath is a brief fury, and for one who does not refrain from it, it's a long fury).

[28] Hamilton, *Structure of Allegory*, pp. 117f.

fire. The *Argonautica* (IV.865f.) records that Thetis nightly surrounded her infant son with fire; she ceased only when discovered by Peleus, who pulled the child out. Both Achilles' wife and son can be called Pyrrhus, and Comes records the tradition that Achilles himself was first called Pyrisous, "saved from the fire."[29] Deidamia, on this account, called the son whom Achilles sired on her Pyrrhus. When Achilles is at the height of his furor in the *Iliad* he enters the river Scamander, and he is in danger of drowning; the revolted river, "muttering in foam and blood and dead bodies," rises against him (*Il.* XXI.325). The timely intervention of the armor-maker Hephaistos, who sets an "inhuman fire" on the waters, blasts the river's strength, allowing Achilles to escape. It is hard not to think of Pyrochles—a despoiler of corpses and a seeker of revenge—trying to extinguish his fires in the glutted Idle Lake, where he thrashes, as Archimago says, "In daunger rather to be drent, then brent" (II.vi.49). He has been set on fire by Furor, and has thus become like him, for Furor, according to Cartari's handbook of images, is nothing other than wrath enflamed.[30] Archimago is able to save the degenerating situation; but not for long. He disarms Pyrochles, and then unintentionally supplies him with the sword of Arthur. The sword was forged in the flames of Aetna, like the sword of Turnus; it was dipped in the waters of Styx, like Achilles himself (*Aen.* XII.90; II.viii.20). Inadvertently, these allusions might tell us, Archimago has armed Pyrochles for his last battle. Pyrochles cannot control the sword, because he cannot control himself.

The son of Achilles, Pyrrhus, is also a part of the classical subject of epic wrath. Like that of Pyrochles, the approach of Pyrrhus is terrible. In the second book of the *Aeneid*, Pyrrhus perpetuates the bloodlust of his father, and Virgil makes him a degraded Achilles. In Seneca's *Troades* he calls for the murder of Polyxena to satisfy his father's ghost, and Agamemnon's counsel of restraint falls on deaf ears. Agamemnon's description of the effects of the conquest of Troy are in Pyrochles' vein: "But wrath, the fiery foeman, victory given to the night's charge, they cannot be kept in check" (Sed regi frenis nequit / et ira et ardens hostis et victoria / commissa noctis). He goes on to explain the Greek barbarity to have been wrought by resentment and darkness, "whereby fury itself is spurred on, and the successful sword, whose lust, once stained [with blood], is madness" (hoc fecit dolor / tenebraeque, per quas ipse se irritat furor / gladiusque felix, cuius infecti semel vecors libido est [279–285]). In the *Aeneid* the hero is told he will have to face yet another Achilles, namely Turnus, whose furor is inspired by Allecto, as Spenser's Furor is

[29] For Pyrrha as Achilles' wife, see Heliodorus, *Ethiopica*, III (in Rev. Roland Smith, trans., *The Greek Romances*, London, 1882, pp. 63f.). For Pyrisous, Comes, *Mythol.*, IX.xii, "De Achille," *edn. cit.*, p. 989.

[30] *Le Imagini* (Venice, 1625), p. 292.

THE ANATOMY OF TEMPERANCE

ignited by Occasion (cf. *Aen.* VII.456-457, with II.v.22; besides the torch, there is the old woman's shape and the goad). Turnus' name, according to Fulgentius, means wrath—Aeneas' own wrath, which the hero must conquer in himself.[31] Turnus also jumps into a river (*Aen.* IX.1085ff.), and one may find anticipations of Pyrochles' seizures in Turnus' working himself up for his *finale*: "his agitur furiis, totque ardentis ab ore scintillae absistunt, oculis micat acribus ignis" (such is the frenzy driving him: from all his face shoot fiery sparks; his eager eyes flash flame [*Aen.* XII.101–102]). He is like a bull before battle, arousing a fearful bellowing, "and essaying to throw wrath into his horns, charges a tree-trunk; . . . ventosque lacessit ictibus aut sparsa ad pugnam proludit harena" (He lashes the winds with his blows, and paws the sand in prelude for the fray [XII. 105-106]). Completing this pattern of associations, Pyrochles dies with a phrase of the dying Turnus—"vse thy fortune," *utere sorte tua* (*Aen.* XII.932; *F.Q.* II.viii.52; cf. stanza 45 with *Aen.* XII.952). The Renaissance reader would have heard this, as he heard Ariosto's allusion to the same death at the end of the *Furioso*.[32]

One other association of Pyrochles may be mentioned. The pagan is said to be the grandson of Phlegethon, and the rivers of hell were sometimes taken for types of the painful and distressful passions. Thus Pyrochles complains that he is consumed: the damned ghost "In flaming Phlegeton does not so felly rost" (II.vi.50). The player's Pyrrhus in *Hamlet* is "roasted in wrath and fire" (II.ii.472), and the violent in Dante's *Inferno*, immersed in Phlegethon, include a Pyrrhus—either this one or a descendant with a similar reputation. Dante's Cocytus, according to Macrobius the river of "what moves us to lamentation and tears," has Judas at its center, and Spenser's Cocytus has Pilate.[33] A similar allegory attached the four cardinal virtues to the four rivers of paradise. It has been suggested that Guyon's name derives from this tradition, which identifies the river Gihon with the virtue of temperance.[34]

[31] *Virgiliana Continentia*, in R. Helm, *Fvlgentivs. Opera*, p. 105.

[32] Williams, *Theory of the Heroic Epic in Italian Criticism* (Baltimore, 1917), p. 11, citing Pigna, *I romanzi*, p. 78. In making the case for a more or less Aristotelian *Furioso*, Pigna notes two pages later that Ariosto begins with an echo of the first line of the *Iliad* and ends with a conclusion like that of the *Aeneid*. This second observation is found in many of the equipped Ariostos, including that of Harington.

[33] Macrobius, *Comm. in Somn. Scip.*, I.x.11. Dante's Satan weeps in Cocytus, and the souls in Spenser's "sad waves" make the shore resound with their "piteous cryes" (II.vii.57); their sight is "ruefull." For a diagram relating the four infernal rivers to the four humours (choler = Phlegethon), see Cornelius Agrippa, *Three Books of Occult Philosophy*, II.vii (London, 1645), pp. 186f. For the bodily channels as rivers cut through a garden, see Plato, *Timaeus* 77c.

[34] The suggestion is Alastair Fowler's, in "The River Guyon," *MLN*, 75 (1960), pp. 289-292. The allegory is as old as Philo, *Questions and Answers on Genesis*, I.12 (in Loeb edn., supp., vol. 1, p. 8). It appears in Ambrose, *De Paradis.*, iii.16; Greg-

This essay began with a brief discussion of the washing of Ruddymane, and we may conclude by noting that the waters of his "font" are logically "Gihonic" also. In Hebrew the word *gihon* simply means "to burst forth," and this etymology is relevant to the occurrences in the Ruddymane episode: Amavia's outburst, the gushing forth of her blood, Guyon's stopping of its "floudgates," the drops congealed in her eyes, the sympathetic tears that rise up in Guyon, and the lachrymous bubbling of the fountain itself, "Welling out streams of tears" (II.ii.8). The name of the river of paradise indicates that "it is always troubled," according to *Mandeville's Travels*, "and Gihon in the language of Ethiopia is to say 'troubled' and in the language of Egypt also."[35] This same river, according to Mandeville, issues in a well under an altar near the sepulchre of Our Lady, just outside of Jerusalem.[36] The Palmer, who elaborates upon the properties and secret virtues infused into such waters, is one who has been to Jerusalem, and therefore he is surely also acquainted with the waters of Siloe that appear in Isaiah 8:6 and John 9:7. Siloe is the place where Jesus tells the man born blind to wash himself, and it is offered by Spenser as a type for the well of life in Book I: it can "the guilt of sinfull crimes cleane wash away," and Redcrosse is accordingly steeped in it (I.xi.30f.). The man born blind also raises theological questions of the kind that are suggested by the stained Ruddymane: "who did sinne, this man, or his parents?" the Apostles ask (John 9:2f.). Jesus answers that neither did, and the Palmer will assert Amavia's innocence too (II.ii.10).

Spenser's virginal fountain is "Shapt like a maid, that such ye may her know" (II.ii.9), and the water supply for Jerusalem is the well just mentioned, which came to be known as the Virgin's Spring; according to Baedeker, "The name is derived from a legend of the fourteenth century to the effect that the Virgin once drew water or washed the swaddling-clothes of her Son here."[37] This spring may be a precursor for the *natatorium* of Ruddymane. The same waters are apparently those tapped for Hezekiah's waterworks in Jerusalem. The Geneva gloss on a text where the project is given notice—II Chronicles 32:30—identifies these waters with the Siloe of the Gospel. The text itself, however, calls them Gihon.

---

ory, *Moral.*, II.xlix.76; and Augustine, *De Gen. contra Manich.*, II.x.13 (here it is the Tigris that stands for temperance).

[35] *Mandeville's Travels*, ed. M. C. Seymour, World's Classics (Oxford, 1968), chap. 33, p. 235.

[36] *Ibid.*, chap. 11, p. 72.

[37] Karl Baedeker, *Palestine and Syria*, 4th edn. (Leipzig, 1906), p. 82. For further on these links, see *Encyclopedia Biblica*, ed. Cheyne and Black (New York, 1901), *sub* En-rogal, Gihon, Jerusalem, and Siloe. For the legend, cf. Palestine Pilgrims' Text Society's Library, 13 vols.: vol. 8: *Wanderings of Felix Fabri*, vol. 1, pt. 2 (London, 1897), pp. 525–533; vol. 6: *Guide-Book to Palestine* (ca. 1350) (London, 1894), pp. 14f.

No less matter of argumentacion ministereth the qualitie of time, which signifieth two thynges. First it is taken playnly for the time present, past, or to come: Second it signifieth opportunitie to a thynge, and so when a man cometh as wold haue it, we say he cometh in time. And in the seuenth of Ihon, when Christ sayth: My tyme is not yet come, tyme is taken for opportunitie of tyme. And lykewyse in the syxt to the Galat. Therfore whyle we haue tyme. &c. The Rhetoriciaes put chaunce under tyme, because the ende of a thynge perteyneth to the time that foloweth: bot of thys wyll we speke in the place called Euent.

  (Richard Sherry, *A treatise of Schemes & Tropes*, on the Aristotelean
  "predicament" time, one of the places of logical invention)

Time is that wherein there is opportunity, and opportunity is that wherein there is no great time.

                        (Hippocrates, *Praeceptione* I, *in init.*)

[i]

One further form of control deserves attention here. Our integrity may be symbolized in space by the coordinate body: the continent man, as we say, can pull himself together. In contrast, Pyrochles and Cymochles tend to reduce themselves in our minds to a human torch and a human slough. Their suicidal tendencies are pronounced, and that *memento mori* Maleger—who seems to acquire an identity as his victim loses one—looks very like the Spenserian version of the death-wish itself. The opposite will is simply the will to live, which we first meet in Amavia, who "loues to liue" (II.i.55). Her care for life includes the rescue of her husband from intemperance; but Mordant's name indicates that he also stands for man in his aspect of a dying animal, and his demise causes his wife's suicide. She loses her will to live.

The maintenance of a continuous identity through time is a larger theme than temperance, but in Spenser this legend supplies the model. Such routines as eating and sleeping are properly governed by temperance, but the whole ordering of time belongs to it. Cicero may speak for the theory on which my commentary relies:

I have next to treat of order and opportunity in our actions (*de opportunitate temporum*). These two duties are comprehended in the science which the Greeks call *eutaxia*, not that which we translate "modestia," a term connoting "modus" or moderation, but that by which we understand the observance of order. Eutaxia in this sense which we may also call

305

"modestia," is defined by the Stoics as the science of accurately disposing our words and deeds. Thus order and disposition appear to have the same sense: for they define order as the disposition of things in their fit and proper places. By the place of an action they mean its fitness in point of time; it is called in Greek *eukairia*, in Latin *occasio*. Consequently, "modestia" in this sense is the science of doing the right thing at the right time. Prudence, of which I spoke at the outset, may also be defined in the same way: but it is self-command, temperance, and similar virtues that concern us here.[38]

The theme song of intemperance is *carpe diem*; the answering watchword is Claudian's *comprime motus*—"subdue occasion," as Elyot translates it.[39]

The control of time is a theme of wide application in Renaissance literature, of which the greatest hero says "The readiness is all." The overhasty Hotspur ends his life as "time's fool," while the carefully matured debut of Prince Hal "redeems the time." Satan in *Paradise Regained* urges the reluctant Christ that "Zeal and Duty are not slow, / But on Occasion's forelock watchful wait" (III.173–174), and he seems to have learned something from Christ's answer, "All things are best fulfill'd in their due time," when he later adds that "each act is rightliest done, / Not when it must, but when it may be best" (IV.475–476). Erasmus' famous essay in the *Adagia* calls *festina lente* (hasten slowly) the "royal" proverb and says that it enjoins the ruler in particular to "rightly combine promptness at the opportune moment with cautious deliberation."[40] Erasmus draws a contrast between the recalcitrance of Agamemnon ("no high deed or show of spirit is recorded of him except that he flew into a rage over the removal of Chryseis") and the "undisciplined impulses" of Achilles. Achilles and Agamemnon are the *bradeōs* and *speude* components of the proverb, Erasmus suggests. The same contrast is at work in Spenser's Huddibras—whose name sounds like the Greek phrase in reverse—and Sansloi. Like Agamemnon, Huddibras is "not so good of deedes, as great

[38] *De Officiis* I.40, trans. by George B. Gardiner, reprinted in Moses Hadas, ed., *Basic Works of Cicero* (New York, 1951), p. 54. Cf. Sir Thomas Elyot, *The Gouernour*, Everyman's Library (London, 1907), I.xxv, p. 106: "Modestie, whiche by Tulli is defined to be the knowledge of opportunitie of thinges to be done or spoken, in appoyntyng and settyng them in tyme or place to them conuenient and propre."

[39] Elyot, *Gouernour*, II.i, *edn. cit.*, p. 120. Quoted in Baldwin's *Treatise of Moral Philosophy* (London, 1620), fol. 55ʳ.

[40] Quotations are taken from Erasmus' article on this adage as translated by Margaret Mann Phillips, in *Erasmus on His Times* (Cambridge, 1967), pp. 3–17. For more on the virtue of maturity as an aspect of prudence, see Elyot, *Gouernour*, I.xxii, *edn. cit.*, pp. 97–99: maturity counsels to "spede the[e] slowly," and it is the "meane or mediocritie betwene slouthe and celeritie"—"do neyther to moche ne to litle, to soone ne to late, to swyftely nor slowely, but in due tyme and measure."

of name," and he seems incapacitated; like Achilles, Sansloi is "encouraged, / Through strong opinion of his matchlesse might," and needs restraining (II.ii.17–18). Medina in turn encourages Huddibras and assuages Sansloi (II.ii.38). "Some natures need the spur, others the rein," as Erasmus says of *festina* and *lente*: ". . . one must be tempered by the other."[41]

One meaning of temperance, then, is good timing—a meaning that its etymology will support. The porter at the Castle of Alma never rings his "larumbell" out of time (II.ix.25); he never sounds the alarm heedlessly, or speaks out of turn. Pyrochles seeks Occasion, but Guyon tempers his rashness with "aduizement *slow*" (II.v.13). We ought not be anxious for the morrow, Phedria alleges by the lilies in her defense of indolence (II.vi.16, Matt. 6:28); rather we should "Gather the Rose of loue, whilest yet is time" (II.xii.75). The same theme of controlling time also gives considerable prominence to the iconography of fortune in this legend. This includes the fortune of Mammon, which can purvey all necessities "in a twinckling of an eye" (II.vii.11), meaning in a "moment of time." Mammon's offer of his daughter Philotime in marriage is an offer of a quick way to success; her name, in this context, means something like "time-serving," or an infatuation with opportunity, as well as honors.

Comes identifies the golden chain that Spenser gives to Philotime with ambition,[42] and Spenser makes it symbolize the whole structure of "degree" as a form of compulsion:

> Those that were vp themselues, kept others low,
> Those that were low themselues, held others hard,
> Ne suffred them to rise or greater grow,
> But euery one did striue his fellow downe to throw.
>
> (II.vii.47)

Competition for a place is analyzed here with remarkable irony: every link of the chain is a "step of dignity," and the suitors are trying to advance themselves to "high degree" (II.vii.46f.); but, as Shakespeare's Ulysses observes in *Troilus and Cressida*, it is exactly this envious "emulation" that takes degree away (I.iii.102ff., esp. 127–134). Degree is "the

---

[41] Phillips, *Erasmus on His Times*, p. 17.

[42] *Mythol.*, II.iv, "De Iunone," *edn. cit.*, p. 139, frequently cited, following Charles Lemmi, "The Symbolism of the Classical Episodes in *The Faerie Queene*," *Philological Quarterly*, 8 (1929), p. 277. Lemmi, however, does not indicate the way in which the myth makes Philotime holding her golden fetters a Juno-figure: Zeus suspended the ambitious and rebellious Hera from heaven by the wrists *by means of a similar golden chain* (Comes, *Mythol.*, p. 135, quotes the account in *Iliad* XV.18–22). Juno's peacocks with their many eyes make her the tutelary goddess of riches (*Mythol.*, p. 138: "the proud are ambitious, desirous of arduous things, who have the goddess of riches as their patroness, for it is necessary that many men watch to guard their things").

ladder of all high designs," in Ulysses' rather ambiguous phrase, but the inordinate desire to excell that Spenser's lines describe is a Scholastic definition of pride,[43] and such a desire threatens to deprive degree of its very power to confer distinction and security: "euery one did striue his fellow downe to throw." Guyon's refusal of an "vnequall fate" (II.vii.50), on the other hand, maintains both degree and his own "tranquility of mind."

The same refusal also leaves Guyon free to act, and here the poet's anxious image of enthrallment might contain another meaning: it could signify a universal submission to fortune, as in the following passage from Seneca's famous essay, "On Tranquility of Mind":

> For we are all of us coupled by fortune, some of us have a golden and easie chaine, some a more base and sordide inthralment. But what skilleth it, what is it? all of us are environed with the same guard, and they that enchaine others are enchained themselves. It may be thou thinkest that the chain which is tied to the left arme waieth not so much as that on the right. Some are enthraled by their honours, othersome by their base estate. There are some made subiect to anothers emperie, others are vassals to themselves; there are some that are confined to one place, others that are arrested by those charges that are committed unto them. All our whole life is a servitude. . . .[44]

There is another analogy between Philotime and Fortune, for being an evil Prays-desire, Philotime can confer upon Guyon a reputation "for workes and merites iust" (II.vii.49): she can reward his virtue with worldly glory. And yet Guyon refuses this honor, presumably on grounds like those discussed in Montaigne's essay "Of Glory":

> Virtue is a very vain and frivolous thing if it derives its recommendation from glory. To no purpose should we undertake to have it keep its rank apart, and disjoin it from fortune: for what is there more fortuitous than reputation? *Truly Fortune rules in all things; she illumines or obscures all things according to her pleasure rather than the truth* [Sallust]. To make actions be known and seen is purely the work of fortune.[45]

The "darksome neather world" that dims Philotime's glory (II.vii.49) also obscures Guyon's virtue in resisting Mammon; his actions in the underworld remain unknown and unglorified among the other characters.

---

[43] The definition is reflected in Dante, *Purg.* XI.86f., XVII.115. See Aquinas, *Summa Theol.*, Pt. II, 1st Pt., q.84, art.2, resp.; also Augustine, *Civ. Dei*, XIV.xxviii, and Albertus Magnus, *In II Sent.*, dist. xlii, art.8.

[44] *De Tranq. Animae* X.3, trans. by Thomas Lodge, in Seneca, *The Workes both Morall and Natural* (London, 1614), p. 645. Spenser translates Seneca's title, ironically, in Amavia's suicide speech, I.i.47, "soules tranquilitee." (It is also a Latin title for an essay in Plutarch's *Moralia*.)

[45] *Essais*, II.xii, trans. Donald Frame, *Complete Essays of Montaigne* (Stanford, Calif., 1965), p. 470.

There are other examples of Fortune's power in Book II. Consider, for example, the following speech of Phedria, in which the lazy girl urges patience to the restless Guyon, during a moment of becalmment:

> Faire Sir (quoth she) be not displeased at all;
> Who fares on sea, may not commaund his way,
> Ne wind and weather at his pleasure call:
> The sea is wide, and easie for to stray;
> The wind vnstable, and doth neuer stay.
>
> (II.vi.23)

Like the golden chain from Seneca, this imagery serves to raise the whole question of man's control over his circumstances, and by implication it denies him any power to assert his will over his fortunes. This becomes more obvious when we think of Phedria not as a siren, but as a *Fortuna* figure.

The evidence that Fortune is a mariner must go back to the idea that fortunes are made and lost at sea, and the idea that the sea is especially hazardous. An important witness is Boethius' *Consolation of Philosophy*, from which it might be deduced, in the words of H. R. Patch, that "Life is . . . a sea of trouble stirred up by Fortuna, and with our light skiff we venture on its waves."[46] Cartari and Giraldus, ignoring this medieval literary tradition, felt that the image of Fortune had taken a novel form in their own times: "Among all the drawings done of Fortune," reports Cartari, "up until now I find none which depict her on the sea sailing between troubled waves: and none which put her on the pinnacle of a high rock, turning with the winds. I think these paintings are modern, because I do not find anything like them mentioned in the ancients, as Giraldi has likewise said."[47] Fortune's light skiff and Fortune-driven sails (related to the windturned Fortune) are both tropes known to the *romanzi*. Boiardo's Elidonia, for example, abandoned the sail of her *navicella* to fortune (*Orl. Inn.* II.i.7); likewise, the pilot of Ariosto's Astolfo

---

[46] H. R. Patch, *The Goddess Fortuna in Medieval Literature* (Cambridge, Mass., 1927), p. 101; see esp. n. 4. The crucial text is Boethius, *De Cons. Phil.* II, prose iv. Mignault, on Alciati's Embl. XCVIII ("Ars naturam adiuuans"), cites the oration *pro tas technas* ("On the Good Arts"), attributed to Galen or the orator Menodatus, for the image of inconstant Fortune as an agitated sea on which a ship tosses with the rudder entrusted to a blind pilot (*Emblemata*, Antwerp edn. of 1581, p. 347). Being a governor, Fortune is given a *gubernaculum* which may be either the handle of her wheel, or the rudder of a ship. See Giraldus, *Hist. Deorum*, Syntag. XVI, in *Op. om.*, I, col. 464A and 456D, citing Lactantius, *Divine Institutes*, III.29. See also Cicero, *De Off.* II.6.

[47] *Le Imagini* (edn. of Venice, 1625), p. 356. I have consulted, besides Patch, Alfred Doren, *Fortuna im Mittelalter und in der Renaissance*, Vorträge der Bibliothek Warburg, ed. Fritz Saxl, vol. 2, 1922–1923, I (Leipzig-Berlin, 1924), pp. 71–144; and Raimond van Marle, *Iconographie de L'Art Profane*, vol. 2, *Allégories et Symbols* (The Hague, 1932), pp. 181–202.

was forced to adapt the course of his bark to the direction in which fortune sped it (*O.F.* XXII.7ff.). A positive example is found in a context
Spenser knew well, the episode of the conveyance of the Christian soldiers
who retrieve Tasso's Rinaldo. The soldiers are specifically called "for-
tunati" (*Ger. Lib.* XV.6), and they are borne to the Fortunate Isles. The
mysterious pilot who provides their transportation over the main wears
her hair in the manner indicated below for Fortuna and Occasio, and she
is dressed in the changeable colors one also finds in Boiardo's Occasio
figure, Morgana (*Orl. Inn.* II.viii.43). Her forelock is not only Occasio's,
but also Fortune's, according to a frequent trope in Ariosto. Her multi-
colored garment is found in Boccaccio and the *Romance of the Rose.*[48]

We read that one Giovanni Rucellai "had an effigy of Fortuna placed
on the arch of his new residence in Florence; a tutelary nymph is seen
steering the boat through perilous seas. In the boat are two figures personi-
fying Virtue (i.e. valor and skill) and Prudentia, signifying a challenge
to the vagaries of chance."[49] This voyage is close to the one in Spenser,
except for the pointed absence in Phedria's boat of the Palmer (the Prudence figure) and a "heedfull Boateman" (a Virtue figure).

The emblem of a ship under the pilotage of a fortune-daemon takes
many forms. The two that are most relevant to the Phedria episode are
the depiction of Fortune with one foot on shore and one foot in the boat,
and the emblem of Fortune herself blowing the wind that fills the sail she
holds.[50] We catch sight of the former image of Fortune's instability in

[48] Boccaccio, *De Casibus,* III.i, VI.i; *Romance of the Rose,* ll. 6146ff. For an illustration, see André Chastel, *The Myth of the Renaissance,* trans. Stuart Gilbert (Skira,
Geneva, 1969), p. 6, which reproduces in color the frontispiece by Jean Fouquet for
a ms. of Martin Le Franc's *L'Estrif de Vertue et de Fortune.* For Fortune as doing
a man a favor in taking him off the sea, and confining him to an island, see Plutarch,
De Exilo, Moralia 603E.

[49] Chastel, *Myth of the Renaissance,* p. 11. For the opposition of Fortune and
Prudence or Virtue, see Lactantius, *Div. Inst.,* III.29, citing Perseus, *Sat.* X.365.
See Mario Santoro, *Fortuna, ragione e prudenza nella civiltà letteraria del Cinque-
cento* (Naples, 1967), p. 7, on their rapport; and Klaus Heitmann, *Fortuna und
Virtus. Ein Studie zu Petrarcas Lebensweisheit* (Cologne, 1957). For a medal on
the theme, see George Francis Hill, *Medals of the Renaissance* (Oxford, 1920), Plate
XXIII, no. 5, "Virtute et Constancia," showing the typical Fortuna-figure with her
sail, standing on a ball-like shell in the middle of the sea.

[50] Doren, *Fortuna im Mittelalter, loc. cit.,* pp. 120ff. and 136f.; van Marle, *Iconographie,* vol. 2, p. 188, fig. 213, figure from the Siena Cathedral pavement. For Fortune
with her foot on the world-ball and with a rudder, fig. 215, engraving of Nicoletta
of Modena. Alciati's emblem shows Fortune with one foot on the ball, on land, and
one out of view, beyond which we see a ship on the sea. "Lymage de Fortune," in
Gilles Corrozet, *Hecatongraphie* (Paris, 1543), fol. vii[b], shows Fortune standing on
a globe and a dolphin in the sea. For Fortune blowing her own sail, see Wind,
Pagan Mysteries, plate 48, reproducing a drawing attributed to Peter Vischer the
Younger; and cf. G. F. Hill, *A Corpus of Italian Medals* (London, 1930), nos. 958,

Guyon's hesitation between land and sea, when the Palmer gets left behind. The latter image might lead us toward the autonomy of Phedria's craft, but its implications are really almost the opposite. This becomes clear when we find a man, or "self," controlling the sail: the image then suggests virtue and the ability to dominate fortune. Phedria's craft, although it seems footloose and fancy-free, is beyond control, and thus not really an image of freedom at all; a free will is a directed one. We are seeing precisely the free conception being asserted over the slavish conception when Guyon's boatman in the last canto manfully exerts himself to avoid the whirlpool of decay, "Whose circled waters rapt with whirling sway, / Like to a restlesse wheele, still running round" (II.xii.20). Guyon's second voyage vindicates the power of the temperate will to avoid being wholly determined by the turning of the restless wheel of the medieval Fortune.

[ii]

Those who catch hold of Philotime's golden chain present a sinister version of taking Time or Occasion or Fortune by the forelock. Cartari's article on Fortune explores this iconography fully; he refers us to two examples that touch on Spenser's overall presentation. One is an epigram of Ausonius that gave to the statue of Occasio a companion, namely *Paenitentia*; the onlooker asks,

"Who is she who bears thee company?" "Let her tell thee." "Tell me, I beg, who thou art." "I am a goddess to whom not even Cicero himself gave a name. I am a goddess who exacts penalties for what is done and what undone, to cause repentance. So I am called *Metanoea* [change of mind]."

The speaker turns again to Occasio:

"Do thou now tell me what does she along with thee?" "When I have flown away, she remains: she is retained by those I have passed by. Thou also whilst thou keepest asking, whilst thou tarriest with questioning wilt say that I have slipped away out of thy hands."[51]

968, 981, 993, 1027, 1065, 1070, 1071. In some examples of the type, Fortune's ball is in the sea, and her sail does double duty as her billowing scarf. There are hints of Venus anadyomene in the figure. Cf. also Hill, *Corpus*, no. 532, where the Fortuna-figure has Occasio's hair, a wind-borne scarf, and stands on a broken wheel; and the synthetic image of Occasio with her own sail, from Corrozet's *Hecatongraphie* (1543), in Arthur Henkel and Albrecht Schöne, eds., *Emblemata* (Stuttgart, 1967), col. 1810.

[51] *Epig.* XXXIII.9–16, trans. H. G. Evelyn-White, in Loeb *Ausonius*, vol. 2, pp. 175–177. (Elsewhere this epigram is numbered 12.) Compare *Distichs of Cato* II.26:

Cartari also mentions the character Penitence in the famous painting of "Calumny" by Apelles, which Lucian described.[52] Calumny drags a young man by the hair, which reminds us of the abuse of Spenser's Phedon by Furor and Occasion; as a railing hag, Occasion is related to Ate and Sclaunder elsewhere in the poem. Occasion, then, is a complex idea that includes fortune, victimization, report, and repentance.[53]

A story told in the *Orlando Innamorato* gives a narrative form to the emblem tradition.[54] To rescue his companions from an enchantment, Orlando at one point enters the submarine garden-world of the fay Morgana. The portal bears an inscription warning him to take her by the forelock while she sleeps, for she is bald behind. This Orlando fails to do, and having missed his opportunity he returns to find Morgana awake. His imprisoned friends have by now told him he must capture the fay if they are to be delivered from her detention. He approaches, but she flies from him. The landscape quickly changes from the garden into a chaotic and tempestuous wilderness, as Orlando gives chase. Then a new character appears on the scene:

> Pur segue Orlando e fortuna non cura,
> E prender vol Morgana a la finita,
> Ma sempre cresce sua disaventura,
> Perchè una dama de una grotta uscita,
> Pallida in faccia e magra di figura
> Che di color di terra era vestita
> Presse un flagello in mano aspero e grosso,
> Battendo a sè le spalle e tutto il dosso.

Still Orlando follows and his fortune gets no better—he would finally catch Morgana, but his misadventure only increases, because a woman emerges from a cave—pallid in face and meagre of figure, clad in the color of earth, she holds a whip in hand, heavy and severe, beating the shoulders with it, and all the back.

(II.ix.5)

"Fronte capillata, post est occasio calva"; *Gr. Anth.* XVI.275, on Lysippus' statue of Time, by Posidippus; and Phaedrus, *Fab.* X.viii, where the Lysippean figure "signifies how brief is Opportunity . . . an effigy of Time, that slothful delay should not hinder the execution of our purposes."

[52] In Loeb *Lucian*, trans. A. M. Harmon, vol. 1, pp. 364–367. For further on the subject, see R. Atrocchi, "The Calumny of Apelles in the Literature of the Quatrocento," *PMLA*, 36 (1921), pp. 454–491.

[53] See R. Wittkower, "Patience and Chance: The Story of an Emblem for Ercole II of Ferrara," *Journal of the Warburg Institute*, vol. 1 (1937–1938), p. 171, and, in the same vol., "Chance, Time and Virtue," pp. 313–321.

[54] *Orl. Inn.* II.viii.13ff. The suggestion that Phedon's account of his victimization by Furor owes something to Boiardo's tale is made by H. H. Blanchard, "Spenser and Boiardo," *PMLA*, 40 (1923), pp. 834f.

Orlando asks who the miserable one is, and she answers that she is Penitence, who always follows those who lose their ventures. So long as Orlando pursues Morgana, she will follow with her scourge, and, therefore, he had better arm himself with patience. Patient he will not be, Orlando insists—quite the contrary. When things fall out as Penitence has warned, Orlando turns on his tormentor:

> Il conte, a lei voltato in mal talento,
> Gli mena un pugno alla sinestra golta.
> Ma, come gionto avesse a mezo il vento,
> O ver nel fumo, o nella nebbia folta,
> Via passò il pugno per mezo la testa
> De un lato ad altro, e cosa non l'arresta.

The count, turning to her with an ill will, dealt a punch to her cheek sinister. But, as if he had struck at the middle of the wind, or truly into smoke, or into a thick cloud, the blow passed through the middle of the head, from one side to the other, and nothing arrested it.

(II.ix.11)

As if he had struck at himself, Orlando feels another stroke of the whip descend. Hardly believing that he has not injured her, Orlando continues to combat "quella dama che una ombra sembrava" (that dame who seemed a shade), but to no avail. He returns to his pursuit of Morgana, but the scourging continues. He turns yet again, but he cannot touch "quella cosa vana" (that vain thing). Finally he learns that the combat is fruitless, but a deep confusion sets in:

> "Se a Dio piace,—diceva—on al demonio
> Ch'io abbi pazïenza, ed io me l'abbia:
> Ma siame il mondo tutto testimonio
> Ch'io la tragualcio con sapor di rabbia.
> Qual frensia di mente o quale insonio
> Me ha qua giuso condutto in questa gabbia?
> Dove entrai io qua dentro, o come e quando?
> Son fatto un altro, o sono ancora Orlando?"

If it pleases God, he said, and not the devil, that I have patience, then I will have it. But let the whole world be witness that I swallow it with a relish of anger. What frenzy of mind or what nightmare has conducted me here into this trap? Where did I enter this, or how, or when? Have I become another, or am I still Orlando?

(II.ix.15)

To conclude this account: Orlando finally does succeed in taking Morgana by the forelock; Penitence withdraws into her cave and the landscape reverts to its original beauty and serenity. Morgana is prevailed upon to release her prisoners.

Despite the intrinsic interest of sources and analogues, I adduce this parallel chiefly to illustrate the latent continuity of Spenser's Occasion and Maleger episodes. The resemblances of Phedon's story to Orlando's are the simpler ones: the infuriated Phedon pursues the treacherous maid Pyrene through woods and plains; as his abstraction deepens he is over-taken by Furor and Occasion, and their abuse of his body only ceases when Occasion has been bound by the temperate Guyon. Spenser's Occasion differs from the traditional figures, however, in being old and lame, or Saturnine. Her "hoare lockes" reappear in the hags serving Maleger, whose names are Impatience and Impotence—Impotence is also lame (II.iv.4; xi.23). The two hags may be understood as vicious counterparts for the honor-figures Prays-desire and Shamefastness: they are forward and froward dispositions in relation to action, an "evil eagerness," and a restraint based upon incapacity. Thus they manifest Erasmus' *festina* and *lente* figures in an ironic form, for impotence includes procrastination, just as Erasmus' *lente* stands for a caution that includes deliberative delay. Arthur is rescued from their domination by his squire, whose name, Timias, comes from the Greek word for honor, *timē*, but also conceivably suggests the English word *time*, in view of the present context.

In the stanzas introducing Arthur's squire, we are told that Arthur is practically defeated by "fierce Fortune" (II.xi.30),[55] and other resemblances to Boiardo's tale have probably occurred to the reader already; we may list them interpretatively. Both episodes feature the baffling and repeated encounter—or non-encounter—with a body that is partly immaterial be-cause the allegory is allowed to play tricks with the fiction. Both Peni-tence and Maleger seem to be the mental shadows of their respective heroes; Boiardo's Penitence is Orlando beside himself, and she will go away when his mind clears of self-hatred. The "vnsound" Maleger is more mysterious, but in some sense he represents a *defect* of nature, a devitalized area that comes into being when resistance fails, as Antaeus conquered when he fell (Ovid, *Ibis* 394). His campaign against the Castle of Alma is renewed when Guyon, the spirit of temperance, departs. (Likewise, when Guyon arrives on Phedria's island, the oblivious Cy-mochles revives.) As something that happens to the mind, as well as to the body, Maleger produces a crisis of doubt. The Renaissance conception

---

[55] For the theme, cf. Boethius, *De Cons. Phil.* IV, prose vii: "You skirmish fiercly with any fortune, lest either affliction oppress you or prosperity corrupt you. Stay yourselves strongly in the mean! For whatsoever cometh either short, or goeth be-yond, may well contemn felicity, but will never obtain the reward of labour. For it is placed in your power to frame to yourselves what fortune you please." (Loeb trans., p. 361.) Cf. *F.Q.* II.v.12.

of pathological melancholy, as *Hamlet* reminds us, includes impairment of the will, remorse of conscience, anxiety about the future state, and a susceptibility to apparitions, as well as an obsession with the imagery of death and corruption. Further, there is a theme of controlling time in *Hamlet*, for Hamlet must set the time right, contrary to the untimely and overhasty action that has set it wrong.[56] Hamlet is compelled to delay, and he is deeply puzzled by the mysterious frustration of his eagerness to act by his proneness to length: he is a man caught between Impatience and Impotence, or Claudius and Polonius.

Directly following his analysis of time, in the passage quoted at the head of this essay, Sherry discusses the limits on the capacity to act:

> Facultie is a power to do the thynge that is taken in hand: and in con-iectures two thinges specially be considered: whether he could or wold. Wyll is gathered of hope to performe it, and is made more probable when the nature of the mynde is ioyned to it: as it is not like he wyl abide [remain satisfied] in his glorie, because he is enuious and ambicious. Also when we counsell one to leaue of vayne mouthynge, when it is not in his power to get agayne that is gone.[57]

Hamlet will not regain that greater sense of possibility that died with his father, and both Spenser's and Boiardo's episodes present the nightmarish pursuit of an antagonist who is obsessively before the pursuer, because something analogous is behind him in time. This is difficult to express iconographically (i.e., in space), without resorting to images like Morgana's forelock and Maleger's arrows. Orlando's *opportunity* is behind him—it has become Penitence or regret. Arthur's *potential* is behind him—it has become Impotence. Both episodes trap the hero in a repeating cycle, and both require patience of him where panic threatens. There are also possible parallels in Spenser's and Boiardo's descriptions: Maleger is "pale and wan . . . leane and meagre," and Penitence is "Pallida in faccia e magra di figura" (*F.Q.* II.xi.23; *Orl. Inn.* II.ix.5). Maleger is also a cave-dweller (as was Antaeus); and perhaps the clothing of Penitence, the color of *earth*, was suggestive as well.

Other parallels can explain Maleger's being modeled on the Tartars or Scythians, and his arrows as the missiles of outrageous Fortune. Turning again to Cartari, we read that Giraldus has remarked the new images of Fortune too: he wrote that "in our time some have made fortune on horseback—with beautiful enough invention—and she runs away, always driven by Fate (indicating to us Destiny, apparently), the retinue holding bow and arrows for wounding. This depiction shows the velocity of

---

[56] For the reading of *Hamlet* here, see Frye, *Fools of Time* (Toronto, 1967), pp. 36, 89f., 93f.

[57] Richard Sherry, *A treatise of Schemes & Tropes* . . . (London, 1550), fol. fiiir.

fortune, because it does not rest, but always runs away, driven by Fate: because where Destiny is, you do not have a place for fortune."[58] Such a difficult image is relevant because in Spenser the pursuit of fortune is followed, or displaced, by the "destiny" of Impotence, who resupplies Maleger with arrows.

Cartari's illustration of this fleeing Fortune is grouped on a plate that also shows another Fortune image, that of a Scythian Fortune, who is distinguished by being footless and winged—"signifying," the caption reads, "her velocity and instability, and that occasion needs to comply, because it swiftly flies from her, and because lost and omitted occasion is followed in vain, and in vain repented."[59] So Maleger, riding "in haste," comes to the aid of his cohorts: "Vpon a Tygre swift . . . he rode, / That as the winde ran vnderneath his lode, / While his long legs nigh raught [nearly reached] vnto the ground" (II.xi.20). Maleger, or his mount, is virtually footless; his "light-foot beast" flies "as the winged wind," and "scarse his feet on ground were seene to tred" (II.xi.25–26).

Cartari's footless Fortune comes from Quintus Curtius' *History of Alexander* (VII.viii), and its context also deserves notice. At this point in the history, Alexander is about to embark upon what appears to be a desperate campaign against the Scythians. In the background is the question whether the hero's fortunes are exhausted; they have taken a decided turn for the worse. Furthermore, the hero is suffering at the time from a debilitating battle-wound. On the eve of battle an embassy from the Scythians comes to impress upon the invader the hazards he will be presently undertaking: "Our arrows we send to our enemies," their leader intones:

Pass now the Jaxartes [River], and you will know how wide the Scythian plains are: never will you overtake the people. Our poverty will be swifter than your army, which carries the spoil of so many great nations. Again; when you imagine us at the greatest distance, you will see us in your camp. With the same rapidity as we fly, we pursue.

I am told, that the Scythian deserts are proverbially derided by the Greeks. But we seek unpeopled and uncultivated tracts in preference to cities and rich provinces.

Henceforth hold Fortune with clenched hands; for she is slippery. Nor will she be detained against her will. Sound advice appears better afterwards, than when it is given. Put a curb on your prosperity; and it will be guarded with less trouble. Our fathers teach us, that Fortune has not

[58] *Le Imagini, edn. cit.*, pp. 351f. The reference is to Giraldus, *Hist. Deorum*, Syntag. XVI, in *Op. om.*, I, col. 457D.

[59] *Le Imagini*, p. 351; Giraldus, *Hist. Deorum*, Syntag. XVI, in *Op. om.*, I, col. 457A.

feet to stand upon: she has hands and wings: when she stretches out her hands, she suffers not her wings to be confined.[60]

In the next chapter Alexander responds to this temperate advice by saying that he will be guided by his fortune, in which he is confident, and the advice of his friends, so that he may not do anything rashly. In the succeeding battle the Scythians are routed, though Alexander himself is too weakened to give chase. The "greedy" Arthur may also be an Alexander, who was notable equally for his magnanimity and for his impatience. And being a symbol of Fortune, the unconquerable and receding Scythian spaces occupied by Maleger ("vew of eye could scarse him ouertake," II.xi.25) may be understood as tracts of time as well.

[iii]

. . . I know not whence I came hither into this—shall I call it dying life or living death?

(Augustine, *Confessions*, I.6)

By describing the resemblances to other texts, one in some measure elicits the themes of Spenser's Maleger episode. However, we might expand somewhat upon the specific meaning of Arthur's battle as a resistance to the very loss of resistance. Let us suppose that the onset of Maleger symbolizes a fit of melancholy, his element being that of "earthly sad despaire," as Donne calls it in "The Dissolution." It is well enough known that the medieval conception analogous to melancholy falls within the sin of accidie: thus the nice paradox that Evil Eagerness should trap Arthur in a condition that otherwise is sloth. But of course accidie takes in an area that the word *sloth* does not adequately describe, namely, the defeat of the spirit. According to the orthodox account of Chaucer's Parson, this sin included wanhope, outrageous sorrow, dread, incapacitation of the will, *tristicia*, and *tarditas* (slowness in turning to God).[61] The remedy,

---

[60] Trans. Peter Pratt (London, 1821), vol. 2, pp. 194ff.

[61] *Parson's Tale*, ll. 676–738 (Robinson edn.). As Siegfried Wenzel shows in *The Sin of Sloth* (Chapel Hill, 1967), acedia originates in a pathological condition of the contemplative life, which is partly what melancholy eventually became: it first appears as an affliction of fourth century hermits. Literally "uncaringness," this acedia was a restless negligence—or tardiness, listlessness, or impotence—respecting the observation of spiritual duties. As described by Evagrius Ponticus and John Cassian (*De Institutione Coenobiorum*, X), it was a noontide feverishness of the cell. In Cassian's scheme of the sins, it corresponds to St. Gregory's *tristicia*, which includes a distracting spiritual sorrow and a sluggishness in obeying the commandments (*Moralia*, XXXI.xlv). The spiritual inappetence of acedia eventually coalesces with the Gregorian *tristicia*: in Aquinas, acedia is *sorrow about*, as well as *aversion to* one's spiritual good (*Summa Theol.*, Pt. II, 2nd Pt., q.35, art.1, resp., and art.2,

according to the Parson again, is fortitude, and in fortitude's species—
magnanimity, magnificence, and constancy—we will recognize the qualities elsewhere indicated as belonging to Arthur. These species derive from
the list, in Macrobius' *Commentary*, of the seven parts of fortitude. Magnificence is one of the four parts of fortitude according to Cicero as well;
the other three are confidence, patience, and perseverance. Magnificence
and fortitude, according to St. Thomas, "both do something difficult," and
Arthur's magnificence, in the sense of the "accomplishment *of great and
lofty undertakings, with a certain broad and noble purpose of mind,*"
might well be undermined by Evil Eagerness. Such undertakings, on the
contrary, require perseverance, i.e., "long persistence in any kind of difficult good," for "it belongs to perseverance to persevere to the end of the
virtuous work."[62] The sheer difficulty in mastering Maleger obtains some
of its point with these descriptions, to which we will want to add St.
Thomas' virtue of "longanimity," or long-sufferance,[63] for the battle is

---

resp.; *ibid.*, Pt. I, q.63, art.2, resp. ad obj.2; and *ibid.*, Pt. II, 2nd Pt., q.54, art.2,
resp. ad obj.1, "an oppressive sorrow"). Cf. Gower, *Confessio Amantis*, IV.3389ff., on
Tristesse as the beginning of wanhope, which is maintained by Obstinacy. (Obstinacy is otherwise an extreme of perseverance, namely, that Pertinacity discussed
by Aquinas in *Summa Theol.*, Pt. II, 2nd Pt., q.138, art.2.) For our theme in
Petrarch, see Klaus Heitmann, *Fortuna und Virtu* (Köln, 1958), pp. 202ff., on
"Fortunas' Wasse: Accidia," and "Virtus' Wasse: Fortitudo," and Wenzel, *op. cit.*,
pp. 155–163; Wenzel notes the identification of acedia with *egritudo* in Petrarch,
and the secularization of the medieval concept there. If, as appears likely, the scheme
of the seven capital sins owes something to tables of the affects of the seven planets,
then the intellectual link between acedia and melancholy would ultimately depend
upon a common astrological inheritance from Saturn: indeed, the Saturnine provenance of acedia might almost qualify as a discovery of the Renaissance. For some
iconographic carry-over from acedia to melancholy, see R. Kiblansky, E. Panofsky,
and F. Saxl, *Saturn and Melancholy* (London, 1964), pp. 300ff. For melancholy's place
among the *causes* of acedia, see Wenzel, pp. 191–194. For the seven sins and the
planets, see below, Chap. VI, nn. 9of. with text. For the source of Dürer's "Melen-
cholia I" in a painting of Acedia by Bellini, see Guy de Tervarent, *Les enigmes de
l'art: l'art savant* (Paris, 1946), pp. 13–20.

[62] The quotations are from *Summa Theol.*, Pt. II, 2nd Pt., q.134, art.4; *ibid.*, q.128,
resp., quoting Cicero, *De Invent.* II. liv; *ibid.*, q.134, art.1, resp. ad obj.1; *ibid.*, q.134,
art.1, resp. ad obj.2. Aquinas also discusses Macrobius, *Comm. in Somn. Scip.*, I.viii.
For the post-Aristotelian interpretation of magnificence, see above, Chap. I, "Arthurian Torso," sec. iii, nn. 115f. with text.

[63] *Summa Theol.*, Pt. II, 2nd Pt., q.136, art.5. The rendering "longanimity" indicates
the relation of this virtue to magnanimity. Laurence of Orleans, in his *Somme le
Roi*, includes among the subdivisions of "evil amendment"—the second of the three
branches of sloth—procrastination, recklessness, and badly motivated religious zeal,
along with the more obvious "default of heart"; and under the third branch of
sloth he includes impatience with spiritual counsel. Opposed to sloth is the spiritual
virtue of "Prowesse," which is activated by a concern for one's spiritual well-being
(see *The Book of the Vices and Virtues*, ed. W. Nelson Francis, EETS, Original

distinctly a protracted one. It comes home to us with renewed force that Maleger is besieging a Castle of Perseverance.

Our identification of Arthur's special quality in this episode as fortitude belongs to the point made earlier concerning Arthur's being characterized in terms of the Platonic spirited element in the soul, otherwise the Scholastic volitive faculty by virtue of which the soul properly moves. St. Thomas says that each of the four cardinal virtues is opposed to one of four "wounds of nature." The "wound" that is specifically opposed to fortitude is the one of *weakness*: "insofar as the irascible is deprived of its ordainment to the arduous, there is the wound of weakness." Further, "when the passions withdraw us from following the dictate of reason, *e.g.*, through fear of danger or toil, . . . then man needs to be strengthened for that which reason dictates, lest he turn back, and to this end there is fortitude."[64] It is this kind of recalcitrance that we might call *tarditas*, and to oppose it we might designate a virtue of promptitude, or responsiveness to good promptings. Thus, in the Maleger episode, Arthur's ardor is rekindled by the example of Timias, which revives in him "thought of glorie and of fame" (II.xi.31). Even more pertinent to our reading, fortitude is particularly "the virtue which strengthens the soul against the dangers of death." Arthur is defending the "*fort* of reason" against the "affections," according to the opening stanza here (II.xi.1), and in fact St. Thomas says that every virtue that strengthens the soul against any passions whatever may be called fortitude. It is of some interest that he demonstrates this principle with respect to the overlap of fortitude and temperance. Patience also overlaps with fortitude: "Patience endures not only the dangers of death, with which fortitude is concerned, without excessive sorrow, but also any other hardships or dangers."[65]

The patience to endure without excessive sorrow brings us back to the nature of accidie, or the medieval kind of melancholy. "Accidie is a ful greet enemy to the lif ode of the body," the Parson tells us, "for it hath no purveaunce agayn temporeel necessitee" (*Parson's Tale*, 684); it brings

---

Series 217, London, 1942, pp. 26ff., pp. 161ff.; the opposition of this kind of prowess to dejection and weariness appears in the Macro Play of *Mankind*). One subdivision of the *Somme*'s Prowesse is Perseverance, for acedia—in the words of Alanus de Insulis—is not only "the torpor of the mind by which one neglects to begin good works," but also that by which one "grows weary in *finishing* them" (Wenzel, *Sin of Sloth*, pp. 80, 218, quoting *De virtutibus et de vitiis et de donis Spiritus Sancti*, ed. O. Lottin, *Mediaeval Studies*, 12 (1950), pp. 20–56, 42; cf. Aquinas, *Summa Theol.*, Pt. II, 2nd Pt., q.35, art.1, resp.) The other subdivisions include Magnificence, Good Hope, Security, Patience, Constancy, and Magnanimity, following Macrobius.

[64] *Summa Theol.*, Pt. II, 1st Pt., q.85, art.3; and *ibid.*, q.61, art.2.

[65] For Thomas's discussion of fortitude, see *Summa Theol.*, Pt. II, 1st Pt., q.61, art.4; *ibid.*, q.61, art.3; and *ibid.*, q.61, art.4, resp. ad obj.1, quoting Cicero, *De Off.* I.20. *Summa Theol.*, Pt. II, 2nd Pt., q.128, resp. ad obj.4.

with it "the synne of wordly sorwe, swich as is cleped *tristicia*, that sleeth man, as seith Seint Paul. / For certes, swich sorwe werketh to the death of the soule and of the body also; for therof comth that a man is annoyed of his owene life. / Wherfore swich sorwe shorteth ful ofte the life of man, er that his tyme be come by wey of Kynde" (724–726). The passage in Paul to which the Parson refers (following *Summa Theol.*, Pt. II, 2nd Pt., q.35, art.3, obj.3, contra) implies two kinds of regret, one good and one evil. "For godlie sorowe causeth repentance unto salvacion, not to be repented of: but the worldlie sorowe causeth death" (II Cor. 7:10, Geneva Bible). This "worldlie sorowe" is classically that evil *aegritude* or distress described in Cicero's *Tusculan Disputations* (IV.viii.18f.) in its varieties of anxiety, mourning, sadness, trouble, lamentation, depression ("aegritudo cum cogitatione"), vexation, pining, and complete despondency or desperation ("aegritudo sine ulla rerum expectatione meliorum"). It is an analogous *aegritude* or "worldlie sorowe" that eventually overtakes Redcrosse in the episode of Despair: in terms of the later episode, the unfortified hero, impotent to redeem his life, becomes impatient to end it. Significantly, this follows upon his separation from Arthur.

The onset of Maleger thus suggests the coming to consciousness of that death we are in, even in the midst of life. Arthur's mind is fixated on "th'vtmost issue of his owne decay," to borrow words with only a slightly different meaning in their context in this episode (II.xi.41). Arthur wrestles, in the idiom of Ephesians, not against flesh and blood (Maleger lacks these), but against an irrational autopathic malaise that gets power over them. If Arthur's fight represents a bout of depression, he might well "pray for desire"—desire in this legend being the mere will to go on living. Expounding the Antaeus myth, Fulgentius cites the instance of one Diogenes, who was racked with pain in his lungs: seeing men flocking to the amphitheatre, Diogenes said, "How great is the stupidity of men; they run off to watch men fighting with beasts, and pass me by, struggling with natural misery."[66] One may note an analogous "mistake" in later editions of Book II: they describe Arthur's antagonist as *"this"* lifeless shadow"; more suggestive of the psychomachia in Book II, the 1590 edition reads *his* (II.xi.44).

If Maleger-Antaeus is Arthur's own natural misery, and the misery is melancholia; and if Maleger is Arthur's shadow-self: then Maleger may also be the inadequate, worthless, or evil self who is the subject of the typical melancholiac's aggrieved self-reflections. Arthur's melancholia derives from his disappointing love of Gloriana, for his Prays-desire is "Pensiue . . . and sad in mind, / Through great desire of glory and of fame" (II.ix.38). According to Freud's "Mourning and Melancholia," the

[66] *Virgiliana Continentia*, in R. Helm, *Fvlgentivs. Opera*, p. 43.

melancholiac's self-abasement proceeds from his having directed toward himself an animosity otherwise directed toward an object of love, which he feels has abandoned or betrayed him. It is this substitution of the self for the love-object that gives melancholy its affinities with narcissism, for, unlike mourning, melancholy does not provide for the full detachment of the ego from the object of grief. Melancholy is pathologically regressive in relation to normal sorrow over loss in the way that narcissism is pathologically regressive in relation to normal erotic object-cathexis. We might say that melancholy is an "allegorical" grief; in the same way, the desire of Britomart, at the outset of Book III, is an "allegorical" love—hence her association with Narcissus there. Maleger, at any rate, is an intensely "allegorical" creation.

An animation peculiar to allegory, Maleger is fashioned (in the words of Donne's "Nocturnall") "From dull privations, and leane emptiness": he can only be "re-begot / Of absence, darknesse, death: things which are not." Created out of the almost pure ecktoplasm of allegorical "otherness," Maleger is free to disappear upon the making whole of Arthur: into his own voidness, so to speak. The presentation of absence, the substantiation of shadow, the embodiment of loss, the animation of death—these are the allegorist's natural *forte*. But it is still a paradox that in creating a vehicle for these things, the allegorist undermines his very claim to have done so.

Maleger's name might make him not only the evil of sickness, but also the sickness of evil. According to Augustine (e.g., *Confessions*, VII.12), evil is a kind of privation of authentic being, which is good. Maleger exhibits some of this original voidness of evil—which itself seems to derive from ideas about the aboriginal evilness of the void. Like evil, at any rate, Maleger is able to extract a being from privation. Herein lies the darker logic of this episode: namely, Maleger's subtle identity with his opposites. For Maleger, "without bloud" and "without spright" (II.xi.40), is nonetheless a kind of "subtle body"; and if he is a "lifelesse shadow," he is also a "dead-liuing swaine" (II.xi.44). Similarly, Spenser's Death looks "like a shade"—"Vnbodied, vnsoul'd, vnheard, vnseene" (VII.vii.46)—and yet a shade is traditionally a "life" or "soul" or "spirit" that survives the death of the body. To lose one's shadow, folklore and the savage mind agree, is to lose a possession scarcely less dear than life itself.

These considerations compel yet a further reading of Arthur's attempt to retrieve his flit and shadowy other, if Maleger is, in a semi-technical sense, the hero's "life." Maleger may be identified with such a life, even though his appearance is also a sign of the loss of life. In the medical sense, the sign is a symptom; the belief that the appearance of a man's double signals the imminence of his death is well attested. In *Of Ghosts and Spirits Walking by Nyght*, Lavater notes that men sick of some deadly disease often hear something moving about their rooms, in the way that they themselves once did; often, before they die, or a little after their deaths, they see either their own shapes, or some other shadows of men. In *Miscellanies upon Various Subjects* John Aubrey quotes Cardanus on the double-image in dreams: in dreams, it is a sign of death, because out of one are made two, when the soul is separated from the body; it is a sign of the disease in sick men.[67]

This dividing person is inevitably the subject of allegory. And yet the ghost or spirit that separates from the dying man does not itself die. Death is "but parting of the breath" (VII.vii.46), and the breath is the breath of life; Cymochles "Breathd out his ghost," but it survives in "th'infernall shade" to which it flies (II.viii.45). In the Maleger episode we witness an allegorizing form of this metempsychosis, where the soul of the dying man animates the personification of his death. Meanwhile, Arthur is contriving "How to take life from that dead-liuing swaine"—in part, how to take it back. Life—whosoever it might be—will prevail, for it seems that the allegorist, *qua* allegorist, commits himself to an animistic poetic theology in which death *qua* death, cannot exist, except in a lively way. Death is a metaphor for a radical discontinuity; allegories are by definition "continuous."

The generalizing of Maleger, which has been the burden of our analysis of the allegory, might prompt one to remark, with Burton's *Anatomy*, that "Melancholy in this sense is the character of mortality" (Pt. I, Sec. 1, memb. 1, subs. 5). If Arthur in this episode successfully confronts the spectre of his own mortality, then there may still be a more recondite sense in which he conquers death itself: in the Apocalypse, Death is also cast into a lake. At the least, one could say that every successful convalescence necessarily entails, as its contrapositive, the termination of a morbid state. In this figurative sense, the demise of Maleger foreshadows the death of Death. Such a conquest will remind us that ultimately the earthy man will rise up to put on incorruption, and that the "graue terrestrial"— to which Maleger cannot otherwise be committed (II.xi.45)—will lose not only its victory, but also its significance. Maleger might finally be discarded as a meaningless sign, one of those "former things"—death, sorrow, pain—that it is promised shall be put away.

Guyon's legend takes its beginning from the mortality of Mordant— from that mortality's being put into effect, as it were. Therefore, in the context of temperance, Arthur's victory might symbolize no more than a temporary remission of an ultimately fatal disease. But the victory is accorded to a greater one than Guyon, and inevitably it will suggest more than a mere recovery of health, or revival of good hope. Within *The*

---

[67] *Of Ghostes* (London, 1572), p. 77; *Miscellanies*, 4th edn. (London, 1857), p. 89, quoting "Cardanus, Synes. Somniorum, lib. ii. cap. 12," *sub* "De seipso duplicato."

Faerie Queene overall, it serves to illustrate a particular aspect of the myth of Arthur's return. In Malory and elsewhere this means the return from Avalon, and in Book II Arthur's survival is logically parallel to the remanding of the heroic persona from the underworld, which is also an apple-land of the dead. The early Church affirmed that God would not let his holy one see corruption, and the victory won in the Maleger episode shows that an analogous expectation exists on the part of Spenser's faerie.

[iv]

If Arthur's defeat of Orgoglio offers an analogy for "revelation" or "un-veiling" in Book I, then his defeat of Maleger ought to offer something comparable in the context of the temperate attitude cultivated in Book II. Arthur solves the deepening riddle of Maleger—"th'vtmost issew of his owne decay"—only when he pauses and *remembers well* that Maleger originated from the earth: the earth is his elemental "natiue seat," to which it is ordained that earth will return (II.xi.45; 32). Good Memory is one of Alma's counselors, and hence the analogy for revelation here is simply "presence of mind," or mental self-possession and its extension into the reaches of experience. Its enemy is distraction.

The intellectual grasp in question is not unrelated to Cicero's theme of doing the right thing at the right time. Such a capacity depends heavily upon foresight, hindsight, and judgment, and these answer to the three dimensions of time. They are the powers belonging to Alma's three sages. They are also the three aspects of prudence, according to an influential passage in Cicero.[68] Prudence is otherwise the special virtue of the Palmer, and within this virtue the Palmer's assistance might especially recall the Aristotelian habit of *euboulia*, "a habit whereby we take good counsel" (*Nich. Ethics* VI.9). Since it belongs to prudence to do this also (*Nich. Ethics* VI.5), Aquinas comments that "it might seem that *euboulia* is not a virtue annexed to prudence, but rather prudence itself"; he responds that prudence excels in commanding, and that *euboulia* is rather a secondary virtue of prudence that perfects counsel.[69] Guyon and the Palmer are sometimes on opposite sides of such a distinction.

We notice something anxious about young Phantastes that corresponds to something "decrepit" about old Eumnestes. In degraded form, these qualities turn up as Maleger's aids, Impatience and Impotence. Similarly,

---

[68] *De Invent. Rhet.* II.liii; so in Aquinas, *Summa Theol.*, Pt. II, 1st Pt., q.57, art.6, obj.4 and resp., and *ibid.*, Pt. II, 2nd Pt., q.48. Cicero's word for foresight, *praesagitio*, turns up in connection with the corresponding figure in Book I, Contemplation, who is able to "presage" Redcrosse's path to the heavenly Jerusalem (I.x.61).

[69] *Summa Theol.*, Pt. II, 1st Pt., q.57, art.6, obj.1 and resp.

we found a trace of rashness in Prays-desire, and a corresponding timidity in Shamefastness. As the temperate man is governed by the desire for praise and the fear of shame, so the distracted man is hagridden by the inability to wait, and the fear of failure in the face of new opportunity. We may conclude that the resemblance of Impatience and Impotence to the harridan Occasio is essential to Spenser's theme.

It is one more paradox of the allegory of this episode that Evil Eagerness should prove to be a master of the tactics of delay: premature action ultimately retards real action, and an insufficient marshaling of force is revealed in a frustration of effect. Erasmus therefore points to the *Maturate fugam* of *Aeneid* I.136 as advice comparable to *festina lente*: "hasten your flight," yes, "but in such a way that you do not anticipate the appointed time."[70] Surely Maleger acts in this way, earlier relenting his pace and giving ground to draw Arthur on (II.xi.27; cf. 36), and later laying low while he recoups his strength from the earth. In his turn, Arthur is well advised to arrest his hasty pursuit, and he waits for Maleger to exhaust his supply of arrows; a little later Maleger is drawn into abandoning his weaponry prematurely. The initiative only finally passes to Arthur when he "gan some other wayes aduize" (II.xi.44), his action thereby transforming itself from the precipitate and *festinata*, to the considered and *maturata*.

Erasmus said that some natures need the "spur" of *festina*, and some the "rein" of *lente*, in other words, "a wise promptness together with moderation, . . . so that nothing is done rashly and then regretted." Maleger's hags resemble the *Metanoia* figures in Ausonius and Boiardo because the impulsive or *festinata* kind of hurry "has companions: error and repentence." "Hasty wrath and heedlesse hazardry," Guyon advises Pyrochles, "Doe breede repentaunce late" (II.v.13). In Guyon's own story, it is the Palmer who has the office of forestalling foolish actions through prior experience, and maturing wise actions through careful planning and preparation. Thus the hero is cautioned and prompted by his elder companion, as Arthur, in the allegorical parody, is hurried by Impatience and delayed by Impotence. The Palmer also acts the part of Shamefastness and Prays-desire, i.e., the part of the tutor, as it is set out in Elyot's *Gouernour*. Elyot's description should complete our comparison between the Palmer and the *anima* figures at the Castle:

> The most necessary thinges to be obserued by a master in his disciples or scholars (as Licon the noble grammarian saide) is Shamefastnes and praise. By shamefastnes, as it were with a bridell, they rule well theyr

---

[70] "Festina lente" is quoted from Phillips' trans., *Erasmus on His Times*, p. 5. Quotes in the following paragraph are from pp. 17, 4, and 17.

dedes as their appetites. And desire of prayse addeth a sharp spurre to their disposition towards lernyng and vertue.[71]

Such "spur" and "rein" imagery also applies to the control of the more feckless characters. Atin pricks the sluggish Cymochles "with spurs of shame and wrong" (II.v.38); Cymochles thereupon pricks his horse. And when the impatient and impetuous Pyrochles spurs into view and bears down on Guyon, the hero arrests his charge by beheading his charger.

It is the theme of mental control that gives some importance in this legend to the handling of abstracted states of mind, and also to handling abstractions themselves. The Palmer has to explain the staining of Ruddymane and the Furor-Occasion complex. Mammon points out the invulnerability of Disdain. Alma feels called upon to explain the strange behavior of Prays-desire and Shamefastness.[72] Maleger's qualities seem inexplicable; he is uncanny by nature. Since these object-lessons in allegore-

[71] I.ix, Everyman's Library, p. 33.

[72] II.ii.5–10; II.iv.10f., II.vii.42; II.ix.39, 42. The case of Ruddymane is particularly obvious, for his stain is specifically a "Symbole," and hence a sign (with a secondary meaning of "testament"); and like all such signs, it is liable to misinterpretation. It symbolizes not "bloudguiltinesse" (II.ii.4), but the "innocence" of Ruddymane's mother (II.ii.10), though the phrase "in lieu of innocence" seems designed to accommodate the contradiction of the literal stain and the figurative declaration of purity. Allegory, in its general impulse towards the defamiliarization of discourse, battens on such discrepancies. (For the word "testament" for the legacy of Mordant, cf. Hebrews 9:15–17: ". . . that death being a meane, unto the redemption of these prevarications which were under the former testament. . . . For where there is a testament: the death of the testatour must of necessitie come betwene. For a testament is confirmed in the dead: otherwise it is yet of no value, whiles he that testeth, liveth" [Rheims].) In discussing the phenomenology of allegory here, I have not fully developed the relation between meaningfulness and time, but the argument can be guessed: some interpretations are not so much wrong, as premature, and thus intemperate—"meaning" develops in the lacuna between what is heard and what is understood, the mediatorial or "mean" time between cognition and re-cognition. This delay in registration is another form of the veil between sign and significance. The episodes in Book II tend to end with the fixing of the issue of the action by the drawing of a moral over some final image—a process still going on in the legend's last line. The memorialization of the action contributes to the importance of Eumnestes as the legend's "eudoxus" figure. The role of the Palmer as interpreter is analogous. The Palmer is a hermeneut by virtue of his caduceus, Hermes' rod. Hermes' mission to Odysseus was of course allegorized as the persuasions of reason in the correction of passion. See Heraclides Ponticus, *Allegoriae Homeri*, in Gale, *Opuscula Mythologica*, pp. 492f., and *Homeri Poetae Vita*, in the same collection, p. 343. Cf. Cornutus, *De Natura Deorum* 16, *ibid.*, p. 167: "Qui affirmant Joven tulisse ex Maia Mercurium, docere videntur, Mercuriam speculationi & sedulae inquisitioni natum esse." See also Comes, *Mythol.*, V.v, "De Mercurio" (Geneva, 1641), p. 442.

sis do not turn up elsewhere in the poem, one presumes that they are meant to illustrate one more activity of the temperate mind.

There may be a deeper lesson as well. In a passage on the phenomenon that psychoanalysis calls "projection," Jung explains that the subject who does not know his own mind will not be able to distinguish its effects on his perception of the objective environment; his perception will be at the mercy of his projections, and he unwittingly will keep encountering his projections in his environment. This subjective reflection is suggested by episodes as different as Cymochles in the Bower and Arthur's encounters with a reluctant Prays-desire and a vacuous Maleger. Imposed upon by such projections, the mind finds in the world representations of its own undiscovered aspect; both the nymphs as perceived by Cymochles, and Maleger as perceived by Arthur have about them something deeply illusory. Jung goes on to say that such projections "lead to an autoerotic or autistic condition in which one dreams a world whose reality remains forever unattainable." He adds that "the resultant *sentiment d'incompletude* and the still worse feeling of sterility are in their turn explained by projection as the malevolence of the environment, and by means of this vicious circle the isolation is intensified."[73] This is certainly true for Arthur in the Maleger episode, and the preceding scenes in the Castle of Alma have stressed the capacity of the heroes for self-consciousness. Allegoresis, too, is a response to a *sentiment d'incompletude* with respect to an object offered for interpretation. We will be presented with just such an object in our next section, namely, those retreating apples of Tantalus, "whose reality remains forever unattainable."

Journey into the Interior

[i]

Nowhere in the poem is the consciousness that the internal environment is potentially or imaginatively external so strong as in Book II, partly because the internal environment of temperance, like the external environment, is particularly physical to begin with. Book II is the most landscaped part of the poem, and its landscapes are the most explicitly allegorical; they are very much the *ob-jectum* of the temperament confronting

---

[73] C. G. Jung, *Psyche and Symbol*, ed. Violet S. de Laszlo (Garden City, 1958), p. 8 (text reprinted from *Aion*, "The Shadow," in *Collected Works*, trans. R.F.C. Hull, vol. 9, Pt. 2). The usefulness of this quotation was suggested to me by Kent van den Berg. To my examples may be added the unshared laughter of Phedria, which seems rather autistic (see II.vi.3f.).

them. Often they obey a principle of allegorical chiasmus, as we might call it, whereby the external features of the environment reflect the internal ones in inverse form. A man in an environment here often stands for the environment in the man. A strong sense of such a chiasmic principle also emerges in the paired imagery of the legend. The bilious cycle of the Gulf of Greediness, alternately engorging itself and regurgitating, seems emblematic of the general tendency in this regard. The fountain, in the "little lake" of the laver where the bathing beauties splash, seems to sail in the sea (II.xii.62), a particularly involuted example of such a chiasmus. Bathing itself, as in the *Odyssey*, seems chiasmatically related to voyaging, since both involve immersion in a vessel and in water. Other examples are the floating and wandering islands, where the island havens have become boats; and the ships caught in the lurking quicksand, where the boat is sinking into land.[74] In the mired lake, the water itself might be described as becoming landlocked. There is also a kind of chiasmus in the conceptualization in this legend: Maleger is strongest in infirmity (II.xi. 40), and the newly aware Mordant dies giving life to sin under the law. One of the most important instances of the chiasmic tendency is the metaphor of interiority, whereby any "interior" or subject is "exterior" and an object from a viewpoint outside of it. The comparison made below between the Cave of Mammon and the Castle of Alma hinges upon just such a chiasmus of internal and external aspects. We meet here, on a smaller scale, the technique that gives *The Faerie Queene* its vast structure of analogy overall.

The significance of the episodes involving the Castle of Alma resides to a large extent in the Castle's having an inside and an outside. One might guess that the child begins to achieve an "interior self" at just that point in his play when he becomes fascinated with hiding things, and especially with secreting things inside containers. In such play the child repeatedly checks on whether the concealed object is to be found where he has deposited it; we may compare Mammon counting his gold. The child thus teaches himself that objects persist in some super-sensible way; they do not disappear altogether, even though they are temporarily not to be seen. The hidden object, in continuing to exist, parallels the thought of the object in the mind of the person remembering that it is "there." Thus develops a kind of reciprocity between the consciousness of interiority and

---

[74] The most notable example is Phedria's boat, which looks "like a litle forrest" with its boughs and arbors (II.vi.2); that is, her boat has exchanged places with her island. By the time of II.xii.10ff. her island is explicitly sea-borne. A phrase like "departing land" shows this chiasmus in little (II.xii.15—Phedria is launching her boat).

the interiority of consciousness. As we will see, the principal scene in which Guyon is encouraged to reach out for an object finds its precise parallel in the retrieval of information in the cell of Memory. It is also significant that the golden apples of Mammon's underworld probably conceal an interior precisely opposed to the exterior they show.

The interiority of the Castle might be taken as a kind of paradigm for all the enclosed spaces in the poem that stand for something inviolate in experience. It is a castle belonging to a virgin (Hebrew *almah*), but it is also a virgin castle, like the "castellum" of Martha and Mary, which, because Christ entered there, is part of the homily for the feast of the Assumption of the Virgin. (Such a castle appears in the Digby play of *Mary Magdalene*, and is attacked by the seven deadly sins.)[75] Guyon is also a virgin, and he carries a shield picturing the virgin queen; a medieval poet would have had the Virgin Mary. This legend also introduces the virginal Belphoebe, the queen's private person, who was raised by Diana.

The Castle of Alma is under siege, and hence it is also a "castle of perseverance." As in the play by that name, it resists attack, a second attack follows, there is a temporary defeat (Arthur's impasse), and a second victory. By means of this relapse, the tradition—as late as Bunyan's *Holy War*—represents the continuing nature of the struggle against a tireless adversary. In the usual medieval allegory, the castle of the soul was kept by the five wits against the devil. One study cites a French poem called *Le Songe du castel* in which seven kings assault such a castle. They enter by the five windows and secure possession; then an eighth dark king on a black horse overcomes the castle for the last time.[76] One may also compare the seven devils in the parable (Matt. 12:43-45) who come back with the expelled spirit to reoccupy his former house, now "empty, swept, & garnyshed." The Geneva Bible comments: "Yf Satan be cast out, we must watche stil, that he enter not againe, for since he was once mans olde gest, he knoweth euerie hole & corner of our house." Spenser allows for this allegory in the seven bands Maleger has assigned to the main entrance of the Castle; perhaps the mouth has been chosen because sin requires consent. Christ says that it is not what enters the mouth but what leaves it that defiles a man (Matt. 15:11-20, Mark 7:16-23).

Spenser is more interested in the ceaseless battery of stimuli on the bulwarks of the five senses. There is a psychomachia theme here, but only when the Castle becomes identified in our minds with the subject of the

[75] *The Digby Plays*, ed. F. J. Furnivall, EETS, Extra Series, no. 70 (London, 1896), pp. 78–83.
[76] Roberta Douglas Cornelius, *The Figurative Castle; a Study in the Medieval Allegory of the Edifice with Especial Reference to Religious Writings* (Bryn Mawr, Pa., 1930), pp. 16f. For a thorough-going example of the soul as a besieged city, with scouts, temptations, and the siege-engines of avarice, see Gregory of Nyssa, *In Ecclesiast. Hom.* VIII, on "There is a time for making war," in PG, XLIV, 743–748.

two major temptations in the legend. A close analogue for Spenser's symbolism, taken as a whole, is the elaborations on the temptation of Buddha in the wilderness by Māra, the Evil One. In an early version Māra's attacking hosts are described:

> Pleasures of sense compose thy foremost ranks;
> dislikes thy second; thirst and hunger form
> thy third array; cravings come fourth; the fifth
> is sloth and torpor; sixth faintheartedness;
> doubts make the seventh; th' eighth, pretense, hard heart,
> and pelf, repute, the pride of place, with fame
> ill-gotten, scorn of others, praise of self.[77]

In one version the Buddha is showered with rains, rocks, spears, arrows, coals, and ashes.[78] In other versions the attacking demons appear with inhuman cries—"some with a thousand mouths, others potbellied and deformed, others drinking blood, all grimacing and laughing horribly."[79] In the West it is St. Anthony who suffers these attacks in the wilderness; he also passes unmoved by some gold.[80] Bosch and Breughel painted the besieged saint, and they could have painted the wonderful army of Maleger.

Maleger's grotesque minions have obvious affinities with the victims of Circe, especially in their resemblance to a similar crew that impedes Rug-

---

[77] The verses are found in Clarence H. Hamilton, ed., *Buddhism . . . Selections from Buddhist Literature*, Library of Liberal Arts (Indianapolis, 1952), p. 19, reprinting the Padhana-sutta from the Sutta-nipāta, trans. Lord Chalmers, in *Buddha's Teachings*, Harvard Oriental Series, XXXVII, pp. 101, 103, 105.

[78] See Edward J. Thomas, *The Life of Buddha* (3rd edn., London, 1956), pp. 71–80, 230–232, 239f., and A. Foucher, *The Life of Buddha*, trans. and abr. by Simone B. Boas (Middletown, Conn., 1963), pp. 110–114.

[79] Oroon Ghosh, *The Dance of Shiva and Other Tales*, Signet Classics (New York, 1965), pp. 200f.

[80] Anastasius, *Life of Anthony*: chap. 9 (animal forms of the devil); chap. 13 (demonic animals that occupy ruins); chap. 12 (the gold in the desert). For the temptation of Christ as an attack on him by the personifications and Furies of the vices of Christian psychomachia tradition, there is a precedent in the "Oratio prima" of Jacobus Strasburgus, *Christi victoris et Satane pugna in deserto* (Leipzig, 1565), a predecessor of *Paradise Regained*; passages from it are translated in Watson Kirconnell, *Awake the Courteous Echo* (Toronto, 1973), pp. 270–286. The Christian's imperilment by the tempting demons of the senses is the theme of the ancient hymn attributed to St. Andrew of Crete and translated by John Neale as "Christian, dost thou see them / On the holy ground" (Presbyterian Hymnal, Philadelphia, 1933, no. 275). The Maleger episode also recalls "The Furies" that attack fallen man in the third part of the first day of DuBartas' second *Week*: these include Sickness, with regiments that assault "the fort of *Adam's* head . . . *Reason's* best Bulwark" (Sylvester trans., ll. 342f.), the vital parts, the natural powers, and the body surface, along with four captains "far more fierce and eager, / That on all sides the Spirit it selfe beleaguer" (ll. 654f.): Sorrow, Joy, Feare, and Desire. The last includes in his band Ambition, and Avarice "all-arm'd in hooking Tenters" (l. 708).

giero on the island of Alcina (*O.F.* VI.6of.). They may also recall the beasts that build in the ruins of Babylon and Edom.[81] This link is not completely unlikely, given the comparison of the Castle to the Tower of Babel (II.ix.21). A collation of the full list of Spenser's beasts with a

Isaiah 13 and 34	Maleger's bands	Phantastes' mind	Guyon's voyage	Alcina's beasts	Malengine
siren (LXX)			mermaid		
lamia (Vulg.)	hags	hags	harpy		
strange	deformed		visages		
visures	creatures		deform		
	fiend	fiend			
owl	owl	owl	owl, stritch		(bird)
raven			raven		
stork					
eagle (LXX)	eagle, gryphon			eagle	
wildcat	lynx, tiger	lion		cat	
ape	ape	ape		ape	
hedgehog	urchin				hedgehog
ass-centaur		centaur		centaur	(Periclymenus)
satyr, faun			sea-satyr	goat	(goat)
jackal	dog			hound	
dragon	snake				snake
	boar, swine				
	toad				
	spider				
	snail				

synthetic list collected out of the various translations of the Bible shows enough correspondences to make Calvin's comment on Isaiah 13 apt: "the place of men is nearly supplied by beasts, which represent the dispositions of those who raised those goodly edifices."[82]

Maleger's bands are specifically ugly, deformed, impoverished-looking, and greedy. Hence it is somewhat ironic that the first crew, appealing to the lust of the eyes, lays siege with the engines of "Beautie, and money," corresponding to the temptations of Acrasia and Mammon. For the self-possessed, or active, or awakened mind, beauty and money are goods, insofar as they are subject to "right vsaunce" (II.vii.7); for the passive mind, they are idols that come to possess all the energies of their be-

---

[81] See the accompanying table. The ostrich-form of the sense of taste is a particular curiosity. It must be a deformation analogous to the cranelike neck of Gluttony at I.iv.21, which in turn answers to the prayer of the gourmand recorded by Aristotle, that his throat become longer than the crane's (*Nich. Ethics* III.x, 1118b).

[82] *Commentary on Isaiah*, trans. Pringle, vol. 3, p. 56.

holders. Frye explains that the Castle of Alma contains both goods: beauty, in the sense of order and proportion; and wealth, in the sense of well-being, or health.[83] The admission of Guyon and Arthur to the Castle symbolizes something like the temperate assimilation of experience, including the admission of others to our confidence. Guyon, being temperate himself, must also be engaged in self-appraisal, or introspection. The exclusion of Maleger's unhealthy crew stands for the insulation of a body of integrity from whatever would break it down. At the bulwark of the sense of hearing, where we might have expected sensual music, Spenser has slander, lies, flattery and bad counsel (II.xi.10), things that corrupt judgment. Likewise, Alma's porter debars "Bablers of folly, and blazers of crime" (II.ix.25)—not so much evil company, but rather the spirit that might prompt the utterance of such things.[84]

Now let us turn to the Cave of Mammon. Guyon throughout his legend is a rather nomadic character, like his companion the Palmer, and his wandering into the desert to be tempted is rather appropriate. Once again we may recall the employment of a travels motif in this legend, a motif that in this instance symbolizes the quest for experience, as opposed to the quest for innocence in Book I. Such a quest is in danger of degenerating into a mere search for novelty, and even of becoming a kind of feckless vagabondage. In allowing Mammon to tempt him, Guyon clearly takes this risk, and yet the form of the adventure as a temptation casts him in the role of resisting worldly experience. Guyon will prove to be a little like Mammon's gold:

> And euery feend his busie paines applide
> To melt the golden metall, ready to be tride.
>
> (II.vii.35)

Mammon is apparently the appropriate spirit. Cornelius Agrippa describes him as the head of the last order of devils: "Moreover the Tempters and Ensnarers have the last place, one of which is present with every man, which we therefore call the evill *Genius*, and their Prince is *Mammon*, which is interpreted covetousness."[85] Agrippa's evil genius will re-

---

[83] "Structure of Imagery" in *Fables of Identity*, p. 81.

[84] For the theme, cf. *The Gouernour*, III.xxvii, *edn. cit.*, p. 290, where Elyot cites Lucian's *Calumny of Apelles* to the effect that "a wise man, when he douteth of the honestie and vertue of the persone accused, he shulde kepe close his eares and nat open them hastely . . . , and put reason for a diligent porter and watche, whiche ought to examine and lette in the reportes that be good, and exlude and prohibite them that be contrary. For it is a thinge . . . very unfittinge to ordeyne for thy house a keper or porter, and thine eares and mynde to leaue to all men wyde open."

[85] *Three Books of Occult Philosophy*, III.xviii, trans. J[ohn] F[rench] (London, 1651), p. 399. Cf. Geo. Victorius, *A Discourse on the Nature of Spirits*: "Also there

mind us of the fiend that stalks Guyon throughout his trial, waiting for a slip.

The temperance previously described has been a virtue corresponding to classical descriptions of temperance and continence. Here temperance takes on a second meaning, expounded in Macrobius and Plotinus, for whom the virtue entails the soul's repudiation of the world.[86] Hence the importance of the analogy to Christ's temptation. In Luke the temptation falls into three parts: the temptation to turn stones into bread (the temptation of material substance); the temptation to assume, at Satan's disposal, the earthly equivalents of the power and the glory; and the temptation to tempt God by Christ's throwing himself off the temple. The third temptation refers to a Psalm prophesying the Messiah, which says that angels will bear him up; when the temptation in Matthew ends, angels indeed do come and minister to Christ. They are not described, but they have the place at the end of the temptation that the other angels at the tomb have at Christ's resurrection. In Matthew, the angel of the tomb descends from heaven, and so does the angel that looks after Guyon at the end of his three-day interment. The canto in question begins with an allusion to the Psalm on the mindfulness of God toward man, a verse in which Erasmus, for example, heard an allusion to the guardian angels of men.[87]

---

are tempters and deceivers that lie in wait to deceive, who are present with every man; and these we term evil Angels, which have Mammon for their King, and they do affect men with an insatiable avarice, and thirsty desire after authority and dominion." (Trans. Robert Turner, 1555, reprint, London, 1783, in *Agrippa's Fourth Book of Occult Philosophy*, p. 187.)

[86] *Comm. in Somn. Scip.*, I.viii; *Enneads* I, VI.6. Plotinus' distinction appears in Aquinas, *Summa Theol.*, Pt. II, 1st Pt., q.61, art.5, resp.: the *perfecting* virtue of temperance, "so far as nature allows, neglects the needs of the body"; the *perfect* virtue "knows no earthly desires." Perfecting virtues are those of the man "who flies from human affairs and devotes himself exclusively to the things of God." In *The Book of Vices and Virtues*, a fourteenth-century English trans. of the *Somme Le Roi* of Lorens d'Orleans, ed. W. Nelson Francis, EETS, no. 217 (London, 1942), p. 123, the three offices of temperance are the shunning of the sins of the flesh, pride of heart, and covetousness; in Dan Michel's *Agenbyte of Inwit*, ed. Richard Morris, EETS, no. 23 (London, 1866), p. 125, the offices are shunning the world, flesh, and devil. In Petrarch's *De Vita Solitaria*, Lib. I, Tract. iv, cap. 5, Plotinus' concept is invoked as an argument in favor of the solitary life; this chapter is directly followed by a discussion of the rewards of unwitnessed spiritual combat in the wilderness, Christ's temptation being the major example. (Guyon's solitary victory also seems unsung, for no one either during or after the ordeal seems to know that Guyon has undertaken it.) Landino, in his exposition of the progress of Aeneas to Italy, speaks of the perfecting of Aeneas' temperance through the three Neo-Platonic grades of virtue: civil, purgatorial, and souls already purged: *Quaestiones Camuldulenses* (Venice, n.d.), fol. hii[r-v], kii[v], liii[v], and mi[r].

[87] Ps. 8:1 Erasmus, *Concerning the Immense Mercy of God*: "The eighth psalm repeats what Moses relates in Genesis, marveling at God's goodness, who has be-

The analogy with the three domains of Mammon's temptation seems fairly pronounced. At the outset Mammon tempts Guyon to worship his "godhead" (II.vii.9), a feature of the second temptation in Luke; Mammon claims to be able to purvey kingdoms "in twinckling of an eye," an exact echo of the earlier translations of Luke's "moment of time" (Luke 4:5, in the Coverdale, Great, and Geneva Bibles; the Bishops' Bible introduces the modern version). Guyon refuses Mammon's offer, but he nonetheless consents to visit his realm. Its three areas are the storeroom and smelter (the temptation to acquire substance); the Temple of Philotime (the temptation to acquire glory); and the garden of Proserpina (a mysterious temptation to "give in" and pick the golden apples from a Hesperidean tree).

This last temptation has been variously explained; the evidence suggests that it is partly to be understood as an intellectual temptation.[88] First, if it were an intellectual temptation, it would enjoin some kind of avarice of knowledge or wisdom.[89] As Mammon's realm is infernal, criminals are being punished in it, and Tantalus is specifically instanced for his "mind intemperate." Tantalus is widely taken for a type of greed because that is how his punishment was traditionally allegorized; he is tantalized because

---

stowed so much mercy on man. 'What is Adam's breed,' it says, 'that it should claim they care? Thou has placed him only a little below the angels. . . .' I will say what is even more sublime: we even owe the angels of heaven to the Lord's mercy. ¶ My word would carry little weight, if Paul did not teach this. . . . Speaking of the angels he says: 'What are they, all of them, but spirits apt for service, whom he sends out when the destined heirs of eternal salvation have need of them?' . . . etc." (Trans. J. P. Dolan, *The Essential Erasmus*, New York, 1964, p. 238.)

[88] In *The Allegorical Temper* (New Haven, 1957), Harry Berger covers much the same ground as I do here, stressing the presence of the motif of curiosity throughout the episode, and noting the indication of the time Guyon spends contemplating the plights of the damned in the third realm (II.vii.63, "too long here to be told"—i.e., too long, period). See n. 10, above.

[89] Besides Berger, the reader is referred to Frank Kermode, Jr., "The Cave of Mammon," in *Elizabethan Poetry: Stratford-Upon-Avon Studies* 2, ed. John Russell Brown and Bernard Harris (London, 1960), pp. 151–173. Kermode's thesis has contributed considerably to my thinking here: he derives it from a note by Upton, and maintains that the episode as a whole describes an initiation procedure, based on classical lore concerning the Eleusinian mysteries. The initiation, Kermode concludes, is designed to strengthen "heroic virtue" in the hero. A novel feature of Kermode's argument is the identification of the fiend stalking Guyon with a particular functionary in the mysteries: he cites Lucian, *Kataplous* 22 and 25, on the guarding of the damned by a torch-bearing Fury—one of Lucian's characters compares the procedure of the Mysteries. Kermode also cites the devouring demon Eurynomus in the picture by Polygnotus which portrayed the underworld, as described in Pausanias, X.xxviii.7. (For the analogous demon in Virgil, *Aen.* VI.601ff., see n. 117 below.) There is also some slight evidence for an initiation procedure in the Tantalus-cup reported in Philostratus, *Vit. Apoll.* III.xxv and VII.xiv, and also *Epist.* LXXVIII, "by the waters of Tantalus in which you initiated me"; the latter is a fragment cited

greedy men, being insatiable, can never get enough.[90] But this merely determines his appropriateness for this whole canto, rather than for a particular place in it. His is the intemperate tongue, for Spenser, "That did the bankets of the Gods bewray" (*Virgil's Gnat*, 386); this crime is surely alluded to here, since Tantalus goes on to "blaspheme" the Jove whom once he feasted (II.vii.59–60). In grislier versions of his dealings with his divine associates, Tantalus sorely tried their divine omniscience with a feast of human flesh, or offered men the divine food. He accuses the gods of injustice, and he is a violater of divine prohibitions. The presence of Tantalus therefore argues, at least to some extent, for an allegory of forbidden knowledge. His companion Pilate also had dealings with a divine person, and he now adjudges himself "the falsest Iudge, alas, / And most vniust" (II.vii.62).[91] Thus we have a second character whose mistake is intellectual, the Pilate who asked, "What is truth?" and then washed his hands of the answer. If Tantalus was too curious, perhaps Pilate was not curious enough.

The evidence of the golden apple tree is ambiguous, but tree and water suggest their redeemed counterparts in Eden. Wisdom is said to be a tree of life to them who lay hold of her,[92] and Spenser's tree in Eden is

---

in Porphyry, *De Styge, sub fin.* More important is the information that in the Eleusinian mysteries of Proserpina and Demeter *it is forbidden to sit.* Spenser would not have known the Homeric *Hymn to Demeter*, but the information is found in Clement of Alexandria, *Exhortation to the Heathen*, ii (ANF, vol. 2, p. 176), with reference to the fatigued Demeter sitting down at a well near Eleusis. Psyche, when she visits Proserpina in Hades, refuses the offer of a *sedile delicatum* and so is enabled to take a box containing a secret from Proserpina back from the underworld (Apulieus, *The Golden Ass* VI.20). See also n. 117 below. For objections to Kermode's view of Tantalus as a revealer of mysteries, see Paul Alpers, *The Poetry of "The Faerie Queene"* (Princeton, 1968), pp. 245–247.

[90] Tantalus is a type of greed in Horace, *Sat.* I.i, ll. 68ff. In Lucretius, *De Rerum* III.98off., Tantalus is a type of the fear of the gods, or superstitious anxiety, and in Cicero, *Tusc. Disp.* IV.xvi.35f., a type of anxiety, especially over possessions. Temperance is being discussed as a kind of frugality there. For other greedy Tantaluses, see Fulgentius, *Mitologiarum*, II.xv, citing Petronius, *Frg.* 82, and *Virgiliana Continentia*, in Helm, *Fvlgentivs. Opera*, p. 101; Servius, *ad. Aen.* VI.603; Macrobius, *Comm. in Somn. Scip.*, I.x.13; Alanus, *De Planctu Naturae*, prose vi; Boccaccio, *G. D. G.*, XII.i (Romano edn., vol. 2, p. 579); Alciati, *Emblemata*, Emb. LXXXIV (edn. of Antwerp, 1581), citing Petronius; Greene, *Whitney's Choice of Emblemes*, p. 74; Fraunce, *Third Part of the Countess of Pembroke's Iuychurche*, fol. 30ʳ (citing Horace, but also Ovid on Tantalus as a teller of secrets); Wilson, *Rhetorique*, ed. Mair, p. 196; Sidney, *Astrophel and Stella*, Son. 24; DuBartas, *Divine Weeks*, in Sylvester's trans., II–I.iii, ll. 709–717; and Comes, *Mythol.*, VI.xviii, *edn. cit.*, pp. 628f. (quoting Horace).

[91] In Lucian, *Kataplous* 28f., a tyrant is punished by not being allowed to drink of Lethe; he must go on remembering what he did in life, and he shares a berth with Tantalus.

[92] Prov. 3:18; see also Prov. 11:30. Cf. Prov. 15:4: "A wholsome tongue is as a tre of life."

closely associated with the tree of the knowledge of good and evil. Eve's sin reaches into all of sin's dimensions, but it certainly included an immoderate desire for knowledge, for something that would make her like God. Proserpina herself is detained in the underworld for eating the fruit of the dead, and of course Proserpina was occasionally compared to mankind in the bondage of the devil.[93] The contrast between the tree in Eden and Proserpina's infernal herber is enforced by the parallel between the heroes: Redcrosse is nourished by the one in the course of his three-day battle, and Guyon eschews the fruit of the other in the course of his. We may compare the diction as well:

> In all the world like was not to be found,
>   Saue in that soile, where all good things did grow,
>   And freely sprong out of the fruitful ground,
>   As incorrupted Nature did them sow,
>
> (I.xi.47)

> . . . a gardin goodly garnished
> With hearbs and fruits, whose kinds mote not be red:
> Not such, as earth out of her fruitful woomb
> Throwes forth to men, sweet and well sauoured,
> But direfull deadly black both leave and bloom
> Fit to adorne the dead, and decke the drery toombe.
>
> (II.vii.51)

The character of Mammon's golden apples cannot be understood without reference to this production of a black and deadly fruit that has lost its savor.

The apples of Mammon are provocative—this is one thing that all the mythological allusions have in common, apart from the letters a, t, l, or n. To a greater or lesser degree the various apples all suggest the use of intelligence or cunning, or the lust of the eye. The apples of the Hesperides were taken for a type of knowledge or learning.[94] The apples of Atalanta,

[93] Dante's Matilda, who reminds us of an unfallen Eve, is compared to Proserpina at *Purg.* XXVIII.49–53. In the *Ovide Moralizé*, V.3041–3144, Ceres looking for Proserpina is the Church seeking to recover the souls of the faithful who have strayed from the fold. (Text in *Verhandelingen de Koninklijke Nederlandse Academie*, vols. 15, 21, 30, 37, 43, ed. C. de Boer and J. van't Sant, Amsterdam, 1915–1938.) In Sandy's commentary on his Ovid, Proserpina's apple is equated with Eve's, and in *Paradise Lost* IX.432 Eve is implicitly compared to Proserpina by way of the Classical simile that made Proserpina herself a gathered flower (see *Par. Lost* IV.268ff.).

[94] Fulgentius, *Virgiliana Continentia*, in *Opera*, ed. Helm, pp. 96–98, explains that the Hesperides are to be understood as study, understanding, memory, and eloquence, in the course of describing the golden bough as "secreta scientiae." In Comes, *Mythol.*, VII.vii, *edn. cit.*, p. 727, the same apples are given a variety of significances, including that of astronomical knowledge and the reward for virtue. Achilles Bocchius, *Symbolcarvm Qvaestionvm*, symb. lv, expounds the dragon as

Acontius, and Até are lures; in the case of Até, there is added a critical judgment. (Até's apple came from the "tree of Proserpina," according to Peele's *Arraignment of Paris*.)[95] "Partial Paris," the judge, chooses the beauty of Venus, and thereby rejects the wisdom offered by Minerva.[96]

Compared to other symbols in the poem, the apples are unexplained by Spenser; it is in their nature to provoke our curiosity, and this in itself is evidence for their character. Curiosity, according to Aquinas, is a vice related to the lust of the eyes.[97] The contrary of curiosity in Aquinas is studiousness, and studiousness is described as a part of the virtue of temperance; it is classified as a kind of restraint, and the whole discussion follows on a consideration of the temptation of our first parents. Curiosity itself has a place in the tradition, presented by E. M. Pope on *Paradise Regained*, of the "triple equation" of Christ's temptation.[98] According to this tradition, Christ was tempted both as a second Adam, and as a worldling. One version of this equation expounded by St. Augustine applies here:

> Now these three kinds of vice, namely the pleasure of the flesh, and pride, and curiosity, include all sins. And they appear to me to be enumerated by the Apostle John, when he says, "Love not the world; for all that is in the world is the lust of the flesh, and the lust of the eyes, and the pride of life." For through the eyes especially prevails curiosity. To what the rest indeed belong is clear. And that temptation of the Lord Man was threefold: by food, that is, by the lust of the flesh, where it is suggested, "com-

---

cupidity, but the apples as wisdom. For dangerous golden apples in the *romanzi*, see Boiardo, *Orl. Inn.* II.v.6ff., the garden of Falerina, and I.xii.26, the Trunk of Treasure in the garden of riches which Prasildo is sent off to conquer. (The tree has "fruit of emerald and branches of gold," rather like the realm of Venus in Politian's *Stanze*, I.94, which includes a plant, "which has branches of emerald and fruit of gold; and fruit that stopped Atalanta still.") These trees all recall the wedding gift that Pluto offers Proserpina in Claudian, *De Raptu* II.290ff.: "a precious tree with curving branches gleaming with vegetable metal in the shady wood" (trans. Platnauer in Loeb edn.)—Pluto promises that his bride will be enriched with golden fruit. For Pluto as avarice, see Giraldus, *Hist. Deorum*, Syntag. VI, in *Op. om.*, I, col. 194A, citing Fulgentius on Pluto as wealth (*Mitologiarum*, I.v; see also Plato, *Cratylus* 403a), and *ibid.*, col. 202G, reporting the god Pluto to be meant by Mammon in Chaldee or Syriac, "who is interpreted riches or lucre."

[95] Prologue, l. 7.

[96] For Paris' rejection of Minerva's wisdom in choosing to award the apple to Venus, see Fulgentius, *Mitol.*, II.i, and Comes, *Mythol.*, VI.xxiii, *edn. cit.*, pp. 654, 660f. See below, "Fables of Green Fields," sec. iii, esp. n. 142.

[97] *Summa Theol.*, Pt. II, 2nd Pt., q.167, art.1–2; for studiousness, see *ibid.*, q.166 (esp. art.2, obj.3 and resp., where studiousness is defined as a kind of restraint). These places are also cited by Berger, *Allegorical Temper*, p. 23.

[98] Elizabeth Marie Pope, *Paradise Regained: The Tradition and the Poem* (New York, 1962), chap. V, "The Triple Equation," pp. 51–69.

mand these stones that they be made bread": by vain boasting, where, when stationed on a mountain, all the kingdoms of this earth are shown Him, and promised if He would worship: by curiosity, where, from the pinnacle of the temple, He is advised to cast Himself down, for the sake of trying whether He would be borne up by Angels.[99]

This patristic identification of Luke's third temptation with curiosity might be compared to the "kingdoms temptation" of Adam: Gregory specifies the first two temptations (as given in Matthew) as gluttony and vainglory; he makes the third an avarice for power, and compares Adam's "knowing good and evil."[100] It would be possible to extrapolate from this an "avarice for knowledge."

Spenser conforms most nearly to the tradition as a whole with regard to the second temptation: Christ's temptation on the temple as Adam's temptation to be like the gods—the temptation of the pride of life, or vainglory. Philotime is exalted to the height of a room resembling a temple, but she is said to have been excluded from the company of the gods. Being the *third* temptation in Ambrose's commentary on Luke, the temple temptation becomes the temptation to ambition, which may better have fit the kingdoms temptation.[101] The effect of the order of temptations in Matthew is also felt in Ambrose's summary. Ambrose states the important principle that "the causes of temptation are the causes of cupidity. Moreover, the causes of cupidity are delight of the flesh, the appearance of glory, and the avidity for power." He also demotes the food temptation;

[99] *Ennar. in Psalmos*, VIII.8, as trans. in NPNF, 1st Series, vol. 8, pp. 31f. With Augustine compare Aquinas, *Summa Theol.*, Pt. II, 1st Pt., q.84, art.1, on covetousness, "which goes by the name of avarice," as being the root of all sins (see also q.79, art.5, resp. ad obj.1), and q.77, art.5, on the threefold division of all sin into *concupiscence of the flesh* (the appetite for food and sex), *the pride of life* ("inordinate appetite of the arduous good . . . for pride is the inordinate appetite of excellence"), and *concupiscence of the eyes* ("whether this be taken as referring to sight itself, of which the eyes are the organ, so as to denote curiosity . . . or to the concupiscence of things which are proposed outwardly to the eyes, so as to denote covetousness"). Cf. also the threefold classification of "man's good" in *Summa Theol.*, Pt. 2, 1st Pt., q.84, art.4, resp.: (1) the good of the soul, excellence of honor and praise; (2) the good of the body, its preservation through food and sexual intercourse; (3) external goods, or riches. The corresponding vices are: (1) vainglory, (2) gluttony and lust, (3) covetousness.

[100] *XL Hom. in Evang.*, Lib. I, Hom. XVI.2, in PL, LXXVI, 1135f. Cf. also Pseudo-Chrysostomon, in Aquinas, *Catena Aurea, St. Matt.*, Parker Society trans., vol. 1, Part I, p. 121: "nets of appetite, ambition, covetousness."

[101] Ambrose, *Expos. Evang. Sec. Lucam*, IV.17, Pl, XV, 1617 (the arrows of *gula*, *jactantia*, and *ambitio*; *jactantia* is varied to *facilitas* at col. 1622). On the second temptation: "is it good to exercise power, to desire honor? Good if it is bestowed upon us, not if it is seized"; "we are taught then to despise ambition because it is subject to the power of the devil" (*ibid.*, IV.28, 30, in PL, XV, 1620f.; quoted in Aquinas, *Catena Aurea*).

Satan did not prevail over Eve through food, "but the attractive ambition of promised honors deceived her."[102]

Augustine's interpretation of the third temptation provides Spenser's reader with the more notable datum. The theme is especially Augustinian: "concupiscence of the eyes," according to *De Vera Religione* (38), "makes men curious," and in *Confessions*, X.30ff., the Saint takes up the three Johannine categories as the temptations offered by the flesh, by curiosity, and by self-esteem, respectively. "Pride of life" is translated as *ambition of the world*, showing the influence of the tradition we have just invoked, and it somewhat anticipates our argument to note that Augustine's discussion turns upon the difficulties in being objective about being the subject of praise. The "lust of the eyes" is explained as follows: "there is present in the soul a kind of empty longing and curiosity which aims not at taking pleasure in the flesh, but at acquiring experience through the flesh, and this empty curiosity is dignified by the names of learning and science." As a temptation, this lust takes in the indulgence of morbid curiosity about, say, pain; curiosity about nature, such as the desire to investigate the courses of the stars; curiosity about sacrilegious mysteries; inquiry of the ghosts of the dead; asking God for a sign; and, in general, curiosity about "things which it does no good to know and which men only want to know for the sake of knowing."[103] Most of these kinds of knowledge can be read into Spenser's third temptation, but not into the first and second, considered by themselves.

Furthermore, we learn from Augustine that this kind of lust of the eyes leads one to make trials and experiments. Ambrose stated the synonymy of the sources of cupidity and temptation, and this synonymy is surely one reason why the two major episodes of the legend take the form they do. Augustine states that there is a temptation to "try," a deduction that also follows from the equation Christ makes between Satan and the Israelites who tempted God. So here we come upon a particular intensification of the temptation subject, a temptation to "attempt." In this peculiar compounding of the subject we also stumble upon a mystery, namely a never-to-be-spoken cooperation—or even alliance—between the tempter and the tempted. This alliance helps account for the strange diffidence or reserve that prevails between the two parties to the temptation. Of course such an alliance is only a temporary appearance, but while Guyon is resisting Mammon's three specific temptations, he is indulging the general temptation to make trial of himself. In refusing the apples of curiosity, however, he would be symbolically declaring a limit on the temptation as

---

[102] Ambrose, *Expos. Evang. Sec. Lucam*, IV.34, in PL, XV, 1622.

[103] *Confessions*, X.36, trans. Rex Warner. This text is also quoted by Berger, *Allegorical Temper*, p. 26, who makes much the same point about Guyon's self-temptation in pursuit of what may be an idle desire to experience his own excellence.

338

a whole, and, as it were, refusing to put the Father to further unnecessary tests. He does not taste the apples, that is, he does not *test* them.

Mammon, on the other hand, is a likely subject for a temptation to evil curiosity. By nature he is secretive, as his first action of hiding his wealth "From the worldes eye" indicates (II.vii.vii); he totals up his wealth "to feed his eye / And covetous desire" (II.vii.4), which means he enjoys tempting himself. His coat, like a dragon's hoard, is richly entailed with "curious mould." Thus Mammon, who is eventually "enmoued" (II.vii.51), may be thought of as an archetypal tempter, as one succumbing to the temptation that is offered whenever temptation is put in harm's way.

The apples may well be a celebrated curiosity in their own right. And this being the case, they may have something further to tell us about the character of the third temptation. In many ways Spenser's apples resemble the famous Dead Sea fruit that grows in the incinerated district of Sodom. St. Augustine describes the region:

> The Land of Sodom was not always as it now is; but once it had the appearance of other lands, and enjoyed equal if not richer fertility; for, in the divine narrative, it was compared to the paradise of God. But after it was touched (by fire) from heaven, as even pagan history testifies, and as is now witnessed by those who visit the spot, it became unnaturally and horribly sooty in appearance; and its apples, under a deceitful appearance of ripeness, contain ashes within.[104]

This description conforms to those of Josephus, Tacitus, and Solinus, but it adds the biblical comparison that makes the apples the fruit of a fallen paradise.[105] Mandeville likewise reports that cinders are found inside the apples, "in token that by wrath of God the cities and the land were burnt *and sunken into Hell.*"[106] If Mammon's apples are those of Sodom, the Renaissance reader would have recognized the fruit offered to Guyon as not only suspicious, but also specious. Guyon himself accuses Mammon of abusing his worldlings with "vaine shewes" (II.vii.39).

[104] *Civ. Dei*, XXI.viii, trans. M. Dods, *edn. cit.*, p. 777. Cf. Wisdom 10:7: ". . . the waste land that smoketh, yet giueth testimonie, and the trees that beare frute that neuer cometh to ripnes" (Geneva Bible). For Sodom as the garden of God, see Gen. 12:10.

[105] Josephus, *Hist.* IV.viii.4; Tacitus, *Hist.* V.6; Solinus, *Polyhistor* xlvii; Justinus, *Hist.* xxxvi.6. Cf. also Pliny, *Nat. Hist.* V.xv.71–73: nothing sinks in the Dead Sea; Engedi, once second only to Jerusalem in fertility and palm groves, is now a *bustum* (a cremated place).

[106] *Travels*, ed. Seymour, chap. 12, p. 77. The apples are also described in Peter Comestor, *Historia Scholastica*, Lib. Gen., cap. liii (PL, CXCVIII. 1102).

The evidence for the character of the apples is stronger than it might at first seem. Descriptions of the apples of Sodom are almost always found in connection with the Dead Sea, for which there is a close analogy in the Idle Lake. *Batman upon Bartholemew* describes the Dead Sea's most notable property: "whensoever thou woldest haue drowned therein any thing that hath lyfe . . . , anone it plungeth and commeth again up, though it be strongly thrust downward."[107] So the Idle Lake: "the waves . . . every weightie thing . . . did upbeare / Ne ought mote euer sinke downe to the bottome there." Phedria's floating island may be compared to the asphalt that floats on the Sea, as may the castle maintained on the Dead Sea by Tasso's Armida (see *Ger. Lib.* X.63). This characteristic extends to the equally pestilential waters of Spenser's River Cocytus: "many damned wights, / In those sad waves which direfull deadly stanke, / Plonged continually of cruell Sprights" (II.vii.57). The passage just quoted from *Batman upon Bartholemew* continues:

> In the brim thereof trees grow, the apples whereof be greene till they be ripe, & if ye cut them when they be ripe, ye shall finde ashes within them. . . . And there growe most faire apples, that make men see them, haue likeing to eate of them, and if one take them, they fade & fall in ashes, and smoke as though they were burning.

The text cites Josephus and the *Glossa* on II Peter; the 1510 edition of Hegesippus (Ambrose's version of Josephus) says, "ut edendi generent spectatibus cupiditatem" (so that they produce in the beholders the desire of eating), as does the *Glossa*.[108] But the 1471 text of Orosius, on the same phenomenon, says, "ut edentibus gignant cupiditatem" (so that they produce cupidity in the eaters).[109]

The linking of these apples with the Hesperidean fruit turns up in a text very close to Spenser, for van der Noot pairs them as images for miserliness:

> Some other become thorough riches like vnto the Dragon which kept the golden apples of the Orchard of the Hesperide, whereof he himself had no commoditie, neyther suffred any other to enjoy any part of it. Tertullian sayeth, that riches resemble and are much lyke vnto the Apples of *Sodome* and *Gomorre*, which seemed goodly and faire to the eye, but being once touched, fell and straightway turned into dust and ashes.[110]

[107] *Battman vppon Bartholeme, His Booke De Proprietatibus Rerum* (London, 1582), XIII.xiii, pp. 193f.

[108] *Historia de Bello Ivdaico*, trans. by Ambrose (edn. of I. Badius Ascensius, Paris, 1510), IV.xviii, Fol. Lᵣ; *Glossa ordinaria*, on II Peter 2:6, PL, CXIV, 692.

[109] *Impressus is liber est . . . Augustae a. 1471*, per Johannem Schüszler, as cited by Rev. Joseph Bosworth in his trans. of *King Alfred's Anglo-Saxon Version of . . . Orosius* (London, 1859), p. 63, n. 1.

[110] *A Theatre for voluptuous wordlings*, fol. 4; Hankins, *Source and Meaning*, p. 131, also quotes this passage. The reference is to Tertullian, *Apolog.*, xl.7. Other

The classical and Christian references alone cannot confirm this identification however. One comes a step closer to the poet with the blighted pleasure garden described by Diana in Lydgate's *Reson and Sensuallyte*; the Latin manuscript gloss (according to the modern text) identifies the poisonous plants there with the Dead Sea fruit.[111] We meet other pleasure gardens in Spenser's poem, and it is significant that the most important of these, the Garden of Adonis, is sometimes paired with the so-called gardens of Tantalus—that is, the "gardens" or fruits dangled in front of the condemned man in hell.[112] These gardens were proverbial for illusion —not only for the unpossessible, but also for the fallacious or specious. This is apparent in Fulgentius, who goes on to say that Tantalus was deposited in a lake in the inferno, and that the hanging apples appeared at his touch *to fly into ashes*.[113] This mysterious link between the tantalizing Dead Sea fruit and the punishments in the underworld is attested by *Paradise Lost*, where the serpents are tempted and tantalized by a fruit tree that worsens their thirst.[114] The appropriate gloss for such a tree would be Isaiah 44:19–20—"Shall I bowe to the stok of a tre. He fedeth of ashes"—on which the Geneva Bible comments that the idolator "is abused as one that wold eat ashes, thinking to satisfie his hungre." Although we

---

early Christian notices of the deceptions wrought by these apples are "A Strain of Jonah the Prophet" and "A Strain of Sodom," poems trans. in ANF, vol. 4, pp. 127, 131 (PL, II, 1108, 1104). It is easy to identify van der Noot's tree-guarding dragon with Mammon, on the basis that both are misers. With van der Noot's idea of the dragon, compare Phaedrus, *Fables* IV.xx (otherwise xix or xxi), "Vulpes et draco," where a dragon in a subterranean den is fated to watch over a hidden treasure that it *neither takes for itself nor allows to others*: a fox who finds the dragon likens him to a tormented miser, under the wrath of the gods. Festus, *De Verborum Significatu* IV, *sub* "Dracones," derives the name *apo tou drakein*, "which is seeing. For they are said to have the clearest sharpness of eyes, on which account the ancients set them to lie watch for the sake of the guardianship of treasures." (Solinus, in *Polyhistor* xxxvi, explains the keeper of the apples as merely a serpentine arm of the sea that formed a protective circle around what would otherwise have been a submarine level of ground: perhaps the encirclement of the subterranean garden of Proserpina owes something to these indications.)

[111] E. Sieper, ed., EETS, Extra Series, no. 84, 89 (London, 1901–1903), vol. 1, p. 103.

[112] For this link, see below, Chap. IV, "Gardens of Pleasure," nn. 146ff. That the Bower of Bliss is a garden of Tantalus is suggested by the fruit on the vine at II.xii.54f., "Some as the Rubine . . . Some like faire Emeraudes . . . some . . . of burnisht gold": its "bounches hanging downe, seemed to entice / All passers by . . . And did themselues into their hands incline, / As freely offering to be gathered" (compare the "loaden" and "ouer-hanging branches of the garden in the underworld, II.vii.53, 56). According to Gongora, *Son.* 82, the roses of love are also "apples of Tantalus."

[113] *Mitologiarum* II.xv, "Fabula Tantali," in Helm, *Opera*, p. 57: "poma quoque fugitiuis cinerescentia tactibus."

[114] X.561ff.; for the tantalizing of the devils prior to the temptation of man, see II.604–614.

341

may still not be sure what, in the allegory, Guyon is being tempted to do, we can begin to say why he should not do it: in some way or other, he would be badly deceived.

Guyon is also enticed by Mammon with a "silver stoole"—a footstool—"To rest thy wearie person" (II.vii.63). Food and sleep are the two supports for the life of man, and if eating the fruit of the dead kept Proserpina in hell, sitting on the silver seat is not likely to prove less dangerous to Guyon. An evil rest in this case would imply a relaxation of vigilance. A comic instance is found in *Iliad* XIV, where Hera lures Zeus to bed. She is aided in her scheme by Sleep, to whom she has promised as a reward not only a golden throne, but also a stool on which the god can rest his shining feet when he is feasting (XIV.231ff.). We have seen the contrast between the watchful Care and Sleep at the entry of Mammon's realm (II.vii.25), and we know that Guyon is stalked by a watchful demon. But for a more exact counterpart of the stool, we will want a seat occupied by a figure like Mnemosyne in the Orphic Hymn, who is fond of waking (*philagrupnos*, translated as *irrequies*, unresting, and *pervigil*, vigilant), and who banishes Lethe from the minds of the initiates.[115]

Mammon's stool is in the underworld, and there is only one such seat in the classical Hades, that being the one to which Theseus was anchored. The most important thing about this seat is that Apollodorus tells us that it was called the "chair of forgetfulness"; Horace's phrase for Theseus' chains, "Lethean bonds," must reflect the same tradition.[116] Apollodorus writes about Theseus and his companion Pirithous, that "on the pretense that they were about to partake of good cheer, Hades bade them first be seated on the Chair of Forgetfulness, to which they grew and were held fast by the coils of serpents."[117] Whatever else it implies, the seat offered to Guyon might well entail this hazard of fixity, "getting stuck," as elsewhere in the quicksand of Unthriftyhead. If the seat is to be associated with idleness, one could also compare Phedria's "wandring Islands": "Whosoeuer once hath *fastened* / *His foot* thereon, may neuer it recure, /

[115] *Orpheos Apanta*, ed. G. C. Hambergerus (Leipzig, 1764), Hymn LXXVI, pp. 274–277.

[116] *Odes* IV.7, l. 27.

[117] *Epitome* i.24, trans. Frazer, in Loeb *Apollodorus*, vol. 2, p. 153. (Other references to Theseus' predicament, without the chair, are Diod. Sic., IV.lxiii.4 seq.; Apol. Rhod., *Argonaut.* I.101ff.; Hyginus, *Fab.* LXXIX, and Pausanias, *Perieg.* X.xxix.9.) Pausanius' report of Polygnotus' pictures does include a representation of Sloth (X.xxix.1). More pertinent to Spenser is *Aen.* VI.617f., describing the eternally sedentary Theseus, and also the torment of his partner Pirithoüs, which is usually assigned to Tantalus: "over whom hangs a black crag that now, yea now, would seem to slip and fall! High festal couches gleam with frames of gold, and before their eyes is spread a banquet in royal splendour. Yet, reclining hard by, the eldest Fury stays their hands from touching of the table, springing forth with uplifted torch and thunderous cries" (*Aen.* VI, 601–605, trans. Fairclough in Loeb edn.). Couch and banquet would seem to pair Spenser's symbols.

But wandreth euer more vncertein and vnsure" (II.xii.12). The comparison to the isle of Delos seems to mean that a loss of stability ends in a loss of free movement as well; the forward or motile foot of a free mind may fall into a restless vagabondage, and then the "firm" or "fixt foot" of a steadfast will becomes correspondingly paralyzed.[118] And as Homer so brilliantly shows in the Lotus Eaters episode, the inability to sustain a continuous will—a genuine purposiveness—presumes an abdication or a numbing of the memory.

Though we have only the two classical references to the Chair of Forgetfulness, its existence is also vouched for by a report of a Chair of Memory found in Pausanias' account of the oracle of Trophonius. Pausanias gives ample indication that consultation at this shrine was the crux of an initiation procedure. The procedure began with a purification at a building sacred to the Good Spirit and Fortune, and it continued on to a spring where the initiate drank of the "Water of Forgetfulness," and thence to another called "the Water of Memory." The latter will cause the initiate to remember the things he has seen during his descent into the cave of Trophonius. Afterwards the priests in charge seat him on the Chair of Memory, where he is interrogated as to what he has seen below. His kindred then take him back to the precinct of Fortune and the Good Spirit, "though he is still paralysed with terror and is wholly unconscious, both of himself and his surroundings." Cartari, in his summary of this report, softens this last detail, though he does say that the initiate returns to himself only little by little.[119]

In all of this it is hard not to think of Guyon, separated from his guide, passing through the hands of a Fortune figure, entering the underworld, returning to the surface of the earth unconscious, guarded by his guardian spirit, and rejoined by his guide. And the stool, with its invitation to sloth, may include mental sloth—forgetfulness or inattention or unretentiveness—just as the apples may excite not only the lust of the eyes, but also curiosity. The corresponding antidotes, the fruits of studiousness and the Chair of Heedfulness, or Memory, are notable for their absence, but we will want to keep them in the back of our minds all the same.

[ii]

The tour of the Castle of Alma also falls into three parts. If the explorations of the world inside the earth and the world inside the body

---

[118] For this interpretation of the *piè fermo* in Dante, *Inf.* I.30, which also applies to the "firmnes" of the "fixt foot" of the compasses described in Donne's departure poem, "A Valediction: Forbidding Mourning," see John Freccero, "Dante's Firm Foot," *Harvard Theological Journal*, 53 (1959), pp. 245-281.

[119] Pausanias, *Perieg.* IX.xxxix.5-14; Cartari, *Le Imagini,* "Apollo" (Venice, 1625), p. 63: "un seggio, che si dimandava la sede della memoria. . . ."

should turn out to be parallel, we would have an interesting confirmation of the nature of the three temptations.

At the entrance to each realm there is a stress on vigilance: anxiety in the case of Mammon's cave, circumspection at Alma's castle. Then there is a tour in three stages; at Alma's castle this tour follows the pattern of the three kinds of "spirits" that, according to contemporary physiology, meditated the link in man between the physical and the intellectual creation. These are the natural, cordial, and animal spirits, which act on the body, the emotions, and the mind respectively. Their seats are the liver, the heart, and the brain. The passage of Guyon through the Castle, as a spirit of temperance, perhaps represents the process by which nutriment passes into these subtler forms.

The first stage of the tour includes the refectory and the kitchen; the first realm of Mammon is his stronghold and his smelter. One should note here that in the Renaissance mind the processing of metals and the digestion of food implied similar changes in matter. "Concoction," the name of Alma's cook, is also a technical process of chemical refining by heat; Milton describes the digestion of his angels in this manner:

> . . . with keen dispatch
> Of real hunger, and concoctive heat
> To transubstantiate; what redounds transpires
> Through spirits with ease; nor wonder, if by fire
> Of sooty coal the empiric alchemist
> Can turn, or holds it possible to turn,
> Metals of drossiest ore to perfect gold,
> As from the mine.
>
> (*Par. Lost* V.436–440)

Alma's kitchen stove is described as a controlled volcanic underground; Alma's cooks skim inedible wastes from the cauldron it heats. Comparably, in the underworld Guyon sees both an accumulating store of dead matter, and the process of creating it. The heated ranges, the ladles for removing the dross, and the bellows—which here inflame, rather than temper, an unruly Vulcan—are closely imitated details. (Mammon's furnaces are open; the one at the Castle is closed.) We may even compare the laborers. The feverish demons who serve as Mammon's colliers exhibit the acquisition of substance as an enslaving compulsion; they panic easily. Alma's equally sweaty but more self-possessed workers exhibit the assimilation of food as a controlled drive.

The second stage of each episode takes place in the emotional rather than the physical domain, and treats the appetite for honor. We have paid some attention to this parallel already. The relations are put in order in John Gay's essay on the *Fundamental Principle of Virtue* (Sec. IV), on the "Law of Esteem":

Ambition is a desire of being esteemed. Hence a desire of being thought an object of esteem; hence of being an object of esteem; hence of doing laudable, i.e. useful actions. . . . Ambition in too great a degree is called pride, of which there are several species. The title to the esteem of others, which ariseth from any meritorious action, is called honor. The pleasure arising from honor being paid to us, i.e. from others acknowledging that we are entitled to their esteem, is without a name. Modesty is the fear of losing esteem. The uneasiness or passion which ariseth from a sense that we have lost it, is called shame. So that ambition, and all those other passions and affections belonging to it, together with shame, arise from the esteem of others.[120]

At the Castle, Guyon enters the parlor of the heart, where Alma's paramours are received, cordially one presumes. While Guyon attempts to hold parley with his own Shamefastness, Arthur aspires to cheer a moody and somewhat disdainful Prays-desire. Although consonant with Arthur's own disposition, the sibylline maiden manages to embarrass the Prince by divining the unsureness of his quest for glory. In other words, these anima figures gently suggest the knights' limitations and perhaps qualify their self-estimates.

We may contrast Shamefastness and Prays-desire with Mammon's arrogant daughter Philotime, to whom Mammon offers Guyon a prestigious marriage. Philotime is kin to the vainglorious Lucifera in Book I, as the allusions here to Lucifera's parents, Pluto and Proserpina, would indicate: ambition is a kind of pride, as indicated in St. Thomas' discussion of vainglory.[121] Love-of-esteem, as we have noted elsewhere, is a fallen Gloriana presiding over a corrupted Cleopolis. The match Mammon proposes subtly takes up Guyon's own theme of "honours suit" (II.vii.10), to which

---

[120] "Approbation and Affection Considered with Regard to Merit, or the Law of Esteem." Text in *The English Philosophers from Bacon to Mill*, ed. E. A. Burtt (New York, 1939), pp. 780f. See also Cicero, *Pro Archias* 11: "True merit asks for no other reward for the effort and danger it undergoes than this token of honorable fame. . . . As things are, a certain noble instinct abides deep in the heart of every worthy man, which animates the soul, day and night, with an incentive toward glory and reminds us that the story of our fame must not be given up when the term of life ends: it must be made coexistent with all future time." (Trans. Palmer Bovie, in *Cicero: Nine Orations and the Dream of Scipio* [New York, 1967], pp. 226f.) So also Scipio, in Petrarch, *Life of Scipio*, chap. xi. All men are actuated by praise, according to Cicero in *Pro Archias* 26; it is won by honorable deeds and great services to the state, according to *Phillipics* I.12.

[121] *Summa Theol.*, Pt. II, 1st Pt., q.84, art.4: praise is sought inordinately by vainglory, the first of the seven capital vices. In *Confessions*, X.36–39, Augustine takes up the question of how the temptation to the "pride of life" or vainglory and the love of praise, is to be distinguished from the pleasure taken in intelligent regard; he wonders if one can know whether one can really despise or do without it. Cf. also *Civ. Dei*, V.xii–xiv.

the knight appealed in refusing Mammon's money. Mammon pursues this hint for his own advantage:

> But since thou hast found fauour in mine eye,
> Thy spouse I will her make, if that thou lust,
> That she may thee aduance for workes and merites iust.
>
> (II.vii.49)

There are overtones of theological error in this offer, not to mention a temptation to a presumptuous self-satisfaction. Classical self-reliance is tempted to believe that favor can be found with the Lord on some basis other than faith. Guyon refuses the match, saying that he is already engaged. Guyon also resists "the excessive view"—described by Montaigne in his essay "Of Glory"—"that virtue itself was desirable only for the honor that always attended it: 'There is little difference "twixt buried idleness / And hidden virtue" (Horace). . . . If that were true, we should be virtuous only in public; and there would be no point in keeping under rule and order the operations of the soul, where lies the true seat of virtue, except in so far as they should come to the knowledge of others.' "[122] Shamefastness, the conscience figure at the Castle of Alma, ought to be the monitor of these same "operations of the soul."

Let us review Guyon's progress up to this point. The first temptation was, according to Augustine, "by food." The body, making bread into flesh, betters the temptation to make stones into bread. The second temptation was "by vain boasting"; far from being tempted in this way, Guyon blushes at his immodesty. This is also the temptation to "the pride of life," in which Christ refuses to worship the devil in return for wordly kingdoms. Guyon refuses to accept the worldly honors and dignities at Mammon's disposal, and he also refuses to affiliate with Mammon. He thus maintains a more exclusive devotion, either to his own Shamefastness, or to Gloriana, she being "the Idole of her makers great magnificence" (II.ii.41), or God's glory. The third temptation was "by curiosity," and while Guyon restrains his curiosity, he will be encouraged to indulge his studiousness.

The third stage of the tour of the Castle takes the knights to the three studies housed under Alma's roof. The sages correspond to the archetype of the three wise men in the service of the Virgin; they might be portrayed as young, middle-aged, and old. (Alma's roof is planted with flowers and herb gardens, and perhaps this planting contrasts with the overhanging

---

[122] *Essais*, II.xiv, trans. Donald Frame, in *Complete Essays, edn. cit.*, p. 470. The "workes and merites iust" recall Mammon's suggestion that Guyon "must wage / [His] workes for wealth," and "life for gold engage" (II.vii.18)—i.e., immerse himself in a Protestant work-ethic and the pursuit of that economic success in which Calvinism recognized evidence of God's favor. I am indebted to Mrs. Patricia Parker for this reading.

tree and poisonous vegetation of the garden in the underworld.) The three sages advise Alma; they do not rule her. It is the business of the temperate mind to take its own counsel. The evil judgments alluded to in Mammon's realm are not those pictured on the walls of the central counselor:

> . . . picturals
> Of Magistrates, of courts, of tribunals,
> Of commen-wealthes, of states, or policy,
> Of lawes, of iudgements, and of decretals;
> All artes, all science, all Philosophy,
> And all that in the world was aye thought wittily.
>
> (II.ix.53)

The other use of the word *philosophy* in this legend is found in the Garden of Proserpina, where the plants are described.

> *Cicuta* bad,
> With which th'vniust *Atheniens* made to dy
> Wise *Socrates*, who thereof quaffing glad
> Pourd out his life, and last Philosophy
> To the faire *Critias* his dearest Belamy,
>
> (II.vii.52)

Pilate and Tantalus are also both guilty of evil judgment. The Athenian court and the Roman magistrate also offer a parallel: each presided over a critical point at which classical civilization failed to receive the truth. Tantalus, like his counterpart Aesculapius in Book I, violated the privileges of a divine and forbidden knowledge. Guyon, in contrast, behaves studiously, for he restrains himself from acting in respect to something the significance of which is concealed from him. He resists a temptation to unwisdom. The three sages at the Castle of Alma, on the other hand, are said to be wiser than Socrates, and Guyon's exploration of the Castle doubtless fulfills the Socratic precept of self-knowledge. This self-knowledge includes the stories of past selves in history, or the collective memory, and Guyon and Arthur settle down to read about their progenitors, in a tribute to their intellectual appetites.

Thus we are brought to the figure of Eumnestes, who corresponds to Contemplation in Book I. As the latter reminded us of St. John, Eumnestes reminds us of Homer. He is older than Nestor (to whom Longinus implicitly compares Homer),[123] half-blind, and his chronicles, being a

---

[123] So I read *On the Sublime* IX, which quotes Nestor from *Od.* III.109ff. ("There lies Ajax . . . [and] there my own dear son"), as Homer in his garrulous old age looking back on the *Iliad* of his youth. Like Homer, Nestor in the *Iliad* compares the present unfavorably with the past, and like the Homeric priest of Apollo (*Il.* I.70; cf. *Georg.* IV.392), he has mental command over three dimensions of time,

patriotic catalogue, contain "Argument worth of Moeonian quill" (II.x.3); the Homeric Muses are the daughters of Memory.

The memory is proverbially "the Threasure of the minde" and it "lieth in the hinder part, the which is made most perfect tempertnesse, and moderation of qualities in the braine."[124] Such a treasury would contrast with Mammon's storehouses, but particularly with the gold-laden boughs of the garden of Proserpina and Tantalus. One finds this link in Fulgentius, who explains Aeneas' descent to Avernus as the mind revisiting scenes of its past. Aeneas deposits the golden bough at the gate of Tartarus, and so enters on the Elysian Fields:

> For *elisis* [cancellation] in Greek means *resolutio* [a turning around], from a wild life after the discipline of fear. For as Proserpina is the queen of the underworld, so the queen of knowledge is memory, which reigns in minds anticipating [*proserpens*] an *elisis*. To her, therefore, the golden bough of learning is dedicated; this memory Cicero was accustomed to call the treasury of knowledge.[125]

Mammon's coat is overgrown with rust, because his "huge threasury" is laid up where thieves break in and rust corrupts.[126] Good Memory's records are less perishable: the old man "laid them vp in his immortal scrine / Where they for euer incorrupted dwell" (II.ix.56). Thus Eumnestes and

---

since he remembers three generations of men. Significantly, the greater part of Nestor's portion of the catalogue of ships is taken up with the poet Thamyris, whom the Muses punished by depriving him of his memory (*Il.* II.594ff.). For Nestor as a type of the temperate man, and the temperate lawgiver, see Plato, *Laws* IV, 711e.

[124] Wilson, *Arte of Rhetorique*, ed. Mair, pp. 210–212. So likewise Spenser's schoolmaster, Richard Mulcaster, in *The Elementarie*, I.vii ("laie up in the threasurie of rememberance," Campagnac edn., p. 38); Sidney, *Defense* ("memory being the only treasure of knowledge"); Ascham, *Scholemaster* ("memory, the only key and keeper of all learning," ed. R. J. Schoeck, Don Mills, Ontario, 1966, p. 37); Vives, *Fable about Man* ("the treasury of all things . . . for the safekeeping of these divine riches, a memory, the storehouse of all that we have enumerated"). For this quality of retentiveness in a scholar, see Ascham, *Scholemaster*, I, *sub* MNEMON, *edn. cit.*, p. 30. For my thought, cf. Hugh Boyd's adaptation of Petrarch's *Triumph of Time*: "Not wealth alone, but mental states decay, / And, like the gifts of Mammon, pass away" (in *The Sonnets, Triumphs and Other Poems*, London, 1907, vol. 2, p. 399).

[125] *Virgiliana Continentia*, in *Opera*, ed. Helm, pp. 99, 101f. The reference is to Cicero, *De Orat.* I.v.18. For Proserpina as wisdom, cf. Giraldus, *Hist. Deorum*, Syntag. VI, in *Op. om.*, I, col. 203G seq., citing Proclus (*Six Books on Platonic Theology*, VI.xi) and Plato (*Cratylus* 404d, which derives the name from *sophe*).

[126] Matt. 6:19f.; II.vii.4. With what follows, compare Augustine, *Confessions*, X.8; "I come to the fields and spacious palaces of memory. . . . When I am in this treasure house, some things are produced at once, some things take longer and have, as it were, to be fetched from a more remote part of the store, and some things come pouring out all together and . . . thrust themselves forward as though they were saying: 'Surely you must be looking for me.' . . . what happens is that the images of things perceived are there ready at hand for thought to recall." (Trans. Rex Warner.)

his records fill the gap in the symbolism left by the apples; the books beguile the knights with "delight of nouelties," and their "studies" keep them from dinner (II.x.77). Guyon refuses to fetch the golden apples for Tantalus, but he looks "greedily" at Eumnestes' book (II.ix.60). In a movement contrary to that of the apples, the proper book for Arthur "chaunced to the Princes hand to rize" (II.ix.59). This last must be the effect of recall, to judge by the parallel offered by Eumnestes himself:

> Amidst them all he in a chaire was set
> Tossing and turning them withouten end;
> But for he was vnhable them to fet,
> A litle boy did on him still atend,
> To reach, when euer he for ought did send;
> And oft when things were lost, or laid amis,
> That boy them sought, and vnto him did lend.
> Therefore he *Anamnestes* cleped is,
> And that old man *Eumenstes*, by their propertis.
>
> (II.ix.58)

Here then, in a single image, is an equivalent for Tantalus reaching for the apples and Theseus struggling in the Chair of Forgetfulness. The eternally sedentary Theseus, "condemned to endlesse slouth by law" (I.v.35), has been replaced by the active mind, tossing and turning its books in "endlesse exercise," rooted to the Chair of Memory.

Mammon's sooty appearance and his rusty coat are somewhat belied by the coat's golden lining (II.vii.4); conversely, the golden fruit envelopes dust and ashes—topologically, all linings are both "inside" and "outside." The specious apples and the cell of memory, the first showy and the second deeply recessive, also enhance this consciousness of interiority, from which our discussion began. In Augustine's remarks upon memory and its immense capacity, interiority is a recurrent and problematic subject: "Everything I have learned is there," Augustine says, "removed somehow to an inner place, which is still no place." Especially with learning, "it is not the case that I retain the image and leave the thing itself outside me." Meanings are possessed by the memory without any physical appropriation whatsoever, "for as I go over all the gateways of my body, I am unable to find by which one they gained access." Rather, intellectual knowledge seems to be gotten through recollection itself, as if it were a prior possession, only requiring to be brought into existence that it be kept in mind, or brought to mind. For "memory itself is mind. . . . Therefore the memory must be, as it were, the stomach of the mind." This comparison between rumination and recollection is not perfect, however, because the virtual experience of remembering allows the mind to even remember its own forgetfulness (*Confessions*, X.9–16). This discussion seems to end by proving that the stool of forgetfulness and the seat of memory belong to nearly the same space, if memory is both the *cavern* (X.16) and *seat* (X.25) of the mental interior. It inevitably leads into Augustine's exposition of the three temptations, cited above, because the argument has ended upon the question of the mind's very act of self-possession. The possibility of the mind's conscription by the three appetites—lust of the eyes, of the flesh, and the pride of life—logically follows.

We have elsewhere described the Scholastic analysis of the will into the concupiscible, irascible, and rational appetites. It will be apparent from the foregoing discussion that the legend of temperance has found room for the same analysis: Spenser, if he is a better teacher than Aquinas, is not essentially a *different* one. The Scholastic classification may be reviewed here by means of a summary from Plato, one of its sources:

> The three parts [of the soul] have . . . three kinds of pleasure, . . . and similarly three appetites and controls. . . . One part, we say, is that with which a man learns, one is that with which he feels anger. But the third part, . . . we could not easily designate . . . , but gave it the name of its chief and strongest element, for we call it the appetitive part because of the intensity of its appetites concerned with food and drink and love . . . , and likewise the money-loving part, because money is the chief instrument for the gratification of such desires. . . . And if we should also say that its pleasure and its love were for gain or profit should we not thus . . . justify our calling it the money-loving and gain-loving part? . . . And again, of the high-spirited element, do we not say that it is wholly set on predominance and victory and good repute? . . . And might we not appropriately designate it as the ambitious part and that which is covetous of honor? . . . But surely it is obvious . . . that all the endeavor of the part by which we learn is ever toward knowledge of the truth of things. . . . And that is why we say that the primary classes of men also are three, the philosopher or lover of wisdom, the lover of victory, and the lover of gain.[127]

The Castle of Alma develops the positive form of this analysis. Thus, while Alma's kitchen on one level represents the actual processes of consumption that go on in the physical person, on another level it represents a state of the will. In the latter case a character like Diet pertains not so much to nutrition, but to the whole order of constraints upon the concupiscible appetite, which could be expressed in forms other than thirst and hunger. The underworld develops its infernal analysis of the will in the same fashion, according to whether inclination is corrupted by cupid-

---

[127] *Republic* IX, 580e–581c, trans. Paul Shorey, in E. Hamilton and H. Cairns, eds., *Collected Dialogues*, Bollingen Series LXXI (1961), pp. 807f. For the Scholastic analysis of the will elsewhere in Book II, see "The Temper of Occasion," sec. iii, nn. 62–68, and Chap. I, "Arthurian Torso," sec. iii, nn. 136–144, with text.

ity, by ambition (an inordinate desire to excell through the overcoming of obstacles), or by a "rational appetite" for an inappropriate knowledge (or an abuse of the understanding). Ultimately the underworld presents a vision of damnation, though this is only explicit in the third temptation, where the souls in question *know* they are in hell.

Milton also arranges the central part of Christ's temptation into the categories of wealth, power, and wisdom—according to a far more complex scheme than we have expounded here—and he specifically says that, in entering Satan's domain, the hero "into himself descended" (*Par. Reg.* II.111). As in Milton, each of the temptations in the underworld is an enticement to expediency, designed to induce in the subject of the temtation a desire to seize or appropriate a power from without, rather than develop it from within. In short, the temptations urge an abdication of the autonomy of the will. When Spenser's hero faints at the end of his trial, we are to understand both the limits upon the kind of resistance temperance by itself can offer and the limits upon self-reliance in general. At just this point Guyon's guardian spirit descends to take over for the senseless knight; the guardian's office in turn passes to Arthur, that is, to a "self" who relies upon more than one virtue. The same pattern may be discerned in canto xi, when Guyon, after a night's sleep, departs from the Castle, and Arthur takes up the burden of its defense against Maleger. This episode does not properly end until—in words like those of the earlier sequence—life has mastered its lifeless foe.[128] The reader may well conclude that the Castle of Alma, far from being the dull and unoriginal allegory that it is sometimes made out to be, rises above its surrounding legend, "hugely politic," and makes its presence felt throughout the symbolism. The Castle is said to be proportioned by the numbers seven and nine; the reasons for these numbers remain rather obscure, but as our comparison of the seventh and ninth cantos of this book indicates, Spenser's "goodly frame of temperance" observes these proportions also.

The Analogy of Good Order

First, this is certain: that like as in every man there is a body and also a soul, in whose flourishing and prosperous state both togidder standeth the weal and felicity of man, so likewise there is in every commonalty, city and country, as it were, a politic body, and another thing also, resembling the soul of man, in whose flourishing both togidder resteth also the true common weal. This body is nothing else but the multitude of people, the number of citizens, in every commonalty, city or country. The things which is resembled to the soul is civil order and politic law administered

---

[128] Comparing "lifelesse shadow" at II.xi.44 with "sencelesse foe" at II.viii.53.

by officers and rulers. For like as the body in every man receiveth his life by the virtue of the soul, and is governed thereby, so doth the multitude of people in every country receive, as it were, civil life by laws well administered by good officers and wise rulers, by whom they be governed and kept in politic order. Wherefore the one may, as meseemeth, right well be compared to the body and the other to the soul.

(Thomas Starkey, *A Dialogue Between Reginald Pole & Thomas Lupset,* II, ed. Kathleen M. Burton, p. 55)

[i]

Spenser conceives temperance as the virtue that secures the private integrity against an unruly physical environment. As a consequence, this virtue is the natural model for personal orderliness and the control of internal power; presumably our allegiance to the institutions of society that maintain law and order is elaborated from the ideal of control established by this early training. This broadening of the virtue seems to be the logic behind Spenser's construction of the legend of justice, where a quest like Guyon's is undertaken on behalf of the social body. So far as I know, the literature on the poem has not given this analogy any detailed exposition, but any criticism of the poem that interests itself in the unity of Spenser's work cannot really afford to neglect at least the possibility of such a relation.[129]

The association of justice and temperance goes back to Plato's proposal in the *Republic* that the just society be organized on the model of the faculties of the well-governed man. The languge of the definition placed at the opening of Elyot's *Gouernour* is characteristic: "A publike weale is a body lyuying, compacte or made of sondry astates and degrees of men, whiche is disposed by the ordre of equite and gouerned by the rule and moderation of reason."[130] In the *Republic* itself, this rule of reason is manifested by the early domination of the other characters by the reasonable Socrates; indeed, after the first book, the theory of the just state takes the form of an anatomy of the mind of its chief exponent. Guyon is similarly dominated by the Palmer. When Guyon visits the Castle of Alma, the Palmer temporarily drops out of the symbolism; the three Socratic sages can be thought of as taking over his role. In the legend of justice,

---

[129] The possibility for a counterpart for Book II in Book V is broached and dismissed in H.S.V. Jones, *Spenser Handbook* (New York, 1937), pp. 249–251; it is directly asserted in Frye, *Anatomy*, p. 201; and strongly implied in Roche, *Kindly Flame* (Princeton, 1964), pp. 200f. Roche hesitantly proposes the comparisons around which the "analogies" of the present book are constructed, though he distrusts their usefulness (*ibid.*, p. 210).

[130] *Gouernour*, I.i, Everyman's Library, p. 1.

we do not see the social body in quite the way we see the physical one, any more than we see social corporation that makes up Arthur as a body. The place of the Castle of Alma is taken by the public person of the queen and her court, the queen being the most obvious representative of the social order she heads. The communist giant and his mob of adherents form the parody of this corporation.

Spenser's conception of justice is hierarchical in its own right. First and at bottom, justice is a matter of securing power, without which authority cannot exist: "For powre is the right hand of Iustice truly hight" (V.iv.2). This is the club of Hercules, or "The club of Iustice dread, with kingly powre endewed" (V.i.2).[131] The possession of force is prior to justice proper, just as the iron man, Talus, goes in advance of Artegall. This *modus operandi* answers directly to the lawless condition of the Hesiodic iron age, where "man's right hand is law" (*Works and Days* 274). Ideally, power is brought into the service of the law, which has a dialectical relation to whatever is outside the law and therefore contests with it for power. In its turn, legal justice is subject to a higher ideal of equity, represented by the control of Isis over the crocodile—the crocodile is identified with Spenser's potentially draconic protagonist, Artegall.[132] The polarization of equity and the will toward retribution is also evidenced in the exclusion of Talus from Isis' domain, where the priests abstain from blood. Further, justice may be tempered with mercy, when a sufficiently established sovereignty exists. Mercy, however, is to be carefully distinguished from pity, which is no mercy to justice; pity can become a kind of capitulation, or partiality to injustice. In the trial of Duessa at the court of Mercilla, Spenser balances these rival claims by having five witnesses appear on Duessa's behalf, and five witnesses against her, with the generous Prince and rigorous Artegall falling on opposite sides of the question.

As with the control of bodily energy in the legend of temperance, the virgin is again an important symbol, this time in relation to savage power. First we have Astraea, or Virgo, "enemy to monsters," as Horace calls her.[133] We have already compared her to Diana with respect to her posture of self-defense. Astraea training Artegall, Isis dominating the crocodile, and Mercilla enthroned above the chained lion show the opposite movement, toward mastery. Artegall himself is trained to tame wild beasts,

---

[131] Cf. Pierre de La Primaudaye, *French Academie*, trans. T[homas] B[owes] (London, 1586), p. 609: "so we may also call those men his [the ruler's] hands, whom he hath appointed to execute such things as are to be don. These are the magistrates & officers established by the souueraigne, & armed with power to compel the subiects to obey his laws, or els to punish them."

[132] For Draco = *drakwn*, see Aristotle, *Rhetoric* II.23, the twenty-eighth topic of proof, arguments from names: "Herodicas said . . . of the legislator Draco that his laws were those not of a human being, but of a dragon, so savage were they."

[133] *Odes* I.12, l.22: "saevis inimica virgo / beluis."

and the first malefactor he encounters is Sir Sanglier (French, "boar"); Talus brings the culprit in, "Bound like a beast appointed to the stall" (V.i.22). And in the second canto Artegall enters a river to wrestle with its evil proprietor, Pollente, "a mirrour to all mighty men, / In whose right hands great power is contayned" (V.ii.19). Similar imagery belongs to Britomart, who defeats Marinell on the shore of his "rich strond" in the third book, and brings her lover Artegall to heel in the fourth. If Artegall is symbolized by the Nile-god Osiris, he too may have an association with a river, and perhaps all these associations are meant to underwrite Britomart's description of her future city dominating its river:

> It *Troynouant* is hight, that with the waues
> Of wealthy *Thamis* washed is along,
> Vpon whose stubborne neck, whereat he raues
> With roring rage, and sore him selfe does throng,
> That all men feare to tempt his billowes strong,
> She fastned hath her foot, which standes so hy,
> That it a wonder of the world is song
> In forreine landes, and all which passen by,
> Beholding it from far, do think it threates the skye.
>
> (III.ix.45)[134]

With this brief background, we may turn to the correspondences with temperance. I apologize for the repetition and paraphrase the following account necessitates; on the other hand, I do not expect the reader to accept mere assertion as evidence, where a demonstration is possible. Both legends naturally fall into four parts of three cantos each—at least when they are compared.

As a kind of prologue to Book II proper, Spenser begins with the "link" between Redcrosse and Guyon. The significant passage here is Guyon's description of Redcrosse's virtual canonization: Redcrosse's name is now "enrolled . . . in heauenly registers aboue the Sunne" (II.i.32), and Guyon thinks of his world as a forsaken one. In Book V the post-lapsarian symbol is the retreat of Astraea to the stars. There she becomes a "sign" in the zodiac which distantly oversees the action of the hero, just as the analogy with Book I exercises its influence over the action of Book II.

The first episode in each book has the hero discover a corpse in a pool of blood, and this victim confirms the hero's dedication. In each case the victim leaves behind him three parties: his murderer, a bereft lover, and a more or less mute survivor who furnishes an object-lesson, but is not a

---

[134] This stanza is quoted to this effect in Frye, "Structure of Imagery," in *Fables of Identity*, p. 84.

fully articulate character. (The babe Ruddymane corresponds to the surviving lady disputed by Sir Sanglier and the abused knight. The lover, like Amavia, is in a suicidal mood, and he would almost admit to the crime, "That I mote drinke the cup, whereof she drank" [V.i.15].) Artegall's failure to ask the lady to which of the knights she belongs would be more logical if she were the child originally disputed in the judgment of Solomon; the episode is based on the biblical story, and of course Spenser could count upon his readers to recognize the divine source of Artegall's wisdom. Each episode seems to show a limit on the given virtue's power of reform. Ruddymane is a child of wrath, and his hands are indelibly stained with the "deep sanguine" of an inherited "bloud-guiltinesse" (II.ii.4). This guilt, baptism cannot remove; perhaps there is some relation to Artegall's foregoing of a trial by sacrament in the case of Sanglier (V.i.25), "That did his hands in Ladies bloud embrew" (V.i.16). Sanglier gets off with more of a judgment than a punishment; his guilt is marked, like Cain's, but no more comes of it. The emphasis is on the *apprehension* of the criminal, just as in Book II the emphasis is on the manifestation of sin in Ruddymane, rather than its removal.

We may defer the comparison of the second cantos to our discussion of equity in Book V, only noting here that Guyon's visit to the golden Medina and Artegall's discussion of the scales of justice with the giant constitute the exposition of the mean for each legend. The washing of Ruddymane's hands and the washing away of Munera's guilty blood extend the symbolism of corruption for both cases—Munera stands for graft, and in the ideal age "Iustice was not for most meed outhyred" (V, proem, 3). The giant's concept of a distempered physical world, like Mordant's legacy in Ruddymane, refers the evidence back to the great mutation of the Fall.

The third canto in the legend of temperance has not so far been discussed because it opens a serial that is not closed until the corresponding point in the legend of justice. Or rather two interlocking serials: one is concerned with true and false claims to honor; the other, with true and false claims to "honesty," or chastity. We may put off a description of this exceedingly Spenserian harmony until we come to the central books, but we should note here that Braggadocchio is introduced in canto iii of Book II, and dismissed in canto iii of Book V.[135] He is a kind of romance equivalent for the *miles gloriosus* of comedy. The romance society of fairyland has only an episodic tolerance for his subversive insolence: the first headnote reports that he "is made the scorne / Of knighthood trew" (II.iii), but this exposure is really reserved for the later canto, in which he "is uncas'd / in all the Ladies sights" (V.iii, rubric). In Book II he acquires his groom Trompart, who proceeds to amplify his master to

[135] See below, Chap. IV, "Perpetual Generations," sec. v.

Belphoebe;[136] Braggadocchio, as he says, is endeavoring to raise his name above the moon. In Book V, at the tournament in honor of Marinell's wedding to Florimell, the trumpets resound with the borrowed accomplishments of the loudmouth, who displays as his own the arms with which Artegall has triumphed—the arms depict the sun.

Braggadocchio's conjunction with Belphoebe may remind us of another knight characterized by preposterous bravado and dubious horsemanship:

> When thou art king, let us not that are squires of the night's body be called thieves of the day's beauty: let us be Diana's foresters, gentlemen of the shade, minions of the moon; and let men say we be men of good government, being governed as the sea is, by our noble and chaste mistress the moon, under whose countenance we steal.
>
> (*Henry IV, Part I*, I.ii.23–30)[137]

Before Guyon sets out for Medina's house—a castle by the sea—his horse is mysteriously stolen. At the same point in Book V, Artegall meets Florimell's dwarf, who advises him of Florimell's coming marriage, which is to be held at a "Castle of the Strond" (V.ii.4; iv.3). Guyon's horse turns up under Braggadocchio, in the canto following its theft—at the same point the dishonorable knight makes an assault on Belphoebe's virginity. The horse duly appears at the wedding in Book V, where the imposter now attempts to impugn the credentials of the bride. Braggadocchio has a Florimell of his own to present, and she is wearing the authenticating cestus, the token of Florimell's chaste government. In the legend of temperance, the chastity of Belphoebe takes the form of celibacy; the chastity of Florimell, in the legend of justice, takes the form of marriage, a specifically legal institution. Justice is now done to temperance: the golden girdle is restored to the lady who can wear it, and the horse with the golden bridle is returned to the knight who can manage it. The analogy here is the analogy of government. Braggadocchio's incontinence has consisted in his inability to resist appropriating the attributes of more noble natures—the chaste, the courageous, and the chivalrous. Like Falstaff's predecessor in *Henry VI, Part I* (IV.i), the coward is stripped of his knighthood.

[136] Trompart's name may remind us of the hypocrites of Matt. 6:2 who sound a trumpet before them when they are giving alms. In Lydgate's trans. of Guillaume de Deguilleville, *Pilgrimage of the Life of Man*, we read about a "horn of boasting" being carried by pride (l. 14336 of the EETS edn., Extra Series, no. 77, Pt. 2, p. 389). Trompart is otherwise the clarion of Fame: see Chaucer, *House of Fame*, III.1237–1250, 1567ff.

[137] This speech deserves comparison with the one in Part II (IV.iii.51ff.), where Falstaff tells Prince John not to be surprised if "I in the clear sky of fame o'ershine you as much as the full moon doth the cinders of the element, which show like pins' heads to her."

[ii]

It is in the third canto that the subterranean relation between Books II and V first surfaces, upon the final appearance of the Arethuse-like Florimell. Thus the interlacement of Books III and IV cedes its functions in organizing the narrative to a more linear kind of parallelism. The revelation of this transfer is oddly right here: Guyon learns who stole his horse, while we learn that the wayfaring patterns of Book II are being appropriated as a vehicle for Book V. The meeting of the two heroes officially recognizes this borrowing as a legitimate importation. In the subsequent three cantos the rationale is further extended, along the otherwise parallel lines suggested by the viatores' juncture. Guyon tempers the ferocity of justice when he restrains the momentarily choleric Artegall; Artegall ajudges that the horse Brigliadoro is the property of Guyon.

The fourth canto of each book goes on to illustrate each hero's resistance to ungoverned action, as a mediator. In both cases the knights act in an advisory capacity to rash young men: each recounts an unhappy tale of "wrath, gelosie, griefe, love" (II.iv.35), involving two couples in a complicated exchange of roles and properties. Phedon's enemy Occasion corresponds to the unpersonified fortune of Bracidas, felt in the action of the sea that has robbed and then enriched him. Artegall places the knights' swords underfoot, as Guyon bound Furor in Book II, and ratifies the just distribution that fortune has already made. (The association of Fortune with the sea is traditional, of course; Horace calls her "dominam aequoris," mistress of the sea.)[138]

In the next episode Artegall encounters Sir Terpine, whom a mob of Amazons is about to lynch. The reprieve provided by Artegall has a rather inexact counterpart in the release of Phedon from the furor of occasion. At any rate, Artegall now proceeds against the Amazon queen Radigund, and at the end of the fourth canto she sends her maid Clarin to the city wall to challenge Artegall to single combat for his offense in releasing Terpine. Similarly in Book II, Atin announces Pyrochles, who seeks out Guyon for his actions regarding Phedon. Two qualities characterize Pyrochles: choler and wrath. The latter, as the classical analogues suggest, tends to make him a spirit of vengeance. Taken together, Pyrochles and Furor suggest the internecine war of the person who cannot control himself. The counterparts for choler and wrath in the legend of justice will be rebellion and revenge—Amazons, by way of their defiance

---

[138] Horace, *Odes* I.35, l. 6. In Boethius, *De Cons. Phil.* II, metre i, Fortune is described as being as unpredictable as the tide of Euripus. Boethius is quoted by Erasmus, in the *Adagia, sub* "FORTVNA estuaria." In Comes, *Mythol.*, IV.ix, *edn. cit.*, p. 334, the goddess is said to be the daughter of Ocean, on the basis of the Homeric *Hymn to Demeter*, l. 420.

of the usual social order, are a logical symbol involving both. As La Primaudaye reports, "Cicero saith, that that which the Latines call Anger, is named of the Grecians desire of revenge."[139] There is one further link between the two: Spenser tells us that a famous Amazon queen defeated Pyrrhus (II.iii.31).

The duels with Pyrochles and Radigund provoke similar imagery. Pyrochles seems to be on fire. He rages like a tiger, but his conqueror abides his wrath. He comes under his conqueror's foot, but his life is spared. Radigund is also compared to a tiger (at V.vii.30); she is of the same implacable stripe, and she too seems to be on fire. Artegall, like Guyon, waits for an advantage. Pyrochles rages: "He hewd, and lasht, and foynd, and thundred blowes" (II.v.9). And so does Radigund: "She hewd, she foynd, she lasht, she laid on euery side" (V.v.6; the same is said again of Pyrochles in his fight with Arthur, II.viii.47). Guyon conquers by careful self-control; Artegall conquers rather in more of a wrath, because righteous indignation has a place in the operations of justice. Guyon, "Tempering the passion with aduizement slow" (II.v.13), allows Pyrochles to live. Artegall is similarly moved by the beauty of Radigund: "At sight thereof his cruell minded hart / Empierced was with pitifull regard" (V.v.13). Both protagonists lose their labor because of this error of misplaced leniency. Pyrochles insists on enlarging Furor, who mortally wounds his foolish benefactor. The Palmer counsels Guyon against showing Pyrochles any second mercy: "Ne let thy stout hart melt in pitty vayne" (II.v.24). The infatuated Artegall throws away his sword and the Amazon repays his mercy with a vengeance, hanging the hapless Terpine and carrying out her contract with Artegall to the letter. In both books the trouble-making messenger has a further part to play in the victimization of the hero. Atin departs at the defeat of Pyrochles by Guyon to arouse the avenging brother Cymochles. Clarin bears false messages between her lovesick mistress and the imprisoned Artegall. The role also appears in Talus, who goes to Britomart at Artegall's demise, because justice has been separated from the law, or from power, and only equity can restore it.

At this point in Book II the scene shifts to the Bower of Bliss, where Cymochles holidays with Acrasia: her victims, we are told, are eventually "captiu'd eternally in yron mewes, / And darksom deñs" (II.v.27). Like Cymochles, Artegall is also disarmed and symbolically emasculated, and he too is eventually subjected to iron chains (V.v.50). The linen he is forced to weave and the feminine garments he wears parody the linen garb of the priests of Isis; Radigund's regimen stands for weakness, rather than restraint. The imagery of Book II tends to be derived from the classical epics, and the effeminization of Cymochles suggests subjec-

---

[139] *French Academie, edn. cit.,* p. 312.

tion to Circe, though Guyon himself goes no further than the isle of Phedria. Book V tends to rely on an analogy to Hercules, and the corresponding area belongs to Omphale, or, alternatively, Iole, to whom Radigund is compared.[140] In both legends there is a period that we might call the "dissociation of the hero," referring to the way in which the heroic role departs from Artegall at this point in Book V, with Britomart having to take over for the champion. In the allegory we may suppose that equity must abrogate the letter of the compact whereby Artegall was tricked, or that equity must correct an error of vain pity. Talus leaves the enfeebled hero and goes to Britomart to report her lover "in harlots bondage tide" (V.vi.11). Guyon is similarly divided from the Palmer by Phedria, and each hero is without his second during cantos six and seven. The same sort of thing happens in the enemy camp. Clarin, Radigund's maid, falls in love with Artegall herself, and works at cross-purposes to her mistress. Atin departs from Pyrochles and goes to Cymochles at the Bower, where he assumes the Palmer's usual role in rousing disarmed valor; then he too is separated from his knight by Phedria.

When Britomart sets out to recover her lover she has the task of self-preservation that Guyon has in Book II. On her way she is lured into the house of the treacherous Dolon, who employs the same trapfalls as did his ally Pollente. As the names tell us, Pollente and Dolon represent the two traditional forms of coercion, force and fraud.[141] Pollente is the master of a powerful river, and Artegall beheads him with the sword Chrysaor; elsewhere Chrysaor is listed among the sea-gods who claim "The powre to rule the billowes, and the waues to tame" (IV.xi.13). In the legend of temperance Pollente's power appears as simply involuntary impulse—such as the laughter of Phedria, whose companions "get carried away." Phedria is met by a river, but the river has soon expanded into the Idle Lake, as natural energy, left to itself, dissipates and becomes dissipated.

To summarize the events of the sixth canto: Britomart is taken for Artegall, and Dolon makes an attempt on her life, thinking to revenge one of his sons, slain in the action at Pollente's bridge. Guyon encounters Cymochles on Phedria's island, and Cymochles attacks him, more or less on general principles.[142] Britomart survives Dolon's trap; Guyon retains

---

[140] The substitution of Iole for Omphale at *F.Q.* V.v.24 is also found in Tasso, *Ger. Lib.* XVI.3, and Boccaccio, *Teseide*, VII.62: in Boccaccio's *Concerning Famous Women*, xxi, Iole is said to have humbled Hercules in revenge for the death of her father. Cf. Cooper's *Dictionary*, appended to the *Thesaurus, sub* "Iole": "the daughter of Eurytus King of Aetolia, whome Hercules loued so much, that he served hir in a womans appareil, and spanne on a distaffe."

[141] *Nich. Ethics* V.ii (1131a). So Elyot, *Gouernour*, III.i, Everyman's Library, p. 196, on the two forms of involuntary interference.

[142] La Primaudaye, *French Academie, edn. cit.*, p. 312: "impatiency and choler, which argue and accompanie for the most part a weake and effeminate hart." The

his sense of direction in Phedria's realm. Britomart reaches the perilous bridge, now manned by Dolon's remaining sons, and they revile her for murder. Guyon, returning from Phedria's island, reaches shore to be reviled by Atin for the supposed death of Pyrochles; then Pyrochles is discovered, thrashing in the Idle Lake. Britomart mows down her accusers on the bridge, and one is thrown into the river below. Thus the sixth canto of each book ends—or almost ends—on the further shore of a scene of violent drowning. The surreptitious Dolon reminds us of Archimago, and it is thus not surprising that Archimago turns up to give Pyrochles one last extension of life, just at the point where Dolon is left to bestow his two dead sons.

It was suggested above that Mammon's cave and the Castle of Alma provide the foci of the symbolism for the legend of temperance. Mammon's cave involves an instructive vision, as does the sixth book of the *Aeneid*, even though the nature of temperance is defined negatively. In Book V the negative symbolism was presented in the second canto—opposite the house of Medina in the parallel with Book II. The positive symbolism is to be found at Isis Church and the palace of Mercilla, and they provide the symbolic foci for the legend of justice. The Isis Church canto, then, ought to contain a parallel to Mercilla's palace, and it ought to provide an instructive vision, if Book II and Book V follow a similar order. This is in fact the case. In the seventh canto Britomart visits Isis Church and then proceeds against her rival Radigund, whom she dispatches. In the ninth canto Artegall visits Mercilla's palace—after the defeat of Malengine—and then witnesses the trial and condemnation of Mercilla's rival, Duessa. Radigund and Duessa may both be regarded as rebels from the authority of the virgin queen; in the historical allegory they represent Mary Queen of Scots. (Or at least Duessa does; she had this part as early as the conclusion of Book I, where she put in a claim for the hand of the Englishman.)

It is the structural parallel between the two books that seems important here; one does not see any real correspondence between Mammon and Radigund. However, we do discern a change of tempo at the opening of each seventh canto, signaling the advent of a more complex understanding of what the virtue in question entails, and an internalization of its properties. Talus is expressly excluded from "That part of Iustice, which is Equity" (V.viii.3). Milton to the contrary, it is made just as clear that

principle is reversible in Spenser, since Cymochles and Pyrochles are brothers. The passivity entailed in the surrender to the passions is implied by Spenser's use of the word "idle" with most of them. See n. 14, above.

Guyon undergoes his ordeal in Mammon's underworld without the support of the Palmer.[143] In Book V, justice is now identified with the restraint placed on power; in Book II, temperance is identified with resistance to temptation. The priests recognize in the chaste Britomart a type of this restraint, and Mammon, although he may not acknowledge Guyon for what he is, surely clarifies what he is not.

The real structural likeness between the two seventh cantos can only emerge from a larger comparison between the two installments of the poem. The premium upon integrity at the center of Book II—the center of the first installment—refers Guyon's temperance to both the righteousness of Book I and the continence of Book III. Guyon seems totally conscripted by the private virtues here. Similarly, the clement equity at the center of the second installment hearkens back to the world harmony promoted by friendship, and forward to the graciousness promoted by courtesy; that is, equity suggests the larger outlines of the *social* contract.

[iii]

The remainder of the analogy between the two books may be more briefly stated, for much of it is a matter of organization. In Book II the space between Mammon's cave and the Castle of Alma is mediated by Arthur; the enemies are Acrates' sons—Pyrochles and Cymochles—and Maleger. In Book V the same space is filled by the Soldan and Adicia, and Malengine. Both heroes have been absent in a sense. Artegall has been in eclipse in Radigund's realm; and Guyon, below the earth.[144] Their restoration is symbolized by the return of their assistants, who rejoin their respective heroes, bringing with them "magnific" characters with greater powers to intercede for their charges. Talus returns with Britomart; the Palmer summons Arthur. After Britomart has restored Artegall's power of action she discreetly withdraws, and Artegall suddenly finds himself acting in concert with Arthur on behalf of the abused Samient.

The case of Guyon is rather different. Restored to the light of day by Mammon, he falls unconscious. He never sees his famous guardian angel because his virtue is not in the area of revelation. Nor is he aware of the battle on his behalf by Arthur against the two brothers. And yet it is probably fair to assert that he is a participant, in the way a patient partic-

[143] In *Areopagitica* Milton mistakenly thinks Guyon has the Palmer guiding him, whereas Spenser implies that the knight is being tested for the strength of his *habit* of temperance, rather than for his reliance on reason.

[144] Alastair Fowler also takes this to be an operant metaphor here, since Radigund's shield is the moon, and since—as we shall see—Artegall's course is solar; *Spenser and the Numbers of Time* (New York, 1964), pp. 219f. For Isis as the moon eclipsing the (Typhonic) sun, see Plutarch, *De Iside* 44, *Moralia* 368D. For the Amazons' lunar shields, see Virgil, *Aen.* I.490f., Statius, *Theb.* V.145.

ipates in his recovery, or in an operation; to borrow an image from another context:

> The genius and the mortal instruments
> Are then in council, and the state of man,
> Like to a little kingdom, suffers then
> The nature of an insurrection.
>
> (*Julius Caesar*, II.i.66–69)

Arthur and Artegall are temporarily unaware of each other's identity as they dispatch the two pagans pursuing a new character, Samient, who brings the knights "together."[145] Her oppressors turn out to have been agents of the Soldan and Adicia; against this tyrant and his consort the two knights now proceed. Any analogy with the two sons of Acrates is not close, though Adicia's rage relates her to both Pyrochles and Radigund; Adicia is not only compared to a tiger, she turns into one. One other detail is worth remarking. Pyrochles tries to fight Arthur with Arthur's sword, and he finds it treacherous—in romance even swords are loyal. The weapon of the Soldan is literally a juggernaut, and it betrays him when the flesh-eating team that draws it is blinded by Arthur's exposed shield. The moral points to reflexive mechanisms that destroy those who use them for evil ends. In both legends, Arthur's eighth canto victory will be repeated in the eleventh canto: in Book II he will engage the diseased humour Maleger, and, in Book V, the tyrant Gerioneo. We may note that these later antagonists are related to the earlier ones. The original Geryon is also said to feed his herd on human flesh (V.viii.28; x.9), and, like the Soldan, he is to be identified with the power of Spain.

The theme of Arthur's battle against Pyrochles and Cymochles is the protection of a beset physical body; in the civic context of Book V, the defended body becomes various territorial and political integrities, but more especially Protestant England in opposition to the alliance of Spain and Rome. In the historical allegory the Soldan's chariot represents the Armada; thus the victorious prince must be the maritime Arthur mentioned in our first chapter. The English attributed the defeat of the Armada to the intervention of divine providence; the winds that bedeviled the Spanish fleet were His couriers—"He blew and they were scattered."[146] Hence the exposure of Arthur's shield corresponds to the invisible aid rendered Guyon by his guardian angel.

The historical allegory of the defeat of the Soldan will be discussed in

---

[145] For "sam" in this sense of oneness, see I.x.56f., where the angels are seen entering the city "As commonly as friend does with his frend," and the elect are "Saints all in that citie sam." I owe my explanation of Samient to A. C. Hamilton.

[146] The motto on the medal commemorating the victory most nearly resembles Ps. 147:18 (*Afflavit Deus*).

another essay. It takes its start from the defense of the queen's ambassador Samient, whose official connection with Mercilla tells us the identity of the endangered person in Book V. Samient goes on to get mixed up with Malengine, and perhaps it is significant that the conspiracy of the Jesuit missionaries in England to murder the queen reached to the Spanish ambassador. Just as the Castle of Alma will someday fall, being subject to decay, so also the palace of Mercilla is susceptible of subversion. The reader is free to make Mercilla an *Astraea redux*, on the basis of the hints in the proem, but the evidence really points, not to Saturn and the Golden Age, but to Saturn's son, Jove, armed with the power that he later threatens to use against Mutabilitie (VII.vi.31). Hence the prominence in this area of the legend of Maleger's Protean counterpart Malengine. His guile recalls Dolon's plot on the life of Britomart, and so it is not illogical to compare his machinations to the plots on the life of the queen.

In our parallel, Malengine is placed opposite the bands of Maleger. The warfare of both enemies reflects Spenser's experience with the guerrilla tactics of the Irish kern. Thus the efforts of Malengine, though they may symbolize plots directed against the heart of the English court, retain the imagery of combat in the hinterlands, where the enemy is difficult to engage, or even to recognize. Maleger's retreat also has this nomadic character; he uses the age-old Parthian tactic of drawing invaders on, which was developed in the ebb and flow of migratory peoples across the steppes. Maleger's men are "all in straunge manner armed"; they employ the makeshift weapons of the underdog. Both Malengine and Maleger are versatile and uncanny—ubiquitous in advance, and, in retreat, almost impossible to pin down.

After clearing their way of the inimical forces (only temporarily in Book II), the heroes enter the house of recognition. The theme in each case is internal order. Alma's porter is the tongue, whose heavy armament symbolizes the kind of restraints to be applied to all conduct, but especially speech:

> Within the Barbican a Porter sate,
>> Day and night duely keeping watch and ward,
>> Nor wight, nor word mote passe out of the gate,
>> But in good order, and with dew regard;
>> Vtterers of secrets he from thence debard,
>> Bablers of folly, and blazers of crime.
>> His larumbell might lowd and wide be hard,
>> When cause requird, but neuer out of time;
>>
>> (II.ix.25)

As the horrible example of Braggadocchio shows, temperate and well-timed speech belongs to Guyon's discipline. (Cicero contrasts decorous

speech with talking about one's self, and playing the braggart soldier.)[147]
Besides binding Occasion, Guyon puts a lock on her tongue, a punishment
like Papageno's in *The Magic Flute*. In the body politic the place of the
teeth is taken by Awe, who corresponds to Reverence at the entrance to the
House of Holiness. "When it opened, no man might it close," Spenser
ironically says of Alma's entryway (II.ix.23). Learning to keep one's
mouth shut is an essential of politic behavior as well. Just beyond Mercilla's porter, at the place where the baptismal font would be in a church,
we encounter a character who was christened Bonfont. He has been re-
named Malfont, "that he likened was to a welhed / Of evill words"
(V.ix.26). It is his punishment that brings home the analogy with Book II.
His tongue is nailed to a post, representing the suppression of the seditious
poet who writes in bad taste—so to speak—about his queen. (The corresponding font-symbol in Book I is perhaps Fidelia's cup, with its brazen
serpent.) This retribution (which was visited on the corpse of Cicero, and
also on Heresy in the *Psychomachia* of Prudentius) makes the point that
Guyon's temperate speech becomes censorship in the world of Artegall.
The virtuous counterpart of the slanderous Malfont is Duessa's accuser
Zele, "That well could charme his tongue, and time his speach" (V.ix.39).

The marshal at Mercilla's palace is named Order. The most frequent
occurrence of this word elsewhere in the poem is in the comparable
stanzas of Book II; Alma's porter enforces the orderly intake of experience,
and her marshal, Appetite, knows how to order a meal. Alma's steward,
Diet, carries the white rod that belongs to Elizabeth in the prophecy
Merlin makes to Britomart in the following book. Isis also has this white
rod, with which she manifests her authority over the insurgent crocodile.
In the prophecy it is said that the white rod will smite "the *Belgicke*
shore" (III.iii.49), and the prophecy is fulfilled after the Mercilla canto
of Book V. At Mercilla's palace the white rod (which was the symbol of office for Elizabeth's ministers)[148] is replaced by the sceptre, "The
sacred pledge of peace and clemencie" (V.ix.30); the crocodile modulates
into a slightly bilious British lion. The visceral rumblings of the lion confined beneath the throne correspond to the activity of the kitchen of the
Castle; the kitchen's furnace threatens to "breake out, and set the whole
on fire" (II.ix.30), an impulse associated with the crocodile and, less ob-
trusively, with the lion:

---

[147] Aristotle treats the boaster at some length, *Nich. Ethics* IV.vii; the military
braggart makes his appearance by name in Cicero's *De Off.* I.xxxviii. See also Aristotle, *Rhet.* II.6.

[148] As reported in *Shakespeare's England*, ed. Sir Walter Raleigh, *et al.* (Oxford,
1916), vol. 1, p. 84, in E. K. Chambers' article, "The Court": "The ordinary mode
of appointing an important household officer [who would have a seat in the Privy
Council] was by delivery of a white staff, which became the symbol of his office."

> Whylest vnderneath her feete, thereas she sate,
> An huge great Lyon lay, that mote appal
> An hardie courage, like captiued thrall,
> With a strong yron chaine and coller bound,
> That once he could not moue, nor quich at all;
> Yet did he murmure with rebellious sound,
> And softly royne, when salvage choler gan redound.
>
> (V.ix.33)

The crocodile and the lion, like Elizabeth's mightiest favorites, "murmure with rebellious sound."

To cool Alma's kitchen dynamo, "goodly ordinaunce" has provided the lungs for ventilation (II.ix.30). In Book V the comparable function perhaps falls to the daughters of Themis, the goddess Order. They traditionally attend on the throne of Zeus, as suppliants or intercessors who cool the wrath of the provoked sky-god. Like Isis, this "beauie of faire Virgins" (V.ix.31) is dressed in white and manifests the principle of restraint. To the traditional three daughters, Spenser has added Reueraunce (for the magistrate is appointed by God), and Temperaunce, whose presence by now is perhaps sufficiently accounted for. The others personify justice proper (Dice, sometimes identified with Astraea),[149] good order (Eunomie), and peace (Eirene). The last-named is Artegall's goal in the pacification of Ireland. Perhaps Eirene deserves to be called the hero's "interior paramour"; she would correspond to Guyon's anima figure,

---

[149] Astraea is identified with Diké in Aratos, *Phaenom.* 96 seq., which retails the story of the departure of the goddess. Themis, Astraea, and Virgo are equated by Calpurnius, *Eclogue* I.42 seq. Martianus Capella, *De Nuptis*, II.174 (Dick edn., p. 71), identifies Astraea with Themis. In Hyginus, *Poet. Astron.* II.25, Hesiod's Diké (the daughter of Zeus and Themis in *Theog.* 901f.) is identified with Virgo, and she is said to flee the earth with the birth of the *brazen* race—this was perhaps a hint for the legacy of Talus to Artegall, for the classical Talos was a member of the brazen race (scholia on Apollon. Rhod., *Argonaut.* IV.1643, and Apollodorus, *Bibl.* I.ix.26), and this race was succeeded by the iron one. Servius, *ad Eclog.* IV.6, also says that Virgo is Justice, the daughter of Themis, and Macrobius, *Saturnalia*, I.xxi.24, says Virgo is a symbol of justice. Pseudo-Eratosthenes, *Catasterismi* 9, says Virgo was called Diké. In the myth of decline in Hesiod's *Works and Days* it is said that Aidos and Nemesis will forsake the earth for the company of gods (197 seq.), and we also learn (256 seq.) that "virgin Diké, the daughter of God," sits beside her father Zeus the son of Kronos and advises him of the doings of unjust princes. The associations are brought together in Plutarch's *To An Ignorant Prince* 4 (*Moralia* 781), where Shame (*aidous*) waits on Zeus' throne with the virginal Diké, Themis, Sophrosuné, and Ophelé (justice, law, wise prudence, and ministration)—therefore kings are called *aidouious*, reverend. Spenser's Temperance is clothed in white garments (like Isis), and so is Hesiod's Aidos. Cf. also Ovid, *Metam.* I.129, where the flight of Astraea is linked to that of *pudor*, shame; and Juvenal, *Sat.* VI.1–20, where Astraea is said to have withdrawn with Chastity. For Britomart in Book V as a returning Astraea, see below, "The Course of Justice," sec. i.

Shamefastness, one of the "bevy of faire Ladies" dwelling in the heart of the Castle. As Eirene is linked to the bashful Irena, so Shamefastness is ironically linked to the blushing bathing beauties at Acrasia's garden.[150] The fountain in which the girls cavort is "over-wrought" with wanton cupidons, and Cupid also has a place in the recognition scene in Alma's parlor (II.xii.60; ix.34). This place is modest, of course, when compared with Cupid's role in the Garden of Adonis or the Temple of Venus. The half-hidden cherubim that suspend Mercilla's cloth of state are the correspondingly reticent figures in the fifth book.

The last stage of the heroes' tour of the Castle saw their elevation to the cells of Alma's three advisors; in Book V, Mercilla's guests are invited to take their place on either side of the queen to hear a case presently being debated. Thus the tripartite arrangement of the tribunal recalls the earlier division of the mind; and the history lesson Arthur read under Eumnestes is replaced by a contemporary example. If contemporary, it ought to show analogies with Alma's second counselor, or Judgment: the walls of the central sage's cell show pictures "Of Magistrates, of courts, of tribunals, . . . Of lawes, of iudgements, and of decretals" (II.ix.53). In the judgment made upon Duessa there is also an exercise of judgment as well as justice, and in fact this part of justice—the more intellectual part—is closely identified with equity. So in Aristotle:

> What is called judgment, in virtue of which men are said to "be sympathetic judges" and to "have judgment," is the right discrimination of the equitable. This is shown by the fact that we say the equitable man is above all others a man of sympathetic judgment, and identify equity with sympathetic judgment about certain facts. And sympathetic judgment is judgment which discriminates what is equitable and does so correctly; and correct judgment is that which judges what is true.[151]

An entertainment by Lyly addresses the queen as she "in whose hands Justice hath left her balance,"[152] and Spenser's trial seems to be intended to realize the imagery of this version of Astraea's legacy. The tribunal, in a sense, stands for the well-balanced mind of the judge:

> But in the mind the doome of right must bee;
> And so likewise of words, the which be spoken,
> The eare must be the ballance, to decree
> And iudge, whether with truth or falsehood they agree.
>
> (V.ii.47)

---

[150] Cf. II.ix.43: Shamefastness, Guyon is told, "is the *fountaine* of your modestee." She is "abasht for shame," while one of the wantons in the fountain is temporarily "Abasht, that her a straunger did avise" (II.xii.66).

[151] *Nich. Ethics* VI.xi (1143a), trans. by W. D. Ross.

[152] "On the Queen's Visit to Theobalds" (May, 1591), in *Complete Works*, ed. Bond (Oxford, 1902), vol. 1, p. 417.

In the trial, the balance is struck between Duessa's just and zealous accusers, and her sympathetic and cautious advocates. The result is the equivalent of a divided jury, six parties for conviction and six against.

We noted earlier that Maleger's bands and Phantastes' fancies had elements in common. We may ask if there is some character at the trial of Duessa who has a similar potentially cooperating relation with Mercilla's enemies. If there is, he must be among the advocates of Duessa. These include Arthur, whose generous nature puts him on the side of "fancies ruth," or "vain pity" (V.ix.45, 49–50). In a way, the changing of Arthur's mind is the point of the trial. Eumnestes' British chronicle was also presented for Arthur's benefit; it describes the foundation of Britain by Brute and its subsequent unification—"reduced . . . to one mans gouernments" (II.ix.59). Such a lesson turns on the accomplishments of Donwallo, which are recounted just halfway through the whole:

> . . . countreis he redus'd to quiet state,
> And shortly brought to ciuill gouernaunce,
> Now one, which earst were many, made through variaunce.
>
> Then made he sacred lawes, which some men say
> Were vnto him reveald in vision,
> By which he freed the Traueilers high way,
> The Churches part, and Ploughmans portion,
> Restraining stealth, and strong extortion;
> The gracious *Numa* of great *Britanie*:
> For till his dayes, the chiefe dominion
> By strength was wielded without pollicie;
> Therefore he first wore crown of gold for dignitie.
>
> (II.x.38–39)

This ordering power also appears in the reasonable ruler of the Castle herself, for hers is the function of the rational soul:

> But in body, which doth freely yeeld
> His partes to reasons rule obedient
> And letteth her that ought the scepter weeld,
> All happy peace and goodly gouernment,
> Is settled there in sure establishment;
> There Alma like a virgin Queene most bright,
> Doth flourish in all beautie excellent:
>
> (II.xi.1)

The balance is tipped against Duessa by Ate; turning queen's evidence, the hag leads off a series of five more witnesses whose accusations seem to be specific offenses against the Litae, also five in number.[153] At this

---

[153] The throne-room dialectic of Ate ("Ruin") and the Litae ("Supplication," Heedfulness) is as old as the allegory of Phoinix in *Iliad* IX.502 seq.

point Arthur comes over to the side represented by Artegall. The first of
the "Many graue persons, that against her pled" is described as

> . . . a sage old *Syre*, that had to name
> The *Kingdomes care*, with a white siluer hed,
> That many high regards and reasons gainst her red
>
> (V.ix.43)

Here is the figure who corresponds to the Johannine Contemplation, and
the Homeric Eumnestes, the treasurer of memory. In Spenser's day the
model for such a personage was William Cecil, Lord Burghley: "The
rugged forhead that with graue foresight / Welds kingdomes causes, and
affaires of state" (IV, proem, 1). In his Dedicatory Sonnet he is addressed
as the "Lord high Threasurer of England,"

> . . . whose carefull brest
> To menage of most graue affaires is bent,
> And on whose mightie shoulders most doth rest
> The burdein of this kingdomes gouernment.

The execution of justice is left suspended between the "iust vengeance"
and "piteous ruth" of the queen. The condemnation of Duessa is "tempred
without griefe or gall, / Till strong constraint did her thereto enforce"
(V.ix.50). The final outcome here alluded to makes the point that however clement the magistrate, his first function is to secure his sovereignty.
This will be the history-lesson which the heroes carry with them to their
final missions.

The theme of Eumnestes' chronicle is the establishment of national
sovereignty; usurpers and foreign invaders crowd its pages, and the Roman
power is among them. In Book V Arthur is engaged on behalf of Belge
against the contemporary Roman power, the Catholic tyranny in the Low
Countries. Belge is a suppliant widow whose husband's murder has the
same result as the departure of Guyon from the Castle: oppression by a
giant modeled on a tyrant defeated by Hercules. Two features of Gerioneo
will remind us of Book II. First there is the giant's triplicity: Maleger
renewed himself three times; Gerioneo has three bodies. Geryon and
Antaeus have a certain natural resemblance, and indeed the older allegory
of the battle with Antaeus as the war of flesh and spirit was also applied
to Geryon.[154] The association seems to have occurred to Claudian, who

[154] For thoroughgoing examples of the older allegory, see Coluccio Salutati, *De
Laboribus Herculis*, III.xxvii.8f., and xxviii.8, in the edition of B. L. Ullman (Zurich,
1951), pp. 289ff., 328. As Salutati elsewhere notes (III.xii.6), both Geryon and
Antaeus may be treated as *libido* (following the lead of Fulgentius, *Mitol.*, II.iv).

says of Hercules, "Thou hast o'erthrown the many limbs of the triple-headed monster and returned thrice victorious from a single foe. Vain the falls of Antaeus. . . ."[155] Aeschylus' Clytemnestra almost seems to be talking about Antaeus in her reference to Geryon: "If he [Agamemnon] had died each time that rumour told his death / he must have been some triple-bodied Geryon / back from the dead with threefold cloak of earth upon / his body, and killed once for every shape assumed."[156] Diodorus Siculus treats the two victories as part of the same expedition.[157] The resemblance to Maleger of an enemy—*pugna triplex*[158]—whose strokes are "Behinde, beside, before" (V.xi.6), perhaps needs no laboring. The connecting link in this symbolism is to be found in the legend of friendship, where the story of the thrice-revived Triamond is based on an allegory customarily attached to Geryon. The allegory in question made Geryon a type of fraternal concord, and thus the tyrannical Gerioneo of Book V is a parody of the brotherhood created by justice and fellow feeling.[159] Secondly, there is the giant's sphinxlike shrine-monster, whose riddles stand for the Inquisition, the terrors of which replace the perplexities caused by Maleger. After recapturing the most important castle of Belge in the tenth canto, Arthur passes through its gates (as he leaves Alma's castle in Book II), prunes down the challenger without, flushes the monster, and destroys it along with Gerioneo's idol. There is a reference to the suicide of the sphinx in Book V at the point in Book II where Impatience and Impotence dispatch themselves, but the more obvious parallel for the allegory of the two hags is in the story of Sir Burbon, the impatient and impotent monarch whose story Spenser appended to the eleventh canto.

Maleger's attack on the Castle of Alma began when Guyon sailed off toward Acrasia's island. In Book V it is Arthur who departs from the queen's domain by sea, during the time that Artegall and Talus encounter Sir Burbon. The text is in some unresolved quandary here, since the Burbon adventure is announced in the quatrain at the opening of the twelfth canto, after the adventure has already been narrated. Perhaps Spenser realized that it fitted better with the eleventh canto analogy with Book II, rather than the twelfth canto analogy, where it would have spoiled the parallel between the two voyages to a dangerous island.

Geryon thus becomes *geos eris eona*, eternal strife with our earthly nature; Antaeus, the giant who draws his powers from the earth of Libya, is our contrary libido.

[155] Claudian, *De Raptu* II.39–41: "tergeminique ducis numerosos deicis artus / et totiens uno victor ab hoste redis. / non cadere Antaeo . . ." (addressing Hercules).

[156] *Agamemnon* 870, trans. Richmond Lattimore.

[157] Diod. Sic., *Bibl.* IV.xvii.4 seq.

[158] Martial, V.lxv.11.

[159] For the allegory of Geryon as Concord, see *infra*, "Single Nature's Double Name," sec. iii.

By the fourth stanza of the last canto both heroes are seaborne, in pursuit of their assigned quests. The sense of mission is strong here, especially in Book II, where the voyage has overtones of the terrific boat-trip that will bring Paul to Rome at the end of the Book of Acts. Both of Spenser's heroes travel to their islands with two assistants; the boatman in the second book has the kind of sergeantlike loyalty to his post for which Sir Sergis is praised in the later book.[160] Before the critical confrontation there are two tasks performed by the chief *aide-de-camp*: one offshore, and one on the island. The Palmer quells first the sea-monsters and then the land-beasts. Talus wades into the water to engage the force holding the shore; then he exterminates the enemy force sent to meet the invaders by land. Guyon passes through the Bower without deviating from his course, the Palmer continuing to act in the role of moral rudder. Artegall goes on to best the giant Grantorto in single combat, avoiding his lethal axe like a "skillful Marriner" who strikes his sails before a storm (V.xii.18). The refined Acrasia and the brutal Grantorto do not resemble each other, except that both are usurpers of a kind; the emphasis in bringing the usurpers to justice is on the destructive aspect of the knights' tasks, rather than on the regeneration of the youthful victims. Guyon liberates Verdant from the succuba-like Acrasia, and Artegall has a similar rejuvenating effect on Irena.

Guyon destroys the Bower after Acrasia's capture; an equally rigorous Artegall punishes those who have collaborated with the dead Grantorto. Each quest concludes with the follow-up actions undertaken by the knight's seconds. The Palmer redeems Acrasia's enchanted victims, and Talus aids in the reform of the savage island by revealing crime and searching out rebels. The operations of both heroes have a rather negative tone. Artegall's armed peace is certainly not the peaceable kingdom. Guyon appears in the "tempest of his wrathfulness" (II.xii.83).

Each book has an epilogue suggesting a relapse into unregenerate experience, perhaps in the absence of something more positive than restraint. The recalcitrant hog Grylle, preferring to remain comfortably sloughed in his brutish nature, reproaches Guyon for restoring him to human form. Here is the minor triumph of Mutabilitie found at the end of each legend. The supremacy of change she so brilliantly argues has reminded one critic of Erasmus' *Praise of Folly*;[161] and one of that parody-goddess's examples of the happiness of the beast state is Plutarch's Gryllus.[162] A similarly

---

[160] Comparing II.xii.29 with V.xi.38 and xii.10.

[161] William Blisset, "Spenser's Mutabilitie," in *Essays in English Literature . . . Presented to A.S.P. Woodhouse*, ed. M. MacLure and F. Watt (Toronto, 1964), pp. 33f. This essay provides many keys to the interpretation of the Mutabilitie Cantos offered in this book.

[162] Had Ulysses drunk Circe's cups, Horace says (*Epist.* I.2, l. 30), "he would have lived a filthy [*immundis*] dog, or a hog delighting in mire." Spenser's Grylle "de-

unsympathetic public opinion backbites Artegall on his return from the savage island: two relatives of the Occasion of Book II, the hags Envy and Detraction, set the Blatant Beast on the disembarking hero. The final word in Book V is not given to judicious or well-tempered speech; instead, we hear the abusive tongues of a collective reproach.

The analogy we have just outlined suggests that Spenser's second installment is not merely a sequel to his first. The second depends on its predecessor, at least in this instance, for scaffolding, and for one kind of order. The analogy also helps to explain the discreteness of individual episodes in Book V, a technical feature of the narrative that gains some significance if Artegall's progress in part depends upon his observing the course laid down by Guyon's legend. Next, the analogy serves to assert the importance of the personal qualities of the governor, and helps maintain justice as an ethical virtue. The self-control of the governor is reflected in his government. Artegall fails to suppress pity, and consequently he fails to suppress rebellion. Artegall suffers, and Terpine and justice suffer much more. Finally, the analogy illustrates the relation between private regimen and public "regiment": both virtues are concerned with turning conscious, or dehumanized, or natural power into conscious mastery. Three further dimensions of this theme of mastery will form the subject of the remainder of our study of Book V.

---

lights in filth" (II.xii.87). Whitney's Circe-emblem (*Choice of Emblemes*, ed., Greene, p. 82), "Homines voluptatis transformator," says of Ulysses' men: "Some had the shape of Goats, and Hogges, some Apes, and Asses weare. / Who, when they might have their former shape againe, / They did refuse, and rather wish'd, still brutish to remain." See the emblem of Petrus Costalius, in *Pegma, Cum narrationibus philosophiciis* (Leiden, 1555), p. 176, "In Grillum. Voluptatem immanissimus quisque sequitur lubens" (anyone very savage follows pleasure willingly). For appetite transforming men into Circe's swine, see Xenophon, *Memorabilia* I.iii.7. For Gryllus himself, see Plutarch, *Bruta animalia uti* (*Moralia* 986ff.). Renaissance references are Erasmus, *Praise of Folly* (in J. P. Dolan, trans., *The Essential Erasmus*, New York, 1964, p. 124), where the pig offers a paradoxical economia of the beast state; Gelli, *Circe*, where Circe's beasts, in a dialogue with Ulysses, prove rational and articulate defenders of irrational instinct as a guide to life; Calvin, *Institutes*, I.iii.3, where Gryllus is offered as philosophic proof that without revelation man's life is no better than a beast's; Calfhill, *Answer to Martiall's Treatise of the Cross*, Parker Society (Cambridge, 1846), p. 248, where Gryllus cannot be, properly speaking, transformed into a beast ("should not I acknowledge and confess with Gryllus, in whom, (bearing the figure of a reasonable creature,) enchantment could take no place, that reason and religion should be preferred to the belly?"). A character named Grillo in *O.F.* XVIII.16f. appears to be dead drunk at the time he is killed by Cloridano and Medoro. Grylle's philosophy is treated at more length below, in Chap. IV, "Gardens of Pleasure," sec. i.

The Art of Equity

Having laid before the reader the inclusive analogy between Spenser's second and fifth books, I now propose to reverse this procedure, and offer some autonomous status for the legend of justice. The reader may ask why he should have to master the analogy with Book II, if it is to be subsequently deconjugated, but our order does do some justice to the fact that in the seriatim reading of the poem the analogies between Books II and V call themselves to our attention before Book V has taken shape by itself. In appending the second three books to the first three Spenser created so deep a fold in his representation of moral being that the "antithetical" or median book of the second installment almost inevitably seeks parity with the corresponding book in the first. Any study that isolates Book V for independent treatment will be limited by the omission of this reference to the twofold nature of the poem.

There are, however, features of Book V that make it unique, and they rightly command independent notice. Spenser's characterization of justice in terms of equity, power, and the national will are convenient topics for this consideration, and they have the added advantage of corresponding roughly to our earlier discussions of Book II in terms of interiority, energy, and the control of time. In short, we can establish the larger relation between the two legends on a basis other than an analogy of episodes.

The institutions of law and order elaborate upon the character strength that is particularly Guyon's; but there are independent psychological prototypes for the virtue of justice. The symbolic child we have elsewhere relied on to provide a clue to these prototypes may be found in Artegall himself, under the training of Astraea. By skipping over the central books, we find our persona older, of school age, ready to leave the family and enter on a society of what are initially strangers. Again, training is the issue, especially objective training in the skills required for survival in the environment. In the social relations of this period, authority as well as friendship is sought; qualities of leadership and organization are important, as they are in schoolyard games. The erotic interest, however, hardly appears as such. In this legend it is expressed in terms of the will-to-power; one can see this in the dream of the crocodile, and in the contest of Britomart and Radigund. Here maidens in distress are not the rewards for their rescue; conquest is its own reward. Thus the legend of justice belongs to the psychological period known as "latency." A tomboy like Radigund is the right competition for the heroic personae.

This derivation seems less fanciful in the light of another character strength developed during latency, namely, the mastery of complicated physical skills and the laws of physical objects.[163] The handbooks for courtier and governor strongly approved of this sort of education; in Book V the most obvious example is perhaps Artegall's skill in swimming.[164] We have mentioned Artegall's being trained to tame wild animals, as Xenophon's Cyrus was educated for justice by means of blood sports. At one point in the preceding book it is said that "savage" Artegall wears the arms of Achilles, and Achilles received a comparable education in the arts of war from Chiron. As Achilles himself tells us at the end of Statius' fragment, the *Achilleid* (II.163-165), "he implanted deep within my heart the precepts of divine justice, whereby he was wont to give revered laws to the tribes that dwelt on Pelion, and tame his own twy-formed folk."[165]

Latency is also the period in which the concept of work becomes meaningful, and in which the pursuit and completion of a task requiring extended application can be understood. The single-mindedness of Talus recognizes that there is no work that is not in part mechanical. Success in this period comes in terms of seeing a plan or project through; the corresponding failure is a failure of competence. Success requires mastery and skill; failure results in a sense of incompetence and inferiority. The communist giant's scheme reveals this frustrating kind of incapacity, and no doubt the issue of the organization of the work in society—as well as the wealth—is involved. The giant's troubles with the scales suggest the problems of manipulating tools and symbols effectively. The failure of Artegall to finish his contract with Radigund is a defeat for competence, as well as justice, and his incarceration in a workhouse, doing women's work at the loom, gives us an ironic version of the virtue of industry. Artegall must also suffer feelings of inferiority in this defeat, though it is left to Britomart to give them voice. Almost every episode contains an example of fruitless industry or thwarted effort. Thus it is partly owing to the theme of work and its frustration that the cumulative defeat in this legend looms so large. Book V subjects heroic endeavour itself to a rather pessimistic assessment. In Spenser's legend about faith, there is naturally more misplaced faith than elsewhere in the poem; in his legend about work, there is rather more lost labor.

The positive version of industry appears cumulatively also, and the prominence given to the analogy with the labors of Hercules deserves comment here.[166] So also does a certain thematic similarity to Virgil's

---

[163] Similarly, Erikson, *Childhood and Society*, 2nd edn., pp. 86, 258-261.

[164] Swimming is commended as a noble skill in Elyot, *Gouernour*, I.xvii, *edn. cit.*, p. 75, and Castiglione, *Courtier*, in Milligan, ed., *Three Renaissance Classics*, p. 281.

[165] Trans. by J. H. Mozley, in Loeb *Statius*, vol. 2, pp. 593-595.

[166] This analogy is developed at length in T. K. Dunseath, *Spenser's Allegory of Justice in Book Five of "The Faerie Queene"* (Princeton, 1968), *passim*. See as well Jane Aptekar, *Icons of Justice* (New York, 1969), chap. 10, "The Champion of True Justice," and chap. 11, "The Choice."

Aeneid. According to the humanist Francesco Filelfo, in a letter to which Don Cameron Allen has drawn attention, the later books of the *Aeneid* show Aeneas, or Justice, overthrowing Turnus, or Injustice.[167] Like the *Aeneid*, Spenser's fifth book shows the art of government as a Herculean labor of shouldering burdens, maintaining vigilance, dominating chaos, suppressing selfish wills, and carrying out the duties of office. Aeneas transmits to Ascanius an example of virtue and true work (*Aen.* XII. 435ff.); it is "the work" as well as the "equal balance" that condemns Turnus to death (XII.725–727); the city-building Dido of Virgil's first book gives laws and ordinances to her people, and equalizes their work and labor in just proportions (I.507–508). In the *Georgics* the "arms" of hardy rustics are agricultural tools, and it is toil that conquers all (*Geo.* I.160, 145). And as in Spenser, there is an analogy between the civic hero of the epic and the laboring Hercules.[168]

The services of Hercules to mankind were connected with the establishment of civilization from classical times. So also were the careers of Bacchus and Osiris—the Egyptian god is associated by syncretists with both of the Greco-Roman demigods, and Artegall is linked to both Hercules and Osiris, along with their human equivalents Samson and Anthony.[169]

---

[167] Allen, *Mysteriously Meant*, p. 155, citing Francesco Filelfo, *Epistolarum libri sedecim* (Paris, 1513), pp. 4ᵛ–7ʳ, letter of Jan. 1427 to Cyriacus of Ancona.

[168] Examples of the analogy are the Cacus-epyllion, *Aen.* VIII.185 seq., and the prophecy of Augustus in VI.801–803. The analogy of Augustus with Atlas belongs here too, because Aeneas is descended from Atlas (VIII.136–142), and because Hercules shouldered Atlas' burden (see VIII.731, IV.247, 481f., VI.791–797, IV.404–407). Augustus is also another Hercules in Horace, *Odes* III.14.

[169] V.i.2, V.vii.2, V.viii.2 (with V.v.24). The stanzas seem to be regularly placed. The identification of Bacchus with Osiris is a commonplace: see Herodotus, II.144; Plutarch, *De Iside* 13; Diod. Sic., I.ix.3, etc.; Giraldus, *Hist. Deorum*, Syntag. VIII, in *Op. om.*, I, col. 280f.; Comes, *Mythol.*, V.xiii, pp. 484, 489, *edn. cit.*; Cartari, *Le Imagini*, pp. 320ff., edn. cit. Comes and Cartari both cite Tibullus, I.vii. Remembering that there is an Egyptian Hercules as well as an Egyptian Bacchus, one may draw Hercules into the equation. Bacchus and Hercules are paired by Diod. Sic., IV.xv.1, as mortal Olympians, and all three demi-gods are grouped together by Plutarch, *De Iside* 27, as comparable euhemerized benefactors of mankind. Cooper's *Dictionary*, *sub* "Hercules," cites pseudo-Berosus to the effect that Hercules was the *son* of Osiris, and adds that St. Jerome, on Gen. 10, writes that it was this Egyptian Hercules who performed the twelve labors. A character like Shakespeare's Antony also belongs here (so Spenser, *F.Q.* V.viii.2—cf. Tasso, *Ger. Lib.* XVI.7) for he is Dionysian (Plutarch compares Antony to Dionysus), Herculean (owing to his guardian deity), and the lover of the chief priestess of Isis. Comes, in *Mythol.*, V.xiii, pp. 489f., compares Bacchus to Hercules: they have the same fatherland, use nearly the same insignia, and were both burned. He cites Sidonius Antipater, who compares the two on the basis of their columns; their arms and skins; the enmity of Hera; their cremation; and their exaltation to the immortal realm. In Spenser's *Teares*,

A series of resemblances to Hercules' tasks can be adduced for Artegall's adventures, though in some episodes the analogy is slight; also, allusions on Spenser's part cannot always be proved. Here is the whole list: the apprehension of Sanglier, the capture of the Erymanthian boar; the struggle with Pollente, the wrestling-match with the river-god Achelous; the cleaning up of Munera's corruption, the cleansing of the Augean stables;[170] the hero's victories in the tournament at Marinell's wedding, Hercules' quelling of the Lapiths and Centaurs at the wedding of Theseus;[171] the period with Radigund, the Omphale-phase or the victory over the Amazons; the episode of the Soldan, the mares of the Thracian tyrant Diomedes; the destruction of Malengine, the killing of Cacus, or of the shape-changing Periclymenus;[172] the service of Mercilla, the service of Hera, or Hera's glory (the etymology of Hercules); the battle with Geryon, the battle with Gerioneo; the rescues of Samient, Belge, and Irena, the rescue of Hesione; the use of Talus, Hercules' use of "The club of Iustice dread, with kingly powre endewed" (V.i.2). As the example of Talus reminds us, the development of physical skills has a corollary in the management of real tools. In later life this kind of competence is elaborated as technological expertise; tools and utensils become machines, and bat and ball become weaponry.

The important thing about this list is the sense it gives of Artegall's operations as a course of tasks, and of Artegall's life as the conscripted one of the public servant. Unlike the Redcrosse knight, Artegall seems

---

l. 461, it is the Muses who raised Bacchus and Hercules to heaven; Osiris is similarly explained at *F.Q.* V.vii.2.

[170] The unrewarded conquest of Troy by Hercules may also be present in the attack on Munera's domain, where Talus takes no gold. For an account of this episode in a readily available form, see William Warner, *Albion's England*, I.iv, in Alexander Chalmers, ed., *English Poets* (London, 1810), vol. 4, pp. 515f.

[171] Hercules' enmity to the Centaurs is well known, and figures in our discussion of Malengine, in "The Course of Justice," sec. i, below. The Centaurs are also notable for disrupting the wedding of Theseus (see *F.Q.* IV.i.22 and VI.x.13), upon which occasion Hercules saved the day. If their name implies that there were a hundred of them, then it is significant that Artegall rescues Marinell from a hundred knights during his wedding celebration. For the etymology *centum*-Centaur, see Comes, *Mythol.*, VI.xvi, *edn. cit.*, p. 615.

[172] Comes mentions Periclymenus as an analogue for Proteus, at *Mythol.*, VIII.viii, *edn. cit.*, p. 843, citing a comparison made by one Ephorion, and the description in Hesiod, *Catalogue of Women* 10. The most important notice of this character would be Ovid, *Metam.* XII.556 seq. See also Apoll. Rhod., *Argonaut.* I.156–160, and Apollodorus, *Bibl.* I.ix.9. Malengine's relation to Proteus is discussed below, in "The Custodian of Europe," n. 296 and text.

unaware of the analogy under which he labors, and Spenser often leaves the Herculean parallel unstated.[173] For example: in the episode of the communist giant, Artegall meets a kind of anti-Artegall, for the giant is a lawgiver, and, should he succeed in establishing his laws, society will derive its benefits from him. Scholars have noted that since the giant has secured his following through oratory, he corresponds to the iconographical type known as the Hercules Gallicus, whose persuasive eloquence drew crowds after him as if by golden chains.[174] Here is part of Budé's version of the description in Lucian:

> And there is a great crowd of people of all kinds who follow him as if by force and constraint; this is how it presents itself to the eye. For he holds all of them with chains of gold and silver attached to their ears: and they let themselves be led by him voluntarily. Hercules holds the end of these chains in his mouth. . . . We Celts [Lucian is told by his guide] signify Eloquence by Hercules, who was not a man of strength and endurance, as is commonly believed, but who was knowledgeable, wise, and spoke so well and with such good grace, that he saw all his great enterprises through to the end by singular prudence, which he demonstrated by his sensible and well-chosen language, called *Suada* by the Romans, since it persuaded everyone it wished to; and called *Psitagogue* by the Greeks, and similarly by the Latins, *Flexanima*: signifying by these well-chosen words the ability to move the minds and hearts of men, to control and change their loyalties at will. . . . This speech twists the minds of audience all around, incites and disperses, stops and constrains choice and free will, in accordance with the aim or whim of him who speaks or writes.[175]

[173] The Blatant Beast has affinities with both the Hydra and Cerberus: Cerberus is traditionally the object of the twelfth labor, and in Spenser it falls to the succeeding hero to accomplish this quest—it is implied that Hercules cannot do everything (see below, "The Beast Enlarged"). The beast of the Inquisition is also compared to the Hydra, and her piercing is described in terms of hydraulic engineering (V.xi. 31f.).

[174] For a useful study, see Robert E. Hallowell, "Ronsard and the Gallic Hercules Myth," *Studies in the Renaissance*, 9 (1962), pp. 242–255. For Comes, see *Mythol.* V.v, "De Mercurio," *edn. cit.*, pp. 435f.; for Cartari, *Le Imagini* (Venice, 1625), "Mercurio," p. 251f. Lucian says this Hercules is the Gallic deity Ogmius, mentioned by Erasmus at the opening of the *Paracelsis*. Again, Book VI takes over for Book V: the power of eloquence to lead a captive audience is ceded to Calidore—he leads the Blatant Beast by a chain through fairyland, and "all the people where so he did go, / Out of their townes did round about him throng" (VI.xii.37).

[175] G. Budé *Institution du Prince* (Paris, 1547; facsimile, Farnborough, Hants, Eng., 1966), cap. xiv, pp. 59f. For the orator's golden chain, cf. Sidney, *Astrophel and Stella*, Son. 58, and La Primaudaye, *French Academie*, Pt. II, chap. 15 (edn. of 1594), pp. 96ff., on the organ of the tongue. Cf. Lucian, *Heracles, ab init.*

We may compare the effects secured by the giant:

> ... the vulgar did about him flocke,
> And cluster thicke vnto his leasings vaine,
> Like foolish flies about an hony crocke
> In hope by him great benefite to gaine,
> And vncontrolled freedome to obtaine.
> All which when *Artegall* did see, and heare,
> How he mis-led the simple peoples traine,
>
> (V.ii.33)

On the Lucianic hieroglyph, Apteker quotes Bodin, who says that the Herculean orator "can excite the most cowardly to overcome the bravest"; the orator "revolutionizes a commonwealth, and plays upon the people at will."[176] Dunseath notes how the demagogue challenges comparison with the hero, being his rival in forensics,[177] and it is therefore significant that their argument gradually comes around to the nature of words themselves. Words, as it proves, are light, and only the informed mind, armed with what Budé calls "the interior word," can give them their due weight. In the same passage, Budé goes on to mention the superficiality of rhetoric without Hercules' arms, which are "probable arguments, the likely reasoning, and well-chosen sayings and phrases" employed by orators.[178] Artegall introduces these, while the giant, an increasingly frustrated orator —not to mention iconographer—tries to force the evidence:

> ... yet did he labour long,
> And swat, and chauf'd and proued euery way:
> Yet all the wrongs could not a little right downe way.
>
> (V.ii.46)

Artegall, employing that Roman *suada* used by the orator, attempts to "asswage" the giant, who proves unbending; Artegall borrows from the wisdom literature of Holy Writ, "For when a speaker rests upon science, no one can crush him":

And to speak otherwise, without natural prudence, or a large amount of acquired knowledge, is a superficial thing, without any depth: in which

---

[176] Jane Aptekar, *Icons of Justice* (New York, 1969), p. 229, quoting Jean Bodin, *Six Books of the Commonwealth*, IV.vii, trans. Tooley, p. 143.

[177] *Spenser's Allegory of Justice*, pp. 99–101.

[178] V.ii.47: "in the mind the doome of right must bee; / And so likewise of words ... The eare must be the ballance, to decree / and judge." Cf. the Geneva gloss on Job 12:11 ("Doth not the eares discerne the wordes"): "He exhorteth them to be wise in iudging, and as wel to know the right vse why God hath giuen them eares as he hathe done a mouth."

377

there is no solidity, and from which one cannot proceed; a vain and useless noise, with superfluous language (not Eloquence) without any fruit,
effect, or vigour, like an empty quiver, or a bow without an arrow.[179]

The giant weighs vanity, and fills his balance with "idle toys" (V.ii.30);
hence the words "fether," "winde," "winged words," and "light" for what
goes in his balance.[180]

The actual emblem of the Hercules Gallicus does not make an appearance in the episode, though as a Herculean orator Artegall logically makes
his other extensive speech to the "mis-trayned" Flourdelis, or Lady France.
And yet, to the informed reader, the confounding of the giant with his
balances—like a tempest-driven ship "spoyling all her geares and goodly
ray" (V.ii.50)—must suggest the potential for entanglement, confusion,
and dismay latent in the very awkward image of leadership the emblem
presents in the first place.

There is one further example of this image of Hercules concealed in
Spenser's legend. The golden chains that went out from the orator's mouth
were, according to Lucian, attached to his pierced tongue. The poet Malfont is also an orator, and he has spoken against the queen in "bold
speaches" (V.ix.25). In Valeriano's *Hieroglyphica* (XXXII.xxxix), under
"Lingua," Hercules' pierced tongue is given as an emblem of eloquence;[181]
Malfont's nailed tongue is such an emblem too—again, an eloquence gone
wrong.

[ii]

The history of the state has the place in the legend of justice that the
history of the Church had in the legend of holiness. Here the *Aeneid*
theme is the Crown's mission to establish the new political dispensation
for the new age. Thus a major idea of Book V is sovereignty, corresponding roughly to unanimity in Book I, and autonomy in Book II. Sovereignty
has a special political extension in the idea of dominion over others, and
the securing of this dominion proves costly in terms of our sympathies: the
book abounds in chopped off heads, lopped extremities, grisly anthropoid
grins, guerrilla warfare, armies of occupation, violent pacifications, and
embittered ends.

Besides the obvious dominion of a sovereign over his country and the
lands he claims, there are a number of other authorities treated in the
legend. There is the lordship of the husband over the wife, a theme felt
both in Sir Burbon's failure to control his trothplight Lady Flourdelis and

---

[179] Budé, *Institution du Prince, edn. cit.*, cap. xiv, pp. 50f.
[180] V.ii.31, 43–45.
[181] Cited by Robert E. Hallowell, *art. cit.* in n. 174, above.

in Artegall's unjust subjection to Radigund. Britomart reclaims this lost dominion on Artegall's behalf, and requires the Amazons to swear fealty to her lord.[182] The dominion enjoyed by the property owner is found in the story of the two brothers and in Artegall's rebuttal of the communist giant. There is also the problematic dominion over the open sea, already symbolically allowed to Britomart in her conquest of Marinell;[183] it also figures in the allegory of the Soldan. The dominion of the master over the slave is revealed in the deep bond between Artegall and Talus. And there is the Erastian dominion of the sovereign over the nation in matters of religion, the establishment of which was commonly understood as a primary responsibility of the ruler. The ruler, in turn, was appointed by God, and serves as his deputy or viceroy. Both the widowed Lady Belge and the feckless Sir Burbon are unable to retain this sovereignty over religion. Various technical dominions include those of the Crown over rivers, certain specified kinds of public revenues, Crown courts, and colonial administrations. Finally, there are more metaphorical jurisdictions, particularly those of law and equity. The dominion of equity especially will concern us here, for justice is served only if this dominion qualifies and rationalizes the others. Equity, in fact,

[182] More precisely, Britomart restores the Amazons to men's subjection, and makes the new-made men swear their fealty to her lord (V.vii.42f.): i.e., she restores the men to superiority, even while preserving her own superior position; and she vicariously subjects herself to Artegall, even while she deepens his obligation to her. (I have condensed the action for the sake of the argument: subjection and fealty are analogous with regard to Christian marriage.) It is pertinent to note here that Radegund was a fifth century saint ("as Saintlike as Saint Radegund" is proverbial in *Mother Hvbberds Tale*, l. 497): she refused to consummate her enforced marriage with a conquering prince. Artegall's contract with Radigund might easily imply an unconsummated marriage-contract, the marriage being one in which the lady is holding out for mastery (see esp. V.vi.32). The nunnery that the saint went on to found and preside over may well appear in the Amazon town that Britomart disestablishes. In this context, Radigund's name would mean not so much "rash woman" (Greek *radios* + *guné*), but "offended wife" (Latin *radere* + *guné*). For St. Radegund, see *The lyf of Seynt Radegunde* [by Henry Bradshaw?] (publ. R. Pynson, ca. 1510). Hankins is the only critic to draw attention to this story (*Source and Meaning*, p. 153). The other source for the name is Rhodogune (V.iv.35, "Radegone"), whom Cooper's *Dictionary* describes as "the daughter of kynge Darius, which kylled hir nurse for persuadynge hir to marie after hir fyrst husbandes death." The role of Radigund's handmaid is only inversely analogous. (For the Rhodogune in question, see Plutarch, *Artaxerxes* 27; Philostratus, *Imagines* II.5, Appian, *Syr.* 67f., and Justin, *Hist.* XXXVIII.ix.3). For this identification, see D. C. Allen, "Spenser's Radigund," *MLN* 67 (1952), pp. 120–122. Philostratus reads: "she prays to conquer men, even as she has now conquered them; for I do not think she loves to be loved" (Loeb edn., p. 147).
[183] Cf. III.iv.18: Britomart admires the booty from the sea, but passes on, "for all was in her powre." The queen, on the contrary, often greeted the ships of her privateers at the docks in person, to exact the Crown's cut on the spot.

is the art or "second nature" of justice, which corrects and justifies all the preestablished social orders that make up a kind of first nature.

There are many ways of describing equity in the terms just proposed. Halfway through the legend Spenser addresses himself to "That part of Iustice, which is Equity, / Whereof I haue to treat here presently" (V.vii. 2), implying that in some mysterious way equity's time has come. He refers partly to the legalized injustice of Radigund, which equity can properly correct. But he also means that equity is the logical secondary development of his subject. Something similar happens at the same point in the legend of temperance, where the understanding of the virtue is decisively interiorized by the temptation of the hero in the underworld. In fact, the identification of temperance with resistance to temptation assimilates the virtue to a Christian or biblical context. The same complication is to be noted here, because of the associations of equity with Christian mercy. In both cases the interior understanding of the virtue fulfills the habit of the virtue by means of the consciousness of it—or by becoming its conscience.[184]

Spenser specifically says that equity is measured out according to the "line of conscience," and that it determines when the magistrate ought to dispense with "rigour" (V.i.7), by which he means "the rigour of the law" (cf. the Geneva gloss on the mother in the judgment of Solomon at I Kings 3:26: "she had rather endure the rigour of the lawe, then se her childe cruelly slaine"). The rigor of the law is represented in Talus, whom both Britomart and Artegall have occasion to restrain. Talus is not allowed within the precincts of Isis, or equity, because unlike equity, the internalization of the law, the ruthless iron man wants "sence / And sorrowes feeling," even if his tears suggest that he has a conscience of a rudimentary sort (V.vi.9).

[184] Although he is arguing a technical position (namely that equity is not a moral virtue above the law which might give the judge the discretion to break the law), and although it was not published in Spenser's time, Edward Hake's *Epieikeia: A Dialogue on Equity in Three Parts* (1599?), nonetheless provides an apt summary of our theme here: ". . . if you will add . . . that this *correctio legis* is not the act of the judge but is the act of Epiekeia, which is the sowle and spyrit of the lawe (and so a part of the same lawe), then what can be more evident then that this wee call *correctio legis* is not indeede as it is termed but is rather in the trewe appellation thereof to be termed *correctio litere legis*, even as the purer part of a man's reason may be said to correct the more sensuall and more corrupte parte of the same reason? . . . for a judge in his exposition of the lawe sometymes to forsake the letter of the lawe or to decline from the same, and to suffer himself to be ledde by the *Equity* thereof which exhybiteth unto him this secreat sense and hidden (but the right and trewe) meaning of the lawe, this is not [to] change the lawe, but is indeede to sett the law in his right place, and rather to give life to the lawe which otherwise in the letter thereof would be dead." (Text ed. D.E.C. Yale, Yale Law Library Publications, no. 13, London, 1953, p. 28.)

An analogous hierarchy of symbols informs the *Oresteia* of Aeschylus. At the bottom of its structure are the Furies, representing the purely violent world of the blood feud and the ancestral curse. These primitive and savage monsters not only stand for indiscriminate vengeance, however, but also for the fear of retribution, and so they are a permanent part of the dialectic of the criminal law. Nonetheless, they are considered a pollution of the temple of Delphi; like Talus, they are associated with both bloodhounds and uncontrolled bloodshed. The next level of justice is the area of revenge taken disinterestedly, on principle, so to speak. Apollo's instrument in carrying out the Greek equivalent of the *lex talionis* is Orestes. Clytemnestra dreams of Orestes as a snake, as Britomart dreams of Artegell as a crocodile. Beyond this level is the rational consideration of circumstances, symbolized by the Areopagus. At Orestes' trial before the future Athenian high court, the equitable Athena asserts that injustice must not win by technicalities (or oaths). The trial ends in a hung jury, and Orestes is acquitted, the decisive vote being cast by the sympathetic Athena. We might say this vote stands for the benefit of the doubt. Spenser's trial, however, leads to the conviction of Duessa, when six further witnesses tip the balance against her. They are introduced by the hag Ate, a spirit of accusation who corresponds to the Furies at the trial of Orestes. The virgin-goddess Athena presides over the Aeschylean structure, but Aeschylus lacks any way to suggest the transvaluation of justice by some higher principle, with the result that the law is declared fulfilled on a basis not far removed from caprice. Spenser is able to complete his symbolism by means of the concept of mercy, educed from justice proper, as he says, "by diuine extreate" (V.x.1).

The contrast between the law of ordinances and the law of conscience was familiar to Spenser's original audience in the biblical context, of course, for the rigor of the law is easily taken for the letter of the law. Jeremiah and Ezekiel promise a change of heart in terms that reverse the metamorphosis described in the Deucalion stanza of Spenser's proem (V, proem, 2):

> I wil take the stone heart out of their bodies, & wil giue them an heart of flesh, That thei maie walke in my statutes
> (Ezekiel 11:19–20 Geneva Bible)

> . . . this shalbe the couenant that I will make with the house of Israel . . .
> I wil put my Law in their inward partes, & write it in their hearts. . . .
> (Jeremiah 31:33, Geneva Bible)

On the latter, the Geneva gloss explains, "In the time of Christ my Law shal instead of tables of stone be written in heartes."

Equity and mercy are associated in the mind of Christian culture because both qualify the law. In Spenser's legend this connection is enforced by the cognate symbolism of Isis and Mercilla. The Puritan William Perkins, in an illuminating essay on equity, advises the magistrate—whose responsibility equity is—that he "should not forget that justice always shakes hands with her sister mercy and that all laws allow of a mitigation."[185] The jurist St. German writes that equity "is the rigtwiseness that considereth all the particular circumstance of the deede, the which also is tempred with the swetnes of mercy."[186] Spenser makes equity responsible for the "clemence" that restrains the sternness of the judgments made by the "righeous" Artegall (V.vii.22). On clemency, the judicial equivalent of mercy, we may quote La Primaudaye at greater length:

> It is true, that gentlenes and clemencie most all become a great and excellent man, and is one principall vertue necessary for a Magistrate. Notwithstanding it must be so rulled, that for the benefite of the Commonwealth, severity and rigour be ioined therewith: because it is unpossible to rule & governe a multitude without this. And yet is not the part sither of a wise Phisition, or of a good governor of an Estate, to set hand to the iron, except in great necessitie, when there is no other remedie. For if they do otherwise, as there is want of discretion in both, so most of all in the Magistrate, bicause iniustice also is ioined with crueltie. So that it is necessarie, both in clemence and rigor to keep some honest meane by right reason, and prudence, to the end that the inconveniencies of both may be eschewed.[187]

A just governor—to paraphrase the above—will join clemency to severity, and seek the mean between them, even while remaining mindful that injustice is joined to cruelty, as Spenser's Adicia is joined to the Soldan. Lodowick Bryskett, in his *Discourse of Ciuill Life* (London, 1606), says that justice "tempereth with equitie (which may be termed a kind of clemency ioyned to iustice) things seuerely established by law, to the end that exact iustice may not proue to be exact wrong" (p. 249). This is how Britomart will "ioyne" Artegall (V.vii.23).

Pity, on the other hand, is a dangerous restraint on the rigor of the law that equity, symbolized by Isis, properly qualifies. St. German says that "in some cases it is necessarie to leaue the woordes of the law, and to

---

[185] My text is the selection from *Epieķeia, or a Treatise of Christian Equity and Moderation* (in Perkins, *Workes*, London, 1626-1631, vol. 2, pp. 437–441), printed in Edmund Morgan, ed., *Puritan Political Ideas* (Indianapolis, 1965), pp. 59–71. The quote is from p. 65.

[186] Christopher Saint German, *The Dyaloges in Englyshe* (London, 1554), I.xvi, fol. 27r-v.

[187] *French Academie, edn. cit.*, p. 592. On p. 583 Isocrates is cited in favor of "governing men more by clemencie and prudence, than by rigor and crueltie."

folowe that reason and iustice requireth, and to that intent equitie is ordeined: that is to saie to temper and mitigate the rigour of the law."[188] Wilson in his *Rhetoric* speaks of the judge using "mercie to mitigate the rigor of the lawe,"[189] and Hooker commends rulers "If . . . they haue tempred rigour with lenitie."[190] Elyot defines mercy as "a temperaunce of the mynde of hym that hath powar to be auenged . . . and is alway ioyne with reason."[191] He distinguishes it from "vaine pitie," which is "a sick-nesse of the mynde . . . wherein is contayned neither iustice nor yet commendable charitie, but rather therby ensueth negligence, contempte, dissobedience, and finally all mischiefe."[192] Lipsius also makes the distinc-tion between pity, "the fault of an abject and base mind, cast down at the show of another's mishap," and mercy, "An inclination of the minde to succour the necessity of miserie of another."[193] This contrast occurs in Spenser's legend, where Mercilla does not save Duessa, but sends aid to Belge. Perkins says that, as "mercy without justice is foolish pittie, so justice without mercy, is crueltie"; those who argue for the general abro-gation of the law are carried away by "a certaine foolish kind of pity," a fault that proceeds from "an effeminateness of Mind."[194] Gower, assimi-lating the contrast of rigor and lenience to a mean of courage, describes a kingly virtue of hardiness that falls between a reckless cruelty and a cowardly pity.[195] These are the virtues that are at issue in the scene where the "cruell minded" Artegall is overwhelmed by pity for Radigund—a scene notably parallel to the one in which he submits to love for Britomart, the representative of equity. "Pittie without equitie," says Lyly in his cele-bration of the virtues of the queen, is "plaine partialitie."[196] So it proves here in the case of the hapless Terpine. "Thextremytees of Justyce ben cruelte and defaulte," according to Caxton's translation of the *Golden Legend*,[197] and Artegall's default costs Terpine's life. In the parallel with

---

[188] *Dialogues, loc. cit.*

[189] *Rhetorique*, ed. Mair, p. 100.

[190] *Laws of Ecclesiastical Polity* (1597), V.lxxvi, sec. 8.

[191] *Gouernour*, II.vii, "Mercifulness," *edn. cit.*, p. 145: "And who that ouer moche correcteth, obserueth none equitie." Similarly at III.xxi, p. 260: "There is also a Moderation to be used agayne wrathe or appetite of vengeaunce," and so the justiciar ought not to be moved by wrath, "but onely by equitie."

[192] *Gouernour*, II.vii, p. 145.

[193] Justus Lipsius, *Two Bookes of Constancie*, I.xii, trans. by Sir John Stradling (1594), ed. Rudolf Kirk (New Brunswick, N.J., 1939), p. 99.

[194] Perkins, *Epiekeia*, in Morgan, ed., *Puritan Political Ideas*, pp. 64f.

[195] *Confessio Amantis*, VII.3572ff.

[196] *Euphues his England*, in *Euphues*, ed. Croll and Clemons, p. 445, on Elizabeth's mitigation of the rigor of the law. (For the phrase, cf. Mirabella at VI.vii.36f.: she "cryde mercie, to abate the extremitie of law," and her judge Cupid "did the rigour of his doome represse.")

[197] Cited in the *OED, sub* extremity[2].

Book II, Guyon is restrained from a similar error of "pittie vayne" (II.v.24) in aiding the willful Pyrochles; the issue recurs in Book V with the "wilfull fall" of Duessa, where Pittie argues on behalf of the accused, and Arthur begins to relent his courage for "ruth"; "piteous ruth" also touches the queen (V.ix.45–50). "Ruth" also affects the compassionate Britomart, when the ruthless and revengeful Talus is making it hot for Radigund's retainers (V.vii.36). The steel in Artegall's revengeful sword feels "ruth" before Britomart's goddesslike beauty (IV.vi.21), just as his severity is later *mollified* by "ruth" for the moonlike beauty of Radigund (V.v.13). According to the physical theory of the Garden of Adonis canto, the moon ministers to earthly matter by *tempering* and *mollifying* it with the lunar humour (III.vi.9, 7), and the clemency mediated by the moon-goddess Isis must have a similar effect upon the sun of justice. Mercy is also a heavenly influence "pour'd down on men" (V.x.1).

Having seen where some of equity's affinities lie, we may try to define more precisely what it is. Not only does the poetic etymology of Isis (Greek *isos*, "equal") refer to equity, but so does the name Artegall (*egal*, "equal"). Thus equity is ideally synonymous with justice. It is included in the law and is not against it, but it is not in the letter but rather in the intention of the law. The "rigour of the law," of course, admits of the prince's construction, "that is, the prince's moderation, interpretation, limitation, or dispensation, lest peradventure that old and accustomed proverbe be rightly applied unto them, 'Law with extremity is extreme injury.' "[198] Narrowly, equity is defined as the "application of ordinances to circumstances,"[199] but what is meant is often the extenuation or abatement of the law's extremity: "mens lawes," says Perkins, "must needs bee executed with a discreet and wise moderation. This moderation is publike equity."[200] Again "publike equity is, namely nothing else, but a moderation and mitigation of the extremity of a law, upon honest and convenient reasons, and in such cases, as were not directly intended in the law."[201] Being defined dialectically, equity may also be understood as a mean of justice; according to Perkins, it is the part of magistrates in executing the laws to "temper them with such discretion, as neither too much mitigation, doe abolish the law, nor too much extremitie leave not place for mitigation."[202] For sometimes the glory of the law "stands in the mitiga-

---

[198] Bullinger, *Decades*, II, Parker Society edn., vol. 1, pp. 339f. Bullinger is defining the prince's epiekeia. The saying is from Eccles. 7:16, also quoted in Hake, *Epieikeia, edn. cit.*, p. 8.

[199] By La Primaudaye, in *French Academie, edn. cit.*, p. 594. So Perkins, *Epieikeia*, in Morgan, *Puritan Political Ideas*, p. 61, says that the extremity of justice is manifested when reason can be shown "why in a Christian consideration of some circumstances, this justice [of the law] should be mitigated, and yet is not."

[200] Perkins, *Epieikeia*, in Morgan, *Puritan Political Ideas*, p. 67.

[201] *Ibid.*, p. 64.　　　　　　　　　　　　　　　　　　[202] *Ibid.*

THE ART OF EQUITY

tion, and not in the extremity, insomuch as the moderation is then the equity of the law, and the extremity is meere injustice."[203]

We are thus to understand that equity is a kind of temperance within the execution of justice, especially since it is associated with seeking a mean between "too much" and "too little"; it tempers the "extremity" of justice. Likewise, the balanced judgment of the just man may be compared to the equilibrium of the temperate man, as in the following passage from a popular medieval handbook:

> And just as to man's body many sicknesses occur on account of the distemperance of these four qualities [love, dread, joy, sorrow] or these four humours, the hearts of men and women also [suffer] on account of the distemperance of these four things.
>
> When the two sides of the body are of one accord and ordained, that is, the reason and the will, then a man or a woman is well ordained within him. These are the boughs of the root of a right faire tree, that is to say, of a right fair virtue that men call equity, evenness.
>
> Evenness is properly [found] when men proceed by judgment right full and true, neither too nicely nor too boisteriously, without bowing to the one side or to the other, when a man goes forth evenly and right as a line, for equity is no other thing than even-hood. Whoever has that virtue, he is a good and wise judge.[204]

The "line" of this passage may be traditional. La Primaudaye says that if the magistrate "live under right, reason, truth and Iustice . . . he is not unlike to a line or rule, which being first right it selfe, afterward [is] corrective [of] all other crooked things that are applied to it."[205] One may compare Isaiah 28:17: "Iudgement also wil I lay to the rule, & righteousnes to the balance." In a passage significant for its combination of theory and imagery, Astraea teaches Artegall

> . . . to weigh both right and wrong
> In equall ballance with due recompence,
> And equitie to measure out along,
> According to the line of conscience
> When so it needs with rigour to dispence.
>
> (V.i.7)

---

[203] *Ibid.*, p. 67. In the light of these considerations, we may translate Radigund's "vnequall might" over Artegall (V.v.32) as *inequitous* might.

[204] Laurence of Orleans, *The Boke of Vices and Virtues*, ed. W. Nelson Francis (London, 1942), p. 152; text modernized. Likewise, "to proporcion the sentence or iugement in an equalitie, it belongeth to temperaunce," according to Elyot, *Gouernour*, III.i, "Of Justyce." Similarly, John Higgins, preface to the *Mirror for Magistrates* (1574), Sig. *iiij: "proportion in judgement and sentence, which pertaineth to Temperance."

[205] *French Academie*, Pt. I, *edn. cit.*, p. 589.

The same accents are heard in what the Palmer teaches Guyon:

> But temperance (said he) with golden squire
> Betwixt them both can measure out a meane
>
> (II.i.58)

The golden squire may be a carpenter's square, and it would symbolize the golden mean.[206] One may compare the description of equity with the scene where the golden Medina herself presides over the deficient Elissa and the excessive Perissa and their respectively disgruntled and outrageous suitors—she reminds us of Alice, trying to maintain her equanimity at the mad tea-party:

> Betwixt them both the faire Medina sate
> With sober grace, and goodly carriage:
> With equal measure she did moderate
> The strong extremities of their outrage;
> That forward paire she ever would asswage,
> When they would striue dew reason to exceed;
> But that same froward twaine would accourage,
> And of her plenty adde vnto their need
> So kept she them in order, and her selfe in heed.
>
> (II.ii.38)

Her measure is "equal," while her sisters are Elissa, "short of equal," and Perissa, "over-equal." In other words, Medina possesses the virtue of "even-hood," or "the right discrimination of the equitable."

Justice also may be defined as a mean between more and less, for the securing of some form of equality is always a traditional function of justice. This equality is often described as taking two forms:

---

[206] See Fowler, "Emblems of Temperance in *The Faerie Queene*," *Review of English Studies*, New Series, vol. 11, no. 42 (1960), p. 143, citing Achillius Bocchius, *Symbolicarvm qvaestionvm* (Bologna, 1574), symb. cxliv. Cf. Wilson, *Rhetorique*, ed. Mair, p. 35: "Temperaunce, is a measuring of affections according to the will of reason, and a subduing of lust vnto the Square of honestie." For "conscience" as equity, see Sir Thomas Smith's description of the purpose of the Court of Chancery: it substitutes for a *praetor* "(which might *moderari illus ius summum*, give actions where none was, mitigate the exactness and rigour of the law written, give exceptions . . . and maintain always *aequum & bonum*). . . . So that he that putteth up his bill in the Chancery . . . has relief as in the solemn *forum*. And for so much as in this case he is without remedy in the common law, therefore he requireth the chancellor according to equity and reason to provide for him and to take such order as to good conscience shall appertain. And the Court of the Chancery is called of the common people the court of conscience, because that the chancellor is not strained by rigour or form of words of law to judge but *ex aequo* and *bono* and according to conscience, as I have said." (Smith, *De Republica Anglorum*, ed. L. Alston, Cambridge, 1906, pp. 7of.) Cf. Fletcher, *Prophetic Moment*, pp. 276ff.

For we find two sorts of equalitie: namely equalitie of quantitie, and of proportion. Equalitie of quantitie is requisite in commutative iustice, that euery one may take as much as he ought. Equalitie of proportion is requisite in distributive iustice, and in rewarding men according to their desert. This equalitie (sayeth *Plato*) giveth the greatest honours to them that excell most in vertue, and the less places of dignitie to such as are inferior in vertue and learning, distributing to both that which belongeth to them by reason.[207]

Cox's *Rhetoric* divides justice into two parts, legality and equity, and names as the two subdivisions of equity distributive and commutative justice (the latter being an equality in exchange); it is "equality" that distributes or apportions rewards for more or less than equal services to the state.[208] In Euripides' *Phoenissae*, Jocasta enjoins Eteocles to accept parity with his brother, in the name of what could probably be classified as commutative justice:

Equality is what is naturally lawful for mankind: the more and the less are in eternal enmity, and herald the day of hatred. Equality it is, that ordained for man measure, and the divisions of weight, and the distinctions of number. Equal, on their yearly course, move the rayless eye of night and the light of the sun, and neither of them grudges the victory to the other. So the sunlight and the night are the servants of men; and can you not bear to hold an equal place with your brother and allow him an equal share?[209]

In a curious parallel to this symbolism, Spenser seems to say that the nocturnal Isis and diurnal Osiris are named on similar principles, "For that they both like race in equall iustice runne" (V.vii.4):[210] we have seen that

[207] La Primaudaye, *French Academie*, Pt. I, *edn. cit.*, p. 727. Cf. V.vi.19: "For equall right in equall things doth stand."

[208] Leonard Cox, *Arte or Crafte of Rhetoryke*, ed. F. I. Carpenter (Chicago, 1899), pp. 45ff. Cf. Elyot, *Gouernour*, III.i, *edn. cit.*, p. 196: "iustyce commutatiue hathe no regarde to the persone, but onely consideryinge the inequalitie wherby the one thynge excedeth the other, indeuoureth to brynge them bothe to an equalitie." And also *Gouernour*, III.iii, *edn. cit.*, pp. 204f., on "equality" as preserved by diversity of degrees—but requiring a recognition of man's common estate. So Plato, *Laws* VI, 757b–e, where it is allowed that the strict equity of unequal rewards for unequal merits must be mitigated by an indulgence of the kind of equality that gives birth to friendship—i.e., the égalité that is paired with fraternité. See also Aristotle, *Nich. Ethics* V.iii–iv, and *Politics* III.ix and V.i.

[209] Ll. 538–551, trans. by F. M. Cornford, in *From Religion to Philosophy* (reprint of New York, 1957), sec. 95, pp. 169f. This book is the source of several subsequent ideas here.

[210] The central stanza of Book V, as Fowler notes, *Numbers of Time*, pp. 219f. Fowler, citing the solar-lunar holidays reported in *De Iside* 52 (*Moralia* 372B), makes the logical deduction that since day and night run an equal race on the

the suffix of Artegall's name contains an "Isis," and Osiris' name contains the syllables of *isos*. Britomart and Artegall will "ioyne in equall portion" (V.vii.23): sun and moon join as equals at an equinoctial juncture.

We may take this opportunity to expound the Egyptain mythography in its own right. The Isis Church episode makes it explicit that the divine pair stand for the extremity of the law and its mitigation. From the Orphic Hymns one may learn that among the beneficiaries of men there is a kingly justice, Dike, that apprehends all misconduct like the eye of the sun, and executes revenge and punishment.[211] And there is also a goddess, *Dikaiosune* (Righteousness), celebrated in a sister hymn, to whom equity belongs; she hates excess (*to pleon*) and prizes *isotāte* (*aequum* in the Latin translation). Her judgments (*isotātos*) are rendered as *Aequitatis* in the Latin, and her honored character is *iustissima virgo*.[212] Spenser means something similar by Isis and Osiris. Pseudo-Eratosthenes reports that some have said that the Virgo or Dike who deserted men is Isis.[213] It is natural to make the connection between the just Virgin and the goddess whose tomb, according to Diodorus Sicilus, was inscribed, "I am Isis, the Queen of every land, she who was taught by Hermes; and whatever laws I have ordained, none is able to annul."[214] The longer declarations in the *Koré Kosmou* also make Isis a lawgiver, but Spenser is likelier to have known the identification of Isis as a goddess of justice in Plutarch (*De Iside* 9). It remains to note that Eusebius' explanation for the name of Isis confirms the identification etymologically: "the power of the earth, they [the Egyptians] called Isis, because of the equality [*isotāta*], which is the source of justice: but they call the moon the celestial earth. . . ." Eusebius also notes here that the Egyptians indicate the sun, who is otherwise called Osiris, by a man embarked on a ship, "the ship set on a croco-

---

equinox, the Isis church episode is to be thought of as taking place at this time within the solar year: "The cult celebrated at Isis Church is thus in some sense a cult of the equinox" (*op. cit.*, p. 219). As we will see, there is a strong argument for accepting Fowler's idea as one more of the traces of a zodiacal scheme for the twelve cantos of this legend. Cf. DuBartas, *Divine Weeks*, trans. Sylvester, I.IV, ll. 262f.: "After the *Maiden*, shines the *Balance* bright, / Equall divider of the Day and Night."

[211] Hymn LXI, in Hambergerus, ed., *Orpheos Apanta*, pp. 261f.; invoked by Demosthenes in his *Oration against Aristogiton* 492A.

[212] Hymn LXII, in *Orpheos Apanta*, pp. 260–263.

[213] *Catasterismi* 9, "Virgo," in Gale, *Opuscula Mythologica*, p. 106, Isis invented laws according to Comes, *Mythol.*, V.xiv, "De Cerere," *edn. cit.*, p. 516, and she stood for justice, according to Giraldus in his article on her, in *Hist. Deorum*, Syntag. XII, in *Op. om.*, I, col. 384E.

[214] Diod. Sic., *Bibl. Hist.* I.xxvii.4. Cf. also the *Koré Kosmou*, 65, 67, 68 (quoted in Stobaeus, *Eclogae* I.41, 44 *ad fin.*); in Scott, ed. and trans., *Hermetica*, vol. 1, p. 493.

dile."[215] The image is duly represented in Cartari's handbook,[216] and Spenser has this crocodile too. If Isis is a Dike and an Aequitatis, then the communist giant is not entirely wrong in attributing the impairment of the estate of the world to a loss of "equality," the retreat of equity to the stars.

[iii]

Some of the above lore may now be reapplied to the poem, and more especially to the complex and somewhat untidy proportion that may be discovered between the second and seventh cantos of Books II and V. The second cantos of both legends show personifications of the virtue measuring out the virtue to its extremes. In Book II Guyon betakes himself to the house of "golden Meane," mediates a peace between Sansloi and Huddibras, is in turn attacked by them, and then is rescued by Medina, who acts as the means to their reconcilement. Then they all go to table, where Medina serves. In Book V Artegall and Talus meet four antagonists who also fall into opposed pairs. The capitalistic monopoly formed by Pollente and Munera represents the combination of power and wealth; the revolution that the giant and the mob are brewing in the sequel intends to reduce all things to equality—the mob expects to be greatly enriched by the redistribution. Like Guyon, Artegall opposes both extremes. Thus the common idea of the two cantos is *measure*: on the one hand, the classical measure which ought to be in all things; on the other hand, the meting out of justice, which is dispensed measure for measure (cf. Luke 6:38).

As temperance is preeminently the virtue of the mean, Medina is partly a version of the hero himself. Within the more ironic context of Book V, the same duplication of the heroic persona may be observed in Artegall's opponent, the egalitarian giant, who experiments with the scales of justice. Nelson directs our attention to the source of Artegall's name in Geoffrey of Monmouth, where we find Arthgallo,[217] an unjust king whom adversity and the good will of a devoted brother eventually reformed. As Nelson's citation indicates, the rule of the early Arthgallo was noteworthy because of his repression of the noble and his promotion of the base; further, he expropriated the property of the rich and heaped up treasure for himself. The reformed Arthgallo reversed his erstwhile policy, and "did begin to abase the baser sort"; he also allowed every man to hold his own. One

---

[215] *Praep. Evang.*, III.xi.115c–d; ed. and trans. Gifford, Tom. 3, Pt. 1, p. 126.

[216] Cartari, *Le Imagini*, "Apollo, Febo: Il Sole" (Venice, 1625), p. 45.

[217] Nelson, *Poetry of Edmund Spenser*, pp. 257f., citing *History of the Kings of Britain*, III.xvii, trans. Sebastian Evans, revsd. Charles W. Dunn (New York, 1958), p. 61.

concludes—as Fletcher recently has[218]—that the giant presents a vicious Arthgallo, with his patronage of the base and garnishment of the rich. Artegall was taught "to weigh both right and wrong / In equall ballance" (V.i.7), and the giant is induced by Artegall to attempt a similar feat.[219] Here we might remember that weighing right and wrong together is elsewhere said to be characteristic of Avarice (I.iv.27), and we have just come from an episode about bribery. The giant's penultimate experiment anticipates the judgment that goes against him:

> . . . but still it downe did slide,
> And by no meane could in the weight by stayd.
> For by no meanes the false will with the truth be wayd.
>
> (V.ii.45)

The imagery tells us that there is no mean between right and wrong, and two wrongs do not make a right. As a final test, Artegall proposes that the giant compare "two falses of each equall share," to illustrate that "right sate in the middest of the beame alone" (V.ii.48). Despite his preponderance of theoretical apparatus, the giant proves a poor judge of the mean:

> But he the right from thence did thrust away
> For it was not the right, which he did seeke;
> But rather strove extremities to way,
> Th'one to diminish, th'other for to eeke:
> For of the meane he greatly did misleek.
>
> (V.ii.49)

The point of all this seems to be that the mean of temperance is not the mean of justice, in the correction of abuses. Unlike Medina, who is able to accommodate her four maladjusted table guests in the same equation, Artegall cannot dissuade the hubristic and malcontented giant, nor pacify the lawless multitude. In the sardonic conclusion, Talus shoulders the leveler into the sea, just as earlier he responded to the extremities of the golden-handed Munera by cutting them off.

The giant's experiments with the balance, as Frye observes, parody the deliberations of equity, symbolized by Isis. Frye indicates an analogous

---

[218] Angus Fletcher, *The Prophetic Moment* (Chicago, 1971), p. 157f. One also notes that this same evil aggrandisement appears in Pollente, for while his groom "pols and pils the poore . . . he him selfe vppon *the rich* doth tyrannize" (V.ii.6).

[219] Cf. Edmund Burke, in his *Reflections upon the French Revolution*: "The pretended rights of those [radical] theorists are all extremes; and in proportion as they are metaphysically true, they are morally and politically false. The rights of men are in a sort of *middle*, incapable of definition, but not impossible to be discerned. The rights of men in government are their advantages; and these are often in balances between good and evil, and sometimes between evil and evil. . . . Men have no rights to what is not reasonable, and to what is not for their benefit."

relation in Book II: "the golden mean of temperance is parodied by the golden means provided by Mammon."[220] The conjunction of these two parodies does not seem accidental, even if the "plenty" from which Medina adds to the "need" of the deficient pair is not like the "plenteous meeds" that Munera showers on Talus to corrupt him (II.ii.38; V.ii.9). Rather, Munera is the connecting link to Mammon, for she is found under a heap of gold. Mammon's wealth is parted from "right vsuance" (II.vii.7); in seeking it, men have abused nature's plenty and exceeded "The measure of her meane" (II.vii.16). Moreover, this wealth is suspect; it may be tainted with blood-guiltiness (II.vii.19). In the same episode, Philotime's suitors resort to bribes in making their way up her ladder, and Pilate, more mysteriously, is offered to us as an unjust judge. It is typical of the relation of these two virtues that there should be a quality of temperance at the heart of the legend of justice, and a parody of the exercise of justice at the heart of the legend of temperance.

The relation between Mammon's cave and Isis Church is structural. It is here that the "mystery" of each virtue seems to be expounded, with each virtue being identified with its abstemious aspect. We may also compare the metal symbolism. Mammon is encountered "sunning" his gold, probably for the purpose of revivifying it.[221] He has some of the characteristics of an alchemist: a blackened visage, a magical furnace, a possible reliance on illusion or "vaine shewes" (II.vii.39). Isis and Osiris might suggest an alchemical mystery too, since the principal work of alchemy was symbolized by the marriage of a solar king—"our gold"—to a lunar queen—"our silver." This process of *conjunction* was followed by *rubification*, the transmutation of the elements to gold by the "red tincture"; both processes find analogues in Britomart's dream of a striking color change and her commixture with a fiery dragon.

If we are at all correct in seeing a parody relation between the second and seventh cantos in each book, there is every chance that Spenser will make Munera a sardonic Isis, or goddess of justice, as he made the giant a sardonic "iudge of equity" (V.iii.36). This proves to be the case. Both Isis and Munera are identified with Egyptian idols, both have silver feet,

---

[220] "Structure of Imagery," in *Fables of Identity*, p. 79.
[221] Cf. Drayton, *The Man in the Moon*, in Chalmers, *The English Poets*, vol. 4, p. 421:

> And the base churl, the Sun that dare not trust,
> With his old gold, yet smelling it doth rust,
> Lays it abroad, but locks himself within
> Three doubled locks, or ere he dare begin
> To ope his bags . . .

Lewis, *The Discarded Image* (Cambridge, 1964), p. 106, points to the same idea of the sun's power to renew gold's luster in *Comus*, ll. 398f.: "You may as well spread out the unsunned heaps / Of miser's treasure by an outlaw's den."

and both have the power to modify the course of justice. But the equitable tempering of the law is not accomplished by *merces*, bribes, but by clemency, the judicial equivalent of *mercedum*, pity or mercy. In Book II the Palmer moralized the bloody hands of Ruddymane as a "sacred Symbole" of incorrigibility; here Talus makes an example of the offending hands. In so doing, he turns Munera into an "icon of justice," for a well-known allegory from Plutarch's *De Iside* represented justice as being without hands.[222]

One further analogy between the two second cantos remains, the analogy between the cleansing of Ruddymane and the operation of Artegall in washing the "filthy bloud" of Pollente and the "guilty blood" of Munera down the river they have exploited. Just as temperance is expressed hygenically, so Artegall's justice is closely identified with the action of the river itself, as in a famous similitude from Amos: "let judgement runne downe as waters, and righteousnes as a mightie river" (Amos 5:24). Munera's name comes from the word for *bribe* in the Vulgate, which Langland quotes in the course of bringing his Lady Meed to justice.[223] Munera's

---

[222] The allegory, from Plutarch, *De Iside* 10, may be found in Lydgate, "Devyse of a Desguysing," ll. 173ff., in *Minor Poems*, ed. McCracken, vol. 2, pp. 682f. See also *Whitney's Choice of Emblemes*, ed. Greene, p. 136, "Abstentia," where the Latin in the margin reads, in part, "Stobaeus from Plutarch's forty-fourth oration relates that the Theban images of judges were without hands. . . . This partly because justice ought not to take bribes. . . ." Given the beheading of Pollente, the *headless* Egyptian justice of Diod. Sic., I.xcvi.9, may be relevant here also.

[223] *Piers Plowman*, B-Text, Passus III.95f. (Job 15:34, "Fire will devour the tabernacle of those who readily accept *bribes*"); Passus III.241f. (Ps. 15:5, "who gave not his money for usury, and *bribes* against the innocent"); Passus III.247f. (Ps. 26:10, "In whose hands [*manibus*] are iniquities, their right hand is filled by bribes [*muneribus*]"—the play on words is recognized in the C-Text, IV.118, "ryche hondes"); Passus III.332f. (Prov. 22:9). The clerk who hails Mede into court "Toke Mede bi the middel" (B-Text, Passus III.10), with which one may compare Spenser, V.ii.27: "Her selfe then tooke he by the sclender wast." Langland has the phrase "mede mesurelees" (B-Text, Passus III.245), Spenser "plenteous meedes" (V.ii.9) and "endlesse riches" (V.ii.23). Munera's slender waist, if it is also her middle, may have some reference to the neglect of the mean here. How regularly Amos' "gihonic" image for justice was glossed, I do not know, but the relevance of the following commentary thereon, by Jerome, will be apparent: "*Et revelabitur quasi aqua judicium, et justicia quasi torrens fortis.* LXX: *Et volvetur sicut aqua judicium, et justicia sicut torrens invius.* As water is borne from a steep—which otherwise mingles together—despoils, and makes all open to the eye: so God's judgment and justice, which he sometimes makes upon his people, will reveal them to all, and bear an image of the strongest torrent. Whatever it seizes, it draws with it, and it does not allow itself to be obstructed. In like manner, moreover, the Septuagint: the judgment of the very evil is turned as water—because it does not abide by one ruling, but is borne about by all the winds of doctrine, tries the unprovable, and would sooner have praised, thinking [judgment] to amount to nothing. The justifications of these are compared not to streams and the purest springs, but to turbid and muddy

heaped-up wealth exceeds that of many princes, and it is called "mucky pelfe" (V.ii.9, 27). Thus Artegall's task finds its Herculean analogue in the labor of cleansing the Augean stables, a story that insists upon the psychological association of increment and excrement. Augeias was the wealthiest man on earth, and, according to Salutati, the name Augean is to be referred to *augmentum*, because manure increases the yield of the field.[224] Hercules cleaned Augeias' pens by diverting a river through them.

Ruddymane's cleansing also alludes to baptism, and the same canto in Book V sees the drowning of the giant, a prophet of biblical pretensions whom the historical allegory, with some show of probability, identifies with the Anabaptists.[225] This would not be the only instance in this legend of a quizzical manifestation of the Reformation, given the unregenerate mob that prevails upon Sir Burbon. Like the Anabaptists, the giant is not only theoretically communist, but also antinomian. He will suppress "Tyrants that make men subject to their law" and the vulgar expect to obtain "vncontrolled freedome" under his dispensation (V.ii.38, 33). Spenser's reader naturally links the giant's description of the mutable lower world back to the degenerating cosmic order described in the proem, but Artegall, in his rebuttal, appeals to the heavens' constancy. He also argues, at least by implication, that the adjustment or restoration of the changeless state of the original creation cannot be the proper subject of human justice; the attempt to make it such would lead—metaphorically, one supposes— to an unbinding of the chains in which the ocean at the time of the crea-

---

torrents, which the waters of judgment do not have, having been collected from rocks and cliffs and briars. One who wants to cross these, is instead carried off headlong, and, his feet having been undermined, it cannot be said by him, *he sets my feet upon the rock* (Vulg. Ps. 39:3); for he treads upon sands [or shores] which have no foundations, and since he has submitted to their danger, he says, as the Hebrews do, *The waters are come over my soul* (Vulg. Ps. 68:1). On the contrary, we read of the just, whose judgment is not turned as water, and whose justice is not carried like an impassable torrent, that *the thoughts of the just are judgments* (Prov. 12:5)." (*Comm. in Amos*, II.v, in PL, 25, 1054D–1055A.) It is the dynamic *evolution* of Pollente's river—from an impassable and irrational gulf of judgment into a purified, purifying, and unobstructed river of justice—which gives this commentary its special interest here.

[224] *De Laboribus Herculis*, IV.vi.5–7, Ullman edn., p. 367. For the classical sources, see Apollodorus, *Bibl.* II.v.5, 7; Diod. Sic., IV.13; Pausanias, V.i.9f., Tzetes on Lycophron 41; and Servius, *ad Aen.* VIII.300, who says the stables had become a threat to fertility: pestilence emanated from them and the mired pastures were unable to be plowed.

[225] See Variorum *Works*, ed. Edwin Greenlaw, *et al., Book V*, Appendix III, pp. 336–345, summarizing the article of F. M. Padelford. As a prophet, the giant echoes the eschatological message that the valleys and hills shall be made equal (Isa. 40:4): this was the burden of John the *Baptist* (Luke 3:5). It was also the ninth of the twelve traditional signs of the coming of the Antichrist. See n. 258, below.

tion was originally confined. In terms of the Ruddymane episode, where moral virtue cannot eradicate original sin, the world order cannot be "anabaptized." Such an allusion lends a certain relevance to the pessimistic reference to Deucalion in the proem; the classical flood-hero survived the deluge only to perpetuate a race as hardhearted as the one that drowned. Genesis agrees: man was as corrupt after the flood as he was before it. Since Deucalion was the just man who consulted the justice-goddess Themis, his unsuccess must be a type of Artegall's own.

The Course of Justice

The Buddhist Wheel of the Law is a transparent solar symbol; when the new emperor . . . performs the ceremony of setting in motion the Wheel of the Law, he is merely launching the sun on an orderly course which beats time for the universe and for man. . . . The general consensus then among the people we have reviewed seems to be that the sun is law in so far as he imposes it upon all things but at the same time law is something distinct from the sun, inasmuch as it governs even him.

(A. M. Hocart, *Kingship*, London, 1927, pp. 53–55)

For one [philosopher] says the sun is justice, for the sun alone governs all things, passing through them and burning them. Then when I am pleased and tell this to someone, thinking it is a fine answer, he laughs at me and asks if I think there is no justice among men when the sun has set.

(Plato, *Cratylus* 413b)

[i]

Spenser apparently makes nothing of the fact that the daughters of Themis, or Order, were sometimes known as the Hours, rather than the Litae, or Prayers. This fact may still belong to the poem because there is an analogy between the daughters of the sky-god in Book V and in the Mutabilitie cantos. The Litae wait on Jove's throne night and day (V.ix.31), and the Hours at heaven's gate "did daily watch, and nightly wake / By euen turnes" (VII.vii.45).[226] The Litae, since they treat for

---

[226] Comes, *Mythol.*, IV.xvi, "De Horis," *edn. cit.*, pp. 412ff., translates the passages from Hesiod (*Theog.* 900f.) and the Orphic Hymn (XLII) that make the Horae *Eunomia, Dice,* and *Irene* ("Leges, Iusticia, & Pax"), as well as giving the texts from Ovid and Homer that place the Horae at the gates of heaven. Allegorically, the daughters of Jove and Themis "are born from the observation of divine things and from civil laws, because—since Themis is equity, instilled in the souls of men by nature itself—her origin is divine, from which laws take their beginning."

pardon and remission, speak for the repeal of an action in time. More obvious reference to the laws governing time derives from the Egyptian wizards mentioned in the proem, horologers who observed the course of the sun. The communist giant's conclusions seem to have been influenced by their results, or rather by the deduction to be made from a comparison with more recent observations; unlike Mutabilitie, however, he does not cite these observations. The Egyptian priests within the legend tend the shrine of the lunar Isis, it is cryptically explained, because of her likeness to the solar Osiris, "For that they both like race in equall iustice runne" (V.vii.4).[227] Here the implication is the opposite of the giant's and Mutabilitie's: the poet implies that the cosmic solar order has not miscarried. Britomart dreams of a sexual metamorphosis that will replace her lunar symbolism with a solar one, and at the same time the solar crocodile becomes decidedly Typhonic: "swolne with pride of his owne peerelesse powre" (V.vii.15).[228] When he is brought to heel, he and Britomart beget a child, which the logic of the symbolism would make a Horus, a hopeful child who is also a solar deity in his own right.[229]

The proem describes the stars as mutable in their courses, or subject to some larger rhythm not yet clearly manifest. The sun has lost thirty "minutes" in fourteen hundred years, and has twice "wested" towards the east. Britomart waits for her hero to return, and anxiously counts the time, but "Each hour did seeme a moneth, and euery moneth a yeare" (V.vi.5).[230] Even the comparison of the loss of Belge's sons to the death of Niobe's children at the hands of Apollo and Diana might seem suggestive; the malefactor is Gerioneo, and "twelue of them he did by times deuoure" (V.x.8). However, all these references to solar time, no matter how con-

---

Reverence is here for the reasons implied in n. 149, on the presence of Shame among those attending the divine throne, and also perhaps because of the definition of reverence as *justice towards the gods* (so Elyot, *Gouernour*, III.ii, *edn. cit.*, p. 198).

[227] See n. 144, above.

[228] It is denied that the drought-producing Typhon is the sun in Plutarch, *De Iside* 51 (*Moralia* 372); at *Moralia* 371D–E, Typhon is said to turn into a crocodile. So also Cartari, *Le Imagini, edn. cit.*, pp. 321f.

[229] The birthday of the "Eyes of Horus" is closely linked in *De Iside* 51, *Moralia* 372B, with the alignment of sun and moon and the birthday of the "staff" of the sun, following the autumnal equinox. Horus is also said to direct the revolution of the sun (*De Iside* 61, *Moralia* 375F). Further, Horus is said to take his name from the Greek *horai*, hours: so Macrobius, *Saturnalia*, I.xxi.13, and so reported by Cartari, *Imagini*, p. 322, and p. 407, *sub* "Le Gratie," where the name of the Horae is derived from the Egyptian name for the sun.

[230] Cf. the word "minute" in the proem (stanza 7), where it means the sixtieth part of a degree. Spenser's stanza is imitated from Harington in his Ariosto, *O.F.* XVI.10, if I am not mistaken: "Where I your comming look'd for long in vaine, / Each houre a day, each moneth did seem a yeare / And of your absence long I did complaine, / Enquiring oft, if I of you could heare."

sistent with one another, do not constitute a theme in themselves, and we may well wonder what they are doing in a legend of justice.

The labors of Hercules, being twelve in number, suggest to mythography an analogy with the sun's passage through the twelve zodiacal signs, or houses.[231] Spenser seems to pursue this correspondence only intermittently, and again the appeal is to a theme, rather than a scheme. The twelve signs develop a complex mythology of their own, and it is rather too heterogenous to integrate with the Hercules analogy. Aries, for example, is the ram that bore Phrixus and Helle; Taurus is the bull that carried off Europa; Gemini are Castor and Pollux; and so forth.[232] But Leo is the lion that Hercules slew (VII.vii.36), and the two patterns cross at this point. Spenser twice compares the loss of Artegall's superiority over Radigund to Hercules' surrender of his lion skin to Omphale.[233] This occurs in the fifth canto, and Leo is the fifth zodiacal sign. Britomart enters the book in the sixth canto, and the sixth sign is Virgo, the Virgin of justice. She visits Isis Church in the seventh canto, and the seventh sign is Libra, the scales of justice, an image we have already had occasion to link to Isis as equity. The eighth sign is Scorpio, and Arthur, with his sunlike shield, meets this image in the Soldan's armed chariot:

> As when the firie-mouthed steeds, which drew
> The Sunnes bright wayne to *Phaetons* decay,
> Soone as they did the monstrous Scorpion vew,
> With vgly craples crawling in their way,
> The dreadfull sight did them so sore affray,
> That their well knowen courses they forwent,
> And leading th'euer-burning lampe astray,
> This lower world nigh all to ashes brent,
> And left their scorched path yet in the firmament.
>
> (V.viii.40)

Even his name must be significant, if the Sol-dan dies the victim of a chariot as unmanageable as the one that the Sun gave his son.

To this torso of an analogy there may or may not be much to add. In Malengine, Artegall possibly meets a "Gote" (V.ix.15) or Capricorn, but actually the evil one ought to correspond to the preceding sign, Sagittarius, the armed Centaur—his weaponry and his resemblance to Maleger might support this. The Centaur is Chiron, a cave-dwelling teacher of justice.[234] Cancer, the fourth sign, ought to be linked to the two quarreling

[231] Comes, *Mythol.*, VII.i, *edn. cit.*, p. 704.
[232] Pseudo-Eratosthenes, *Catasterismi* 19, 14, 10; Mutabilitie cantos, VII.vii.23–25, and V, proem, 5f.
[233] V.v.24, viii.2. The hero may be identified with the lion at V.ix.33.
[234] *Catasterismi* 40.

brothers; but it would be easier to make the brothers Gemini, the third sign. The third canto may also contain Gemini imagery; Artegall and Guyon are both present, and each knight acts on behalf of the other. There is also the rival sun Braggadocchio: the canto begins with an allusion to the strengthening and return of the sun in the course of time, and the appearance of the two Florimells together—like the conjunction of Artegall and Guyon—is decidedly geminate:

> As when two sunnes appeare in the azure skye,
>   Mounted in Phebus charet fierie bright,
>   Both darting forth faire beames to each mans eye,
>   And both adorn'd with lampes of flaming light,
>   (V.iii.19)

The solstice actually falls in the next sign (Cancer), though Spenser's symbolism makes this seem like the longest day. Artegall's surrender to the lunar Radigund suggests the gradual shortening of the hours of daylight thereafter. The winter solstice, if there were one, ought to be Artegall's judgment against Duessa, the moment of his reasserting the sovereignty he formerly lost to Radigund. The vernal equinox, which occurs in Aries, would simply correspond to the commencement of the legend, or rather with the end of the preceding legend, which does indeed seem to take place in the spring. The summerlike heats of the Radigund episode seem to support this hypothesis, but what Mercilla might have to do with December (which is "chill"—VII.vii.41) remains a mystery.

We may develop this analogy, not only through the Herculean correspondences, but also by reference to the traditional zodiacal mythology, as it is embedded in the Mutabilitie cantos. The fuller scheme may be outlined as follows:

Cantos 1–2: Aries or the Ram	
Talus	Mars or Ares
Pollente and Artegall in the river	Phrixus and Helle on the ram's back
Munera	The Golden Fleece
Cantos 2–3: Taurus or the Bull	
The return of Florimell	The arrival of the Cretan Bull with Europa
Cantos 3–4: Gemini or the Twins	
The two Florimells	The doubling of the sun
Amidas and Bracidas	The alternating lives of Castor and Pollux
Canto 4: Cancer or the Crab	
Artegall's putting the swords of the two brothers underfoot	Hercules crushing the crab underfoot in the Labor of the Hydra

397

Cantos 5–6: Leo or the Lion

Radigund's depriving the hero
of his armour

Hercules surrendering the skin
of the Nemean Lion to Omphale

Cantos 6–7: Virgo or the Virgin

The return of Britomart to redeem the hero of justice

The eventual return of Astraea
to earth

Canto 7: Libra or the Scales

Isis Church and the introduction of Equity

Virgo holding the scales of justice

Canto 8: Scorpio or the Scorpion

The Soldan's chariot and its
demise

The Scorpion that spooked
Phaeton's horses

Canto 9: Sagittarius or the Archer

Malengine and his retreat

The Centaur

Cantos 9–10: Capricorn or the
Goat

Malengine

The Goat

Mercilla's palace

The nurture of Jove

Cantos 10–11: Aquarius or the
Water-Carrier

Gerioneo

[————]

The Inquisition

"the Roman floud" (Tiber) (?)

Canto 12: Pisces or the Fishes

Grantorto

[————]

Envy and Detraction

The Fishes

This list is by no means self-explanatory, and it may seem rather fanciful
in places. My procedure in allowing the image assigned to any one canto
to encroach upon its neighbouring canto is vouched for in the proem, however. We are told that the "creatures" in the sky, like those on the earth
below, are doing just that (V, proem, 5–6, V.i.7).

Going over the particulars of the table, we find Talus as *Aries*: Ares is
another name of Mars, and Talus—both armiger and armament—is introduced here, as the martial aspect of Artegall. In the Mutabilitie cantos
Aries bears the month to which Mars gives his name, and accordingly
March is "armed strongly" (VII.vii.32). Aries is also the ram that Phrixus
and Helle rode over the Hellespont, and Pollente and Artegall resemble
them in struggling on Pollente's horse in the river—like Helle, Pollente
is precipitated into the water. The same ram in time becomes the golden
fleece, which Medea helped Jason to win. The golden Munera prevents
Artegall from reaching her treasure, but she is like Medea in her attempt
to bring Talos-Talus down by means of witchcraft.[235] *Taurus* (identified

[235] See V.ii.22: "powr of charms, which she against him wrought," and Apoll.
Rhod., *Argonaut.* IV.1639ff.

as the Cretan Bull that Hercules conquered as the seventh labor) is said by Apollodorus and Spenser to be the bull that abducted Europa.[236] Since she is both an Angelica and a flower maiden carried off by sea, Florimell is a Europa figure too. In the Mutabilitie cantos Europa's progress is associated with the return of spring and the flourishing of flowers in April (VII.vii.33). The *Twins* are Castor and Pollux, whom Amidas and Bracidas resemble, not in their friendship, but in their alternating fortunes. Artegall puts their swords underfoot, and (for what it is worth) Hercules had to crush the *Crab* underfoot in the course of his labor against the Hydra.[237] A slight echo of this story is preserved in the proem, where we read that the Bull has so displaced "those two Twinnes of Jove, / That they have *crusht* the Crab" (V, proem, 6). As Fowler notes, the two brothers are the sons of one Milesio, whose name is one of the epithets of Jove.[238] *Leo* the Lion, according to the Mutabilitie cantos, is still angry (VII.vii.36), and we have observed the element of anger in Artegall's conquest of the tigerish Radigund. In the sequel the hero loses his ireful virtue, and with it his lion skin. The return of Britomart to rectify this mistaken indulgence, according to my tabulation, suggests a covert *Astraea redux* motif, as Britomart's canto position aligns her with *Virgo*. Britomart also belongs to an erotic convention that has one of its poles in a Virgo tradition. Virgo's month is August, the same month in which the Roman Church celebrates the Virgin Mary's assumption into heaven. This coordination of pagan and Christian ascension myths might seem a purely adventitious piece of design here, but it may appear less accidental when we explain the relation of December to Capricorn and Mercilla. The August-Virgo of the Mutabilitie cantos is crowned with ears of corn (VII.vii.37); Spenser would have known this as a feature of the image of Isis, though in Book V he substitutes a crown of gold.[239]

Traditionally, Virgo holds *Libra* in her hand, as Justice suspends the scales. In the Libra canto, Britomart-Isis redresses the balance between Artegall and the other sex, and deals out justice like a "Goddesse" (V.vii.42). Besides the scales, Justice typically holds a sword, like the one with which Mercilla is endowed. Britomart, in putting down rebellion with her "faulchin," is acting the part of Justice (see V.i.9); significantly, she completes her victory over Radigund by rearming the knight of equity. In a zodiacal scheme the symbols of sword and scales would be attached to September: in the Mutabilitie cantos September holds in one hand a

---

[236] *Bibl.* II.v.7; and also Pseudo-Eratosthenes, *Catasterismi* 14. So Spenser, V, proem, 5, and VII.vii.33.

[237] *Castasterismi* 11.   [238] *Numbers of Time*, p. 207.

[239] For the image of Isis, see Apuleius, *Golden Ass* XI.3. In Macrobius, Virgo, the symbol of justice, carries an ear of corn in her hand (*Saturnalia*, I.xxi.24); so also in DuBartas, *Divine Weeks*, Sylvester trans., I.IV.261. For Britomart-Virgo-Diana, see below, Chap. IV, "Heroic Eros," sec. i.

knife hook and in the other a pair of weights "with which he did assoyle /
Both more and lesse, where it in doubt did stand, / And equall gave to
each as justice duly scann'd" (VII.vii.38). To paraphrase in terms of
Book V: he proceeded equitably, adjusting the claims of more-than-*isos*
and less-than-*isos*. We have noted Spenser's apparent allusion here to the
equinox, which occurs in *Libra*, as Virgil says, "When the Scales make
daylight and sleep equal in hours and just halve the globe between light
and shadow."[240]

The "dreadfull scorpion," we have already met (VII.vii.39; cf. V.viii.40).
This creature slew great Orion, "by Dianaes doom unjust," but the unjust
judgments of the Soldan's consort Adicia do not ultimately overtake the
heroes of justice. Beyond Scorpio is the *Archer*, the sign usually identified
with a Centaur. A vague suitability of this image for Malengine may be
discerned at the outset, since legend implies that the Centaurs are a race
of wild, cave-dwelling mountaineers with a considerable hostility to Hercules. Like Malengine also, they are reminiscent of shaggy satyrs and the
onocentauroi in the LXX Isaiah, and they are by nature fantastic (see
II.ix.50). However, Spenser's Malengine is more obviously modeled on
Virgil's evil thief Cacus, who would not appear to be a Centaur. Virgil
does make Cacus *semihomo* (*Aen.* VIII.194), and in the *Metamorphoses*
Ovid uses this exact word for the species in question. In the "evil pouch"
of the thieves in Dante's *Inferno*, accordingly, we meet a Cacus who is
explicitly a Centaur.[241] This link is stronger than it at first looks. In the
place in Ovid the subject is *Hercules'* relations to the centaurs, and it is
here that the story of the centaur Periclymenus is told. As remarked above,
Periclymenus is very likely one of the less obvious models for Malengine.

The remainder of this analogy is rather more quizzical. Even if Malengine is also in some sense a *Capricorn*, or Goat, it is not clear how Mercilla's palace might accord with the scheme. Here we should look at the
time of year that this sign identifies, which is December, or the season
of Advent. Spenser duly commemorates this datum in the Mutabilitie
cantos (as he does in the course of the British history read at the Castle
of Alma), but then he shifts to the pagan parallel, referring the Goat to
the one by means of which "th'Idaean mayd" nursed the infant Jove
(VII.vii.41). As we have seen, Mercilla is partly enthroned as a Jove,
because all monarchs symbolically occupy "Joves judgement seat" (V.ix.
31). However not only Justice, but also Mercy is originally bred "in
th'Almighties euerlasting seat" (V.x.1f.; proem, 10f.): there is thus a
sense in which both Jovian rule and Christian mercy are given under the

[240] *Georgics* I.208–209. See above, n. 210 and text.
[241] *Metam.* XII.536; *Inf.* XXV.17–34. Dante's Cacus torments the phoenix-like
Vanni Fucci, and all of the thieves are characterized as shape-changers. How Cacus
became a centaur, apart from my indications, remains mysterious.

sign of Capricorn. The traditional debate between Justice and Mercy, staged at the time of the Incarnation, turns on the question of whether man merits salvation; in Spenser it is replaced by the question of the *relation* of justice to mercy.

So far as I can see, there is no connection between *Aquarius* and Gerioneo, though the Tiber—the water that Aquarius normally pours—might conceivably have something to do with the Inquisition under Gerioneo's patronage. Nor does Grantorto, at the end of the cycle, seem to be a *Pisces*. Envy and Detraction, however, are "two griesly creatures" ("creatures" is the technical term Spenser uses for the *zoion* of the zodiac), and they combine together even though they are opposed. Iconography shows the Fish linked together by a reversing line between their mouths. One shows dull eyes askew, while the other has a "mouth distort / Foming with poyson round about the gils" (V.xii.28, 33–36). Somewhat more germane, as it turns out, would be a comparison to the labors of the twelve months, which Spenser integrates with his presentation of the zodiac in the Mutabilitie cantos. Radigund's scimitar need not remind us of the sickle carried by July, nor the Soldan's armed chariot of the plowshares of October; but the hatchets and pruning-tools that characterize the agricultural activity at the year's end seem to make the weaponry of Gerioneo and Grantorto what it is. The possible significance of this alteration will meet us in the technological context of the following essay, in our remarks about the conversion of swords into pruning-hooks.

Perhaps another reason for not making Gerioneo a zodiacal sign is the solar character of his received mythography. Comes, having remarked the interpretation of Hercules as the sun, explicitly makes the Geryon voyage stand for the sun's decline into winter, corresponding to Hercules' departure into Spain, or the west.[242] According to some accounts, Hercules sailed to this adventure in a golden vessel lent by Helios himself.[243] Hesiod names Geryon's island Erutheie, or "red island," locating it "in the dim stead out beyond glorious Ocean" (*Theog.* 290, 294): the land of the sunset. Spenser agrees with Hesiod in calling Geryon's cattle-keeper

[242] *Mythol.*, VII.i, *edn. cit.*, p. 704: "Dictus est enim Geryon *apo to garuein*, quod fremere significat, quod proprium est hyemis." Melanchthon, *Ennaratio Libri IX Metamorphoseon Ovidii*, in Bretschneider and Bindseil, eds., *Works*, vol. 19 (Brunswig, 1853), cols. 593f., also makes Geryon stand for winter, deriving the name from *gěruō*, Lat. *clamo*, the thunder of winter storms. Giraldus also has the defeat of Geryon as the sun's breaking up of thunder-clouds, in *Herculis Vita*, in *Op. om.*, I, col. 580A. Spenser's Gerioneo, however, produces "furious heats" (V.xi.13); he "brayd aloud" and "laught . . . loud" (V.xi.8, 9). The knights who come to aid Gerioneo's seneschal, on the other hand, *thunder* on Arthur (V.x.34f.).

[243] *Mythol.*, VII.i, *edn. cit.*, p. 681, citing Pherecydes, and therefore Athenaeus, *Deipnosophistae* XI.39. See also Apollodorus, *Bibl.* II.v.10, and Servius, *ad Aen.* VIII.300.

Eurytion and his Typhoëan dog Othrus; and he makes the cattle *purple* in color (V.x.9–10). Helios, as we know from Homer, is also a keeper of kine. There is one small indication that the poet may think of Gerioneo's kine—"The fayrest kyne alive"—as like those Helios rejoiced in at his rising and setting (*Od*. XII.379–381). Arthur sets out to make the voyage that will bring him to Gerioneo's domain,

> The morrow next appear'd, with *purple* hayre
> Yet dropping fresh out of the Indian fount,
> And bringing light into the heauens fayre,
> When he was readie to his steede to mount,
>
> (V.x.16)

Thus Belge rejoices at his coming: "Alreadie seemes that fortunes headlong wheele / Begins to turne, and sunne to shine more bright, / Then it was wont" (V.x.20).

The analogy between the heroic personae and the sun is not very strong on the periphery of the complete cycle. It is stronger when the sun itself is stronger, during the "midday" of the legend. During this time, Artegall is rather weaker, and so there may be a sense in which the sun—whose eye no deed escapes—takes over for the hero. The analogy might then express a kind of solar regard for justice.

The lights in the firmament were fixed for signs (Gen. 1:14), and in Book V they are signs pointing to the nature of the subject. The sun is a symbol of justice or rule, but it remains to say why. The shorter answer is that the sun represents the *course* of justice; the word *course* is repeated, from the first and seventh stanzas of the proem, in the final stanza of the legend. The sun is expressed in Book V by shields and wheels (iii.1, 14; viii.40–41); the same form must determine the cycle of the legend itself, the twelve cantos being, as it were, the rays of a solar disc, or the spokes of a solar wheel. It follows from Artegall's passage through this pattern that the longer answer to our question is to be framed in terms of the relation of justice to the requirements of regularity, customary order, and even punctuality: in the relation of justice to time.[244]

In the second essay of the present chapter, we treated the idea of temperance as temporal control; we are predisposed to seek a similar conception in Book V. As we have seen, Spenser naturally thinks of justice as a form of good order, and order has a temporal aspect. This aspect is the burden of a notable formulation assigned to Anaximander:

[244] Remarks somewhat similar to mine here are found in Angus Fletcher, *The Prophetic Moment* (Chicago, 1971), pp. 135–146.

Things perish into those things out of which they have their birth, according to that which is ordained; for they give reparation to one another and pay the penalty of their injustice according to the disposition of time [*taxin kronou*].[245]

One finds just such a process taking place in the exchange of chattels between the two brothers—the place of their story corresponds to that of the Occasio episode in Book II. Artegall invokes comparable imagery for reparation in arguing with the giant:

> For whatsoeuer from one place doth fall
> Is with the tide vnto an other brought:
> For there is nothing lost, that may be found, if sought.
>
> (V.ii.39)

Thus there is a principle of redress in all natural exchange, "according to the disposition of time." This principle constitutes a kind of law or justice. Everything that happens is not just, but is subject to correction by justice. Spenser expresses this sense of things in the defeat of the Soldan, which we are to compare to the defeat of the Armada: "Iustice that day of wrong her selfe had wroken" (V.viii.44). Heraclitus' twenty-ninth fragment asserts that the sun itself "will not overstep his measures, or the Spirits of Vengeance, the ministers of Justice, would find him out."[246] We can see that the sun's decline in the proem is unsettling because it is not clear what correction it is liable to. There are enough references to Artegall's incarceration in the West to draw him into this solar orbit too. It is Talus and Britomart who take the part of "ministers of justice," and seek out the errant solar hero. As Horace says, "Often does the Father of day [*Diespiter*, or Jupiter], having been neglected, confound the innocent with the guilty"; and yet, he adds, "rarely does punishment, with her lame foot, abandon the villain who flies before her [*antecedentem*]" (*Odes* III.2, ll. 29–32).

Time is an important element in the calculation of justice, then, because corrective justice follows upon injustice in time. Many of the larger movements of the poem that are determined by a rhythm of reformation and

[245] Simplicius, *Phys.* XXIV.17, quoting Theophrastus, as trans. in Cornford, *From Religion to Philosophy*, p. 8. For a discussion, see G. S. Kirk and J. E. Raven, *The PreSocratic Philosophers* (Cambridge, 1966), pp. 117-121, and especially the citation there of Solon, Frg. 24 Diehl, ll. 1-7, where *en diké Kronou* is translated as "trial conducted by Time" ("The great Olympian deities would be my best supporting witness for this in the court of Time"), with reference to failure of perseverance.

[246] Trans. in Cornford, *From Religion to Philosophy*, p. 19, and cited by Plutarch in *De Iside* 47, *Moralia* 370D. Cf. V.ii.35f.: the heavens contain the lower elements and guide them in their courses: "Such heauenly iustice doth among them raine, / That euery one doe know their certaine bound, / In which they doe these many yeares remaine."

renovation are thus prominent in this particular legend. Their primary symbol is in the return of Arthur, and we have noted that Artegall's name promotes him as Arthur's equal. Such movements include the recovery of the national basis of the English Church, the Reformation of the Church generally, and the renewal of the historical Troy—and its imperial descendant—in a New Troy. The legend of justice contains Spenser's most explicit reference to the Reformation, and his nearest approach to Troynovant. Mercilla's palace is a realization of the long sequence of allusions to Cleopolis and Troynovant, that is, of a capital city—no such court or city appears in the poem hereafter. Justice is finally done to Florimell in this legend; and Duessa, passing into her historical embodiment, is also given her just due. Like Truth, Justice must be a daughter of Time,[247] as well as of God, if only because God repays in God's own time: "Iustice, though her dome she doe prolong, / Yet at the last she will her owne cause right" (V.xi.1). The justiciar might also trust in God, because he acts in God's place, "his cause to end"; justice is God's own peculiar cause (V, proem, 10). Thus in his fight against the Soldan, Arthur—being in the right—"More in his causes truth . . . trusted than in might" (V.viii.30). Deeds, Arthur tells Belge, ought to be judged "by their trueth and by the causes right," and these, rather than the prince himself, have fought in her behalf (V.xi.17). Talus also may serve in the same "cause"; two of his assigned functions are the reformation of evils and the eliciting of truth. The cause of truth also includes the overthrow of the Sphinx monster, an image of the Inquisition that presents an evil counterpart for the interrogations conducted by Talus.

The cause of truth and justice receives ironic treatment in the dénouement of the legend. Artegall falls victim to Detraction, a form of evil accusation that speaks against the hero, as Ate formerly spoke against Duessa. Artegall now revokes the reform he has been instituting in Ireland: "His course of Iustice he was forst to stay," the poet writes (V.xii. 27), where "stay" has its technical overtone of a suspension of judicial proceedings. Talus and Artegall are thus recalled before they have had time to finish their inquiry, or to see that justice takes its course. Similarly,

---

[247] For classical, Christian, and Renaissance sources, see Arthur Henkel and Albrecht Schöne, eds., *Emblemata* (Stuttgart, 1967), col. 1816. Studies are: Fritz Saxl, "Veritas Filia Temporis," in *Philosophy and History: Essays presented to Ernst Cassirer*, ed. R. Kiblansky and H. R. Paton (Oxford, 1936), pp. 197–222; Donald Gordon, "Veritas Filia Temporis," in *Journal of the Warburg Institute*, 3 (1939-1940); and Samuel Chew, *The Pilgrimage of Life* (New Haven and London, 1962), esp. pp. 18f. Chew cites images of Time as the executioner of justice, bearing the scales, and in a somewhat different connection, Time armed with a scourge or whip (see Chew's fig. 25, the title page of Giovanni Andrea Gilio's *Topica Poetica*, 1580). The idea that Talus is the "scourge of folly" is not entirely false to Spenser's presentation, as indicated below.

the accusations against Artegall are allowed to stand by default, for truth is vindicated by time—"time in her iust terme the truth to light should bring" (I.ix.5)—and in the legend of justice no more time remains.

[ii]

As the casuality just cited might remind us, there is an *occasio* theme in this legend as well. Here the question of man's capacity to assert his will over his personal fortunes, as we met it in Book II, is translated into the issue of the nation's will to assert its destiny in the dimension of history. As a result, this legend moves from the exercise of the just will of the magistrate to the presentation of an epitome of current history. This epitome is confined to a single legend, thus reducing the historical destinies of England to the status of an episode, in the context of the whole poem. But at the same time this procedure makes the legend of justice the chief focus of the critical historical moment. The legend begins with allusions to the retreat of Astraea, which Hesiod places at the beginning of the Bronze Age, and there is the sense throughout that justice takes the form of a dispensation, or an ideal era over which a personification of justice would preside. In the case of a monarchy, dynastic ambitions will inevitably hedge such a patriotic theme, just as they do in Shakespeare's history plays and Virgil's *Aeneid*. Spenser already presented in Book II the chronicles of Eumnestes and Philotime's court of ambitious time-servers trying to raise themselves out of obscurity.

When the idea of justice asserting itself in time—as reprisal, redress, repeal, reparation, correction, amendment, and reform—combines with the idea of a reign of justice, that is, a historical manifestation of conceptual justice, then England itself comes to embody a justice of a sort. It is not too much to say that Spenser's legend ends by making England the Talus of Europe, the islander who disciplines the central nation-states and prevents the success of the Continental drive for hegemony (the Catholic League) from tyrannizing the smaller states on the periphery.[248] It is to suggest that conceptual justice seeks this historical expression that Spenser constructs the following double sequence:

Defeat of fraud:

Overthrow of Dolon's sons, who try to kill Britomart	Defeat of Malengine, who tries to abduct Samient

Locus of recognition of justice figure:

Isis Church, crocodile, Instruction of Britomart	Mercilla's palace, lion, Instruction of Artegall

[248] See esp. Ludwig Dehio, *The Precarious Balance* (*Gleichgewicht order Hegemonie*), trans. Charles Fullman (New York, 1962), *passim*.

Execution of the rebel queen:

Britomart's duel with Radigund;   Mercilla's trial of Duessa;
Freeing of Artegall   Disabusement of Arthur

Arthurian intervention against Spanish power:

Artegall's and Arthur's defeat of   Arthur's defeat of Gerioneo on
the Soldan on Samient's behalf   Belge's behalf

Doom of the oppressor's female complement:

Flight of Adicia   Flushing of the monster under
                            the idol

Having made the point that justice is manifested historically, we may proceed to a correlative notion, namely, that justice can take the form of a response to historical occasion. The theme is felt whenever the knights of this legend retreat or dissemble to gain an advantage, but two episodes here ought to concern us particularly. The episodes involving the Soldan and Sir Burbon present the Impatience-Impotence theme of Book II in its "public" form.

The historical allegory of Samient has not, to my knowledge, been explained. It could conceivably refer to English sea power. The ambassador Samient, in this interpretation, would represent the English merchant marine bent on peaceful trade; the two pagans who chase her on horseback across the foreground of the eighth canto would be piratical military ships, and Arthur and Artegall would be English privateers. "Safe passage," in this allegory, would refer to England's contest with Spain for the privilege of the seas, which the Spanish monopoly on the New World had more or less denied. The abuse of Samient then falls into place as the attack on Hawkins' fleet in the Mexican port of San Juan de Ulloa in 1568, or such provocations thereafter as the seizure of an English corn fleet in Spanish ports in 1585. Samient's treating for peace on Mercilla's behalf ought to refer to late peace-feelers toward the Prince of Parma, made even as the Armada was being prepared. Her abuse, especially by the Soldan's consort, might recall the delivery of English merchants in Philip's dominions to the Inquisition. The historical allegory of the penetration of the Soldan's defenses by Artegall in the disguise of the dead pagan is more difficult to guess, but surely there is a slight analogy to Elizabeth's policy of encouraging privateers while officially disapproving of them—that is, the strategy of not admitting that their activities belonged to English policy. More specifically, one thinks of Drake's famous raid on Cadiz, and his seizure of the fortress on Cape St. Vincent, which made it possible for him to block the mobilization of the Armada in the harbor at Lisbon. "El Draque" became a legend with the enemy; he seemed to have an uncanny foreknowledge and was rumored to be able to control the winds themselves.[249] Drake's strategy was essentially to anticipate and prevent the consolidation of the Spanish war effort—Artegall's actions are preventive also. Elizabeth's own strategy, of delaying the war with Spain until the initiative genuinely passed into her hands, might also be compared with Artegall's forestalling action. Artegall returns Samient to the Soldan's domain, as though she, like peace or negotiation (*sam*, "together"), were still within the enemy's compass. (Negotiations for peace continued after the Cadiz raid, and Elizabeth disavowed any intention of taking Cape St. Vincent.) Finally, Artegall's concluding attack on the Soldan's adherents may refer to either the picking to pieces of the remains of the Armada, or to the follow-up blows that England delivered against Spain's Atlantic ports. Sir John Norris—one of Artegall's embodiments in the Ireland of the last canto—commanded the first of these. Artegall's operations, of course, are rather more effective than the expedition against Portugal was, but Spenser also saw fit to ignore this fact in his reference to the mission in the Dedicatory Sonnet to Norris.

Whatever the historical allegory here, the description we have offered shows the importance of time in the action. Prudence, risk, forethought, and delay—all give Arthur and Artegall the control over action that the Soldan finally loses. The Soldan is destroyed in a sun chariot that departs from its wonted track. His horses are like Phaeton's: "their well knowen courses they forwent, / . . . leading th'euer-burning lampe astray" (V.viii. 40). The Scorpion, "With vgly craples crawling in their way," is seconded by Arthur's "sunlike shield" (V.viii.41), and the lawless beasts drag their master "amongst the yron hookes and graples keene." The chariot itself has become the Scorpion, while Arthur has taken over its function as the minister of justice who finds out the sun if it oversteps its measures. Thus the Soldan's catastrophe repeats from the proem the image of the sun that has lost its course.

Another action in this legend also illustrates the government of time, namely, the temporizing of Sir Burbon. As noted earlier, this episode is placed parallel to the defeat of Maleger's auxiliaries, Impatience and Impotence. In the British chronicle, Arthur read about the "greedy thirst of royall crowne" and the "hideous hunger of dominion" (II.x.35, 47); Burbon is possessed by a similar "greedie great desire" of winning France (V.xi.61). To do so, he has abandoned the red-cross shield of his Protestant identity to the mob. (In Book II Arthur throws away his shield as useless in his battle with Maleger; II.xi.41.) Burbon opportunely argues that he may resume his shield "when time doth serue." He believes that "to temporise is not from truth to swerue, / Ne for aduantage terme to entertaine" (V.xi.56). France has been successfully "tempted" by bribes. The Refor-

[249] So J. E. Neale, *Queen Elizabeth I: A Biography* (reprint, New York, 1957), p. 304.

mation thought that Truth had indeed shown herself to be the daughter of Time, but here it has proved otherwise. Burbon carries France off, and Spenser reflects upon apostasy as the result of "sacred hunger of ambitious mindes, / And impotent desire of men to raine" (V.xii.1).[250]

The end of the legend implies that retreat of justice from men's affairs with which the legend in fact began. The degeneration of men into stones in the proem, where Deucalion is invoked, recurs in the last stanza, where Detraction is still, as it were, casting the first stone. Detraction seems to be the triumphant Envy of Hesiod's *Works and Days* (255 seq.) spreading calumnious rumours and driving out the virgin Justice: she and Envy will take away from Artegall whatever he may have accomplished. Artegall is called away from the execution of justice "through occasion," and the furor of Occasion, as we know, shares motifs with the triumph of Calumny and the triumph of Mutabilitie. It is as if justice, as an ideal form, can only exist in its purity in a world beyond ours, an empyreal realm to which it now returns. The theme of a lapsed golden age from which Spenser begins traps the cycle of the legend in a kind of paradoxical tautology: where justice truly obtains, no justice is required; and, where there is no justice, no justice can be done.

As we have just noted, this circularity appears in the alignment of the Detraction episode with the proem and the Astraea myth of the first canto. The space allotted to each is considerable, and may have an effect on the solar "course" we have observed in the progress of the hero. The prologue tells us that the sun's course has "miscaried" (7), the sun having declined "nigh thirtie minutes" from the measurement recorded by Ptolemy. Since a minute is a measure of time (as well as a sixtieth of a degree of space), we might wonder what it would mean if the sun should be, not half a degree off, but half an hour. If we were to suppose that the twelve cantos of the legend constitute its "day," then the period in question would be half a canto. Now in point of fact the sun has not declined thirty minutes from its Ptolemaic measurement, but *thirteen*; Spenser is "wrong." It is a curious fact also, that the effect of the precession of the equinoxes—and we remember that the arithmetical center of the book is equinoctial—is to make the sun rise in the house adjacent to the one assigned it in the Ptolemaic system, i.e., thirty degrees off its proper position. Either the prologue material, or the epilogue material, or both together, might seem to usurp some such portion of the whole; the prologue discusses just this encroachment. We have already noted a slippage in the coordination of the incidents of the legend and the signs: Florimell ought to be Europa, but she is next door, in Gemini; Isis ought to be Virgo, but she is found in Libra; and so forth. One further source of evidence is the rubric of the

[250] These are the only uses of the word "impotent" in the poem, minor evidence of the alignment of the two episodes.

last canto; it announces an adventure that has actually backslid half a canto, and has already transpired. This failure of synchronization may be quite meaningless. Or it may be one more sign that Book V is to issue in a miscarriage of justice.

The Custodian of Europe

> . . . prepare warre, wake vp the mightie men: let all the men of warre drawe nere & come vp.
> Breake your ploweshares into swordes, and your sieths into speares. . . .
> (Joel 3:9–10, Geneva Bible)

To conclude our study of the legend of justice, we may focus on its most prominent symbol, the iron man Talus. Talus, as much as anything else in Book V, insists upon some autonomous status for the legend, and his circuit through this book is also essential in the characterization of justice as a "course." Conforming to the analogy with the Palmer in Book II, Artegall's second is described as the "true guide of his way and vertuous gouernment" (V.viii.3), but he is really as much a bodyguard as a guardian; he takes direction, rather than giving it. Both the Palmer and Talus are full-sized characters; unlike the dwarf that lags behind Redcrosse and Una, they precede the knights on their travels. This forward station indicates that the rule of reason and the authority of law loom large in the operations of the knights in question.

The relation of Talus and Artegall, however, is not the parental relation elsewhere discernible in the typical hero's assistant, for Talus is basically a slave. The theme of work—its discipline and mechanics—especially appears in Talus' servitude. Artegall and Talus are deeply interdependent, and their cooperation might seem susceptible of the Hegelian-Marxist analysis of the master-slave relation. Nothing in the text says that Talus is afraid of Artegall, but he clearly fears no one else. He serves no one except Artegall and Artegall's surrogate Britomart, and in his master's stead he inspires the fear inspired by an overseer. Just as we might see in Artegall's control over Talus the master's conscription of the desire of the slave, so in Talus we might see the alienation of the slave from his work (he does his master's work) and the resulting objectification of the laborer into the class of a *thing*: a Promethean robot. We also find the dialectic whereby master and slave each become the negation of the other. Artegall is no less occupied than Talus—consciousness needs work—and Artegall depends on Talus. In a way, then, Artegall is as enslaved as Talus. On the other side of the equation, Talus might recognize in Artegall's dependence his own latent *independence*, a lesson the slave can learn from his existence as one deprived of all the things on which his master depends. The expendability of the master is more properly the theme of the communist giant, who has thrown off the fear of "Lordings" and imagined for himself the possibility of an unconditioned freedom. The potential transposition of master and slave consciousnesses might be the burden of another episode as well, namely, the enslavement of Artegall by Radigund, which results in the emancipation of Talus. This incident occasions the only revelation of the iron man's sensitivity, while Artegall endures domestic subservience—Radigund's charges are compelled "to spin, to card, to sew, to wring" (V.iv.31). In the conflict with the giant, Talus remains a loyal "slave," identifying with his ruling-class master; but this particular conscription of Talus should not prevent us from seeing that the giant is a Talus too, that is, a Talus in rebellion, a "slave" who is determined to be an obstacle to himself no longer, and hence to be an Artegall as well.

Talus' obedience, I need hardly say, is never explicitly characterized in terms of the class relation just described. We must reason back to such a relation from indirect evidence. We might also reason forward, from the same relation, to the significances that are actually assigned to Talus. First, the classical Talos was the servant of the lawgiver Minos, who came to be judge of the dead, and thus a "discerner of sin," as Dante calls him (*Inf.* V.9). Until the slave judges for himself, he is under a kind of judgment, or perpetual sentence; his life is led entirely under the law. Secondly, the slave is the subject of regimentation, and indeed his first motions toward mastery require the establishment of solidarity with other slaves, that is, a continuation of his regimentation in the form of an army or a union. Thirdly, the slave is an instrument of the will of the master, and so a commodity and a chattel, as well as a producer of other commodities. Out of these three conditions we may derive the three most obvious categories of Talus' significance. First is the legalistic Talus, who classically bore the tables of the laws of Minos, and who in Spenser disposes of Munera as Moses did the golden calf (the biblical episode is bracketed by the giving of the law). Then there is the martial Talus, whose invulnerability simply represents armed force. And last is the technological Talus, the ingenious machine or machine-maker. Within the purview of the magistrate, the three Taluses form the whole police power of surveillance, investigation, detection, apprehension, arrest, arraignment, and punishment—the more or less unidealized mechanics of justice instrumental to the enforcement and execution of the law.[251] This description by no

[251] See note 131 above, and cf. John Hughes' *Remarks*, in his edn. of Spenser's *Works* (1715), p. xc: "Talus with his Iron Flail . . . is a bold Allegorical Figure, to signify the Execution of Justice."

means exhausts Talus' full significance, however: he also suggests the mechanics of force, and the laws of mechanics.

Artegall and Talus are said to be sufficient to deal with a whole regiment (V.i.30), and this makes Talus something of a regiment himself. The iron man bears a resemblance to the medieval Mars, who is often portrayed as encased in armor.[252] Talus' flail, and the comparisons that make him a wolf, also belong to Mars' iconography, respectively symbolizing the scourge of war and the rapine of the soldiery.[253] Jean Seznec refers us to the influential medieval tradition promulgated by Albericus, who gives Mars the wolf and the whip, and he notes that *flagellum* (whip) shares an etymology with *flayeu* (flail), the rendering of the French *Ovide moralisé*.[254] Mars carries a whip in Petrarch's *Africa*, in a passage describing the images of the gods.[255] Somewhat confusingly, Spenser says that Talus does not use his flail in war,[256] which can only be right if for the moment the poet means that the use of the flail as a weapon is restricted to "police actions" within a preestablished jurisdiction. Many indications might contradict this limitation of the use of the weapon; it is true, however, that Talus does not generally participate in martial actions initiated against foreign countries, and he is thus more like a militia than an army. In terms of the securing of the sovereignty prerequisite to justice, we might think of him as standing for something minimal, like martial law.

Embodying the organized response of the law to those outside it, Talus is a reactionary in the basic sense of the word. He appears as such in his interaction with the communist giant, for example. When the giant refuses to yield to the reason of Artegall, Talus becomes gigantic himself, and "Approching nigh vnto him cheeke by cheeke, / He shouldered him

[252] Cf. Chaucer, *Knight's Tale*, ll. 1982f., "the temple of Mars armypotent, / Wrought al of burned steel"; l. 2441, "the stierne god armypotent"; l. 2046, the "god of arms."

[253] For the heroic personae as a wolf, see V.iv.44, V.vi.30, V.xii.38; for the wolf with Mars, Cartari, *Imagini, edn. cit.*, pp. 299f. (The wolf is of course sacred to Mars, as in Horace, *Odes* I.17.) See also Boccaccio, *G.D.G.*, IX.iii, Romano edn., vol. 2, p. 449, for the wolf as the voracity of military camps.

[254] *The Survival of the Pagan Gods*, trans. Barbara Sessions (reprint, New York, 1961), pp. 190–193. Cf. Chaucer, *Knight's Tale*, ll. 2047f., on the statue of Mars, "A wolf ther stood biforn nym at his feet / With eyen rede, and of a man he eet."

[255] *Africa*, III.186ff. The whip is surely related to Mars' team. In Statius, *Thebiad* VII.73f., the team-driving Bellona tires his horses with a long *cuspide*, which must be a goad. Discord holds "bloody iron" in Boccaccio, *Teseida*, VII.34, describing Mars' temple. A source for the tradition must be *Aen.* VIII.700ff.: "In the middle Mavors storms, embossed in iron, . . . and with rent robe Discord strides rejoicing, whom Bellona follows with bloody *flagello*."

[256] V.iv.44, "neuer wont in warre"; and yet this proscription is found in the same stanza that evokes Mars' emblem the wolf—the "deuouring enemie" of the sheep—during what is patently a war involving troops and "shooting."

from off the higher ground" (V.ii.49). In its turn, the *mobile vulgus* that had gathered around the prophet suddenly mobilizes: "They rose in armes, and all in battell order stood" (V.ii.51). When Artegall sends Talus to treat for peace, the mob attacks him; the mob having largely forfeited any consideration by such an action, Talus lays into it with the terrific iron flail. We see in these incidents the way in which lawlessness provokes the equal and opposite force of the law. The polarization seems to obey physical principles, as the mob is radicalized and Talus alienated. Such a reciprocity of countervailing forces exhibits a relation between the laws of the physical world and the moral law of *talio*, "an equall or like payne in recompense of an hurt."[257] The discovery of such an analogy has been one of the claims made by the giant; he argues from the original equality of *the elements* for a redistribution of *the wealth*. Artegall does not admit the analogy and argues that it is only the nature of the giant that has "run awry"; it is the giant leveler, rather than the landscape, who gets "equalized"—he is dumped from the "higher ground" into the sea.[258] The mutilation of the hands of the grafter and the tongue of the slanderer also express this mechanism of reprisal in kind.

The association of Spenser's Talus with the law is also suggested by the legend of the classical Talos, the bronze roundsman of Crete who displayed in the villages the laws of Minos, which were engraved on brazen tablets.[259] Spenser's character has a similar function in the Ireland of the last canto:

> And that same yron man which could reueale
> All hidden crimes, through all that realme he sent
> To search out those, that vsd to rob and steale,
> Or did rebell gainst lawfull gouernment;
> On whom he did inflict most grieuous punishment.
>
> (V.xii.26)

[257] Thomas Cooper, *Thesavrus Lingvae Romanae & Britannicae . . . Accessit dictionarivm historicvm et poëticum . . .* (London, 1565), *sub* "Talio."

[258] The image of the exalted valley is primeval-eschatological: see Isa. 40:4, Luke 3:5. For a similar pagan idea, see Plutarch, *De Iside* 47, *Moralia* 370B. For a study, see D. C. Allen, *The Legend of Noah*, Illinois Studies in Language and Literature, vol. 33, no. 3f. (Urbana, Ill., 1949), pp. 94–96, citing Bede, Alcuin, Rabanus Maurus, Peter Comestor, *Glossa ordinaria* on Gen. 7, David Pareus, and Antonio de Torquemada, with *F.Q.* V.ii.28, on the levelness of the antedeluvian landscape.

[259] Pseudo-Platonic *Minos* 320C; Apollodorus, *Bibl.* I.ix.26; Zenobius, *Cent.* V.85, citing Simonides, *Frg.* 204 (see Loeb *Lyra Graeca*, ed. J. M. Edmonds, vol. 2, pp. 404–406); Comes, *Mythol.*, III.vii, "De Minoe," *edn. cit.*, p. 209: "Vsus est (vt aiunt) Minos Rhadamanti opera, viri quidem boni, sed qui tamen regias artes non prorsus fuerat edoctus, quem Minos in vrbe habuit legum custodem, cum extra vrbem Talais opera vteretur, qui vocatus fuit Æreus, quia tabulas aereas per vicos circumferret." Cf. Athenaeus, *Deipnosoph.* XIII, p. 603D: "Rhadamanthus the Just was beloved by Talos," quoting Ibycus, *Frg.* 32. Simonides, "Ex auctore Prouerbiorum," is printed in Fulvius Ursinus, ed., *Carmina novem illvstrivm feminarvm . . . Et Lyricorvm . . . Simonidis . . .* (Antwerp, 1548), p. 185.

Perhaps a comic example of the Talos role is to be found in Sancho Panza, a lawgiver and a deputy-governor who makes evening rounds of his "island," and remarks that judges and governors ought to be made of (insensible) brass. The provenance of the remark of the proverb-loving Sancho is confirmed by Erasmus' *Adagia*, where *Chalcenterus* (brass-intestines) is said to apply to the endurance of those who undertake labors as if they possessed "innards of brass, as was feigned of Talos, the custodian of the island of Crete."[260]

Spenser's iron man has been conceived with some appreciation for Hooker's observation that "laws of arms" are "built upon depraved nature." Similarly,

> Laws politic, ordained for external order and regiment amongst men, are never formed as they should be, unless presuming the will of man to be inwardly obstinate, rebellious, and averse from all obedience unto the sacred laws of his nature; in a word, unless presuming man to be in regard of his depraved mind little better than a wild beast. . . .[261]

In the *Vewe* (1022–1023) Spenser argues against leaving the sense of the law to the will of the judge: rather, "the lawes oughte to be like stonye tables playne stedfaste and vnmoueable." Talos is said to be "Immoueable, resistlesse, without end" (V.i.12). According to Comes, Astraea at her departure left behind a *testamentum*. Astraea traditionally departed with the coming of the iron age, and Spenser's goddess leaves Talos as a legacy to Artegall.[262] That it was *law* she left behind is implied by at least one classical poet, Claudian, in a political panegyric on the consulship of Manlius Theodorus. There, Justice-Virgo recalls her "pupil" Manlius to public office, because she looked down from heaven and saw *law* deprived of its proper interpreter.[263]

The classical Talos is also a guardian per se. In the *Argonautica*, he throws stones at the voyagers as they approach the shore of Crete. Spenser's Talos throws rocks at Malengine (V.ix.17).[264] Perhaps Spenser is thinking

[260] *Don Quixote*, Pt. II, chap. xlix. Erasmus, *Adagia* (edn. of Antwerp, 1646), *sub* "Chalcenterus," *sub* TOLERENTIA, p. 696, applied to the grammarian Didymus, with reference to his indefatigable endurance.

[261] *Laws of Ecclesiastical Polity*, I.x.1, Everyman's Library, vol. 1, p. 188.

[262] *Mythol.*, II.ii, *edn. cit.*, pp. 115f. (As remarked above, the departure of Astraea is followed by the iron age, in Aratus, *Phaen.* 96ff.)

[263] *Panegyricus Dictus Manlio* 166ff., in Loeb *Claudian*, ed. M. Platnauer, vol. 1, pp. 346f. For the theme here we may compare Lactantius, *Epitome of the Divine Institutes*, lix (in ANF, vol. 7, pp. 246f.): justice having been put to flight, as poets relate, men instituted *laws*. See also *Div. Inst.*, V.v–vi (*vol. cit.*, pp. 140–142). For the retreat and return of Astraea in relation to law and the labor of plowing, see Claudian, *In Rufinum* I.50–57, 354–387.

[264] *Argonaut.* IV.1637ff. Cacus, the original of one of Talos' opposites, Malengine, is also a rock-thrower, according to Ovid, *Fasti* I.569. The burning of Munera's gold might remind us that Talos is said to have burned his victims to death: Suidas, *sub*

of capital punishment under the Old Law, which was by stoning.[265] Given the dialectical relation of Talus to his antagonists, it is not surprising to find features of his legend displaced to them on occasion. Malengine actually turns into a stone, and the enemies on the shore in the final canto shower the approaching force with stones. The communist giant is tumbled from a promontory to his death, and this is also the fate of the classical Talos. (Similarly, the Talos who was a nephew of Daedalus was either toppled over the edge of the Acropolis or flung into the sea.) The final canto also shows Munera's retainers throwing stones at Talus, and Munera attempting to prevail over him by "powr of charms, which she against him wrought" (V.ii.22). These last sound like the charms that Medea used to bring down the Talos of the *Argonautica*.

Whether or not it is engraved on the biblical stone or the classical bronze, the tables of the law are a kind of record or monument of the law's having been brought into existence, and also a future denunciatory witness against those who break it—those whom the law will "overtake." Talus, if he is an immovable giant who is also an iron "testament," is perhaps monumental in several senses. As a suit of armour like the one worn by Mars, he bears some resemblance to the empty shield and armour of the Soldan, all that remains of the warmonger after his disastrous campaign against Arthur. Artegall causes these arms to be "hung in all mens sight, / To be a moniment for euermoure" (V.viii.45), even though of the Soldan himself the poet writes "That of his shape appear'd no litle moniment" (V.viii.43). Artegall leaves many such remainders in his course; the effect is to suggest that the present social order is founded on the defeat of earlier and less just orders, and may partly depend for peaceful continuance upon maintaining the memory of their violent ends. As a result, the legend comes to resemble a commemorative monument like the House of Ate, which is described very near the opening of Spenser's social installment:

> And all within the riuen walls were hung
>> With ragged monuments of times forepast,
>> All which the sad effects of discord sung:
>> There were rent robes, and broken sceptres plast,
>> Altars defyl'd, and holy things defast,
>> Disshiuered speares, and shields ytorne in twaine,

"Sardanios gelous"; Photius, *Lexicon* 500.24; scholia on Plato's *Rep.* 337a; Zenobius, *Cent.* V.85. The liquidation of the gold might also remind us of Talos' own mode of death, by the pulling of a pin from his heel, draining from him his life-blood (*Argonaut.* IV.1677ff., "like melted lead"; Apollodorus, *Bibl.* I.ix.26).

[265] Lev. 24:14–23; Num. 15:32–36; Deut. 13:6–10, 17:2–7, 22:20f.; John 8:4–7. Hercules bombards one of Malengine's originals—namely Cacus—with mill-stones, at *Aen.* VIII.250.

Great cities ransackt, and strong castles rast,
Nations captiued, and huge armies slaine:
Of all which ruines there some relicks did remain.

(IV.i.21)

In Book V these signs, relics, and monuments (Spenser uses these terms interchangeably at IV.i.21ff.) include the heads of Sanglier's lady and of Pollente, Munera's hands and feet, Braggadocchio's and Artegall's broken swords, Artegall's arms hung "With moniments of many knights decay" (V.v.22), the Soldan's arms, and Malfont's tongue. Other witnesses to Ate's domination are Belge's "ruinate" city with Gerioneo's castle in its neck; Gerioneo's idol, desecrated by Arthur, and its temple, which "nigh asunder brast" (V.xi.28); and Burbon's shield, broken into pieces. From the outset Talus is allegorical not only of such siege-engines as bring about this destruction, but also of those that *might* bring it about; he too has the symbolic and admonitory function of a sign.

Many of the acts of defilement and disfiguration in this legend are done symbolically, to make or unmake a sign. We note the razing of the foundations of Munera's castle, the official baffling of Braggadocchio and the blotting out of his shield, and the erasure of the first part of Bonfont's name. In these cases the fixing of the monument's or sign's significance in part consists in the eradication of a prior monument or sign—as Spenser says of Munera's castle—"That there mote be no hope of reparation, / Nor memory thereof to any nation" (V.ii.28).

Talus' admonitory role is broad. As a symbol of armaments, he performs a service merely by being seen, like the military hardware on display in a Moscow May Day parade. As a witness to the law, he functions like the pre-incriminatory recital of the Mosaic legislation in Deuteronomy. As a sign, he prophecies and threatens a debacle; as a monument, he commemorates this debacle—we may compare the horses of Phaëthon that "This lower world nigh all to ashes brent, / And left their scorched path yet in the firmament" (V.viii.40). Talus comes into operation with the creation of the sign of justice, when Astraea retreats into this same firmament, "Mongst those twelue signes which nightly we doe see" (V.i.11). The iron man is left on earth as a heavy monument to the departure of Justice into the heavens.[266]

It will be obvious from the foregoing that Talus brings us very close to the "epic" commemoration of strife touched upon in the first essay in this book. Talus and Artegall show epic tendencies, in terms of our dis-

[266] I owe this formulation of Talus' place among the signs and monuments of Book V to a paper on this topic by my student Walter Stiller.

cussion there, because of their particular associations with a historical epoch and its passing. One of the first things we learn about Artegall is that he seemed to be "one of th'old Heroes" (III.iii.32), and Hesiod, in his version of the myth of the Four Ages, interpolates the generation of the heroes between the vanished brazen race (whose arms seemed to grow from their shoulders and who were destroyed by their own hands) and the present iron race. It is significant for the theme of the *Works and Days* that the iron race never rests from labor by day (ll. 175f.). The original of Talus was a bronze man; being iron, then, Talus is naturally his successor. He is also the member of a successor-race, whether a race of epic heroes, or a race of enslaved laborers. He exhibits the surpassing strength of the former, and the iron endurance of the latter.

Apart from these considerations, Talus is also a creation of "romance," if only because he is *animate* hardware. As a metal guard, he belongs to a whole class of such automata; his kind survives in the haunted castles of gothic romance down to the current movie era. The example closest to Spenser seems to be in the romance of *Virgilius*, where the magician Virgil invents a copper horseman with an iron flail, for the purposes of discouraging "night-runners and thieves" and enforcing a curfew at Rome.[267] Spenser's character "vsed in times of jeopardy / To keepe a nightly watch" (V.iv.46). The same *Virgilius* elsewhere describes a gate guarded by copper porters with iron mallets or sledges; and similar porters are met with in other medieval romances.[268] Conformably, Talus is associated with various entryways in the course of his duties. He attacks the door of Munera, and he is denied entrance to Isis Church. He guards Britomart's door at Dolon's house like a faithful watchdog, and he also

[267] The parallel is first noted in C. G. Leland, *The Unpublished Legends of Virgil* (New York, 1900), p. 152, and again in John Steadman, "Spenser and the *Virgilius* Legend: Another Talus Parallel," *MLN*, 73 (1958), pp. 412f. For the text, see Henry Morley, ed., *Early Prose Romances* (London, 1889). My citations are from pp. 223f., 233.

[268] For other metallic porters or guards, see *The High History of The Holy Grail* (*Perlesvaus*), trans. Sebastian Evans (London, 1907), Branch XVII, title xiv, and Branch XVIII, title i (Virgil's "Turning Castle"); and Branch XVIII, title x (two copper porters with iron mallets); vol. 2, *edn. cit.*, pp. 22f., 25ff., 33. In Lord Berners' *Huon of Bordeaux*, ed. S. L. Lee, EETS, Extra Series, nos. 40, 41, 43, 50 (London, 1882–1887), vol. 1, pp. 98f., the palace of Dunostre is made impregnable by two brass guards armed with iron flails. In *Partenay*, XXII, 2999, a giant arms himself with "flaelles thre of yre" and "thre gret slegges wrought" (ed. Skeat, EETS, Original Series, no. 22, London, 1866). In the prose *Melusine*, xxxviii, ed. A. K. Donald, EETS, Extra Series 68 (London, 1895), p. 303, cited in OED, *sub* flail³, the same giant wields a "flayel of yron" with which he gives Geoffrey "a gret buffet," and he also has three hammers of iron, one of which he throws at Geoffrey. Aptekar, *Icons of Justice*, pp. 44–52, cites much of this material.

guards the entrance to her tent in the field. Spenser has thus made Talus a kind of vigilant "two-handed engine at the door."[269]

Talos is the name not only of an invention, but also of an inventor. Spenser writes that Artegall "bad his seruant *Talus* to inuent . . ." (V.ii.20). This second Talos was the nephew of the inventor Daedalus, to whom he was apprenticed. (The first Talos was a gift to King Minos from the smith Hephaestos; Daedalus, the master of the second Talos, invented in Minos' service. The two stories seem to be saying the same thing.) Talos proved an apt pupil of his uncle; his most famous invention was the saw, which he copied in iron from the backbone of a fish. His precocity, in fact, caused the jealous Daedalus to murder him.[270] Daedalus, caught with the corpse, claimed to be inhuming a snake.[271] In the Latin version of the story (where the victim was called Calos, or Perdix), the nephew flew away from Daedalus in the form of a *perdix*, or partridge.[272] We will meet some of these details presently.

Given the iron man and this smith of the same name, we can see the affinities of Spenser's Talus not only with law enforcement, but also with technological power. He resembles the statues of Daedalus, which Aristotle mentions in a passage on automata as instrumental means (*Politics* 1253b), and which Plato says are only worthwhile to own if you have them tethered (*Meno* 97d)—otherwise they are like escaped slaves.[273] Hence Talus, besides being the helpful giant who aids the hero on his quest, is also the sorcerer's dangerous apprentice. His actions require the

[269] *Lycidas*, l. 130. In his Rinehart edn. of Milton (New York, 1962), Frye suggests this idea. Similarly, Frye compares the "narrow bridge of licensing where the challenger should pass" to *F.Q.* V.ii.4, an especially apt comparison if Pollente alludes to monopoly patents granted to corporations. In any case, the guarding of the door and the harassment at the bridge are related images of the keeping of the narrow place in this legend.

[270] For Daedalus' relations with his nephew, see Apollodorus, *Bibl.* III.xv.8; Diodorus Sic., *Bibl.* IV.lxxvi; Ovid, *Metam.* VIII.236ff.; Hyginus, *Fab.* XXXIX, CXLIV; Servius, *ad Aen.* VI.14; Isidore, *Orig.*, XIX.xix.9; Suidas and Photius, *sub* "Perdikos hieron"; Lactantius Placidus, *Nar. fab.* VIII.3.

[271] Diodorus Sic., *Bibl.* IV.lxxvi: Talos is pushed off a cliff here. (See also Apollodorus, *Bibl.* III.xv.8; Pausanias, *Perieg.* VII.iv.5 and I.xxi.4; Hyginus, *Fab.* XXXIX.) The death in question is reported in Comes, *Mythol.*, VII.xvi, "De Daedalo," *edn. cit.*, p. 799.

[272] For Perdix as a partridge, see Ovid, *Metam.* VIII.251ff., and also Lactantius Placidus, *Narr. fab.* VIII.3. Perdix is listed among the inventors in Hyginus, *Fab.* CCLXXIV.

[273] Other sources for the statues of Daedalus are scholia on Catullus, 57, "Non Castor si fingar ille Cretam," and Callistratus, *Descriptiones* 8: "Daedalus, if one is to place credence in the Cretan marvel, had the power to construct statues endowed with motion." In this last, of course, there is a specific allusion to Talus. See also Palaephatus, *De Incred.* 22; Zenobius, p. 55; Hesychius and Suidas, *sub* "Daidaleia."

strict supervision of Artegall, for he represents the kind of automatic process that, once set in motion, cannot reverse or stop itself. The potentially runaway energies of such a mechanism cannot really determine a course of action, only pursue an action more or less to death. The obvious example of the possessed mechanism is the chariot of the Soldan, where the horses run amuck, carrying chariot and driver to their doom. Talus himself has a tendency to go slightly berserk in the pursuit of justice, and his activities easily degenerate into an anarchy of killing for the sake of killing—thus carrying out Artegall's motto of *Saluagesse sans finesse* (IV.iv.39). In the following book the same quality of overeagerness shows up in the Salvage Man on occasion;[274] he also lacks finesse.

Artegall's suitability for the management of Talus is suggested by the following simile from his battle with Radigund:

> Like as a Smith that to his cunning feat
> The stubborne mettall seeketh to subdew,
> Soone as he feeles it mollifide with heat,
> With his great yron sledge doth strongly on it beat.
>
> So did Sir *Artegall* vpon her lay,
> As if she had an yron anduile beene,
> That flakes of fire, bright as sunny ray,
> Out of her steely armes were flashing seene,
> That all on fire ye would her surely weene.
>
> (V.v.7–8)

Artegall lays upon the stubborn Radigund "As if she had an yron anduile beene" (V.v.8): under the influence of Mars, according to Chaucer's description of the god's iron-pillared temple, is the smith, who forges keen blades upon his anvil.[275] In some examples from medieval romance the smith's iron sledge is a mate for the flail. The comparison of the golden sword, Chrysaor, to a sledge, reminds one of the golden sword given to Judas Maccabaeus by Jeremiah in a vision—"Maccabaeus" may mean "the hammerer."[276]

In a legend full of hardware, great symbolic importance attaches to the terrific iron flail with which Talus is armed. This implement has apocalyptic overtones. The fan of an impending destruction appears in the

[274] Cf. VI.vi.22 and 38 with V.vi.30.

[275] Chaucer, in *The Knight's Tale*, ll. 2025f., "the smyth, / That forgeth sharpe swerdes on his styth." During the golden age of Saturn, before justice had left the earth, the old Sabines had heard "neither war trumpets nor yet the sword-blade clink, imposed on the hard anvil" (Virgil, *Georgics* II.473–475, 536–540). For the comparison to Pyrochles, see Horace, *Odes* IV.15, l. 19, *ira, quae procudit enses* ("wrath, which forges weapons").

[276] See William Patten, *The Calender of Scripture* (London, 1575), fol. 128ᵛ: "Machabaeus. *Heb. Xim*[*inez*]. Percutiens: Stryking."

prophets and the gospel, and it is in the hand of the Messiah who will separate the wheat from the chaff.[277] Talus' weapon varies from a machine for separating truth from falsehood to a homely fly-swatter for extirpating pests (V.i.12; ii.53; xi.58–59). It is "thunderous," as Renaissance weaponry had become, and therefore it resembles "the flashing Leuin," which Spenser calls an "Engin" (V.vi.40).[278] Mythologically, Artegall's iron man joins a class with Thor's returning hammer (since Talus can be recalled), and Zeus' iron thunderbolts (with which he is said to *flog* the rebellious Typhon).[279] These thunderbolts were forged by the armorer Hephaestos, or Vulcan, and mythography suggests that Talus is owed to a similar manufacture. In *Areopagitica*, Milton compares London, as a host for Reformation thinkers, to a forge: "the shop of war hath not there more anvils and hammers waking, to fashion out the plates and instruments of armed justice in defense of beleaguered truth." Talus is employed in the same cause.

As an instrument for dividing truth from falsehood, Talus' flail must correspond to the "dividers" of a just judge, and therefore to the giant's balances. Spenser is not very clear on this point, but the balances seem to be a scientific measuring-device, and the giant apparently intends a quantitative evaluation of the material world. Taking a somewhat sacramental view of the established natural order, Artegall asserts, in a quasi-biblical refutation of the fault-finder, ungainsayable limitations on natural knowledge.[280] The shipwreck of the scales (V.ii.50) reverberates in the wreck of the Soldan's inherently self-confounding contraption.

[277] Matt. 3:11f., Isa. 41:16; Jer. 15:7.

[278] See V.ii.21 (with his flail Talus "thundred strokes"), and V.v.19 ("He with his yron flaile amongst them thondred"). Cf. "recoyle" in V.xi.65, and IV.ii.16, "heare the ordenance thonder." Cannonade is also implied by the battery and thunder of the Seneschal's knights at V.x.34f.

[279] Hesiod, *Theog.* 853. This must be the ultimate source for the endowment of the image of Jove with a *flagro*, in Macrobius, *Saturnalia*, I.xxiii, cited by Aptekar in *Icons of Justice*, p. 48. Thor's hammer Mjöllnir ("Crusher"), with which he defends men and gods against the giants, is paired by Snori Sturluson with Thor's iron gauntlets. The hammer is sometimes said to have been made by subterranean dwarfs, as Zeus' thunderbolts are forged by the Cyclopes. The incident with Geirröth in the *Prose Edda* may imply Thor's own mastery of the forge.

[280] See esp. the angel speaking to Esdras at II Esd. 4:5: "weigh me the weight of fire, or measure me the blast of wind, or call me againe the day that is past." Other important passages are Job: 23–25, 37:16, 38:2–18; Isa. 40:6, 12, 34; Jer. 10:10, 51:15, 32:17; Wisd. 11:19f.: II Esd. 4:36f. ("he hath weighed the worlde in the balance. The measure of the times is measured: the ages are counted by number, and they shal not be moued or shaken, til the measure thereof be fulfilled"—cf. V.ii.35f.); Rom. 11:33; Hab. 3:6; Jer. 33:22; Jer. 31:37 ("Thus saith the Lord, If the heauens can be measured, or the fundacions of the earth be searched out beneath, then wil I cast of[f] all the sede of Israél, for all that they haue done"; Geneva gloss: "The one and the other is impossible").

The motif of evil tools, frequently agricultural implements, meets us often enough in this legend. As a result, the action seems to be carried out in what is *technologically* an iron age. For when the Golden Age departed,

> Then men found how to snare game in toils, to cheat with bird-lime, and to circle great glades with hounds. And now one lashes a broad stream with a casting net, seeking the depths, and another through the sea trails his dripping drag-net. Then came iron's stiffness and the shrill saw-blade —for early man cleft the splitting wood with wedges; then came divers arts. Toil conquered the world, unrelenting toil. . . .[281]

The tools in Book V include the huge iron-studded "Polaxe" of Grantorto, the "bils and glayues" of his friends in France, the "huge great yron axe" of Gerioneo, the iron hooks and fishnets of Malengine, and the Soldan's scythed chariot with its "yron hookes and graples keene."[282] Other evil mechanisms include the trapfalls of Dolon and the treacherous bridge of Pollente, and the iron fetters and entrapping contract of Radigund. Gerioneo himself is such a war machine—and nearly an image of Shiva the Destroyer:

> Thereto a great aduantage eke he has
> > Through his three double hands thrise multiplyde,
> > Besides the double strength, which in them was:
> > For stil when fit occasion did betyde,
> > He could his weapon shift from side to syde,
> > From hand to hand, and with such nimblesse sly
> > Could wield about, that ere it were espide,
> > The wicked stroke did wound his enemy,
> Behinde, beside, before, as he it list apply.
>
> (V.xi.6)

Gerioneo loses two of his arms, in a significant simile, "Like fruitlesse braunches, which the hatchets slight / Hath pruned from the natiue tree, and cropped quight" (V.xi.11).

"The embattled cart," or the Armada, becomes almost literally a juggernaut, and it is also a rather specifically martial image, the image of Mars as carter.[283] The chariot is filled with military inventions ("all other weap-

---

[281] Virgil, *Georgics* I.139–146, trans. Fairclough, in Loeb *Virgil*, vol. 1, p. 91. It is worth recalling here that Talos invented the saw by copying a serpent's teeth or a fish's backbone in iron—so Comes on Calos, *Mythol.*, VII.xvi, *edn. cit.*, p. 798, and Stephanus, *Dictionarium* (Leiden, 1686), *sub* "Talus."

[282] The places are V.xii.14, ix.58, ix.5, xi.9ff., viii.42. For Malengine's gins, see Hab. 1:13–17, where it is said that the wicked "take vp all with the angle: thei catche it in their net, and gather it in their yarne" (vs. 15, Geneva Bible).

[283] In Mars' shrine in Chaucer's *Knight's Tale*, ll. 2041f., "The statue of Mars upon a carte stood / Armed, and looked grym as he were wood [mad]." For the

ons lesse or more, / which warlike vses had deuiz'd of yore," V.viii.38). From it the Soldan throws a "wicked shaft guyded through th'ayrie wyde, / By some bad spirit." The malign influence at work may well be that of Ares, the god not only of war, but also of mischance. It follows that the Soldan, armed in rusty plate (V.viii.29), is the god of arms in his iron chariot, holding the reins of war or "Of armes al the brydel."[284] According to Chaucer's description, on which one may rely here, Mars' principal temple is in Thrace,[285] and Spenser's mythography makes the Soldan a "Thracian Tyrant" (V.viii.31). But if the embattled charioteer is a Mars, he is also Mars' luckless victim, for the untoward accidents and casualties to which this god's patronage extends include the carter overridden by his cart, laid low under the wheel, and reeling ships burning on the sea.[286] Mars' affects, likewise, reach to madness,[287] as it is seen in the frenzy of the Soldan's wife. She manifests the human form of the gales that in Chaucer blow out of Mars' doors,[288] and that also overthrew the Armada.

Talus' activity also has an agricultural cast.[289] The rebels, in the wake of his flail, "lay scattred ouer all the land, / As thicke as doth the seede after the sowers hand" (V.xii.7). This comparison, coming late in the legend, may even express the hope that the sword can be beaten into the plow-share, for sowing is a "martial" image in a special sense. In the cycle of the months, March, "with brows full sternly bent," is a Mars, "armed strongly," as noted earlier:

---

medieval Mars in a peasant's heavy cart (which in the Renaissance became the battle chariot of a Roman legionary), see Seznec, *Survival of the Pagan Gods, edn. cit.*, pp. 190–194, with illustrations. In a German calendar of 1498, the labor of the month of March is illustrated by plowing; the team for the plowman's wheeled implement is driven by a plowboy with a whip. Apropos the Soldan, Mars' second zodiacal house is Scorpio; Aries and Scorpio, in the language of a Renaissance planetary iconography, are the two wheels of Mars' car. (For the images, see Von A. Schramm, ed., *Der Bilderschmuck der Frühdrucke*, vol. 7, Leipzig, 1923, *Deutsch kalender* of Johann Schaeffler, Table 111, no. 350; and *ibid.*, vol. 22, Leipzig, 1943, *Planeten-bilder, 1 Serie*, by Erhard Ratdolt, Table 29, no. 121.) The best illustration of Mars with cart and flail is Taddeo di Bartolo's wall-painting in the ante-chapel of the Palazzo Pubblico, Seina.

[284] *Knight's Tale*, l. 2009, describing the temple of Mars.

[285] *Ibid.*, l. 1972 (cf. Boccaccio, *Teseida*, VII.30).

[286] *Knight's Tale*, l. 2022.

[287] *Ibid.*, l. 2021, "Woodnesse, laughynge in his rage."

[288] *Ibid.*, ll. 1983–1986, 2422f.

[289] Given the appearance of Talos in the *Minos*, it may be significant that justice is defined there as a literal dispensation: "The farmer dispenses (*dianemei*) to each soil the seed it deserves. . . . The farmer, then, is a good dispenser (*nomeus*), and for these matters his laws and dispensations (*nomoi kai dianomai*) are right" (317). For the trans. and discussion, see Cornford, *From Religion to Philosophy*, p. 29.

Yet in his hand a spade he also hent,
And in a bag all sorts of seeds ysame,
Which on the earth he strowed as he went,
(VII.vii.32)

Thus the imagery makes Talus a *rustic* Mars, the god of husbandmen. At this point the labors of the Herculean hero would become identical with the labors of the months; this is exactly what the imagery of hatchets and tree-pruning suggests may be happening as the legend's course passes from February to March.

The lesson that technological power may be turned equally to good or evil account is illustrated by one of Spenser's most memorable episodes, that of Malengine. In the analogy with Book II, Malengine was said to occupy the place of the bands of Maleger, encountered before the Castle of Alma. Maleger himself does not actually appear until after Guyon leaves the Castle, in the place that the Gerioneo episode occupies in Book V. Malengine and Gerioneo also show some continuity, for Malengine resembles the famous thief Cacus, a villain Hercules killed on his return through Italy with Geryon's cattle. One variant, it may be noted, gives Cacus himself Geryon's three heads.[290] Cacus' story is told in the *Aeneid* by Evander, when Aeneas visits him; the story, apparently, is meant to suggest to the wandering hero that, like his earlier type Hercules, he give the old king aid against a local enemy. The mission against Malengine is undertaken under somewhat similar auspices.

Cacus in particular stole cattle, and this must have suggested him to Spenser as the type of the Irish kern, whose cattle rustling was notorious. In the *Vewe* Spenser argues that countries of nomadic cattle drovers are always found to be barbarous, and he mentions the Tartars, to whom Maleger was compared.[291] He proposes the interruption and eventual destruction of the comings and goings of this way of life, partly by means of garrisons: "As for his [the kerns'] / Create [livestock] they cannot be above grounde but they must nedes fall into their hands [the garrisons] or starve for he hath no fastenes nor refuge for them. And as for his partakers of the Moores Butlers and Cavanghes [Anglo-Irish sympathizers] they will sone leaue him when they see his fastenes and strong places thus taken from him" (3733-3737). An essential element in the plan of

[290] Propertius, IV.ix.10; so Comes, *Mythol.*, VII.i, *edn. cit.*, p. 683, "Cacus the *tricipitem* son of Vulcan." In Virgil, the defeat of Cacus is a triple effort; see *Aen.* VIII.230-232.
[291] *Vewe* 4932; II.xi.26.

Arthur and Artegall is to interpose themselves between Malengine and his cave. Malengine is very much a thief: he "robbed all the countrie thereabout"; he is "light of hand," and is armed with a long, hooked staff, "Fit to catch hold of all that he could weld, / Or in the compass of his clouches tooke" (V.ix.4–5, 11); "And of legierdemayne [sleight of hand] did know" (V.ix.13). Injustice enriches itself "by hook and crooke" (V.ii.27), and Giotto's painting of Injustice accordingly shows him holding a long pole hooked exactly like Malengine's.[292] In the classical authors, Cacus' particular trick depends on Hercules' misreading the tracks of his cattle, for the thief brings them into his dwelling backwards. There is a hint of this kind of dealing in Spenser's account of the cave:

> And all within, it full of wyndings is,
> And hidden wayes, that scarse an hound by smell
> Can follow out those *false footsteps* of his
> Ne none can backe returne, that once are gone amis.
>
> (V.ix.6)

This hiding place is another Daedalean invention, for Daedalus invented the labyrinth. We may compare the description of its recesses with the retreat of Munera:

> But Talus, that could like a limehound winde her,
> And all things secrete wisely could bewray,
> At length found out, whereas she hidden lay. . . .
>
> (V.ii.25)

Malengine being a Cacus, Talus becomes a Hercules with his lever, prying the malefactor from his cover, but also exposing the truth. Thus we read in Solinus that "when Cacus had been punished, Hercules dedicated an altar to Father Inventor, which he had promised if he found the lost cattle."[293] Talus is an *Inventor* in this additional sense, in that he is a patron of discovery and detection, and the enemy of the cunning evasions of "evil ingenuity."

The antagonist of such a Talus steals more than cattle; he is "smooth of tongue, and subtile in his tale," and with his "guilefull words" he would even steal Samient from herself (V.ix.5, 12). His fraud includes the seductive manipulation of words. We may compare Fulgentius on the evil Cacus: "This same one is double because malice is multiform, not simple. Malice harms even in a triple mode: either obviously, as the more powerful do; or subtly, as false friends; or secretly, as by an unavoidable brigand

---

[292] Arena Chapel frescoes in Padua, North Wall, bottom register. The resemblance seems striking.

[293] *Polyhistor* i.

[*impossibilis latro*]."[294] In the *Inferno,* Dante puts the thief Cacus after the hypocrites and before the false counselors; the latter suffer in "the thievish fire" (*Inf.* XXXVII.127), because they steal a man's reason. In the light of this association, it is significant that the original form of the eighth commandment may well have been, "Thou shalt not steal *a man*" (cf. Exod. 21:16). Thus Spenser's episode is characterized throughout by stealing. When Malengine tries to steal away, he violates the commandment against the furtive action in yet one more way.

Another of Malengine's types is found in Proteus—the deceptive speech and the subsequent shape-changing under pressure confirm this. Hook and net might also remind us that Proteus is the shepherd of the seas; Malengine is at least a fisherman (V.ix.11). There are traces in Malengine's legerdemain of Lucian's Proteus. Lucian, in his essay on the dance, explains Proteus' transformations as the arts of the juggler and the resourceful dancer-mime:[295]

> Vp to the rocke he ran, and thereon flew
> Like a wyld Gote, leaping from hill to hill;
> And dauncing on the craggy cliffes at will;
>
> (V.ix.15)

Proteus could symbolize man's capacity for self-transformation (in Pico's *Oration*), for playing many roles (in Vives' *Fable*), and for accommodation to the conditions of civil life (in Comes).[296] Malengine is a criminal version of these possibilities—fugitive, unaccountable, evasive, surreptitious.

Like Cacus, the Irish renegades retreated to their mountain fastness, but Talus pursues, adapting himself to the nimbleness of the goat, the speed of the fox, and the succeeding transformations as they require. The more Malengine changes, the more he declares what he is. As the shape-changer goes through his chameleonlike repertoire it becomes increasingly clear

[294] *Mitologiarum,* II.iii; in Helm edn., p. 42. For emphasis on Cacus' guile, see Virgil, *Aen.* VIII.206 (*intractatum scelerisve dolive*), 226f. (a rock overhangs his entryway, hung in iron by his father Vulcan's art); Propertius, IV.ix.10; and Martial, V.45. For the translation of his name as Latin *malum,* see Ovid, *Fasti* 551f. ("Cacus . . . to strangers and neighbours no slight *malum*"); Fulgentius, *Virgiliana Continentia,* ed. Helm, p. 105; and Servius, *ad Aen.* VIII.190.

[295] *De Saltibus* 19, cited by Comes, *Mythol.,* VIII.viii, *edn. cit.,* p. 843.

[296] Pico, *Oration* 4; Vives, *Fable* (trans. Nancy Lenkeith, in Cassirer, *et al.,* eds., *Renaissance Philosophy of Man,* p. 389); Comes, *Mythol.,* VIII.viii, *edn. cit.,* p. 845. For the canny civic Proteus, either adaptable ruler or spineless shape-shifter, see Diod. Sic., *Bibl.* I.lxii.1ff. Cartari, *Le Imagini, edn. cit.,* pp. 188f., says that Proteus' adaptations were dictated by prudence. See Julian, *Epist.* LXXIX (cited in note 66 to Chapter II, *supra*) and Libanius, *Orat.* XVIII.176, on Julian's outdoing Proteus in the number of civic functions he performed (Loeb *Libanius,* ed. Norman, vol. 1, pp. 394f.). For a negative Renaissance example, see Camoëns, *Os Lusiadas,* VII.85.

that he changes in relation to Talus. He is Talus outside the law, man the inventive tool-maker, continually discovering new shifts and weapons in the analogy of nature. That the two engines are in some sense equals is attested by Malengine's "*Sardonian* smyle"; the *risus sardonicus* was said to be on the face of the Cretan Talos when he embraced his victims. (This derivation of the phrase, along with others, is to be found in Erasmus' *Adagia*, where a substantial account of Talos is given.)[297] The transformations into bird and snake—in which form he is scotched—might recall the death of Talos the inventor. It is this series of metamorphoses that corresponds to the bestial bands of Maleger in Book II: dancing goat (in the imagery), fox, bush, bird, stone, and hedgehog.[298] Malengine thus reverts to the sterile terrain we have elsewhere associated with those demon-haunted landscapes in Isaiah. This domain was introduced with the flight of Adicia, who turned into a tigress; she makes her den here at the opening of Malengine's canto. Like the victim of Mars in Chaucer, "the carrion in the bush with the throat y-carved,"[299] Malengine's remains are "left a carrion outcast / For beasts and foules to feed vpon" (V.ix.19). He becomes one with that blasted wilderness where thorns, porcupines, satyrs, wild beasts, and birds of prey endlessly generate in the ruined strongholds of a cursed civilization.

This is perhaps the proper note on which to end a discussion of Book V. Talus is a fine instance of Spenser's "curious universal scholarship," embodying diverse traditions and bringing a unified interpretation out of them. One variant of the Talos myth records that the bronze giant was a gift from Zeus to Europa, rather than a gift to Minos.[300] Spenser does not utilize this detail, but whether we think of his invention in terms of military-industrial technology, in terms of the rule of law, or in terms of the policing of the Continent by England, Talus does indeed seem to have been an essential part of the European endowment.

[297] *Adagia, sub* "RISUS Sardonius" (edn. of Frankfurt, 1646), pp. 620–622. The sources are Suidas, *sub* "Sardanios gelous," where the phrase is said to be proverbial for those who laugh at their own destruction; Photius, *Lexicon* 500.24; Zenobius, *Cent.* V.85; scholia on *Rep.* 337a. Both Photius and Zenobius cite Simonides, *Frg.* 204.

[298] See n. 81, above, and Chap. II, "The Beginning of Idolatry," sec. ii.

[299] *Knight's Tale*, l. 2013.

[300] The variant is found in Eustathius, *Comm. on Od.* XX.302, p. 1893 (and also scholia on *Od.* XX.312), and recorded in Stephanus, *Dictionarium historicum, geographicum, poeticum* . . . (Leiden, 1686), *sub* "Talos." This Talos was fabricated by Vulcan, and Vulcan is also the father of Malengine's Virgilian counterpart Cacus (*Aen.* VIII.227).

IV

THE CONJUGATION OF THE WORLD

Since Zeus, having composed the world from opposites, led it into agreement and peace and sowed sameness in all things, and unity that interpenetrates the universe, Pherecydes used to say that when he was about to create, Zeus had changed into Eros.

(Proclus, *in Tim.* II, p. 54 Diehl; trans. adapted from G. S. Kirk and J. E. Raven, *The Presocratic Philosophers*, Cambridge, 1966, no. 55.)

To live humanly means never to escape the astonishment of one's own sex at the other, and the desire of one's sex to understand the other. . . . As they consider one another and necessarily realise that they question each other, they become mutually, not the law of each other's being (for each must be true to his particularity), but the measure or criterion of their inner right to live in their sexual distinctiveness. Man can be and speak and act as a true man only as he realizes that in so doing he must answer the question of woman, i.e., give her an account of his humanity. Much that is typically masculine would have to be left unsaid and undone, or said and done quite differently, if man remembered that in it, if it is to be truly masculine, he must prove his humanity in the eyes of woman, to whom he constitutes so great a question mark. . . . When man excuses himself from this recollection, he strengthens rather than dispels woman's natural doubt of his humanity. And the more he strengthens her doubt, and the bond of fellowship between them is therefore weakened, so much the more doubtful does his humanity become even objectively, and so much the more is humanity as such called in question for both sides. . . . Woman, too, is challenged by the natural criticism of man to prove herself human in his eyes. If she may and must live out her life as woman, she too must consider that she has to render an account to man as he must render an account to her, that she is measured by his norms as he by hers. For this reason all the movements of man and woman in which there is an open or secret attempt to escape this reciprocal responsibility are suspect at least from the very outset. . . . They are not to elude their mutual responsibility, but to fulfil it. And, of course, they must fulfil it even when no representative of the opposite sex is present. As a norm and criterion the opposite sex is always and everywhere present. The divine decision that it is not good for man to be alone has been taken irrevocably; and it applies to woman as well as to man. For both, therefore, there is only an incidental, external, provisional and transient isolation and autonomy. They elude themselves if they try to escape their orientation on one another, i.e., the fact they are ordered, related and directed to one another. Their being is always and in all circumstances a being with the other.

(Karl Barth, *Church Dogmatics*, Vol. III, *The Doctrine of Creation*, Part IV, English trans. ed. G. W. Bromily and T. F. Torrance, Edinburgh, 1961, pp. 167f.)

Friendship is a virtue, or ioyneth vertues. . . . [It] is none other thing, but a perfect consent of all things.

(William Baldwin, *A Treatise of Morrall Philosophie*, IV.iii)

The Hard Begin: Thresholds of Desire

. . . in all the affairs of man's life the first step holds the place of God himself and makes all the rest right, if but approached with proper reverence by all concerned.

(Plato, *Laws* VI, 775e, concerning the nuptial bed)

Now we also find that in some places in Italy the bride stepping beyond the paternal house lifts up her foot, and does not touch the threshold. For this practice diverse causes are assigned. It seems quite right to me, lest she possibly be hurt by magic potions, which are customarily buried under the threshold by witches, to the destruction of marriage, or harmony, or the power of generation.

("Cur limen non tangat sponsa," in J. C. Scaliger, *Poetices*, III.c, "Epithalamion," p. 352, *edn. cit.*)

ter pedis offensi signo est revocata
(Thrice was Myrrha stopped by the omen of the stumbling foot)

(Ovid, *Metam.* X.452)

> Most noble Virgin, that by fatall lore
> Hast learn'd to loue, let no whit thee dismay
> The hard begin, that meets thee in the dore,

(III.iii.21)

As in the naturall generation and formation made of the seed in the womb of a woman, the body is joynted and organized about the 28 day, and so it begins to be no more an *Embrion*, but capable as a matter prepared to its form to receive the soule, which faileth not to insinuate and innest it selfe into the body about the fortieth day; about the third month it hath motion and sense: Even so *Virginity* is an *Embrion*, an unfashioned lump, till it attain to a certain time, which is about twelve years of age in women, fourteen in men, and then it beginneth to have the soule of *Love* infused into it, and to become a *vertue:* . . .

(John Donne, Paradox XII, "That Virginity Is A Vertue")

[i]

In discussing Book I we touched on two larger principles of romance: its cyclical structure, and its dialectical characterization. We noticed that both the biblical saving history and the romance quest were redundant in structure, and that both the Simon Magus legend and the protagonist and antagonist of romance express a contest between two magics. In our dis-

429

cussion of Book III, we will consider the form these two principles take in a context that remains heroic, but has become erotic as well.

The characters that set the mood in romance are often close to nature-spirits,[1] like the satyrs in the woodland of Book I, or the water-nymphs that lead into the pleasant places of Book II. Animals with putative human sympathies, elemental spirits, and spirits per se all belong here. Spenser has many such characters in minor roles, and sometimes treats even major characters as the "spirits" of the virtues they represent. Pyrochles, for example, might be understood as an untamed fire-demon under the nominal control of Archimago, the False Florimell would be a cloud-fairy, and so forth. There is a sense in which all natural magic is also fertility magic, and this sense helps to explain why the pure or healthy kind of magic in romance is so often the magic of chastity. The impure kind of magic is of course susceptible of a sexual characterization also, and thus we find that much of what is broadly called romance—including the True Life Romance variety—dwells rather insistently upon the corrupting power of adultery. Apparently, an ideal of chastity cannot be very adequately characterized without reference to purity on the one hand, and unchastity on the other.

The varieties of chastity in romance might give us pause at the outset. A rough conspectus would begin with the identification of chastity with innocence; examples are the chastity of Una, and, less theologically, that of Shakespeare's Miranda. Somewhere in this same area of innocence is the male purity of a character like Galahad, in whom the virtue of chastity is also a physical strength. To a lesser extent this is also true of Guyon, whose continence is a part of his health. The female attribute corresponding to male strength is beauty, which may be characterized as "set apart," like the beauty of Una—hers is chiefly the beauty of holiness. Or beauty may be unadulterated and virginal, like that of Dante's Matilda in the earthly paradise, or Spenser's Belphoebe, who also enjoys an earthly paradise (II.v.40). Well within the hallowed ideal is the laudable purity of Petrarch's Laura; her sanctity is almost Christological—despite something quizzical in its being ultimately guaranteed by death. While Laura is alive its preservation is typified by the retreat of the mythical Daphne, who resisted Apollo, the god of poets laureate, and was changed into a laurel. Next comes the more clearly threatened chastity of the heroines of the Greek romances, such as that of Pericles' daughter; she prevails even in a brothel. Other examples are Joseph in the Bible, the Lady in *Comus*, and the repeatedly imperiled Fanny of *Joseph Andrews*. The corresponding characters in Spenser are Belphoebe (in the Braggadocchio episode),[2] Britomart (at the House of Busirane), and Florimell. Lighter-

---

[1] Frye, *Anatomy of Criticism*, pp. 196f.

[2] Belphoebe's flight from Braggadocchio momentarily crosses with the flight of Joseph from Potiphar's wife: compare II.iii.42, "So turned her about, and fled away

hearted instances of threatened chastity on the male side include Joseph
Andrews himself, and the Sir Gawain of *Sir Gawain and the Green
Knight*—Gawain is typically known for his appreciation of the ladies, and
his hostess in this poem can hardly believe that her husband's guest is the
same man. Again the hero's invulnerability is linked to his chastity.

Miranda is remarkable for both innocence and beauty, but she is also
specifically said to be fourteen years old, which is the same age that Shakespeare assigned to Juliet; thus her marriageability agrees exactly with her
sexual awakening. In the case of Juliet, the heroine is not technically less
chaste because of the potentially devouring carnality of her speeches; the
displacement of the salacious aspect of her anticipation to the Nurse tells
us that Juliet is still an innocent.

More obviously in the realm of experience, we have the married constancy of Odysseus' wife, Penelope, along with the Circean destruction of
the suitors that its preservation seems to entail. The traditional genealogy
makes Penelope first cousin to Helen, and the analogy between Penelope
and Circe, which Homer's poem itself urges, also suggests that married
chastity requires our adopting a kind of double perspective, if not exactly
a double standard. One thinks of Helena, in *All's Well That Ends Well*,
where the future wife doubles as her husband's whore; perhaps postnup-
tial chastity, in its differentiation from virginity, always implicitly contains
such a paradox. So, in a very different way, does the chastity of the coy
mistress; in the paradoxical, teasing, or malicious chastity of Ariosto's
Angelica, for example, unavailability or disinclination is the only real chastity involved. More explicitly specious is the chastity of the False Florimell;
her beauties are stolen from Petrarch, and her "Spright," so to speak, is a
fallen Angelica.

The narcissism properly imputed to a character like Marinell may also
be understood as a specious chastity. Marinell resembles Narcissus because
"many ladies fayre did oft complaine, / That they for loue of him would
algates dy" (III.iv.26), and because of "his too haughtie hardines" (III.iv.
24)—his pride.[3] As Ovid says of Narcissus, "Many youths and many maidens sought his love; but in that slender form was pride so hard that no
youth, no maiden touched his heart" (*Metam.* III.353ff.). Like Narcissus,
Marinell is the offspring of water folk, and he is lamented by Cymoent's
sister nymphs, as Narcissus was by his sisters the Naiades (*Metam.*
III.505f.). There is a homosexual aspect to Narcissus' love; Spenser implies
that Marinell's aversion to women may be the function of a secluding

---

apace," with Gen. 39:12ff., "he left his garment in her hand, & was fled out. . . . &
fled away, and got him out . . . & fled out" (Geneva Bible).

[3] Cf. Politian's Julio, in the *Stanze per la Giostra*, I.10: "How many nymphs sighed
for him! But the amorous nymphs could never bend the arrogant youth, nor could
his proud heart be warmed." For further on this analogy, see below, "The Analogy
of Natural Plenitude," sec. ii, *ad fin.*

parental love that is itself narcissistic, for Marinell's mother laments her "sweetest sweet" as the "Deare image of my selfe" (III.iv.39, 36). Rather differently, the last canto of Book IV shows the languishing of Marinell and Florimell, in an episode that reconstructs the myth of Narcissus and Echo.

The "friendship romance," as we will be calling it, also educes an ideal analogous to chastity. Friends are also "lovers," and their relation is hardly less exclusive. Platonic love is of course an ideal of chastity. Spenser touches on this analogy whenever Britomart in her male disguise befriends another male. The parody ideal would be homosexuality, corresponding to the narcissism just named.

Another paradoxical form of chastity is brother-sister love. It could be that such a love belongs among our images of innocence, along with the "my sister, my bride" motif of the Song of Songs. One notes the invitation into the closed paradisal garden, and the addendum concerning the virginal little sister. We may also quote the bride as follows:

> O that you were like a brother to me,
>   that nursed at my mother's breast!
> If I met you outside, I would kiss you,
>   and none would despise me.
> I would lead and bring you
>   into the house of my mother,
>   and into the chamber of her that conceived me.
>   (Song 8:1–2, Revised Standard Version)

This love might easily lend itself to a kind of parody of chastity by frustration, should the figure become literal. An example from a work already cited is the final hindrance thrown in the way of the marriage of the chaste Fanny and Joseph Andrews, when Pamela Andrews comes on the scene and Fanny is apparently revealed to be Joseph's sister too. Rather more sardonic is Thomas Mann's story, "The Blood of the Walsungs." Here the brother and sister move easily from adolescent narcissism to literal incest; the familiarities of the pair culminate during the week before the marriage of the sister to a successful bourgeois. The incestuous couple regard their intimacy as a form of purity (racial purity is implied by the story's title), and the impending marriage as a corruption of that purity. An extreme in this kind is reached in Spenser's Argante and Ollyphant; the mythic prototype of this pair may be Isis and Osiris—both have shared an incestuous womb. It could be argued that we are no longer talking about the varieties of chastity, but perhaps incest has some claim to being a kind of intentional chastity, or at least an inversion of promiscuity.

Mythography recognizes the interchangeability of narcissism and incest in one variant of the Narcissus myth itself. Typically, Narcissus' "Paramour" (III.ii.45) is merely the spectral "echo" or "shadow" of the boy's substance, but in the variant he is said to expire contemplating the death of his beloved twin sister.[4] As Carol Schreier Rupprecht has pointed out in this connection, Britomart's mirror similarly substitutes the image of the other sex for the "semblant" of the self. Such a mirror might symbolize not so much the threat of incest, as the heroine's endangerment by an ultimately imprisoning absorption in her own adolescent bisexuality.

The principals in the story by Mann, its title advises us, play out their destinies under the Wagnerian archetype of incest, namely, the love of the twins Siegmund and Sieglinde. One may compare their inspiration to that of Dante's Paolo and Francesca, whose lust is prompted by the Arthurian archetype of adultery; Spenser's Paridell and Hellenore are likewise ruled by the Homeric archetype. The romance theme of a secondhand romance might at first seem to have no more appreciable relation to chastity than incest did, but such a theme does suggest—however inadvertently —the conforming of the erotic life to an ideal. In the *Iliad* (VI.357f.) Helen says that her life is doomed to become the subject of song and story. This *imitatio* motif therefore takes shape very early: Helen envisages her own life as designing itself in the form of literature, in a surprising prolepsis of the tradition that so often invokes the authority of her example.

While discussing this tendency towards the typification of romance by romance, it is probably worth noting the kind of determination to which the copy is subject. In her famous account of the scene between Lancelot and Guinevere, Francesca retells the details incorrectly, it appears. In the book from which it is likely that the lovers are reading, it is not the knight, but the queen herself, who offers the famous corrupting kiss;[5] basically, Francesca seems no less forward. More distant images oversee the action as well. In the *Paradiso* the canto that corresponds to Francesca's in the *Inferno* will find the pilgrim in the heaven of the moon—the moon is both a pure and a mutable (or spotty) body—where Dante berths those who have broken their marriage vows to Christ.

This kind of discrepant archetype is found in a different way in the

[4] So Comes, *Mythol.*, IX.xvi, "De Narcisso," pp. 1002f., *edn. cit.*, referring to Pausanias, *Perieg.* IX.xxxi.8. Comes' account reads: "Evanthus in his *Fables* wrote that there was a twin sister for him [Narcissus], for the form of the face, and the hair, the clothes, and all the parts of the body were alike. Inasmuch as they hunted together, these made the sister beloved to the boy. Upon her death, he is said to have come to a fountain alone, and suffering from desire, gazed upon his own image there. But although that seemed somewhat of a solace, he at length perished with great desire, or, as is more pleasing to others, threw himself into the fountain and perished." I owe my knowledge of this crucial variant to Carol Schreier Rupprecht, who points out its significance for Spenser in "The Martial Maid and the Challenge of Androgeny (Notes on an Unbefriended Archetype)," in *Spring: An Annual of Archetypal Psychology and Jungian Thought* (Zurich, 1974).

[5] For the evidence, see *Parad.* XVI.13–15 and the Old French *Lancelot du Lac*, as presented and discussed in Paget Toynbee, *Dante Studies and Researches* (London, 1902), chap. I.

recent pornographic novel *The Story of O*. We would not call O's life chaste, but surely no vow of chastity could demand a greater self-abnegation. There are obvious resemblances between the house of discipline, to which O is spirited off by her lover, and a convent; O's existence is lived out under what is unmistakably the tyranny of a saint's life, in a nunnery of Venus. There are no close analogies in Spenser, though one may compare at various points the sacrifice of Amoret, the bondage enforced by Argante, and the fate of Hellenore among the satyrs.

The remainder of our conspectus must be labeled "evil chastity," allowing the Spenserian oxymoron the full force of its ambiguity. The most obvious example is a surreptitious unchastity, that is, a chastity consisting merely of appearances. The immortality of a goddess who becomes a mortal's mistress might belong here too, when the goddess' incorruption contrasts with the degradation or undoing of her partner. Age cannot wither such a goddess, but it may make her seem somewhat heartless. There are a few hints of such a contrast in Spenser's portrayal of the relation of Timias and Belphoebe. The human example of this kind of evil chastity is the untrue Guinevere, who, though not anything like a goddess, occupies an analogous social position—on her chastity depends the preservation of an entire social order. Guinevere is not chaste, but in Malory she is cold. She also gains a kind of putative chastity from Malory's studied indirection in his account of her terrible betrayal. In Spenser, the type in question must be represented by Duessa, who has affinities with Circe, in Book I, and Guinevere, in Book V. At the opening of Book I, Duessa claims to be undeflowered, and near the end of Book V she is charged with "foule Adulterie," where the accusing Ate has the place of Morgan le Fay in Malory.

The reader may well suspect that Spenser's poem contains a development similar to our conspectus. At one end of it we placed the exceptionally pure daughter of an ethical magician; at the other, the sorceress or witch who leads her lovers to their deaths. Midway in our scheme we find a chaste and beautiful girl—a Juliet, an Amoret, or perhaps a Clarissa—awakening into life and womanhood, and yet temporarily put into a deathlike trance or under an evil spell. In each case the girl is in a sense ravished, and yet no one can doubt that she also remains inviolate and pure.

Malecasta, or "evil chastity," is the name of the character with whom Britomart shares an uneasy bed in the first canto of Book III. Romance characterizes chastity dialectically, and we might take the bed in question to symbolize the idea that chastity embraces its own contrary, so to speak. The same bed reminds us that not a few beds in romance are occupied by lovers who for one reason or another are forbidden to enjoy their love, or are sundered by being brought together. Without some such rudimentary principle of a dialectical characterization of erotic energy, we cannot account for the phenomenon of a love story like that of Tristan and Iseult, where the adulterous queen has a double in the inviolate Iseult of the White Hands.[6] Spenser has a version of this motif in the story of the snowy Florimell, though in this story the moral polarities of the imagery are reversed.

Our conspectus of chastities illustrates a further point. Chastity, conceived in purely physical terms, would be merely a pagan scruple, no more binding on the spiritual liberty of a Christian than a Jewish dietary restriction; the law of charity alone might well dictate the restriction's being discarded. The taboo observed by the selfish Marinell seems like this kind of inhibition; Marinell in Book III reminds us a little of the chaste pagan Hippolytus in the same area of Book I. Further, Marinell's treasure tends to suggest that he is guilty of an avarice of seed. Avarice never gives to charity, but Charity multiplies her babes—Spenser conceives of chastity as no less fertile, or generous, than Charity. We reach a similar conclusion if we conceive of chastity as wholly spiritual, for although no physical violation could then touch or sully it, neither could any but a virtual sexuality attach to it. A chastity that only generates ideas, Spenser's treatment implies, makes a monster of its mind (see III.ii.40) and is not really more virtuous or viable than a wholly physical chastity. The truth lies somewhere between: chastity is both a spiritual virtue and a physical virtue. It recognizes the body as a temple, and analogizes its consecration to Christ with the presentation of a pure offering to the spouse (see I Cor. 6:15ff.). Conversely, Malbecco's wife Hellenore, with her adulterous eyes and corrupt intentions, presents a spouse essentially no more chaste than the woman who becomes the mistress of the licentious satyrs.

Our other principle of romance concerned its cyclical structure. The quest movement may be presented reiteratively by multiplying the questers, rather than the stations of the quest—we are familiar with this procedure from the overall plan of the poem. Book III begins with a movement designed to scatter the heroic personae in several directions, the implication being that there are many forms of chastity. Book III takes the romance initiative in the pursuit of private phantoms that are erotic distractions from the consolidating military action of the epic: the knights are scattered away from Britomart, as the questers of the larger plan are dispersed from the court of Britomart's allegorical "other," the fairy queen. This provenance for the present quest strongly enhances one's sense of Book III as marking a new beginning for the poem as a whole.

---

[6] For a discussion of this phenomenon from a rather different point of view, see Denis de Rougemont, *Love in the Western World* (Pantheon Books trans., 1956; rprnt. of New York, 1957), I.2–9, pp. 4–36.

[ii]

We said comparatively little about the Bower of Bliss in our preceding discussion of the second book. The most important thing about it for now is the transition it provides from Book II to Book III. The Bower is no doubt a temptation to dissipation of all kinds, but sexual temptation is predominant, and the hero's temperance is called upon as the basis for his chastity. In other words, the sexual nature of the heroic persona is now coming into its own. Guyon's resistance depends on willpower marshaled by reason; and chastity, as much as any of the virtues, requires purity, self-government and restraint. However, the control of natural energy is properly a prerequisite for its *use*, and Spenser's idea of chastity is closely associated in his mind with pursuit, or purposiveness. The question, then, is no longer the achievement of autonomy, but the establishment of permissible goals. In Spenser, chastity anticipates fulfillment in fruitful marriage; nevertheless, the honorable deeds of Belphoebe are equally expressions of this drive to reproduce. Belphoebe fosters both love and admiration, and like the barren woman of Wisdom 3:15, who has known no guilty bed, "she shall have fruit in the visitation of holy souls" (Douay).

The psychological archetypes for the third book come from the third Freudian phase, the genital phase. Just as the Castle of Alma represented the body as a structure for intake and elimination, so the Garden of Adonis suggests the female organs of generation. The Castle, like the Garden, possessed two gates, one for the recruitment of what would be green and raw, the other for the retirement of what has become decayed and moribund. The Garden reverses this pattern of ingress and egress; the body grows old and dies, but in the Garden the moribund return and grow young.

The virtue of chastity could hardly exist without sexual consciousness; it might therefore be described as an elaboration of the conditions surrounding the emergence of sexual impulses, which are originally directed toward the parent of the opposite sex. "Un-chastity," so to speak, is incest, in its psychogenesis. Adult chastity is also sexual attachment to a parent of the opposite sex, but the potential parent of one's own children. Failure in this phase involves perverse or paralyzing attachments, along with the inability to free one's self from a dominating parent or parental imago, or the inability to defeat the older rival of the same sex. Hence the prominence given in this legend to the Oedipal triangle, whereby an older person imprisons or incapacitates a younger person of the opposite sex. Borrowing our schemata from Erikson again, we may say that the tension between autonomy and shame from the last legend has been replaced by a tension between an enterprising initiative and guilty fixées.

The initiative is taken by Britomart, who is setting out in search of a husband. Here we may quote Erikson at some length:

> The ambulatory and infantile genital stage adds to the inventory of basic social modalities in both sexes that of "making" in the sense of "being on the make." There is no simple, stronger word to match the social modalities previously enumerated. The word suggests head-on attack, enjoyment of competition, insistence on goal, pleasure of conquest. In the boy, the emphasis remains on "making" by phallic-intrusive modes: in the girl it sooner or later changes to making by teasing and provoking or by milder forms of "snaring"—i.e., by making herself attractive and endearing. The child thus develops the prerequisite for *initiative*, i.e., for the selection of goals and perseverance in approaching them.[7]

One feels in Britomart a surplus of energy, said to be characteristic of the stage in question. Her exuberant unhorsing of various challengers suggests this, as does the fact that her drive carries her through two books, and into a third, in search of her lover. The greatly enlarged cast and wider range of characterization in this legend also may be partly attributable to this expansive quality.

With the diversification of the characters in Book III goes a certain decided imbalance, when they are taken in isolation. Britomart is capable of large emotional swings, and she seems at times precipitous and overbold. Amoret is clearly unnerved, Florimell high-strung, and Marinell obtusely self-enclosed—first in his aggressive beeline across the beach, and then in the moody aftermath of his comedown. Amoret is particularly a product of narrow ideas of femininity, which are perhaps her own: women do not enjoy sexual love, but submit to it as inferior beings, like sheep led to the slaughter; women are helpless creatures in constant need of rescue and reassurance; and women, when they "love," do so in the context of the religion of courtly love, a superstitious devotion of which they are properly the idols. One supposes that Spenser's Venus laughs at all of this as so much fantasy (IV.x.56), but it takes its toll on Amoret. It is partly Britomart's quest to free in herself the capacity to love. This theme of deliverance is found at the climax of her legend in the House of Busirane, where she is advised, on behalf of Amoret, to be bold, but not too bold.

All the women have moments when they may be described as overwrought; all the men, moments when they are unmanned. We notice that the balance in these relations is frequently restored in the following book, to which the conclusions of many stories in Book III are deferred. Without

---

[7] Erikson, *Childhood and Society*, p. 90. On the third Freudian phase and Erikson's interpretation, see *ibid.*, pp. 85–108, 251–258. Some aspects of the Eriksonian theme here are treated at greater length in Stephen Barney's essay on Books III and IV, where this passage is also cited, to similar effect.

unduly pressing this observation, one may mention that the sexual nature actually comes into its own not once, but twice in life: when the child discovers his sex and the sexuality of his parents, and again with the onset of puberty, when unchastity is for the first time a biological possibility. Chastity is thus preeminently a virtue of self-realization, simply because it coincides, as a real virtue, with "coming of age."[8] Accordingly, there is considerable logic in the sequence of events that makes Britomart meet Florimell flying from court before Britomart has wounded Marinell, even though his fall caused her flight. Florimell's sexuality appears to be of the precocious kind; thus she flies "early." Marinell is more of a late-bloomer, if not a case of arrested development; he falls "late." Britomart is able to step into the Florimell-Marinell continuum twice. Similarly, there is a large structure of recurrence at the center of the present poem, whereby the virtue of chastity achieves its natural complement in the virtue of friendship; the latter for Spenser may be defined as the virtue of proper or natural affiliation.

This doubling is not unrelated to the appearance of the poem in two installments, a "private" and a "public" one. The most obvious instance of doubling is found in the two enlargements of Amoret. The story of her courtship is told *after* the story of her deliverance from the anxiety represented by Busirane, who has the place of the father imago. Likewise, Britomart falls in love with Artegall before she meets him (when they meet, they fall in love again), and Florimell and Marinell are separated lovers before they are formally introduced. Amoret, if her name is any clue, also ought to be our symbolic child, and therefore she ought to be raised twice. In Book III she is nurtured in the Garden of Adonis with the babes; in Book IV she is transplanted to the Temple of Venus. At the Garden it is said that she is "trained vp in true feminitee" and "lessoned / In all the lore of loue, and goodly womanhead" (III.vi.51). At the Temple of

---

[8] Cf. Frye, "Structure of Imagery," in *Fables of Identity*, p. 80: "What Diana stands for is resistance to corruption, which is the beginning, and of course always an essential part of moral realization." With this I wish to combine Erikson, *Childhood and Society*, rev. ed., p. 258: "the 'oedipal' stage results not only in the oppressive establishment of a moral sense restricting the horizon of the permissible; it also sets the direction toward the possible and tangible which permits the dreams of early childhood to be attached to the goals of active adult life. Social institutions, therefore, offer children of this age an *economic ethos*, in the form of ideal adults recognizable by their uniforms and their functions, and fascinating enough to replace, the heroes of picture book and fairy tale." Britomart's continuance in the poem into later stages of it may be referred to this directedness. The exceptional span of Britomart's career is anticipated at III.iii.4, where the poet invokes the aid of Memory to recount the queen's ancestry until it issues in the queen herself, "by dew degrees and long protense." The considerable future that Britomart will have in the narrative in part reflects the length of the reign of Queen Elizabeth.

Venus she is found in the lap of the matron Womanhood, as Cupid himself is elsewhere found in the lap of Venus, in Spenser's greater genesis myth. This recurrence of sexuality will meet us once again, in our discussion of the sixth book, also decidedly erotic in character; there it is not a question of the cast in Book III coming of age in Book IV, but a question of the heroic persona of the whole poem coming of age.

The objection that the Garden of Adonis, being a realm of preexistence, can hardly symbolize later thresholds as well, fails to consider that Amoret is placed here *after* she is born. The Garden is a womb of unborn seeds, and Amoret's womanhood presumably depends in part on her identfying herself with the womanly or parental role—that is, becoming herself the womb, or "kindergarten," for other seeds. The Garden symbolizes a love that leads to matrimony, and thence to maternity.

The ideas in Book III are properly "seminal"; they are realized or materialized through a *mater*. The conception of her future lover, as it is fostered by Britomart, shows this train of thought perfectly. When Britomart hears Artegall magnified by Redcrosse, she is pleased to discover "that euer she affixed had / Her hart on knight so goodly glorified" (cf. the "transfixed" heart of Amoret at III.xiii.31, and her "wounded mind" at IV.i.7). But Britomart is also relieved that some part of her secret is "out"—an utterance shared with another:

> The louing mother, that nine monethes did beare,
> In the deare closet of her painefull side,
> Her tender babe, it seeing safe appeare,
> Doth not so much reioyce, as she reioyced there.
>
> (III.ii.11)

In other words, Britomart's love *follows* upon her submitting to the invasion of her mind by the idea of another; and it is followed *by* her submitting to the acceptable pain of pregnancy and labor. (We are to compare both the maternal joy of John 16:21, which does not remember the travail of childbirth, and the "louing side" of Chrysogonee at III.vi.27.) The mother of an idea of the beloved, Britomart inevitably becomes the idea—or fore-conceit—of a loving mother.

The theme of a young woman on the threshold of sexual consciousness makes itself felt especially in the opening cantos of Book III. We are introduced to the legend of chastity by the unhorsing of Guyon and the flight of Florimell, which indicate the so-called genital-locomotor behaviors of thrust and enticement. The flight of Florimell, one of Spenser's inspired metaphors for the nature of this virtue, is of course borrowed from Ariosto's opening canto. This has suggested that the poet, if he began *The Faerie Queene* by imitating Ariosto, must have begun here, rather than with Book I.[9] But the *artistic* reason for beginning with Ariosto, given the logic of the present poem, is to announce not an Ariostan imitation, but an Ariostan theme, the attractions and distractions of chivalric love. Doubtless Spenser thought that in the moral allegory Florimell's flight enjoined the reader to "fly fornication" (I Cor. 6:18), but his Ariostan original especially suggests a paradigm for the diversification of the one into the many that is a characteristic of the romance form of epic. In Spenser one might expect such a theme to have philosophic overtones. The connection between the flight of Florimell and the birth of the babes from the Garden might be the Neo-Platonic conception of the "descent of the soul" to the world of "generation"—in Plotinine language, the "sewing to birth."[10] Florimell's story is given a decidedly annual shape, and the Genius upon the threshold of the Garden is a Janus figure; he is the same daemon, functionally speaking, as the issue-god who gives his name to January.

The Bower of Bliss, because of its miragelike resemblance to the Garden, and its threshold position regarding Book III, ought to contain parodies of the Neo-Platonic symbolism. The ivory gate, the pseudo-genius, and the intoxicating cup offered to the initiate may all be so construed. The gate, being ivory, is the kind of gate associated with the triumph of Petrarch's Cupid, a triumph held in the vale of an isle beyond the Aegean and sacred to Venus:

> Errori e sogni ed imagini smorte
> eran d'intorno a l'arco trionfale
> e false opinioni in su le porte
> (*Trionfo d'amore*, IV.139–141)

> Errors and dreams and vain imaginings
> were gathered at his triumphal arch,
> and false opinions in his gates.

The earthly paradise in Trissino's epic—presided over by the sorceress Acratia—is specifically approached through an ivory gate.[11] The other

---

[9] For example, Josephine Waters Bennett, *The Evolution of "The Faerie Queene"* (Chicago, 1942), *passim*, esp. pp. 231–244, and J. B. Owen, "The Structure of the *Faerie Queene*," *PMLA*, 68 (1943), pp. 1079–1100, esp. pp. 1095f. Both authors believe that something in the poem wants revising, and both distinguish between Ariostan and Virgilian strata and structure. Both believe that the Ariostan material preceded the material of the first two books, but Bennett also believes this Ariostan material to have been subsequently revised, the material from the Ur-poem thereby becoming considerably confused with respect to narrative consistency. I take Book III to be just as well organized as its predecessors, but on different principles.

[10] Plotinus, *Enneads* IV, VIII.5, with *Enn.* I, VI.7.

[11] *L'Italia Liberata da Gotti*, V.155; in Trissino, *Opere* (Verona, 1729), I, p. 45.

two ingresses to Acratia's realm are by way of fountains where the traveler is offered unmanning drinks. The various cups associated with Spenser's Acrasia and Trissino's Acratia have their original in the cup of Ariosto's Alcina. Ariosto's commentator Fornari links the cup offered to Ruggiero by one of Alcina's ladies (*O.F.* X.39, 45) with the drugs of Circe, on the strong evidence of the text itself.[12] Here the *romanzi* tradition is also in agreement. Boiardo's fay Dragontina offers a cup, and she is also a "Circella."[13] Berni, in his *refacimento* of Boiardo's poem, explains the drink in terms that could have been taken from Petrarch's picture of the fantasies thronging Cupid's triumphal gate.[14] Fornari has a second explanation for Alcina's cup: it is the drink of deception or illusion offered the newborn in the *Table of Cebes*,[15] that is, a soul drink like the one in Plato's myth of Er. Since the Genius also appears in the *Table*, the link between the thresholds of the Bower and the Garden takes on a decidedly Neo-Platonic cast.

To cross that threshold is to undertake experience, however unwisely. The unborn, we are told elsewhere in English literature,

> . . . ought to be an exceedingly happy people, for they have no extremes of good or ill fortune, never marrying, but living in a state much like that fabled by the poets as the primitive condition of mankind. In spite of this, however, they are incessantly complaining; they know that we in this world have bodies, and indeed they know everything else about us, for they move among us whethersoever they will. . . . One would think that this should be enough for them; and most of them are indeed alive to the desperate risk which they run by indulging themselves in that body with "sensible warm motion" which they so much desire; nevertheless, there are some to whom the *ennui* of a disembodied existence is so intolerable that they will venture anything for a change; so they resolve to quit. The conditions which they must accept are so uncertain, that none but the most

[12] *La Spositione* (Florence, 1549–1550), II, p. 168.

[13] *Orl. Inn.* II.vi.52.

[14] Quoted below, in "Gardens of Pleasure," sec. ii, n. 192 and text.

[15] *La Spositione*, II, p. 168. Besides *Cebes' Table*, see Plato, *Phaedrus* 250a, *Rep.* X, 621; Plotinus, *Enn.* IV, III.26; Irenaeus, *Contra Haer.*, II.59; for the cup, Iamblichus, *De Myst.* III.xx; Servius, *ad Aen.* VI.725 and 743. See below, notes 257–260, on the Bacchic character of the bowl, and cf. Macrobius, *Comm. in Somn. Scip.*, I.xii.7f.: "When the soul is being drawn towards a body in this first protraction of itself it begins to experience a tumultuous influx of matter rushing in upon it. This is what Plato alludes to when he speaks in the *Phaedo* [79c] of a soul suddenly staggering as if drunk as it is being drawn into the body. . . . Another clue to this secret is the location of the constellation of the Bowl of Bacchus in the region between Cancer and Leo, indicating that there for the first time intoxication overtakes descending souls. . . ." (Trans. W. H. Stahl, New York, 1952, p. 135.)

foolish will consent to them; and it from these, and these only, that our own ranks are recruited. . . .[16]

Having resolved upon this birth, the unborn one takes a potion that obliterates memory and the sense of identity, and then "he becomes a bare vital principle": "He has but one instinct, which is that he is to go to such and such a place, where he will find two persons whom he is to importune till they consent to undertake him."[17] That is, he must find two persons who are similarly inclined to indulge themselves in that body with sensible warm motion, and who—venturing anything for a change—are willing to become parents.

[iii]

With this start on a general theory for Book III, we may examine the first three cantos of the legend to assess the emerging theme. Britomart, the only child of a king whom we never see, goes into her father's closet and finds a magic mirror, in which she sees the man she desires. In passing, one notes that the safety of the kingdom depends upon this mirror, where it often depends upon the king himself. The girl discovers herself acutely susceptible of erotic emotions, which she associates with her "bleeding bowels" (III.ii.39). She confesses her feelings to her nurse, Glauce, claiming that her "crime (if crime it be)" is atypical, since she has only fallen in love with an image—that is, entertained a fantasy. What this fantasy might be is implicit in the comparisons disavowed by Glauce:

> Daughter (said she) what need ye be dismayd,
>   Or why make ye such Monster of your mind?
>   Of much more vncouth thing I was affrayd;
>   Of filthy lust, contrarie vnto kind:
>   For who with reason can you aye reproue,
>   To loue the semblant pleasing most your mind,
>   And yield your heart, whence ye cannot remoue?
> No guilt in you, but in the tyranny of loue.
>
> Not so th'*Arabian Myrrhe* did set her mind;
>   Nor so did *Biblis* spend her pining hart,
>   But lou'd their natiue flesh against all kind, . . .
>   (III.ii.40–41)

The distracted heroine takes to her bed, while her owlish companion keeps nocturnal watch. "Nor herbes, nor charms, nor counsell" (III.iii.5) avail to dispel the new fixée, and a consultation with Merlin is sought,

---

[16] Samuel Butler, *Erewhon*, chap. 19, "The World of the Unborn" (New York, 1927), p. 183.
[17] *Erewhon, edn. cit.*, p. 189.

> Least that it should her turne to foule repriefe
> And sore reproch, when so her father deare
> Should of his dearest daughters hard misfortune
> heare.
>
> (III.iii.5)

The pair venture forth to Merlin's cave, hesitate without, and then, daring to "offend," make "entrance bold" through his "darkesome dore"—"with loue to frend" (III.iii.14-15). There is some reluctance to discuss the problem, but Merlin penetrates Britomart's attempt at anonymity:

> The doubtfull Mayd, seeing her selfe descryde,
>   Was all abasht, and her pure yuory
>   Into a cleare Carnation suddeine dyde;
>   As faire *Aurora* rising hastily,
>   Doth by her blushing tell, that she did lye
>   All night in old *Tithonus* frosen bed
>   Whereof she seemes ashamed inwardly.
>
> (III.iii.20)

In the light of the allusions to Myrrha and her father, the comparison is rather diagnostic. Britomart's reaction to Merlin, psychoanalytic interpreters would point out, exhibits the phenomenon known as transference.

Britomart merely blushes, but the imagery just quoted makes the color change rather more intense. Such a change, associated with Britomart on three further occasions, comes to signal an irreversible metamorphosis into sexual consciousness. One may compare the flower in *A Midsummer Night's Dream*, which is changed from white to red when it is struck by Cupid's arrow. In an elegiac context this flower would be identical with the mulberry stained by the blood of Pyramus; in Spenser, the comparable symbolism attaches to the transmutation of Adonis.

Merlin advises Britomart to accept her new role—"do by all dew meanes thy destiny fulfill"—and shows her the line destined to emerge from her marriage. This progeny culminates in a "royall virgin" with a white rod, and the Isis toward whom the progress of the poem carries the heroine—and with whom her symbolism finally merges—is also identified by this white rod. Merlin's prophecy in Book III corresponds to that of Contemplation in Book I, and the early and late placing of the respective predictions tells us something about the differences between the two virtues for which the prophets speak. The holiness that will make Redcrosse a saint is a transcendent virtue, while the chastity that will make Britomart a mother is an immanent virtue. Hence Merlin can advise Britomart simply to accept a natural development, in spite of the accompanying efflorescence of fantasies. It is her fortune to fall in love; and falling in love, in terms of our comparison, is a *fortunate* fall.

The presence of Redcrosse in the first canto here brings us back to the subject of the initiative for Britomart's quest. Even without the Malecasta episode, Britomart's insomnia recalls the troubled sleep of the earlier hero at the House of Archimago:

> And if that any drop of slombring rest
> Did chaunce to still into her weary spright
> When feeble nature felt her selfe opprest,
> Streight way with dreames, and with fantastick sight
> Of dreadfull things, the same was put to flight,
> That oft out of her bed she did astart,
> As one with vew of ghastly feends affright:
> Tho gan she to renew her former smart,
> And thinke of that faire visage, written in her hart.
>
> (III.ii.29)

Thus the fantasizing of the erotic life in Book III offers a parallel for the genesis of idolatry in Book I. We can compare Archimago's creation of the false Una with the origination of Merlin himself in Book III. Merlin was "begotten . . . By false illusion of a guilefull spright / On a faire Lady Nonne . . . daughter to Pubidus" (III.iii.13; cf. Latin *pubes, pubidis,* "adult"). Such an Archimagesque generation might give Merlin a rather apocryphal relation to chastity; along with Merlin's entrapment underground by the seductive Lady of the Lake, it offers commentary on the ultimate sterility of mere suggestibility.

Britomart now takes up arms, and enters both the poem and fairyland at the same time, leaving behind the realm of her father and becoming her own man, so to speak. After the initial encounters with Guyon and Florimell, she meets Redcrosse, who is beset by the six knights of Castle Joyous. Champions of Malecasta, the knights represent the forces of seduction—a seduction that would involve Redcrosse's dividing his loyalty to Una. Britomart frustrates their attempt on the faithful knight, and the rubric for the canto informs us that "Duessaes traines," as well as Malecasta's knights, "are defaced" here. Duessa, in fact, never appears in the canto. The canto does, however, depict the nocturnal visit of an unchaste woman in a scarlet robe to the bed of the sleeping heroic persona, and we can hardly doubt that in some obscure way Duessa is present here, just as she was in the first canto of Book I.

Malecasta's walls depict the legend of Adonis,

> Deadly engored of a great wild Bore,
> And by his side the Goddesse groueling
> Makes for him endlesse mone, and euermore
> With her soft garment wipes away the gore,
> Which staines his snowy skin . . .
>
> (III.i.38)

444

Malecasta is smitten by the fairness of her guest, and, taking Britomart to be something of an Adonis herself, approaches in the dead of night to offer her services in the part of Venus. She lies down beside the disarmed maid. Britomart awakens, and, fearing the worst, "She lightly lept out of her filed bed, / And to her weapon ran, in minde to gride / The loathed leachour" (III.i.62). We note a subtle exchange here: Britomart has now made the same mistake about Malecasta that Malecasta has made about Britomart. Each believes *the other* to be *a male*. Malecasta's outcry summons assistance on both sides, Redcrosse arriving to remind us of his original encounter with the false Una. In the ensuing scuffle Britomart receives an arrow wound from Gardante:

> The mortall steele stayed not, till it was seene
> To gore her side, yet was the wound not deepe,
> But lightly rased her soft silken skin,
> That drops of purple bloud thereout did weepe
> Which did her lilly smock with staines of vermeil
> steep.
>
> (III.i.65)

This light wound expresses the extent of Britomart's vulnerability. We are to contrast it with the condition of Amoret in the last canto. Amoret, being Love, seems to be all wound; her very heart is exposed and taken from her in the Masque of Cupid. Amoret's oppressor inadvertently wounds Britomart as well, and the Adonis imagery is carefully repeated:

> From her, to whom his fury first he ment,
> The wicked weapon rashly he did wrest,
> Vnawares it strooke into her snowie chest,
> That little drops empurpled her faire brest.
>
> (III.xii.33)

The wound is "unawares," we may suppose, because Busirane preys on women, and Britomart, though she appears to Busirane to be a knight, is a woman. Conversely, Malecasta preys on men. It is less obvious what particular erotic susceptibility is symbolized by the wound Britomart takes in her domain.

Two themes that we have already mentioned stand out here: the theme of a sexual awakening involving Oedipal fantasies, and the theme of adopting a sexual role and goal that will lead to one's replacing one's own parent.[18] That is, one becomes the parent of one's own children, but also, with the adoption of the parental role, the parent from one's own childhood. Britomart expends considerable care on her charge, Amoret, thus

---

[18] Lewis, I take it, is not quite right, where he says that "The only thing Spenser does not know is that Britomart is the daughter of Busirane—that his ideal of married love grew out of courtly love." (*Allegory of Love*, Oxford, 1938, p. 341.)

anticipating her future role as a mother. A third theme, so far not mentioned, is also present in the Malecasta episode, namely, a theme of "gender clarification."

These themes are more explicit in Spenser's sources, which he has somewhat chastened, so to speak. The relation of Britomart to her nurse has been imitated from the *Ciris*, a quasi-Ovidian epyllion formerly attributed to Virgil.[19] This poem is haunted by the example of Ovid's story of Myrrha, who slept with her father. The heroine of the *Ciris*, Scylla, approaches the same paternal bed, though only to secure a lock of her father's crimson hair, in which resides the safety of the state and her father's power on the field of battle. The girl has fallen in love, not with her father, but his enemy, King Minos, to whom her father refuses to give her in marriage. The lock of hair, then, corresponds to the mysterious mirror to which Spenser's Britomart is said to be "hayre" (III.ii.22); the lock suggests a talisman of potency. The same poem makes the girl's nurse the mother of one Britomartis, whom King Minos had once attempted to outrage. This Britomartis escaped from Minos by fleeing to the sea; other accounts of her tell us that her flight ended in a fishing smack.[20] Thus one part of the Britomartis story appears in the flight of Spenser's Florimell; fleeing from a lustful beast, she ends up in the same situation.

Being an ideal beauty, and therefore a descendant of Petrarch's Laura, Florimell is compared to Daphne; but being an aspect of the chastity of Britomartis—an earlier and purer Scylla—she is also compared to the impure and criminal Scylla, or Myrrha:

> Not halfe so fast the wicked Myrrha fled
> From dread of her reuenging fathers hond:
> Nor halfe so fast to saue her maidenhed,
> Fled fearefull *Daphne* on th'*Ægaean* strond,

[19] For example, III.ii.47, "The drunken lampe downe in the oyle did steepe," freely renders *Ciris* 344: "inverso bibulum restinguens lumen olivo." Ovid implies that the story of the *Ciris* is his kind of subject at *Amores* III.xii.21f.

[20] Pausanias, *Perieg.* II.xxx.3; Callimachus, *Hymn* III.189–200; Comes, *Mythol.*, III.viii, *edn. cit.*, p. 262; Giraldus, *Hist. Deorum*, Syntag. XII, on *Op. om.*, I, col. 365G (where the name Britomartis, following Solinus, is interpreted *dulcis virgo*); Antoninus Liberalis, *Fab.* 40, as cited by Emil Koeppel in his article, "Spenser's Florimell und die Britomartis-Sage des Antoninus Liberalis," in *Herrig's Archiv*, 107 (1901), pp. 394–396, summarized in the Variorum *Works, Book III*, pp. 332f.: the sea-peril of Britomartis-Dictynna in *Ciris* 294–305 appears in that aspect of Britomart represented by Florimell. A significant variant of the myth appears in Boccaccio, *G.D.G.*, II.xxxv, "De Brictona Martis VIIII^a filia" (Romano edn., vol. 2, p. 477), where the virgin vowed to perpetual virginity is a daughter of Mars. She is "Britona" in the Italian translation of Boccaccio, and "Bryten, Martis filiam," in the 2nd Vatican Mythographer (in Bode, ed., *Scriptores rerum mythicarum latini*, II.26, p. 83). Spenser, who makes Britomart a "mayd martiall" (III.iii.53), must know this tradition, for reasons that will emerge below, in "Heroic Eros," sec. i.

As Florimell fled from that Monster yond,
To reach the sea, ere she of him were raught:
For in the sea to drowne her selfe she fond
Rather then of the tyrant to be caught:

(III.vii.26)

Although Spenser has taken Glauce's reference to Myrrha from the *Ciris* (238f.) (Myrrha having made a monster of her mind as Scylla, Britomart, and Florimell have not) he has nonetheless imitated Ovid's story as well. In the first canto Florimell is "chased" by a "griesly Foster"; other uses of the word "foster" make it mean a parent, in which case *this* parent would be the father who chases Myrrha—the aroused Cinyras. Further, there are broad hints of Myrrha's passion in the nocturnal fraud of Malecasta. The midnight hour and the cosmic backdrop suggest Ovidian originals (cf. III.i.57–59 and *Metam.* X.368–372, 446f.), and Britomart goes for her sword, as King Cinyras, discovering the filial identity of his bedmate, goes for his. Ovid is telling his story in connection with the birth of Myrrha's child Adonis, who otherwise appears in Malecasta's tapestry. Venus falls in love with Adonis owing to a glancing chest-wound from Cupid's arrow (*Metam.* X.525f.). Thus Malecasta's tapestry, the attraction toward illicit nocturnal congress, and the wound from Gardant's arrow, all suggest the same complex in Ovid.

Besides the resemblances between Myrrha and Malecasta, there are resemblances between Myrrha and Britomart. As we have seen, the Scylla of the *Ciris* is partly a Myrrha and partly a Britomartis. Particularly analogous are the speeches of Britomart's and Myrrha's nurses (III.ii.30–36; *Metam.* X.395–418); the nurses both command healing charms, herbs, and magic rites. Even Britomart's seemingly idiosyncratic line, "my crime (if crime it be)," reflects the prayer of Ovid's lovesick Myrrha: "scelerique resistite nostro, / si tamen noc scelus est" (resist this crime in us, if indeed this is a crime [*Metam.* X.322f.]). The same equation authorizes a set of resemblances between the situations of Britomart and Malecasta. Britomart sleeps in the same bed as her nurse, makes the nurse's rest uneasy, and leaps out of this "loathed nest" as she leaps out of her "soft fethered nest" with the "loathed leachour" (III.ii.30; i.58, 62). And where Malecasta ministers to Britomart, so does the nurse (cf. "She softly felt, if any member mooued" with "She softly felt, and rubbed busily"—III.i.60, ii.34).

A second story of frustrated passion to which Spenser seems to have had recourse is the tale of Ricciardetto, told in the twenty-fifth canto of the *Furioso.* The story is a kind of fabliau on the theme of Iphis and Ianthe. Ariosto in fact echoes Ovid's verses in the monologue of Fiordispina.[21]

---

[21] See *Metam.* IX.726–744, comparing *O.F.* XXV.35–37, for the imitation. Ovid's story is as follows. Iphis, raised as a boy, but actually an unwanted girl in disguise—

This lady conceives a passion for Bradamante at a point when the latter appears to be a knight in arms. Behaving much like Malecasta, she loses no time in communicating her desires; but Bradamante, unlike the naive Britomart, apprises the enamored one of her mistake, and attempts to divert the passion, which has become quite fixed despite the inappropriateness of its object. Again there is a reference (*O.F.* XXV.36) to Ovidian examples of perverse passions, including Myrrha's. Bradamante is persuaded to spend the night in the castle of the family of the lovesick maid, and the two share a bed made restless by the afflicted party. In the morning the embarrassed lady knight gladly departs. Spenser apparently ceases to follow the story at this point; it goes on to recount how Ricciardetto, Bradamante's scapegrace twin, returns in his sister's place, and, once in bed with the lady, reveals a sexual metamorphosis highly gratifying to both parties. But here, quite unexpectedly, one may compare Spenser's "She softly felt, if any member moooued," with Ariosto's "she found with her hand the express truth. . . . She touched and saw she had what she so much desired" (III.i.60; *O.F.* XXV.66–67). Ariosto allows the fraud to continue for several months, until it is discovered by the pregnant Fiordispina's outraged family. Though the point need not be overstressed, the rather confused attractions in Spenser's opening canto do suggest the theme of sorting out the sexual identity of the heroine.[22] Perhaps the fear of incest and female homosexuality in Spenser's sources (however lightly treated) accounts for the feeling in the opening canto that the dangers that hedge chastity are *unconscious* dangers, which take one by surprise. In what is almost her last appearance, Britomart is found in a bedroom (in Book V), where she is mistaken for her male counterpart, Artegall. She is the guest of Dolon—that is, she is still endangered by a bedroom fraud.

We are told that there is a period in the Oedipal phase when little girls temporarily want to be little boys, and Britomart's disguise might well remind us of this.[23] In itself, the disguise merely symbolizes the adoption of a

the fraud includes her being given a name of common gender (*Metam.* IX.710f.)— is betrothed to the beautiful Ianthe, whom Iphis passionately desires to possess. On the day before her wedding she goes to Isis' temple to pray to the goddess for help; the goddess is moved, and upon leaving the temple the girl is transformed into a boy. Britomart also visits Isis' temple, before her reunion with Artegall, where she receives a sign of the goddess' favor, and dreams of a metamorphosis that in part identifies her with the male Osiris.

[22] Cf. Alpers, in *Poetry of "The Faerie Queene,"* p. 185, where he is discussing Ariosto's description of the divided mind of Fiordispina as she contemplates the dual sexuality of Bradamante at *O.F.* XXV.33: "Rather than presenting her as suffering a special fate because of the circumstances of her case, he presents these circumstances as if they were part of the oscillations of hope and despair that occur in any of love's victims." It is not actually a case of "rather than": Ariosto has it both ways.

[23] *Three Contributions to the Theory of Sex*, in *Basic Writings of Sigmund Freud*, trans. A. A. Brill (New York, 1938), p. 565, and "Some Psychical Consequences of

truculent exterior; but that exterior is one that secures the heroine an equality with the other sex. Britomart's irritability also partly derives from Spenser's conception of chastity as the specifically human form taken by natural energy. Dealing with this energy makes Britomart rather intense, if not actually fractious; its more extreme effects on Florimell and Amoret are an uncontrollable flight and a paralyzing fixation.

These extremes are modulated in Britomart—and in responses to Britomart—partly because she herself is not polarized by sexuality. Rather, she is polarized *as* sexuality:

> . . . shee was full of amiable grace,
> And manly terror mixed therewithall,
> That as the one stird vp affections bace,
> So th'other did mens rash desires apall,
> And hold them backe, that would in error fall;
>
> (III.i.46)

In this description, Spenser takes from the Italian virago-type the idea of a superior economy of wrath and charity that is metaphorically androgynous. Britomart may not have the curling lip of a Bradamante, but subsequent events do show her to be all care and concern toward her beloved, and much correction and reproof—and little tolerance—toward weaker natures.

It is significant for the virago characterization that Ariosto's Bradamante and his Marfisa both have brothers who are their twins (Ricciardetto and Ruggiero respectively). Britomart, as we have seen, is a complex "double" too: she is "male" to Malecasta, her evil counterpart, and "female" to Artegall, her semblant in the mirror; later she will enter on a rivalry with a mannish woman—Radigund—who emasculates her future husband. As Carol Schreier Rupprecht points out, the relations of Marfisa, Bradamante, and Ruggiero may be understood as those of rival selves competing for dominance within a basically androgynous sexual nature; the same explanation may be offered for the character of Britomart. The more superficial diagnosis, that Britomart is basically a transvestite, is perhaps better reserved for the sprite whom the witch decks in the clothes left behind by Florimell. This impersonator is definitely male, and he seems to be a very mincing sort of fellow—"he in counterfeisance did excell, / And all the wyles of wemens wits knew passing well" (III.viii.8). Such a creature might well be rather indifferent to a lover, and there is a sense in which his self-sufficiency parodies the independence of the heroine.

---

the Anatomical Distinction Between the Sexes," in Freud, *The Standard Edition*, vol. 19 (London, 1925), pp. 248–258; also Robert Fliess on female inferiority feelings, in *Erogeneity and Libido: addenda to the theory of the psychological development of the human* (New York, 1967), pp. 147–150, 171–176.

The verses quoted above, describing Britomart's effect, also suggest that her chastity casts a magic circle or *temenos* about her; the invulnerability that her virtue confers is otherwise symbolized by her enchanted lance. The preserved area appears in a number of parietal symbols that modulate the threshold symbol. The most important of these symbols is the barrier of fire that seals off Amoret from her lover, Scudamour. Amoret is the sleeping beauty of the Brunhilde myth, as it were, to whom only a sufficiently pure champion is able to gain access. Spenser compares Britomart to a rose hedged by thorns (III.i.46), which reminds us of the fairytale version of the same myth. The triple circle with which Glauce somewhat unintentionally seals off her charge repeats the symbolism in a more jocose form. There may also be a fire barrier at the end of the first canto, where Britomart lays about her with a "flaming sword": "Here, there, and euery where about her sawyd / Her wrathful steele" (III.i.66). In Book III, of course, a virgin is a paradisal *hortus conclusus*, and the original closed garden was also sealed off by a fiery revolving sword. In Dante this same fire barrier is specifically mediated by an angel of chastity, and the beloved is met beyond it.

The theme of crossing a sexual threshold is implied in each of the clashes of Britomart in Book III. Nowhere is the motif of trespass stronger than in the Busirane episode, where the heroine invades the fullest field of demonic force; she invades Love itself, which, according to Diotima in the *Symposium*, is a great demon. Busirane, as a magician, has conjured this demon. Busirane is also a father figure, and thus his porch ought to recall the "threshold of the chamber" that Cinyras' daughter trod (*Metam.* X.456, "thalami iam limina tangit"—note the possibly technical use of "chamber" at III.i.62). The "monstrous enmity" that the advance of Scudamour and Britomart provokes "Enforced them their forward footing to reuoke" (III.xi.22, 21); their retreat seems to echo Ovid's "ter pedis offensi signo est revocata," the signal of the "offended" foot that thrice revokes the advancing Myhrra (*Metam.* X.452; cf. III.iii.14f.).

Britomart refuses to abandon Scudamour's quest "without venturing," dreading "enterprised prayse . . . to disauaunce" (III.xi.24). In her two remaining clashes the emphasis also falls on this forward and antagonistic quality; she will not be deflected. In the Marinell episode she dares to cross the "pretious shore," apparently flooring a previously unsusceptible bachelor. In what one takes to be an erotic image, Marinell is spilled among his accumulated wealth with a wound like that of Adonis—though his "pearles and pretious stones" (III.vv.18) may suggest that his vulnerability more properly belongs to Onan. Marinell's charge across the beach also gives him something of the character of a spent wave. The collision seems in part to be precipitated by Britomart's extreme moodiness. At the time she is in a particularly stormy state of mind. The seashore marks a threshold for Florimell also; the goring of her horse and the loss of her cestus there anticipate the subsequent assault upon her virginity by the fisherman and Proteus.

Britomart's later encounter with Paridell, the seducer, is actually accompanied by a storm. In this case the clash is the result of a quarrel outside the closed gates of the castle of the jealous Malbecco. Both knight and lady knight are overturned, which might suggest that the upcoming contest between chastity and adultery could go either way; a further meaning is that jealousy is inimical to both, for Britomart and Paridell now make common cause against Malbecco. Malbecco has denied a whole group of knights shelter in his castle because he fears for the virtue of his young wife, Hellenore. All the knights resolve to fire the gates, which makes this threshold rather like the entrance to the Castle of Jealousy in *The Romance of the Rose*, under the assault of Love's barons.[24] That the castle is to be associated with the cloistered virtue of Malbecco's wife the following comparison makes clear:

> No fort so fensible, no wals so strong,
> But that continuall battery will riue,
> Or daily siege, through dispuruayance long,
> And lacke of reskewes will to parley driue;
> And Peece, that vnto parley eare will giue,
> Will shortly yeeld it selfe, and will be made
> The vassall of the victors will byliue:
> That stratageme had oftentimes assayd
> This crafty Paramoure, and now it plaine displayd.
>
> (III.x.10)

In an image that conflates the whole cycle of the Trojan War, Malbecco admits the knights as the Trojans admitted the Trojan horse, and the crafty Paridell fires Hellenore's libidinous desires, as the Greeks fired Troy.

At both the castle of Malecasta and the castle of Malbecco Britomart's beauty is revealed, once she is inside. This motif, the epiphany of the triumphant virago, is taken from the Italians, and it will appear twice more in the following legend.[25] It occurs in connection with Britomart's military

[24] Ll. 20667ff., in the trans. of Harry W. Robbins, ed. Charles Dunn (New York, 1962). My references throughout are to line numbers of this translation.

[25] The word epiphany is partly suggested to me by the Homeric *Hymn to Athena* (Hymn XXVIII in the Loeb edn.), where the astonishment and tumult caused in heaven by the newborn goddess is ended when she removes her heavenly armor from her shoulders. Even more suggestive, however, is a passage from Quintus Smyrnaeus' *Fall of Troy*, I.656–668, which Carol Rupprecht cites in the study referred to in n. 4, above. The passage describes the events after Achilles has killed the Amazon Penthesileia: "Now from her head he plucked / The helmet splendour flashing like the beams / Of the great sun, or Zeus' own glory-light. / Then, there

encounters, for she stands in the same relation to her rash antagonists as to her abashed admirers. In Spenser the motif derives its importance from the theme of Britomart's emergence as a woman, out of the shadows of girlhood: Britomart "vented vp her vmbriere" (III.i.42) at the outset of her legend. *Epiphany* would seem to be the right word here, for the motif in Spenser always entails three ideas: the manifestation of new or prodigious light, the equation of the heroine with a divine being, and the securing of devotion.

Heroic Eros

Hermogenes: . . . but what is the meaning of the word *hero* (*hēros*, in the old writing *heros*)?

Socrates: I think that there is no difficulty in explaining, for the name is not much altered, and signifies that they were born of love.

Hermogenes: What do you mean?

Socrates: Do you not know that the heroes are demigods?

Hermogenes: What then?

Socrates: All of them sprang either from the love of a god for a mortal woman, or of a mortal man for a goddess. Think of the word in the old

---

as fallen in dust and blood she lay, / Rose, like the breaking of the dawn, to view / 'Neath dainty-pencilled brows a lovely face, / Lovely in death. The Argives thronged around, / And all they saw and marvelled, for she seemed / Like an Immortal. In her armour there / Upon the earth she lay, and seemed the Child / Of Zeus, the tireless Huntress Artemis / Sleeping, what time her feet forwearied are / With following lions with her flying shafts / Over the hills far-stretching. She was made / A wonder of beauty even in her death / By Aphrodite glorious-crowned, the Bride / Of the strong War-god, to the end that he, / The son of noble Peleus, might be pierced / With the sharp arrow of repentant love." (Trans. Arthur S. Way, Loeb edn., p. 55.) The Aldine text of this poem, composed in the fourth century, was published in 1504. Rupprecht is surely right in seeing here a remarkable anticipation of the Italian motif, and the mythology especially reminds us of Britomart: the incarnation of Venus triumphing over Mars, the enamoring of Achilles by Penthesileia, and the comparison to Diana. Examples in the *romanzi* are Ariosto, *O.F.* XXXII.79f., Bradamante at the Castle of Tristram (= Britomart at the Castle of Malebecco; cf. *F.Q.* III.ix.20); Boiardo, *Orl. Inn.* III.v.40–42, the enamoring of Ruggiero (= enamoring of Artegall; cf. *F.Q.* IV.vi.19ff.); Pulci, *Morgante Maggiore*, III.17, the revelation of an enemy virago to Orlando when he pierces her armor; Tasso, *Ger. Lib.* IV.28–30, the revelation of Armida, who is compared to a comet (cf. *F.Q.* III.l.16 and IV.i.13). For an essay on the transformations of this motif, which points rather to the Virgilian prototype in Book I of the *Aeneid*, see A. Bartlett Giamatti, "From Magic to Miracle," in Herschel Baker, ed., *Four Essays on Romance* (Cambridge, Mass., 1971), pp. 15–31.

Attic, and you will see better that the name *heros* is only a slight alteration of Eros, from whom the heroes sprang.

(Plato. *Cratylus* 398c–d, trans. Jowett)

the loveris maladye / Of Hereos
(Chaucer, *The Knight's
Tale*, 1373–1374)

The fatall purpose of diuine foresight,
Thou doest effect in destined descents,
Through deepe impression of thy secret might,
And stirredst vp th'Heroes high intents
(III.iii.2, on the Ancients' attribution of
divinity to Love)

[i]

The epiphany of Venus constitutes a major motif for the whole of *The
Faerie Queene*. In Book I there is Charissa, accompanied by her doves and
putti; even though she hates Cupid's snare as she hates hell, she fosters in
her progeny the Christian form of that emotion which she otherwise repre-
hends. Belphoebe in Book II does not at first remind us of Venus, but
rather of that virginal Diana to whom Horace dedicates the blood of a
wild boar that is just aiming its first sidelong thrust (*Odes* III.22); Belphoebe carries a boar spear and uses a bow and arrow. In Book III, however, she renounces love only to arouse it, and both her gait and her laurel
and myrtle bower might tell us that she is a Venus incognito, like Virgil's
goddess at the opening of the *Aeneid*, who appears as a huntress and a
nymph of Diana. (Spenser also applies to Belphoebe a comparison of Dido
to Diana: all the Tyrian girls, Venus explained to Aeneas, dress as Venus
does—that is, like Diana.)[26] The Venus armed with a quiver and a bow
might suggest the attraction and incitement of frigid beauty,[27] and such
a figure, as a passage in Bembo's *Gli Asolani* reminds us, is not far removed
from Petrarchan erotic convention:

[26] *Aen.* I.336f.; *F.Q.* II.iii.31. Belphoebe's first appearance—to Braggadocchio—
also depends on Dido's first appearance to Aeneas, *Aen.* I.498–502, Dido being Elissa,
and hence Elizabeth. For the comparable Homeric echo, see "Perpetual Generations,"
sec. v, below, where Belphoebe and Braggadocchio are equated with Nausicaa and
Odysseus.

[27] See André Chastel, "Diana and Venus" and "The Eros of Frigid Beauty," in
The Crisis of the Renaissance 1520–1600, trans. Peter Price (Skira, Geneva, 1968),
pp. 148–158; Edgar Wind, *Pagan Mysteries in the Renaissance*, rev. edn. (New York,
1968), pp. 77–79. For the first Venus-Diana modulation in *The Faerie Queene*, see
I.vi.16.

Who cannot in a moment convert his ladylove into an archeress who wounds men with the pointed arrows of her eyes? a thing which the ancients perhaps more slily feigned when they would often speak of huntresses and of their woodland prey, by lovely nymphs intending lovely women who with the barbs of penetrating glances slew the hearts of savage men.[28]

Julio, in Politian's *Stanze*, accordingly addresses the nymph he comes upon while hunting a doe put in his way by Venus: "Whatever you are, sovereign virgin, nymph, or goddess (but certainly you seem a goddess to me); if a goddess, perhaps you are my Diana; if mortal, tell me who you are, for your appearance surpasses human nature."[29] A poem in the *Greek Anthology* lends slight classical authority to this interpretation of Venus as Diana. The subject is the so-called Lacedaemonian or Spartan Venus, who was said to be armed: "Cypris has ever learnt to carry a quiver and bow, and to ply the far-shooting archer's craft. Is it from reverence for the laws of warlike Lycurgus that, bringing her love-charms to Sparta, she comes clad in armour for close combat?"[30] The venery of Venus appears in the *Romance of the Rose* when Venus hunts with Adonis (ll. 15671ff.), and later when she tucks up her skirts and shoots her bow against the Tower of Shame, whose columns rather resemble the legs of Belphoebe (ll. 20785ff., 21248ff.).

The figure who mediates the Venus-Diana opposition in Spenser is obviously Britomart; her name is one of Diana's,[31] and Glauce, her nurse, bears the name of a mother of Diana.[32] Britomart's iconographical prototype, on the other hand, is the variation of Venus we have just met, the figure otherwise known as *Venus armata*. In his notice of the *armata* epithet for Venus, Giraldus cites Quintillian to the effect that the armed or Lacedaemonian Venus—who is also found in Pausanias—provided a stock subject for the student of rhetoric to practice on.[33] The *Greek Anthology* has a

---

[28] Trans. Rudolf Gottfried (Urbana, Ill., 1957), p. 87.

[29] *Stanze per la Giostra*, I.45.

[30] *Gr. Anth.* XVI.173, trans. by W. R. Paton in the Loeb edn., vol. 5, p. 259.

[31] See the references in n. 20, above. The Britomartis-Dictynna of *Ciris* 294–305 is not, of course, Diana herself, but one of Diana's nymphs. Giraldus, *Hist. Deorum*, Syntag. XII, in *Op. om.*, I, col. 366C, cites Phavorinus for Britomartis as the cognomen of Diana. (For the epithet Dictynna, see *ibid.*, cols. 365G–366E.) Britomartis is Diana in Solinus, *Polyhistor* xv, where the name is interpreted to mean *virginem dulcem*.

[32] Cicero, *De Nat. Deo.* III.xxiii.58, mentioned by Giraldus, *Hist. Deorum*, Syntag. XII, in *Op. om.*, I, col. 356E.

[33] Giraldus, *Hist. Deorum*, Syntag. XIII, in *Op. om.*, I, col. 394C–F. Quintillian, *Institut.* II.iv.26. (Armed Venuses are mentioned in Pausanias at II.v.1, III.xv.10, xxiii.1.) See Cartari, *Le Imagini* (Venice, 1625), pp. 397–399.

collection of examples, the most important of which ranks, according to Hutton, as the thirteenth most translated poem of the collection. The original reads:

> Pallas, seeing Cytherea in arms, said "Cypris, wouldst thou that we went to the judgment so?" But she, with a gentle smile, answered "Why should I lift up a shield in combat? If I conquer when naked, how will it be when I arm myself?"[34]

Ausonius' Latin version doubtless helped give the poem its wide currency.[35]

Comes cites a nearby poem from the *Anthology* to explain the type of the *Venus victrix*,[36] who is also recorded in Giraldus:[37] "Leonidas said that armed Venus to have armed among men in vain, since she had conquered the god of war himself, even Mars, in the nude."[38] Comes' linking of the Roman goddess of victory with the armed Venus merely underlines what seems to be implicit in the sources, namely, the treatment of Venus as a Mars: "Cypris belongs to Sparta too," explains another *Anthology* piece, "but her statue is not, as in other cities, draped in soft folds. No, on her head she wears a helmet instead of a veil, and bears a spear instead of golden branches. For it is not meet that she should be without arms, who is the spouse of Thracian Ares and a Lacedaemonian."[39] Yet another epigram in the same series asks the marriage goddess why she has put on murderous

---

[34] *Gr. Anth.* XVI.174, trans. W. R. Paton, Loeb edn., vol. 5, p. 261. See James Hutton, *The Greek Anthology in Italy* (Ithaca, New York, 1935), p. 77. Ariosto's pastiche, which is taken from *Gr. Anth.* XVI.177, ll. 5f.; 173, ll. 3f.; and 176, may be offered as an example of its kind: "—The arms, Venus, are those of Mars; what weight do you go under uselessly, as if you contemplated war with a mortal? It is no work for iron, when you yourself, nude, stripped the powerful god of iron of his spoils. —The god has his arms, stranger, do not mistake; this is Sparta, where they are given to me according to a custom of the fathers. And they become me, who was born in a savage wave from blood; who am the love of Mars, who am Lacedaemonian."

[35] Ausonius, *Epig.* LXIV, "Armatam vidit Venerem" (trans. in H. G. Evelyn-White, in Loeb *Ausonius*, vol. 2, p. 193). Ausonius' version is quoted in Giraldus (*Op. om.*, I, col. 394E) and trans. in Cartari, *Le Imagini, edn. cit.*, pp. 397, 399. Others depending on the poem are J. C. Scaliger, in his reply, "Imbelli imbellis" (quoted in Hutton, *Greek Anthology in Italy*, p. 194), Minturno, "Armatam Venerem aspiceret" (in Hutton, p. 233), and Elio Giulo Crotti, "In Veneram Armatam" (in Hutton, p. 229).

[36] *Mythol.* IV.xiii, *edn. cit.*, p. 383.

[37] *Hist. Deorum*, Syntag. XIII, in *Op. om.*, I, col. 394F; and Cartari, *Le Imagini, edn. cit.*, p. 399. See Varro, *De Lingua Latina* V.62.

[38] *Gr. Anth.* XVI.171, also the basis for Sannazaro, "Induerat thoraca humeris, galeamque decoro" (quoted in Hutton, *Greek Anthology in Italy*, p. 141), and for Politian's own Greek exercise on the theme (quoted and trans. in Hutton, p. 136).

[39] *Gr. Anth.* XVI.176, trans. by W. R. Paton, in Loeb edn., vol. 5, p. 261.

engines: "Is it that thou hast despoiled bold Ares to boast how great is the might of Cypris?"[40] When Phedria quells the anger of Cymochles she asserts that Mars is Cupid's friend, and Mars will also appear at the House of Busirane in an unmanned state resembling Amoret's own ("full of burning darts, / And many wide wounds launched through his inner parts," III.xi.41). The conquest of Mars by love explains why the child of Mars and Venus should be called Harmonia. In Spenser too, Concord harmonizes Love and Hate, according to that principle whereby union is expressed by the commensuration of opposites. Mars is attracted to Venus —in the conceit of Claudian—as iron is attracted to a magnet.[41]

The most important of the epigrams on the armed Venus paradox also implied a comparison of Venus to Pallas, or Minerva, another goddess of victory. Rudolf Wittkower cites examples of the *Venus victrix* armed with a shield bearing Minerva's Gorgoneion, along with evidence for a type that he refers to as a "Minerva Pudica."[42] The Lady in *Comus*, for example, invokes the Gorgonian shield of chastity (ll. 447–452). The cause of chastity in Spenser has a patron in the lady-knight Palladine, and Britomart herself lays aside her armour,

> Like as *Minerua*, being late returnd
> From slaughter of the Giaunts conquered; . . .
>
> . . . .
>
> Hath loosd her helmet from her lofty hed,
> And her *Gorgonian* shield gins to vntye
> From her left arme, to rest in glorious victorye.
>
> (III.ix.22)

Britomart has just overthrown Paridell, and the comparison reminds us that, in the same battle with the giants, the giant Pallas threatened Athena with rape. Thus Comes says that the shield abashes Minerva's admirers.[43]

---

[40] *Ibid.*, XVI.177, trans. Paton, Loeb edn., vol. 5, p. 261.

[41] *Magnes*, ll. 22–39, in Loeb *Claudian*, ed. Platnauer, vol. 2, pp. 236f., for the nuptials of the god and goddess in a common temple. For Harmonia, see n. 51, below.

[42] "Transformations of Minerva in Renaissance Imagery," *Journal of the Warburg Institute*, 2 (1938–1939), pp. 194–205.

[43] *Mythol.*, IV.v, "De Pallade," p. 306, *edn. cit.*, where the opposition of the virginal Pallas to the voluptuous Venus is followed by remarks on the Gorgon on Pallas' chest as implying the formidable aspect of the wise, vigilant, and temperate with respect to outlaws. For Minerva's Gorgonian shield opposing the arrows of Cupid, see the emblem of Gilles Corrozet, in *Hecatongraphie* (Paris, 1543), Sig. C^v, "Chasteté vainc Cupido" ("Against Pallas Cupid darted his lance, / But she opposed her shield, and did so well / That she made a conquest of him, / Completely stripped of arms, and power"), reproduced in Arthur Henkel and Albrecht Schöne, eds., *Emblemata* (Stuttgart, 1967), cols. 1733f. It is the Minerva pudica who triumphs in the "inward beauty"—"that which no eyes can see"—of the bride in the *Epithalamion*: "But if ye saw . . . Much more then would ye wonder . . . And stand astonisht

The admiration that Britomart secures on this occasion might deserve the question Ovid asks in the first poem of the *Amores*: "What if Venus should snatch the arms of fair-haired Minerva, / What if Minerva should fan torches of love into flame?"[44]

The whole characterization of Britomart may be thought of as taking its beginnings from the introduction of Belphoebe into the poem, then passing through the Venerean and amorous loci of the central books, and finally modulating into its original form in the legend of justice with the implied comparison of Britomart to her rival Radigund. Despite their opposed moral affiliations, it is no accident that the independent Belphoebe and the rebellious Radigund share imagery. Radigund is a virago dressed in buskins barred with golden bands, and a silver camise. Belphoebe's dress is the same.[45]

Radigund is specifically an Amazon queen, and thus an original for the characterization in question. Her ferocity recalls the "martial nature" of a character like Marfisa in the Orlando epics. Marfisa's name, in fact, may be a doublet for that of the Amazon queen Marpesia or Martesia, a "daughter of Mars."[46] All Amazons are of course "daughters of Mars," and Britomart, who is also Boccaccio's Britona, is in some sense their sister. Another of her prototypes is the Amazon Penthesileia (III.iv.2), whose Amazon mother Otrerae was the wife of Mars,[47] and with whom Achilles fell in love. Ariosto's Marfisa is herself potentially an Amazon, and like Britomart she liberates a knight from bondage to Amazons[48]—we may want to understand an act of fealty here, or a deliverance from an Amazonian fixée. Artegall, as we have already seen, is a Mars—and also an Achilles—and hence potentially the husband or lover of an Amazon.

---

lyke to those which red / Medusaes mazeful hed. / There dwels sweet loue and constant chastity, / Vnspotted fayth and comely womanhood, / Regard of honour and mild modesty" (ll. 185–193). "Medusaes mazeful hed" can be a genital image, suitably labyrinthine; one should therefore compare this description with Spenser's rhetoric for the beauteous maidenhead of Belphoebe, at III.v.54f.

[44] *Amores* I.i.7f., trans. Rolfe Humphries.

[45] *F.Q.* II.iii.26f. ("Silken Camvs," "gilden buskins . . . with golden bendes," "Below her ham"—the last line of stanza 26 falls short, as does the Camus); V.v.2f. ("Camus light of . . . silk," "Vp to her ham," "bends of gold").

[46] Orosius, *Hist. adv. Paganos*, I.15 (Marpesia); Justin, *Hist.* ii.4; Boccaccio, *Concerning Famous Women*, chap. xi, Martesia and Lampedo, Queens of the Amazons: "daughters of Mars."

[47] Hyginus, *Fab.* CCIII and CCXXV: "Otrera, an Amazon, wife of Mars" (see *Iliad* III.186–189, where Helen is marshalled among the Amazons, "the people of Otreus"); Penthesileia's parents: Servius, *ad Aen.* I.491, and Hyginus, *Fab.* CXII. For Britomartis-Britona, see n. 20, above. For Amazons as "daughters of Mars," see Euripides, *Heracles* 413.

[48] *O.F.* XIX.88–XX.92; see stanzas 77–78 for Marfisa's rejection of a position of rank among the Amazons.

In the epiphany of Britomart at the opening of Book IV, Britomart is compared to Bellona, a female Mars, suggesting at the outset that the legend will have specific occasion to present the heroine as a Lacedaemonian Venus, quite apart from the more "hermetic" Venus of the Temple. Spenser places the Garden of Adonis, and the encounter of Venus with Diana, at the center of Book III. He arranges the meeting of Britomart and Artegall at the center of the following book. To this scheme one might compare the Cytherea of the *Hypnerotomachia*, which centers on two shrine-like fountains. One is sacred to Adonis, and contains a tomb bearing panels on each side: one panel shows Adonis killed by the boar, and it is inscribed "Impvra Svavitas"; the other panel shows the killing of Adonis by Mars. The second fountain turns out to be the scene of the copulation of Venus and the aggressor himself.[49] In Spenser's narrative at the center of Book IV, Artegall is seeking out the unknown knight to revenge his mysterious defeat at his (her) hands. He is accompanied by Scudamour—Mars is Cupid's friend[50]—and Scudamour has a part to play in reconciling the two warriors. In the combat, Britomart overcomes Artegall as an armed Venus, by being exposed to her lover as "That peereless paterne of Dame natures pride" (IV.vi.24). And Artegall capitulates as a disarmed Mars, losing that "yron courage" (IV.vi.17) or that iron boldness that Britomart has already made hers at the House of Busirane.

We may take the union of Britomart and Artegall, here in the offing, to portend some ideal combination of concupiscent and irascible faculties; such a balance is implied by Spenser's having compensated each character for what would ordinarily be a characteristic deficiency. The amorous maiden is fiery and irascible, and the martial warrior proves concupiscent and appassionated. Ficino allegorizes the typal union in similar terms: "Moreover there are concupiscent and irascible men, just as if kindred proclivities towards passion: there are even *things* with a propensity to wrath, and to the contrary, so that the poets do not unworthily conjoin Mars with Venus."[51] Artegall, who formerly thought to conquer Brito-

[49] *Hypnerotomachia*, Methuen facsimile (London, 1904), Sig. Zvii[r]; for the Adonis-lament, Sig. Zviii[v].

[50] *F.Q.* II.vi.35: "And is for *Venus* loues renowmed more, / Then all his wars and spoiles, the which he did of yore."

[51] *In Plotinum*, In Librum De Dubiis Animae Primum (*Enn.* IV, III), in cap. xxviii, in Ficino, *Op. om.* (reprint, Torino, 1957), II-2, p. 1754. The interpretation of Mars as the irascible and Venus as the concupiscible appetite is also found in Boccaccio's glosses on the temples in the *Teseide*, VII.30, 50. Cf. the *discordia concors* and amicable enmity discussed by Pico in his definition of beauty: it is said by the poets that "Venus loves Mars, because Beauty, which we call Venus, cannot subsist without contrariety; and that Venus tames and mitigates Mars, because the tempering power restrains and overcomes the strife and hate which persist between con-

mart, now applies himself to the conquest of his own passion. Ficino notes that "It is in this that the power of Cupid differs from the force of Mars; indeed it is in this way that military power and love differ: the general possesses others through himself; the lover takes possession of himself through another."[52]

The emphasis in the lovers' encounter is not obviously iconographic. Nevertheless, we will want to know the sources for the figure of the Lacedaemonian Venus. Both Cartari and Giraldus cite a story told by Lactantius.[53] The Lacedaemonians built a temple to Venus, and the image of the armed goddess that it contained commemorated a unique event. Once, when the Spartans were besieging Messene, the enemy secretly made off to Sparta, with the purpose of sacking the city in the absence of its warriors. They were foiled, however, when the Spartan women, seeing the danger, armed themselves and put the Messenians to rout. "Meanwhile," Cartari reports, "the Lacedaemonians, seeing that they had been tricked by the enemy, pursued them, and because they were returning by another road, did not meet them, but met instead their wives, all armed, and thinking that *they* were the enemy, prepared to fight: but they revealed themselves to their husbands, who knew them incontinently, and went abruptly to embrace them: and because time did not permit that each find his own, thus armed the way they were, each took his pleasure in whomever he met with. . . ." As Spenser says, when Artegall relents before the unhelmeted Radigund, "No hand so cruell, nor hart so hard, / But ruth of beautie will it mollifie" (V.v.13). Unlike the Spartans and their wives, Britomart and Artegall are not yet married, but it is at this meeting that their marriage is contracted. As in Lactantius' story, the warrior seeking to revenge himself on his enemy meets his wife in arms; she is revealed to him, and their enmity modulates into its opposite, even though the lovers cannot presently know each other as individuals. This comparison, however acrobatic, does show that when an etiological tale is adduced to explain the *Venus armata* image, the events leading up to its formation will resemble those that unite Spenser's Venus and Mars.

---

trary elements." (*Commento*, II.vi, trans. Wind, *Pagan Mysteries*, p. 89.) For the marriage of Mars and Venus issuing in their child Harmony, see Comes, *Mythol.*, IX.xiv edn. cit., p. 995; and Hesiod, *Theog.* 975; Pausanias, IX.v.2; Ovid, *Metam.* III.132; Statius, *Theb.* III.283.

[52] *De Amore*, VII.ii, trans. Sears Jayne, *Marsilio Ficino's Commentary on Plato's Symposium; the text and translation* . . . , University of Missouri Studies, vol. 19, no. 1 (Columbia, Missouri, 1944), p. 142.

[53] Giraldus, *Hist. Deorum*, Syntag. XIII, in *Op. om.*, I, col. 394C–F, and Cartari, *Le Imagini*, p. 397; edn. cit. (I am translating Verdier's French however: *Les Images des Dieux des Anciens*, Lyon, 1581, p. 615). The source is Lactantius, *Divine Instit.*, I.20.

Britomart adopts her arms when she has determined to search for her husband, and if we were to try to explain the *Venus armata* image psycho-analytically, we should refer it to the stays and gussets of female clothing in general. Its psychogenesis would then reside in an attempt to add or reconstruct something that the woman is originally without. This is per-haps another way of saying that Britomart arms herself partly in a bid for equality with her husband. Alpers' reading of these opening episodes of Britomart's quest stresses the comedy that keeps showing through, and George Meredith observes that comedy "comes of some degree of social equality of the sexes." It flourishes "where women are on the road to an equal footing with men, in attainments and in liberty—in what they have won for themselves, and what has been granted them by a fair civiliza-tion."[54] This may not be the whole truth, but it might be variously applied to the *Odyssey, Lysistrata, Much Ado About Nothing, Pride and Preju-dice*, and the plays of Shaw. One of Shaw's heroines, in fact, is Major Bar-bara, a child of Lady Britomart and Captain Undershaft, who is an armaments manufacturer, and so a Vulcan as well as a Mars. Meredith writes:

> The heroines of comedy are like women of the world, not necessarily heartless from being clear-sighted; they seem so to the sentimentally reared, only for the reason that they use their wits, and are not wandering vessels crying for a captain or a pilot. Comedy is an exhibition of their battle with men, and that of men with them; and as the two, however divergent, both look on one object, namely, life, the gradual similarity of their im-pressions must bring them to some resemblance. The comic poet dares to show us men and women coming to this mutual likeness; he is for saying that when they draw together in social life their minds grow liker; just as the Philosopher discerns the similarity of boy and girl, until the girl is marched away to the nursery.[55]

There is little in this passage that will not bear comparison with the emergent relation of Britomart and Artegall.

---

[54] "An Essay on Comedy," in *Comedy* (reprint, with Bergson's essay on "Laugh-ter," Garden City, New York, 1965), p. 32. Cf. p. 31: "Where the veil is over women's faces, you cannot have society, without which the senses are barbarous and the Comic Spirit is driven to the gutters of grossness to slake its thirst. Arabs in this respect are worse than Italians—much worse than Germans—just in the degree that their system of treating women is worse." For Alpers, see *Poetry of "The Faerie Queene,"* pp. 180–185. For the equality secured by armour, cf. *F.Q.* III.iii.61, where Glauce is the subject. For the psychoanalysis of women's clothing, cf. Freud, "Fetish-ism," in *International Journal of Psycho-analysis*, 9 (1928), pp. 161–166, on the origin of fetishism in a substitution for the phallus and as expressing an aversion to the character of the female genitalia.

[55] "An Essay on Comedy," in *Comedy*, p. 15.

Of course the heroism of chastity is not only expressed in the image of the armed virgin. In his study of the symbolism we have just covered, Edgar Wind cites two Italian medals, made for one Giovanna Tuorbuoni, both of which portray the lady herself on one side. On the reverse, one of the medals shows Virgil's Venus-Virgo, armed with bow and arrow. The reverse of the other also shows a combination of chastity and love, but this time by means of an altogether different image, that of the three Graces. It is to this second symbolism that we now turn, even if it should entail our heroine's being marched away to the nursery.

[ii]

ter vocata . . . diva triformis
(Horace, *Odes* III.22)

The beame of beautie sparkled from aboue,
The floure of vertue and pure chastitie,
The blossome of sweet ioy and perfect loue.
(*Colin Clovt*, ll. 468–470)

If Britomart presents the heroine of chastity as a *Venus armata*, we may inquire as to what aspects of Venus are presented by Belphoebe, Florimell, and Amoret. Their relations to Venus are marked: Belphoebe is the Venus-Virgo, Florimell wears Venus' cestus, and Amoret has Venus for her sponsor. But Spenser's three examples of womanhood have been configured in such a way that one cannot avoid a constantly revolving *comparison* of their honesty, beauty, and love—stressed now in one, and now in another. Heroic eros, Spenser says, "doth *true beautie loue*, / And chooseth vertue for his dearest Dame" (III.iii.1). The secret of this relation is apparently to be framed in terms of a triform Venus. There is such a Venus, expounded in Renaissance Neo-Platonic theology, namely, the Orphic Venus of Pico. Pico asserts that this Venus is properly unfolded or diversified in her three companions, the Graces.[56] An example is found in the passage in Ficino that describes this unfolding process. In explaining the Neo-Platonic dialectic of proceeding, conversion, and enrapture, Ficino adduces the "trinity" of Apollo, Mercury, and Venus. Venus is Beauty, of which the true and harmonious idea is also a *ternario*: "the beautiful, suggesting itself to us in the way that Venus is closely accompanied by the three Graces, accosts [*aggreditur*] the soul by wonderment, while it meets [*congreditur*] it by loving, while it engages [*ingreditur*] it by being pleasing." Here then, the three Graces pertaining to Venus (or beauty), are admiration, love,

---

[56] "Conclusiones . . . de modo intelligendi hymnos Orphei," no. 8, in *Op. om.* (Basel, 1572), vol. 1, p. 106. Wind, in his *Pagan Mysteries in the Renaissance*, discusses many of the texts which I cite here, and I am following his argument.

and enjoyment. An alternative Ficinian explanation of this sort makes the ternario stand for Truth, Concord, and Beauty: "true beautie loue," as Spenser says.[57]

It may strike one as curious that Spenser names Mount Acidale—the haunt of the Graces—as the nursery of Florimell (IV.v.5). Like the Graces in Book VI, Florimell manifests the charm exercised by beauty. And though it is Diana who adopted the infant Belphoebe, the Graces also rocked her cradle (III.vi.2), and "Vpon her eyelids *many Graces* sate" (II.ii.25): E. K.'s gloss on the phrase in "Ivne" explains that "though there be indeede but three Graces or Charites . . . yet in respect of many gyftes of bounty, there may be sayde more. And so Musaeus sayeth, that in Heroes eyther eye there satte a hundred graces." (Spenser's outer-ring of Graces also numbers a hundred, at VI.x.11.) An emblem in Achilles Bocchius' collection shows Venus entrusting newborn twins, Eros and Anteros, to the Graces for upbringing,[58] and so there may be room in the same symbolism for Amoret, who is brought up as a child of Cupid and a sister of Pleasure in the favorite earthly haunt of Venus. Distributing these associations, we arrive at the following array:

Belphoebe	Florimell	Amoret
Diana or Virgo	Graces	Venus or Cupid
Chastity	Beauty	Love or Pleasure

As Ficino's explanation implies, the central figure in such a pattern may be both the class of the figures, and a member of the class; hence the Graces may be unfolded into the contrary figures of Venus and Diana.[59]

To arrive at such an interpretation of the three Graces, we may begin with the Orphic *Hymn*, where the Graces are named Thalia, Aglaia, and Euphrosyne. In the Latin translation these names are rendered as Flora, Maiesta, and—oddly—Virgo. They are "young mothers of pure pleasures" ("Laetitiae matres purae vitulantes"), lovely and always flourishing ("semper virideis"), and desired by mortals.[60] Wind compares the similar inter-

---

[57] *In Plotinum* (*Enn.* I, III), "De Triplici reditu animae ad divinum, ad divinum praeludium Argumentum," in *Op. om.*, II-2, p. 1559.

[58] *Symbolicarvm qvaestionvm* (Bologna, 1574), symb. LXXX, pp. CLXX seq.

[59] See Wind, *Pagan Mysteries*, pp. 39f., 196f. For the first example in *The Faerie Queene*, see *F.Q.* I.i.48, where Una, "the chastest flowre," modulates into the protégée of Venus, to the accompaniment of Flora and the Graces; cf. I.vi.16, where Una appears as a sober Venus and a disarmed Diana.

[60] Hymn LIX, in *Orpheos Apanta*, ed. Hambergerus, pp. 258f., trans. J. J. Scaliger. This trans. was added to Stephanus' 1570 edn. of the Hymns. For the history, see Guilemus Quandt, ed., *Orphei Hymni* (Berlin, 1962), Prolegomena, p. 34*: the young Scaliger later referred to the translation as a *mendosum opus*. The use of Flora for Thalia, elsewhere translated as *viriditas*, may be compared with E. K.'s gloss on the Chloris who became Flora, in "Aprill," l. 122: "The name of a Nymph,

pretation of the Graces through their names implied in a passage in Plutarch on the Graces as benefits. The Latin of Xylander's translation makes the Graces *pulchrius* (which sounds like Aglaia), *iucundius* (from Euphrosyne), and *gaudii* (from *thalea*, good cheer, rather than *thaleia*, blooming).[61] Cartari makes them *maestà* and *venustà, allegrezza giocondità*, and *piacevolezza* (majesty or beauty, jocundity, and pleasantry).[62] Comes, on the other hand, gives *splendor, laetitia*, and *pullulare* (to burgeon, flourish), as the etymologies. Abraham Fraunce conforms to Comes.[63] Spenser, in Book VI, avoids the Flora tradition for Thalia:

> mylde *Euphrosyne*
> Next faire *Aglaia*, last *Thalia* merry:
> Sweete Goddesses all three which me in mirth do cherry.
> (VI.x.22)

The Neo-Platonic tradition also has interpretations of the names. In an epistle to Lorenzo the Magnificent, under "De tribus Gratijs & Genio," Ficino gives the names as Viriditas, Lux, and Laetitia; and under "Tres Gratiae, & tres Planetae" he associates the radiant Grace with Phoebus.[64] Pico concludes that the same Verdure, Splendor, and Gladness "are nothing but the three properties appertaining to that Ideal Beauty" that is symbolized by Venus. He goes on to maintain that Verdure represents the permanence and "integra" of beauty; Splendor represents the illumination of beauty; and Gladness, "the desire which it [beauty] arouses in the will for the possession of that ineffable gladness."[65] In a letter to Lorenzo di Pierfrancesco, cited by Gombrich, Ficino maintains that beauty is nothing but grace—a grace composed of the three Graces, which attract, enrapture, and turn contemplation toward itself, kindling it "with the love

---

and signifieth greenesse, of whom is sayd, that Zephyrus the Westerne wind being in loue with her, and coueting her to wyfe, gaue her for a dowrie, the chiefdome and souraigntye of al flowres and greene herbes, growing on earth."

[61] *Pagan Mysteries*, p. 35; Plutarch, *Cum principibus philosphandum esse* 3, *Moralia* 778E (the same names are found in Hesiod, *Theog.* 907, and Pausanias, *Perieg.* IX.xxxv.5).

[62] *Le Imagini, edn. cit.*, p. 411. For Giraldus on the Graces as cheer, see *De Ingrati Crimen Vitando*, in *Op. om.*, II, col. 731D; and *Hist. Deorum*, Syntag. III, in *Op. om.*, I, col. 419C–D: "amiable hilarity is reciprocal, that is, it ought to be shared back and forth and ought to be flourishing." The traditional significance of the Graces as cheer flourishes throughout Book VI; see Chap. V, n. 52 with preceding text.

[63] *Mythol.*, IV.xv, "De Gratiis," p. 411, *edn. cit.; Third part of the Countess of Pembrokes Iuychurche*, fol. 45ᵛ–46ʳ.

[64] *Epistolae*, Lib. VI, in *Op. om.*, I–2, p. 846 (the letter is dated Oct. 18, 1491).

[65] *A Platonic Discourse Upon Love*, Thomas Stanley's seventeenth century trans. of Pico's *Commentary* on Benivieni's *Canzone d'Amore* (Venice, 1522); text in Pico, *Op. om.* (Basel, 1587), where the place is II.xv.

of divine contemplation and beauty."[66] I have left out Ficino's references to Apollo, who attracts by music; Venus, who enraptures the eye; and Mercury, who acts through intellect. Ficino also refers to these in his *Commento*:

> This pleasing quality, whether of virtue, shape, or sound, which summons and attracts the soul to itself through reason, sight, or hearing, is most rightly called Beauty. These are the three graces about which Orpheus speaks thus: "Splendor, Youth, and Abundant Happiness" [*Splendor, viriditas, laetitiaque uberrima*].
>
> He calls "splendor" that charm and beauty of the soul which consists of brightness of truth and virtue; "youth" he applies to charm of shape and color, for this shines especially in the greeness of youth; and finally, by "happiness," he means that pure, salutary and perpetual delight which we feel in Music.[67]

In this passage, Ficino may intend a circulation of gifts among his three Graces, for it is his Viriditas that shines, his Splendor that is the beauty of an honest soul; and the delight of his Joyfulness that is pure. Once again, one of the Graces stands for an integrity that might be truth or chastity, or, in Spenser's words, "the *vertue* of chast loue," which is conferred by Venus' cestus (IV.v.3). Yet one more passage advances this Ficinian theme of the graces of true beauty:

> According to a widespread notion we think of beauty as being something graceful, or as certain graces that attract us through sight, hearing, or reason. This thing is truly called Beauty, insofar as it is present in things that are seen, heard, and thought; and it manifests the three Graces to us. Truly, as much as it consists in sight, hearing, and in reason, it is called delectation and pleasure; pleasure, in which things [it is] *decorous*, for it properly follows on seemly things of itself, and seemly *pleasure*, [in that] a seemly appetite follows on this also, love itself of course.[68]

Giraldus' notice of the Graces also makes the *venustas* of the "majestic" Aglaia honest, and the festive Thalia, beautiful (*concinnitas* and *lepiditasve*).[69]

We may compare the last passage cited from Ficino, which moves from decorum in the appreciation of Beauty to the pleasure of love, to the *Com-*

---

[66] *Symbolic Images* (London, New York, 1972), p. 59. Ficino, *Epistolae*, Lib. VII, in *Op. om.*, I–2, p. 862 (the letter is addressed "Domino Matthaeo Forlivensi clarissimo Pontificis commissario").

[67] *De Amore*, II.iii, trans. Jayne, p. 167.

[68] *In Plotinum*, In Lib. de Pulchritudine (*Enn.* I, VI), in Ficino, *Op. om.*, II–2, p. 1574.

[69] *Hist. Deorum*, Syntag, XIII, in *Op. om.*, I, col. 420E.

mento passage adduced by Wind to explain a medal of Pico's that labels the three Graces Pulchritudo, Amor, and Voluptas. Ficino describes the love created in everything by the Divine Beauty, which draws the world to itself in a way that illustrates the formula that "Love begins in Beauty and ends in Pleasure"; the whole process is described as "an attraction which returns to the same place where it began as though in a kind of circle," and the circle is to be "identified by the three names of Love, Beauty, and Pleasure."[70]

The passage we have quoted on the appropriateness of our response to beauty, with its emphasis on *decora* as much as *voluptas* in any delectation, might lead us to a second medal, answering to the first in Wind's opinion, where the same three Graces have become Castitas, Pulchritudo, and Amor.[71] Wind professes to find the iconography of these three attributes in the coiffure of Botticelli's Graces, the jewelry of those of Raphael, and the emblems of the Graces in the pack of cards known as the Tarochi. The emblems in the Tarochi are flame, flower, and loincloth, and the Castitas Grace in Raphael also wears the loincloth. The Tarochi card shows the Graces with Venus, and the three attributes seem to be Venerean to begin with. The torch belongs to a type known as the Saxon Venus, the Graces deck Venus with flowers when she comes ashore at Cytherea, and the loincloth looks like a medieval version of Venus' cestus. We have only the tradition of the purity of the pleasures of the Graces, or the honesty of their beauty, to authorize the presence of a Grace of Castitas on the medal. There is no reason the Graces should not be chaste: Comes translates a poem of Meleager to the effect that they were.[72] But the pictorial Castitas tradition—found even in Alciati's "Gratia" print—is very dim in the lists of the Graces' epithets. The meaning of the substitution on the second medal is clear, however. As Wind explains, the first medal il-

---

[70] *De Amore*, II.ii; trans. Jayne, pp. 133f. Wind, *Pagan Mysteries*, p. 43. Cf. Sebastiano Erizzo, in Ruscelli, *Lettere di XIII uomini illustri* (Venice, 1560), pp. 627ff., cited in Garin, *Italian Humanism* (New York, 1965), p. 120: "Beauty is nothing but a certain gracefulness which fills the emotions with pleasure, and the knowledge of which stimulates love." For the rotating triplicity being discussed here, cf. *Gr. Anth.* V.196: "Zenophilia's beauty is Love's gift, Cypris charmed her bed, and the Graces gave her grace"; and V.260, which describes three different coiffures for the beloved: "The three Graces dwell in the three aspects of your beauty." Cf. also V.195: "The Graces wove a triple crown for Zenophilia, a badge of her triple beauty," assigned to Love, Cypris, and Persuasion.

[71] *Pagan Mysteries*, pp. 75, 83f., 117–119. Cf. Petrarch, *Canz.* CCXV: "Love is in her with honesty joined, with natural beauty her habit adorned."

[72] *Mythol.*, IV.xv, p. 409: "The Charites are three in number, the Horae three; and both are chaste." Often the Graces are stated to be virgins—so Giraldus' article, in *Op. om.*, I, Syntag. XIII, col. 419E, on the epithet *Parthenoi*: "i.e., the Graces are called virgins and maidens, and cheerful and laughing, because it accords with thanks to be without fraud and cunning, but rather clean and pure."

lustrates that Love is the desire to enjoy Beauty, and the second, that Beauty is the mean term between Chastity and Love—what is attractive must also be honest to be beautiful.[73] When Spenser comes to his description of the fourth Grace, he graces her with three graces that depart markedly from the tradition of the names he has just invoked:

> Another Grace she well deserues to be,
> In whom so many Graces gathered are,
> Excelling much the meane of her degree;
> *Diuine resemblaunce, beauty soueraine rare,*
> *Firme Chastity,* that spight ne blemish dare;
> (VI.x.27, italics mine)

To which Spenser adds a fourth grace of courtesy. Having expanded upon his lady's radiance in the preceding stanza, Spenser then offers an apology to the "Sunne of the world," Gloriana, the "greatest Maiesty" whom he has sung in so many lays before. Here it is hard not to think of the Grace who is called *Maiesta, Pulchrius,* and *Splendor;* or of the celebration of the chastity of the radiant Belphoebe, "as faire as *Phoebus* sunne" (II. v.27).[74] And we will not miss the point that Chastity here is one of the Graces, paired with Beauty.

We may now return to Belphoebe's happy horoscope, which is detailed, and which makes her chastity a gift, or grace:

> . . . to this faire *Belphoebe* in her berth
> The heauens so fauorable were and free,
> Looking with myld aspect vpon the earth,
> In th' *Horoscope* of her natiuitee,
> That all the gifts of grace and chastitee
> On her they poured forth of plenteous horne;
> *Ioue* laught on *Venus* from his soueraigne see,
> And *Phoebus* with faire beames did her adorne,
> And all the Graces rockt her cradle being borne.
> (III.vi.2)

What interests us here is the easy passage from the three gods to the Graces. In the passage already mentioned, Ficino says that the Graces betoken three aspects of Venus, just as Venus forms one member of the trinity of Venus, Apollo, and Mercury. But in one chapter of a treatise specifically devoted to the influence of astral powers, Ficino explains "How the three Graces and their ideal combination are Jupiter, and Sol, and Venus, and how Jupiter is the middle Grace of the twins." He says that

---

[73] *Pagan Mysteries*, pp. 73f.

[74] For "brightness" as the significance of the name Phoebus, see Macrobius, *Saturnalia*, I.xvii.33.

"this Venus herself is the most beloved of Jove, even just as Jupiter is of the Sun, as if there were among them the harmonies of the three Graces—and the conjunctions."[75] And in Ficino's letter, "On the Three Graces and the Genius," the Graces of Viriditas, Lux, and Laetitia are again identified as Jove, Phoebus, and Venus.[76]

With ample evidence for the tri-formation of the loveliness of Venus, we may study the interrelation of Belphoebe, Florimell, and Amoret. First, Belphoebe and Amoret are twins, and yet the parallel adventures in love belong to Amoret and Florimell. Similarly, in the *dos-à-dos* configuration of the Graces, where the middle Grace faces away from us, the Graces may be paired according to either their similarity of direction, or their proximity. This alternative gives a certain rightness to Horace's description of "the Grace" as having *geminisque sororibus* (twin-born sisters);[77] so Spenser's reference to them as "three Twins to light by *Venus* brought" (*Teares*, l. 403).

Second, the Graces are often pictured as moving in a linked circle. Over the course of Books II and III, Spenser's three figures each appear twice, and in the same order:

1st appearance: Belphoebe	Florimell		Amoret		
2nd appearance:		Belphoebe		Florimell	Amoret
Book and canto: II.iii	III.i	III.v	III.vi	III.viif.	III.xii

Simply taking the appearances in order, one could say that the first cycle (Belphoebe-Florimell-Belphoebe) shows Florimell in the context of chastity, and the second (Amoret-Florimell-Amoret) shows her in the context of amorous experience. Or, studying the relation of the two registers, one could note that Belphoebe's second appearance interrupts the round of first appearances, and Amoret's first appearance is interpolated into the second

---

[75] *De Triplici Vita*, III.v, in *Op. om.*, I-I, p. 536.

[76] *Loc. cit.*, note 64, above. The citation of Ficino is supported now by Richard J. Berleth, in his article "Heavens favorable and free: Belphoebe's Nativity in *The Faerie Queene*," in *ELH*, 40 (Winter, 1973), pp. 479–500, which also cites the following suggestive passage from Ptolemy, *Tetrabiblos* III.7, from a chapter on the horoscope "Of Twins": ". . . whenever such an arrangement of the planets does not include the horoscopic angle with the luminaries, but rather that of the mid-heaven, mothers with such genitures generally conceive twins or even more; and in particular, they give multiple birth . . . , to two or three females, by the geniture of the Graces, when Venus and the moon, with Mercury made feminine, are so arranged." (Trans. F. E. Robbins in Loeb edn.—with *Manetho*, ed. and trans. W. G. Waddell—p. 259.) Berleth compares the maternity of Chrysogonee.

[77] *Odes* IV.7, l. 5; cited in Comes, *Mythol.*, IV.xv, pp. 409f.

round, this design signifying the transfer of emphasis from chastity to love at the center of Book III.

Third, just as the outer Graces form a much allegorized ratio of one to two with the inner Grace, so each of Spenser's figures may be paired with one of the other two in a respect that excludes or "averts" the third. Florimell and Amoret are in love, Belphoebe is not. Unlike the other two, who are marriageable, the celibate Belphoebe has no occasion to wear the cestus of Venus. And although Florimell and Amoret are perfectly chaste, the shadow of a defloration symbolism is allowed to pass over both of them, and not over Belphoebe. Again, Florimell and Belphoebe each attract a lover who resembles a wounded Adonis; Amoret, who is raised in the Garden of Adonis, does not—rather, *she* is the wounded one. Again, Amoret and Belphoebe are twins; they are opposed as Venus and Diana, even as late as Belphoebe's encounter with Timias and Amoret in the fourth book; Florimell is not shown in this opposed relation. Remembering what we have learned about Castitas, Pulchritudo, and Amor, we may now schematize the relations described in this revolving ratio:

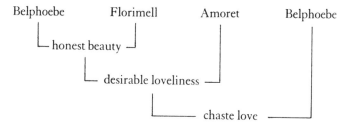

The first medal paired love with pleasure, and therefore we should also read:

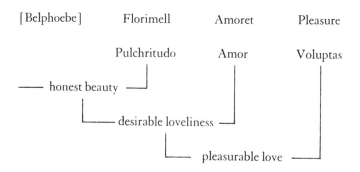

468

In a way, the second medal merely turns the first medal back a step. Spenser allows for both possibilities, for, as well as being Belphoebe's twin, Amoret is a stepsister to Pleasure.

For a similar reading of a popular triad of goddesses, one should compare Bruno on the judgment of Paris, which he says represents a choice between physical beauty, intelligence, and "worthy splendor of majesty." Bruno's argument is much like the reading of Spenser's triad proposed here. Bruno explains that the lover "compares his object, which contains and unites the qualities, characteristics and species of beauty to other objects which can only offer one, and besides, each one distributed among diverse individuals."[78]

> Now it happens that here there are three species of beauty, although all three are found in each of the three goddesses; for Venus is not deficient in wisdom and majesty, and Juno is not wanting in beauty and wisdom any more than Athena is wanting in majesty and beauty. Nevertheless, in each of the three goddesses one of these qualities happens to surpass the others and for that reason is considered proper to her, while the other qualities are considered mere accidents; moreover, with respect to the qualities which predominate in her, each goddess appears sovereign and outweighs her rivals.[79]

This is the way we have learned to relate Belphoebe, Florimell, and Amoret; the reason for their difference, in Bruno's words, "is that certain qualities do not belong to each goddess primarily and according to its essence, but according to participation and derivation."[80] And, as it turns out in Book VI, a comparison of Paris' three goddesses to the three Graces is not only plausible iconography, but also a specifically Spenserian association.[81]

Politian, speaking of the three Horae (whom he has substituted for the three Graces), says in the *Stanze* that "Their face [*sic*] are not the same, not diverse, / As for sisters well befits."[82] In phrases like those of Sidney's

---

[78] *Heroic Frenzies*, I.v.11, trans. Paul Eugene Memmo, University of North Carolina Studies in Romance Language and Literature, no. 50 (Chapel Hill, 1964), pp. 167f. Cf. Politian's *Stanze per la Giostra*, I.45, where the poet says Simonetta "would resemble Thalia if she took lute in hand; she would resemble Minerva if she had a spear; if she had a bow in hand and quiver at her side, you would swear she was chaste Diana." It seems possible that the three *divae* of the choice of Paris may have affected the Graces tradition: Venus-Love, Juno-Majesty, and Pallas-Virginity.

[79] *Heroic Frenzies*, I.v.11, *edn. cit.*, pp. 167f.

[80] *Ibid.*

[81] See "Fables of Green Fields," sec. iii, below.

[82] *Stanze per la Giostra*, I.100, echoing Ovid, *Metam.* II.13f. Politian implies the Graces. The Graces also traditionally welcome the anadyomene-figure ashore (*Od.* VIII.364; cf. also Flora's welcome in Ovid, *Fasti* V.217–220).

Cecropia, counseling Pamela to marry, Spenser joins beauty to love, and youth to delight, for love is the honoring and preserving of beauty.[83] Belphoebe has the name suggesting radiant beauty, and Florimell has the name suggesting attraction and juvenescence (Flower-honey), and yet Florimell is the preeminent beauty, like her prototype Helen, the "flowre of beautie" (III.ix.35). Florimell's flight merits comparison with that divine radiation so much discussed in orthodox Ficinian treatments of beauty's visual character.[84] The beauty of Amoret, on the other hand, is not sufficient to carry the day against the False Florimell. Belphoebe should be the Grace of Castitas, but the cestus, corresponding to Chastity's loincloth, is given to Florimell. It is also worn by Amoret, and appropriated by the False Florimell, "that shone as Phebes light" (IV.v.14). Thus the compounding of any two of the three figures may be compensated for by the imputation of a double excellence to the third. Belphoebe is twice chaste, for she is not only chaste, but virginal. Florimell is twice beautiful, insofar as the only greater beauty that can be imagined takes the form of a second Florimell. Amoret is doubled with respect to love. Belphoebe, though loved by Timias, does not suffer an erotic passion herself, and Florimell's love for Marinell is not soon reciprocated; but as the pairing of their names is meant to indicate, Scudamour and Amoret are both beloved, and in love.

The Triumph of Chastity

> . . . Nothing may help or heal
> While Amor incensed remembers wrong.
> Vindictive, not himself he'll spare;
> For scope to give his vengeance play
> Himself he'll blaspheme and betray.
> (Melville, "Lines Traced Under an
> Image of Amor Threatening")

> O, I have bought the mansion of a love,
> But not possessed it; and though I am sold,
> Not yet enjoyed. So tedious is this day
> As is the night before some festival. . . .
> (*Romeo and Juliet*, III.ii.26–29)

[83] *Arcadia*, III.x, in Feuillerat, ed., *Works*, vol. 1, p. 405.
[84] See Eugenio Garin, *Italian Humanism: Philosophy and Civic Life in the Renaissance*, trans. Peter Munz (New York, 1965), pp. 114ff. Florimell's effulgence beautifies the fisher's boat with "blazing beauties beame" at III.viii.22.

[i]

When we compare the two episodes in which Britomart is wounded, we perceive a certain obvious similarity in outline. Both Castle Joyous and the House of Busirane are a locus of profane love. Britomart encounters a knight stymied before each place. In both cases the knight's dedication, symbolized by the shield that identifies him, is endangered. The pure lady-knight is able to overcome the obstacle, and to enter each domain unscathed. Each interior presents a mythological tapestry. The first tells the story of Venus and Adonis; the second depicts the triumph of Venus' son Cupid, and is bordered by the "long bloody river" that is traditionally associated with the worship of Adonis in Syria.[85] In each house Britomart is entertained by a sixfold company that personifies something presently taking place. Thus glances, talk, jocularity, kissing, drinking, and darkness all accompany Malecasta's attempt to attract Britomart. Likewise the conturbations of love symbolized in the Masque of Cupid are the emotions Amoret and Scudamour have been going through, which even now torture the maid. They are Amoret's personal experience of the possible "phantasies / In wauering wemens wit" (III.xii.26). Both these formal structures have a tradition outside of Spenser.[86] Each episode leads to the

[85] Lucian, *Syrian Goddess* 8. For the annual character of the god's obsequies, see Jerome, *Comm. in Ezech.*, III.viii (on Ezk. 8:13f., in PL, XXV, 82f.); Stephanus, *Diction. Hist. Geo. Poet., sub* "Adonis" (2); Giraldus, *Hist. Deorum,* Styntag XIII, in *Op. om.*, I, col. 413B. See also Claudian, *De Raptu* II, Praef., l. 43, where it is said that the Nile ran red with Busiris' blood when Hercules put him to death.

[86] For the formal structure at Castle Joyous, see Allan H. Gilbert, "The Ladder of Lechery, the *Faerie Queene* III, i, 45," *MLN*, 56 (1941), pp. 594–597, citing especially Lucian, *Amores* 53, and James M. Hutton, "Spenser and the 'Cinq Points en Amours,'" *MLN*, 57 (1942), pp. 657–661, citing a number of medieval love poems. See also John Charles Nelson, *Renaissance Theory of Love* (New York, 1958), p. 52, who quotes Lorenzo di Medici, *In comento sopra alcuni de suoi sonetti* (from *Opera*, vol. 1, Bari, 1913, p. 120), where Lorenzo refers to a ladder of increasing involvements: seeing, singing, talking, laughing, sighing, and ultimately touching. Nelson, *Theory of Love*, p. 41, also provides a parallel for the formal structure of the paired masquers at the House of Busirane, which we may identify with the scale of the "conturbations of love" described in the pseudo-Egidio Colonna's commentary on Guido Calvacanti's *Donna mi prega*: the text is found in Gino Lega, ed., *Il Canzoniere Vatican Barbarin Latino* (Bologna, 1905), pp. 94f. Nelson writes that the lover experiences "'contrary steps' of hope and desperation, repose and anxiety, confidence and fear, pleasure and displeasure, joy and bitterness"; these steps are "so many manifestations of love's darkness, which is so powerful that it causes the domination of the negative emotions by their positive opposites." Cf. the list in Politian's *Stanze per la Giostra*, I.74–76: "Sweet Fear and timid Pleasure, sweet Angers and sweet Truces, Tears . . . deathly Pallor and Fearful Affection . . . with Leanness and Trouble; vigilant suspicion . . . Happiness," etc. For the theme in Ariosto, see the passage from *O.F.* XXI.1–3 cited below. With Amoret's womanly fantasies, compare Hellenore's at III.ix.52, and the False Florimell's at III.viii.8.

confrontation of Britomart with an embodiment of lust, and in both cases Britomart is superficially wounded.

For Britomart's conquest at the House of Busirane there is some precedent in Petrarch's second *Triumph*, the triumph of chastity over love.[87] Petrarch's figure wears a white gown and carries the shield that brought Medusa to her death; the arms of Britomart are likened to a "*Gorgonian shield*" (III.ix.22). Love moves to strike the heroine down, but "never was there fencer so adept / at turning blows aside." The poet, like Scudamour, awaits the outcome; expecting that the beloved will be conquered by the love-god, he hopes to be bound to her as a fellow captive:

> Io era al fin cogli occhi e col cor fiso,
> sperando la vittoria ond'esser sole
> e di non esser piu da lei diviso

> I watched to the end, with eyes and heart fixed,
> hoping the victory to be where it is usually
> and I to be divided from her no longer
> (*Trionfo della Pudicizia*, 55–57)

He expects, in other words, to be joined to the beloved by Love, as Scudamour is eventually united with Amoret—Britomart, rather than Cupid, brings together the latter pair. Contrary to expectation, however, Love's shafts are extinguished by this greater Camilla, her van including Desirefor-Honor and Fear-of-Shame. The distracted and overwhelmed love-god is then bound to a column with a chain of diamond and topaz, "such as women used to wear, but wear no more." The new captive is apparently suitably chastised—though the "vengeances" are not spelled out—and his former prisoners released.

The possible fate of Petrarch's bound Cupid is the subject of the *Cupid Crucified* of Ausonius.[88] This poem describes the bad dream that Cupid had, in which the shades of his female victims revenge their wounds.

---

[87] *Trionfo della Pudicizia*, ll. 18f. The parallel is perhaps first suggested by E. B. Fowler, *Spenser and the Courts of Love* (Menasha, Wisc., 1921), pp. 114–116. Petrarch's *Triumphs* were a favorite subject for Renaissance tapestries, and the tapestry of the triumph of love here surely is meant to apprise us of this extension of the Petrarchan tradition. For the iconographic tradition, see Raimond van Marle, *Iconographie de L'Art Profane* (The Hague, 1932), vol. 2, *Allegories et Symboles*, pp. 111–132, esp. fig. 142 and pl. 128 (Flemish Tapestry, Victoria and Albert Museum, London).

[88] The poem is translated entire in Cartari, *Le Imagini, edn. cit.*, pp. 380–386. (Text in Loeb *Ausonius*, vol. 1, pp. 206ff.) The links to Petrarch's *Triumph* and Hellenistic art and literature have also been noted by Panofsky, *Studies in Iconology* (reprint, New York, 1962), p. 176, n. 79. Also compare Petrarch's Son. 243 (*Canz.* CCLXXIV), "Amor, who tied me and keeps me on this cross, / Trembles when he sees her"; remembering that the poet became enamored on Good Friday.

Cupid, caught in the grove of the lovers in the underworld, is bound to the myrtle tree to which Adonis was once bound (for a slight to Proserpina), and blood is drawn. As an Adonis, Cupid must be a "dying god," and there is death in the face of Amoret too.[89] We will meet again the suggestion that a scourging subject belongs to the pagan god of love as well as the Christian one.

More explicit recognition of a relation between Petrarch's and Ausonius' poems is implied by an episode in Politian's *Stanze*, where the lover Julio dreams about his beloved Simonetta:

> He seemed to see his lady, cruel, arrogant, and obdurate in countenance, tie Cupid to the green trunk of Minerva's happy tree; armed with the Gorgon shield over her white gown, she protected her chaste breast, and seemed to tear the feathers from his wings: and she broke the bows and arrows of the wretch.

> Alas, how he had changed from the Love who just now had joyfully returned! He was not haughtily and nimbly soaring, he was not at all gloating over his triumph; rather the little wretch cried miserably for mercy, and called to Julio with a piteous face: "Have pity on me, defend me from her, fair Julio."

> And Julio inside his false sleep seemed to answer him with confused mind: "How may I do this, my sweet lord? For she is enclosed in the armour of Pallas. You see my spirits cannot endure the terrible face of Medusa, the angry hiss of vipers, the face, the helmet, and the flashing of lances."[90]

This lover also has some of the problems of Scudamour, though it will be Amoret, rather than Cupid, who is initially bound at the House of Busirane.

There is the suggestion in the passage quoted from Politian that when the lover is frustrated as a spectator, the love object is bound as an actor. Similar ratios seem to obtain at the House of Busirane, where the theatrical proceedings (rather than Julio's anxious dream) formalize the metaphor of the spectator as an alienated performer. One may even feel that Britomart's protracted contemplation of the erotic shows at the House possesses a skeptophilic quality. Caught in the interval between the lover outside and the beloved within, Britomart seems to share a little of her situation with both parties: she gets a taste of Amoret's experience of fascinated horror, and a taste of Scudamour's carefully harbored anticipation of the disrobing

---

[89] III.xii.19. See the following section for an analysis.

[90] *Stanze per la Giostra*, II.28–30. David Quint has kindly allowed me to use his unpublished translation of this poem here.

of the bride. Cupid has removed his blindfold, and Leda peeks at the Swan's ruffled "pryde" (III.xi.32).

Perhaps we are still not fully equipped to explain Spenser's analysis of the situation represented at the House of Busirane as an interaction of four personae, but we can begin to see that Spenser has established a scheme such that the *animus* of each sex is understood as the *anima* of the other. The result is a kind of "quadrature" of the characterization:

	Male	*Female*
Animus	Busirane (oppressive)	Britomart (intrusive)
Anima	Scudamour (appassionated, oppressed)	Amoret (appassionated, traumatized)

That Britomart is an honorary knight acknowledges that a lady may be a lover; and, just as there is a sense in which the armed Venus that she presents is masculine, so there is also a sense in which the eros or passion presented by Scudamour is feminine. But, besides establishing a kind of parity between the sexes, this analysis also inculcates a special lesson in allegory, a lesson that a legend of love might well offer in any case: the "likeness" to which love brings the sexes. In Book III the male's allegorical "other" will be female, and the woman's will be male. One of the symbols of allegorical otherness is the mirror, and the mirror from which Britomart's legend begins exchanges sex for sex, like the rationalization of the Narcissus myth cited from Pausanias. The comparison of Britomart's lovelorn state to that of Narcissus is ironically disavowed (III.ii.45), but it is not entirely surprising that the reversal in which the final episode of the legend issues takes the form of reuniting the separated lovers as a hermaphrodite. The bath replaces Narcissus' pool—the Ovidian hermaphrodite was formed in a pool also. In such a union each of the lovers can recover his or her own sexual nature from the other, and at the same time be made psychosexually whole.

Petrarchan love unmans the lover, as it unmans Scudamour. It is mixed with lust, as illustrated in Busirane. Its beloved rejects the advances of the lover, as Amoret and Britomart resist the old enchanter. But Amoret, who makes a fourth in this equation, hardly seems to resemble Laura. Before attempting to explain her personal trauma, we must recur to the tradition of the "defeat of Love."

There is an Ariostan predecessor for the House of Busirane. The text is the first victory of Ariosto's virago heroine Bradamante. In this adventure

474

the lady knight binds the old enchanter Atlante with his own chain.[91] She forces Atlante to disenchant the prison palace that confines her lover Ruggiero—a disenchantment that requires the extinguishing of pots of fire concealed beneath the palace threshold. In Spenser, then, Britomart has the place of Bradamante; and Busirane, of Atlante. This analogy would make Atlante a bound "elder Eros," and it was just such a Petrarchan interpretation of the story that Ariosto's commentators in fact supplied. Porcacchi and Fornari both equate Atlante with Love. Fornari understands Bradamante "as the goddess of chastity, which conquers Cupid, god of love." He also explains the location of Atlante's palace in the Pyrenees as an allusion to love's fiery nature.[92] A fiery barrier for Cupid's realm subsequently appears in the *Rinaldo* of Tasso; true lovers can pass it, and the oracle of love within includes a representation of Cupid's triumphs with which Tasso's hero is uneasy (V.58ff.).

Amoret still remains outside the circle of the symbolism, though one can see that Ariosto's Bradamante, in freeing her lover, also frees a part of herself. Similarly, Amoret's experience resembles the nightmarish sufferings of Cupid as described by Ausonius and Politian, except that Cupid is the opposite sex. To further explain Amoret's torment, we must presume to enter Amoret's mind. To herself, we might suppose, she is a female "Cupid crucified," that is, the object of a vengeance taken in terms of the very passion that she has inspired.[93] The trouble begins on Amoret's wedding-night. As a student of Renaissance epithalamia, Spenser would have been well aware of the tradition of sexual violence that had surfaced in the wedding-poems of his time. The conceits include a bedroom combat in which it is anticipated that the bride will be roughly used, the engagement to culminate in a traumatic thrust.[94] Concerning this epithalamium motif, we may note that the wounding of Britomart occupies the symbolic place of the rupturing of Amoret's hymen; the wound is much slighter than Amoret's fantasies of male domination would have suggested—apparently she anticipates virtual disembowelment.[95]

[91] *O.F.* IV.7–38. Atlante's chain is easily equated with the chain of love, a trope found elsewhere in Ariosto: e.g., *O.F.* X.97, XLII.1, 64.

[92] Fornari, *La Spositione . . . sopra l'Orlando furioso* (Florence, 1549–1550), I, pp. 180ff.; cf. *Orlando Furioso . . . le nuoue argomenti di . . . Dolce: . . . the nuoue allegorie, & annotationi di M. Tomaso Porcacchi . . .* (Vinegia: Polo, 1583), canto IV.

[93] Wind, *Pagan Mysteries*, pp. 146f., n. 19, cites an antique lovespell that "prescribes that a gem be engraved on one side with the tortures of Psyche imposed by Eros and Aphrodite, on the other with the group of Eros and Psyche embracing."

[94] See Scaliger, *Poetices*, III.c, *edn. cit.*, p. 346; the epithalamic convention includes the storming of the bride, *lascivia lususque*, and the bride's fear of the impending struggle. See Leonard Forster, *The Icy Fire* (Cambridge, 1969), pp. 104–144.

[95] A symbol of the hymen also occurs—as Steven Barney has pointed out to me—at the Temple of Venus, where the goddess' veil may be interpreted as the veil of the flesh, and the fragile, quintessential substance of the stone on which she stands

A folktale analogue dramatically illustrates Amoret's terrible surmise. This is the story of Mr. Fox, which Malone first records in his variorum Shakespeare of 1790 (via a communication from Mr. Blakeway), in explanation of the line from the "old tale" quoted in *Much Ado* (I.i.216). In this story, a certain Lady Mary and her brothers repair to a castle of theirs where a neighborhood bachelor, Mr. Fox, becomes a frequent guest. Being much taken with the lady, Mr. Fox invites her to visit *his* castle. One day she does so. Mr. Fox is not at home, but she nonetheless enters, and comes upon doors marked "Be Bold" and "Be Not Too Bold—Lest Your Heart's Blood Run Cold." Hazarding this consequence—and committing the trespass typically enjoined by folktale for the ultimate rectification of some past misdeed—the lady opens the door to behold a roomful of the remains (including tubs of blood) of Mr. Fox's former victims. Thus the forbidding portal common to Spenser and this old tale originally discovered a Bluebeard's closet of horrors. Mr. Fox returns with another lady. Hiding herself, Lady Mary secretly witnesses her evil host's violent way with his unfortunate guest, and then escapes home. Her brothers thereafter take vengeance upon Mr. Fox. As a spectator in the lonely castle, Lady Mary resembles Britomart. But as the one who only narrowly avoids the fate in store for those women who put themselves in the power of such a suitor, Mr. Fox's "intended" more nearly resembles Amoret.

The retributive relations between guest and host in this story recall Roche's fine suggestion that Busirane owes his name to a passage in Ovid's *Art of Love* that asserts that Venus favors the bold;[96] the lover is advised to take the part of Busiris, the Egyptian king who was told that the shedding of a stranger's blood would restore Egypt's lost fertility. Busiris sacrifices the very seer who came to impart this intelligence. It is right (Ovid says) that the woman should grieve, feeling the wound that she gives.[97] Elsewhere Ovid reports that Busiris painted his walls with pilgrims'

---

as the same thing. For the latter, cf. Shakespeare, *Pericles*, IV.vi.142f., "crack the glass of her virginity and make the rest malleable." Considerable support for the interpretation is offered by the *Hypnerotomachia*, where the fountain of Venus is veiled by a curtain embroidered HYMEN, and domed by pure crystal. When the lover rends this veil, the goddess is disclosed anadyomene (Methuen facsimile, London, 1904, Sig. Zi^r). See n. 111 below. In general, however, Scudamour at the Temple of Venus invades the beloved's *mind*, not her body.

[96] Thomas Roche, *The Kindly Flame* (Princeton, 1964), pp. 81ff., citing Thomas Warton from the Variorum *Works, Book III*, p. 287.

[97] *Ars Amat.* I.643ff. For the vengeance-theme and the anteros motif developed below, cf. Ficino, *De Amore*, II.viii, Jayne trans., p. 145: "Certainly there is a most just vengeance in reciprocal love, for a homicide must be punished by death, and who will deny that a man who is loved is a homicide since he robs the loving one of his soul?" For the vindictive Cupid-statue of Melville's poem, cf. Theocritus, *Idyl* XXIII.

blood[98]—here we may compare Busirane's tapestry. Roche's suggestion is further supported by the story that makes Busiris the instigator of an attempt by pirates to abduct and rape the Hesperides.[99]

If Venus favors the bold, and Busiris is their type, then Britomart, who is also advised to be bold, must be a Busiris too. And if the abusive Cupid is also a Busiris, and the crucified Cupid appears in Amoret, there are at least three Amor figures at the House; Scudamour, the protégé of Cupid, makes four. We may now address ourselves more directly to the recurrent question of this essay, that of the formal generation of the dialectic of the Busirane episode: from what unity of concept does it proceed?

The name of the comatose princess in the fairytale—the figure to whom we have compared the enchanted Amoret—is Briar-rose. Briar-rose, as her name implies, sleeps behind a wall of thorns. Furthermore, the spell laid upon her at christening is only activated when, at fifteen years, she pricks her finger; it is then that she feels the curse laid upon roses. The princess wounds herself during the newly discovered activity of spinning, which is taboo in the kingdom, and which an older woman shows her in a remote place in the royal castle. There are, of course, several psychoanalytically related meanings for the forbidden spinning. Along with the datum of the onset of the curse, the interpreter must also consider a conflation of "lance" and "distaff" symbols. Britomart substitutes as much as she rejects when she refuses to lead her life "As Ladies *wont*, in pleasures *want*on lap, / To *finger* the fine needle and nyce thread, / Me *leuer* were with point of foemans speare be dead" (III.ii.6). The Malecasta episode may be feasibly recast in terms of this abreaction to a suppressed impulse toward self-excitement: Malecasta is "Of euery finest fingers touch affrayd" (III.i.61).

Briar-rose is vulnerable to herself; the same thing is true of Amoret. In the course of the Busirane episode Spenser has occasion to tell us that the god also spared not to wound himself (III.xi.45). (The reference is to the complaint of the wounded Cupid in Apulieus, *The Golden Ass* V.24 and 28; at V.30, the chastisement of Cupid is anticipated by his mother. At line 28 of the fourth of the intercalated addenda to the *Amoretti*, the bee-stung Cupid complains "I wounded am full sore.") This might be only

---

[98] *Metam.* IX.182f.

[99] See Diodorus Sic., *Bibl.* IV.xxvii.2, and Comes' notice of the story, *Mythol.* VII.vii, pp. 726ff., *edn. cit.*: "In this region Atlas begot six daughters, who were called Atlantides, and on account of their mother, Hesperides. Smitten by desire for their beauties, Busiris sent brigands and pirates after them on account of their swiftness. These raped them and carried them off for themselves. At the time Hercules fought against Antaeus, the robbers ravished the girls in a certain garden and forced them aboard ship. Hercules, seeing the case of the virgins—where the robbers were perhaps eating by the shore—killed the brigands to a man, and returned the daughters to their father." For further on this rape, see n. 549, below.

a way of saying that love spares no one; but, when the conceit is read back into the overall context in which it occurs, it may be found to contain the whole basis of the symbolism. Amoret and Busirane become differentiations of the same being, a little like Britomart and Malecasta. We might call the one an *Amor Vulneratus*, and the other an *Amor Vindictus*.

The examples so far cited have perhaps already suggested that Cupid's vulnerability to love must be reflexive. Because she causes desire, the beloved may be conceived as a Cupid. But because she is independent of the wound that she gives, and is susceptible to no power of attraction other than her own, the beloved, as such a Cupid, is potentially a Narcissus, and therefore liable to an analogous fate. The self-regard implicit in Cupid's solity has been aptly remarked. Cupid has been called "the One": "Marcianus after Aristotle affirmeth that Cupid is so named because it is one alone, & wold euer haue himselfe to be sought, & hath nothing besides, but being voide of all elation or couple, doth wrest his owne heates to himselfe: . . ."[100] Amoret is not finally "voide of all elation or couple": quite the contrary. But her isolation is marked, and it seems logical to suppose it to be a form of introversion. Amoret is deeply in love, and nothing indicates that she is fascinated by herself, or even by her capacity to inspire love. But she does seem fairly oblivious to the *actuality* of Scudamour beyond the walls, and the passion that she has inspired in him seems to have driven her deep into her own fantasies. It follows that, in her ecstasy, Amoret may be partly self-ravished, and her wound partly self-inflicted.

Once we have conflated the episode in this way—a way that makes it all Amoret—we will want to restore the differentia of our earlier analysis, along the lines of the polarization that the episode actually presents. Is there a less claustrophobic reading that nonetheless preserves a theme of Love against Himself? What does this theme mean in a legend of chastity? And what are its antecedents?

Ausonius' poem goes back to a *topos* in the *Greek Anthology*, namely, the bound Cupid of Hellenistic statuary.[101] Of the six *Anthology* poems

---

[100] The quote is from a passage discussing the Concord or Friendship signified by the number one; basically, it makes Cupid hermaphroditic. It is from *Batman vppon Bartholome* (1582), fol. 2ʳ⁻ᵛ, citing Agrippa, *De Occulta Phil.* (II.iv; in the J. French trans. of 1651, p. 174). For the hermaphroditic Cupid, cf. the text from *Asclepius*, xx seq., cited at n. 467, below.

[101] *Gr. Anth.* XVI.195–199. The Loeb edn., ed. Paton, vol. 5, pp. 272–277, illustrates the monuments. Renaissance medals show the type, as noted in Wind, *Pagan Mysteries*, p. 147. Examples reproduced in G. F. Hill, *A Corpus of Italian Medals* (London, 1930), fall into three categories, illustrating the evolution of our topic: (1) bound Cupid *solus*: nos. 233, 234, 235; (2) adolescent Cupid bound by a virgin:

upon this image, four have a retribution motif. Antipater of Sidon writes an epigram that taunts the captive: "Who took captive fire by fire and guile by guile? My boy, bedew not thy sweet face with tears, for thou dost take delight in the tears of young men."[102] An inscription on a statue is not only an epigram, but also the motto for an image. Comparably, the House of Busirane is quite explicitly emblematic, with its idol, dumbshow, quizzical images, and labels. Thus genre as well as subject matter relates the Busirane episode to an Alciati emblem titled "Virtuous Love Conquering Vicious Love." One version of the emblem depicts a conflagration, next to which a winged Venus has bound Cupid to a post. (Other versions show two Cupids.) The verses read:

> Nemesis painted a Love, winged, and an enemy to the winged one; dominating a bow by a bow, and fire by fire. So that what he did to others he suffered: and hereupon the intrepid, weapon-bearing boy— wretched—wept. Thrice he spits against the last windings: a wonderful thing, fire was consumed by fire, love hated the furies of Love.[103]

The French translation is expansive: "From her he suffered and endured / The hard and painful passion / He made others suffer. . . . He almost

---

nos. 992 and 1011, both titled "Virginitas Amoris Frenum" (Virginity with respect to the Frenzy of Love)—but the Petrarchan subject of the second category is implicit in the first, given the title of nos. 233, "Virtuti ac formae pudicitia praeciosissimum," and 235, "Dea militati stat"; and (3), no. 919, an impassioned young man kneeling bound on an altar, with Cupid blowing flames beneath him, and facing a full grown woman seated in the chair of a chariot—the whole drawn by horses, which a second Cupid mounts while a second man brings these horses under control. The medal may be supplemented by the two paintings reproduced in Hill, *Corpus of Italian Medals*, vol. 1, plate between pp. 242f., one of which is Wallace Collection, no. 556; apparently all portray a triumph of chastity subject, especially if the woman in the chariot holds the broken bow that is found on the bottom register of the medal. The tableau is particularly interesting to Spenser students because of the sense of its becoming a scenario: love inflames, while chastity restrains —love drives the horses of passion, which must yet be bridled.

[102] *Gr. Anth.* XVI.197, trans. W. R. Paton, Loeb edn., vol. 5, p. 275.

[103] Emb. CX, "*Anteros*, Amor virtutis aliun Cupiden superans," in *Omnia . . . Alciati . . . Emblemata cum commentariis . . . per Claudium Minoem* (Antwerp, 1581), pp. 386–390. The title leads me to identify the winged victor with Venus, rather than a swift Nemesis, as in the poem. That Venus and Nemesis are essentially the same in this context is the purport of Pausanias, *Perieg.* I.xxxiii.7, which makes Nemesis the mother of Anteros: Nemesis has wings, like Love, because the goddess most often manifests herself as a consequence of love. For the theme of the emblem, cf. Sidney, *Astrophel and Stella*, Son. 42, on Stella's eyes, which, "while they make Love conquer, conquer Love; / The schools where Venus hath learned chastity." The source of the emblem is *Gr. Anth.* XVI.251. See also *Gr. Anth.* IX.440 (=Moschus, *Idyl* I), cited in n. 361, below.

died of weeping. . . . Devoured by excess of grief . . . Love by love was chastised. . . .[104]

The spellbinding of the heroine (III.ii.50), has a parallel in the *Aeneid*, in the place where Venus tells Cupid that she will put a ring of fire around Dido, and hold her fast, such that no god will be able to change her.[105] To explain Alciati's "furias odit Amoris amor," his commentator cites Ovid's "Causa fuit multis noster amoris amore" (our love has been the cause for many loves). Mignault thinks of the two loves of the emblem as an Eros and an Anteros, according to an ambiguity whereby Anteros can be anti-erotic.[106] And for the Nemesis theme he is able to cite a short passage from Boethius: "Indeed, what can any man do to another which another man may not do to him? We recall that Busiris, who was accustomed to kill his guests, was himself slain by his guest Hercules."[107] According to the same principle, the greater Love represented by Britomart releases Amoret and binds the evil host in her place. Mignault cites the example of Hippolytus' resistance to Phaedra, which is also found in Petrarch's *Triumph*, and he specifically understands Alciati's emblem to record "the triumph of chastity."

Iconographically, then, the Busirane episode presents an extended emblem of the polarization of love. Since either Chastity or Anteros conquers love, both Britomart and Amoret are shown as opposed to Busirane. The rivalry between the two meanings of Anteros—"love in return" and "contrary to love"—is a large part of the dialectic. Amoret must learn to reciprocate love, and yet retain her resistance to corruption. For this dialectic we may recur to our earlier point, apropos Archimago, that the contest in romance is between two magics. For in Book III, the "false Archimage" who pursues the heroine is hardly to be distinguished from the "false Archer" that wounds her (III.iv.45, ii.26).

Busirane is a magician because Love is a magician. Plato, in *Symposium* 203, describes love as "terrible as an enchanter, sorcerer, sophist." For Love

[104] *Emblemata* (Latinogallica) (Paris, 1584), Emb. CX, p. 152: the "Virtuous Love" is a winged lady here.

[105] *Aen.* I.673–675. For the triple binding of such an amorous spell cf. esp. *Eclogue* VIII.73–78, where the "bonds of Venus" are invoked.

[106] Ovid, *Amores* III.xi.20; Alciati (Antwerp, 1581), p. 390. The word *anteros* (counter-love) means "love in return," as in Cartari's depiction in *Le Imagini, edn. cit.*, p. 364, which gives a long citation from Porphyry on the source of the image. The Alciati emblem often shows two Cupids—as in the Basel edn. of 1534, p. 76— but Anteros here means contrary-to-love, or love's antidote. See also Achilles Bocchius, *Symbolicarvm qvaestionvm*, Symb. LXXX: "Hic Anteros quid est nisi verum esse amorem mutuum?" and contrast Alciati, Emb. CIX (Antwerp edn.), p. 382, "*Anteros, id est amor virtutis*" (two Venuses).

[107] *De Cons. Phil.* II, prose vi; Alciati, *edn. cit.*, p. 388.

as a sophist we will want to refer to the Proteus of this legend, but Busirane is undoubtedly Love the Enchanter; as Ficino says, "in love there is all the power of enchantment," for "the work of enchantment is the attraction of one thing to another because of a certain similarity of one thing to another."[108] Ficino's explanation might owe something to Plotinus, who wrote on this same "primary wizard and enchanter":

> How do magic spells work? By sympathy, and by the natural concord of things that are alike and opposition of things that are different. . . . For many things are done and enchanted without any other contrivance. The true magic is the "Love and Strife in the All." This is the primary wizard and enchanter, from observing whom men come to use philtres and spells on each other. For because desire is natural and things that cause desire attract each other, there has grown up an art of attraction by desire through magic, used by those who add by magic touches various natures designed to draw different people together and with a force of desire implanted in them: they join one soul to another. . . . They use as well figures with power in them. . . .[109]

But, though Busirane exerts compulsion on desire through magic spells, he is Strife rather than Love insofar as he causes the opposition of Scudamour and Amoret. For their very love seemingly polarizes them into aggressor and victim. Britomart, in bringing them together, takes the part of the rival magician, and the rival Love.

The signs over which Busirane labors remind one a little of the ceremonies in the *Hypnerotomachia*; the beloved Polia and the high-priestess write characters with the cinders of sacrificial swans and doves, charms for the preservation of love.[110] The scene is unimportant except as a prologue to another, in which Venus commends the mutual love of Polia and Poliphilus to four personifications, one of whom is called Henosis. Each of the lovers is to be an Anteros to the other, and their *henosis* is shortly realized; the lover reports:

> When the goddess had finished her orders, her son took an arrow and pulled his bow with such force that he touched his breast with one hand and the iron of the arrow with the other: then shot upon us with such power as it is impossible to describe. Barely had he let go the string, than I felt the arrow pass right through my heart, and in the same movement (still red and steaming with my blood) enter the breast of Polia, where it stayed fixed, having given me a wound for which there was no need for medicine. This done, Cupid approached Polia, and removed the arrow resting half-way into her breast.

[108] *De Amore*, Vi.x, Jayne trans., p. 200.
[109] *Enn.* IV, IV.40, trans. by A. H. Armstrong, in *Plotinus* (London, 1953), p. 110.
[110] Methuen facsimile (London, 1904), Sig. o viii^r-v.

The lover apparently faints as the image of his beloved takes possession of his heart; he is lost in an ecstasy of metamorphosis:

> Here was not a nerve or vein in me that did not burn like dry straw in a huge furnace, so that I barely recognized myself any longer, and thought that I had been changed into another shape. I was also uncertain as to the state of my soul. I think it was like Hermaphroditus taking his beloved in his arms in a fountain, feeling and seeing two bodies become one. For my pulse had changed and I drew deep breaths like someone who while sleeping dreams of being so weighed down that he can hardly breathe, and then catching his breath in great gasps.[111]

Like Cupid here, Britomart takes the action that removes Love's arrow, or sting, and in the subsequent *henosis* the lovers share a kind of seizure.

In Ficino's *Commento*, we hear that bewitching lovers "win over and snare their loved ones with the powers of rhetoric and the metres of poetry, as though with some incantation; moreover, they overcome and take possession of them with worship and rewards exactly as though with magic potions. Therefore, no one doubts that Love is an enchanter, since the whole power of enchantment rests in love, and the work of love is effected by bewitchment, magic spells, and potions."[112] These are Busirane's "thousand charmes," which Britomart is able to "reuerse" in Amoret (III.xii.31, 36), but which on an earlier occasion the backward Glauce—with a considerable effort of witchcraft and "many an idle verse—could not "reuerse" in Britomart (III.ii.48). As Steven Barney points out,[113] the means employed by Glauce—the herbs, charms, and counsel—are the same ones that the witch employs in trying to dispel her son's fascination with Florimell. The witch goes on to fabricate the Stesichoran False Florimell, who is Petrarchan as well. As the description by Ficino implies, Love the enchanter is also Love the poet; and, whatever the conjured surrogate may be, the House of Busirane is the work of a major artist. Indeed, Busirane

---

[111] Trans. from the French of Ian Martin, *Discours du songe de Poliphile* (Paris, 1561), fol. 128^v. The original is found on Sig. ziij^v–ziiij^r, in the Methuen facsimile of the first edition. The French omits a reference to the transformation of Biblis, and substitutes the oppressed sleeper for the state of seizure, or "Epilipsia." For the painful wound given at the beginning of marriage, which leads to the *holōn krasis* or "integral amalgamation" of the married pair, see Plutarch, *Amatorius* 24, *Moralia* 769E–F.

[112] *De Amore*, VI.x, Jayne trans., p. 200.

[113] In a forthcoming chapter in a study of allegory, comparing III.iii.5 ("Nor herbes, nor charmes nor counsell, that is chief") with III.vii.21 ("With herbs, with charms, with counsell, and with teares"). Cf. *O.F.* XXXI.5, on the wound made by lover's jealousy, which I take to be the source: "This is the cruel and poisoned wound for which neither potion nor salve avails, nor muttering, nor image from a wiseman, nor long observing of favorable stars, nor great experience of magic art, nor anything its inventor Zoraster did. . . ."

almost seems to have grown old in the service of a craft at once literary and erotic: an art inevitably characterized as "so long to learn." As Lewis originally pointed out, Busirane stands for an oppressive tradition; Spenser implies it wants unlearning.

In reversing the mage's spell, it may be added, Britomart engages yet one more of the epithets of Venus, namely, that of the temple goddess known to classical authors as *Venus Verticordia*.[114] This Venus was said to have reversed the corruption of Roman women by licentious love and to have made honest wives of them again. Cartari adds to this report the notice that "there was a Venus similar to this one of the Romans, whom the Greeks called Apostrophia, and whom we would want to call *Avertrice*, because she was opposed to dishonest lusts and took from the human mind libidinous desires."[115] Such a Venus, the protector of marriage, must surely be included in that line that leads from Petrarch's Pudicizia, who was adept at averting blows, to this greater Avertrice, who parries the elder Love, and maintains the younger one a "virgin wife" (IV.i.6).

It remains to indicate Britomart's own relation to the experience of the House of Busirane. We might call her personal theme the vigil of Venus. As Greenlaw saw, the atmosphere and appurtenances of the House pertain to a Grail initiation.[116] In the Grail stories, the quester beholds the sacred objects—lance and dish—in the presence of a mysteriously stricken being. Thus the sacrificial silver dish (or basin), the steel darts, and Amoret's chronic wound. The deeply oppressive watching at closed doors belongs to the same theme, though this imagery is not peculiar to the Grail romance; the night-vigil in a dreadful place is found in "gothic" romance as a general rule. A strong scene early in Chretien de Troye's *Ywain* combines the gothic cryptic place with the erotic theme. Ywain has followed a wounded antagonist into his castle and been trapped in a sealed

---

[114] See Valerius Maximus, *Fact. et Dict.* VIII.15; Ovid, *Fasti* IV.160, Pausanias, *Perieg.* IX.xvi.2 seq.

[115] *Le Imagini, edn. cit.*, p. 395. So also Comes, *Mythol.*, IV.xiii, p. 395, *edn. cit.*, on Venus Apostraphia or Epistropha: "she turns men from outrageous unchastity." Also noted in Giraldus, *Hist. Deorum*, Syntag. XIII, in *Op. om.*, I, col. 390.

[116] Edwin A. Greenlaw, "Britomart at the House of Busirane," *Studies in Philology*, 26 (1929), pp. 117-130. Compare the following from Malory: Balin attempts to rescue a damsel that has been riding with him from the armed attack of many men at a castle: "And they . . . all seyde nay, they wolde nat fyght with hym, for they did nothynge but the olde custom of theys castell, and tolde hym that hir lady was syke and had leyne many yeres, and she mygt nat be hole but yf she had bloode in a sylver dysshe full, of a clene mayde and a kynges doughter. ¶ 'And therefore the custom of thys castell ys that there shall no damesell passe thys way but she shall blede of hir bloode a sylver dysshefull.'" (Vinaver, ed., *Malory: Works*, 2nd edn., London, 1971, p. 51.)

room between the portcullis and the entryway to a further apartment. The wounded knight shortly dies within the inner chamber, and his corpse is borne through the outer room, under the direction of his distraught lady, to its burial. Ywain remains unseen. He has been able to render himself invisible by means of a magic ring, and the dead man's retainers fail to discover their master's enemy—though the corpse bleeds afresh in his presence. Ywain in fact has betaken himself to a bed in the room, from which he beholds the knight's lady for the first time. He falls precipitously in love, and the "sweet enemy" theme is launched at once:

> Love had conducted a raid on his land and had succeeded completely in taking her quarry. His enemy had led away his heart, for he loved that one who most detested him. Although she did not realize it, the lady had fully vindicated her lord's death. She had received a greater requital than she could ever have achieved had Love not avenged her by assailing him so sweetly, piercing his heart through his eyes. This wound would last longer than any wound made by lance or sword. A sword cut heals and becomes whole very soon when a physician attends to it, but the wound made by Love becomes worse the nearer it is to its physician. My Lord Ywain had received a hurt which would never be healed, for Love had devoted herself wholly to him.[117]

There is a sense in which the Petrarchan conventions anticipated here are reintegrated into their chivalric context in Spenser's episode: *Ywain* already has the sealed room, the exchange of wounds, the modulation of the vulnerability of a dying-god figure into an erotic context, and the antagonism that leads to a new union.

Britomart's vigil on behalf of Amoret portends a kind of keeping watch over love. A parody of the theme is the guard that Malbecco jealously maintains over young Hellenore. In Gascoigne's version of Ariosto's story of Sospetto—a story that lies behind Spenser's—Gascoigne allegorizes the six gates of the suspicious man by giving them porters: Dread, Mistrust, Wrath, Desperation, Frenzy, and Fury.[118] These Gascoigne has taken

[117] *Ywain, the Knight of the Lion*, trans. Robert Ackerman and Frederick Locke (New York, 1957), pp. 23f.

[118] Gascoigne, *The Adventures of Master F. J.*, rev. edn. from *The Posies*, ed. J. W. Cunliffe (Cambridge, 1907), reprinted in *Elizabethan Fiction*, ed. Robert Ashley and Edwin Moseley (New York, 1953), pp. 50f. See William Nelson, "A Source for Spenser's Malbecco," in *MLN*, 68 (1953), pp. 226–229, and Waldo F. McNeir, "Ariosto's Sospetto, Gascoigne's Suspicion, and Spenser's Malbecco," in *Festschrift für Walther Fischer* (Heidelberg, 1959), pp. 33–48. The story of Sospetto, without Gascoigne's Elenore, is told in Ariosto's *Cinque Canti*, II.8–20, where the theme of paranoid insecurity more nearly reflects Plutarch, *To an Ignorant Prince* 4, *Moralia* 781E. Sources for Sospetto's self-enclosure include stories told of Dionysius of Syracuse (see Cicero, *De Off.* II.xii.25, *Tusc. Disp.* V.xx.59; Valerius Maximus, *Dict. Fact.* IX.xiii.4; Ammianus Marcellinus, *Rerum Gest.* XVI.viii.10).

from a description of jealousy elsewhere in Ariosto, from a passage Gascoigne's young lover will himself recite a few pages later. Ariosto has Sospetto, Timore, Martir, Frenesia, Rabbia, and Gelosia; Gascoigne's version makes the emotions of dread, fear, care, cold suspect, deep despair, and furious frenzy into Jealousy's handmaids. Just as we can find the six champions of Malecasta in the Malbecco episode, so we can also find the six porters of Sospetto there. Several of these personifications also appear in the Masque of Cupid at the House of Busirane: Suspect, Fear, Fury, Grief, and Doubt. Ideally, the Masque would illustrate Ariosto's assertion that *amore* is advanced by an alteration of delight and *amaro*, the bitterness that disposes the palate for pleasure. These bitternesses, according to the same place in Ariosto, are the disdains, the repulses, and finally all the *martir* of love. Jealousy is the one exception.[119] It is a wound inflicted by false or true suspicions, which darkens reason and poisons the mind. Britomart's function at the House of Busirane entails the dispelling of this broad kind of jealousy, a nameless fear of betrayal in surrendering to love. Paradoxically, Britomart's chaperonage of Amoret restores to her something that at the end of the legend allows her to lose herself in pleasure.

Britomart's vigil over love may be observed as late as the house of Dolon, in Book V, where Britomart herself is in an anxious mood, fearing that Artegall has betrayed her for Radigund. Turning to self-reproach, the weary yet wary heroine addresses her own beguiled and momentarily traitorous eyes in words echoing those of Christ to Peter at Gethsemane— Peter's eyes were also heavy (V.vi.25, with 27; Matt. 26:40–43). This rather emphatic animadversion upon Britomart's eyes suggests one last way of locating the vigil theme, again iconographically: by means of the striking image of the blinded dragon.

It is Cupid who has blinded the dragon, just as he has transfixed Amoret, and also as Gardant has glanced Britomart. The dragon here has a rather long tradition, but he is not the traditional evil dragon. Rather, he is an aspect of Britomart as Minerva or Pallas. In the Orphic Hymn to her, the Minerva who conquered the Titans in the Phlegrean plain is addressed as a wily-formed dragon.[120] The dragons of *Aeneid* II.225–227 seek the shrine of the savage Tritonia, where they take up their post under the feet of the goddess and the circle of her shield. In Cornutus' article on Minerva, we read that owls and serpents are sacred to the goddess, because of the prop-

---

[119] *O.F.* XXXI 1–3: Bradamante feigns sick, but it is not corporeal pain that afflicts her: "It was desire that disabled her soul from within / And made it suffer the alteration of Love." See n. 86, above. Britomart conquers this affliction in Merlin's cave, where the Ariosto passage is also echoed (see n. 113).

[120] Orphic Hymn XXXI, l. 11, in Hambergerus, ed., *Orpheos Apanta*, with the trans. of Joseph Scaliger. The Latin makes the goddess "Bellona virago" and "Gorgonitruda": in Spenser the "Minerva" of III.iv.22 was "Bellona" in the 1590 edn. of the poem.

erties of their eyes: Minerva has gray (*glaucos*) eyes herself. "For a fierce dragon guards her, accommodated, it is asserted, in like manner to a vigilant guardian: he is not easily able to be surprised. Her eyes' gray color represent animosity and truculence towards men."[121] The dragon, we are told by Claude Mignault, gets its Greek name from its eyes; thus the blinded dragon at the House of Busirane is no less an oxymoron than the triumph of a Cupid defeated by love. Mignault is commenting on Alciati's emblem, *Custodiendas Virgines* (The Guardianship of Virgins):

> This is the true effigy of the maiden Pallas: hers this dragon is, who stands posted before the feet of his mistress. Why this animal for the companion of the goddess? Because to this one is committed the guardianship of things: thus he watches over groves and sacred precincts. His task is to guard unmarried girls with ever-vigilant pains: Love sets his traps everywhere.[122]

Spenser's Cupid has blinded the very symbol of vigilance. It is Britomart who takes the part of Love defeating Love; Alciati's emblem formulates her charge. Although Love sets his traps everywhere, the watchful guardian of a virgin takes up her post, and the pervigilium of the unmarried girl goes on.

[ii]

The foregoing establishes the scenario for one of the two or three most memorable episodes in *The Faerie Queene*. But the scenario does not explain the dreadful image of Amoret herself, on which so much of the episode turns. Amoret may be a Cupid crucified, but, being a deathly Cupid as a consequence, she is also something more.

The antitheses of the masque symbolize the pains in the pleasure of love. Alciati symbolized these by the Anacreonic story of Cupid's being stung by bees while tasting honey;[123] Spenser's Displeasure and Pleasure carry a

---

[121] *De Nat. Deorum*, 20, "De Minerva," in Gale, *Opscula Mythologica*, p. 186.

[122] Emb. XXII, *Omnia Andreae Alciati v.c. Emblemata cum commentariis . . . per Claudium Minoem* (Antwerp, 1581), pp. 104–107. Minerva's *cernuus Draco* or discerning dragon appears underfoot in Hadrianus Junius, *Emblemata* (Antwerp, 1565), no. 24, "Virginem Pudicitiae, Matronam Domus satagere" ("the Virgin secures her chastity, the Matron her house"): the emblem shows Minerva on a dragon, paired with Venus standing on the house-carrying turtle. Minerva stands on the dragon because "the well-provided Virgin occupies herself with decorum." But the source of the emblem in Plutarch, *De Iside* 75, *Moralia* 381E, says that it is because "maidens need watching." I was unaware when I wrote my essay that C. S. Lewis, in *Images of Life* (Cambridge, 1967), pp. 22f., quotes the same emblem of Alciati to the same effect.

[123] Emb. LXXXIX in *edn. cit. Anacreonta* 35, "The Wounded Cupid." For the ratio of gall and honey in love, see IV.x.i.

wasp and a honeybee to symbolize the same bittersweet quality of love.[124] But Amoret's extremity clearly presses this paradox to its limit, which is the point where the intensity of love, or Amor, touches on death, or Mors.[125] Perfect love was often understood to demand a kind of *ecstasis*, or death to the world, as one can see in the discourse set at the end of Castiglione's *Courtier*.[126] Amoret is literally outside of herself, and though Spenser may intend no such mystery of the divine *raptus*, our knowledge of its tradition complicates our response to the possessed maid. For example, Spenser compares Fancy, one of the masquers, to Ganymede, "that ympe of Troy, / Whom Ioue did loue" (III.xii.7), and to Hylas, who took the fancy of Hercules. Ganymede can also be a type for abduction by the divine love, and Hylas appears just after a reference to the ravishing effect of the music for the masque—"the fraile soul in deepe delight nigh dround" (III.xii.6).[127] Ficino says that whoever loves also dies, and the presence of death in love is very much the secret burden of Cupid's triumph.[128]

The masque interweaves at least four strands of imagery for death. First are the images of ravishment, just mentioned. Amoret's abduction and enchantment belong here too. Second are those images that imply death because they refer to a dreadful end for passion. Dissemblance walks in feare of "hid mischaunce." Daunger carries a rusty blade called Mishap— the same blade, one may say, effects the deaths of Romeo and Juliet. And Fury tosses a firebrand about her head,

> . . . still roming here and there;
> As a dismayed Deare in chace embost,
> Forgetfull of his safety, hath his right way lost.
>
> (III.xii.17)

The image recalls Dido's *furor*. Dido is compared to a wounded deer, wandering in pain, as well as a Fury-hounded tragic actor,[129] and her distracted course also ends in suicide. Thirdly, there are the images that anticipate Amoret's own condition: Doubt advances with feeble steps; Fear is as pale as ashes; Grief is "Dying each day with inward wounds of dol-

---

[124] On the literary transmission of this bittersweetness from Sappho, Frg. 137 (Diehl), see Wind, *Pagan Mysteries*, pp. 161–163. For Amore:Amaro, see Petrarch, *Trionfo d'Amore*, I.75f.

[125] The following is largely suggested by Wind, *Pagan Mysteries*, chap. 10, "Amor as a God of Death." Wind does not treat Apulieus, Spenser, or Shakespeare. For Amore and Morte in Petrarch, see Sonnets 29, 32, and 72 (*Canz.* XXXVI, XL, XCIII); also Son. 162, 163 (*Canz.* CXCV, CXCVI).

[126] See Wind, *Pagan Mysteries*, pp. 154–160.

[127] Wind, *Pagan Mysteries*, pp. 154, 159.

[128] *De Amore*, II.viii.

[129] *Aen.* IV.66–73, 465–473. Cf. Scudamour at IV.i.49.

ours dart" (III.xii.16). Grief's pincers are also those that will torment Scudamour at the House of Care. Daunger's blade directs us to Amoret's side, "Entrenched deepe with knife accursed keene" (III.xii.20). Finally, there are the images that suggest that, though Amoret was absent from her own wedding, she may be present at her own funeral. Grief appears to be dressed in mourning, and Hope sprinkles a holy water dipped in the dew that we have elsewhere associated with the hope of the resurrection (III.xii.13).

In attempting to explain this kind of imagery for love, Edgar Wind directs us to the Eros figures sculpted on Roman sarcophagi, where conventionally Cupid holds his torch downwards. In one classical text—the image of Komos in Philostrates—such a gesture is also made at the doorway to a wedding celebration.[130] The result of making Cupid party to a funeral will be to make Amoret an *Éros funèbre*.[131] Sarcophagi subjects included the loves of the gods for mortals, such as the love of Cupid for Psyche and Jove for Ganymede,[132] and the loves of the gods also decorate the walls of Busirane's mausoleum-like interior. Fancy and Desire, in the masque, suggest the elder and younger Cupids, though it is hard to tell which is which, as Spenser notes. They come at the beginning of the procession, and yet the few sparks that Desire holds in his hands and blows into new life, if the context is funerary, are not so much the original *semina* of love, as its remains.[133]

To describe the extinction of the lover in his movement towards the beloved, Pico in his *Commento* resorts to the myths of Alcestis and Orpheus: "Alcestis achieved the perfection of love because she longed to go to the beloved through death; and dying through love, she was by the grace of the gods revived."[134] Using the evidence of the monuments, Wind compares Psyche:[135] according to Apulieus she braved the underworld for the sake of love also.[136] Amoret, whose train includes as many maladies

---

[130] *Imagines* I.2. (*Riotise* is found at the end of the masque, III.xii.25.)

[131] Wind, *Pagan Mysteries*, pp. 157–160, esp. n. 19. Wind cites A. D. Nock, Sarcophagi and Symbolism," *American Journal of Archaeology*, 50 (1946), p. 160, Collignon, in Daremberg-Saglio, ed., *Dictionaire*, vol. 1, pp. 1609f., *sub* "Éros funèbre," and the link of Hymen to death in Servius, *ad Aen.* I.651.

[132] Wind, *Pagan Mysteries*, p. 160, citing a Roman sarcophagus from Tarsus, Metropolitan Museum of Art, New York.

[133] III.xii.9. Fancy's painted plumes are the rainbow wings of Petrarch's Amore (*Trionfo d'Amore*, I.26f.), and Desire's sparks are the "secret sparks of his [Love's] infused fire," in Spenser's *Hymn to Love*, l. 97. With his laurel branch, Ease is perhaps specifically Petrarchan also: see *Trionfo d'Amore*, I.82, where love is "nacque d'ozio," born of ease, or idleness.

[134] *Commento*, III.viii, trans. by Wind, *Pagan Mysteries*, p. 157.

[135] *Pagan Mysteries*, p. 160.

[136] *The Golden Ass* VI.16–20. Wind does not mention the fact that the movement in Apulieus that ends in Psyche's assumption into heaven begins with her *feralium*

as there are "paines in loue, or punishments in hell" (III.xii.26), may also belong in this mythological company. Pico, following Plato, found the love of Orpheus an imperfect one,[137] since Orpheus did not fully assent to death —and therefore only saw a spectre of the beloved. Since he cannot bring his beloved out, Scudamour is a kind of Orpheus,[138] and there are surely traces of both Alcestis and the spectral Eurydice in the benighted Amoret:

> She doleful Lady, like a dreary Spright,
> Cald by strong charmes out of eternall night,
> Had deathes owne image figurd in her face,
> Full of sad signes, fearefull to liuing sight;
> Yet in that horror shewd a seemely grace,
> And with her feeble feet did moue a comely pace.
>
> (III.xii.19)

Thus Amoret's marriage and her pathos are equated in a way that suggests both the self-extinction implicit in the surrender to love and the terrible curse that may be contained in love. Such a theme is "fit for tragicke Stage" (III.xii.3), as the poet says, and we may conclude our analysis by comparing *Romeo and Juliet*. In Shakespeare's play too, the marriage and death sequences are disposed in such a way as to suggest that Juliet is doomed before she enjoys her wedding-night, and that she is married to death before she takes her husband. Next to the passage just quoted from Spenser, we may set the image of Romeo's drugged and finally suicidal bride. "Death," Romeo tells her,

> Hath had no power yet upon thy beauty.
> Thou are not conquered. Beauty's ensign yet
> Is crimson in thy lips and in thy cheeks,
> And death's pale flag is not advanced.
>
> (V.iii.93ff.)[139]

And yet death in this play is amorous: Romeo's metaphor of the kiss of death will seem almost conventional[140] after Capulet's suggestion that

---

nuptiarum, her "funeral marriage" to Cupid, where funeral preparations, processionals, and ceremonies are substituted for the nuptial celebration. (*Golden Ass* IV.33-35.)

[137] *Symposium* 179d. See Wind, *Pagan Mysteries*, p. 160.

[138] Scudamour is specifically compared to Orpheus retrieving Eurydice at the Temple of Venus, at IV.x.58.

[139] For the *signs* in both Shakespeare and Spenser, cf. Petrarch, *Canz.* CCLXX, where, after the death of Laura, the poet begs Amore to "Retrieve from Death (*Morte*) what he stole, and replace your ensigns on the beautiful face."

[140] For this pure and intimate kiss, the *mors osculi* of Pico, see Wind, *Pagan Mysteries*, p. 155, which translates *Commento*, III.viii, and cites, among others, Leone

THE CONJUGATION OF THE WORLD

death has enjoyed the "right of the first night."[141] Both Paris and Romeo
come to the tomb with a torch, and Romeo has already been a torch-carry-
ing Cupid in a masque. The part of the elder Cupid has been taken by
the Friar—the part of Love the Enchanter, and the Love that works for
concord. But, unlike Britomart, the Friar cannot take the curse off love.
He tells Juliet that "A greater power than we can contradict / Hath
thwarted our intents" (V.iii.153f.), and he abandons the maid in the tomb.

Despite the irony of Shakespeare's treatment, the play does offer an
image for ideal love. It is an image that is found at the close of the
Hypnerotomachia, where the beloved is entombed in the mind of the
lover, because that is where the beloved properly lives: there is a sense
in which she is entombed alive.[142] Like Amoret, Juliet is "Cald by strong
charmes out of eternall night," and the theme of the play is essentially the
nocturnal awakening of Romeo's bride. "When his lover dies," we are
told, the lover "will likewise die, and when his lover returns to life a second
time, he will also." Love, according to Ficino, wakes the drowsy and revives the dead.[143]

Gardens of Pleasure

A Paradise in Greeke signifieth a Garden of pleasure, or place of delights.
(E. K. on "Jvne," l. 10)

And paradise is between corruptibility and incorruptibility. And two
springs come out . . . and they separate into four parts, and go round with
quiet course, and go down into the paradise of Eden, between corruptibility and incorruptibility. And thence they go forth along the earth, and

---

Hebraeo, *Dialoghi d'amore* (Friedeberg-Seeley and Barnes trans., pp. 49–51); Cas-
tiglioni, *Courtier*, IV.lxx; and Bruno, *Heroic Frenzies*, II.i.7. In taking such a kiss,
the lover is not readily dissociated from death itself: see *Romeo and Juliet*, V.iii.92
("Death, that hath suck'd the honey of thy breath"), and 113ff. ("and, lips, O you /
The doors of breath, seal with a righteous kiss / A dateless bargain to engrossing
death!").

[141] *Romeo and Juliet*, IV.v.35-38.

[142] *Hypnerotomachia Poliphili* (London, 1904), Sig. Fiii[v], the epitaph for Polia,
Felix Polia quae sepulta vivis, cited by Wind, *Pagan Mysteries*, p. 163; with which
one may compare the lover falling into pieces like an incinerated cadaver and being
consoled by Polia, Sig. rv[v], and the mysterious urn in the fourth triumph, where
the chariot that bears it portrays the incineration of Semele and also carries Cupid
wounded by Psyche's lamp, Sig. li[r]–lii[v]. The extinguishing of the torch in the sar-
cophagus-like cistern also seems to resemble the *Hypnoeros* gesture.

[143] *De Amore*, II.viii, Jayne trans., p. 145, on love as a voluntary death; and the
passage from *ibid.*, I.iii, cited in n. 355, below. Cf. the *De Charitate* of Giovanni Nesi
(1487), as quoted in Eugenio Garin, *Italian Humanism*, trans. Munz (New York,
1963), p. 112: "The lover becomes the beloved because the lover, dying, lives in the
beloved."

have a revolution to their circle even as other elements. And here there
is no unfruitful tree, and every place is blessed.

(The Book of the Secrets of Enoch 8:5–7, trans. R. H. Charles, ed.,
Apocrypha and Pseudepigrapha of the Old Testament, vol. 2, p. 434)

[i]

In laying out a garden, the first and chief thing to be considered is the
genius of the place.

(Alexander Pope, in Joseph Spence, *Observations, Anecdotes, and
Characters of Books and Men*, no. 609, Osborn edn., vol. 1, p. 253)

Our first essay attempted to establish the theme of the sexual threshold
for the legend of chastity. A related theme is the retreat from a sexual
threshold, or behind one, depending on whether withdrawal or intimacy
is being celebrated. The symbol of this theme is the secluded bower where
Venus keeps her vigil over Adonis. The hovering of Acrasia over Verdant
in the Bower of Bliss is the evil counterpart.

Spenser has carefully anticipated Verdant's condition earlier in Book II.
In the first canto we discover Mordant with Acrasia's cup:

> . . . vpon the soiled gras
> The dead corse of an armed knight was spred,
> Whose armour all with bloud besprinkled was;
> His ruddie lips did smile, and rosy red
> Did paint his chearefull cheekes, yet being ded:
> Seemd to haue beene a goodly personage,
> Now in his freshest flowre of lustie hed,
> Fit to inflame faire Lady with loues rage,
> But that fiers fate did crop the blossome of his age.
>
> (II.i.41)

As a prematurely dead youth Mordant is an expired Adonis; as a de-
bauchee, he is more clearly Dionysian, with the marks of a ruinous satia-
tion on his florid face. Near the middle of the legend Atin finds Cymochles
in the Bower of Bliss itself. Peeping at the beauties who are conquering
him with their nakedness, "made drunk with drugs of deare voluptuous
receipt" (II.v.34), Cymochles is a disarmed Mars. The debauched Mordant
and the disarmed Cymochles recur in Verdant, who is found asleep under
the devouring eyes of Acrasia. Verdant "seemed to bee / Some goodly
swayne":

> A sweet regard, and amiable grace,
> Mixed with manly sternnesse did appeare
> Yet sleeping, in his well proportiond face,
> And on his tender lips the downy heare
> Did now but freshly spring, and silken blossomes beare.
>
> (II.xii.79)

Likewise, the Venus of Malecasta's tapestry leads her Adonis to a secret shade, "Where him to sleepe she gently would persuade" (III.i.35).

The victim of the Bower is anticipated by Mordant and Cymochles, and a similar trail of victims leads to the Garden of Adonis. In the tapestry, the subversive eyes of Venus remind us of those of Cymochles and Acrasia. Marinell is wounded in the left side, on his "pretious shore" (III.iv.17); he *wallows* in his gore like a sacrificial ox; he is lamented by nymphs; and he is conveyed to his mother's protective bower on a wagon strewn with flowers stained with his blood. Timias is wounded, also in the left thigh, when he is attacked from ambush in his pursuit of a forester armed with a boar spear. He swoons; he lies "wallowd all in his owne gore"; and he is found by Belphoebe, who also carries a boar spear (II.iii.29). Belphoebe is herself in pursuit of "some wild beast, which with her arrowes keene / She wounded had" (III.v.28). She is led to Timias:

> His locks, like faded leaues fallen to ground,
> Knotted with bloud, in bounches rudely ran,
> And his sweete lips, on which before that stownd
> The bud of youth to blossome faire began,
> Spoild of their rosie red, were woxen pale and wan.
>
> (III.v.29)

The imagery is as old as Bion: "His dark blood drips down his skin of snow . . . and the rose flees from his lip."[144] As Marinell was "laid in easie couch" (III.iv.43), so Timias, in the "earthly Paradize" of Belphoebe, is "layed / In easy couch" (III.v.41). Both youths are eventually cured by the ministrations of mother and mistress, though not without complications and, in the following book, a kind of relapse. The renewable quality of their wounds, like the annual reddening of the Syrian river that bears his name, reinforces the comparison to Adonis or Thammuz "yearly wounded" (*Par. Lost* I.452). These wounds are actually not so much cured as indulged, or *fostered*; this pious maternal care, reflecting ideas about the feeding and starving of sickness, preserves the Adonis-victims as pietà-like emblems of love-stricken youth.

The brief description of Belphoebe's bower leads into the Garden of Adonis itself. The other Bower and the Garden are carefully paralleled, as has been frequently noted. Each has a solicitous genius at the gate: the one "a double nature has," the other is effeminate. Each excludes bestial violence. Each discovers at its center the languishing youth. Both are earthly paradises, enjoying perfectly temperate weather; both are affluent, plenteous, and diversified. Both feature laurel shade, luxuriant vegetation, and brimming humours and juices. Both descriptions lead to the inner

---

[144] *Lament for Adonis*, 9–11, trans. Andrew Lang, *Theocritus, Bion and Moschus* (London, 1907), p. 172.

bower: in the one Acrasia "depastures" on the sight of Verdant, in the other Venus "reaps" her pleasure of Adonis (II.xii.73; III.vi.5). There is an elegiac element in both descriptions; the song of *carpe diem* in the Bower is balanced by the lamentation of the mother-mistress and the elegiac flowers in the Garden. Finally, in both cases the youth is revived: Verdant is awakened and released; and it is asserted that Adonis "may not / For euer die . . . All be he subiect to mortalitie" (III.vi.47).

The result of this correspondence is the suggestion that the elaborate artifice of the Bower is designed to produce the illusion for which the Garden is the actual reality.[145] The beauties of the Bower tease, and there are hints that they cannot be fully possessed:

> Her snowy brest was bare to readie spoyle
> Of hungry eies, *which n'ote therewith be fild,*
>
> . . . .
>
> . . . her faire eyes sweet smyling in delight,
> Moystened their fierie beames, with which she thrild
> Fraile harts, *yet quenched not;*
>
> (II.xii.78, italics mine)

The love-nest therefore becomes a garden of Tantalus, to which Erasmus refers his reader in his explanation of the proverbial use of *horti Adoni*.[146] Philostratus equates "lamia's gold" with the *horti Tantali*. In the same author a sage is reported as follows: " 'I have ceased to take these matters seriously, for I now know that I used to feed on the gardens of Tantalus.' Thus he indicated to his questioner that all pleasures are a shadow and a dream."[147] We have already mentioned the other indications of the illusory nature of the Bower: the ivory gate of false dreams, the cup of Circe, and the emphasis on dissimulated contrivance.

Erasmus explains that the gardens of Adonis refer to "things vain, and scarcely fruitful, and only fit for pleasure brief and at hand. Pausanias attests that the gardens of Adonis referred to delicacies, chiefly lettuce and numerous herbs, in which [gardens] the seeds were conserved not otherwise than by being placed in pots." Hence it is that the proverb rebukes "futile and trifling men, and those fitted for foolish pleasures: which includes minstrels, sophists, lascivious poets, *cupidiarii*, and others of that

[145] The phrasing echoes Frye, "Structure of Imagery," in *Fables of Identity*, p. 82.

[146] Erasmus, *Adagia, sub* "INTEMPERANTIA, ET LIBIDO—Adonidis horti," in Frankfurt edn. of 1646, p. 410. See also p. 698, "VANITAS—Tantalus horti": "of goods, of which it is not licit to enjoy; or of those things which seem to be something when they are nothing." (See also "Tantali mensa," p. 700.)

[147] Philostratus, *Vita Apolloni* IV.xxv. See also *Lives of the Sophists* I.19 (Loeb edn. of *Philostratus and Eunapius*, ed. and trans. W. C. Wright, p. 69), and II.14 (*ibid.*, p. 243) where the gardens of Tantalus are described as "some visionary image which both is and is not."

kind." Erasmus adds, rather oddly, that there were *two* gardens sacred to Venus, "because Adonis was her lover, torn away in the first flower of age, and changed into a flower."[148] Spenser's second Venerean garden is "called by her lost louers name" (III.vi.29). The psalm of Adonis in Theocritus speaks of two beds: "Another bed is strewn for beautiful Adonis, one bed Cypris keeps."[149] At any rate, there is the phrase "as fruitless as the gardens of Adonis"; "by a not dissimilar figure Isaeus following Philostratus calls juvenile pleasures *tantalo kipous*: because they are very much like shades and sleep, nor do they satisfy the soul of men, but they provoke it further. Similarly Pollux called the speech of the sophist Athenodorus the gardens of Tantalos because it was juvenile and light, displaying an appearance as if it were something, when it was nothing."[150] Spenser has displaced these associations from the Garden to the Bower. The transitory quality of the gardens prompts Erasmus to compare the life of man to them.[151] This agrees with a suggestion in Plutarch that defends the immortality of the soul. Plutarch asks if God would "tend souls of a day grown in a frail vessel of flesh that admits of no strong root of life, only to be presently extinguished on the slightest occasion"—"like the women who nurse and tend their 'gardens of Adonis'?"[152] One further Erasmian association should be recorded. Folly says that she was born in the Fortunate Isles, which she describes as the earthly paradise: "where all things grow without plowing or planting. In these islands there is no labor, or old age, or any sickness"; its delightful flora include moly (she compares herself to Circe a little further on), and the list ends with rose, violet, hyacinth, and the gardens of Adonis. Her followers include *Hedonai* and *Komos*.[153] We will have more to say about the interpretation of the classical gardens of Adonis below. For the moment, we have demonstrated their association with transitory, or foolish, or illusory pleasure.

Both the Bower and the Garden are described in an order meant to represent a process. The Bower is ordered—if that is the word—by incontinence. Beyond the gate are the wild animals; similarly, the perimeters of Alcina's realm in Ariosto are barred by the Circean beasts already mentioned in connection with the armies of Maleger.[154] Without trying to

---

[148] Erasmus, *Adagia, sub* "Adonidis horti."

[149] *Idyl* XV.126–129, trans. Lang, *Theocritus* . . . , p. 83.

[150] Erasmus, *Adagia, sub* "Adonidis horti."

[151] *Ibid.*

[152] Plutarch, *De sera numinis vindicta* 17, *Moralia* 560, trans. P. H. De Lacey and B. Einarson, in Loeb edn., vol. 7, p. 253.

[153] *Praise of Folly*, trans. J. P. Dolan, in *The Essential Erasmus* (New York, 1964), pp. 104f.

[154] *O.F.* VI.60–63, VII.80, VII.10–13. Cf. Chap. II, n. 342, above.

specify any one meaning, we note that in Ariosto the crew of beasts opposes the departure of Alcina's guests; it is as if the break with Alcina involves the defeat of passions that become rebellious at the threat of a change of life. Perhaps a certain spiritedness or indignation is required in response. We feel a similar conflict in the encounter of the reproachful Grylle and the wrathful Guyon. The beasts in Spenser are barred from the Bower of Acrasia by a fence, which is weak: incontinence apparently has only superficial objections to more bestial or violent passions.

At the gate is the *genius loci*, whom we might call Pleasure. His garments may owe something to the tradition of the effeminating clothing worn in such realms, going back to the gift of Dido to Aeneas; more likely they are Bacchic. Pleasure has the garden's "gouernall," but his staff, unlike the controlling rod of Diet at the Castle of Alma, is a "formalitie" (II.xii.48). As in Milton's *Comus*, the host's staff has the power of enchantment, and the enchanter offers his potion to travelers (II.xii.46, 49). Comus is the son of Circe and Bacchus, the god of release, and Fowler has demonstrated the presence of a Bacchic strain in both of Acrasia's victims, Mordant and Verdant.[155] This Bacchic theme is worth illustrating here to characterize in a preliminary way the intemperance of the Bower as a whole.

The death of Mordant commences the theme. The origin of the phrase about mixing Bacchus with the Nymph insists upon an allegory of intemperance. At one point in the *Laws* Plato discusses tempering the drunkenness of youth with the sobriety of age in affairs of state. He alludes in passing to the chastening of the heat of wine with another, soberer divinity (773d). Plutarch explains that this reference is to mixing pure wine with water (*Moralia* 791 B–C). Alciati has an emblem, "On a Statute of Bacchus," alluding to the theme, and to the story in Athenaeus about the inventor of the mixing of wine.[156] This benefactor of mankind founded an altar to the "upright" Dionysus, in gratitude for the discovery that restored men formerly doubled over with drink. "Near it, he also built an altar to the Nymphs to remind devotees of the mixing; for the Nymphs are said to be the nurses of Dionysus."[157] Cartari, in his article on Bacchus, tells the same story; the Nymph there serves to remind us "that the use of wine ought to be temperate."[158] Mignault, in his commentary on the emblem, translates a poem of Maleger of Gadara in this vein, which says

[155] "Emblems of Temperance in *The Faerie Queene*, Book II," *Review of English Studies*, New Series, vol. 11, no. 42 (May, 1960), pp. 144–149.

[156] Emb. XXV, "In Statuam Bacchi," edn. of Antwerp, 1581, pp. 115–123; Mignault on Bacchus and the Nymph, p. 120; on Plato and Plutarch, p. 121.

[157] Athenaeus, *Deipnosophistae* II.38. Compare John Cleveland, "Upon an Hermaphrodite," ll. 5–8: "Thus we chastise the God of Wine / With Water that is Feminine, / Until the cooler Nymph abate / His wrath, and so concorporate."

[158] *Le Imagini* (Venice, 1625), *sub* "Baccho," p. 306.

that "When Bacchus sprang from the fire, the Nymphs bathed him since he was covered with ashes. For this reason Bacchus is the Nymphs' friend and if you hinder them from mingling you will taste his burning fire."[159] Two pages over, in the passage from the *Laws*, Plato remarks on the drunken man who on his wedding night begets a feckless progeny: "he cannot but imprint its color and impress on the souls and bodies of the unborn and become sire to a sorely degenerate brood" (775).[160] Mordant's unwashable son perhaps falls into this category; his reddened hands might remind us of the hands of Excesse, who squeezes grapes. It may be that Ruddymane is a purple Bacchus—the infant Bacchus in the care of the Nymph—and that his hands are stained with the blood of the grape. If so, it is a wine that proves immiscible in water. Some evidence in favor of this interpretation is found in the report of Solinus concerning a unique fountain of Diana: "If any man that is not of chast & cleane life take of ye water of ye fountain Diana, which runneth by Camerine, the liquor of the wine, and the liquor of the water will not ioyne in one substance." Golding's translation does not explain what wine is meant, but the original indicates blood, the wine of the body.[161] Mordant himself has proved incapable of surviving this draught, so it may be that his cup has this wine— his old intemperance—still in it.

The Bacchic character of the Bower is first focused on the Genius with his wine bowl, as a result of the associations just reviewed. There is, of course, the convivial link between love-making and wine-drinking, the Anacreonic crowning of the cup with the rose. Indeed, the wine-god created the rose when he distilled nectar on the thorn plant, according to *Anacreonta* 55, where a rite involving roses is said to be required by Dionysus. The vines and ivy in the Bower are more specifically Bacchic. The ivy is here, as Comes says, because "it is always *viridis* and *iuvenis*, as the god himself is feigned to be."[162] The beardless Verdant, in this reading, becomes the florid son of the Nymph, hidden in the *locus amoenus* that Comes generously indites:

> . . . a region pleasurable throughout, a meadow notable for softness, and
> for the irrigation of the many gushing limpid waters the place abounded

[159] *Epig.* 113 in Graefe edn. (Leipzig, 1821), trans. Richard Aldington, *The Poems of Meleager of Gadara* (London, 1920). (Quoted by Mignault in Alciati, *edn. cit.*, p. 120.)

[160] Trans. A. E. Taylor in Hamilton and Cairnes, eds., *Collected Dialogues* (New York, 1961), p. 1350.

[161] *The Excellent & Pleasant Worke*, Scholars' Facsimiles and Reprints (Gainesville, Florida, 1955); Solinus, *Polyhistor* x: "Diana qui ad Camerinam fluit si habitus impudice hauserit, non coibunt in corpus unum latex vineus et latex aquae."

[162] *Mythol.*, V.xiii, pp. 487f., *edn. cit.* Also cited by Fowler in *art. cit.* Cf. Comes, p. 477, "semper iuvenen," and Cartari, *Le Imagini*, p. 38.

in, planted with all species of fruit-bearing trees, for many vines were even born there spontaneously. The place was blown by many very pleasant and salubrious breezes, on account of which the uncultivated fields bore fruit over the greatest period of time, since the entrance to the region was enclosed with many dense and high trees, and the valleys with a deep forest, so the sun could not easily penetrate. . . . At all the entries were fountains of sweet water, wherefore the flourishing and odiferous trees were many—and pleasurable flowers, and a variety of birdsong. And to conclude in a word, nothing further could be desired there for the absolute pleasure of the inhabitant.[163]

It was on an analogous inaccessible florid mount that Bacchus taught certain men the use of wine. The description has a certain interest in its own right, but it especially interests the student of *locus amoenus* tradition because of the placing of the fountains.

Acrasia's porter, the *genius loci* and an evil genius as well, is also a minor subaltern of the wine-god. According to Comes, wine used moderately is a Good Demon. However, Comes also says that among the companions of Bacchus was the *genius* Acratus. Further, "sorrowful demons accompany this god [Bacchus], among whom Acratus obtains chief place, because there are many [intemperances] which follow upon immoderate usage in drinking: loquacity certainly, and boldness, and a profusion of household things—impudence, with clamor and obstreperousness, hostility, and many such." These the ancients call evil demons and cobalts.[164] It is equally likely that the porter is also that other member of Bacchus' retinue, Como, who, according to Cartari, resembles the beardless Bacchus: Como is the god of conviviality, holds a staff, occupies a threshold, is adorned with flowers, and has a pot. Cartari's depiction is taken from the elder Philostratus' *Imagines* (I.2), where we also learn that the revel permits men to put on women's garb. Significantly, Como keeps the door of a place where a wedding-celebration is in progress: the lovers, Cartari says, are already in bed.[165]

Beyond the porter, pleasure of indulgence leads to Excesse, who also offers the Bacchic-Circean drink. Her threshold is marked by a grape arbor. The wanton wreathings of its vine are one instance of a landscape that keeps threatening to assimilate the subjects in it—here, for an Apollonian poet, is an aesthetic problem in addition to the problem of self-definition. The spontaneity of the Bacchic vine is a commonplace of

---

[163] *Mythol.*, pp. 503f.

[164] *Ibid.*, p. 479 ("Cobali daemones . . . inter comites fuit Acratus genius"); pp. 499f. ("daemones . . . Acratus principem"); p. 485 (wine used moderately is a Good Demon).

[165] *Le Imagini, sub* "Baccho," pp. 305f. See Philostratus, *Imagines* I.2, "Komos" (Carousal).

the god's imagery from the Homeric *Hymn* on. There may also be a reference to the grapevine that framed the entrance to Calypso's cave in Homer[166]—Calypso was easily confused with Circe.[167]

Indulgence opens into a paradise "too lauishly" adorned (II.xii.50); Excesse leads to the fountain graced by two girls, where excess can be seen turning into abandon. A responsive chord is struck in Guyon, and we sense that the loss of inhibition anticipates the act of incontinence itself. Thus we arrive at the innermost Bower. The rose song is placed precisely here, as a final incitement and justification, because any act of this kind is partly prompted by a desire to seize an opportunity or "occasion." What follows the fatal indulgence is variously represented: by the sleeping Verdant, whose passion has yielded to passivity; by Grylle, who has happily renounced "the excellence / Of his creation"; and by the Palmer with his net, who represents the Shakespearean "waste of shame," the awakening to a feeling of degradation and entrapment.[168] Spenser's sequence—through pleasure, indulgence, excess, abandon, consent, passion, awakening, and self-reproach—reveals the logic of surrender beneath the profusion of the Bower, and inevitably guides us to its destruction. Moments after Verdant awakes his garden is in shambles; as the rose song itself acknowledges, juvenile pleasures are transitory.

Guyon's fury, which represents the will's self-recovery, is also Bacchic. Guyon begins his conquest of the Bower by spilling wine, a gesture that can be recognized as part of the god's cult. In freeing Verdant, Guyon is also the kind of Bacchus who was said to liberate, on the basis of a pun on his name Liber.[169] Finally, Grylle, the strongest evidence for the presence of Circe in this place, may well be drunk—*swine* drunk. This drunkenness is that "wherewith bothe the body and soule is deformed, and the figure of man is as it were by inchauntement transformed in to an ugly and lothesome ymage," as Elyot's *Gouernour* (III.xxii) explains it. In terms of the progress through the Bower, Grylle has the place of a hangover.

---

[166] *Od.* V.63–70.

[167] As in Aristotle, *Nich. Ethics* II.ix, the passage on the mean that has presumably influenced Spenser's use of Scylla and Charybdis imagery, as Comes cites it, *Mythol.*, X, "De Scylla" (*edn. cit.*, pp. 1052f.). In Gower, *Confessio Amantis*, VI.1426ff., Circe and Calypso are co-regents of Sicily who turn Ulysses' men into beasts and both fall in love with him. In Plotinus, *Enn.* I, VI.8, Circe and Calypso together stand for the "delights of sensation," and so in Pico, *Oration*, 5, "if you see one blinded by the vain illusions of imagery, as it were of Calypso, and softened by their gnawing allurement, delivered over to his senses, it is a beast and not a man you see" (trans. Forbes, in Cassirer, *et al.*, eds., *Renaissance Philosophy of Man*, p. 226).

[168] *F.Q.* II.xii.80 ("his bodie he did spend") and 86 ("did vnmanly looke . . . some for inward shame"); with Shakespeare, Son. 129.

[169] Comes, *Mythol.*, V.xiii, p. 497, *edn. cit.*: Bacchus derives his name from *furor*; Cartari, *art. cit.*, p. 312: Bacchus the liberator.

Scholars have studied the debt to Tasso and Trissino in these episodes.[170] It is particularly to Trissino that Spenser owes the "design" we have just outlined. A brief resort to his realm of Acratia can help us with the nature of Spenser's dénouement. Acratia's quarters lead to a vivarium of harmless beasts, and a park from which no trees are missing: there are fruits of all kinds; the flowers never fade, and neither does the spring. Clearly we are in the earthly paradise. The entrances to the pleasant meadow in which this *palazzo* is situated are appointed with fountains, and the proffered drinks from the one soften the taker, and from the other make him hate all manly deeds—they provide a choice without an alternative. The third portal, as noted above, is made of ivory. Acratia's buildings bring one from four courtyards adorned with sculpted loges to a grand salon, and then another where the vista takes in fruit gardens, and thence to the personal apartments of Acratia, diverse little rooms with beds and mirrors and *ignudi* and softening baths; thence one descends to two grand galleries, columned with silver and gold, each overlooking gardens adorned with fountains and lakelets. Galleries, bays, and courts succeed one another in a bewildering proliferation, as wall after wall yields to reveal new interiors and new vistas. Here, one could easily lose oneself. All, in a way, is designed to postpone the encounter of the cavalier with the furthest reaches of Acratia's apartment, where there is a small exit that is never seen. It is covered with gold, but it is made of iron and ebony. It is closed night and day, and only poverty sometimes manages to unlock it. One is retired through this door when he goes broke. Beyond, one is drawn into an appalling forest where the grass is bruised and the stench of *assfoetid* and sulphur comes forth:

> E questa orribil selva è circondata
> D' un gran muro di ferro, e quindi s' esce
> Per un sol uscio picciolo, e coperto
> Di amare ortiche, e di pungenti spine;
> Ove una vecchia imperiosa siede
> Con una sferza in man, ch' ognun percuote;
> E le percosse sue son tanto amare,
> Che vanno infino a le midolle, e a gli ossi.

And this horrible wood is surrounded with a great wall of iron, and thence one issues through a lone small exit, covered with bitter nettles,

---

[170] Charles W. Lemmi, "The Influence of Trissino on *The Faerie Queene*," *Philological Quarterly*, 7 (1928), pp. 220–223, and A. Bartlett Giamatti, *The Earthly Paradise and the Renaissance Epic* (Princeton, 1966), pp. 171–179. I am much indebted to the latter. My paraphrase of the *Italia Liberata da Gotti*, Books IV and V concerning Acratia's realm, depends on Trissino, *Opere* (Verona, 1729), pp. 39–48; my quotes are from pp. 46 and 47.

and stinging spines; there sits an imperious old woman, lash in hand, who strikes all; and her blows are so harsh that they reach to the marrow, and the bone.

(Book V, ll. 239–246)

We have met the old woman before, and this is the route the rescue mission is advised to take to expose Acratia. Her name is *Metanea*, that Repentance that follows upon fleeting occasion.

The cavaliers, coming through the backyard, apprehend the mage, retain her through her Protean repertory of shape-changes, and hail her into the wood. She cries for help, and a cloud of armed men, "full of bitter hail and tempest," descends upon the rescue party. The leader of the sober band of rescuers addresses his bewitched friend:

> Ove correte, o cari miei fratelli?
> Non ci vedete qui? che siam venuti
> Per selve, e spine, e per sentieri amari
> A trarvi fuor di questo orribil nodo?

If I am right, O brothers dear to me—if not ourselves, whom do you see? Newcomers, who come through woods, and thorns, and through better paths to draw you out of this horrible knot?

(Book V, ll. 359–362)

One knight fails to respond, and his rescuer exposes Acratia's nether parts, the stench of which makes them analogous to the recess of the horrible wood itself. At this the hostile knight is able to recognize his friends, and he takes a drink of the water of reclamation that will restore his transmuted mind. Curiously, his illumination is compared to the kindling of a new fire with dry wood in a dark room where the good Vulcan has been covered with cinders, or let dry over the andirons, for the night. Perhaps in this simile there is just a hint of the enlightenment of Vulcan by the sun at dawn, concerning the adultery of Venus and Mars.

Like the shape-changes of Acratia, all the scenery finally parts to reveal that barren and angry place, from which the only exit is by way of repentance. Similar deductions in Spenser are much less explicit, but the amazement of the beasts transformed back into men, the "tempest" of Guyon's wrath, the defacement of the Bower—"of the fairest late, now made the fowlest place" (II.xii.83), the attack on Guyon by Acratia's victims, and the sorrow of the better-advised Verdant, all find equivalents in Trissino.

Spenser follows up his version of the disabusement theme with the recalcitrance of Grylle. The two stanzas devoted to this character, at least as much as the wreckage of the Bower, function as a counterweight to all that has gone before. Plutarch's essay on Gryllus belongs in the tradition of the paradoxical *economia*, like Erasmus' Folly, who adduced Gryllus' example in her praise of the happiness of the beast-state. "All beasts are happy," according to Doctor Faustus.[171] Ten out of eleven of Ulysses' men in Gelli's dialogue *Circe* prefer not to be changed back into men. It is Gelli's dialogue that Spenser's phrase "the excellence of his creation" seems to echo, and that gives his allusion, despite Grylle's comic and earthy propensities, considerable seriousness. Book II, with its two sets of animal transformations, emphasizes a theme of the Hermetic *Asclepius*, the capacity of man for self-transformation into whatever he attaches himself to. Man may put his mind everywhere, divinely apprehending truth and virtually becoming a terrestrial god—or he may become a beast.[172] We may compare Grylle to Maleger's bands,

> . . . some fashioned in the wast
> Like swine; for so deforme is luxury,
> Surfeat, misdiet, and vnthriftie wast,
> Vaine feasts, and idle superfluity
>
> (II.xi.12)

Gelli took this theme from Pico's *Oration on the Dignity of Man*, including Pico's comparison of man to Proteus.[173] Gelli's Ulysses argues that among the creatures the particular excellence of man's nature lies in his unique faculties of understanding (by which the mind can become all things) and will (by which it can make the better choice). The noble elephant Aglaphemus chooses to become a man—" 'How much more I can appreciate the human condition,' " he says, " 'since I made trial of the other.' "[174] Most men, however, want the life of the beast, at least if Circe is right in her insistence that her animals have the same understandings that they had when they wore the human shape.[175] On the whole, however, Gelli argues that those who choose the state of beasts have already become incapable of the alternative; he does admit that the perfection belonging

---

[171] Scene xv, l. 128. Faustus wishes that upon his death he could "be changed / Into some brutish beast."

[172] *Asclepius*, i.5–7.

[173] Gelli, *Circe*, trans. H. Iden (1557). I refer to the version of Thomas Brown, corr. and ed. by Robert M. Adams (Ithaca, New York, 1963), p. 168. (For Proteus, see Pico, *Oration*, 4, and Adams' edn. of *Circe*, p. 3.) For more on Grylle's literary descent, see Chap. III, n. 159, above. (The boar is also a Venerean image: the piglike among Maleger's followers are deformed by *luxury*, and Venus rides a "swine savage" in Guillaume de Deguilleville's *Pilgrimage of Life*, l. 13091, Lydgate's trans.)

[174] Gelli, *Circe*, Adams edn., pp. 168ff., 176.

[175] *Ibid.*, p. 82.

to man's nature is the hardest to obtain.[176] A not too distant relative of
Gelli's Aglaphemus is Mill's Socratic pig:

Few human creatures would consent to be changed into any of the lower
animals, for a promise of the fullest allowance of a beast's pleasures; . . .
a being of higher faculties requires more to make him happy . . . in spite
of these liabilities [of the human condition], he can never really wish to
sink into what he feels to be a lower grade of existence. We may give what
explanation we please of this unwillingness: . . . but its most appropriate
apellation is a sense of dignity. . . . It is better to be a human being dis-
satisfied than a pig satisfied. And if the fool, or the pig, are of a different
opinion, it is because they only know their own side of the question. The
other party to the comparison knows both sides.[177]

The excellence of man's creation consists in his capacity to make the comparison in question. In giving Grylle his will, the poet dignifies Grylle's
will as free and human, for he is allowed the exercise of his power of
choice. But in making the Palmer say that Grylle has *forgotten* the being
with which he started out in life—he surely cannot have *renounced* it—
the poet seriously questions Grylle's understanding.

[ii]

The thresholds of the Bower mark stages in the subversion of the temperate will. The Garden of Adonis is constructed very differently, and
represents an accommodation of mutability, rather than its triumph. The
description is in three sections: the first includes the Genius, the babes, and
the unborn forms; the second, the figure of Time and the lament of Venus
over his depredations; the third, the inner bower, and the triumphant
assertion that Adonis survives, "by succession made perpetuall" (III.vi.47).
This order in a sense recapitulates the legend up to this point, moving from
the thresholds of the opening cantos, to the wounded youths of the following cantos, and ending here in a vision of the power of nature to renew life.
The Garden contains "the seeds of time" or "timely seed"—i.e., that
growth-nurturing and generational time peculiar to the action of Book
III. Therefore it encapsulates the action, being the episodic germ out of
which the preceding narrative has been, as it were, "backward bred"
(V, proem, 2).

Behind the two gardens lies Spenser's dialectical treatment of the tradition of the *locus amoenus* and the earthly paradise. Anything like an adequate treatment of Spenser's predecessors is beyond the scope of this book,
but even a cursory and selective discussion may hope to illuminate the

[176] *Ibid.*, pp. 31, 40–45, 78, 82, 101, 107f., 113, 123f., 127, 155f., 175f.
[177] John Stuart Mill, *Utilitarianism*, ii.

tradition in which Spenser is working, so rich are the resources. The technical use of the term *locus amoenus*, or pleasance, we owe to Curtius, who revives it from Servius, in the latter's commentary on a landscape in Virgil's *Georgics*.[178] The term itself, Curtius implies, may owe something to a line of Virgil's describing the Elysian Fields: "devenere locos laestos et amoena virecta" (they came to joyful places and green pleasances).[179] Peter Comester describes Eden as a *locus amoenissimus*, for example,[180] and E. K. describes the Elysian Fields as "a place of pleasure like Paradise."[181] Spenser's Garden of Adonis excels all other "pleasant places" (III. vi.29), and the phrase echoes in the descriptions of both Venus' park and Mount Acidale (IV.x.21; VI.x.5, 30). Servius connects the Virgilian *amoena* with *amor*. He also suggests an etymology with *a-moenis* (fruitless):[182] the two etymologies almost symbolize the opposition of the two gardens in Spenser.

An example of this species of landscape description is the following well-known passage from Ovid, describing the bower of Diana:

> Vallis erat piceis et acuta densa cupressu,
> nomine Gargaphie succinctae sacra Dianae,
> cuius in extremo est antrum nemorale recessu
> arte laboratum nulla: simulaverat artem
> ingenio natura suo; nam pumice vivo et
> levibus tofis nativum duxerat arcum;
> fons sonat a dextra tenui perlucidus unda,
> margine gramineo patulos incinctus hiatus.
>
> (*Metam.* III.155–165)

Golding's translation is, as usual, expansive:

> There was a valley thicke
> With Pinaple and Cipresse trees that armed be with pricke.
> Gargaphie hight this shadie plot, it was a sacred place
> To chaste *Diana* and the Nymphes that wayted on hir grace.

---

[178] E. R. Curtius, *European Literature and the Latin Middle Ages* (New York, 1953), p. 199, citing Servius, *ad Georg.* II.470; and p. 192, citing Isidore, *Etym.*, XIV.vii.33 (see n. 182, below).

[179] *Aen.* VI.638.

[180] *Hist. Scholastica*, Lib. Gen., cap. xiii (PL, CLIX, 1067); cf. *Paradisum voluptatis* in Gen. 2:8; and Gen. 2:10: "And a river issued out of the place of pleasure (*loco voluptatis*) to water Paradise," and Gen. 2:15: "Our Lord God therefore took man, and put him the Paradise of pleasure (*paradiso voluptatis*)."

[181] E. K. on "Elysian fieldes," in "November," l. 179.

[182] Servius, *ad Aen.* VI.638. Isidore has much the same, in *Etym.*, XIV.viii.33: "Amoena loca Verrius Flaccus dicta ait, eo quod solum amorem praestent, et ad se amanda alliciant. Varro, quod sine munere sunt, nec quidquam in his officii, quasi amunia, hoc est, sine fructu, unde et nullus fructus exsolvitur." (PL, LXXXII, 524.)

Within the furthest end thereof there was a pleasant Bowre
So vaulted with the leavie trees, the Sunne had there no powre:
Not made by hand nor mans devise, and yet no man alive,
A trimmer piece of worke than that could for his life contrive.
With flint and Pommy was it wallde by nature halfe about,
And on the right side of the same full freshly flowed out
A lively spring with Christall streame: whereof the upper brim
Was greene with grasse and matted herbes that smelled verie trim.

(178–189)

The question of the relative contributions of "nature" and "art" in the creation of such places tells us that they are basically gardens, for gardens always pose this question, being the work of both together.

The interesting phrase *pomice vivo* occurs once elsewhere in Ovid, in his description of the trysting place of Hercules and Omphale (*Fasti* II.315). It also appears in Claudian's landscape of Enna (*De Raptu* II.103), where the sun-proof shade of the two Ovidian examples is also found. Ovid and Claudian would seem to be the sources of an interesting stanza in Politian's *Stanze*. Following Claudian, Politian describes the mountaintop domain sacred to Venus and secured with a wall of gold. The foliage there also screens a living fountain from the heat of the sun:

L'acqua da viva pomice zampilla,
Che con suo arco il bel monte sospende;
E per fiorito solco indi tranquilla
Pingendo ogni sua orma al fonte scende:
Dalle cui labra un grato umor distilla,
Che 'l premio di lor ombre agli arbor rende:
Ciascun si pasce a mensa non avara;
E par che l'un dell'altro cresca a gara.

The water burst from living pumice, which the beautiful mount suspended within its arch; and thence through flowery rills painting all its tranquil track descends to the fount. From its lip a gracious humour is distilled, which renders to the trees the reward of their shade: each feeds itself a not illiberal measure, and by this one with the other flourishes in rivalry.

(I.81)

With this we may compare the Bower of Bliss with its green arbor, where art strives to compare with nature:

And all within with flowres was garnished,
That when myld *Zephyrus* emongst them blew,
Did breath out bounteous smels, and painted colors shew.

And fast beside, there trickled softly downe
  A gentle streame, whose murmuring waue did play
  Emongst the pumy stones, and made a sowne,
  To lull him soft a sleepe, that by it lay;

(II.v.30)

Spenser's "pumy stones," then, are Italian; furthermore, they recur in the paradise of Belphoebe and her nymphs:

  Into that forest farre they thence him led,
    Where was their dwelling, in a pleasant glade,
    With mountaines round about enuironed,
    And mighty woods, which did the valley shade,
    And like a stately Theatre it made,
    Spreading it selfe into a spatious plaine
    And in the midst a little riuer plaide
    Emongst the pumy stones, which seemd to plaine
  With gentle murmure, that his course they did restraine.

(III.v.39)

Here we should notice not only the similarity, but also the difference. The murmur of the stream in the Bower of Bliss is a narcotic; in Belphoebe's bower, the stream is active and restless. The difference is between a passive dissipation and a lively energy, between a drugged Cymochles and an impatient Timias.

As a late classical example of the *locus amoenus*, Curtius quotes the river poem by Tiberianus.[183] It might also be used to illustrate the continuity of the conventions of this genre. The lush description ends with the following:

  has per umbras omnis ales plus canora quam putes
  cantibus vernis strepebat et susurris dulcibus;
  hic loquentis murmur amnis concinebat frondibus,
  quis melos vocalis aurae musa Zephyri moverat.
  sic euntem per virecta pulchra odora et musica
  ales amnis aura lucus flos et umbra iuverat.

---

[183] Curtius, *European Literature*, pp. 196f. Latin text from Loeb *Minor Latin Poets*, ed. and trans. J. W. and A. M. Duff, pp. 558, 560. Cf. the poem of Asmenius (fl. c. 400), "Adeste Musae," which catalogues the praiseworthy features of gardens (produce, pleasure, refreshment, flowers, bees, shade, birdsong), and sums up: "oblectat hortus, avocat pascit tenet / Animoque maesto demit angores graves" (a garden delights, it distracts, feeds, supports, and dismisses heavy cares from the sad mind). (*Anthologia Latina*, "de laude horti," in Baehrens, ed., *Poeta Latini Minores*, vol. 4, p. 152.)

In these shadows all the birds murmured and warbled with sweet songs of spring more melodiously than you could conceive; this murmur of the loquacious river harmonized with the leaves, which the singing muse of the Zephyr moved to the melody of the breeze. Thus one going through the verdure, the beauty, the odor, and the music—the birds, the stream, the air, the grove, and the shade delighted.

(15-20)

The poem, it would seem, has been designed to make the concluding résumé possible. The same rhetorical feature turns up in Spenser in Phedria's garden:

> No daintie flowre or herbe, that growes on ground,
> No arboret with painted blossomes drest,
> And smelling sweet, but there might be found
> To bud out faire, and her sweet smels throw all around.

> No tree, whose braunches did not brauely spring
> No braunch, whereon a fine bird did not sit:
> No bird, but did her shrill notes sweetly sing:
> No song, but did containe a louely dit:
> Trees, braunches, birds, and songs were framed fit,

(II.vi.13)

Here is an art that plainly fails to conceal art; it is somewhat canned—the shrill Phedria is none too subtle either.

The ideal of a coordinated and harmonious appeal to the senses is carried much further in the Bower of Bliss. Music, with its "divine respondence meet," is an apt symbol for this concordance:

> Eftsoones they heard a most melodious sound,
>   Of all that mote delight a daintie eare
>   Such as attonce might not on liuing ground,
>   Saue in this Paradise, be heard elswhere:
>   Right hard it was, for wight, which did it heare,
>   To read, what manner musicke that mote bee:
>   For all that pleasing is to liuing eare,
>   Was there consorted in one harmonee,
> Birdes, voyces, instruments, windes, waters, all agree.

(II.xii.70)

Curtius suggests, on the basis of Horace's remark about detached purple patches (which include "the winding stream gliding through the *amoenos agros*"), that the tendency of the *locus amoenus* to become a rhetorical showpiece unto itself was recognized early.[184] We have already noticed

---

[184] Horace, *Ars Poetica* 17; Curtius, *European Literature*, p. 195.

the separating tendency of the enlarged *locus amoenus* in the epic of Tasso, where Armida's paradise contributes equally to the problems of unifying the epic army and the problems of unifying the "arms" epic. Spenser's Bower of Bliss, as its frequent culling for anthologies shows, might raise similar problems. These are anticipated in Phedria's island, which is clearly a kind of detached purple patch, wandering through Book II from canto vi to canto xii. The Bower itself suggests a host of related aesthetic issues, both in the area of artistic imitation and illusion, and in the area of artistic balance and proportion. The Bower is, in both areas, something of a muchness. It is the work of an inspired beautician, who has left nothing to chance or nature. In such a case, art "undermines" nature, and like the fountain and the girls it holds, the Bower's contrivance seems both shallow and "ouer-wrought" (II.xii.59, 62). Bagehot's strictures on ornate poetry may be applied to it verbatim:

> The first defect which strikes a student of ornate art—the first which arrests the mere reader of it—is what is called a want of simplicity. Nothing is described as it is, everything has about it an atmosphere of *something else*. . . . Even in the highest cases ornate art leaves upon a cultured and delicate taste, the conviction that it is in an unexplained manner unsatisfactory, "a thing in which we feel there is some hidden want!"[185]

Ornateness shares this nature with prolixity. The Bower of Bliss is described in the longest canto of *The Faerie Queene*; the presiding genius is explicitly named Excesse.

[iii]

A broader avenue of approach to Spenser's gardens is by way of the tradition of the earthly paradise. The earthly paradise is a *locus amoenus* writ large, as it were. Often it is not practical to distinguish the one from the other, as in the following description, which is rhetorically in the *locus amoenus* convention, but at the same time describes the paradisal Fields of the Blest:

> . . . a place dedicated to the happie, without anie stub or tree, but the fielde was a plaine coequate medow of sweete hearbes and pleasunt flowers, of all sorts of colours, and sundry varieng fashions, yeelding so fragrant a smell as is possible to speake of, not burnt with the extreme heat of the

---

[185] "Wordsworth, Tennyson, and Browning, or Pure, Ornate, and Grotesque Art in English Poetry," in Edmund D. Jones, ed., *English Critical Essays*, World's Classics (London, 1916), p. 416. An example of the kind of art Bagehot indicts would be Phedria's boat, "bedecked trim / With boughes and arbours wouen cunningly, / That like a forrest seemed outwardly" (II.vi.2): i.e., her boat has changed places with her island.

sunne, but moderate, the ground moystened with sweete ryuers, the aire pure and cleane, the daies all alike, the earth continually like a painting, remaining alwaies vnhurt, with their deawie freshnesse, reseruing and holding their colours without interdict of time.[186]

Spenser would have learned from the Italian poems the practice of having the narrative touch upon a conspectus of such paradisal places, scattered over the reaches of the story as were the Cyclades in the Western Ocean, which these places often resemble.[187] Ariosto, for example, has not only the garden of Alcina and the Garden of Eden, but also the isle of Venus and the realm of Gloricia.[188]

An important strand of the tradition concerns the penetration of the enchanted garden of deceit or illusion. To the domain of Trissino's Acratia may be added those of Tasso's Armida and Ariosto's Alcina, and Boiardo's fays Morgana, Falerina, and Dragontina, all *femmes fatales*. Pre-*romanzi* examples of a specifically entrapping garden may be found in Chretien de Troyes' *Erec and Enide*, and in the *Gesta Romanorum*.[189] The garden in Chretien, for example, is a labyrinth where knights in quest of a king's daughter lose their lives to a champion waiting within its mysterious confines. The garden is flowery and fruitful throughout the year; it abounds in every healing plant; and every bird song may be heard there. It reminds the hero Erec of his "Joy"—that is, the consummation of his love—at least until he encounters a number of sharpened stakes adorned with the heads of his predecessors. The theme of the imprisoning mistress is also to be met here, for the hero next comes upon a comely maiden on a couch; it is her knight who, at her behest, has slain all who have previously undertaken the adventure. The knight explains to his conqueror Erec that the lady thought to detain him with her there all the days of his life, since previously none could defeat him.

Similar themes are treated in Boiardo, where the conquest of enchanted gardens becomes a regular knightly occupation. One such garden, maintained by Dragontina, enjoys the eternal spring; its air is perfumed by all the flowers; and the usual brightly colored and richly adorned palazzo is attached.[190] (The "cabinets" and banquet houses of Spenser's Bower go

---

[186] *The Strife of Love in a Dream*, the partial Elizabethan trans. of the *Hypnerotomachia Poliphili* of Francesco Colonna, ed. A. Lang (London, 1890), p. 232.

[187] Cf. Tasso, *Ger. Lib.* XV.37, 41, on the number of the Fortunate Isles, and Spenser, *F.Q.* II.xii.10, for the wandering islands.

[188] *O.F.* XVIII.136–139; *Cinque Canti*, I.71–81.

[189] *Erec and Enide*, vv. 5739ff., in *Arthurian Romances*, trans. W. W. Comfort, Everyman's Library (London and New York, 1967), pp. 75–80. *Gesta Romanorum*, ed. Sidney Herrtage, EETS, Extra Series 33 (London, 1879), pp. 111ff. (In the Latin versions this is number 33; here it is 31.)

[190] *Orl. Inn.* II.vi.44ff.

back to the *gabinetti* and architectural wonders of his predecessors.)[191]
The association of such a garden with Circe is perhaps original with
Boiardo; his nymph is linked with the goddess by both her enchanting
cup and a tapestry depicting a rather un-Homeric version of Circe's
legend. Men are not turned to animals by Dragontina's beverage, but they
lose their memories and their sense of chivalric direction. On Dragontina's
behalf the enchanted Orlando attacks his would-be rescuers Brandimart
and Astolfo. Berni, in his version of the poem, is at pains to explain the
drink:

> Io ho pensato a questa acqua incantata
> A questo fiume della oblivione,
> Ed holla ad una cosa assomigliata,
> Ch'alcun mi par che chiami passione,
> Alcuni opinione hanno chiamata,
> Ed altri affetto, ed altri impressione
> Che l'uom lascia venirsi, buona o trista,
> Per detto d'attri, o per fede o per vista.

I have meant by this enchanted water, by this river of oblivion, this cup,
to represent a thing which some, like me, call passion: some have called it
opinion, and others affection, and others impression, which man allows
himself to take—whether good or bad—from the word of others, either
upon trust or at sight.[192]

Berni's interpretation is possible, because the theme of illusion is in the
original of Boiardo. Such themes appear in all Boiardo's successors, and
the idea that one under an illusion or a mistaken impression has drunk
from Circe's cup is a commonplace by the time the Duke uses it in *The
Comedy of Errors*.[193]

---

[191] Cf. the "greene cabinet" of "December," l. 17. The *Hypnerotomachia* carries
this tradition to an extreme, but Trissino's description of the palace of Acratia is
architecturally complex, and the angel who describes it is named Palladio. The
palace of Ariosto's Gloricia compares favorably with the work of Alberti, Bramante,
and Vitruvius (*Cinque Canti*, I.78). Marvell's "Upon Appleton House" promotes a
whole school of architectural domestications of pastoral in English literature.

[192] *Orlando Innamorato di Matteo Maria Boiardo, rifatto da Francesco Berni*, ed.
Severino Ferrari (Florence, 1911), I.x.1. Cf. Domenichi's allegory on *Orl. In.* I.vi,
in his 1546 edn. of Boiardo's original (p. 23): the drink given to the count "shows
how quick the fantasy is to change one's thought."

[193] V.i.271. (Cf. Stephen Gosson, *The School of Abuse*, ed. Edward Arber, English
Reprints, Westminster, 1895, p. 20: the poets' inventions are "the Cuppes of *Circes*,
that turne reasonable creatures into brute Beastes.") At the gate Spenser displaces
the allusion to Circe to Medea (II.xii.44f.) for many reasons: because the object
of conquest is approached by a voyage that passes by both argosies and wandering
rocks; and because of the literary relations of Circe and Medea. Circe, in one gene-

The *locus amoenus* is a natural meeting-place for lovers as well as pastoral figures. This erotic possibility is made official when such a pleasance is placed under the guardianship of Venus, or becomes the scene of one of her amours. Venus is a garden-goddess in a scattering of classical texts that dimly anticipate descriptions like Ariosto's of her gardens on the Cyprian isle.[194] A *carpe diem* poem of Ausonius makes the available rose garden belong to Venus.[195] In Lydgate's *Reson and Sensuallyte*, the chaste Diana describes Venus' garden of pleasure. In passing she characterizes it as Vulcan's bed and Circe's cup,[196] which is a surprisingly apt summary of the mythology of the Bower of Bliss. The bed of Mars and Venus was not originally a garden, but one may cite a precedent in a minor Latin poet, Reposianus.[197] This poet creates a very complete *locus amoenus* around the famous adultery and the lovers' apprehension, and thus the theme of the entrapping garden of romance appears before "romance." In Reposianus' garden "rich Nature toils for Venus' luxury" (l. 47), and it seems to the poet that Venus made the grove for love alone. The flora

---

alogy, is Medea's aunt, and Apollonius, according to Comes, "calls Medea herself Aeian, either because she resorted to Circean arts, or because she appeared dangerous to several." (*Mythol.*, VI.vii, "De Medea," *edn. cit.*, p. 569.) Tasso, *Ger. Lib.* IV.86, compares Armida to both witches because both changed men's shapes. In Valerius Flaccus, *Arg.* VII.210ff., Medea is persuaded by Circe, who is Venus in disguise.

[194] Pliny, *Nat. Hist.* XIX.xix.20: "Plautus speaks of gardens as being under the guardianship of Venus"; Varro, *On Agriculture*, I.i.6: "I beseech Minerva and Venus, of whom the one protects the olive yard, and the other the garden; and in her honour the rustic Vinalia has been established"; Varro, *Frg.* 4 (= *On the Latin Language* VI.20), on the gardens set aside for Venus during the Vinalia: "Prolubium and lubido 'desire' are derived from lubet 'it is pleasing'; whence also *the grove of Venus Lubentina gets its name*"; Pausanias, I.xix.2: "Concerning the district called The Gardens, and the temple of Aphrodite, there is no story that is told by them, nor yet about the Aphrodite which stands near the temple. Now the shape of it is square, like that of the Hermae, and the inscription declares that the Heavenly Aphrodite is the oldest of those called Fates. But the statue of Aphrodite in the Gardens is the work of Alcamenes, and one of the most noteworthy things in Athens." (All translations from the Loeb Classical Library.)

[195] In the Loeb *Ausonius*, ed. and trans. H. G. Evelyn-White, vol. 2, Appendix II, pp. 276-281. (Herrick's "Gather ye rosebuds" is a version.)

[196] *Reson and Sensuallyte*, ed. E. Sieper, EETS, Extra Series, 84, 89 (London, 1901–1903): Circe's cup, ll. 3421, 4093; Vulcan's bed, ll. 3762, 4136. This garden is specifically the place where Adonis died (l. 3690, "the forest of cytheron"); its enticements should be avoided like the Sirens (l. 4098).

[197] *De Concubitu Martis et Veneris*, in Loeb *Minor Latin Poets*, ed. and trans. J. Wright Duff and Arnold M. Duff, pp. 524ff. The earliest edition of the poet is listed here as P. Burman, *Anthol. Lat.*, Amsterdam, 1759—the ms. on which this text depends is said to be the Codex Salmasianus of the Latin Anthologia. Since earlier notice of this piece is lacking, one cannot adduce its example for any other purpose than that of showing the late classical formation of the tradition to which Spenser's Bower belongs.

include laurel, myrtle, and flower beds on which the lovers lie; there are also fountains, shade, and every fragrance. Reposianus' description of Mars in the garden anticipates Spenser's description of Cymochles in the Bower: "He in his covering of flowers with stealthy eye [*furtivo lumine*] gazes agape at Venus and he trembles with the full fire" (ll. 103–104). We may compare Spenser's expansion of the idea:

> He, like an Adder, lurking in the weeds,
>> His wandring thought in deepe desire does steepe,
>> And his fraile eye with spoile of beautie feedes;
>> Sometimes he falsely faines himself to sleepe,
>> Whiles through their lids his wanton eies do peepe,
>> To steale a snatch of amorous conceipt,
>> Whereby close fire into his heart does creepe:
>>> (II.v.34)

The motif, in both Spenser and Reposianus, seems to go back to Lucretius' hymn to Alma Venus, though the literal disarming of the war-god is not found in the earlier poet: "Mars . . . gazes on you [Venus] and feeds his greedy eyes with love" [pascit amore avidos inhians in te, dea, visus].[198] Lucretius' description must be the source of the similar picture of the supine Mars, reclining on Venus' breast, in Politian's *Stanze*: the war-god "*Pascendo* gli occhi pur della sua faccia" (I.122). The same description occurs in Tasso, with the kisses from Politian and the suspiration from Lucretius; only now it is Armida, with "humid eyes," hanging over Rinaldo:

> e i famelici sguardi avidamente
> in lei *pascendo* si consuma e strugge.
> S'inchina, e i dolci baci ella sovente
> liba or da gli occhi e da le labra or sugge,
> ed in quel punto ei sospirar si sente
> profondo sí che pensi: "Or l'alma fugge
> e 'n lei trapassa peregrina." . . .

And his famished glances avidly on her feed, thus consumed and melted. And she, bending over, frequently now tastes the sweet kisses from his

---

[198] *De Rerum Natura* I.36. The whole passage reads: "Mars . . . often throws himself into your bosom, overpowered by the eternal wound of love; then bending back his shapely neck and looking upward, gazes upon you and feeds his greedy eyes with love; and as he lies there his breath hangs on your lips. Bend down your sacred body above the reclining god, O glorious Goddess, and pour forth sweet words from your mouth. . . ." (Trans. Russel M. Geer.) With this pose compare Milton's Adam and Eve, in *Par. Lost* IV.493–501: Milton restores the male to superiority. My subsequent citation of Politian and Tasso I owe to Giamatti, *Earthly Paradise*, pp. 133, 278.

eyes and from his lips now sucks; and at this point he feels himself breathing profoundly—as if he thought, "the soul now flies and passes, pilgrim-like, into her."

(XVI.19)

As a slight echo of *pascendo* elsewhere indicates, the martial hero is among the mares, put out to pasture (XVI.28).

Spenser omits nothing from the tradition:

> And all that while, right ouer him she hong,
>   With her false eyes fast fixed on his sight,
>   As seeking medicine, whence she was stong,
>   Or greedily depasturing delight:
>   And oft inclining downe with kisses light,
>   For feare of waking him, his lips bedewd,
>   And through his humid eyes did sucke his spright,
>   Quite molten into lust and pleasure lewd;
> Wherewith she sighed soft, as if his case she rewd,
>
> (II.xii.73)

Spenser's is the most fully developed picture; self-abandon here implies the surrender of the spirit to something more sinister than Tasso's queen of hearts. Acrasia, unlike Armida, cannot love; more like Ariosto's Alcina, she can only use her lovers, which means using them up. The languishing Verdant, "his dayes, his goods, his bodie he did spend" (II.xii.80). In the end, Acrasia's victims become milling beasts. The man in them is elsewhere represented by the debilitated Mordant, pitifully susceptible to that collapse, externally induced, which seems to coincide with the exhaustion of his inner resources. Despite his youth, Mordant is a derelict.

The baneful pleasure-garden occurs elsewhere in the Spenser canon. The *Mviopotomos* tells the story of a butterfly who seemed to be lord of all creation:

> To the gay gardins of his vnstaid desire
> Him wholly caried, to refresh his sprights;
> There lauish Nature in her best attire,
> Powres forth sweete odors, and alluring sights;
> And Arte with her contending, doth aspire
> T'excell the naturall, with made delights:
> And all that faire or pleasant may be found,
> In riotous excesse doth there abound.
>
> (161–168)

The net that Acrasia wears is compared to "the subtile web" woven by Arachne, and there is a relative of Arachne in the butterfly's garden too.

"Regardless of his gouernaunce," the seemingly free spirit is carried by a hostile wind into the spider's net. He struggles, but only worsens his plight:

> ... in the ende he breathelesse did remaine,
> And all his yougthly forces idly spent,
> Him to the mercie of th'auenger lent.

$$(430-432)$$

If the tale is cautionary, or at least parabolic, it seems to tell the story of a garden of plenty and delight that became an entrapping and paralyzing Bower of Bliss.

The sensuous grove of Reposianus, where Venus trysts with Mars, is also, by implication, a Garden of Adonis. Mars has taken the youth's place in the grove, "adorned by the love of the goddess after the wound of Adonis." The place is "meet for worship from Byblos," a center of the Adonis cult.[199] Apart from this poem, Adonis appears as a minor but semistandard denizen of the earthly paradise. A typical *locus amoenus* is a wedding gift to Ovid's Flora (who enjoys perpetual spring); it includes the elegiac flower collection—Narcissus, Attis, and the son of Cinyras from whose wounds, by Flora's art, beauty springs (*Fasti* V.205ff.). The description of the grove of lovers in the afterlife, in Ausonius' *Cupid Crucified*, includes a list of elegiac flowers, that is, the florifications of beloved youths, and Adonis is included among them (ll. 1-15, 57-61). A poem by Dioscorides on Sappho places the dead love-poet in a paradise for immortalized lovers; we learn that Venus laments Adonis while in this "holy grove of the Blessed."[200] The tomb of Adonis is found on the island of Cythera, which the lovers of the *Hypnerotomachia* reach. This island is in the tradition of the lovers' paradise, with gardens, groves, labyrinths, baths, and the fount of Venus.[201] In Politian's *Stanze*, the list of flowers in Venus' realm includes "Adon rinfresca a Venere il suo pianto" (Adonis renewing his plaint to Venus) (I.79). The *locus amoenus* hallowed by the presence of Courtesy, in Tasso's *Rinaldo*, includes a flowery bank where Hyacinthus, Narcissus, and Adonis are rep-

---

[199] *De Conubitu Martis et Veneris*, ll. 33-36.

[200] *Gr. Anth.* VII.407.

[201] *Poliphili Hypnerotomachia*, Methuen facsimile reproduction of the first edn. (London, 1904), Sig. zi^rff. It should be noted that the tomb is technically a garden of Adonis because Venus laments Adonis here during an eight day period that commences the first of May; the roses scattered on the tomb are replenished overnight, and they are stained with Venus' blood—she cut her foot coming to the aid of Adonis when he was struck down by Mars (sig. zviii^v).

resented.[202] Theocritus' festival psalm to Adonis includes the miniature gardens, but some larger grove also seems to be referred to, one that could accommodate children, Cupids, and nightingales. References like those of Pliny to the gardens of Adonis as equivalent to the gardens of the Hesperides and Alcinous do not imply anything merely embryonic or ephemeral.[203]

The association of Venus with the earthly paradise is well known. Tibullus declares that Venus will personally escort him to the paradisal Elysian Fields, where lovers sport together.[204] Comes, in his article on the Elysian Fields, quotes this passage.[205] As Servius points out, the Elysian Fields in Virgil allude to the Fortunate Isles,[206] and the paradisal afterlife that is promised to Menelaus in the *Odyssey* is not the only Elysian-romantic isle in the Homeric poem. In Claudian's influential *Epithalamium*, the Cyprian isle is described as an earthly paradise consecrated to Venus and love. Venus dwells there on the summit; Cupid dips his arrows alternately in two springs; and Youth shuts out Age from the grove.[207] (In the grove of Reposianus the reeds at the fountain supply Cupid with shafts.) Claudian's description has obvious connections with the garden of Mirth in *The Romance of the Rose*, which Chaucer calls Venus' garden. Venus' temple includes a garden in Boccaccio's *Teseide*, to which the lover's personified prayer takes flight—the machinery is from Claudian.[208] Claudian has also supplied the conceit for Politian's *Stanze*, as well as details. However, it is really in Petrarch's *Triumph* that one first finds the Renaissance conception of the enchanted isle of Venus to which Cupid's captives are themselves transported.[209] As in Ariosto later, it is an isle which unmans the prisoner.

The gardens of Adonis, as noted above, are to be associated with pleasure, negatively in Erasmus, positively in Spenser. Spenser's gardens are

---

[202] *Rinaldo*, VII.54 (Adonis is "chi di dolce amor t'are e t'avinse, / o bella diva, il cor molle e cortese"). The motif of the florified youths in the *ver perpetuum* of the Elysian Fields is classical: an example is Lucian, *True History* II.17, where Hylas, Narcissus, and Hyacinthus are grouped together.

[203] *Nat. Hist.* XIX.xix.4.

[204] Tibullus, I.iii.57–66.

[205] Comes, *Mythol.*, III.xix, *edn. cit.*, pp. 272f. Indexed under "Elysiorum camporum amoenitas." Spenser's Temple of Venus, with its groves of friends and lovers, has also been influenced by the Elysian Fields tradition.

[206] Servius, *ad Aen.* VI.640, citing his preceding notice at *Aen.* V.735, which reads: "Philosophers have taught that Elysium is in the Fortunate Isles"—rather than either underground or in the circle of the moon. Cf. *peirata gaiës* of *Od.* IV.563.

[207] *Epithalamium de nuptiis Honorii Augusti*, ll. 49ff. (in Loeb *Claudian*, ed. M. Platnauer, vol. 1, pp. 246–249).

[208] *Teseide*, VII.50f.

[209] Petrarch, *Trionfo d'Amore*, IV, ll. 100–105. Giamatti, *Earthly Paradise, passim*, documents the line of descent most fully.

"fraught / With pleasures manifold" (III.vi, rubric). Cupid was nursed here (*Colin Clout*, 803–804), as will be his namesake Amoret (III.vi.28). The daughter of Cupid, Pleasure, is a denizen. In Claudian, the allegorical figures within the walls include *non secura Voluptas*;[210] in Politian, timid Pleasure and *Volutta con Bellezza* (Will with Beauty);[211] in the garden in Chaucer's *Parliament of Foules*, Cupid's daughter "Wille," going back to a pun on *Voluptas* and *Voluntas*;[212] in the gardens of Queen Eleuterilia, in the *Hypnerotomachia*, within the portal of the Mother of Love, Thelemia and Voluptuousness.[213] The personnel are well established, and even Rabelais calls his *locus amoenus* the Abbey of Theleme, where one does what one wants. Spenser's Garden contains a Voluptas, too, for Fulgentius derives Adonis' name itself from *hedonai*, and identifies him with the pleasurable balm exuded by the myrrh tree (see I.i.9).[214]

Besides representing the pleasure of love, Spenser's Garden represents the fruitfulness and fullness of time that love implies. The Garden features continual spring and harvest, "both meeting at one time" (III.vi.42), and as in Botticelli's *Primavera* the boughs bear flower and fruit at once. Shakespeare alludes to the classical example: "Thy promises are like Adonis' garden / That one day bloom'd and fruitful were the next" (*Henry VI, Part I*, I.vi.6f.). In the apocalypse, we are told in Amos 9:13,

---

[210] *Epithalamium de nuptiis Honorii Augusti*, l. 82. Note also Licentia at l. 78.

[211] *Stanze per la Giostra*, I.75.

[212] *Parliament of Foules*, l. 214. For the pun, see Dante, *Convivio*, iv.6. In Boccaccio, *Teseida*, VII.54, Cupid's daughter Voluttà selects arrows to temper among those her father is manufacturing.

[213] *Hypnerotomachia* (London, 1904), sig. hii^r; when, at sig. i ii^r, the dreamer makes Paris' choice of the sensual life, Logistilla departs in a snit (Greek *thellos*, "will"). Logistilla the reader will recognize from Ariosto (*O.F.* VI.43, etc.). Cf. Virgil in Dante, *Purg.* XXVII.130f.: "I have brought you here with reason . . . ; now take pleasure as your guide"; and ll. 140f.: "free, upright, and whole is your *will*; it would be wrong not to do as it pleases." It is of some significance that the next character Dante meets is the active, Eve-like Matelda (cf. Greek *teleos*, "complete, fulfilled"). The pleasance-symbol of a mediate fulfillment also appears in the Middle English *Pearl*, where the criterion of repleteness or maturity appears both in the form and *telos* of the poem, and in the theological issue raised there. Blake's *Book of Thel* seems to reflect the same convention, as it might appear in the context of Donne's remarks on the Paradox (XII) "That Virginity is a Vertue": "All other *Vertues* lodge in the *Will* (it is the will that makes them vertues). But it is the unwillingnesse to keep it, the desire to forsake it, that makes this a vertue." The poem features as its heroine a "daughter of beauty" who leads a wishful and ultimately willful existence in an Edenic garden, to which she retreats "unhindered" in the poem's last line: her *inclinations* fail to fulfill themselves in *pleasure*.

[214] *Mitologiarum*, III.viii, "Fabula Mirrae et Adonis," in *Fvlgentivs: Opera*, ed. R. Helm, pp. 72f.

the plowman will overtake the reaper; and the treader of the vintage, him who sows the seed. In the Eden of Revelation the twelve trees bear fruit twelve times a year. If it were not for time, everything that grows in the Garden "Should happie be, and haue immortall blis" (III.vi.41); thus the Garden suggests a state in which time would follow the rhythm of human desires, rather than merely date them. Waller's description of the Summer-Islands deftly remarks each of these desiderata, including the accelerated growth of vegetation:

> For the king Spring which but salutes us here,
> Inhabits there, and courts them all the year:
> Ripe Fruits and blossoms on the same Trees live;
> At once they promise, what at once they give:
> So sweet the Air, so moderate the Clime;
> None sickly lives, or dies before his time.
> Heaven sure has kept this spot of earth uncurst,
> To shew how all things were Created first.
>
> (Canto I, 40–47)

The Bower of Bliss is compared to Eden, "if ought with Eden mote compaire" (II.xii.52); it follows that the Garden of Adonis involves the same comparison. Like the name Adonis, the name of the biblical paradise of pleasure was said to derive from the word for pleasure, whether Greek or Hebrew. E. K.'s note on "Jvne" says that Eden is named for its being situated in "the most fertile and pleasaunte country of the world." Paulus Fagius, on *gan bǝ ēden* of Genesis 2:8, writes that "Eden, in Hebrew, means *voluptatem* and *delitias*; hence this garden receives the term Eden on account of pleasure, amenity, and delights." Or it may be the name of a region mentioned in Isaiah 37, "in which the Lord has planted a garden most pleasant and full of delights"; however, "the author of the Latin edition for the people everywhere explains Eden as paradise of pleasure. And moreover paradise the Persian word, as even Xenophon attests, means garden, which they call paradises. . . ."[215] In the light of these traditions, even Paeana's very minor "gardens of delight" (IV.viii.54) have their etymological prototype in Eden.

The link between the Garden of Adonis and Eden has already figured in our discussion of Redcrosse's garden. It proves harder to document outside of Spenser's poem, but Josephine Waters Bennett cites a note in the *Aethici Cosmographia* of Joshua Simmler of 1575:

> I have no doubt that this name [Adonis] is corrupt, nor do I find anywhere a province of this name. It is strongly possible [that it is put] for

[215] *Pirosh hamǝloth al dabar . . . id est, Exegesis . . . in . . . Geneseos* (Isnae, 1542).

Eden: by this name Holy Writ denominates the oriental region where the Paradise of God was. And he confirms this opinion of ours, because he afterwards writes that the river Armodium waters the region of Adonis and Mesopotamia . . . showing Mesopotamia [as] the locale for Eden.

A somewhat more complicated account of a similar place-name is found in Raleigh's *History* (I.iii.10), where he discusses the popular question of Eden's Eastern locale.[216] In editions of Comes' *Mythologiae* after 1596 (though not before, so far as I have been able to determine), the notes of an "anonymus lector" have been appended; this "lector" proposes to illuminate the sources of ethnic superstition, and his first article treats the *Adonidis horti*. Perhaps he provides a summary of then current opinion:

Of the garden of Eden or earthly paradise, which Moses describes, Genes. 2, there are extant most certain testimonies and vestiges in Ethnic writers. And first from the name itself, Eden (which in Hebrew is the same as both pleasure and delight) the garden of delights is designated. And Xenophon in this sense writes in the books of the education and expedition of Cyrus, they call *Pardeis* that which the Greeks call *paradeison*, and which the Latins have truly named by a change from the Greeks *Paradisum*. Further, Paradise is a place the most pleasant of all, and most full of pleasures: as A. Gellius also defines it—which he thinks to be called *vivaria* [parks] by the Latins, lib. 2 *Noct. Attic.* cap. 20. From whence, being Blessed after this life, those most happy seats are subsequently called Paradise in the Word of God. Luc. 23:44, 2 Corinth. 12:4, and Apoc. 2:7. These all also allude to the Hebrew name Eden, the meaning of which they refer to, and retain. Now this Greek word *hedonai*, which signifies pleasure, seems to derive from the Hebrew Eden. And so also Adonis the fiction of the poets and the region of Adonis or Edonis (which is Eden), but corrupt by the wayward Greek pronunciation for Edenis, rather Edene. Indeed, according to Lactantius, the Sybil remembers these delicious gardens, that is, of Eden and the abandoned Paradise, lib. 2. cap. 12. Homer, from old tradition, writes of the Elysian Fields, that is, a certain place the most happy on this orb, and a site even at the farthest end of the orb, in which the most blessed good and pious men live; lib. 5. *Odyss.* And from Homer thereafter, the others, first poets, then philosophers, took it over. In turn [we have] the *Adonis horti* and Hesperidean gardens, so celebrated in Ethnic writers, and some resembling these. And they were able to be regarded as a certain trace of this

---

[216] Josephine Waters Bennett, "Spenser's Garden of Adonis," *PMLA*, 47 (1932), p. 48, n. 11, where the Latin is given from the *Aethici Cosmographica* of 1575. Raleigh cites the same supposed corruption of Eden on the part of Aethicus, and cites Stephanus, *De Urbibus*, for a city of Adana upon the Euphrates.

garden: from which Pliny, lib. 19. *Hist. Natur.* cap. 4. [The identity of the gardens of Adonis and Eden is reiterated, with reference to Simmler's scholia, and finally even the name Adam is said to express the relation obscurely.][217]

This may be the source of similar remarks in Henry Reynoldes' *Myth-omystes.*[218]

Our anonymous "lector" remembered his Lactantius, while dropping the emphasis of the Christian apologist on the unreliability of classical authority. Lactantius actually is eager to refute the Lucretian genesis myth, which he reports accurately.[219] According to Lactantius, the myth includes the notion of the primavera of the world; the native generative power of the unaided earth, which endows its births with their subsequent reproductive capacities; perpetual spring and the absence of seasonal vicissitudes; and the eventual passing of this condition of things. Thus one further relation between the Garden of Adonis and the primal garden is the conception of the biblical earthly paradise as a place of origins, "the first seminarie / Of all things, that are borne to liue and die, / According to their kinds" —like Noah's ark, stocked with two of each kind and preserving "sede of generacion vnto the world" (Gen. 6:20; Wisdom 14:6, Geneva Bible; *F.Q.* III.vi.30). More properly, the first creation, of which Eden was only a part, is the "original" of this world. The classical *locus amoenus* was blessed with perpetual spring, and so was the Golden Age. The Bible, in that it makes labor in the fields subsequent to the loss of Eden, and mentions winter only after the Flood, seems to be saying the same things.

The idea of the earthly paradise as a "creation" also meets us whenever its flora and fauna are stressed as being representative. The garden of Mirth in the *Romance of the Rose* contains at least one or two of every fruitful tree—only unattractive trees have been excluded. The park at Spenser's Temple of Venus lacks "No tree, that is of count" (IV.x.22); the wood at Mt. Acidale is formed by "all trees of honour" (VI.x.6). Thus the rhetorical *topos* of the replete grove, or park, or vivarium easily becomes a metaphor for the productivity of nature. The catalogue of natural objects, *natura naturata*, soon suggests nature creating, *natura naturans*. The presence of Nature or Venus Genetrix in these places is the logical fulfillment of a semirhetorical ideal of *copia* or plenitude.

We need to know how such a reservoir came to have Adonis for its patron. Perhaps the poet took a hint from the island paradise of Alcina

---

[217] This supplement to Comes' *Mythologiae* is listed in the *Catalogue* of the British Museum as first appearing in the 1596 edn. In my text, the Geneva edn. of 1641, the article translated here is found at Sigs. Ii^v–Iii^r.

[218] *Mythomystes*, in Spingarn, *Critical Essays*, vol. 1, p. 179.

[219] *Divine Institutes*, II.xii (trans. in ANF, vol. 7, pp. 60f.).

in Ariosto. It is a *locus amoenus*; it seems that Love was born here, and, again as in Claudian, he dips his arrows in its stream to sharpen them. Ruggiero, the successor of Astolfo, puts himself at the disposal of the bewitching one, and here the lovers tryst. The dalliance comes to an end when Melissa, disguised as Ruggiero's magician-uncle, arrives to dispel the illusion. Ruggiero's uncle taught him to disarm wild beasts and to draw the teeth of the boar, and he might well rebuke Ruggiero for having become Alcina's Attis or Adonis.[220] Like Virgil's Mercury, Melissa exhorts the hero to live up to his Trojan-Italian destiny, which includes marrying her mistress and siring the ancestors of the poet's benefactor:

> Deh non vietar che le più nobile alme
> Che sian formate no l'eterne idee,
> De temp in temp abbian corporee salme
> Del ceppo che radice in te aver dee:

O do not forbid the most noble souls which are formed in the eternal ideas—from age to age to habit in corporeal bodies—to be given from the stock which has root in you.

(O.F. VII.61)

Clearly this Adonis is in the wrong *locus amoenus*, the transcient or fruit-less one. Melissa's brief suggestion that we turn to a contrasting realm, from which ours is from time to time replenished, will doubtless prove a proper course.

Seminarium Mundi: The Pregnancy and
Primavera of the World

On thy Calends, Paphian Queen, plant the Paphian lettuce. While the plant desires its mother-earth's embrace, who longs for it, and she most soft beneath the yielding field lies waiting, grant her increase. Now the times are the genitalia of the world, now when love to union hastes; the spirit of the world revels in Venus, and urged by the stimuli of Cupid, itself embraces its parturitions, and fills with conceptions. The father of the sea his Tethys now allures, and now the lord of all the waves his Amphitrite; each anon displays to her caerulean lord a new-born breed, and fills the sea with swimmers. King of gods himself lays down his thunder and repeats, as once by craft with the Acrisian maid, his ancient loves and in impetuous rain descends into the lap of Mother Earth; nor

---

[220] *O.F.* VII.57: "Acciò che dopo tanta disciplina / Tu sii l'Adone o l'Atide d'Al-cina?"

does the genetrix her son's love refuse, but, inflamed by Cupid, permits his embrace. Hence seas, hence hills, hence even the whole wide world is celebrating Spring; hence comes desire to man and beast and bird, and flames of love burn in the heart, and in the marrow rage, till Venus, satiated, impregnates their fruitful members, and generates a various brood, and ever fills the world with new progeny, lest it grow tired with empty age.

> (Columella, *De re rustica* X, "On the Care of Gardens," ll. 192–214; trans. adapted from Forster's and Heffner's in the Loeb edn.)

[i]

The physical allegories of Adonis are well known. Comes quotes the commentator on Theocritus to the effect that Adonis is a seed of wheat, passing from Venus to Proserpina, and back again, "because Adonis is sown fruit, on which account he spends six months under the earth, six months Venus possesses him in the temperate air, from which the reapers evidently collect him."[221] Cornutus, in his article on Ceres, says that Adonis is seeds,[222] and Eusebius contrasts him with Attis, "the symbol of the blossoms which appear early in the spring, and fall off before complete fertilization." Attis is castrated "from the fruits not having attained to seminal perfection: but Adonis was the symbol of the cutting of the perfect fruits."[223] Such an Adonis would be a male Koré, a role implied by the Orphic Hymn when it calls Adonis "korē, kai kore," a male and female vegetation deity.[224] The scholia of Hermeas on the gardens of Adonis in Plato's *Phaedrus* says Adonis "presides over everything that grows and perishes in the earth."[225]

The allegory of the solar Adonis merely extends this symbolism for the annual cycle of vegetation. This Adonis is found in the Orphic Hymn, where the "semper viridescens" god is also the lamp of the turning year. Macrobius expands this interpretation; in lamenting Adonis, Venus laments the decline of the sun.[226] The third Vatican mythographer records

[221] *Mythol.*, V.xvi, "De Adoni," p. 525, *edn. cit.*; scholia on Theocritus, III.48. Cf. Jerome, *Comm. in Ezch.*, VIII.13f. (PL, XXV, 83).

[222] *De Nat. Deorum*, 28, "De Cerere," in Gale, *Opuscula Mythologica*, p. 210.

[223] *Praep. Evang.*, XV.xi (p. 110b), in Gifford edn. and trans., Tom. III, Pars I, p. 120. Cf. Augustine, *Civ. Dei*, VII.xxv.

[224] Orphic Hymn LIV, cited by Comes, *Mythol.*, p. 525: "Orpheus thinks that Adonis is the sun, since he says *illum rebus omnibus praebere nutrimetum, & esse germinandi autorem.*" Cf. III.vi.9: the sun is "father . . . of generation . . . th'author of life and light."

[225] Hermeas Alexandrinus, *In Phaedrum* 276b; in I. N. Theodorakopglos, ed., *Platonis Phaedrus* (Athens, 1948), p. 453.

[226] *Saturnalia*, I.xxi.1–6: the upper signs of the zodiac, or the upper hemisphere, are Venus; the lower, Proserpina; Venus laments the onset of winter. (This is the

this reading of the myth,[227] and it is found in Melanchthon on Ovid,[228] citing Pontano's *Urania*.[229] Comes explains the boar as winter, "because winter is savagely bestial and bristling, on account of which the powers of the sun are gradually eclipsed." "Without the power of the Sun, Venus is nothing. . . . They say he is extinguished with respect to winter, because the generation of herbs and many things ceases at that time."[230] Comes' article on Adonis is followed directly by his article on the sun, which opens with these words: "The sun, whom we take to be the author of generation and properly of all good things, as God commanded it. . . ."[231] Circe is the daughter of the Sun and "the humour of the Ocean." The Ocean refers to "the succession of matter or to the female"; the Sun, to "the artifex or male, who is the author of form in the generation of natural things."[232] The Sun "is the source of light in the whole sky, and the author of benefits in all natural things."[233] Elsewhere Comes allegorizes Priapus as "the seeds of natural things," conceived from heat and humour, that is, his parents the Naiads or Venus and Adonis—Adonis, like Dionysus, being "another one of the names for the sun."[234] Spenser's terminology is well attested.

---

source of the ideas in the passage from Equicola, *Di Natura d'Amore*, quoted in Ellrodt, *Neoplatonism*, p. 88.)

[227] Bode, *Scriptores rerum mythicarum latini*, III.ll.17, pp. 238f.

[228] Melanchthon, *Enar. in librum X Metamorph.*, in *Opera*, ed. Bretschneider and Bindseil, vol. 19 (Brunswig, 1853), col. 608: "Pontanus transfers the fable to physics, and understands by Adonis the sun, than which nothing is more beautiful; by his virility, the solar rays, through which all things born in the earth are generated; by the boar, the zodiacal sign of Capricorn; for this cuts off the solar rays, when the days are contracted into gloom; by Venus, the earth herself, which loves the sun, and, bereaved of it, laments."

[229] As quoted in Melanchthon, *ibid.*, from "primo de stellis," the passage from Pontanus reads: "And indeed deserted earth laments the falling sun, whom gloomy winter casts a glaring eye at, and at whom his more savage face of a boar bristles with hoary frost, and whose hair much rain steeps, and foully beats down on both his shoulders. And just as when a maid alone sighs for her absent husband to transform sterile life in the bed, the restless one anticipating his dear embrace with her curves full and disclosed, so earth opens its breathing places, in order that he come, through whom there is sap in her herbs, and that he pile up the snows and lash the wind with hail;—for when the sun, himself the creating father of things, so transforms himself, or the mid-winter spirits beneath the cold, then the bereaved earth covers the furrows in her womb with mud and at last gladdens in the embrace her Adonis."

[230] *Mythol.*, V.xvi, "De Adoni," *edn. cit.*, pp. 525f.

[231] *Mythol.*, V.xvii, "De Sole," p. 526.

[232] *Mythol.*, VI.vi, "De Circe," p. 564.

[233] *Mythol.*, V.xvii, "De Sole," p. 529. Cf. n. 223, above.

[234] *Mythol.*, V.xx, "De Priapo," p. 521.

> Great father he of generation
>   Is rightly cald, th'author of life and light;
>   And his faire sister for creation
>   Ministreth matter fit, which tempred right
> With heate and humour, breedes the liuing wight.
>
> (III.vi.9)

It is the *moon* that "administers" to matter, or prepares it by moistening it, as Fowler's definitive citation from Ficino shows.[235] That is why a trace of the motif of the bath of the moon-goddess Diana crosses the imagery for Chrysogonee's impregnation ("In a fresh fountaine, farre from all men's vew," III.vi.6). The sun, however, confers upon matter its "formall feature," according to a related passage in *Colin Clout* (859–862).

There is a further physical meaning for Adonis, partly related to the form-giving sun. The Orphic Hymn describes Adonis as *polumorphe*, much-formed, and *Aglaomorphe*, of splendid form. Adonis is "beautiful" because he is under the influence of the planet Venus:

> The house of goodly formes and faire aspects,
> Whence all the world deriues the glorious
> Features of beautie, and all shapes select,
> With which high God his workmanship hath deckt;
>
> (III.vi.12)

In Latin what is beautiful is *formosus*, or *speciosus*, words that mean "shapely" and "good-looking." Augustine, for example, in discussing the nature of the good, has occasion to remark upon the capacity of matter (*hyle*) for good form: "if form is some good, whence those who excel in it are called beautiful [*formosus*], as from appearance [*species*] they are called handsome [*speciosus*], even the capacity of form is undoubtedly something good."[236] In the *Anticlaudianus* of Alanus de Insulis, where Nature has determined upon the creation of a somewhat Platonic perfect man (virtually a philosophical second Adam), we are twice told that the new being is provided with a body on which Nature has lavished all the riches of form: "Narcissus breathes in this form, and another Adonis

---

[235] Alastair Fowler, *Spenser and the Numbers of Time*, p. 141, citing Ficino, *Comm. in Timaeum*, Appendix, chap. 20 (in *Op. om.*, I-2, p. 1468). For the moon's contribution to generation, see Aristotle, *De Partibus Animalium* IV.v; Cicero, *De Divinatione* II.33; *De Nat. Deorum* II.xix; Horace, *Sat.* II.iv.30; Pliny, *Nat. Hist.* II.cii.221, XI.lxix.149; Aulus Gellius, *Att. Noct.* XX.viii. See Hankins, *Source and Meaning*, p. 245.

[236] *The Nature of the Good*, 18, trans. A. H. Newman, in NPNF, 1st Series, vol. 4, p. 354. For beauty as "feature," cf. Shakespeare, *Son.* 11: "Let those whom Nature hath not made for store, / Harsh featureless, and rude, barrenly perish. . . . Thou shouldst print more, not let that copy die." (The poet speaks to the beautiful youth, "beauty's pattern to succeeding men," *Son.* 19.)

breathes in this *specie*."[237] Such a form must reflect one of the things that Prudence has beheld in heaven (elsewhere in the poem) among "engendered shapes, . . . the forms of men, the primordial origins of things, the cause of causes, the seeds of motives,"[238] and the answers to such questions as "Why the *species* purged of form makes Adonis clear" ("Cur formae species purgata sernat Adonim").[239] Hankins draws attention to this passage,[240] because the poet seems to mean that the typal or essential form— the revealed or serene Adonis—is shown when it is detached from the perishable or changeable physical form. So Spenser's Adonis:

> . . . for he may not
> For euer die, and euer buried bee
> In balefull night, where all things are forgot;
> All be he subiect to mortalitie,
> Yet is eterne in mutabilitie,
> And by succession made perpetuall,
> Transformed oft, and chaunged diuerslie:
> For him the Father of all formes they call;
>
> (III.vi.47)

A clue for the interpretation of Adonis in Alanus is found elsewhere in his poem, where Reason "peers into the abyss of things." There she sees:

> . . . the form which creates of the subject, achieves its being, contributes to the event or guides it into existence, which generates, changes it, preserves it in being; . . . subjects deprived of forms, return to antique chaos and seek again the proper matrix, and she sees the pure form regain strength in its own state, nor does it lament the loss of the loathesome qualities of its degenerate substance, but the form, rejoicing, takes repose in its own being . . . it returns . . . to its own place of birth. . . . Young, it is not deflowered by the old age of substance but always creates maiden forms out of forms.[241]

The passage from Spenser about the survival of Adonis applies equally well to the death and rebirth of seed, the revival of the all-fathering sun, and the perpetuation of form. However, the "seminarie of all things that

---

[237] *Anticlaudianus*, VII, l. 42: "So that another Venus might discern him returned."

[238] *Anticlaudianus*, VI, ll. 214–216: "ingenitas species . . . hominum formas, primordia rerum, / Causarum causas, racionum semina." The list also includes "ydeas / Celestes." (Text ed. Bossuat, Testes Philosophiques du Moyen Age 1, Paris, 1955.)

[239] *Anticlaudianus*, VI, l. 226.

[240] Hankins, *Source and Meaning*, p. 247.

[241] *Anticlaudianus*, I, ll. 460–463, 468–472, 474, 476f., trans. W. H. Cornog (Philadelphia, 1935), p. 63.

are born and die" is placed in a legend about a heroine headed toward marriage, and the Renaissance reader would have understood its special application to that theme. The petulant Adonis in Shakespeare's poem, for example, rebuffs the approaches of the love-goddess in a way that begs comparison with the "beautiful youth" of the Sonnets—the minion of Nature's pleasure—who refuses to perpetuate himself through progeny. He refuses to set the "many maiden gardens" that would bear him flowers.[242] An ultimately less self-enclosed youth, on the other hand, concludes that the world must be peopled.[243]

La Primaudaye says "The society of wedlocke is the seminarie and preservation of all societie."[244] For Augustine, "The crown of marriage is the chastity of procreation and faithfulness in rendering the carnal debt."[245] A topic for rhetorical training, this theme appears in Wilson's *Rhetoric*, which translates an epistle of Erasmus, and in Rainoldes' *Foundacion of Rhetoricke*, which translates a piece by Apothonius.[246] According to Erasmus, marriage supplies issue, "the which through mortalitie doe from tyme to tyme decaie"; marriage purposes to keep our "own kinde from decaye, and throughe encrease of issue, to make the whole kinde immortall"; "throughe Mariage, all thinges are, and do styll continue, and withoute the same all things do decaye, and come to noughte."[247] As Spenser says,

> For all that liues, is subiect to that law:
> All things decay in time, and to their end do draw.
>   (III.vi.40)

Rainoldes explains that God's power is set forth not only in his creation and original workmanship, "but also from tyme to tyme, the posteritiee of men, in their offspring and procreacion, doe aboundantlie commonstrate the same":

> How sone would the whole worlde be dissolved, and in perpetuall ruine
> if that God from tymes and ages, had not by godlie procreacion, blessed
> this infinite issue of mankinde. The dignitie of man in his creacion,
> showeth the worthie succession, maintained by procreacion.[248]

[242] *Son.* 16. Cf. *Son.* 3, "the tillage of thy husbandry." For Shakespeare's fair young patron as the solar Adonis, see *Son.* 18, "Shall I compare thee to a summer's day."
[243] *Much Ado About Nothing*, II.iii.242.
[244] *French Academie* (London, 1586), p. 480.
[245] *De Bono Conjugali*, xi.12.
[246] Richard Rainolde, *The Foundacion of Rhetoricke*, Scholars Facsimiles and Reprints (Gainesville, Fla., 1945); for Apothonius' *Progymnastica* and its history, see the translation of Ray Nadeau, in *Speech Monographs*, vol. 19, no. 4 (Ann Arbor, Mich., 1952), pp. 264ff.
[247] Thomas Wilson, *The Arte of Rhetorique*, Scholars Facsimiles and Reprints (Gainesville, Fla., 1962), "An Epistle to Persuade a young ientleman to Mariage, deuised by Erasmus."
[248] Rainolde, *Foundacion of Rhetoricke*, fol. iv^r. Cf. Erasmus in Wilson, *Arte of*

This language was often echoed:

So man, as if divine, preserves the human species by a perpetual succession. As if thankful, he renders to nature what he received in borrowing—and often with interest.[249]

. . . man shulde render to nature, that he had borowed of her, and to the image of God, shulde brynge forth and nourysshe chyldren lyke himselfe, and restore the comon felowshyp of mankinde with a certayne succession, and to kepe it perpetual. . . .[250]

Thus Spenser's "by succession made perpetual" echoes the standard Renaissance encomium of marriage: through marriage man maintains his being in its extenuation over time.

This institution, it remains to add, was sanctified in a garden. Milton might well hail wedded Love not only as the "true source / Of human offspring," but also as the "mysterious Law" and "sole propriety / In Paradise" (*Par. Lost* IV.750-752). "Love's fruitful Grove," as Sylvester translates DuBartas, also belongs to the machinery of pagan epithalamia, thanks to the example of Claudian's poem: Claudian's conceit is still in service in the *Divine Weeks*, where the embassy of two Cupidons from the Venerean oasis is prefixed to the nuptials of King Solomon. Despite the opportunity for biblical echoes, DuBartas describes the grove, "clad in eternall green, / Where all the year long lusty *May* is seen," as a typical classical *locus amoenus* (II.IV.ii, ll. 655ff.). Claudian's idea of Cupid's mission is, in turn, as old as Theognis, 1275-1278, for which Edmonds' Loeb translation is "Love himself riseth in due season, when the earth swelleth and bloweth with the flowers of Spring; ay, then cometh Love from Cyprus' beauteous isle with joy for man throughout the world" (*Elegy and Iambus*, vol. 1, p. 387). But the word that Edmonds emends to joy (*charma*), in the Greek text is actually seed (*sperma*).

The emblem of Adonis in Alciati—"The Amulet of Venus"—also sheds light on the sexuality of Spenser's Garden. The picture shows the ministration of Venus to the slain lover: "the Cyprian preserved [or concealed] the lifeless Adonis—his groin suffused by the tooth of the wild beast—

Rhetorique, fol. 24[r]: "assured destruction muste here needes folowe excepte men through the benefite of Mariage supplie issue, the which through mortalitie doe from tyme to tyme decaie." Cf. Shakespeare, *Son.* 11: "If all were minded so, *the times* should perish."

[249] Ficino, *Op. om.*, I-2, p. 778: *Epist.* Lib. IV, "Matrimonij laus." For the lending metaphor, cf. Shakespeare, *Son.* 4.

[250] *The Commendation of Matrimony, made by Cornelius Agrippa, & translated into englishe by David Clapam* (London, 1509), fol. Bii[v].

with leaves of lettuce. Henceforth, as much as lettuce opposes the genital field, that much the lustful eruca can scarcely stimulate it."[251] According to this little *aetion*, the lettuce gets its power as an anti-aphrodisiac from its association with the demise of Adonis. The death of Adonis, one might conclude, is impotence. Mignault explains that by "genital field" the organs of generation are meant, and he points to the source of the phrase in a passage of Virgil, where it is a poeticism for the animal womb. Hankins, following up this clue, observes that the fertilizing seminal fluid in the same passage is called "Venus"[252]—presumably because of an identification, like that found in Cornutus, of the foam-born Aphrodite with "ta spermata tōn Zōōn" (the seed of the animals).[253] Mignault adds that "the genital field is called *kepos* in Greek and *hortus* in Latin." In sum, the sterilizing of the "garden" of the genital area is poetically synonymous with the death or burial of Adonis. If Spenser's Garden is also genital in character, then Adonis preserved within it corresponds to the male member or seed, and the *mons veneris* with its uncut foliage and enclosing grove stands for the female pudenda. The likelihood that a vale of preexistence symbolizes "the chaste womb informed with timely seed"—in the words of Spenser's marriage poem—is strong at the outset, quite apart from the impregnation of Chrysogonee by the sun in the passage immediately preceding. Spenser uses the word *informed* there in the same sense as in the *Epithalamion*.[254]

The Greek word for the "shameful parts," *aidoion* (usually the plural *aidoia*) may possibly have been suggestive in making the identification of the Garden of Adonis with the genital area. Hesychius explains a very similar-looking word, *aydonos*, as meaning *neossos* (youngling), according to Stephanus' Greek dictionary. (Hesychius means "the young nightingale.") Stephanus also includes Hesychius' statement that "the female genitals are called by the same name by Archilochus." Phavorinus (as the enlarged Stephanus reports), glosses the same word as a place or workshop where the nightingales sang, or the youngling birds, or the female shameful parts. As it happens, the word *aydonos* appears in Theocritus' description of the gardens of Adonis: "Here are built for him shadowy bowers of green, all laden [*gravata* in the Latin trans. of Stephanus] with tender anise, and children flit overhead—the little Loves—as the young nightingales perched upon the trees fly forth and try their wings from bough to bough."[255] One may compare the amoretti in the grove we have cited from DuBartas: "These frolick Lovelings fraighted Nests do make / The balmy Trees' o'r-laden Boughs to crack. . . . Some are but kindled yet, some

[251] Emb. LXXVII, "Amuletum Veneris," pp. 288f., Antwerp edn. of 1581.
[252] *Georg.* III.136; Hankins, *Source and Meaning*, pp. 241f.
[253] *De Nat. Deorum*, 24, "De Venere," in Gale, ed., *Opuscula Mythologica*, p. 197. Cf. Fulgentius, *Mitologiarum*, II, "De Venere," ed. Helm, p. 39.
[254] *Epithal.*, l. 386; *F.Q.* III.vi.8.
[255] *Idyl* XV.119-122, trans. A. Lang, *Theocritus*, p. 83.

quick appeare. . . . Some douny-clad, some (fledger) take a twig / To pearch-upon, some hop from sprig to sprig" (ll. 692–699). Besides the gardens, the offerings to Adonis also include "all ripe fruit that the tall trees' branches bear." As Spenser's text nears the grove given to Adonis, it seems to become Theocritian:

> . . . the boughes doe laughing blossomes beare,
> And with fresh colours decke the wanton Prime,
> And eke attonce the heauy trees they clime,
> Which seeme to labour vnder their fruits lode:
> The whiles the ioyous birdes make their pastime
> Emongst the shadie leaues, their sweet abode,
> And their true loues without suspition tell abrode.
>
> (III.vi.42)

This is the central stanza of Book III, and it immediately anticipates the stately Mount of Venus that, in the next line rises "Right in the middest of that Paradise." If the birds among its leaves are the amorous *aydonoi* from Theocritus, then they might well have taken up their abode here: in the intimate center, or omphalos, to which the structure of the symmetrically disposed legend of pudicity seems inevitably ordained.

The image of the womb as a garden is well explained by Paracelsus:

God willed that the seed of man should not be sown in the body of the elements—not in the earth—but in woman; that his image should be conceived in her and brought forth through her and not from the field of the world. And yet woman in her own way is also a field of the earth and not at all different from it. She replaces it, so to speak, she is the field and the garden mould in which the child is sown and planted, then growing up to be a man.[256]

The link between sowing or gardening and procreation was especially strong in the case of Adam, for, according to Augustine, "in Paradise men were able to sow in the genital fields [*arvis genitalibus*] of women with the genital members of males, just as grain is sown in fields by the hands of farmers."[257] There are also interpretations of Eden that make it a womb. In Gregory's *Moralia*, "Paradise is the womb of the human race," which was opened by the serpent, etc.[258] Such an allegory is at least implied in all

---

[256] Trans. by Norbert Guterman from Jolande Jacobi, *Paracelsus. Selected Writings* (New York, 1951), pp. 99f., from *Astronomia Magna* (1537–38), in Sudhof and Matthiessen, ed., *Sämtliche Werke* (Munich, Berlin, 1928–1933), Pt. I, vol. 12, p. 46.

[257] Augustine, *Contra Julianum*, 14 (PL, XLV, 1444–1445).

[258] *Moralia*, III.xii.22, on the *ostia* of Job 3:10 (PL, LXXV, 649). (Also quoted in Hankins, *Source and Meaning*, p. 283.) Origen, *Contra Celsum*, IV.xl, makes the

the imagery that makes the Virgin Mary a paradisal *hortus conclusus.*[259] There is also a strong trace of this allegory in one interpretation of the leaves and skins in which Adam and Eve were clothed; according to certain Churchmen these clothes were the flesh—others make them a symbol of man's acquiring mortality.[260] Neither interpretation is inconsistent with Plotinus' usage in speaking of the degrading "muddy vesture" in which souls are clothed in their descent.[261] The "fleshly weeds" that the babes adopt upon leaving the garden are identical with such a symbol. A further

---

entry into the garden of Zeus by Penia (in Plato's *Symposium*) analogous to the serpent's prevailing upon Eve, and the expulsion from Eden the Platonic notion of the soul's loss of its wings and acquisition of a mortal body.

[259] Since the Genius here is the "Selfe" (II.xii.47), we may compare Ps. 139:13: "It was you who created my inmost self / and put me together in my mother's womb." This self is also the rational soul, or co-operates with it, on the evidence of *Summa Theol.*, Pt. I, q.113, art.4, resp., where Aquinas assigns the guardian angel especial care over the rational soul in man, because the guardianship in question is exercised not only toward the common species, but also toward the proper form of each individual, which is the rational soul. See *Summa Theol.*, Pt. I, q.113, art.2, resp.: "Now it is manifest that the providence of God is chiefly expressed towards what remains forever; whereas as regards things which pass away, the providence of God acts so as to order their existence to the things which are perpetual. Hence, the providence of God is related to each man as it is to every genus or species of things corruptible." Further, *Summa Theol.*, Pt. I, q.113, art.5, resp. ad obj.3, "As long as the child is in the mother's womb, it is not entirely separate, but by reason of a certain intimate tie is still part of her; just as the fruit while hanging on the tree is part of the tree. And therefore it can be said with some degree of probability, that the angel who guards the mother guards the child while in the womb. But when the child becomes separate from the mother at birth, an angel guardian is appointed to it, as Jerome says (*Comm. In Matt.*, III, *super* 18:10 [PL, XXVI, 130B])." (Trans. Anton C. Pegis.) Spenser's genius must also be the first of the two mentioned by Servius, *ad Aen.* VI.743, since the Virgil text contributes to the cycle of the soul-forms; Servius writes that "when we are born, we are alloted two geniuses, one which exhorts us to good, the other which depraves us to evil."

[260] Gregory Nazianzen, *Orat.*, 38 (NPNF, 2nd Series, vol. 7, p. 348); Gregory of Nyssa, *Orat. Cat.*, viii; Cyril of Jerusalem, *Cat. Lect.* XIII.18; Philo, *Questions and Answers*, I.53. For the body as clothing, cf. Origen, *De Principis*, III.iii.2; Methodius, *De Resurrect.*, I.iv.2, I.xxiii.3; Augustine, *De Trin.*, XII.xi: "being naked of their first garment, they earned by mortality coats of skins"; Bede, *In Gen.*, I.iii.21. Bede says mortality is insinuated by the putting on of the skins; the term *induere*, "to put on," may recall I Cor. 15:53, to put on the new man; cf. *F.Q.* III.vi.35, "Some fit for reasonable soules t'indew."

[261] *Enn.* I, VI.7: "only those reach it [the Good] who rise to the intelligible realm, face it fully, stripped of the muddy vesture with which they were clothed in their descent, just as those who mount to the temple sanctuaries must purify themselves and leave aside their old clothing, and enter in nakedness, having cast off in the ascent all that is alien to the divine." (Trans. Elmer O'Brien, ed., *The Essential Plotinus*, New York, 1964, p. 40: the *muddiness* of the garment is inferred by the translator from the preceding chapter in Plotinus, on the soilure belonging to matter.)

Spenserian example of the biblical association is found in the charity of the third hospitaler in Book I:

> The third had of their wardrobe custodie, . . .
> . . . clothes meet to keepe keene could away,
> And naked nature seemely to aray;
> With which bare wretched wights he dayly clad,
> The images of God in earthly clay;
>
> (I.x.39)

As God clothed Adam, so the parent clothes the child. In this respect, at least, phylogeny repeats ontogeny.

The tradition of the unborn realm is found in English literature after Spenser. Butler's *Erewhon*, states that the future is "in the loins of the past," that a man of forty would gladly return to the unborn world, and that this is what is meant by the pairing of womb and tomb in Job 3. For the comparison of the "doors of the womb" (Job 3:10) to egress from the world, one may also cite Solomon on his birth:

> I myself am also mortal and a man like all other and am come of him that was first made of the earth.
> And in my mothers wome was I facioned to be flesh in ten moneths:
> I was broght together into blood of the sede of man, and by pleasure that cometh with slepe.
> And when I was borne, I receiued the commune aire, and fel vpon the earth, which is of like nature, crying & weping at the first as all other do. . . .
> For there is no King that had anie other beginning of birth.
> All men then haue one entrance unto life, and a like going out.
>
> (Wisdom 7:1–3, 5–6, Geneva Bible)

Cyclically conceived, departure from life may be compared to re-entering the womb. Thus there is a certain logic in Spenser's locating Chaos in "the wide wombe of the world." Likewise, the Garden of Adonis is a realm of postexistence, though a man cannot enter his mother's womb again, except symbolically, as would the old man in Chaucer's *Pardoner's Tale*, who demands to be readmitted to his mother the earth. Job compares the slumber of the tomb to the state of the stillborn child (Job 3:11–19, 10:8–11, 18–22), and imagines a moratorium in a grave where the worm will be his mother (Job 14:13–14, 17:13, 14). Spenser's Garden also proves to be a very inclusive image, that is, one that almost comprehends its own contrary.

The resemblance of the "entrance unto life" to the "like going out" appears in another way: annually. The gate is manned by the Genius, whose "double nature" tells us that he is also Janus. This identification is critical for the relation between the life cycle of the year and any other cycle. In his argument to the *Calender*, E. K. notes that January is the "gate and entraunce of the yere," and that Janus is the god to whom the pagans "attributed the byrth and beginning of all creatures new comming into the world." More generally, in Porphyry's treatise on Homer's cave of the nymphs, it is said that all twin-gated enclosures symbolize nature.[262]

It is easy to visualize the Garden in Porphyry's terms:

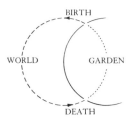

The presence of Time within this enclosure, and the Table of Cebes— where it is the *enclosed* space that is entered at birth—tend to enforce the symbolic reversibility of the garden-world into a world-garden. The world is also the seminary of all things that live and die; thus, insofar as the world offers care and support for "being," it is represented by the Garden. Paracelsus speaks to this point when he says that God "made heaven and earth and formed them into a matrix, in which man is conceived, born, and nourished as though in an outer mother, when he no longer rests in his own mother. Thus life in the world is like life in the matrix. . . ."[263] With only a slight extension of the symbolism, one may say that every youth that is lived in the shadow of a protective parent is lived within a Garden of Adonis. The garden is to be met with in a lying-in hospital, or a kindergarten, or a nursery, or even in a supermarket:

> And euery sort is in a sundry bed
> Set by it selfe, and ranckt in comely rew: . . .
>
> Daily they grow, and daily forth are sent
> Into the world, to it replenish more;
> Yet is the stocke not lessened, nor spent,
> But still remains in euerlasting store.
>
> (III.vi.35–36)

---

[262] *De Nymph. Antro*, 13.

[263] Trans. Norbert Guterman, in Jacobi, ed., *Paracelsus. Selected Writings*, p. 99. Text from *Von hinfallenden Siechtagen der Mutter (Hysterie)*, in Sudhoff and Matthiessen, eds., *Sämtliche Werke*, Pt. I, vol. 8, p. 327.

ERRATUM

The order of the diagrams presented on pages 530-531 should be as shown below:

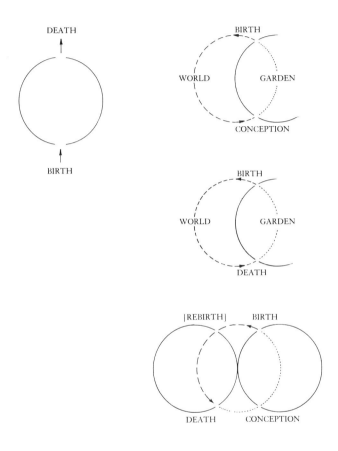

To read the Garden accurately, however, we must integrate this image with that of the salvage yard.

It is logical to suppose that one enters the Garden when one is "sown."

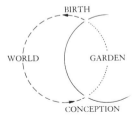

But this is not strictly correct. One's potential form may lie in the Garden for a thousand years before conception. In this respect the form is rather like a recessive gene. One's typal form passes through the hinder gate of the Garden when it ceases to "inform" its material substrate, and it is conserved there until the time of a new conception. Thus:

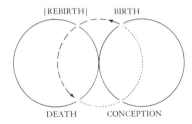

Since preexistence in the womb overlaps with postexistence in the tomb, we may represent the fuller scheme thus:

Three thresholds are established: the gates of death, conception, and parturition. One place remains in the cycle. Although a man cannot re-enter the womb except symbolically, he can do so seminally. The "rebirth" or "conception" that follows parturition and precedes death is the engendering of a second generation. The parent becomes a Garden of Adonis himself. The four phases of such a cycle are: (1) maturation within the womb; (2) maturation outside the womb; (3) parenthood and the nurture of children; (4) retirement back into the Garden. Spenser does not characterize this last-named aspect of the Garden at all, except in its double, the Chaos, but the *ascesis* of form doubtless has its poetry too—one thinks of the legend of the elephants' graveyard, or Ezekiel's valley of dry bones. The limbo of children shares its place with the limbo of fathers: Old Genius with his babes is a slightly dissociated *puer senex*, like the old man and babe shown on the threshold of the Old and New Year in the traditional iconography of the typical first of January cartoon.

A rough analogy exists between the four thresholds of life and the four thresholds of romance: "initiative" (the desire of the babes to enter the world); "exile" (parturition, separation from the "paradise" of the womb); "initiation" (the consciousness or fructification of sexuality); "impasse" (Time with his scythe, loss of form, or any impeded growth). The point is not to seek a full correspondence, but to develop an appreciation for the shared impetus of two seemingly different things: the cycle of physical growth and maturation, and the quest on behalf of chastity. This parallelism develops from the concept of a virgin bride, or the nexus of the cult of virginity with the cultivation of a virgin.

We must ask why there is an analogy between the cardinal points of the natural cycle, and the stations of the quest. The babes "invade" the state of life, though an iron wall circumvents the garden; Britomart "invades" Busirane's inner sanctum, though inhibited by an iron door (III.xi.22, vi.37). Amoret loses the iron chain binding her waist (an image suspiciously like that of the cestus falling loose from the False Florimell) on the very occasion when the preservation of her virginity is assured. Britomart also enters upon the private reserve of Marinell, and advances upon the enchanted cave of Merlin and the jealously guarded castle of Malbecco. Her attraction toward cloistered interiors—closet, cave, castle, inner room—is logical since she is a virgin, but it is somewhat paradoxical that Britomart is also the penetrating agent.

It is in Chrysogonee that we meet the essential paradox of a fruitful virgin, and also the consequence that rationalizes the paradox: the *propagation* of a virgin. The incarnation of Belphoebe and Amoret within the "louing side" of Chrysogonee prefigures the assumption of Amoret into the Garden of the nurturing and cherishing Venus—or perhaps the nursery has been read back into the pre-natal state. In a similar way, the immaculate conception of Mary was read back into the life of St. Anne, so that it could be reproduced in the engendering of Jesus. An analogous duplication appears in the description of the flourishing rose of Belphoebe's maiden-head, which Spenser treats as Belphoebe's *child*. He calls it "the daughter of her Morne" (III.v.51), that is, the offspring of her virginal girlhood. Belphoebe was herself born "of the wombe of Morning dew" (III.vi.3), and the rhetoric thus places her virginity in the second generation. To maintain itself generically—or allegorically—Virginity must assume into itself its own succeeding issue. This way of putting it might bring to mind the incest prototypes that figure so notably elsewhere in this legend, if only because mother and child, at the stage of the child's pre-natal nurture, really do constitute an incestuous union. Closer to the case of Amoret is the receptivity of the *Venus Genetrix* to the approaches of her son Amor, as described in the epigraph to the present essay. In his twelfth Paradox, Donne argues that the virtue of Virginity must consume itself to remain a virtue:

> The Paracelsians (curing like by like) say, That if the lives of living Creatures could be taken down, they would make us immortall. By this Rule, female *Virgins* by a discreet marriage should swallow down into their *Virginity* another *Virginity*, and devour such a life and spirit into their womb, that it might make them, as it were, immortall here on earth, besides their perfect immortality in heaven: And that *Vertue* which other-wise would putrifie and corrupt, shall then be compleat; and shall be recorded in Heaven, and enrolled here on Earth; and the name of *Virgin* shal be exchanged for a farre more honorable name, *A Wife*.

This symbolic invagination or invasion of Virginity by itself offers a clue for interpreting the original ending of Book III. At the center of the legend, Amoret has been brought into the Garden. At the end—if her union with Scudamour has the coital significance it seems to have—the Garden is brought into Amoret.

[ii]

The poem waxes philosophical at the thresholds of the "experimental or-der." An exposition of the philosophy in question may commence with the garden goddess Venus. Venus inspires "natures fruitfull progenyes" to gen-erate, and according to Ficino the Earthly Venus is "the power of genera-tion with which the World-Soul is endowed," or "the power of generation in us" that desires that beauty be propagated.[264] Elsewhere in Ficino's com-

---

[264] *De Amore*, II.vii; Jayne trans., pp. 142f. Cf. also VI.v (Jayne, p. 187): the second of three loves "is placed in the earthly Venus, in that power of generation which the World-Soul has." Many of these passages are also cited by Hankins, *Source and Meaning*, p. 237.

mentary the World-Soul is called the soul of "prime matter,"[265] and Venus is said to have a *mater* because she is "thought to be related to matter, since she is incorporated in the matter of the world."[266] Furthermore, Ficino says that the beauty seen by the Heavenly Venus (analogous to the "heauenly hous" of the planet in Spenser), is that which the Earthly Venus "tries to prepare in earthly matter"; this she does by means of "the fertility of the divine seeds."[267] The epithet indicates that these seeds are in some sense not natural. They may be understood as a productive capacity conferred on earthly matter rather than inherent in it. In the same treatise, each of the four realms of being is said to contain its characteristic capacity: Ideas in the divine Mind, "Reasons" in the Soul, Seeds in Nature, and Forms in matter.[268]

Pico, in his commentary on the poem of Bienvieni, explicitly cites Plotinus for the doctrine that the Ideas of Plato are infused from the Angelic Mind into the rational Soul, and from this infusion springs human love. Pico asserts that Plotinus, "by the same Argument whereby he proves Ideas not accidental but substantial in the Angelick Minde, evinceth likewise the specifical Reasons, the Ideas in the Soul, to be substantial, terming the Soul *Venus*, as having a specious splendid Love in respect of these specifical Reasons."[269] Ficino's Venus prepares beauty in earthly matter by means of

[265] *De Amore*, VI.iii (Jayne trans., p. 185).

[266] *De Amore*, II.vii (Jayne, p. 142).

[267] *De Amore*, VI.vii (Jayne, p. 192).

[268] *De Amore*, II.iii: "Huius modo radius omnes rerum species in quattuor illis effingit: species illas in mente, ideas; in anima, rationes; in natura, semina; in materia, formas appellare solemus. Idcirco quattuor in circulis quattuor splendores esse in primo, rationem in secundo; in tertio seminum, formarum in ultimo." (Jayne text, pp. 30f.) Cf. II.iv, Jayne trans., p. 139: "[Plato] posits three categories of divine Forms: Ideas, Concepts, and Seeds. . . . The third type revolves around the third, that is, the Seeds of things around the Soul, for they go through the Soul into Nature, that is, into the power of generation, and again join Nature to the Soul. In the same order forms descend from Nature into Matter. . . ." There are further references in II.v and V.iv. For the prototypal ideas in the divine mind as forms or species or *logoi* or reasons (as in "the reason of a horse"), see Augustine, *Eighty-three Different Questions*, art.46, 2 (in PL, XL, 30).

[269] *Commento*, II.xxii, in *Opera omnia* (Basel, 1586), p. 908; II.xviii, the trans. of Thomas Stanley, *A Platonick Discourse upon Love by Pico della Mirandola*, ed. Edmund G. Gardner (Boston, 1914), p. 41. The Italian reads: ". . . Che è la prima Venere, non sieno accidentale, ma sustantiale alla mente angelica. Uuo le etiamdio che queste ragioni specifiche che sono nellanima, come le idee nella mente, siena sustantali allanima, & per queste tale: hora dira Plotino che Venere celeste è quella prima anima rationale, & divina. Et per non dare occasione ad alcuna di errare, che per queste paroli si mouessi ad credare che la natura dellanima, in quanto natura di anima rationale, fussi Venere, soggiunge de sotto, che questa anima è chiamata Venere, inquanto in lei è certo splendide & specioso amore, disegnando per questo

divine seeds; Pico's Venus is enamored of the reasons of the species. In another passage of the same commentary Pico says that the opacity of the First Mind eclipses the luster of the ideas that God has placed there, and that this Mind desires the beauty the ideas have lost in their descent from God: "This desire is Love; begot when Porus, the affluence of Ideas, mixeth with Penia, the indigence of that inform nature we termed Jupiter, in whose Garden the Ideas are planted; with these the first Minde adorned, was by the ancients named Paradise. . . ."[270] This over-dense passage seems to mean that the Ideas are implanted in an otherwise barren or formless nature; whether or not this process is identical with the adorning of the first Mind is not clearly stated. Pico of course alludes to the begetting of Eros in Plato's *Symposium*, to which Plotinus attached an allegory of the production of the world. For Plotinus the garden of Zeus, where the drunken Porus impregnates Penia, represents the "Reason-Principles," derived from a higher intellectual principle, breaking into the garden of Zeus on the birthday of Aphrodite, or of the World-Soul. He says that the splendors contained in the World-Soul "are thought of as a garden of Zeus with reference to their existing within Life; and Porus sleeps in the garden in the sense of being heavy with its produce."[271]

These same "Reason-Principles" are apparently implied in a text that Spenser cannot have known, Julian's *Hymn to the Mother of the Gods*, a notable analogy for Spenser's philosophical myth. Julian expounds Attis, "who resembles the sun's rays,"[272] where Spenser expounds Adonis. The philosopher calls upon the myth to illustrate "how the cyclic substance can contain the incorporeal causes of the forms that are embodied in matter":

> For that, apart from these causes, it is not possible for generation to take place is, I think, clear and manifest. For why are there so many kinds of generated things? . . . Whence the distinguishing characteristics of things according to their species in well-defined types, if there are not pre-existing and pre-established concepts, and causes which existed beforehand to serve as a pattern?[273]

---

quelle specifiche rationi dellequali habbia me parlato, ad che ritornando dico che cosi come quello primo amore che è nella mente si chiama angelica & divino, cosi questaltro che è la principale parte della natura de lhuomo."

[270] *Commento*, II.xi, in *Op. om.*, p. 905; Stanley trans., II.x, p. 31. "Affluence" is a property of the Bower of Bliss (II.xii.42, II.v.28, etc.), it being a place "In which all pleasures plenteously abound" (II.xii.58); likewise, in the Garden of Adonis, "all plentie, and all pleasure flowes" (III.vi.41). For the garden of Zeus as Eden, see n. 258, above.

[271] *Enn.* III, V.ix.

[272] *Orat.* V, trans. Wilmer Cave Wright, in Loeb *Julian*, vol. 1, p. 463.

[273] *Ibid.*, 162D–163A (Wright trans., pp. 453, 455).

As in the mind forms exist not actually but potentially, so in the World-Soul the *logoi* are contained not potentially, but actually, as causes.[274] "Our souls must subsist in dependence on these and come forth together with them, and so receive from them the concepts of the forms. . . ." These forms are bestowed "on matter and on these material bodies of our world."[275] As Platonic forms, they are distinguished from the compound of form and matter, which is more specifically compared to the god Attis, "the cause which descends even unto matter." Attis is "the connecting link between forms embodied in matter beneath the region of the moon" and "the cause that is set over matter."[276] He is the beloved of the mother-goddess, who loves "not only the forms embodied in matter, but to a still greater degree the causes of those forms"; this goddess "preserves all that is subject to generation and decay," and loves "their creative and generative cause" which, contrary to her will "descended even to the lowest limits of matter."[277] Attis' love for a nymph and his death at the spring equinox both stand for the descent of the forms into matter.[278]

Closer to Spenser's own intellectual milieu is the poem that Nesca Robb quotes from a Florentine manuscript dated about 1490.[279] The poet describes a chaos where

> . . . every seed combined
> And every form that was or is to be,
> Shaped by the Creator, is enclosed,
> And the sun's rays bring them to maturity.[280]

In the same poem the poet visits the dwelling of Venus Urania, which is the birthplace of love, and is located in the garden of Ideas. The poet salutes the goddess as the power through which all things are brought into being and preserved,[281] and then expands upon the garden that contains all the forms known on the earth. Here the Ideas hide "immortal forms," which await birth "ascose nel suo lembo" (hidden in its border, or limbo).[282] It is these images that are the means whereby form adorns the rude

---

[274] *Ibid.*, 163C (pp. 455–457).

[275] *Ibid.*, 164B (p. 459).

[276] *Ibid.*, 165B (p. 461); 165D (p. 463).

[277] *Ibid.*, 166B–C (p. 465); 167B (p. 467).

[278] *Ibid.*; at 165D (p. 463), the nymph is the dampness of matter; at 168C (p. 471), Attis' concealment and descent into the cave are his inclination toward matter; at 171B (p. 479) the same is found.

[279] Nesca Robb, *Neoplatonism in the Renaissance* (reprint, New York, 1968), citing the *Poema Visione* of Giovanni Nesi, in Codici Riccardiani 2750.

[280] *Poema Visione*, cap. iii, p. 10ᵛ, as cited in Robb, *Neoplatonism*, p. 154.

[281] *Poema Visione*, cap. xxiii, pp. 75, 77ᵛ; as cited in Robb, *Neoplatonism*, p. 158: "Salve, . . . dea / Per cui e cio e et per cui vive / Ogni vita vivente in tua idea."

[282] *Poema Visione*, cap. xxvi, p. 86; in Robb, *Neoplatonism*, p. 158.

and barren first nurse ("inform matter," one can assume). What on the earth is nourished by the sun or moon "has its seed from the forms." All that is, is found here.[283]

Ficino's "seeds," Pico's "specifical Reasons," Plotinus' Reason-Principles, Julian's *logoi* that the World-Soul contains "not potentially, but actually, as causes," and the conservatories of seminal forms in the Florentine's poem —all share a common idea with the poet of the Garden of Adonis. Spenser scholars have identified the idea as the seminal reasons (*logoi spermatikoi* or *rationes seminales*) of later classical philosophy. My own researches were suggested by Nelson, and supplemented by Ellrodt, to whom credit for the essential discovery goes.[284]

The tradition behind the seeds is useful in that it tends to break down the barriers between the explanations of the Garden as a realm of pre-existent souls, or of Platonic forms, separate from matter, and a realm of natural seeds in which form and matter are already compounded.[285] The seminal principles, or reasons, are briefly suggested in Marcus Aurelius; the passage does not figure in the tradition, but provides us with a convenient definition of the essential concept: the existence of "germs of future existences, endowed with productive capacities of realization, change, and phenomenal succession."[286] Diogenes Laertius, in his history of the philosophers, explains the terminology of Zeno's school:

[283] *Ibid.*: "Cio che nutre quaggiu o sole o luna / Da le forme celeste han lor semente / Et che dal fonte ove ogni ben s'aduna. Cio che e si truova in quello; . . . Ogni alma ivi; ogni vita . . . Essere albergo, et fuor di lui niente." And: "Nel ampia vesta sua l'imago à sculpta / Dello exemplar divino: onde ella adorna / La nuda pria nutrice arida et inculta."

[284] Nelson, *Poetry of Edmund Spenser* (New York, 1962), pp. 210ff., esp. 211–218; Robert Ellrodt, *Neoplatonism in Spenser* (Geneva, 1960), pp. 77–84, 176–182. My own work was done before the remarkable sub-chapter of Hankins on the Garden, in *Source and Meaning*, pp. 234–293, but I have benefited from it retrospectively and in revision. Hankins' chapter is definitive so far as Spenser is concerned, and I adjudge it a unique achievement in Renaissance studies besides. I have retained my treatment—even though I duplicate much of Hankins' extensive citation of Ficino— not in defiance of what is a common enterprise, but to preserve the completeness of my arguments concerning the coherence of the allegories for the descent of Florimell with those for the Garden. I have noted some places where I corroborate Hankins, and also specific indebtednesses.

[285] Compare Hooker, *Laws of Eccl. Pol.*, I.iii.4, on the maintenance of form by natural things: "Form in other creatures is a thing proportionable unto soul in living creatures. Sensible it is not, nor otherwise discernible, than only by effects. According to the diversity of inward forms, things of the world are distinguished into their kinds."

[286] *To Himself* IX.1.

Now the term Nature is used by them to mean sometimes that which holds the world together, sometimes that which causes terrestrial things to spring up. Nature is defined as a force moving of itself, producing and preserving in being its offspring in accordance with seminal principles within definite periods, and effecting results homogeneous with their sources.[287]

In Plotinus the conception is more fully developed, and provides a kind of philosophic anticipation of the "gene pool." The begetting parent contains more than one rational form, and both parents furnish the totality of rational forms in the determining of a new form; moreover, "the number of these [seminal] reasons would be infinite if the world did not traverse identical series of existence in cycles of eternal recurrence."[288] These cycles are found in a poem that Spenser translates from DuBellay, in which the seeds of all things are mentioned,[289] and Spenser's babes return and abide in the Garden for a millennial interval before going into the world again: "So like a wheele around they runne from old to new" (III.vi.33). According to Plotinus, men generate due to the activity within them of the seminal reasons.[290] That speaks for the physical side of the notion; on the metaphysical side, the seed principles remain invisible, continuously producing the many out of the one. A good summary of Plotinus' theory as a whole is the following:

Considered in its totality Intelligence contains all entities, as the genus contains all species and as the whole contains all parts. The powers contained in seeds provide an illustration. Each seed, considered in its totality, is a center which contains all the parts of the organism in an undivided form. Nevertheless in this seed the seminal reason of the eye differs from that of the hands, and this diversity is manifested in the organs begotten through the seminal reasons. The powers that are contained in seeds thus constitute each a unified seminal form with the parts implied in it. What in the seed is corporeal, its humidity, for instance, contains matter; but the seminal reason is entirely form. It is identical with the generative kind of soul, a soul which herself is the image of a superior soul. This generative power contained in seeds is sometimes called Nature. Proceeding from the superior powers as light radiates from the fire, it alters and fashions matter by imparting to matter its seminal reasons. . . .[291]

[287] *Lives* VII.148; trans. R. D. Hicks in the Loeb edn., vol. 2, p. 253.
[288] *Enn.* V, VI.1f.; trans. Joseph Katz, in *The Philosophy of Plotinus.* Representative Books from the *Enneads* (New York, 1950), p. 134.
[289] *Rvines of Rome: by Bellay*, Son. 22.
[290] *Enn.* III, VIII.7.
[291] *Enn.* V, IX.6; trans. Katz, p. 134.

Further, "the simultaneous presence of the seminal reason of an animal and of matter fit to receive it, must necessarily result in the birth of a new animal." This last agrees with Spenser on the Chaos of substance:

> All things from thence doe their first being fetch,
> And borrow matter, whereof they are made,
> Which when as forme and feature it does ketch,
> Becomes a bodie, and doth then inuade
> The state of life, out of the griesly shade.
>
> (III.vi.37)

For us the critical point in the history of the doctrine is the assimilation of the seminal reasons to Christian theories about the creation recorded in Genesis. We owe this development chiefly to Saint Augustine, but Augustine was preceded by Greek Fathers on the Hexameral theme. Basil, for example, says that the Lord's command to the earth gave it its natural and permanent law, and its power to produce thereafter.[292] The Geneva Bible does not greatly differ: "it is the onely power of Gods worde that maketh ye earth fruteful, which else naturally is barren" (gloss on Gen. 1:11). We may compare Spenser:

> . . . for of their owne accord
> All things, as they created were doe grow,
> And yet remember well the mightie word,
> Which first was spoken by th'Almightie lord,
> That bad them to increase and multiply:
>
> (III.vi.34)

If all things grow in the order in which they were created, there is a hint that phylogeny repeats ontogeny. Basil says: "God did not command the

---

[292] Basil, *Hex.*, V.i, trans. in NPNF, 2nd Series, vol. 8, p. 76. For the thought, compare Hooker, *Laws of Eccl. Pol.*, I.iii.2: "His commanding those things to be which are . . . it seemeth that Moses had herein . . . a further purpose, namely, first, to teach that God did not work as a necessary, but a voluntary Agent, intending beforehand and decreeing with himself that which did outwardly proceed from him; Secondly, to shew that God did then institute a Law general to be observed by creatures, and therfore according to the manner of Lawes, the Institution therof is described as being established by solemne injunction. His commanding those things to be which are, and to be in such sort as they are, to keepe that tenure and course which they doe, importeth the establishment of Nature's Law." At I.iii.4, Hooker rejects the idea that Nature works through observing certain exemplary drafts or patterns, but says that, in observing the laws and keeping those forms which give them being, the works of nature are no less exact. Cf. also Augustine, *De Gen. ad Lit.*, II.8 (PL, XXXIV, 269): "the model, according to which the creature is fashioned, is in the Word of God before the creature is fashioned."

539

earth immediately to give forth seed and fruit, but to produce germs, to grow green, and to arrive at maturity in the seed; so that this command teaches nature what she has to do in the course of the ages."[293] Gregory of Nyssa, in his *Hexameron*, says that what is meant by "in the beginning" is that all the beginnings (or "principles"), causes, and powers of things were made by God. Heaven, ether, stars, fire, air, sea, earth, animals, and plants—existed from the first motion of his will, even though they appear consecutively, according to a certain necessary series. The world develops from the working of each thing's *logos* in it.[294] The earth was unseen and formless, everything having been advanced to procreating at the start by the power of God, just as if by means of a certain power of a seed projected into the procreation of the world.[295]

Augustine's own words contain much of the patristic tradition thereafter stemming from him. The whole tendency of his discussion illustrates an idea well expressed by Sir Thomas Browne: "The exiguity and smallnesse of some seed extending to large productions is one of the magnalities of nature, somewhat illustrating the work of the Creation, and vast production from nothing."[296] Again, phylogeny repeats ontogeny: such is the result of assimilating the seminal reasons to the theory of the creation. The world is created *ex nihilo*, for with God nothing is impossible; a seed breeds from "next to nothing," and seems similarly potent. The fifth book of Augustine's *Commentary on Genesis according to the Literal Sense* is devoted to explaining the verses near the opening of the second chapter of Genesis, which say that the Lord made the plants of the field *before* they arose in the earth.[297] Augustine explains that the sacred writer refers to the first creation, which took place on the first "day," because God created all things in his Word from the beginning, "in the day that the Lord God made the earth and heavens" (Gen. 2:4). Augustine invites the reader to consider the causality anterior to a seed, on the analogy of the seed's relation to a tree. The tree was not thrown up at a blow, but grew in the familiar order from a root that a seed fixed in the earth. Only later was the tree in all its parts formed and articulated:

> Now this seed comes from a grain: the grain contains all these parts originally, not in the state of corporal mass, but in potentiality and causality. For the magnitude [of the tree] is compounded of earth and water. But what is more wonderful and important in this small grain, is the

[293] *Hex.*, V.v, trans. cit., p. 78.
[294] *In Hexameron Liber*, PG, XLIV, 71B-C.
[295] *Ibid.*, 78D.
[296] *Garden of Cyrus*, III.
[297] *De Gen. ad Lit.*, V.i–xiii, esp. sect. 12 of this book. (Sections are numbered continuously through books.) My reading has been greatly aided by MM. Peronne, *et al.*, eds. and trans., *Oeuvres Completes de Saint Augustine* (Paris, 1873), vol. 7.

power through which the nearby moisture, mixed with the earth, has the power to change so much into the quality of that tree—into the division of the branches, into the greenness and figure of the leaves, into the form and corpulence of the fruit, and the order and distinction of all. For what arises from the tree, or hangs from it, which has not been extracted and grown from the treasure hidden in this seed? Now this seed comes from a tree, not from this tree, but from another tree which itself came from another seed.[298]

The seeds, or the trees, were preceded by the earth that produced them:

Now just as all that developed into the tree, with time, was comprised in the invisible seed, so it is believed that the world, when God created everything at the same time, at that time comprised in it all which was made in him and with him; not only the sky with the sun, moon, and stars, whose order is maintained in a cyclic course, and the earth and the deep which are subject rather to an inconsistent movement, and which, set lower, make a second part of the world; but *even those things which the water and the earth produced potentially and in their causes, before the course of time made them appear* as they are observed by us now in those works that God continues in even until now [italics mine].

Hence this: "This is the book of the creatures of heaven and earth; when the day was made, God made heaven and earth, and all the greenery of the field before it was on the earth, and all the grass of the field before it was risen" (Gen. 2:4): he did not make this happen in such a way as it continues [to happen] now, by means of rain and the cultivation of men; for to this it is added, "for there was no man who worked the earth" (Gen. 2:5): but in that way in which he created everything together, and finished the sixfold number of days, when he presented the day which he represented six times, on account of those things which he made, not temporally with alternations of spaces, but in causality according to an orderly knowledge. From which works he rested on the seventh day, even his rest on that same day acknowledged and hallowed for joy. And he blessed and sanctified this day, not for something in his works, but in his rest. Thereafter he created no further creatures, but what he had made he maintained, actively administering, governing, and moving, without cessation, resting and at the same time working, as was already treated. Concerning these works of his which are now continuing—explaining their unfolding through time—Scripture has: "Now a fountain ascended from earth and watered all the face of the earth" (Gen. 2:6).[299]

In the course of considering whether the phrase "male and female he created them" implies Eve's preexistence in the seminal reasons (since this

---

[298] *De Gen. ad Lit.*, V.xxiii.44. [299] *Ibid.*, V.xxiii.45.

creation occurs in the account of the sixth day, prior to God's "rest"), Augustine has occasion to explain:

> All the most usual course of nature has its precise natural law, by which the spirit of life (which is a creature) has its appetites determined, so that it cannot produce an evil will. And the elements of the world have their force and quality, what each can or cannot do, what can be done from what or not done. From these, as the primordial [principles] of things, all that is generated takes its going forth and process, in its proper time, and its ends and deceases according to kind. Thus it is that from a grain of wheat a bean is not born, or wheat from a bean, or a man from a beast, or a beast from a man. Beyond this natural movement and course of things the power of the Creator reserves to itself the power to make from all of these something other than what those seminal reasons, as it were, reserve, but not that which he did not place in them, so that he could make it from these or by himself. For he is omnipotent not by virtue of ignorant power, but by the virtue of wisdom. And on this account he makes from each thing, in time, what he put in it before, so that he was able to.[300]

Augustine's answer to the question about Eve, however, is no, more or less: Eve was not, as it were, hidden in the first creation, as the Levites were hidden in the loins of Abraham (Heb. 7:9-10); and yet it is possible to say that Abraham was in Adam, and Adam in the original creation. Nothing was made that was not first in the "causes" of things; God has, however, reserved to himself certain of these, which appear in such mysteries as the creation of Eve and the bringing of salvation out of sin. Nonetheless, such prodigies as Aaron's rod, Balaam's ass, and Sarah's conceiving imply the creation *in them* of these possibilities, as well as in God: "Horum et talius modoram rationes, non tantum in Deo sunt, sed ab illo etiam rebus creatis inditae atque concreatae."[301] On the basis of Augustine's usage, Saint Thomas Aquinas, in his article on the seminal reasons, distinguishes three categories: seminal virtues, causal virtues, and typal ideas originally in the Word. Miracles are the province of the two last-named potencies. On the causal virtues he also refers us to another Augustinian text, *De Trinitate*, III.ix: "As a mother is pregnant with unborn offspring, so is the world itself pregnant with the causes of unborn beings."[302]

Commentary on the creation story in Genesis notes that whereas God himself made the heavens and the earth, the light, and also man, he commanded the earth and the waters to produce the plants and animals. That

---

[300] *Ibid.*, IX.xvii.32; trans. in Vernon J. Bourke, ed., *The Essential Augustine* (New York, 1964), p. 103.

[301] *De Gen. ad Lit.*, IX.xvii.32.

[302] *Summa Theol.*, Pt. I, q.115, art.2, resp. ad obj.4.

is, the earth seems to concur in the production of that part of the creation that can, in turn, reproduce its kind. Here too, then, is evidence of a creation through second causes. Such causes, according to *De Trinitate*, account for the production of frogs and serpents by the Egyptian magicians.

> For those seeds that are visible now to our eyes from fruits and living things, are quite distinct from the hidden seeds of those former seeds; from which, at the bidding of the Creator, the water produced the first swimming creatures and fowl, and the earth the first buds after their kind, and the first living creatures after their kind. For neither at that time were those seeds so drawn forth into products of their several kinds, as that the power of production was exhausted in those products; but oftentimes, suitable combinations of circumstances are wanting, whereby they may be enabled to burst forth and complete their species. For, consider, the very least shoot is a seed; for, if fitly consigned to the earth, it produces a tree. But of this shoot there is yet a more subtle seed in some grain of the same species, and this is visible even to us. But of this grain also there is further still a seed, which, although we are unable to see with our eyes, yet we can conjecture its existence from our reason; because, except there were some such power in those elements, there would not so frequently be produced from the earth things which had not been sown there; nor yet so many animals, without any previous commixture of male and female, whether on the land, or in the water, which yet grow, and by commingling bring forth others, while themselves sprang up without any union of parents.[303]

The trees of paradise—apparently so numerous—were similarly produced out of this original endowment.

The question about Eve seemed to pose the problem of the potentiality of the creation in its sharpest form. Gregory explicitly says that Eve was in Adam as every plant of the field was made before it sprang up in the earth. Saint Bonaventura, on the contrary, asserts that the body of the woman was not in the man's side seminally, in the proper acceptation of that idea;[304] but, if we merely mean that a certain active potential exists in matter, we can say that the seminal reason was in Adam's side. One

[303] *De Trin.*, III.viii.13; trans. from NPNF, 1st Series, vol. 3, pp. 6of. Also cited by Bonaventura, *Sent. Lib. II*, Dist. XV, Pt. I, q.1, resp.

[304] Gregory, *Moralia*, XXXII.xii.16, Library of the Fathers trans., vol. 3, pp. 522f. Bonaventura, *Sent. Lib. II*, Dist. XVIII, Art. 1, q.2, resp. ("Utrum mulier formata fuerit de costa viri secundum rationem seminalem"). My text is *Opera Theologica Selecta*, ed. Fathers of the College of St. Bonaventura, vol. 2 (Quaracchi, Florence, 1938).

could add that the whole race was, as it were, produced out of the side of the sleeping Adam. The identification of Spenser's Garden with such a repository explains why it was here that the first Elf found the first Fay. An interpretation of this sort may be found in La Primaudaye's discussion of God's provision for the "defect of nature" through the "vertue of Generation":

> For as God hath created all things by his mightie word, so by the selfe same word hee hath created and placed in the first kinds of the creatures that he hath created, those seedes whereby he would haue every one preserved both in the whole and in his severall kindes, hee did there—withall endue it with vertue to doeso, as it hath alwaies done so hitherto, doeth so daily, and will doe so to the end of the world: . . . For hee created us all in *Adam* and *Eve*, and shut us up as it were in a store-house, or in a spring or fountaine, or as in one stocke of mankinde, out of which he produceth man continually.[305]

A little later La Primaudaye speaks of the reins as "the seede vessels serving for Generation, . . . and as it were the seminary of mankind."[306]

The name "Elf," we are told, means "quick," and the Garden may well claim to be the bed where "the fruitfull seades / Of all things liuing . . . Doe life conceiue, and quickned are by kynd" (III.vi.8), in the poet's words describing the preternatural Nile mud. Though any reservoir of potential new life is meant by the Garden, it particularly stands for the "genial bed" of the newly wed couple. Cupid was presumably nursed here —after a birth as sinless as Amoret's—not only because human love was fostered in the Garden of Eden, with Elf and Fay, but also because it is fostered in marriage generally. Conjugal love is the mother of all living.

Bonaventura, like Thomas, wants to distinguish causalities; the seminal reasons are neither ordinary seeds, nor exemplary forms:

> . . . cause and causal reason differ, because the cause refers to the productive principle, while the causal reason truly refers to the rule directing that principle in its operation. Similarly, through this mode the seed and the seminal reason differ. However, the uncreated rule of development [*agentis*] is the exemplary or ideal form, while the created rule of development is the natural form; and so the rational causes are ideal forms or exemplars, while the seminal reasons are natural forms.[307]

As they are forms, and the soul is also a form, the seminal reasons also appear in Bonaventura's discussion of the production of the sensible soul.

---

[305] *French Academie*, Pt. II, chap. 69 (edn. of London, 1594), pp. 386f.

[306] *Ibid.*, chap. 70, p. 390: "Therefore it is written in the Hebrewes, that *Leui was yet in the loins of his father Abraham*."

[307] *Sent. Lib. II*, Dist. XVIII, Art. 1, q.2, resp. (2nd para.); *Opera Theologica Selecta*, vol. 2, p. 449.

There are four ways in which the souls of brutes may have been produced: (1) from nothing; (2) from something, materially and seminally, i.e., from spiritual matter, which would be a preexistent seminary of forms; (3) from something materially; (4) seminally and not materially. Bonaventura writes on this last mode:

> And here is the fourth mode of speaking of how souls, which are purely *sensibiles*, are produced from something *seminaliter* but not materially. Seminally, I say, because forms are generables and corruptibles by nature: and here, just as other natural forms are not produced *ex nihilo*, but there is other power active in matter from which they become, as if from a *seminario*; so even it is understood in respect to sensible souls, which are forms only, in which mode they exist in brutish souls. . . .[308]

Bonaventura explains that "since the sensible soul is the form, it does not have a material part in itself, but only comes into being from the active potential of matter, which is excited by an agent":

> However, they [sensible souls] are either produced from that seminary and otherwise in the beginning, because now they are produced from a pre-existent seminary according to a sufficient actuality—in the beginning truly they were also produced from that seminary; or, if that seminary in some way pre-existed before the fifth day, on which the production of the animals was accomplished, on the fifth day it is at the point of the complete developed reason, in such a way that the soul is given the active virtue of nature, so that it can successively propagate and multiply into so much soul and so much body.[309]

Just as a humour becomes a seed through the generative potential, and afterward an organic body in the matrix, so the sensible soul, "which was in potentiality, is drawn forth into act through the virtue of a particular agent and the assistance of a celestial body"; ". . . it is itself that seminary in the earth," as certain seeds also become, that brings active potentiality into existence. Thus the informing sensible soul of the animal derives from a seminary of such forms, and this seminary, however it may have come into being *ex nihilo*, was the source of the production of the animals on the fifth day of creation. Bonaventura's other mode of production of forms, from a seminary of *matter*, we will discuss somewhat further on.

The earthly paradise of Dante, atop the mountain of Purgatory, possesses very much the powers ascribed to the original creation by Augustine and the tradition. Dante learns that an otherwise uninterrupted gale circles the earth and encounters the "dense wood" on the other side:

[308] *Sent. Lib. II*, Dist. XV, Art. 1, q.1, resp.; *edn. cit.*, p. 382.
[309] *Ibid.*; the following quotations are from the Ad obiecta, 4; *edn. cit.*, p. 384.

And the smitten plants have such power
    that they impregnate the breeze with their virtues,
    and the air, revolving, scatters them,
and the land elsewhere, according as it is suited
    in itself and in its climate, conceives
    and produces from different virtues different growths.
Having heard this, it should not appear
    a marvel to you when some plant
    without apparent seed takes root.
And you must know that the sacred land
    where you are is full of every seed
    and has fruit not plucked in your world.
The water you see does not come from a spring
    restored by vapour condensed by cold,
    like rivers which rise and fall,
but comes from a stable and certain source
    since it takes its will from the will of God
    what is poured forth in two streams.[310]

Dante's hypothesis implies the replenishment of the creation from a prior creation; it also accounts for the production of new species, and touches on the interaction of the virtue or seed with its earthly conditions.

Dante's "source" (Ital. *vena*, spring) of the two rivers may in part refer to the mysterious fructifying *fons* of the Vulgate for Genesis 2:6: "But a *fons* rose up from the earth, and watered the whole face of the earth." Augustine devoted considerable attention to this verse. He suggests that the *fons* could be the original source of the four rivers of paradise, which were later reduced by the fall. Since the source does not depend on the present water cycle, it is not conformable to the usual explanations of the rise and fall of rivers, though it does remind Augustine of the Nile, which waters rainless Egypt.[311] (Augustine has just a little earlier remarked that since Genesis 2:5f. implies that the seminal creation required no rain, one may say of it quite literally that it is God who giveth the increase—I Cor. 3:7.)[312] Finally, the sacred author "rightly began with this element [water], from which all species are born, either animal or herbs and trees, in order to accomplish the varied temporal numbers of their proper natures. For all the primordial seeds, whether they generate according to all flesh, or according to all fruits, are moist and are increased by moisture."[313]

---

[310] *Purg.* XXVIII.109–126; trans. H. R. Huse Rinehart edn. (New York, 1961), p. 300. Being, as it were, the sempiternal reasons of the flowers *here*, the flowers *there* are produced by "the high land" *without seed* (*Purg.* XXVIII.69).

[311] *De Gen. ad Lit.*, V.vii.19, 21, and V.x.25.

[312] *Ibid.*, V.vi.18.   [313] *Ibid.*, V.vii.20.

Hence Augustine associates the *fons* with the fecundating power and the providence of God, by means of which God originally brought the present creation out of the first one, and now maintains it.[314]

With this background, stanzas like the following from Spenser gain considerable depth, as the Logos modulates into the *logoi spermatikoi*:

> Ne needs there Gardiner to set, or sow,
>> To plant or prune: for of their owne accord
>> All things, as they created were, doe grow,
>> And yet remember well the mightie word,
>> Which first was spoken by th'Almightie lord,
>> That bad them to increase and multiply:
>> Ne doe they need with water of the ford,
>> Or of the clouds to moysten their roots dry;
> For in themselues eternall moisture they imply.

(III.vi.34)

The behest here is the one made to the earth and the oceans in Genesis. The unaided nature of the production may remind us of other accounts of the creation than the one found in the Bible, but, as Ellrodt pointed out, the specific dispensability of human cultivation, irrigation, and rain, would seem to reflect the exact verses Augustine adopted to exemplify the doctrine of the creation of nature in its causes. Spenser's "eternall moisture" suggests that metaphysical humidity or divine endowment we have met in Augustine; it stands for the inexhaustible maintenance implied in the original creation. A similar feature is found in the sixth-century Christian Latin poet Avitius, who describes the Garden of Eden in classical terms: the place is perpetually green; winter never comes there; autumn with its fruits and spring with its flowers fill its year, and the yearly cycle of planting and harvest is condensed to a month. "Nor does the nature of the place ask for rains, which it does not have; but the contented buds are endowed with their own dew."[315] The *Cursor Mundi* records the tradition

---

[314] *Ibid.*, V.xxiii.45.

[315] *Poematum de Mosaicae Historiae Gestis*, ll. 226f. Text in PL, LIX, 328–329A. Not so different is found in the *Romance of the Rose*, ll. 19949–19955, where Jean de Meung describes the paradisal Shepherd's Park; in the Robbins trans.:

> Nor are these flowers either immature
> Or overblown, but in the herbage glow
> In full perfection of their perfect age.
> They're never scorched by too-bright shining sun
> Or drowned by dewdrops bathing them at dawn,
> But e'er their roots the sweetest sap provide
> To keep them in their perfect loveliness.

that there was no rain on earth until the Flood; until then the earth bore spontaneously.[316] Presumably the latter idea derives from the fact that the Bible does not mention seedtime and harvest until the covenant with Noah, the first tiller of the soil (Gen. 8:22; 9:20). At the time of the rising of the mist, God had sent no rain, nor was there any man present to till the soil (Gen. 2:5). The same moisture may water the *conceptus of* Belphoebe, whose "berth was of the wombe of Morning dew," and who was bred "Till to her dew perfection she was ripened" (III.vi.3).

Spenser's next stanza describes the Garden as the source of the species. It is here, in the language of I Corinthians 15, that all living things are sown as physical bodies:

> Infinite shapes of creatures there are bred,
>   And vncouth formes, which none yet euer knew,
>   And euery sort is in a sundry bed
>   Set by it selfe, and ranckt in comely rew:
>   Some fit for reasonable soules t'indew,
>   Some made for beasts, some made for birds to weare,
>   And all the fruitfull spawne of fishes hew
>   In endlesse rancks along enraunged were,
> That seem'd the *Ocean* could not containe them there.
>
> (III.vi.35)

As in Augustine, this preexistent creation explains prodigies; as in Dante, it explains new species. It also accounts for the production of things "According to their kindes" (III.vi.30). Colet explains this "unvarying recurrence and reproduction" as an indication of a certain exhaustion of limit on the begetting power of the seminal reasons once they are drawn into actual kinds of plants and animals. A similar limit is described by Lucretius in a passage quoted below. The Genesis account itself seems to imply a double creation, the first imposing its limits on the second:[317]

> Then God said, Let the earth budde forthe the budde of the herbe, that sedeth sede, the fruteful tre, which beareth frute according to his kinde, which maie haue his sede in it self vpon the earth. & it was so.

[316] *Cursor Mundi*, ed. Morris, EETS, nos. 57, 59, 62, 66, 68, 90, 101 (London, 1874-1893), ll. 1988-1992: "the time was euer ilik grene . . . And thof no rain on erth fell."

[317] For exactly this idea, reading the Augustinian interpretation of Gen. 2:4 into Gen. 1:11, see Aquinas, *Summa Theol.*, Pt. I, q.69, art.2, resp.: "it may be said that the first constitution of species belongs to the work of the six days, but the reproduction among them of like from like, to the government of the universe. And Scripture indicates this in the words, *before it sprung up in the earth*, and *before it grew*, that is, before like was produced from like; just as now happens in the order of nature through seeds. Wherefore Scripture says pointedly (Gen. 1:11): *Let the earth bring forth the green herb, and such as may seed*, as indicating the production of perfect species, from which the seeds of others should arise."

And the earth broght forthe the budde of the herbe, that sedeth sede according to his kinde, also the tre that yeldeth frute, which hathe his sede in it selfe according to his kinde. . . .

(Gen. 1:11–12, Geneva Bible)

The shapes in the Garden are also ranked according to their kinds, and they recall the different kinds of flesh in I Corinthians 15:37–39:

And that which thou sowest, thou sowest not that body that shalbe, but bare corne, as it falleth, of wheat, or of some other.

But God giueth it a bodie at his pleasure, euen to eurie sede his owne bodie.

All flesh is not the same flesh, but there is one flesh of men, and another flesh of beastes, and another of fishes, and another of birdes.

(Geneva Bible)

Once again we meet the anteriority of the "seed" to the conferral on it of a material body: a soul or form prior to the compound of form and substance. Thus Spenser's "fruitful spawne of fishes," however literal it sounds, also casts a metaphysical shadow; the numerousness of the ocean kind suggests the fecundity of the *logoi spermatikoi* themselves.

In Spenser's own time, the "seminarie virtues," as Nashe calls them,[318] were well enough known. A concise and orthodox account is found in Timothy Bright's *Treatise of Melancholy* (1586):

You knowe, God first created all things subject to the course of times, and corruption of the earth, after that hee had distinguished the confused masse of thinges, into the heavens, and the foure elements. This earth he had endued with a fecunditye of infinite seeds of all things: which hee comaunded it, as a mother, to bring forth, and as it is most agreable to their nature, to entertaine with nourishment all the furniture of this inferioure worlde, of these creatures, some he fixed there still, and maintaineth the seedes, till the end of al thinges, and that determinate time, which he hath ordained, for the emptying of those seeds of creatures, which he first endued the earth withall. Other some, that is to say, the animals, hee drewe wholly from the earth at the beginning, and planted seede in them onely, and food from other creatures: as beasts, and man in respect of his bodie: the difference only this: that likely it is mans body was made of purer mould as a most precious tabernacle and temple, wherein the image of god should afterward be inshrined. . . .[319]

[318] Nashe, *Works*, ed. R. B. McKerrow (London, 1904–1910), vol. 1, p. 228.
[319] I quote from the selections from Bright's *Treatise* in James Winny, ed., *The Frame of Order: An Outline of Elizabethan Belief Taken from Treatises of the Late Sixteenth Century* (New York, 1957), p. 56.

As Spenser says, "Some [forms] fit for reasonable soules t'indew" (III.vi. 35).

The passage from Bright is perhaps the minimum necessary to establish the relevance of the tradition to Spenser, and it is Hexameral in its emphasis. We began, however, from the *Neo-Platonic* tradition, and Renaissance Neo-Platonism has things to say here of comparable relevance. The question of how the seminal reasons are imposed from the elements is one that Pico, in his *Heptaplus*, prefers to pass over,[320] but Colet, in his *Letters to Radulphus on the Mosaic Account of the Creation*, expounds them at some length. The connecting link is probably Ficino.

In Ficino's *Commento*, which is the text that first suggests to a student of Spenser that the seminal reasons belong to a "myth of love," we heard that there were three categories of divine forms, in addition to the shapes in ordinary matter: Ideas in the Mind, Concepts in the Soul, and Seeds in Nature. "The third type revolves around the third, that is the Seeds of things around the Soul, for they go through the Soul into Nature, that is, into the power of generation, and again join Nature to the Soul."[321] When Ficino comes to the seminal reasons in his commentary on Plotinus, he briefs the reader on what to expect:

Among these things about the seminal reason—that is, about universal nature—you will note four. First, indeed, this is the efficient principle of all generable things. Second, it is all of that, just insofar as the seed of all things is comprehensive. Third, single things which are generated through it are made *sigillatim* [impressed with a characterizing marking]: namely, in accordance with their efficient and exemplary virtue. Fourth, in it is prescribed the universal disposition and vicissitude of natural things in the interim: and so it will be expressed forth, according to how it is impressed within, in such a way that nothing remains beyond providence.[322]

The seminal reasons are contained in the World-Soul, which Ficino reports Plotinus to describe as "the natural seminary of the universe," "the living seminary of the world," and "the soul of the world flourishing omniformly from itself as a certain soul."[323]

A passage in Ficino's *De Triplici Vita* names the seminal reasons as instrumental in reforming the "individual species" when it has degenerated

[320] *Heptaplus*, V.v.
[321] See n. 268, above.
[322] *In Plotinum* (*Enn.* III, II, "In Librvm De Providentia. Comment.," xv), in Ficino, *Op. om.*, II-2, p. 1695.
[323] *In Plotinum* (*Enn.* III, III, "In Librvm secundvm de Providentia comment," i, "Quomodo machina mundi congruat cum natura . . ."), in *Op. om.*, II-2, p. 1701. Cf. Ficino *in Plat. Tim.*, cap. i: "Therefore the subject of this book is universal nature itself, that is, a certain seminary and unific virtue infused into the whole world." Cf. also Plotinus, *Enn. V*, IX.6: nature is the name given to the seminal power.

from its proper form. Here Ficino recurs to the dormant potencies of the reasons for the purposes of magic:

> . . . because the soul of the world possesses, through divine influence, the seminal reasons of things—as many ideas as are in the divine mind; by means of which reasons it fashions just as many species in matter. Wherefore each individual species properly answers to an idea through the appropriate seminal reason: and often it can easily accept through this middle something from that place. When, indeed, it is effected through this middle from there, and if on that account it degenerates from proper form, it can be formed afresh [*rursus*] by this middle nearest to itself, through which middle it is easily reformed. And certainly [this is so] if you correctly concentrate on the species of a thing, rather than the individuals of it—which are scattered—conforming to the image of the idea. In this way you draw this so opportunely prepared endowment [*munus*] uniquely into matter: clearly the seminal [endowment] of the soul.[324]

The *rursus* here is similar to the return of the babes in Spenser's Garden, "where first they grew: / So like a wheele around they runne from old to new" (III.vi.33).

Ficino attributes analogous productive powers to the imagination. But before the imagination creates anything, "the forms of things already exist in the world by way of a movement clearly there by virtue of the fruitful generated world, through the seminal reasons of course."

> On this account the prime forms of things are procreated in the world from the reasons of its nature infused in it: while the singular things generated from the beholding imagination, through singular movements, are, in a certain way, daily movements, and singular, by which the forms of things are stirred towards mutual change. By this perpetual alteration, in fact, matter is properly prepared far and wide for the daily receiving of new forms, in accordance with the reasons.[325]

The seeds of things in nature are much more numerous than the ideas in the mind, the former compensating for their comparative debility by their comparative numerousness: "For the same reason matter is spread through more, under the forms by an individual seed." Ficino describes the multiplicity of matter, and goes on to add: "And then whenever the species of mutable things perish, the number of single things is augmented by substances—now through succession, now at the same time—through divine

---

[324] *Libri de Vita III* ("De Vita Coelitus Comparanda"), i, in *Op. om.*, I-1, p. 531. Hankins has the same citation, *Source and Meaning*, p. 261.

[325] *In Plotinum* (*Enn.* III, III.xvii), in *Op. om.*, II-2, p. 1640. For this idea, which parallels Plotinus' doctrine that contemplation is a generation in a more than figurative sense, see *Enn.* III, VIII.4–7, and Chap. V, n. 4 and text, below.

influence—beyond the abiding multitude."[326] This providential maintenance of the stock in the world by a supplemental stock that is both within
the process of succession and beyond it is also found in Spenser. The Garden is never depleted, "But still remaines in euerlasting store, / As it at
the first created was" (III.vi.36). The Garden replenishes the world, yet
the "huge eternall Chaos" in the world supplies the substance on which
it draws for a new creation. In the passage quoted above on mutual change,
Ficino goes on to add that "alteration and generation are always companions in the universe—generation is really no less than alteration. Further,
change relates generation, after nature, to the imagination." It may be important then, that art plays "second natures part" (IV.x.21) at the Temple
of Venus. It does so again on Mount Acidale, the seminary of Spenser's
own art, and the nursery of Florimell, or beauty.

Ficino supplies one further idea for the interpretation of the Garden of
Adonis as a seminary of forms. Adonis, as we have seen, is the father of
forms, even as the sun is the author of generation. The two offices are
apparently comparable. Ficino says that the genital power flourishes in
matter due to the intellectual soul, which he calls the *ratio seminaria
mundi*, the seminary reason of the world:

> Likewise it is customarily said, the Sun generates natural things, because
> it creates by an abiding light. And there is the light of the sun and the
> light of the sun is effecting these things at the same time through heat.
> It truly matches the intellect and the male in both respects: for it generates
> as if separated from the generated thing. Truly, [it generates] the seminal
> nature of the world through the virtue of the male seminary. For it acts
> intrinsically on both. Indeed, [it acts] on the world by the fruit of genera-
> tion.[327]

One last passage from Ficino rings the changes on most of the themes of
the others. In discussing the repleteness of the *anima mundi* and its determination of the world, the solar analogy is again invoked:

> Either there is nothing in it [the world-soul], or apart from it, or made
> by accident: according to the reasons. For all things are referred to it—

[326] *In Plotinum* (*Enn.* III, II "De Providentia," xvii), in *Op. om.*, II-2, p. 1697.
Also quoted by Hankins, *Source and Meaning*, pp. 261f.

[327] *In Plotinum* (*Enn.* III, II.ii), in *Op. om.*, II-2, p. 1687. See also on *Enn.* III,
IV.xiv, p. 1742. The *Genius* might also be identified with the sun, on the basis of
Macrobius, *Saturnalia*, I.xix.17: the Egyptians say that there are four deities that
preside over a man's birth: the first is his Genius, by which the Egyptians understood the sun, "because the sun, the author of spirit, heat, and light, is the generator
and guardian of human life, and therefore, it is believed, is the daemon, that is the
god of those being born." For the Genius as part of the world-soul, specifically the
intellectual part, see Varro as cited by Augustine, *Civ. Dei*, VII.xxiii.

552

implanted [*insitas*] seeds, and also the higher exemplars. Whereby single things either originate successively, or are unyieldingly brought into an order. The sun of the world, the substance of natural life, completely possesses and bears that which the rest of the world has parts of. Therefore some have placed the soul of the world itself in it, on account of its rays being everywhere diffused: all virtues of natural things are first in the seminal reasons of common nature. These are presently translated into the sphere of the world, and into their shapes—shapes rather more changeable than stable. These are the species of natural things, in which thereafter lie the wonderful powers beyond the elements, and—from figures themselves of heaven—also lower powers.[328]

Spenser does not insist that Adonis is the sun. He merely shows us, as Ficino does here, that the "natural seminary of the universe" deserves comparison with what in *De Sole* is called "the efficacy of the Sun in generation; in determination of times of birth; and of all else."[329]

It is generally affirmed that Spenser takes the thousand-year cycle of generation from Virgil's Anchises, who explains to his son the purging of the souls in the afterlife—souls who are also the unborn. Preliminary to this teaching, Anchises describes the animation of the world by spirit and mind, from which life is derived:

> igneus est ollis vigor et caelestis origo
> seminibus, quantum non noxia corpora tardant

> Fiery is the vigor and celestial the origin
> of those seeds, insofar as harmful bodies do not detain them
>
> (*Aen.* VI.730–731)

Apparently Anchises refers to the souls or lives; however, the seeds might also be referred to the animating principles of the cosmos that Anchises has just been expounding. In *Batman upon Bartholomew*, we are told that the seeds in the Virgil passage are found in the *anima mundi* as ideas are found in the divine mind: they are the seminal reasons of things in the world.[330] The same place gives definitions of the Genius: there is the good Genius assigned to the direction of the reasonable soul, "continually work-

---

[328] *In Plotinum* (*Enn.* IV, IV.xxxv), in *Op. om.*, II-2, p. 1746.

[329] *De Sole*, rubric for Chap. v.

[330] *Batman vppon Bartholome, his booke De Proprietatibus Rerum* (London, 1582), XI.xi. The "secret sparks of his [Cupid's] infused fire," which inspire generation in *Hymn of Love*, l. 97, would otherwise be seeds like these. See *Aen.* VI.6, "seeds of flame in flinty veins," and the seeds of the four elements in *Eclogue* VI.32; cf. also Cicero, *De Finibus* V.vii, "seeds and sparks of virtue." I believe that the words "seed," in which the "reasons" of things are contained, and the phrase *vigor vitae*, in Ficino, *De Amore*, VI.vii, on the birth of love from a spark born of Poverty and Plenty, must reflect Virgil's passage.

ing in us by illumining, although we do not alwaies mark him" (cf. II.xii.47); and there is the demon of our begetting that descends from the starry circuit, "ye executor & keeper of life."

Something of a synthesis meets us in Colet's *Letters* on the creation. To the works of the days Colet assigns typical Neo-Platonic significances: the first stand for eternity; the second, for perpetuity; the third for the productiveness of the earth.[331] By "earth" Colet means something analogous to Pico's "indigence of . . . inform nature." Nonetheless, the earth, "the parent of vegetation," has a "native fecundity of its own," an "innate power, derived from its own seminal principles, of producing a numerous and varied offspring," such that it can bring forth without help from the sun.[332] This power derives from God:

> But among corporeal things, the nearer any are by nature to the fountainhead (such as the elements and the heaven), the fuller they naturally are of conceptive power, and the greater their productiveness. For these, which give birth to all the rest, have derived, together with their own origin, seminal principles from the Sower and Planter, God, even as the female does after impregnation. God, who is greatest and best, and the fulness of all things, contained all in Himself (that we may observe due order), before he had diffused them abroad. It was inevitable, therefore, that in the bosom and embrace of so great and so fruitful a Progenitor, the female, so to speak (namely Matter), should be let go from the Father of all, teeming with every kind of increase, and should bring with her the seeds of all things, called by philosophers *seminal principles*.[333]

We will want to know if Spenser also has this remarkably inseminated matter.

[iii]

No garden is complete without a compost heap, and Spenser's is no exception:

> For in the wide wombe of the world there lyes,
> In hatefull darkenesse and in deepe horrore,
> An huge eternall *Chaos* which supplyes
> The substances of natures fruitfull progenyes.
>
> (III.vi.36)

The horror of the scrap pile and the loss of being is here, and yet matter without form is merely the reverse of form without matter, and both are

---

[331] John Colet, *Letters to Radulphus on the Mosaic Account of the Creation together with other treatises*, ed. and trans. J. H. Lupton (London, 1876), pp. 16–20.
[332] *Ibid.*, p. 18. [333] *Ibid.*, p. 16.

a kind of limbo. Hence forms are clothed in matter, and matter "dons" sundry forms. Spenser can say that all the flowers with which Nature decks herself are originally "fetched" from the garden, and yet that all things "fetch" their first being from chaos; at the same time he draws a contrast between the ranked or speciated order of the garden and the formlessness of the first matter. At some point the unformed matter of the Chaos and the immaterial forms of the Garden must unite in order for the compound to be born:

> . . . when as forme and feature it does ketch,
> Becomes a bodie, and doth then inuade
> The state of life, out of the griesly shade
> (III.vi.37)

In terms of the tradition of the seminal reasons, such a "wombe" of unformed matter requires something akin to impregnation.

Thus the logic whereby a Garden of Forms must enjoy a liminal relation with a Chaos of Matter. Each functions as the other's allegorical "other," for in the actualizing of the potential of each, each must recruit, or "reap," the other. This reciprocity helps to account for the sense of desertion that haunts the Garden, even amidst its plenitude. For the plenishment of the Garden—its stocking—only partly answers to resourceful Nature's abhorrence of a vacuum. The womb itself is a type of this vacuum; in its barren state it is like Sheol, or the thirsty earth: it is insatiable, and never says, "Enough" (Prov. 30:15f.). The Garden, if it is a space devoid of matter, must also be a kind of vacuum.

In the *Rvines of Rome*, it is predicted that at the completion of the Platonic Great Year, the "seedes, of which all things at first were bred, / Shall in great Chaos womb again be hid" (XXII). Sir Thomas Browne places the seeds in the same repository, in the *Garden of Cyrus*, where he writes that "Legions of seminall Idaea's lye in their second Chaos and *Orcus* of Hippocrates; till putting on the habits of their forms, they show themselves on the stage of the world."[334] Browne's account is remarkably confused in some ways, since it seems to have forms putting on forms, and we may object, with Bonaventura concerning the production of the sensible soul, that if the seminal idea *is* the form, "it does not have a material part in itself, but only comes into being from the active potential

---

[334] *Garden of Cyrus*, IV. Browne may also be quoted from *Pseudodoxia Epidemica*, VI.vii: "God . . . hath with variety disposed the principles of all things; wisely contriving them in their proper seminaries, and where they best maintaine the intention of their species." (For this "intention," see Boethius, *De Cons. Phil.* III, prose xi, quoted in Chap. I, n. 199, above.) For a remarkable parody, depending on Samuel Garth's *Dispensary*, canto vi, see the seminal Chaos of literary conceptions in Pope's *Dunciad*, I.51–76, "Where nameless somethings in their causes sleep"—the fructifying heat of Pope's "warm Third-day" might be posited for the third day in Genesis 1 also.

of matter, which is excited by an agent."[335] And yet a seminary of matter, a "second Chaos," is not impossible if we imagine the seeds planted in matter as being matter's potential for form. Bonaventura once says that forms are in matter *seminaliter*, as are the seminal reasons, even though they are remote from complete actualization.[336] Colet, in the passage quoted above, also thinks of the prime matter as impregnated with the seminal reasons. Pico, in his *Commento*, explains that Orpheus placed Love, of all the gods, in the womb (or bosom) of Chaos, "because Chaos means nothing other than matter, full of all the forms, but confused and imperfect."[337] The Orcus of Hippocrates, to which Browne refers, may be the Hades of the following passage concerning the differentiation of phenomena from the flux of elemental fire and water. These two basic elements

> . . . separate off from themselves many forms of many kinds, both of seeds and of living creatures, which are like to one another neither in their appearance nor in their power. For as they never stay in the same condition, but are always changing to this or to that, from these elements too are separated off things which are necessarily unlike. So of all things nothing perishes, and nothing comes into being that did not exist before. Things change merely by mingling and being separated. But the current belief among men is that one thing increases and comes to light from Hades, while another thing diminishes and perishes from the light into Hades.[338]

In this men are mistaken: "For there is life in the things of the other world, as well as in those of this. If there be life, there cannot be death, unless all things die with it. For whither will death take place? Nor can what is not come into being. For whence will it come? . . . Whenever I speak of 'becoming' or 'perishing' I am merely using popular expressions; what I really mean is 'mingling' or 'separating.' The facts are these. 'Becoming' and 'perishing' are the same thing. . . ." Closer to Browne is a passage in Iamblichos, in which the Monad is discussed:

> . . . they also call it matter and universal receptacle, insomuch as not only is it capable of producing the dyad, which is matter in the proper sense, but in that it is the receptacle of all the seminal reasons [*logōn*], at

---

[335] *Sent. Lib. II*, Dist. XV, Art. 1, q.1, resp. ad obj. 4; p. 384, *edn. cit.*

[336] *Sent. Lib. II*, Dist. VII; Pars II, Art. 2, q.2, ad obj. 5; p. 196, *edn. cit.*

[337] *Commento*, II.xii: "Per qual cagione sia posito da Orpheo Amore nel seno di Chaos." (*Op. om.*, Basel, 1587, p. 905.) *Seno* may also mean bosom—this more figurative usage accords with Ficino's "gremium" ("lap") as cited in n. 353, below. Cf. Leone Hebraeo, *Dialoghi d'Amore*, Caramella edn., pp. 75, 109f., who says the first matter is also called chaos, the common mother of generation. For the seeds of things in the aboriginal chaos (Ovid, *Metam.* I.7–9) as "specious effigies lacking certain form," see Boccaccio, *G.D.G.*, I.ii.

[338] *Regimen* I.vi, trans. W.H.S. Jones, in Loeb *Hippocrates*, vol. 4, pp. 233, 235.

least if it is true that it is the purveyour and universal dispensatrice. Similarly they call it Chaos, meaning the first-born Chaos of Hesiod, out of which all the rest is come forth, as from the Monad.[339]

On the basis of this tradition, one may assert that Chaos contains the seminal reasons also.

Spenser has no extensive representation of this Chaos as such, and yet the imagery makes his sea an alternative reservoir of "the substances of natures fruitfull progenies" (III.vi.36). Robbins cites an interesting passage in Erigina's *De divisione naturae*, where the sea that God created in Genesis is said to symbolize the "mutability of matter endowed with quality and substance subject to generation and decay, while dry land signifies the substantial forms which suffer no change."[340] Spenser's Proteus invites a similar interpretation; and, therefore, the ripening of Amoret in the Garden of Adonis and the eduction of Florimell from the House of Proteus are two versions of the same process. In Genesis the sea, like the earth, was commanded to bear; Spenser notes that it bore not only fish but also fowl—an observation very much in the Hexameral tradition (IV.xii.1, Gen. 1:20, and Geneva gloss thereon). Spenser echoes his "Long worke it were to account the endlesse progenie" that buds and blossoms in the Garden, when he later says that it is an "endlesse worke" "To count the seas abundant progeny" (IV.xii.1):

> Therefore the antique wisards will inuented,
>   That *Venus* of the fomy sea was bred;
>   For that the seas by her are most augmented.
>
> (IV.xii.2)

The exposition of these waters is properly the business of our next essay, but the link between the Venus of the Garden and the Venus of the sea is worth establishing now, because it helps clarify one of the more vexed topics in Spenser criticism: the presence of Time in the Garden.

Lucretius, in a passage we have already mentioned, says that the earth, as a mother, eventually lost the power to bear:

> . . . she has ceased, like a woman overcome by old age. For time changes the nature of the whole world, and everything must pass from one stage to another, nor does anything remain like to itself; everything moves about; Nature alters everything and forces everything to change. . . .

[339] *Theological Principles of Arithmetic*, IV.17, as quoted in A.-J. Festugière, *La Révélation d'Hermés Trismégiste* (Paris, 1950–1954), vol. 4, p. 44.

[340] F. E. Robbins' paraphrase, in *The Hexaemeral Literature* (Chicago, 1912), p. 76, from PL, CXXII, 701D–703C (*De Div. Nat.*, III.27).

Thus then the passage of time alters the whole world and the earth enters upon one state after another, so that it is not able to produce what once it did, and can produce what it once could not.[341]

Spenser's Garden may resemble the Mother Earth of Lucretius (and not his Nature): in putting Time in the Garden, the poet endows it with the seed of its own destruction. The nurturing matrix from which life springs ought not to be the place where life is cut off. With the presence of Time, the genital field is seemingly aborted, or castrated. Time as the grim reaper may be included in the Garden either because certain potentialities fail to come into actuality, as does the untimely birth in Job 3:16 that does not see the light; or because certain things die prematurely, "before their time," as do the youths commemorated by the flowers.

Spenser may simply be reflecting on the rueful conditions that obtain *after* birth, advancing from topic to topic with no effort at consistency, or with a sense of *discordia concors*: Time and death are in the Garden as Hate and Love are conjoined by Concord at the Temple of Venus. This explanation is correct, as far as it goes, but it neglects the method of the mythographers of Spenser's own day, which was to capitalize upon such an anomaly.

The critical debate about Time in the Garden—i.e., rhetorical cogency versus a logical inconsistency—loses some of its point if the seminal reasons are also understood to be "seeds of time," the principles that pre-scribe "the universal disposition and vicissitude of natural things." The seminal reasons control a thing's time, its finite period: they *are* the pro-verbial seeds of its destruction. In the definition in *Batman upon Bartholo-mew*, "time is the dimension of changeable things,"[342] and if generation is also change, then Time at least belongs in the Garden with respect to the developmental or dynamic aspect of the forms. Time is a condition of Becoming. Plotinus tries to answer the question naturally posed by time for Platonic philosophy, namely, "how did time first come out?" He posits an expansive nature, restless in itself, that sought wider horizons: "and so, always moving on to what comes after and is not the same, but one thing after another, we made a long stretch of our journey and constructed

---

[341] *De Rerum Natura* V.826–836, trans. Russell M. Geer, Library of Liberal Arts (Indianapolis, 1965).

[342] *Batman vppon Bartholome*, IX.ii, which attributes the statement to Rabanus Maurus. In Rabanus' *De Universo*, I.i. (PL, CXI, 15–16), the immutability and abid-ingness of God, *sine tempore*, is contrasted with the mutability of the creatures. Cf. Isidore, *Sent.*, I.vi–vii (PL, LXXXIII, 547f.), which discusses the subjection of created beings (with the exception of the angels and unformed matter) to time and times. Times come into existence with created beings, and none may be properly ascribed to God. See also Augustine, *Conf.*, XIII.8, on the enumeration of times as evidencing the mutability of the things in which the created world consists.

time." This nature "did not want the whole to be present to it altogether; and as from a quiet seed the *logos*, unfolding itself, advances, as it thinks to largeness . . . in the same way Soul, . . . moved with a motion . . . and put itself into time . . . and then handed over that which came into being as a slave to time, by making the whole of it exist in time and encompassing all its ways with time." The motion made by the Nous is duplicated by the Soul; the result is

> . . . instead of sameness and self-identity and abiding, that which does not abide in the same but does one act after another; and, instead of that which is one without distance or separation, an image of unity, one by continuity; and, instead of a complete unbounded whole, a continuous unbounded succession and, instead of a whole all together, a whole which is and always will be going to come into being part by part.[343]

Time, Spenser says, is a relentless killjoy: he cannot be slowed by pity; and yet the gods are often "relented," or softened, "To see so faire things mard, and spoyled quight" (III.vi.39–40). Then the poet introduces Venus, lamenting over her "brood" and walking through the Garden, like God in Genesis 3:8 ("Afterwards they heard the voyce of the Lord God walking in the garden in the coole of the day"). A curious etymology, recorded in William Patten's *Calender of Scripture*, makes Eden the Syriac word for time.[344] Time's depredations are linked with Venus' solicitude for "faire things mard" *by a scythe*. It is this scythe that brings Venus into the Garden: if the logic of the topics is associative, the most logical association will be the birth of Venus.

Venus stands for the power of generation with which the World-Soul is endowed, and which is incorporated in the matter of the world. Therefore Time is in the Garden partly because of the Aristotelean link between generation and corruption. Unless a seed "die," it cannot bear fruit: "For all of us are sprung from what is perishable and mortal, and are born just as if by the procreation of Saturn, who in his generation puts forth all sorts of forms and colours, of which not a single one shows visibly in himself."[345] This passage, from Paracelsus, is less cryptic if "the procreation of Saturn" refers not to Saturn's children but to the "separation" of his or his father's seed, which, falling on the sea, generated the beautiful form of Venus. Paracelsus goes on to say that uncreated primal matter will also be found to contain this same mystery. The meaning of the "procreation

[343] *Enn.* III, VII.11, trans. A. H. Armstrong, in *Plotinus* (London, 1953), pp. 114–116.

[344] *The Calender of Scripture* (London, 1575), *sub* "Eden," fol. 61r, citing Archbishop Ximinez.

[345] *Philos. Add. to the Athenians*, I, Text V, trans. in A. E. Waite, ed. and trans., *Hermetic and Alchemical Writings of Paracelsus* (London, 1894), vol. 2, p. 251.

of Saturn" probably depends upon the tradition that makes Saturn with his sickle an image of time.

Leone Hebraeo expounds the mythographical dialectic of Venus and Time at considerable length:

> The testicles of Caelus represent the generative powers which flow from heaven into the lower world, and of these Venus is the appropriate instrument, as being that [planet] which peculiarly infuses generative appetite and power into animals. Saturn is said to have cut them with a scythe, because Saturn in Greek is called Cronus, that means "Time," which is the cause of generation in this lower world, since things existing in time must have a beginning and be generated; and moreover because time destroys the things subject to it, and whatsoever is corruptible must needs be generated. This time, symbolized by Saturn, conveyed generation by means of Venus from heaven to the lower world, which is called a "sea," because of the continual generation and decay. And this is the meaning of generation with a scythe: generation in the world originates in destruction. Again the proper nature of Saturn is to destroy, as that of Venus is to generate, since the one is the cause of birth, the other of death.[346]

Abraham Fraunce includes the same allegory in his exposition of Venus, where he also explains Adonis as the sun, and the boar as winter. Venus and Saturn stand for the cycle of propagation and destruction, and Saturn is "Tyme, with his scythe."[347] It thus appears that Time is found in the Garden not only because forms decay and perish, but also because of the contrary: "whatsoever is corruptible must needs be generated." What is latent in the Garden must be reaped *there*, if it is to be sown *here*.

Boccaccio, in his article, on the same sea-born Venus, gives a variant interpretation, which derives from Fulgentius. Venus was born from the blood of the testicles cut by Saturn from heaven,

> ... because, as one can assume from Macrobius, there were no times when there was chaos. For time is a certain measure which is collected from the circling of heaven, and it is thus born, as time, from the circling of heaven, and thereafter born from itself, of Flesh (*Caronos*), who is Cronus, whom we call Saturn; when the seeds of all things sown beyond heaven flow out from heaven, and the universal elements that cause the abundance of the world are founded from those seeds, in which the world is perfected in all its parts and members, then there comes an end to the cutting off

[346] *Dialoghi d'Amore*, ed. Santino Caramella (Bari, 1929), pp. 131f.; trans. as *The Philosophy of Love*, by F. Friedeberg-Seeley and Jean H. Barnes (London, 1937), p. 150.

[347] *Third part of the Countesse of Pembrokes Iuychurche* (London, 1592), fol. 45ʳ.

of the seeds from heaven, at a certain time. And on this account the genitals seem cut by Saturn, that is, by time, and thrown into the sea, so that he appears as the faculty of begetting and propagating which is assumed, through Venus, into the humour transferred by the coitus of the male and by the female means, which are understood by foam.[348]

If this is not an allegory for the seminal disposition in which the world was created, it is not far removed from it. Ficino's interpretation of the myth makes use of the same themes:

> The story told by Hesiod in the Theogony of how Saturn castrated Heaven and threw the testicles into the sea, out of the agitated foam of which Venus was born, we should perhaps understand as referring to the potential fecundity of all things which lies latent in the first principle. This the divine spirit drinks and first unfolds within himself; after which he pours it forth in the soul and matter, which is called the sea, because of the motion, time, and humour of generation.[349]

The Third Vatican Mythographer explains the myth more simply. Physically the myth asserts that unless the humour of heaven descend to the earth, nothing is intrinsically created, and Venus is the beauty of the earth. He adds that Venus may have been born from the virile blood and spume of the sea because venerean use is debilitating: whence it is feigned that Venus is born through loss.[350] Thus Spenser's Venus might be said to

---

[348] *G.D.G.*, III.xxiii; Romano edn., vol. 1, pp. 149f.; "cut by Saturn" could perhaps be "from Saturn." Fulgentius, *Mitologia*, II, "De Venere." For early notices of this allegory, see Macrobius, *Saturnalia*, I.viii.6, and Cicero, *De Nat. Deorum* II.xxv.64. Cf. also the Saturnian "sickle of fate" in Alanus, *De Planctu*, prose v, where it is said that Venus "permits the sickle of fate to run out far into the grain of the human race, and does not repair the loss with any renewed birth from any fresh seed"—i.e., she assents to her own demise. (The same text of Macrobius will help explain the scythe that is placed just under the line of circumcision in the phallic canopy over Priapus in the illustration for the *Hypnerotomachia*: Macrobius' authorities derive the name Saturn "from the Greek word *sathé*, which means male member. . . . As for the god's attribute of a sickle, it is held by some to indicate that time reaps, cuts off, and cuts short all things." Trans. Percival Vaughn Davies, New York, 1969, p. 65.) The allegory of Saturn's genitals thrown into the sea as the generative virtue reserved to time and infused in the humours of the earth is also found in the *Bible of the Poets*. For further on the deposition in the sea, see below, sec. iv, *ad fin.*, and "Perpetual Generations," sec. iii.

[349] *Comm. in Philebus*, in *Op. om.*, I–2, p. 637; cited and trans. in E. H. Gombrich, *Symbolic Images* (London, 1972), p. 72.

[350] Bode, *Scriptores rerum mythicarum latini tres*, III.i.7, p. 155. The mythographer is unsure whether Venus was generated from the genitals cut from Caelus, or from those of Saturn himself. Jeun de Meung, for whom the myth is very important, believes they were Saturn's (*Romance of the Rose*, ll. 5411f., 10989ff.).

"reape sweet pleasure of the wanton boy" in the way that the Time of the mythographers releases the potential fecundity of all things into matter. The lovely boy of Shakespeare's sonnets, who is unwilling to be reaped in this way, thereby defines himself as a recalcitrant Adonis; he is last seen holding "Time's fickle glass, his sickle hour," in a sonnet that ends prematurely, an ominous two lines short.

In the Garden there were so many kinds of fish, "That seem'd the *Ocean* could not containe them there" (III.vi.35). The same problem comes up with the ocean itself in Book IV, where the "fruitfull seede" of the "seas abundant progeny" seems past counting (IV.xii.1). Nonetheless, the poet matches nature in this feat of *copia* when he recounts the vast convocation of the rivers at the House of Proteus. The rivers are backed up "euen to the door" (IV.xii.3). A comparison with similar underwater vaults and nether waters in other texts shows that Spenser's river-congress also implies a "seminary" of rivers. Thus the descent of the waters to the Ocean, no less than the descent of forms from the Garden, suggests the maintenance of a perpetual succession. In their very nature, rivers are always proceeding toward their dissolution, while at the same time they are "dilating" their being, and even reverting to their site of origin—for "from the Ocean all rivers spring" (VI, proem, 7). Homeric tradition, however, makes more than rivers originate from Oceanus. The sea proves to be the Chaos of prime matter; implicit in its welter are the seeds of time or Venus, from which "the universal elements that cause the abundance of the world are founded."

[iv]

It remains to characterize Spenser's myth of love as a whole, in order to see the Garden of Adonis in terms of the larger cycle to which it belongs. In respect to this larger cycle, the Garden is significant primarily in that it is the nursery of Amoret, whose name makes her an infant Cupid or Eros. Being female, being a twin, and reciprocating the love of Scudamour, Amoret is an Anteros as well, and there are traditions that make Cupid hermaphroditic. As Cupid, Amoret is the protégée of Venus, and Venus finds her in the search for her lost son. Diana has scornfully advised Venus to "goe seeke your boy, / Where you him left, in *Mars* his bed" (III.vi.24). Instead—we remember that Venus has two beds—Venus retires with the newly discovered Amoret to that most excellent of "pleasant places," the Garden of Adonis, so called "by her lost louers name" (III. vi.29). Comparably, Venus names the child she finds Amoretta, "in her litle loues stead" (III.vi.28).[351] The twins are born "pure and vnspotted," as was Cupid; the passage is of paramount importance:

> For him the greatest of the Gods we deeme,
> Borne without Syre or couples, of one kynd,
> For *Venus* selfe doth soly couples seeme,
> Both male and female, through commixture joynd,
> So pure and spotlesse *Cupid* forth she brought,
> And in the gardens of *Adonis* nurst:
> Where growing, he his own perfection wrought,
> And shortly was of all the Gods the first.
>
> (*Colin Clout*, ll. 799–806)

This condensed version of Spenser's myth of love establishes two of its cardinal points: the virgin birth and the emergence of the god from obscurity to preeminence. In terms of the divine analogy for the *Hymn of Love*, the one would correspond to Advent; the other, to the proclamation of the gospel. Cupid releases his arrows into the world as the new divinity announces the coming of his kingdom.

There are two other points in the myth, which correspond to the Creation and the Passion. In the *Hymn* Cupid is "Begot of Plentie and Penurie," and then borne by Venus; but, as with the other infant god, one might distinguish his literal generation from a prior metaphorical one, for Cupid is also "elder than his own nativity" and co-eternal with the Creation (50–57). In fact, "the world ... was not, till he did it make," and he wings over its "great wide waste" like the Spirit that broods on the face of the deep in Genesis (58–75).[352] He awakens from the "lap" of the mother that Ficino associates with matter.[353] Thereafter his activities correspond to those assigned the demiurge in the *Timaeus*. The Timaeic terminology finds its way into Wisdom, where it is said that God created the world

---

[351] Spenser's line also engages Apulieus, *The Golden Ass* V.29, where Venus threatens to "bear another son, better than you [Cupid]," or to "adopt one of my little servants."

[352] For the early accommodation of the Orphic creation-myth to the Genesis account, cf. Lactantius, *Divine Institutes*, I.v (ANF. vol. 7, pp. 13f.).

[353] For the meaning of the "lap," see the remarkable identification of the "naked lap" of matter from Ficino (*In Plotinum, Enn.* VI, i.xxviii, *Op. om.*, II–2, p. 1773), in Hankins, *Source and Meaning*, pp. 257f. Ficino's *gremium* can also mean *bosom*, in which case the term connects with *Timaeus* 49a, where formless matter is the "receptacle, and in a manner the nurse of all becoming." Cf. the "nuda pria nutrice" in the *Poema Visione* cited above, n. 283. Cf. also the lap (*grembo*) of Thetis on which the "genital sack" of Uranus falls, and from which Venus is generated, in Politian, *Stanze per la Giostra*, I.99.

from unformed matter.[354] In giving Cupid this creative function, Spenser more nearly reflects the Orphic creation myth, where Cupid emerges from an egg in the womb of Darkness and proceeds to set nature in motion.[355] Lyly's version is synthetic, and even closer to Spenser: "it is feigned by the poets that love sat upon the chaos and created the world."[356]

The Ovidian flood story and the spontaneous Lucretian genesis are both recalled in the generation and delivery of Chrysogonee's twins. She conceives after a mollifying bath under the impregnating influence of the sun. Lactantius maintained that the earth could not bear spontaneously, without the sun; Colet read the Genesis account as implying the contrary, since the sun was created after the plants were brought forth.[357] Echoing Ovid, Spenser compares Chrysogonee's fruitfulness to that of the Nile mud, quickened by heat and moisture. Such a phrase as "fruitfull seades / Of all things liuing" (III.vi.8) slightly expands Ovid's "fecundaque semina rerum" (*Metam*. I.419). The impregnation of Chrysogonee in part reminds us of the story of Danae, whose tale is told in the tapestry at the House of Busirane, but with Chrysogonee it is the refinement of sexual contact—rather than its ubiquity—that is stressed. Images of incubation and embryonic life naturally follow.

Chrysogonee, then, is fructified as the earth is, by warmth and moisture; and, like the earth, she is endowed with seeds of future existences, which she brings forth according to both her chaste and fruitful kind. Belphoebe is virginal, like Mary ("Her berth was of the wombe of Morning dew," III.vi.3, echoing Ps. 110:3). Amoret is a "little love," like Cupid. Thus Diana and Venus meet in Chrysogonee, as they meet over her. Women cry out to Diana in childbirth, but Chrysogonee's name especially dedicates her to Venus, in her pure form, as the following Theocritean epigram, for a statue of Aphrodite, suggests:

> This is Cypris,—not she of the people; nay, venerate the goddess by her name—the Heavenly Aphrodite. The statue is the offering of chaste Chrysogone, even in the house of Amphicles, whose children and whose life were hers! And always year by year went well with them, who began

---

[354] Wisdom 11:18 (Vulgate); *Timaeus* 51a. For reflections on the potential formity and the horror-producing effect of the mutability of this formless matter, see Augustine, *Conf*., IV.6 and VII.8, and cf. *F.Q.* III.vi.36f. See also *Conf*. XII.12–29.

[355] Aristophanes, *Birds* 691–704, with Hesiod, *Theog.* 115–122. (Cf. also *Clem. Recog*., X.xvii.) So Ficino, *De Amore*, I.iii: "it is that still formless substance which we mean by Chaos. . . . Love accompanies the chaos, precedes the world, wakens the drowsy, lights the obscure, revives the dead, gives form to the formless, and finishes [perfects] the incomplete." (Jayne trans., pp. 128f.) For Love the perfector, see below, n. 528.

[356] *Loves Metamorphoses*, I.i.1.

[357] Lactantius, *Divine Institutes*, II.xii (ANF, vol. 7, pp. 6of.); Colet, *Letters to Radulphus*, trans. Lupton, p. 18.

each year with thy worship, Lady, for mortals who care for the Immortals
have themselves thereby the better fortune.[358]

Spenser's Chrysogonee is the daughter of Amphisa (rather than Amphicles); and the name Amphisa implies the "double nature" that emerges in Chrysogonee's offspring.

The symbolism for Cupid's passion must be supplied from human counterparts, for Cupid himself is usually unaffected—though Spenser tells us, at the House of Busirane, that Cupid has not spared to wound himself (III.xi.45), a theme we have already explored. The lover who sacrifices his heart in the temple of his goddess in the first Easter sonnet (*Amoretti*, XXII), and the sexually interpreted Adonis of Book III both express the passion in question. Frye has remarked that Venus and Cupid form an erotic Madonna, and Venus and Adonis an erotic Pietà.[359] Thus in Malecasta's tapestry the queen of heaven wraps her Love-lies-bleeding with the traditional starry mantle (III.i.36, 38). The motifs combine in the iconography of the *Hypnerotomachia*. Venus' effigy there sits within the mysteriously blooming arbor containing the grave of Adonis; she nurses Cupid, and the inscription reads, "Nay cruel child, it is not milk thou suckst from thy mother's breast, but many a tear that thou must render back again, that she may weep for dead Adonis."[360] Love is mysteriously nursed on sorrow, and the newborn god must learn to weep.

The story of Amoret entails a female imitation of the cycle of Cupid. Both are born "immaculately," both are raised in the Garden of Adonis, and both are objects of a search by a Venus figure.[361] The marriages of both are vexed, and involve a period of slander and exile. Finally, both

---

[358] Epig. XIII, trans. Lang. *Theocritus*, p. 164. (Hankins has made the same identification, *Source and Meaning*, p. 278, n. 2, and adds that Giraldus, *Hist. Deorum*, Syntagma XIII, records that the couple lived platonically, with Chrysogonee remaining a virgin.) Chrysogonee is a Venus in being the *Alma . . . geminorum mater Amorum*, "Gracious Mother of the Twin Loves" (Ovid, *Fasti* IV.1). Belphoebe is a twin Anteros of the anti-erotic kind.

[359] Frye, "Structure of Imagery," in *Fables of Identity*, p. 82. Cf. also "How true a twain," p. 92, and "Recognition in *The Winter's Tale*," pp. 117f.; and *Anatomy of Criticism*, p. 205. See further, Leo Steinberg, "The Metaphors of Love and Birth in Michelangelo's *Pietàs*," in *Studies in Erotic Art*, ed. Theodore Bowie and Cornelia V. Christenson (New York, 1970).

[360] Trans. by Mary Hottinger from Linda Fierz-David's Jungian paraphrase, *The Dream of Poliphilo* (New York, 1950), p. 168. For Cupid's nourishment on the lover's tears, see Petrarch, Son. 72 (*Canz.* XCIII).

[361] For the analogy between the discovery of Amoret in the "hue and cry after Cupid" and her rediscovery as a bound Cupid in the House of Busirane, cf. Moschus, *Idyl* I (=*Gr. Anth.* IX.440), ll. 24f.: "And if thou catch Love, *bind him*, and bring him, *and have no pity*, and if thou see him weeping, take heed lest he give thee the slip" (Lang trans., *Theocritus*, p. 188.)

return latterly, in the symbolism, in a climactic temple episode. Cupid, of course, is always in advance of his timid namesake. When Amoret was born, Cupid was already at large—we assume that the missing child of Venus is about his mother's business. While Amoret is maturing in the garden, Cupid is already old enough to be married and to have become a father. Amoret is next presented at the fairy court. We are told that many there are enamored of her, and thus this period must also be cognate with her service at the Temple of Venus. Cupid, meanwhile, is again abroad in the world, enjoying his preeminence. Then comes Amoret's marriage, from which she is more or less absent. Here Cupid is consolidating his triumph as a jealous god—his apotheosis—while Amoret is suffering the god's pathos and *sparagmos* as love's martyr.

Cupid's return at the end of the second half of this legend repeats the return of Adonis at the end of the first half. When matter loses its given form—forms being mutable and subject to decay—Adonis dies. Thus Spenser's sixth canto leads up to the "gloomy grove" of the dying god, which the elegiac flowers indicate to be a grave plot. At the same time, we are told that both seedtime and harvest meet here, and Venus "reaps" the boy in a special sense. Spenser describes their bower as a delectable *mons veneris* where Adonis is preserved like a seed in a furrow. His death thus becomes a seed's death, the prerequisite for new life.

Anatomically, Adonis in the Garden is not only the seed in the womb, but also the phallus. Wounded in the thigh, he is the phallus by synecdoche, similar to the way in which the essential Osiris is that god's missing organ. Further, it may be argued that the boar alternates with Adonis. Like Time, the boar out of the wood traditionally wreaks havoc in the planted place (Psalm 80:13); but, like Adonis, this particular boar is a kind of prisoner of Venus, paradoxically excluded from the garden, by being subsumed into the mount. Since it is the continuous divine copulation within this mount that keeps the garden from declining into the sterility of winter, there may be a sense in which the boar's frustrated phallic thrust is finally and consummately embedded in that thigh toward which his aggression is otherwise so dangerously directed. For the nonce, lust, like winter, has lost its sting.

Spenser's legend supports the idea that lust *is* wintry, in contrast to the temperate Garden, where the boar of winter has been properly bound. Shakespeare implies the same thing about jealousy, in *The Winter's Tale*; in the "spring" part of the play the dead Mamillius seems to reappear in the form of Florizell. Substances find new forms; Adonis is renewed. At the same time the mutability of Adonis can be assimilated to a theme of

566

metamorphosis. Metamorphosis may be described as the charity of the pagan gods.[362] One may even compare the transformation that Nature promises at the end of the Mutabilitie cantos: "all shall changed bee" (VII.vii.59). Conversely, the passage in I Corinthians 15, which this seems to echo, expounds the Christian metamorphosis myth: "we shall all be changed." The character of this change—the raising of the spiritual body and its glorification—may be deduced from Nature's first appearance, for she is introduced with an allusion to the Transfiguration.

In Spenser's elegy for Astrophel, who dies from a thigh wound, the beloved youth is transmuted into flower and star; simultaneously, he is translated into the Christian paradise. Adonis, buried in a garden, and carried through the successive transformations of his substance as if borne on the back of a kind of organic dynamism or *demi-ourgos*, eventually becomes the patron of these changes—and thus he qualifies for a poetic promotion that makes him the "Father of all formes," or a Demiurge himself (see *Timaeus* 28–29). The vegetated mortal who is sown as a body in Ovid's tale and Malecasta's tapestry will be raised in the Garden of Adonis as a life-giving spirit. It is, of course, only a generic immortality that Adonis enjoys, as all of the characters in allegory are somewhat generic. Nonetheless, the rebirth imagery of Book III aligns itself with the ressurrection imagery of Book I: Spenser has revived a pagan fertility god. The allegory of Adonis makes him stand for the survival and perpetuation of all created forms. This interpretation is not a fantastic rationalization of the story, but an imaginative reconstruction of what the story originally meant.

Spenser ends the description of the Garden by sketching in the rest of its population—though on the whole the Garden gives an impression of semi-desertion, for life there is automatic, unconscious, and embryonic. After Amoret grows to "perfect ripeness," Psyche's daughter Pleasure introduces her to the fairy court. The Garden thus represents a kind of chrysalis stage in her psychological development. The poet then turns from the Garden to Florimell, whose cycle seems to be moving away from the fairy court and its chevaliers toward the disorganized and mutable sea. And yet, in its turn, the sea becomes a natural complement for the Garden, as Spenser's symbolism evolves with the revolving year. In the fourth book

---

[362] So Frye, "The Structure of Imagery," in *Fables of Identity,* p. 82: "the theme of metamorphosis, which is the central symbol of love as the pagans conceived it." *A Midsummer Night's Dream* contains at least three such transformations (the ass beloved by the moon-goddess, the exchange of the changeling boy, the empurpled flower).

his sea contains the stuff of a new creation, and it has been endowed with a seminal disposition at least equal to the one placed in the loins of Abraham:

> O what an endlesse worke haue I in hand,
>   To count the seas abundant progeny
>   Whose fruitfull seede farre passeth those in land,
>   And also those which wonne in th'azure sky?
>   For much more eath to tell the stars on hy,
>   Albe they endlesse seeme in estimation,
>   Then to recount the Seas posterity.
>   So fertile be the floods in generation,
> So huge their numbers, and so numberlesse their nation.

(IV.xii.1)

Perpetual Generations

The eel, the siren of cold seas that leaves the Baltic to reach our seas, our estuaries, the rivers which, deep down, it follows upwards, under the opposing spate, from branch to branch, from tendril to tendril, thinned down, ever more inland, ever more into the heart of rock, slipping through little channels of slime, until one day the light glancing from chestnut-trees illuminates its Streak in the stagnant pools, in the hollows that go down from the steeps of the Appennines to the Romagna; the eel, torch, lash, arrow of Love upon earth, which our gullies and fiery, dried-up streams alone lead back to paradises of fertility; the green soul that looks for life in places where only heat and desolation gnaw, the spark which says everything begins when everything seems blackened, a buried stump, the brief rainbow, twin-sister to the one which you set in the middle of your eye, and let shine in the midst of the sons of men, sunk in your mud,—can you not believe her a sister?
(Eugenio Montale, "L'anguilla," trans. George M. Kay in *The Penguin Book of Italian Verse*)

. . . let us not longer omit our homage to Efficient Nature, *natura naturans*, the quick cause before which all forms flee as the driven snows; itself secret, its works driven before it in flocks and multitudes, (as the ancients represented nature by Proteus, a shepherd,) and in indescribable variety.
(Emerson, in "Nature," *Essays, Second Series*)

. . . we must posit a matter common to all the elements and underlying all these transformations of theirs . . . by philosophers called first matter;

or by the more ancient of them "chaos" . . . , because potentially and originally all things inhere therein in promiscuity and confusion; and thereof all things are made separately and successively. . . . [This matter] desires and loves the forms of all created things with a love like a woman's for a man. And as this love, appetite, and desire are not to be appeased by the actual presence of any one form, it is ever enamoured of another that is absent and, abandoning the one, seizes on the other; so that, as it cannot be actualized in all forms at once, it assumes them all successively one after the other. Its many parts do indeed embrace all forms simultaneously, but since each part desires to enjoy the love of all the forms, they must needs be transmuted into one another in continual succession. . . . no one form can fulfil this insatiable appetite. Thus first matter causes both the continual production of those forms which it lacks, and the continual destruction of those which it possesses. Hence some call it a harlot, because of the variety and inconstancy of its loves; for no sooner does it love one than it desires to leave it for another. Yet it is this adulterous love which beautifies the lower world with such and so wondrous variety of fair-formed things.

(Leone Hebraeo, *Dialoghi d'Amore*, Caramella edn., pp. 75f.; trans. Friedeberg-Seeley and Barnes)

[i]

The gardens of Adonis are a symbol both of the order of nature and of its powers of renewal. Stones, mud, oceans, and the atmosphere are relatively formless, and the way in which dead or inorganic matter originates life is, as it were, a birth-mystery in itself. There is something in nature that refuses to decline into an endless and chaotic winter night, and poets continue to identify its annual victory with love.[363] This power of renewal is involved in the mysterious parity that obtains between Amoret and Florimell.

The story of Florimell, like the year, has four turning-points. The first is the news of Marinell's demise (III.v.10), if that is what precipitates Florimell's flight from the fairy court. Florimell pauses at the witch's cottage, from which she intends to retrace her steps; but the witch's pursuing hyena-monster sets her in motion once again, and she arrives at the seashore, a second turning-point. This threshold is marked by the goring of her horse and the loss of her girdle. Horse and cottage are replaced by fishing-smack, sea-chariot, and the submarine cave to which Proteus consigns her. The third turning-point is the visit of the water-gods to the House of Proteus to celebrate the marriage of the Thames and Medway;

[363] Cf. Frye, *A Natural Perspective* (New York, 1965), pp. 112–114, 121.

on this occasion Florimell's lachrymose captivity is discovered by Marinell, for whom she professes her unrequited and inalienable love. Thus Florimell is present at a wedding at the end of Book IV, but, like Amoret, only as love's martyr. The analogy with the situation of Amoret at the end of Book III will be obvious. Marinell's mother proceeds to procure Florimell's release, on behalf of her smitten son, and the fourth point is reached with the marriage of the lovers in the following book.

The reader will recall the description of Cupid's being a step in advance of the cycle of Amoret. Florimell is similarly in and out of phase with Marinell, for fluctuations in the water cycle eventuate in fluctuations in the cycle of vegetation—April showers bring May flowers. Florimell flees the court after the fall of Marinell, if we follow the report of Canto v (III.v. 10); or she is in flight before, if we follow the sequence of Cantos ii and iv. The recurrence of Marinell's old wound at the marriage of the Thames and Medway again delays the lovers' union, and thus the contracted but deferred marriage duplicates the ambiguous synchronization of the two cycles with which the story begins.

The ironic cycle of the False Florimell also moves through four points, forming a kind of converse pattern for the other cycle. The points are: (1) her creation; (2) her climb from obscurity to eminence in fairyland; (3) her apotheosis as the beauty queen at Satyrane's tournament in honor of the real Florimell; (4) her dissolution at Marinell's wedding. Her congealment and dissolution are marked by contact with the true Florimell; her climb and apotheosis are delimited by her conjunction with Braggadocchio. Florimell moves out of society—from court to cottage to cave— and is eventually restored to it. The counterfeit moves into society to replace her, and then dissolves into the waters from which Florimell returns. Marinell's mother arranges his match to Florimell; the witch, failing to recapture the escaping Florimell, fashions an image of the beauty for *her* boy, who is equally infatuated. Florimell repulses the suit of the god Proteus, while the False Florimell honors the claim and accepts the service of the foot-soldier Braggadocchio.

The complex of the two Florimells, as we noted in our chapter on Book I, parallels the relation of Una and Duessa. The correspondence is extensive. Both Una and Florimell are equipped with a "palfrey" and a dwarf. Both are separated from their proper lover and sojourn in the wilderness before rejoining him. There Una is idolized by the satyrs, Florimell by the churl. (The comparison of the decorated goddess Flora to the paganized Una is suggestive here.) Like Una, Florimell enters a suspicious but apparently cozy retreat where the host makes an image of her for purposes of erotic delectation. Both women are threatened by lustful assaults and both are honored and defended by the chivalrous Sir Satyrane. In each case the good-natured knight is only approximately equal to the challenge that the evil represents. Both heroines find themselves in the hands of a Protean shape-changer who would be their knight. The chivalry of both Archimago and Proteus, however, proves unreliable.

There are also obvious similarities between the doubles. Like the false Una, the False Florimell is created out of liquid air by an evil magician, and she is animated by a spright. She passes from hand to hand, like the social climber she is, and at one point she seems to more or less replace Duessa—with the arrival of the False Florimell at the opening of Book IV Duessa simply drops out of view. Both counterfeits are coy mistresses, and for each a tournament is fought. Both are unprotesting vassals of the victor's might, in Spenser's phrase (IV.viii.32). Both raise doubts in the lover's mind about the desirability of "the thing it selfe," and in both cases the virtual image successfully supplants the virtuous one. Both are exposed and shamed in various contexts, and at the hero's marriage celebration a fit spokesman for the counterfeit—a liar—enters her rival claim for the honors enjoyed by the true bride. Both are brought to justice in the presence of the rightful claimant in Book V. Both are cosmetic duplications of the true image, hiding their guilty front with innocent snow, as Milton says of Nature in the *Nativity Ode* (1.39).[364] Both slander the true image merely by passing for it; this slander is felt particularly in the claims made by Archimago and Braggadocchio. Perhaps Shakespeare had Spenser's allegory in mind when he wrote:

> Truth may seem, but cannot be;
> Beauty brag, but 'tis not she,
> Truth and beauty buried be.
> (*The Phoenix and the Turtle*,
> 62–64)

The False Florimell is particularly like Duessa in respect of being a *fantastic* imitation. Her beauty is hallucinatory in a way that suggests how the schismatic perception has come into existence in the first place, for she is "fairer than her selfe, if ought algate / Might fairer be" (III.viii.9). As such, she is a parody of ideal beauty:

> Whose like on earth was neuer framed yit,
> That euen Nature selfe envide the same,
> And grudg'd to see the counterfet should shame
> The thing it selfe.
> (III.viii.5)

---

[364] Protestant commentary, influenced by Lactantius, *Divine Instit.*, I.20, sometimes referred to the Roman worship of the goddess Flora—reputedly a former prostitute—as a precedent for latter-day Roman devotional practice. Cf. E. K. on "March," l. 20, with Bale, *Votaryes*, Pt. II, preface, fol. iii^v. Note the comparison of the two Florimells at V.iii.24, where Florimell is "Like the true saint beside the image set."

We have already mentioned, with Roche, a model for Spenser's tale in the story of the idol of Helen that went to Troy in Helen's place.[365] When, in Euripides' *Helen*, Menelaus meets his real wife, the same dramatic point is made as in the recognition scene at Marinell's wedding festival. The Greeks in Euripides' tale have been keeping the cloud-image of Helen in a sea-cave; while the doubtful Menelaus is confronting the real Helen (who seems to him like a hallucination), it is reported that the supposedly secure object of the whole Trojan War has mysteriously disappeared, returning to the skies from which she came.[366] Comparably, the False Florimell seems to evaporate in the presence of the true Florimell.

Spenser has yet another Helen, Hellenore, whom her lovers the satyrs decorate as a May-lady, after her escape from a marriage to a December-like husband. In the eighteenth *Idyl* of Theocritus we can read about the marriage of a Helen who is likened to the spring and to the growth of the spring crops. The maidens in the poem decorate a tree sacred to her with vegetation. A Helen Dendritus, or Helen of the Tree, is known to Pausanias also—apparently she was the object of a Rhodian cult.[367] Both Euripides' play and Theocritus' idyl celebrate an admirable married Helen; thus Spenser's theme of a virtuous Helen has authoritative classical precedents.

Just as Stesichorus' Helen myth preserves Helen's essential chastity, Spenser's distinction between a true and false Florimell preserves Florimell's chastity. The doubling of Florimell—to look at the matter only slightly differently—makes Florimell herself temporarily *Die Frau Ohne Schatten*: the woman without a shadow in the Strauss opera.[368] As long as her proxy is on the scene, Florimell is not only singular for her purity, but for her isolation. This isolation does suggest in Florimell a loneliness that parallels the single life of Marinell, or that "unwillingness to marry"

---

[365] Roche, *Kindly Flame*, pp. 153–155, marshals classical and Renaissance references. See Chap. II, esp. "The Beginning of Idolatry," sec. iv, *ad fin.*, and nn. 69, 70–74, above. Alanus, *De Planctu*, prose ix, describes Helen among the drawings of Genius: "There Helen, half a goddess in her loveliness, the brilliancy of her beauty interposing for her, could be called beauty" (trans. Moffat, New York, 1908, p. 91). The basic idea here, that the *specious* Helen might divide from her actual person, is part of Spenser's allegory. So also is the offer of Horace, *Epod.* XVII.42, where the poet advances his willingness to lie, in order to re-establish the beloved's reputation for chastity, in return for something comparable to the relief afforded the blind Stesichorus for his palinode. I.e., the poet will purify her name, if permitted to corrupt her person.

[366] *Helena* 31–67, 546–624.

[367] *Perieg.* III.xv.3.

[368] The sought-for shadow confers fertility on a fairy princess otherwise made sterile by her marriage to a mortal: she gains a shadow as a reward for her selfless renunciation of an opportunity to rob a mortal wife of hers. Hoffmansthal, who wrote the libretto, followed with another on the two Helens, *Die ägyptische Helena*.

imported by his name.[369] The "shadow" figure is created at the time when Florimell herself is falling into the hands of the lustful fisherman and Proteus. Proteus presses his suit by means of various transformations while the shadow-Florimell entertains a bewildering succession of lovers. Thus there is a feeling that the fantasy-Florimell can do what the true one cannot. Proteus' changes before Florimell may be interpreted as a riot of promiscuous fantasies in the mind of a young woman on the threshold of marriageability. She has the devotion of many "louers," and only the monstrous waves that surround her prison keep them from abducting her by "force, or secret theft" (IV.xi.3). She is protected from chaos by her own inhibitions; even without "yron barres" or "brasen locke" she is scarcely less bound than Amoret. Her bondage comes to an end after Proteus has retired back into his more properly parental role as the sponsor-host at the marriage of the Thames and Medway. It is psychologically significant that the shadow figure is enabled to disappear only when the true husband and wife finally meet on their wedding-day. The False Florimell is also an evil Florimell. She is chaste because she is sterile, and she secures the devotions of her lovers because she encourages them in adulterous fantasies. She is exorcised when the pure Florimell assumes the contrary responsibilities of married love.

Like Helen and Angelica, Florimell is a celebrated beauty. The Renaissance never tired of saying that it is beauty that enamours and that the lover desires to enjoy. The comparison of Florimell's first appearance to a comet implies this, since a comet can represent the awakening of love, according to E. K.'s argument for "December." In short, Florimell is a prodigy of vernal loveliness, as is the Helen of Proclus, "all the beauty subsisting about generation."[370] Arthur hopes that the fairy queen will resemble her because he hopes that his lady will be beautiful. It is particularly sensible or natural beauty that Florimell comes to symbolize, and this beauty is elusive and fleeting. Nature, as Heraclitus says, loves to hide.[371]

There is a sense in which Florimell is also ideal beauty. The parallel

---

[369] I owe this interpretation of Marinell's name to Stephen Barney's unpublished essay on Books III–IV; once seen, it seems to me an inevitable interpretation of the name's significance. The wealthy bachelor encounters Britomart when she is seeking out a husband: i.e., the proper rejoinder to Marinell's name is, "It is a truth universally acknowledged that a single man in possession of a good fortune, must be in want of a wife."

[370] See above, Chap. II, n. 70.

[371] Frg. 211: *Physis kruptesthai philei.* Cf. Diana as a type of Nature in the Mutabilitie cantos, and Emerson on *natura naturata*: "There is nothing so wonderful in any particular landscape as the necessity of being beautiful under which every landscape lies. Nature cannot be surprised in undress. Beauty breaks in everywhere." (*Essays, Second Series,* "Nature.")

with Book I tells us that Florimell's beauty is true, while that of the False Florimell is a persuasive duplication. Beauty, as we noted in regard to Adonis, may be form, or specious, and this opens up a possible antithesis between an ideal form and a degraded "copy." The story of the two Helens lends itself to the sort of Neo-Platonic exegesis that the two Venuses attract. We have already noted the Simonian myth of Helen, where the earthly Helen is the degenerate embodiment of the Thought of the divine mind. As late as Part II of Goethe's *Faust* there is speculation on the problematic ideality of Helen's beauty.[372] Chiron answers Faust's question about the most beautiful of women:

> Female beauty is a nothing,
> Often a frigid image
> Only grace and vitality
> Make beauty attractive. . .[373]

Chiron then names Helen as an example of this living kind of beauty. The False Florimell, on the other hand, is more like the *starres Bild* or numb form, since she is made from snow.

The False Florimell's authentic descendant is found in the heavily made-up high fashion model, who is valued not so much as she is real, but as she is photogenic. It is possible to confuse such a model, in the flesh, with a store mannikin. Marinell, at his wedding, does such a double-take, even as he realizes just how beautiful his wife is. The False Florimell is also contrasted with Amoret: in the context of Book IV, the meaning is that while the model-Florimell has made herself attractive, she has not made herself endearing.

One notes that the False Florimell shares her aesthetics with the Bower of Bliss, with its emphasis on artifice and illusion. There is a more technical reference, as her specific composition is meant to indicate. Her damask and pale coloring, achieved by vermilion and wax, her hair of golden wire, her eyes like stars, and her flesh of snow—the sum of these charms makes her a "portrait" like the one described in Trissino's essay of that name. The artist proceeds like Petrarch:

> . . . who will first color the hair . . . making it of fine gold, and fairer than burnished gold; and he will make the face of warm snow, or rather of those white roses mixed with *vermiglie* in a vessel of gold; similarly, he will take the lips from the *vermiglie* rose, and the eyebrows from ebony; and the beautiful, sweet, smooth white and black of the eyes he

---

[372] The myth of the alternate Helen is of some importance in *Faust*, Pt. II: it is explicitly recognized at ll. 8872f. and 8879ff.

[373] *Faust*, Pt. II, ll. 7399–7402.

will liken to two brilliant stars, with that I know not what within, which in short "can make the night light, the day dark, / And the honey bitter [*mele amaro*], and sweeten wormwood."[374]

Unlike the speaker here, we do know "what within," but aside from the demon that animates them, the sum of these adornments makes the False Florimell a dead Petrarchanism. If the lady's virtue is specious, then Spenser's treatment implies that a good deal of the sentiment expressed in Petrarchan form is only superficially chaste.

[ii]

The stories of Hellenore and Florimell seem to follow up the suggestion of the Theocritian idyll that Helen is to be identified with an abducted and recovered vegetation-spirit. In reverting to her original place in the cycle we described, Florimell cannot "come of age" in quite the definitive way of a Britomart or Amoret. Neither her birth nor her introduction into faerie are described, but her wedding is. Her mystery is that she can only come of age *again*. Goethe speaks to precisely this point when he has Chiron explain the long sequence of lovers with which fable has provided Helen:

> *Chiron*: It's queer about women in mythology. A poet does what he likes with them. They never grow up, they're never old, they're always enticing, they're carried off in youth, courted in old age. Chronology means nothing to a poet.
>
> *Faust*: Then let chronology mean nothing to her [Helen]. Didn't Achilles find her on the island of Pherae, quite outside of time?[375]

Helen is timeless, but as her emergence into Goethe's poem suggests, she is also perennial. The latter quality is more properly the characterization of the Koré figure, to whom we may now turn.

That Florimell is a spirit of flowers is clear from her name. In Ovid's *Fasti* (V.183f.), Flora tells us that she has given seeds to countless peoples;

---

[374] *I Ritratti*, in Trissino, *Opera* (Verona, 1729), I, p. 272. The tissue of quotations is from *Canz*. CXCVI, CXXVII, CXXXI, CLVII, CCXV. Cited in Leonard Forster, *The Icy Fire. Five Studies in European Petrarchanism* (Cambridge, 1969), p. 125. With the False Florimell cf. esp. Laura's "gelata mente" (frozen mind) and "le rose vermiglie in fra le neve" of her lips (the vermilion roses in the snow), in *Canz*, CXXXI (Son. 101).

[375] *Faust*, Pt. II, ll. 7428–7436. Trans. Barker Farley (Toronto, 1971). "Pherae" should in fact be Leuce, following Pausanias, III.xix.11-13 (see Roche, *Kindly Flame*, p. 186).

she presides over a flower garden, and she enjoys perpetual spring. Further on she says: "Honey is my gift. 'Tis I who call the winged creatures, which yield honey [*mellem*], to the violet, and the clover, and the grey thyme" (271–272).[376] Florimell has a similar attraction for her pursuers.

Florimell's cycle also has analogies with that of Proserpina, another flower maiden.[377] The missing Florimell is sought in the same manner as the Angelica of Orlando (III.viii.28; cf. *O. F.* VIII.68); if he had had the car of the Eleusinian deity—Ceres—Orlando would have searched wood, field, pond, river, valley, mountain, plain, earth, sea, sky, and the depth of eternal oblivion (XII.1–3).[378] The places searched, combined with Angelica's unique invisibility, give Ariosto's somewhat spooky heroine some of the qualities of an elusive nature-spirit. Proserpina held Adonis in the underworld for six months each year, and she herself was confined there for the same period. Spenser's story entails both cycles by making Marinell, his Adonis, a figure for the annual refreshing of waters. The coordination of the two stories is perhaps signalized in the name of Florimell's dwarf, Doni.[379] If additional evidence is wanted for Florimell as a female Adonis, one may add that the binding of the boar sent after her is a feature of a poetic variant of the myth.[380]

While Florimell is undersea she is replaced on land by a "snowy" Florimell, and the Proteus of the eighth canto of Book III is also described as a winter persona. His beard is sprinkled with frost, and at his approach Florimell's "faint heart was with the frozen cold / Benumbed so inly" that she swoons:

[376] Trans. J. G. Frazer, Loeb edn., p. 281. For the idea that Florimell represents something like "honey of generation," we also need Porphyry, *On the Cave of the Nymphs*, 7: "But the sweetness of honey signifies, with theologists, the same thing as the pleasure arising from copulation." In the following section Porphyry reports that the ancients called Proserpina *honied*. See n. 385, below.

[377] An important study here is William Blisset, "Florimell and Marinell," *Studies in English Literature 1500–1900* (Rice University Press), 5 (1965), pp. 87–104. For the link between Florimell and the Florence of *Arthur of Little Britain*—who substitutes a persuasive image of herself in a pavilion, for viewing by the knights at a tournament, and who is impersonated by her look-alike queen Proserpina (who in turn disappears at her wedding ceremonies, thereby permitting Arthur's rescue of the true Florence)—see Hankins, *Source and Meaning*, pp. 165f.

[378] See Milton, Letter to Diodati, 1637 (in Columbia edn. of *Works*, vol. 12, p. 26): "Ceres never sought her daughter Proserpina . . . with greater ardor than I do this idea of Beauty."

[379] So Blisset, "Florimell and Marinell," p. 103.

[380] For the poem, "The Dead Adonis," see J. M. Edmonds, ed. and trans., *The Greek Bucolic Poets*, Loeb Classical Library, pp. 480–483. The poem was first printed in the 1495 Aldine edn. of these poets, and is translated as "The Thirty-first Idyllion of Theocritus," in A. H. Bullen, ed., *Some Longer Elizabethan Poems* (Westminster, 1903), pp. 145f. In the poem the bound and repentant boar confesses he only charged Adonis through mad desire to kiss his thigh.

> Her vp betwixt his rugged hands he reard,
>   And with his frory lips full softly kist,
>   While the cold ysickles from his rough beard. . . .
>   (III.viii.35)

The fisherman who precedes Proteus also belongs to this seasonal metaphor. His "frozen spright," "congealed flesh," and "dry withered stocke"
are quickened by the sight of what is now described as Florimell's "snowy
skin" (III.vii.23–25).

Why the rape of Proserpina should be given a nautical-piscatorial treatment will be touched on below. The abductor's chariot is still present in
Spenser's version; the abduction itself involved a flight across seas, according to the relevant Orphic *Hymn* and the Orphic *Argonautica*.[381] The
latter is quoted to this effect in Comes, and the passage has Proserpina
carried over the *sterile* waves to a cave.[382] The loss of Florimell's girdle at
the seashore may reflect a detail of Ovid's version of the story: Ceres discovers her abducted daughter's *zona* floating on the waters of Cyane
(*Metam.* V.470).

Florimell's long flight is not part of the Proserpina tale, but Ovid's narration of this tale is intermingled with his account of Alpheus and Arethusa; this parallel is suggestive, when we consider the eventual union of
Florimell with Marinell. Arethusa tells Ceres how she fled through plains,
mountains, rocks and cliffs, "and where there was no way at all":

> The sun was at my back. I saw my pursuer's long shadow stretching
> out ahead of me—unless it was my fear that saw it—but surely I heard
> the terrifying sound of feet, and his deep-panting breath fanned my hair.
> Then, forspent with the toil of flight, I cried aloud: "O help me or I
> am caught, help thy armour-bearer, goddess of the nets [Dictynna]. . . ."[383]

Florimell, fleeing her pursuers like a frightened deer,

>   . . . flyes away of her owne feet affeard,
>   And euery leafe, that shaketh with the least

---

[381] Orphic Hymn XVIII; *Orphic Argonautica*, ll. 1189–1194. Cf. Julius Firmicus
Maternus' account of the rape, in *De Errore Profanarum Relig.*, vii (PL, XII, 999f.):
"He put in line the team of four which drew the vehicle through the middle of the
lake. He was plunged into a profound depth . . ."; and Ovid, *Metam.* V.405f.: "and
through deep lakes he galloped, through the stagnations of the Palici. . . ."

[382] *Mythol.*, III.xvi, pp. 244f., *edn. cit.* (Less definitely, Giraldus, *Hist. Deorum*,
Synt. VI, in *Op. om.*, I, col. 205D: Proserpina was rapt, according to Orpheus, "from
a place near the Ocean.")

[383] *Metam.* V.614–619, trans. by F. J. Miller in Loeb edn. In Florimell's case, such
a wind might well be Zephyrus, Flora's pursuer in *Fasti* V.202f.

Murmure of winde her terror hath encreast;

. . . .

Each shade she saw, and each noyse she did heare,
Did seeme to be the same, which she escapt whyleare.

(III.vii.1)

Diana changes Arethusa into the waters with which her shape-changing
lover mingles, even as the girl plunges underground and undersea; so
Florimell escapes the land, and falls into the hands of the fisherman with
his nets. Then, in the care of her would-be lover Proteus, she too sinks
beneath the sea.

The whole cycle may be put together as follows. Florimell's departure
from court signalizes either the onset of the year's decline and the plants
going to seed or the shedding of spring blossoms. (The latter accords well
with Florimell's surpassing loveliness.) If her flight is precipitated by
Marinell's demise, it may be caused by a change in the water cycle, though
Spenser may also symbolize something like the "death" of rivers in the
sea. (Marinell's despairing mother incontinently "threw her selfe downe
on the Continent" [III.iv.30].) The loss of Florimell's girdle may represent
the defoliation that marks the coming of winter. We do not see Marinell
again until he visits the House of Proteus, on the occasion of the marriage
of the Thames and Medway. Being partly mortal, Marinell does not enter
the sea-god's actual hall; he remains on one of those thresholds described
in our first essay. We are told that the guests, among whom rivers are
the most prominent, are backed up to the door (IV.xii.4). The imagery
implies spring floods, and the bride herself appears like "a new spring"
(IV.xi.46), attended by fifty-two Nereids. With the sighting of Florimell
by Marinell, the contact of fresh water and the flower-spirit is renewed.
Marinell falls in love with the captive, and he appears to relapse temporarily into his former decayed state. His mother, "Leauing watery gods,"
hies to Apollo, the healing sun. Apollo informs her that her son's latest
affliction is love, "that leads each liuing kind" (IV.xii.25). The sun raises
water to the skies. Marinell being assured of Florimell's hand in marriage
—Cymodoce demands that Neptune "repleuie" the girl (IV.xii.31)—his
spirits revive:

As withered weed through cruel winters tine,
That feeles the warmth of sunny beames reflection,
Liftes vp his head, that did before decline
And gins to spread his leafe before the faire sunshine.

(IV.xii.34)

The union of the lovers is officialized in the legend of justice, when
Marinell has fully regained his strength, and when rivers have stabilized

their levels after a thaw. Artegall is presumably the justice of the peace. Spenser marks both the legal occasion and the natural one with the dissolution of the snowy Florimell; an evanescent rainbow passes through the imagery (V.iii.25). Like the author of the story of Noah, the poet suggests that the order of nature also participates in contractual relations:

> Then God said, This is the token of the couenant which I make betwene me and you, & betwene euerie liuing thing, that is with you vnto perpetual generacions. I have set my bowe in the cloude, and it shalbe for a signe of the couenant betwene me and the earth.
>
> (Gen. 9:12f., Geneva Bible)

It is significant for our theme that Noah removes the covering from the ark and beholds the decline of the waters from the dry parts of the earth on the first day of the first month of spring—New Year's Day.[384]

[iii]

> That from which generation arises is matter; that to which it proceeds is form.
>
> (Aquinas, *Principles of Nature*, ii.15)

In coordinating the imagery of Book III, we had occasion to suggest that the flight of Florimell bore some relation to the egress from the Garden of Adonis. To the Neo-Platonic exegete, both might symbolize the descent of the soul and its attachment to the "wheel of birth," but there is no substantial evidence for such an allegory in anything we have so far reported. Florimell does end up in a submarine cave, and caves and grottoes for Plotinus represent the sensible or material world into which the soul falls when it loses its "wings." And of course there is the general resemblance of the stories of Florimell and Amoret to the Psyche myth. Psyche was "reuyld" by her future mother-in-law, Venus (III.vi.50), and Cupid was exiled from her presence; perhaps a similar mother-in-law motif underlies the otherwise unexplained lines in the description of Florimell's escape to the sea:

> Yet there that cruell Queene auengeresse,
> Not satisfide so farre her to estraunge
> From courtly blisse and wonted happinesse,
> Did heape on her new waues of weary wretchednesse.
>
> (III.viii.20)

---

[384] Gen. 8:13, Geneva Bible, with gloss. For Abib as the first month, cf. E. K. in the argument to the *Calender* with Exod. 12:2, etc. For God's covenant with the diurnal cycle, see Jer. 31:35 and 33:20; for the covenant with God as a marriage contract, see Hos. 1:9 with 2:18–25.

An allegory of the soul's experience would also suit the Proserpina story, though perhaps only a Neo-Platonist could have been counted on to explain it this way.[385] The flight of the soul from the one into the many makes the realm of Proteus an apt destination. Proclus says that Proserpina "contains in herself the fountains of virtue and soul, which the maker of all things imparts to the world," and that the mediating aspect of the triform goddess "leads all things into an origin": "For it is proper to the grown soul that it generate itself and lead into an origin." Proclus also says that the rape of Proserpina is perfectly arranged: ". . . she also imparts to the extremes [of the virginal and the unmixed] the procreation of living creatures, which takes its origin from herself." This middle aspect of the goddess is adapted to "contact with generated things," and it "rejoices in progressions and multiplications."[386]

More conventionally, the Orphic *Hymn* makes Proserpina the bringer of springtime; in the spring, her form is seen in the green, fruit-bearing growth of the field.[387] The typical allegories of Proserpina derive from this function. Eusebius reports that Porphyry's interpretation expounded the passage of Pluto under the earth as equivalent to the sun drawing into the earth a certain power from the seeds cast there, at the time of the winter solstice: for "Koré is the seminal power."[388] Comes says that Pluto stands for the virtue of the earth because all things arise from the earth and sink back into it: "Therefore the power of the earth draws to itself below the roots of the fruits of the earth, wherefore it is said that Pluto abducts Proserpina under the earth."[389] Proclus was more metaphysical, but perhaps not so different. Bacon, in his *Wisdom of the Ancients*, refers Proserpina confined in Pluto's realm to the spirits trapped in matter.[390] There is no exact parallel for the Spenserian result of compounding Proserpina with Proteus, namely, the drawing of a "seminal power" into a generable nature. Marinell finds Florimell after the pouring of all the rivers into the House of Proteus. An earlier passage might be adduced as commentary:

[385] Besides Proclus, cited below, there is Sallustius, *De dis et mundo*, iv, in Gale, *Opuscula Mythologica*, p. 251: "Certainly the rape of Kore is said to have taken place near the other equinox [than the one associated with Attis], and this signifies the descent of souls." Spenser could not have known this text, but he could have read in Porphyry's *Cave of the Nymphs* that the corporalization of the soul is analogous to being initiated into the mysteries of the terrene Goddess Ceres, and that souls proceeding into generation are called bees, as Proserpina was called honied (sec. 5 and 8).

[386] *On the Theology of Plato*, VI.xi, in *Procli Svccessoris Platonci in Platonis Theologiam Libri Sex*, trans. Aemilius Portus (Hamburg, 1618), p. 374.

[387] Orphic Hymn XXIX.

[388] *Praep. Evang.*, III.xi, p. 109c, trans. Gifford, vol. 3, pt. 1, p. 120.

[389] *Mythol.*, II.ix, *edn. cit.*, p. 176. There is much the same at III.xvi, "De Proserpina," pp. 248f.

[390] "Proserpina or spirit"; see also *Sylva Sylvarum*, IV.219.

> . . . reason teacheth that the fruitfull seades
> Of all things liuing, through impression
> Of the sunbeames in moyst complexion,
> Doe life conceiue and quickned are by kynd:
> So after Nilus invndation,
> Infinite shapes of creatures men do fynd,
> Informed in the mud, on which the Sunne hath shynd.
>
> (III.vi.8)

We may compare a passage from *Colin Clout* (859–862):

> . . . everie liuing wight
> Crept forth like wormes out of her slimie nature [the earth's],
> Soone as on them the suns life giuing light
> Had powred kindly heat and formall feature

Proteus' realm, on this reading, presents that "second Chaos" of Sir Thomas Browne, seeded with the potential forms, or the capacity for "formall feature." Florimell sheds into the realm of her captor that Ficinian Venus in the World-Soul, namely "formes and faire aspects, / Whence all the world deriues the glorious / Features of beautie" (III.vi.12). If Florimell is Beauty, her name suggests its quality of "formality."

This reading is recommended to us through Porphyry's treatise on Homer's cave of the nymphs, with which one may compare the cave that confines Florimell. Porphyry's version of Homer's cave is exceedingly moist, even though not submarine. Spenser's cave is eaten out of the rock, "That seemes rough Masons hand with engines keene / Had long while laboured it to engraue" (III.viii.37). Homer's cave contains wine bowls and amphorae hollowed in the rock, and also looms of stone. Homer's cave is the resort of immortal nymphs; Spenser's cave is kept by an old nymph who is also an "immortall." Homer's cave is a kind of treasury (honey is found there, and richly dyed fabrics are woven there), and Odysseus will cache his treasure in it; Spenser's nymph is named Panope, "All-wealth," and Proteus offers Florimell "kingdomes vnto her vew" (III.viii.40). Homer's cave has two entrances, one for mortals and one for immortals; Spenser says Panope entertained Proteus' guest "As an immortall mote a mortall wight" (III.viii.38). Homer's cave, Porphyry asserts, may well stand for matter:

> . . . which, according to a secret signification, is denominated a stone
> and a rock, on account of its sluggish and repercussive nature with re-
> spect to form: the ancients, at the same time, asserting that matter is
> infinite through its privation of form. Since, however, it is continually
> flowing, and is itself destitute of the supervening investments of form,
> through which it participates in the *morphe*, and becomes visible, the

flowing waters, darkness, or, as the poet says, obscurity of the cavern, were considered by the ancients as apt symbols of what the world contains, on account of the matter with which it is connected. Through matter, therefore, the world is obscure and dark; but through the connecting power, and orderly distribution of form, from which also it is called the world, it is beautiful and delightful. Hence it may very properly be denominated a cave; as being lovely indeed to him who first enters into it, through its participation of forms, but obscure to him who surveys its foundation, and examines it with an intellectual eye.[391]

Perhaps it is such a survey that Marinell makes at the end of Book IV.

Our reading gains considerable authority from the mythography for Proteus. If the Florimell cycle is generated from the symbol of the Garden of Adonis, the realm of Proteus ought to be the chaos of unformed matter. It is from the Ocean River that gods and men arose, according to Homer,[392] and following the *Life of Homer* it was not unusual in the Renaissance to assert that the poet intimated the doctrine of Thales, that water was the universal father of all things.[393] The allegory of Proteus belongs to this school.

The identification of Proteus is impressively represented. Giraldus quotes Proclus on the god: "in se complectentem omnes rerum formas in mundo genitarum" (in him are comprised all forms of things in the world of generation): that is why he enumerates his flock of seals.[394] Fraunce says that Proteus is a "type of nature"[395] and Stephanus speaks similarly.[396]

---

[391] *De Antro Nympharum*, 2, trans. Thomas Taylor, *Select Works of Porphyry* (London, 1823), pp. 174f.

[392] *Il.* XIV.246 (and 201).

[393] *Vita Homeri*, in Gale, *Opuscula Mythologica*, p. 324. Thales' dependence on Homer is also asserted in Heraclides Ponticus, in Gale, pp. 438f.; in Sextus Empiricus, *Adv. Math.* X.313–318; and in Aristotle, *Metaphysics* I.iii, 983b. So also Cartari, *Le Imagini* (Venice, 1625), p. 188, and Comes, *Mythol.*, VIII.i, *edn. cit.*, p. 811. Cf. Plato, *Theaetetus* 152e: "Homer, who by saying 'Oceanos begetter of gods and mother of Tethys' declared all things to be the offspring of flux and motion."

[394] Giraldus, *Hist. Deorum*, Syntag. V, in *Op. om.*, I, col. 168E, citing Proclus on Plato's *Laws*. One may compare Proclus, *In Platonis Rem. Pub.*, 379f. (ed. W. Kroll, vol. 1, pp. 109–114), where Proteus is said to represent by his changes the progression of the one into the many; or else he is a certain intellect "possessing and comprehending in himself all the forms of generated natures" ("echoun te kai periechoun en eautou ta eidai panta toun geneitoun")—on this account he numbers his seals. (My source is Thomas Taylor, trans., *Works of Plato*, London, 1804, vol. 1, pp. 161–167.)

[395] *Third part of the Countesse of Pembrokes Iuychurche*, fol. 22ᵛ. citing Cornelius Gemma, *De Naturae divinis characterismis . . .* (Antwerp, 1575), 2 vols. in one, II, p. 195. In the course of introducing an exposition of the myth of Orpheus and Eurydice, in Virgil's fourth *Georgic*, as an allegory about the darkness of the human mind sunken in the senses, with Orpheus as the power of the agent intellect to dispel the idols that stupefy it and to effect its rescue, Gemma writes: "Why, fixed upon

Heraclides says that by Proteus, Homer meant *matter*, the most ancient substance:

> For truly this fable comprehends the original genesis of the universe, from which all parts of the established world were produced which we presently behold. For originally the world was unformed and muddy, and it had not yet attained the integrity of the discreet, distinct things of its forms. For neither was the earth stable on its center, as the foundation of all things, nor was there the perpetual movement of the heaven turning with certain faith. . . .[397]

The Homerist explains that the various transformations of Proteus allegorize the four elements; Eidothea, Proteus' helpful daughter, represents that Providence that impressed forms on matter.

> Consequently it agrees [with Homer] that Proteus be called unformed matter: Eidothea is certainly Providence, which alone causes its form and shape: and the shapeless universe was separated—a discreet whole—from both, into its own parts, hanging together and finished. And doubtless he called the island Pharos where these things happened, for *phersai* means to generate: and Callimachus calls the sterile earth *apharaton, apharatos hoion gunai*, i.e., like a sterile woman. And so naturally this place, the parent of all things, he names *Pharos*, implying through the sound an etymology from fecundity, insinuating what he means. . . . The age [of Proteus] indeed denotes the oldest and primal substance, and that unformed matter has been committed to the polity of time (?). *Halios* certainly is not recognized as belonging to a marine demon—we do not understand it as *apo tais halos*, i.e., in the sea: but something heaped up and combined from many and various things. For *halidzein* in Greek means to congregate. Also he is rightly said to be truthful, for what could be adjudged more true than this substance, from which all is generated?[398]

For Sextus Empiricus, Proteus stands for the first cause, his daughter for the particulars of matter.[399] The Orphic *Hymn* addressed Proteus as "first-

---

present things, we examine these [notions deriving from the intellect] so slowly, and, so far from judging them truly as they are, are entangled in infinite snares of errors, Proteus—representing a symbol of multiform nature—in the presence of Aristaeus, or the human race, reveals"; Gemma then quotes *Georg.* IV.453–459 on Orpheus' enmity to Aristaeus for the loss of his wife.

[396] Carolo Stephanus, *Dictionarium historicum, geographicum, poeticum* (Leiden, 1686), *sub* "Proteus."

[397] Gesner trans., reprinted in Gale, *Opuscula Mythologica*, pp. 488–491.

[398] *Loc. cit.*   [399] *Adv. Math.* IX.5.

born," the one who exhibits all of nature's principles, and who turns holy matter into various forms (*ideais polymorphois*); nature assigned all beginnings to this god.[400] Eustathius, on *Odyssey* IV, also says that Proteus is the primitive matter.[401] As late as Gothe's *Faust* (II.ii) and the third episode of Joyce's *Ulysses*, Proteus has this significance.[402] In Goethe the somewhat ambiguous sea-god appears with Thales; Proteus shatters the one into the many, seeding the sea with that bare vital principle or homunculus who is surely the seed principle of the species. In Joyce's *Ulysses*, "Proteus" in part stands for the "ineluctable modality of the visible," the sensible or material world; Stephen's ironic reference to the *Prix de Paris*—i.e., Helen —shows that this Proteus is Egyptian too.[403]

As the variety of citations will have suggested, we are dealing here with a kind of orthodoxy. In the seventeenth century, as a "Symbole of the first Matter," Proteus appears in Bacon's *Wisdom of the Ancients*, and in Browne and Milton.[404] An important influence on such authors is likely to have been Comes, who introduces an otherwise unidentified text from a supposedly Orphic *Hymn* into his article. In the poem he quotes, Proteus is addressed as the one "by whom the *primordia* of nature were elicited":

[400] Orphic Hymn XXIV, in Hambergerus, ed., *Orpheos Apanta*, pp. 216f. Giraldus quotes this Hymn on Proteus being said "to hold the keys to the Bridges, and the beginnings of all nature, and to change matter into multiform species" (*Hist. Deorum*, Syntag. V, in *Op. om.*, I, col. 169D).

[401] On *Ody.* IV.465, p. 1503.21, *protogonon hylēn; Eustathius Commentarii ad Homeri Odysseam*, vol. 1 (Leipzig, 1825), p. 174. So also scholia E on *Od.* IV.456, in W. Dindorf, ed., *Scholia Graeca in Homeri Odysseam* (Oxford, 1855), vol. 1, p. 214: the animals are allegorized as the four elements, and Eidothea as all the moulded forms.

[402] So Joyce, in his schemata for the symbolism; see Hugh Kenner, *Dublin's Joyce* (Indiana, 1956), p. 226, for the chart.

[403] *Ulysses* (New York, 1961), pp. 37, 50 ("*Prix de Paris*: beware of imitations. Just you give it a fair trial.").

[404] Bacon, *De Sapientia Veterum*, XIII, "Proteus, or Matter"; Browne, *Garden of Cyrus*, V, the source of the quotation here; Milton, *Par. Lost* V.603–605, where Proteus is the alchemical original matter, and his multiformity, it is implied, matter's diversity. Bacon says that "the universe with its several species according to their ordinary frame and structure, is merely the face of matter unconstrained and at liberty, with its flock of materiate creatures. Nevertheless if any skilful servant of Nature shall bring force to bear on matter, and shall vex it and drive it to extremities ... then will matter ... finding itself in these straits, turn and transform itself into strange shapes ... till it has gone through the whole circle ... when, if the force be continued, it returns at last to itself." This passage is presumably the source of Shelley's Rousseau, in *The Triumph of Life*, describing Bacon: "he compelled / The Proteus shape of Nature, as it slept / To wake, and lead him to the caves that held / The treasure of the secrets of its reign" (ll. 270ff.).

"You know how to turn sacred matter into many forms—prudent, venerable, and knowing the wholes which are, which have been, and the *ventura* that are to be drawn out."[405] Comes has probably been imposed upon, for the last line is a slightly abbreviated version of Virgil's line (*Georg*. IV.393) about Proteus' vatic powers. The mythographer then quotes the Homeric passage on the transformations, and comments:

> For from the same matter, from a hidden principle of atmospheric heat, either trees or animals are born, or matter itself is converted into elements, which [is what] the ancients mean by so many and such multiple changes of forms; whence Proteus is undoubtedly almost *to protonon*, first in existence. For all matter exists first in the intellect, and it always seeks various forms, impelled by nature. Whence Proteus is said to turn himself into so many forms. For it belongs to a completely foolish man to think that there was indeed some man or other who turned himself into so many forms.[406]

Further on in the same article Comes treats Proteus as a learned natural philosopher, who, conforming himself to his subject matter, wrote "de mutatione elementorum, & quo pacto illa principia sint omnium nascentium, quae vt uires singula sumpserint" (about the reciprocal changes of the elements; and how there are nascent in all things those principles which they [the changes?] enter into as singular forces).[407] Other examples of this tradition in the Renaissance are found in Melanchthon's gloss on his edition of Virgil's *Georgics*, Cardanus in the first book of his *De Subtilitate*, and DuBartas in his creation poem. Melanchthon explains that "various bodies were created from humid matter. All bodies are resolved to this extreme in their first state, that is, the elemental state. So they were created from this as well—this is perhaps what Proteus signifies."[408] Cardanus argues for the conservation of the primal matter, but in a variable quantity, for it occupies different volumes in different forms: "Nevertheless, matter has definite limits of greatness and smallness within which, like some Proteus, it assumes an indefinite number of magnitudes."[409] DuBartas calls the first matter the first thing made:

[405] *Mythol.* VIII.viii, *edn.* cit., p. 841. So far as I know, there is no such Orphic hymn, though Comes has a Greek text as well as the Latin translation. The same text is cited by Jean De Sponde, in his notes on *Od.* IV, in *Homeri qvae extant omnia* (Basel, 1583), II, p. 53.

[406] *Mythol.* VIII.viii, p. 842.

[407] *Mythol.* VIII.viii, p. 844.

[408] *Opera*, ed. Bretschneider and Bindseil, vol. 19, "Ennaratio Georgicon Virgilii" (in *Georg.* IV.388), col. 430.

[409] *De Subtilitate*, Lib. I, trans. Myrtle Marguerite Cass (Williamsport, Penn., 1934), p. 84.

Table of the All-Powerful, true corpus of the universe,
Common receptacle of diverse accidents,
Entirely parallel to itself, entirely contained in itself
Without being increased or diminished by the will of time,
Immutable of essence, and mutable of frontal aspect,
More than not a Proteus. . . .[410]

The rhetoric, as well as the theme, is that of an Orphic *Hymn*.

Proteus, in sum, represents matter in its infinite receptivity to form, espe-cially generable form. He stands for that "sea," met with earlier, endowed with "the potential fecundity of all things which lies latent in the first prin-ciple," as Ficino described it in his comment on the generation of Venus. There are two complementary ways of understanding Florimell's detention in this realm. When we look forward to her emergence from the ocean, she is the seed of heaven out of which Venus will be born, that is, the forms im-plicit in the prime matter, waiting to be elicited from it. When we look backward over the decay of her fortunes, they suggest the corruption of form; it is then significant that she is replaced in the upper world by a snowy copy, as if that world preserved a memory of her form, or a prototype on the model of which she might be re-formed. The relation of the two Flor-imells may be loosely compared to that of forms inside the Garden and outside: inside, a typal form maintains the species according to its kind; outside, the visible form is subject to variation and decay. And yet Flor-imell proves to be the real conserver of form: her rival is made of wax and snow and mercury, a list of amorphous substances that are all natural shape-changers, oscillating between the conditions of a solid and a liquid. They are all fundamentally *promiscuous*, we might say. Thus the False Florimell is the mutable Protean, in our sense of the term, while the true Florimell, despite her many "louers" (IV.xi.3), remains true to her virtue, and so true to form. Because Proteus symbolizes not only "inform matter," but also seasonal change, Florimell's confinement in his realm stands for that annual obliteration of form that occurs every winter, when nature, deprived of "kindly heat and formall feature," seems bent on returning to something like her "unformed and muddy" original.

[iv]

The physical myth of Proteus does not provide the only reason for the detainment of Spenser's Koré figure underwater. The poet is also making his contribution to the vogue for discovering piscatorial equiv-

---

[410] I.II; ll. 223–228 in the Sylvester trans.; quoted in a different context in Ellrodt, *Neoplatonism*, p. 73.

alents for the motifs of pastoral poetry.[411] In this convention the shepherds' god Pan finds his counterpart in Proteus, "the shepherd of the seas." Colin Clout provides an extensive example in his description of Proteus in the poem bearing his name, but *The Faerie Queene* offers more of a conspectus. Most pastoral stories have an amorous subject. This characteristic does not exclude Marinell; like Belphoebe, or Marcella in an early episode of *Don Quixote*, he is the pastoral figure who withdraws into the pastoral world not to experience love, but to avoid experiencing it.[412]

Marinell is something of an experiment in many ways. He is an aquatic Adonis. There are classical and mythological reasons for connecting Adonis with water. In Ovid's account of Adonis' death the body is laid out on the seashore, and other stories have him borne or thrown into the water like Osiris.[413] The identification of Adonis with the river in Syria that reddens in the spring more specifically entails a relation with a water cycle.[414]

Another prototype for Marinell is found in Achilles, the sea-nymph's son, kept out of battle by his loving mother. "Why does he live in safety, as they say the marine son of Thetis did?" Horace asks about a young man effeminated by love and reluctant to join in athletics.[415] The inverse reluctance, in a legend where the engagement is erotic, is expressed in Marinell's name; he "will not marry," or be a *mari*, a husband.[416] The love-life of Achilles is a regular feature of the post-Homeric material concerning the hero. Achilles traditionally becomes a lover because of his vulnerability to the charms of the Amazon Pentheseleia, who defeats him

[411] Accounts of this convention may be found in Henry M. Hall, *Idylls of Fishermen* (New York, 1912), and Leonard Grant, *Neo-Latin Literature and the Pastoral* (Chapel Hill, 1965), pp. 205–228. An inspiration was Theocritus, *Idyl* XXI.

[412] See Renato Poggiolli, "The Oaten Flute," *Harvard Library Bulletin*, 11, no. 2 (1957), pp. 147–184.

[413] Ovid, *Metam.* X.716, and Theocritus, *Idyl* XV.132–136: "But lo, in the morning we will all of us gather with the dew, and carry him forth among the waves that break upon the beach, and with locks unloosed, and ungirt raiment falling to the ankles, and bosoms bare will we begin our shrill sweet song." (Trans. Lang.) See Lucian, *Syrian Goddess* 8, for the reception of the floating head of the Egyptian Adonis at Byblos.

[414] For the river, see Lucian, *Syrian Goddess* 8, and n. 85 above.

[415] *Odes* I.8, ll. 15f.: in dressing her son Achilles as a woman, Thetis emasculates him.

[416] See n. 369, above. Thus Marinell belongs to a class of reluctant males who are the objects of an amorous female—Shakespeare's Adonis, Drayton's Endymion, Francis Beaumont's Hermaphroditus, Phineas Fletcher's Anchises, and the Narcissus of Thomas Edwards (1595) and James Shirley (1618). Like Marlowe's Leander, these males are all notable for their effeminate beauty, and for the projection, as it were, of a post-coital passivity onto foreplay. See n. 436, below.

in battle; Pentheseleia is therefore cited as a type for Britomart at the opening of the canto in which she topples Marinell. The arrow of Paris that gives Achilles his fatal wound is said by E. K. to be allegorically love,[417] and generations later Spenser's Paridell is still unloosing such arrows at Hellenore. The classical Achilles is the last of Helen's lovers, according to the variant of the story referred to in Goethe: Achilles replaces Paris when he marries Helen in the afterlife. Marinell's late or "epilogic" marriage to Florimell thus fulfills a final term in the Helen story, as Roche points out.[418]

The elegiac treatment of Marinell and the lamentation of Britomart beside the sea presumably owe something to the example of Sannazaro's first *Piscatorial Eclogue*. Here the wretched Lycidas asks where he shall follow his beloved Phyllis, now that she is dead.

For your sake once the land was pleasing to me and crowds and cheerful cities with their walls; now it is my pleasure to wander the borders of the vasty deep and to roam freely over the stormy waves mingled with crowds of Tritons and amid the monsters of the rocks and rude-shaped seals with fearful forms, where I can never see land.[419]

This is the rocky and grievous world through which Marinell roams upon the thresholds of Proteus (IV.xii.4) when he happens upon Florimell; her prison groans with her lament and with billows beating from the main (IV.xii.5). She is like the birds in Sannazaro's sea-caves, "filling the sad rocks with their querulous complaints."[420]

> In this sad plight he walked here and there,
> And romed round about the rocke in vaine,
> As he had lost himselfe, he wist not where;
> Oft listening if he mote her heare againe;
> And still bemoning her vnworthy paine.
>
> (IV.xii.17)

The "Huge sea of sorrows" on which Britomart tosses—as did her ancestor Britomartis—pointedly aligns her with the imperiled Florimell:

> Far from the hoped hauen of reliefe,
> Why do thy cruell billowes beat so strong,
> And thy moyst mountaines each on others throng,
> Threatning to swallow vp my fearefull life?
>
> (IV.iv.8)

[417] E. K. on "March," l. 97, and Argument, with reference to Fulgentius, *Mitologiarum*, III.7 (Helm edn., pp. 71f.).

[418] Roche, *Kindly Flame*, p. 186, citing Pausanias, III.xix. 11–13; also Tzetzes on Lychophron, 143 and 171–173, and Servius, *ad Aen.* I.34.

[419] Ll. 72–76, trans. in Ralph Nash, *Arcadia and Piscatorial Eclogues* (Detroit, 1966), p. 161.

[420] *Eclogue* I.4f. (Nash, p. 156).

These are the love-laments poured out beside the "wave-resounding sea" (*maris undisoni*) of Sannazaro:[421] "far and wide re-echoes the whole stretch of wave-resounding waters."[422] The Glauce beside Britomart is momentarily the Glaucus of the same poet, "a watcher of the sands beside the sea."[423]

The bereaved Lycidas of Sannazaro's first example promises the beloved annual obsequies:

> Here for you Nisaea and Cymodoce with yellow hair unbound and gentle Palaemon with his virtuous mother Panope and Galatea, protectoress of the Sicilian deep, will weave their solemn dances and sing the songs which Proteus the seer once taught them, being divinely inspired, when he bewailed the death of great Achilles and comforted Thetis' bitter lamentations.[424]

Cymodoce will sing the songs taught (*edocuit*) to her by Proteus, who himself lamented Achilles and comforted Achilles' mother. Marinell's mother, who is also named Cymodoce, consults the same seer, and bewails her son in company like that kept by Homer's Thetis. The sea-elegy, Sannazaro seems to be saying, has its prototype in the lament of Homer's mother-goddess.

Thus, the complaints of Spenser's fourth canto—Britomart's, Cymodoce's, and Arthur's as well—are conventional. They seem indulged, and perhaps even indulged solipsistically. In Homer, when Patrocles dies, the handmaidens' lament modulates into the prophetic mourning of Thetis and her nymphs for Achilles. Homer says that the captive women really did not lament Patrocles, but each lamented her own woes; the complaints of Spenser's nymphs are marked by a certain stock-responsiveness also.[425]

In the consolation of Sannazaro's poem, Lycidas imagines his betrothed pursuing fish along the streams of Elysium, and the unwithering flowers that she plucks there blend seaweed with the more traditional violets.[426] Although there is no mention of Adonis-flowers (the others are the narcissus and the ever-living amaranth), much of the rest of Spenser's sea-pastoral machinery is anticipated here. Spenser's Proteus, of course, does not lament the sea-nymph's son: Sannazaro must be reflecting Ovid, who has Proteus foresee a great son for the goddess of the waves, and urges her to conceive. The Proteus of Ovid also counsels Peleus on the way to capture the nymph, who can herself take a hundred forms.[427] Spenser's Cymodoce is not obviously Protean, but she is shown to be adaptable and

---

[421] *Eclogue* II.75 (Nash, p. 168).   [422] *Frg.*, l. 12 (Nash, p. 190).

[423] *Eclogue* II.54 (Nash, p. 166).

[424] *Eclogue* I.84–90, trans. Nash, pp. 161, 163.

[425] See *Iliad* XVIII.28-31, 50ff., and XIX.301f. For the descent of Thetis' nymphs to the "old man of the sea," their father Nereus, see *Il.* XVIII.140f.

[426] *Eclogue* I.91–96 (in Nash, p. 162).   [427] *Metam.* XI.221–223, 250–256.

resourceful. Her name changes from Cymoent, and the later form can be interpreted *cursus fluctuum*, as Boccaccio reports, citing Servius.[428] Cymodoce is among the standard names of the nymphs, from Homer on, and in Silius Italicus' *Punica* she is the nymph who asks Proteus to prophesy the future of the Italian shore. To do so, he must tell a story that includes Achilles (VII.409ff.).

For those in a quandary, a consultation with Proteus is a conventional way of proceeding, but a very prominent classical instance, the epyllion of Aristaeus in Virgil's fourth *Georgic*, particularly recalls the story of Marinell and his mother. A little like Flora in Ovid's *Fasti*, Aristaeus is the poet's eponymous beekeeper. He loses his flock of bees for mysterious reasons, according to Virgil, and in despair he complains to his mother Cyrene, a river-nymph. The mother and her companions (who include Cymodoce and Arethuse) become aware of the lad's lament, and at Arethuse's instance the swain is conveyed by a mountain-wave beneath the waters; there, significantly, one nymph "was enumerating the gods' myriad loves from Chaos on" (*Georg.* IV.347). For Aristaeus it is lawful to tread the divine threshold; for Marinell, apparently, it is not. Aristaeus is thus enabled to visit the sources of all the rivers, along with his mother's comforting bower. Cyrene then sends her son to visit the cave of Proteus to wrest an oracle from him. Proteus tells him that the decayed state of his fortunes is owing to his part in the confinement of Eurydice in the underworld—here Virgil reverts to an unfamiliar story of Eurydice's flight from Aristaeus to avoid rape. Aristaeus makes sacrifices to the offended party, and his flock is restored to him—a new swarm of bees emerges from the side of one of the slain bullocks.

Whether or not this story is Spenser's source, it does represent the *kind* of tale that the poet intends to tell. Even the link with Eurydice reminds one of Spenser's overall theme. The escaping maiden at the beginning of Virgil's story and the returning bees at the end more nearly belong to one cycle in Spenser. The motif of the elegiac figure who visits the undersea sources of the rivers with a nymph is also found in the solemn conclusion to Sannazaro's *Arcadia*.[429] The amazement of the sea-folk at the passing

[428] *G.D.G.*, VII.xv (Romano edn., vol. 1, p. 350). Cf. Giraldus, *Hist. Deorum*, Syntag. V, in *Op. om.*, I, col. 174E: "Cymodoce, hac est qua fluctus per caerula Ponti, Ventorum & celeres flatus." Landino, *Quaestiones Camuldenses* (Venice, n.d.), fol. i ii^v, interprets Cymothoe, "per undas currens."

[429] *Arcadia*, chap. 12 (in Nash, pp. 136f.): an allusion to Virgil's fourth *Georgic* seems patent, and Homer's cave of the nymphs may also be a source. In turn, Sannazaro has probably influenced the seminary of the rivers under Ascalona, in Tasso, *Ger. Lib.* XIV.36f., 41, with which compare *F.Q.* IV.xi.20f., and also Fairfax's translation of the Tasso passage. An example of the underwater congress of rivers which is more local in scope is found in Peter Bembo's Latin epyllion *Benacus* (i.e., Lago di Garda), which celebrates the elevation of Matteo Giberti to the local bishopric:

of Marinell's funeral cortege is even more conventional; it figures in the keelhauling of the lustful Scylla of the *Ciris*, and in Catullus' epithalamion for Peleus and Thetis.[430] The *Ciris*, with its motif of flight to the sea, is another example of the kind of tale with which Spenser is concerned.

Another motif belonging to the sea-progress is the submission of the waves in sympathy (III.iv.32). There is an analogy in Moschus' second *Idyl*, which re-creates the abduction of Europa by Zeus: "the sea, as he came, grew smooth, and the sea-monsters gambolled around."[431] Like the punishment of Scylla (it turns up in the keelhauling of the lustful fishermen at the hands of Proteus), the Europa motif more properly belongs to the story of the abduction of Florimell. Europa was a flower girl too; she carried a flower basket,[432] and Politian has her leave her companions on the flowery shore in a scene that suggests the abduction of Proserpina.[433] Moschus' Europa, carried off by the metamorphosed god, "was not for long to set her heart's delight upon the flowers, nay, nor long to keep untouched her maiden girdle."[434] Horace (in *Odes* III.27) pictures the girl as being preoccupied with picking flowers and suddenly finding herself in the middle of the sea, endangered by fraudulent monsters. Florimell inherits this Europa motif particularly from Angelica, who flies to the shore to cross the sea. Ariosto says that so long as she is *in Europe* she is not secure. Thus her demon-possessed horse plunges into the deep; the rider collects her garments and gathers up her feet to avoid the water, and the greater winds, along with the ocean, are hushed by her beauty; the land appears smaller and smaller. Most of these details are taken from Ovid's account of Europa (*Metam.* II.846ff. and VI.103–106); some are found in Politian's *Stanze* (I.105–106). Lucian's highly pictorial treatment in the *Dialogues of the Sea-Gods* XV develops into a pageant, with the accompaniment of the Nereids and the calming of the sea. Spenser does not follow Ariosto in attaching all of this to Florimell, but he does betray his heroine into the

---

the tutelary gods of all the rivers in Northern Italy are assembled here, to hear Neptune announce Giberti's coming achievements. Two texts may have been influential: Dante, *Inf.* XX.61-81, where the lap of Lake Benaco pools the "mille fonti" that bathe the Apennines, and Catullus, 64, ll. 267 seq., esp. 285–293, on the gods and rivers attending the marriage of Peleus and Thetis. That Spenser knows the latter seems clear from *F.Q.* VII.vii. 11–12, for the description of Mole there reminds us of Peneios in Catullus' poem, and a reference to the "spousall hymne" of Peleus and Thetis follows directly. (Bembo's poem was printed in *Carmina Quinque Illustrium Poetarum*, 1548; text in *Opere*, Venice, 1729, vol. 4, pp. 349–351.) For the concept of a primordial river-vault, see Plato, *Phaedo* 111c–112e.

[430] *Ciris*, ll. 391–399. Catullus, 64, ll. 12–21.

[431] *Idyl* II, "Europa," ll. 115–124.   [432] Moschus, *Idyl* II.34.

[433] *Stanze per la Giostra*, I.106. Jove's other transformations, following the will of Love, succeed.

[434] *Idyl* II.72f.

power of the shape-changing god, and Angelica falls victim to a Proteus also.[435]

The result of these comparisons seems clear: Spenser is consciously re-creating the marine motifs of the Mediterranean epyllion.[436] The poet is showing us that the power of love extends to the kingdom of the sea. That is why, according to an emblematic poem in the *Greek Anthology*, Cupid holds a flower in one hand—Florimell—and a dolphin in the other—Marinell.[437]

The flux of analogies and comparisons makes a related point as well: love takes many forms. As Ovid says, explaining his attraction to every girl that he encounters, "my love suits itself to all the stories."[438] To ex-press this, one needs an enriched mythology: its principal symbol will be metamorphosis, signifying the capacity of love to change—and to change persons. Hence the great importance attaching to the intervention of Proteus in the affairs of Florimell and Marinell, where the mutable god symbolizes love's vicissitude. Perhaps at least as important is the parity that emerges between Busirane and Proteus in the overall structure of the

[435] *O.F.* VIII.30, 35–37. Cf. Moschus, *Idyl* II.125–134. For Spenser's more explicit Europan mythology, note the lust-driven bulls that dare to tempt the deepest flood at the coming of Spring, in IV.x.46, and the Taurus that bears April in VII.vii.33. See also *Mviopotomos*, ll. 277–296. For Florimell's association with Taurus, cf. Chap. III, "The Course of Justice," sec. i, above.

[436] The term *epyllion* is adopted here advisedly, to indicate a comparison between Spenser's narrative and that of poems like the *Ciris* and Lodge's *Glaucus and Scylla* (1584). The English species, of which *Hero and Leander* is the most famous exam-ple, includes the poems referred to in n. 416, above; philosophical interpretations of the genre are Drayton's *Endymion and Phoebe* and Chapman's *Ovid's Banquet of Sense*. The generic tendency persists in English in Keats' *Endymion* (cf. Drayton), and less obviously, in Tennyson's *Lucretius* (cf. Chapman). These poems feature a myth of erotic connoisseurship or erotic possession (Hero's name is derived from *eros* by Fulgentius and the tradition following him); a rich sensual preoccupation; a theme of metamorphosis (often in connection with the metamorphic element of water); and frequent erotic *pietàs*. Subfeatures are a deliberate mythopoetic digres-siveness and the accommodation of extended "monodramatic" complaints by the narrative. The Ovidian subplot of the Mutabilitie Cantos is epyllionic on the first account, and the laments of III.iv are epyllionic on the second.

[437] *Gr. Anth.* XVI.207. Roche, *Kindly Flame*, pp. 190–192, cites this emblem conceit from Alciati, *Emblemata* (Antwerp, 1581), "Potentia Amoris," p. 81, and Green, *Whitney's Choice of Emblemes*, p. 182. Roche says that "Marinell is never compared to a fish," but he is born by a dolphin, like Arion at the marriage of Thames and Medway. Aelian, *Hist. anim.* IX.36, records a fish called Adonis: "People like to call it 'Adonis' because it loves both land and sea and those who first gave it this name were hinting . . . at the son of Cinyras, whose life was divided between the two goddesses." (Trans. Scholfield, in Loeb *Aelian*, vol. 2, p. 257.) This fish appears in Renaissance dictionaries.

[438] *Amores* II.iv.44.

two books. To account for this parity we need to know how Proteus, like Busiris, came to be a lover. *Two Gentlemen of Verona*, for example, features a Proteus in the part of the hero's unworthy friend, who becomes a decidedly uncouth rival for the love of the heroine. The tradition behind the choice of name for false friend and lust-driven lover is worth educing.[439]

Two classical authors strongly hint that Proteus may be a type of the lover. Lucian, after describing the many forms taken by Jove in pursuit of mortal loves, summarizes by saying that Jove showed himself to be more changeable than even Proteus.[440] In Busirane's tapestry, Jove and the other gods subject to the power of Cupid appear in many forms. Roche derived Busirane's name from a passage in Ovid's *Art of Love*; further on in Ovid's argument Proteus appears as a type of the seducer:

> I was about to end, but various are the hearts of women; use a thousand means to waylay as many hearts. The same earth bears not everything; this soil suits vines, that olives; in that, wheat thrives. Hearts have as many fashions as the world has shapes; the wise man will suit himself to countless fashions, and like Proteus will now resolve himself into light waves, and now will be a lion, now a tree, now a shaggy boar. Here fish are caught with spears, there with hooks; here they are dragged with taut ropes in hollow nets. . . . And so it comes that she who has feared to commit herself to an honorable lover degrades herself to the embraces of a mean one.[441]

In the tapestry of Cupid's triumphs all the gods have "degraded" themselves in this way, in that they have all subjected themselves to the Protean conditions of matter and its forms.

In the story of Vertumnus, Ovid gives fictional form to this theme. Vertumnus is the god who gained access to Pomona by means of a variety of disguises—reaper, herdsman, farmer, soldier, fisherman—and in the end resorted to a theophany that procured his acceptance as a lover. Erasmus, in his article on "Protein mutabilior," associates Proteus with Vertumnus, "for this god varied himself into all the *species* of things," and Harington, in the index to his translation of Ariosto, writes that Proteus is "counted a God of the sea called Vertumnus, because he is said to turn himself into all shapes."[442] Harington seems to mean that Vertumnus gets his name from *vertere* (to turn).

[439] Giamatti, in his essay "Proteus Unbound," in Demetz, *et al.*, eds., *Disciplines of Criticism* (New Haven, 1968), proceeds along similar lines.

[440] *De Sacrificiis* 5, trans. A. M. Harmon, in Loeb *Lucian*, vol. 3, p. 161.

[441] *Ars Amat.* I.755–770, trans. J. H. Mozely in the Loeb edn., p. 65.

[442] *Metam.* XIV.628ff. Erasmus pairs Proteus and Vertumnus as examples of inconstancy in *On Copy*, II, "Method of Collecting *Exempla*," and in the *Adagia, sub* "Proteus mutabilior," cites "Vertumno inconstantior" as comparable. For Harington's index entry, *Orlando Furioso in English Heroical Verse* (London, 1607), Sig. Ooij.[r]

Earlier we noted that Busirane was Love the Enchanter. Plato also compared Love to a sophist. Ovid's Proteus (in the passage just quoted) is Love the Sophist. Expanding on Plato's identification, Ficino compares the sophist, as a pretentious and crafty debater, to the wiles and changes of mind of the lover.[443] Spenser's Proteus is also a sophist (III.iv.28), and so this nexus is virtually complete. Moreover, there is a second route to it.

A *psychomachia* tradition found in Clement of Alexandria, Servius, Boccaccio, Erasmus, and, to a lesser degree, Alciati, makes Proteus a type of libido, passion, or *cupiditas*. The key text in Clement identifies the concupiscible element in the Platonic analysis of the soul with Proteus because it "allures to adulteries, to licentiousness, to seductions. . . . For lust becomes and fabricates all things."[444] Servius, in a passage that is repeated by the Third Vatican Mythographer, explains the fettering of the vatic god's wiles, which are his variety of forms: "for man has within him *libido, stulticia, ferocitas*, and *dolum* [fraud]." Because this Proteus can be fettered by prudence, Virgil says that, like a priest, he "is able to prophesy and to take upon himself divinity, since thereupon there will have been banished from him the fire of cupidity, the harshness of the wilds [*silvestris*], the sliding of the soul [*animi*], [and] the resemblance to the inconstancy of the waters."[445] The ferocity of man's elemental nature is represented in the Proteus of Ariosto; and Erasmus, in the *Enchiridion*, makes the struggle with Proteus the Christian's battle for self-control.[446]

Spenser insists upon Proteus' use of flattery in his wooing (III.viii.38), as the god who has befriended Florimell enters into an increasingly hypocritical relation with her. This, too, is traditional. The *Metamorphosis Moraliter* compares Proteus to Achelous (a shape-changing antagonist of Hercules), as "a flatterer and a false, double-dealing and destructive friend guilty of inconstancy."[447] Erasmus, in the *Adagia*, compares Proteus'

---

[443] *De Amore*, VI.x (Jayne trans., p. 199).

[444] *Paedagog.*, III.i, trans. in ANF, vol. 2, p. 271. Cited by Mignault, in Alciati, *Emblemata* (Antwerp, 1581), p. 633. Clement in particular refers to wanton love of bodily adornment, in contrast to being "arrayed in chastity, the sacred stole of the body."

[445] *Ad Georg.* IV.400, in Thilo-Hagen, ed., *Servii Grammatici*, vol. 3, p. 351; Bode, ed., *Scriptores mythicarum rerum latini*, III.xi.25, p. 242. Cf. Boccaccio, *G.D.G.*, Vii.ix (Romano edn., vol. 1, p. 344). So also Giraldus on Proteus, in *Hist. Deorum*, Syntag. V, *Op. om.*, I, col. 168G.

[446] Erasmus, *Enchiridion*, vii; trans. Himelick, pp. 76f.

[447] *Metamorphosis Ovidiana Moraliter* (Paris, 1515), fol. lxxiiiᵛ. Cf. Alexander Pope, in his note on line 521 of his trans. of *Od.* IV, where he is following Eustathius, p. 1503.14–16, fairly closely: "others make him an emblem of true friendship, which ought not to be settled till it has been tried in all shapes: others make Proteus a picture of a flatterer, who takes up all shapes, and suits himself to all forms, in compliance to the temper of the person whom he courts."

changeability to the proverbial mutability of the chameleon, and under *Chameleonte mutabilior* he refers the phrase to the vice of inconstancy (cf. Duessa at IV.i.18). These associations, which Spenser must have helped to keep current in England, are reflected in the conduct of Shakespeare's Proteus, who is a changeable lover, an inconstant friend, and finally a would-be rapist. This Proteus says that he must forgo Julia and Valentine to be constant to himself; Silvia tells him that falsehood becomes him, since he is a worshiper of shadows and false shapes.[448] His attachment to Silvia may remind us that the physical Proteus was the symbol of that anarchic prime matter, or *silva*; it was common to assert that profane love is immersed in matter. At any rate, the love of this play is specifically "the Chameleon Love."

Spenser's character, if not Shakespeare's, must also reflect the Proteus of Ariosto.[449] The narrative in question begins with the rape of the Princess of Eduba by the sea-god; subsequently, the Edubans mistreat the pregnant girl, and Proteus punishes them by sending the Orco monster to devour, on a regular basis, the most beautiful maidens the Edubans have to offer in compensation for the princess. Having exhausted their own resources, the Edubans one day happen on the wayward Angelica. At the time, she is the object of a pursuit by a lustful but impotent hermit, who has caught up with her in a seaside cave. The Edubans take over the prize, and proceed to expose the maid for the delectation of the Orco. Spenser's account of the lustful fisherman and the possessive sea-god clearly owes its theme of successive sea-peril to Ariosto.

Florimell's voyage in the "Fishers wandring bote, / That went at will, withouten carde or sayle" (III.viii.31), is another version of Guyon's voyage with Phedria. When Proteus takes over, Florimell's pilot changes, but not his uncontrollable tendency. Florimell has merely "chaunged from one to other fear" (III.vii.33), as Angelica exchanged a sterile lust for a lust for destruction. Commentary on the whole trip is offered by Britomart's speech from shore, which addresses her own "Huge sea of sorrow," and takes up the same Europa-like conceits:

[448] *Two Gentlemen of Verona*, II.vi.31f.; IV.ii.129f. For the protean chameleon, cf. OED, *sub* chameleon[1], citing Baldwin, *Moral Philosophy*,1564 edn., vii.8: "As a camelion hath all colors save white, so hath a flatterer all points save honestie." So the chameleonic Duessa of Book IV: "all colours, saue the trew."

[449] For an account of the Ariostan episode, with emphasis on its civic theme, see Giamatti, "Proteus Unbound," in Demetz, *et al.*, eds., *Disciplines of Criticism*, pp. 468–470. For the relation to Spenser, see Alpers, *Poetry of "The Faerie Queene,"* p. 195, and Hankins, *Source and Meaning*, p. 231. A verbal echo appears in *F.Q.* IV.xii.28, "Whether old Proteus true or false had sayd," which is close to *O.F.* VIII.58, "O vera o falsa che fosse la cosa / Di Proteo, ch'io non so che me ne dica."

> . . . my feeble vessell crazd, and crackt
> Through thy strong buffets and outrageous blowes,
> Cannot endure, but needs it must be wrackt
> On the rough rocks, or on the sandy shallowes,
> The whiles that loue it steres, and fortune rowes;
> Loue my lewd Pilot hath a restlesse mind
> And fortune Boteswaine no assurance knowes, . . .
>
> (III.iv.9)

Florimell's pilot, then, stands for the "restlesse mind" or fickleness of the lover, the psychological obverse of Florimell's own, otherwise unexpressed, dread of promiscuity.

It remains to state why, *moraliter*, the Proteus of lust should also be, in the same poem, *physice*, the Proteus of seasonal change and winter. There is a sense in which lust is wintry and sterile, of course, and a sense in which abandon to such a Proteus entails—on several levels—"going to seed." Clement described libido as more multiform than Proteus, who becomes and fabricates all things and attempts to defraud through his appearances. Clement also suggests that the rioting will of such a Proteus brings with it the corruption not so much of chastity as of form: "Passions break out, pleasures overflow, beauty fades, and falls quicker than the leaf on the ground, when the amorous storms of lust blow on it before the coming of autumn; and it is withered by destruction." Beauty is a flower, and Florimell, who has a flowerlike beauty, has good reason to fear such an agent of destruction.

The extensive interference of the sea-god in the affairs of Florimell and Marinell makes Proteus a "type of nature," in the sense of natural succession. Such a Proteus is not committed to any one moral role. At the outset, he is responsible for the Platonic "subtle sophisms" about Marinell's fate; near the end, he is the accommodating host at the wedding of Thames and Medway. His significance thus varies from a spirit of vicissitude and decay to a spirit of new combinations and renewal; he can represent change for the better, as well as the worse. Likewise, the Proteus of Comes may be an accommodating and adaptable ruler, exemplifying virtues of tolerance, compliance, and civic concord.[450] By the time we come to this late version of the sea-god, we may also have become aware of a kind of "harmony" or "concordance" emerging from the central books of

---

[450] *Mythol.*, VIII.viii, *edn. cit.*, p. 845. Quoted to the same effect by Giamatti, "Proteus Unbound."

Spenser's poem. This concordance is more properly the subject of the concluding essay in this chapter.

[v]

In our study of the stories that run through the center of Spenser's poem, it remains here to indicate one further serial. It regularly turns up in the third, fifth, and eighth cantos. Starting from the introduction of Belphoebe in the second book, and continuing through the wounding of Timias by the Blatant Beast in the sixth book, the elements of this serial are interlaced rather like a Spenserian rhyme scheme. An outline of the conjunctions of the characters involved helps to indicate this:

Braggadocchio and Belphoebe	(II, iii; woods)
Timias and Belphoebe	(III, v; bower)
Braggadocchio and the False Florimell	(III, viii; woods)
Braggadocchio and the False Florimell	(IV, v; tourney)
Timias and Belphoebe	(IV, viii; woods)
Braggadocchio and the False Florimell	(V, iii; tourney at Marinell's wedding)
Timias alone	(VI, v; woods)

A double cycle emerges. In the Belphoebe cycle, the virgin is introduced in the woods with Braggadocchio; celebrated in her paradisal bower with Timias; and separated from, and reconciled to, Timias. In the alternate cycle, the False Florimell is created and then won and lost by Braggadocchio. To the aristocracy of fairyland, the False Florimell is something of a vulgar *arriviste*. Her social climb culminates in her triumph in the beauty contest at the tournament of Satyrane; then, at a second tourney, she is dismissed from the poem. As a comparison shows, the discovery of Braggadocchio and Timias by Belphoebe offers a contrast in heroic endeavor. While hunting in the woods, Belphoebe comes upon the trumpery knight cowering in the bushes. Appropriately, he pretends he has been asleep. (There is possibly an allusion here to the discovery of Odysseus by Nausicaa; she too is compared to Artemis and addressed as a goddess, and she wishes good fortune to the man before her. Odysseus, like Braggadocchio, has been asleep, and he approaches, in his speech at least, on his knees.)[451] Belphoebe is again pursuing the chase when she discovers Ti-

---

[451] *Od.* VI.126–169. Cf. also Rosalind in *As You Like It*, I.iii.118–121: "A gallant curtle-ax upon my thigh, / A boar-spear in my hand; and in my heart / Lie there what hidden woman's fear there will, / We'll have a swashing and a martial outside, as many other mannish cowards have / That do outface it."

mias, languishing from his near-mortal wound (received in defense of Florimell). The wound suggests an erotic susceptibility, for it is afflicted by kin of the lustful forester. In the earlier episode, Braggadocchio, taking courage from his own bluff, boorishly attempts an assault on Belphoebe's honor. Timias, taking a new wound from his fair physician, becomes party to a noble (though not oversolemn) compliment to that honor.

In his next appearance, Braggadocchio wins and loses the False Florimell. He is shamefully cowed out of his possession, which he won by mere words from the churl. Nonetheless, the same lady later honors this base champion above any other, and awards herself to him as the prize for a tourney in which he has not distinguished himself—nor even participated, so far as one can tell. The False Florimell does not appear to much greater advantage in the trial involving the cestus of the true Florimell: shallow calls unto shallow, and deflation is followed by deflation.

Later, the dedicated and reckless Timias, again in a battle with a personification of lust, dishonors himself—at least in the eyes of Belphoebe. His rustication follows, but eventually he is returned to his mistress' friendship and favor. The last Braggadocchio episode shows the feckless knight offending both justice and temperance; he is publicly disgraced and thereupon deprived of his bogus knighthood. Finally, in Book VI, Timias is unjustly slandered by three brothers who ambush him in a way reminiscent of the attack of the foresters in Book III; his wounds require yet another withdrawal.

Spenser intends an allegory of two attachments that contrasts aspiration to true honor with the false pretension to it. The allegory is suggested by Aristotelian theory about the vanity of friendships between ignoble natures, and the tensions in friendships between unequals.[452] The preferment of Braggadocchio by the False Florimell and the rescue of Timias by his *dea*, or "Angell," are contrasting interpretations—ironic and panegyrical—of Angelica's famous choice of the wounded foot-soldier Medoro, in preference to Orlando. We need to recognize the interlocking pattern if we are to fully acknowledge the theme. One then observes that the fanfaronade for the False Florimell, along with Trompart's similar efforts on behalf of his patron, form a parody of the celebration devoted by the poet to the honorable chastity of Belphoebe. Belphoebe, in turn, veils the glory of the queen (II, proem, 5), whom the poet, at the outset of his poem, heralded with "trumpets sterne" and "afflicted stile." In Book V Trompart veils the snowy Florimell (V.iii.17), and Braggadocchio hopes to hear his name sounded in fame's "eternall trompe" (II.iii.38)—but the Trompart that announces the blowhard shares the etymology of his name with the French *tromper* (to deceive). His master is "trumpery," showy but worthless.

452 *Nich. Ethics* VII.vii, and VII.iv.

Single Nature's Double Name

> But Man by number is to manifest
> His single imperfection, and beget
> Like of his like, his Image multipli'd,
> In unity defective, which requires
> Collateral love, and dearest amity.
> (*Paradise Lost* VIII.422–425)

> . . . so ancient is the desire of one another which is implanted in us, reuniting our original nature, making one of two, and healing the state of man.
> (Plato, *Symposium* 191c–d, trans. Jowett)

[i]

The following two essays describe some relations between the central books. Very simple observations demonstrate that a parallelism such as that described for Books II and V also exists for Books III and IV. Of course, a sequel as well as an analogy is often involved here, and it is sometimes merely a matter of emphasis that determines which is which. For example, the third book begins with the flight of Florimell, and ends with the deliverance of Amoret seven months after her abduction by Busirane. The fourth book begins with the wanderings of Amoret, and ends with the deliverance of Florimell seven months after her imprisonment by Proteus. The seventh canto of the earlier book shows Florimell escaping from the hyena-monster and falling into the clutches of Proteus; the same canto of the later book shows Amoret escaping from the savage identified as "greedie Lust" (IV.vii, rubric). Both the monster and the savage resemble the Orco monster of the Italians. Boiardo's Orco is blind, spotted, and sharpscented, and those he pursues escape by sea.[453] In Ariosto, the Orco belongs to Proteus' realm, and elsewhere in the same poem he keeps Norandino's wife in a cave, as Spenser's Lust keeps Aemylia.[454]

The organization of symbols in the two books is also similar. Together the two legends offer a variety of loves and lovers of varying degrees of purity. This range gives Frye occasion to remark that the society of Book III lends itself to a moral stratification: "the true lovers are on top of what

[453] *Orl. Inr.* III.iii.27–50; for this Orc as Polyphemus, see *ibid.*, III.iii.55f.
[454] *O.F.* VII.51, 54; X.100–109; XI.28–48. Spenser's Lust is much closer, however, to the orc of XVII.27ff. (27: Carpathian Sea—Proteus is Carpathian too; 30: tusks; 31: snout, sense of smell; 32: scrip; 33: *awe* of old and young women; 34: herd; 35: cannibalism; 40: he does *not* eat women; 59: wide throat).

might be called a hierarchy of erotic imitations."[455] Belphoebe and her mother Chrysogonee ought to be included in the elite group also. Chaste love is an erotic imitation of virginity, so to speak; conversely, Belphoebe can be thought of as an honorary lover, given her charity to the more susceptible Timias.[456]

Presiding over the hierarchy as a whole is Venus, whom Spenser, adopting the gender of a noted crux in Virgil, calls "Great *God* of men and women" (IV.x.47).[457] Like virginity, chaste love seeks a pure body, the "one flesh" of biblical marriage, or a union of pure spirits. It was not unusual in the Renaissance to associate Aristophanes' myth of the sexes (in Plato's *Symposium*) with the bisexual Adam that rabbinical speculation found hinted at in the Genesis accounts of the creation of man.[458] The corollary idea, that the married couple also forms Aristophanes' androgyne, dovetails with the understanding of Adam's union as the prototype of all marriages. So John Cleveland:

> Adam, till his Rib was lost,
> Had the Sexes thus ingrost,
> When Providence our Sire did cleave,
> And out of *Adam* carved Eve,
> Then did Man 'bout Wedlock treat
> To make his Body up compleat.

[455] *Anatomy of Criticism*, p. 202, on romances that present experience as comprehensible, and take a comprehensive view of it.

[456] For the first steps of this hierarchy, see William Baldwin, *A treatise of Morall Philosophie* (London, 1620), Fol. 115ᵛ: "Chastity and purity of life, consisteth either in sincere virginity, or in faithfull matrimony. The first degree of Chastity, is pure virginity, and the second faithfull matrimony." (Also cited in Hankins, *Source and Meaning*, p. 148.) Belphoebe stands on the "highest staire" of the hierarchy (III.v.54), while Amoret is born "in the second place" (III.vi.4). Cf. also Wilson, *Rhetorique* (facsimile reprint, Gainesville, Fla., 1962), fol. 29, translating Erasmus' epistle: "I would wishe nowe, that thei, whiche exhort yong folke euery where . . . to liue a single life, and to professe virginitie: that thei would bestowe the same labour in setting furth the description of chast and pure wedlocke." Cf. also La Primaudaye's classification of conjunctions in *French Academie*, p. 492, on the marriage of honor, to God, and the marriage of love, "for the preservation of the image of man."

[457] *Aen.* II.632: "the *god* [presumed to be Venus] leads Aeneas down before the retiring flames" of the conflagration of Troy. See n. 468, below.

[458] See Leone Hebraeo, *Philosophy of Love*, the *Dialoghi d'Amore* trans. by Friedeberg-Seeley and Barnes, pp. 343f. (in the Carmella edn., pp. 291f.). For the androgynous Adam see also Origen, *In Gen.*, I.15 (PG, XII, 158); *In Cant. Cant.*, II.11 (PG, XIII, 134); and Philo, *De opificio mundi*, 76; *Quis rerum divinarum heres*, 164. For the Renaissance biblical commentaries, see Arnold Williams, *The Common Expositor* (Chapel Hill, 1948), p. 92, n. 92. The agreement of Moses and Plato on the biform man may also be found in Eusebius, *Praep. Evang.*, XII.xii, p. 585c (in Gifford edn., Tom. III, Pt. 2, p. 633).

> Thus Matrimony speaks but thee
> In a Grave Solemnity:
> For Man and Wife make but one right
> Canonical Hermaphrodite.[459]

Marriage, in turn, is the original of all social bonds, according to La Primaudaye:

> Now because there is no conjunction or communion in any humane societie, wherein that holy bonde, which ought to knitt all men together, and ioyne them one to another, is better declared, that in that whereby man & wife are conjoyned and united, as it were in one selfe same bodie, and in one soule, therefore it pleased God not without cause to beginne this holie societie by that coniounction, which is the bonde and foundation of all the rest, and as it were the spring-head and fountayne of all mankinde.[460]

DuBartas' epithalamium of Adam and Eve universalizes the same conjunction:

> Source of all joyes! sweet Hee-Shee-Coupled-One!
> Thy sacred Birth I never think upon,
> But (ravisht) I admire how God did them
> Make two of One, One of Two again.
> O blessed Bond! O happy marriage!
> Which dost the match 'twixt Christ and us presage!
> O chastest friendship, whose pure flames impart
> Two Soules in one, two Hearts into one Heart![461]

[459] "Upon an Hermaphrodite," ll. 9–18.

[460] *French Academie*, p. 23.

[461] Sylvester trans., I.VI.1062–1069, in A. B. Grosart, ed., *Complete Works of Joshua Sylvester*, vol. I, p. 81. Another summary of our theme may be found in the emblem of Barthelemy Anneu in his *Picta Poesis* (Leiden, 1552), emb. no. 14, "Matrimonii Typus," reproduced in Arthur Henkel and Albrecht Schöne, eds., *Emblemata* (Stuttgart, 1967), cols. 1631f. The picture centers on an elaborate conjugal knot that veils the shameful parts of an embracing hermaphrodite or androgyne; on the one side is the approving horned Moses, who indicated that the married pair would be one flesh. On the other side is a foolish horned satyr, who ridicules the folly of being divided by quarrels. The lovers also form a tree, or stock, bearing fruit by way of the "genital fields" (*genitalibus aruis*) that we have met before. Cf. Spenser, *F.Q.* III.xii.47, 1590 edn.: "Thus doe those louers with sweet counteruayle, / Each other of loues bitter fruit despoile." The making one of two, and the abolition of the distinction between the sexes, is a minor theme of early Christian incorporation sayings: see II Clement 12:2 ("when the Lord was asked by someone when his kingdom would come, he said, When the two will be one, and the outside like the inside, and the male with the female neither male nor female"); Clement of Alexandria, *Strom.*,

The language is conventional, and might also be used for friendship. Helena's description of her girlhood with Hermia, from Shakespeare's marriage-play, has the same theme:

> We Hermia, like two artificial gods,
> Have with our needles created both one flower,
> Both on one sampler, sitting on one cushion,
> Both warbling one song, both in one key;
> As if our hands, our sides, voices, and minds,
> Had been incorporate. So we grew together,
> Like to a double cherry, seeming parted,
> But yet an union in partition;
>
> (*M.N.D.*, III.ii.203–210)

The word "partition" is echoed by the wall of the mechanicals' play (with perhaps an echo of Ephesians 2:14, where it is said that Christ "hathe made of bothe one, and hathe broken the stoppe of the particion wall").

The hermaphrodite is the symbol of the ideal union in Spenser; the juncture it represents is somewhat unique, though a character like Britomart, who does duty for both sexes at the opening of Book IV, also expresses the ideal. The love of Scudamour and Amoret is more typically at an impasse. Below this level of a frustrated ideal, one might postulate a "natural" love, where there would be no impediments. An intimation of this kind of fulfillment is present in the story of Hellenore and the satyrs. A relation of "natural" love is not ordinarily accessible to waking experience, where sexuality does not remain morally neutral, like stimulus and response, but either degrades or elevates. The Squire of Dames, for example, is subject to shame, though apparently not to any great extent. He offers Sir Satyrane a slightly cynical report of his Ariosto-like amours: the only impediments this handsome Don Juan has met have been lack of opportunity and fear of getting caught. The freedom from restraint apparently offered by such uninhibited gratification is somewhat belied by the giantess Argante, for whom the Squire has proved easy prey. The implication may be that the Squire's appetite has turned to less normal forms of satisfaction.

The Squire is fit company for Paridell, who is Spenser's representation of the knowing Ovidian seducer, particularly the adulterer. Paridell has this role in the story of Hellenore and Malbecco, which comes from Ariosto; and a detail from Ovid's letter of Helen—the kisses and signs exchanged by way of the wine—duly appears in Paridell's technique.[462] The

---

III.xcii.2; Hippolytus, *Refut.*, V.vii.15; Gospel of Thomas, 23. The unity of Adam and Eve at Ephesians 5:32 is not as important as Galatians 3:28: "there is neither Jew nor Greek, . . . neither male nor female; for you are all one in Christ Jesus."

[462] Ovid, *Heroides* XVII.79f., 87f.; *Ars Amat.* I.575f.; *Amores* I.iv.29–32; see also Lucian, *True History* II.25, and a similar device in Achilles Tatius, II.9. Cf. *As You*

first book of Ovid's *Art of Love* teaches the lover the arts of the pleader and flatterer, the use of Bacchus or wine, prayer to the god of night, and the use of tears and kisses, and it mentions Troy as a model of broken resistance. We have seen these arts formally described at the Castle of Malecasta.[463] Ovid illustrates the use of wine by retailing the story of the abandoned Ariadne who was taken up by the Bacchic satyrs;[464] this reminds us of Hellenore's eventual home, as it reminded us of Una's woodland refuge.

Lower levels of passion are occupied by the churls and the possessive old men. Then come the monsters already mentioned. The bottom level, Frye suggests, belongs to Argante and Ollyphant. Like Amoret and Belphoebe, the giants are twins. They are conceived in sin—the offspring of an incestuous union of mother and son. United in the womb, they too manifest the "one flesh" of an ideal union. Plutarch attributes such a birth to Isis and Osiris; like Spenser's Venus, Isis is also said to be bisexual and to represent nature.[465] Both giant and giantess are given to "bestiality," and are thus a kind of personified Sodom and Gomorrah.

In accordance with the "structure of recurrence" at the center of *The Faerie Queene*, much of this classification continues to obtain in the context of friendship; the capacity to form an ideal concord replaces degrees of purity as the classifying criterion. True friends, with their "one soul in bodies twain," take their place at the top of the hierarchy. So do members of the "marriage *quaternio*," which is discussed below. Next come unions based on natural affinity: the marriage of the Thames and Medway is the obvious example. Family love, and also the sympathy between Timias and the

---

Like It, III.v.72f.: "I pray you do not fall in love with me, / For I am falser than vows made in wine."

[463] *Ars Amat.* I. *Flattery*: 439, 445, 480, 619; *tears*: 659; *prayers*: 440, 442, 735; *kisses*: 663; *Troy*: 363. Ovidian equivalents for Spenser's characters are: Gardante: 109 (*Respiciunt, oculisque notant*), 499f.; Parlante: 143, 569, 607; Jocante: 238; Basciomani: 663; Bacchante: 189, 233 (*Bacchi*), 237, 244 (*Venus in vinis ignis in igne fuit*), 523; Noctante: 246, 735. Spenser does not mention touching, 606 (*pede tange pedem*, "footsies"), which is reserved for the bedroom episode: Malecasta is "Of euery finest fingers touch affrayd," and Britomart and Redcrosse join "foot to foot" (III.i.61, 66).

[464] *Ars Amat.* I.525–564. See Chap. II, n. 464 with text.

[465] *De Iside* 12, *Moralia* 356A, for the birth mystery. For Isis as "the female principle of nature," *De Iside* 53; for the lunar Isis as "generation" and "the mother of the world," having a nature both male and female, *De Iside* 43. *Typhoeus* being the father of the twins is a further hint of an Egyptian mythography here. The father apparently raped his mother the earth, with which we may compare the generation of the Typhonic Orgoglio at I.vii.9. The monstrosity of a mother's congress with a son is a theme of the Phaedra-Pasiphae complex, and Argante's ultimate bestiality is Pasiphaean: compare the "natiue flesh" of III.ii.41 with III.vii.49. The evidence that Ollyphant's bestiality is homosexual is circumstantial: see "The Analogy of Natural Plenitude," sec. i, below.

dove, might be placed here too. Further down the scale is the relation of Braggadocchio and the False Florimell—the parvenus provide a kind of parody of natural affinity. Then there are the ignoble partnerships based on a temporary identity of selfish interests: Paridell is again a member of such a combination, with Blandamour. (Together they form a "paramour.")[466] With their consorts at the opening of Book IV, Paridell and Blandamour constitute a kind of parody of the marriage quaternio. The False Florimell, in her conjunction with Paridell here, is that "idol" Paris brought home to Troy. Strictly antisocial behaviour is more properly the subject of the last two books; it is represented in the action of Book IV by Sclaunder and Ate.

[ii]

Before describing the parallels in the disposition of the central books, we may enlarge somewhat on the symbolism. Three symbols for the union of friends and lovers may be mentioned: the marriage quaternio, the comity of Triamond and his brothers, and the hermaphrodite. Each of the symbols expresses love's power to unite and to multiply: to consolidate a community, and to expand one. This creative function of love determines Spenser's choice of a hermaphroditic Venus to receive the homage of the Lucretian hymn. The androgyny of the gods is a well-known and often-remarked feature of late classical religiosity, probably not unrelated to other syncretistic phenomena. A notable example, for our purposes, is found in the Hermetic treatise known as the *Asclepius*. Apropos the mystery of the eternal production of the world, the treatise explains that God contains both sexes. Hence the maintenance of the world with all its contents. Not only God, but all beings are filled by the fecundity of the sexes:

> . . . for take away the fecundity of all things which have being, and it will be impossible for them to be what they always are. . . . For I say that the world contains nature in itself and conserves all that is born. For by procreation each thing is full of the sexes and the conjunction of each of them; or—what is more true—there exists a unity past understanding which you can rightly call either Cupid or Venus or both.[467]

Spenser's Nature, it is hinted by the description in the Mutabilitie cantos, is also androgynous. Like the Nature of the Orphic *Hymn* (IX), she would be both father and mother of all.

The mythological compendiums of Spenser's own time derived their

---

[466] See IV.i.36, "Her fayned Paramour" (Paridell's advance upon Britomart and Amoret at the instigation of Blandamour); III.x.10 (Paris as Paramour); IV.v.8, 24 (aspirants to False Florimell as her paramours); III.ii.45, "idle *Paramoure*" (Narcissus, but also hints of idle Paridell as the idolatrous lover of the image of Helen).

[467] *Asclepius*, xx seq., in *Corpus Hermeticum*, ed. A. D. Nock and trans. A.-J. Festugière (Paris, 1945), vol. 2, pp. 321f.

accounts of an androgynous Venus from Servius' note on Virgil's masculine goddess (just mentioned), and from Macrobius' citations on the Cyprian bearded Venus who was both male and female.[468] Cartari explains that the Roman Venus was bearded, in order that this goddess should have the insignia of man and woman, as the one to whom pertained "the universal generation of animals: and from the middle, above, she was made in the form of a man, and the remainder, below, was of a woman."[469] Giraldus cites Suidas for the bearded statue: "and to the same goddess [the Roman votresses] also affixed a beard, so that the Goddess had masculine and femine equipment, since she was believed to be in charge of all generation."[470] Giraldus also cites Eusebius' *Preparation for the Gospel*, a popular source among the learned: "her fruitful and creative parts are covered, because they are the cause of seed and nourishment."[471] The later allegory of Alexander Ross is in the same vein: "An Hermaphrodite also may be called *Venus barbarata*: besides, in love there is both action and suffering, neither can there be procreation, but when the male and female are united in one."[472]

It is not surprising, then, that Spenser makes his Venus hermaphroditic, "For *Venus* selfe doth soly couples seeme" (*Colin Clovt*, 810). In embracing, the reunited Scudamour and Amoret also form a hermaphrodite. The link between the Temple of Venus and the hermaphrodite must ultimately depend upon those texts that make Hermes and Aphrodite share in the patronage of marriage.[473] The Spenserian symbolism, as has been pointed out, finds a precedent in the poet Deschampes, who places a "most majestic lord" in a pleasance resorted to by lovers:

> I saw there people I did not know
> Making their plea to God on their knees
> Demanding that their prayer be heard
> And that he send his grace to them
> And his love to this earthly place.

[468] Servius, *ad Aen.* II.632; Macrobius, *Saturnalia*, III.viii.1–3. See also Plato, *Symposium* 181c: "the younger Aphrodite, whose nature partakes of both male and female"; and cf. the Amathusian Venus of Catullus, LXVIII.51: she is "duplex."

[469] *Le Imagini, edn. cit.*, pp. 401, 403.

[470] *Hist. Deorum*, Syntag. XIII, *sub* "Venus babarata," in *Op. om.*, I, col. 394G–395C; both Giraldus and Cartari cite an account in Suidas of a Roman Venus with a beard and comb. Giraldus also cites a "Venus biformis" from Julius Firmicus [Maternus].

[471] *Praep. Evang.*, III.xi, p. 114b–c (Gifford edn. and trans., vol. 3, p. 125); Giraldus, *Hist. Deorum*, Syntag. XIII, in *Op. om.*, I, col. 395B.

[472] *Mystagogvs Poeticvs, or the Muses Interpreter*, 2nd edn. (London, 1648), *sub* "Hermaphrodite."

[473] Plutarch, *Conjugalia praecepta*, Pref., *Moralia* 138D, cited in Cartari, *Le Imagini*, p. 396; Julian, *Orat.* V.1790, on "Hermes Epaphroditus": "through Hermes and Aphrodite are invoked all generated things everywhere."

Then the better to see him convening
I hid under a hawthorne.
And I saw that those gods had given to them
A lord and a lady in one union.
Hermaphrodite declines him.
And the gods had also determined him
Half man and half woman,
And said to them: "This love inclines
To both that I have made you—
The one and the other will form you,
And without him no man can have
Sense or good doctrine,
Valor, honor, nor discipline,
Or will ever be perfect
In the renown which this one will have:
Now guard those to whom he is inclined."[474]

Deschampes' spelling of his name, Hermofondricus, does not encourage one to believe that the poet understood the relation of the love-god to Aphrodite, however. Spenser, on the other hand, refers Scudamour and Amoret to "that faire Hermaphrodite, / Which that rich Romane of white marble wrought, / And in his costly Bath causd to bee site" (III.xii.46, 1590 edn.). The *Greek Anthology* contains an epigram that may explain the site: "To men I am Hermes, but to women appear to be Aphrodite, and I bear the tokens of both my parents. Therefore not inappropriately they put me, the Hermaphrodite, the child of ambiguous sex, in a bath for both sexes."[475] Even this last piece of statuary in the Busirane cantos proves to have an epigram attaching to it.

A relative of the *Anthology* poem among the epigrams of Ausonius may have contributed to Spenser's notion that the bath was Roman, as well as have supported his identification of the Hermaphrodite with Venus: "By Mercury begotten, conceived by Cytherea, Hermaphroditus, compound alike in name as in body, combining either sex, but not complete in either; having the power of neither love of an ambiguous Venus."[476] Ausonius also has an epigram on the paradoxical one flesh of Hermaphroditus and the possible pleasures of being two in one.[477] The story of Salamicis is told in Ovid, and Ovid is probably the source of the word play, in Ausonius' Latin, on *neutro* and *utroque*. Ovid's lines are:

[474] *Ille Lay: Le Lay Amoureux,* ll. 109ff., in Eustace Deschampes, *Oeuvres Compketes,* Société des Anciens Textes François (Paris, 1880), vol. 2, pp. 196f. This text is cited by E. B. Fowler, *Spenser and the Courts of Love,* p. 60.

[475] *Gr. Anth.* IX.783, trans. by W. R. Paton, ed., Loeb *Lyra Graeca,* vol. 3, p. 423.

[476] *Epig.* CII, "De Hermaphrodito et eius Natura."

[477] *Epig.* CIII, "De Coniunctione Salmacis cum Hermaphrodito."

nec duo sunt forma duplex, nec femina dici
nec puer ut possit, neutrumque et utrumque videntur

They were no longer the duplex form of two, nor could either one be
called woman or man; they seemed neither and both

(*Metam.* IV.378–379)

Ovid also describes Hermaphroditus as having become a whole body; he
is one "*amborum nomen habenti*" (having the names of both) (IV.384).
Spenser says that Venus "hath both kinds in one, / Both male and female,
both vnder one name" (IV.x.41), and hence his lovers' names also manifest
their impending mutualization: Scudamoret, Britomartegall, Osirisis, Pari-
dellenore, Thamedway, and, in Book VI, Claribellamour. The rivers
Thame and Isis have also joined to produce Thamis, their offspring, which
extends the symbolism into a second generation. The names, in the idiom
of Sylvester's DuBartas, foresee the lovers' incorporation into "Hee-Shee
Coupled Ones."

As said before, the union of lovers is an ideal, as well as a desire, and
therefore it is not without frustrations. The hermaphrodite symbol is often
slightly ironic, as in Shakespeare's *Phoenix and the Turtle*, which belongs
to this tradition. In Ovid's vein, the compounded birds were to themselves
"yet either neither," and for them "the self was not the same." The latter
phrase recalls the phoenix of Lactantius:

> Happy being, whether male or female or neither one
> nor the other, who knows nothing of the bonds of Venus.
> His Venus is death, in death alone is pleasure. . . .
> He is he and not he, the same and not the same. . . .[478]

To A. Bartlett Giamatti I owe the observation that such a virginal union
seems to be offered to Olindo and Sophronia in the second book of Tasso's
Jerusalem Delivered. The two Christians are tied back to back to the stake,
and they are also engaged to be married. The martyrs therefore form an
extroverted version of a union that would properly be reversed. In Plato's
Symposium, Aristophanes fables that the sexes were created by the severing
of the similarly misallied androgyne. Olindo requests that, so long as they
must burn together, he and Sophronia also be allowed to face one another.
Tasso works the concettist changes on this rather Petrarchan impasse, including the one alluded to below that has Cupid and Death exchange arrows. The divisive and consuming love of Scudamour and Amoret at the

---

[478] *Carmen de ave phoenixe*, ll. 161–165, 169: note "Femina seu mas sit neutrum
seu sit utrumque." Also cp. the phoenix of Tertullian in *De resurrect. carnis*, xiii:
"another, yet the same" (PL, II, 857B).

House of Busirane obeys similar principles. It is a union in which there is always a threat of extinction, and, as in Tasso, the lovers are delivered through the intervention of an armed virgin.

Improbable as it might at first seem, Aristophanes' ironic myth also haunts the opening episode of Book III, especially in the form of the analogy with Genesis mentioned above. First, when Malecasta beds down with Britomart, it is "by her side." Britomart, awakening from her slumber, "chaungd her weary side" (III.i.61), a change that might suggest both the reversibility of Britomart's sex role, and that realignment necessary to truly integrate the Aristophanic androgyne. "Feeling one close couched by her side" (III.i.62), the maid leaps from the "filed" bed, and is about to "gride" her sleeping partner—who duly faints, like Duessa at the impending alienation of Redcrosse. The seemingly innocent word "side" continues to echo in the remainder of the episode: Britomart stands off from Malecasta, "on th'other side," and then Gardante's arrow is seen "to gore her side" (III.i.63, 65). Thus opens that wound in human nature, or severance of sides, which Britomart herself now experiences, and which will only close at the close of the legend, in the symbol of the embracing lovers. And yet this conclusion in an honorable union is provided for, if only momentarily, even at the end of the first canto: Britomart unites with Redcrosse, "Ay ioyning foot to foot, and side to side."

[iii]

Like the Vision of Dame Kind, the Vision of Agape is multiple, but it is a multiplicity of persons; like the Vision of Eros, it involves human persons only; like the Vision of God it is of a mutual relation; but unlike any of the others, this relation is a relation between equals.

(W. H. Auden, in *The Protestant Mystics*, introduction, sec. V; ed. Anne Freemantle, Boston, 1964)

Since friendship strives by mutual consent of the lovers to cultivate the Soul through virtue, it is apparently nothing but a perfect concordance of two Souls in the worship of God. Those who worship God with a pious mind, however, are loved by God. Therefore there are not two friends only, but always necessarily three, two human beings and one God. . . . He unites us into one; He is the indissoluble bond and perpetual guardian of friendship.

(Ficino, *Epistolae*, Lib. I, "Amicitia illa stabilis, quae à Deo constatur," in *Op. om.*, I-1, p. 634, trans. P. O. Kristeller)

A second symbol of the same general type as the hermaphrodite provides the *donnée* for the allegory of Priamond, Diamond, and Triamond, Agape's triplets. The fiction carries out the theme of friendship as a unity of souls; Spenser's treatment proceeds to incorporate a plurality of souls in a single body. (Presumably he ignores Aristotle's apt remark in the *Politics* that such a conception as Aristophanes' hermaphrodite tends to be rather watery when extended beyond two persons.)[479] Like Argante and Ollyphant, the three brothers shared one womb. Owing to a promise that Agape extracts from the Fates, their loving souls are rejoined, at death, to the body of the third brother. This transfusion twice renews Triamond's life in the third combat with Camballo.

A similar symbol of friendship existed in the story of Castor and Pollux, the Twins of Jove who share one soul between them, "redeemed by an alternate death," as Virgil says.[480] Accordingly the Twins are the patron deities of fraternal love. Eratosthenes tells us that it was through fraternal love that they conquered all men.[481] For Spenser's version of this idea, Nelson has proposed a source in Virgil's Erulus, "whom at his birth his mother Feronia had given (awful to tell!) three lives with threefold armour to wear—thrice had he to be laid low in death."[482] Erulus is mentioned by King Evander as a conquest of his youth. Servius remarks that the old king tells the story in the way of self-justification, to hint at his own equivalence with the Hercules who killed Geryon. On his return from the west, Hercules killed Cacus on Evander's behalf. Aeneas is being asked to make a third in this illustrious company, by undertaking Evander's cause against the Latin princes. Servius further explains that the three souls of Erulus are the physical, the fiery, and the intellectual souls. Spenser's legend suggests that love survives, not only the death of the other

[479] *Politics* II.i.16f. (1262b).

[480] *Aen.* VI.121. We may regard the self-subjugation required by friendship as creating the conditions for Axel Olrik's "Law of Two": "whenever two people appear in the same role," according to this rule of folk narrative, "both are depicted as being small and weak. In this type of close association, two people can evade the Law of Contrast and become subjugated instead to the *Law of Twins*. . . . Beings of subordinate rank appear in duplicate: two Dioscuri are messengers of Zeus. . . . If, however, the twins are elevated to major roles, then they will be pitted against one another. This may be illustrated by the myths of the Dioscuri. One is bright and one is gloomy; one immortal and the other mortal. They fight over the same woman and eventually kill each other." The story, however, has in Spenser added a third "twin," according to Olrik's *Law of Repetition*: "The repetition is almost always tied to the number three. . . . Nothing distinguishes the great bulk of folk narrative from modern literature and from reality as much as does the number three." (Quotes taken from the trans. of "Epische Gesetze der Volksdichtung," by Jeanne P. Steager, in Alan Dundes, ed., *The Study of Folklore*, Englewood Cliffs, N.J., 1965, pp. 133, 135f.)

[481] Eratosthenes Cyrrenaei, *Catasterismi* 10, "Gemini," in Gale, *Opuscula Mythologica*, p. 106.

[482] *Poetry of Edmund Spenser*, p. 244. Trans. of *Aen.* VIII.564ff. taken from Fairclough, ed., Loeb *Virgil*, vol. 2, p. 99.

self, but also the death of the nutritive and animal souls: the love of the intellectual soul, like the intellectual soul itself, is immortal.

Geryon proves to be an equally suggestive source. Silius Italicus, for example, tells us that Geryon was furnished with *tres animae*: "Never did earth see another man whom a single death could not destroy—for whom the stern Sisters spun a third lease of life when the thread had twice been snapped" (*Punica* I.278–282). The details of the Fates and the souls is very close to Spenser. At Spenser's end of an honored tradition, Comes reports: "It is said that Geryon when ruling Spain had three sons, remarkable for strength and skill in warfare, who were accustomed to protect the reign of their father by counsel and concord."[483] This information probably derives from Diodorus Siculus.[484] Similarly, Arrianus explains Geryon as three friends acting in concert.[485] In the *Vewe*, Spenser mentions Lucian's *Toxarius*, a collection of friendship novelle that concludes on just such an example: friends have two of everything, "for the union of two or three friends is like the pictures of Geryon that artists exhibit—a man with six hands and three heads."[486] To Lucian, "Geryon was three persons acting together in all things, as is right if they really are friends." Renaissance sources come even closer to Spenser's allegory. In his essay on Hercules, Giraldus says that Geryon is fashioned as triple-bodied, "quod unanimes atque concordes tres essent fratres."[487] The *Dictionary* of Stephanus informs us that Geryon is credited with three bodies, "because there were three brothers of the same name, living in such concord of soul, that they were thought to be ruled by one soul." The explanation probably comes from the *Adagia* of Erasmus, who subjoins it to his description of *Tryceps Geryon* as proverbial for *asperitas*.[488] Erasmus' report, in turn, echoes the late classical historian Justinus, who is also quoted in Salutati's chapter on this labor of Hercules.[489] Erasmus would probably be the source of Alciati's emblem, "Concordia Insuperabilis," for Erasmus' other Geryon

[483] *Mythol.*, VII.i, "De Hercule," *edn. cit.*, p. 681. Geryon is an alliance of three brothers in the extended Hercules legend presented in William Warner, *Albion's England*, II.viii.

[484] Diod. Sic., *Bibl.* IV.xvii.1f.

[485] *Hist.* II.xvi.2–6.

[486] *Toxarius* 62; Spenser, *Vewe*, 1805f. Cf. also Eunapius on the mutuality of the impoverished friends Prohaeresius and Hephaestion, who had only one cloak between them: "Their only resource therefore was to be two men in one, just as the myths say that Geryon was made up of three bodies; so these students were two men in one" (*Lives of the Philosophers* 487, trans. W. C. Wright, ed., Loeb *Philostratus and Eunapius*, pp. 485, 487).

[487] *Herculis Vita*, on *Op. om.*, I, col. 580A–B.

[488] Stephanus, *Dictionarium historicum . . . poeticum, sub* "Geryon"; Erasmus, *Adagia, sub* ASPERITAS, "Tryceps Geryon" (edn. of Frankfurt, 1646), p. 74.

[489] *Hist.* XLIV.iv.6; Salutati, *De Laboribus Herculis*, III.xvii, ed. B. L. Ullman (Zurich, 1951), p. 327.

was indomitable. Alciati's legend reads, "Among three brothers was such concord, along with mutual justice and one love, that unconquered they held ample reigns by means of human strength, being called by one name, Geryon."[490] The emblem appears in the famous "Seasons" tapestry at Hatfield, and is also recorded in Ripa's *Iconology*.[491] Sabinus' Renaissance Ovid explains Geryon's triplicity as either three brothers or three souls;[492] Landino also mentions the allegory of the three souls.[493] Finally, the *Etymologies* of Isidore tell us that Geryon is reported to have had a triple form, because "there were three brothers of such harmonious spirit that it was, as it were, one soul in three bodies."[494] In Spenser's own words, "never discord did amongst them fall" (IV.ii.54):

> These three did loue each other dearely well,
> And with so firme affection were allyde,
> As if but one soule in them all did dwell,
> Which did her powre into three parts diuyde;
>
> (IV.ii.43)

A trace of the story of the three brothers is found in Boiardo, where a few stanzas sketch the ancestry of Agramante.[495] Ultimately Agramante is derived from Alexander, who when he died left Elidonia pregnant. The mother abandons herself to a pilotless boat that lands on the Barbary coast. Here she gives birth to three sons—Tripoli is named after them. The sons prove inseparable, and in time they attract all to their leadership by virtue of their courteous nature and their generosity. Furnished by the heavens with such valor that they are able to grasp the rule of all the neighborhood, they nonetheless conquer chiefly through the attraction of their goodness. Two of the brothers die without heirs, leaving the third to reign over all of Africa. As the parallels might suggest, the appeal of this kind of story

---

[490] Emb. XL, "Concordia insuperabilis," *edn. cit.*, pp. 178–180, first cited for the three brothers by Roche, *Kindly Flame*, pp. 17f. The material here is partly duplicated in Aptekar, *Icons of Justice* (New York, 1969), pp. 145–149 (my project was done independently). Mignault on Alciati cites the proverbial sons of Molione, originally from *Iliad* XI.708, whose bodies were described as grown together in Plutarch, *Brotherly Love* I (*Moralia* 478A) and Apollodorus, *Bibl.* II.vii.2. Cf. Gregory Nazianzen, *Panegyric on St. Basil*, xxii (NPNF, 2nd Series, vol. 7, pp. 402f.), cited in Erasmus, *Adagia, sub* DIGNITATIS EXCELLENTIA, "Molones" (Frankfurt edn. of 1646), p. 192.

[491] Cesar Ripa, *Della novissima Iconologia* (Padua, 1625), *sub* "Concordia militaire," p. 115.

[492] Georg Sabini, marginalia on *Metam.* IX.184, in *P. Ovidii Metamorphosis, seu fabulae poeticae: earumque interpretatio* (Frankfurt, 1593), p. 315.

[493] *Quaestiones Camuldulenses . . . In P. Virgilii Maronis allegorias. liber tertius . . . quartus* (Venice, n.d.), Sig. niij^v.

[494] *Etymol.*, XI.iii.28 (PL, LXXXII, 422).

[495] *Orl. Inn.* II.i.6–14.

THE CONJUGATION OF THE WORLD

is popular; the triple fellowship of the noble-minded and the courageous wins hearts as well as victories. We are not far from the Geryon friendship myth in a story like *The Three Musketeers*, whose famous motto in fact appears to be one further manifestation of the emblem tradition of *Concord Insuperabilis* as Fraternité.

The allegory of Geryon as "three souls," found above in Servius, Isidore, Landino, and Sabinus' Ovid, forms a strong minority report on the meaning of the myth. Such an interpretation has something in common with the myth of Castor and Pollux, and also with primitive theories about the distribution of the life-stuff. Lévi-Strauss draws attention to a myth of the Winnebagos reported by Paul Radin, which he suggests is to be explained by the following hypothesis:

> Every individual is entitled to a specific quota of years of life and experience. If a person dies before his time, his relatives can ask the spirits to distribute among them what he has failed to utilize. But there is more in this theory than meets the eye. The unspent life-span given up by the hero, when he lets himself be killed by his enemies, will be added to the capital of life, set up in trust for the group. Nevertheless, his act of dedication is not entirely without personal profit: by becoming a hero, an individual makes a choice, he exchanges a full life-span for a shortened one, but while the full life-span is unique, granted once and for all, the shortened one appears as a kind of lease taken on eternity. That is, by giving up one full life, an indefinite succession of half-lives is gained.[496]

Agape's request, then, is not unlike the idea here; the heroically short life is extended in a trust for the group on whose behalf it is sacrificed.

The Scholastic doctrine of the three souls in the generation of an individual bears a curious analogy to this process. The first and the second souls are drawn into the third soul, which, being the rational soul, is immortal:

> ... when a more perfect form supervenes the previous form is corrupted: yet so that the supervening form contains the perfection of the previous form, and something in addition. . . . We concluded therefore that the intellectual soul is created by God at the end of human generation, and

---

[496] "Four Winnebago Myths: A Structural Sketch," reprint in *Myth and Cosmos*, ed. John Middleton (Garden City, N.Y., 1967), p. 16; citing Paul Radin, *The Culture of the Winnebago*: as described by themselves, Special Publications of the Bollingen Foundation, No. 1 (Bloomington, Indiana, 1949), p. 41, entry no. 32. Lévi-Strauss has proceeded upon suggestive, but comparatively slim evidence.

this soul is at the same time sensitive and nutritive, for the preexisting forms have been corrupted.[497]

The assimilation of the powers of the sensitive and nutritive souls to the incorruptible soul means, according to Aquinas, that "the intellectual soul contains virtually whatever belongs to the sensitive soul of brute animals, and to the nutritive soul of plants," both of which it supplants; it does not, however, acquire the corruptibility of the lesser souls.[498] Thus the appropriateness to Spenser of the physical allegory reported in Melanchthon, from the proemium of Pontano's *Urania*:

> Poets [Pontano says], who first writing of the nature of things fabulously, so to speak, according to Peter Bembo treat Geryon, a certain ruler in the Spanish Ocean, as three souls having even three bodies; and this *tribus* to have been a usage: they intended to teach by these wonder-causing words that the genus of the body is triplex, even as the genus of the soul is triplex. Since there is one genus of the body proper to trees and herbs, and it is called that from vegetation and the sole sustenance and vegetable nutrition of the body itself. . . .[499]

And so forth, through the other two bodies or souls. According to Dante, "When Lachesis has no more thread" (*Purg.* XXV.79), that is, at death, the intellectual soul carries off from the body the faculties of the animal and vegetable souls. Thus Agape, in procuring the union of her three sons from the Fates, obtains for them something very like the immortality of the soul.

In her solicitation of the Fates, Agape makes them the allies of her maternity, as it were, for it is during pregnancy that the vegetal and sensitive souls of the unborn child are endowed with the higher soul. Agape is herself a "Fay," and this is emphasized. Spenser probably associated the fays with the Fates because of the three fays that come before Demogorgon at the opening of Ariosto's *Cinque Canti*. In making the Fates more of her mind, Agape turns them back from their function of drawing out and cutting the "thrids" of life, to their function in relation to the primordial Demogorgon. We may quote Boccaccio:

[497] *Summa Theol.*, Pt. I, q.118, art.2, resp. ad obj.2.

[498] *Summa Theol.*, Pt. I, q.76, art.3. The second brother receives his soul *through traduction* (IV.iii.13), a semi-technical terminology, for which see Augustine, *De Gen. ad Lit.*, X.iii and xxiv. We may compare Sir John Davies, *Nosce Teipsum*, in Bullett, ed., *Silver Poets of the Sixteenth Century*, p. 363, where Davies reproves the belief of the old fathers in the soul's having taken its beginning *ex traduce*, from other souls.

[499] *Ennaratio Libri IX Metamorphoseon Ovidii*, in *Opera*, ed. Bretschneider and Bindseil, vol. 19, cols. 593f.

I think the fiction that the Fates are produced in the same parturition and are given as attendant to the brother [i.e., Demogorgon], is to be understood [to mean that] as he procreates or begets, he nourishes, and finally he draws out by birth a nature extended by means of their law. These are the three offices of the three Fates.[500]

Begetting, nourishing, and giving birth are also the three productive offices of Agape herself.[501]

They are also her metaphorical offices. Ficino, for example, says that the angel of the heaven of Venus, the third heaven, fosters charity in worthy men. The derivation is complex:

Charity, I say, [fostered] by the threefold supercelestial heaven, in the third heaven and the angel of it, as the influence in our soul. This, if in fact the holy Spirit of God first brands it on the Seraphim. Secondly, these chiefly join their mystery and allegiance to the Principalities. Those ruling the third sphere ascend to Venus there, where the charity infused in you by God is continually nourished, increased, and perfected [alitur, adolescit, atque perficitur].[502]

The pseudo-Dionysian machinery aside, one can see that Ficino thinks of charity's operation as involving a threefold sequence, or a threefold transfer of power from the supercelestial, to the celestial, to the psychical worlds.

In prevailing upon the Fates, and in obtaining secret benefits for her sons, Agape almost seems to illustrate the "three-fold advantage" and the "harmonious friendship of the gods" that are described by Iamblichos as the things gained by prayer:

. . . the first kind of prayer is that which brings [God and man] together, since it brings about the association with the divine and gives us knowledge thereof. The second establishes a bond of fellowship founded upon like-mindedness and calls down the gifts sent by the gods, which arrive before we can ask for them and perfect our efforts even without our knowledge. The third and most perfect form finally seals

---

[500] G.D.G., I.iv; Romano edn., vol. 1, p. 23. The Fates are the three dimensions of time at G.D.G., I.v, p. 27. For the seniority of Demogorgon to all the fays, see also Boiardo, Orl. Inn. II.xiii.26–29. For the etymological equation Fatum, Fay, Faerie, see Antonio Panizzi's introduction to his edn. of Boiardo and Ariosto (London, 1830–1834), vol. 1, pp. 13f.

[501] Somewhat similarly, Sir John Davies says that the three kinds of soul are answerable to three kinds of life: pre-existence in the womb (vegetative soul); earthly life (animal soul); and eternal life (rational soul). (Nosce Teipsum, in Bullett, ed., Silver Poets of the Sixteenth Century, p. 400.)

[502] De Raptu Pauli, in E. Garin, ed., Prosatori Latini del Quattrocento (Milan, 1952), p. 934.

the secret union, which hands over every decision privately to the gods and leaves our souls completely at rest in them.[503]

Iamblichos further explains that the three stages have to do with illumination, fellowship in a common task, and "the state of being filled with the [divine] fire." It is an analogous "three-fold advantage" that Agape secures from the Fates.

Agape is not, as might at first be supposed, a mistake for Philia. The analogy between the divine love and brotherly feeling is a New Testament commonplace, and Agape brings up her children to love one another, even as she has loved them. The ecclesiastical community is a fellowship; its members are urged "to love brotherly without faining" (I Peter 1:22), and to forgive and forebear mutually on the Lord's model (Colossians 3:13). Spenser's allegory derives some of its meaning from Paul's exhortation:

> And aboue all these things put on loue [*agape*], which is the bonde of perfectnes [*telieotes*]. and let the peace of God rule in your hearts, to the which ye are called in one bodie, and be ye amiable [*eucharistos*].
> (Col. 3:14-15, Geneva Bible)

In the course of illustrating the trinitarian nature of love, Augustine turns to that brotherly love in which the Apostle placed the perfection of righteousness (I John 2:10):

> . . . this same brotherly love itself . . . is set forth by so great authority, not only to be from God, but also to be God. When, therefore, we love our brother from love, we love our brother from God; neither can it be that we do not love above all else that same love by which we love our brother: whence it may be gathered that these two commandments cannot exist unless interchangeably. For since "God is love," he who loves love certainly loves God; but he must needs love love, who loves his brother.[504]

Ficino defines charity as the religious sentiment embracing one's fellow men as brothers for the sake of God and of celestial beatitude, and expressing itself concretely in active assistance to one's neighbour.[505] La

[503] *De Mysteriis*, V.26, as trans. by R. M. Grant, ed., *Hellenistic Religions* (Bloomington, Ind., 1953), p. 175. For the Latin trans. by Ficino, see *Op. om.*, II-2, p. 1908ff.
[504] *De Trinitate*, VIII.viii.12, in PL, XLII, 958; trans. from NPNF, 1st Series, vol. 3, p. 123. The reading of the three brothers that follows owes some of its emphases to Wind, *Pagan Mysteries*, pp. 41f., 209f., 241-255; I differ in taking Spenser's allegory to be more interesting than Wind supposes.
[505] So Kristeller, *The Philosophy of Marsilio Ficino* (New York, 1953), p. 277. Cf.

Primaudaye speaks similarly in his discussion of the "principall cause and end of all true friendship": "First we say with *Socrates*, that true friendship cannot be framed but by the helpe and grace of God, who draweth like to the love of his like: that everie perfect friendship is to bee linked with the bond of charitie, and ought to be referred to God, as to our soveraigne Good and cheefest friend."[506] Further, "Friendship ought to be free, as charitie is, from whence he hath his beginning."[507] Milton uses the word charity in this way in his salute to wedded love, through which "Relations dear, and all the Charities / Of Father, Son, and Brother first were known" (*Par. Lost* IV.756f.).

The three-ness of Agape's progeny might also suggest that love is trinitarian. Paul says that *agape* is the "bond of perfection," and the Neo-Platonic–Pythagorean symbolism of the number three also makes it a kind of bond of perfection. According to Porphyry's *Life of Pythagoras*, the Pythagoreans taught that forms endowed with a beginning, a middle, and an "end"—a perfecting—ought to be attributed to the ternary number: anything perfect and complete, i.e., produced, having a middle, and being self-joined, had its principle in the ternary.[508] The same author, in his *Commentary* on Euclid's first book, reports the productive virtues of triangles in Pythagorean thought: they "bring into unity things that are in every way divided and changeable," because they bring their lines together "and provide them an imported fellowship and contact with one another."[509] Thus to the Pythagoreanism of metempsychosis, the episode adds the Pythagorean doctrine of the perfection belonging to the triad. Ficino, whom we have quoted on the three realms through which love

---

Baldwin, *Treatise*, III.iii (London, 1620), fol. 79ᵛ: "Friendship is none other thing, but a perfect consent of all things, appertaining as well to God as to man, with benevolence and Charitie."

[506] *French Academie* (London, 1586), p. 138.

[507] *Ibid.*, p. 142.

[508] *De Vita Pythagore*, trans. into Latin by Hieron. Wolfe (Cambridge, 1655), publ. with Epectitus as *Stoici Philosophi*; pp. 202–204. Cf. Aristotle, *De Caelo* I, 268a, for the same Pythagoreanism. Similarly Proclus, *Plat. Theol. Libri VI*, IV.xvi, in Aemilius Portus' edn. and trans. (Hamburg, 1618), p. 219, on the triple nature and source of a perfected unity that *abides, turns*, and *gathers*: three perfections are the source of unity, or pre-exist it, and the thing-perfecting Trinity is an image of the perfected Trinity of the One. *Teliotes* is thus equated with *triadic* conceptualization: "perfection is triplex, the parts before, from the parts, and in the parts."

[509] Glenn R. Morrow, trans., *A Commentary on the First Book of Euclid's Elements* (Princeton, 1970), Definitions xxiv–xxix (166), pp. 131f.

descends, also thinks of love as observing a circular progression through efflux, retroversion, and a return to inherence. One of Ficino's followers describes this progression:

> We say that God is the beginning, the middle and the end. By "begin-ning" we mean that everything stems from Him; "middle" signifies that everything turns towards Him; and "end" means that everything is do-nated by Him for the sake of ultimate perfection, which consists in union with Him. This much had already been hinted by the Pythago-reans when they said that the Trinity is the measure of all things.

Proclus, in his *Commentary on the Timaeus* (83.265), says that "There are three sorts of 'wholes'—the first, anterior to the parts; the second, composed of the parts; the third, knitting into one stuff the parts and the whole." Such a progression is necessarily observed by the story of the conception, fraternity, and amalgamation of the three brothers: Aristotle's *Poetics* (chap. vii) asserts that the poet's fable, or plot, if it is a com-plete thing or whole, "is what has a beginning, a middle, and an end." There are, then, good reasons for agreeing with Roche that Spenser is right in making Telamond, on the title page of the legend, an alias for Tria-mond, for a "perfect" world would also be a triplex one.[510]

The triple character of love is especially a theme of Augustine, who asserts that "there are three things in *Caritas*, as it were a vestige of the Trinity":

> But what is love or charity, which divine Scripture so greatly praises and proclaims, except the love of good? But love is *of* some one that loves, and *with* love something *is* loved. Behold, then, there are three things: he that loves, and that which is loved, and love. . . . What does the mind love in a friend except the mind? There, then, also are three things: he that loves, and that which is loved, and love.

Augustine discusses the ternary of mind, love, and knowledge in the same terms: "these things are severally in themselves. But so are they in each other."[511] Augustine's arguments seem to recur in Leone Hebraeo, where

---

[510] *Kindly Flame*, pp. 16f. See below, nn. 527f. Ficino's follower is Francesco Cattani da Diacceto, in *I tre libri d'amore* (Vinegia, 1566), as quoted in Eugenio Garin, *Italian Humanism*, trans. Munz (New York, 1963), pp. 115f.

[511] *De Trinitate*, VIII.x.14; and IX.v.8. Trans. H. W. Haddan, rev. William G. T. Shedd, in NPNF, 1st Series, vol. 3, pp. 124, 129. Cf. *ibid.*, IX.iv.7, in the same vein: "I cannot see how those other three [mind, knowledge, love] are not of the same substance, since the mind loves itself, and itself knows itself; and these three so exist, as that the mind is neither known or loved by any other things at all. These three therefore must needs be of one and the same essence." And *ibid.*, IX.v.8: "And each severally is . . . in each two, because the mind which knows and loves itself, is in

they are not tied to a specifically Christian trinity of love. Leone explains the character of the love that God has, which divides him neither from himself, nor from love. The lover, the beloved, and their love are, in God, all one, and share the same essence, as also the knower, the known, and the act of knowing are, in God, three in one. Justifying the intellect's conversion of absolute unity into three, or its apprehension of "this unity of love in the threefold form of beloved, lover and love," Leone explains that, though it is impossible "to conceive of the multiplication of unity if that unity is not preserved within the product," there is still a creative procession in the realization of love, analogous to that efflux from God that produced chaos and the universe that issued out of it. "The potential lover is other than the potential beloved and they are two persons, while potential love makes a third which exists neither in the beloved nor in the lover; but when the potential lover becomes actual he is made one and the same with the beloved and with love." The union of these three different natures forms "one pure and single nature without division of any kind."[512]

The marriage of true minds does not admit impediments, and there is therefore nothing to prevent the migration of the souls of Priamond and Diamond into Triamond. The loss of their individuality—an objection on the realistic level—is no loss for friendship, which depends upon a common "bond of virtue." "Such a bond," according to Leone, "is indissoluble and begets a friendship stable and wholly perfect." The cause of the union and intimacy of friends

> . . . is the reciprocal virtue and wisdom of the friends, which by its spiritual character and separateness from matter and freedom from corporeal conditions, removes the diversity of persons from corporeal individuality, and generates in the friends a common mental essence sustained by wisdom and by their common love and volition.[513]

As Shakespeare says of the phoenix and the turtle, they "had the essence but in one."

---

its own love and knowledge. . . . And . . . also each two is in each severally. . . . But in what way all are in all, we have already shown . . . ; since the mind loves itself as a whole, and knows its own love wholly, and loves its own knowledge wholly, when these three things are perfect in respect to themselves. Therefore these three things are marvellously inseparable from each other, and yet each of them is severally a substance, and all together are one substance or essence, whilst they are mutually predicated relatively." (Trans. cit., pp. 128f.)

[512] *Dialoghi d'Amore*, ed. Caramella, pp. 253–257; trans. Friedeberg-Seeley and Barnes, *Philosophy of Love*, pp. 299–304.

[513] *Dialoghi d'Amore*, ed. Caramella, pp. 29f.; trans. in Nesca Robb, *Neoplatonism of the Italian Renaissance* (London, 1935), p. 210.

The translator of the passages quoted from Augustine notes that the mutuality of the three "substances" of mind, love, and knowledge, illustrates "what the Greek Trinitarians denominate the *perichoresis* of the divine essence. By the figure of circulation, they describe the eternal in-being and indwelling of one person in another." He adds:

> This is founded on John 14:10–11, 17:21–23: "Believest thou not that I am in the father, and the Father in Me? I pray that they all may be one, as thou Father art in Me, and I in Thee." Athanasius (*Oratio*, iii.21) remarks that Christ here prays that the disciples may imitate the trinitarian unity of *essence*, in their unity of *affection*.[514]

In short, the love of the three brothers is a vestige of the Trinity's unity of essence.[515]

One further manifestation in the legend of friendship of the theme of *caritas* is the House of Care, which follows the story of Agape's care for her sons. Care means worry here, but the sorrows of love are blended with a Virgilian kind of *Cura*, which includes sympathy, sensitivity, and painstakingness.[516] Spenser expresses this not so much through Scudamour as through the care that Britomart takes over Amoret, but the theme also comes through in Spenser's particular technique. To this reader's mind, at least, the allegory in this episode is deliberately labored and pedantic; it elaborates a conceit somewhat overcarefully.

As earlier noted, the conceit in question makes the smithy of Vulcan emblematic of the anxieties of a lover. This Vulcan is typically an artisan,

---

[514] William G. T. Shedd, in NPNF, 1st Series, vol. 3, p. 129, n. 1.

[515] Some readers will want to quote St. Augustine, *De Trinitate*, VIII.ii: "Of whom [God] we endeavour to think, so far as He Himself permits and grants, let us not think of any touch or embrace in local space, as if of three bodies, or of any compactness of conjunction, as fables tell us of three-bodied Geryon; but let whatsoever may occur to the mind, that is of such as to be greater in three than in each singly, and less in one than in two, be rejected without any doubt; for so everything corporeal is rejected." (Trans. Haddan, *op. cit.*, p. 116.) But others will recall Sir John Davies, *Nosce Teipsum*, in Bullett, ed., *Silver Poets*, p. 381: "Yet these three powers [of the soul] are not three souls, but one / As one and two are both contain'd in three / Three being one number by itself alone: / A shadow of the blessed Trinity." For Geryon as a parody of the Trinity, one may compare Dante's triplex Satan, in *Inf.* XXXIV.37–57.

[516] For this quality in Virgil, see Viktor Pöschl, *The Art of Virgil*, trans. Gerda Seligson (Ann Arbor, 1962), pp. 44, 53f., and esp. p. 184, n. 15, on *Aen.* IV.332, *obnixus curam*: "It is characteristic of the tenderness of Roman feeling and simultaneously of Roman practical moralism that 'love' in Latin has the connotation of 'sorrow, care, worry.'" For the Vulcanic emblem of Care, see above, Chap. II, n. 20.

especially in a passage Spenser would have known from Virgil, where Vulcan commits himself to forging arms for Aeneas with "quidquid in arte mea possum promittere curae" (whatever care I can promise in my art) (*Aen.* VIII.401). To confine the art of this episode by implying that it is merely a careful piece of work—or merely an episode, or merely a conceit—does it a great injustice, however. The episode itself warns us against such a careless foreshortening of attention, and to understand it fully, we must look beyond it.

Care is first offered as a laborer obsessed by his work; we can infer that his appearance in the narrative is generated out of Scudamour's own very large capacity for care. Spenser clearly echoes Virgil's description of the Cyclopean forges commandeered by Vulcan, with their thundering cave, reverberating groans, and panting bellows (*Aen.* VIII.416–421, 449). Scudamour's cares are simply a lover's worst suspicions about the fidelity of the beloved, and therefore Care is in part Vulcanic because Vulcan is husband to a faithless wife. Spenser's Vulcan presumably suspects the worst; perhaps his work is a way of keeping his mind off his betrayal. In Virgil, however, Vulcan forges at Venus' behest, as an act of love. The classical smith also signalized his devotion by making the cestus for Venus. Spenser draws our attention to the gift—"wrought in *Lemno* with vnquenched fire" (IV.v.3)—at the opening of this canto. Indeed, it is this same cestus that fits Amoret in the canto's *alter* half, in direct refutation of Scudamour's worst suspicions; like the two lovers, the two halves of this canto only *appear* to be divided. And however peculiar to Scudamour, a care for the fidelity of the beloved is a symptom of the more general concern of a lover.

Scudamour cares for Amoret, of course, but more complexly, the lover cares to be, himself, cared for. The lover worries over whether he is beloved, and takes pains, or care, to be lovable. In this respect, Scudamour's "carefull mind" might well contrast with the outward appearance of Care, who is content with his ragged garment, "ne for better cared" (IV.v.35). It may seem a subtle point, but it appears that caring about one thing can cause one to become careless about another. Such an antithesis between anxiety and neglect is near the heart of Spenser's picture of caring. This emerges when we compare Care to a quite different figure in this book, namely, the self-abandoned Timias. In the parallel between Books III and IV outlined in the following essay, Scudamour at the House of Care will be referred to Timias in the care or *cura* of Belphoebe; both of the lovers are notably heartsick. But it is only later in Book IV that the fullness of the relation between Timias and Scudamour is actually indicated—after Timias has become separated from his offended mistress. Fearing that Belphoebe can never again care for him, Timias falls into that antithetical state of self-neglect that specifically belongs to the preoccupied and hirsute Care (cf. IV.v.35f., IV.vii.40f., 43).

Much of Scudamour's experience of his cares takes place at night, because "The things that day most minds, at night doe most appear" (IV.v.43). Thus care, since it entails an intensification of *minding*, helps to explain why this particular episode is maintained on so insistently an allegorical plane. Night allegorically veils that truth which is oftentimes intimated, or "minded," by dreaming; Scudamour's restless night is at least partly a bad dream. This emphasis on minding per se, however, will not tell us what kind of minding might be peculiar to a legend of friendship.

A friend, for our purposes here, is one "that mindes *anothers* cares," and in so doing is able to some extent to forget his own (I.v.18). The episode of Care is placed just before the disabusement of Scudamour in his encounter with Britomart; she is finally revealed to him to be female. Scudamour's enlightenment coincides with the relieving of allegoricalness here. As Britomart becomes *her*self, Scudamour is freed from considering her *his* rival. Relations are restored, more or less according to the complementary distribution discussed in our essay on the Busirane episode. Thus the restless night partly serves to prepare Scudamour's mind for the transfer of the lover's self-regard to regard for a sympathetic alter ego. It does not matter so much whether this be Britomart or Amoret, only that it be someone with whom Scudamour can share his care, and thus in some measure defenestrate and disinfest it.

[iv]

A last symbol of concord expands the harmonized company to four. A notion found in the treatises of Leone Hebraeo and Ficino makes the relation of lover and beloved involve not two but four persons, the two parties in question gaining both a self and an alter ego by their love.[517] A spokesman in Plutarch's *Dialogue on Love* asserts that "It is to Love, my friend, that you should suppose the familiar lines of Empedocles to refer: 'Foursquare Friendship, equal in breadth and length, thou perceivest in thy mind, thine eyes may not descry him.' "[518] A stable grouping

[517] Leone Hebraeo, *Philosophy of Love*, trans. Friedeberg-Seeley and Barnes, pp. 260, 343; Ficino, *De Amore*, VII.ii, pp. 142ff., Jayne trans. See also Castiglione, *The Courtier*, IV.lxiv: lovers kissing pour themselves into each other so that each has two souls. See J. C. Nelson, *Renaissance Theory of Love* (New York, 1958), p. 91, for the information that "this apparently inconsequential statement was widely repeated after Leone."

[518] *Amatorious* 13, *Moralia* 756D, as trans. by Moses Hadas, *On Love, the Family and the Good Life: Sel. Essays of Plutarch* (New York, 1957), p. 91. A more literal translation will not yield anything like "Foursquare Friendship" (see W. C. Helmbold's translation in Loeb *Moralia*, vol. 9, p. 349), but Hadas is reading into his version the context of Plutarch's citation, Empedocles, Frg. 17, in part: "at one time

of friends and lovers often numbers four in Renaissance treatments of these themes. Spenser's *Prothalamion*, incidentally, celebrates such a union, and the male parties are compared to Castor and Pollux, "the twins of *Ioue*" (l. 173). An obvious instance forms the basis for Sidney's *Arcadia*, where the two protagonists are friends and suitors, and the ladies whose hands they seek are sisters. Such quartets are also found in *Two Gentlemen of Verona* and *A Midsummer Night's Dream*, where there is no previous blood relation among the parties, though Helena and Hermia have been like sisters to one another. Both plays are said to owe the intrigue of the lovers to Montemayor's *Diana*.[519] Similar motifs in the novelle of Cardenio and Dorotea in Part I of *Don Quixote* suggest the importance of the Spanish model.[520] *The Comedy of Errors, As You Like It, Much Ado About Nothing, All's Well That Ends Well*, and *Twelfth Night*, all end in double unions in which at least two of the persons are related by blood.

Spenser's story of Triamond and Cambel, more obviously than any of of the above, conforms to Jung's description of the "marriage quaternio," a configuration of two exogamous males, each married to the other's sister.[521] In the folk tales that Jung discusses, the double marriage realigns sexual and sibling alliances in a way that suggests deliverance from a threat of incest between brother and sister. Spenser's tale does not say anything like that, but the classical story of the incestuous Canacee is told at length

---

it [the universe?] grew to be one only from many, at another it divided again to be many from one, fire and water and earth and the vast height of air, dread Strife too, apart from these, everywhere equally balanced, and Love in their midst, equal in length and breadth. On her do thou gaze with thy mind, and sit not with dazed eyes; for she is recognized as inborn in mortal limbs; by her they think kind thoughts and do the works of concord, calling her Joy by name and Aphrodite." (Trans. in Kirk and Raven, *PreSocratic Philosophers*, pp. 327f.) Cf. also Plutarch, *Brotherly Love* 1: "the ancient representations of the Dioscuri are called by the Spartans 'beam figures': they consist of two parallel wooden beams joined by two other traverse beams placed across them; and this common and indivisible character of offering appears entirely suitable to the brotherly love of these gods." (Trans. W. C. Helmbold, Loeb *Moralia*, vol. 6, p. 247.) The figure is illustrated in Giraldus, *Hist. Deorum*, Syntag. V, in *Op. om.*, I, col. 185C.

[519] See Judith M. Kennedy, ed., *Critical Edition of Yong's Translation of George of Montemayor's Diana* (Oxford, 1968), introduction, pp. xlvi–l, and the studies cited in n. 3, p. xlvii.

[520] The recognitions in the scenes at the inn produce a quadrangular pattern, with Quixote, as a kind of Strife-figure, excluded. (Cardenio and Dorotea are guilty of "evil trust"—too little faith and misplaced credulity, respectively; Zoraida and the runaway "muleteer" may be faulted for filial ingratitude.)

[521] *The Psychology of the Transference*, trans. R.F.C. Hull (Princeton, 1969), pp. 58–67 (taken from *Collected Works*, vol. 16, *The Practice of Psychotherapy*).

in Gower's *Confessio Amantis*, and Chaucer breaks off *The Squire's Tale* with what appears to be a forecast of the same development between Canacee and her brother Cambalo.[522] In Spenser's sequel, Cambel and Canacee do indeed marry, but Canacee is provided with a new brother, Triamond, and Cambel's sister is named Cambina. A wearying amount of anxiety and bloodshed precede the resolution, which the new arrangement allows for from the start; why Cambel should be so unwilling to yield up Cambina is not well explained, unless we assume that he simply does not want to be divided from his sister by an unworthy marriage on her part.

In the light of our overall theme of the conjugation of the world, the point about the marriage quaternio is that it forms a *proportion*. In such a proportion the foursome is united by a double bond: one of kin, and one of kind. The security and coherence of this proportion is sanctioned by the *Timaeus*, where Plato argues that the stability and unification of the creation required not one, but two "means" between the "extreme" elements of fire and earth. The text implies that these two means properly belong to a theory of friendship:

> . . . solid bodies are always compacted not by one mean but by two. . . . out of such elements which are in number four, the body of the world was created, and it was harmonized by proportion, and therefore has the spirit of friendship, and having been reconciled to itself, it was indissoluble by the hand of any other than the framer.[523]

The legend of friendship, one concludes, might well occupy Spenser's fourth book.

In the allegory of the formation of a friendship, it is perhaps the death of self-attachment that is symbolized by the prolonged combat in which Priamond and Diamond die, and Cambel loses Cambina. Aristotle remarks that firm friendships are not necessarily easily formed.[524] The names of Agape's three sons might also be referred to a process of outgrowing successive worlds of affection: first, the family love of Agape herself; second, the erotic love of the quest for Cambina; and, third, the male friendship between Cambel and Triamond, which absorbs the first two. These three orders or spheres of love are specifically said to be illustrated by a

[522] *Confessio Amantis*, III.142ff. Link to the *Man of Law's Tale*, "The Wordes of the Hoost to the compaignye," ll. 78f.

[523] *Tim.* 32b–c, trans. F. M. Cornford. Cf. Fowler's discussion of the tetrad as a stable "double mean" in *Numbers of Time*, pp. 24–33, 166–169.

[524] *Nich. Ethics* VIII.iii (1156b); cf. IX.x (1171a).

second quaternio that appears in the second half of this book (IV.ix.1–2). In place of the sibling tie, one finds the Platonized physical resemblance of the friends Amyas and Placidas. The motif is well explained by Pater in his description of the thirteenth-century French *Friendship of Amis and Amile*:

> The friendship of Amis and Amile is deepened by the romantic circumstance of an entire personal resemblance between the two heroes, so that they pass for each other again and again, and thereby into many strange adventures; that curious interest of the Doppelgänger, which begins among the stars with the Dioscuri, being entwined in and out through all the incidents of the story, like an outward token of the inward similitude of their souls.[525]

The names Amyas and Placidas conceivably reflect the "twins" of Concord, namely, Friendship and Peace (IV.x.34). In the story one finds an indicative confusion over who marries whom: the rubric reports that Amyas, rather than Placidas, marries Paeana. If so, Amyas must have ceded his beloved Aemylia to his friend, a not unheard of procedure in the friendship-romance; friends have all things in common. Boccaccio's Gisippus makes such a gesture, as do Boiardo's Iroldo, Ariosto's Leone, and Shakespeare's Valentine.[526] The description of the former "lewd loues" of the fair wife of the "trusty squire" would seem to fit the fair Paeana (IV.ix.15–16). If, on the other hand, Spenser has suddenly switched to Aemylia in this passage, the conclusion that Arthur "had perfectly compylde / These paires of friends in peace" (IV.ix.17) is surely as well supported. (The switch would entail our believing that Aemylia's abduction by the ogre of Lust was not without some compromise to Aemylia's own moral character—and that the "trusty squire" is Amyas.) Nothing in the story itself has prepared us to believe that Aemylia will not be reunited with Amyas. In any case, the fiction seems designed to establish an equivalence among the characters: all are imprisoned at one point or another, and Arthur aids each character in turn.

The title page of this legend states that the exemplary friends are named Cambel and Telamond, but Triamond is the name used in the story proper. The alternate name is nonetheless suggestive, for it would mean

---

[525] *The Renaissance*, chap. 1, "Two Early French Stories."

[526] *Decameron*, Tenth Day, Eighth Tale (and thereafter, Elyot, *Gouernour*, II.xii, at length; cf. also *Decameron*, X.5 and *Filocolo*, IV, Question 4a, the story of Tarolfo); *Orl. Inn.* I.xii.87–89; *O.F.* XLV.52–60, 82, 90, XLVI.36. The suddenness of Valentine's offer in *Two Gentlemen of Verona*, V.iv.82f., is not meant to make him a Proteus, but rather to show the constancy of his own friendship, in the face of his friend's inconstancy.

a "finished" or "perfected" world. A character named Telia is the last of sixteen dancers introduced in Jonson's marriage-masque *Hymenai*, and Jonson has a note explaining that Telia derives from an epithet for Juno as "Perfectrix," because she presides over and perfects marriages. "Telia," the masque says, "for Hymen, perfects all, and ends" (l. 265). Jonson cites Julius Pollux, Servius, and a Greek scholia on Pindar (*Nem. Odes* X): "'nuptials are therefore called *teleioi* because they bring about perfection of life,' and so note the maturity which should be in matrimony."[527] Love works his own perfection in Spenser also.[528] We may note the word *perfectly* in the conclusion to the story of Amyas, quoted above, and the word *finish* in the plans of Artegall and Britomart:

> . . . she yeelded her consent
> To be his loue, and take him for her Lord,
> Till they with marriage might finish that accord.
>
> (IV.vi.41)

At the end of Book IV Spenser anticipates the same marriage for Florimell and Marinell. The last word of the book is "perfected." The poet says that the ending yet remains, "Which to another place I leaue to be perfected." The stanza that concludes the story of Triamond and Cambel includes the same ideas:

> . . . their daies they spent
> In perfect loue, deuoide of hatefull strife,
> Allide with bands of mutuall couplement;
>
> (IV.iii.52)[529]

Thus Telamond-Triamond is a thrice-perfected character, by virtue of his capacity for three unions; his fraternity, his friendship, and his membership in the final *quaternio*.

---

[527] Jonson, *Complete Masques*, ed. Stephen Orgel (New Haven, 1969), p. 520, where the following references are supplied: Pollux, III.38; Photius, *sub* "Teleon"; Plutarch, *Moralia* 264B; 2nd schol. on Pindar, *Nem. Odes* X.18; Aeschylus, *Eumenides* 214; *Gr. Anth.* VI.44; Aristophanes, *Thesmorph.* 973. For a Renaissance discussion, see Scaliger, *Poetices* (Heidelberg, 1617), III.c, p. 349, on the personnel of the epithalamium.

[528] *Colin Clovts Come Home Againe*, l. 805. See n. 355, for the Amore of Ficino, which *perfecit imperfecta* (*De Amore*, I.iii); in the same place Love is "perfect in himself" and "self-completing."

[529] Compare with this stanza Aristotle, *Nich. Ethics* IX.x (1171a), on the limit to the number of friends a person can have: "perhaps the largest number with whom one can live together (for that, we found, is thought to be very characteristic of friendship); . . . . Further, they too must be friends of one another, if they are to spend all their days together." (Trans. Ross.) Cf. IV.ii.54: ". . . during all their dayes, / And neuer discord did amongst them fall."

Let then no doubt, *Celinda*, touch,
  Much less your fairest mind invade,
  Were not our souls immortal made
Our equal loves can make them such.

So when one wing can make no way,
  Two joyned can themselves dilate,
  So can two persons propagate
When singly either would decay.

So when from hence we shall be gone,
  And be no more, nor you, nor I,
  As one anothers mystery,
Each shall be both, yet both but one.

(Lord Herbert of Cherbury, *An Ode*
upon a Question moved, Whether
Love should continue for ever?)

[i]

To conclude the consideration of Spenser's central books, I would like to describe how the fourth legend perfects the third by engaging the earlier themes in a social context. One's sense that Spenser inclined toward such an interpretation is based on such features as the displacement of the symbol of the hermaphrodite, and supported by the parallel ordering of materials in the two books. I have elsewhere suggested that such a parallel, psychologically speaking, would correspond to the relation between the self's original awakening to sexual consciousness and the rejoining of the issue at the end of latency, with the formation of permanent loves between equals. Examples of this "structure of recurrence" include Marinell's relapse; the two adventures of Timias involving Belphoebe and personifications of lust (one in relation to Florimell, the other in relation to Amoret); Britomart's two meetings with Scudamour (III.xi, IV.vi–ix), and with Paridell (III.ix, IV.ix); the repeated peril of Florimell and Amoret; and the two paradises where Venus presides. We also noted that Spenser tells the story of the original affiliation of Scudamour and Amoret *after* the impasse of the House of Busirane has been disposed of. Britomart falls in love with Artegall, and also defeats him, *before* she has met him. Florimell flees from court owing to the demise of Marinell, prior to their introduction at the end of Book IV. Marinell is said to have "despised" Florimell

626

(IV.xi.5; see III.v.9); Artegall is said to have been "rebellious vnto loue" (IV.vi.31). Clearly, one of the obstacles in the way of love has been in the nature of the lover, whoever he may be.

Without insisting on its logical Freudian interpretation, we may note that the structure of recurrence naturally entails a "moratorium" on sexual fulfillment; the moratorium lasts until the *proper* lover appears.[530] Amoret, at the House of Busirane, is awaiting such a lover; so is Florimell in the cave of Proteus. Both Busirane and Proteus are older men, as is the impotent Malbecco, in the same area of the poem. On his natural level, Malbecco reminds us of Mammon. When Malbecco enlists Braggadocchio's aid: "forth he drew / Great store of treasure, therewith him to tempt" (III.x.29). The hell-scene, we recall, was hedged with references to Pluto and Proserpina, who are prototypes for Mammon and his daughter: the male old and dusky, the female aspiring and golden. We have noted traces of the same myth in the abduction of Florimell.[531] Spenser says that Florimell and Amoret each waited seven months. Perhaps there is an allusion here to the number of years between the poet's two installments.

In Spenser's revision of the conclusion of the third book, Amoret gets Britomart instead of Scudamour. At first she thinks Britomart is one more abducting male, and her doubts about both the sex and intentions of her champion parallel the ambiguities of the scenes at Malecasta's Castle at the opening of Britomart's quest. As in the earlier canto, these doubts are resolved, and Amoret is safe until the chaperonage extended by the patroness of chastity is mysteriously withdrawn. Thereafter, Amoret is on her own until she is joined by Arthur. In the first two books the Arthurian intervention signaled the termination of the hero's period of dissociation; perhaps Amoret's conjunction with Arthur here indicates her renewed readiness for espousal.

No doubt Spenser intends us to understand by the structure of recurrence that the constancy of lovers is preordained: it exists before the actual person with whom the lover affiliates presents himself. Nature made the two friends Amyas and Placidas amazingly alike: "As if that by one patterne seene somewhere, / She had them made a paragone to be" (III.ix.11). Nonetheless, a story like Marinell's does not really seem to have been made to fall into this convenient Platonic mould. Marinell is a recluse from love who receives a wound from a knight who is apparently a male, and every-

---

[530] The term is Erikson's, *Childhood and Society*, pp. 262f., where it is used in a somewhat different sense for the interim of adolescence, "a psychological stage between childhood and adulthood." *This* kind of moratorium is more correctly the subject of our first essay on Book VI, "The Quest for the Faerie Queene," below.

[531] Comparing "kingdoms" in III.viii.40 with II.vii.11.

thing else in this legend prepares us to believe that this is a love-wound. Up until this point, Marinell has avoided women, on the advice of his mother. She fears woman's *love*; she does not know to fear woman's *force* (III.iv.27). Presumably the reference is to the emasculating effect of Marinell's unnatural chastity, but we can hardly separate this, in the fiction, from his apparent vulnerability to maternal domination. Retired to his mother's bower, he becomes the unwilling object of her anxious solicitation —"like her thrall" (IV.xi.7). Seven months later, Marinell falls in love with the girl next door; the mother is replaced by the "other."

In the parallel between the two books, presently to be developed, it is interesting to compare Marinell at the House of Proteus to Scudamour at the House of Busirane. Scudamour is not precisely threatened by "woman's force," but he is rather emasculated by his failure to reach Amoret. Like the Adonis-figures, he is "all wallowed / Vpon the grassy ground," and he is "groueling" (III.xi.7–8) in the same way as the sacrificial ox to which Marinell is compared (III.iv.17), and also like Venus beside the dying Adonis in the tapestry (III.i.38). Britomart encounters Scudamour in this state while she is chasing Ollyphant. Ollyphant, in turn, has been forced to leave off chasing a "fearefull boy" (III.xi.4). The "beastly vse" to which the giant intends to subject the young man is presumably homosexual. By means of the proximity of Ollyphant to Scudamour Spenser reminds us of the range of sexual experience. Defeat is a part of this range, and Spenser's representation is faithful to this possibility. At the House of Proteus, Marinell's mother accomplishes what Britomart does at the House of Busirane: the deliverance of the lady. But as the analogy with Book III can suggest, there is a sense in which Cymoent threatens the sexual wholeness of Marinell as surely as Ollyphant would.

In passing we may remark that it is this plenitude of representation that confers on the erotic vision of the poem its reputation for health, vitality, and sanity. The total of Spenser's examples, on balance, makes him something like a spokesman for a kind of high norm of naturalness in erotic relations. This is the opposite of the impression one might take from the overstrained and neurotic figure of Amoret at the House of Busirane. And yet this is the figure Spenser places at the center of the whole. Milton must have had some such paradox of constrained energy in mind when he conceived the unmoved Lady on whom *Comus* turns.

The legend of chastity is organized symmetrically.[532] At the center of the book Spenser places the cool and shady Garden of Adonis, which rep-

[532] Frye, "Structure of Imagery," in *Fables of Identity*, p. 83; see also Lewis, *Allegory of Love*, pp. 339–344.

resents the chaste heroine's potential for self-realization, as the presence of the Genius might indicate. The periphery of the book is hedged by the nocturnal life of the loci of Malecasta and Busirane, which represent an overheated erotic desire. Britomart passes through the last two loci chastened but unhindered; she does not visit the locus of recognition, however, because the realization of her love is deferred to another legend. Amoret, on the contrary, is nurtured in the Garden, and Britomart's identification with her interests emerges at the juncture of the two books. Thus the legend as a whole has the entrance-exit pattern of its own locus of recognition.

Britomart achieves the quest meant for Scudamour, and in the sequel, Scudamour visits the locus of recognition perhaps in some sense meant for Britomart. It is Britomart who requests Scudamour's account of the Temple of Venus. The two eductions of Amoret, then, must be another instance of the structure of recurrence. Just as Britomart enterprises the field version of this eduction (at the House of Busirane), she also experiences a field version of the scene of recognition, when she is acknowledged as a Venus figure by Artegall.[533] As the poem stands, this acknowledgment signals the effective accomplishment of her quest: the enamoring of her future spouse. Their meeting is placed at the center of Book IV; that is, halfway between the lovers' respective legends, and also halfway between the symbols of Venus and Adonis, and Isis and Osiris.

Britomart then turns back to Amoret, "her second care"; likewise, Spenser himself turned to Florimell at the end of the Garden of Adonis canto.[534] Hence the concluding stanzas of the two sixth cantos show the same movement. On the earlier occasion Spenser predicts the reunion of Scudamour and Amoret. At the end of the book it is a fact, and Britomart resolves to bring the same to pass for herself. On the later occasion she has done so.

Starting with the initial cantos, we can point to further analogies in organization and theme. Both cantos describe a mythological set-piece that the fiction subsequently reflects. In Book III, there is the tapestry of Adonis; in Book IV, the relics of Ate. The relics on Ate's walls—where mementos of destructiveness are ironically preserved—include broken bands, torn shields, rent robes, and broken weapons: emblems of civic ruptures have replaced the earlier engoring of Adonis. In the fiction, Britomart's wound from Gardante is replaced by the slandering of Britomart to Scudamour. Britomart is wounded in spite of her immunity to Male-

---

[533] On the Mars-Venus myth here, see above, "Heroic Eros," sec. i.

[534] IV.vi.46f., III.vi.53–55. Amoret's being Britomart's "second care" corresponds to her being born "in the second place" (III.vi.4). Britomart's primary care is her chastity, or her Belphoebe-aspect; see n. 456, above.

casta; we note the parallel success of Ate's slander, despite Scudamour's decisive repulse of the adulterous Paridell. (The equivalence between Gardante and Paridell depends upon Paridell's employment of the seduction technique of Malecasta's champions; Paris wounded Achilles with the arrow of lustful love, according to E. K.'s note on what he calls "the dart of some beautifull regard, which is Cupides arrowe.")[535] The Adonis tapestry also provides advance notice of the disasters of Marinell and Timias. Like the wounding of Timias by the foul forester, the consequences of Scudamour's susceptibility emerge in the fifth canto: as Timias festers in Belphoebe's bower, so Scudamour spends a tormenting night at the House of Care. Among Ate's relics is the golden apple that led to the adultery of Helen and the fall of Troy. The comparable provoking objects in the fourth and fifth cantos are Florimell's cestus, and the False Florimell. The cestus unfastens when it is worn by the unchaste; it becomes a symbol of infidelity. (Ate, one recalls, tries to sunder the golden chain of Concord.) The False Florimell is an ersatz-Helen who arouses lust and dissension wherever she turns up. Both the cestus and the counterfeit are prizes at Satyrane's tournament, and the occasion provides notable examples of discord.

Spenser indicates a number of common points of reference for the opening cantos which we have not mentioned. In both cantos Britomart is seen lending aid to the chastity of which she is the patron by preserving an endangered loyalty. In Book III she comes to the aid of the stymied Redcrosse. He is harassed by six knights who represent an attempt to seduce him from Una. Duessa is promised in the rubric because the nocturnal approaches of the false Una in Book I parallel the seductions of Malecasta. (Hence Malecasta wears a red robe at night, and her palace exhibits the luxury of the "proud *Persian* Queenes" that is also linked to Duessa [III.i.41; I.ii.13].) Redcrosse, though typically disarrayed, brings his sword to Britomart's support in the skirmish. Duessa appears in her proper person in Book IV, where she adds her voice to the slander of Britomart, claiming that Amoret has slept with Britomart in the castle of couples the night before. It was Malecasta who shared Britomart's bed in Book III; the overtones of lesbian love in the earlier book have disappeared from the parallel offered by the sequel, where the sex of the lady's sleeping partner is known. When homosexual attachments are in the offing, the sex of the partner is in some sense *not* known.

In both opening cantos Britomart accommodates the requirements of an arbitrary castle custom. Malecasta's law requires that the passing knight take her as his mistress if he does not serve another. If the knight has a mistress, he must defend or forswear his allegiance. When Britomart in-

---

[535] E. K. on "March," Argument, and on l. 97.

quires as to the compensation for the successful defender, she is told that
it is again the love of Malecasta. The choice is hard, as Britomart remarks
(III.i.27); any compelling seduction takes this form of a choice without
an alternative. Owing to her disguise, Britomart is able to counter with
a riddle of her own:

> Loue haue I sure, (quoth she) but Lady none;
> Yet will I not fro mine owne loue remoue,
> Ne to your Lady will I seruice done,
>
> (III.i.28)

She humbles the six knights on Redcrosse's behalf, and the two enter
Malecasta's domain for the night.

A less amplified incident of the same design occurs in the first canto of
the sequel. Here the custom requires that every knight who would join
the fellowship of the castle must be paired with a lady. A knight with no
lady of his own (corresponding to the singular Redcrosse) attempts to
claim Amoret, and Britomart takes up the challenge of the odd-man-out.
Again she riddles on her identity, balancing positive and negative:

> And sayd, her loue to lose she was full loth
> But either he should neither of them haue, or both.
>
> (IV.i.10)

Having unhorsed the challenger, she graciously reveals her sex and offers
herself as his lady, thereby reconciling the claims of both a would-be
Scudamour and her fearful charge Amoret. The allegory implies that the
aspiring lover must learn to respect the integrity (the Una-aspect) of the
beloved. In the symbolism, as the lady of the knight and the knight of
the lady, Britomart has taken on the character of both halves of the
hermaphrodite formed by the lovers in the original ending of the preceding legend: as we have seen, it is the hermaphrodite that is "either
. . . neither . . . both."

The virtuous characters in Book IV are now replaced in the poet's
attention by Paridell and Blandamour, and their paramours, Duessa and
Ate. With Blandamour's acquisition of the False Florimell, Duessa ceases
to be mentioned as a member of the company, as if the two counterfeits
were roughly interchangeable in the story, as well as in the symbolism.
At the point where Paridell is quarreling with Blandamour over the new
prize, Britomart in the earlier book converses with her riding companion
Redcrosse about Artegall. In Book IV the unstable quaternio now comes
upon Cambel and Triamond with their wives, and the poet in both books
steps back from the foreground narrative to tell the story of the titular
heroes' destinies.

Britomart's quest begins with her discovering Artegall's reflection in the hermaphroditic looking-glass of Venus. (It was perhaps suggested by *The Squire's Tale*, the starting point for the story of Cambel and Triamond also.)[536] The quest continues into the underworld where Merlin allays Britomart's anxieties about falling in love, and insists that she set out to establish the line that will get Elizabeth Tudor born. Britomart arms herself to enter fairyland in disguise, her disguise including her adoption of a truculent exterior.

In Book IV Agape's three sons undertake the quest for Canacee. Agape's visit to the subterranean realm of the Fates to inquire about the future of her sons corresponds to Britomart's visit to Merlin's cave. Britomart's line will climax in the Tudor dynasty:

> Thenceforth eternall vnion shall be made
> Betweene the nations different afore,
> And sacred Peace shall louingly perswade
> The warlike minds, to learne her goodly lore,
> And ciuile armes to exercise no more:
> Then shall a royall virgin raine, which shall
> Stretch her white rod ouer the *Belgicke* shore,
> And the great Castle smite so sore with all,
> That it shall make him shake, and shortly learne to fall.
>
> (III.iii.49)

Such an "eternall vnion" will be the work of Concord and Peace, and the comparable reconciliation in Book IV is effected by the peacemaker Canacee. She enters the field of battle like the civic Cybele, armed with a "rod of peace": "Shee smote them lightly with her powerfull wand" (IV.iii.42, 48), an emblem of Concord.[537] As a consequence Cambel and Triamond are "faithfully affrended" (IV.iii.52). At this point in Book III, Britomart and Redcrosse are parting in "Friendship professed with vnfained hart" (III.iii.62).

The souls of Priamond and Diamond are destined to appear in Tria-

---

[536] *Squire's Tale*, ll. 132ff. For the wife as mirror to the husband, see Plutarch, *Marriage Counsel* 14, or Edmund Tilney, *Flower of Friendship* (i.e. "spousall amity") (London, 1568), Sig. E4ᵛ. Or perhaps we are to think of Ficino, *De Amore*, II.vii, trans. Jayne, p. 146: "a lover imprints a likeness of a loved one upon his soul, and so the soul of the lover becomes a mirror in which is reflected the image of the loved one. Thereupon, when the loved one recognizes himself in the lover, he is forced to love him." Being a world of glass, the mirror is also like the moon, for the wife should reflect the husband, as the moon does the sun—so DuBartas, *Weeks*, I.IV.722–731 (Sylvester trans.), on the moon as a glass ball.

[537] For Cambina as Cybele, see Roche, *Kindly Flame*, pp. 25–27, and for Thames as Cybele at IV.ix.27f., see ibid., p. 182. (For a pre-Spenserean link between Cybele and a river—the Tiber—see Virgil, *Aen.* X.219–235.) For Cybele generally, see below, "The Analogy of Natural Plenitude," sec. iii.

mond. In a more abstract descent, the chastity of Britomart is destined to appear in Spenser's queen. Thus both the lengthened life of the third brother and the "Briton bloud" of the Tudors are critically involved in a theme of ideal succession.[538] Spenser addressed Cupid: "The fatall purpose of diuine foresight, / Thou does effect in destined descents" (III.iii.2), and the love of the three brothers proves as strong as death. In the stanza following the one quoted above, Merlin baulks at a further prevision of a catastrophic development. Similarly, although it is left to us to reflect upon it, the two extra lives of Triamond have been used up, and his own was not destined to be long.[539] The poet does not draw much attention to these qualifications, but they are evidence of the unacknowledged presence of mutability in even the happiest of endings.

In Book IV the theme of a nationally manifested destiny is transferred from the chastity of the queen to the literary friendships of her chief poet. Spenser describes himself as the successor to Chaucer, a second author of the English epos. The lines describing the quasi-Pythagorean survival of Chaucer's spirit in Spenser, "through infusion sweete," relate the fellowship of the poets to the fraternity of the three brothers.

The theme of Spenser's poetic lineage also has an international dimension: in the next canto Spenser somewhat inaccurately claims that he has overgone Ariosto, in describing a drink which turns hate to love (IV.iii.45). This mention enlists Spenser as the third in a series of writers of romance. He is returning preeminence in the genre to England—a part of the general migration northward of the Italian Renaissance. Britomart's quest involves the same theme of the passing of an ascendancy from the Latin world to the English one. Like Bradamante's lover, Ruggiero, Britomart is "lineally extract" from Trojan stock, and Britomart will reiterate the theme of an ideal succession in response to Paridell's description of his Trojan lineage. Merlin has told Britomart:

> For from thy wombe a famous Progenie
> Shall spring, out of the auncient *Troian* blood,
> Of those same antique Peres the heauens brood, . . .

[538] The idea of human cooperation in a heavenly ordained or caused destiny (end, purpose, intention) obtains throughout the third canto of Book III. It is reflected in a plethora of variations on such words as *spring* (1, 16, 22, 26, 27); *cause* (15, 18, 19, 25); *begin* (4, 21, 22); *emprise, enterprise* (35, 51, 53); *purpose* (2, 17, 25, 36, 51, 60); *intend, intent* (2, 41); *protense* (4); *portend* (14); *end* (3, 14, 15, 50); *fatall end* (15); *fattal Instrument* (38); *fate, fates* (19, 24, 28, 44); *last fate* (28); *issue* (29, 39); *long time* (28, 30, 31); *full time* (40); *closure* (27); *term* (25, 44, 48); *dew* (4, 25, 52). For the correspondence with Book IV the reader will want to compare Agape's enterprise with Merlin's doctrine: "'Indeede the Fates are firme, / And may not shrink, . . . Yet ought mens good endevours them confirme, / And guyde the heauenly causes to their constant terme'" (III.iii.25).

[539] According to the evidence of IV.ii.50, Priamond's was the shortest of the three lives. This seems to be forgotten at IV.iii.52, l. 5: "he ledd a long and happie life."

It was not, *Britomart*, thy wandring eye
　　Glauncing vnwares in charmed looking glas,
　　But the streight course of heauenly destiny,
　　Led with eternall prouidence, that has
　　Guided thy glaunce, to bring his will to pass:
　　　　　　　　　　　　　　　　　(III.iii.22, 24)

In the ninth canto Paridell describes the wanderings of Aeneas in slightly
different terms: "he through fatall errour long was led" (III.ix.41). Paridell also recalls Mnemon's tale of the wanderings of Brute: "At last by
fatall course they driuen were" (III.ix.49)—"Driuen by fatall error" as
Eumnestes elsewhere records (II.x.9). Thus "*Troynouant* was built of old
Troyes ashes cold" (III.ix.38). Britomart is then able to add:

　　. . . a third kingdome yet is to arise,
　　Out of the *Troians* scattered of-spring,
　　That in all glory and great enterprise
　　Both first and second *Troy* shall dare to equalize.
　　　　　　　　　　　　　　　　　(III.ix.44)

The wandering Paridell is still attached to the adulterous cycle of the first
Troy, and the events of the next canto are a drastically foreshortened account of his Trojan lineage. Later he is seen with Duessa, whom Spenser
has identified with the second Troy, or Rome, and we ultimately hear
that he dies as her victim (V.ix.41).

In the ninth canto of the fourth book Spenser completes the story of the
Amyas-Placidas quaternio. Britomart's dialogue with Paridell is replaced
by her request to Scudamour, who tells the story of *his* courtship.

Any parallel between the second quarters of the two legends will not be
close. The sections in question are both busy panels of repeating motifs:
in Book III the presiding mythological character is Adonis; in Book IV
it is Ate. The three bowers of the earlier book become metaphors for erotic
sensitivities; the three jousts suggest imperfect social encounter. In the
fourth canto of Book III Britomart overturns the undefeated Marinell in
his charge across the beach; the same "stranger knight" robs the savage
Artegall of his victories in Book IV. (Both of her antagonists are newly
introduced; both are related to Achilles, as she is to Penthesilea.) In the
earlier book Arthur loses track of Florimell; in the later book the honors
of the tournament are settled on her counterfeit. Timias, with his lovesick
heart, languishes in Belphoebe's bower; Scudamour tosses and turns at the
House of Care. (Later in Book IV, Timias himself falls into the unkempt
or careless condition of Scudamour's heartless host.) Timias in Book III

becomes part of the celebration of the chastity of Belphoebe; the tournament in Book IV ends by honoring the hallucinatory beauty—whom everyone supposes to be Florimell—"That shone as Phebes light" (IV.v.14). It is Amoret who actually qualifies for the prize for chastity; Amoret is Belphoebe's twin sister. It would clearly be a mistake, given the plethora of divergent details, to insist upon specific correspondences: it is mainly the sense of confusion and cross-purposes that these cantos have in common.

The two sixth cantos lead to a new beginning. In Book III we find the flyting of Venus and Diana during the search for Cupid: in Book IV there is the conflict of Scudamour and Britomart, that is, "Cupid's man" and Diana's namesake. In the earlier book Cupid is missing, and the newborn Amoret is discovered in his place. In the later book Amoret is missing, Britomart is revealed, and the love of Britomart and Artegall is born. The Garden of Adonis of the earlier book is the paradise of fulfillment, or "louers heauen," which Spenser's heroine now blushingly experiences (IV.vi.32). Britomart is revealed as "That peerelesse patern of Dame natures pride" (IV.iv.24). The phrase may indicate that, like the Garden of Adonis, Britomart mediates an unspoiled perfection to natures that ordinarily fall far short of it. Artegall's response to her beauty distinctly echoes the satyrs' worship of Una. Artegall "fell humbly downe vpon his knee, / And of his wonder made religion" (IV.vi.22). *O dea certe.*[540]

We may now summarize the place of the two sixth cantos. Midway between the Bower of Bliss and the House of Busirane Spenser describes the Garden of Adonis, his vision of fruitful chastity, as opposed to either the sterile promiscuity of the Bower, or the traumatized virginity of the House. The meeting of Britomart and Artegall is similarly placed. It belongs to the pattern of reconciling conflicts in this legend—here a conflict in which Britomart appeases the jealous Scudamour and tames the savage Artegall. It is therefore placed midway between the legends of chastity and justice. Friendship exists chiefly among the virtuous. Thus this canto forms a principal link in that golden chain of concord that is also the Arthurian chain of the virtues.

[ii]

In canvassing the second halves of the two legends, we may start with the notable conceit of Spenser's day that takes as its emblem an exchange of arrows between Cupid and Death. The emblem explains why all the

---

[540] *Aen.* I.328, the motto for the virgin queen at the end of Spenser's "April." The scene in Virgil is used to introduce Belphoebe at II.iii: stanzas 21, 33, and 44 all broach her celestial descent. So does III.v.34–36, where Belphoebe claims to be not Virgil's *dea*, but "the Mayd," or Virgo.

young men are dying and all the old men are falling in love.[541] A comparable situation obtains in Book III. The "morbid" first half of the legend shows us the "deaths" of Marinell, Timias, and Adonis; the "sterile" second half presents the unavailing loves of Proteus, Malbecco, and Busirane. Each of these last-named is a possessive older man to whom an unwilling younger woman is subject. What the three stories have in common, besides the Oedipal theme already noted, is the motif of metamorphosis: Proteus' changes for Florimell; Malbecco's reduction to a goat and his transformation into an abstraction; and Busirane's abduction of Amoret by means of the disguises of a masque. Just as the Adonis tapestry apprised us of a mythological type prominent in the first half of the legend, the tapestry of Busirane summarizes the metamorphosis motif. It portrays the force of Eros driving through the Protean disguises of the gods in their pursuit of nymphs and mortals—a possession by love that the stern and sullen gods are not spared.

The second half of Book IV progresses beyond these hindering attachments to proper and apt espousals, and young men accordingly displace the older ones. Instead of Busirane's tapestry—which is "entrayld" with the "long bloody river" (III.xi.46)—the poet catalogues the guests at the wedding of the Thames and Medway, a voluminous recital of the rivers and water-nymphs who descend to the House of Proteus. In place of the Masque of Cupid, with its coercion of the distraught wife, Spenser describes the ceremonial approach of the relenting bride and collected groom to the sea. One is reminded of the allegorizing of Leone Hebraeo, who tells us that the adulterous loves of the gods stand for unnatural combinations, while the gods' marriages stand for natural combinations.[542] The river-union also illustrates a theme of metamorphosis: as in marriage generally, the bride takes her lover's name and thenceforth shares his bed.

A comparison between Amoret and Florimell seems obvious enough at the end of the two books, and there is clearly an analogy between their perils in the seventh cantos as well. Florimell flies from the hyena beast that

<hr/>

[541] Alciati, *Emblemata*, Emb. CLIV and CLV, "De Morte & Amore" and "In formosam fato praereptam," *edn. cit.*, pp. 545–548; and thereafter, Green, *Whitney's Choice of Emblems*, pp. 132f. Green also gives the Latin of the poem by DuBellay based on Alciati, pp. lxiif. For Tasso's use of the conceit, see *Ger. Lib.* II.34. For Alciati's sources, see Panofsky, *Studies in Iconology* (reprint, New York, 1962), p. 125, n. 76. Cf. also the theme of Thomas Watson's "My love is past," in Hebel and Hudson, eds., *Poetry of the English Renaissance* (New York, 1957), p. 148, said to be partly adopted from M. Girolamo Parabosco's *Epitaph of Love*, "In cenere giace qui sepolo Amore,/Colpa di quella, che morir, mi face."

[542] *Philosophy of Love*, trans. Friedeberg-Seeley and Barnes, p. 122. Cf. also *ibid.*, p. 77, on affinity as one of the five causes of love: "rivers . . . hasten, as soon as they attain sufficient volume, to reach the sea and [mingle with] all the watery element, because of the love they bear their kind."

"feeds on womens flesh as others feede on gras" (III.vii.22); she flees much faster than Myrrha or fearful Daphne (III.vii.26). Amoret flees the ogre, also a devourer, with teeth "like to a tusked Bore" (IV.vii.5). She "makes her feare a spur to hast her flight":

> More swift then Myrrh' or Daphne in her race,
> Or any of the Thracian Nimphes in saluage chase.
> (IV.vii.22)

The beast disembowels Florimell's horse before Satyrane arrives to bind him. Amoret, in the clutches of the ogre, is wounded by her would-be rescuer Timias, before Belphoebe arrives and dispatches the savage. Florimell's essential nature is not touched. Amoret's vulnerability we are familliar with.

There may be other similarities between the monsters. The decidedly Priapan physiognomy of the ogre includes "eares . . . More great than th'eares of Elephants" (IV.vii.5), Spenser's one mention of this animal.[543] The ogre seems to belong to the same genre as Argante and *Ollyphant*, who are introduced just after the beast in Book III. As we know from Roland's horn, Olifante, the name may refer to the elephant's tusks, which in this context are chosen for their phallic overtones. Like Ollyphant, the ogre is swift as a roebuck (III.xi.5, IV.vii.22); and, like Argante, he trusses his victims (III.vii.37, IV.vii.18). The original quest against Ollyphant belonged to Sir Thopas, as the 1590 edition indicates (III.vii.48)—Chaucer's Sir Thopas was notable for his chastity. The corresponding quest against Argante belongs to the lady knight Palladine. As the poem now stands, Britomart has the only quest against Ollyphant in Book III, while it is Belphoebe who dispatches the ogre in Book IV. Satyrane is thoroughly incapacitated by Argante; Timias does not fare well against the ogre. The two male knights seem to illustrate the limitations on the heroism of natural virtue and inexperience respectively. In Book III the Squire of Dames is also introduced as the victim of Argante. In the morally polarized world of the poem, he lacks an identifying name, being of too weak a moral character. On the scale of sexual degradations, perhaps his place is occupied in the following book by the somewhat soiled Aemylia. We naturally contrast her with Amoret, who escapes from the ogre's cave without Aemylia's delay. Both Amoret and Aemylia eventually come under the protection of Arthur. Similarly, Florimell escapes to the realm of Proteus.

---

[543] That is, the scrip-like ears of the Lust-monster are the scrotum, according to a well-established usage, e.g., *Romance of the Rose*, ll. 19638–19641 and 21245, where staff and scrip mean phallus and genital sack. (Cf. the purse and bill of Chaucer's *Merchant's Tale*, l. 1937, and the "nether purs" of the Wife of Bath's Prologue, l. 44b; and OED, "purse," *sub* II.8b, citing R. Androse, trans. *Alexis' Secrets*, "the itch of the purse of the testicles.")

Proteus himself lays siege to the prize, and Spenser warns us against our slanderously assuming a similar low attraction between the prince and Amoret. Florimell resists Proteus' "flattering words" (III.viii.38), and "losse of chastity, or chaunge of loue" (III.viii.42). In canto viii Proteus imprisons Florimell beneath the sea, thus rhyming her fate with that of Marinell, who was carried off to his mother's bower back in the fourth canto:

> . . . the late ruine of proud *Marinell*,
> And suddein parture of faire *Florimell*,
> (III.viii.46)

An analogous symmetry emerges in the sequel when, in canto viii, Amoret enters the House of the hag Sclaunder; for Scudamour's insomnia at the House of Care, in canto v, is the result of slanders by the hag Ate. Sclaunder's "words were not, as common words are ment, / T'expresse the meaning of the inward mind" (IV.viii.26). That is, they were not meant to express truth, but rancor. Sclaunder reviles Amoret and Aemylia as whores, and we are reminded of the slandering of Truth by Abessa in Book I. A long passage expounds the confusion in the human mind of good and evil, fair and foul, love and lust (IV.viii.29–33). The slanderous and the salacious have a close relation in that both exploit the resources of innuendo and *double-entendre*. The pairing of Duessa and Ate at the opening of this legend is meant to express this connection. Sclaunder depends on our assuming the worst about Amoret, projecting the workings of our own lust onto a time of "simple truth and blameless chastity" (IV.viii.30). The Fall has confirmed this corruption, which is basically a corruption of our attractions by our appetites:

> Then beautie, which was made to represent
>   The great Creatours owne resemblance bright,
>   Vnto abuse of lawlesse lust was lent,
>   And made the baite of bestiall delight:
>   Then faire grew foule, and foule grew faire in sight,
>   And that which wont to vanquish God and man,
>   Was made the vassall of the victors might;
>   Then did her glorious flowre wex dead and wan,
> Despisd and troden downe of all that ouerran.
>
> (IV.viii.32)

Beauty is thus defined in terms of an apparent willingness to be debauched. This stanza clarifies the parallel with Florimell in Book III, where the flower of true beauty is supplanted by the suggestive counterfeit. Meanwhile, Satyrane has been hearing the lascivious stories of the Squire of

Dames—stories that do not slander the ladies so much as the teller (III.viii.44).

Spenser then runs this risk himself, in the story of Malbecco, which is told in the following two cantos. It is an extended fabliau, and the satyrs are an apt choice for its personnel. The fabliau is a genre of canny experience and harsh reprisals; the trusting and the vulnerable rarely do well there. Placed in the romance context of Book III, the Malbecco story suggests a society failing to form, and the loneliness of its conclusion leads the reader directly to the fearsome isolation of the House of Busirane.

The story is introduced with Paridell, who wears a flaming heart on his chest. In Book I the flaming heart was the emblem of the sin of Lechery (I.iv.25). The corresponding character in the fourth book must be Corflambo, if his name is any indication. He defeats men and women with his fierce eyebeams, which put "secret flakes of lustfull fire" into hearts (IV.viii.49). In Book III Paridell and Hellenore exchange significant glances; Hellenore sends her husband's guest a "firie dart whose hed / Empoisned was with privy lust" and the "wicked engine" finds ready tinder: Helen was the loose "Tindarid lass" (IV.xi.19).

Arthur beheads Corflambo (Paeana's sire), and the rest of the story is devoted to the forming of the Amyas-Placidas quaternio. The Prince then proceeds with Amoret until he meets with Britomart and Scudamour, where the symbolism might suggest the joining of another quaternio. Our attention is directed, however, to a gang of quarrelsome sexual humours—Paridell among them—whom Spenser compares to the four elements at war.[544] Paridell is about to attack Britomart, but peace is made, and Britomart asks Scudamour to relate the story of his courtship. In the earlier book Paridell also crosses with Britomart, and when matters have been patched up at Malbecco's castle we hear the story of his Trojan lineage.

In Book IV the first quaternio consolidates in the third canto; the second quaternio, in the ninth. In Book III we might look for some parallel in the story of Britomart, in terms of the sexual thresholds earlier discussed. In these cantos Britomart is seen in conjunction with Merlin and Malbecco respectively. Both Merlin and Malbecco are tricked by women, and both are condemned to live in a cave forever. Merlin made the mirror that Britomart found in her father's closet, and Hellenore invades Malbecco's closet to steal and burn his money. Britomart hesitates before Merlin in the same way that Aurora hesitates before Tithonus. Spenser first introduced this

---

[544] Fowler's analysis of the foursome into its factors, in *Numbers of Time*, pp. 31f., recalls the similar factoring of the four humours, and the comparison of these to four enemies in *Romance of the Rose*, ll. 16905f. In Spenser ardor and cold-heartedness would have the place of hot and cold, and constancy and inconstancy of dry and moist. (Druon: constant diffidence; Blandamour: inconstant ardor; Claribell: constant ardor; Paridell: inconstant diffidence).

myth when Una left the House of Archimago at daybreak (I.ii.7). Aurora is mentioned again at the opening of the tenth canto, when Britomart leaves Malbecco's castle. Merlin says that Britomart is no more hidden from him "then Sunne in cloudy vele" (III.iii.19), and at Malbecco's castle she is revealed with her hair "like sunny beames / That in a cloud their light did long time stay" (III.ix.20). Both hosts, in other words, supply the Tithonus-like shadows from which the heroine emerges; we have already noted the reiteration of her British-Trojan destiny in the later canto.

In our account of a running analogy between Books III and IV we are now at the tenth canto. Any parallel between the seduction of Hellenore from the castle of Malbecco and the eduction of Amoret from the Temple of Venus seems fanciful at best. And yet it is clear that the castle of Malbecco shares features with the Castle of Malecasta and the House of Busirane; likewise, the Temple of Venus is related to the castle of couples and the House of Proteus. We have also seen a number of places where one legend gives a more symbolical or thematic account of the fiction or narrative in the other legend. For example, the true and false Florimells correspond to the chaste and slandered Amoret: the false Florimell is the reified form of a slandered reputation. (Amoret is paired with Aemylia, but the latter is more a weak sister than a slanderous double.)

We may sense an analogy if we come to the castle and the Temple by way of the *Romance of the Rose*. In the campaign of Love's barons against the Castle of Jealousy, Venus herself leads the attack, sending a fiery arrow against the Tower of Shame.[545] In Spenser's story, Britomart—along with Satyrane, Paridell, and the Squire of Dames—conspires to fire Malbecco's gates. Like Paridell, Scudamour penetrates a building of difficult access, and evades the guardians of the young lady he seeks. The fears and suspicions of Malbecco correspond to the porter figures in the later book—Doubt, Delay, and Daunger. Spenser says that Cupid secretly smiled to see the prospering of Paridell's suit; Venus frankly favors Scudamour with amiable laughter (III.x.5; IV.x.56). Paridell wears a burning heart, and Hellenore burns the idolatrous Malbecco's money; Scudamour claims Amoret in the name of a sacrifice to Venus, and presumably the altars of the goddess flame with hearts like the one sacrificed by the lover in the twenty-second *Amoretti* sonnet. Paridell steals Hellenore from under the one miserly eye of Malbecco; Scudamour leads Amoret from the Temple under the liberal gaze of Venus. Paridell eventually abandons Hellenore to the satyrs, who treat her as common property, in contrast to Malbecco's seclu-

---

[545] *Romance of the Rose*, ll. 15779ff., 20683ff.

sion of her. Scudamour will lose Amoret to Busirane; and, like Malbecco, he will be unable to redeem his wife.

It is paradoxical, of course, to treat Malbecco's castle as a temple of Venus. Yet behind Paridell and Hellenore lie their prototypes in Paris and Helen, and a standard episode of the medieval tale of Troy had Paris abduct Helen from the temple of Venus. The Trojan's robbing of the temple is found in the tradition extending from Benoit de Sainte More's *Roman de Troie*: in Caxton's *Recuyell*, in Lydgate's *Troybook* and *Fall of Princes*, and in Gower's *Confessio Amantis*.[546] Both Hellenore and Amoret, as Paridell says of the first Helen, are gifts of Venus (III.ix.34). Paridell's emblem is appropriately Venerean: the mythological compendiums of Cartari and Giraldus both report the type known as the Saxon Venus, who bears a flaming torch on her chest. The *fax pectoris* is also specifically Parisian.[547]

Malbecco attempts to redeem his wife, and he hazards both his wealth and safety to do so. In return he is fleeced by Braggadocchio and given the horn by the satyrs' herd of goats. (The goat is the zodiacal sign for December and the emblem of the lechery and jealousy of old men [I.iv.24].) After his failure Malbecco falls into a cave while trying to commit suicide. Consumed with his passion to the point of abstraction, he "Forgot he was a man, and *Gealosie* is hight" (III.x.60). Thus he is granted a kind of

[546] The basis for the medieval account is Dares the Phrygian, *Hist.*, 9f., where we learn that Helen was abducted from the isle of Cytherea while she sacrificed to Diana at the temple of Venus. This last anomaly is strikingly explained by R. M. Frazer, Jr., in his trans. of Darys and Dictys, *The Trojan War* (Bloomington, Ind., 1966), by reference to Dares' source, Dracontius' *Romulea* VIII.435, where the text has *Dione* rather than Diana. For the story, see "De raptu Helenae," ll. 498–515 in Bachrens, ed., *Poeta Latini Minores*, vol. 5. In Guido de Columnis, *Historia Destructionis Troiae*, Lib. VII, ed. Nathaniel Edward Griffen (Cambridge, Mass., 1936), pp. 69–76, Paris and Helen exchange secret signs in the temple in question. For the subsequent medieval versions the references are: *The Recuyell of The Historyes of Troye of Raoul Lefever*, trans. Wm. Caxton, ed. H. Oskar Sommer (London, 1894), vol. 2, pp. 529–534, where the temple is on the "ysle of Cythare"; Lydgate, *Troybook*, ll. 1412–1420, and *Fall of Troy*, I, ll. 5986ff.; Gower, *Confessio Amantis*, Book V, ll. 7469–7590. Gower's account is not the least important for Spenser, because the temple incident is his reason for telling the story: not as an example of adulterous love, but of a sub-species of *avarice*, namely sacrilege. Comparably, Scudamour fears committing "sacrilege . . . the Church to rob" (IV.x.53) at the Temple. Another instance of the sack of Troy-temple of Venus complex is Samuel Daniel's *Delia*, Son. 39.

[547] It originates in the dream of Hecuba. See Ovid, *Heroides* XVI.50; Dictys, *Ephemerido Belli Troiani*, III.26; Hyginus, *Fab.* XCI; Servius, *ad Aen.* VII.320, X.750; Apollodorus, *Bibl.* III.xii.5. For the *fax pectoris* as an image for Venus herself, see the Saxon Venus noticed in Giraldus, *Hist. Deorum*, Synt. XIII, *Op. om.*, I, col. 387F, "ardentem facem pectore," and Cartari, *Le Imagini, edn. cit.*, p. 391. In Chaucer, *Merchant's Tale*, l. 1727f., Venus dances at January's marriage with a firebrand, with which she burns the lover Damian (l. 1777f.).

parody of immortality, like Tithonus. The sterility that has overtaken this sombre story may be set against the plenitude manifested by the environs of Venus. Malbecco's castle is a place where wealth is hoarded, and he is robbed; Venus' grounds are "lauishly enricht with natures threasure" (IV.x.23), and the quester is correspondingly enriched:

> For all that nature by her mother wit
> Could frame in earth, and forme of substance base,
> Was there, and all that nature did omit
> Art playing second natures part, supplyed it.
>
> No tree, that is of count, . . .
>
> . . . .
> But there was planted, or grew naturall
> No sense of man so coy and curious nice,
> But there mote find to please itself withall;
>
> (IV.x.21–22)

Man's special nature is acknowledged here by the presence of his arts, which play "second natures part": Venus brings persons as well as bodies together. Nature without nurture, on the other hand, is represented by the world of Hellenore's satyrs. As said before, it is a world of stimulus and response: its denizens may not be capable of a friendship like that of Jonathan and David, but neither is there any evidence among them of the knowing selfishness of a Paridell.

In both legends the two concluding cantos comprise a clearly defined unit. Each describes the events leading to the deliverance of a heroine from her principal oppressor. Both Amoret and Florimell have been holding out for seven months; both are confined to a "dongeon deep" guarded by fiends, before which a helpless lover is presently situated. Each victim is divided from the mortal male by a barrier element (Scudamour cannot pass through fire, Marinell is apparently not at home under water). Each captor has a name that seems to refer to an Egyptian host, Egypt being a symbol for bondage in Book I. (Busiris is the Pharaoh of the Exodus according to both Raleigh and Milton.)[548] In both stories a deliverer is brought on the scene in order to behold the processional celebration of a wedding—the evil host is the master of the revels. As noted above, Busirane

[548] Raleigh, *History*, II.ii.7. See Otto of Freising, *The Two Cities*, I.18f., for the Pharaoh as "King Bochoris," who was urged to eliminate foreigners from Egypt and who lived at the same time as the tyrant Busiris, who put foreigners to death. Busiris is the name of the Pharaoh in *Par. Lost* I.307: see D. C. Allen in *MLN*, 65 (1950), p. 115.

and Proteus are types of Love the magician and Love the sophist. At the same time that they are hosts, they are also abductors. Busiris, in a legend to which Spenser glancingly refers in his first canto (III.i.57), sent pirates to kidnap the beautiful daughters of Atlas.[549] Here Busirane's band of masquers correspond to the gang of friends who steal a bride on behalf of a rejected suitor.[550] Proteus is more obviously piratical, though in the traditional story he *rescues* Helen from pirates; here he has rescued Florimell from the fisherman. In Busirane's tapestry Britomart sees the shifts to which Eros has driven the gods. In the orderly momentum of the rivers' march to the sea, Marinell witnesses the gods as they celebrate a marriage. In either case the poetic principle is mythological: the identification of a natural manifestation with a divine one. On the one hand we may recognize the god concealed in a golden shower, or a bull, or a dolphin. On the other, we may see a divine being revealed in the character of an ocean, or a river, or a countryside.

It is Cupid with his arrows who has the place of honor in Busirane's ante-chamber and the Masque; the emphasis falls on the ferocity and coercive power of Eros. At the House of Proteus violent attraction is replaced by natural affinity, and the abusive Cupid is succeeded by the more harmonious Arion. As the volatile Cupid surmounts the dragon that his arrows have blinded, Arion is accompanied by the dolphin his music

---

[549] See n. 99, above. Besides the Ovid text that makes Busiris the type of the ruthless seducer and Proteus the type of the mendacious one, the tyranny of Busiris and the reign of Proteus form matching halves in Plutarch, *On the Malice of Herodotus* 12 (*Moralia* 857). Plutarch is condemning Herodotus for being "such a pro-barbarian that he acquits Busiris of the charge of human sacrifice and murder of strangers. He . . . turns this charge . . . back against the Greeks. His story, in his second book [II.119], is that Menelaus after recovering Helen from Proteus and being honoured with rich presents behaved like the most shocking criminal." (Trans. L. Pearson and E. H. Sandbach, eds., Loeb *Moralia*, vol. 11, p. 25.) But in fact Herodotus does not mention Busiris here. Valerius Probus, in a note on the text of Virgil in which Servius has allegorized Proteus as the passions, says (at *Ecl.* IV.390) that Proteus is both Egyptian and Greek (or Carpathian and *Pallenen*) because "Proteus was born in Egypt, and it is said that on account of the cruelty of Busiris that he sought *Pallenen* and made his way back into Egypt." (Text in Thilo-Hagen, ed., *Servii*, vol. 3, Appendix Serviana, p. 386; Servius Danielis also has this explanation, *vol.* 3, p. 350.) Mignault, in Alciati, *edn. cit.*, p. 634, writes: "Valerius Probus makes Proteus an Egyptian, whom he states to be so denominated on account of a certain remarkable cruelty of Busiris; Virgil notwithstanding." Cf. the alexandrine of III.xi.22 (". . . so we a God inuade") and IV.xii.16 ("Yet had refusde a God . . .") for the analogy between the two dominions.

[550] For an example that has some of the contours of Spenser's episode, see Alciphron, *Epist.* II.35 (Schlepes edn.), Loeb *Alciphron, Aelian, Philostratus: The Letters*, ed. Benner and Fobes, pp. 138f., reading Hermaphrodite for *erma phaidrion*.

has enamored and compelled.[551] Spenser repeats the Busirane image of Cupid in the enamoring of Marinell:

> Thus whilst his stony heart with tender ruth
> Was toucht, and mighty courage mollifide,
> Dame *Venus* sonne that tameth stubborn youth
> With iron bit, and maketh him abide,
> Till like a victor on his backe he ride,
> Into his mouth his maystring bridle threw,
> That made him stoupe, till he did him bestride:
>
> (IV.xii.13)

What Britomart sees in the Masque took place seven months earlier, at Amoret's wedding. What Marinell sees causes him to suffer an apparent relapse; his wound is seven months old. Busirane is fettered, and Proteus overruled. Neptune's warrant for the release of Florimell corresponds to Busirane's un-spellbinding of Amoret; the revival of Marinell, to the closing of Amoret's wound. In his second edition Spenser postponed the reunion of Scudamour and Amoret, and the marriage of Florimell and Marinell is similarly delayed at the end of Book IV. The union is not solemnized until the legend of justice, as we noted, because wedlock is a public and legal institution, as well as a personal and natural one.

At the end of Book IV Cymodoce makes her appeal to the sea's sovereign, Neptune, basing her case for Florimell's release on considerations of "equitie" (IV.xii.31), thus anticipating the subject of Spenser's next legend. But in fact the whole preceding canto is a triumph of order; each of the sub-processionals at the wedding of Thames and Medway is led by an order figure. First is Neptune himself, "That rules the Seas" (IV.xi.10); he and the other sea-gods who claim the power to rule the waves are announced by Triton, whose trumpet revoked the floods, according to Ovid (*Metam.* I.334ff.). Then, heading the rivers, comes Nereus, a trustworthy prophet and a teacher of righteousness (IV.xi.18). And then Arion, whose music calmed the raging seas (IV.xi.23); he leads the

---

[551] For the motif of *Cupid* on the dolphin's back, see *Anacreonta* 57, which describes a vase depicting a swimming Venus accompanied by a convoy of revelers mounted on the backs of dolphins—Eros, Himeros, and Pothos (Love, Desire, and Longing); in Edmonds, ed. and trans., Loeb *Elegy and Iambus*, vol. 2, Pt. 2, pp. 94f. Cf. also Apuleius, *The Golden Ass* IV.31, where the servitors of Venus traveling over the sea include Palaemon the "little driver of the dolphin," a motif Raphael incorporates into his Galatea fresco. Politian's Galatea, in *Stanze* I.118, is towed by dolphins and encircled by a "lascivious flock," one of which sports for love. See Wind, "Raphael: The Dead Child on a Dolphin," in *Times Literary Supplement*, 25 (Oct. 1963), p. 874. For Arion's music as erotic persuasion, see *Amoretti* XXXVIII.

groom's party, with the groom wearing the capital or crown city on his head, followed by the English and Irish rivers. And last the bride, leading the daughters of Nereus who are assigned "To rule his tides" (IV.xi.52).[552] The Nereids include Cymodoce herself, "that with her least word can asswage / The surging seas" (IV.xi.50), and it is on her name that the canto ends.

With this culminating *exemplum* of orderliness for its preface, most of the last canto of the book is devoted to the rectification of the relations of Florimell and Marinell, and thus the canto proves rather retrospective in character. There is a sense in which Marinell has returned to his origins. Book III began with Britomart's mirror, or, we might say, with the differentiation of Narcissus. It would be appropriate if Book IV should end with something cognate. A brief study of Marinell's discovery there shows that the theme of the last canto is "the mortification of Narcissus."

Like Marinell, Narcissus was the subject of a prophecy made to his mother: in Ovid's story Tiresias tells her that the attractive boy will live to a ripe old age, but only "if he never knows himself" (*Metam.* III.348). Marinell, in contrast, comes to know his "other"—Florimell—but he is still like Narcissus in being separated from his desire by a barrier of water. Like Narcissus, he fades into a shadow of his former self, so that "nothing like himselfe he seemd in sight" (IV.xii.20; cf. *Metam.* III.489–493). The fixity of Marinell's grief over the impasse is also rather reminiscent of the *dolor* of Ovid's account. Further, Florimell's frustrated imprecation—"let him liue vnlou'd, or loue him selfe alone" (IV.xii.9)—recalls the prayer of the scorned youth in Ovid, who exclaimed, "sic amet ipse licet, sic non potiatur amato!" (so let him love himself, and not possess the beloved one [*Metam.* III. 405]). In Ovid, Nemesis will fulfill this prayer.

Among those whom Narcissus spurned, the only one Ovid actually names is Echo, and there are several senses in which Florimell also becomes a wasted shadow, a mere echo, of herself. One thinks of her relation to the False Florimell. Spenser differs from Ovid's tale, however, in making Florimell's complaint awaken a sympathetic echo in the heart of the formerly hardhearted Marinell. Thus the phrases describing the girl's complaint, in the fifth stanza ("to her selfe her sorrow did bemone"); the stone seemed "to feele her grieuous paine, / And oft to grone") reverberate in the twelfth stanza, where Marinell's response to hearing this complaint is described: "He could no more but her great misery bemone," and he "euen for griefe of mind . . . oft did grone." As this "no more but" suggests, there is a sense in which Marinell has changed places with the incapacitated Echo figure—the original story is reversed when Marinell hovers

[552] Spenser may allude to their mother's name, Eurynome, "wide rule." I am indebted to a paper of my student Erroll McDonald for the analysis of the processionals in IV.xi offered here.

around the imprisoned other, "As he had lost him selfe . . . Oft listening if he mote her heare againe" (IV.xii.17). This not only makes Marinell a repentant Narcissus, hearkening to and heeding the Echo figure, but it also shows us where his rehabilitation will lie: in his capacity to reverse a Narcissistic introversion. Unlike the grief that reduces Ovid's Echo to the haunting of lonely caves (*Metam*. III.393–395), Florimell's complaint is not ignored by her young man; likewise, the infatuation that saps the manhood of Narcissus in Ovid—where the boy pleads with his image when it seems to have deserted him (*Metam*. III.475–478)—becomes in Spenser's story response to a more authentic other. The consequent socializing of Narcissus provides an apt conclusion for a legend of friendship, even while it ends Narcissus as Narcissus. Thus the Narcissus myth proves to have the place at the end of Book IV that the symbol of the hermaphrodite has at the end of Book III.

A different way of understanding the end of the legend of friendship depends on Cymodoce's decision to ignore the possible consequences of Marinell's infatuation with a mortal bride. "Me too the nymphs have loved!" cries Ovid's lovelorn boy (*Metam*. III.456), and in becoming a flower he remains among them. Marinell's mother promises her son that she will procure for him any nymph he pleases: "For loue of Nymphes she thought she need not care" (IV.xii.27). But Marinell has fallen in love with "mortall creatures sead," and it is really the surrender of a precariously maintained state of privacy and perfection—a state of arrested development—that will humanize his character. Friendship in particular humanizes love, and a specifically human love entails an acceptance of mortality and self-surrender. Marinell, who in spite of his name will finally become a husband, will also cease in some ways to be that pure water-spirit and perfect ephebe that is his former character. This consideration might seem to work against the more typical reading of Marinell's revival at the end of Book IV as the cyclic regeneration of a water-spirit, but in fact Spenser's last comparison makes Marinell a reviving plant, that is, more like Florimell than Marinell. In a fairytale by Mary de Morgan called "Through the Fire," a fire-princess and a water-prince fall in love, yet they dread to be united, for fear that each will be the end of the other. But when the match is made, the lovers do not perish; each loses that wild and impersonal nature that in part defines an elemental spirit, but their mutualization also results in their becoming persons. As we will see in our concluding essay, this surrender of a generic existence for a personal one de-allegorizes the agents in fiction, and so marks an end of the animism that made them allegorical. Perhaps the seemingly excessive emphasis on Marinell's "engrieued minde" is partly attributable to this impending separation of consciousness out of nature, for such a separation subjects a nature-spirit to a kind of mortalism. This suggestion takes us somewhat beyond our present subject, however, and in fact inclines toward the "death of Pan" motif that we find in the Mutabilitie cantos. Another relation of Books III and IV to these same cantos will bring us to the conclusion of our consideration here.

[iii]

As we advance through the second three books of Spenser's poem, we encounter a continual reversion of the poem to its own antecedents. The large parallel just outlined suggests a great "fold" in the world of the poem. The two installments, lying together in this full complement of being, insinuate that large congruity of the world with itself that Spenser elsewhere expresses by the androgyny of Nature. The overall theme of the second installment is concord; thus the larger analogy that the second installment discovers with the first manifests Spenser's second subject through nothing less basic than a conjugation of the poem with itself.

In works of literature that present themselves as "works-in-progress," the midpoint that we earlier discussed in epic and romance may take the form of the introduction of a "second subject." Often this subject is marriage, for the obvious reason that such a subject allows the author to expand his matter into a new social context without merely repeating himself. It seems clear that whatever organization might have ultimately been supplied for the *Canterbury Tales* the "marriage-group" would have occupied such a position. The marriage, of course, need never take place. The marriage proposal may itself generate much of the new interest—this is the case in Rabelais' third book, the Widow Wadman episodes of *Tristram Shandy*, and the suit of the Widow Bardell in *The Pickwick Papers*. A more unconventional example of the second subject is found in Virginia Woolf's *Orlando*, where the decisive turning-point in the hero's progress is marked by his transformation into a heroine. Structurally, this is not very different from the continuation device of *Pilgrim's Progress*, where Christian is replaced by Christiana; as a psychological development, however, its affinities are with the poet whose central books show us a lady knight in the Orlando-Rosalind tradition, and a Venus who is hermaphroditic.

Venus is the Alma Mater in both legends: the mistress of Adonis and center of Book III, and the biform sponsor of Cupid's man and Cupid's woman near the end of Book IV. We have already invoked the tradition that makes her a nature-goddess, and here we should reemphasize her universal character in *The Faerie Queene*.[553] The garden-Venus of Book

---

[553] For the identity of Venus and Nature, see Apuleius, *Golden Ass* IV.30, where Venus says: "Behold I, the primeval parent of nature, the original beginning of the elements, the *alma* Venus of the whole world. . . ." In the *Romance of the Rose*,

III is like the *Natura querellis* of Claudian's *De Raptu Proserpina*, weeping like Ceres or Rachel over her children who are not.[554] The Temple-Venus is like the Natura of Alanus, *genetrix rerum*, "at whose nod the world grows young."[555] No reading of any part of the poem seems complete without some reference to the Mutabilitie cantos, and it is especially this continuity of "Great *Nature*" and "Great *Venus*" (VII.vii.13, IV.x.44) that serves to establish these cantos' centrality to the present poem.

Indeed, the major proportions of the Mutabilitie cantos themselves may be at the center of the poem, in the two cantos treating the House of Busirane. There too we have the invading beauty, the tyranny of the sovereign principle, the processional spectacle of the principle's triumph, the dialectical personification of the presiding deity, and even the qualified or revisionary ending. The Mutabilitie cantos also reflect the periphery of Books III and IV. The initial fiction of these cantos supposes an assault on an integrity symbolized by the chaste moon; the convocation in the sequel expands into an epiphany of Nature in which all her works bear her witness. As its opening canto attests, Spenser's central massif begins by proposing an analogous subject; Britomart's name, like that of Cynthia, is a cognomen of Diana. And the closing cantos bring out of that subject an equivalent testimony of natural plenitude; both the bridal at the House of Proteus and the congregation on Arlo Hill arrive at something like a concordat of the entire creation.

Venus is not the only figure from Book IV whom Nature recalls. The "greatest goddess," the peacemaker with the possibly terrible face, the indifferent justiciar in whom all contraries are reconciled, who treats the gods as gods treat men—this figure also merges with a sequence of Cybele figures from the same book, standing for the same broad sovereignties. Like Venus, the Asiatic Ceres is bisexual in her Agdistes-Attis aspect; significantly, Agdistes suffers the fate of castration, which Spenser's Faunus, another type of nature, is only just spared. Spenser's own Agdistes, in the Garden of the slain Adonis, cannot be presumed to be entirely innocent of this story either.

Zeuxis, famous for his portrait of Venus, is instead described trying to draw Nature, "when employed to make / An image for her temple." Like Spenser, Jean de Meung retreats from attempting the description of her beauty himself (" 'Twere not right / That I should give account of Nature's form / Or of her face.' "). (Trans. Robbins, ll. 16153f., 16197ff.) Some of the materials in the following section are discussed in Josephine Waters Bennett, "Spenser's Venus and the *Cantos of Mutabilitie*," *Studies in Philology*, 30 (1933), pp. 160–192.

[554] *De Raptu Proserpina* III.33.

[555] *De Planctu Naturae*, metre iv: "Cujus ad nutum juvenescit orbis" (PL, CCX, 447).

The least obvious of the Cybeline relatives of Nature is Dame Concord:

> By her the heauen is in his course contained,
> And all the world in state vnmoued stands,
> As their Almightie maker first ordained,
> And bound them with inuiolable bands;
>
> (IV.x.35)

Comparably, Nature is "the equall mother, / And knittest each to each, as brother unto brother" (VII.vii.14). Concord might seem to resemble Cybele only in respect to the oddity of her head-dress, which is both a "crown" and a bejewelled "Danisk hood" (perhaps a gabelled "French hood" of Danish material?); Cybele wears a turreted or mural crown, which is her distinctive emblem. But Concord's relation to Cambina also makes her a link between Cybele and Nature. Cambina ends strife in "friendships bond," the "mightier band" that is otherwise the "bonds of peace"; these restrain the lions that draw Cambina's chariot (IV.iii, rubric; 48; 40). Paradoxically, the peacemaker arrives amid the greatest clamor, in a Corybantic car, "with speedie whirling pace . . . driuing like a storm out sent" (IV.iii.38). The Corybants were "whirlers" and noisemakers; and, like the lions, they were part of the goddess' traditional entourage. Cambina's cup of Nepenthe probably recalls the blessings of inebriation celebrated by Cybele's rout, or "communion."

The one explicit instance of "Old *Cybele*" in Book IV is the river Thames with his turreted crown; cities are also the work of concord. Virgil's Trojans tried to found their new town on hundred-citied Crete, where Mt. Ida is sacred to Cybele. Virgil implies that the founders of the first Troy originally emigrated from Crete, bringing the worship of the goddess with them (*Aen.* III.99–113). Thames' crown is also a renovated Troy, Troynovant, and thus the advance of the river harmonizes with the advance of civilization:

> Like as the mother of the Gods, they say,
> In her great iron charet wonts to ride,
> When to *Ioues* pallace she doth take her way:
> Old *Cybele*, arayd with pompous pride,
>
> (IV.xi.28)

Spenser can use this same image negatively. According to Macrobius' *Saturnalia* (I.xxiii.20), Cybele's lion-drawn chariot was the earth. Mutability, "th'Earth's daughter," takes a similar route "To *Ioues* high Palace," on an inspiration we know from Book I to be analogous to Luciferan pride (VII.vi.22f.; I.iv.17). Mutability is presented by means of a processional; Nature is accorded a kind of throne-triumph and may conceal a lion's face behind her veil, and she gives her judgment in a moment of suspense exactly analogous to the moment in which Cambina intervenes as arbitrator between Cambel and Triamond (VII.vii.47; IV.iii.27). And yet the poet has placed neither Nature nor Mutabilitie in a chariot. However, the Orphic *Hymn* to Nature says that Nature giddily whirls [*dineousa*] a rapid chariot everlastingly, and the Mutabilitie cantos begin from "the euerwhirling wheele / Of Change" (VII.vi.1). The indications that Nature is Cybeline are therefore strong. The Nature that "knittest each to each, as brother vnto brother" (VII.vii.14) is also Orphic. Orpheus himself is a patron of friendship, partly on account of his having once made friends out of enemies (IV.ii.1).

Some of Spenser's most characteristic eloquence seems to be inspired by the approach of Nature, the *Magna Mater*:

> This great Grandmother of all creatures bred
> Great *Nature*, euer young yet full of eld,
> Still moouing, yet vnmoued from her sted;
> Vnseene of any, yet of all beheld;
>
> (VII.vii.13)

And yet a long tradition lies behind these lines, exemplified by such personifications as Claudian's Natura, *vultu longaeva decoro* (with the aged beautiful face).[556] Nature is in fact often described by means of contrary or dialectically arranged epithets. This rhetorical usage is particularly notable in the case of the enthroned goddess of the Orphic *Hymn*; for example, she is *autopater, apator* (self-fathered, without a father).

The *Hymn* has an essential contribution to make to our sense of Spenser's Nature as both the sum of phenomena, and the mysterious noumenon behind them. In the Latin translation:

> infinitaque finis
> Nulli communis, communiter officiosa,
>
> . . . .
>
> . . . regina potestas
> Aprilis adolescentum indidem adulta resolvans.
> Omnium tu pater et mater, nutrix quoque et altrix,
>
> . . . .
>
> Omniparens, figula, et multarurum perfica rerum
> Aeterna et motans, . . .
> Pilentum rapidum aeterna vortigine torquens

. . . infinite finite [unending yet bringing to an end], common to none, commonly obliging, . . . queen power releasing the young of April,

---

[556] *De Consulatu Stilichonis* II.431. For the whole tradition, with reference to Claudian esp., see Curtius, *European Literature*, pp. 106–127.

and from the same place the full-grown. You, father and mother of all, even nurse and foster-mother, . . . All-bearing, fashioner and finisher of the multitude of things, eternal and moving, . . . whirling giddily a rapid car everlastingly.[557]

The poet's "Still moouing, yet vnmoued from her sted," plainly translates the "Aeterna et motans" of the *Hymn*, and manages to put stillness and steadiness on both sides of the distinction at the same time. But the phrase "unseene of any, yet of all beheld" would seem to offer a rather inexact version of "common to all, yet not shared, alone." Spenser has apparently fused this motif with another one, namely, "visible, yet invisible." There is no exact equivalent in this *Hymn*, though perhaps *aidia*, the Latin *aeterna*, might also mean unseen. But the missing phrase is actually to be found in the Orphic *Hymn* to Venus: Venus is "phainomenai t' aphanais."[558] Conversely, the Orphic Nature is "father and mother of all, even nurse and foster-mother," while Spenser's Venus is "syre and mother . . . her selfe alone," and she "Begets and eke conceiues, ne needeth other none" (IV.x.41). Spenser has equated the two *Hymns*, and the two goddesses. In the *Hymn* to Nature, the goddess is also saluted as *pandoteira* (all-giving), which the Latin mysteriously translates as *omnidua*; if this means "all two," the universal androgyny of the goddess is again suggested. In the same place, Nature also receives the cognomen *Philia*, which we would normally render as *amicitia*. But in fact the Latin translates it as "Venus," which implies the assignment of a wider and ultimately more pacific dominion to the mother of Eros. With this typical Renaissance interpretation the author of the legend of friendship has repeatedly concurred.

[557] Orphic Hymn IX.8f., 17f., 20–23; cited by H. G. Lotspeich, *Classical Mythology in the Poetry of Edm. Spenser* (Princeton, 1932), p. 87. Latin trans. by Joseph J. Scaliger, added to Stephanus' 1570 edn. of the Hymns. For the rhetoric, see below, Chap. VI, "The Triumph of Time," and compare Augustine, *Confessions*, I.4, describing God: "most hidden and most near; most beauteous and most strong; constant yet not comprehended; changeless, yet changing all things; never new, never old; making all things new, yet bringing the proud to decay and they know it not; always working, yet ever at rest; still gathering, yet needing nothing; sustaining, pervading, and protecting; creating, nourishing, and bringing to perfection; seeking, and yet possessing all things." (Trans. adapted from Rex Warner and James Pilkington.)

[558] Orphic Hymn LIV.10; in the trans., "Visa, inuisa" (in Hambergerus, ed., *Orpheos Apanta*, pp. 250f.). A negative, of course, is also "seen, yet unseen," and in the Mutabilitie cantos, Death, "with most grim and griesly visage *seene*," is at the same time "Vnbodied, vnsoul'd, vnheard, *vnseene*" (VII.vii.46). The analogous figure is not so much Nature as her mutable shadow: in this case Night, who is also veiled. For the "still moving" paradox, cf. William Cartwright's description of the annual cycle: "Motion as in a Mill / Is busie standing still" ("A New-years-gift," stanza 3, in *Poems*, 1651).

V

THE WORD OF GOD AND THE
WORDS OF MEN

"As time goes on the Vinaya-Pitaka will disappear, but as long as a four-line stanza remains among men, so long the disappearance of learning will not have occurred. But when a pious king shall cause a purse containing a thousand pieces of money to be placed in a golden casket on the back of an elephant, and shall cause proclamation up to the second and third time to be made throughout the city to the sound of the drum, as follows: 'Any one who knows a single stanza spoken by The Buddhas, let him take these thousand coins together with this elephant,' and yet shall fail to find any one who knows a four-line stanza, and shall receive again the purse containing the thousand pieces into the royal palace, then the disappearance of learning will have occurred.

"This, O Sāriputta, is the disappearance of learning.

"Now as time goes on the last of the priests will carry their robes, their bowls, and their tooth-sticks after the manner of the naked ascetics. They will take a bottle-gourd, make of it a begging-bowl, and carry it in their arms, or in their hands, or in the balance of a carrying-pole. And as time goes on a priest will say, 'What is the good of this yellow robe?' and cut a small piece of yellow cloth, and tie it around his neck, or his ears, or his hair, and devote himself to husbandry or trade and the like, and to taking care of wife and children. Then he will give gifts to the southern congregation. And the fruit of this gift, say I, will be a myriadfold. As time goes on the priests will say, 'What do we want with this?' and they will throw away the piece of yellow cloth and persecute the wild animals and birds of the forest, and thus the disappearance of the symbols will have occurred.

"This, O Sāriputta, is *the disappearance of the symbols*."

("The Buddhist Apocalypse," from Henry Clark Warren, *Buddhism in Translations*, sec. 102.)

[i]

THE formal education of a child starts by introducing him to a very hypothetical construction: a fairyland of letters and numbers and the rules for their grammars. To some extent all early training has this arbitrary character, at least when it is considered from the point of view of unconditioned impulse and natural energy. Eventually our experience and our education become more or less synonymous; we begin to inhabit the world we have made. Our fairyland becomes "second nature" to us, a *habitus* in the Scholastic sense, and this second nature occupies virtually the entire available space of our conscious faculties. Our education may very well continue beyond this point, but it no longer has as its primary object the introduction of the cultural matrix into our minds. Instead, we begin to explore our identifications with that matrix: alterations and revisions have to be made introspectively, so to speak, from the inside.

By the end of the fifth book, an analogous establishment or formation or institution has come into existence for *The Faerie Queene*—or so Spenser's confidence that he cannot go astray in the sixth book seems to indicate. If the poem is not complete, something in it is; the opening stanza of the proem tells us as much:

> The waies, through which my weary steps I guyde,
>> In this delightfull land of Faery,
>> Are so exceeding spacious and wyde,
>> And sprinckled with such sweet variety,
>> Of all that pleasant is to eare or eye,
>> That I nigh rauisht with rare thoughts delight,
>> My tedious trauell doe forget thereby;
>> And when I gin to feele decay of might,
> It strength to me supplies, and chears my dulled spright.
>
> (VI, proem, 1)

Spenser's poem has been graduated to one of his resources; it has become "second nature" to the poet and the reader. This development argues not only for its magnitude, but also for a measure of repleteness.

In comparison to its predecessors, Calidore's legend in Book VI exhibits a devaluation of explicit programs of allegorical significance; along with this devaluation comes a corresponding efflorescence of such romance motifs as the mysterious foundling, the woodland nonage, the noble savage, the rustication of the chivalric personae, and the knight's retirement from worldly endeavour. These motifs are evidently phases of some fuller cycle. Other romance motifs in Book VI are the talking beast, the pirate cave, and the narrow escape from cannibals. Delight seems to have been given precedence over instruction here, and often enough we find ourselves experiencing not the romance of faith or chastity, but the romance of romance itself.

The subversive element in this kind of romance, as we noted in the case of Ariosto, is not so much the antagonist, as it is irony: the timeless Arcadia proves transitory—Death has been in this Arcadia too; the hero's chief virtue, being somewhat superficial, makes him seem slightly "hollow"; and the Arcadian context of the quest resigns the quest itself to a perfunctory performance.[1] The burden of the following commentary is mainly on the other side, but even our sustained comparison between this book and the legend of holiness may be taken to be ironical.

Despite the differences in tone, there are many moral allegories in the sixth book that do not differ in their essential structure from the general practice of the poem. For Sansfoy, Sansjoy, and Sansloi of the first book, the last can offer Decetto, Despetto, and Defetto. For the rebellious Radigund of the legend of justice, the legend of courtesy has the rebellious Mirabella. Nonetheless, characters like the giant Disdain impress one as "quotations" from the poem's earlier moral allegory, and Spenser's own reference to the giant's brother, Orgoglio, lends this impression substance. A more typical enemy in this legend is the hostile and inhospitable Turpine: he does so many shameful things that it is hard to characterize his significance beyond saying that he represents the capacity to do shameful things. Much of his time is spent harassing decent persons, especially the inoffensive Calepine, to whom he refuses assistance and shelter. He is simply a difficult or intractable person of the kind recognized in Della Casa's popular handbook of manners: "Surly people seem like strangers everywhere—you might even say like intruders—whereas amiable people on the other hand seem to have friends and acquaintances wherever they go."[2] This citation explains precisely the contrast between Turpine and Calidore, and it also helps to explain why Turpine seems so inscrutable.

---

[1] Calidore begins by suggesting that the lowly quest of courtesy will go unnoticed ("Yet shall it not by none be testifyde," VI.i.6), though in point of fact the hero will be admired by throngs of people at the conclusion of the legend. More typically, it is the part of courtesy to be somewhat self-effacing, which makes the quest for glory in this legend decidedly quizzical at the outset.

[2] *Galateo*, chap. ix, trans. R. S. Pine-Coffin, Penguin Classics (Harmondsworth, Middlesex, 1958), p. 38. The rudimentary character of the threat posed by Turpine is of course part of the point—Turpine is rude. This quality is given its name in Crudor (raw, unrefined), and appears in a positive form in the "ruder hart" of the untutored Salvage Man: lacking the refinements of speech, he communicates by "rude tokens" (VI.vi.4, 11).

THE QUEST FOR THE FAERIE QUEENE

Still, such an allegory is a form of the "exemplarist" reading of fiction to be found in the apparatus that is printed with the Renaissance Ariosto. The legend is full of such "examples."

Perhaps the reassimilation of the allegory by the fiction is not altogether unanticipated. Book V has shown us the "greater" Arthur spoken of in our first essay, and he is a visitor in the court of a queen closely identified with Gloriana. The condemnation of Duessa as Mary Queen of Scots on this occasion effectively terminates her allegorical "otherness," and the reader will remember that the emergence of Duessa more or less coincided with the beginning of the poem. Her demise might serve to mark the passing of an allegory that we translate into a series of alternate significances, a point like that reached in learning another language, where we cease to match and parse and interpolate.

There are a number of other evidences of the terminal character of the present book. Like Britomart, Calidore is a character whose presence is not continuously required by his legend. A comparatively disengaged view of the action of the quest is taken by the poet, and the themes of holiday and contemplative withdrawal bulk large. We have Calidore's retirement to the world of the shepherds, and, within that, Colin's seclusion on Mount Acidale: arts and letters qualify as a recreation and an adornment of leisure. Colin apologizes for a singular dereliction of duty—he is not celebrating the fairy queen; the Graces themselves were begot while Jove was on holiday (VI.x.22). Meliboe is a retired court gardener, and the Hermit is a retired knight errant. Related themes are the privacy sought by lovers and the rustication of Timias and Serena after the bites of the Blatant Beast. There are briefer indications of the same withdrawal movement in the retreat of the cannibals to the little grove, and the harboring of Pastorella by the pirate captain underground. Calepine's retreat from Turpine extends the theme to the withdrawal of knights from ruinous engagements. Perhaps the motif of uninterrupted or unmolested sleep belongs here as well, for sleep is also a withdrawal from the world.

The theme of cynosure, another aspect of the theme of contemplation, is important in this legend. Serena is found on her altar of green turfs, Pastorella on her hillock, and the three Graces on Mount Acidale. In their various contexts, all these scenes suggest the contemplation or worship of beauty through the noble sense of the eyes. Why this should be appropriate to the virtue of courtesy will concern us further on. We may note here that these scenes have the effect of arresting forward progress to allow Spenser's audience to reflect upon the beauties of the poem itself.

Mount Acidale has the place in Book VI that the Garden of Adonis has in Book III. It is the source out of which the legend seems to "well," and the place on which the poet has expended the greatest amount of "learnings threasures" (VI, proem, 2). Having been the nursery of Florimell and the haunt of Venus, it is also "seminal," as Spenser implies in a critical stanza that invokes the Muse:

> Reuele to me the sacred noursery
> Of vertue, which with you doth there remaine,
> Where it in siluer bowre does hidden ly
> From view of men, and wicked worlds disdaine.
> Since it at first was by the Gods with paine
> Planted in earth, being deriu'd at furst
> From heauenly seedes of bounty soueraine,
> And by them long with carefull labour nurst,
> Till it to ripenesse grew, and forth to honour burst.
>
> (VI, proem, 3)

The reader who comes to this from Ficino's discussion of the insiting of the *logoi spermatikoi* in the World-Soul will recognize some of the sources of this gracious endowment. Since the seminary abides with the Muses, we may recall that Ficino attributes analogous generative powers to the imagination. In doing so he is greatly influenced by Plotinus' doctrine of the procreativity of Mind, and especially of contemplation.[3] The following sentences from Plotinus offer as much commentary on Book VI as on Book III:

> Begetting originates in contemplation and ends in the production of a form, that is, a new object of contemplation. In general, all things as they are images of their generating principles produce forms and objects of contemplation. . . . Moreover, animals generate due to the activity within them of seminal reasons. Generation is a contemplation. It results from the longing of pregnancy to produce a multiplicity of forms and objects of contemplation, to fill everything with reason, and never to cease from contemplation. Begetting means to produce some form; and this means to spread contemplation everywhere. All the faults met with in begotten things or in actions are due to the fact that one did stray from the object of one's contemplation. The poor workman resembles the producer of bad forms. Also lovers must be counted among those who contemplate and pursue forms.[4]

There is, then, a chain of analogies between Calepine seeking Serena, the cannibals contemplating her rape, Calidore and the shepherds gazing on Pastorella, Calidore gazing on the Graces, Colin piping to his beloved

[3] See above, Chap. IV, n. 325 and accompanying text, Ficino, *In Plotinum, Enn.* II, III.xvii (in *Op. om.*, II-2, p. 1640).

[4] *Enn.* III, VIII.7, trans. Joseph Katz, in *The Philosophy of Plotinus* (New York, 1950), p. 50.

fourth Grace, and the poet seeking the pattern for his legend "deepe within the mynd." The ripeness of the seeds in the sacred nursery is reflected in the swelling belly of Serena, the "timely frute" that Calidore comes to enjoy in his courtship of Pastorella (VI.x.38), the Graces begotten by Jove on Mount Acidale, and the secret pregnancy of Pastorella's mother. All recall Serena's being allowed to "Sleepe out her *fill*" (VI.viii.38), and dimly suggest that Plotinine extension of contemplation into the promulgation of forms, even if some of this issue is merely "lustfull fantasyes" (VI.viii.47).

Very closely related to both the themes of privacy and contemplative cynosure is what one might call the "embowerment" of the open landscapes found throughout this legend. I owe much of my final sense of this phenomenon in Book VI to an essay by my student Eric Rosenberg, to whose work I will refer here.[5] Rosenberg also begins from the "siluer bowre" of the proem, where the seeds of virtue are said to be hidden and nurtured—we may compare the "Heroicke seed" represented by Sir Tristram, who is concealed from the world's view "amongst the woodie Gods" (VI.ii.25, 26). Not far away is the "couert" into which the besieged Priscilla disappears (VI.ii.43); it is apparently adjacent to the "glade" and "secret shade" where she trysts with Aladine (VI.iii.8). Aladine's bower is invaded by a nameless knight who has caught sight of the lovers. (We never do learn his name; he remains what intruders always are so long as they are intruders, which is a kind of stranger.) Not much different, in that it also symbolizes the private community formed by lovers, is the "couert shade" in which Calepine and Serena safely rest; here it is Calidore who inadvertently interrupts the "quiet" enjoyed by the pair (VI.iii.20, 21). Almost immediately thereafter follows the eruption of the Blatant Beast, which attacks Serena. The Beast's epithet has partly defined him as being loud, or outspoken, or noisily explicit;[6] as elsewhere suggested, Serena has

---

[5] In the following section of this essay I am deeply indebted to Mr. Rosenberg's study of bowers as a key to the theme and organization of Book VI. His work was submitted in Yale College as a Senior Project, for which I was the director. Rosenberg's piece has supplied me with critical links between the theme of contemplative withdrawal and the theme of origins by describing the symbolism—as I am taking it to be—for the reserved and manifested self. He derives this symbolism from the inner-outer configuration of space in Book VI. Mr. Rosenberg is presently preparing his study for publication.

[6] The evidence for this overtone must be found in Spenser's own usage, if the OED is right in listing his as the first instance. The editors derive "blatant" from *bleating*, after the Scottish form *blaitand*, and Latin *blatire*, to babble. Certainly the strong trend of usage after Spenser inclines one to find the idea of clamor and offensive outrightness in the original meaning of the word.

suddenly become the object not only of unwanted scrutiny, but also of unwanted talk.

Deeper in the same woods is the dwelling of the Salvage Man, in which Calepine will convalesce, "Farre in the forrest by a hollow glade, / Couered with mossie shrubs . . . Where foot of liuing creature neuer trode" (VI.iv.13). Serena, for her restoration, will be retired to the grovelike green chapel in which the Hermit abides, a recluse from the annoyance of the neighborhood (VI.v.34f.). She also receives counsel in his "cell." In addition to these retreats, we may mention the modulation of the "silver bowre" of the proem in the "siluer slomber" that keeps Arthur temporarily oblivious to treachery, and the "siluer sleepe" enjoyed by Meliboe as a consequence of his "minds vnmoued quiet" (VI.vii.19, ix.22). The ground on which the Graces dance (partly owing to a description in Horace, *Odes* I.4, ll. 6f.) is "hollow" (VI.x.10).

The sense of Book VI, then, is of a variety of separate individuals, set apart from one another throughout a common landscape in which each occupies his own "discreet" space—like so many eremites in so many niches. One thinks of paintings of the desert saints in their caves and hollows, and we might also compare the sequestration of the Israelites in the booths in the wilderness. The Hermit's arbor resembles a leafy "cage" (VI.v.38), an image that characterizes the kind of penetrable screen interposed between viewer and view in many of these places. Calidore, for example, spies the shepherds for the first time in among "the budded broomes" (VI.ix.5). The defenses these places provide are often merely provisional, like "the litle cots, where shepherds lie" (VI.ix.4), which especially offer shelter during the wintertime. Other examples are the bushes in which the nurse Melissa hides the infant Pastorella, and the place "vnder the forrests syde" where Matilda bemoans her childlessness (IV.iv.26). In Matilda's case Calepine becomes the intruder, though ultimately a welcome one; thanks to his gift of the foundling, he is enabled to make a graceful retreat.

There are also several parodies of this circumscription and "in-scaping" of the terrain in this legend. Rosenberg draws our attention to perhaps the most notable, the "woody glade"—in the midst of "thicke woods and brakes and briers" (VI.v.17)—where a beset Timias fights his lonely battle against a myriad bent on slandering him. The implication is that Timias has been too frank or forthright for his own good; the "couert" impedes his line of vision, shrouding his enemies, and thus exposing him to ambush and enclosure, i.e., to his foes' innuendo and indirection (VI.v.20). The garment with which Blandina covers the shameful Turpine is another example of an evil use of discretion to "cloke" malevolence.

There are "deeper" examples of recalcitrance as well. The thieves' "little

Island . . . couered with shrubby woods" (VI.x.41) appears at one point to be without any access whatsoever, though otherwise it is simply a hollow cave concealed by thick shrubs (VI.x.42). The hero's bold entrance upon this sequestered underworld is preceded by a respectful delay and much indirection, leading to another welcome intrusion. We have noted the cannibals' deflection into the "litle groue," where it is Calepine who "thrusts into the thickest throng" (VI.viii.49). For a parody of the Hermit's bower we might compare the "Cloysters" of the monks, with their dread of exposing their "cels and secrets neare" (VI.xii.24). Such "bowers," to use Rosenberg's term, are really dens: his apt example is the foul lair in which the Blatant Beast—in a parallel with the seeds of virtue in the silver bower of the proem—"to perfect ripeness grew" (VI.i.8).

Rosenberg has suggested another way in which the spaces of Book VI are enclosed. The ring the cannibals form around Serena must correspond to the secondary ring of lusty shepherds around Pastorella, which in turn anticipates the outer ring of the Graces on Mount Acidale. We could argue that Mirabella, being a center of attention, is another object of cynosure: at least her lovers are said to adore her, and she is hailed before the assembled court of Cupid. In the light of these configurations, Calepine's loss of direction confronts us with a significant impasse:

> For nought but woods and forrests farre and nye
> That all about did close the compasse of his eye.
> (VI.iv.24)

With this we may compare the outer ring of the Graces enclosing the inner ring: ". . . round about did hemme, / and like a girlond did in *compasse* stemme" (VI.x.12). These two uses of the word *compass* are dimly echoed by a third; in the stanza introducing his last canto, the poet says that although his narrative has been at sea, he has not lost his compass. This seems to be correct in a special sense, for the narrative itself is encompassed by a kind of double ring. The outer ring is formed by the disappearance and return of Calidore, and the inner ring by the disappearance and return of his surrogate, Calepine; thus the encircled Serena and Pastorella turn up on the periphery of the two narrative rings. Mirabella, along with the Hermit, is found within the inner ring.

One may also think of the narrative as digressing inward toward the dwelling of the Hermit, and then, starting from Mirabella's isolation by Scorn and Disdain, digressing outward toward Serena and Pastorella. Spenser may partly acknowledge such a quasi-topographical pattern in his account of Calidore's chase after the Blatant Beast, which shows the hero moving outward across a series of frontiers, each at a further remove from the court from which courtesy seems to have taken its name (VI.i.1):

Him first from court he to the citties coursed,
And from the citties to the townes him prest,
And from the townes into the countrie forsed,
And from the country back to priuate farmes he scorsed.

From thence into the open fields he fled, . . .

(VI.ix.3-4)

The slight reversion in the movement "back to priuate farmes"—back toward the center—becomes more marked at the end of the legend. The hero returns to a castle, then chases the Beast into the cloisters, and thereafter compels his captive to follow him through the towns—presumably on the way back to the court of the queen who sent him. It is from this court that courtesy ideally wells (VI, proem, 7), but there is something ironic in the hero's never penetrating to the deeper recesses of the forest where the bowers of the Salvage Man and the Hermit lie; Calidore is perhaps too much the courtier ever to be found apart from some society or other for any length of time. The inward and outward oscillation for the narrative tends, finally, to make the legend itself an object of centripetal gaze, and thus a focus for contemplation.

The Hermit tells his guests to "Shun secresie" and to "talk in open sight," but he also counsels them to isolate the senses and contain their impulses (VI.vi.14, 7). The two counsels are by no means wholly contradictory, but the difference between them expresses a tension peculiar to courtesy. "Evil communications corrupt good manners" (I Cor. 15:33), the Hermit implies, "For in much speaking thou shalt not escape sin" (Proverbs 10:19). The Hermit may shun secrecy; but, nevertheless, he dwells apart, and his past history remains undisclosed. Courtesy, which depends on fair speech, also requires that many things be left unsaid. This tension is also felt in the hospitality and retrenchment exhibited in different combinations by Aldus, the Hermit, and Meliboe—and also in the cannibals and the thieves. One will recall that the words *guest* and *host* are both derived from words meaning stranger.

The retention and guarding of some secret core of being seems essential to this legend; the theme is taken beyond the requirements of mere modesty or the dictates of natural reticence, though these are its ostensible sources. The meaning of the self is the larger issue here. A self ought to be, almost by definition, something inviolable. Courtesy is shown in the respect accorded to another person's determination upon inward possession. The devouring eyes of the cannibals, which symbolically violate Serena, also violate this respect for privacy. The cannibals are very bad hosts, since they plan to eat their guest; but they also show some minimal respect for her privacy in that they let her "Sleepe out her fill" (VI.viii.38). In a parallel with this scene, the hospitably treated Calidore gazes on Pastorella with "hungry eye" (VI.ix.26), but he makes his first approaches indirectly, through her more accessible sponsor.

Further, the courteous person is not once, but twice, circumspect; if only out of fear of imposing on others, he reserves some part of his own inner being from others. It is partly this economy of self-reservation that is suggested by Meliboe's frugality. It must also be symbolized by the creation of the protective or cellular spaces immediately around so many of the figures in the legend's landscape. Thus the more shallow hollows and temporary recesses in this landscape simply imply that moment in the day that Satan cannot find, when one shuts out the world in order to enjoy the delights of revery. The more deeply embedded loci suggest longer pauses for refreshment and recuperation of the sense of the self. Deeper still are those places that symbolize the actual maintenance of the self out of a reserve as continuously generative as the Garden of Adonis.

Much self-respecting behavior, it could be argued, is rooted in this sense of possessing an inner being, and courtesy in particular mediates between such self-possession and other persons. Perhaps Turpine's inscrutability may be seen as taking this reserve to an extreme; like the thieves' den, his person is without any real access. We are meant to contrast the Salvage Man, who led a completely private existence until his discovery of Calepine and Serena, but who then develops accessibility and compassion directly as occasion offers. Courtesy is thus preeminently a virtue that *manifests* itself; the legend is full of examples of this emergence, as well as the emergencies that prompt it. In the more genuine of its manifestations, courtesy expresses the inwardly conceived generous or kind thought, as opposed to the motivation disguised by "fayned" or "forged shows" (VI, proem, 4; v.38). Externally considered, Mount Acidale is just such a delusive "show" on the part of the poet (VI.x.17); at the same time, however, it is a gracious answer to the prayer made in the proem, that the Muses reveal to the poet the inward seat of virtue. There is a sense in which Mount Acidale is "deep within the mynd," that deeper reservoir of "thought" from which the thoughtful or considerate action originates.

An important aspect of the theme of the reserved and manifested self is the frequent motif of secret or concealed *origins*. We note the prominence of the *enfance* motif in the stories of Tristram and Pastorella. The bower of the proem is specifically a nursery and a flower-bed, from which virtue "forth to honour burst." The broad hints about the noble blood of the Salvage Man and the bear baby point back to this same place: as Rosenberg notes, Tristram is like a flower enclosed in its bud, which "At length breakes forth," and the Salvage Man's nobility will "at the last breake forth" (VI.ii.35, v.1). This emphasis on beginnings gives precedence to the origins of heroism, as opposed to the derivations from it; once Tristram has acquired his knighthood, horse, and arms, the poet ceases to follow his story.

The flower of courtesy, the poet says, bowers "on a lowly stalke" (VI, proem, 4), and the theme of origins is appropriate to Book VI because there is a sense in which all beginnings are necessarily *humble*. The reversion to humble origins is met in the activity of Colin Clout. In the self-depiction of Pastorella's favorite poet we hearken back to the pre-chivalric beginnings of Spenser's own poetic canon; following the example of Virgil, poets were supposed to *begin*, not end, with the meanness of pastoral. This notable reversal of the order established by Virgil gives a special cast to Calidore's pursuit of the Blatant Beast, which takes the hero from cities to farms, and from farms into open fields. Calidore's course reverses the development of civilization, which the development of Virgil's poetic canon was alleged to have recapitulated.[7]

Rather more quizzical, but scarcely less suggestive of the theme of origins, are the two discoveries in the legend of the Freudian primal scene. The viewing of the fairies on Mount Acidale strikes one as a sublimation of the same scene. Surreptitiously observed, such scenes suggest the origins of speculation; they provoke curiosity and want interpretation. And perhaps these scenes also preserve some faint memory of their paradisal originals. In the future that God plans for Israel, there will be no more wild animals in the land, and the people "shal dwell safely in the wildernes, and slepe in the woods" (Ezk. 34:25, Geneva Bible).

The cells and coverts and fairy rings that enclose the space of this legend are not the only features that make Book VI markedly romantic. The narrator tends to digress from the chivalric to the unchivalric upon any occasion that offers. Calepine, for example, refuses Matilda's offer of a horse and arms, and apparently prefers roaming through the greenwood

---

[7] Servius, following Donatus at the end of his *Life of Virgil*, believes that the *Bucolics*, *Georgics*, and *Aeneid* follow a natural order, from verse written by men in the wilds ("in montibus"), to verse dealing with agricultural communities, to verse on the imperial theme of war. Thus arose the opinion that the ontogeny of the individual poetic oeuvre might follow the phylogeny of literature as a whole, from the humble to the grand style. Servius' proemiums to each of Virgil's kinds may be consulted here, especially *In Vergilii Bucolicon*, in Thilo-Hagen, eds., *Servii*, vol. 3, pp. 1–3. Spenser refers to the Servian tradition in "October," ll. 55–60: the "laboured lands" that Virgil cultivated come from Servius' derivation of the title *Georgics* from Grk. *gais ergon*: "id est terrae operam" (Thilo-Hagen, eds., *Servii*, vol. 3, p. 129).

without them in search of his lost Serena (VI.iv.39f.). We have already remarked the tendency to go beyond the "heroic" fiction in search of "romance" origins. As a court poet, of course, Spenser is anxious to justi the breeding of his more noble and gentle characters, but as a writer of romances he feels free to discover that breeding in some fairly out-of-the-way places.

The intensification of romance is especially evident in the two brigand episodes. The sacrifice of Serena by the cannibals may recall an episode in the second book of the Greek romance of *Clitopho and Leucippe*, by Achilles Tatius. There the hero beholds brigands sacrificing the heroine on a rude altar of earth—they are performing a religious observance, and they appear to stab the victim and feast upon her innards. The scene turns out to be a staged deception, and Leucippe is later brought out of her coffin alive. By the end of this particular romance we have learned the wisdom of the hero's friend, who at another crisis advises Clitopho not to despair of Leucippe's survival: " 'Consider,' he said, 'how often she has died and come to life again; who knows but what she may do the same on this occasion also?' "⁸ Elsewhere in the same story, a gang of pirates slays their commander—who has fallen in love with Leucippe—during a quarrel over whether or not she shall be sold to slavers.⁹ Pastorella's story owes its central episode to this motif. In Heliodorus, similarly, the captain Trachinus fights with his subordinate Pelorus over possession of the heroine; the consequent falling out among the pirates leads to a battle in which they all destroy each other.¹⁰ In Ariosto, Orlando rescues Isabella from a cave where she is captive to slave-traders; they are trying to make arrangements to sell her, and again there is havoc in the cave (*O.F.* XIII.29–39).

In the genre in question, the preservation of the heroine's physical integrity is an important consideration in maintaining the fiction itself. The heroine generally puts off a number of inappropriate suitors whose importunate advances alternate with lurid threats of ritual sacrifice or burial alive. The reader comes to regard the violation of the heroine's body by the wrong lover as approximately equivalent to death itself. The dénouement of such a fiction entails recognition scenes that lead to the heroine's losing her virginity under the proper auspices. Spenser's episodes of Serena and Pastorella are roughly parallel, and both heroines are brought as close to death as possible. Serena is all but sacrificed when Calepine

---

⁸ Achilles Tatius, VII.6, trans. by Rev. Roland Smith, in *The Greek Romances* (*Scriptores Erotici Graeci*) (London, 1882), p. 478.

⁹ Achilles Tatius, VIII.16; in Smith, *Greek Romances*, p. 507.

¹⁰ *Ethiopica* V; Smith, *Greek Romances*, pp. 127–129. An allusion to Sidney is not out of the question here, since this episode has inspired the opening scene of Sidney's *Arcadia*. Sidney is an appropriate pattern for Spenser's hero, because the *Defense of Poetry* opposes not merely slander, but the slander of the office of the poet.

arrives, and she is said to be "alreadie dead with fearefull fright" (VI.viii. 45). Likewise, when Calidore rescues Pastorella, she is being held captive in a tomblike cave where death is said to walk at large (VI.xi.16). As part of her ordeal she is trapped in the embrace of her dead protector, the pirate-captain, and she shares his wound. Afterwards she is recovered from under a pile of corpses. When Calidore finally reaches her, she is "Looking each houre into deathes mouth to fall" (VI.xi.44). Serena has already fallen into the mouth of the slanderous Blatant Beast, and the Beast's affinities with Cerberus, the corpse-devouring dog of Hades, suggest the connection between the monster of the legend and the pirates' underworld. The dog is a veritable confusion of tongues, and the quarrel among the pirates is "the frute of too much talk":

> Like as a sort of hungry dogs ymet
> About some carcase by the common way,
> Doe fall together, stryuing each to get
> The greatest portion of the greedie pray;
> All on confused heapes themselues assay,
> And snatch, and byte, and rend, and tug, and teare;
> That who them sees, would wonder at their fray,
> And who sees not, would be affrayd to heare.
>
> (VI.xi.17)

So the harried Beast of the following canto: "He grind, hee bit, he scratcht, he venim threw" (VI.xii.31). The two brigand episodes occupy the same canto-positions as the two dragons in Book I, where the theme of death and revival is sacramental in character. Thus the sixth book supplies romance analogues for the martyr's altar and the accusing dragon; presumably they are not there only for the sake of design, but for the sake of some deeper ironic resonance as well.

[ii]

Our first chapter mentioned some ways in which the sixth book completes the poem. It is the terminal legend in the "social" installment, and its virtue reconciles the antithesis of friendship and justice. Hence Artegall is last seen making friends with Calidore, and Calidore's own quest serves both the interests of friendship and justice. The socialization of the personality in this installment has proceeded through a sequence of widening allegiances: parents and family, friends, nation, and now "humanity"— other persons in general. One's courtesy, in Book VI, is the outward sign of one's own humanity. Calidore owes his virtue to "gentlenesse of spright / And manners mylde" (VI.i.2); thus his courtesy corresponds to the Latin *mansuetudo*, that is, mildness or gentleness. *Mansuetudo* may also be defined as "tameness," and its effects are recognized in the object of Calidore's quest, which is the *taming* of the Blatant Beast, as opposed to merely capturing him. The quality of mansuetude is associated with *clementia* in Latin usage, but also with *humanitas*. Spenser directly links Calidore's virtue with his "gracious speach" (VI.i.26), and *humanitas* has a second meaning of "polished speech."[11] It is to *humanitas* that Calidore appeals in his rebuke of the coarse Crudor: "No greater shame to man then inhumanitie" (VI.i.26). The Salvage Man's designation emphasizes that he is a man, and he is remarkable precisely for his "mild humanity, and perfect gentle mynd" (VI.v.29). One feels the patness here of the marginal comment in the English translation of La Primaudaye's chapter "Of Meekenes, Clemencie, Mildnes, Gentlenes, and Humanitie": "This word man is in the Latin Homo, from whence is derived *humanitas*, which signifieth curtesie or gentleness."[12] The virtue is acknowledged, as both the discussions of La Primaudaye and Elyot indicate, in the doing of services for—benefiting—our fellow man. Elyot divides the virtue into three parts: benevolence, beneficence, and liberality.[13] It is thus a link to the three Graces, because of the famous allegory in Seneca's *De Beneficiis*, where the circle of the Graces symbolizes "the bestowying, receiving, & requyting of benefits."[14]

Calidore's virtue demands that he be personable, but, like Britomart, he also seems to have a personality or personal humanity. Artegall's virtue may be "Most sacred vertue . . . of all the rest," but it is Calidore, as a person, who is "beloued ouer all" (V, proem, 10; VI.i.2). The ideal Arthur of the poem as a whole would be a continent Christian knight, dedicated to the service of his mistress, attracted to fellow noble spirits, and a defender of the weak and wronged. But beyond these requirements of the chivalric conception, there is the spirit of chivalry itself, and Calidore possesses this in a preeminent degree. There is a kind of overlap here, since

[11] For examples of the overlapping of the two meanings, see Cicero, *Laws* III.i.1; *Verr.* II.iii.4, sec. 8; see also *De Orat.* II.xvii.72 and I.xvi.71. For *humanitas* with *mansuetudo*, *Rep.* II.xiv, and esp. *Epist. ad Q. Fr.* I.i.8, "omnia plena clementiae, mansuetudinis, humanitatis."

[12] *French Academie* (London, 1586), "Of Meekenes, Clemencie, Mildnes, Gentlenes, and Humanitie," p. 319. On this virtue in Ficino, see Kristeller, *Philosophy of Marsilio Ficino*, pp. 113f.; see Ficino, *Epistolae*, Lib. I, *Op. om.* I–2, p. 635, for *humanitas* as opposed to *crudelitas* and as the virtue bidding us love all men as members of one family.

[13] *Gouernour*, II.viii, "The thre principall partes of humanitie," Everyman's Library, pp. 147ff. Cf. Cornutus, *De Nat. Deorum* 15, "De Gratiis," in Gale, *Opuscula Mythologica*, p. 163: "Formosae esse narrantur, quod insigni forma vigeant, & formae decorum liberalitatem exercentibus tribuant, & facile ad benefaciendum impellantur."

[14] *De Beneficiis* I.iii; trans. Arthur Golding, *Concerning Benefyting* (London, 1578), p. 4.

both Calidore and the traditional Arthur are notable for their generous spirit. In part because of an ambiguity in the meaning of the word gentleman, Calidore may claim to be very much that gentleman that the poem conceives to be its end.

It is, of course, easy to criticize Calidore for his limitations—in the allegory, limitations peculiar to courtesy.[15] In the terms adopted below, the supervenient may turn out to be the merely superficial. The art of pleasing is implicitly condemned by the last stanza of the legend, and we may well be troubled by Calidore's artfulness: his willingness to use others and to manage everything to his own advantage (as in his wangling of invitations), and his skill in ingratiating himself with the "best" sort of people.[16] He commits a number of *faux pas*; there is his offer of money to Meliboe, for example; and his forwardness to present himself in situations where retreat might actually have been the better part of courtesy.[17] We accept his rather sly condescension to Coridon, but at the same time we note that Coridon does not disguise his selfish impulses under a host of disarming strategies that are essentially insincere. Blandina is an enemy to the true form of the virtue, but apparently there is a good deal of blandness, or affected serenity, in the practice of courtesy itself.

This is the place to note that the allegorically veiled truth of a legend of courtesy will be the polite white lie; subtlety, indirection, the disguise of ulterior motives, and the studied use of misrepresentation may all serve its cause. In such a legend the truth will seldom be wholly simple, and the polarization of truth and falsehood will dissolve into questions of essential and feigned sincerity. The reader is not kept overlong in doubt about the nature of hypocrisy in Book I, but in Book VI we will have to say, with Raleigh in his *History* (II.vi.7), that "some virtues and some vices are so nicely distinguished, and so resembling each other as they are often confounded."

[15] For this critique, see Richard Neuse, "Book VI as Conclusion to *The Faerie Queene*," ELH, 35 (Sept. 1968), reprinted in *Critical Essays on Spenser from ELH* (Baltimore, 1970), pp. 222–246. The emphasis of my essays here, however, is very much on the side of Harry Berger, Jr., "A Secret Discipline: *The Faerie Queene*, Book VI," in William Nelson, ed., *Form and Convention in the Poetry of Edmund Spenser*, English Institute Essays (New York, 1961), pp. 35–75. My thinking on Book VI is much indebted to Berger.

[16] VI.i.3 ("with the greatest *purchast* greatest grace / Which he could wisely *vse*, and well *apply*, / To please the best"); VI.ix.27 ("to occasion *meanes*, to *worke* his mind, / And to *insinuate* his harts desire, / He thus replyde"); VI.x.37 ("But *vsde* him friendly for further intent, / That by his fellowship, he *colour* might . . ."); VI.x.38 ("so well he *wrought* her . . ."); VI.xi.35 ("so well him *wrought with meed*, / And faire bespoke with words"). These are hardly examples of "the unbought grace of life."

[17] VI.ix.32; VI.iii.20f.; VI.x.17–19.

Logically, the emergence of a "gentleman" ought to mark the end of the allegories of the virtues as early character strengths that have been pedagogically reconstructed. And it is true that courtesy, superficially speaking at least, seems to be an added thing. The loves in this legend are curiously unprojected into an allegorical dimension: they do not impress us as "interpreted" forms of early psychological attachments. Doubtless Calepine loves serenity as well as Serena, and Calidore is fond of pastoral as well as Pastorella, but on the whole these heroines are not much more allegorized than Priscilla or the unnamed victim of discourtesy who has lost some of her clothes in the first canto.

Further, the hero of this legend has no guardian, and thus we lose the usual parental overtones noticeable in the care of the hero. (Talus is more of a Big Brother.) The general freedom of the legend from iconography is also suggestive. The hero lacks his usual complement of symbolic equipage: Calidore is so short on weaponry that he has to hew off the head of an attacking tiger with a shepherd's crook; Calepine stops the mouth of an angry bear with a handy rock. In current parlance, Calidore is free of cumbersome "character armor," and both the Salvage Man and the Graces go naked.

Finally, when we go to look for our symbolic child—usually a foundling or changeling on whom the educational themes of the legend are focused —we find two candidates, separated by about a generation. These are the bear baby and Sir Tristram. There is something particularly posthumous about the baby, for we know virtually nothing about his antecedents. He is a type-case for all the others; psychologically speaking, they are all orphaned, like those "seeds of virtue" deposited in the natural world, which in fact they partly represent. The bear baby differs from the others in that Spenser appears to attach no symbolic significance to it. The infant is *tabula rasa*, and the woman who adopts him is told that she may bring him up for either chivalry or philosophy.

The bear is not moralized either. He is not even a romance bear like those who "do offices of pity" for foundlings.[18] Rather, he is one of those that threatens the foundling, like the bear in *Mucedorus*. And yet the bear has a significance for the theme of nurture either way, since the child is conveyed to the wife of one Sir Bruin for its upbringing. Bears in general belong to this theme, for a reason that Erasmus makes clear in his essay on early education:

It is sayde that beares caste oute a lumpe of fleshe wythout anye fashion, whych wyth longe lyckyng, they forme and brynge into a fashyon, but there is no beares yonge one so euyll fauored as a manne is, borne of a rude mynde.

[18] *Winter's Tale*, II.iii.189.

Except with much studye ye forme and fashion this, thou shalt be a father of monster, and not of a man.[19]

Erasmus addresses the father of the child in question in terms that will remind us of the future of the bear baby, and the barrenness of Matilda, who adopts it:

> After the longe despayred fruitfulnes of thy wyfe, I hearesay thou art made a father, and that wyth a man chyle, whyche sheweth in it self a meruelous towardnes, and euen to be lyke the parentes: and that if so be we maye by such markes and tokens pronosticatiue anye thyng, maye seeme to promise perfite vertue. And that therefore thoe doest entend, to se thys chylde of so grete hope, assone as he shalbe some what of age to be begonne in good letters, and to be taught in very honest learnynge, to be instructed and fashioned with the very wholesome precepts of philosophy.[20]

Beasts, Erasmus says, "folowe onely the affectes of nature, a manne except he be fashioned wyth learning, and preceptes of philosophy, is rawght in affections more then beastlike."[21] He argues throughout the essay that it is man's nature to be learned, and says that this learning may well begin with the art of the poets. In other words, the theme of virtue focused on the child is education itself. The alternative of arms or letters is traditional,[22] but its appearance in this legend in particular suggests alternative responses to the present poem: the romance of chivalry might be extended, or the time may be arriving for the poet to disengage himself from the quest and take a philosophical view of it.

Although he is not precisely a symbolic child, the naked Salvage Man is at least a child of nature. He corresponds in this legend to Sir Satyrane in Book I; he is an apt pupil for the lessons of the virtue in question, even though he must get on by speaking signs. He is also another of our more or less pure romance denizens, invulnerable by magic, incapable of fear, compassionate by nature, and adept in natural healing. He belongs to the line of Enkidu in the Epic of Gilgamesh. Enkidu is likewise a hairy wildman, innocent of civilization, and he is adopted by the hero's mother. A

---

[19] *De pueris ad virtutem instituendis*, trans. by Richard Sherry in *A treatise of Schemes & Tropes . . . whervnto is added a declamacion, That chyldren euen strayt from their infancie should be well and gently brought vp in learninge* (London, 1550), fol. Diiij[r-v]. (See Pliny, *Nat. Hist.* VIII.liv.126.)

[20] *De pueris*, fol. Bii[r-v].   [21] *Ibid.*, fol. Ciii[v].

[22] For the topos, see Curtius, *European Literature*, pp. 178f., citing Boiardo, *Orl. Inn.* I.xviii.41–45 and *Don Quixote*, I.xxxviii, among other examples. Curtius points out the similarity to the *sapientia et fortitudo* topic. Spenser would know it from Castiglione's *Courtier*. Other Spenserean instances are the title page of the *Calender* and *F.Q.* II.iii.40.

similar relation between the Salvage Man and Arthur may well be in the offing. Closer to Spenser is the romance of *Valentine and Orson*.[23] Orson is carried off at birth in the mouth of a bear. The bear raises the babe and at maturity he is brought back into society. Like Enkidu, Orson engages his civilized brother in combat; like the Salvage Man, he is fearless, fights tooth and nail, and speaks by means of signs. If *Valentine and Orson* is Spenser's source, it provides a link between the bear baby and the Salvage Man dwelling in the same forest. In classical fable it is Paris who is said to have been suckled by a bear,[24] and curiously enough Calidore is compared to Paris in a stanza that seems to demand parity with its counterpart in Book III (VI.ix.36, III.ix.36). Calidore, too, is drawn into that orbit of motifs that center on a foundling.

The remaining candidate for the role of symbolic child is the seventeen-year-old Sir Tristram. Tristram calls our attention to the number of young persons in this legend. It seems as if the psychogenic period for Book VI ought to be "adolescence," Erikson's fifth stage, where the basic opposition is said to be between "identity" and "role confusion." Role-playing is an essential element in courtesy, and in Calidore's conduct overall. The loves in this legend also seem to fall under Erikson's remarks on adolescent courtship, where role-playing is also important: "To a considerable extent adolescent love is an attempt to arrive at a definition of one's identity by projecting one's diffused ego image on another and by seeing it there reflected and gradually clarified. This is why so much of young love is conversation."[25] Calidore's love, being that of an older man, may seem a more wistful form of solace, but nonetheless one governed by a somewhat similar need. The adolescent period also provides the moratorium "between the morality learned by the child and the ethics to be developed by the adult";[26] Book VI, with its muting of the allegory, suggests a comparable transition for the poem. The pressure on the adolescent to focus on a choice of occupation makes itself felt in Book VI too; Calidore's sojourn among the shepherds, for example, implies a choice of "lives." Even more important is the new definition of occupation vouchsafed Sir Tristram.

[23] The parallels to Spenser are set out by Arthur Dickson in his edition of *Valentine and Orson*, trans. from the French by Henry Watson (2nd edn., ca. 1548–1558), EETS, Original Series, no. 204 (London, 1937), pp. li–lix. I reached the same conclusions on the basis of the summary and excerpts in John Ashton, ed., *Romances of Chivalry* (London, 1887), pp. 235–256. This romance contains an interesting "green man" motif as well.

[24] Apollodorus, *Bibl.* III.xii.5; Lychophron, *Alexandreis* 138. For the strong evidence for a "Parisian" Calidore, see "Fables of Green Fields," sec. ii, and nn. 134–145, below.

[25] *Childhood and Society*, p. 262; see pp. 261–263.

[26] *Ibid.*, pp. 262f.

Tristram is the only character who is actually knighted in the poem—doubtless such a ceremony particularly belongs to courtesy, since this virtue includes "friendly offices that bynde" (VI.x.23). Tristram is a stripling who resents being treated like a child (VI.ii.11), and who, in becoming a Sir, becomes eligible for what is otherwise a term of courteous address. His being knighted makes him the only "Childe" in the poem, aside from the royal Child or Infant, namely, Prince Arthur. Tristram, in fact, is the only other "Arthurian" character in the entire *Faerie Queene*. Spenser would seem to be anticipating future needs for a new cast. At the same time we may be meant to recognize the emergence of a heroic generation that has had its nativity and education in the wilderness, like the Israelites who eventually possess the promised land. The evidence we have adduced is at least suggestive, as if some mysterious coming of age were taking place in that greater personage whom the poem sets out to fashion.

The intensification of romance in this legend seems to reflect the theme of a "realized faerie." The Arcadian landscape suggests such a theme, partly because Sidney's *Arcadia* places the pastoral excursion at the heart of the romance subject. Framing this subject in Sidney are the chivalric adventures and, beyond them, the princely vocation of the protagonists—the heroes have a different name for each of their three identities. Similarly, the immersion of Calidore and Pastorella in the shepherds' world provides an intensification of the rustication and return pattern that prevails in the poem as a whole. As the fairies glimpsed on Mount Acidale suggest, this is a faerie within faerie.

The poet himself is found enjoying his art in this pastoral setting. He reminds us of Horace in his first ode, playing the pipes of Euterpe—the pastoral Muse, according to Spenser's *Teares*. Horace is screened from men by the nymphs, satyrs, and Muses. According to Servius and Vida, and confirmed by established practice, the pastoral was the genre with which the poet should begin.[27] Vida elsewhere tells the poet in general that to fulfill his mission he ought to withdraw to an *amoenus locus* frequented by Pan, Faunus, Sylvanus, and the nymphs.[28] Quintillian contradicts this advice in a passage important for its lengthy statement of the positive ideal.[29] The maidens dancing around Colin Clout seem to be

---

[27] See above, n. 7. For Vida, see A. S. Cook, ed., *The Art of Poetry* (New York, 1926), p. 71, reprinting Vida's *Art*, I.486–496.

[28] Vida, *Art of Poetry*, I.489f.: ". . . et amoena silentis / Accedat loca ruris. . . ."

[29] *Institutes* X.iii.22, trans. H. E. Butler, ed., Loeb edn., vol. 4, pp. 102ff. A most important text here is Boccaccio, *G.D.G.* XIV.xi, Romano edn., vol. 2, pp. 711ff., where the preference of the poet for lonely haunts as favorable to contemplation is treated at length. Tacitus, *Dial. de Orat.* 13, invokes the rural retreat of Virgil, and

fairies or nymphs, and Elyot's dictionary reports that "Nymphe doth signify the bryde or spouse new married, a nymphe or fayrie."[30] Hence this is a potentially erotic realm, as well as the seedbed of poetic activity, and Colin places his mistress at the very center of his vision. If she is also to be identified with Spenser's recently espoused wife, the theme of a realized faerie makes itself felt in an autobiographical dimension as well.

The same theme of course entails meanings particular to courtesy. Calidore has a daily beauty in his life that makes a rival ugly, yet Calidore's worthiest exertions have as their goal the eliciting of the other person's best. In theological terms this best would be something not far removed from his innocence. "Faerie" can be described as Spenser's symbol for the aims of education; the "end" of learning, according to Sidney's *Apology*, "is to lead and draw us to as high a perfection as our degenerate souls, made worse by their clay lodgings, can be capable of."[31] As a consequence, symbols of regeneration are not wanting here. The noble Salvage Man "neither plough'd nor sowed," nor does he kill for his food (VI.iv.14). The bear baby is said to be "whole" and a "spotlesse spirit" (VI.iv.35); and, unlike Ruddymane, he can be washed. Other auguries of innocence in this legend are copulation without concupiscence, and nakedness without shame—or at least without culpability or blemish. There is encouragement and consolation in the renewal of chivalric hope in a new generation, and there are a number of stories that imply that characters *can* go home again (Aladine and Priscilla; Pastorella; and perhaps the bear baby, if his new father's name is any indication). An atmosphere of secular redemption is suggested by the repentance or conversion of characters from evil to good. The changes of heart in such figures as Briana, Crudor, Sir

---

quotes the poet as singing, "Me let the sweet Muses lead to their soft retreats, their living fountains, and melodious groves, where I may dwell remote from care, master of myself, and under no necessity of doing what my heart condemns" (see *Georg.* II.475-494). The weary poet wandering through faerie and being refreshed by it, in *F.Q.* VI, proem, 1, may remind us of Horace, *Epist.* II.2, ll. 65ff., which Boccaccio quotes: Horace asks how the poet in the city can "in noise unceasing tune the lay, / Or tread, where others hardly find their way?" Calidore, like the poet in many ways, begins in a similar perplexity, "To tread an endlesse trace, withouten guyde, / Or good direction, how to enter in" (VI.i.6). For the Horace passage again, see Petrarch, *De Vita Solitaria*, Lib. II, Tract. viii, cap. 2, and also cf. the rural inspiration invoked for Petrarch's *Africa*, I.5-13. See also n. 144, below.

[30] *Bibliotheca Eliotae* (London, 1559), *sub* "Nympha."

[31] Text from Gilbert, *Literary Criticism*, p. 417. Echoes of this passage seem to be heard in Bacon, *Advancement of Learning*, II.i.13, and Milton, *Of Education*. Milton is in turn echoed in John Dennis' *Grounds of Criticism in Poetry* (1704): "The great design of the arts is to restore the decays that happened to human nature by the Fall, by restoring order" (in Scott Elledge, ed., *Eighteenth Century Critical Essays*, vol. 1, p. 102).

Enias, and perhaps Mirabella are unprecedented elsewhere in the poem. Reverence is discovered among savages, and chivalry among thieves. Minor evidence of a promising development is the sense of refuge in the legend, which combines with the safe-conducts offered various characters; a Good Samaritan theme belongs to courtesy. In the older generation we may cite the hospitality and content of Meliboe and the Hermit, which answers to the hopefulness inspired by the young. Finally, there is the ambiguity between the origins of courtesy and the "nursery of vertue" in general; we meet both noble (or prelapsarian) origins disguised by humble circumstances, and humble (or postlapsarian) origins ennobled by growth or refinement. In the Salvage Man and the bear baby, the origins of heroism are broached; in the knighting of Sir Tristram, the origins of chivalry and Arthurianism; in the cynosure of Serena, the origins of sacramental religion; and in the celebration of Colin's mistress among the rustics, the origins of poetry and the present poem. In the Arcadia of the legend Pastorella is found dressed in green, like Sir Tristram in the woods. With the discovery of the red rose on the foundling's breast the color symbolism of the poem modulates into something like its home key. The discovery of Pastorella's parents suggests a counterpart in Book VI for the doctrine of election in Book I—"predestination to life," as Spenser's church called it.[32]

The virtue of courtesy is said to be a kind of gift (VI.ii.2). The legend of Calidore impresses us as a gift to the reader, and analogies between the contribution of courtesy to the heroic persona and the contribution of the last book to Spenser's poem come very easily. As Spenser's usage shows, a grace is a gift, and it is also something added, like a grace note— a charm or adornment. The social graces and the literary graces both entail gracious speech or fair words. Thus Cooper's *Dictionary*: "where in speaking or writing appereth to bee a mervaylous delectation or sweetnesse, it was sayde, that therein was a grace, in Greeke *Charis*."[33] Courtesy endows the hero with his "finish," and the sixth book seems to confer a like benefit upon our poem. It is gratuitous in the most positive sense.

The reader of Book VI is not surprised that the festive Thalia is both Grace and Muse—the Muse of comedy, and of idyllic poetry as well (in *Teares*, l. 180, she masks "in mirth with Graces well beseene"). Courtesy is an art; so is the writing of poetry, and Spenser's Graces are frequently associated with the Muses. Courtesy is especially shown in recognizing benefits, in returning thanks; the scene on Mount Acidale seems to call for the recognition of the poet—the Graces, according to E. K.'s

---

[32] Article XVII of the thirty-nine *Articles of Religion.*

[33] Thomas Cooper, *Thesavrvs Lingvae Romanae & Britannicae . . . Acessit dictionarivm historicvm et poëticum* (London, 1565), *sub* "Charites."

famous note, stand for thanks. Graciousness cannot be forced; neither can Colin's inspiration: the wind bloweth where it listeth, and the Graces visit whom they will. As St. Augustine says of the divine favor, echoing Romans 11:6, "Because gratuitously, therefore by grace; for grace is no grace unless it is gratuitous."[34] Like the other nymphs of faerie, the Graces are elusive, but their epiphany near the end of the legend—even as they vanish—provides Spenser's canon with a definitive expression of that "second nature" that art sets out to manifest.

Finally, in Book VI the quest of the hero and the effort of the poet come into that alignment from which they departed at the opening of the poem. Both hero and poet serve the fairy queen, and yet the parallel between them is most marked in an analogous dereliction; thus the poet begins the last movement of Book VI by returning to plow his furrow (Lat. *versus*, "furrow"), in order to reap "rich frute": he follows Calidore, "Sewing the Blatant Beast" over the countryside and "Reaping eternall glorie" (VI.ix.1f.). But when georgic turns to pastoral, he asks,

> Who now does follow the foule *Blatant Beast,*
> Whiles *Calidore* does follow that faire Mayd,
> Vnmindfull of his vow and high beheast,
> Which by the Faery Queene was on him layd,
> That he should neuer leaue, nor be delayd
> From chacing him, till he had it attchiued?
>> (VI.x.1)

The poet seems to be asking himself the same question in the poems celebrating his mistress:

> Great wrong I doe, I can it not deny,
>> to that most sacred Empresse my dear dred,
> not finishing her Queene of faëry,
>> that mote enlarge her liuing prayses dead:
>>> (*Amoretti* XXXIII)

Calidore chased the Beast so fast, "That he nould let him breath nor gather spright" (VI.iii.26), but the winded poet asks leave from his *bête noire,* to "gather to my selfe new breath awhile," after so long a "race" as he has run (*Amoretti* LXXX); and eventually the sweaty Calidore also sits down to rest. The parallel cuts two ways: the quest on behalf of Gloriana remains problematic and unsure; the quest for *The Faerie Queene* no longer is in question.

[34] Second Discourse on Ps. 18:1, in *St. Augustine on the Psalms,* trans. Dames Scholastica Hebgin and Felicitas Corrigan, Ancient Christian Writers, 29 (Westminster, Md., 1960), vol. 1, p. 183. (Augustine is discussing the justification of the sinner through Christ's blood.)

> The greatest scholars tell us that the learning of other things rests on methodical study . . . whereas nature herself endows the poet . . . by a kind of divine inspiration. . . . Ennius rightly called poets sacred, as if committed to us by some gift and dispensation of the gods. Let the name of poet also be revered by you—no savage race ever desecrates it. Hills, rocks, and solitudes resound to the human voice; beasts are halted, controlled by its cadence. And shall we, in our highly civilized state, be insensible to the voice of poets?
>
> (Cicero, *Pro Archias* 8)

[i]

If Book I of *The Faerie Queene* may be said to present the romance of the gospel, Book VI presents the gospel of romance. Much of the remainder of my commentary examines this closure in the poem. Book I we described as a romance analogy for revelation, or the Word of God. The sixth book offers a romance analogy for "ciuill conuersation." Faith takes its learning and its vision from God's Word; the practice of civility seems to take the same things from the humanities, especially humane letters.

The relation between the logos and the art of words is an old and honored one. In his *Christian Doctrine* Augustine maintains the legitimacy of applying the science of *oratio*—rhetorical analysis—to the sacred page; he has occasion to remark that "the condition of men would be lowered if God had not wished to have men"—rather than angels—"supply his word to men" (cf. Heb. 1:1f.; I Pet. 1:12).[35] In the epistle prefixed to the Vulgate, Jerome maintains the literary supremacy of the Bible by means of comparisons to classical authors,[36] but his arguments were often used in the defense of poetry since the comparisons seemed to prove that the revelation also came through poets. The early humanists thought of theology as the poetry that pertained to God; inversely, they thought of fiction as full of mysteries and quasi-religious truths. Sidney says that he follows Aristotle in believing that poets were "the ancient treasurers of the Grecians' divinity,"[37] and Spenser's Polyhymnia reports that priests once expressed their laws and oracles in verse (*Teares*, 599).

In his *Replication*, Skelton says that if we may trust the example of David, poets do more than merely feign; God dwells in the poet, and the

---

[35] "Prologue," 6, trans. D. W. Robertson (Bloomington, Ind., 1958), p. 5.
[36] *Epist.* LIII.7 (PL, XXII, 547).   [37] *Defense*: Gilbert, *Criticism*, p. 457.

poet is instigated and inspired by the Holy Ghost.[38] The convention may be treated flippantly, as when Ariosto's Saint John accounts himself an author;[39] or nostalgically, as when Sidney says that David is shown by the Psalms to have been "a passionate lover of that unspeakable and ever-lasting beauty to be seen by the eyes of the mind only cleared by faith."[40] In the *Ruines of Time* (309–315) Spenser invokes Sidney's inspiration, asking for "that sacred breath" that Sidney now breathes in heaven.

Renaissance poetics observed that, like God, the poet creates a world,[41] and also like Him, the poet has the power to bestow an immortality. It is the Muses who redeemed Eurydice:

> The seuen fold yron gates of grislie Hell,
> And horrid house of sad *Proserpina*,
> They able are with power of mightie spell
> To breake, and thence the soules to bring awaie
> Out of dread darkenesse, to eternall day,
> And them immortall make, which els would die
> In foule forgetfulnesse, and nameles lie.
>
> (*Ruines*, 372–378)

The same power is attributed by Jerome to the "spiritual poetry" of David: "David . . . Christum lyra personat, et in decachordo psalterio ab inferis excitat resurgentem."[42] Skelton's version is:

> For David, our poet, harped so melodiously
> Of our Saviour Christ in his decachord psaltry,
> That at his resurrection he harped out of hell
> Old patriarchs and prophets in heaven with him to dwell.[43]

---

[38] *Complete Poems of John Skelton*, ed. Philip Henderson (New York, 1966), p. 427. For an authoritative presentation of the traditional relation of poet to prophet, see William Kerrigan, *The Prophetic Milton* (Charlottesville, Va., 1974), chap. i.

[39] *O.F.* XXXV.29.

[40] *Defense*, in Gilbert, ed., *Literary Criticism*, p. 411.

[41] For the comparison of the poet to the Creator, see Sidney, *Defense*, in Gilbert, *Literary Criticism*, pp. 412–414; Puttenham, *Arte*, I.i, in Smith, *Elizabethan Critical Essays*, vol. 2, p. 3; Scaliger, *Poetices*, I.i (Heidelberg edn. of 1617, p. 6); Tasso, *Discourses on the Heroic Poem*, III, in *Prose*, ed. Mazzali, p. 562. An important source for the Italian tradition is probably Landino's prefatory matter to his edition of the *Commedia*.

[42] *Loc. cit.* in n. 36.

[43] *Complete Poems*, ed. Henderson, p. 426. Perhaps there are very minor hints of the shepherd-musician David in the portrait of Spenser's hero: VI.ix, rubric, to return evil for good in a sexual rivalry (I Sam. 25:21); VI.i.3, to win favor in the eyes of men (I Sam. 16:6); VI.i.2, to steal men's hearts (David's son Absalom at II Sam. 5:6, 13); VI.x.35f. (I Sam. 17:34–37, David's contests with wild animals). Sidney, a likely model for Calidore, translated the Psalms of David.

Horace describes the powers of Orpheus in analogous terms: the hundred-headed beast was disarmed by poetry (*Odes* II.13); the lyre once blandished the Cerberus whose head is fortified by a hundred serpents (III.11).[44] Spenser's Piers attributes the same powers to the piping of the poet Cuddy:

> Soone as thou gynst to sette thy notes in frame,
> O how the rurall routes to thee doe cleaue:
> Seemeth thou dost their soule of sence bereaue,
> All as the shepheard, that did fetch his dame
> From *Plutoes* balefull bowre withouten leave:
> His musicks might the hellish hound did tame.
>
> ("October," 25-30)

We can hardly miss the genesis of the quest of Calidore here—the Calidore whose comely speech so readily gains him a following, who rescues Pastorella from the "hellish dens" of the thieves, and who tames the Blatant Beast.[45] The enemies of poetry are the enemies of courtesy, and courtesy and humane letters make common cause against rude speech. Thus Calidore and Colin Clout act in concert: Calidore leads the dancers' ring, while Colin calls the tune (VI.ix.41).

If theology is the poetry of divinity, perhaps poetry supplies a comparable "theology" or testament of humanity. Castiglione says that "besides goodness the true and principall ornament of the minde in every man ... are letters"; undoubtedly they "have beene graunted of God unto men for a soveraigne gift."[46] It is a commonplace of Spenser's culture that human nature is greatly benefited by good letters. Thus the art of words itself may belong to our symbols of regeneration. On the negative side, for example, the unregenerate impostor in *Mother Hvbberds Tale* scorns learning and the "love of letters." Following his natural course he goes on to mock "Gods holie Ministers":

> What else did he by progression
> But mock high God himselfe, whom they professe?
>
> (842-843)

[44] In the latter case the reference is also to the lyre invented by Mercury.

[45] VI.i.2; xi.41; xii.38. For an inverse relation between poetic apprehension and the quest of courtesy, see the rubric for canto x: "Calidore sees the Graces daunce, / To Colins melody: / The whiles his Pastorell is led, / Into captiuity." For the relation itself, see William V. Nestrick, "The Virtuous and Gentle Discipline of Gentlemen and Poets," reprinted in Harry Berger, Jr., ed., *Spenser: A Collection of Critical Essays*, Twentieth Century Views (Englewood Cliffs, N.J., 1968), pp. 132-145.

[46] Hoby trans., in *Three Renaissance Classics*, ed. Burton A. Milligan (New York, 1953), pp. 312f.

The Blatant Beast of the last canto, comparably, proceeds through blasphemy and despoliation of the Clergy—"Regarding nought religion, nor their holy heast"—to an attack on "learned wits" and the "gentle Poets rime" (VI.xii.23; 40). The state of poetry and the state of the ministry are equally concerns of the *Calender*, where the pastor and the pastoral poet share the same symbol. In *The Teares of the Mvses*, poetry is conceived of as "the Learneds taske" (l. 216), and the state of learning is the essential subject of the "satire." The imagery for ignorance and error in this poem leads directly to Book I of *The Faerie Queene*: ignorance, Urania declares, is "the enemie of grace" (l. 497). As the satire on ignorant clerics in the *Tale* shows, Spenser thinks of the ministry as being the learned's task also.

Thus what Fidelia teaches Redcrosse from her book—"Wherein darke things were writ, hard to be vnderstood" (I.x.14)—has counterparts in Book VI, such as the learned allegorical commentary with which Colin Clout invests Calidore's vision of the otherwise naked Graces. The mount of Contemplation is not only compared to Sinai and Olivet, but also to Parnassus,

> On which the thrise three learned Ladies play
> Their heauenly notes, and make full many a louely lay.
>
> (I.x.54)

Spenser's Graces sing, and in *The Teares* they are invited to join the Muses' lament—a lament that ends, as we noted elsewhere, with the breaking of the Muses' "learned instruments."

The Muses' appearance in the proem to this legend foreshadows the Graces on Mount Acidale, and links the Graces to the humanities. So also does Erasmus in his explanation of the joining of honesty to delectation, in the pursuit of humane studies:

> And I am deceyued except the old men [the Ancients] ment that also, whyche ascribed to the Muses beynge virgins, excellent beutye, harpe songes, daunses, and playes in the pleasaunt fieldes, and ioyned to them as felowes the Ladies of loue [the Graces]: and that increase of studies dyd stande specially in mutual loue of mindes, and therefore the olde men called it the lernyng that perteined to man.[47]

"Wherefore lernynyng is called humanitie," the margin directs us. The Muses and the Graces together, we may deduce from Erasmus, stand for the community formed by educated men. To this explanation of "humanitie," we may subjoin a passage from Guarino:

[47] *De pueris ad virtutem instituendi*, Sherry trans. in *op. cit.*, n. 18, above; Sig. Nviii[v]-Oi[r], "The meaning of ye poets deuise touching the Muses & Charites." See n. 155, below.

To each species of creature has been allotted a peculiar and instinctive gift. . . . To man only is given the desire to learn. Hence what the Greeks called "*paideia*," we call "studia humanitatis." For learning and training in virtue are peculiar to man: therefore our forefathers summarized as "humanitas" the pursuits and activities proper to mankind.[48]

Guarino, in turn, echoes Aullus Gellius, who says that the word *humanitas*, meaning "a kind of friendly spirit and good-feeling towards all men without distinction," more correctly means "education and training in the good arts." He cites the first sentence of Varro's *Human Antiquities*, explaining that Varro did not use *humanior* "in its usual sense of *facile et tractabile et benivolo*, although without knowledge of letters"; rather, he meant a man "of some cultivation and education":

> Those who earnestly desire and seek after these [the liberal arts] are most highly humanized. For the pursuit of that kind of knowledge, and the training given by it, have been granted to man alone of all the animals, and for that reason it is termed *humanitas* or "humanity."[49]

Given that good letters have the place in Book VI that the Word of God has in Book I, we might expect Calidore to be a patron of fair speech as Redcrosse is the champion of the Word. Conviction, represented by Fidelia, is replaced by persuasion, and there is a tradition that names Persuasion as one of the Graces.[50] Hence it comes about that Calidore is a courtier,

[48] *De Ordine Docendi et Studendi*, vi, trans. in William Harrison Woodward, *Vittorino da Feltre and Other Humanist Educators*, Classics in Education, no. 18 (New York, 1963), p. 177.

[49] *Noctes Att.* XIII.xvii, trans. by J. C. Rolfe in Loeb edn., vol. 2, pp. 457, 459.

[50] Hesiod, *Works and Days* 73 ("Both the Charites the goddesses and revered Persuasion"); Orphic *Hymn* to Nature (IX), l. 13 (*Charitōn poluōnume peitho*; Latin of 1586 edn., "venustatumque Suada"); Plutarch, *Conjugal Precepts*, Preface, *Moralia* 138D ("Persuasion and the Graces"); Quintillian, *Inst.* X.i.82 ("Why should I speak of the unaffected charm of Xenophon, so far beyond the power of affectation to attain? The Graces themselves seem to have moulded his style, and we may with the utmost justice say of him . . . that the goddess of persuasion sat enthroned upon his lips"—trans. Butler); Cornutus, *De Natura Deo.* 24, "Venus," in Gale, *Opuscula Mythologica*, p. 197 ("Moreover the Graces attend on Venus, and Persuasion and Mercury are companions and followers"); *Gr. Anth.* V.195 (quoted in n. 70, Chap. IV, above) and XVI.288 ("thy body is the Graces', thy spirit is Peitho's"); Martianus Capella, *De Nuptis*, IX, Dick edn., p. 480 ("Pitho, Voluptas et Gratiae"); Cartari, *Le Imagini*, "Venere" (Venice, 1625), p. 396, on the pairing of Venus with Mercury ("That is why they also put among the Graces who accompany Venus the one which was called Pitho by the Greeks, and Suadela by the Latins, and who was the goddess of persuading"); Comes, *Mythol.*, IV.xv, *edn. cit.*, p. 409, and also IV.xiii, p. 386, where Suadela is a daughter of Venus; Giraldus, *Hist. Deorum*, in Syntag. XIII, in *Op. om.*, I, col. 420E ("Hermesianax and Proclus say Pitho to be one among the Graces. Sappho, as one reads in the scholia on Hesiod, makes Pitho a daughter of

like the one described in a long passage in *Mother Hvbberds Tale* (717–793). His prototype is found in Castiglione, and perhaps the most important thing about this celebrated ideal is Castiglione's resolve to form a courtier in words. Thus the graces of the courtier tend to develop analogies with the graces of literary style. Discussions of the courtier's conduct become discussions of his speech. His usefulness to his prince becomes his power to offer persuasive advice, properly spoken; his oratory is his finest accomplishment. His education is in the humanities—especially letters. The whole book, being the dialogue of an elite, offers itself as a demonstration of the kind of thing in which he will excel. As its title promises, the treatise becomes the ideal courtier in book form, an urbane ambassador that courts its international readership as the courtier inspires his prince: by means of example, good will, and becoming speech.

The hero of the legend of courtesy is short of weaponry, but he makes up the deficiency with his fair words. The uses of speech in this legend perhaps require no detailed enumeration. It is possible that the overlapping narrative in the opening cantos is largely contrived to get Calidore into as many conversations as possible. On the side of the heroic personae we find salutation, welcome, invitation, sympathetic inquiry, counsel, commiseration, thanks, apology, appeasement, suasion, and entreaty. The cannibal-priest mutters over Serena—saying grace perhaps—and the Salvage Man murmurs before the same lady. The grateful Calepine and Serena thank God for the food their rescuer presents them, and Meliboe praises God for his prosperity. The brigands fall to blows, "the frute of too much talk" (VI.xi.16). The principal offenses to courtesy are offered by insult, reproach, and detraction; the Blatant Beast runs a gamut from scandal-mongering to blasphemy.

The function of speech in offering comfort, cheer, and encouragement finds its way into almost every story in Book VI. Arthur's rescue of Timias is followed by the exchange of "gracious speaches" (VI.v.24). The hospitable Aldus puts a good face on his own loss of hope, "and turned it to cheare, / To cheare his guests" (VI.iii.6). Calidore "vpcheard" the dismayed Briana with news of her acceptance by Crudor (VI.i.44). His solicitude also heartens the distraught Priscilla: "The Ladie hearing his so courteous speach / Gan reare her eyes as to the chearefull light" (VI.ii.42). Calepine, on the other hand, sorrows that he has no means to comfort Serena, but with the dawn she "Vprear'd her head to

---

Venus: for this reason he writes in that place in the *Works and Days* that Pandora was decorated by the Graces and Pitho"); Alciati, *Emblemata* (Augsburg, 1550), Emb. CLXXV, "Gratiae" ("Euphrosyne is joy, Aglaia formal beauty, Pithus is Persuasion, charming and witty in speech. Why nude? Because the beauty of a mind is established by candor and pleases by exceptional straight-forwardness.").

see that chearefull sight" (VI.iv.45). Later he is able to cheer Matilda, and he commends the bear baby to her care with comforting counsel and "sensefull speach" (VI.iv.27; 34; 37). When he at last rescues Serena from the cannibals he proceeds "to question of her present woe; / And afterwards to cheare with speaches kind" (VI.viii.50). In contrast, she is speechless with embarrassment. This is Calepine's last action in the present poem, and it is possible that we are to derive his name from the Greek for "beautiful speech" (*kalos-epos*).[51] Likewise, when Calidore rescues Pastorella, "He her gan to recomfort, all he might, / With gladfull speaches, and with louely cheare" (VI.xi.5). Calidore also consoles Colin for the loss of his vision: "And to recomfort him, all comely meanes did frame" (VI.x.29). And Colin explains that the Graces are "sweete Goddesses all three, which me in mirth do cherry" (VI.x.22), with a glance at jocund Euphrosyne and Thalia-*thalea*.[52] Even the Salvage Man, with his "senseless words" and speaking signs, manages to convey compassion and commiseration (VI.iv.11).

A purely ingratiating speech is not the only antidote to a purely malicious one, and Calidore's persuasions include words of censure, as when he tries to shame Crudor into better conduct. Like the Roman censor, Calidore is granted a discretionary power over public morals: it takes an Artegall to deal with homicide, but Calidore would be better suited for a case of indecent exposure. (Another Roman office having surveillance over morals was that of *aedile*; the aedile's duties included the repair of public buildings, and their protection from desecration—especially temples.) According to Cicero (*Rep.* IV.iv), the only penalty imposed by the censor is a red face and a bad name (*ignomia*, or *infamia*). On the whole, however, Calidore is shown hushing up whatever might be embarrassing, or defamatory, or injurious to another's reputation.

We have suggested that the prototype of courteous speech is humane letters, and there are hints in Book VI of the Pygmalion-theme found in *The Courtier*, where the description of the thing gradually becomes the thing itself, as the courtier's life becomes a work of art. Since Calidore's heroism shares an Orphic model with the vocation of the poet, the taming of the Beast by the hero has a counterpart in the poet's control over his words. The noise of the Beast is also somewhat Orphic, for it makes the rocks and trees shake with dismay (V.xii.41), as Orpheus' song made them follow him. In Ovid, the description of this effect calls forth the poet's own catalogue of trees (*Metam.* X.88ff.), and Spenser's poem began with a similar poetic act. At the end of the poem, the Beast inspires an-

---

[51] The derivation is suggested by Pauline Parker, *The Allegory of the "Faerie Queene"* (Oxford, 1962), p. 223, and after her, by Arnold Williams, *Flower on a Lowly Stalk* (Michigan State University Press, 1967), p. 70.

[52] For the Graces of cheerfulness and merriment, see Chap. IV, nn. 60–63, above.

other such act, namely, the poet's catalogue of the creatures heard in the Beast's many voices (VI.xii.27f.). The catalogue is the poetic form in which *thesis* yields back all its ground to *taxis*: thus the Beast threatens the poet with the "snowballing redundancy" that was a danger in his project from the outset. The full enumeration of the rivers at Thames' marriage, for example, would have needed "an hundred tongues to tell, / And hundred mouthes" (IV.xi.9). Here is the monstrosity that might overtake a poet who did not know when to stop.

There are other minor evidences of the transformation of the subject of the book into the book-as-subject. The Hermit not only knows "the art of words," he also explains the lineage of the Beast "as in books is taught" (VI.v.9). He might have been reading the present poem, since he echoes it fairly closely: Calidore says that the Beast "was begot . . . in . . . darkesom den, . . . Where he was festered long in *Stygian* fen"; the Hermit says the Beast was "long in *Stygian* den vpbrought" (VI.i.7f.; vi.9). "Begot of hellishe race," Calidore says; "bred of hellish strene," the Hermit echoes. The absorption of this book in the world of other books may also appear in some of the characters' names. Calepine is a name for a standard Latin dictionary; Aldus is the name of the great printer of classical texts whom Erasmus made proverbial for the labors of scholars.[53] The pastourelle is the name of a romance literary form in which a knight encounters an attractive shepherd lass in an erotic context.[54] Calidore, in becoming a shepherd, seems to enter a secondary or literary world, the world of the pastourelle as well as of Pastorella. Access to such a world is thus gained by becoming a poet, and this Calidore apparently does also. In his Arcadian sojourn he reminds us not only of Sidney's Mucedorus in shepherd guise, but also of Sidney's introduction of himself

[53] In both the adage "Herculei Labores" and *The Praise of Folly*. The suggestions for Calepine and Aldus are Berger's, in "A Secret Discipline," in Nelson, *Form and Convention*, p. 171, n. 6. Donald Cheney, *Spenser's Image of Nature* (New Haven, 1966), pp. 202–204, derives Calepine from Ariosto's Pinabello, a type for Turpine (= *pine* + *bellus* [= Gk. *kalos*], beautiful).

[54] So in the vernacular; in the Latin dialogues adduced as an analogue, the place of the knight is taken by a scholar. The knight may or may not win the lass, and by fair means or by foul: in his wooing he employs gifts, promises, suasion, and may resort to force. The maid's relations may interfere. In expanded forms, for example in the play of Adam de la Hall, *Robin et Marion* (ed. K. Vartz, 1962), and as late as Shakespeare's *Winter's Tale*, scenes of rustic revelry or games complicate the encounter; and this is also true in Spenser. The earliest example of the pastourelle is Marcabru's Provençal "L'autrier jost' una sebissa," but an analogy may be seen with Theocritus, *Idyl* 27, the story of Apollo's courtship of Admetus' daughter. The Song of Songs also supplies analogies, if it is treated as a dialogue. See W. P. Jones, *The Pastourelle* (Cambridge, Mass., 1931), E. Piguet, *L'Evolution de La Pastourelle* (Basel, 1927), and M. Delbouiller, *Les origines de la pastourelle* (Brussels, 1926).

into his romance as the shepherd knight.[55] Meliboe is a name from both Chaucer and Virgil, in each case a name closely associated with the poet's own persona. (Meliboeus begins the *Eclogues* with the story of his farm, which tradition made Virgil's own; it is Chaucer who tells the *Tale* of Melibee.) Colin Clout appears as Spenser's own persona, and Colin was also a spokesman for Skelton. The Blatant Beast is a rather markedly Skeltonic creation too. The "quotations" from Malory's saga, especially those at the end of the poem, refer the Arthurian subject back to its literary tradition, as if Spenser's poem had begun to take up membership in some larger canon than even Spenser can manifest. Here again we meet the theme of "realized faerie," a faerie realized by speech.

[ii]

The analogy of the Word is not the only one to be considered here. The mythography of the Graces suggests another, namely, the analogy of truth and sincerity. According to Seneca, the Graces "weare looce garmentes, howbeit very sheere and thin, because weldooinges are willing too bee seene."[56] The Third Vatican Mythographer reports that the Graces "are painted naked, because grace ought to be without paint [*fuco*, "pretense"], i.e., not simulated and feigned, but pure and sincere."[57] Cartari applies the idea to the allegory of benefits: "They say that the Graces are virgins, joyful and laughing, to show that whoever does benefits, need not make use of any deception, but may do so cheerfully and with a sincere heart."[58] Further, "They are virgins because doing well by others needs to be done with a pure soul, and a sincere one, and without any ties of obligation: as they show even in the separated and loose garments, which are lucid and transparent, because the soul by which benefits are done possesses such [qualities] inwardly through its being."[59] Though the dedication of the defenders of civil conversation is less exclusive than Redcrosse's dedication to truth, there are hints of an analogy. Tristram is made to swear "Faith to his knight, and truth to Ladies all" (VI.ii.35). Crudor is made to swear a "faithfull oth" of "true fealtie" to Calidore, "by his owne sword, and by the crosse thereon" (VI.i.43-44). Calidore himself inspires confidence. To Aladine he appears to be "full of faithfull trust," and he pledges his faith to Aladine to safely convey Priscilla home (VI.iii.13; 15-16). Calidore loves "simple truth and stedfast honesty," and he is said to hate flattery and lies (VI.i.3). His courtesy is unfeigned and sincere. (He can engage

---

[55] *Arcadia*, II.21, in *Prose Works*, ed. Feuillerat, vol. 1, pp. 284f.

[56] *Concerning Benefyting* I.iii; Golding trans., pp. 3f.

[57] Bode, *Scriptores rerum mythicarum latini*, III.11.2, p. 229.

[58] *Le Imagini*, "Le Gratie," *edn. cit.*, p. 409.

[59] *Le Imagini*, p. 412.

in deception, and does so to preserve Priscilla's reputation, and also to retain Coridon's assistance—candor and courtesy do not make synonymous demands.) There is also the idea here that courtesy involves a kind of faith in other people's good nature.

Sincerity always seems to involve good will, just as detraction always seems to be prompted by ill-will, rather than the love of the truth. Archimago employs slander to separate the Redcrosse knight from Truth, and for a period running from the opening of the third canto to the end of the eighth we follow Una's adventures without her rightful protector. Similar consequences follow upon the success of detraction in Book VI. If there is a character in the legend of courtesy who corresponds to Una, it is surely Serena. Her adventures are threaded through the corresponding area of the sixth book. Calidore rescues her from the Blatant Beast in the third canto, and then disappears from the poem until the opening of the ninth. He is replaced by Calepine and Arthur. The period of his absence corresponds to what we elsewhere called the dissociation of the hero. Duessa is exposed and Redcrosse is therefore rejoined with Una; Serena is found, and then Calidore mysteriously enters the peaceful world of the shepherds.

The comparison of the stories of the two ladies, Una and Serena, begins in the third cantos. Here Una appears about to be attacked by a lion, but the lion is tamed by her presence, and she proceeds with the lion to the house of Corceca, where she spends an uncomfortable night. The next day Una is joined by Redcrosse—except that he is not Redcrosse, but Archimago in disguise. They are pursued by a vengeance-seeking Sansloi, and Archimago, trapped in his own hypocrisy, is forced to give the fanatic battle. At the end of the third canto Sansloi kills the lion, exposes Archimago, and is ready to outrage Una. Serena's plight at the end of the third canto of the later book is similar. She has been attacked by the Blatant Beast; she has spent the night with Calepine outside the castle of the inhospitable Turpine, and the next day the pair are pursued by the same knight in the name of an inscrutable vengeance. Like Redcrosse-Archimago, Calepine is forced to stand, and at the end of the canto he is badly wounded. His only refuge is behind his lady. Later, at the end of the sixth canto, we find the shameful Turpine hiding behind the skirts of the exculpatory Blandina. This echo suggests a possible interpretation for the earlier scene: faced with Turpine's outrage, the best Calepine can do is maintain a serene front. Serena pleads with Turpine for her lover, as Una pleads with Sansloi for the fallen Redcrosse-Archimago. Unlike Archimago's, Calepine's conduct does not make him a hypocrite, but it does expose the limitations of the social mask. Without some such allegorizing, it is not easy to explain how Calepine could be reduced to such a discourteous shift. Even the most courteous are liable to be caught out by a really rude person. Calepine says "ladies first" just where he ought not to have. We are often tempted to expose another, rather than ourself, in an uncomfortable situation. In putting serenity first, he may also foreshadow the truancy of Calidore. His last action, significantly, is to offer Serena cover.

At this point in the parallel between the two legends, both Una and Serena break down in tears. Una is suddenly delivered from Sansloi, however, by the timely arrival of a flock of fauns and satyrs. The same providential intervention is provided for the imperiled Serena and Calepine, when the Salvage Man appears from the woods to drive off the relentless Turpine. Both the satyrs and the savage are struck with compassion; both "fawn" in the service of their new guests, whom they do their best to entertain.

With the ladies apparently safe, the woodlanders theme is expanded. In the earlier book we hear the story of the newly arrived Sir Satyrane, the son of a satyr and a noblewoman. It is intimated that the savage is of noble birth also. In his nonage Satyrane subdued wild animals—he used to tear bear cubs from their mothers' teats. In Book VI the unarmed Calepine achieves a similar feat in his rescue of the bear baby. Meanwhile, as Calepine's adventure has separated him from Serena, the Salvage Man undertakes to lead the lady out of the woods; Sir Satyrane performs the same office for Una, whereupon the deceits of Archimago and the violence of Sansloi again make their appearance. Una takes flight to Arthur; in Book VI Serena and the savage also join Arthur. In the later book Spenser goes on to tell the story of Timias and the Blatant Beast—the "De" brothers correspond to Sansloi.

To summarize: both Una and Serena retreat to a woodland in which wild animals do not harm spotless spirits, where savages are noble or reverent. It is a childlike or naive world, and the satyrs' good nature does not prevent their falling into idolatry. Their capacity for receiving the Word is limited. Likewise, the Salvage Man, lacking articulate speech, is confined to the blurred and random eloquence of "speaking signs" and emotive murmurs and moans. The point is not that one can be human without language, but that being truly human implies a certain content for one's speech: the Salvage Man's generous spirit seeks expression simultaneously in acts of humanity and feelingful sounds. Similarly, though the satyrs are only capable of natural religion, their impulses make them religious by nature, and therefore human.

As we are meant to contrast the true Una and the counterfeit Duessa in Book I, so we are meant to contrast Serena and Blandina in Book VI. Blandina is related to her husband, Turpine, in somewhat the way Duessa is related to her secret love, Sansjoy. In both cases the deceptive female *shrouds* the disabled knight and secures his reprieve from the *coup de grace.* There are overtones of a sinister parody when we are told that "Duessa wept":

> As when a wearie traueller that strayes
> By muddy shore of broad seuen-mouth *Nile*,
> Vnweeting of the perillous wandring wayes,
> Doth meet a cruell craftie Crocodile,
> Which in false griefe hyding his harmefull guile,
> Doth weepe full sore, and sheddeth tender teares:
> The foolish man, that pitties all this while
> His mournefull plight, is swallowd vp vnawares,
> Forgetfull of his owne, that mindes anothers cares.
>
>   (I.v.17–18)

"So wept Duessa, . . ." "cloked with *Fidessaes* name" (I.v.19; vii.1). The same sort of things are said of Blandina, who can imitate serene weather:

> Yet were her words and lookes but false and fayned,
>   To some hid end to make more easie way,
>   Or to allure such fondlings, whom she trayned
>   Into her trap vnto their owne decay:
>   Thereto, when needed, she could weepe and pray,
>   And when her listed, she could fawne and flatter;
>   Now smyling smoothly, like to sommers day,
>   Now glooming sadly, to cloke her matter
> Yet were her words but wynd, and her teares but water.
>
>   (VI.vi.42)

As there is a Grace of Persuasion, so there is a Siren of flattery. The Sirens were a traditional type for persuasive rhetoric, and Erasmus asks, "What is the song of the Sirens, except an insincere, ready assent [*assentationem*], as the most blandishing [*blandissimam*] of all things, yea, and the most pestiferous."[60] Comes explains the Sirens as an allegory of flatterers: "They induce in princes a most deep sleep, and the greater part of them do not see what distinguishes a friend from a flatterer."[61] Comparably, Blandina persuades Prince Arthur to sleep in Turpine's castle. We may isolate less comely forms of evil speech for separate treatment, though the Blatant Beast, being a dog, might under some circumstances fawn and flatter also.[62]

---

[60] *De Copia,* in *Opera om.,* ed. Jean le Clerc (Leiden, 1703), vol. 1, p. 91D–E.

[61] *Mythol.,* VII.xiii, *edn. cit.,* p. 755. A formal example of a Siren representing the power of rhetoric to persuade is found in Philostratus, *Lives of the Sophists* 17, describing the monument for the grave of the orator Isocrates.

[62] Cf. Bruno, *Spectacle of the Triumphant Beast,* I.ii, trans. A. Imerti (New Brunswick, N.J., 1964), p. 115: "Let us remove from the heaven of our mind . . . the

ra·nkle, v.i. (Of wound, sore, &c.) fester, continue painful, (archaic);
(of envy, disappointment, &c., or their cause) be bitter, give intermit-
tent or constant pain. [f. OF *rancler* (*rancle, drancle, draoncle*, festering
sore = med. L. *dranunculus* dim. of *draco* serpent)]

(The Concise Oxford Dictionary, third edn.)

Rancorous speech in Book VI is represented by the Blatant Beast, a Cer-
berus-like "dog" or "curre" in the service of Envy and Detraction, and also
employed by Despetto, Decetto, and Defetto ("spite," "deceit," and "defect" or "blemish").[63] The latter trio are, as it were, Cerberus' three heads,
for in their attack on Timias they are compared to "a mastiffe, and a
hound, / And a curre-dog" (VI.v.19). This symbol of collective malig-
nancy emerges out of Artegall's experience with the mobs of Book V—
proverbially, the multitude is a beast with many heads. One hears overtones of that experience in the reports of the *Vewe*, which is partly a
defense of Lord Grey against those who are heard "slaunderouslye to
barke" at Grey's Irish policy (3613–3615). "Evill tonges backbite and
slaunder" the memory of Spenser's former employer (3388–3390). Spenser
maintains Grey's honorableness, "how ever envye liste to *batter* against
him"; other texts have *blatter*. Grey's detractors have been oftentimes
moved to malign him out of "malicious minde or priuate grevaunce . . .
euen those which did backebite him are Choked with their owne fenim"
(600–611). The Beast shares its tongues with Virgil's Fama, full of tongues,
and its teeth with Ovid's "biting Envy," which rants and rails at the
Roman poet in an envoi.[64] The Envy-envoi tradition is found in Alanus'
Anticlaudianus, where the poet is compared to a sailor safe on shore at

---

Canis Major of murmuring, the Canis Minor of Adulation." For the tamed or servile
Cerberus, cf. Horace, *Odes* II.19 (last stanza) and *Odes* III.11 (l. 15, *blandienti*).
Cf. the "fearefull dog" of *F.Q.* VI.xii.36–38: "he follow'd so, / As if he learned
had obedience long"; and cf. the captive and abashed dog to which the bound
Timias is compared at VI.viii.5—Timias has attacked Disdain like a "Mastiffe"
(VI.vii.47). Arthur reviles the pusillanimous Turpine as a "vile cowheard dogge"
(VI.vi.33).

[63] For the association of "spight" and "blemish" see VI.x.27, and also the frequent
imagery of defacement throughout the legend. "Deface" is often opposed to "grace"
in the rhymes. The marking or mutilation of buildings, for example, might qualify
as a form of discourtesy: the Blatant Beast is guilty of this kind of aesthetic offense
at VI.xii.25.

[64] *Aen.* IV.174ff.; *Ars Amat.* I.xv.1. Cf. Achilles Tatius, VI.10: "Rumour and
Slander are two kindred Furies: Rumour is Slander's daughter. Slander is sharper
than any sword, stronger than fire, more persuasive than a Siren." (Trans. Gaselee,
Loeb edn., p. 325.)

last, who nonetheless "fears attacks by land . . . lest envy rage against him, or slander fix its teeth in him."⁶⁵ Artegall hazards such a shore on his return from the savage island. Spenser's *Calender* has this kind of envoi also; he commends his book to the protection of Sidney, the gentleman "worthy all titles both of learning and cheualrie"—i.e., arms and letters. Book VI, by making Calidore its hero, commends the greater poem to the same sort of nobleman.

It is Calidore's task, in Shakespeare's words, "to tie up envy, evermore enlarged" (*Son.* 70). The Beast is part of a long line of figures for malign and antisocial speech in *The Faerie Queene*, running back through Envy, Detraction, Malfont, Sclaunder, Ate, and Occasion. The Envy of Book I is the first of these—like Fama, he is "ypainted full of eyes" (I.iv.31; *Aen.* IV.181f.). The Blatant Beast attacks religious houses, and Envy accuses those who do good works of lacking faith:

> He hated all good workes and vertuous deeds,
>> And him no lesse, that any like did vse,
>> And who with gracious bread the hungry feeds,
>> His almes for want of faith he doth accuse;
>> So euery good to bad he doth abuse:
>> And eke the verse of famous Poets witt
>> He does backebite, and spightfull poison spues
> From leprous mouth on all, that euer writt:
>> (I.iv.32)

Thus Envy has taken the same course as the Beast. We may also compare the troops that mount their attack on the bulwark of the sense of hearing, at the Castle of Alma:

> . . . some like to Snakes,
> Some like wild Bores late rouzed out of the brakes;
> Slaunderous reproches, and fowle infamies,
> Leasings, backbytings, and vaine-glorious crakes,
> Bad counsels, prayses, and false flatteries.
>> (II.xi.10)⁶⁶

As a mythological conception, the Blatant Beast has important classical antecedents, especially among the monsters encountered by Hercules. The Erymanthean boar, said to have wasted *Arcadia*,⁶⁷ was taken alive by

---

⁶⁵ *Anticlaudianus*, IX.ix, ll. 415ff., trans. Cornung, p. 161.

⁶⁶ Cf. the advice of Lucian, *Calumny of Apelles*, cited in n. 84, Chap. III, above.

⁶⁷ So Cooper's *Dictionariṽm* appended to the *Thesaṽrvs Lingṽuae Romanae & Britannicae, sub* "Hercules"—presumably because Erymanthus is the name of a river and a mountain in Arcadia. See Pausanias, *Perieg.* I.xxvii.9 and VIII.xxiv.5; Apollodorus, *Bibl.* II.v.4; Servius, *ad Aen.* VI.802; Ovid, *Metam.* IX.191f.

Hercules. According to Apollodorus, the dragon of the Hesperides had many sorts of voices and a hundred heads.[68] Cerberus, as we have noted, is also said to have a hundred heads. So is the Hydra, which Horace says Hercules could conquer—in contrast to envy, which remained to be conquered at the end (*Epist.* II.i.10-11). Horace's report reflects Artegall's experience, and Erasmus' treatment of the labors of Hercules in the *Adagia* focuses on this text.[69] Envy "is not one monstrosity only, but armed with a hundred heads, and if one head is struck off two more grow in its place"; struggling with it only makes it swell out the worse against you. It "is hardly ever abolished. That is the victory of very few, and even Hercules himself barely achieved it. . . . The people who carp and slander in secret against those who are trying with the noblest efforts to do good to the world, are just spitting poison, a deadly poison at that." The only antidote is selflessness: "if your merit is rewarded by evil report, if secret envy hisses at you, if the Lernaean Hydra shoots poison from its three hundred heads, then it will be proof of a lofty and undaunted mind" to persevere, despite ingratitude.[70] Erasmus' discussion of the adage then turns to an apology for the labor of the author; the Blatant Beast ultimately finds the same context. Under the heading "Calumny," the *Adagia* lists *Frustra Herculi*.[71] " 'in vain about Hercules'—There is to be understood you have contrived calumny. Those who so conduct all their work, that no man may be able or dare to slander: about them this is customarily said. For the nature of Hercules was to take away hostile things by strength, not by fraud."[72] However, the story of the frustrated Hercules of Book V ends in a triumph not of fame, but of infamy: it is Calidore, not Artegall, who is able to "crop" the Hydra-headed evil of *calumnia* (cf. V.i.1, VI.xii.32).

Romance antecedents for the Blatant Beast include the three-headed monster named "malice privy" that is contrived by Disdain, Strangeness, and Envy in Hawes' *Pastime of Pleasure*;[73] and the cacophonous Questing

---

[68] *Bibl.* II.v.11: "an immortal dragon with a hundred heads, offspring of Typhon and Echidna," etc. Cerberus is *centiceps* in Horace, *Odes* II.13, l. 34; cf. III.11, l. 17.

[69] The Herculean parallel might make Artegall's defeat an ironic triumph of fame: the retrieval of Cerberus was traditionally the final labor, and it sometimes implied the hero's triumph over death; fame also triumphs over death.

[70] Trans. of "Herculei Labores," in Philips, *Erasmus on His Times*, pp. 18–20.

[71] *Adagia* (Frankfurt, 1646), p. 113 (*sub* CALUMNIA).

[72] Artegall, on the other hand, is accused of treachery (V.xii.40). We are told that "he past afore, withouten dread," and "he past on, and seem'd of them [his accusers] to take no keepe" (V:xii.39, 42); cf. John 8:59: "And he passed through the middes of them and so went his way." If the mark the serpent leaves on Artegall when it bites him from behind is a heelwound, Artegall is put in a class with other heroes with feet made of clay, especially Adam and Talos (who was killed through the removal of a pin in his heel).

[73] Ed. W. E. Mead, EETS, no. 173 (London, 1928), ll. 4548, 4949, 5009, 5111.

Beast near the opening of Malory. In the *Pilgrimage of Life*, the *dogs* of the Scylla of Conspiracy are named Envy and Detraction.[74] Finally, from the Renaissance, one may cite the description of the Furies that ascend to earth at the Fall in DuBartas—these include a Typhonic Cerberus:

> Ther dreadful *Hydra*, and dire *Cerberus*
> Which on one body, beareth (monsterous)
> The heads of Dragon, Dog, Ounse, Bear, and Bull,
> Wolfe, Lion, Horse (of strength and stomach full)
> Lifting his lungs, he hisses, barks and brayes,
> He howls, he yels, he bellowes, roars, and neighs:
> Such a back sant, such a confused sound
> From many-headed bodies doth rebound.[75]

Spenser's description of the mouth of slander also develops from Cerberus into a bestiary—and into one last lair as well:

> And therein were a thousand tongs empight,
>   Of sundry kindes, and sundry quality,
>   Some were of dogs, that barked day and night,
>   And some of cats, that wrawling still did cry,
>   And some of Beares, that groynd continually,
>   And some of Tygres, that did seeme to gren,
>   And snar at all, that euer passed by:
> But most of them were tongues of mortall men,
> Which spake reprochfully, not caring where nor when.
>
> And them amongst were mingled here and there
>   The tongues of Serpents with three forked stings,
>   That spat out poyson . . . .
>   (VI.xii.27–28)

Milton places both Rumour and "Discord with a thousand various mouths" (*Par. Lost* II.967) with Demogorgon in Chaos, and Boccaccio assigns "Litigation, vulgarly called Discord," to the same place.[76] In Rabelais the strident and confused noise of Hearsay emanates from a stunted old man who is polylingual: "In his throat were seven tongues, and each tongue was slit into seven parts. Nevertheless, he spoke on different subjects and in different languages, with all seven at the same time. He had also, spread over his head and the rest of his body, as many ears as Argus of old had

---

[74] Guillaume de Deguileville, *Pilgrimage of the Life of Man*, Englished by John Lydgate, ed. F. J. Furnivall, EETS, Extra Series, nos. 77, 83, 102 (London, 1899–1904), ll. 21672ff.

[75] II.I.iii.272–279, trans. Sylvester; in *Works*, ed. Grosart, vol. 1, p. 116.

[76] *G.D.G.*, I.iii (Romano edn., vol. 1, p. 18): Litigation is the first to emerge from the womb of Chaos.

eyes."[77] Hearsay's relation to litigation is suggested by his being engaged in training witnesses for hire.

Two genealogies are given for the Beast. Calidore derives him from the Chimaera and Cerberus. The Chimaera signifies the arts of rhetoric in Comes and Bocchius.[78] (The Beast is also compared to the Hydra, which has an association with the abuse of words going back to Plato's sophists.)[79] Being a dog, the Beast's philosophical affinities are with the Cynics, "a sect . . . which signifyeth doggish, . . . For they barked at all men";[80] apparently the Beast has nothing good to say about anyone either (VI.xii.28). It is the tradition attaching to Cerberus that is the more decisive here. Petronius identified the dog with lawyers, according to the evidence of Fulgentius, who cites Petronius' reference while explaining the *tricerberus* in Virgil's underworld. Fulgentius continues from Petronius' explanation: "Therefore, then, the calumny of quarrels is taught here, and a saleable tongue used in other business when the application of learning is profitable, just as nowadays is constantly seen in lawyers. But a rancor flavored by the honey of wisdom savors of scandal."[81] In Fulgentius' *Mitologiarum*, Cerberus has three heads "because the envies of mortal quarrels are

[77] "The Fifth Book," chap. 31, trans. J. M. Cohen, Penguin Classics (Harmondsworth, England, 1970), p. 679.

[78] Achilles Bocchius, *Symbolicarvm Qvaestionvm*, symb. cxxxvii, "Ars Rhetor. Triplex movet, iuvat, ducet, / Sed praepotens est veritas divinitas" (the emblem shows Perseus conquering the triform monster in a configuration like that of Carpaccio's painting of St. George); Comes, *Mythol.*, IX.iii, *edn. cit.*, p. 950. According to John Steadman, "Spenser's *Errour* and the Renaissance Allegorical Tradition," in *Neuphilologische Mitteilungen*, 62 (1961), pp. 22–38, the allegory derives from a scholia of Demetrius Trinculius on Hesiod's Echidna (the dam of the Chimaera), found in Richerius' *Lectionum Antiquarum*. For the Chimaera Steadman also cites Valeriano, *Hieroglyphica* (Basel, 1575), p. 16. In both Richerius and Valeriano the dragon's coils stand for erudition and deviousness of mind. Alciati's emblem of Perseus conquering the Chimaera is titled "Consilio & virtute chimaerum superari, id est, fortiores & deceptores" (*Emblemata*, Emb. XIV, edn. of Antwerp, 1581, p. 77), but the triform beast is allegorized by Mignault as the three ages of love. In *The Praise of Folly*, the mixed rhetorical materials of monkish sermons are compared to the Chimaera.

[79] *Euthydemus* 297c. For examples of the argumentative hydra, see John of Salisbury, *Policraticus*, II.26; Boccaccio, *G.D.G.*, XIII.i; Salutati, *De Laboribus Herculis*, III.ix; William Warner, *Albion's England*, II.viii, stanzas 22–25, 28.

[80] Cooper, *Thesavrvs . . . Dictionarivm historicvm et poëticum, sub* "Cynici." See VI.xii.28. Greek *kuneos*, doglike, also means impudent or shameless, and traditionally a dog's life is cheap and expendable, or low or mean. For the link to the Cynics, see Diog. Laer., *Vitae* VI.19 and 60. Shakespeare's Thersites has Cynic blood, and is addressed as dog, bitch-wolf's son, and whoreson cur (*T.&C.*, II.1.7, 10, 38, 48, 50, and see l. 32 for Cerberus).

[81] Petronius, *Frg.* 8; Fulgentius, *Virgiliana Continentia*, in Helm, *Opera. Fulgentivs*, pp. 98f.

instigated by three conditions, i.e. natural, causal, accidental."[82] The *Meta-morphoses Moraliter* comes even closer to Spenser: "Let us say that Cerberus is a detractor: because he is known to have three heads and three barking dogs to emit three kinds of evil detraction; moreover by evil words he is used to alarming the whole earth with strife and contention. And because he delights in the dark, i.e. the adversities of others: . . . it is usual with him to lament: and then he usually emits a spittle of venom of evil words, and poisons with aconite fertile fields, i.e. good persons."[83] The Beast has his venom-dripping jaws from such a Cerberus, but of course we meet his like in any embittered or rabid partisan, like the anonymous Citizen who works himself into a lather in *Ulysses*; here too we have a talking dog, "the hydrophobia dropping from his jaws."[84]

A related characteristic of the beast is its looseness: it is at large, and it is guilty of sacrilege; it wreaks havoc and leaves desecration in its path. "That cur, rumour," Greville writes, "runs in every place."[85] Like the Questing Beast in Malory, its errant course makes it a parody of the quest itself.[86] As a mythological conception, both Spenser's and Malory's beasts may be compared to the Celtic "spectral pack," reported by British my-thographers, which pursues the damned.[87] Similar conceptions related to Spenser's figure are the hell-hound in the first chorus of Seneca's *Oedipus* ("Some say the Hound of Hell has broken his iron chains / And is at large in our land");[88] the *harrying* of hell by Hercules, which means the running down of Cerberus; Dante's Envy, at the opening of the *Inferno*, let loose from hell and to be driven back there by a savior figure identified with a greyhound;[89] and the runaway hybrid beast in Ariosto, which rages through history and has recently attacked the Holy Faith.[90] All these

[82] *Mitologiarum*, I.vi; in Helm edn., p. 20.

[83] *Metamorphoseos Ouidiana Moraliter a Magistro Thomas vvaleys Anglico* (Paris, 1515), fol. lxiii[v].

[84] Random House edn. (New York, 1961), p. 311.

[85] *Caelica*, 38.

[86] Thus the Beast would bring the secrets of the monks' cloisters to light (VI.xii. 24), while Calidore similarly attempts to expose the Beast (VI.xii.35). See n. 163, below.

[87] See K. M. Briggs, *The Faeries in Tradition and Literature* (London, 1967), chap. 5, "The Host of the Dead," pp. 48ff., and p. 224, "The Spectral Pack which hunts for souls"; and, for the Wild Hunt, Brian Branston, *The Last Gods of England* (London, 1957), p. 89, which cites the account in the *Anglo-Saxon Chronicle* for A.D. 1127. Also Robert Graves, *The White Goddess* (New York, 1948), pp. 33, 68f., 124.

[88] *Oed.* 171–173.

[89] *Inf.* I.109–111. In *Inf.* VI.22, Cerberus is the *gran verm*. For Hercules as harrowing hell, see *Inf.* IX.98f.

[90] *O.F.* XXVI.31–33, 35f., 40–46. The beast came into the world with weights and measures; one day it will be slain by Ariosto's patrons, but being slain many times it is virtually deathless.

runaways share with the Beast its "liberty" (VI.xii.36), which is really license (VI.xii.28);[91] thus the captive Beast may be compared to Horace's *evaganti frena licentia*, that mad vagrant license on which the reign of Augustus enforced straight order (*Odes* IV.15).

Lastly, one may mention a link between Cerberus and the slander of the poet. Skelton wrote a poem "Against Venomous Tongues—Empoisoned with Slander and False Detraction":

> Such tongues unhappy hath made great division
> In realms, in cities, by such false abusion;
> Of false fickle tongues such cloaked collusion
> Hath brought noble princes to extreme confusion.

Like Spenser at the end of the poem, Skelton had been brought into a mighty peer's displeasure—Wolsey's. He prays that Cerberus may devour his betrayer, *lingua dolosa*, for "A false double tongue is more fierce and fell / Then Cerberus the cur couching in the kennel of hell."[92]

Hesiod's Typhon has a hundred serpent heads, and he too emits a multitude of noises: the bellowing of bulls, the roar of lions, the braying of dogs, and hissing (*Theog.* 825, 829–835). There is a sense in which the Beast is a wind-monster, and Spenser's other genealogy makes the dog the offspring of Typhon and Echidna (VI.vi.9–11). This genealogy recalls the mythology of the first book. Error was an Echidna-monster, and there are echoes of the imagery at the opening of Book I, when Calidore at the opening of Book VI sets out on his quest of the Beast:

> . . . now I begin
> To tread an endlesse trace, withouten guyde,
> Or good direction, how to enter in,
> Or how to issue forth in waies vntryde
> (VI.i.6)

Redcrosse and Una, lost in the wood of Error, forge blindly ahead, "Till that some end they finde or in or out" (I.i.11). The relation of Error to

---

[91] For this license, cf. Bullinger, *Decades*, III, Sermon IV, in Parker Society edn., vol. 2, p. 117: "in this law are forbidden tale-bearings, privy slanders, back bitings, close whisperings, and all suspicions which rise by such occasions. Despiteful quips therefore, and heads that are ready to speak evil of all men, are plainly condemned. For some there are which are without honestie, not sticking to slander all estates and conditions, both high and low, private and public, and people of all ages: . . . And to themselves they seem very eloquent, while with bitter words they check and find fault with all sorts of men: yea, they account the malapert prattling of their unbridled tongues to be a commendation of uncontrolled liberty and free licence of speaking; that is, which carry about a tongue full of bitterness, curses, and deceit: even as they also are not without sin that love a-life to hear envenomed speech and hurtful talking." Cf. VI.xii.28.

[92] *Complete Poems*, ed. Henderson, p. 249.

Fama is a staple of critical thinking in the English Renaissance, which possessed a strong sense of "what hazard truth is in when it passeth through the hands of report, how maimed and deformed it becometh."[93] While trying to trace the Beast, the hero comes on the young man corresponding to Fradubio, caught in the "guilefull traines" of Briana and her seneschal Maleffort. (Calidore brushes away Briana's retainers like a steer molested by flies; Redcrosse is compared to a shepherd brushing away gnats.)[94] The allegory in the later book is certainly faint enough, but perverted effort in the service of an evil custom is a fertile source of error. Milton comes late in a line of reformers, such as Bilson, who often quoted phrases such as Cyprian's: "custom without truth is but the long continuance of error." Bilson also quotes Tertullian: "whatsover [is] against the truth must be accounted error, even though old custom"; and the Council of Carthage: "Christ says I am the truth, not I am custom."[95] The New Testament itself associates hypocrisy with tradition (e.g., Matt. 15:6-7). Much of the lore of courtesy is contained in "usage," and some usage may be evil; besides Briana's custom, and the similar usage attributed to Turpine (VI.vi.34), there are the "accursed order" and "ceremonies" observed by the religious cannibals. This episode in particular seems to denote common grounds between ignorant superstition and barbarous custom. One further instance of evil custom might be discerned in Mirabella, the conventional coy mistress, since, like Briana, she is capable of reform.

There is also clearly a sense in which the Beast corresponds to the dragons of the first book, as a part of that satanic dragon who accuses men night and day (Rev. 12:10). Like Duessa's beast, he is rampant (I.viii.12; VI.xii.29), which perhaps means rife. The Beast's mouth is "All set with yron teeth in raunges twaine, . . . Appearing like the mouth of *Orcus* griesly grim" (VI.xii.26). Similarly, the dragon's "deepe deuouring iawes / Wide gaped, like the griesly mouth of hell"; "in either iaw / Three ranckes of yron teeth enraunged were" (I.xi.12-13, echoing Isa. 5:14).

With equal propriety the Beast might be compared to Archimago; rumour is no less a "beast that was, and is not, and yet is." They turn up at comparable points in the narrative, and they both traffic in lies and half-truths. The idol-makers in the first chapter of Romans who turned the truth into a lie became "full of envy, . . . of debate, of disceite, taking all things in the euil parte, whisperers, Backebiters, haters of God, doers of

---

[93] Hooker, in *Laws of Ecclesiastical Polity*, I.xiii.2. See also I.viii.11, on custom as a support for idolatry.

[94] The nuisance presented by locusts and flies may be that of detractors: so Alciati, *Emblemata*, Emb. CLXIII, "In detractores" (Antwerp, 1581), p. 564.

[95] The quotes are from Thomas Bilson, *The True Difference Between Christian Subjection and Unchristian Rebellion* (London, 1585), p. 603. These belong to a common Reformation stock—Milton cites Cyprian's seventy-fourth epistle in *Of Reformation*, for example. The relation between custom and error is incisively expounded in the preface to the *Doctrine and Discipline of Divorce*.

wrong, proude, boasters, inuenters of euil things" (2:28–29). Thus the Beast wounds Serena, as Archimago slanders Una. Later the Beast is part of the ambush of Timias, as Archimago waylays Satyrane and Una with a lie about Redcrosse. And finally the capture of the Beast follows on Calidore's harrowing of the thieves' underworld, as the capture of the accusing Archimago follows on Redcrosse's Easter victory.

Before he can be captured, of course, the hypocrisy of Archimago must be exposed by the person of Truth. At the corresponding point in Book VI, ironically, the Beast, in the part of a slanderous Protestant muckraker, exposes the filth of the cloisters. We will meet this inversion of the theme of exposure in the two books again, but here the parallel is restored; the Beast, compelled by Calidore, is compared to Cerberus resisting exposure to the revealing light of the sun. Cerberus, according to Spenser, was forced to tell in Hades "what on earth was donne" (VI.xii.35). Giraldus likens Hercules' conquest of Cerberus to the sun's dissipating infection and pestilence, and then adds that "there are others who want to understand by Cerberus truth, which, as if stinking in a deep place, and—as Democritus said—hidden away, Hercules brought out among men by exposing it."[96] Spenser understands his Cerberus this way too.

Finally, like Archimago, the Beast escapes his chains—both malefactors seem to be "evermore enlarged." Thus Archimago will be found at the opening of Book II, as the Beast was discovered at the end of Book V, that is, slandering the righteous hero of the preceding quest.

The lengthy epigraph from the "Buddhist Apocalypse," at the opening of the present chapter, represents the resigned cadences that prevail in Spenser's last book. The Beast, however, seems somewhat out of place in such an ending—as if he had become separated from the noisier ending of, say, the *Völuspá*, from which he could be a renegade. The above testimonies go some way toward showing that the Beast is legion, and in the noisier ending, where presently only the Beast breaks loose, all hell would be breaking loose with him. Comparison shows that the Beast's iron chain may be classified with ligatures that are cosmological elsewhere in both Spenser and the tradition.[97] It follows that when this leash is broken, there

[96] *Herculis Vita*, in *Op. om.*, I, col. 587F.

[97] For the chain, see I.ix.1, IV.i.30, IV.x.35, V.ii.42, V.ix.30, VI.xii.35, and, above all, VII.vi.14, "Fearing least *Chaos* broken had his chaine." Cf. *Hymne of Love*, ll. 78–89, and the cosmic iron and adamantine chains cited in James Hutton, "Spenser's 'Adamantine chains': A Cosmological Metaphor," in *The Classical Tradition*, ed. Luitpold Wallach (Ithaca, New York, 1966), pp. 572–594, a complete study. For the association between the knots that hold the universe together with the chains on wild animals, see Boethius, *De Cons. Phil.* III, metre ii. See below, Chap. VI, nn. 46f. In Ovid, *Metam.* VII.412, Hercules drags Cerberus bound with an adamantine chain; cf. Spenser's Acrasia (II.xii.82).

are overtones of some cataclysmic time-to-come, when the forces of chaos will have their terrible hour, and, in the words of Snori Sturluson, "all fetters and bonds will be snapped and severed."

In the Northern tradition, the age of the gods is terminated by a universal insurgency of giants and monsters. Principal among these are the Norse Behemoth, the wolf Fenrir; and the Norse Leviathan, the Midgard Serpent. The latter "will blow so much poison that the whole sky and earth will be spattered with it," and while Thor is doing battle with this monster, "the hound Garm, which was bound in front of the cliff-cave of hell, will also get free." Rising to occasion, the heroic gods do their last services to men:

> Odin will ride first . . . , and he will make for the wolf Fenrir. Thor will advance at his side but will be unable to help him, because he will have his hands full fighting the Midgard Serpent. Thor will slay the Midgard Serpent, but stagger back only nine paces before he falls down dead, on account of the poison blown upon him by the serpent.[98]

Book VI of *The Faerie Queene* closes with a kind of twilight of the gods over several generations, and we have already met such a defeat in the terminus of Book V. Mythologically speaking, then, the fate of the slandered Artegall somewhat resembles that of Thor here, because the poison of slander is nearly fatal for an agent of Gloriana—an agent animated by the desire for praise. The hound Garm, however, is readily dispatched. Not so the Blatant Beast—quite the contrary. For those rumours that have been started up about the dastardliness of the former hero and the licentiousness of the retiring poet may never be laid to rest.

The Analogy of Sufficient Grace

> Where iustice growes there eke grows greater grace
>
> (I. ix. 53)

> Where sinne abounded, there grace abounded much more.
>
> (Romans 5:20)

> If he be innocent and ignorant of ill, they say he is rude, and hath no grace: so ungraciously do some graceless men misuse the fair and godly word *grace*.
>
> (Ascham, *The Scholemaster*, ed. Schoeck, p. 43)

---

[98] All quotations taken from Snori Sturluson, *The Prose Edda*, trans. Jean I. Young (Berkeley and Los Angeles, 1966), pp. 86–88.

[i]

The word *grace* meets us everywhere in the sixth book, and when we come to the epiphany of the Graces themselves, late in the legend, we are likely to feel that it has been precipitated out of a ubiquity of lesser, lower-case manifestations. There is an analogy here with what the theologians call "prevenient grace"; as if Spenser has deliberately made much of the argument of the legend turn upon this sole word, the qualities of grace—its influence, its sufficiency, its numinous omnipresence—seem to be imitated at the level of the diction. The wide variety of meanings possible to the word, in itself, contributes to the sense of the plenitude of grace. The same variety also extends the poet's ideal of *copia*, or rhetorical sufficiency and generosity. Further, graciousness helps define the kind of Arthurian magnanimity belonging specifically to this legend, just as the divine condescension did in Book I. Some of the meanings of grace in Book VI are also vaguely theological; this analogy with Book I introduces the almost inevitable idea that grace supplies the "poetic theology" for this legend.

Calidore's gift, as we have said, is a grace. This gift may be a sign of the divine favor; if the tutor's charge "be of nature curtaise, piteouse, and of a free and liberall harte," writes Elyot, "it is a principall token of grace, (as hit is by all scripture determined)."[99] Conversely, "A humble and gentle nature," according to Erasmus' *Enchiridion*, "obtains not only God's favor but the good will and respect of your fellow man."[100] Spenser similarly remarks Calidore's deference to his rustic rivals: "Courtesie amongst the rudest breeds / Good will and favour" (VI.ix.45). Thus Book VI is related to the first not only by the analogy of the Word, but also by an analogy of grace. In the context of the later book, we think more immediately of two meanings for grace, depending on whether it is taken to be a property of good manners (one may behave graciously, or disgracefully), or a property of good manner (one may move or write gracefully, or gracelessly). Both good manners and good manner are ingratiating: they win favor, or grace. Hence the analogy with divine grace, for the gracious thing seems to have been the beneficiary of a divine bestowal: it pleases because it has already obtained the favor it seems to deserve of us. It enjoys, once again, prevenient grace, which, theologically speaking, anticipates the well-disposed will and is a prerequisite for it. However, since such grace is not earned, it might also seem like an adornment or

---

[99] *Gouernour*, I.vi, *edn. cit.*, p. 24.

[100] *Enchiridion*, xxxviii; trans. Dolan, in *The Essential Erasmus* (New York, 1964), pp. 89f.

augmentation of the spiritual life—a bonus or gratuity, rather than a strict necessity. These are the paradoxes that sustain the Augustinian-Pelagian controversy, and they are not far from our minds when Colin explains that heavenly graces abound in England:

> There learned arts do florish in great honor,
> And Poets wits are had in peerlesse price:
> Religion hath lay powre to rest vpon her.
> Aduancing vertue and suppressing vice.
> For end, all good, all grace there freely growes,
> Had people grace it gratefully to vse:
> For God his gifts there plenteously bestowes
> But graceless men them greatly do abuse.
>
> (*Colin Clout*, 320–327)

Insofar as their wills are free, men may sue for grace, and also may refuse it. It "freely growes," and yet sufficient conditions for its acceptance may be wanting; people do not always have the grace to receive it. There are theological overtones of the circulation of grace between man and heaven in *The Courtier*, too. On the subject of acquiring grace, one of Castiglione's speakers says, "by vertue of the word a man may say, that who so hath grace is gracious" (Singleton translates this, "by the very meaning of the word, it can be said that he who has grace, finds grace").[101]

In Book I it is God who graces, as Redcrosse acknowledges (I.x.64—"So God me grace"—is a characteristic expression). Heavenly grace is an essential support of the faith. It is seen in Una's face (I.iii.4; vi.18); it prevents Orgoglio from destroying Redcrosse (I.vii.12); it is felt in Arthur's office (I.viii.1); it gives Contemplation his vision, as the Graces give Colin his (I.x.47; VI.x.20); it is present in the sacraments (I.xi.48). (Compare the eucharist in *Tale*, 437–438: "God it is that feedes them with his grace, / The bread of life powr'd downe from heauenly place"; the context is ironic, but the doctrine is sound enough.)

There are signs that the sixth book is touched by the same providence. Calidore wishes that the heavens had graced him with a low degree (VI.ix.28). It is perhaps heaven's grace that provided help for the infant Pastorella; now the heavens have graced her mother with the same child's return—"The same is yonder Lady, whom high God did saue," says the nurse (VI.xii.8; 16–17). The Graces themselves have favored Colin; he in turn graces his mistress. She is "a goddesse graced / With heauenly gifts from heuen first enraced" (VI.x.20; 25). Even the cannibals prove suscep-

---

[101] *The Courtier*, I.xxiv. Cf. I.xiv: "some there are borne indued with such graces, that they seeme not to have beene borne, but rather fashioned with the verie hand of some God, and abound in all goodnes both of bodie and minde" (Hoby trans.).

tible, in their way; they decide to devote Serena to their god, "since by grace of God she there was sent" (VI.viii.38).[102]

In Pico's *Commento* the Graces stand for what comes from God to us, and returns from us to God[103]—a similar allegory appears in the Englishman Stephen Batman.[104] The eucharistic theology devised by the cannibals, who take Serena to be an instance of "heauenly grace" (VI.viii.37), exhibits the same circulation of gifts. Landino, in the opening pages of his commentary on Dante's *Commedia*, explained the three ladies that initiate the pilgrim's salvation as prevenient, illuminating, and proficient grace. Then he digresses:

> It seems to me possible that the poets have written about this. Because one possessed with genius readily grasped something that does not differ so very much from what I have recounted from true theology. Thus Hesiod writes in his *Theogony* that the Graces are three, and the number does not disagree. They are the daughters of Jove. This signifies nothing other than that from God alone proceeds all grace. . . . They were begot by Jove on Eurymone: and Eurymone in Greek means wide field: because nothing is a more bountiful field to us than the divine grace. . . . These are their names: . . . Aglaia in Greek means splendour, and certainly only the divine grace ends our darkness. Because it illuminates it. Euphrosyne means making joy, because it is this alone which makes joyous. Thalia signifies flowery, and making green: because it makes flourish and refreshes us in all virtue.[105]

Spenser's Graces—"daughters of sky-ruling Ioue, / By him begot of faire *Eurynome*" (VI.x.22)—share their parentage with Landino's. In the par-

[102] The power of fortune is in no way minimized in Book VI: on the contrary, the eventual triumph of Mutabilitie seems to be in the making throughout. Fortune has undone the victim of Maleffort (VI.i.41), brought the Salvage Man to aid Serena (VI.iv.2), fulfilled the prophecy about Sir Bruin's son (VI.iv.35), caused Serena's capture by thieves and allowed her release (VI.viii.34, 46), discovered Pastorella to Meliboe (VI.ix.14), exposed her to the tiger's attack and the brigands (VI.x.34, 38), and caused her rescue by Calidore and her return to her parents (VI.xi.8, xii.20); and it is "chance" that has saved Calepine from Turpine (VI.iii.51). Meliboe teaches that the riches of the temperate mind allow each to "fortunize" his life (VI.ix.30), and thus to neutralize want, or perhaps more broadly, vicissitude.

[103] *Commento*, II.xv; in the Stanley trans., II.xii (edn. of Boston, 1914), p. 35.

[104] Stephen Batman, *The new ariual of the three Gracis into Anglia* (London, ca. 1580). The book is a graceless medley, offered as a gift to the author's father. The dedication explains the courtesy of returning benefits (Sig. A2[r]ff.). Batman begins with a Somnius (Sig. A5[r]) in which one *Charites* comes to aid him in writing: she is from Elohim, and came into being with man's creation (Sig. Bii[r-v]). Charites gives the writer three graces to guide his pen: Thankfulness (Sig. B3[v]), who gives one the grace to seek virtue; Plenteousness (Sig. C2[r]), God's plentiful grace; and Liberality (Sig. C4[r]), who is particularly God's mercy.

[105] *Dante con l'espositione di Cristoforo Landino* (Venice, 1564), fol. 13[r], trans. by C. W. Lemmi in his study, *The Classic Deities in Bacon* (Baltimore, 1933), p. 23.

allel with Book I they are placed opposite the heavenly graces bestowed on Redcrosse at the House of Holiness. Within Book VI they are found on a hill "plaste in an open plaine" (VI.x.6). This open plain must reflect the etymology for "Eurymone," and so might the "open fields" in which Calidore discovers Pastorella, as Meliboe did in times past (VI.ix.4, 14; xii.16). There is a sense, then, in which these fields have been graced.

The configuration of the Graces themselves, we are told, illustrates "That good should from vs goe, then come in greater store" (VI.x.24). The "then" is decidedly ambiguous: will we receive more than we have given, or should we give more than we may expect to receive? Yet another paradox of grace may be here. Grace is multiplied for those who are not intent upon benefiting themselves: those who expect little will receive much.[106] Good turns and benefits in Book VI correspond to the various "charities" inculcated at the Holy Hospital in Book I. Although inspired by it, these charities are not the divine charity of God's grace, nor can they compel it; and gift-giving, however genuine the courtesy that prompts it, does not bestow Calidore's mysterious gift.

Apart from the the divine bestowal, the sixth book has been especially graced in an aesthetic sense. Just as the theologian debates the place of grace in the scheme of salvation, the aesthetician debates whether graceful-ness is a supervenient property.[107] We have cited a number of passages that actually identify the Graces with beauty, but some of the Renaissance discussion of beauty turns on precisely the question whether beauty neces-sarily involves grace, or whether grace is more like an accident or augmen-tation of beauty, and not completely essential to it.[108] *The Courtier* ends

[106] This ambiguity meets us in Meliboe, who, "hauing small," does not "wish for more it to augment." Yet the little that he has "growes dayly more"; "What haue I," he asks, "but to praise th'Almighty, that doth send it?" (VI.ix.20f.). Cf. Pas-torella's "gracing small" of the pirate captain: "a little well is lent," the poet mor-alizes, "that gaineth more withall" (VI.xi.6). After Calidore dispatches the tiger, Pastorella thanks him a thousand times: "From that day forth she gan him to affect, / And daily more her favour to augment" (VI.x.36f.). The allegory that makes the two returning Graces the double requital due for benefits derives from Servius, *ad Aen.* I.720, and is found in Fulgentius, *Mitologiarum*, II.iv; the 2nd and 3rd Vatican Mythographers (in Bode, *Opuscula Mythologica*, II.36, III.11.2); and Boccaccio, *G.D.G.*, V.xxxv.

[107] So Peter Burkholder, "Is Gracefulness a Supervenient Property?," in *Aesthetics II, Tulane Studies in Philosophy*, vol. 20 (New Orleans, 1971), pp. 19–35.

[108] Cf. the description of Pastorella: "soothly sure she was full fayre of face, / And perfectly well shapt in euery lim, / Which she did more augment with modest grace" (VI.ix.9). For the Renaissance discussion, see Eugenio Garin, "The Problem of Gracefulness," in *Italian Humanism, Philosophy and Civic Life in the Renais-sance*, trans. Peter Munz (New York, 1965), pp. 117–122. Cf. Balthasar Gracián, *Art of Worldly Wisdom* (1647), cxxvii: "Grace is the ornament of ornament. With-out it, beauty is lifeless."

by describing beauty as "a flow of divine goodness" or a divine ray; when this ray finds a harmoniously colored and configured object, gracefulness occurs.[109] Della Casa thinks of gracefulness as synonymous with beauty only some of the time. Gracefulness is the persuasive aspect of beauty, as it were; good proportions make goodness beautiful, and they make beauty graceful.[110] The "evolution of the graceful in art" has become a historical subject in Schelling, and we may apply his remarks to the development marked by Spenser's sixth book as well:

> In the beginning, . . . the creative spirit shows itself entirely lost in the Form, inaccessibly shut up, and even in its grandeur still harsh. But the more it succeeds in uniting its entire fulness in one product, the more it gradually relaxes from its severity; and where it has fully developed the form, so as to rest contented and self-collected in it, it seems to become cheerful and begins to move in gentle lines. . . . the rigid outlines melt and temper themselves into flexibility; a lovely essence, neither sensuous nor spiritual, but which cannot be grasped, diffuses itself over the form, and intwines itself with every outline, every vibration of the frame.
>
> This essence, not to be seized, as we have already remarked, but yet perceptible to all, is what the language of the Greeks designated by the name *Charis*, ours as Grace.
>
> Wherever, in a fully developed form, Grace appears, the work is complete on the side of Nature; nothing more is wanting; all demands are satisfied. Here, already, soul and body are in complete harmony; Body is Form, Grace is Soul, although not Soul in itself, but the Soul of Form, or the Soul of Nature.
>
> Art may linger, and remain stationary at this point; for already, on one side at least, its whole task is finished.[111]

The supervenience of grace is rather notably suggested by the revels on Mount Acidale, and by the mythology of the Graces themselves, in the superimposition of a fourth Grace on the traditional threesome—she is an added grace. Spenser does not tell us who this Grace is, precisely, but she is said to have inspired the piping of Colin Clout, and therefore she corresponds to the Grace of Art. Such a Grace, we may learn from the

[109] *The Courtier*, IV.lii. Cf. Hoby trans., ed. Milligan, *Three Renaissance Classics*, p. 593: " an influence of the heavenly bountifulnesse, the which for all it stretcheth over all things that be created (like the light of the sunne) yet when it findeth out a face well proportioned, and framed with a certain lively agreement of several colours, . . . thereinto it distilleth it selfe and appeareth most wellfavoured, and decketh out and lightneth the subject where it shineth with a marvellous grace."

[110] *Galateo*, chap. 28; Pine-Coffin trans., p. 93.

[111] *On the Relation of the Plastic Arts to Nature*, trans. J. Elliott Cabot, in *The German Classics* (New York, 1913), vol. 5, pp. 106–136; sec. iv, "The Evolution of the Graceful in Art."

mythographers, is as old as Homer, for he makes Charis the wife of the artisan Hephaestos.[112] She is unnamed, because in the arts there are always "nameless graces which no methods teach," as Pope puts it (*Essay on Criticism*, l. 144). On Mount Acidale poetic intuition and poetic innovation vault past the artifice of rationalized form, surprise the poet's end, and obtain "a grace beyond the reach of art" (l. 153).

Castiglione conceives of grace as being characterized by informality and an apearance of nonchalance, that studied neglect of method that makes an art of artlessness. The Bower of Bliss failed in exactly this respect: there Flora was decked—like a pompous bride—by "her mother Art, as halfe in scorne / Of niggard Nature" (II.xii.50). It ought to have been something like the reverse. Book VI, on the other hand, is the least formal of Spenser's legends, the most inconclusive, and seemingly the most effortless. In this respect one might think it more like the original of the Bower in Tasso:

> E quel che 'l bello e 'l carro a accresce a l'opre,
> l'arte, che tutto fa, nulla si scopre.
>
> (*Ger. Lib.* XVI.9)

And that which increased the beauty and the appreciation of the work, was that the art which made it all, disclosed itself nowhere.

But on Mount Acidale the suspicion that art made the work is curiously dispelled by having the artist inside it; his creation appears to be Nature's work alone.

The sense of a numinous presence, which we have associated with grace in this legend, may be illustrated in other ways, too, especially by the "imagery" of air. New developments in the narrative are announced by voices in the air: shrieks, grieving, music, and caroling. The legend seems almost overheard in this regard. The story evinces a rather barometric sensitivity, if you will: Serena strays into the vicinity of the Blatant Beast, "Allur'd with myldnesse of the gentle wether" (VI.iii.23); Calepine parts from Serena when he enters the woods "to take the ayre, and heare the thrushes song" (VI.iv.17); Calidore surrenders to becalment among the shepherds, rather than submit to agitation by vain hopes "Of courtly favour, fed with light report / Of euery blayst" (VI.x.2). The cynosures of Serena, Pastorella, and the Graces are all accompanied by the sound of bagpipes, which are notably wind instruments. The words of Blandina are

---

[112] Cornutus, *De Natura Deo.* 15, in Bode, *Opuscula Mythologica*, p. 163: "Homerus in suo poëmate perhibet, unam è Gratiarum numero cohabitare Vulcano. Quare hoc? Quod artificum opera plurimum gratiae obtineant." Giraldus, *Hist. Deorum*, in *Op. om.*, I, col. 420F; cf. Comes, *Mythol.* IV.xv, *edn. cit.*, p. 411.

mere wind and water, whereas gracious speech—the poet's in particular—
is more truly of the spirit. The same imagery has its demotic counterpart
in the Blatant Beast, whose mythology makes his speech Typhonic. He
too is a wind instrument, as in the following passage where Calidore
outstrips his adversary:

> Through woods and hils he follow'd him so fast,
> That he nould let him breath nor gather spright,
> But forst him gape and gaspe, with dread aghast,
> As if his lungs and lites were nigh asunder brast.
>
> (VI.iii.26)

The Beast, one might guess, has been reduced to the extremity of pure
billingsgate.

[ii]

Man requires grace because he has been disgraced. In Book I he is disgraced before God: he cannot please God through his own efforts alone.
There are analogies with courtesy, for society also may threaten us with
shame or disgrace. And yet the humiliation of the disgraced party may still
prepare for grace. A rather inexact and somewhat ironic parallel for the
humility that wins theological grace also turns up in the realm of sensibility, namely, that disarming neglect, or *sprezzatura*, that ingratiates by
means of a "certain disgracing to cover arte withall."[113] Hoby's translation
makes the analogy easier to see.

Redcrosse is "disgrast" when he meets Orgoglio; Duessa has also disgraced Fraelissa (I.vii.11; ii.38). In his fight with Error, the knight is
"fearefull more of shame / Then of the certaine perill" (I.i.24); the same
emotion is still influential when Calidore undertakes his final quest,
"Asham'd to thinke" of his truancy:

> That he much feared, least reprochfull blame
> With foule dishonour him mote blot therefore;
>
> (VI.xii.12)

Shame belongs to the experience of the disgraced Adam, and it may be
thought of as the emotion at the bottom of the Fall, as pride was somewhere near the top. The last sight at the House of Pride is the heap of
corpses of those who "came to shamefull end" (I.vi.53). The Orgoglio

---

[113] *Courtier*, IV.xxvi, in the Hoby trans., *op. cit.*, p. 286: "and (to speake a new
word) to use in everye thing a certaine disgracing [= *sprezzatura*] to cover arte
withall, and seeme whatsoever he doth and saith, to doe it without paine, and (as
it were) not minding it."

episode ends with Redcrosse speechless with dismay, and is followed by the shaming of Duessa. Redcrosse is said to be "inwardly dismaid" at the approach of Orgoglio, and we have already described the symbolism pertaining to the triumph of pride: under the domineering giant there is a humiliated captive. The same emotion takes its extroverted form in attempts to shame or demean or insult others. Redcrosse is exposed to something like this kind of shame at the House of Pride, where he shows himself sensitive to Lucifera's contempt. "Him selfe estraunging from their ioyaunce vaine" (I.iv.37), he suddenly finds himself faced with the accusations of Sansjoy; in their contest, "each to deadly shame would driue his foe" (I.v.9). Duessa is the daughter of Deceit and Shame, and the two names turn up as personifications in Book VI, in Decetto and Turpine.

The faithful and true in Book I are attacked by Sansfoy, Sansjoy, and Sansloi (infidelity, lack of Christian cheer, and a spirit of disobedience). One suspects that Redcrosse wins his technical victory over Sansjoy because he *is* estranged from the House of Pride. Christians are strangers and pilgrims on the earth; it offers them "no lasting city," and their hopes are elsewhere.[114] The comparable themes in Book VI are focused on Timias, who is attacked by Despetto, Decetto, and Defetto. The wounded hero is eventually retired to the lodging of the Hermit—the Beast's wounds "rankle" and the Hermit is a master of healing speech. The Hermit is compared to Podalyrius, the son of Aesculapius, and physician to the festering and ostracized Philoctetes. The Hermit can heal the passions, and his "holesome reede of sad sobriety" (VI.vi.5) may remind us of the sober mood of the Catholic epistles in the New Testament. There we are told that friendship with the world is enmity to God, for the world is filled with the lust of the eyes, and of the flesh, and the pride of life (I John 2:15–16; James 4:4). God opposes the proud, but gives grace to the humble; we are men of double mind, and we should purify our hearts, mortify our spirits (James 4:1f.), and abstain from the passions of the flesh (II Peter 2:11). We should keep our tongue from evil and speaking guile (I Pet. 3:9, after Ps. 34), like Christ on whose lips no guile was found (I Pet. 2:22). We are told to put away insincerity and slander (I Pet. 2:1), to bridle the passions, especially the untamable tongue (James 3:2f.). We ought to seek an unblemished life, keeping our "conversation" blameless, to belie the accusations of the Gentiles (II Pet. 3:14; I Pet. 2:12; 3:16). It is perhaps implied that it is best to ignore the contempt of the profligate, as well as to avoid the insobriety of their lives (I Pet. 4:2–7). Thus the Hermit:

[114] Heb. 11:13 (cf. Gen. 23:4, Heb. 11:9); Heb. 13:14. Redcrosse is protected by the otherworldliness of the Christian, in other words.

First learne your outward sences to refraine
From things, that stirre vp fraile affection;
Your eies, your eares, your tongue, your talk restraine
From that they most affect, and in due termes containe.
(VI.vi.7)

And again:

The best (sayd he) that I can you aduize,
Is to auoide the occasion of the ill:

. . . .

Abstaine from pleasure, and restraine your will.
Subdue desire, and bridle loose delight,
Vse scanted diet, and forbeare your fill,
Shun secresie, and talke in open sight:
(VI.vi.14)

Like the Redcrosse knight at the House of Holiness, the Hermit "From all this worlds incombraunce did himselfe assoyle" (VI.vi.37; cf. I.x.52). This self-mortifying discipline answers to the emotions that characterize discourtesy, of which perhaps the most important is contempt. Spenser's stories all insist that contempt is opposed to courtesy, as pride to holiness. The "difficult" person is often a case of embittered self-love, and there are many difficult persons in the sixth book, though frequently what we see of them is their envy.[115] Both arrogance and envy make one want to shame others. The unnamed knight who envies Aladine's lovemaking relieves his frustration by demeaning his own lady. The proud or offended or rankled person cannot be courteous. No one is prouder than Briana, who heaps indignities on Calidore "with scornfull pride" (VI.i.30). She is responding to Crudor, who has rejected her "through high disdaine / And proud despight of his selfe pleasing mynd" (VI.i.14–15). Calidore accepts Briana's challenge, "for aye me to disgrace / With all those shames that erst ye spake me to deface" (VI.i.28), and he reproaches the humbled Crudor for his pride (VI.i.41). The discourteous knight whom Tristram dispatches has shamed his lady; he is "full of proud disdaine" and scorns Tristram's rebuke (VI.ii.11). Earlier he wounded the unarmed Aladine "in his dispiteous pryde" (VI.ii.40). Turpine abuses and shames Calepine with "scornefull pryde" (VI.iii.47); he is described as "that proud / And shamefull knight" (VI.vi.34). Timias' enemies are proud Despetto and "spightfullest Defetto," and they conspire "to worke his utter shame, and him

---

[115] On this class of person, see now Hankins, *Source and Meaning*, pp. 178f., where Calepine's name is derived from *chalepoi*, the "difficult," on the basis of a technical usage in Francesco Piccolomini's *Vniuersa Philosphia de Moribus* (1583), IV.29, p. 202D; see n. 2 and text, above.

confound" (VI.v.14). The self-infatuated Mirabella is condemned to suffer under Scorn and Disdain—Disdain is brother to Orgoglio. Mirabella is under the wrath of Cupid. According to Horace, Venus hates pride ("ingratum Veneri pone superbiam"—put off pride, ungrateful to Venus [*Odes* III.10, l. 9]). "Despight" himself gives evidence at Mirabella's trial (VI.vii.34). The envious Coridon schemes to shame Calidore (VI.ix.43).

Adam first experiences shame when he becomes conscious of his nakedness; as Spenser says, "Shame would be hid" (VI.viii.5). Thus the attempt to shame other persons in this legend is symbolized by various kinds of exposure. Maleffort has half-stripped the character corresponding to Fraelissa in Book I; the tree-bound victim, corresponding to Fradubio, appears in her lover, who is due to lose his beard. Maleffort is attempting to cut off the lady's hair—the hair that is a woman's praise or glory and is given her for a covering (I Cor. 11:15). Turpine has a reputation for a similar usage; he is accustomed to despoiling knights and ladies of their arms or their upper garments. The unnamed intruder-knight takes advantage of the disarmed Aladine and the disarrayed Priscilla. Calidore twice stumbles onto scenes of undress, and the cannibals strip Serena. Ironically, the trophies or princely spoils that adorn the triumph of Serena's beauty in the imagery or diction are basically the clothes and jewels of which she has just been divested in the fiction.[116]

Where pride dreads humiliation, and would humiliate others, courtesy is expressed in a willingness to risk its own humiliation. The courteous act is the deferential one; the courteous person takes on burdens, starting from the rendering of obeisance. So Priscilla helps Calidore bear Aladine; and, like the Good Samaritan, Calidore pours balm in the victim's wounds. Shaming others especially involves abasing or disparaging or demeaning them. Arthur sets out to repay "the vile demeane and vsage bad" that Turpine has offered Calepine (VI.vi.18); Disdain and Scorn "demeane" Mirabella (VI.vii.39). The Graces, on the contrary, teach us "how to each degree and kynde / We should our selues demeane, to low and hie" (VI.x.23). The Beast disregards this sort of ranking, and speaks licentiously "Of good and bad alike, of low and hie" (VI.xii.28). Calidore professes his courtesy "Euen vnto the lowest and the least" (VI.xii.2). This is just what the caste-proud snob cannot bring himself to do.

---

[116] Cf. "they spoile her of her jewels deare, / And afterwards of all her rich array" with "Her goodly thighes, whose glorie did appeare / Like a triumphall arch, and thereupon / The spoiles of princes hang'd, which were in battel won" (VI.viii.41, 42). See Herbert Spencer, *Principles of Sociology*, vol. II-1, pp. 128–143, in the Westminster edn. of the *Synthetic Philosophy* (New York and London, n.d.), on the surrender of clothing, and pp. 36–51, *vol. cit.*, on the taking of trophies: Spencer classifies both as forms of symbolic obeisance, humiliation, or abasement, along with mutilation.

But different ranks merit different courtesies, and Calidore conforms to decorum even when he arms himself to attack the brigands. He provides himself with "a sword of meanest sort," and only when victory is in sight does he employ "a sword of better say" (VI.xi.42, 47). The "demeanure" of the aspiring Pastorella sets her above the shepherds from the start: "Though meane her lot, yet higher did her mind ascend" (VI.ix.10). Nonetheless, she is accustomed "to loue the lowly things" (VI.ix.35), including the unpretentious art of Colin Clout. Therefore Calidore adopts the clothes and manners of the shepherds, as did Apollo when he courted the daughter of the herder Admetus.[117] Apollo's courtship is mentioned in the tapestry of Cupid's triumphs (III.xi.39). (It is Tibullus who describes how Love bid Apollo house himself in a lowly cottage and take up duties in the dairy. The god's verse is interrupted by the herd; Calidore's courtly inventions do not fare well with Pastorella either.) "The gentle heart scornes base disparagement" (VI.x.37), but Calidore does not utterly repudiate the company of the cowardly Coridon. By modestly taking second place to Coridon, the hero silences would-be maligners (VI.ix.45); modesty is an antidote to pride.[118] Calidore seems to say that he accepts Briana's shames; in turn, in his engagement with Crudor, Calidore "made him to stoupe to ground with meeke humilitie" (VI.i.28; 38). Arthur likewise compels Disdain to bend the knee.

There is a sense in which courtesy is a form of reverence, Reverence being the official greeter at the House of Holiness. Reverence possesses the graces, as a comparison of the following passage with Colin's commentary on his vision of the Graces will show:

> There fairely them receiues a gentle Squire,
>   Of milde demeanure, and rare courtesie,
>   Right cleanly clad in comely sad attire;
>   In word and deede that shew'd great modestie,
>   And knew his good to all of each degree,
>   Hight *Reuerence*. He them with speeches meet
> Does faire entreat; no courting nicetie,
>   But simple true, and eke vnfained sweet,
> As might become a Squire so great persons to greet.

(I.x.7)

---

[117] Tibullus, II.iii.11ff.; Theocritus, *Idyl* 27; Politian, *Stanze*, I.108; Ovid, *Metam.* VI.122. If Apollo or Calidore wrote bucolics, on the other hand, he would have adopted a "lowly gate" (Envoi to the *Calender*): the pastoral style is a humble style, in contrast to that of the epic, "which consists in praising by elevated speech and great sentences" (Thilo-Hagen, eds., *Servii*, vol. 1, p. 4). It is the poet's own humility that makes him appear in this legend in his pastoral persona.

[118] According to Erasmus, *Enchiridion*, xxxviii.

The House of Holiness is entered "stouping low" (I.x.5), and Reverence appears just after *Humilitá*. The Christian, of course, imitates the Christ who humbled himself, taking the form of a servant, and yet a servant at whose name every knee will bow (Phil. 2:8–10). The association of courtesy and reverence is classical as well, as in Cicero:

> For, as physical beauty with harmonious symmetry of the limbs engages the attention and delights the eye, for the very reason that all the parts combine in harmony and grace, so this propriety, which shines out in our conduct, engages the approbation of our fellow men by the order, consistency, and self-control it imposes upon every word and deed.
>
> We should, therefore, in our dealings with people show what I may almost call reverence [*reverentia*] toward all men—not only towards the men who are the best, but towards others as well. For indifference to public opinion implies not merely self-sufficiency, but even total lack of principle. There is, too, a difference between justice and considerateness in one's relations to one's fellow-men. It is the function of justice not to do wrong to one's fellow-men; of considerateness, not to wound their feelings; and in this the essence of propriety is best seen.[119]

As the above account suggests, the legend is filled with the mysterious reciprocities of deference and demeanor, the subtle ways in which we acknowledge the duty and respect we owe to our superiors, and assert the privileges we enjoy as the superiors of others.[120] Crudor considers himself superior to Briana, and his eventual acceptance of her implies a generous condescension on his part. The "meaner borne" Aladine (VI.iii.7) is similarly dependent upon the condescension of Priscilla. Calidore's superior position in society is felt in all those instances in which he takes for granted that others will receive him deferentially, even though his company is not necessarily wanted. Coridon is helpless in his rivalry with Calidore because he can never really impugn the privilege to condescend that belongs to his superior. The disdain that Mirabella feels, on the other hand, is pretentious; she arrogates to herself a highborn demeanor not properly hers: she is "of meane parentage" and Disdain might well "demeane" her in turn (VI.vii.28, 39). All the evil efforts of detraction in this book might be said to evince a rebellion against this code of proper deference. Detraction, as its etymology suggests, is the "taking away" from those to whom deference is seemingly owed. If it is owed, then it cannot be bought, or paid for; thus the paradox that whenever Calidore defers to Coridon (to whom deference is not owed), he further obligates Coridon to remember his

---

[119] *De Officiis*, I.xxix.99, trans. Walter Miller in the Loeb edn., pp. 101, 103.
[120] For the following analysis, see Erving Goffman, *Interaction Ritual* (New York, 1967), "The Nature of Deference and Demeanour," pp. 47–95.

unworthiness. Far from implying that Coridon is an equal, Calidore's treatment of his rival must further impress upon him that he is not. Calidore has a demeanor of superiority to depart from; Coridon, who must accept this condescension with good grace, loses even the power to detract. This is one more instance of grace in Book VI, for, as Boccaccio explains in his article on the Graces, "Grace is a certain liberal disposition of the mind, particularly of the greater towards the lesser, by which benefits and compliances are sometimes bestowed even without being called for, on no precedent merit, by indulgence."[121] Coridon does not particularly merit the indulgence he receives, and his own considerable claims to a grievance are somewhat undermined thereby. This knowing condescension on Calidore's part, of course, will lose him friends wherever it is felt that Coridon has been merely outsmarted, rather than genuinely graced.

Fables of Green Fields

If we may be allowed the expression, *it is not the resemblances, but the differences, which resemble each other.*
(Claude Lévi-Strauss, *Totemism*, trans. Rodney Needham, Boston, 1963, p. 77)

[i]

Our comparisons between Book I and Book VI have not depended very much upon the kind of detailed canto analysis that we have elsewhere developed to expound the analogy between the private and public books of the poem. Certain of our concluding themes can be illuminated by such an analysis, however, though nothing like the parallel between the second and fifth books obtains here.

We have seen some analogy in the disposition of the materials of the two legends, in the course of the preceding discussion. In order, we have compared the following: Error and the Blatant Beast; the dedications of the hero; the symbolic victims; the wilderness sojourns of the heroines Una and Serena; the satyrs and Sir Satyrane, and the Salvage Man; and the "dissociation" and disappearance of the heroic personae. This brings us up to the seventh canto, which is the point at which Spenser first alerts us to the possibility of an analogy between the two installments: he points out that Disdain is a blood relation to Orgoglio.

At the opening of the seventh canto in Book I, Redcrosse has just escaped

[121] *G.D.G.*, I.xvi, Romano edn., vol. I, pp. 47f.

the dangerous House of Pride; but Duessa, cloaked as Fidessa, catches up to the guileless knight, and he is soon "Pourd out in loosenesse on the grassy ground" (I.vii.7). At this point in Book VI, Arthur has escaped the castle of the treacherous Turpine, but the ingrate's hired assassins also catch up to the prince, who is equally oblivious to *his* peril. Turpine has seduced his men with the arts of Duessa's counterpart, Turpine's wife Blandina, "comming courteously, / To cloke the mischief, which he inly ment" (VI.vii.4). His men fail, and Turpine himself approaches the sleeping Arthur, "Loosely displayed vpon the grassie ground" (VI.vii.18). In Book I the hero is thoroughly shamed by the approach of Orgoglio, but in Book VI the disgrace falls instead upon Turpine, and then Mirabella. Arthur is partly saved by the "shame" of Sir Enias (VI.vii.23).

In the later book the victimization of the hero is transferred to Timias, who attempts to rescue Mirabella from the giant Disdain. Instead, he is bound and shamed in his turn. Orgoglio and Disdain are conceived along similar allegorical lines. Both are oversized. Orgoglio could never pass into the House of Holiness, for its gate is low. The haughty gait and rigid postures of Disdain prevent his genuflection before the superior might of Arthur—his knees crack, rather than bend. His disparaging language would never allow him to experience the Graces, which, as we noted before, teach us "how to each degree and kynde / We should our selues demeane, to low, to hie" (VI.x.23). Although Disdain can see his golden feet, he remains unaware of the ridiculous figure he finally makes. One recalls that Ignaro is the foster father of Pride.

Lesser parallels may be noted. When Orgoglio strikes, Redcrosse is almost "pouldred all, as thin as floure"; when Disdain brings his club down on Arthur, he "Thought sure [to] haue pownded him to powder soft" (I.vii.12; VI.viii.15). In each battle Arthur's groom is jeopardized by the giant's second. (In the earlier book Timias is menaced by Duessa's beast; in the later book Sir Enias is oppressed by Scorn.) The fall of Duessa stands for God's judgment on the promiscuous "great citie" of Revelation; Mirabella's humiliation is the judgment of Cupid on the cruel mistress convention, and her salvation depends on the mortification of her pride. Duessa bears the golden cup filled with the blood of the saints; Mirabella carries a bottle of tears—she must wander through the world until she has saved as many as she has slain (VI.viii.22).

The sequel to the deflation of Orgoglio in Book I has two sections: the exploration of Orgoglio's palace-prison, with Arthur's rescue of Redcrosse; and the vindication of Una, with the shaming of Duessa. Matters are more complicated in Book VI. Corresponding to Redcrosse, Timias is the victim enlarged by Arthur. (The reunions of Arthur and Timias partly suggest the reintegration of the heroic persona, elsewhere symbolized by Arthur's friendships.) This reunion is followed by the episode of Serena and the cannibals; she is the "wonderous beauty" who replaces Mirabella in the narrative as Una replaces Duessa. Serena, appropriately enough, departed from Timias at his fall before Disdain; at the corresponding point in Book I, Una's faithful dwarf fled from Redcrosse, the victim of Orgoglio.

There is possibly an analogy between the chalice administered by Duessa and the equipment of the cannibal priest; the altars would belong to this analogy too. The Christian innocents of Book I, victims of Duessa's beast, have been slain on the altar like "sheepe out of the fold" (I.viii.35). Una's iconology includes a lamb; she is like a "seely Lambe" herself (I.vi.10). Serena is like "a sheepe astray" when the cannibals discover her (VI.viii.36). Elsewhere the wandering heroine has been the victim of the Blatant Beast; here she is compared to a sacrificial altar, and the Beast will prove to be a desecrater of altars. Unlikely as it at first seems, the imagery implies some agreement here, though how we are to relate the exposure of Duessa to that of Serena is hardly clear.

One might begin by noting a parallel with the biblical ritual of atonement. In the scapegoat ritual outlined in the sixteenth chapter of Leviticus there are two victims. One, like Duessa, is cursed and polluted, and is driven into the wilderness to be received by the demon Azazel, as Duessa will be received by Archimago. The other scapegoat is innocent, and is offered on the priestly altar. Calepine, however, slays the priest instead of the sacrifice, sacrificing him "to th'infernall feends" who presumably have inspired him (VI.viii.49).

If Duessa with her cup in part stands for the Mass, the religious thieves may also be celebrating a kind of Mass—one in which the table guest becomes, as it were, the "host." Reginald Scot, in his *Discovery of Witchcraft*, for example, takes a swipe at "The Canibals crueltie of popish sacrifices exceeding in tyrannie the Jewes or Gentiles,"[122] and the more unbuttoned Protestant polemic turns up the same comparison: the Real Presence, according to Ridley, "confirmeth and maintaineth that beastly kind of cruelty of the 'Anthropophagi,' that is devourers of man's flesh."[123] This is actually the technical position of Zwingli, in his *Commentary on True and False Religion*, where he opposes spiritual to corporeal manducation:

> I have now refuted, I hope, this senseless notion about bodily flesh. In doing that my only object was to prove that to teach that the bodily flesh and sensible flesh of Christ is eaten when we give thanks to God is not only impious but also foolish and monstrous, unless perhaps one is living among the Anthropophagi.[124]

[122] XI.iii; Montague Summers edn., p. 109.

[123] "Disputation at Oxford," in *Works*, ed. Rev. Henry Christmas, Parker Society (Cambridge, 1853), p. 199 (taken from Foxe's *Acts and Monuments*).

[124] *Commentary on True and False Religion*, excerpted in Hans J. Hillerbrand, ed., *The Protestant Reformation* (New York, 1968), p. 112. Similarly, *Exposition of*

The Eucharist here is defined as a giving of thanks. Spenser implies that the cannibals are giving thanks also. The "ceremonies," the consecration of the sacrifice, the "common feast," the "bloudy vessels," the devotion of Serena's "guiltelesse blood" to religious purposes, the divided garment, and the muttering of the priest all argue for the representation of a degenerate version of the sacrament. In particular the Protestant might have noted analogies for the unintelligible Latin of the Roman service, and the practice known as the "reservation of the cup."[125] In the historical allegory the "salvage nation" of thieves is probably Irish, and therefore popish; despite his admiration for its dedication, the author of the *Vewe* is scandalized by the Irish priesthood's ignorance, and there may be an allusion to that condition here.

There is another apposition in the two episodes, in the descriptions of Duessa and Serena—especially in the aesthetics of those descriptions. The analogy is between truth and beauty, and is an extension of the analogy between the Word of God and the words of the poets. Both descriptions are sensational physical anatomies, unparalleled elsewhere in the poem for graphic detail. Both transform the conventional catalogue of the beauties of the ideal mistress into something rich and strange. And both seem to be under a mounting pressure for psychological release. Already known to us as the sinister coy mistress who leads her lovers to hell, Duessa is now exposed as the loathly lady from whom knights in romance are happily delivered. "Spoile her of her scarlot robe," Una commands:

> So as she bad, that witch they disaraid,
>   And robd of royall robes, and purple pall,
>   And ornaments richly were displaid;
>   Ne spared they to strip her naked all.
>   Then when they had despoild her tire and call,
>   Such as she was, their eyes might her behold,
>   That her misshaped parts did them appall,
>   A loathly, wrinckled hag, ill fauoured, old,
> Whose secret filth good manners biddeth not be told.
>
> (I.viii.46)

Serena is likewise "spoyld of all attire" (VI.viii.48):

> But all boots not, they hands vpon her lay;
>   At first they spoile her of her iewels deare,
>   And afterwards of all her rich array;
>   The which amongst them they in peeces teare,

---

the Faith, in G. W. Bromily, ed. and trans., *Zwingli and Bullinger* (Philadelphia, 1953), p. 261.

[125] Duessa's cup—"Death and despeyre did many thereof sup" (I.viii.14)—also perverts the Lord's Supper.

> And of the pray each one a part doth beare.
> Now being naked to their sordid eyes
> The goodly threasures of nature appeare:
> Which as they view with lustfull fantasyes,
> Each wisheth to him selfe, and to the rest enuyes.
>
> (VI.viii.41)

The *topos* of modesty that causes Spenser's "chaster Muse" to blush at the foulness of Duessa also controls the impulse of the cannibals, since they are prevented from raping the sacrifice:

> Her neather parts, the shame of all her kind,
>   My chaster Muse for shame doth blush to write;
>
> (I.viii.48)

> Those daintie parts, the dearlings of delight,
>   Which mote not be prophan'd of common eyes,
>
> (VI.viii.43)

Spenser nevertheless *does* write, and the cannibals each have their fantasies. Serena's paps "like white silken pillowes were"; Duessa's are "dried dugs, like bladders lacking wind" (VI.viii.42; I.viii.47). Serena's skin is silken; Duessa's, "rough, as maple rind." Serena almost seems to be pregnant ("her bellie white and clere, / Which like an Altar did it selfe vprere"); Duessa is a kind of parody of a nursing mother ("Her dried dugs . . . Hong downe, and filthy matter from them weld"). About the one figure there is a tense expectancy; about the other, a savage disillusionment. On the one hand, a spellbinding fairness; on the other, an appalling deformity.

Is there anything here beyond an edifying exercise in rhetorical analysis? If the comparison also illustrates an analogy of discovery and shame, then exposure in the context of courtesy means a very different thing from exposure in the context of revelation. The "secret filth" of Duessa is also that of such institutions as the monasteries; but where the truth exposes the one in the legend of holiness, the Blatant Beast, or scandal, ravages the other in the legend devoted to civility.

The order of the description of Duessa resembles that of Solomon's bride (Song 2:1-7). As her tail indicates, Duessa is one of the foxes that spoil the bride's vineyard (2:15). Coming to the same point in the anatomy of Serena, Spenser describes

> Her goodly thighes, whose glorie did appeare
> Like a triumphal Arch, and thereupon
> The spoiles of Princes hang'd, which were in battel won.
>
> (VI.viii.42)

714

So the anatomy of the bride: "Thy necke is as the towre of Dauid buylt for defense: a thousand shields hang therein, and all the targates of the strong men" (Song 4:4, Geneva Bible).[126]

Serena is ideally a still unravished bride of quietness, so to speak, and her perfection is set off by the mounting pitch of the cannibals' whooping, shrieks, and bagpipes. The cacophony supplies a kind of parody of the shepherds piping to the bride figures in Arcadia. While she is still composed in sleep, Serena's beauty does impose itself upon her viewers, and, when she is stripped, the same comeliness temporarily diverts them from their more usual appetite. Thus the theme of the corresponding episode in Book I—namely, the recognition and vindication of truth—has its counterpart here in the revelation and discrimination of beauty. Hence the emphasis on appreciative beholding. In the one legend, the naked Duessa becomes the biblical gazingstock among the nations (Nahum 3:5-6). In the other, the naked Serena becomes a kind of *omphalos* for the focusing of imaginative reverie:

> How beautiful are thy goings with shoes, o princes daughter: the iointes of thy thighs are like iewels: the worke of the hand of a cunning workeman.
>
> Thy navel is as a rownde cuppe that wanteth not lickour: thy belly is as an heape of wheat compassed about with lilies.
>
> (Song 7:1-2, Geneva Bible)

The biblical bride appears to be a kind of altar too.

We said that the import of this area of Book I was the imminence of revelation. The lights are not nearly so dazzling in Book VI, but perhaps there is an analogous theme for courtesy—namely, the refinement of sensibility, through the contemplation of beauty. Calidore sees the fair and comely Graces because he is the considerate or responsive person; he is also sensitive to the art of Colin Clout. As Della Casa suggests in his courtesy book, the capacity for the discrimination of beauty is in itself a kind of gift or grace.[127] Thus the reception of truth in Book I finds its counterpart in Book VI in the appreciation of the beautiful.

---

[126] Belphoebe also attracts the imagery of the bride, of course. Compare II.iii.24 with Song 4:11 (with a hint of the trophy imagery of vs. 4), and II.iii.28 with Song 5:15.

[127] *Galateo*, chap. 26: "This is a special gift of man, for the other animals can recognize neither beauty nor any form at all; and since the sense of beauty is ours alone . . . , we ought to appreciate it for its own value and hold it very dear, especially those of us who are more sensitive and therefore recognize beauty more readily." (Trans. Pine-Coffin.) In passing we may note that the remark of the unnamed lady about the beauty of the exposed Priscilla ("Faire was the Ladie sure, that mote content / An hart, not carried with too curious eyes," VI.ii.16) implies that it might not satisfy a connoisseur. The remark, which seems gratuitous in the bad sense, is at any rate peculiar to Book VI.

Calidore's name reminds us of Ficino's derivation of the Greek word for beauty from the word meaning "to call," and the sexuality of the revelation in Book VI is meant to suggest that beauty is partly defined by its being "comely," or attractive.[128] As the treatment of Duessa's repulsiveness shows, our sensibilities are closely related to our senses, and we often describe what appeals to or offends the one in terms borrowed from the other.[129] Duessa is physically unseemly, foul, and coarse, and the passage describing her may be thought to be distasteful as well. The description of Serena—just as deliberately, one feels—is presented as a model of chaste and decorous eloquence. There are no revealing veils, like Acrasia's; Serena's beauties, like the Graces themselves,

> . . . also naked are, that without guile
> Or false dissemblaunce all them plaine may see,
> Simple and true from couert malice free:
>
> (VI.x.24)

Serena cannot be expected to feel this way herself, however. Duessa flies into the darkness to hide her "open shame" (I.viii.50), and in the most ironic of counterpoints, Serena, overcome with "inward shame," cowers before the dawn that will expose her nakedness to her lover.

[ii]

The reunion of Redcrosse with Una at the end of the eighth canto signals the end of the theme of ungodliness in the legend, though it can hardly terminate the enmity of Satan or the "man of sin" (I.ix.46) to the godly. Redcrosse's reunification seems to result in a dramatic simplification in the allegory of Book I from this point on. In the sixth book the discovery of Serena provides the equivalent prognosis of an upward turn in the fortunes of courtesy. Calidore now returns to the legend, crossing into the happy Arcadia of the shepherds in the hue and cry after the Blatant Beast. The Arcadian episode also seems to clarify and simplify the life of the virtue in question.

In each book the four remaining cantos present the same sequence: the formation of a friendship followed by an extended colloquy; the visitation of

---

[128] *De Amore*, V.i. (The suffix to Calidore's name means "gift," which Spenser translates as "grace" in his etymologizing of Pandora in *Teares*, l. 578.) It is hard to believe that Spenser did not know of Cale (or Kalé) as one of the names of the Graces. This is found in Eustathius, p. 1665.58, in *Comm. in Od.* (Leipzig, 1825), p. 390; see n. 144, below. Ficino's discussion of the etymology is immediately followed by his treatment of the Graces as beauty.

[129] For these remarks, see Della Casa, *Galateo*, chap. 27, "How things which are repulsive to the senses also upset the mind," and chap. 2, "Definition of obnoxious behavior according to the senses which it offends."

the locus of recognition and the beholding of the vision pertaining to the virtue; the deliverance by the hero of the wasted kingdom of the "princess"; the reunion of the heroine with her original parents; and the capture of the last enemy. No doubt such a parallel ought to be offered tactfully, but merely to ignore it would deprive the poem of an important sense of kept appointment. Where Redcrosse overcomes an enemy who would see him "damnifyde" (I.xi.52), Calidore civilizes the Beast, "That neuer more he mote endammadge wight" (VI.xii.38). In these cantos Redcrosse accomplishes the promise of his election, if that is theologically the correct description: his sanctification enrolls him among the saints (II.i.32). It is probably no more than a typographical accident that makes Book VI "The Legend of S. Calidore." The S. is ambiguous, but Spenser's headings have proved imaginatively misleading elsewhere.

In the ninth canto of Book I, Redcrosse makes the major friendship of the legend, linking with his benefactor Arthur in the golden chain of concord. In exchange for a golden box of precious liquor, Redcrosse gives Arthur a Gospel written in golden letters. In the legend of courtesy, Calidore is befriended by Meliboe, but Meliboe declines Calidore's rather ill-advised offer of gold. Arthur recounts his pastoral upbringing by Timon (whose name suggests "honor"), his ignorance of his true parentage, and his conveyance to fairyland. A similar story belongs to the "georgic" Redcrosse. In Book VI Meliboe tells Calidore the story of his metropolitan experience, and the foundling motifs are attached to his foster child Pastorella. In Book I Arthur describes his miraculous conceit of the fairy queen, and in Book VI Calidore abandons his service to the same queen and takes up the quest for Pastorella: thus Arthur's entry on faerie has a likeness with a difference to Calidore's service among the shepherds. Calidore's sight of a "soueraigne goddesse" (VI.ix.9) is present to his sense as well as his fancy; in the two legends where other men see visions, Arthur's own quest remains a dream (VI.vii.6).

The second subject of the ninth canto in Book I, the temptation of Redcrosse by Despair, hardly seems like a parallel for the conversation of Calidore and Meliboe. Yet in fact each episode belongs to an analysis of the hero's unheroic state of mind. Despair, for example, does not attack Redcrosse; Redcrosse comes to Despair. Both heroes are somewhat truant here, even while their inward movement suggests that last character strength in life, the power of renunciation.[130] They are weary of strife, they long for repose and release, and they seem to doubt the reality of the quest. In both legends the hero is thinking of peaceful havens: Redcrosse wants to die, and Calidore wishes the heavens had bestowed on him some

---

[130] So Erikson, in "The Roots of Virtue," in Huxley, *Humanist Frame*. On reasons for dying and ways of effecting an end to life, compare Spenser's Despair with Seneca, *Epist.* LXX.

lower station in life (VI.ix.28). We are warned to beware of the "charmed speeches" of Despair:

> His subtill tongue, like dropping honny, mealt'th
> Into the hart, and searcheth euery vaine,
> That ere one be aware, by secret stealth
> His powre is reft, and weakenesse doth remaine.
>
> (I.ix.31)

An analogous suasion belongs to Meliboe:

>   the knight with greedy eare
> Hong still vpon his melting mouth attent;
> Whose sensefull words empierst his hart so neare,
> That he was rapt with double rauishment,
>
> . . . .
>
> He lost himselfe, and like one halfe entraunced grew.
>
> (VI.ix.26)

Meliboe's name suggests honey, and he dispenses consoling doctrine in the counsel-of-prudence tradition to which Chaucer's *Tale* belongs. (Also, like the family of Chaucer's character, Meliboe's family will be victimized by thieves.) One could say that Despair argues for a depressing kind of prudence as well, since he claims to be urging the hero to flee the wrath to come. Despair is an accuser of sin, though he imputes this character to God. In Book VI Meliboe warns that men "In vaine . . . The heauens of their fortunes fault accuse." "It is the mynd, that maketh good or ill, / That maketh wretch or happie"; "each vnto himselfe his life may fortunize" (VI.ix.29–30). In Book I this confidence comes rather dearer; it corresponds to a trust in God's grace. If Despair is wrong in arguing that man, compelled to sin, is compelled to damn himself, perhaps Meliboe is hardly more right in arguing that man is not compelled to be unhappy. Fortune's power over lives is not belittled by succeeding events in Book VI.

Whereas Redcrosse is seeking the grace of God, Calidore is only seeking the favor of his fellows, and especially the grace of Pastorella. At the end of the Despair episode, Una intervenes to assert God's providence, and Despair, rather than the hero, attempts suicide. In the later book, Calidore commends himself to Pastorella's grace by dispatching an attacking tiger, but more important for the theme, he defeats his rivals' envy. He graces the jealous Coridon, "for ill rewards him well" (VI.ix, rubric), and by such means prevents in Pastorella's other suitors any desire to malign him.

The temptation of Redcrosse, although purely demonic in its immediate effect, nonetheless contains the germ of the hero's regeneration, for it demonstrates his conviction of his own sinfulness. It is therefore a kind of grace in disguise, and it leads to the penitential House of Holiness. For a counterpart, Book VI offers the humbling of Calidore's spirit among the shepherds; as Coridon's envy loses its sting, the hero mysteriously happens upon the vision of the three Graces.

[iii]

The two loci of recognition differ markedly. Whereas holiness depends on sacramental discipline, courtesy depends on an unaffected and almost careless demeanor, an art that affects to neglect art. The symbolism reflects the difference. The House of Holiness is emblematic, formal, and full of graduation procedures and Sunday schooling. Mount Acidale is a *locus amoenus*, that is, a carefree landscape.[131] It does not suggest a remembering of the Sabbath, only a sabbatical, and it provides a hauntingly beautiful obbligato in the upper registers of the poem. Perhaps it ought to be left at that—and then again, perhaps not.

At the House of Holiness Una places her knight under the tuition of Fidelia, Speranza, and Charissa; they are the three daughters of Coelia, "called, in the argument of the canto, Holiness, but properly, Heavenly Grace," according to Ruskin.[132] "Heauenly grace" and "celestial grace" are Spenserian phrases, but how Ruskin arrived at his conclusion deserves investigation. The word *grace* is used frequently in this canto, and it is applied to the three sisters as well as to the progress of the knight:

> The faithfull knight now grew in little space,
> By hearing her, and by her sisters lore,
> To such perfection of all heauenly grace,
> That wretched world he gan for to abhore,
> And mortall life gan loath, . . .
>
> (I.x.21)

On Mount Acidale, this grievance corresponds to Calidore's sorrow for having interrupted Colin's communion with the Graces. In each case, the regret of the hero attests to his devotion to the virtue.

The summit in the House of Holiness canto is the mount of Contem-

---

[131] Giraldus, *Hist. Deorum*, Syntag. XIII, in *Op. om.*, I, col. 401F, derives the Acidalian fountain in which the Graces bathe from a-kēdes, "which displaces care." So also Mythographus II.36, in Bode, ed., *Scriptores*, p. 86. One notes the bathing-motif in the parallel scene which Faunus interrupts in the Mutabilitie cantos.

[132] *Stones of Venice*, app. 2, reprinted in the *Variorum*, ed. Greenlaw *et al.*, *Book I*, pp. 422–424. Grace is the cause of the love of God, of faith, and of hope, according to Aquinas, *Summa Contra Gent.*, III, Pt. II, cap. cli–cliii. See also n. 149, below.

plation, and it is here that the vision proper is vouchsafed the hero. When Redcrosse beholds the celestial city from Revelation, he pleads in accents that echo the earlier temptation of Despair:

> O let me not (quoth he) then turne againe
>> Backe to the world, whose ioyes so fruitlesse are;
>> But let me here for aye in peace remaine,
>> Or streight way on that last long voyage fare,
>> That nothing may my present hope empare.

(I.x.63)

Calidore, enchanted by the words of Colin Clout on Mount Acidale, also "had no will away to fare" (VI.x.30). But Redcrosse has a mission to accomplish, and Calidore leaves the mountain to continue his courtship. The vision confers on the hero his aspirations, but, for a knight, having visions is not an end in itself.

Such visions are a symbol for an end. They are signs presented to the quester so that he may learn to ask the right questions: failure to do so causes the knight to revert to his errant phase. The grail romances suggest that the symbols only gain their proper significance when they are beheld again; only then do they prove recognizable, and therefore instructive. At that point—effectively the occasion of the knight's initiation—they become disclosures of the power or the grace to complete the quest.

The symbols for the vocation of Redcrosse, such as the difficult text, the mortified serpent, the anchor, and the newborn babe, have been explained. In the *Calender* Colin's emblem was also the anchor of hope, and since Colin is reunited with his mistress on Mount Acidale, this hope seems to have been at last fulfilled. Apart from the garlands in the imagery, however, there apparently are no explicit emblems of Calidore's vocation to be seen. The garlands recognize Calidore's first encounter with Pastorella and his gift to Coridon, but the symbol for Calidore's quest also must somehow be implicit in the images for *literary* vocation: the broken pipes, the vanishing Graces, the "unfinished" text itself.

What relation do the Graces have to Calidore's Arcadian rustication as a whole? Calidore is particularly compared to Paris, in the days when Paris courted the nymph Oenone (VI.ix.36). Brief study of the parallels may convince us that Calidore's legend conforms to a not very well known branch of the medieval Troy legend, which describes the youth and education of Paris among shepherds or cowherds.[133] I owe my acquaintance with the more recondite parts of this material to the modern edition of the thirteenth-century *Excidium Troiae* prepared by Bagby Atwood and

---

[133] Classical sources include: Ovid, *Heroides* XVI.90–92; Ennius, as cited in Varro, *De Ling. Lat.* VII.82; Aelian, *Hist.* XII.42; Lychophron, *Alex.* 138; Tzetzes, on *Alex.* 86 and 138; schol. on *Iliad* III.325, XII.93, XV.341; Hyginus, *Fab.* XCI and CCLXXIII.

Virgil Whitaker,[134] though I had already arrived at the conclusion that a Paris legend was in the making from prominent indications in the text. Donald Cheney has come to a similar conclusion.[135]

In their introduction, Atwood and Whitaker indicate three categories for the pertinent matter here: first, the status of Paris as a foundling; second, his life as a herdsman, Alexander, "the protector of the flocks," and as the lover of Oenone, a divinely derived shepherdess; and third, his deeds of prowess during this pre-Trojan period. Authority for the last category is by far the weakest, but Spenser could have known that Paris gets his name Alexander for his routing of cattle thieves.[136] It seems less likely that Spenser would have been familiar with any of the medieval texts that the editors cite for Paris' dispatch of a she-bear and a lion, and his athletic contests with his brothers.[137] However, Servius reports these last contests briefly, and so does Hyginus (*Fab.* XCI) in a slightly different form. Servius (*ad Aen.* V.370) writes:

> According to the *Troica* of Nero [a lost poem by the Emperor], this Paris was certainly exceedingly valorous, for indeed on the occasion of the Trojan match of the festival of Agonalia he excelled everyone, even Hector himself. Whom, when he drew his sword on him in anger, he said to be a brother: which he proved by baby-toys brought forth—he who up until now was escaping notice in a rustic habit.

This report is rather unclear as to who made the identification of the disguised Paris. In the *Excidium Troiae*, where this occasion is also treated, Paris is identified by the shepherd who is Paris' foster parent. Closer to Spenser are two sources cited for Paris' staging of contests between bulls: the Middle English *Story of England* by Robert Mannyng, and the anonymous *Seege or Batyle of Troye*.[138] Atwood and Whitaker summarize the

[134] *Excidium Troiae*, ed. E. Bagby Atwood and Virgil K. Whitaker, Medieval Academy of America (Cambridge, Mass., 1944), "Introduction," II–IV, pp. xxi–lviii.

[135] *Spenser's Image of Nature* (New Haven, 1966), pp. 218–227. Cheney says that in leaving Acidale to pursue Pastorella, Calidore makes Paris' choice of Venus.

[136] For this meaning of the name, see Apollodorus, *Bibl.* III.x.9, and Ovid, *Heroides* XVI.51f., 359f.

[137] How Spenser came by this material may be less important than accounting for his use of it. One possible source is Boccaccio, *G.D.G.*, VI.xxii (Romano edn., vol. 1, p. 303), which reports Paris' deposition with the royal shepherd, his attaining great fame for his justice among litigants, his judging the goddesses, and the story quoted from Servius. Boccaccio identifies the mysterious intervention as that of the shepherd. The family reunion follows. The reader will see that Spenser has displaced the *termini* of the tale to Pastorella.

[138] *The Seege or Batyle of Troye*, ed. M. E. Barnicle, EETS, Original Series, no. 172 (London, 1927), pp. 22–24; see pp. lx–lxi, lxiv–lxxx for analysis of analogues quoted from the *Trojanska Prica* and *Trojumanns Saga*. In this noteworthy version Paris relates that in the forest he had acted as arbiter between four ladies of *Elfin land*

story: Paris "likes to watch fights between the bulls, and gives the winner a golden crown. One day Mars takes the likeness of a bull and overcomes Paris' favorite. Paris removes the crown from his bull and awards it to Mars. For this reason he wins a wide reputation for justice."[139] In the *Seege* Paris crowns the winner with a garland.[140] It seems that Spenser has combined the athletic contest with the bull contest. There is a slight precedent for this conflation in Hyginus, who has Paris' favorite bull led off as a prize for funeral games being held by Priam in honor of his supposedly dead son. Paris himself attends in disguise, and, out of fondness for the bull, wins the games even over his own brothers.[141] Here Paris has the place in the human contests that Mars had in the bull contest: he is the winner in disguise. In many versions of the story, it is on account of this demonstration of fairness that Paris is called upon to choose among the three goddesses. This tale confirms what one might take to be the case anyway, that Calidore's awarding the crown to Coridon (an act of graciousness toward a rival, corresponding to Paris' impartiality) establishes the precondition for Calidore's vision of the three Graces.

If the three Graces correspond to the three goddesses on Mount Ida, what symbolic "choice of Paris" confronts the hero on Mount Acidale? In Calidore's sojourn among the shepherds, the necessity is felt of the hero's choosing between the active and contemplative life; the choice is another version of the alternative of chivalry or philosophy proposed for the bear baby. The courting of Pastorella argues for the presence of a third alternative, a life of pleasure. According to the tradition deriving from Fulgentius, Paris, in choosing between the beauties of the three goddesses, passed judgment on the same three lives.[142] The goddesses' favors show

---

for the possession of a golden ball that they had found (Barnicle edn., pp. 40ff.). (See also *Seege of Troy*, ed. C.H.A. Wager, New York, 1899, pp. lxv–lxxi, for discussion of sources and analogues.)

[139] Atwood and Whitaker, eds., *Excidium Troiae*, p. xliii. In Mannyng's *Story of England*, ed. F. J. Furnivall, 2 vols. (London, 1887), vol. 1, pp. 16–19, the bullfights are watched by the goddesses. See ll. 499f.: "& that was gret curtesye / To gyue the bole the maistrie," on the awarding of the crown.

[140] Atwood and Whitaker, p. xliii, cite eight sources for flowers, as opposed to the gold crown: *Seege*, ll. 281–288, is quoted on p. xxvi. The garland has some classical authority in the *stephanos Alexandrou* ("crown of Alexander"), a species of laurel suitable for making crowns and found on Mount Ida, so named because Paris used to crown himself with it after games in the fields. See Theophrastus, *Hist. plant.* I.x.8, III.xvii.4; Pliny, *Nat. Hist.* XV.xxxix.131f.; Dioscorides, *Materia medica* IV.147.

[141] *Fab.* XCI. That these contests were wrestling matches is implied by *Excidium Troiae*, ed. Bagby and Whitaker, p. 5, l. 8.

[142] *Mitologiarum*, II.i, in Helm, *Fvlgentivs. Opera*, pp. 36–40. The allegory is based on the three lives in Plutarch, *De liberis educandis* 10, *Moralia* 8, and goes back to the three classes of men in Plato, *Rep.* IX, 580 seq. In Ficino, *Epistolae*, Lib. X, in *Op. om.*, I–2, pp. 919f., the three lives are equated with Pallas as *sapientia*, Juno as *potentia*, and Venus as *gratia*. Minerva offers knowledge to Paris for the first time in

this: Venus offered Helen, or any woman, i.e., sensual gratification; Juno offered power, or wealth in the medieval tradition; Minerva offered prowess, or, in the medieval tradition, wisdom. In the seventy-fourth *Amoretti* sonnet Spenser ascribes his life to three women: his mother, his sovereign, and his wife. They have given him "guifts of body, fortune and of mind." These ought to be the gifts of the three goddesses, but in fact Spenser calls his benefactors the three graces. Conversely, Colin calls the Graces "Goddesses all three," though neither Venus nor Gloriana is among them:

> These three on men all gracious gifts bestow,
> Which decke the body or adorne the mynde,
> (VI.x.22)

Calidore is compared to Paris not only because he is confronted by three divine beauties,[143] but also because he is confronted by a *diva triformis* who symbolizes, as in Book III, the choice of three lives.

Hyginus, *Fab.* XCII; so also in Boccaccio, *G.D.G.*, VI.xxii; she offers *wisdom* in Comes, *Mythol.*, VI.xxiii, *edn. cit.*, p. 654. The commendation of the theoretic or unproductive philosophical life—necessarily a life of leisure—is found in the genre of intellectual prose known as "protreptic." Beginnings are visible in Plato, *Rep.* 441 and 580 seq., and *Theaetetus* 172c–177c; Aristotle, *Metaphysics* I.i; Cicero, *De Off.* III.i. The Graces are *anima, corpus, fortuna*, in Ficino, *Op. om.*, I-I, p. 890.

[143] Some provision for this migration of motif is found in Sosostratus' lost *Teiresias*, as reported by Eustathius, p. 1665.58, which says that Aphrodite and the three Charites—by name Pasithea, Cale, and Euphrosyne—disputed as to which of the four was most beautiful: the judge was Teiresias, whom Aphrodite turned into an old woman for choosing in favor of Cale. (*Comm. in Od.*, vol. 1, Leipzig, 1825, p. 390.) The choice would seem to have been inevitable. This legend does not appear in Comes, Cartari, or Giraldus. Iconographical study can offer us support here however: for example, in Cranach's painting of the judgment of Paris, the three naked goddesses look like a quotation from representations of the Graces— the Cupid poised to shoot from above recalls the same motif for the Graces of Botticelli's *Primavera*. Raphael's Graces may be the *verso* for his Dream of Scipio (see Silius Italicus, *Punica* XV.18ff., and Petrarch, *Africa*, I-II), which is a version of the dream of Paris of the goddesses (so Wind, *Pagan Mysteries*, pp. 81–85). Elizabeth ought to have been the fourth Grace, as in Spenser's "Aprill," and a similar conceit made her a fourth goddess, namely Diana. See Lyly, "Iouis Elizabeth," in *Euphues and his England*; Peele, *Arraignment of Paris*; and Sabie, *Pan's Pipe*, all cited in E. C. Wilson, *England's Eliza* (Cambridge, Mass., 1939), pp. 136, 147f. Wilson cites C. H. Collins Baker, *Catalogue of Pictures at Hampton Court* (1929), p. 47, for Elizabeth as combining the gifts of the three goddesses; pp. 238f., n. 16. Bush reports that the pageants for Anne Boleyn in 1533 included both the three Graces and the judgment of the three goddesses (*Mythology and the Renaissance Tradition*, rev. edn., New York, 1963, p. 79). See J. D. Reeves, "The Judgment of Paris as a device of Tudor Flattery," *Notes and Queries*, 199 (1954), pp. 7–11, for an extended listing, including Nicholas Udall, "The Judgemente of Paris" (1553); Harington, *O.F.* XI.53; Greene, *Menaphon*, Doran's description of Samela, ll. 18–24 (Juno = "shew of maiestie," and later in the same work, *'Iuno* for maiestie").

Returning now to the comparison with Book I, we may start from the House of Holiness as a symbol for the Christian life, especially in its contemplative dimension. Mount Acidale suggests something analogous for the creative life, since the election of such a life implies the solitary life as well. Quintillian writes that "Everyone . . . will agree that the absence of company and deep silence are most conducive to writing," but then he demurs:

> though I would not go so far as to concur in the opinion of those who think woods and groves the most suitable localities for the purpose, on the ground that the freedom of the sky and the charm of the surroundings produce sublimity of thought and wealth of inspiration. For whatever causes us delight, must necessarily distract us from the concentration due to our work. The mind cannot devote its undivided and sincere attention to a number of things at the same time, and wherever it turns its gaze it must cease to contemplate its appointed task.[144]

The extended *locus amoenus* with which Quintillian follows up this advice suggests that there is as much to be said on the other side—Quintillian hardly lets us trust what he is saying. Similarly, Redcrosse works hard at the House, making the steady sacrifice that Christian living requires, but it emerges that the most important thing about this life is the grace to surrender to it. The creative life, with its combination of effort and leisure, contains a similar paradox.[145] Thus it is that six great efforts of concentration precede the recreations on Mount Acidale, and yet the poet's finest utterance comes almost unbidden, and shows him to be inspired. Here, if

[144] Loeb *Institutes* X.iii.22, trans. H. E. Butler. Cf. Boccaccio, *G.D.G.*, XIV.xi, Romano edn., vol. 2, p. 711, where the poet's retreat to such pleasant solitudes is for the contemplation of things divine. For the choice of the *solitary* life, see Petrarch, *Ad Familiares*, XIX.3, "To Laelius," where the poet adduces his own *De Vita Solitaria*. There the choice is between the active or public life and the contemplative one—the latter seeks "the paradise of solitude" (II.iii.3), in which one can say, with Ambrose to Sabinus, "I am never less lonely when I seem to be alone. . . . I summon whom I wish according to my pleasure and attach to myself those whom I like best and consider most congenial" (II.iii.2). Here the murmuring stream is especially grateful to the Muses, and one enjoys "an active rest and a restful work" (I.v.2). Compare the poet in Tacitus, *De Orat.* 12: "But woods, and groves, and solitude itself . . . to me afford such delight, that I reckon it among the chief blessings of poetry that it is cultivated far from the noise and bustle of the world. . . . The poet retires to scenes of solitude where peace and innocence reside, and there he treads on consecrated ground. It was there that Eloquence first grew up, and there she reared her temple. In such retreats she first adorned herself with those graces which have made mankind enamoured of her charms; and there she inspired the hearts of the blameless and the good." The speaker goes on to say that oracles first spoke in woods and sacred groves, and that the Golden Age abounded with inspired poets, than whom no character was more highly honored.

[145] Echoing Frye, *Return of Eden*, p. 7.

anywhere, we will say that Spenser's poetry is "no arte, but a diuine gift and heauenly instinct not to bee gotten by laboure and learning, but adorned with both."[146] As Saint Augustine said, "Because gratuitously, so by grace; for grace is no grace unless it is gratuitous."

To complete the comparison of the House of Holiness to Mount Acidale, we will want to know about a tradition that makes the three theological virtues the Christian Graces. In the *Marriage of Philology and Mercury* of Martianus Capella, the preparations of the bride for admission into heaven are attended by the four cardinal virtues, who are seconded by the three Graces.[147] At the top of the mountain of purgatory in Dante the bride figure is accompanied by the four cardinal virtues, now with the three theological virtues. The latter, like the Graces, dance in a ring ("Tre donne in giro" [*Purg.* XXIX.131]).[148] As with the Graces, this circulation is allegorically accounted for: Faith and Love alternately take the lead, over their weaker sister Hope. Dante's salvation begins from the *tre donne* that Landino, in a passage already cited, identified with three aspects of divine grace. The *Metamorphoses Moraliter*, in the article "De Venere," predictably identifies the three Graces with the theological virtues, in the allegory *in bono*: "Rather say that these three maids are the three theological virtues. . . . The first two are turned towards us, because we believe and hope well together. But the third doubtless averts her face, inasmuch as we cleave to God and love those near to us."[149] The allegory makes faith

---

[146] E. K., "Argument" to "October." Cf. Sidney, *Defense of Poetry*: "the ancient learned affirm it was a divine gift and no human skill" (Gilbert, *Literary Criticism*, p. 447). Some will object that such a reading is naive, and that this is the most contrived scene in the whole poem: "Doe you not marke," they will ask, "this that you call . . . disgracing, is a verie curiositie? for it is well knowne that hee enforceth himselfe with all diligence possible to make a shew not to minde it, and that is to minde it too much. ¶ And because hee passeth certaine limits of a meane, that disgracing of his is curious, and not comely, and is a thing that commeth cleane contrary to passe from the drift, (that is to wit) to cover arte." (*The Courtier*, I.xxvii, trans. Hoby, in Milligan, ed., *Three Renaissance Classics*, p. 287.) This objection is crucial to the meaning of Book VI: there is a sense in which Spenser has it both ways.

[147] *De Nuptis*, II, 33G–34G, Dick edn., pp. 56–58.

[148] In William Goodyear's trans. of Jean Cartigny's *Wandering Knight*, ed. Dorothy Atkinson Evans (Seattle, 1951), p. 108, the three theological virtues also join hands. Evans argues for Spenser's use of this work.

[149] *Metamorphosis Ovidiana Moraliter*, "Prologus," fol. viiiᵛ. This same allegory of the Graces is found as late as Ross' article on them, in his *Mystagogvs Poeticvs* (London, 1648), p. 143. According to Aquinas, the theological virtues are a form of divine assistance: they come from God, and by them God directs us to himself (*Summa Theol.*, Pt. II, 1st Pt., q.62, art.1). Pico says almost the same thing of the Graces, in the text cited in n. 103, above.

and hope the reflection upon things unseen; and love, the charitably disposed and outwardly directed will. (From Saint Paul on, discussion of the three virtues almost inevitably refers to this dialectic: Augustine, for example, says that "Faith believes, Hope and Love pray," and "there is no love without hope, no hope without love, and neither love nor hope without faith.")[150] Though there is no circular configuration in Spenser, Fidelia and Speranza do approach, while Charissa is approached. The averted gaze appears in Speranza, who has her hopes fixed on heaven. In Peele's *Descensus Astraea*, the three Graces and the three theological virtues appear in sequence in the retinue of the title figure. With this tradition in mind, we may ask if there is any parallel between the Graces in Book VI and the three sister virtues in Book I.

One text of the Third Vatican Mythographer reads "Tres ei Gratiae quae *caritates* dicuntur," where the others read *Charites*.[151] Spenser seems to cross his *Charites* with the charities too, though the verbal means are more complex. Una brings her knight from the cave of Despair to the House of Holiness to "cherish him with diets daint, . . . where he chearen might" (I.x.2). Speranza is not so "chearefull" as Fidelia. Una beseeches Redcrosse, after he has been made whole again, "Himselfe to chearish," and then brings him to Charissa, who entertains him "with friendly chearefull mood" (I.x.29, 32). And courtesies are frequently exchanged at the House; they are specifically extended by Reverence, Celia, Una, and Charissa— "who them requites with court'sies seeming meet" (I.x.32). On the other side, the importance of cheer in the endeavors of courtesy has met us already. Colin explains the Graces as "Sweete Goddesses all three which me in mirth do cherry" (VI.x.22). The divine condescension is strongly implied in the scene on Mount Acidale; the equations of cheer and charity, and the Graces and the Virtues, can do little more than appeal to the correctness of this original impression.

It is Charissa in Book I who corresponds to the Alma Mater of the poem as a whole; her nursery and generativity or maternity indicate this. She is "Full of great Loue," though she has nothing to do with Cupid; her turtle doves and "multitude of babes" remind us of the cupidons that flock around Venus (I.x.31). In Book VI it is the Graces who correspond to Venus, though they are only her handmaids. But just as Charissa signifies the fostering of a higher love than eros, so the gifts of the Graces transcend

---

[150] *Enchiridion*, vii–viii. Aquinas says that "both faith and hope are quickened by charity" (*Summa Theol.*, Pt. II, 1st Pt., q.62, art.4), while hope and love pertain to the appetite (*ibid.*, art.3).

[151] Bode, ed., *Scriptores rerum mythicarum latini*, III.11.2, p. 229.

even the provision of the queen of beauty, with her "house of goodly formes and faire aspects" (III.vi.11):

> Those three to men all gifts of grace do graunt
> And all, that Venus in her selfe doth vaunt
> Is borrowed of them. . . .
>
> (VI.x.15)

Schelling, whom we quoted earlier on the grace that emerges in art to transfigure form, says that "the pure image of Beauty arrested at this point is the Goddess of Love." And yet he notes that such a grace is even more suggestive, when it is united with goodness:

> Here Art, as it were, transcends itself, and again becomes means only. On this summit sensuous Grace becomes in turn the husk and body of a higher life; what was before a whole is treated as a part, and the highest relation of Art and Nature is reached in this—that it makes Nature the medium of manifesting the soul which it contains.[152]

This transumption of the aesthetic also governs the equation between the Graces and their counterparts in Book I: the Graces that emerge to transfigure the art of Book VI modulate into symbols of renewed innocence like Charissa's babes.

There are other approaches to the relation between Venus and the Graces. We have already discussed the paradoxical distinction between grace and beauty, and Venus is notably absent from the scene on Mount Acidale, even though the bare female form is found nowhere else in the poem in such abundance. The poet hints at another transformation of Venus when he writes, ". . . Such was the beauty of this goodly band, / Whose *sundry parts* were here too long to tell," and then refers us to the excelling beauty of the figure of the fourth Grace in the center (VI.x.14); in a way, this figure has taken Venus' place. The poet in his revery has apparently resorted to the stratagem of Zeuxis; "the painter for whom the girls of Calabria posed in the nude did no more than recognize which of Venus' limbs each of them had appropriated to herself, and when he had restored each limb to the goddess, she was there ready to be painted, for he could picture to himself her beauty and how it was composed." A reversal appears in the case of the uncomely woman, whose parts are really those "of different beautiful women and not only of the one who seems to have borrowed them on loan from all the others."[153] Traditionally, then,

---

[152] *Loc. cit.*, in n. 111, above.

[153] *Galateo*, chap. 26; Pine-Coffin trans., p. 91. The "Frieze of Girls" in the concluding section of Proust's *L'Ombre des Jeunes Filles en Fleurs* (*A La Recherche du Temps Perdu*, I.II), is conceived as precisely this kind of Zeuxian epiphany.

beautiful women are indebted for their beauty to *Venus*, but in Book VI (x.15) Venus is the *borrower*. Spenser's formulation makes the ideal beauty the one composed of the parts of different beautiful women; Venus is the one whose beauties are on loan from the Graces.

Confronted with only one beauty, the isolated Serena, the poet does enumerate her "sundry parts." This time his procedure finds its counterpart directly in the text, for the cannibals are also connoisseurs of beauty:

> Some with their eyes the daintest morsels chose;
> Some praise her paps, some praise her lips and nose;
>
> (VI.viii.39)

One doubts that Serena's beauty will survive their murderous dissection. Pastorella is merely said to be "well shapt in euery lim" (VI.ix.8), but here the analogy of the hero with Paris serves again, for, as a judge, "partial Paris" discriminates among the goddesses' gifts and beauties, and hence among their parts and graces. This brings us back to Calidore's viewing of the Graces on Mount Acidale, but there the fourth Grace is endowed with many graces, and hence, Colin seems to warn, eludes just such an analysis—she is Juno, Venus, and Pallas, and a fourth as well:

> Diuine resemblaunce, beauty soueraine rare,
> Firme Chastity, that spight ne blemish dare;
> All which she with such courtesie doth grace
> That all her peres cannot with her compare,
>
> (VI.x.27)

The fourth Grace combined the other three—so Giraldus' remarks suggest.[154] In such a Grace there is no place for Deffeto and Despetto; hers is a beauty without defect, and one from which detraction can take nothing away.

In the *Greek Anthology* we read that "The Graces wove a triple crown for Zenophilia, a badge of her triple beauty" (V.195). On Mount Acidale the poet has done as much for the unnamed Grace at the center of his rings. Because the mood of Book VI is contemplative, the stories in Book VI are inconclusive, for contemplation is either prior or posterior to action.

---

[154] *Hist. Deorum*, Syntag. XIII, in *Op. om.*, I, col. 420E: "some write that Pasithea is one of the Graces, which are three: . . . Pasithea, as if to say, completely divine, who ought to be majesty, exhuberance, and charm in herself, and also combines the others." With this *unique diva*, compare the ideal of Shakespeare's Benedict, in *Much Ado*, II.i.32: "Till all graces be in one woman, one woman shall not come in my grace." For beauty, chastity, love, and "peerlesse grace" in his mistress, cf. *Colin Clout*, ll. 468–470. I owe this citation to David Burchmore, "The Image of the Center in *Colin Clout*," paper for 1976 Southeastern Renaissance Conference (University of South Carolina).

The symbol of the ring, however, is conclusive; the stories seem designed to lead up to it. Since the ring also appears when the poet returns to complete the story of Calepine and Serena, and again when he returns to complete the account of Calidore, we must ask what larger cycle is being closed when the poet himself is found, on the periphery of the poem, in conjunction with the same terminal symbol. If Book VI taken as a whole has the pattern of a triple ring, the poet may have woven a garland for himself, as Serena did before she was interrupted by the Blatant Beast (VI.iii.23). It would be a crown of laurel.

When Mount Acidale is seen as this kind of culminating vision, it is almost inevitable that the breaking of the visionary's chosen instrument should be read as his unobtrusive valedictory. As Spenser signed his Latin verse epistle to Harvey, "Plura vellem per Charites, sed non licet Musas": that is, it would be gracious to write more, but lack of poetic inspiration forbids it. By this point in Book VI, the Muses and the Graces have virtually traded places: the Muses would more, but the disappearing Graces have mysteriously prevented it.[155] Because the poignancy and special character of the vision owe so much to the vision's being interrupted, however, the interruption, no less than the vision itself, may constitute a gift of grace. It proves to be an *inspired* interruption. One wonders if this subversion of the vision is not a part of the meaning of the rubric to canto x, which conflates the action similarly:

> Calidore sees the Graces daunce,
> To Colins melody:
> The whiles his Pastorell is led,
> Into captiuity.

The poet, having lost his pastoral vision, turns to the task of interpreting it to his audience: "Tho gan that shepheard thus for to dilate" (VI.x.21). The word *dilate* seems unexceptional here, but Spenser uses it only once again in the poem, at the end of the Mutabilitie cantos, where it turns up as a semi-technical term employed in Nature's explanation of the way in which all mutable things fulfill the law of their being—through dilation. Its use on Mount Acidale thus suggests the way in which Spenser's poem —or Colin's vision—fulfills the law of *its* being: through that delay, or dilation, during which an interpretation is allowed to emerge.

As an interpreter, the poet functions as the *eudoxus* figure that we have met in the other loci of recognition, and especially as the Johannine Con-

---

[155] The "thrise three learned Ladies" of I.x.54 are easily associated with the three Graces by way of Horace, *Odes* III.19: "Let our goblets be mixed up with three or nine cups, according to everyone's disposition. The enraptured bard, who delights in the odd-numbered Muses, shall call for brimmers thrice three. Each of the Graces, in conjunction with her naked sisters, fearful of broils, prohibits upwards of three." That the inspired poet is aided by the Graces as well as the Muses appears from Plato, *Laws* III, 682a.

templation of Book I, who mediated a divine communication to men. At the same time, the exegete is no longer strictly the inspired poet, no longer Apollo, the leader of the Muses or Graces; the Graces are gone, and his has become a somewhat ungrateful task. As Shakespeare says in another context, "The words of Mercury are harsh after the songs of Apollo."[156]

However, even if the words of Mercury are not so pleasing as the music of Apollo, neither can the song be fully expressed without them. In his civic and courtly function, in the value he gives to order and harmony, and in his classical learning, Spenser is a decidedly Apollonian poet. But Colin Clout does not play the lyre; he plays the pipes, like the woody god Pan. Another god with an association with the pipes is the rustic Hermes—Hermes in fact invented them. Old and honorable traditions also connect Hermes with the *logos*; he is the interpreter of the gods, and the inventor of "letters." There is a sense in which Spenser is also a Hermetic poet: in his partiality to mediated interpretations and recondite learning, in his preoccupation with the language of poetry and the poetry of etymology, and in his patronage of arts with an analogy to magic.

Like Apollo, Hermes is painted with the Graces,[157] and it is significant for the scene on Mount Acidale that it is Hermes who brings the three goddesses before Paris. Curiously enough, the Homeric *Hymn* to Hermes, in which the god's mythologum is found, is largely devoted to the mischievous theft by the infant Hermes of Apollo's cattle.[158] The same displacement of Apollo by Hermes meets us on Mount Acidale, when the Apollonian poet turns his back on the "Great sunne of the universe," and the Hermetic interpreter gives his garland to a mere country lass. Once again, it is Hobgoblin run away with the garland from Apollo.[159]

---

[156] *Love's Labour Lost*, V.ii.930: a messenger interrupts a dramatic performance with bad news.

[157] For Mercury with the Graces, see Horace, *Odes* I.30, *Ad Venerem*; Seneca, *De Benefic.* I.iii; Cornutus, *De Nat. Deo* 24. Mercury leading the Graces: Giraldus, *Hist. Deorum*, in *Op. om.*, I, 419F, and Cartari, *Le Imagini, edn. cit.*, p. 410. Golding translates Seneca: "Yea and Mercurie standeth with them: not because reason commendeth benefites, but because it so pleased the Peinter." The medieval image of Apollo with the three Graces in his right hand (alternatively a lyre) derives from Macrobius, *Saturnalia*, I.xvii.13; it is reported in Comes, *Mythol.*, IV.x, *edn. cit.*, p. 363. Behind Macrobius are Callimachus, *Aetia*, Frg. 114; Plutarch, *De Musica* 14, *Moralia* 644; Pausanias, *Perieg.* IX.xxxv.3; Philo, *Legatis ad Caium* XIII, 95. For discussions, see Rudolf Pfeiffer, "The Image of the Delian Apollo and Apolline Ethics," *Journal of the Warburg and Courtauld Institutes*, 15 (1952), pp. 20–32, and Ernst Kantorowicz, "On transformations of Apolline ethics," in *Charites: Studien zur Alterumswissenschaft*, ed. K. Schauenburg (Bonn, 1957), pp. 265–274.

[158] Mercury's theft from Apollo is also found in Horace, *Odes* I.10; it is reported in Comes, *Mythol.*, IV.x, *edn. cit.*, pp. 343f.

[159] We meet the same myth in Raleigh's "Vision vpon this conceipt of the Faery Queene," where the graces have abandoned Laura's tomb to attend the mistress of

The place occupied by the dragon in Book I is taken by the brigands in Book VI. The heroes respectively recover Eden and deliver Arcadia. Christian iconography for the harrowing of hell shows the triumphant Christ leading a procession headed by Adam and Eve out of the jaws of death. The same Messiah is also the Good Shepherd of Israel, who leads his flock to safety and abundant pastures; the gospel explains his mission in terms of the shepherd who goes in search of the missing lamb and lays down his life for his sheep. Book VI, which shows Calidore bringing Pastorella and the shepherds' flocks out of the "hellish dens" of the thieves, seems to be broaching a non-theological treatment of the same theme of the pastoral care. Coridon weeps with pity when he sees his stolen sheep, and when the thieves hire Calidore and Coridon to perform their duties, they confess that "they themselues were euill groomes, . . . Vnwont with heards to watch, or pasture sheepe" (VI.xi.40). One recalls the bad shepherds of John 10:12, for Spenser the type of English clerics with plural livings ("Maye," 37–54).

More than sheep, at any rate, are at issue. The cave of the thieves has the cryptlike quality of Limbo; the darkness affords only "A doubtfull sense of things, not so well seene, as felt" (VI.x.42). Spenser seems to echo the three-day plague of darkness in the Exodus, "euen darcknes that may be felt" (21:10). The thieves are slave traders, and one may add, with the Wisdom of Solomon, that their underworld is "an image of that darkeness that was to come vpon them: yea, they were vnto them selues more grieuous then darkenes" (17:20).[160] Overtones of a passion are heard in the prolonged ordeal of Pastorella. In the falling out in the cave, she is pinioned between the arms of the thief, "Like a sweet Angell twixt two clouds vphild" (VI.xi.21).[161] The clouds in the imagery refer to the loss of an unclouded serenity, but some greater darkness seems to have settled on the narrative as well. Coridon escapes craftily, "Ne stayeth leaue to take, before his friends doe dye" (VI.xi.18).[162]

---

the new poet, and where Homer himself "curst th'accesse of that celestiall theife." I owe the suggestion that the Homeric *Hymn* is the ultimate source for Harvey's remark about *The Faerie Queene*—in the second of the *Three Proper and Wittie Familiar Letters*—to Geoffrey Hartman, "The Interpreter: A Self-Analysis," *New Literary History*, 4 (1972–1973), p. 223.

[160] Curiously, Shakespeare's *Twelfth Night* mentions both the Egyptian thief ("Like to th'Egyptian thief at point of death / Kill what I love," V.i.118f.) and the Egyptian darkness ("I say there is no darkness but ignorance, in which thou art more puzzled than the Egyptians in their fog," IV.ii.43ff.).

[161] See the *Hymne of Heavenly Love* on the prolonged ordeal of the disgraced Christ: "And lastly how twixt robbers crucifyde, / With bitter wounds through hands . . ." (ll. 244f.).

[162] The defection of Peter is linked to craftiness at V.vi.27, where the apostle's betrayal shadows the attempt of Dolon on Britomart's life. Cf. Coridon's cowardice at VI.x.35: "His life he steemed dearer than his friend."

The interment in the cave is deathly three times over: the thieves' fight and the death of Meliboe; the revival and relapse of Pastorella; and the mission of Calidore. Calidore sets out, "God before," and he comes like a thief in the night. His entry into the cave prompts the diction that elsewhere characterizes the harrowing of hell; he "with huge resistlesse might, / The dores assayled, and the locks vpbrast" (VI.xi.43; cf. I.viii.4).

In the sequel, Pastorella acquires new parents. They seem to replace Meliboe and his wife, and perhaps Pastorella's nurse Melissa. Like Adam and Eve in Book I, Bellamour and Claribell have also experienced incarceration; since their union was consummated in a prison, the orphaned Pastorella slightly resembles the Una who wears the black stole, "As one that inly mournd" (I.i.4). Pastorella is recognized for who she is and presented to her mother; her identity is confirmed with tears and kisses. Likewise, Una is brought into the presence of her parents; she is kissed by the King of Eden and revealed to Redcrosse without her veil. Thus the first book, focusing on man's potential adoption as a son of God, restores to Adam his divinely granted birthright in paradise. The last book, where the issue is man's potential for gentleness and civility, creates a fragile literary pastoral for the society that Spenser's poem sets out to educate.

Spenser plans to leave Una in Eden in the last canto, which means, in practice, that she will not reappear in the poem. We can argue that the same disengagement obtains in the case of Pastorella and her return to *her* parents, for there is no hint that Calidore plans to marry the girl. And yet we are told that the knight had his will of her (VI.x.38). Such amours are a part of life, and courtesy requires their being kept secret; but there is something knowing and blasé here, which obviously contrasts with the declaring of the bans in Book I. The difference is also reflected in the circumstances under which Una and Pastorella were conceived: Una is the fruit of a union instituted in paradise, and truth is the daughter of God (III.iv.59); Pastorella's conception—however unjustly—was furtive and unpublishable.

With Una safely back in Eden, the poet ends his re-veiling of the truths revealed by divinity. Something essential is lost to the poet's allegory thereafter, for allegory veils truth. Perhaps something just as consequential for Spenser's fiction is lost at the end of Book VI, since fairyland is inconceivable without its origins in pastoral. Within the fiction, it is Coridon who deserts Pastorella, but at the end of Book VI, the poet himself steals away for the sake of his personal safety, abandoning any further plans for publication.

At the end of Book I Archimago reappears, bringing letters to slander Redcrosse, and forbid the bans. However, Archimago is exposed and bound, and the hero is not ultimately disgraced. At the end of the last book Calidore is also in danger of "reprochfull blame" (VI.xii.12), but he goes on to win the admiration of fairyland in his capture and exhibition of the Beast.[163] Nonetheless, both of the calumniators make good their escape, and no one has been in on the death of either. The sudden "echelonment" of Calidore's successors at the very end of the poem rushes us out of fairie space and time: the "Faery land" of the thirty-seventh stanza becomes the "Britane land" of the thirty-ninth, and two stanzas later the poem is over. At the beginning of the poem the hero compelled Error to disgorge a mess of foul papers. At the end of the poem the text itself is threatened by the foul-mouthed utterance of the Beast. Spenser's serial thus closes with a symbol not unlike the one that opened it, as if the quest as a whole had accomplished nothing. The quest does not quite end where it began, however.

All of Spenser's knights renew the quest. Nonetheless, as with any extended work of literature, later parts of Spenser's poem increasingly presuppose a protagonist of a rather different order. The word *quest* has both a subjective and an objective meaning. It may refer to the ongoing search, or *mutatis mutandi*, to the object that will end the search. Each of the knights is seeking a realized faerie, even as he gradually brings it into existence in the course of the quest. At the house of recognition each knight encounters another self, a rendezvous that anticipates the closing of the gap between the two senses of the quest. But on Mount Acidale we catch a glimpse of the completed ring of faerie itself. If it is the completion of *The Faerie Queene* that has now become the object of the quest, with whom should we identify the subjective quester—who follows that quest? Not Colin Clout, it would appear; and, as the conclusion of the sixth book seems designed to warn us, not the good Sir Pelleus, nor Sir Lamoracke of yore.

[163] For the comparison, see n. 96 and text, above.

VI

IN DAEMOGORGON'S HALL: THE FORMING-POWER OF A RENAISSANCE IMAGINATION

I have smiled, I confess, when contemplating coming to record this folly of the ancients who supposed that there was this eternal being lurking in the bowels of the earth, generated by nobody, and the father of all things. . . . Theodontius said that the reason for their foolish opinion was their not having their principles from learned men, but from the most ancient of the rustics of Arcady. These stolidly believed it, since they were inland men and mountain-dwellers and half-woodmen, and saw the earth by itself spontaneously producing forests and all the trees, and sending forth flowers, fruits, and seeds, rearing up animals and then receiving them when they died. And they saw mountains belching up flames, casting off rocks from hard flint, and exhaling winds from concave places and valleys; and they perceived that earth to be moved sometimes, and even to emit a roaring sound—and to pour forth from its bowels springs, lakes, and rivers, as if ethereal fire and clear air sprang up from it; and it made water from having drunk deep from the great sea of the ocean, and from fiery collisions discharged globes into the heights from the ashes of the sun and from the moon, and fixed them deeply in the everlasting stars as the sky. Those who followed after them, considering this a little further, were decided not to say that the earth alone was the author of these things, but, implicit in it, a divine mind, by the intellect and will of which the same things were done; and that this mind had its seat beneath the earth.

(Boccaccio, *Genealogie Deorum Gentilium*, I, introductory remarks to cap. i, on the mansion of Demogorgon being in the bowels of the earth: Romano edn., vol. 1, pp. 13f.)

I will tell you what I have heard about the progeny of Demogorgon. The poet Pronapis says in his "Protocosmos" that Demogorgon was alone save for Eternity and Chaos, and as he rested in his eternity, he felt a disturbance in the womb of Chaos. So that to relieve Chaos, Demogorgon stretched forth his hand and opened its womb, whence issued Strife, making hubbub, ugly and unseemly to look upon; who would fain have flown aloft, but that Demogorgon hurled him downward. And as the sweats and fiery groans of Chaos abated not, Demogorgon did not withdraw his hand till he had drawn from its womb Pan and three sisters called Fates; and, deeming Pan the fairest of all things born, Demogorgon made him his steward and gave him the three sisters as a retinue, that is as servants and companions. And Chaos, seeing itself divested of its burden, by order of Demogorgon set Pan on his father's throne. . . . It is said of Pan that he was enthroned by order of Demogorgon, because Nature administers the divine order and governance to things.

(Leone Hebraeo, *Dialoghi d'Amore*, Caramella edn., pp. 108f., 112; trans. Friedeberg-Seeley and Barnes)

haec super imposita est caeli fulgentis imago,
signaque sex foribus destris totidemque sinistras.

Above these is placed the image of the shining sky,
six signs on the right-hand doors, and just as many
  on the left.
  (Ovid, *Metam.* II.17f., the Palace of the Sun)

Our infancie is compared to the Moon, in which we seem only to live
and grow, as plants; the second age to Mercury, wherein we are taught
and instructed; our third age to Venus, the days of love, desire, and
vanity; the fourth to the Sun, the strong, flourishing, and beautiful age
of man's life; the fifth to Mars, in which we seek honor and victory, and
in which our thoughts travail to ambitious ends; the sixth age is ascribed
to Jupiter, in which we begin to take accompt of our times, judge of
ourselves, and grow to the perfection of our understanding; the last and
seventh to Saturn, wherein our days are sad and overcast, and in which we
find by dear and lamentable experience, and by the loss which can never
be repaired, that of all our vain passions and affections past, the sorrow
only abideth.
  (Sir Walter Raleigh, *The History of the World*, I.ii.5)

| i |

TURNING the page from the end of Spenser's sixth book to the Mutabilitie
cantos may remind one of the Renaissance Ariosto edited by Ruscelli;
there the *Orlando Furioso* is succeeded by the *Cinque Canti*, an undigested
block of narrative that seems to belong to the subject of the larger poem,
and yet to go beyond it. These additional cantos show a sane Orlando and
presume a married and Christian Ruggiero, though a landless one. They
pause to recount Astolfo's penitential sojourn inside of Alcina's whale, and
they end with Charlemagne's siege of Prague, the rebellion of Rinaldo,
and the desperate conflict between Rinaldo's forces and the army of Orlando—a portent of a greater breakdown anticipated at the outset. Above
all, the *Cinque Canti* look forward to an *Iliad*-like destruction of Charlemagne's court, the second subject of Pulci's Orlando poem. Thus they offer a new epic cause, a new answer to the question that the bard traditionally addresses to the Muse: "What god was it then?" Who precipitated
the action of the poem?
  At the outset we are referred to the quinquennial convocation of all the
fays, a Great Consult convened in a Himalayan fastness otherwise beyond

the reaches of the poem's geography. After many injuries and insults—
recorded most fully in Boiardo—the fays meet in council in their kingdom
and plot the ruin of the court of Charlemagne. Thus the backdrop lifts
to reveal the genesis of the Roland saga in the inspired enmity of Gano.
Above the steeps at the remote ends of the earth a glittering palace rises
tier on tier before the reader's eye, a palace that resembles the palace of
the Sun in Ovid:

> To right and left stood Day and Month and Year
> And Century, and the Hours set at equal distances[1]

To the mount of assembly come all the fays—through the dark air, borne
by demons, in ships of glass, carried by Pegasi, Griffins, and winged cars—
to present themselves to the high consistory summoned by their governor.
All are prompt, and all are decked in their finery, except Morgana. She
arrives late and dishevelled, in the same dress she wore on the day when
Orlando took her captive in Boiardo's poem. Alcina too is here; she too
has been offended, and she becomes a prime mover of the action, inspiring
the jealousy of Gano. We are in the palace of Demogorgon, and the fays,
disseminated throughout nature's works—by the ancients "sometimes
called Nymphs, and Goddesses with less lovely names"—are clearly also
the Fates. Ruscelli draws the moral in the allegory that heads the piece:

> In continuing with the five cantos, along with all that which is already
> known, you ought to appreciate, in order to comprehend them clearly,
> that the author wants to represent the great instability, and the little
> stedfastness of mundane felicity, and that no one ought to trust very
> much in it—but always ought to keep the heart on God's word, in which
> alone is found perpetual stability, all true good. Thus, in the last cantos
> of the *Furioso*, having described the great victory of Charles, the author
> comes with this new subject to show how quickly and with what furor
> Fortune revolves herself into the contrary. . . .[2]

If we trust Ruscelli's placing of the *Cinque Canti*, then Demogorgon, the
alpha-figure of Renaissance theogony, was also to have been an omega fig-

---

[1] *Metam.* II.25f. For the comparable splendor of the two palaces, see *Metam.* II.1–4,
16f., 23ff., and *Cinque Canti*, I.1–3. For Ariosto's Demogorgon, see Boiardo, *Orl. Inn.*
II.xiii.26–28: ". . . This Demogorgon is superior to every fairy (I don't know if you've
ever heard tell of him), and he judges and decides among them, and he can make
them do whatever he wants. At night he rides upon a ram, crossing over mountains
and sea, and every morning he scourges witches, fairies, and empty phantasms
with living serpents; if he finds them in the world in the morning—because they
may not appear during the day—he beats them with such furious blows that they
would gladly die if they could. Now he chains them down in the deep sea, now
he makes them go barefoot upon the wind, now he leads them into the fire behind
him, to some he gives this punishment, to some he gives another."
[2] Edition of Venice, 1603, p. 535; argument to Canto I.

ure, the AIŌN, as it were, into which the poem was to have ultimately gathered itself.

Demogorgon is the god of the primordial and the aboriginal, "the God of the earth," as Cooper's *Dictionary* defines him, following Boccaccio, and the "first creatour of the earth," the addition showing that the derivation of this figure from the demiurge has not been essentially lost. In Boccaccio, Demogorgon has two companions from of old: Eternity and Chaos.[3] These are the poles, roughly speaking, of the symbolism of the Mutabilitie cantos. That is, we may think of Demogorgon as either Eternity or Chaos, and as either enthroning or dethroning Jupiter.

In Spenser, Demogorgon is coexistent with Night, that theogonic Night, the most ancient grandmother of all, whose existence antedates the genesis of the house of the celestial gods, or the heavens, "which men call Skye" (*HHB*, 52). Like Night, Demogorgon "sawst the secrets of the world vnmade" (I.v.22), for Demogorgon "The hideous Chaos keepes," "Farre from the view of Gods, and heauens bliss" (IV.ii.47). It is this state—"eternall night" (VII.vi.14)—to which Mutabilitie, given her head, would willingly return the cosmos. Mutabilitie has the witch's or conjurer's traditional power to molest the moon in her sphere, but her real effect is closer

---

[3] *G.D.G.*, I, preface following the "Prohemium" to chap. 1; in Romano edn., vol. 1, p. 15. Spenser substitutes Boccaccio's Eternity for Hesiod's Chaos in the genealogy at *F.Q.* II.iv.42. The following lines by Conrad Celtis (publ. 1473) give a fair picture of Demogorgon: "It is recorded that all things were produced out of ancient chaos through the commotion of Demogorgon, when by chance the belly of the old man swelled up and, carrying the whole world in his body, he distended his womb heavy with a ripe weight, which was conceived from the beginning of the eternal world; impatient of his load, and at length desirous to put down the inert weight and the unformed mass pressing down upon his stomach, he cried out, indignant: 'I offer you to the empty air, O deformed chaos of the world shameful to the gods, and you discordant seeds of all things, which have lain slothful, hidden for so great a time in our limbs, often causing bitter pains, while you waged wars buried in my viscera: Go, go, immediately, I exhort you, and fashion with comely decorum the ruddy stars of the light-flowing heavens, and stand before me now empty with your tumult, while you build the workings of the world, which the eternal world binds into a concordant pact in perennial peace!'" The world then separates out into spaces and the courses of the planets are fixed, "which now impede the onrushing time with a retrograde motion and retard the wandering courses from proceeding and delay backwards their flowing by standing still, in order that the fates may pass with a fixed and stable course, while the flying seeds mix with a refluent motion that will turn about through different alternatives in order that at length through the ages the world may complete its centuries with an eternal course, this ordered by the god, who rules the rapid stars." Trans. by David Quint, from Kurt Adel, ed., *Conradi Celtis Qvae Vindobonae Prelo Svbicienda Cvravit Opvscvla* (Leipzig, 1964), "De Origine et Sitv Germanorum," "Fabula Demogorgonis de creatione mundi praefatio," ll. 1–18, 48–55; pp. 55–57. Giraldus, *Hist. Deorum*, Syntag. IV, prefatory letter, in *Op. om.*, I, col. 157, explains the first god of Boccaccio as a misreading of *demiourgon* in Plato: "the creatour of all."

to that of those conjurers mentioned in Job who are skilled to rouse up Leviathan.[4] The same accents are heard in Renaissance literature whenever the great dynamo of a morally ambivalent Nature rumbles and threatens to undo itself.[5]

Like Demogorgon, Mutabilitie is chthonic. Her father is Titan, and thus she is an aspiring Titaness, like Prometheus; her adversary is Jove, the son of Titan's younger brother Saturn, whom Jove dethroned. But she is also the daughter of a Cybelean mother, and granddaughter of the great Anarch:

> . . . a daughter, by the mothers side,
> Of her that is Grand-mother magnifide
> of all the Gods, great Earth, great *Chaos* child.
> (VII.vi.26)

But if Mutabilitie shows affinities to Demogorgon, through her descent from Chaos, so does Nature through her own claims to priority and, ultimately, through her proximity to Eternity. Nature is "great Grandmother of all creatures bred" (VII.vii.13), while Jove, though he may be the "father of gods and men" in Homer, is only a creature when compared to the higher principle to which Mutabilitie appeals:

> . . . the highest him, that is behight
> Father of God and man by equall might;
> To weet, the God of Nature,
> (VII.vi.35)

These lines do not refer precisely to the Christian God, for the case is actually tried before Nature herself. Rather closer is the Timaeic demiurge, who made the gods by making the Hesiodic Heaven and Earth from which they were generated. These gods are especially the planetary deities. In calling Nature "God," Spenser is playing upon an old and tolerated confusion, no doubt related to the question in classical literature of whether nature made the gods or the gods made nature. Calvin comments: "I admit, indeed, that the expression, 'Nature is God,' may be piously used, if dictated by a pious mind." Calvin does, however, object to this usage, "as it is inaccurate and harsh (Nature being more properly *the order which has been established by God*)."[6] A similar ambiguity attaches to Boccac-

---

[4] Job 3:8, a passage specifically invoking the elimination of a day from the calendar.

[5] Compare the passages from Boccaccio quoted below and *King Lear*, II.iv.280f., "What they are, yet I know not; but they shall be / The terrors of the earth." Gorgon may be either *terre*, earth, or *terribilis*, terrible, according to Boccaccio, *loc. cit.*

[6] *Institutes*, I.v.5, trans. Beveridge (edn. cit., Chap. II, n. 415), p. 8, on *Aen.* VI.724 and *Georg.* IV.220. Cf. also Ovid, *Metam.* I.21. (Ovid does not decide whether the strife of chaos was composed by a god or "kindlier Nature.")

cio's Demogorgon, which Boccaccio considers a recondite poetic fiction, "But since the naked sense of these deities is in error, it remains to explain what name of his seems so terrible to utter."

> Therefore [the writer] says, as I suppose, Demogorgon in Greek, god of the earth in Latin. . . . Or rather, the wisdom of the earth, since often demon is expounded as knowing, or wisdom. Or, as it is more pleasing to others, terrible god, because of the true God who dwells in heaven it is written: Holy and terrible is his name.[7]

It is also an easy step from Demogorgon's subterranean dwelling-place to the cave of Claudian's Eternity, in Boccaccio's next article. Before that cave sits Nature, surrounded by the souls (or babes, in Cartari's illustration of the scene) who desire to come into the world.[8]

As the above suggests, Nature and Mutabilitie are differentiations out of a single theogonic principle. Further, at the end of the eon, their difference may be resolved back into a single, undifferentiated principle. That is, either into Chaos,

> . . . when the compast course of the vniuerse
> In sixe and thirtie thousand yeares is ronne,
> The bands of th' elements shall backe reuerse
> To their first discord, and be quite undonne:
> > The seedes, of which all things at first were bred,
> > Shall in great Chaos wombe againe be hid.
> > > (*Ruines of Rome* 22)

Or Eternity,

> . . . that same time when no more change shall be,
> But stedfast rest of all things firmely stayd
> Vpon the pillours of Eternity,
> > (VII.viii.2)

Thus Spenser's two goddesses represent two natures, the one tending toward Chaos, and the other tending toward Eternity, but both occupying a middle ground of generation and corruption. This brings us to an essential theorem in the interpretation of these cantos, namely, that Nature and Mutabilitie are related to each other dialectically.

Many ways of illustrating this dialectic suggest themselves. In challenging to herself "the whole worlds raigne" (VII.vii.15), or "the worlds

---

[7] *G.D.G.*, I, preface to chap. 1; Romano edn., vol. 1, p. 15.

[8] *De Cons. Stil.* II.431, translated in Cartari, *Le Imagini* (Venice, 1625), pp. 16–18; see p. 19 for the illustration.

whole souerainty" (VII.vii.16), Mutabilitie is really claiming that *she* is Nature, "greatest godesse, onely great" (VII.vii.14), for she frankly allows that this universal dominion is otherwise owed to Nature. She begins her claims by offering the Earth in evidence:

> And first, the Earth (great mother of vs all)
> That only seems vnmou'd and permanent,
> And vnto Mutability not thrall;
> Yet is she chang'd in part, and eeke in generall.
>
> (VII.vi.17)

Here the rhetorical forms for describing movement and permanency, part and whole, are in fact borrowed from the conventional language for Nature, "Still moouing, yet vnmoued from her sted" (VII.vii.3). When Nature puts Mutabilitie down ("They are not changed from their first estate / But by their change their being doe dilate"), she calls Mutabilitie "daughter."[9] Mutabilitie is otherwise the daughter of Earth, and the final apellation, even if it is only generic, subtly recovers the earth for abidingness and steadiness, by making Nature and Earth both "mother." As the stable earth-mother and the earth's mutable daughter, the Nature-Mutabilitie pair then falls into the ancient pattern of Demeter-Koré.

A more extended example of the rhetoric for Nature is found in Pliny's description at the opening of his second book:

> . . . sacer est, aeternus, immensus, totus in tota, immo ver ipse totum, finitus et infinito similis, omnium rerum certus et similis incerto, extra intra cuncta conplexus in se, idemque rerum naturae opus et rerum ipsa natura.[10]

"Sacred, everlasting, boundless, the whole within the whole, yea rather the whole itself, finite and like the infinite, of all things certain, and like the uncertain, beyond the combination in itself, and within the all, at the same time the work of nature and the nature of things itself."

Pliny's passage reconciles two kinds of nature. Likewise the Nature who sits before the doors of Eternity in Boccaccio is a *janitrix*; Boccaccio says that we ought to understand her as *natura naturata*, "for what *natura naturans* sends in [to the world] never goes out."[11] The distinction here is between what in nature is perishable, and what is sustaining.

---

[9] The filial relation is apparent in one of Spenser's models, the suit of Ovid's Phaëthon to his father Apollo; see *Metam.* II.32, 56–58, 99f.

[10] *Nat. hist.* II.i.2. For the rhetoric, see Chap. IV, n. 410 and text.

[11] *G.D.G.*, I.i; Romano edn., vol. 1, p. 17. For the two natures, see Aquinas, *Summa Theol.*, Pt. II, Pt. 1, q.85, art.6, resp., where *Natura naturans* is identified with the God who preserves the universe through the alteration of generation and corruption.

La Primaudaye also describes two kinds of nature:

> . . . the one spiritual, intelligible, and the unchangeable beginning of motion and rest, or rather the vertue, efficient, and preserving cause of all things: the other, sinsible [*sic*] mutable, and subject to generation and corruption, respecting all things that have life, and shall have end.[12]

Spenser implies the same dialectic of the intelligible and sensible Nature when he adopts the Orphic description, "Vnseene of any, yet of all beheld" (VII.vii.13), a description suggested in another way by Nature's wearing a veil.[13] Mutabilitie will ask, "But what we see not, who shall vs persuade?" (VII.vii.49) and she dismisses the planetary gods (or the intelligences of the planetary spheres) as noumena for which there is no phenomenal evidence. This might tell us that Nature and Mutabilitie are related as an intrinsic and extrinsic nature. One could even say that Mutabilitie—who is beautiful—*is* Nature's veil. Her beauty imposes on Jove, as poetic variety imposes on the contemplative intellect:

> And very often things cheerfully change their distinguishing marks, and continuously help and continuously transform their interchanged appearances into the one of the other. For it often is brought to pass, with respect to the mind, that diverse images of many successive things separate from the same thing.[14]

The poem that began with Truth veiled in opinion and fiction ends with Nature veiled in mutable appearances.

A further step in the study of the dialectic of Mutabilitie and Nature depends upon an analysis of Mutabilitie's claims. In arrogating all of Nature to herself, Mutabilitie attempts to show the court that she already has it: the eclipse with which she opens her campaign portends the extension of her title to the heavens. If, however, her assertion of title were unequivocally supportable, she would have no real occasion to assert it.

[12] *French Academie* (London, 1586), p. 171.

[13] Cf. Proclus, in A.-J. Festugière, trans., *Commentaire sur le Timée* (Paris, 1966), Livre I, pp. 181–183, where the *peplon* worn by Athena, the goddess of weaving, is allegorized as the tissue formed by the order of things, especially since the robe portrayed a theomachy—i.e., a cosmogonic myth. Proclus also speaks of mythmakers showing "Athena, who presides over the Nature comprehended by the goddess who weaves the beautiful order of intelligible forms. . . ." (Livre I, p. 264). I assume the veil is Nature's virtually indescribable garment, and that this is also identical with the flowers that the "daedale earth" throws forth at the spreading of Venus' mantle at IV.x.44f. The flowers the nymphs offer under Nature's throne "richer seem'd then any tapestry." Spenser refers us to Alanus, *De Planctu*, where Nature's garment is decorated with her various works. (Cf. Athena's art in Hesiod, *Works and Days* 64, *poludaidalon histon huphainein*, "to weave the variegated web.") For a further instance of Athena's peplon, see n. 79, below.

[14] Vida, *The Art of Poetry*, III.58–63.

743

She should have no need to call upon another nature to make good on something her triumph still wants: Nature cannot give her what she already supposedly has. Mutabilitie is eager to press her claim for sovereignty by trying to show that she already possesses it, so her suit can only be an attempt to establish better title to the possession that she alleges to be already nine parts hers. The plaintiff "overeaches," if she allows that she has anything more than merely nominal to reach for.

By appealing to the *de jure* authority of Nature, Mutabilitie inevitably recognizes the existence of a "nature" other than her own, a nature characterized as a lawgiver, rather than a lawbreaker. Mutabilitie's claim of universal sway might also end up endorsing the conception of a consistent or unified nature. Mutabilitie says that the four elements are not only changed, but also are changed "Into themselues" (VII.vii.25). Here Mutabilitie means "changed into each other," but the passage in the *Timaeus* (49c–d) that she inadvertently echoes continues, "and thus generation appears to be transmitted from one [element] to the other in a circle." The cyclical nature of Becoming and of the transformations of the four elements is also a theme of Aristotle in his treatise *On Generation and Corruption* (II.10, 337a). The common idea seems decidedly like Nature's own at the end of the debate. If the sergeant at the trial succeeds in presenting all the evidence of mutability that Mutabilitie has amassed, it will be, paradoxically, evidence of order—Order is the sergeant's name.

Mutabilitie's relation to Jove is also dialectical. Their particular dialectic is indicated by their being cousins. Jove at one point asserts that might makes right (VII.vi.33), and Mutabilitie's might, should it make her another Jove, would eventuate in one final irony of mutation: she would become something that she supposedly is not. For Jove stands for constancy, or the inherence of order in things. At least he tries to stand for this; but in the presence of Mutabilitie's beauty, he "chang'd his cheere" (VII.vi.31). Jove always had a weakness for a pretty girl, and his constancy seems to be flexible, if not in fact somewhat mutable. (The cataclysm that he abjures might have turned out to be another triumph for Mutabilitie, and so perhaps he is less irresolute than at first appears.) Mutabilitie, in contrast, almost ends up displaying an exemplary constancy: her perseverance is one of its species. The same thing happens to her evidence for the ubiquity of change, which may be construed as evidence for *regular* change. Every month that she introduces, beyond the sixth, weighs down the scales—the seventh zodiacal sign—in favor of orderliness, as the year reverts to its beginning.

Another of the dialectical relations that lie behind the Mutabilitie cantos opposes Nature to Fortune. In expounding this relation one is led to some further observations on the form taken by a fiction about constancy. If Spenser had written a legend for constancy, it might well have shown a constant nature submitted to the inconstancy of Fortune; Elizabethans were fond of construing man's life as the product of the interaction of Fortune and Nature[15]—we would say environment and heredity. One may suspect that the two cantos have grown out of schemes like the debate between Nature and Fortune in Hawes' *Example of Virtue*, though clearly they have outgrown it as well.

The identification of Fortune and Mutabilitie is a natural one: "Thou pinchest at my mutability," says Chaucer's Fortune, and Spenser speaks of "fortunes mutabilitie" (*Virgil's Gnat*, 560). La Primaudaye, coming closer to the balance struck at the end of Spenser's poem, says that Fortune is constant in her very inconstancy.[16] Stories are told about Fortune that parallel the "plot" (VII.vi.23) of Mutabilitie. In *The Rare Triumphs of Love and Fortune* (1589), Tysiphone in Act I interrupts the wrangling gods with an ultimatum from Pluto on behalf of his daughter Fortune, and she herself asserts that "Of all things heer beneath the Moone, I should the ruler be."[17] In Bruno's *Triumphant Beast*, Jove celebrates the anniversary of the expulsion of the giants by instituting a new heaven to symbolize the self-renovation of the gods. In a minor episode Hercules returns to earth, and Fortune sues for the vacancy he leaves among the constellations. She is denied, since all the stars are already regarded as her seats, and as being at her disposal: "For all which is governed by the fate of mutation passes through the urn, through its revolution, and through the hand of your Excellency."[18] Similar paradoxes have met us in our

---

[15] My phrasing echoes Arthur Gilman's introduction to the Signet edn. of *As You Like It* (New York, 1963), p. xxiv. The theme is Boethian: see *De Cons. Phil.* II, prose v.

[16] *French Academie* (London, 1586), chap. 44, p. 468. Cf. Boethius, *De Cons. Phil.* II, prose 1: "She [fortune] has in your affairs persevered in that constancy proper to her by her mutability itself." See also *ibid.*, II, prose viii: "in adversity when she showeth herself inconstant by changing, then is she even true." (Loeb trans.) Cf. the moon's "*constant* Change-fulness" in DuBartas, Sylvester trans., *Wks.* I.IV, rub. ("constant course with most unconstant face," Pembroke, Ps. 104:19).

[17] *The Rare Triumphs of Love and Fortune* (1589; perhaps played 1582–3), ed. W. W. Greg, Malone Society Reprint (London, 1931), I.i.134, Sig. Aiiii[v]. Cf. ll. 163–169 (Sig. Aiiii[r]): "But should I reckon up what thinges I can confound, / what is it then, . . . Is not the wonder of the World a woork that soon decayes: / therfore ye see all earthly thinges, are wearing out alwaies / As brittle as the glasse, unconstant like the minde: / as fickle as the whirling wheele, as wauering as the winde. / Loe, such am I that ouerthrowes the hiest reared towre: / that changeth and supporteth Realmes in twinkling of an hower." Cf. also "Antropos" in Lydgate, *Reson and Sensualyte*, l. 369, and Allecto in Alanus *Anticlaudianus*, VIII, ll. 139–211.

[18] *The Expulsion of the Triumphant Beast*, II.ii, trans. Arthur D. Imerti (New Brunswick, N.J., 1964), p. 177.

analysis of Mutabilitie's claims. More simply, Comes reports that Fortune almost ousted Jove from his throne.[19]

The frontispiece of Robert Record's *Castle of Knowledge* (1556), an exposition of astronomy, loosely conforms to Spenser. Fortune is shown standing under the sign of the moon, on her ball, and turning her wheel, "whose ruler is Ignorance." Opposite her is Urania, under the sign of the sun, standing on a stable cube, supporting and taking the measure of the "Sphere of Destinye," an astronomical sphere that the book will teach. The picture shows that the two share a certain morphology of symbols, but the rubric suggests that they turn their spheres in opposite directions:

> Though spitefull Fortune turned her wheele
> > To staye the Sphere of Vranye,
> Yet dooth this Sphere resist that welle,
> > And fleeyth all fortunes villanye.
> Though earthe do honour Fortunes balle,
> > And bytells [= battles] blynde hyr wheele aduance,
> The heauens to fortune are not thralle,
> > These Spheres surmount all fortunes chance.

Mutabilitie, of course, argues that this is not so—aside from her sister Bellona's sway on the earth, the heavens are thrall to unpredictable change. The incursion of Mutabilitie into the heavens is a dire portent at the opening of Book V too. In the *Timaeus* the stars are gods; and in Spenser's two passages, it is the twilight of the gods.

Mutabilitie is characterized as an analogy for fallen nature, somewhat in the way that Fortune is typically characterized as *mis*fortune or adversity. Mutabilitie is also a Strife figure, unwelcome to the society of the gods. In Leone Hebraeo we find an allegory of Strife's exclusion from heaven: either Demogorgon or Jupiter hurled her to earth, where continual opposition gives rise to the sequence of procreation.[20] The allusion is to the story told in Homer, of how Ate came among men. Comes reports the almost opposite story of how Strife or *Eris* came among the gods when she tossed the apple of Discord among them at the wedding celebration of Peleus and Thetis. Comes explains that "When discord, indeed, and the inequality of men by birth, came on, then not only did the temper

---

[19] *Mythol.*, IV.ix, *edn. cit.*, p. 339: "Haec eadem tantum existimationis, tantúmque imperium ab Homeri temporibus accepit, vt Iupiter de coelo ab ea propè fuerit detrusus, omnémque rerum administrationem & sceptrum ipsum è manibus illa Ioui propè extorserit, sicut crediderunt insulsi homines."

[20] *The Philosophy of Love*, trans. Friedeberg-Seeley and Barnes, p. 126; *Dialoghi d'Amore*, ed. Santino Caramella (Bari, 1929), p. 110. Demogorgon is discussed at length in the terms proposed here, pp. 108-111, Caramella edn. For Ate ("Ruin"), see *Iliad* XIX.91-130, and cf. Ares' sister Eris at *Iliad* IV.440ff.

THE TRIUMPH OF TIME

of things perish, but everything was in fact ruined: for as friendship is the principle of generation, so quarreling is of corruption."[21] But the union in question assured that Thetis' offspring, being mortal, would not overthrow Jove. Spenser's allusion to this wedding feast (VII.vii.12) thus encompasses both the commencement and the resolution of the altercation that is his subject.

Bacon says that Saturn's dethronement by Jupiter represents the rejection of mutability by the heavens,[22] and this is part of Spenser's meaning in alluding to the same myth (VII.vi.27). Comes, expounding the myth of Saturn's attack on *his* father, Uranus, makes it stand for the attempt of corruption on heaven.[23] Should she succeed, Mutabilitie would also become part of a dethronement myth. The lunar eclipse with which Mutabilitie begins her ascent is surely one of those eclipses that "disastrous twilight sheds / On half the Nations, and with fear of change / Perplexes monarchs," and of course Spenser's monarch was England's "mortal moon," just as the moon was England's national planet.[24] We are told that much ancient enthronement symbolism depends upon the ritual recital of the defeat of the powers of chaos by the powers of order or creation,[25] and Jove's confirmation here is not basically different. Any triumph —as the *Dunciad* reminds us—might take this form, with the "mighty mother" enthroning her champion and protégé. Furthermore, a triumph over Mutabilitie on Jove's part will also be a kind of triumph over time, and hence over Saturn, or Father Time, and thus a renewal of Jove's original accession to power. The following interpretation of the Cronos myth might therefore commend itself to our attention:

[21] *Mythol.*, VI.xxiii, "De Paride," p. 660 ("Hanc fabulam confictam fuisse de generatione . . ."). For the story, see Hyginus, *Fab.* XCII, and Lucian, *Dialogues of the Sea-Gods* 5 (7 in Loeb edn.).

[22] *De Sapientia Veterum*, "Coelum, or Beginnings." See n. 26, below.

[23] *Mythol.*, X, "Saturno," *edn. cit.*, p. 1020: "[Saturnus] deiectus de regno idcirco fuit, quod aetheris natura credita sit immunis ab omni corruptione, cum non sentiat vim temporis, quod inferiùs extra suum regnum destrusit."

[24] *Par. Lost* I.596–599. For the English national planet, see Gower, *Confessio Amantis*, VII.749–754. The link is played on by the gravediggers in *Hamlet* and by Donne in *Ignatius His Conclave*.

[25] Theodor Gaster, *Thespis: Ritual, Myth and Drama in the Ancient Near East* (New York, 1950); Engnell, *Studies in Divine Kingship in the Ancient Near East* (2nd edn., Uppsala, 1965); Mowinckel, *Psalmenstudien, II: Das Thronbesteigungsfest Jahwäs und der Ursprung der Eschatologie* (1922); A. R. Johnson, *Sacral Kingship in Ancient Israel* (Wales Univ. Press, 1967); H. Frankfort, *Kingship and the Gods* (Cambridge, 1948). I have not dwelled upon the political theme, but the annualization of Elizabeth's enthronement in Accession Day tournaments may be noted here: the queen's champion had the symbolic function of Marduk in the Babylonian creation-liturgy. For the constancy theme in the ceremonies upon the occasion of the retirement of this champion in 1590, see E. K. Chambers, *Sir Henry Lee* (Oxford, 1936), pp. 135–149, where we read about a pillar of constancy, and two years later, a debate between constancy and inconstancy.

For Jupiter put Cronos headlong into Tartarus, ejecting him from the supremacy. In this, therefore, as if under a veil, is treated the universal process of generation or order, which we deduce is to be called, customarily, *apo tou krainein*, i.e., by mixing together. . . . Saturn hindered the flow of heaven into a more abundant earth, and caused meaner vapours. Moreover, the nature of the world, which we called Jove, spreading infusions, checked that so great mutation of things, and fettered it with chains, extending and drawing it out over a long time for the world.[26]

This passage reads rather like those that we have cited for the presence of Time in the Garden, on the relation of time and generation,[27] except that here the action of time does not advance generation; rather, the retardation of change checks corruption, and, in effect, slows time. In delaying Mutabilitie, Jove gives Nature time to appear. All things—even Mutabilitie—dilate their being, and this dilation takes place in time.

The procession of the times, as Mutabilitie indicates (VII.vii.56), is a "triumph," whosever triumph it may be. In part it is merely the triumph of that Saturnine Time of the Garden; the labors of the months show June with plow-irons, July with scythe and sickle, September with a knife-hook, October with plowing share and colter, November riding "The seed of *Saturne*" (the Centaur, VII.vii.40), January with a hatchet, and February with plow and pruning tools. Autumn holds a reaping sickle, Sir Saturn with his "turning cranks" and "crookes" (VII.vii.52) is the only knight mentioned in the piece, and Time with his consuming scythe brings up the penultimate stanza. The successive and "extrinsic" time represented here seems to belong to Mutabilitie:

> For, who sees not, that *Time* on all doth pray?
> But *Times* do change and moue continually.
> So nothing here long standeth in one stay:
> (VII.vii.47)

Eventually we will want to know if Nature, in contrast, entails some sort of "intrinsic" time, like the one Jove lays claim to:

> . . . who is it (to me tell)
> That *Time* himselfe doth moue and still compell
> To keepe his course? Is not that namely wee
> Which poure that vertue from our heauenly cell
> That moues them all and makes them changed be?
> (VII.vii.48)

[26] Cornutus, *De Nat. Deo.* 7, "De Saturno," in Gale, *Opuscula Mythologica*, pp. 148f.
[27] See Chap. IV, "Seminarium Mundi," sec. iii, above.

[ii]

One form of dialectic is parody, and it is possible to see in Mutabilitie a parody of the Nature-goddess found in Alanus and Bernard Silvestris. The Nature of these poets presides over the making of man; Mutabilitie would then be an ironic *Natura querellis*, that Nature of Claudian and Alanus who complains before high authority that her works are in decay. The dialogue form, as we said earlier, makes the Mutabilitie cantos resemble a brief epic, but an ironic debate in which the issue remains in doubt indicates affinities with intellectual satire, especially the kind of satire attributed to Mennipius. The Mennipean point of view, we may gather from Lucian, is represented by the moon.[28]

Lucian also introduces us to the figure of the sardonic critic at the council of the gods, the carper Momus, a kind of spokesman for the satirist's point of view.[29] Mutabilitie is decidedly a relative of Momus, for Momus may be defined as a comic Prometheus, an embodiment of the rebellious and exuberant spirit of dialectical or Aristophanic comedy.[30] Here Mutabilitie's lawsuit falls into place as the hatching of a harebrained scheme in which the "plot" of this kind of comedy typically consists. The argument with Jove and the appeal to Nature form the binary comic *agon*, and the assault of Mutabilitie parallels the attempts on the comic society made by the imposters or *alazon*. Jove's confirmation has the place of the promotion of a "new Zeus," with which an Aristophanes comedy may conclude. In Sidonius (*Carmina* I.1-4), it is Nature who raises the young Jupiter to power in the first place.

Spenser does not seem to mention Momus, but four texts that do involve him help to characterize Mutabilitie in the terms we have just proposed. Momus is described in the *Koré Kosmou*, which Patrizi translated from Stobaeus' anthology in 1591. Here Momus is a spirit powerful in both body and mind, who "was comely and stately to look on, but exceeding fierce and terrible." This Momus rises to the occasion at the first creation of man:

---

[28] See Lucian's *Icaromennipus*. For a somewhat parallel Icaromennipean ascent, see William Basse's *Urania or the Woman in the Moone*, in *Works*, ed. R. Warwick Bond (London, 1893), pp. 267–314. For the classical-medieval complaint of Nature, see above all Curtius, *European Literature*, chap. 6.

[29] For Momus in Lucian, see *Zeus Tragoedus* 19–23, 26–31, 42–45; *Consistory of the Gods, passim; Hermotimus* 20; also references in *Dionysus* 8, *Judgment of the Goddesses* 2, *Icaromenippus* 31; *Wisdom of Nigrinus* 32.

[30] My description is indebted to Frye, "Old and New Comedy," in *Shakespeare Survey* 22, ed. Kenneth Muir (Cambridge, 1969), pp. 1–5; Frye asserts that *Prometheus* has the symbolic place in the Old Comedy which Cupid has in the New. For the form, see F. M. Cornford, *The Origin of Attic Comedy* (Cambridge, 1914).

When these things had come to pass . . . there arose from the earth a mighty spirit, named Momus. . . . Then Momus said, "Hermes, you are doing a rash thing in making man. . . . Tell me, you that are the author of his being, is it your settled purpose to leave him free from care, this being that is going to look with audacious gaze upon the beauteous mysteries of nature? Is it your will to let him be exempt from sorrow, this man that is going to send forth his designing thoughts to the very ends of the earth? . . . And all this might be borne, but they will do more: they will press on to the world above, seeking to discover by observation the laws and movement of the heavens. Are they then to meet with no impediment? . . ."[31]

It is to this jealous Momus that we owe "this state of life so tickle" (VII.viii.1):

"Let their presumptuous eagerness be disappointed of its expectations. Let their souls be a prey to a succession of varying hopes, sometimes fulfilled, at other times frustrated, so that even the sweetness of attainment may be but a bait to lure the wretches on to more unmitigated miseries. . . ."[32]

Hermes is pleased by this counsel, and he devises the means to accomplish it.

Mutabilitie has the kind of high-aspiring mind that Momus refers to, and she is a measurer of nature who appeals to those stargazers that the poet mentions in the prologue to Book V. Clearly Spenser's argument is divided very differently, however, for Mutabilitie is like the thing that Momus opposes, man's questioning spirit, and also like the thing that Momus represents, the obstacles to man's happiness. Spenser does definitely suggest that Mutabilitie, in her aspiration and presumption, is typically mortal. The divine retaliation for this presumption might well take the form of a race-destroying cataclysm:

> But ah! if Gods should striue with flesh yfere,
> Then shortly should the progeny of Man
> Be rooted out, if *Ioue* should doe still what he can:
>
> (VII.vi.31)

In the ironic parallel to this threat in Spenser's sub-plot, Mutabilitie's foolish counterpart Faunus will be menaced with gelding.

The Hermetic Momus, Frances Yates has suggested,[33] might have in-

---

[31] *Stobaei Hermetica* Exc. XXIII, Isis to Horus, 43–48, trans. by W. W. Scott, *Hermetica*, vol. 1, pp. 480–485.
[32] *Ibid.*
[33] *Giordano Bruno and the Hermetic Tradition*, pp. 215–217.

fluenced the Momus who is a character in Bruno's *Expulsion of the Triumphant Beast.* Jove's reform of the heavens in that work commemorates the anniversary of the gigantomachia, and it is initiated when Jove convenes the gods in the presence of a recalled Momus:

> Momus, who had spoken against the gods, and had argued, as it seemed to them, too severely against their errors, therefore had been banished from their consistory, and from conversation with them, and relegated to the star which is at the tip of Callisto's tail, without the privilege of passing the limit of that parallel under which Mount Caucus lies. There the poor god was weakened by the rigors of cold and of hunger, but now is recalled, vindicated, restored to his pristine state, and made ordinary and extraordinary herald, with the most ample privilege of being able to reprehend vices without any regard to the title or dignity of any person.[34]

Momus, in the office of Jove's conscience, directs much of the reform.

It is more likely that Bruno owes something to the *Momus* of Alberti, where the son of Night gives the work its title. Here Momus is cast down to earth in retribution for disturbing the peace in heaven. However, his earthly success as a philosopher and a demagogue makes him a new menace to the gods and the universe. He is recalled and Jove binds him to a rock in the sea forever. As a last insult, Juno deprives him of his masculinity. However, this Prometheus-gone-wrong is ultimately remembered as Jove's only honest counselor, and Jove settles down to read Momus' surviving treatise on the subject of the just prince.[35] Clearly Bruno has followed Alberti's revisionary ending; Spenser is much closer to the expulsion motif that otherwise predominates.

We said that there seemed to be no Momus in Spenser's actual text, but there is the "Foolish God," Faunus, who laughs at Diana's "some-what" and almost loses his own. Presumably Spenser would have known the derivation of the god's name from *momos* (ridicule, blame). In the hands of Spenser's nymphs, Faunus is decidedly a silenced Momus:

---

[34] Imerti trans., p. 95. The punishment of Bruno's Momus makes him a Callisto, the nymph of Diana brutalized into a bear for her amour with Jove. She was hunted by her own son. Jove raised her to the stars, giving her the highest place in the heavens, while Juno forbade that she ever bathe in the Ocean. The Callisto figure in the Mutabilitie cantos appears in the subplot, distributed between Faunus (who is hounded out of Arlo), and Molanna (the nymph whom Faunus corrupts to procure a view of Diana bathing, "for *loue* a likely pray" [VII.vi.45], referring to Callisto herself in Ovid, *Metam.* II.417–421; see also 450–465 and 489–492). The limit imposed on Momus refers his punishment to that of a second offender, namely Prometheus, who was fettered to Mount Caucus. Mutabilitie is a potential Prometheus, at VII.vi. 29.

[35] *Momus; o del Principe*, ed. and trans. Giuseppi Martini (Bologna, 1942).

They mocke and scorne him, and him foule miscall;

. . . .

Ne ought he said what euer did heare;
But hanging downe his head, did like a Mome appeare.

At length, when they had flouted him their fill,
They gan to cast what penaunce him to giue.
Some would haue gelt him, . . .
Others would through the riuer him haue driue,
And ducked deepe: . . .

(VII.vi.49–50)

The OED gives Mome[3] as an anglicized form of Momus, and cites *Mirror for Magistrates, Wilful Fall Blacksmith* xiv: "I dare be bolde a while to play the mome, Out of my sacke some others faultes to lease, And let my own behind my backe to peyse" (1563). It also gives usages from the next century: "to play the Mome . . . to reprehend," "censorious Momes," "the Censure of Detracting Momes." More typically, of course, a mome is a bemused blockhead, an "Idiot" (*Comedy of Errors*, III.i.32). Faunus is that too, but behind him stands Mutabilitie, a greater Mome who mocks the gods.[36] Indeed, it is scarcely too much to cite that doubter, mentioned in the coda to Sidney's *Defense*, who, "by a certain rustical disdain," should "become such a mome as to be a Momus of poetry."

It is a Momus like Alberti's to whom Erasmus' Folly refers, when speaking of the folly of the gods:

> I should prefer that their deeds be narrated by a certain Momus, by whom they used to be narrated often until recently when the gods angrily threw him down to earth for continually disturbing their pleasure with his sagacious interruptions. However, mortals do not think the exile worthy of hospitality, especially since there is no place for him at the royal court were my Flattery holds first place; and Momus could no more get along with her than a wolf with a lamb. So with him out of

---

[36] We may add that Mutability is the kind of satyr-satirist, who does not fear to attack exalted personages, envisaged by Milton in the *Apology for Smectymnuus*. And like Sir Saturn, she is a kind of "crank" (see VII.vii.52), and claims priority to Jove. Saturn, according to the early definition of Thomas Drant, may give his name to satire (*A Medicinable Morall*, London, 1566, sig. a iiii^v: "Satyre of writhled waspysche Saturne may be namde"). Mutabilitie is equated with Faunus in the subplot, and satyrs were understood from late classical times to be satirists (see, for example, Evanthius, "De Fabula," II.5, at the head of Donatus' commentary on Terrence). She undertakes a lawsuit, a potentially satiric procedure—Roman satire knows of a figure called the Adversarius, who is not the satirist himself, but an interlocutor or special audience provided for the satirist. The Adversarius may engage in rejoinder, as Jove does here. At any rate, a quasi-juridical format is not inappropriate to the controversial stance of satire.

the way, the gods can play the fool more freely and pleasantly, doing what they please, as Homer says, without a censor.[37]

As her own narration of the gods' peccadilloes follows, Folly is something of a Momus herself, the canny fool at the court of the gods.

Folly is also a paradoxical economiast, that is, a praiser of something of dubious value. Mutabilitie has affinities with the type, if only because of the high value she puts on herself. The resemblance goes further, however; like Momus and Mutabilitie, Folly is neither dull nor stultifying. Indeed, she may end up persuading us of the wisdom of folly, for in her enumeration of the widespread instances of her worship, she gradually turns folly into a kind of law—or wisdom—at work in the world. Her presumption even leads her to talk about her sapient aspect in scriptural terms. The devil quotes Scripture, of course, but there is some truth in this comparison all the same: "For in her is the spirit of understanding, which is . . . manifolde, subtil, moueable, . . . without care, hauing all power, . . . and passing through all, intellectual, . . . For wisdome is nimbler then all nimble things" (Wisdom 7:22-24, Geneva Bible).

If Folly can be a kind of inverse Wisdom, then in the divided characterization of the Mutabilitie cantos, Nature ought to represent Wisdom right side out. Like the biblical Wisdom, Nature is a creatrix, and like Truth (and also like the bride of the Solomon who chose wisdom), Nature wears a veil. One may take these parallels to mean that Nature stands for the "truth" of nature, or for the wisdom that governs nature. These are interpretations that we have already arrived at by other means. To summarize: Spenser's debate poem, with its assembly of gods and its ironic view of their reliability—or their constancy—has affinities with classical Mennipean satire; and yet on its scriptural side it may have a relation to the wisdom literature. The resulting combination is a kind of Lucianic treatment of the cosmogonic theme in Job.

The subject of the debate leagues the Mutabilitie cantos with the argument between Artegall and the giant in Book V. The giant is both a critic of the established natural order, and a would-be measurer of it. We have noted the recourse to wisdom in that argument. Apart from the general recommendation of prudence, two frequent wisdom subjects are the knowledge of "the times," especially as they govern the rhythms of life, and the critique of wisdom itself. Thus the wisdom literature of the Bible not only includes Job, with its exploration of the limits of the "experimental" order and our knowledge of it, but also the two creation-teachings in Genesis. The story of the seven days tells how a creating word first

[37] Trans. John P. Dolan, in *The Essential Erasmus*, p. 109.

brought the times into being, and the almost contrary story of the Fall derives the inauspicious origins of the mind's power of discrimination.

It is Wisdom that possesses mental control over the times. By now we are familiar with the rhetoric with which Solomon expresses Wisdom's intrinsic kind of relation to temporality:

> Et cum sit una, omnia potest:
> et in se permanens omnia innovat,
> initia, et consummationem,
> et medielatem temporum,
> vicissitudinem permutationes,
> et commutationes temporum, . . .

And since she is one, she is capable of all; and abiding in herself, innovates all—beginning, and consummation, and the middle of times; changes of vicissitudes, and changes of times.[38]

This co-present time is the subject of Nature as a whole, so to speak. Nature is the "unchangeable beginning of motion and rest," and also "the order and continuance of the works of God,"[39] or the "manner of working which God hath set for each created being to keep."[40] If Nature *is*, she has an existence in conjunction with present time: thus she is "euer young yet full of eld" (VII.vii.13). An argument from Plato's *Parmenides* (152ab) takes a similar form: the One, if it exists at all, exists in present time:

> Time, moreover, is advancing. Hence since the one moves forward temporally, it is always becoming older than itself. And we remember that what is becoming older becomes older than something that is becoming younger. So, since the one is becoming older than itself, that self must be becoming younger.[41]

"Therefore," it is concluded, the One "is becoming both younger and older than itself."

What the Bible says of Wisdom's self-reversion in time, Spenser's Nature says of "all things":

> They are not changed from their first estate;
> But by their change their being doe dilate:
> And turning to themselues at length againe,

---

[38] Wisdom of Solomon 7:27, Vulgate. For further on the biblical Wisdom as a goddess, and more particularly as Isis, see Hans Conzelmann, "The Mother of Wisdom," in James M. Robinson, ed., *The Future of Our Religious Past*, trans. Charles E. Carlston and Robert P. Scharlemann (New York, 1971), pp. 230–243.

[39] La Primaudaye, *French Academie* (London, 1586), p. 172.

[40] Hooker, *Laws of Ecclesiastical Polity*, I.iii; Everyman's Library, vol. 1, p. 155.

[41] Trans. F. M. Cornford, in *Collected Dialogues of Plato*, ed. Hamilton and Cairns (New York, 1961), p. 944.

754

> Doe worke their own perfection so by fate:
> Then ouer them Change doth not rule and raigne;
> But they raigne ouer change, and doe their states maintaine.
>
> (VII.vii.58)

The existence of the creature seems fleeting and unstayed, but in its aging it renews the law of nature, and the law abides; therefore "the obedience of creatures unto the law of nature is the stay of the whole world."[42] As a Wisdom-goddess, Nature is a sibyl who did not forget to ask for renewed youth.

Nature's final wisdom consists in her acceding to a time when all shall be changed, "And from thenceforth, none no more change shall see" (VII.vii.59). Nature then vanishes, as if putting her prediction into effect. The poet repeats that this would be a time "when no more Change shalle be, / But stedfast rest of all things firmely stayd / Vpon the pillours of Eternity" (VII.viii.2). We do not have much else by way of Spenser's characterization of Eternity, but Nature, in ceding her dominion to it, partakes of it at a distance—just as Mutabilitie, in seeking her own decay, partakes of Chaos.

Eternity, "contrayr to *Mutabilitie*" and all her ruinous "work," resembles Wisdom: Wisdom was present with God before the world was made, being "set up from everlasting," "before His works of old" (Prov. 8:23, 22). In his last stanza the poet leans less on the traditional pillar of constancy, and more on the Biblical pillar of truth: Nature almost quotes I Corinthians 15:51f. ("we shall all be changed"), and the poet prays to the Author of all life that this promise be fulfilled, and he be raised up on the last day. The concluding stanza effectuates the poem's virtual Amen, which is to say, "this is fixed, this is firm and most certain" (cf. Hebrew *aman*). All creatures have their beginning in such an Amen, which is Truth (so Rev. 3:14, with Geneva gloss). And while the pillars of the earth may be destroyed (Ps. 75:3, Job 9:6), Spenser's "pillours of Eternity" imply a foundation subject to no unreliability or infirmity. Here Wisdom has raised her seven pillars (Prov. 9:1). The poem ends by referring us to this prior eternal verity or firmament, and anticipates its ultimate reestablishment.

From Spenser we may turn to Marullus, whose "natural hymn" to Eternity enables us to study this final relation.[43] The position of Nature in the retinue of Eternity is symbolic:

---

[42] Hooker, *Laws*, I.iii, *edn. cit.*, vol. 1, p. 157.

[43] *Michaelis Marulli Carmina*, ed. A. Perosa (Zurich, 1951), pp. 113f. I am indebted to Fred Nichols for the use of his translation in making mine. Marullus' poem is a principal source of the first of Ronsard's *Hymni*: Spenser surely knew it.

Behind, however, by an exceedingly long interval, all-bearing Nature comes on, and the terrible old man with the curved scythe, and the brief Hours at equal intervals, and also the Year, passing and re-passing the same so many times, retracing the well-oiled tracks with servile tread.[44]

We are nearing, once again, the palace of Demogorgon.

Spenser ends by affirming that all things will be firmly stayed—one might almost say enthroned—upon the pillars of eternity. "All that moueth, doth in *Change* delight: / But thence-forth all shall rest eternally": all will rest with the God of rest, the Lord of the Sabbath. We may compare Marullus' Eternity:

> . . . raised high up on your perpetual throne, you give laws and rights to the heavens, you divide what is celestial from what is infirm and you secure [*firmas*] it eternally in steady rest, free from evil hardships, free from perils.[45]

Further, Eternity excludes senility from her domain, and binds the fleeing ages in perpetual adamantine.[46] The same adamantine links the elements in Spenser's creation (*HL*, 89), and constitutes the pillars on which the earth is founded (*HHB*, 36). In the Mutabilitie cantos a comparable chain ties down the Typhon-like Chaos.[47] Eternity thus re-collects that drawn out Boethean-Plotinine time: "Gathering the various turnings of age, what is to come intermixed with what has passed away, and enclosing them in the true present, you collect the divers days in a single ken." Then come the lines that by now we have learned to expect in this kind of poetry, by whatever hand:

> Yourself at the same time the part, at the same time the whole.
>   Without end, without beginning,
> All beginning, and equally end. With no distinction
> All rounded: and there is nothing not consonant with any part
>   of you.[48]

The poem ends with an appeal for favor toward men, who were originally created of a celestial and holy stock: "O stand nearer and bring unto

---

[44] *Aeternitate*, ll. 13–17.

[45] Ll. 20–23. Cf. Petrarch, *Trionfo dell'Eternita*, ll. 20f., 28f.: "un mondo novo, in etate immobile ed eterna, . . . Et le tres parti sue vidi ristrette ad una sola, e quella una esser ferma."

[46] Ll. 24f. For the adamantine, see Chap. V, n. 97, above.

[47] VII.vi.14f. Bacon has Typhon tied down with adamantine chains in *De Sapientia Veterum, sub* "Pan or Nature." Bacon follows a text like Valerius Flaccus, *Argonautica* III.224f., which describes the insurgency of the Titan Coeus in the lowest pit, "having broken the bonds of Jove and trailing adamantine chains."

[48] Ll. 26–28, 29–31. For the "all rounded," see Boethius, *De Cons. Phil.* III, prose xii, on the undivided sphere of the divine substance, quoting Parmenides, *Frg.* 8:43 (Diels), "In a body like a sphere well-rounded on all sides."

kindred heaven."[49] In the Mutabilitie cantos it is ultimately toward this Eternity that both Nature and the poet turn. Man fleeth as a shadow and never continueth in one stay, while God is from everlasting to everlasting. A Sabbath rest remains for the people of that God, with whom there is no transmutation, nor shadow of alteration.[50]

The Death of Pan

"Can death be the end of these heroes and demi-gods you tell us about? By Our Lady, in my ruminations I thought that they were immortal, like lovely angels—may the Lord pardon my ignorance. But this most reverend Macrobe says that they die once and for all."

"Not all of them," answered Pantagruel. "The Stoics said that they were immortal, incapable of suffering, and invisible. Pindar clearly says that those hard-hearted sisters the Fates spin no more thread—that is to say life—from their flax and spindles for the Hamadryads than for the trees whose guardian godesses they are. These are the oaks which, according to Callimachus and Pausanias, *in Phoci*, gave them birth. Martianus Capella, by the way, concurs in this opinion. As for the Demigods, Pans, Satyrs, Sylvans, Will-o'-the-Wisps, Aegipans, Nymphs, Heroes, and Demons, many men have from the sum total of the different aeons calculated by Hesiod, reckoned their lives to last 9,720 years. This figure was reached by raising the unity to Quadrinity, multiplying the quadrinity by four, and then multiplying the sum five times by solid triangles. See Plutarch in his book *On the Obsolescence of Oracles*."

"That's no breviary stuff," said Friar John. "I'll only believe so much of it as you wish me to."

(Rabelais, Book Four, xxvii, trans. J. M. Cohen)

[i]

In the final movement of Spenser's last book there occurs a marked exchange between "subject" and "object." On the one hand, the artist paints himself into his picture, which is the picture of an Arcadia that will shortly be destroyed. We are not told how Colin Clout fares in the general decimation of the shepherds' society, and it may be (as the epigraph for the tenth canto implies) that he is safely out of the way at the time. On the other hand, the poem shows the Blatant Beast escaping from the pic-

[49] Ll. 34–36. Cf. the final prayer to see the god at rest who sustains the motion of the universe, *De Cons. Phil.* III, metre ix, ll. 22–28.

[50] Anglican Burial Service (see Ps. 144:4; Eccl. 6:12, 8:3; Job 14:2); Heb. 4:10; James 1:17, Vulgate.

ture frame formed by faerie space and time, and violently intruding upon Spenser's England. In the former case, then, the poem is symbolically destroyed from within; in the latter case, it bursts through its own limits. As the poem has become more fully realized as an object, the poet has objectified himself within it; meanwhile, the object has migrated into the world of the subject, and has taken on a life beyond the command of the mind that created it.

These symbolic exchanges greatly enhance our sense of the poem's achievement of autonomy, even while they also imply the poem's recession into itself, and its dependence upon fictional parameters and premises that are subject to arbitrary alteration, suspension, or termination. A poem that is both autonomous and "zodiacal"—in the sense of comprehending an all-inclusive cosmos—constitutes a kind of poetic universe. The projection of a number of such universes is a special feature of Renaissance fiction, and the large, heterocosmic outlines of these domains have probably contributed substantially to our conception of literature itself as a surrogate universe. The "second nature" manifested in works such as *The Faerie Queene* may also have been instrumental in suggesting the existence of literature as an independent object of study, with all literary works forming a kind of faerie, a field susceptible of investigation and synoptic apprehension.

The student is also engaged in *The Faerie Queene* by the frequent covert reflection throughout its narrative of the processes that bring poems into being. It is the conspiracy of the subject of the poem with the poem as an object that engenders the idea that Spenser is "the poet's poet": the vocation of the poet obtains a regular parity with the actions represented in his poem. This change in position presents one version of what we may call the "subject-object" problem of Renaissance literature: the subjective process of bringing the poem into existence is not fully or practically dissociable from seeing the poem as an objective artifact. The longest canto in the poem is presided over by a character named Excesse; a labored and pedantic allegory describes Care; a character representing "twoness" is introduced in the poem's second canto, reappears at the opening of the second book and again at the opening of the second installment, and disappears from the poem near the end of its second to last book. The poem's self-reflexiveness leads one to frame a description of the poem as enfolding its own running commentary.

We may review the major points of such a commentary, as they lead to the Mutabilitie cantos. After some spilled ink in the preliminary episode of Error, the allegory of Archimago initiates the poem—even while Archimago is engaged in operations that look suspiciously like those whereby allegories are created. Archimago swears by Demogorgon; this deity, appearing at the head of the first humanist defense of poetry, and being senior to all the fays, serves to symbolize the emergence of the large-scale fictional heterocosms of the Renaissance. Archimago moves his arts again at the beginning of the second book, where he is an "Architect" (II.i.1), though much of his supervisory function passes to the Palmer. Archimago's rehabilitation of Duessa upon this occasion might suggest the anxieties of the serial artist, especially his fear of merely repeating himself.

The Demogorgon of Boccaccio may also symbolize the demand of poetic theology for parity with the more absolute kind. Thus the poet in Book I might seem to be working at an obtuse angle to his subject, if not precisely at cross-purposes: he is veiling the very truths that religion ultimately reveals. In Book II we may also postulate a chiasmic relation between the poet's activity and that of the protagonist: while Guyon is trying to integrate his psyche, the poet is analyzing it into its component elements. Many of the phenomena with which Guyon has to deal behave like unacknowledged mental projections, and his virtue includes the achievement of self-consciousness, or a reasonable objectivity about the self. In Book III the allegorical "other" becomes the other sex, but especially the male's femininity and the female's maleness: Amoret is wounded as Cupid, Britomart as Adonis, and so forth. It is Merlin who, as it were, sends Britomart through the looking glass; his resemblance to Archimago is marked.

The central books of the poem are presided over by the goddess of love. Love is the conjugation of the world, and the goddess is accordingly androgynous; thus the crucial juncture between the two halves of the poem is mediated by an unstable hermaphrodite. Indeed, it is the subject's act of joining—or marrying—the two installments that replaces the deleted symbol. Thereafter, the second installment advances upon the first by substantiating its ideals in the world of other persons. It becomes, thereby, the creation, or *ob-jectum* of the first three books themselves. Each of its three topics seems to advance the goal of the completion of the poem as well.

The fourth book, the legend of friendship, affiliates the second installment with its predecessor. Friendship seeks a stability of relation, which it expresses proportionately or tetradically, and the poet establishes an extended proportion between this book and Book III. It is just such a collateral dilation of the self that also defines friendship. The fifth book, the legend of justice, likewise shows us an art that equates the interests of Guyon and Artegall, and so "justifies" the poem, in the sense of bringing it even with its own margins. The last book, the legend of courtesy, treats a "supervenient" quality of grace, the counterpart for the prevenient grace of the first book, and a quality that gives the heroic persona and the heroic poem their finish simultaneously. Then, as the "poetry of conduct" oscillates into the conduct of poetry, the uncontainable enemy of well-meaning and circumspect speech breaks loose from the text, and the poet falls mysteriously silent. Whereas the poet began with his hero expunging Error from his first pages, he ends with the tongues of rumor and calumny fairly drowning him out. The Beast, in fact, suggests a kind of cancer of redundancy that might overtake the poet, were he to continue. In the epilogue, the figure of Nature—a unity in duality—comes forth to argue that self-reversion of all things to their original form in the course of dilating their being; this development has been manifested in the course of the poem itself. Thus Nature emerges at that point where the poem has become an objective order in its own right, and can speak for itself.

The Mutabilitie cantos offer us a Nature, like the Nature saluted by Pliny, "the whole within the whole, yea rather the whole itself, . . . beyond the total in itself, and within the all"; or, like the Eternity of Marullus, "at the same time the part, at the same time the whole."[51] The typical seventh canto of a legend in *The Faerie Queene* arrests the quest movement of that legend, and the Mutabilitie cantos, being the seventh book of the anticipated twelve, impose a similar impasse upon the larger poem. But even while they mark the end of the overall quest, they suggest the fulfilling of the "amphictyonic" design by presenting the pageant of the twelve months and the twelve signs. We are reminded by such a symbol that every year consists of two half-years. As the *Epithalamion* might also imply, the year, simply in reversing itself, re-begins midway. On the evidence of the Mutabilitie cantos, *The Faerie Queene*'s year would re-begin in Libra, at the onset of Autumn, a natural highpoint at which seedtime and harvest both meet at one time.[52] Indeed, the precise symbol of the Jewish feast of Ingathering, or Tabernacles, appears in the cantos; the natural pavillion that rises to enthrone Nature is very much like the Israelite harvest booth—during any harvest there is a sense in which Nature tabernacles among us. This feast is celebrated in the seventh month, which is also the New Year. In every symmetrical structure there exists a half that is sufficient to stand for the whole, and the "half" already before us has turned out to be subdivided symmetrically itself. Thus the bare numeration of the Mutabilitie cantos—vi and vii—might tell us that the poem we have represents not only half the poem, but also—allegorically—the balance remaining to be written.

The most important symbol of the Mutabilitie cantos may be the zodiac. It gives the cantos their numbers, along with their astral prototypes in the

---

[51] Pliny, *Nat. Hist.* II.i.2; Marullus, *Aeternitate*, ll. 29f.
[52] *F.Q.* III.vi.42.

retreating virgin and the balanced judgment. The zodiac also supplies the greater poem with a natural symbol of allness,

> . . . that mightie shining christall wall,
> Wherewith he hath encompassed this All
> (*HHB*, 41–42)

Spenser abridges his larger design, even while he assumes its symbol into his smaller one: the whole is not only present in the part, but the macrocosm has been drawn into the microcosm. Such a symbol expands Spenser's poetic cosmos to its greatest conceivable physical limits, and replaces —if it does not in effect preempt—any further extension of the poem.

The zodiac is an apt symbol for the kind of poem Spenser has written. Renaissance critics either defend or decry the characteristic profusion of fantastic beings spawned by such a poem; Spenser's inventory of Phantastes' mental contents retails a fairly standard list:

> Infernall Hags, *Centaurs*, feends, *Hippodames*,
> Apes, Lions, Ægles, Owles, fooles, louers, children, Dames.
> (II.ix.50)

Tasso, for example, insists that "the Centaurs, the Harpies, and the Cyclopes are not the adequate or principal subject of poetry, nor the flying horses and the other monsters that fill the romances"; he objects that Mazzoni's idols, "as Suidas defines them, are effigies of things that do not subsist, as Tritons, Sphinxes, and Centaurs."[53] Sidney, however, says that the poet creates "forms such as never were in nature, as the heroes, demigods, cyclops, chimeras, furies, and such like; so as he goeth hand in hand with nature, not enclosed within the narrow warrant of her gifts but freely ranging within the zodiac of his own wit."[54] Ariosto, who married the horse to the griffin—creatures traditionally enemies—to produce the hippogriff, clearly favors Phantastes' school.[55]

The zodiac can symbolize the poet's imaginative population of physical nature with creatures of his own begetting. These creatures, however, need not be purely fantastic; they may fictionalize nature in the way that poetry veils truth. Poetry, we remember, does not mean what it says, and yet intends, or dissimulates, something nigh and like. "Being" itself is dis-

---

[53] *Discourses on the Heroic Poem*, II, trans. in Gilbert, *Literary Criticism*, p. 475.

[54] *Defense*, in Gilbert, *Literary Criticism*, p. 412.

[55] *O.F.* IV.18f. See Virgil, *Eclog.* VIII.27: "Griffins shall now be joined with horses." Tasso, in contrast, confines the traditional fantastic menagerie—centaurs, sphinxes, and chimaeras—to the inferno; *Ger. Lib.* IV.5: "e in novi mostri, e non più intesi o visti, / diversi aspetti in un confusi e misti." Ariosto, it might be argued, makes the Hippogriff a kind of Pegasus, since it is the mount of both his Perseus-figure and the ironic Astolfo.

simulated by a poem that presents a virtual zodiac of being, but we must add that the "being" is *animate*, since the zodiac is alive.

The zodiac could stand for the comprehensive aims of Renaissance *Pansophia*, since its images united the stars with the creatures, and the human operator with the periphery of the cosmos.[56] The zodiac is likewise an appropriate symbol for the hylozoism expounded in the name of Renaissance nature-philosophy. Both Renaissance magic and philosophy postulated a cosmos pervaded by a universal spirit or dynamism that preconnected all of nature, including mind, in a vast sympathy of continuous being.[57] The elucidation of the various natural magics, a striking feature of the intellectual life of the age, is consistent with this Renaissance theory of nature. It is sound scholarship that has Goethe's Faust summon up the Erd-geist—the "demon of the earth" surely—where Marlowe's doctor invoked Demogorgon:

> In the floods of life and creative storm
> To and fro I wave.
> Weave eternally.
> And birth and grave,
> An eternal sea,
> A changeful strife,
> A glowing life:
> At the roaring loom of the ages I plod
> And fashion the life-giving garment of God.[58]

Man is understood by the philosophy of the age to enjoy a unique position for taking advantage of this turbulent situation, being himself at the center of creation, and thus its most vital participant.[59] The rebuke of the

---

[56] For this idea, see André Chastel, *The Myth of the Renaissance, 1420–1520*, trans. Stuart Gilbert (Skira, Geneva, 1969), pp. 73f., 78, 89, and also Chastel, *The Crisis of the Renaissance, 1520–1600*, trans. Peter Price (Skira, Geneva, 1968), pp. 133f. For the circumscription of the zodiac, planets, and the thirty-six decans by the All, see Nock, ed., and Festugière, trans., *Corpus Hermeticum* (Paris, 1954), vol. 3, pp. 34f.

[57] I am thinking here particularly of the *anima mundi* in Ficino, esp. the speculations in *De Amore*, VI.iii, but also of the description of other authors on the same theme in Cassirer, *The Individual and the Cosmos in Renaissance Philosophy*, trans. Mario Domandi (reprint, Philadelphia, 1972), pp. 165–170; F. Copplestone, *A History of Philosophy*, vol. 3, *Late Medieval and Renaissance Philosophy*, Pt. II (Garden City, N.Y., 1963), pp. 56–60, 64f., 67, 69f., 74–76; R. G. Collingwood, *The Idea of Nature* (reprint, New York, 1960), pp. 94–96; W. Peuckert, *Pansophia* (Berlin, 1956), pp. 38–41. Spenser's Genius presides over double gates that in Macrobius, *Comm. in Somn. Scip.*, I.xii.1–3, are the gates of Capricorn and Cancer in the zodiac, and the Genius may be the World-Soul.

[58] *Faust*, Pt. I, ll. 501–509, trans. by Walter Kaufmann.

[59] E.g., Pico, *Oration*, 1, 3, 17, 33; Ficino, *Theologica Platonica*, III.ii (man is the mean between heaven and earth, and the bond of the universe possessing the power of all things); Agrippa, *De Occulta Philosophia*, I.i–ii.

Erd-geist—"you are like the spirit you comprehend, not me"[60]—often fell on deaf ears.

Francis Cornford, in his study of the growth of classical scientific philosophy, once argued that the Milesian nature-philosophers, in order to explain natural phenomena, reverted to a hylozoism that was, in its essential character, animism—animism being defined as the primitive conception "of a continuum of living fluid, portioned out into the distinct forms of whatever classification is taken to be important."[61] This conception, Cornford assumed, antedated Olympian representations of the gods; the representations themselves had long since ceased to be assigned responsibility for departments in nature. Such an animism also revived in the more explicit "polydaemonism" of the later Neo-Platonic tradition. The parallel with Renaissance nature-philosophy has been occasionally remarked: this philosophy also experiments with quasi-Ionian animistic conceptions, like Telesio's principle of heat.[62] In its earlier phase this philosophy had recourse to theurgy,[63] and much of Renaissance magic entails a conscious revival of a kind of "polydaemonism." Spenser's kind of allegory is perhaps a literary relative of revived animistic conceptions in philosophy. The more elemental factor in Spenser, however, is the continuing survival in romance of such conceptions.

Polydaemonism not only surfaces in Neo-Platonism, but also passes from folk magic into such a phenomenon as the cults of the saints, who were popularly supposed to effect miracles, after their deaths, within their various jurisdictions—either their particular departments of nature, or the sanctified precincts of their cult's center. The magical landscape of romance is also animistic or daemonological in character: nymphs and

---

[60] *Faust*, Pt. I, ll. 512f.: "Du gleichst dem Geist, den du begreifst, / Nicht mir!"

[61] *From Religion to Philosophy* (reprint of 1912 edn., New York, 1957), p. 81. The following argument is not foreign to Renaissance thinking about poetry. Leone Hebraeo, in *Dialoghi d'Amore*, Caramella edn., pp. 104f., anticipates it fully: the poet's animation of the inanimate (rivers, elements, planets) and his deification of abstractions (passions, vices, virtues) are alike based on the mind's referring each of these things to its essential "formal incorporeal principle, participation in which constitutes its own nature. Such principles [Plato] calls 'ideas,' and considers that the Idea of fire is the true fire, as its formal essence, and that elemental fire is fire in virtue of its partaking of the Idea. . . . Hence it is not odd to attribute a godhead to the ideas of things." Similarly, the ancients numbered Love, Grace, Cupidity, etc., among the gods, because "each of the virtues, vices, and passions of men in general has its own Idea, and manifests itself in them with more or less intensity in proportion as it partakes of the idea." (Trans. Friedeberg-Seeley and Barnes.)

[62] For Telesio, see *De Rerum Natura*, Lib. I, cap. i–xvi, trans. in Arturo B. Fallico and Herman Shapiro, eds., *Renaissance Philosophy: The Italian Philosophers* (New York, 1967), pp. 301ff.

[63] See D. P. Walker, *Spiritual and Demonic Magic from Ficino to Campanella* (London, 1958), and Frances Yates, *Giordano Bruno and the Hermetic Tradition* (Chicago, 1964).

fairies resort to its springs; geniuses guard its groves and fertile places; its trees shed a circle of malign or beneficent influence; its wells dispenses crippling or healing virtues; its forests are haunted by sympathetic or offended beasts, and witches keep their fires there; its caves form the cells of legendary magicians or hermit-healers, the shrines of oracles, or the dwelling-places of unpropitiated ogres; and its summits are visited by visions of spiritual creatures. In short, all the remarkable features of this landscape function as places where the spirits gather, or issue, or make themselves felt or known. The powers of such places may be considered ultimately to derive from some deeper, undepartmentalized theogonic principle; this untapped nature, in which the seeds of things lie undisclosed, is the proper subject of the science of magic. There is a sense, then, in which Demogorgon always underlies the landscape of romance. His surface manifestation, however, is the more easily identified Pan, whom Boccaccio identifies with *natura naturata* and makes Demogorgon's progeny.[64]

The Mount of Contemplation to which Redcrosse comes is an example of the spiritual place. Redcrosse is compared to Jacob at Bethel (Gen. 28:11ff.), and in the Bible story Bethel is both the gate of heaven and the gate of dreams; it is sacramentalized by the ministrations of blessings and oil. Such a place localizes the juncture of the natural and spiritual worlds. In the Mutabilitie cantos it is the sphere of the moon that has the function of the gate of heaven. Time sits by its silver gates; and, if he is comparable to the Hours that keep heaven's gate later in the same text, these gates are also those through which the gods issue (VII.vii.45). The divine influence that passes through these gates is said to be time, which the gods pour down from their heavenly cell (VII.vii.48). A notable juncture, then is marked by the starting of the action of the Mutabilitie cantos from an eclipse. By making the spiritual issue-point cosmic, and the subject of a great impasse, the poet effects two things: he closes the spiritual world out of the poem, and he terminates its *saeculum*.

No less symbolic is the ending of the Mutabilitie cantos with the disappearance of Nature. As with Milton's *Nativity Ode*, there is a way of studying the overall symbolism here as elegiac. In both cases, the elegy is over the death of Pan, that is, the daemonological power implicit in an animistically conceived natural landscape. Something similar may be found in Donne's *First Anniversary*; the burden of that poem is almost an elegy over the pathetic fallacy found in so many elegies. The pantheistic conceptions that Milton exorcises are that same fallacy as it extends to the divine sphere.

---

[64] *G.D.G.*, I.iv; Romano edn., vol. I, p. 22.

Pan, the daemon of universal nature, is ingeniously allegorized by tradition as the anatomy of landscape—mountains with their hairy sides, the sky with the horns of the sun and the moon, the vesture of the heavens spotted with the stars, the music of the spheres issuing from Pan's seven pipes, and so forth.[65] He may not be present in his own person in the Mutabilitie cantos, but kindred personae are. Faunus, with his "goatish beard" is decidedly a pan, and perhaps Pan's protégé—Spenser elsewhere alludes to a story of Pan's violence toward an unidentified type of shamefastness (VII.vi.49; II.ix.40). The zodiac, encompassing the "all" of both time and space, is presented, as are the seven planets, including the horned moon. The month of December thinks on his Saviour's birth, but ironically rides the "shaggy-bearded Goat" associated with the infancy of a different universal lord, "The same wherewith Dan Ioue in tender yeares, They say, was nourisht by th' *Idaean* mayd" (VII.vii.41). Universal Nature herself appears, wearing a veil through which the poet seems to see the theophany on Mount Tabor: the image of the glorified god at whose advent the oracles grew dumb and the pans and satyrs forsook their wonted haunts. Finally, there is the desertion of Arlo Hill after the Faunus incident; Spenser shares with Milton the treatment of the exile of the nature-spirits as a kind of departure of an antimasque.

For Milton, the separation of God out of nature is essential to the characterization of God's authority as prior to any primordial theogonic principle, and to the characterization of God's will as uncontingent and unconditional. The falling Satan in *Paradise Lost* goes the other way, combining with nature and behaving like an emerging pagan deity: he derives his origins from necessity and fate; he submits himself to the sexual conditions that are found throughout nature; he seeks to overthrow his prior rival in his father; he creates a pantheon around him; and he imposes himself upon—even while they impose upon him—Chaos and Demogorgon.[66] In the Mutabilitie cantos the separation of God from nature is reserved from us until the very end, when the poet points to a time when there will be no more nature. This is, however, a perspective that the characters cannot take themselves, except by indirection, as when Mutabilitie appeals from Jove to the "God of Nature" above him. But as it turns out, this god is represented by a goddess.

[65] For the allegory of Pan, see Chap. II, above, n. 296, citing Alciati, Emb. XCVII; Giraldus, *Hist. Deorum*, Syntag. XV, in *Op. om.*, I, col. 451D, citing Servius on *Bucolics* and identifying Pan with Faunus; Leone Hebraeo, *Dialoghi d'Amore*, Caramella edn., pp. 109, 112, 114–116; Mythographus III.8.1; Eusebius, *Praep. Evang.*, III.xi, p. 115a; Macrobius, *Saturnalia*, I.xxii.4–6. Cf. Milton's Eden with its "hairy sides" and "Universal *Pan*" (*Par. Lost* IV.135, 266).

[66] Cf. Yehezkel Kaufmann, *The Religion of Israel*, trans. and abr. Moshe Greenberg (Chicago, 1960), chap. 2, "Pagan Religion."

The elegy over the animate landscape of romance parallels the absence of the hero from the Mutabilitie cantos. While daemons may be nature-spirits, they may also be demigods. We have already suggested that the mediation of spiritual power passes from the cult of the heroes, in the classical world, to the cult of the saints, in the Christian one. The myth of Pan's death commands the attention of the student of the Mutabilitie cantos not as a symbol of the end of demonology, as it appealed to earlier Christian and then to Protestant apologists, but as a symbol of the death of the hero. Rabelais' version of the death of Pan is presented first as a kind of pagan pathos-mystery, and then is attached to the death of Christ; the sequence almost makes Christ the last of the dying nature-spirits. The preface to this passage is quoted in part at the head of the present essay. It is an account of the noble race of the heroes, who dwell apart in the western islands; the heroes' deaths, at great intervals of time, are accompanied by obscure natural convulsions throughout the vicinity. Rabelais' own heroes are notable for their longevity, but such a story may offer commentary on other Renaissance heroes as well. One thinks of a scene like the desertion of Antony by the demigod Hercules in Shakespeare's play, where the parting genius of the protagonist is yielding to the superior power of the genius of Augustus Caesar. Off-stage, in the realm of Herod of Jewry, the way is being prepared for the announcement of the reign of a yet greater prince of peace.

It is the desertion of the Roman by his genius that we remember when we think of the demise of Antony, and it brings his tragedy closer to romance than other Shakespearean tragedies. The element of romance is partly present because insofar as Antony is identified with a demigod he does not die, but, like the proverbial old soldier, merely fades away. Heroes, as the passages quoted from both Rabelais and Sidney might remind us, are not of the race of men, but rather form a race of their own, somewhere between men and demigods and daemons.[67] This older sense of the term *hero* is consciously revived in the Renaissance, and the set-apartness of the heroic genus is perhaps to be connected with the isolation of the protagonist in tragedy.

To get a sense of this daemonic dimension of the tragic hero, one may consider his character elsewhere in Shakespeare: he is a psychological

---

[67] For the classification of the heroes with the daemons, see Plato, *Cratylus* 397e, quoting Hesiod, *Works and Days* 121ff.; *Repub.* 540c; Iamblichos, *De Mysteriis*, ii3; Macrobius, *Saturnalia*, I.xxiii.7, citing Posidonius, *On Heroes and Spirits*; Burton, *Anatomy of Melancholy*, Pt. 1, Sect. 2, Memb. 1, subsec. 2, with Ficino, *De Amore*, VI.iii–iv. The daemon is very like a genius: *Phaedo* 107d, a soul-guide; *Laws* 906a, the warrior's guardian spirit; *Statesman* 217d, tutelary deity of a tribe. The daemons are a superior race (*Laws* 713d); elemental star-spirits who fashion men and animals (*Timaeus* 40d–41d); or elemental spirits *per se* (Platonic *Epinomis* 984f.).

orphan, in a sense not of woman born, but fed instead on witch's milk; he is an "erring barbarian" from off a haunted desert, from a race that differs in "clime, complexion, and degree"; he is an epileptic whose spirit survives as the Roman genius, "constant as the Northern star"; he is come from overseas and is landed naked on the shore of Denmark; he is a king so terrible in his wrath and misery that all of nature is convulsed with storm when he rages. He often has some channel of access to a world of spirits, and part of our concern with his fall might express an anxiety lest he not prove scrutable and human after all. Even the fact that he is found in a play might be relevant. Augustine has a very curious passage on the daemons in which he ascribes to them a passionate attachment to theatrical performances.[68] It was not forgotten that the heroes were another race before they became accommodated to our more prosaic conception of them as men remarkable for some show of valor and service. Otherwise there would have been no point in Plato's expounding of the hero as an allegory of the good man.[69] Isabel Rathborne is quite correct in seeing that Spenser's champions are Fays not only because they are virtuous, but also because they are heroes in the outmoded technical sense of belonging to a heroic race.[70] If the loss of the hero's heroism is in part the loss of his daemonological nature, then it is crucial to an understanding of the Mutabilitie cantos to observe that no champion of faerie makes his presence felt there. On the divine plane, Mutabilitie herself is insisting that we dispense with the fiction of the invisible planetary gods, and in the subplot Faunus is expelled—the comic symbol for the supersession of the whole clan of

[68] *Civ. Dei*, VIII.xiv: with Antony's passion for plays, a motif in *Julius Caesar*, cf. "The demons, therefore, who hold the middle place, as they are inferior to the gods, than whom they inhabit a lower region, so they are superior to men, than whom they inhabit a loftier one. For they have immortality of body in common with the gods, but passions of the mind in common with men. On which account, say they, it is not wonderful that they are delighted with the obscenities of the theatre, and the fictions of the poets, since they are also subject to human passions, from which the gods are far removed, and to which they are altogether strangers. Whence we conclude that it was not the gods, who are all good and highly exalted, that Plato deprived of the pleasure of theatric plays, by reprobating and prohibiting the fictions of the poets, but the demons." (Trans. M. Dods.)

[69] *Cratylus* 397f.: "[Hesiod] means by the golden men, not men literally made of gold, but good and noble. . . . when a good man dies he has honor and a mighty portion among the dead, and becomes a daemon. . . . every wise man who happens to be a good man is *daimonion* both in life and death, and is rightly called a daemon." Cf. *Rep.* 540c, and Augustine, *Civ. Dei*, IX.x and xiii, citing Apuleius, *De Deo Socrat.*, on the blessed or good as *eudaemons*.

[70] Isabel E. Rathborne, *The Meaning of Spenser's Fairyland* (New York, 1937), pp. 142–149, 206. See now Hankins, *Source and Meaning*, pp. 46–50, which very usefully quotes Piccolomini, *Vniuersa Philosophia de Moribus* (Venice, 1583), pp. 328–330, where a synthesis of Platonic and Plutarchan themes is found.

"the Demi-gods, Pans, Satyrs, Sylvans, Will-o'-the-Wisps, Aegipans, Nymphs, Heroes, and Demons."

That the full celebration of the hero is only activated by his demise is an implicitly elegiac theme at least as old as the double ending of the *Iliad*. It is a paradox that, as a literary symbol, heroes in part exist to be superseded; they are supplanted by a lesser, postheroic race whose unheroic stature thereby defines its predecessor as heroic. Such a successor-race can only aspire to be heroic allegorically. The translation of the saint, discussed by Guyon at the opening of Book II, functions similarly: Una is left to "mourn" a departed hero, Guyon is left to imitate his "race." It is out of this same paradox that the concept of the antiheroic takes its beginning. One does not imagine that Spenser originally expected the glorification of his heroes to be finally effected by the mutability of the heroic condition, but the hero's return to the fairy queen at the end of Book V has already anticipated that possibility fully, and the "heaviness" in which Artegall leaves Irena forecasts the poet's own mood at the end of Book VI. Thus the absence of the hero from Spenser's sequel has the odd effect of authenticating the heroism exhibited in what is thus defined as a former time. Where there is no more heroism, we may add, there is no more faerie either.

We have described the effects of Mutabilitie on the landscape of the poem, and on the heroic characterization: the landscape settles into mere landscape, and the heroic "animus" that sustains the quest disappears. These remarks may be extended beyond the animation of the hero and the landscape to a consideration of the effects of Mutabilitie upon the technique of the allegory itself. Many of my conclusions, formulated independently, have been made less tentative by the work of other scholars, and in some places the argument may sound familiar.[71] My application of the argument to the Mutabilitie cantos hopes to supply some of the novelty that the following otherwise wants.

The character of the daemon has a wider application than we have so far indicated, for the daemon shares its otherness not only with the ro-

---

[71] My argument inadvertently duplicates that of Roger Hinks, *Myth and Allegory in Ancient Art* (Warburg Institute, London, 1939), pp. 4–20, 106–113—Hinks also cites *Symp.* 202e. Hinks believes, as I do not, that the "daemonic quality" of later— i.e., medieval and Renaissance—allegory is lost, an idea that is somewhat controverted by Hinks' own remarks on the necessary co-presence in any allegory of archaic or dynamistic elements and conceptual ones. Other work on the theme may be found in Harry Berger, *The Allegorical Temper* (New Haven, 1957), "The Demonic Allegorist," pp. 211–225, and especially Angus Fletcher, *Allegory* (Ithaca, N.Y., 1964), chap. 1, "The Daemonic Agent," pp. 25–69.

mance hero and landscape, but also with a whole range of allegorical personifications. A succinct statement, which has the advantage of not mentioning allegory at all, comes from Cornford:

> The fire-daemon is manifested in all fire; for all fire has the same specific behaviour. It is for this reason that daemons, in Greek theology as elsewhere, remain impersonal; they consist of will and force without individuality, because they are each the soul, not of an individual object, but of a species or kind (*genos*), to which they are related exactly as the daemon of a human kindred (*genos*) is related to his group.[72]

Similarly, because the allegorical personification embodies the type or species of the thing, its life is continuous, like that of the genus. Like the species-demon, it does not die, but fades away, as the interest of the allegorist moves to a different department than the one over which the personification presides. Despair, Sansjoy, Malbecco, Adonis, and the Genius do not die, and Pyrochles, Cymochles, and Maleger die very hard—out of their element. A hero like Triamond dies twice symbolically, in his two brothers; and the two brothers, a little like the Sans brothers in Book I, survive in their survivor. Duessa, who can be executed as Mary Queen of Scots, cannot be executed as Duessa—especially if she also implies the "double sense" of allegory itself. Offices too can have this kind of life in perpetuity: Elizabeth Tudor, as a "mortal moon," can be eclipsed, but the throne of England, like its planetary guardian the moon, survives changes of house. Like the shades Aeneas learns about in the underworld, "Each suffers his own peculiar ghost": his *Manes*, as Anchises says (*Aen.* VI.753), explaining the remains of lives being purged in wind, water, and fire in the afterlife—these lives are the future Roman *gens*.

Romance characterization originates in the treatment of species-demons, demigods, or natural forces—and this includes forces like libido and psychical entities like Synesius' imaginative faculty—as if they were individuals or persons. Likewise, allegorical personifications are also analogous to species-demons, being subtle bodies that have been attenuated into concepts.

Two seemingly studied examples of the nexus just described may be offered. In both cases the transformation of the character by the demon or the concept forms part of the theme. In Ovid's story of Echo and Narcissus, Echo, though once an overtalkative girl, has been reduced to merely repeating the last of what someone else has said; when we meet her she is a fit audience for a born monologist like Narcissus. She tries to enter into a love relation with him, but her suit is rejected, as in a sense an echo always is. As her sleepless cares waste away her form she is left with

---

[72] *From Religion to Philosophy,* edn. *cit.,* p. 97.

only bones and voice, and then her bones turn to rock. She retreats into lonely caves, and she is never seen, only heard; she is no longer Echo, if you will, but merely the phenomenon of the disembodied echo. She has become a kind of spirit in the landscape. Likewise, the image of Narcissus, as Narcissus describes it himself, takes on a kind of eerie mocking life that drains his own. One might call this image the "demon of subjectivity," but it is anyone's guess whether the emphasis should be on the animate demon or the conceptual subjectivity. Similarly, the force or desiderium that keeps the narcissus flower rooted beside the pools over which it hovers may be personified as Narcissus, or conceptualized as narcissism.

Spenser's Malbecco is a somewhat realistic character for an allegory, and almost as a consequence, he is finally hagridden out of the poem by his own latent capacity for allegoricalness; the poet has him followed hard by a band of animated abstractions, "Griefe, and despight, and jealosie, and scorne" (III.x.55). Alienated from his own sameness ("he himselfe himselfe loath'd"), he is overtaken by his own allegorical other: an "aery Spright" that is not only Malbecco's jealousy, but his peculiar evil genius, or demon. This takes place at just the point where he throws himself from a precipice. As in the parallel scene of Gloucester's suicide in *Lear*, Malbecco's capacity for a further fall is actually already exhausted. Malbecco is thus taken into faerie at last, just as his wife has been taken into the world of the satyrs. But Malbecco is fey in more than the old sense of fated to join the fays, or to die: his fey-state is identical with that "selfe-murdring thought" that consumes his substance (III.x.57). In the analogous process that we have been describing, an abstraction dematerializes what it represents and—in representing it dianoetically or generically—what it replaces. In one sense the Genius in Spenser is indeed the "Selfe," as the poet tells us (II.xii.47); but in its division from the self, the Genius is also the other, the other in allegory tending to be the *genus*. Hellenore joins the *genus* satyr, and Malbecco is generalized as Jealousy.

Such a process as these examples illustrate might support the general proposition made by Owen Barfield in his chapter in *Poetic Diction* (1928) on the rational powers of "The Poet": "It is from the Gorgon's head, petrifying life into the stone of abstraction, that Pegasus is born." And yet this process apart from poetry, if it is merely the mind becoming more conscious of its categories, also ought to be potentially fatal to poetry: the *poetic* abstraction, it appears, retains the memory of a vital spirit transversing the whole range of creative and created being—including intellectual being.

In sum, the romance landscape is inherently animate or hylozoic, and romance characterization is demonological; allegorical personifications may be these things too. If the romance hero and the romance landscape are both characterized by the "otherness" of the daemon, there is a sense in which, while the one travels through the other, each will be allegorical of the other.

It takes us only a little apart from our present argument to add that desiderata analogous to those that Cornford indicates for the daemon also apply to the animals so often found in folktale, fairytale, and romance. Particularly in romance, animals are often nature-spirits. And animals often turn up in allegories, where they are useful as typifications of classes as well as personifications. In children's literature, seemingly intent upon acquainting its audience with a society of giraffes and kangeroos, animals serve a double function. They supply a cast that is, as it were, type-cast; to a child, perhaps, human beings seem all alike, whereas the animals are pre-individualized and differentiated from one another by their being members of the various species. The same literature also trains the child to recognize the species, and hence to classify; it does not seem unlikely that animal classification is the model for specification in general. One animal is distinguished from another by its species, but it is the reverse with the person, where each individual almost constitutes a distinct species.[73] As a result, one can make approximately the same point about the allegorical personification, in its relation to the individual person, as Bergson makes about the animal:

> At the same time as the nature of the animal seems to be concentrated into a unique quality, we might say that its individuality is dissolved in a genus. To recognize a man means to distinguish him from other men; but to recognize an animal is normally to decide what species it belongs to. . . . An animal lacks concreteness and individuality, it appears essentially as a quality, and thus essentially as a class.[74]

Animal species, it follows from this description, present a model for abstractions; it may also follow that the first abstractions were more or less animate.

[73] The point is Scholastic: see Aquinas, *Summa Theol.*, Pt. I, q.98, art.1, resp., where the chief purpose of nature is the multiplication of individuals, even though the individual otherwise exists in nature to perpetuate the species; q.74, art.1, obj.3, where man differs from all other animals more than they do from each other; and q.75, art.3, resp. ad obj.1, where man is of the same genus as the animals, but a different species. According to Etienne Gilson, *The Spirit of Medieval Philosophy*, trans. Downes (New York, 1940), p. 195, Duns Scotus went on to maintain that each human individual was a species unto itself—a position that Aquinas advanced only with regard to the angels (*Summa Theol.*, Pt. I, q.50, art.4).

[74] *Les Deux Sources de la morale de la religion* (edn. of Paris, 1958), p. 192; quoted to similar effect in Lévi-Strauss, *Totemism*, trans. Rodney Needham (Boston, 1963), p. 93.

Let us retrace our steps. The romance hero is an agent energized by a not fully personal animus, one resembling a daemon. The romance landscape, similarly, is a "daemonized" field. The next step in the argument would recognize that the daemonizing agent—hero, landscape, concept—may be the daemonized element in the others. That is, the romance hero may be animated by an ideal or abstraction—like holiness—or by the energies otherwise running through nature—the strength of Malory's Gawain, for example, was as that of three at noonday, and the power of the Red Knight waxed and waned under a similar enchantment.[75] Hence the magician among the personnel of romance; he formalizes the course of this energy through a person. The romance landscape is a natural setting under some form of spell; ideas, like the "grace" and "law" of Spenser's first book, may conduce to the same effect. Finally, the allegorized abstraction is also animated. A telling example in Spenser is Talus, who stands for "martial law," but acts like a medieval suit of armor that has been possessed by a demon. The figure belongs to gothic romance, though one may also compare the robots of science fiction, or the character known as the Incredible Hulk, who is found in the current Superman comic books. Another example from the same legend in Spenser is Pollente. Pollente stands for "power," and he monopolizes a river-crossing; his is specifically the power localized in that juncture of the romance topography that we have elsewhere described by means of words like *threshold* and *impasse*, and the associated concept of trespass. We might compare the limitary river-god Scamander in the *Iliad*, since the hero wrestles with him in the water; but Pollente and the sons of Guizor are equally kin of the folktale bridge-troll in the story of Billy Goat Gruff. Like the bridge-troll, Pollente is a threshold-demon.

Implicit in the foregoing argument are two basic ideas: first, that "polydaemonism" is the "poetic theology" proper to romance; second, that there is a "poetic epistemology" for romance, namely the eliciting of the "otherness" of a somewhat improbable fiction by means of an allegory. This need not mean that all romances are allegorical, or that all romances are about demons; but it does imply that the "daemon" is the "other" of romance. That is, a romance may reveal some of its intrinsic nature when it is read as a translation from the tale, or nature, or dwelling-place of a daemon or dynamism. This is no less true of Legatt, in Conrad's *Secret Sharer*, than of Rumpelstiltskin in the fairy tale. The character of Virgil in the *Commedia*, of Heathcliff in *Wuthering Heights*, and of Batman or the Human Torch in the comic books, are all equally illustrations of the same general principle, on different levels of sophistication. More complexly, the daemonic

---

[75] *Morte d'Arthur*, Winchester ms. version, *Tale of Arthur*, 6, and *Morte d'Arthur*, 3; similarly the Red Knight of the Tale of Sir Gareth (Caxton version, Book VII, chaps. xv–xvii).

"other" may be studied in much of the characterization in Dickens' later fiction, where both persons and interiors often seem to behave like suppressed or abstracted parts of other characters, or like parts of dissociated personalities. To borrow the response of Goethe's Faust to Mephistopheles, after Mephistopheles has declared his allegorical meaning, they may be parts who present themselves to us as wholes.[76]

The interdependence of romance, polydaemonism, and allegory is essential to *The Faerie Queene* as to no other work known to English literature. If one does not feel that this nexus is a historical accident, and if romance and animism be set aside as somewhat atavistic in a Renaissance author, then Spenser's kind of allegory—his poetic epistemology—must constitute his period's determinative contribution to his poem. What this epistemological contribution might be our conclusion hopes to suggest.

It remains here to reiterate the implications of the passing of the poem as it is marked by the Mutabilitie cantos. As we have said, daemonic characters do not really die, though they may gradually lose their hold on existence, like a vanishing species, or the fading dream-images described by Synesius. At that point they recede, like Pan, into the landscape out of which they were differentiated by the landscape's having been personified in the first place. One may be reminded of the allegorical extension that Donne allows to the immanent good world-demon in the *First Anniversary*:

> For there's a kinde of World remaining still,
> Though shee which did inanimate and fill
> The world, be gone, yet in this last long night,
> Her Ghost doth walke; that is, a glimmering light,
> A faint weake love of vertue, and of good,
> Reflects from her, on them which understood
> Her worth; and though she have shut in all day,
> The twilight of her memory doth stay;
> Which, from the carcasse of the old world, free,
> Creates a new world, and new creatures bee
> Produc'd: the matter and the stuffe of this,
> Her vertue, and the forme our practice is:[77]

Faunus, after all, does not precisely die; he is only symbolically metamorphosed into a deer; and, driven out, he also returns. Thus the desertion of Arlo Hill and the survival of Faunus make the complex point that land-

---

[76] *Faust*, Pt. I, l. 1345.
[77] *The First Anniversarie*, ll. 67–78.

scape becomes mere landscape after its having been something other than that; and yet that same "something other" is no more than an epiphanization of its own implicit natural energies.

Faunus is punished for what is an offense, not only to Diana, but also to the fairy queen. "Saucy mortals must not view / What the Queen of Stars is doing," say the fairies in Lyly's *Endymion* (IV.iii). Their counterparts in Shakespeare's *Merry Wives* add that "Our radiant queen hates sluts and sluttery" (V.v.46). Two of Diana's victims were the hunters Actaeon and Orion, and the lustful Falstaff of Shakespeare's play is scapegoated as "Herne the hunter," in the guise of a deer. Spenser also alludes to the classical victims of Diana (VII.vi.45, vii.39), and Faunus' expulsion from the valley of the Arlo takes the form of Actaeon's expulsion from Gargaphie, as told in Ovid's *Metamorphoses*. Gargaphie was our specifically Ovidian example of a *locus amoenus* (*Metam*. III.155-164). The parallel of Gargaphie and Diana's Irish retreat at Arlo indicates that Arlo is one more of *The Faerie Queene*'s secret bowers (VII.vi.39-42); Faunus takes his place as the last of the poem's skeptophiliacs.

Ovid's unfortunate hunter was an ordinary mortal; Diana dashed water in his face, and he was metamorphosed into a deer (*Metam*. III.189ff.). Falstaff is metamorphosed several times, and in his "buck-washing" he suffers "three several deaths." Faunus' impulses are naturalized at the outset, however. Faunus is a faun or nature-spirit to begin with: it is the nature of fauns and satyrs to love the flying nymphs,[78] and perhaps to spy on them as well. It follows that Faunus typifies what we have been meaning by a species-demon. Diana judges ducking too good for him, but despite the offense he has offered to chastity, the foolish deity may not be gelded:

> . . . that same would spill
> The Wood-gods breed, which must foreuer liue:
> (VII.vi.50)

We have heard these accents before, in the poet's description of the survival of Adonis (III.vi.47). Every death of a nature-spirit declares that a nature-spirit "cannot foreuer die": "Therefore needs mote he liue, that liuing giues to all."

[ii]

Near the conclusion of Chapter I, it was observed that Faunus interrupts Diana's toilette in the way that Calidore intrudes upon Colin's private reverie; the implication is that Mutabilitie similarly threatens the conti-

---

[78] Horace, *Odes* III.18.

nuity of the poet's production as a whole. We could argue here that Mutabilitie, like those who would violate Una in Book I, seeks to de-mystify the truth of the poem; in other words, to take away Nature's veil. Faunus, however, only succeeds in driving Diana deeper into the poem's landscape, in the form of stones and wolves and water, just as the satyrs, to whose "barbarous truth" Una is committed between her encounters with Sansloi, preserved the maid even while they idolized her beast. At the end of the poem, when Nature might seem to have lifted her veil at last, Nature disappears; she is not so much exposed behind her veil as shown to be impossible to see without it. In retrospect, it is Mutabilitie who has manifested Nature; Faunus, though in no sense a manifestation of Diana, also seems to belong to some larger preservative principle. After he is driven off (in the form of the game that Diana hunts, and in a state of pure animal panic), he returns once more to effect the union of the two rivers Molanna and Fanchin; such a "conjugation" would otherwise be the office of a nature-goddess, like the Venus of Book IV who draws all things together with desire (IV.x.46). Thus the end of the poem both puts the question of the poem's completion, and abides it; the full poem is "unseene of any, yet of all beheld." We will not find another six books, beyond the first six; and in explanation of them the poem might say to us—with Plutarch's report of the epigraph on the statue of the Egyptian wisdom-goddess Isis—"I am all that is and that was and that shall be, and no mortal hath lifted my veil."[79]

In essaying to represent Nature, the noumenon behind so many of the manifestations in the poem as a whole, the poet almost seems to be guilty of the very attempt that comes to grief in Faunus. To represent a noumenon is in some sense to annul it. Thus what in the legend of courtesy would be a failure of tactful address might, in this instance, be a failure of *poetic* tact: a premature attempt to unveil the fiction of the poem and to expose the philosophical significance behind it; or, in the words of Sidney, to remove from "mistress Philosophy" the "masking raiment of Poesy."[80] Given the existence of a Nature that is "unseene of any," it is of some moment that Mutabilitie urges the nonexistence of the invisible

---

[79] *De Iside* 9, *Moralia* 354: more correctly, "no mortal has yet uncovered [*apekalupsen*] my *peplon*." Plutarch is reporting the Egyptian philosophy, "which, for the most part, is veiled in myths and words containing dim reflexions and adumbrations of the truth, as they themselves intimate beyond question by appropriately placing sphinxes before their shrines to indicate that their religious teaching has an enigmatical sort of wisdom." (Trans. F. C. Babbitt, Loeb *Moralia*, vol. 5, pp. 23, 25.)

[80] *Defense*, in Gilbert, *Literary Criticism*, p. 428; cf. p. 458: "it pleased the heavenly Deity, by Hesiod and Homer, under the veil of fables, to give us all knowledge, logic, rhetoric, philosophy, natural and moral." Sidney is citing "Clauserus, the translator of Cornutus" (*De Natura Deorum*).

planetary gods. Mutabilitie, it appears, is the enemy, not only of Jove, but also of poetry; she has "become such a mome as to be a Momus of poetry."

And yet the poet might well concede such a Momus half the argument, for if the gods be not gods, they may still be allegories. Out of this discrepant awareness emerges a theory of allegory itself, with its *raison d'être* in the extension of the life of the gods in the name of their occult significance. What the gods lose in immediacy, they gain in a succession of half-lives, a lease taken upon successive realms of meaning. And even if our Momus of poetry is lifting a veil, and so endangering the mediated vision of allegory, she is also revealing Spenser's poem to be a poem; it is precisely some capacity to betray, or qualify, or call into question its own mode of existence, that characterizes fictionality in literature. Allegory especially functions in this capacity, for, if it is a built-in commentary on a literary work, it is also an intensifier of the work's problematic character.

Of course the inclusion of Mutabilitie in the poem also includes the critic —the Momus at the court of letters. Names like Nature and Mutabilitie, in fact, seem relatively explicit when compared to their "mythologized" counterparts in Book III. It is critical commentary that objectifies poems in this way, and the rather deflationary synopsis of Spenser's ideas found in the Mutabilitie cantos has a decidedly critical effect. Just as the unveiling of Una marked the end of Book I, and at the same time ended Una's presence in the poem, so the representation of great creating Nature proves terminal for the poem as a whole.

In seeking to elicit Nature, especially Nature as an objective order, the poet compels an epiphany of the goddess that mysteriously issues in her departure—an epiphany of a noumenon, we might conclude, cannot really take any other form. Such an epiphany is inevitably ironic, like the one we have already met in Book VI: Nature, being made to speak, pointedly terminates her utterance by her disappearance, as if to tell the poet that he has surrendered any further claims upon her as a subject of poetic speculation. As Donne writes of the old earth, at the death of Elizabeth Drury:

> T'was heavey then to heare thy voyce of mone,
> But this is worse, that thou art speechlesse growne.
> Thou hast forgot thy name, thou hadst; thou wast
> Nothing but she, and her thou hast o'repast. . . .[81]

---

[81] *The First Anniversarie*, ll. 29–32. Curtius writes of the Orphic *Physis*: "This universal goddess is not the personification of an intellectual concept. She is one of the last religious experiences of the late-pagan world." (*European Literature*, p. 107.) However, neither the religious experience of nature nor the cultural experience of lateness are the exclusive property of a period: rather the two experiences seem interdependent. And a wisdom-goddess must personify an intellectual concept of *some* kind.

In Alanus' *De Planctu*, Nature speaks to bewail her own demise; in *Paradise Lost*, Nature sighs through all her works, the burden of her chorus being much the same. Nature need not always speak in this way, of course, and in Spenser's poem she does not; but the finality of her utterance may work in a similar fashion to imply the extremity of her significance, as if, in speaking, Nature exhausts her spirit to do so.

This breaking of the spell of the poem can be taken as evidence for a decisive separation of the "mind" behind the contemplative subject in the poem, from its union with the "nature" behind the contemplated object; at such a juncture nature recedes into the wholly other or purely objective, and the mind is left wholly self-possessed or purely subjective. If it is precisely the contrary participation of the mind in nature in which the World-Soul or "seminary of the world" consists, then the termination of this occult immersion of the one within the other also terminates both Mind and Nature as the poem has known them. This secession of "mind" out of nature entails the end of the technique of Spenser's allegory.

We may take this opportunity to recapitulate the coherence that obtains in Spenser's poem before Mutabilitie intervenes. Nature argues for the abidingness of being. The heavens are shown resisting change, and the year is shown reverting to itself even as it changes. Spenser's poem has shown something similar for the human identity. The theme of the first installment is self-integration. The theme of the second is social coherence, the harmonizing or mutualizing of the elements of society. The first installment treats the making whole of faith, the containing and continuing power of continence, and the self-preserving and self-realizing energy of chastity. The second installment treats the sodalities formed by natural affection, the securing of the public order, and the affirming of the invisible unity of men in their common *humanitas*.

The themes of both installments lend themselves to allegorical treatment, because the allegorical perception is in the perception of "otherness."[82] Such a perception constitutes a kind of reclamation of that which is "other." For the subjective ego, the experience of otherness may take the form of perceiving others as distinct from itself, or it may take the form of perceiving itself in a state of dissociation. The self-conscious person experiences a part of himself as separated into his world; so, in a converse way, does the socialized person. As Shakespeare says in *The Phoenix and the Turtle*:

[82] A collection of the derivatives of the Indo-European root *al-*, "beyond," in fact, sounds like a catalogue of the basic concepts for any theory of allegory: *also, alternate, alteration, parallel, alien, else, ulterior, as* (= *eal swā*, Ger. *als*), *alibi* (Latin "elsewhere").

> Property was thus appalled
> That the self was not the same;
> Single nature's double name
> Neither two nor one was called.

Thus the danger of self-division in the first half of the poem forms the *verso* for the mutual benefits of self-multiplication in the second half. As Herbert of Cherbury writes in his *Ode upon a Question moved*: "So when one wing can make no way, / Two joyned can themselves dilate, / So can two persons propagate / When singly either would decay." The integration of the self that makes possible the transfer of its loyalties to another person is symbolized, with epigrammatic concision, in the figure of the hermaphrodite between the two installments:[83]

> Reason, in itself confounded,
> Saw division grow together,
> To themselves yet either neither
> Simple were so well compounded.

The reader may want to ask why—"If what parts can so remain"—the Spenserian counterpart of this "concordant one" should prove unstable. Why is this symbol dropped from the first installment, with the advent of the second?

Placed in the context of self-preservation, in the first installment, the hermaphrodite suggests either a peculiar imprecision about self-definition, or the failure of self-assertion that is present in any surrender to passivity: hence the Salamicis myth that lurks in the background of Redcrosse's metamorphic enfeeblement by Duessa. In the context of the second installment, where the theme is the extending of the social order, a hermaphroditic attachment would suggest a premature or too exclusive or too introverted fusion. This would be a kind of social narcissism, or a self-reliance that allows no need for others—one thinks of Britomart's mirror, in which she sees her lover no doubt partly as herself. Thus if one approaches the image from the first half of the poem, it looks like a symbol of a self-dissipating extroversion; looking back from the second half, one sees the image as a symbol of narcissistic or incestuous introversion. Where it stands—or stood—it is suitably embracive, though hedged with significant qualifications. The private self does not want to wholly melt into

---

[83] In passing we may note the occurrence of such a mediating symbol at the opening of the second part of *Whitney's Choice of Emblemes*, ed. Green, p. 108, where the first emblem is Janus, shown regarding a sceptre and a mirror: "Respice, & prospice"—he surveys what is past so that he may take in hand what remains to do with greater heed. The symbolism is trivial, but it contains the germ of Spenser's idea, the interface of two installments.

another, until it is quite sure of its own identity; the social self does not want to remain forever fixed, like a senseless stock, but desires to extend itself.

It is not sufficient to observe that Una—"like one that inly mourned"—is a contemplative introvert, whereas Calidore—whose manners "in all mens liking gayned place"—is an ingratiating extrovert. In the first installment, "other persons" are really externalized aspects of the self; therefore they are qualitatively different from other persons in the second installment, though it is clear that they are interchangeable in the fiction. The plurality of the cast tends to be figurative in the legends about the virtues peculiar to the individual, whereas this plurality in the case of the social virtues is more nearly literal—and correspondingly less allegorical. Therefore there is room for the second half of the poem to recover a lost psychological dimension by means of the extended parallel with the first half. The extroverts of the second installment seek in society what the introverts of the first installment seek in themselves, namely unity of being. Hence the extroverts seek something that externalizes the earlier knights' internal objectives. The renewed objectives are a pure love in Book IV, a sense of order in Book V, and the bestowal of another's grace in Book VI. The virtues that integrate the individual are now projected outward in the virtues that integrate the social body. It is a somewhat more difficult point, but we have argued that these secondary virtues emulate the primary ones: friendship is the "chastity" of the social body, or the capacity in it for a pure love; justice is its "goodly frame of temperance," or its ideal constitution; and courtesy is its "holiness," meaning its capacity for hallowing, for reverence, for acts of faith in others, and for the reception of grace. In moving from the first to the second installment, we watch the extension of the virtues of the first three legends into their social context, but we also watch the poem finding itself in its other half, as like envelops like.

The second installment emulates the first. *Aemulatio* is in fact one of the forms of similitude by means of which Michel Foucault, in his study of the representation of the world, categorizes the assimilative mental habits of the Renaissance *epistemé*:

> The relation of emulation enables things to imitate one another from one end of the universe to the other without connection or proximity: by duplicating itself in a mirror the world abolishes the distance proper to it; in this way it overcomes the place allotted to each thing. But which of these reflections coursing through space are the original images? Which is the reality and which the projection? It is often not possible to say, for emulation is a sort of natural twinship existing in things; it arises from a fold in being, the two sides of which stand immediately

opposite to one another. Paracelsus compares this fundamental duplication of the world to the image of two twins who resemble one another completely, without its being possible for anyone to say which of them brought its similitude to the other.[84]

With this "fold in being" the reader is by now very familiar.

The personae of the first three books are "other selves"; those of the second three are "other persons." Over the course of the poem the interest in the idea of the faerie as the other self diminishes as the idea of membership in society as the other self is emphasized. Hence, in the second installment, the number of symbols for the joining of the self to society: such scenes as Marinell's introduction to the festivals of the water gods, Artegall's participation in the deliberations of Mercilla's court, and Calidore's reception into the society of the shepherds. These societies are markedly not the heroes' own. Very roughly speaking, then, the faerie society of the first installment forms that kind of secret society or fraternity that preserves atavistic or totemic identifications. But relations between this fraternity and English society also resemble the relations between the moieties in a tribe divided into two exogamous groups. First faerie promotes the solidarity of the group with its best self, like the "knights of maidenhead" within it; but secondly it offers itself as a coequal moiety, with which the English society can intermarry. One may compare the relations between the Welsh, or British, and the English, or Saxons. Britomart, who is Welsh, i.e., half faerie, seeks out a knight for a husband who is both English and a hero from the other installment, or the other moiety. Cornford asks the question, when does the tribe become aware of otherness? He could answer, from another page in the same book: when it divides into two exogamous phratries.[85]

The answer contained in Cornford's book gives us a sense of the way in which the faerie is an allegorical Englishman, and the Englishman an honorary faerie. It does not quite explain why the best self of the group is symbolized by a race, like that of the hero, different from our own. The

[84] *The Order of Things* (trans. of *Les Mots et les Choses*) (New York, 1970), pp. 19f.

[85] *From Religion to Philosophy, edn. cit.*, pp. 58, 67–69, 210. The idea is more properly found in Émile Durkheim and Marcel Mauss, "De quelques formes primitives de classification: contribution à l'étude des représentations collectives," *Année Sociologique*, 6 (1901–1902; publ. Paris, 1903), pp. 1–72; trans. as *Primitive Classification* by Rodney Needham (Chicago, 1963). Apart from rhetorical considerations, there is no need to assert, with Durkheim and Mauss, which came first, the bipartition of society (or the conjugation of two societies), or the parallel division of the *epistemé*. Neither one came first, if the two phenomena are truly interdependent, or if their congruence is owed to their being informed by a common classificatory principle.

answer might be clearer if the elves and fays were totemic animals, that is, representations to the group of its group character, and its symbiosis with, and dependence on, a department in nature. Originally, it is proposed, the tribe did not distinguish between itself and such a totem. Levy-Bruhl describes a doubling of awareness when this kind of identification—or "participation"—breaks down. He understands being then to divide two ways, between individual and group, and between one species-group and another. Like Cornford, he thinks that the fission of the unitary group-consciousness teaches otherness, especially the otherness of the totem, and thus the otherness of the categories of nature in general:

> . . . as soon as individual consciousness begins to grasp itself as such and consequently to distinguish individuals as such in the surrounding groups of beings, these ideas also define, more or less distinctly, that of the groups as such, and as a further consequence, an idea of the mystic relations uniting the individuals of the group, and the different groups in their turn. The communion which is no longer actually lived, the need for which still appears just as pressing, will be obtained by means of intermediaries. The bororo tribe will no longer declare that they *are* araras [parrots]. They will say that their ancestors were araras, that they are of the same substance as the araras, that they will become araras after death, that it is forbidden to kill and eat araras, except under conditions which are rigidly defined, such as totemic sacrifice, etc.[86]

Such a tribe, we might conclude, comes to lead a perpetual life of allegory.

Allegory, then, is analogous to the *fonction mentale* that allows the Bororo to both be the araras, and to be distinguished from it. The relation implies a partially decomposed participation, or animism, whereby "ego" is in the araras in some form or other. But it also implies a kind of incipient nominalism: ego is ultimately in the araras in name only.

If we think of a concept as either the name of a class, or an abstract "entity," then allegorical thinking offers an intermediate state in the processes of conceptualization. Likewise, if its etymology is any clue, generalization is an intellectual characterization by means of classes, or a *genos*. The concept becomes a universal predicate by way of losing the dynamistic component that also made it, so to speak, a name to conjure with. One may talk about Plato's idea of love, but Plato talks about it as a daemon, "halfway between god and man":

> [Daemons] are the envoys and interpreters that ply between heaven and earth, flying upward with our worship and our prayers, and descending with the heavenly answers and commandments, and since they are between the two estates they weld both sides together and merge them into

---

[86] *How Natives Think* (*Les Fonctions Mentales dans les Sociétés Inférieures*, Paris, 1910), trans. Lilian A. Clare (reprint, New York, 1966), p. 328.

one great whole. They form the medium of the prophetic arts, of the
priestly rites of sacrifice, initiation, and incantation, of divination and of
sorcery, for the divine will not mingle directly with the human, and it
is only through the mediation of the spirit world that man can have any
intercourse, whether waking or sleeping, with the gods. And the man
who is versed in such matters is said to have spiritual powers, as opposed
to the mechanical powers of the man who is expert in the more mundane
arts. There are many spirits, and many kinds of spirits, too, and Love is
one of them.[87]

Plato follows this description with his own allegory of the birth of Love,
moving easily from the account of the daemon to the animation of abstractions.

The mediation performed by the daemon is analogous to that performed
by an allegory. Edwin Goodenough describes the making of a "mystery"
in this way, having defined the common denominator of all mysteries as
"the miraculous elevation of the soul through its assimilation of and by
the immaterial":

> The basic elements in the transformation of a traditional myth and cultus
> into a mystery were twofold: the traditional myth was allegorized into
> a story of the saving approach of divinity to humanity, of the breaking
> down by divine act of the barrier between the immaterial and the material;
> the traditional rite became a representation in matter of the divine
> life and being, so that immaterial reality, the only true reality, became
> accessible for man increasingly to appropriate it.[88]

Allegory also breaches a barrier between the material and the immaterial,
and hence itself provides a mode and a model of this rapprochement with,
or appropriation of, a noumenal realm.

A noteworthy feature of the Hesiodic theogonic tradition—somewhat
self-consciously preserved by Virgil in the vestibule to Hades in the
Aeneid—is the company kept by the archaic gods with abstractions like
Cunning and Force. It seems likely that originally no great distinction
was felt: the divinities were more impersonal than we are wont to imagine,
and the abstractions were less abstract. Numina and abstractions were
both more nearly "vital principles" in a literal sense. Theognis calls Hope
and Danger *difficult daemons*, and the Romans raised temples to Peace
and Fever.[89] Who is to say whether the Hesiodic Erebus is a place, a

---

[87] *Symposium* 202e–203a, trans. Michael Joyce, Everyman's Library.

[88] *An Introduction to Philo Judaeus* (New Haven, 1948), pp. 184f.

[89] Theognis, 1135ff., cited in Hinks, *Myth and Allegory in Ancient Art*, p. 108; Lactantius, *Divine Institutes*, I.20, with Clement of Alexandria, *Exhortation to the Heathen*, ii.

numen, or an abstract entity? More likely, it is an unanalyzed compound of being and a category of being, the *genos*-daemon Darkness.

A later example of the daemonological abstraction commends itself to our attention here. The seven cardinal sins seem like a table of evil affects that only incidentally became a frequent subject of allegorical treatment. There would seem to be no necessary reason for regarding them as beings, except insofar as they dominate a particular human life. But the very insistence of this tradition on taking this particular form might tell us that this sevenfold personification of powerful influences reports the presence of mythical constitutive elements in the scheme. In terms of our earlier discussion, the sins would be daemonological. There are hints of this in Dante, where admission to the earthly paradise is achieved by passing upward through seven levels of sin, each elevation of which is presided over by a singing angel, the beneficent soul-guiding siren, as it were, of its circle. As Morton Bloomfield has pointed out, there is a resemblance here to the Hermetic text in which seven influential and malign beings, identified with the planets, keep the prison-house of the cosmos that the soul seeks to escape.[90] A tabulation of the various powers exercised over mortals by the planetary beings suffices to show that the sins—with the exception of gluttony—are planetary affects. In short, it is not easy to say whether the cardinal sins are beings in the disguise of affects, or vice versa.[91]

Plato's description of the daemon shows it to be both an external force and a kind of mental operator. Figurative speech in general is full of analogous operators. To become enamorable and to be grazed by Amor's arrow seem to be merely two ways of saying approximately the same thing. But perhaps they are really two different ways of conceiving it. In terms consonant with Spenser's allegory, the more "participated" description does not readily discriminate between being struck by a darting glance, and being struck by a glancing dart.

Allegory, then, if it is a form of conceptualization, is a somewhat atavistic one, accompanied by a marked tendency on the part of the allegorist to revert to magical thinking. Holiness, for example, is the concept of spiritual wholeness, and in the levitical legislation it is partly secured by means of avoiding contact with, and pollution by, what is unclean. What

[90] For the gate-keepers or archons of the cosmos as angels, see Origen, *Contra Celsus*, VI.30–32. Cf. also II Esdras 7:75–99.

[91] Sources: *Poimandres* (Libellus I), 25f.; Stobaeus, *Eclogae*, I.v.15; Servius, *ad Aen.* VI.714 and XI.51; and Mythographus III.6.8, in Bode, ed., *Scriptores*, p. 178: "torporem a Saturno, a Marte iracundiam, a Venere libidinem, a Mercurio lucri cupiditatem, a Jove regni desiderium. Quae res, ut ajunt, perturbationem ipsi faciunt, ne suo vigore et viribus propriis uti possit." Bloomfield, *The Seven Deadly Sins* (East Lansing, Mich., 1952), pp. 13, 18, 23, 34, 47–50; see also pp. 53f., 343.

one now normally means by holiness emerged from an allegory of a purity that was once also physical purity. Physical purity, in its turn, now has the allegorical relation to true holiness. To whichever of the meanings of holiness one gives priority, it seems typical of allegory that the patron of holiness in Spenser puts to death what is technically an unclean beast, the dead carcass of which fearful mothers will not let their children touch.

Both a concept and a potency, a class and an entity, what it is and something else, a part and yet a part that presents itself as a whole: the allegorical being resembles the compounding of the Soul as described in the *Timaeus* (35): a "mixed being" of the Same and the Difference. This brings us to yet one further way of understanding allegory as a mental function of an intermediate character. If, on the one hand, allegory implies a departicipation of consciousness in nature; and, on the other hand, it implies a daemonization of discourse, then it might also be construed as a mediate stage in the attenuation of the participation of the subject in the object.

In Renaissance literature, a large paradigm for such a participation may be found in *King Lear*. Lear rages like the storm, and the storm, conjured to crack its cheeks, rages like Lear. In interpreting the implications of this reciprocity, one tries to steer between saying that Lear is a storm-god, and saying that the storm is merely an expressive symbol for Lear's state of mind. We can strike a better balance by way of the standard physico-medical comparison of the course of apoplexy to the action of a tempest: a tempest is apoplectic, and apoplexy is tempestuous.[92] The symptomatology of the king and the storm are analogical because of a dynamistic force or preternatural play of sympathy interanimating them both. Lear's influence on the weather is, as it were, pan-psychic in character: he almost broadcasts the storm. The storm behaves "hylozoically," that is, as if matter were a fellow creature. This reciprocity Ernst Cassirer denominated the subject-object problem of Renaissance thought.[93] Its literary projection, it seems to me, can be studied in some fairly obvious places, even where it is not so nearly the poet's actual theme.

The storm in *Lear* bespeaks a traumatized or breaking subject-object relation as well. Lear has lost his self-control and his control over his situation; meanwhile, his loss seems to have gained control over all of nature, like the atomizing "Hectique fever" that possesses the world of Donne's *Anniversarie*. In other words, Lear not only *has* a relation to the storm,

---

[92] For the reciprocity of tempest and apoplexy, Foucault cites O. Crollius, *Traité des signatures* (trans. of Lyon, 1624), p. 4.
[93] *The Individual and the Cosmos in Ren. Phil.*, chap. 4.

he is also *losing* one. Somewhere out in the chaotic depths of the universe of the play, Pan is dying, and we are made to feel that we are overhearing nothing less than the death agonies of the World-Soul. This breaking of "relation" issues in a storm so elemental that, at the end of it, one could truly say, "the Element of fire is quite put out."

Cassirer calls these relations a "problem," because the Renaissance thinkers relate consciousness and nature substantively, or consubstantially, rather than functionally. Far from being ideally discriminated, and thus neutral each with respect to the other, subject and object in the standard Renaissance epistemology are adequated sympathetically. Cassirer cites the example of Telesio, who defended the use of analogy as a source of knowledge, on the basis of the unity of being underlying all analogies; as a result, Cassirer says, in Telesio "all conception, every mediating ratiocination goes back to an original act of empathy by which we assure ourselves of the community that binds us with all being."[94] Hence also the likeness between Ficino's universe-uniting love and the cognitive faculty as it is described by Patrizzi: both love and the cognitive faculty are said to proceed by an intercourse that assimilates them to their object.[95] The same universal bond of sympathy, according to Pico in his *Apologia*, is the subject of magic; a similar statement is found in the opening pages of the notable compendium of della Porta.[96] At this level of generalization, it is not overbold to say that the protean Archimago and the fascinated Busirane are two instances of the same mental operator.

When the bond of the universe is conceived of as "sympathy" as well as "love," the epistemological consequence is an enriched sense of the significance of analogy. The result is that checkless proliferation of correspondences to which Shakespeare's Fluellen fell comic prey, and which so much preoccupies the mind of Donne's *Anniversarie*. In Donne's poem, the hypertrophy of this analogical elasticity—as one may call it—is set within the context of a late Renaissance agony over the demise of the spirit or principle that informs correspondence itself.

The theme of the death of Pan overshadows Donne's poem as surely as it does Milton's *Nativity Ode*. In Donne's poem, however, the true universal spirit—even though it is identified with an immaculate young child in a cradle—is the heir figure only in an ironical sense. The death of Elizabeth Drury, apparently so insignificant when considered in itself,

---

[94] *Individual and Cosmos, edn. cit.,* p. 142.

[95] *Ibid.,* pp. 131, 134f., citing Francisco Patrizzi, *Panarchia*, xv, "De Intellectu" (*Nova de universis philosophia*, Ferrara, 1591, fol. 31): "cognition is nothing else than a certain coitus with what it knows." Cf. Ficino, *De Amore*, II.viii: similarity is a sameness of nature existent in several beings that obligates them to love.

[96] Pico, *Apologia*, in *Op. om.* (Basel, 1587), p. 121; Giambattista della Porta, *Magiae naturalis*, I.iii.

becomes a particularly poignant symbol of the passing from the world of the whole animating power of sympathy. The symbol is effective precisely because the death is remote: the play of sympathy properly works by magnetically abolishing the distances and differences between the members of an otherwise atomized world. This drawing power is effective even when it is withdrawn. Funneled out of the world through an elegiac subject, it gathers together the universal evidence for the decay of order in the world into one last testimonial to the analogical coherence belonging to all of being. The anxiety attendant upon the death of the child proves scarcely less contagious than sympathy itself. As a result, the Elizabeth of Donne's poem is not only a type of Astraea, retreating before the corruption of the world, and taking its goodness with her: her capacious soul also is enabled to embrace what is much like the traditional idea of the World-Soul. This rejoinder of the poem to itself obeys nearly the same dialectical principle as the one imposed upon the apparent triumph of Mutabilitie—a problematic re-statement of the correspondence, relation, and proportion that have made a poem like *The Faerie Queene* possible.

We may conclude with a question. If the Mutabilitie cantos, like the works mentioned above, suggest an end of those conditions that have made the Spenserian kind of allegory especially telling—in our own words, the passing of "a mediate stage in the attenuation of the participation of the subject in the object"—where is that stage reflected in Renaissance literature itself? There are certain obvious places to look, of course. We have already examined the relation between Spenser's two installments in this light, and a similar relation makes itself felt in the conjugation of the cast in a typical Shakespearean play. This cast is very frequently dichotomous, and its moieties often seem to be governed by subject-object relations. In the resolution to the Shakespearean comic movement, stemming from the *Comedy of Errors*, the lovers find their proper complement and their proper other in the exogamous half of the personae. In the corresponding tragic movement, stemming from the history plays, the hero is isolated in his faction by his rival or his nemesis. The exorcism of the double is notable, for example, in the contest of Hal and Hotspur in *Henry IV, Part I*: though each son aspires to distinguish himself, each also strives for the other's place—they might almost be competing to be alike. Shakespeare seems to indicate this mythologically: Harry Percy will pluck drowned honor up by her Medusan locks; Harry Monmouth mounts his steed like a Perseus upon Pegasus. Once again, "Single nature's double name, / Neither two nor one was called."

To study the subject-object problem as a problem of perception, however, we need examples that specifically point to subjectivity. Twice in

Ariosto's *Orlando Furioso* a major hero advances upon the nude form of a beautiful maiden fettered beside the shore for the delectation of the terrible Orco.[97] It is convenient for the heroism of the hero—not to mention the modesty of the heroine—that each time the knight comes in for a closer look, the monster stirs itself to action also. The fray impends, and the Orco, incomprehensively large and formless, bent on destruction and bearing down upon the prey, somehow gets himself enlisted in that same furious company that will include Rodomonte, and eventually Orlando himself. Apparently a sufficiently aroused hero raises up a comparable monster; and, in entering the Orco, as Orlando does, it may be that the Orco also enters him.

The attractions and antipathies of the scenes from Ariosto seem mutual. Their "poetic epistemology" might be cast in the Spenserian mould, for Spenser's kind of allegory is a great equivocator, objectifying the subject in the object, and subjectivising the object in the subject. An early example in *The Faerie Queene* is the encounter of Redcrosse with "the living tree" Fradubio. On the one hand, the tree cries out in the fearful accents that the reader already has heard in the speech of Redcrosse's dwarf. On the other hand, the knight finds himself paralyzed with fear and unable to move his limbs. Stockstill, Redcrosse has temporarily turned into a tree. "Or man, or tree," he says, addressing Fradubio, but also addressing—the syntax implies—the problem in question (I.ii.31, 34). We may compare Guyon's situation, when he encounters his own bashfulness in the person of Shamefastness. Insofar as the scene presents two individuals, the separateness of the maiden stands for that self-division whereby consciousness divides from itself to achieve a measure of objectivity, or self-consciousness. And insofar as the scene is staged in the parlor of a single heart, Guyon's movement in the maiden's direction suggests a contrary inclination to accommodate or temper feelings of self-consciousness.

With such encounters one may cite the scene in *Macbeth*, where the future murderer sees a dagger before his eyes, and responds to this figment of his imagination by bringing forth a more palpable dagger of his own. Macbeth's dagger of the mind hovers out of reach, like a garden of Tantalus, suspended in the objective space before him, while the physical dagger seems to be drawn from some subjective recess within him. He does not exorcise the fantastical dagger; rather, he substantiates it. And in the process, he also fantasizes the real one. Lady Macbeth calls the dagger the very painting of his fear in the banquet scene (III.iv.62), by which time the phantasmal and the substantial have thoroughly usurped each other's place. Similar exchanges take place throughout the range of Renaissance fictions.

[97] *O.F.* X.92–115, XI.28–60.

The scenes in *Macbeth* might lead us to a more obvious garden of Tantalus in *Paradise Lost*, where it is the devil himself who submits to the temptation of the fruit—*"imagining / For one forbidden Tree a multitude"* (X.553f.)—and so condemns himself to eat the dust and ashes that are properly a serpent's food. The scene is closely related to the one of Satan's metamorphosis, in which Satan falls down "supplanted . . . punisht in the shape he sinn'd" (X.513–516). The grove springs into existence at the analogous moment when the lesser devils undergo their transformation, overtaken by a "horrid sympathy" with their leader: "For what they saw, / They felt themselves now changing . . . the dire form / Catcht by Contagion" (X.540–544). It is the same kind of horrid sympathy—with his rival, as it were—that overtook the new-made Thane of Cawdor.

Men in all ages have known that the mote in the other fellow's eye may reflect the beam that is in one's own. But in the Renaissance the commerce between two subjects is often found, as if the theme of subjectivity had received a kind of enhanced valuation. Each subject's perception modifies the other's: the process of mutual observation objectifies a given subjectivity, and subjectivizes a given objectivity. Mambrino's helmet is either half a helmet, as Quixote would claim, or an inverted barber's basin, as Sancho would claim; but in either case each claim is subtly undermined by incorporating the other: their accommodation does not so much end in a truth as in a truce—or rather a more or less stable oscillation between rival ideas. Thus the reciprocity between two subjects suffers the condition of Dante's fascinated thieves, who, merely by staring at each other, are compelled to change and interchange their ballast: "Property was thus appalled, / That the self was not the same." From this point of view, a conventional observation found in Sylvester's DuBartas uses loaded terms: "as *Chameleons* vary with their object, / So *Princes' manners do transform the subject*" (I.II, ll. 103f.). It is man who is the prince of chameleons, but perhaps the only prince here is the chameleonic principle.

If we were to attempt to summarize the burden of Renaissance literature as a whole, we might say that it takes its birth from an expansionary ideal of human virtuosity, and then exposes the resulting myth—the myth of an awakening or potential godhood as available to man—to the profound critique of human subjectivity that seems to emerge as a rival for the myth itself. Almost before the Renaissance begins, we meet Dante's conquistador Ulysses, who dared his men into going beyond the limits. Many would agree that this journey does not end until we come to the end of the Renaissance, where we meet the figure of Milton's Satan. If Satan is compared to a Renaissance prince, Milton's portrayal would constitute a final indictment of the offer of an uncontingent secular godhood to the creature. The spectacle of Satan's virtuosity—leader, general, inventor, orator, architect, explorer, and conquistador—finds its sinister *verso* in his dangerous mutability and his ultimate inauthenticity—angel of light, mist, toad, beast of prey, and snake. The parabola of Satan's career traces a Faustian hero-icization of the will upward toward divinity, and then through its free fall into chaos and its final entrapment in the specious forms to which its resourcefulness has committed it. Because his changes of being lack authority other than his own, Satan proves to be a deeply unsound and virtually apocryphal being. His capacity for every role compromises any attempt to fix his nature, or even to verify an essential existence for him. Thus Satan can be described as a victim of that constant recasting of the self by the self, which, if it makes the Renaissance man fashionable throughout each of his manifestations, must also make him fashionable to the deprivation of his very core. From our point of view, the most important thing to be said about such a being is what God says in Book III, namely, that the archangel fell by his own suggestion.[98]

The observation of "human subjectivity," of course, is not the privilege of one particular period, any more than it is of a given literary technique. The great exploration of this theme that commences with Petrarch will only remind some readers that Petrarch was a devoted student of St. Augustine. And yet Petrarch and St. Augustine are two radically different "subjects." It is of considerable interest that in earlier philosophical tradition, and in the Renaissance, the quasi-technical term *subject* means "that in which attributes inhere," or even a substance "having its own independent existence." *Subjective* could therefore mean "inherent," hence "real, essential." The term *subject* has since come to mean the conscious or thinking subject, that is, the subject's mind, of which the chief inherent attribute is its own ideas. Hence "subjective" often means merely idiosyncratic, that is, deriving from the particular turn of mind or preconceptions of the individual thinking subject. In *Measure for Measure*, Isabella argues on behalf of the incriminated subject Angelo that "Thoughts are no subjects; / Intents, but merely thoughts" (V.i.453f.); but the preceding riot of subjectivity in the play does not wholly bear her out, and neither does the subsequent history of the word in question.

The allegory of a poem like the *Divine Comedy* is ultimately determined by the likeness or unlikeness that obtains between God as final cause and supreme being, and all of the other causes and beings that derive from him. The "otherness" of the various medieval senses of Scripture is ontological, as their dim resemblance to the four Aristotelian-Scholastic causes suggests. The otherness of Renaissance allegory is more decidedly epistemological: it is determined by the likeness or unlikeness that obtains between the knower and the known. At issue in the scenes from Renaissance literature that we have just discussed are opposed derivations for the

[98] *Par. Lost* III.129.

contingency of being. The question is, to which are we to give the mastery: to the ontological derivation, or the epistemological one? It is the exacerbation of their rivalry, rather than any obvious resolution of it, which characterizes what I take to be the typical Renaissance text.

These generalizations cannot hope to speak to every case. However, the foregoing description does offer a traditional focus in the Hermetic assertion that the mind of man can achieve parity with all things, and, through the mirific and manifold capacity of its understanding, can freely and deliberately metamorphose itself into any one of them. It is a brave new world that finds such a paragon in it, and yet the admirer, considering the evidence that this literature accumulates *per contra*, may be laboring under an illusion.[99] Should the vision of man's potential for universal stature or a supremely elevating self-transformation prove to be a temporary impression, then Miranda might be found awakening not on Prospero's isle, but on Circe's. To the Renaissance, Circe's cup symbolized the power of desire, appetite, infatuation, fancy, surmise, opinion, anxiety, vanity, and ignorance to impose upon that same creature's mind, and to impose a kind of isolating privacy upon it as well. It may well be, the poets warn us, that the shape of everything man beholds, either beyond himself, or within, is subject to an irrational determination by his very suggestibility. In that case, man's celebrated virtuosity would prove to be nothing other than the strongest evidence of his changeableness—and his bottomless capacities for self-delusion. Such a creature would be little more than Caliban, a poor credulous monster, foolishly making a wonder and a god out of what is only a fellow drunkard.

In the texts we have cited pertaining to the creation of Duessa, the effective superstition is credited with the power of realizing for itself at least a partly objective existence. It could hardly be otherwise, where the philosophy of nature maintains the unity of nature and spirit in the name of the vital principle that pervades them both, and where the philosophy of mind urges the mind's power to extend itself into all things.[100] The subject-object problem that results only ceases to be a "problem" when the object contemplated by consciousness becomes truly autonomous, and the

[99] See the conclusion to Montaigne's "Apology for Raymond Sebond," where it is said that it is delusory to imagine that man can add a cubit to his stature: "Nor can man raise himself above himself and humanity; for he can see only with his own eyes, and seize only with his own grasp. . . . It is for our Christian faith, not for his Stoical virtue, to aspire to that divine and miraculous metamorphosis." (Trans. Donald Frame, *Complete Essays of Montaigne, edn. cit.*, p. 457.) The passage is somewhat different in the editions of the *Essays* published in Montaigne's lifetime. Montaigne's objections are fully anticipated in Augustine, *Civ. Dei.* VIII.xxiii.

[100] See Ficino, *Five Questions Concerning the Mind, Epistolae,* Lib. II, i, in *Op. om.*, I–2, pp. 675ff., trans. Josephine L. Burroughs in Cassirer *et al.*, eds., *Renaissance Philosophy of Man* (Chicago, 1948), p. 200.

empathetic relations subsisting between it and the subject no longer obtain. At that point the object would cease to be regarded as covert testimony to the nature of the subject, or as the foil for the subject's peculiar preoccupation. The purely "participated" consciousness would not admit such a distinction, but even where the act of knowing is defined as an act of assimilation, the distinction will arise. In the meantime, the object of contemplation is always becoming the subject of the beholder's mental condition, or of the investigator's mental powers.

On the first pages of some ideal anthology of the period he does so much to initiate, one might find the poet Petrarch, confessing that he has made a holy thing of his beloved Laura—in other words, an idol.[101] The last pages of this same anthology would bring the reader up against a crazed hidalgo posted on a road in Spain—the mad one is trying to compel a group of traveling merchants to confess with him the supereminent beauty of a partly nonexistent lady whom he may never have seen.[102] Behold, this dreamer cometh. Renaissance literature, though it can hardly be said to put the relation of subject and object on that ideal basis of independence that leads from Descartes to Kant, might well be described as a critical engine for insinuating the unavoidable subjectivity of the mind's construction of both the object of knowledge and the object of love. After all, it is not Shakespeare, but Don Quixote, of whom one could truly say that his whole life was a life of allegory. And it is the like of Archimago that puts the giants on the knight's horizon, and the windmills in his head.

---

[101] Son, 192 (*Canz.* CCVIII): "e con preghiere onest / L'adoro, e 'nchino come cosa santa." See *Canz.* XXX, l. 27: "L'idolo mio scolpito in vivo lauro" (my idol carved in living laurel).

[102] *Don Quixote*, Pt. I, chap. 4.

ANALYTICAL TABLE OF CONTENTS

Chapter I (pp. 3–86)

Chapter II (pp. 87–282)

Chapter III (pp. 283–425)

Chapter V (pp. 653–733)

Chapter VI (pp. 735-791)

INDEX

The index was prepared with the dedicated assistance of Greg Colomb and Sue Ellen Campbell; we were also assisted by Gary Walton and Beverly Smolinski: to all my deep thanks. The general index of names and matters is followed by an index to Scriptures cited or alluded to. Proverbs, tropes, topoi, and emblems are entered under those categories.

ho Zeus kateide chronios eis tys diphtheras

Aaron, 40, 63, 222, 542

Abel, 232

Abessa, 213, 218n, 281n, 638

Abraham, 94, 98n, 155, 156, 159, 199, 201, 207, 278, 542, 544n, 568; and Isaac, 155, (156)

acedia, accidie, 242–43, 317–20, 343; *see* idleness, Maleger

Achelous, 375, 594

Achilles, 9, 11, 13, 18, 31, 61, 63, 301–2, 306–7, 373, 451, 452n, 457, 587–89, 590, 630, 634, 772; distraction of, 9; and Helen, 575, 588; individuation of, 9; and love, 587–88; vs. Scamander, 14, 302, 772; shield of, 11; tent of, 21; wrath of, 14; see Marinell, Pyrochles

Achilles Bocchius, *Symb. Quaest.*, 112–13, 335n, 386n, 462, 480n, 692

Achilles Tatius, *Clitopho and Leucippe*, 602n, 665, 588n

Acidale, Mount, 76, 78, 105, 462, 503, 518, 552, 657–59, 661, 663, 664, 672, 674, 702–3, 719–33; name of, 719n; *see* Colin Clout, Graces, topoi: *locus amoenus*

Acontius, 336

Acrasia, 288, 292n, 294n, 301, 330, 358, 366, 369, 441, 491–93, 512, 696n; bower of, 495; and Grantorto, 370; veil of, 716; *see* Acratia, Bower of Bliss, paradise: earthly, topoi: *locus amoenus*

Acrates, 361–62, 497

Acratia (Trissino's), 10, 244, 245, 440–41, 499–500, 508, 509n

Actaeon, 774

Adam, 19n, 30, 67, 133, 159–64, 166–67, 178–79, 185, 186–88, 201, 234, 246, 261, 262, 275, 278, 287, 288, 329n, 333n, 337, 518, 528, 542–44, 602n, 690n, 731–32; androgynous, 232, 600; clothing of, 528–29; in Milton, 8, 133, 511n; other wife of, 228–30; royal, 8, 162–63, 198, 732; second, 140, 159, 161, 178–79, 188, 336, 522; shame of, 704, 707; sleep of, 197, 544; as tree, 161–62; *see* Fradubio, *Life of Adam and Eve*, Lilith, Redcrosse: as Adam

Adam and Eve, 133, 134, 160, 182, 183, 228–32, 544

Adapa, 188

Adicia, 361–62, 382, 400, 406, 421, 425

Admetus, his daughter, 683n, 708

Adonis, 21, 184, 443, 445–46, 447, 454, 458, 471, 473, 491–94, 502, 510n, 513, 517, 519, 521, 535, 562, 565–67, 574, 576, 579, 582, 628–30, 634, 636, 647, 759, 769; emblem of, 525–26; and form, 522–23, 567; as father of form, 552–53; as fish, 592n; flowers, 589; (classical) gardens of, 493, 494, 514–16, 517–18, 520, and gardens of Tantalus, 493–94, taken for Eden, 517–18; marine, 587; phallic identifi-

721; and interior self, 327; of nature, 670; and parents, 436, 439, 442, 445, 530, 532–33, 628; of school age, 372; symbols of, 197, 221; two-year old, 294–95; *see* bear baby, birth: the unborn, Chrysogonee, cupidons, Freud, Erikson, romance motifs: foundling, Ruddymane

Chimaera, 692

Chiron the Centaur, 373, 396, 574–75

chivalry, 5n, 41, 44, 189, 356, 667, 669, 672, 722

Chloris, 462n; *see* Flora

Chretien de Troye, *Erec and Enide*, 508; *Ywain*, 483–84

Christ, 39, 41, 42, 54, 119, 127, 134n, 139, 145, 152–53, 154–56, 159, 165, 167, 170, 172, 179, 180, 183, 188, 189, 190, 196n, 199n, 213, 247n, 248, 254, 261, 265n, 270, 271, 274, 276–80, 292, 300n, 305, 328, 338, 430, 433, 435, 485, 601–2, 619, 677, 695, 705, 709, 731n; as anti-venom, 172–73, 173n, 185; and Apollo, 141n, 142, 144; banner of, 170–71, 195; blood of, 281; body of, 173, 175, 176–77, 184, 247, 270, 277, 278; conception of, 533; entombment of, 170, 187, 270–71; and epic, 20; false, 252, 253, 254; as gardener, 159, 178–79, 191; as Good Shepherd, 731; Incarnation of, 401; Jesus, 201, 304, name of, 180, 185; the Jouster, 190; Kingdom of, 259; the Messiah, 140, 186, 189, 193, 200, 272, 274, 275, 332, 419; in Milton, 58, 306; Passion of, 139, 563; temptation of, 300, 329, 332, 336; tomb of, 209, 277; as tree, 163–64, 166; *see* Adam, advent, Church, Cross, crucifixion, hell: harrowing of, Redcrosse, resurrection, tree

Christendom, 213, 290; *see* Church

Christian, Christiana, *see* Bunyan: *Pilgrim's Progress*

Chrysaor, 359

Chrysogonee, 439, 467n, 522, 526, 532, 564–65, 600; as Venerean, 564–65

Church, the, 44, 52, 67, 105, 126, 130, 134, 139, 145, 148, 151n, 156n, 165, 178, 184, 194, 195, 198, 211, 212, 214, 233, 270–71, 273, 277, 282; as bride, 20, 140, 193, 198, 204, 205, 279; cycle

of, 215–17, 246; divided, 212–13; early, 147–48, 323; Eastern and Western, 213; edifice, 178, 204, 230; English, 171, 217–18, 273, 674; of Ephesus, 130, 159; as fellowship, 615; as garden, 196; holy, 128n, 185; Jerusalem, 213; as Jerusalem (in Tasso), 20; maternal, 134; the old, 228; paradise of, 181, 222; purification of, 45; the reform, 107, 145, 204, 217, 222, 282, 393, 403–4, 419; the Roman, 116, 145n, 175–76, 204, 205, 213, 216–17, 218, 238, 243, 244, 246, 270, 362, 368, 398, 399, 405, 571n, 634; true, 207; unity of, 128, 276, 279–81, 290, 601n–602n; in the wilderness, 196, 210, 211n, 272; *see* bride, Christ, Eve, holiness, legend of: cycle of the Church, Israel, Truth, Temple, Una

Cicero, 26, 27, 28, 358; tongue of, 364; *Brutus*, 23n; *De Divinatione*, 146, 522n; *De Finibus*, 293; *De Invent. Rhet.*, 46n, 77, 318, 323; *De Nat. Deo.*, 220n, 454n, 522n, 561n; *De Off.*, 305–6, 309n, 319n, 323, 363, 484n, 709, 723n; *De opt. gen. orat.*, 23n; *De Oratore*, 26n, (27), (28), 291n, 348, 667n; *Epist. ad Fratrem*, 26n, 667n; *Laws*, 287, 667n; *Orator*, 23n; *Pro Archias*, 345n, 676; *Rep.*, 667n, 682; *Tusc. Displ.*, 293n, 320, 334n, 484n; *Verr.*, 667n; *see Rhetorica ad Herennium*

Cinthio, Giraldi, on romances, 11, 24n

Cinyras, 447, 450, 513, 592n; *see* Myhrra

Circe, Circean, 63, 123, 245, 294n, 329, 359, 370n–371n, 431, 434, 441, 494, 495, 498, 501, 509–10, 521, 790; Aeian, 510n; cup of, 493, 497, 509n, 510; in Ariosto, 14, 244; *see* Acrasia, Duessa

Ciris (Ovidian poem attributed to Virgil), *see* Virgil

Claribell, 639n, 659, 699, 732; name of, 607; *see* Bellamour

Clarin, 357, 358, 359

Claudian (Claudius Claudianus), 306, 519; *De Cons. Stil.*, 650, 741; *De Raptu Pros.*, 241n, 336n, 368, 369n, 471n, 504, 648; *Epithalamion*, 514–15, 525; *In Rufinum*, 292n; *Magnes*, 456; *Panegyr. Dictus Manilio*, 413

815

INDEX

de Meung, Jean, *see Romance of the Rose*
de Montenay, Georgette, *Emblemes*, 123n
de Morgan, Mary, "Through the Fire," 646
"De Raptu Helenae," 641n
De' Rossi, Bastiano, *Descrizione dell'Alparato*, 143n
De Sponde, Jean, Prol. to edn. of Homer, 142n, 585n
Dead Sea, the, 199, 201, 266n, 294, 340; fruit (apples of Sodom), 339–41; *see* apples, Idle Lake
Death, death, allegorical life of, 99, 166, 298, 321–22, 769–70; personified, 321–22, 489–90, 607, 635, 651n, 666; premature, 161–62, 612
debate poems, 79, 749
Deborah, the prophetess, 67, 217–18
deference and demeanor (in Bk. VI), 707–10, 711
Deguilleville, Guillaume de, *Pilgrimage of the Life of Man*, 137n, 356n, 501n, 691
Dehio, Ludwig, 405n
Delbouiller, M., 683n
Della Casa, Giovanni, *Galateo*, 656, 702, 715, 716n, 727n
Del Rio, Martin, *Disq. magic.*, 103, 126n, 233
Demeter, 334n, 742; *see* Ceres
"Demetrius" (Demetrius Phalerus, so-called), *On Style*, 49n, 90
Demetrius Trinculius, 692n
demiurge, 29, 563, 567; and Demogorgon, 739
Democritus, 93n, 696
Demogorgon, 104, 247, 613–14, 691, 735–36, 738–41, 746, 756; and demiurge, 739; as Erd-geist, 762; and Eternity, 739, 741; name of, 740–41; and poetic theology, 758–59; as theogonic principle, 741, 764, 765
demons, daemons, 103, 115, 127, 221, 229–31, 241n, 243n, 248, 249n, 252, 253n, 329, 342, 344, 449, 450, 571, 575, 591, 738, 757, 761, 766–72, 781–83; Azazel, 712; generation of, 230; good, 497; and images, 120; incubus, succuba, 102, 122, 231–33, 235n, 243, 370; Legion, 105; lillim,

236; of the noonday, 241–42; passing of, 773; and personification, 768–70; sorrowful, 497; spirits, 430; of subjectivity, 255, 770; *see* Acratus, lamia, Lilith, Sirens
Demosthenes, *Oration*, 388n
Dennis, John, *Grounds of Criticism in Poetry*, 673n
Descartes, 791
Deschampes, *Le Lay Amoureaux IV*, 605–6
Desert Fathers, 217, 242; *see* St. Anthony
Despair, 99, 134, 152–55, 165, 203, 279, 317, 717–18, 720, 726, 769; in Bunyan, 137; episode of, 203, 217, 320; and Meliboe, 717–18
Despetto, Decetto, Defetto, 598, 656, 660, 686, 688, 705, 706–7, 728
Detraction, 371, 398, 401, 404, 408, 688–97, 709
Deucalion, 289, 381, 394, 408
Deuteronomistic cycle, 200–201
devil, the, 119–20, 122, 129, 166, 167n, 172, 186n, 227, 234, 240, 244, 255, 268, 271, 275, 328, 341n; *see* Satan
dew, 131, 167–69, 184, 275n, 547; *see* manna
Diacceto, Francesco Cattani da, *I tre libri d'amore*, 617n
Diamond, 608, 618, 623, 632–33; *see* Agape's triplets, Priamond, Triamond
Diana, Artemis, 597; bath of, 522, 751, 774; bower of, 503; fountain of, 288–89, 304, 496 (*see also* 172, 263); mythography of, 138, 173, 341, 356, 395, 399n, 400, 452, 453, 454, 469n, 510, 562, 577, 641n; in Spenser, 78, 288–89, 328, 438n, 458, 462, 468, 564, 573, 635, 648, 774; *see* Belphoebe, Cynthia, Dictynna
Di Cesare, Mario A., 26n
Dickens, Charles, 773; *Great Expectations*, 196; *Pickwick Papers*, 647
Dickson, Arthur, 671n
Dictynna, 446n, 454n, 577
Dictys, *Ephemerido Belli Troiani*, 641n; *see* Troy
Dido, 62n, 63, 374, 453, 480, 487; and Aeneas, 48, 495
Diet (Alma's steward), 350, 364, 495

Old Testament; deutero-canonical books, OT apocrypha;
New Testament; and early writings used
in the Church

Library of Congress Cataloging in Publication Data

Nohrnberg, James Carson, 1941-
  The analogy of The Faerie queene.

  Includes index.
  1. Spenser, Edmund, 1552?-1599. The Faerie queene.
I. Spenser, Edmund, 1552?-1599. The Faerie queene.
II. Title.
PR2358.N6   821'.3   76-3795
ISBN 0-691-06307-9